Child and Adolescent Development for Educators

Third Edition

Judith L. Meece
*University of North Carolina
at Chapel Hill*

Denise H. Daniels
*California Polytechnic State University
at San Luis Obispo*

Mc
Graw
Hill

Boston   Burr Ridge, IL   Dubuque, IA   New York   San Francisco   St. Louis
Bangkok   Bogotá   Caracas   Kuala Lumpur   Lisbon   London   Madrid   Mexico City
Milan   Montreal   New Delhi   Santiago   Seoul   Singapore   Sydney   Taipei   Toronto

CHILD AND ADOLESCENT DEVELOPMENT FOR EDUCATORS
Published by McGraw-Hill, an imprint of The McGraw-Hill Companies, Inc., 1221 Avenue of the Americas, New York, NY 10020.

This book is printed on acid-free paper.

1 2 3 4 5 6 7 8 9 0 DOW/DOW 0 9 8 7

ISBN: 978-0-07-352576-1
MHID: 0-07-352576-6

Editor in chief: Emily Barrosse
Executive editor: David S. Patterson
Senior marketing manager: Sarah Martin
Development editor: Vicki Malinee, Van Brien and Associates
Project manager: Val Heffernan, Carlisle Publishing Services
Manuscript editor: Kirsten Balayti
Interior design: Carlisle Publishing Services
Cover design: Preston Thomas
Cover images: © Blend Images
Photo research: Natalia Peschiera/Nancy Null, Van Brien and Associates
Senior production supervisor: Rich DeVitto
Media producer: Jocelyn Spielberger
Media project manager: Magdalena Corona

The text was set in 10/12 Times Roman by Carlisle Publishing Service and Printed on 45# Publishers Matte
By R.R. Donnelley & Sons.

The credits section for this book begins on page C-1 following the References and is considered an extension of the copyright page.

Library of Congress Cataloging-in-Publication Data

Meece, Judith L.
Child and Adolescent Development for Educators/Judith L. Meece, Denise H. Daniels.—3rd ed.
  p. cm.
ISBN 978-0-07-352576-1
  1. Child Development. 2. Adolescence. 3. Constructivism (Education) 4. Cognition in Children. 5. Children—Language. I. Daniels, Denise H. (Denise Honeycutt) - II. Title.
LB1115.M266 2007
370.15′1—dc22

2007003644

www.mhhe.com

Contents in Brief

Contents

CHAPTER 3
Cognitive Development: Piaget's and Vygotsky's Theories 126

CHAPTER 4
Cognitive Development: Information Processing
and Intelligence Theories 185

CHAPTER 7
Peer Relations and Moral Development 400

List of Features

Focus on Development

Preface

The first edition of *Child and Adolescent Development for Educators* was motivated by a desire to create positive school environments for children and adolescents. Young people spend more than 15,000 hours in some form of school setting. Research now shows that the experiences and interactions they have in those settings have a lasting influence on almost every aspect of their development. Moreover, for many young people today, schools play an influential role in protecting them from the adverse effects of poverty, dangerous neighborhoods, or difficult home environments.

The first edition was also based on Judith Meece's work as an educator and researcher. Until the first edition of this text was published, instructors working with educational professionals relied on child and adolescent texts written for psychology students. Although there are many fine texts available, few focus on children's development in school settings. When the first edition was published, there was a growing research literature on child and adolescent development within schools, and the many ways this research can be applied in educational settings. Thus, the first edition of *Child and Adolescent Development for Educators* was written with the intention of designing a text appropriate for educators that included a strong research base on schooling and development. Most important, this text was written to reflect the important role of teachers and schools in children's lives. It was the first book of this type in education.

This new third edition of *Child and Adolescent Development for Educators* brings together two authors who share the same concern about the role that schools play in children's development. Both authors have a strong background in developmental psychology and applications to school settings. Whereas Meece specializes in middle childhood and adolescence, Denise Daniels provides added expertise in early development in schools and other settings. Thus, the authors' collaboration has resulted in a revision that will serve the spectrum of students preparing to enter education. The text is written to appeal to both new educational professionals as well as those returning for a graduate degree in education.

OVERALL APPROACH: A DEVELOPMENT TEXT FOR FUTURE TEACHERS

Child and Adolescent Development for Educators is a text written for teachers as well as school psychologists, counselors, principals, and other educational professionals working in school settings. It presents the content future educators need to know in order to understand the development of their students. From its inception, this book was designed to meet the special interests of teacher education students. For example, in addition to focusing primarily on school-age development, each chapter opens with a school or classroom vignette that sets the stage for the material that follows and then punctuates each discussion with an abundance of school and classroom examples. The *Focus on Research* and *Focus on Teaching* features show students how to connect and apply developmental research to the classroom. Charts and other visual displays are included to summarize key developmental trends. In addition, each chapter includes an assortment of observation, interview, and reflection activities designed to apply key topics. Topic coverage reflects the realities of teaching as well, with over one-third of the text devoted to cognitive and language development. The important influence of social and cultural context on development is also emphasized throughout the book.

COVERAGE AND ORGANIZATION

The text takes a topical approach. The content is focused on those topics of most interest to educators—cognitive development, literacy, social and emotional development, and family involvement in education. Because of its teaching focus and concise discussions, it can be used as a core text with supplemental readings and materials.

The text is organized into nine chapters. Chapter 1 stresses the importance of studying children's development in education and provides an overview of the theories and the methods used in child development research. This chapter emphasizes the important role that schools and teachers play in children's development. Chapter 2 examines children's physical development, with a focus on brain development, puberty, genetic and environmental risk factors, and special health concerns in childhood and adolescence. A special section discusses the implications of brain research for education. There are two chapters on cognitive development, and each provides suggestions for using cognitive theories in the classroom. Chapter 3 focuses on Piaget's cognitive development theory and Vygotsky's sociocultural theory. Both theories serve as theoretical foundations for constructivist approaches in education. Chapter 4 presents information processing and psychometric approaches to understanding children's intellectual development and discusses how individual variations in cognitive development are measured and explained. A special section focuses on the influence of computers on children's learning. The focus of Chapter 5 is children's language and literacy development, and new approaches to teaching reading and writing are highlighted. This chapter also contains information on literacy development in non-English-speaking children. The next two chapters focus on children's emotional and social development. Chapter 6 addresses the development of emotional competence, conceptions of the self, and motivation. It begins with an overview of Erikson's theory of psychosocial development, and each section concludes with a set of suggestions for how teachers can help to foster emotional competence, positive self-conceptions, and academic motivation. Chapter 7 turns to children's social understanding and relations, focusing on the development of social cognition, peer relations, peer groups, and moral development. The chapter addresses how educators can create a caring and supportive environment that promotes social understanding and acceptance. The next chapter, Chapter 8, is devoted to the important role of the family in children's development, including a discussion of family diversity and transitions. For educators, it includes important information on child care, helping children cope with divorce, child maltreatment, and media influences. Most important, the chapter concludes by suggesting some ways educators can form partnerships with parents and other family members. The text ends with a chapter focusing on methods that teachers and educational professionals can use to support children's and adolescents' development in school settings. Chapter 9, new to this third edition, focuses on how educators can establish positive interpersonal relations with their students,

integrate children with special needs in the classroom, and create successful schools for children, youth, and families.

NEW TO THE THIRD EDITION

The first and second editions of *Child and Adolescent Development for Educators* were enthusiastically embraced by instructors of future teachers because of their emphasis on classroom application and the content that teachers need to know. The third edition underwent another major revision based on substantial feedback from instructors using the text as well as other instructors of education majors. All of the feedback was closely considered and used to revise the text to best meet the needs of instructors of future teachers.

Key revisions in the third edition include the following:

Expanded Content and Depth. Each chapter is heavily revised to ensure complete coverage of the topics future teachers need to understand. At least three to four new sections are added to each chapter. Specific added content includes new research on brain development, health and nutrition, neo-Piagiatian and social constructivist perspectives on cognitive development, development of mathematical and scientific concepts, social cognition, computers and learning, language-minority students, development precursors of learning disabilities, emotional competence, ethnic identity development, peer groups, quality preschool programs, teacher–student relations, family influences on development, parental involvement in education, school transitions, resources for child advocacy, and creating school environments that promote positive youth development. The text is also expanded to include more information on early childhood and adolescent development.

New Chapter on Schooling. The new Chapter 9, "Supporting the Development of Children and Youth in School," highlights important topics such as fostering resiliency in youth, establishing positive interpersonal relationships in the classroom, teaching students with special learning needs, and creating successful schools for children, youth, and families.

Integration of Diversity Perspectives. Whereas the first and second editions included a separate chapter on children with special learning needs, this information has been completely integrated throughout the text for the third edition. Each chapter contains information that will enable educators to better understand some of the needs of children with physical disabilities, learning disabilities, and emotional disorders. Chapter 9 discusses approaches teachers can use for differentiating instruction, which reinforces current practices for inclusion today. Additionally, integration of cultural perspectives and differences throughout the text ensures that educational professionals have some background information for working with diverse populations of students.

Pedagogical Features. All of the features have been updated to support the new topics and discussions presented throughout the text and to encourage putting the information into practice, such as:

- Many new *opening vignettes* have been added to provide real-life scenarios that offer opportunities for critical thinking and discussion.
- Highlights in the margins entitled *Understanding Children* have been added to link the text to the accompanying activities in *Understanding Children: An Interview and Observation Guide for Educators*, helping the reader to apply ideas and theories to real children in school.
- Three key discussion features—*Focus on Teaching, Focus on Development*, and *Focus on Research*—have all been revised and updated to relay the latest information and research in the field. The *Focus on Teaching* feature highlights important classroom applications; the *Focus on Development* feature serves as a chronological summary to aid students' understanding of key developmental concepts; and the *Focus on Research* feature reviews critical research in child and adolescent development.

Updated and Expanded Scholarship. The scholarship of the third edition is updated and expanded to reflect new studies. More than 600 new references were added to highlight the most recent research in the field of child and adolescent development. Twelve new feature boxes have been added in the third edition to provide an updated account on research and teaching applications. The relevant *Focus on Research* feature and the solid foundation of scholarship that supports the text make *Child and Adolescent Development for Educators* the most research-based development text for educators.

SUCCESSFUL FEATURES

Supporting Student Learning

The third edition maintains the same *student-friendly writing style* as the first and second editions. The pedagogical structure was developed to support and guide the student's learning. Each chapter begins with an *outline* listing the key topics covered in the chapter. An *opening vignette* set in a school or classroom invites the student into the chapter by providing an immediate engagement. *Focus on Development* boxes provide chronological summaries to help clarify types of development. Bolded *key terms* help students focus on the most important aspects of the chapter. At the end of the chapter, a comprehensive *summary* and *listing of key terms* with page references aid the student's review.

Applying Knowledge

Several features were developed to encourage students to apply their reading about developmental theory and research. Each chapter contains at least one section that discusses the educational implications and applications of the highlighted theories. Several charts and tables are included that also describe educational implications for the various theories discussed. A set of *Activities* at the end of each chapter provides opportunities for the student to use and apply the learning material as well. Additionally:

- The *Focus on Research* feature summarizes developmental research and shows how the research can be applied—and the importance of that application—to the classroom.
- The *Focus on Teaching* boxes provide students with a look inside classrooms, give examples of how teachers approach different situations, and take a look at the role development plays in the classroom setting.
- The *Understanding Children* margin notes provide a link from the text to the accompanying *Understanding Children: An Interview and Observation Guide for Educators* to help readers apply what they are learning to "real" children and youth in educational settings.

SUPPLEMENTS

The text is accompanied by effective supplements developed to support both the instructor and student.

For the Instructor

Online Learning Center Website (www.mhhe.com/meece3e). Available free to users of the text, the accompanying Online Learning Center website provides numerous teaching resources, including a downloadable Instructor's Manual; a test bank of questions; text-specific PowerPoint slides; suggested research topics; and supplemental lecture topics, activities, critical thinking exercises, and audiovisual suggestions.

Additional Child and Adolescent Development Resources. A number of additional useful resources are available for the instructor, including the *McGraw-Hill Overhead Transparencies for Child Development,* the *McGraw-Hill Video Cases in Human Development: Childhood,* and *McGraw-Hill's Multimedia Courseware for Child Development.* Please contact your McGraw-Hill sales representative regarding the most recent offerings for child and adolescent development.

PageOut (www.pageout.net). Create your own course website! Simply plug your course information into a template and click on one of 16 designs, and you can create your own professional-looking website. Powerful features include an interactive course syllabus that lets you post content and links, an online gradebook, lecture notes, bookmarks, and even a discussion board where students can discuss course-related topics.

For the Student

Online Learning Center Website (www.mhhe.com/ meece3e). Available free, the Online Learning Center website provides students with a number of study aids including chapter objectives, chapter overviews, multiple-choice questions, essay questions, key terms, critical thinking exercises, annotated Web links, and additional resources.

Understanding Children: Interview and Observation Guide for Educators **(ISBN 0-07-337857-7).** Authored by Denise Daniels, Florence Beaumont, and Carol Doolin, this convenient and practical resource provides guidelines for observing children in the school setting. Each chapter includes several observation activities and sample forms, and concludes with a "Tips for Teachers" section that discusses the implications of the observations for the future teacher. *Understanding Children* notes appear throughout the margins of *Child and Adolescent Development for Educators* to point out related activities from the guide. Contact your McGraw-Hill sales representative for details on packaging the observation guide with the textbook.

ACKNOWLEDGMENTS

With great appreciation, we would like to thank the many individuals who assisted with the third edition for their generous support and encouragement. First, we would like to thank Billy Gordon, Karl Askew, Alicia Franks, Beverly Glienke, Crystal Hill, Shannon Gibbons, and Ashley Whittaker for their assistance with research, and Sharon Powell and Patricia Ayers-Phillips for their assistance with references. Vicki Malinee, who managed the revision process, kept everything running smoothly. We are grateful to all.

Many individuals have helped to strengthen this text over the years by reviewing one or several chapters. For the *third edition,* the contributions of the following reviewers are gratefully acknowledged:

J'anne Affeld, Northern Arizona University;
Michael Casey, The College of Wooster;
Teresa DeBacker, University of Oklahoma;
Maribeth Downing, Harding University;
Kathleen Fite, Southwest Texas State University;
Dana Fusco, York College;
Jennifer Gordon, George Mason University;
Michele Gregoire, University of Florida;
Charles Guest, University of South Alabama;
Michelle Haney, Berry College;
Joyce Hemphill, University of Wisconsin-Madison;
Catharine Knight, University of Akron;
Deborah Margolis, Merrimack College;
Deborah McMakin, Framingham State College;
Deanna Nekovei, Texas A&M University at Kingsville;
Donna Phillips, Niagara University;
Vincent Rinaldo, Niagara University;
Douglas Sauber, Arcadia University;
Elisabeth Steenken, Bluefield State College;
Bruce Torff, Hofstra University;
Meghan Twiest, Indiana University of Pennsylvania;
Shawn Ward, LeMoyne College; and
Roger Wise, Utah Valley State College.

A special thank-you is also extended to reviewers of the *second edition,* whose comments led to important improvements and refinements: Julie Alexandrin, Eastern Connecticut State University; Kay Alderman, University of Akron; David Andrews, Indiana State University; Rosenna Bakari, State University of New York at Oneonta; Audrey W. Beard, Albany State University;

Katherine Benson, University of Minnesota, Morris; Navaz Bhavnagri, Wayne State University; J. T. Binfet, California State University, San Bernardino; James P. Byrnes, University of Maryland; Clara Carroll, Harding University; Heather Davis, University of Georgia; Sandra Deemer, Millersville University; Darlene DeMarie, University of South Florida; C. Timothy Dickel, Creighton University; Maribeth Downing, Harding University; Saralee S. Goodman, Goucher College; Michele Gregoire, University of Florida; Mary Anne Hannibal, Indiana University of Pennsylvania; Susan Hegland, Iowa State University; Young Suk Hwang, California State University, San Bernardino; Wilsie G. Jenkins, Fort Valley State University; Evelyn Jordan, LaGrange College; Deborah L. Kalkman, Northern Illinois University; Carol R. Keyes, Pace University; Gary W. Ladd, University of Illinois; Sheila Marino, Lander University; Kathy Morrison, University of Texas, Arlington; Jack Piel, University of North Carolina, Charlotte; Evan R. Powell, University of Georgia; F. Thomas Scappaticci, King's College; Shereen F. Sheehan, University of Houston, Clear Lake; Stephen Sherblom, University of Missouri, St. Louis; Susan Sze, Niagara University; Dennis Thompson, Georgia State University; Theresa Thorkildsen, University of Illinois, Chicago; Jayne White, Drury College; Allan Wigfield, University of Maryland; and Barbara Yunker, Jacksonville State University.

And a continued thanks goes to those reviewers who helped shape the *first edition*: Kay Alderman, University of Akron; Linda Anderson, Michigan State University; Hilda Borko, University of Colorado; Carol Anne Kardash, University of Missouri; Paul Pintrich, University of Michigan; Gary Stuck, University of North Carolina; and Allan Wigfield, University of Maryland.

Finally, we would like to acknowledge the generous support of our family, friends, and students. Judith acknowledges the encouragement and support of Susan Griffith, Kate Scantlebury, Ann Schulte, and Gregory Parker. She is especially grateful for the long-distance support from her sister, Cheryl Meece. Denise would like to thank her family members—her husband for assuming more family responsibilities while she worked, and her children for sharing their perspectives on the lives of students in school. Both Denise and Judith would also like to thank their university students over the years for sharing their experiences as classroom observers and educators. A heartfelt thanks to you all.

Judith L. Meece

Denise H. Daniels

About The Authors

Judith L. Meece is a professor of education at the University of North Carolina—Chapel Hill, where she teaches in the School of Education. *Child and Adolescent Development for Educators* draws on her more than 25 years of experience teaching child and adolescent development courses to preservice teachers and graduate students. Before coming to Chapel Hill, Meece taught at Purdue University and completed a postdoctoral fellowship at the Learning Research and Development Center of the University of Pittsburgh. She received her PhD in educational psychology from the University of Michigan in 1981. Meece's research focuses on academic motivation, gender differences in mathematics and science achievement, and schooling influences on development. She has authored or coauthored numerous articles and chapters on these topics. Currently she is involved in two research projects focusing on rural youth as part of the National Research Center of Rural Education Support. She is also co-editing a book on schooling and development.

Denise H. Daniels is an associate professor of child development at California Polytechnic State University at San Luis Obispo. Before coming to Cal Poly, she was an associate professor of educational psychology at Northern Illinois University. Like Meece, she also draws from considerable experience (14 years) teaching prospective and experienced educators and child professionals at undergraduate and graduate levels. She received her PhD in education and developmental studies from UCLA in 1992. Daniels's research focuses on children's motivation to learn in diverse educational settings, and children's and teachers' psychological understandings. She is also involved with children and families as a consultant for a variety of school readiness projects in the local community, and is a parent of two teenagers.

Studying Child and Adolescent Development

STANLEY ROGERS HAS JUST STARTED AT A NEW MIDDLE SCHOOL; HE AND *his family recently moved from a rural area in North Carolina to Cleveland Heights, Ohio. He has a slight build, with red hair and freckles, and dresses oddly compared to students at his new school. Considered a "geek" by other boys in his class, Stanley's favorite subject is social studies. He has a particular passion for the history of the Civil War, to the point that his social studies teacher learns obscure facts from him. In other subjects besides social studies, Stanley shows less interest and refuses to do homework. Although highly capable, he does poorly on tests unless the topic interests him. Stanley's English teacher is frustrated by his work habits and his lack of achievement, when obviously he is so capable. However, what is particularly bothersome to Stanley's teacher is that he disturbs other students when he is not interested in a particular lesson. During small-group work, a study period, or even a group lesson, Stanley will wander around the classroom, make wisecracks, talk with other students, or put his head down to nap. Stanley's teacher has tried several different approaches to change his behavior, such as reminding him about classroom rules, giving him a leadership role in small-group discussions, offering him special rewards for completing assignments, calling him out for disruptive behavior, assigning extra homework, keeping him after class, and talking with his parents. None of these strategies appear to be working. Stanley's teacher is frustrated and feels her authority in the classroom is being challenged by this student.*

Source: *Adapted from Campoy, R. (2005).* Case study analysis in the classroom. Becoming a reflective teacher. *San Francisco: See pp. 147–148.*

Teachers are easily frustrated when challenged by a student like Stanley. He is capable, and passionate about his interests. Stanley also wants to be accepted by his new classmates. What is the problem? Why is it difficult to keep Stanley engaged in classroom activities? What would you do if you were Stanley's teacher?

To reach students like Stanley, teachers need to draw on their knowledge of children's development. Student behavior in the classroom is often a complex interplay of many different individual characteristics (e.g., maturity, gender, ability) and family background, as well as classroom dynamics. For example, children entering a new school may feel vulnerable and uneasy. As young people enter early adolescence, peers can also exert considerable influence on classroom behavior. Most children can handle adjusting to new classrooms with competence, but others may need a good deal of support from teachers and other school personnel (Daniels, Beaumont, & Doolin, 2002). Problem behaviors, as with Stanley, can arise when teachers do not respond appropriately to the developmental needs of their students. As we will learn, the importance of developing a positive relationship with students is critical for children's learning and adjustment in school (Comer, 2004; Pianta, 1999; Wentzel, 2002).

In this chapter, we begin to explore different theories of child development and their implications for teaching. This research can help teachers answer questions about how thinking processes unfold, how children determine right from wrong, when children begin to understand the feelings of others, why children lose interest in learning, how children learn self-discipline, why some adolescents are rejected by their peers, why some youths become aggressive and violent, and so forth. More important, child and adolescent development research can help educators to identify those behaviors that place children at risk for not succeeding in school. Last, child development research can help educators to create an educational environment that promotes the healthy development of all children. The Focus on Research box on page 4 describes how child development research can help guide school reform efforts.

The first two sections of this chapter focus on the question: Why study children's development? Subsequent sections discuss the status of children in school today. We then turn to the theories of development that serve as the focus for this book, and the methods used to study children's development.

Why Study Child and Adolescent Development?

Teachers' Understanding of Development

Teachers hold varying points of view about children's development. Look at the photo below showing two classrooms—one from the 1950s (left) and one from the 1990s (right). What beliefs about children are guiding the teaching practices shown here? On the right, children appear to passive learners, with the teacher as the main transmitter and source of knowledge. On the left, however, children are working in small groups, helping each other, and taking a more active role in their learning. Think about your own beliefs. Which of the two pictures best fits how you think children learn? How did you form these ideas?

Some teachers may have taken a formal course on child psychology, whereas others may construct a naive or commonsense theory of development from their own personal experiences and observations. For example, many prospective teachers believe that children primarily learn through the "teacher as teller" mode (see photo on left), and base those beliefs about learning from their own experiences (Kagan, 1992; Richardson, 1996). In other words, "teachers teach the way the way they were taught" (Nettle, 1998, p. 193). Other studies suggest that teachers' beliefs about their students are influenced by societal beliefs. For example, adolescents are often portrayed in the media as troubled, emotional, rebellious, and out of control due to hormonal changes. If teachers accept these societal views, it is likely to affect the way they teach and interact with adolescents.

Compare these two images of classrooms from the 1950s (left) and 1990s (right). What changes do you see in teaching practices?
Source: Jack Moebes/CORBIS and Will Hart/Photo Edit.

Focus on
Research

Dr. James P. Comer is considered one of America's leading architects of school reform and perhaps the only prominent reformer who views children's development as the center of all educational programs. In a 1997 interview for *Phi Delta Kappan*, Dr. Comer stated, "I have maintained a steady focus on child development and this is what I have tried to bring to education. Even people in education who are sensitive to child development focus on curriculum/instruction/assessment first, and I argue that it should be development first and that development should guide everything else" (Goldberg, 1997, p. 599).

For more than 25 years, Comer has been working with schools using a collaborative process of reform that brings together teachers, principals, parents, health professionals, and community members to create educational programs that foster the development of children. The basic premise of Comer's School Development Program (SDP) is that "all children have the potential to succeed in school and in life, and that the realization of this potential depends on how well educators, families, and communities work together to create environments that support child development; children who are developing well can learn adequately" (Comer & Haynes, 1999, p. 601). The SDP has three important components: (a) a governance and management team that develops a comprehensive school plan, assessment strategy, and staff development program; (b) a mental health or school support team; and (c) a parents' program (Comer, Haynes, Joyner, & Ben Avie, 1996). These three teams work together to promote students' learning and development using

Dr. James P. Comer: Putting Children First

Comer's guiding principles of collaboration, consensus, and no-fault problem solving to create a climate of competence, mutual respect, and trust in the school. Additionally, the SDP team uses six developmental pathways as a framework for making decisions that benefit students. These are physical, cognitive, language arts, social, psychological, and ethical. To educate the whole child, Comer believes that schools must develop a balanced curriculum that is not only focused on cognitive development but also addresses a broad spectrum of children's developmental needs.

One of the first schools to implement the Comer program was Martin Luther King Jr. Elementary School in New Haven, Connecticut—a predominantly African American, low-income, inner-city school. At the beginning of the project in 1968, its students were an average of 19 months below grade level in language arts and 18 months below grade level in reading. Students' scores in both areas were at grade level in 1979 and were 12 months above grade level in 1984. Additionally, parent involvement had increased, school absences and behavior problems had decreased, and staff turnover was nearly zero. These changes occurred without any dramatic change in the socioeconomic backgrounds of the children attending the school.

Today, Comer's School Development Program is operating in more than 700 elementary, middle, and high schools across the United States, and in Trinidad and Tobago. *For Dr. James Comer, education and development are one in the same.*

The connection between teacher beliefs about children's development and instructional practices is demonstrated in a study of school readiness by Mary Lee Smith and Lorrie Shepard (1988). Using a set of open-ended questions, the researchers asked 40 kindergarten teachers in one school district to think about particular children who were not ready for school and to speculate about the reasons for their lack of readiness. The researchers then examined teachers' statements to identify beliefs about (a) the nature of development and early learning, (b) rates of development, (c) causes of unreadiness, and (d) methods of remediation. In this study, the concept of teachers' beliefs referred to those propositions a teacher "holds to be true" (p. 309).

The study showed several noteworthy findings. First, the teachers differed in the extent to which they viewed the development of school readiness as influenced by internal or environmental processes. Nearly half the teachers were labeled "nativists" because they construed development as a maturational process that was "largely or completely outside the influence of parents or teachers" (p. 314). The remaining teachers all believed that school readiness could be influenced by teachers, parents, and other environmental forces, but they differed with respect to the sort of intervention they would recommend for a child who was not ready for school. A large majority of this group believed that additional instruction would increase readiness or would correct specific deficits in readiness. Only 3 of the 40 teachers viewed the development of school readiness as a complex interaction between the child's characteristics and the environment provided by the caregivers. Second, the results of this study indicated that teachers' beliefs about the development of school readiness influenced their decisions to recommend an extra year of kindergarten. Teachers who held nativist beliefs were the most likely to recommend retention, whereas teachers with nonnativist views reported lower rates of retention.

In summary, many studies indicate that teachers' beliefs about children and how they develop have important implications for how they teach and interact with students (Borko & Putnam, 1996; Kagan, 1992; Smith & Shepard, 1988). Research further suggests that teachers are most effective in their teaching when they attempt to understand their students as individuals (Kagan, 1992). Thus, one of the most important reasons to study children's development is to become a teacher who makes a difference in young people's lives.

Most states require a course on child and adolescent development to meet teacher licensing and certification standards. Additionally, a growing number of states are basing their requirements for new teacher certification on the 10 principles of effective teaching identified by INTASC (Interstate New Teacher Assessment and Support Consortium). We have listed the 10 principles in Figure 1.1 on page 6. As you can see, several of these principles require a strong foundation in child and adolescent development.

Schools as a Context for Development

Another very important reason for studying and understanding the development of children and adolescents is the critical role that schools play in their lives (Eccles, 2004; Pianta, 2006; Roeser, Eccles, & Sameroff, 2000; Rutter, Maughan, Mortimore, Ouston, & Smith, 1979). Along with the family and the peer group, schools are one of the most influential contexts for children's development in our society.

By the time young people graduate from high school they will have spent more than 10,000 hours in school. Figure 1.2 on page 6 indicates that approximately one-third of an adolescent's waking life is spent in some type of school environment (Csikszentmihalyi & Larson, 1984). Furthermore, students start school earlier and stay in school longer than young people in past generations. Since the early 1900s, there also have been significant increases in the percentage of young children who attend school. Figure 1.3 on page 7 shows that the percentage of 3- and 4-year-olds enrolled in preprimary programs since 1965. An important feature of this trend is the number of young children in full-day programs. In 2003, approximately 56 percent of children between the ages of 3 and 5 attended a preprimary school all day (National Center of Educational Statistics, 2004). Along with the increase in the number of young children attending school, high school completion rates have also steadily increased over the last 20 years, from 80 to 84 percent of young people between the ages of 18 and 24 years (Federal Interagency Forum on Child and Family Statistics, 2005).

Thus, the fact that children and adolescents spend so much time at school makes this context a potentially powerful influence on their development. Teachers, classmates, and

---

INTASC Standards

The teacher understands the central concepts, tools, and structures of the discipline(s) he or she teaches and can create meaningful learning experiences of subject matter.

The teacher understands how children learn and develop and can provide for their intellectual, social, and personal development.

The teacher understands how students differ in their approaches to learning and creates instructional opportunities that are adapted for diverse learners.

The teacher understands and uses a varirety of instructional strategies to encourage students' development of critical thinking, problem solving, and performance skills.

The teacher uses an understanding of individual and group motivation and behavior to create a learning environment that encourages positive social interactions, active encouragement in learning, and self-motivation.

The teacher uses knowledge of effective verbal, nonverbal, and media communication techniques to foster active inquiry, collaboration, and supportive interaction in the classroom.

The teacher plans instruction based on knowledge of subject matter, students, and community and curriculum goals.

The teacher understands and uses formal and informal assessment strategies to ensure the continuous intellectual, social, and physical development of the learner.

The teacher is a reflective practitioner who continually evaluates the effects of his or her choices and actions on others. (students, parents, and other professionals in the learning community) and who actively seeks opportunity to grow professionally.

The teacher fosters relationships with school colleagues, parents, and agencies in the larger community to support student's learning and well-being.

■ FIGURE 1.1
Overview of INTASC Standards
A strong foundation in child and adolescent development is central for meeting professional teaching standards.
Source: www.ccsso.org/intsct.html.

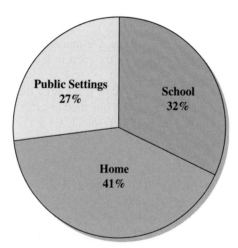

■ FIGURE 1.2
Percentage of Time Adolescents Spend in Different Settings
Adolescents spend approximately one-third of their waking hours in school.
Source: Csikszentmihalyi & Larson (1984).

Public Settings
27%

School
32%

Home
41%

curricula all play an important role in a child's development. When children and youth are not connected with adults or communities who are concerned about their well-being, then school plays an even greater role as a primary socializing influence in the lives of young people (Comer et al., 1996).

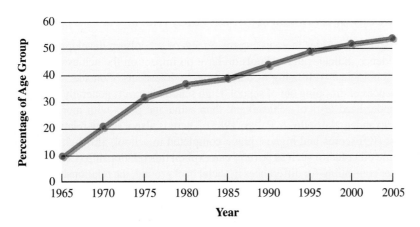

■ FIGURE 1.3
Percent of 3- and 4-Year-Olds Enrolled in Early Education Programs
Over the last 40 years there has been a steady increase in the number of young children attending preschool programs. The quality of early education programs can have a lasting effect on the development of children.
Source: National Center of Educational Statistics (2005a).

Assessing the Effects of Schools on Children's Development

The effects of schools on children's development are not easy to assess. Since schools were first established, there has been no clear consensus concerning what should be the purpose and function of schools in children's lives. Should schools focus exclusively on students' intellectual development? Should schools be concerned about students' social and emotional lives? Should schools teach health, sex education, family life, personal finance, driver's education, and other courses to prepare students for adulthood? Should schools help solve social problems such as poverty, drug abuse, and racism? Ask your classmates and friends these questions, and you will find a wide range of opinions.

For the most part, the debate has focused on whether schools should train basic intellectual skills or provide a more comprehensive training for life that includes both intellectual and emotional development. The school environment changes as one set of goals is emphasized over the other. In the 1960s, for example, educational reformers claimed that schools were not providing learning experiences that were relevant to students' lives. Programs were implemented so that students could receive more "hands-on" and "real world" learning experiences. Since the 1980s, the "back-to-basics" movement has gained momentum because policy makers believe we are losing our competitive edge in the world economic market. Some proposals call for more demanding academic curricula, tougher academic standards, more homework, more tests, longer school days, and the end of social promotion. At times, the school has been viewed as an agent of social reform, as seen in the desegregation and mainstreaming movements of the 1970s, which continue to have an influence on schools today.

It also is difficult to assess the effects of schools on children's development because schools differ greatly with respect to philosophy, resources, learning opportunities, and social climate. Some students have well-equipped classrooms, large libraries, the latest computer technology, small classes, modern school facilities, and access to two or more gymnasiums. Other students are expected to learn in schools with outdated textbooks, overcrowded classrooms, poorly paid teachers, and metal detectors at the front door. Many of these students come from poor families who cannot provide additional resources to support their children's learning at home. Because of tremendous disparities in the way public schools are funded in this country, the poor get a poorer quality of education. In his book *Savage Inequalities,* Jonathan Kozol (1991) speculated that some children have a better chance of learning math and reading on the street than they do in school. For some students, the conditions of schooling have not improved much in the last 10 years.

Effects of Schooling on Development

Despite difficulties in assessing the effects of schools on development, a growing body of evidence indicates that schools do have on impact on the achievement, socialization, and psychological well-being of children and adolescents. Consider, for example, the consequences of dropping out of school. High school dropouts generally perform more poorly on standardized tests of achievement than same-age peers with more years of schooling do (Alexander, Natriello, & Pallas, 1985). There is also a strong relation between intelligence test (IQ) scores and highest grade completed in school, although it is quite possible that some other factor such as poverty can explain this relationship (Ceci, 1991). However, even after controlling for differences in social background, the relationship between IQ and years of school is still fairly strong. According to Stephen Ceci (1990), this relationship is partly explained by the fact that schools teach the basic skills and cultural knowledge that are included in standardized tests of achievement and intelligence (e.g., "What is the boiling point of water?" "What is the capital of the United States?").

A good example of schooling effects on academic development comes from international assessments of mathematics and science achievement. In general, children in the United States do not perform as well as children from Singapore, Hong Kong, or Japan on international assessments. These discrepancies are not simply due to innate differences in cognitive abilities (i.e., Asians do not have better math genes). Researchers have found that American and Japanese students perform equally well on general tests of cognitive functioning (Stevenson & Stigler, 1992). The differences result in part from the instructional practices of teachers in different countries. Japanese teachers, for example, spend more time than American teachers on mathematics instruction (Stevenson & Stigler, 1992). Additionally, U.S. mathematics teachers tend to teach students how to solve a particular problem, then ask the students to solve it on their own. In contrast, Japanese teachers often give students problems that they have not seen before to develop their thinking skills and to prepare them for later instruction (Stigler & Hiebert, 1999). As you can see in Figure 1.4, teachers in Japan also spend more time explaining and developing new concepts in mathematics lessons (Stigler, Gallimore, & Hiebert, 2000). Some important lessons that can be learned from international studies of teaching are described in the Focus on Teaching box on page 10 and 11.

▓ FIGURE 1.4

Average Percentages of Concepts in Eighth-Grade Mathematics Lessons That Were Stated vs. Developed
International studies show that teachers differ in the amount of time spent developing and explaining. Differences in instructional approaches may explain why Japanese children perform better on international assessments than American children.
Source: National Center of Educational Statistics (1995).

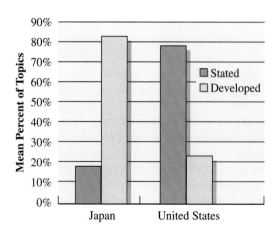

Schools not only affect students' academic achievement but also influence the way they organize their thoughts and cognition. Cross-cultural research has helped psychologists to disentangle the extent to which advances in cognitive functioning are related to formal schooling or to age differences (Cole, 2006). Individuals with more formal schooling are better at remembering disconnected bits of information, and they spontaneously engage in cognitive processes that lead to better recall of information, such as rehearsal and organizational strategies. Additionally, schooled individuals are more likely to sort objects into abstract categories (tools and food items) than into functional groups (e.g., knife with apple, shovel with potato). Schooling also influences the ability of individuals to perceive abstract visual-spatial relations (e.g., mental rotation of objects) and to make figure-ground discriminations (e.g., find hidden objects in puzzles). Taken together, cross-cultural research suggests that formal, Western-style schooling fosters a certain way of thinking, reasoning, and problem solving (Cole, 2006; Rogoff, 1981).

In addition to cognitive development, schools have a strong influence on students' social and emotional development. The quality of children's school experiences influences a wide range of outcomes, including vocational aspirations, feelings of competency and self-worth, academic motivation, identity formation, peer relations, racial attitudes, gender-role beliefs, and even standards of right and wrong. We will discuss many of these influences in later chapters. A few examples include:

- Head Start programs for economically disadvantaged preschool children can help offset some of the effects of poverty, such as truancy, high school dropout, teenage pregnancy, and unemployment.
- Children who are rejected by their peers in school are at greater risk for later psychological disturbance and criminal behavior.
- Children become less intrinsically motivated to learn and less confident of their abilities as they progress in school.
- Cooperative learning programs, if properly implemented, can promote positive race relations and increase acceptance of handicapped students.
- Schools that foster high self-esteem, academic success, and sense of belonging can reduce the likelihood of emotional problems, behavioral disturbance, and delinquency.

At this point in the history of child development research, the question is no longer *whether* schools influence children's development, but rather *what* types of schools or schooling experiences exert a positive influence. Many educational professionals enter education to make a difference in the lives of young people. As we shall see, there is a large knowledge base that can help educators create a learning environment that promotes young people's academic achievement and well-being.

Current Status of Children and Adolescents

Increases in the Population of Schoolchildren

During what was know as the "baby boom" period following World War II (1946 to 1964), there was a dramatic increase in the number of children in the United States. Fluctuations in child population over the last 50 years can be seen in Figure 1.5 on page 12. Enrollment in public schools peaked in the early 1970s. From 1971 to 1984, the school-age population declined by 10 percent, but enrollment in public schools started to increase again and hit record enrollment levels. In 2003, the number of children under the age of 18 was estimated to be about 73 million (Federal Interagency Forum of Child and Family Statistics, 2005).

Focus on
Teaching

Learning from the World's Teachers

James Stigler and his colleagues conducted a videotape study of mathematics classrooms as part of the Third International Mathematics and Science Study (TIMSS) (Stigler, Gonzales, Kawanaka, Knoll, & Serrano, 1999). Previous large-scale international studies relied on questionnaires to collect information about teaching practices and student learning. The TIMSS Videotape Study was the first of its kind to videotape national samples of teachers teaching in their classrooms. The study focused on eighth-grade mathematics classrooms in three countries: Germany (50 classrooms), Japan (50 classrooms), and the United States (100 classrooms). The summary that follows focuses on comparisons between American and Japanese classes and presents some important lessons for educators. For a more detailed account of this study, see *The Teaching Gap* (1999) by J. W. Stigler and J. Hiebert. As you read these lessons, it is important to keep in mind that Japan and the United States have very different economic, political, and educational systems that need to be considered when making cross-cultural comparisons. For a critique of cross-national comparisons, see *Manufactured Crisis* (1995) by D. C. Berliner and D. J. Biddle.

Lesson One: A Focus on Teaching Methods Is Essential for Improving Education

Many policy makers and educational reformers in the United States view improvements in the quality and competence of teachers as critical for improving student achievement and learning. Although variability in teacher competence within countries was evident in the TIMSS Videotape Study, cultural differences in *teach-*

ing methods were considerably greater and more influential. Students' daily experiences in the classroom are mainly determined by the quality of the teaching methods used. Many highly trained and competent American teachers of mathematics employ limited methods that, for the most part, focus on a narrow range of *procedural skills*. As a result, American students spend most of their time in mathematics classes acquiring isolated skills through repeated practice. In contrast, teachers in Japan teach mathematics in a deeper way: They teach for *conceptual understanding*. Their students spend as much time solving challenging problems as they do practicing skills.

Lesson Two: Teaching Is a Cultural Activity

Teaching is influenced by a small and tacit set of cultural beliefs about how students learn, about what role teachers play in the classroom, and about the nature of their subject matter. Although teaching methods may vary within a culture, there is a shared set of cultural beliefs and expectations that underlie teaching. In part, this is explained by the fact that teachers enter their profession with an image of teaching that they have constructed from their many years as a student.

The Videotape Study revealed that mathematics in American classrooms is taught as a set of isolated facts, procedures, or skills to be learned incrementally, piece by piece. The teacher's role is to break down complex tasks into manageable pieces and to provide plenty of opportunities for practice. When students get confused or frustrated, teachers must quickly assist students by providing information to get them back on track. Many teachers

The number of children under the age of 18 in the United States is expected to rise to approximately 80 million by the year 2020.

Increases in the Ethnic Diversity of Schoolchildren

One of the most important demographic trends in the last 25 years is the increased racial and ethnic diversity of America's children. In 1980, nearly 75 percent of all children in this country were non-Hispanic whites. By the year 2010, this group is expected to constitute just over learned mathematics this way, and many parents expect their children to learn mathematics the same way they did.

By contrast, mathematics teaching in Japan reflects a different set of cultural beliefs. Japanese teachers want their students to see relationships between mathematical ideas and concepts. They believe that students learn best by first struggling to solve mathematics problems, then participating in discussions about different problem solutions. The teacher's role in the classroom is to find challenging problems to begin a lesson and to observe how their students solve problems on their own for follow-up discussions. Frustration and confusion are viewed as a natural part of the learning process, and Japanese teachers encourage students to keep struggling in the face of difficulty. They may offer hints to support students' progress, but they refrain from telling or showing students how to solve the problem.

Lesson Three: There Are No "Quick Fixes" for Improving Education

Perhaps the most important lesson of the TIMMS Videotape Study is that there are no "quick fixes" or "magic bullets" to improve education. Despite decades of educational reform in the United States, research suggests that classroom teaching has changed little during this time. By contrast, teaching practices in Japan have changed markedly over the last 50 years. What accounts for this difference?

Whereas American educators have sought major changes within a short period of time, Japanese educators have instituted a system of educational reform that leads to gradual, incremental improvement over time. In Japan,

teachers are not considered competent because they have graduated from college or have completed a standardized test of teacher competency. Japanese teachers are expected to participate in school-based professional development once they enter the teaching profession. *Kounaikenshuu* is the word used to describe the continuous process of school-based professional development in Japan.

One of the most important components of *Kounaikenshuu* is what is known as "lesson study" (*jugyou kenkyuu*), in which groups of teachers work on improving one or several "research lessons." Lesson study involves identifying a problem that poses a challenge to students, and planning, with teacher colleagues, a lesson to achieve a particular learning goal. The lesson is taught by one of the teachers in the lesson-study group, after the other teachers have helped to prepare the design and materials for the lesson. The lesson is then observed by other members of the group. On the basis of the group's observations and discussion of the lesson, the lesson may be revised and taught again. Rather than focusing on a particular weakness of a teacher, group discussions focus on lesson design and teaching methods. Once the lesson-study group has successfully designed and implemented a lesson, it is then shared with other educators. Some Japanese schools may host a "lesson fair" at the end of the school year and invite teachers from other schools to observe the research lessons they have produced in different subjects. Compared with teachers in the United States, Japanese teachers who participate in lesson studies view themselves as contributing to the development of knowledge about teaching as well as contributing to their own professional development.

Source: Adapted from Stigler & Hiebert (1999).

half (60 percent) of the U.S. child population. Prior to 1997, African Americans were the largest minority group in the United States. Currently, African Americans and Latinos represent approximately 35 percent of the child population in the United States (Federal Interagency Forum on Child and Family Statistics, 2005). These numbers are followed by Asian Americans at 4 percent and Native Americans at 1 percent. The number of Latino children has increased faster than that of any other racial or ethnic group. Figure 1.6 on page 12 presents a portrait of the kindergarten class of 1998/1999. As you can see, there is considerable diversity in the children coming to school. By the year 2020, more than one

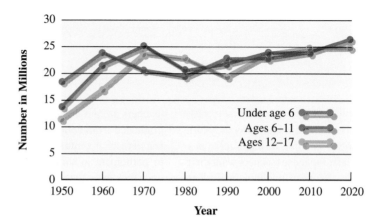

■ FIGURE 1.5

Number of Children in the United States: 1950 to 2020 (Projected)

Student enrollments in schools have fluctuated over the last 50 years.

Source: Federal Interagency Forum on Child and Family Statistics (2005).

Portrait of America's Kindergartners: Class of 1998/1999

In the fall of 1998, approximately 4 million children were attending kindergarten in the United States, many for the first time. According to a national study by the U.S. Department of Education, the ethnic backgrounds of the kindergarten class of 1998/1999 were 58 percent white, 19 percent Latino, 15 percent African American, 3 percent Asian, 2 percent American Indian or Alaskan Native, and 1 percent Hawaiian Native or Pacific Islander. A majority of America's kindergartners (75 percent) live with two parents, and nearly half have mothers with some college education or a college degree. Other key findings of this study were:

- Prior to kindergarten, 3 out of 5 children received care on a regular basis from someone other than a parent.

- As children enter kindergarten for the first time, parents report that 92 percent are eager to learn and 75 percent persist at tasks very often.

- Nearly half of parents report that a family member reads or sings to their kindergarten-age child on a regular basis.

- Approximately 66 percent of first-time kindergarten students can recognize their letters, and 94 percent can recognize numbers and count to 10.

- Teachers report that 75 percent of kindergartners are able to make friends, to join others in play, and to form friendships. Fewer than 10 percent have difficulty getting along with others.

- About 12 percent of boys and 11 percent of girls have a body mass index that places them at risk for becoming overweight.

It is important to note that the above characteristics varied by family type, income level, ethnicity, language spoken at home, and maternal education.

■ FIGURE 1.6

Portrait of America's Kindergartners: Class of 1998/1999

Source: National Center for Educational Statistics (2000a).

in five children in the United States will be of Hispanic origin. The Asian American child population is also expected to increase from 4 percent to 5 percent by 2010 (Federal Interagency Forum on Child and Family Statistics, 2005). Figure 1.7 shows the growing diversity of the school-age population.

A major contributor to the increased diversity of America's schoolchildren is immigration. The United States is a nation of immigrants, but rates of immigration have varied considerably over different periods of our history. Currently, the United States is experiencing a period of high immigration, which began in the 1960s. By 1995, the number of foreign-born persons residing in the United States reached 25 million, and this figure has now risen to 33.5 million (Larsen, 2004). Before 1965, the majority of legal immigrants came from Canada and Europe. However, Asia and Latin America are now the major sources of immigration into the United States.

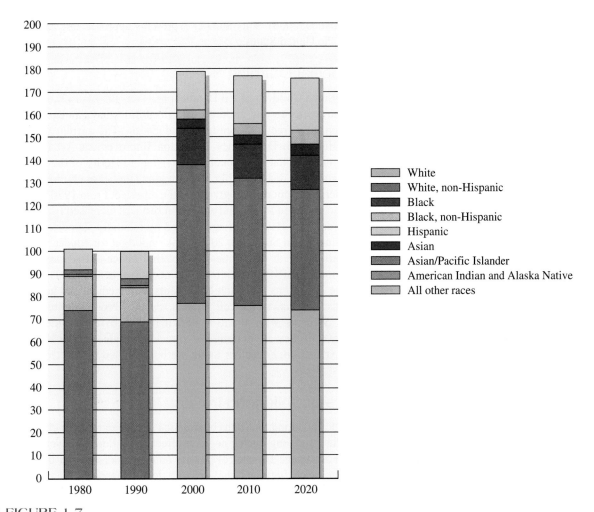

■ FIGURE 1.7
Changing Demographics of U.S. School Population
There is a growing diversity in America's school population. By the year 2020, one out of five children will be of Hispanic origin.
Sources: Federal Interagency Forum on Child and Family Statistics (2005).

Immigrants tend to settle in areas where there are people of similar backgrounds and nationalities. In the 1990s, the majority of the immigrants who arrived in the United States settled in only six states: California, New York, Texas, Florida, New Jersey, and Illinois. In addition, according to 1990 census data, more than 90 percent of the foreign-born population resides in metropolitan areas, including Los Angeles, New York, Miami, Anaheim, Chicago, Washington, D.C., Houston, and San Francisco (National Research Council, 1997). However, geographic concentrations of immigrants are not static. One recent study of foreign-born settlement patterns suggests a decline in concentrated immigrant urban enclaves and more integration into native-born communities (Lichter & Johnson, 2006). For example, the 2000 U.S. Census noted that 297 counties across the United States had foreign-born populations exceeding 5 percent for the first time (Lichter & Johnson, 2006).

Due to recent increases in the number of immigrants living in the United States, schools are becoming more culturally and linguistically diverse. The number of children who spoke a language other than English at home or who had difficulty speaking English was 3 million in 2003, an increase from 1.3 million in 1979 (Federal Interagency Forum on Child and Family Statistics, 2005). This number represents approximately 5 percent of school-age children in the United States.

Children with Special Learning Needs

Beginning in 1975, with the Children of All Handicapped Act (PL 94–142), a number of laws have been enacted to ensure that children with disabilities have an equal opportunity, like other children, to a free and appropriate education. The current form of this legislation, the Individual with Disabilities Education Improvement Act (IDEA), includes a zero-reject mandate. That is, no matter the type and severity of the disability, a free public education cannot be denied. Table 1.1 shows the number of children (ages 3 to 21 years) served in federally supported programs for the disabled. From 1976 to 2004, the number of children who qualified for special education services increased from 8 percent to 14 percent of children, 3 to 21 years of age, served by federally supported programs (National Center of Educational Statistics, 2005). It is important for educators to understand that not only children with disabilities are covered under IDEA. As part of the Vocational Rehabilitation Act of 1973, children with medical or health needs are covered under Section 504. The conditions may include students with medical and health conditions, such as diabetes, asthma, sickle-cell anemia, cystic fibrosis, depression, drug addiction, and so on. Students with attention deficit hyperactivity disorders are also served under Section 504, if they are not eligible to receive services under IDEA. Thus, as discussed in the next section, educators today are being called to work with a more diverse population of students.

Changes in Rates of Childhood Poverty

Another significant factor affecting the status of America's children today is child poverty, which has both immediate and long-lasting negative effects on children's development. As you can see in Figure 1.8 on page 16, rates of poverty among children under the age of 18 have fluctuated since the early 1980s, and these poverty levels depend on the racial or ethnic background of the child. Childhood poverty reached a peak in 1993, when more than 22 percent of children under the age of 18 lived in poverty. In 2004, 13 million children (18 percent) were poor. Children continue to represent a large portion (35 percent) of the poor population in the United States. Poverty rates are the highest for children under the age of 18 than for any other age group. Additionally, 8 percent of children in 2003 lived in families

TABLE 1.1 Children with Disabilities, Ages 3 to 21, Served in Federally Supported Programs for the Disabled, 2003–2004

Disability	Number	Percent of Identified Students
Specific learning disability	2,831,000	42.7
Speech or language impairment	1,441,000	21.7
Mental retardation	593,000	8.9
Emotional disturbance	489,000	7.4
Hearing impairments	79,000	1.2
Orthopedic impairments	77,000	1.2
Other health impairments	464,000	7.0
Visual impairments	28,000	.4
Multiple disabilities	140,000	2.1
Deaf-blindness	2,000	0.0
Autism and traumatic brain injury	166,000	2.8
Developmental delay	305,000	4.6
All disabilities	6,633,000	100.0

Source: National Center of Educational Statistics (2005).

Approximately 14 percent of young people between the ages of 3 and 21 years are served by federally supported programs for the disabled. Students with a specific learning disability represent the largest group served by federal programs.

with total incomes of less than half of the poverty line, or $9,403 a year for a family of four (Federal Interagency Forum on Child and Family Statistics, 2005). Overall, the United States has the highest child poverty rate of any industrialized country. U.S. child poverty rates are two to three times higher than those reported by the United Kingdom, Canada, Germany, Sweden, or France.

Contrary to cultural stereotypes, a majority of poor children are non-Hispanic whites. In actual numbers, approximately 9 million white children live in poverty. Poverty rates, however, tend to be higher among African American and Hispanic populations. Because African American and Hispanic children make up a smaller proportion of the total child population, the percentage of poor children in these groups is considerably higher than that of non-Hispanic whites, as shown in Figure 1.8 on page 16. Whereas 10 percent of the total population of white children in 2003 were poor, the comparable figures were 34 percent for African American children and 30 percent for Latino children (Federal Interagency Forum on Child and Family Statistics, 2005).

Changes in Family Structures

Another significant change affecting the status of children today is the rise of single-headed households. The number of parents living with a child is generally linked to quality of care and amount of economic resources available to that child. Research indicates that children who live with just one parent are more likely to have family incomes below the poverty line. The percentage of American children living with two parents has declined from 85 percent in 1970 to 68 percent in 2004 (Federal Interagency Forum on Child and Family Statistics, 2005). We will examine some of these changes more closely in Chapter 8.

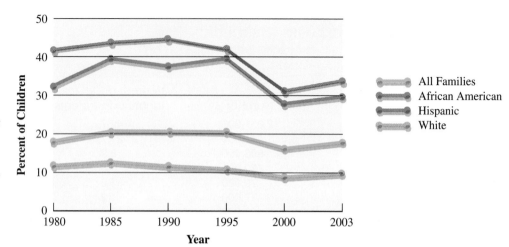

■ FIGURE 1.8
*Percent of U.S.
Children Living
in Poverty by
Ethnic Group*
Poverty rates for children
differ by ethnic group.
Poverty rates are 34 percent
for African American
children and 30 percent for
Latino children.
Source: Federal Interagency
Forum on Child and Family
Statistics (2005).

Implications for Schools

A summary portrait of America's children today is presented in Figure 1.9. How will the current status of children and youth affect schools? First, as mentioned, there are record numbers of elementary and secondary students enrolling in private and public schools today. Since 1990 school enrollment figures have increased by 19 percent. Between 2002 and 2014, a further increase of 4 percent is expected, with increases projected in both public and private schools (Hussar, 2005). Increases in the school population are placing an added burden on schools that are already dealing with overcrowded classrooms, rundown facilities, and teacher shortages. In addition, statistics indicate that the majority of teachers today are in their mid-forties, and this group of teachers is expected to retire within the next 5 to 10 years (National Governor's Association, 2000).

As described, an increasingly diverse group of schoolchildren is coming to school. One of the challenges for educators will be to provide equal educational opportunities to students from various cultural backgrounds. Despite 30 years of desegregation and bilingual education legislation, national test scores of Hispanic and African American students lag behind those of white and Asian students. For example, the most recent NAEP assessment showed that the average scores of 17-year-old African American students were about the same as those of 13-year-old white students in mathematics and reading (Perie & Moran, 2005). Compared with white and Asian students, African American and Hispanic students are less likely to take advanced courses in mathematics and science (National Center for Educational Statistics, 2000b), and they have lower graduation rates.

The educational progress of some students is complicated by language barriers. As has been mentioned, approximately 5 percent of schoolchildren speak a language other than English at home. The majority of these children speak Spanish at home, and most language-minority children, approximately 3 million, are found in the elementary grades (Kindler, 2002; Federal Interagency Forum on Child and Family Statistics, 2005). As the Latino population expands, more and more teachers will be working with students with limited English proficiency, or English-language learners. However, only 12.5 percent of teachers possess 8 hours of more of recent training to work with this population (Reeves, 2006). At present, teachers and administrators are not sufficiently prepared to teach these language-minority children.

More important, as has been discussed, a disproportionate number of both Hispanic and African American families are poor. Poverty rates also tend to be more persistent

A Portrait of America's Children

One in two preschoolers has a mother in the labor force.

One in two will live in a single-parent family at some point in his or her childhood.

One in two will never complete college.

One in three is born to unmarried parents.

One in three will be poor at some point in his or her childhood.

One in three is behind a year or more in school.

One in four lives with only one parent.

One in four was born poor.

One in five is poor now.

One in five was born to a mother who did not graduate from high school.

One in five has a foreign-born mother.

One in six is born to a mother who did not receive prenatal care in the first 3 months of her pregnancy.

One in six has no health insurance.

One in eight will never graduate from high school.

One in eight was born to a teenage mother.

One in 12 lives at less than half the poverty level.

One in 12 has a disability.

One in 13 was born with low birth weight.

One in 24 lives with neither parent.

■ FIGURE 1.9
A Portrait of America's Children
Source: Children's Defense Fund (2000).

among ethnic minority families. One study showed that 24 percent of African American children who were under age 4 in 1968 lived in poverty for 10 of 15 years. The comparable figure for white children was less than 1 percent (McLoyd, 1990).

The negative consequences of poverty on children's development are well documented (Bradley & Corwyn, 2002; Duncan & Brooks-Gunn, 1997; Sherman, 1997). Poor children are more likely to be born prematurely or at a low birth weight, and they are at greater risk for malnutrition and health problems during early development. Poor children are twice as likely as other children to have impaired vision, hearing problems, and anemia. Many poor children live in substandard houses where they are exposed daily to structural, electrical, and sanitation hazards.

Poor families also make up a large percentage of homeless people in the United States. It is estimated that 1.35 million school-aged children are homeless (Institute for Children and Poverty, 2005), but only 77 percent attend school regularly (U.S. Department of Education, 2002). The Focus on Teaching box on the next page presents a summary of different school programs for homeless children.

In terms of school performance, poor children are likely to experience many educational setbacks. By the time they enter school, poor children are already behind their

Focus on
Teaching

School Programs for Homeless Children

The homeless population, once stereotyped as the fate of unemployed alcoholics or schizophrenic bag ladies, has experienced a demographic shift, leaving an estimated over half a million children sleeping homeless each night (U.S. Department of Education, 2000). Homeless families face a number of barriers upon enrolling their school-age children in school, and if enrollment is in fact allowed, the children may experience difficulties of acceptance, misplacement, and misunderstanding among peers and teachers.

The U.S. Congress passed the Stewart B. McKinney Homeless Assistance Act of 1987 to facilitate the enrollment of homeless children in public schools. The act makes provisions for each state to have an Office for Coordination of Education of Homeless Children and Youth, and to review and revise practices that impede homeless children's access to public school. Each state is also required to have an approved plan for addressing problems associated with the children's enrollment, attendance, and success in school (U.S. Department of Education, 1999). With the increasing prevalence of homeless children in schools today, it is essential that comprehensive support programs are available to help schools address the emotional, social, developmental, educational, or health problems that often afflict homeless children. Some examples of such school programs that can serve as models for further development include:

- **City Park School in Dallas, Texas.** Staff members have been successful in assisting new students in feeling accepted, and they provide support for academic

and psychosocial needs. There is a strong emphasis on basic skills. School supplies are given to the students, and parents are referred to medical and social services.

- **Our House, in Decatur, Georgia.** This agency provides free, quality day care to homeless children between the ages of 2 months and 6 years who live in shelters in the county. Children are cared for on an emergency basis until they can begin school. The program provides a safe space, a healthy diet, health care, cognitive stimulation, and emotional support to young children.
- **Grace Hill Family Center in St. Louis, Missouri.** This program provides shelter-based educational services for homeless parents and children. The program's first priority is to enroll shelter children in school. A peer counselor works with school officials and families to place children in preferred schools, ensuring that records are transferred, transportation is arranged, and teachers are informed of any special needs. Volunteers provide child care for children or parents looking for employment and tutoring for school-aged children.
- **First Place in Seattle, Washington.** This elementary school project is designed to meet the educational and emotional needs of homeless children. Space as well as transportation from shelters is provided by the Seattle public schools. The program operates in two classrooms for children from kindergarten through sixth grade. The program offers nutritious meals, academic work, and a quiet time for reading. Teachers give individual attention, counseling, and extra help with schoolwork when needed.

Source: Stronge & Reed-Victor (2000).

middle-class classmates on scores in standardized tests of achievement and intelligence (Children's Defense Fund, 2005, National Center for Educational Statistics, 2000b). Illness and malnutrition can cause children to be less attentive, less motivated, and more irritable, which can lead to behavioral and learning problems in the classroom. As a result, a disproportionate number of low-income children are placed in special education or are retained in a grade.

The educational problems of poor children are further complicated by schools they attend. A relatively high percent attend poor schools with fewer financial and material resources to help these students. For example, teachers in poor schools are two to four times more likely to report inadequate supplies of books, learning materials, and audiovisual equipment, including computers (Sherman, 1997). By the time they reach adolescence, children from low-income families are more likely to drop out of school early. Rates of school truancy, juvenile delinquency, and teenage pregnancy are also higher among children from poor families.

It is clear that poverty can have negative pervasive effects on children. However, many children are resilient and able to overcome tremendous obstacles. That is, not all poor children grow up to be high school dropouts, juvenile delinquents, or teenage parents. As we shall see later, some children are less vulnerable than others to the effects of poverty. Parents, schools, and resources in the community can protect children from the devastating effects of poverty.

Perspectives on Children's Development

So far we have discussed various reasons why teachers need a working knowledge of children's development and of the status of children today. In this section, we will begin to examine the theories child development experts use to explain children's development. First, we will discuss how theorists define development and what they view as the important issues of debate. Next, we will look at five different perspectives on children's development: biological, psychoanalytic, behavioral, cognitive, and contextual. This section serves as an introduction to the theories that will be discussed in later chapters.

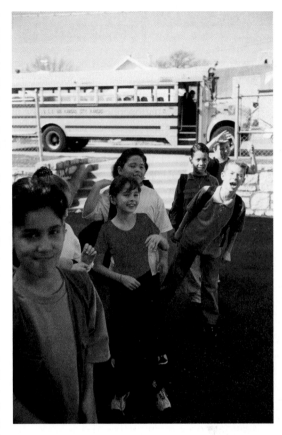

The school population in the United Stated is more diverse than ever before.
Source: © O'Brien Productions/CORBIS.

Why so many theories of development? Suppose you have a girl in your classroom who frequently starts fights with classmates. How would you explain her behavior? There are a number of possible explanations. Perhaps she is not getting enough care and affection at home and is therefore acting out to get attention. Perhaps she has not learned how to control her emotions. Perhaps she has not learned more socially acceptable ways of relating to others. Or, it may be that this student is watching too many violent television shows and is simply imitating the behavior of television characters. Each of these explanations suggests a different form of intervention. Developmental theories provide several frameworks for understanding and interpreting children's behavior. Generally, there are multiple explanations for a particular pattern of behavior, and most theorists agree that one theory of development is not sufficient to explain all we know and observe about children. Therefore, it is best to have a repertoire of different child development theories from which to draw.

Definitions and Issues

Development as used in this text refers to changes in the child that occur *over time*. Although there are differences among theorists, most agree that development represents systematic and successive changes that enhance a child's overall adaptation to the environment. Development is not just any change that occurs as the child matures. To be labeled *developmental,*

Focus on
Research

Two early philosophers, John Locke and Jean-Jacques Rousseau, are considered the philosophical forefathers of developmental psychology. From the eighteenth century until today, these philosophers have greatly influenced our beliefs about the nature of children and how they should be educated. Current debates concerning the role of education in children's lives can be traced back to these early philosophers.

John Locke (1632–1704)

English philosopher John Locke proposed that the child's mind is a blank slate, or *tabula rasa*, on which experience makes its imprint. Children are neither good nor bad; they become that way by virtue of how they are treated. In his book *Some Thoughts Concerning Education,* Locke (1902) compared the formation of the child's mind and attitudes to the "fountains of some rivers, when a gentle application of the hand turns the flexible waters into channels, that make them take quite contrary courses" (pp. 1–2). Locke recognized that children were born with different temperaments and propensities, but he believed that a child could be infinitely improved and perfected through experience, humane treatment, and education. Locke further believed that adults could mold children's moral character and intellect by conditioning them to have the right habits. In Locke's conception of children we find the roots of behavioral approaches to education, which emphasize the importance of reward and punishment in shaping children's behavior. Key to this perspective is the assumption that children are mostly a product of their environment.

Jean-Jacques Rousseau (1712–1778)

Jean-Jacques Rousseau, a Swiss-born philosopher, introduced a romantic conception of childhood. For Rousseau, a child is born in a state of natural goodness. Adults should not shape children forcibly but protect them from the pressures of society and allow them to develop naturally. Rousseau (1762/1911) presented his views on education in *Emile*, a story about a boy and his tutor. Emile passes through several stages of development, and the tutor provides experiences that are appropriate to his needs at the time. Rousseau believed that each dimension of development (physical, mental, social, and moral) followed a particular schedule that should be respected and protected. According to Rousseau, children

The Educational Legacy of Locke and Rousseau

are incapable of true reasoning until the age of 12. During the early period of development, children should be permitted to learn through discovery and experience. In Rousseau's conception of the child, we find the roots of child-centered approaches to education. Key to this perspective is the assumption that the curriculum must evolve from the natural capacities and interests of the child, and it must foster the child's progression toward higher stages of development.

Locke, Rousseau, and Education Today

Locke and Rousseau expressed very different views about the role of education in children's lives. The concept of the child as a blank slate allowed early educational reformers to "dream of schools as institutions for creating a perfect society" (Spring, 1994, p. 29). Because Locke's conception of the child stressed the role of the environment in children's development, it continues to have a powerful influence on education. Today, traces of Locke's "malleable child" can be found in educational reforms that call for higher test scores, tougher promotion standards, stricter discipline, more homework, and better-trained workers.

Rousseau's romantic view of children had the most influence on educational reformers of the twentieth century who rejected the emphasis on passivity, conformity, and authority in schools (Spring, 1994). Elements of Rousseau can be found in the writing of John Dewey (1859–1952), one of the most influential educational reformers of this century. In *The Child and Curriculum*, Dewey expressed the basic principles of child-centered education:

> The child is the starting point, the center, and the end. His development, his growth, is the ideal. It alone furnishes the standard. (Archambault, 1964, pp. 342–343)

Dewey's approach to education emphasized student interest, student activity, group work, real-life learning experiences, and cooperation. Dewey's philosophy influenced educational reforms in the progressive period of the early 1900s and in the mid-1960s to early 1970s, when open classrooms, discovery learning, and other activity-based curricula were introduced. In recent years, the view that education should be appropriate to a child's stage of development has influenced efforts to reform public school programs for young children (Bredekamp & Copple, 1997) and young adolescents (Carnegie Council on Adolescent Development, 1989).

the changes must follow a logical or orderly pattern that moves toward greater complexity and enhances survival. Developmental changes in language, for example, involve more complex forms of speech and language that enable children to better communicate with people in their environment.

For the purposes of this discussion, we define a **theory** as a set of general statements (rules, assumptions, propositions, or principles) used to explain facts. When applied to child development, a theory provides a framework for observing, interpreting, and explaining changes in the child over time. More specifically stated, the three purposes of a developmental theory are to describe how children differ from one age to the next, describe how different aspects of development are interrelated (e.g., influence of cognitive development on peer relations), and explain why development proceeds in a certain direction.

It would be easy to understand children's development if there were just one overarching theory. But, as suggested earlier, there are several different theories of development. Each theory gives the "facts" of development a different meaning by organizing them differently, focusing on different aspects of development, and emphasizing different causal factors. For example, some theories focus on intellectual development, whereas other theories focus on physical or social development. Theories of development also differ with respect to the position they take on certain basic core issues. Among the issues most relevant to educators are the following:

Nature versus nurture. To what extent is development a function of innate biological processes, environmental conditions, or some interaction of the two?

Stability versus plasticity. Are there critical periods in which a child must have certain social or cognitive experiences in order to develop normally? Are developmental processes highly malleable and open to change at any point in the course of development?

Continuity versus discontinuity. Is development a continuous process that occurs gradually in small increments? Is development a series of discrete stages that represent major and abrupt transformations in functioning?

Passive versus active child. What is a child's role in the developmental process? Is the child a passive organism that is simply shaped by genetic or environmental influences? Are children active agents who shape, control, and direct their own development?

Endpoint versus no endpoint. What is it that develops? Is there an endpoint to development? Do all children follow a universal sequence of development?

As a general introduction to the theories that will be discussed in later chapters, we will compare different theoretical perspectives on development with regard to their positions on the basic issues just described. An understanding of these issues is important for two reasons. First, debates about children's development often play a major role in educational reform movements. As described in the Focus on Research box on the previous page, educational reformers often share different beliefs about the nature of children and how they should be educated. Second, we have seen that teachers use different theories to explain children's behavior and to make instructional decisions. These theories, in turn, involve different assumptions about the nature of the child, the sources of development, the nature of development, and so forth. In adopting one or the other view, teachers need to be cognizant of the assumptions they are making about children's development.

Biological Theories

Early pioneers in developmental psychology explained children's development in terms of innate biological processes. Human characteristics "bloom" like a flower according to a predetermined biological timetable. A child goes through invariant, predictable stages of growth and development. According to this perspective, the environment provides the basic nutrients for growth, but it plays little or no role in determining the sequence of development. Moreover, children passively respond and adjust to the changes that occur with age.

Biological theories have been used to explain changes in height, weight, language, mental abilities, motor skills, and many other characteristics. One of the most influential maturational theorists in education is Arnold Gesell (1880–1961) who, along with his colleagues at the Yale Child Development Clinic, established age norms for growth and behavioral change in 10 major areas of development (Gesell & Ilg, 1946; Gesell, Ilg, & Ames, 1956). Gesell and his colleagues also introduced the concept of *readiness.* Learning could occur only if a child was biologically "ready." If a child is unable to perform the activities predicted to be achievable at a specific age, he or she simply needs more time to mature. This view comes closest to the *nativist* theory of development described previously in the section on teachers' beliefs.

A more contemporary version of this biological perspective on development can be found in the study of **behavioral genetics.** Geneticists tell us that many of our physical characteristics (e.g., body type, eye and hair color, skin color) are inherited. Moreover, many of the traits that make us uniquely human (e.g., ability to stand on two legs, speak, think abstractly) are also inherited. We also know that some forms of mental retardation, such as Down syndrome, are caused by chromosomal abnormalities. Behavioral geneticists study the degree to which psychological traits (sociability, aggression, criminality, affective disorders) and mental abilities (intelligence or creative talents) are inherited. Just as many of our physical characteristics are determined by heredity, behavioral geneticists argue that many of our psychological attributes also have a genetic component. For example, as we will discuss in Chapter 4, some researchers have argued that as much as 60 percent of the variation in intelligence within a given population is due to genetic differences (Hernnstein & Murray, 1994). The comparable statistic for personality traits can range from 5 to 40 percent. In reviewing research on behavioral genetics, one researcher concluded: "Genetic influence is so ubiquitous and pervasive that a shift in emphasis is warranted: Ask not what is heritable, ask what is not heritable" (Plomin, 1989, p. 108).

Although research on behavioral genetics suggests that many of a child's traits and abilities may be influenced by biological factors, most theorists today recognize the important roles of the environment and experience in this developmental process. A child born with a genetic predisposition, such as shyness, may not necessarily grow up to be a shy adult. The actual emergence or appearance of this genetic trait will depend on the child's environment. However, a child's genetic traits can shape that environment in several interesting ways. Shy children, for example, may elicit different reactions from others or choose to engage in more solitary activities than highly sociable children. Therefore, the child's genotype and environment are often strongly related (Plomin, DeFries, & Loehlin, 1977; Scarr & McCartney, 1983). In Chapter 2, we will discuss in more detail how genetic and environmental factors can work together to influence children's development. Current research on behavioral genetics suggests that development is a complex interplay between genes and the environment (Plomin, 1990).

Psychoanalytic Theories

Psychoanalytic theories focus on developmental changes in the self and personality. Psychoanalytic theorists such as Sigmund Freud (1856–1939) and Erik Erikson (1902–1994) saw development as a *discontinuous process* that follows a series of discrete stages. At each stage of maturation, certain drives, needs, or conflicts emerge that influence the way a child relates to the environment. These stages are summarized in Table 1.2. Each stage builds on the previous one and represents *qualitative changes* in the child's personality structures or sense of self.

According to psychoanalytic theories, the ways in which children deal with their needs at different ages set the patterns for personality development. For example, toddlers who are harshly punished for accidents during toilet training could develop feelings of shame and self-doubt that affect later development. Erikson, more than Freud, recognized that societies have agreed-upon ways of meeting a child's needs, but maturation still determines when certain personality dimensions emerge. In addition, Erikson believed that development is a lifelong process, whereas Freud maintained that the basic structures of the child's personality are laid down within the first 5 years of life. In other words, there is a **critical period** for personality development.

Behavioral Theories

At the opposite end of the nature–nurture continuum are behaviorist perspectives on development. Behaviorists maintain that developmental changes in behavior are influenced by the environment, and the major mechanisms of development are principles of learning. A child's level of maturation was of little importance to early theorists, but most behaviorists today take a more moderate position, which recognizes certain biological constraints on development (P. Miller, 1993).

Behavioral theories have been used to explain children's development in several areas. John Watson (1878–1958), known as the father of behaviorism, examined the role of **classical conditioning** in the development of children's emotions. Watson conditioned a young boy, Albert, to be afraid of a white rat by making a loud noise whenever the rat appeared. The child's innate fear of loud noises (unconditioned response) became associated with the rat (conditioned response). After several learning trials, Albert showed the same fearful reaction when the rat alone appeared.

B. F. Skinner (1904–1990) argued that parents influence their child's language development through the principles of **instrumental** or **operant conditioning.** When babies

TABLE 1.2   Stage Views of Development

Age	Freud	Erikson	Piaget
Infancy	Oral Anal	Trust vs. mistrust Autonomy vs. shame	Sensorimotor
Early childhood	Phallic	Initiative vs. guilt	Preoperations
Middle childhood	Latency	Industry vs. inferiority	Concrete operations
Adolescence	Genital	Identity vs. role confusion Intimacy vs. isolation	Formal operations

begin to babble, parents react positively, repeat sounds, and reinforce the child for attempting to communicate. Parents respond more positively to sounds that resemble words than to sounds they cannot recognize as words. According to Skinner, this differential reinforcement increases the likelihood that certain sounds will be made again by the child. Behaviorists argue that the meaning of words and rules of grammar are acquired through the same principles of reinforcement.

Behaviorists also believe that children acquire new behaviors through the processes of *observation* and *imitation*. That is, children do not have to be explicitly reinforced for a behavior; they can simply observe a model, remember the behavior, and repeat it later. Observational or social learning theories have been used to explain developmental changes in aggression, social skills, sex-role behavior, attitudes, moral judgments, and standards of conduct (Bandura, 1989).

Behaviorists believe development is a gradual, *continuous* process. It represents small, *quantitative changes,* as the child acquires new skills and behaviors. Similar to maturational theories, children have a *passive role* in this developmental process. They simply respond to environmental inputs and store them away for later use. In addition, there is *no critical stage* for developing various cognitive, language, or social skills. If children are deprived of certain experiences early in development, they can acquire these skills later on. According to this view, there is a good deal of plasticity in development. Furthermore, there are no universal patterns of development because inputs are provided by the environment, which can vary from child to child.

Cognitive Theories

Cognitive theorists focus on the ways children construct their own understandings of their environment. Development occurs through the interplay between a child's emerging mental capabilities and his or her environmental experiences. These theories support the belief that both nature and nurture explain children's development. For this reason, the cognitive theories that we will examine represent an *interactional perspective*. That is, development takes place through the interaction of innate and environmental theories. In subsequent chapters, we will study three different cognitive theories of development: cognitive developmental theory, information processing theory, and social learning theory. Each of these theoretical perspectives is introduced here.

Cognitive Developmental Theory

Jean Piaget (1896–1980) is probably the best-known developmental psychologist in education. Piaget proposed that children pass through an invariant sequence of stages, each characterized by qualitatively different ways of organizing information and learning about the world. He divided cognitive development into four distinct stages, which were presented in Table 1.2. Key to this sequence is the development of symbolic thought, which begins in infancy and continues until thought processes are governed by principles of formal logic.

Piaget believed development represented *qualitative changes* in children's cognitive processes and structures. He also believed that all children pass through these cognitive stages in the same order, but not necessarily at the same age. That is, there is a *universal pattern* to children's cognitive development. In keeping with an interactional perspective, Piaget proposed that development takes place through the interaction of innate and environmental factors. As a child matures, new possibilities become available that stimulate further development. These experiences, in turn, are interpreted in terms of what the child already knows. In this way, children play an *active role* in their own development.

Information Processing Theory

Information processing theories provide another interactional view of development. Rather than focusing on how knowledge is organized at various stages of development, these theories focus on the precise steps involved in performing mental tasks. Information processing theorists use the computer as a model of human thinking. As with the computer, data must be entered, processed, and stored in a child's memory. The components of this information processing system are shown in Figure 1.10. The sense organs receive and pass along information, which is then transformed and recorded into memory by the child for later retrieval. According to this perspective, cognitive advances in thinking result from gradual improvements in children's attention, memory, and strategies for acquiring and using information. Therefore, development involves both *quantitative* (increases in amount of information stored) and *qualitative* (new strategies for information storage and retrieval) changes.

In a view similar to Piaget's, information processing theorists maintain that development results from an interplay between information from the environment and the state of a child's information processing system. The child's existing knowledge and cognitive skills influence his or her ability to acquire new understandings. Although information processing theorists recognize the importance of neurological development, they assume that the development of some cognitive skills can be accelerated with training. Numerous investigations have examined how children can be taught to use more sophisticated memory and learning strategies, but the positive effects of this training for young children are often short lived.

Social Learning Theories

Social learning theories help explain how children learn social behaviors, such as acts of helping and caring for others, aggressive tendencies, and behaviors appropriate for their

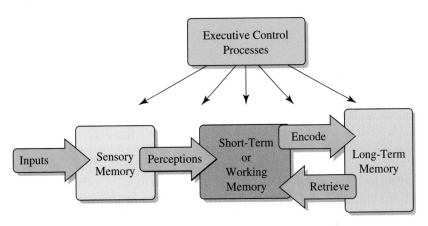

■ FIGURE 1.10
Model of Human Information Processing System

gender. Early social learning theories proposed that children learn new behaviors through observation and imitation. In a reformulation of this theory, referred to as *social-cognitive theory,* Albert Bandura (b. 1925) specified a number of cognitive factors that influence the process of social learning. In order to imitate models, children must be able to process and store information about social behaviors, to anticipate consequences for certain actions, and to regulate their own behavior. As these cognitive processes change with age, children become better able to learn from their social environments.

Similar to Piagetian and information processing approaches, social-cognitive theory maintains that children form mental representations of their social world. For this reason, a child has as much influence on the environment as the environment has on the child. This interplay between the child and the environment is captured in Bandura's concept of **reciprocal determinism** (Bandura, 1986). Children's mental representations of a situation or event influence the way they act and feel, which determines how others perceive and respond to them. These reactions, in turn, influence children's thinking and behavior in subsequent situations. Because social cognitive theory stresses reciprocal relations between a child's internal states (mental representations, perceptions, and emotions) and the environment, it represents an interactional perspective.

Contextual Theories

This last group of theories focuses on the influence of the social and cultural context on children's development. We know from cross-cultural research that there is considerable variability from culture to culture in what children are expected to learn, how they are expected to acquire information and skills, what types of activities children participate in, when children are allowed to participate in those activities, and so on. Contextual theories help to explain these social influences on children's development.

Contextual theorists assume a child has an *active role* in shaping his or her own development. As children mature, they actively seek different social and physical contexts. Activities within these contexts, in turn, change the children, which subsequently changes how they select and respond to activities in the future. However, in contrast to the interactional theories discussed earlier, contextualists emphasize that both the child and the environment are constantly changing, and changes in one often lead to changes in the other. Therefore, there can be *no universal patterns or endpoints* for development. Contextual theories offer a more complex view of development than other developmental theories. According to this perspective, development cannot be separated from the context in which it takes place. A brief description of two theories that fit the contextual framework—social-cultural theory and ecological theory—are presented here.

Social-Cultural Theory

Lev Vygotsky (1896–1934) was one of the first developmentalists to consider the influence of a child's social and cultural context. In his social-cultural theory of language and cognitive development, knowledge is not individually constructed; rather, it is co-constructed between people. Vygotsky believed that children are endowed with certain "elementary functions" (perception, memory, attention, and language) that are transformed into higher mental functions through interactions with others. Vygotsky proposed that talking, thinking, remembering, and problem solving occur first on a social plane between two people. As a child gains new skills and knowledge, the other person involved in an interaction adjusts his or her level of guidance and assistance, which allows the child to assume more and more responsibility for the activity. These social exchanges are subsequently transformed and organized by the child into internal actions and thoughts the child uses to regulate his or her own behavior. Vygotsky believed that development involved *qualitative changes* as the child moves from elementary to higher forms of mental functioning, but he did not specify a set of developmental stages. There are no universal patterns of development in Vygotsky's theory, because cultures differ with respect to goals for children's development.

Vygotsky believed that people structure a child's environment and provide the tools (e.g., language, mathematical symbols, art, writing) for making sense of it. Observe some mothers talking with their 3-year-olds, and you can see Vygotsky's ideas in action. The mothers' speech is slow, simple, and repetitive so that the children can understand what they are saying. Such children are fortunate, because not all mothers talk "baby talk" to their children. When one does, the mother and child are trying to negotiate a shared understanding of language. The child can understand simple sentences under these conditions, but this understanding may not generalize to other language contexts. A key assumption of Vygotsky's theory is that children may be able to demonstrate a higher level of cognitive competence under the guidance of more capable peers and adults.

Ecological Theories

Urie Bronfenbrenner (1917–2005) offers another contextual model of development. He envisions development as embedded in multiple contexts. In his view, "a child's world is organized as a set of nested structures, each inside the next, like a set of Russian dolls" (Bronfenbrenner, 1979, p. 22). As shown in Figure 1.11 on page 28 the child is at the center of this model; the child is born with certain temperamental, mental, and physical characteristics that create the biological context for his or her development. The child, however, does not develop in a vacuum. The next circle represents the child's immediate physical and social environment. It includes physical objects (toys, books, television, computer, etc.), as well as the family, school, peer group, and neighborhood. These settings are all embedded in a broader social and economic context. The outermost circle is the cultural context. It represents the shared beliefs, values, and customs of a culture, as well as subgroups within the culture. This larger context also includes major historical events, such as wars and natural disasters, that affect other ecological contexts.

A major assumption of Bronfenbrenner's bioecological model is that various subsystems (family, school, economic conditions) of this ecological scheme change over the course of development. Change can originate from within the child, as when the child enters puberty or suffers from a severe accident, or it can originate outside the child, as when there is a change in family status or a major historical event such as the Great Depression. Bronfenbrenner (1979) stated, "Whatever the origin, the critical feature of such events is that they alter the existing relation between the person and environment, thus creating a dynamic that may instigate developmental change" (p. 201).

Another major assumption of Bronfenbrenner's ecological model is that changes at one level of the context can influence what occurs at other levels. For example, physical changes at puberty can lead to changes in the child's social relationships with peers, parents, and teachers, but these changes are also influenced by social conditions and by cultural expectations. We mentioned how in different cultures children are expected to assume adult responsibilities when they reach puberty. However, the specific nature of those expectations

■ FIGURE 1.11

Bronfenbrenner's
Bioecological Model
Source: After Bronfenbrenner
(1979).

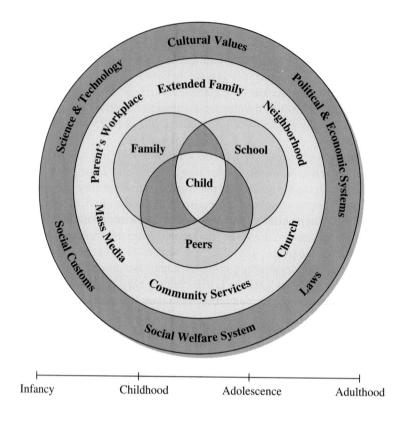

varies depending on the child's gender and economic situation within a particular culture as well. Bronfenbrenner's theory is useful for understanding complex interactions between biological and environmental effects, as well as relations between different environmental contexts (e.g., home and school). It also helps us understand that the environment in which children live is so complex and intertwined that development cannot be reduced to any one single source.

Importance of Multiple Theories

We have just described some of the theoretical assumptions underlying the various developmental theories that will be discussed in subsequent chapters. The specifics of each theory will be described in more detail later. For now, it is enough to recognize the importance of examining children's development from different theoretical perspectives. Some theories may provide a more adequate explanation than others, but all have a place in a teacher's repertoire. In combination they provide a better explanation of children's behavior than any single theory alone can.

Think back to Stanley's teacher. Most of the approaches she tried involved rewards and punishments, which are based on behavioral views of development. Although these approaches work for some students, they tend to be short lived because they do little to create a community of learning in the classroom. In subsequent chapters, we will draw on other child development theories to promote students' learning and engagement in the classroom.

Before moving to the next section, it is important to recognize that the theories presented in this chapter are themselves human constructions that reflect a certain situation, time, and place. Because theories are human constructions, many of the "facts" of development discussed in subsequent chapters are open to question and further interpretation. It is helpful to think of these theories not as statements of "essential truths," but as ways of thinking and talking about children's and adolescents' development in the classroom.

Studying Children's Development

We have just discussed some different theoretical frameworks for understanding children's development. Now let's examine how researchers actually study various aspects of children's development. An understanding of research methods is important for prospective teachers for two reasons. First, as a professional teacher you will attend conferences and read articles that focus on different aspects of children's development. To be a critical consumer of this research, you must be able to judge the quality and validity of different studies. Some methods of study are thought to be more valid and reliable when compared to other methods. Second, as a teacher you will function as a researcher in your own classroom. For example, a teacher might be interested in the following sorts of questions: Are students more involved in learning when I give them a choice of activities? Does concept mapping help students to organize and retain information? Does peer tutoring have a negative or positive effect on children's learning and confidence? Does peer tutoring have the same effect on both low- and high-achieving students?

Observations, interviews, experiments, and surveys can help teachers understand how best to facilitate children's learning and development in their own classrooms. In this last section, we will examine the various research designs and methods researchers use to describe and to explain children's development. After reading this section, you will better understand the research findings discussed in later chapters. We will also discuss how to judge the quality of a study. And, finally, we will consider ethical issues in child development research.

UNDERSTANDING CHILDREN
Observation Guide, Chapter 2

Research Designs

A **research design** is the plan or structure of an investigation. The type of design selected depends, in part, on the investigator's research question. The first step in any scientific study is to define the question to be studied. For example, a researcher may want to know, Does aggression increase or decrease with age? The researcher then reads existing research on this topic and formulates a hypothesis. A **hypothesis** is a statement derived from theory that has not yet been validated. With the exception of case studies or other descriptive types of studies (observations and interviews), the researcher is examining associations between sets of variables. An **independent variable** is defined as the behavior or characteristic believed to influence a particular outcome or result, which is called the **dependent variable.** In the example here, the researcher may hypothesize that children become more aggressive as they get older. Age is the independent variable, and aggression is the dependent variable. Having formulated a research hypothesis based on previous studies, the next step is to choose an appropriate design for testing the hypothesis.

The six most commonly used research designs in developmental research are single-subject cases, correlational studies, longitudinal designs, cross-sectional designs, cross-sequential designs, and experimental interventions. These research designs for describing and explaining children's development differ with respect to complexity, efficiency, and the

TABLE 1.3   Advantages and Disadvantages of Different Research Designs

Type of Design	Advantages	Disadvantages
Case study	Provides detailed information of one person's behavior. Can be used as starting place for future investigations.	May reflect observer bias. May not generalize to other situations.
Correlational studies	Can be used with large samples for testing associations between different variables. (e.g., age and self-esteem).	Cannot be used to test cause-and-effect relations.
Longitudinal studies	Provides information on changes in individual behavior over time. Can be used to test the stability of behaviors and cause-and-effect relations.	Very costly and take years to complete. If study spans several years, participants can become test-wise or drop out of the study, biasing results.
Cross-sectional studies	Can be used with large samples to examine developmental changes. May be completed within a few months. Useful for establishing age norms.	Cannot establish cause-and-effect relations. Do not provide information on the stability of behavior.
Cross-sequential studies	Combine the advantages of longitudinal and cross-sectional designs.	Not frequently used or well understood.
Experimental studies	Conditions of study are well controlled. Degree of control is highest in laboratory studies; study participants are randomly assigned to treatment and control groups.	Involve small samples and if conducted in the laboratory may not generalize to other settings.
Quasi-experimental studies	Utilize comparison groups without random assignment.	Difficult to control for all possible differences between groups.

kinds of questions they can answer. As summarized in Table 1.3, each has its own advantages and disadvantages.

Case Studies

A **case study** is an in-depth investigation of one person or a small group of individuals (e.g., a family, a peer group). Some of the earliest discoveries about children's development have been based on case studies. In the 1800s, for example, Charles Darwin kept a detailed diary of his son's emotional expressions. This diary became the basis for his theory of emotional development in infants and children. Freud kept detailed notes of individual patients that he and other psychoanalysts relied on heavily in their research. Piaget recorded the developmental progress of his children and incorporated his findings into his theory of children's cognitive development.

A case study that has helped researchers understand language development is the story of Genie (Curtiss, 1977). Genie (not her real name) was confined to a small room where no one spoke to her from the age of 20 months until a caseworker found her when she was 13½ years old. When she was discovered, she weighed only 59 pounds and could not speak. During the next 9 years, Genie received intensive therapy to help her learn to speak. However, her language development never approached that of a normal adult. At last report, Genie, in her 30s, was living in a group home for retarded adults, and her language was still not normal.

Case studies provide useful, in-depth information about an aspect of development, such as language or cognition. From studies on subjects such as Genie, we have learned much about the effects of social isolation on language acquisition. This case study also suggests that there may be a critical period for language development, because Genie was never able to acquire normal language taught to her as an adolescent and adult. The chief limitation of a case study is that it is difficult to make general statements about development from a single case: The results may be unique to the individual being studied. In Genie's case, for example, it may be that poor nutrition and physical abuse, both of which can cause brain damage, prevented her from acquiring a language. It is not possible to make conclusions about cause-and-effect relationships. Furthermore, case studies are vulnerable to "observer bias." That is, the researcher may emphasize one aspect of development and ignore other areas. Thus, case studies may provide valuable information about an individual child, but their results may not tell us much about children in general.

Correlational Studies

Correlational studies are perhaps the most widely used design in developmental research. These studies tell us what factors influence or are associated in a positive or negative way. For example, it is commonly believed that school achievement is positively related to self-esteem; students who do well in school feel good about themselves. A researcher could test this hypothesis by administering a measure of self-esteem to a large sample of children and collecting information on their school achievement (grades, tests scores, teacher ratings, etc.). In this example, self-esteem is the independent variable, and achievement is the dependent variable. After collecting these data, the researcher would then examine relations between the measures of self-esteem and school achievement.

The strength of relations between measures is expressed by a statistic called a **correlation coefficient.** Correlations can vary from -1.0 to $+1.0$. If two measures are unrelated, then the correlation would be near zero. This finding would be interpreted to mean that higher or lower scores on one measure did not correspond with higher or lower scores on the other. If higher scores on the self-esteem measure corresponded with higher achievement test scores, then the correlation would be positive, somewhere between 0 and 1.0. If, however, higher scores on one measure were associated with lower scores on the second measure, then the correlation would be negative, somewhere between 0 and -1.0. This finding means that as one score goes up, the second score goes down. A correlation is *statistically significant* when the relation between the two measures is stronger than would be predicted by chance alone.

As an example, most studies report a significant positive correlation between self-esteem and school achievement. However, a positive correlation does not mean that there is a **causal relationship** between the two factors (i.e., changes in one factor *cause* changes in the other). The results merely tell us the two factors are related in some systematic manner. We cannot tell whether higher self-esteem contributes to better school achievement or whether better school achievement contributes to higher self-esteem. That is, the direction of causality is unclear. In fact, both statements of causality could be correct. Moreover, a third variable, the home environment, could have a causal effect on both self-esteem and school achievement (see Figure 1.12 on page 32). *Therefore, correlational studies cannot be used to establish cause-and-effect relationships.* They are simply used to establish relations or associations among different measures.

Longitudinal, Cross-Sectional, and Cross-Sequential Studies

Recall that development involves changes in behavior over time. We discussed how correlational studies can be used to examine relations between age and various behaviors, such as aggression or self-esteem. Two other research designs are widely used to study changes in behavior over time: longitudinal and cross-sectional designs.

■ FIGURE 1.12

Model of Positive Correlation Between School Achievement and Self-Esteem

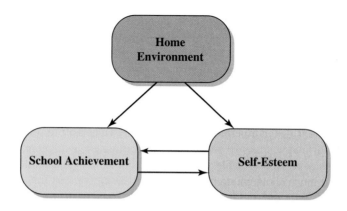

A positive correlation does not mean that positive achievement *causes* children to have self-esteem. It is possible that positive self-esteem can lead to higher school achievement. In addition, a positive or negative home environment can affect both self-esteem and school achievement and explain their positive correlation.

In a **longitudinal study,** the development of one group of children is tracked over several years. Data of different aspects of development are collected on a regular basis. One well-known longitudinal study is Lewis Terman's *Genetic Studies of Genius* (Terman, 1925; Terman & Oden, 1959), which began in 1922 and followed the lives of 1,500 individuals for 70 years. The initial selection criteria for this study was a superior score (top 1 percent of range) on an intelligence test at age 11. During the next 70 years, researchers collected data on the child's early childhood experiences, education, personality characteristics, careers, families, physical and mental health, and adjustment to retirement.

Longitudinal studies can provide valuable information about individual development over time, so it is possible to examine the impact of early events on later development. For example, many working parents want to know how infant day care may affect their child's development in the long run. Longitudinal studies also allow researchers to identify differences in behavior at different points of development (e.g., increases or decreases in aggression with age). In addition, it is possible to examine the stability of a behavior for individual children. For example, do shy children become lonely adults? In Chapter 4, we will discuss the stability of intelligence from childhood to adulthood. This information is drawn from longitudinal studies.

Although longitudinal studies have several advantages, there are several disadvantages that must be considered as well. First, longitudinal studies are costly and take years to complete. A researcher would need to wait 5 years or more, for example, to determine whether aggression increases or decreases during childhood. It is often difficult to keep the sample group intact, especially in our mobile society. There is also the danger that individuals become very "test-wise" if they are repeatedly assessed. And finally, the conclusions drawn from longitudinal studies must be considered in relation to when the study was completed. For example, the Great Depression and World War II probably had a strong influence on the lives of both men and women in the Terman study. Also, gender roles have changed a great deal since the 1940s, when most of the participants probably raised their families. The experiences of children and adults today are likely to be very different from those of children in the 1920s.

Another well-known design for studying developmental changes in children is a **cross-sectional study.** In a cross-sectional study, researchers select children of different ages and measure the factor under study. To use our familiar example, a researcher could study whether the nature and frequency of aggressive acts differ with age by measuring aggression in children of different ages (e.g., 5, 7, 9, and 11 years). Each age group should have a similar profile with regard to ethnic and gender ratios, socioeconomic background, schooling experiences, and so forth. The researcher would then compare groups in terms of their scores on some measure of aggression, such as frequency of fights at school as reported by peers and teachers. If the results showed a greater incidence of fighting among 9- and 11-year-olds than younger children, then the researcher would have evidence to suggest that aggression increases with age. Before drawing this conclusion, the researcher might check to make sure the finding was consistent for boys and girls and for different ethnic groups.

Cross-sectional studies are certainly faster and less costly than longitudinal studies. They can involve a wide age range of subjects and be completed within a couple of months. Cross-sectional studies are therefore useful for establishing **age norms**—the age at which certain characteristics emerge. Because the participants are sampled only once, there is less chance that the assessments will affect their behavior.

As with correlational and longitudinal studies, cross-sectional studies have some disadvantages that must be considered. First, this design does not actually study changes in behavior over time; it provides only an estimate of those changes. In addition, cross-sectional studies cannot provide information on early determinants of behavior. For example, it would not be possible to establish the effects of early cognitive stimulation on later intellectual development. Furthermore, as suggested, the participants for each age group must be carefully selected in order to rule out differences, other than age, that could bias the results. Last, a cross-sectional study cannot provide information about the stability of behaviors over time, because the same children are not followed over time. If you recall, one of the issues of debate in developmental research is the continuity versus discontinuity of development. To answer this question, longitudinal assessments of the same children are needed.

A compromise between longitudinal and cross-sectional studies is the **cross-sequential study.** In a cross-sequential study, children of different ages are selected and then followed for 2 to 3 years. Because there is a wide range of ages to begin with, this design is more efficient than a longitudinal study. By studying the same group of children over time, it is also possible to identify antecedents of behavior, as well as to assess the stability of behavioral patterns. Although sequential designs blend the best features of cross-sectional and longitudinal designs, they are not widely used. Most of the findings related to children's development over time come from either longitudinal or cross-sectional studies.

Experimental Studies

For testing cause-and-effect relations, most researchers rely on experimental designs. These studies are believed to yield the most conclusive cause-effect evidence. For this type of study, participants may be randomly or carefully selected and matched on a number of variables that could potentially affect the results (gender, ethnicity, family background, school achievement, etc.). In an **experimental study,** participants are randomly selected and randomly assigned to either of two conditions: an experimental or a control group. In the experimental condition, the children receive a treatment or intervention of some type. This condition is presumed to cause a certain behavior or outcome. In the control condition, the children do not receive the treatment. After the experiment, children are measured on some

■ FIGURE 1.13
*Model of the Bobo
Doll Experiment*

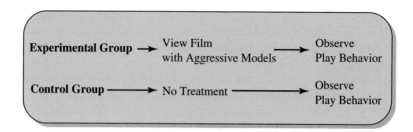

outcome measure. If there is a significant difference between the two groups on this outcome measure, then the results support the hypothesis that the treatment *caused* a change in behavior.

Returning to our question about what causes childhood aggression, let's look at an example of an experimental study. In a classic study, a group of researchers examined the effects of adult models on children's aggression (Bandura, Ross, & Ross, 1963). The research design is outlined in Figure 1.13. Children who were assigned to the experimental condition observed a film in which adults showed aggressive behaviors toward a plastic "Bobo doll" or clown. After watching the film, the children played in a room that contained the doll and some other toys. Children in the control condition did not observe the film but were allowed to play in the room with the Bobo doll. The researchers observed the behavior of each child for 20 minutes through a one-way mirror. They used a behavioral checklist to assess children's aggressive and nonaggressive behaviors. The researchers hypothesized that children who viewed the aggressive model would act more aggressively afterward. In this example, the treatment, viewing a film with an aggressive model, is the independent variable, and aggressive play behavior is the dependent variable. The results confirmed the researchers' hypothesis that children can become more aggressive when they are exposed to aggressive models.

Experiments with randomized control trials are considered to be the "gold standard" in educational and psychological research today (National Research Council [NRC], 2002). However, in school settings random selection and assignment of students to different groups for research purposes is sometimes not possible, practical, or desirable. Under these conditions, researchers employ what is called **quasi-experimental,** or *causal-comparative,* **design,** which involves comparing groups of interest without random assignment to different conditions. To make comparisons between groups possible, participants are matched on key characteristics (gender, ethnicity, socioeconomic status, and so on.) or statistical procedures are used to adjust for differences between groups (NRC, 2002).

As an example, let's consider a school district that is in the process of evaluating the effectiveness of an after-school tutoring program for struggling adolescent readers. The program is implemented in one middle school, and students are drawn from other middle schools in the district to serve as the comparison group. The schools selected do not offer the tutoring program, and the evaluation team is careful to create comparison groups of the same ages, gender, ability levels, and ethnicity. So far, so good! However, other factors such as the amount of time students read at home, their motivation to participate in the program, or some other unmeasured factor could explain differences found between the intervention and comparison groups. In quasi-experimental studies, it is necessary to control and rule out other possible explanations for the differences found between comparison groups. Otherwise, results from these studies can be misleading (NRC, 2002, p. 114). An example of a well-regarded quasi-experimental study examining the effects of age and education is described in the Focus on Research box on the next page.

Focus on Research

Age and Education Effects on Cognitive Development: A Natural Experiment

Frederick Morrison and his colleagues (1995) have conducted a "natural experiment" to assess the effects of age and education on children's cognitive development. The study uses what is known as the *school cut-off method.* Each school system specifies a certain cut-off date to determine when children can enter kindergarten or first grade. A child's birthday must precede this date. For some schools, this cut-off date is December 31, whereas for other schools the date can be as early as March 1.

In Morrison's research, "old kindergarten" children, who just missed the March school-entry date, were compared with "young first-grade" children, who just made the cut-off date. On average, this second group of children were 41 days older than the first group, but they had received an additional year of schooling. The two groups were carefully matched in terms of IQ, parental and occupational similarities, and day care experience at the time of school entry. Morrison's cut-off method provides a way to separate the effects of age (maturation) and experience (education) on cognitive development. If the two groups are equal on cognitive measures, then age is assumed to be the primary driving force. On the other hand, if the young first graders outperform the old kindergartners, then educational experiences can be assumed to play a primary role in cognitive development.

The results of Morrison's natural experiment suggested that school-related experiences rather than age alone have a major impact on cognitive development. The young first graders showed better recall on a memory task than did the old kindergartners. The young first graders also showed greater improvement in their memory skills and performance during the school year than did the old kindergartners. In addition, the young first graders demonstrated greater phonemic awareness (i.e., ability to divide words into syllables or to differentiate sounds within one-syllable words) than did the old kindergartners. Both groups showed improvements in this area during the school year, but the young first graders made greater gains.

Because the two groups of children were about the same age, the development of memory and reading skills is not simply due to growing older. Rather, the results of this natural experiment clearly suggest that experience is an important factor in this developmental process. The young first graders performed better on memory and reading tasks than old kindergartners because they had more formal schooling. That is, their performance on these cognitive tasks was directly enhanced by schooling experiences that emphasized memorization and beginning reading skills. This research supports the conclusion that schools can have a powerful influence on children's cognitive development.

Action Research

Before we turn to data collection methods, it is important to discuss another form of inquiry found in schools today. **Action research** is carried out by teachers, administrators, and other change agents in the school to improve the educational environment for their students. The goal of action research is not to understand general principles of children's development and learning but to understand a specific problem or to improve teaching practices within a specific classroom or school setting. The Japanese "lesson study," discussed earlier, is a form of action research.

Action research has many benefits for teachers. It empowers them to think critically about their own teaching practices, to identify areas in need of change, to find effective solutions, and to improve learning conditions for children under their care. Rather than to function as the recipients of research and knowledge, action research encourages teachers to be problem solvers and continuous learners.

Although there are a number of different models of action research, the basic process involves four steps. These are (1) selecting an area of focus and inquiry, (2) collecting data and information, (3) analyzing and interpreting the data, and (4) developing and implementing a plan for action.

The first step of the process involves *selecting an area of focus or inquiry*. It is recommended that educators choose areas that involve a topic or problem related to teaching and learning they can change or improve, and then state a specific purpose or objective for their investigation. This statement should include the specific research questions that will be addressed, a definitions of variables, and the types of data to be collected (Mills, 2000). For example, a middle school teacher might want to study the social networks of her classroom to determine if students are interacting across ethnic or gender lines. She would need to define the type of interactions of interest and to identify some ways to collect information on interactions in her classroom.

The second step is to *collect data and information* that is appropriate and accessible. Several different data collection methods are described below and may be used in an action research plan. Generally, the nature of research problem or question determines the types of data collected, but sources may include archival records, interviews, focus groups, performance assessments, classroom observations, classroom maps or videos, surveys, journals, and other artifacts. It is best not to rely on one single source of data but to use multiple sources of information to identify common themes across data sources. The use of multiple data collect methods to compare findings across sources is known as **triangulation.**

Having collected relevant data and information, the next step is to *analyze and interpret* those data. The goal of analysis and interpretation is to summarize the data in a reliable and accurate manner. It is important to use the research questions to guide this analysis process, but new questions may emerge during data analysis that require additional data collection. Figure 1.14 portrays the spiral nature of action research. In interpreting the data, it is important to relate the results to findings in the literature or to theories of teaching and learning. The Focus on Teaching box on page 38 describes an action research study in which learning theories were used to interpret the influence of technology on mathematics learning.

The final step of action research is to articulate a *plan for action*. In developing an action plan, the teacher-researcher specifies what needs to be done related to the findings, who is responsible for carrying out the actions, who needs to be consulted or informed about these recommended actions, and how the effects of the actions will be monitored or evaluated. As we suggested in Figure 1.14, the implementation of an action plan can lead to additional research and data collection. Throughout the action research process it is important to keep in mind that the overall goal is to change or improve the educational environment for children.

Data Collection Methods

We have just discussed different designs for describing and explaining children's development. In this discussion, several methods for collecting data on children were mentioned (e.g., standardized performance measures,

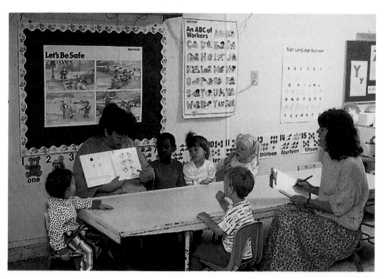

This teacher is sharing her classroom with an educational researcher. Classroom observations provide valuable and rich information about how children learn.
Source: *David Young-Wolff/PhotoEdit.*

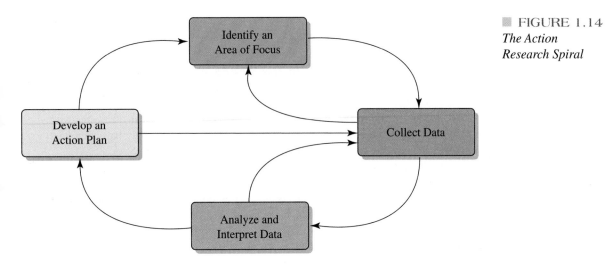

behavioral checklists, self-ratings). The choice of a specific collection method will depend on the hypotheses being tested by the investigator. As we have seen with different research designs, each method of data collection has advantages and disadvantages.

Observations

Information on the development of young children is often collected through *direct observation,* a technique that is very important for teachers to master. When a child is observed in a controlled environment, such as a laboratory, this method is called a **structured observation.** Bandura's experiment with the Bobo doll involved a structured observation of children in a carefully controlled setting. When children are observed in their own environments, these data are called **naturalistic observations.** Regardless of which method of observation is used, observers must record their observations in some way. In some cases, the observer writes down everything the child is doing. In other cases, the observer may only be interested in, and therefore record, certain behaviors, such as acts of aggression. This technique is known as **event sampling.** Alternatively, the observer may use an observation coding sheet that contains a list of behaviors. The observer then checks off the behaviors that occurred within a predetermined time frame (e.g., every 5 minutes). This technique is known as **time sampling.** One disadvantage of this observation method is that the behavior of interest (e.g., fighting) may be so infrequent that the observer may have to wait a long time before seeing it. For this reason, some researchers may try to structure the situation so that the behavior is more likely to occur. For example, the researcher may place a very attractive toy in the toddler unit of a day care center as a way to increase the chances that children may fight over the toy. But as suggested earlier, this modification could make the observation situation more contrived.

In general, some type of time sampling is generally used in most observational studies. The main advantage is that it provides a systematic way of collecting observational data, making it possible to compare different children's behavior. The main disadvantage is that the coding procedure may not pick up infrequent behaviors. In addition, most time-sampling coding procedures provide only counts of behaviors. In some cases, researchers may want to know what preceded or followed a particular behavior. Figure 1.15 on page 39 presents a very simple set of procedures that teachers can use to observe their students' behavior in the classroom.

Focus on
Teaching

Using Technology to Enhance Mathematics Learning

Billabong Elementary School is a large K–7 school that has embraced the use of technology as a key component of its mathematics curriculum reform efforts. The principal of this school is described by his teachers as a visionary leader, and the school has a large collection of computer hardware and software because of the principal's grant-writing efforts. The principal is committed to the use of technology at Billabong because he believes that it is necessary to prepare children for the twenty-first century.

A team of teachers at Billabong decided to conduct an action research project focusing on the impact of technology on student achievement. They decided to observe each others' classrooms, interview teachers and children, analyze test data, and compare the mathematics curriculum taught with the teaching and learning standards proposed by the National Council of Teachers of Mathematics (NCTM). When the team presented its project to the rest of the faculty, all the teachers and the principal indicated that they would cooperate with the research team's request for access to classrooms, curriculum materials, and so on.

The team's initial visits to classrooms revealed that students had good access to computers, scanners, and printers. Most classrooms had at least six computers, and all children in one classroom had laptop computers to use for the year. The students were observed using the computers for their class assignments, creating hypercard stacks for creative writing, playing math games, and so on. Math centers featured different math manipulatives: base-10 blocks, place-value charts, colored chips, tangrams, geo-boards, and so on.

However, a closer look at the classrooms revealed a different story. In many of the classrooms, for example, children busily engaged with computers were playing math mazes. For the most part, the children were engaged in low-level activities, and the purpose of the learning activity was lost. Many children were also engaged in "drill-and-kill" activities that had little relevance to their math learning. In these classrooms, the computers seemed to function as an electronic worksheet to keep the students busy once they had completed their math assignments.

Interviews with children were equally revealing. When conducting the interviews, the research team asked the children to be honest and assured them that their responses would be strictly confidential. As it turns out, some children were brutally honest, telling in great detail the kinds of math activities their teachers used on the computers. Some activities were singled out by the children as a "waste of time," and some children described teachers as "not having a clue" about how the computers were really being used.

Interviews with teachers revealed other problems. Many of the teachers knew very little about the NCTM standards and continued to use their "tried and proven" curriculum in spite of a new textbook adoption by the principal. In fact, some of the teachers were very unhappy about the textbook adoption because no teachers had been consulted in the process.

Compared to those at other schools in the district, Billabong's students performed below average on statewide assessments. This information surprised teachers, who thought that their pupils were doing well in most math strands, with the exception of open-ended problem solving and algebraic relationships. These teachers thought the problem was with the appropriateness of the tests, not the use of technology to enhance teaching and learning.

Before the research team could share its results with the rest of the faculty, a number of issues needed to be considered. The team wanted to share its results without hurting individual teachers and without alienating the teachers from the principal. They decided to adopt a "hold harmless" approach. The team shared the general findings at a faculty meeting and then invited teachers, on a voluntary basis, to meet with team members to discuss the data for their classrooms. Similarly, they invited the principal to meet with them to discuss the implications of the findings for future professional development opportunities.

Source: Adapted from Mills (2001).

Suggestions for Collecting Observations in the Classroom

Time	Activity	Observation	Interpretations/Questions

■ FIGURE 1.15
Suggestions for Collecting Observations in the Classroom
Source: After Brophy & Good (1974) and Florio-Ruane (1985)

1. When collecting observations of students, be sure to note the time and setting of the observation. Record facts about what is happening. Try to write down as much as you can about what the student(s) is/are saying and doing. Look for behaviors that precede or follow a particular event. Do not try to interpret what the student(s) is/are doing; pretend you are a video camera recording the event. Many teachers and researchers find the above format useful for collecting observational records. Note that there is space in the right margin for interpretations and questions.

2. After completing a set of observations, begin to interpret what might be going on in the situation and what the actions might mean to the people involved. Also, record any questions this observation might provoke for further investigation. Begin to look for patterns and consistencies in behavior and record them in the interpretation section. Begin to formulate hypotheses to explain the events you are observing.

3. In drawing conclusions from your observations, look for consistencies in behavior across situations. Identify events that preceded and followed the behavior of interest. Formulate a theory to explain the students' behavior. What type of evidence do you have to support your theory? Finally, consider alternative explanations and interpretations for what you are observing. What type of information might you need to either confirm or reject this explanation?

4. In collecting and analyzing observational records, be careful to avoid some common pitfalls. First, we have a tendency to see "what we want to see." If, for example, we assume teachers treat high and low achievers differently, then we are likely to bias our observations in this way. That is, our own beliefs, expectations, and past experiences can lead us to select and interpret our observations according to prior assumptions. It is important to remove these "perceptual blinders" as much as possible. Be objective. When observing, be sure to collect information that might counter preexisting assumptions and expectations. Second, avoid premature conclusions or interpretations. As suggested earlier, look for patterns of behavior across time and situations. In making a conclusion or interpretation, be sure to cite concrete examples that support your statements. Conclusions are more trustworthy if you can cite several instances of a behavior to support them. Last, be aware of how the situation can influence a student's behavior. In observing other people, we have a tendency to attribute behavior to stable dispositions (i.e., she is shy), rather than to the situation (i.e., she is quiet in class). For this reason, it is important to collect information about a student across situations. If a behavior pattern (i.e., shyness) appears in several settings with different people, then it is appropriate to make inferences about underlying dispositions.

Self-Reports

Another method of collecting information on children is **self-reports.** Children can report on their own behavior, their parents' and teachers' behavior, or their peers' behavior. Parents, teachers, and friends can also report on the child's behavior. Self-reports can take several different forms. The individuals being studied can complete a *questionnaire* that contains a number of carefully structured questions that they must answer. Another type of self-report measure is the *rating scale.* Here individuals are given a set of behaviors or attributes to rate. For example, teachers may be asked to rate a child's effort, persistence, or ability to work independently in the classroom. An example of a rating scale is shown in Figure 1.16 on page 41. Clearly these two self-report measures—questionnaires and rating scales—can be used only with children and adults who can read. These measures are generally less reliable for children under the age of 8 or 9. For younger children, an *interview* may be more appropriate. Using this method, children or adults are asked a set of questions. Some interviews are highly structured and standardized, whereas others are more loosely organized. Interviews are useful for understanding why a person is acting or feeling a certain way.

Because questionnaires and rating scales are efficient ways of collecting information about children, they are widely used in research on children's development, especially if the researcher is collecting information on a large sample of children. However, these data collection methods have some serious disadvantages. First, it's not clear that all children and adults interpret rating scale and questionnaire items in the same way. For example, "works independently" may be interpreted as working alone by one teacher and as completing independent assignments by another teacher. Second, children and adults may not be motivated to complete questionnaires, particularly if they are time-consuming. They may leave answers blank or respond to questions randomly. In addition, children and adults may not be good reporters of their own behaviors. They sometimes answer questions according to how they think you want them to respond. This problem is most likely to occur if children are asked to report on undesirable behaviors, such as fighting, cheating, stealing, and so forth. Similarly, adults are not likely to provide accurate reports of behaviors that are inappropriate or undesirable, such as hitting a child. In general, individuals have a tendency to overestimate desirable behaviors and to underestimate undesirable behaviors. This problem is known as **social desirability.**

Interview questions are less likely to be misinterpreted than questionnaire questions. The interviewer can also probe an individual's responses. Interviews can provide more elaborate and richer data about different events. However, interviews are very time-consuming. Children are more difficult to interview than adults because they are less attentive, slower to respond, and have difficulty understanding questions. In addition, the interview must be transcribed and analyzed according to a coding scheme. Also, the problem of social desirability may be more likely to occur in face-to-face interviews, in which individuals are not likely to divulge feelings, attitudes, or behaviors that others may view as undesirable or inappropriate.

When self-report measures are used, it is best to gather additional information. For example, researchers often collect information about a child's behavior from multiple sources, such as teachers, parents, and peers. If there is a convergence in the information collected from these various sources (e.g., a child is rated as popular by two or more sources), then results are more likely to be accurate. In addition, self-report measures are often used in conjunction with other data collection strategies, such as observations and performance assessments.

■ FIGURE 1.16

Examples of Rating Scale Items

Examples of Rating Scale Items

Directions: Rate how often each student exhibits the following behaviors in class. Rate each behavior on a 1 to 4 scale. Circle 1 if the student *never* shows the behavior, 2 if the student *sometimes* shows the behavior, 3 if the student usually shows the behavior, 4 if the student *frequently* shows the behavior.

	Never	Sometimes	Usually	Frequently
Gets along with others	1	2	3	4
Enjoys challenging activities	1	2	3	4
Works independently	1	2	3	4
Helps others	1	2	3	4
Gives up easily	1	2	3	4

Performance Assessments

Sometimes the best way to collect information about children's development is through **performance assessments,** which seek to measure children's ability to perform specific tasks correctly. These methods are generally used to assess children's physical and cognitive development. For example, asking a group of preschool children to skip around the gym is one way to assess their large motor skills. Intelligence and achievement tests are also performance assessments in which individuals are given a set of cognitive tasks to perform. For example, a subtest of the *Wechsler Scale of Intelligence for Children* (Wechsler, 1991) asks children to make designs with blocks that match a model. Achievement tests also include a standard set of problems for students to solve. In recent years, however, educators have moved away from multiple-choice tests of achievement toward performance assessments in which students are given authentic tasks to perform. Asking fifth-grade students to use their mathematical knowledge to design and to furnish a "dream house" is an example of a performance assessment.

In Chapter 3, we will learn that Piaget used performance assessments in much of his research on children's cognitive development. One of his most famous tasks involved the conservation of water. As shown in Figure 1.17 on page 42, children are first shown two glasses of water and asked if the two glasses contain the same amount of water. Next, the water from one glass is poured into a taller, thinner glass, and the children are again asked if the two glasses contain the same amount of water. A child who does not understand the concept of conservation would say, "No, the taller glass has more." In Piaget's research, children were then asked to explain their answers. This technique of probing children's reasoning processes was known as the **clinical interview method.** It is a good example of how performance assessments can be combined with interviews to assess children's cognitive functioning.

Performance assessments have several advantages. First, they provide a behavioral measure of a child's level of development in a certain area. These assessments are likely to be more accurate than self-reports. Second, performance assessments can show which tasks and problems children can solve at specific ages. Because the tasks, procedures, and conditions can be standardized across situations, the child's performance can be compared with previously established norms. For example, standardized achievement tests have national or state norms, which allow teachers to compare their students' performance with other students of the same age. The

1. Do both glasses have the same amount of water?   2. Now do the glasses have the same amount of water?

■ FIGURE 1.17
Conservation of Liquid Problem

disadvantage of performance assessments, particularly standardized tests, is that they do not provide information on the cognitive processes children use to solve problems. This information must be inferred from the child's performance. However, Piaget's method of combining performance assessments and clinical interviews may be a way of overcoming this problem.

Judging the Quality of a Study

You have just read about different approaches for studying children's development and their various strengths and limitations. The next question is, How do you know whether research findings can be trusted? To answer this question, several important criteria should be considered.

Generalizability

In judging the quality of a study, it is important to examine how the sample was selected. If the sample is limited in some way (e.g., all white males), then the findings should not be generalized to other groups of children. The **generalizability** of research findings has to do with how well the findings apply to another sample or to the general population. Case studies, for example, have limited generalizability because they involve one individual or a small group of individuals. In addition, many developmental studies have been criticized because they are based on white, middle-class samples. Results from these investigations cannot be applied to poor or ethnic minority children. Because a child's social and cultural context can influence behavior, care must be taken to select a representative group of children who vary with respect to ethnicity, social class, and sex. When findings are consistent across different samples of children, then we can be more confident that the results apply to a broad range of children.

Reliability and Validity

In judging the quality of a study, it is also important to examine the reliability and validity of the measures used. **Reliability** refers to the consistency or precision of a measurement when repeated under similar circumstances. For example, there are numerous measures of self-esteem. In choosing a scale, the researcher wants one that provides a reliable estimate. One method for assessing the reliability of a measure is to administer it several times within a short interval of time (a few weeks is acceptable) and to examine the consistency of scores across time. Of course, the same group of individuals should complete the measure each time. Reliable measures yield more consistent scores within a short interval of time. This measure of consistency is called *test-retest* reliability. Studies that use a test, performance measure, or questionnaire should report this information.

A different reliability estimate is used in interview and observation studies. When analyzing observation or interview data, researchers typically identify different categories or patterns of behavior. This analysis process involves subjective interpretations and judgments. To establish the reliability of coding procedures, researchers generally ask two or more people to observe or code the same events. The researcher then computes the degree of agreement between the observers or the raters. Whereas one observer may interpret an intense look as a threat, another observer may not interpret it that way. This estimate of agreement is called *interobserver* or *interrater* reliability. When observers agree in their assessments, the resulting measures are more reliable.

Along with providing a reliable measure of a behavior, a research instrument must provide a valid measure. The **validity** of a measure refers to whether or not it provides an accurate measure of the phenomenon being studied. That is, does the instrument really measure what it purports to measure? It is possible to get a reliable estimate of a behavior, but the instrument used to obtain this assessment may not really assess what it is supposed to. This point is often confusing to many readers. Suppose a researcher thinks, as early researchers did, that the size of a person's head was a measure of intelligence. It is possible to obtain a reliable estimate of an individual's head size, but who today believes that head size is a valid measure of intelligence? This simple example should help clarify the difference between the reliability and validity of a measure.

Many factors can threaten the validity of a measure. In Chapter 4, we will discuss the validity of contemporary tests of intelligence. Although there are many different definitions of intelligence, IQ tests are currently based on a narrow definition of intelligence. If a child does not perform well on these tests, is it correct for the researcher to conclude that the child has low intelligence? Perhaps, as some critics argue, these tests are really a measure of a child's familiarity with white, middle-class American culture since this is the cultural background of most testmakers. Given that children's abilities to focus and concentrate for long periods of time can affect how well they perform on IQ tests, perhaps these tests are really measuring attention span. To establish the validity of a measure such as an IQ test, a researcher must relate it to other valid and reliable measures of the same attribute or behavior. In the case of IQ tests, the scores could be related to other valid tests of intelligence, cognitive abilities, or academic achievement. If a measure is valid, it should show strong relations with these other measures.

Replication

Ultimately in the scientific community, the quality of a research study is judged in terms of its ability to be replicated. Replication involves testing a hypothesis with multiple samples and with different but parallel methods. If the findings replicate, then it is unlikely that the results are due to a particular group of individuals or to a certain research method. Research findings are more trustworthy when they are found across studies that use different samples and methods of collecting data, as well as conducted by different researchers.

Research Ethics

As a prospective teacher or parent, you and your children may at some point be asked to participate in a study. It is important, therefore, that you understand **research ethics,** the ethical standards that researchers must follow when conducting research on human subjects. The guidelines shown in Figure 1.18 have been developed to protect you and your children from dangerous procedures. Because children are often too young to understand

Guidelines for Conducting Research with Children

1. In most cases, researchers must have their study reviewed by a school or institutional review board. Researchers must reveal all relevant information about the study.

2. Researchers must not use any methods or procedures that would cause physical or psychological harm to the child. The benefits of the study must outweigh its possible risks.

3. If participants are under the age of 18, researchers must inform the parents, guardians, or others responsible for the child's care about the research procedures and obtain their written consent before beginning the study.

4. If participants are old enough to understand the research procedures, they must be informed and asked for their verbal consent before participating in the study. Participants must be informed that they can withdraw from the study at any time.

5. Researchers must keep all information about the participants confidential. In all reports of the investigation and in casual conversations about the study, the identities of the participants cannot be revealed.

6. Researchers must inform parents, guardians, or other responsible adults if they obtain information that threatens the child's well-being. For example, if during the study, the researcher discovers that a child is seriously depressed, the researcher must contact a person who can help the child obtain psychological treatment.

7. Each participant has a right to the results of the study. Researchers are obligated to share their research findings with interested parties (e.g., participants, parents, guardians, school officials, and staff). As stated previously, the identities of the participants must be protected in research summaries.

8. Each child participant has the right to the benefits of a treatment provided to other participants. For example, if the experimental treatment is shown to be beneficial, then participants in the control group who did not receive the treatment have a right to beneficial treatments at some later time.

■ FIGURE 1.18
Guidelines for Conducting Research with Children
Source: Society for Research in Child Development (1990).

the issues involved in a study, parents must provide informed consent for their child to participate. Even when children have parental consent to participate in a study, the child can still refuse to participate or can withdraw from the study at any point without penalty. More important, the participants and their parents have a right to information about the results of the study. If you participate in a study, do not hesitate to ask for its results. The information should be presented in a way that protects the identities of the individual participants.

Teachers and parents are often reluctant to participate in a study because of the amount of time involved. However, it is important to keep in mind that researchers continue to make new discoveries about children's development. They are turning more and more to natural environments, such as the classroom or home, as the setting for their studies to ensure their research is a valid description of children's development. All research projects conducted by individuals from institutions who receive federal funds must be reviewed by an ethics review board. In order for a research project to be approved, the perceived benefits of the study for children must outweigh the costs of their time and effort. In any research study, the needs of children and their families should come first.

■ Chapter Summary

Why Study Child and Adolescent Development?

- Child development research can help teachers understand how children change over time and what explains the observed changes.
- Several recent studies have raised questions about teachers' understanding of child and adolescent development. Teachers with a solid foundation of knowledge of children's development are more effective teachers.
- Schools play an important role in children's intellectual, social, and emotional development. Schooling not only affects children's level of intellectual development, but also influences their ways of thinking, problem solving, and reasoning. Schooling experiences shape children's feelings of competency, sense of self, peer relations, and social attitudes, as well as many other aspects of social development.

Perspectives on Children's Development

- Most theorists believe that development involves systematic and orderly changes that enhance a child's overall adaptation to his or her environment. Theories of development provide a coherent framework for interpreting, explaining, and understanding those changes. Developmental theories make different assumptions concerning the nature of child, the nature of development, and the sources of development.
- Biological theories assume that human characteristics unfold according to a biological timetable. The environment plays little role in shaping the course of development. Development is viewed as either continuous or discontinuous, depending on the theorist. Two early maturational theorists were Hall and Gesell.
- Psychoanalytic theories focus on changes in the self and personality. At different stages of physical development, new drives, needs, and conflicts emerge that influence the way children relate to the environment. Key psychoanalytic theorists are Freud and Erikson.
- Behavioral theories emphasize the role of the environment in determining the course of development. Development is gradual and continuous, as a child acquires new skills and behavior through various principles of learning (conditioning, reinforcement, imitation). Some well-known behavioral theorists who have studied children's development are Watson and Skinner.

- In Piagetian, information processing, and social-cognitive theories, development results from an interplay between a child's developing mental abilities and environmental experiences. Children actively seek out information about their environment and attempt to make sense of it using existing knowledge and cognitive processes. Piaget's theory emphasizes qualitative changes in how children organize information, whereas information processing and social-cognitive approaches emphasize developmental changes in the efficiency of children's cognitive processes.
- Contextual theories emphasize relations between a developing child and a changing environment. In Vygotsky's theory, people structure the environment in ways that facilitate children's cognitive development. Brofenbrenner proposed that children's development is embedded in multiple environments. Changes in one system (e.g., parents' divorce) can influence changes that occur in other systems (e.g., child loses interest in schoolwork).
- There are multiple perspectives on children's development. Because no single theory alone can explain all that we know and observe about children, it is important to acquire a repertoire of different theories.

Studying Children's Development

- Studies of children can take several different forms. The most commonly used research designs in child development are case studies, correlational studies, longitudinal and cross-sectional studies, and experimental studies. Correlational and cross-sectional studies can be conducted with large samples. Longitudinal studies are the most useful for identifying antecedents of developmental changes and for establishing the stability of individual behavior. Experiments are used to test cause-and-effect relations, but their findings may not generalize to other settings.
- There are numerous methods for collecting data on children's development. Children can be observed in a structured or unstructured environment, and various behaviors can be recorded and analyzed for frequency of occurrence.
- Information on children can also be collected through rating scales, questionnaires, and interviews. These methods are efficient, but participants may not be accurate or truthful in their reporting. Like observations, performance assessments provide behavioral data.
- There are several criteria for judging the quality of a study. The reliability (precision) and validity (accuracy) of a measure or instrument are also important for judging the quality of a study. Most theorists, however, judge a study in terms of its ability to be replicated and quality of sampling procedures. Research findings are more trustworthy when they are found across studies that use different samples and methods.
- Research studies involving children and adults must follow a set of ethical guidelines. The perceived benefits of a study must outweigh its potential risks and costs in terms of time and effort. Informed consent must be obtained before the study is conducted, and the identities of all participants must remain confidential.

■ Key Terms

action research *(p. 35)*	dependent variable *(p. 29)*	quasi-experimental design *(p. 34)*
age norms *(p. 33)*	development *(p. 19)*	reciprocal determinism *(p. 26)*
behavioral genetics *(p. 22)*	event sampling *(p. 37)*	reliability *(p. 42)*
case study *(p. 30)*	experimental study *(p. 33)*	research design *(p. 29)*
causal relationship *(p. 31)*	generalizability *(p. 42)*	research ethics *(p. 44)*
classical conditioning *(p. 23)*	hypothesis *(p. 29)*	self-reports *(p. 40)*
clinical interview method *(p. 41)*	independent variable *(p. 29)*	social desirability *(p. 40)*
correlation coefficient *(p. 31)*	instrumental conditioning *(p. 23)*	structured observation *(p. 37)*
correlation study *(p. 31)*	longitudinal study *(p. 32)*	theory *(p. 21)*
critical period *(p. 23)*	naturalistic observation *(p. 37)*	time sampling *(p. 37)*
cross-sectional study *(p. 33)*	operant conditioning *(p. 23)*	triangulation *(p. 36)*
cross-sequential study *(p. 33)*	performance assessment *(p. 41)*	validity *(p. 43)*

■ Activities

1. Interview two to five teachers of different grade levels about their knowledge of child or adolescent development. Were they required to take a child or adolescent psychology course as part of their teacher preparation program? What type of issues or concerns do they have about children's development? How do they use information about children's development in planning learning activities, organizing the classroom, identifying students with special learning needs, and disciplining a child? Try to determine the extent to which the teachers' instructional decisions are based on child development research or their own experiences and intuitions. Summarize your findings in a paper you can share with your classmates.

2. Following are questions about children's development (adapted from Martin & Johnson, 1992). Read each item and mark the item you think provides the best answer.

   a. When do children follow rules?
      ____ They reach a stage when they can do things alone.
      ____ Parents praise them for doing things on their own.
      ____ They have a desire to experiment with new ideas and actions.

   b. How do children come to understand differences between plants and animals?
      ____ The distinction is obvious when children reach a certain stage.
      ____ They formulate the concept by observing and analyzing differences between the two groups.
      ____ They are taught the important characteristics of each group.

   c. Why do children's misconceptions about the world eventually change?
      ____ Adults present the correct information.
      ____ As they get older they outgrow immature ideas.
      ____ Their curiosity motivates them to find out more about their ideas.

   d. Why do children make up imaginative stories?
      ____ Make-believe is a natural part of childhood.
      ____ Adults encourage the child's imagination.
      ____ The child's imagination develops from playing with others and thinking about objects.

   e. How do children know that a candy bar broken into pieces is still the same amount of candy?
      ____ While playing with objects, children discover the relationship between parts and wholes.
      ____ Adults tell them the amounts are the same.
      ____ Children naturally know this when they reach a certain age.

   f. How do children learn to resolve conflicts with their friends?
      ____ Some children are naturally more agreeable or cooperative than others.
      ____ Through interacting with others, they discover that cooperation reduces conflicts.
      ____ They are encouraged by adults to get along.

   g. How do young children come to understand that cartoon characters are not real?
      ____ Adults tell them that the stories are make-believe.
      ____ The difference is obvious to children when they reach a certain stage.
      ____ Their everyday experiences help them to figure out that cartoon characters cannot be real.

   h. How do children acquire a desire to learn?
      ____ Children have a natural curiosity about things.
      ____ They imitate parents who like to learn.
      ____ As children learn ideas and skills, they seek out new learning experiences.

   i. How do children come to realize the consequences of their actions?
      ____ Children gradually become more aware of how things happen as they grow older.

_____ They discover through interactions with others that it is important to consider the possible outcomes of different actions.

_____ Adults praise their good behavior or ignore their bad behavior.

After answering the questions, decide with a classmate which of the statements for each item represent the following points of view discussed in this chapter (see pages 22–26):

Biological. Characteristics of the child naturally unfold as the child matures; changes in development are independent of training or experience.

Behavioral. Changes in the child are determined by the environment. The mechanisms that lead to change are direct instruction, reward, punishment, imitation, and so forth.

Cognitive. Changes in the child are due to a dynamic interaction between the child's existing knowledge and the environment. The child plays an active role in his or her own development through the construction of knowledge.

Review your answers to examine which of these points of views you used most frequently to explain children's behavior. Discuss with your classmates how your beliefs might influence the way you teach.

3. For the last century, two major approaches have dominated children's educational programs. Some teachers favor a child-oriented approach in which knowledge is "discovered" or "constructed," and others favor a teacher-oriented approach in which knowledge is "transmitted" or "presented." These approaches can be traced back to the views of Locke and Rousseau on children's development and education. Observe at least two classrooms, focusing on the types of materials used, instructional and discipline practices, and classroom organization. Make a list of characteristics that would be associated with a child-oriented or teacher-oriented approach. How would you characterize the classrooms you observed? Compare your findings with the rest of the class.

4. If you have access to a classroom, you can do your own action research project. Consult with the teacher to find a problem or issue of mutual interest. Review pages 35 and 36 to develop a plan for your project. Be sure to define the problem and identify appropriate data collection methods. After collecting and analyzing the information, develop an action plan and share it with your teacher and classmates.

Physical Development

CHAPTER OUTLINE

L ISA'S WEIGHT BEGAN TO ESCALATE AT 7 YEARS OF AGE WHEN HER *parents separated, and a lengthy and contentious custody battle threw her life into alternating times of chaos and neglect. Food was a source of comfort until Lisa's family members and friends started teasing her about her extra weight, calling her "Little Chubs."*

Lisa entered middle school fragile and without support, longing for peer acceptance. She tried entering a few cliques, and finally found a fit with a group of "headbangers" known for their love of heavy-metal music, drugs, and rejection of adults. Desperate for acceptance, she began cutting classes, smoking, and hanging out with boys, experimenting with marijuana and "crank" (methamphetamine). She took pride in becoming a "loser" and devaluing achievement; thus, her grades fell dramatically. "I'm not supposed to do well anymore. . . . And no one expects it of me—Not the teachers, not the other kids, no one. . . . I don't like to think about what will happen to me and my friends in the future anymore, because if we keep on like this, it might not be good" (p. 105).

Eventually, Lisa's behavior put her at risk for being held back in eighth grade. She began poking pins in her fingers and making designs on her arms and legs with cigarette lighters and razor blades, boasting that she just wants to be different to impress her friends. She says, "I know I have no self-esteem . . . but I can take everything—being stupid, being a dumb blonde— just not people saying stuff about my weight, I can't take that. All my life I've been teased about being fat. . . . Skinny and pretty . . . that's just the way to be" (pp. 108–109).

Source: Adapted from School Girls: Young Women, Self-Esteem, and the Confidence Gap, *by Orenstein, 1994.*

This vignette describes the feelings of a young adolescent girl in middle school. Orenstein (1994) claims that "girls slice and burn themselves for much the same reasons that they deny themselves [or indulge in] food: to alleviate anxiety and depression, to express powerlessness, and to restore a sense of control" (p. 107). Her behavior illustrates how physical changes, such as puberty and weight gain, intersect with social, emotional, and intellectual changes within different ecological contexts. In this case, Lisa did not have a supportive home or school context, like many adolescents do, to intervene and redirect her toward positive development during a time of dramatic change and vulnerability. Fortunately, most adolescents do adjust and develop a healthy sense of well-being despite multiple challenges. Teachers and other school personnel are becoming more aware of how children's and adolescents' physical health affects their academic and social lives. Schools are implementing nutrition and physical activity programs, along with education about healthy living habits, from the early grades. Through these efforts, we hope to help prevent the Lisas in our classrooms from developing unhealthy physical habits that intensify their other struggles in life.

In this chapter, we examine the influence of biological changes on child and adolescent development. The chapter focuses on many different questions of interest to educators: How does heredity influence a child's development? Why are boys more likely than girls to develop inherited diseases or disorders? How does the brain develop? When can children hold a pencil or hit a ball like an adult? When do young people begin puberty? How can parents and teachers help support young people as they make the transition into adolescence?

Because some physical and cognitive problems have a biological basis, the chapter begins with a discussion of the role of heredity in development. We then look at the process of prenatal development and the factors that can place a child at risk for later development. The following sections describe the development of the brain, perceptual abilities, and motor skills, and causes and consequence of some specific learning disabilities. Next, we explore various aspects of physical development, including changes in height and weight in childhood and at the onset of puberty. Here we will examine the psychological impact of puberty and what can be done to support young people through this transition. In the last section, we discuss eating disorders, drug and alcohol abuse, adolescent sexuality, and other health concerns.

 # Prenatal Development

Developmental processes are set into motion at the moment of human conception, when a male sperm penetrates and fertilizes a female egg. Within this fertilized egg, there are complete instructions for creating a new human being. The time from conception to birth is known as the *prenatal development period*. Similar to other developmental processes, prenatal development follows a universal sequence that is mainly directed by genetic influences. However, the environment can still influence what takes place during prenatal development. A variety of adverse conditions and agents, such as dietary deficiencies, radiation, drugs, and maternal diseases, can contribute to variations in the development of an unborn child.

In this section, we examine the developmental processes that give birth to a child. The first section describes the role of genes and chromosomes. Next, we examine the stages of prenatal development. We also discuss the effects of genetic and environmental factors on the unborn child. In the final section, we consider the effects of birth complications (e.g., low birth weight and prematurity) that can affect a child's status at birth and during later development.

Genes and Chromosomes

Human development begins, as mentioned previously, when a male sperm penetrates a female ovum at the point of conception. The sperm and ovum each contain over 1 billion chemically coded genetic messages that, when combined, serve as the blueprint for human life. The *human zygote* is the cell that is formed by the union of the sperm and ovum. It contains one set of 23 **chromosomes** from the mother and another set of 23 chromosomes from the father. As shown in Figure 2.1 on page 52, the 46 chromosomes are arranged into 23 pairs. At birth, an infant has approximately 10 trillion cells, with each cell containing the same 23 pairs of chromosomes as the one-cell zygote. Chromosomes are composed of long, threadlike molecules of deoxyribonucleic acid (DNA), which twist around to form a spiral staircase or a double helix, as pictured in Figure 2.2 on page 52. This DNA contains approximately 20,000 to 25,000 genes, the basic units of heredity (Human Genome Project, 2004). The Human Genome Project has produced a map of our 3 billion DNA sequences that psychologists are just beginning to learn to use to discover genetic risk indicators (Plomin, 2005). Psychologists hope that these discoveries will eventually help prevent or reduce childhood disorders, such as reading disabilities and hyperactivity (Plomin, 1999; 2005), as discussed later in the chapter.

Whereas some traits, such as Huntington's disease, are caused by a single gene, most human traits result from a combined effect of many different genes. Human characteristics, such as skin color or height, that result from the interplay of multiple genes are called **polygenetic traits.** Some genes are not always expressed, because their genetic directions are

■ FIGURE 2.1
Human Chromosomes
Source: After Hetherington & Parke (1993).

■ FIGURE 2.2
A DNA Molecule

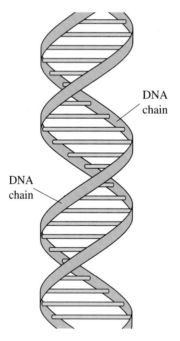

DNA chain

DNA chain

masked by the genes of the other parent. For example, a child who inherits a gene for blonde hair from one parent and a brown-hair gene from the other parent will have brown hair. In this case, the trait not expressed—blonde hair—is the *recessive gene,* whereas brown hair is caused by a *dominant gene.* To produce blonde hair, a recessive gene must be inherited from each parent. Some traits that are caused by recessive genes include blue eyes, baldness, color blindness, hemophilia, and sickle-cell anemia. Abnormalities caused by recessive genes will be discussed in a later section. Other examples of traits caused by dominant genes are curly hair, color vision, and farsightedness.

A child's sex is determined by the twenty-third chromosomes, which are known as the sex chromosomes. Males have two types of sex chromosomes: an X and a Y chromosome, whereas females have two X chromosomes. At the point of conception, if an X-bearing sperm fertilizes an ovum that contains an X chromosome, the fertilized egg will develop as a female (XX). If the sperm contains a Y chromosome, the fertilized egg will develop into a male (XY).

It is believed that sperm that are genetically coded to create male offspring have a greater likelihood of penetrating the ovum than sperm coded to produce females. Approximately 160 males are conceived for every 100 females. However, only 105 boys for every 100 girls are born. Some theorists speculate that females may be better equipped than males to survive the process of prenatal development.

Another interesting fact is that some recessive genes are carried on the sex chromosome. These traits are called *sex-linked characteristics,* because they are carried on the female sex chromosome. For example, baldness, color blindness, and hemophilia are all sex-linked characteristics. Females are the carriers of these disorders, but males have a higher likelihood of inheriting them. The greater genetic vulnerability of males occurs because a recessive gene on the X chromosomes has no matching dominant gene on the Y chromosome to mask its expression. The higher rate of miscarriage and infant mortality for male offspring is partly attributable to their greater vulnerability to sex-linked disorders.

Generally, most pregnancies result in a single birth, but multiple births are becoming more and more frequent, due to the use of hormones to treat infertility problems. There are two ways multiple births occur. First, during the early stages of cell division, a fertilized egg can divide into two clusters that develop into two different fetuses. These are called identical or **monozygotic twins,** because they come from the same fertilized egg and contain the same genetic instructions. Sometimes more than one egg or ova are released from a woman's ovaries at the same time, and both are fertilized. The babies that develop under these conditions are called fraternal or **dizygotic twins,** because they develop from two different eggs. Genetically, dizygotic twins are only as similar as biological siblings, but they share a similar prenatal and postnatal environment. Dizygotic twins (8 per 1,000 births) are more common than monozygotic twins (4 per 1,000 births). The factors linked to fraternal twinning are maternal age, ethnicity, nutrition, number of births, and exposure to fertility drugs (Cohen, 1984).

Genetic and Chromosomal Abnormalities

Every person is the carrier of at least 20 genes that could produce genetic disorders or diseases in their offspring (Milunsky, 1989). Many of these disorders are attributable to recessive genes, so that a person will not inherit a particular condition unless both parents are carriers of the disease. Table 2.1 on page 54 presents a list of common genetic diseases and conditions caused by recessive genes. The disorder Huntington's disease, mentioned earlier, is caused by a dominant gene, but its occurrence is rare (1 out of 18,000 to 25,000 births). Some, but not all, genetic disorders can be detected through genetic counseling or prenatal diagnosis. Couples who already have a child with a genetic disorder, who belong to an ethnic group known to be at risk for a genetic disorder, or who have experienced a series of miscarriages should seek genetic counseling. By taking the couple's genetic history and examining tissue samples, experts are able to determine the risk of genetic disorders that can be identified this way (e.g., sickle-cell anemia, hemophilia, and phenylketonuria—known as PKU). As will be discussed, prenatal tests performed in the third and fourth month of a pregnancy can also reveal a small number of serious genetic disorders. Some parents then have to decide whether or not to continue the pregnancy, which is not an easy decision for any parent.

Some genetic disorders are caused by defects in a chromosome. Most developmental problems of this type occur when genetic instructions go awry during early pregnancy. A chromosome pair does not separate properly, or part of a chromosome breaks off or is damaged. Since the problem does not involve just a single gene, these chromosomal abnormalities usually cause disorders with many physical and mental symptoms.

The best-known genetic disorder of this type is trisomy-21, or **Down syndrome.** A child with Down syndrome has an extra twenty-first chromosome or a piece of one. This disorder occurs in 1 out of 1,000 live births. As shown in Table 2.2 on page 54, incidence of Down syndrome has been linked to the age of the mother. The risk of conceiving a child with Down syndrome is higher among mothers over 35 years old, because there is a greater likelihood that a woman's ova has been exposed to diseases, environmental pollutants, and other damaging effects. Children with Down syndrome have a very characteristic appearance.

TABLE 2.1   Common Genetic Diseases and Disorders

Name	Mode of Inheritance	Incidence	Description	Test Available
Cystic fibrosis	Recessive gene	1 in 3,000 Caucasians; 1 in 16,000 African Americans; 1 in 10,000 Hispanic Americans	Mucous obstructions in lungs and digestive organs that lead to breathing difficulties	Yes
Congenital diabetes	Recessive gene	1 in 2,500 males	Abnormal metabolism of sugar; body does not produce enough insulin	No
Hemophilia	Recessive gene	1 in 10,000 males	Absence of clotting factor in blood	Yes
Huntington's disease	Dominant gene	1 in 18,000 births	Degeneration of central nervous system; symptoms do not appear until age 35 or later	Yes
Muscular dystrophy	Recessive gene	1 in 3,000 males	Degenerative muscular disease	Yes
Phenylketonuria (PKU)	Recessive gene	1 in 15,000 births	Inability to neutralize amino acid phenylalanine, which is present in many proteins; causes severe damage to central nervous system	Yes
Sickle-cell anemia	Recessive gene	1 in 500 African Americans	Abnormal red blood cells cause oxygen deprivation, tissue damage, and susceptibility to infections	Yes
Tay-Sachs disease	Recessive gene	1 in 3,600 births to Jews of European descent	Inability to metabolize fatty substances in neural tissue, which leads to death by age 3 or 4	Yes

TABLE 2.2   Risk Rates of Down Syndrome

Maternal Age (Years)	Rate of Risk
20	1 in 1,900 births
25	1 in 1,200 births
30	1 in 900 births
33	1 in 600 births
36	1 in 300 births
39	1 in 140 births
42	1 in 70 births
45	1 in 30 births

Their heads tend to be smaller and rounder than other children, their eyes are almond shaped, and their limbs are short. Children with Down syndrome often have sweet dispositions, and a range of physical and mental handicaps. They are susceptible to heart defects, infectious diseases, and other health problems. Although most children with Down syndrome have below-average intelligence, they have more learning potential than was assumed 15 to 20 years ago, when the majority of such children were institutionalized. It is important to remember that not all children with Down syndrome are alike. Depending on how much extra genetic material is present, some children with this disorder exhibit practically normal characteristics (Rosenberg & Pettigrew, 1983). About 20 percent of children with Down syndrome die by age 10, but many live until middle adulthood.

Another chromosomal disorder, **fragile-X syndrome,** is one of the leading causes of mental retardation and developmental disabilities (Bailey & Nelson, 1995). Caused by a single gene, fragile-X syndrome is more common in males than females: 1 in 1,000 males versus 1 in 5,000 females. Males with this disorder have more serious symptoms than females, perhaps because the female carries another normal X chromosome. In females, fragile-X syndrome may result in mild forms of retardation, but about 25 percent of females who have this disorder have normal intelligence (Barnes, 1989). Of the males who inherit a fragile-X chromosome, 20 percent will have normal intelligence, 33 percent will be mildly retarded, and the rest will be severely retarded. Delays are generally evident in all developmental domains, although cognitive and communication skills tend to be the most affected. In both boys and girls, fragile-X syndrome is associated with cleft palate, abnormal EEGs, disorders of the eyes,

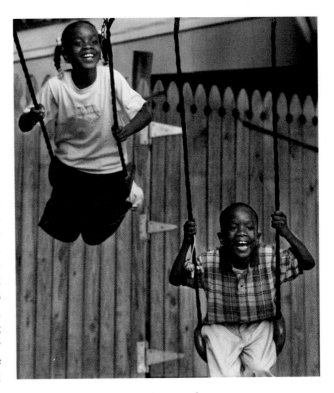

Fraternal twins with fragile-X syndrome.
Source: Chuck Liddy/News & Observer.

and a characteristic facial appearance. It is also associated with attention deficits, hyperactivity, language deficits in males, and increased depression in females. The social relationships of children with fragile-X syndrome are often affected due to poor communication skills. Boys with fragile-X syndrome may display an unusual style of interacting with other people. They tend to avoid direct eye contact during conversation and hand-flapping or hand-biting is common (Hagerman & Silverman, 1991). Compared with Down syndrome, this chromosomal abnormality appears to have more variable effects, which may depend partly on the influence of the environment. It is important to keep in mind that the quality of the family and school environment can moderate the effects of chromosomal anomalies (Bender, Linden, & Robinson, 1987).

Fragile-X syndrome can be detected through genetic screening and DNA analysis. Down syndrome can also be detected, and older mothers are generally counseled to have prenatal tests to identify any unexpected chromosomal abnormalities. The tests used for a prenatal diagnosis are described in Table 2.3. Amniocentesis is the most widely used procedure, but it cannot be performed before the fourth month of pregnancy. It involves inserting a needle through the abdominal wall to withdraw a small amount of amniotic fluid. The fetal cells are then examined for abnormalities. There are several newer tests for detecting genetic defects, but they cannot identify all disorders, and they may be less reliable. Scientists are currently working on methods for correcting some genetic defects before the fetus is born.

From Genotype to Phenotype

To understand the effects of genetic influences on development, it is important to distinguish between a person's genotype and phenotype. The genes a person inherits from both parents for any particular trait make up his or her **genotype.** The actual expression of these traits is his or

TABLE 2.3	Description of Prenatal Tests
Type of Test	**Description**
Ultrasound	High-frequency sound waves used to form electronic picture of fetus; may have long-term effects on mother and fetal tissue
Amniocentesis	Sample of fluid extracted from amniotic sac; procedure typically performed at 15 to 18 weeks, can detect presence of over 100 disorders and sex of fetus; may result in uterine cramping and miscarriage
Chorionic villi sampling	Hollow tube inserted into the chorion, which surrounds the embryo in early weeks of gestation; procedure performed between twelfth and eighteenth week; scope of analysis is limited; some risk of infection
Alpha fetoprotein (AFP) testing	Sample of mother's blood tested for AFP substance between week 15 and 18; procedure can detect defects in neural tube (e.g., spina bifida); recommended for all pregnancies, especially if there is a history of neural tube defect

her **phenotype.** We have already learned that some traits are only expressed when both parents donate a recessive gene, such as with blonde hair. When individuals receive a recessive gene from one parent and a dominant gene from another parent, their genotype will be different from their phenotype. That is, they may have a recessive gene for the disease PKU, but because it is paired with a normal gene it is not expressed. Genes can also interact in an additive fashion to influence a person's phenotype. The several genes that influence height, temperament, intellectual abilities, and many other human traits are believed to interact in an additive way. Thus, genes interact among themselves to influence the actual expression of inherited traits.

A person's observable characteristics are also influenced by ongoing interactions between the genes and the environment. Some genes are not expressed, because the environment does not facilitate their appearance. For instance, a person may have inherited a set of genes for high intellectual ability, but if that talent is not encouraged or stimulated, it may not develop to its fullest. In other cases, the environment can modify the expression of some genes so that the inherited genes do not affect a person's phenotype. The disease PKU, for example, is associated with mental retardation. If a child with PKU is placed on a special diet from birth, mental retardation will not occur. In this case, the environmental effect of a special diet modifies the effects of a particular genotype (PKU), caused by two recessive genes.

Researchers use the concept of **reaction range** to understand genetic and environmental influences. This concept refers to a person's unique, genetically determined response to environmental influences. Two people with the same set of genetic instructions (genotypes) can develop different characteristics (phenotypes) if reared in vastly different environments. Conversely, people with different genotypes will respond differently to the same environments. The concept of reaction range helps us to understand that children differ in their responses to the environment. Our genes determine the upper and lower boundaries for our development, but the environment can facilitate or impede that development. The reaction range defines the degree to which the environment can affect the development. Figure 2.3

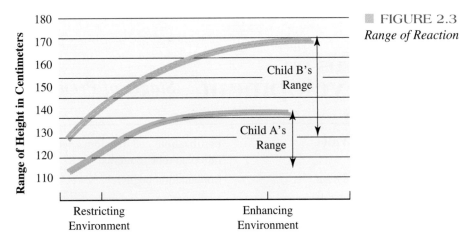

■ FIGURE 2.3
Range of Reaction

A child's genetic inheritance establishes the range of reaction within which environmental influences can affect development.

shows a graphic representation of the reaction range concept. In the diagram, Child A and Child B differ in their genetic inheritance for height. Child A can benefit more from an enriching environment than Child B.

Stages of Prenatal Development

The average period of human gestation is 38 weeks. Within the first weeks of prenatal development, the head, limbs, vital organs, central nervous system, and skeleton are all formed. This period of development is the most rapid in the human life span. The Focus on Development box on page 58 shows the stages of prenatal development. It is divided into three major stages: the *germinal period,* the *embryonic period,* and the *fetal period.* Developmental processes are most susceptible to disruption when the basic human structures are developing. The important changes that occur in each stage are briefly summarized here.

The first stage of prenatal development, the germinal period, encompasses the first 2 weeks of fetal development. In this stage, the fertilized ovum, or zygote, travels down the fallopian tube to the uterus, making new cells through the process of **mitosis.** During mitosis, chromosomes produce duplicate copies of themselves and divide into new cells. Within approximately 4 days, the zygote reaches the uterus, and the fertilized egg now contains 60 to 70 cells formed into a hollow ball. Before the zygote attaches itself to the uterine wall, cell differentiation takes place. The outer edge of the zygote will develop into the embryo, while other cells become the structures that protect and nourish the embryo, such as the placenta, the umbilical cord, and the amniotic sac. By day 6, the zygote develops threadlike structures or villi that enable it to draw nourishment from the uterine wall. Full implantation to the uterine wall does not occur until 12 days after conception, and it is not automatic. An estimated 58 percent of all zygotes fail to implant properly, thereby terminating pregnancy. Only 31 percent of all conceptions become living newborns.

Implantation of the zygote marks the beginning of the next stage of prenatal development, the *embryonic period.* From weeks 2 to 8, all the basic structures of the child are established. During the early days of the embryonic period, the placenta, umbilical cord, and amniotic sac, which were present at implantation, mature and begin to function. These structures are the life-support system for the developing embryo. At the same time, the embryonic structure develops three distinctive layers of cells. The outermost layer, the *ectoderm,* will become the nervous system and skin. The middle layer, the *mesoderm,* will become the

Focus on
Development
Stages of Prenatal Development

Stage	Time	Changes
Germinal	0 to 4 days	Fertilization; cell division; zygote travels down fallopian tube to uterus
	4 to 8 days	Implantation begins
	12 to 13 days	Implantation completed
Embryonic	2 weeks	Placenta begins to form
	3 to 4 weeks	Heart begins to beat; eyes, blood vessels, and nervous system begin to develop
	5 to 6 weeks	Arms and legs begin to form; gonads begin to form
	8 weeks	Development of major organs completed; pregnancy detectable by physical exam
Fetal	8 to 12 weeks	Appearance of genitals; leg and arm movements occur; circulation system functions
	10 weeks	Responds to stimulation
	13 to 16 weeks	Skin and hair develop; skeleton hardens
	20 weeks	Heartbeat can be heard; vigorous movement
	25 to 28 weeks	Begins to gain weight; sucking movements visible
	26 weeks	Eyes open
	28 weeks	Respiratory system matures; survival outside womb possible
	30 weeks	Gains layer of fat under skin
	32 to 26 weeks	Survival outside womb probable
	38 weeks	Normal birth

skeleton and muscles, and the innermost layer, the *endoderm,* will become the digestive tract and vital organs. This remarkable process of cell differentiation appears to be regulated by chemical reactions around the cells. Before differentiation, every cell of the embryo is virtually identical, but some cells will become brain cells while others will become the lining of the stomach, due to their location in the embryo and to the chemical messages they receive from their surrounding environment. In other words, genetic and environmental interactions are already taking place that will influence the process of human development.

During the third and fourth weeks of prenatal development, the heart and neural tube that will become the central nervous system begin to form, and ears and teeth buds under the gums appear in week 6. Between weeks 6 and 8, sex differentiation occurs. If a Y chromosome is present, gonadal tissue begins to differentiate into testes, the male sex organ. If no Y chromosome is present, the gonadal tissue begins to form into female ovaries. The sex chromosomes have now completed their mission; prenatal hormones secreted by the male and female sex organs (testes and ovaries) shape sexual differentiation from here on, including the formation of external genitalia.

By the end of week 8, all the embryo's basic organs and structures (heart, liver, digestive system) are in place, and some begin to function. All this development takes place when the embryo is barely 1 inch long! The rapid development of new organs and systems makes the embryonic period particularly vulnerable to environmental agents that can cause congenital anomalies (see Focus on Development box on page 58). Most miscarriages, or spontaneous abortions, occur within this period. It is nature's way of eliminating the embryos with gross chromosomal or genetic abnormalities that are not likely to survive on their own.

The last and longest stage of prenatal development is called the *fetal period.* During this time (from 8 weeks until birth), the size of the fetus increases. In the fourth and fifth months, the weight of the fetus increases tenfold! Eyelids, fingernails, taste buds, and hair form. By the fifth month, the fetus is generally active and gains another 3 to 4 pounds in the eighth and ninth months. At this time, the respiratory system matures to enable breathing after birth. If the baby is born in the seventh month, it can often survive but will need special support systems. By the ninth month, the fetus is cramped for space, and it is an uncomfortable time for mother and baby alike. Toward the end of this month, the baby moves to a head-down position. When this happens, birth is very near.

Fetus in womb.
Source: Alex Bartel/Science Photo Library/Photo Researchers, Inc.

Environmental Effects on Prenatal Development

Prenatal development, for the most part, is directed by genetic factors. However, as mentioned previously, environmental conditions can interfere with normal fetal development. For this reason, radiologists generally ask women if they are pregnant before taking an X-ray. Doctors and pharmacists also inquire about a woman's status before prescribing a drug. In some work environments, women of child-bearing ages are protected from areas that would expose them to toxic agents.

Any environmental substance or disease that causes abnormal development of the fetus is called a **teratogen.** Forty years ago, many women continued smoke cigarettes and drink alcohol while pregnant. Scientists have now shown that nicotine, alcohol, opiates, and cocaine all can have harmful effects on the development of a fetus (e.g., Mayes & Fahy, 2001). The frequent use of alcohol during pregnancy is one of the leading causes of mental retardation in industrialized countries (Cramer & Davidhizar, 1999). Other substances that can negatively affect the development of the fetus are prescription drugs, radiation, environmental pollutants (e.g., lead, mercury, PCBs), illegal drugs, and synthetic hormones. The effects of selected teratogens are summarized in Table 2.4 on page 60.

Certain diseases contracted by the mother during pregnancy, such as rubella, mumps, chicken pox, and malaria, also can have harmful effects on a developing fetus. Similarly, sexually transmitted diseases, such as chlamydia, syphilis, genital herpes, and gonorrhea, are dangerous as well. These diseases, caused by a viral or bacterial infection, are passed to the fetus through the placenta, infecting the fetus. Genital herpes is not passed to the fetus unless the infection is active at the time of delivery. Acquired immune deficiency syndrome (AIDS), which destroys the immune system, is another deadly disease that can be passed on to an unborn child. The Focus on Research box on page 61 describes new methods for reducing the transmission of HIV to infants.

The effects of these teratogens on prenatal development are neither simple nor straightforward. As discussed earlier, a fetus is most vulnerable to environmental influences

TABLE 2.4   Effects of Selected Drugs and Chemicals on Prenatal Development

Agent or Substance	Possible Effects
Analgesics (painkillers)	Respiratory problems
Anesthetics	Respiratory problems
Aspirin (large quantities)	Respiratory problems; low birth weight; poor motor development; fetal or infant death
Alcohol	Fetal alcohol syndrome (FAS): facial abnormalities; lower IQ; heart problems; developmental lag; poor attention and social skills
Antihistamines	Malformations; fetal death
Caffeine	Increased risk of retarded fetal growth and low birth weight
Cocaine	Structural damage; delayed growth; prematurity and low birth weight; hypersensitivity to stimuli; convulsions and seizures that can cause brain damage; poor attention and social skills
Diethylstilbestrol (DES)	In female offspring, increased risk of vaginal cancer, abnormal uterus, and high-risk pregnancies; in male offspring, increased risk of genital abnormalities and cancer of the testes
Heroin, morphine	Newborn withdrawal symptoms; prematurity and low birth weight; convulsions and tremors; developmental delays; infant death
Marijuana	Impairment of central nervous system; retarded fetal growth; prematurity and low birth weight; fetal or infant death; poor language and memory skills
Nicotine	Stunted fetal growth; prematurity and low birth weight; respiratory problems;convulsions; abnormal heart rate; cleft palate and lip; reduced head size; increased risk of infant death; learning problems
Oral contraceptives	Increased risk of heart and limb deformities
Streptomycin	Hearing loss
Tetracycline	Discolored teeth, slow bone growth
Valium	Cleft palate and lip

during sensitive periods when the body parts and major organs are rapidly developing. In the 1950s, the drug thalidomide was prescribed to expectant women to prevent nausea and sleeplessness. It was used in 28 countries other than the United States, because it did not receive approval from the U.S. Food and Drug Administration (FDA). Women who took the drug between 38 to 46 days after conception gave birth to babies with deformed arms. If exposed to the drug between 46 to 48 days, the babies were born with deformed legs. In contrast, women who took the drug after 50 days gave birth to babies with normal limbs. This tragic example clearly shows the varying influence of teratogens on unborn babies as well as sensitive periods for development.

Besides the timing of exposure, the level of dosage moderates the effects of teratogens on the fetus. In general, the more frequent the exposure and the higher the dose, the more severe the damage. Some teratogenic agents have a cumulative effect. For example, every

Focus on
Research

Preventing AIDS in Infants

Recent statistics indicate that over 1 million children under the age of 15 are living with HIV/AIDS, and approximately 3.2 million children have died from the virus or associated causes. It is also estimated that 7,000 young people between the ages of 10 and 24 become infected with HIV every day—five new cases per minute. More than 95 percent of all HIV-infected people live in developing countries. The United States has a relatively small percentage of the world's children living with HIV/AIDS. The latest available data, which were compiled in 1996, indicated that HIV was the seventh leading cause of death for U.S. children through age 14.

How is HIV transmitted to infants? Nearly 90 percent of infections worldwide occur during pregnancy or birth. Although the precise mechanism is not yet known, scientists believe HIV may be transmitted when the mother's blood enters the fetal circulation or when the infant is exposed to the mucous lining during the birth process. The risk of maternal-infant transmission is significantly increased if the mother has advanced HIV disease. The disease also may be transmitted from a nursing mother to her infant. In developing countries, approximately one-third to one-half of HIV infections occur through breast-feeding. Before blood was routinely screened for HIV in 1995,

some infants were infected with AIDS through blood transfusions or blood products contaminated with HIV.

What can be done to stop the transmission of AIDS to infants? The best way to prevent pediatric HIV infections is to prevent AIDS in adults or to prevent pregnancies in HIV-infected women. Unfortunately, HIV has a long incubation period (up to 10 years or more), during which mothers can transmit the disease without knowing they were infected. If HIV is detected through screening, it is possible to reduce the risk of mother-infant transmission through the use of the drug AZT. A landmark study in 1994 showed that AZT can reduce the transmission of HIV from 25 percent to 8 percent (Centers for Disease Control and Prevention, 1994). In this study, AZT was given to the mother in the second or third trimester and through delivery, and the infants were treated for 6 weeks following birth. The AZT produced no serious side effects in the mothers and infants. The use of AZT has dramatically reduced the incidence of perinatal AIDS in the United States and Europe. However, this treatment is not available to developing countries due to its high cost (approximately $1,000 per pregnancy, not counting counseling and testing). International organizations are studying ways to provide the AZT treatment to developing countries at lower costs.

Source: National Institutes of Health (2000a).

cigarette smoked by a pregnant woman reduces an infant's birth weight by several milligrams. Other teratogens have a threshold effect; the substance is harmless unless its use reaches a certain frequency or dosage level. One or two aspirins during pregnancy may not harm a fetus, but frequent use of aspirin can lower a baby's birth weight, increase fetal or infant death, and impair motor development after birth (Barr, Streissguth, Darby, & Sampson, 1990). Finally, a woman's health status can reduce or increase the effects of teratogens. Poor nutrition, lack of prenatal care, poor health, or the presence of other teratogens can worsen the effects of a single harmful agent. On the other hand, doctors now know for certain that ensuring the level of some nutrients, such as folic acid, can prevent some common birth defects, such as cleft lip and palate and spina bifida.

High-Risk Infants

Most babies are born between 38 and 42 weeks after conception and weigh between 5 and 10 pounds at birth. Babies within both this time period and weight range tend to be at minimal risk for complications. However, 7.7 percent of babies born in the United States weigh less than 5.5 pounds, or 2,500 grams, and 12 percent are born preterm (U.S. Department of Health and Human Services, 2003). Babies who are small for gestation are called **low birth weight** (LBW). Not all low-birth-weight babies are premature or preterm; some full-term babies are classified as low birth weight. In general, a baby's risk factors increase as its period of gestation and weight decrease. A short gestation period or low birth weight is one of the leading causes of infant mortality. These babies die before the age of 1 year. Despite declines in infant mortality over the last decades, the U.S. infant mortality rate ranks highest of industrial countries (see Figure 2.4). In the United States, infant mortality rates are almost twice as high for black infants (13.3 deaths per 1,000 live births) as for Hispanic and white infants (U.S. Department of Health and Human Services, 2003). The statistics are difficult to accept when the United States has one of the most advanced medical systems in the world.

It is also interesting to note that the United States has one of the highest low-birth-weight rates among many industrialized countries, including Canada, Germany, France, Japan, Sweden, and Norway. Moreover, the proportion of U.S. babies born at low birth weight is at its highest level since 1976 (Children's Defense Fund, 1999). As with infant mortality rates, preterm and low-birth-weight deliveries vary by the infant's ethnic background. Asian populations have the lowest preterm delivery rates, while Hispanic and Native Americans have slightly higher rates than do white populations. African Americans have the highest rates of preterm and low-birth-weight deliveries of any major ethnic group in the United States (U.S. Department of Health and Human Services, 2001). African American babies are twice as likely as white or Asian babies to be born preterm, to be born low birth weight, and to die at birth (Shino & Behrman, 1995).

What are the causes of prematurity and low birth weight? The causes of prematurity are not well understood. In some cases, problems with the placenta or cervix are associated with a premature birth. In the third trimester, toxemia (characterized by water retention, high blood pressure, and urine in the blood) can also lead to a premature birth.

The causes of low birth weight are much clearer. The most common and direct cause is poor nutrition. Within the United States, the rates of low birth weight are higher in some areas than in others. In the District of Columbia, for example, rates of low-birth-weight births are around 13 percent for all ethnic groups, whereas 5.5 percent of babies born in Oregon are of low birth weight (Children's Defense Fund, 2000).

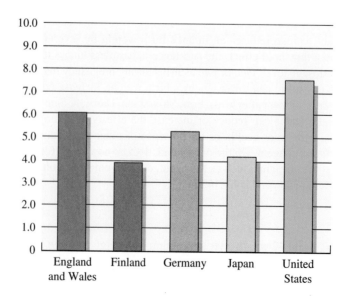

■ FIGURE 2.4
Cross-National Comparisons of Infant Mortality Rates per 1,000 Live Births
Source: U.S. Department of Health and Human Services, *Trends in the Well-being of America's Children and Youth* (2000).

Another common cause of low birth weight is poor prenatal care. It is estimated that one in six American children is born to a mother who did not receive prenatal care in the first trimester (Children's Defense Fund, 2004). Mothers who receive no prenatal care are three times more likely to produce low-birth-weight babies than mothers who receive care in the first trimester. As with proper nutrition, access to prenatal care is related to socioeconomic status. Low-income mothers are less likely to receive prenatal care in the first months of pregnancy than higher-income mothers. Other factors that can increase the risk of low birth weight are substance abuse (including smoking cigarettes, drinking alcohol, and using drugs), maternal age (see Figure 2.5), multiple pregnancies, short time between pregnancies, and the mother's general health condition.

Through the use of modern medical technology, many preterm and low-birth-weight babies survive, but they are at risk for developing a number of complications. Birth weight is the most reliable predictor of infant survival and healthy development. A low birth weight is associated with an increased risk for infections, cerebral palsy, visual impairments, brain damage, and lung and liver disease. As they enter school, children born with a low birth weight are more likely than children of normal birth weight to have mild learning disabilities, attention problems, poor concentration, language delays, and asthma. Low-birth-weight infants are three to five more times more likely to be placed into special education classes or retained in school (Hack, Klein, & Taylor, 1995).

As a nation, we spend about $15 billion per year on neonatal intensive care. We seem to focus more on keeping low-birth-weight babies alive than on preventing this problem. It is estimated that for every dollar we spend on prenatal care, we could save $3.00 in postnatal intensive care and more than $4.60 in long-term health costs for low-birth-weight or preterm babies (Lu, Lin, Prietto, & Garite, 2000). Smoking prevention and cessation programs and the Special Supplement Food Program for Women, Infants, and Children (WIC) have been helpful in improving maternal weight gain (Shino & Behrman, 1995). Although prevention is preferred, it is heartening to learn that some early intervention programs for low-birth-weight premature infants have been effective in enhancing cognitive skills through age 8, especially for those who participated regularly (Hill, Brooks-Gunn, & Wald-fogel, 2003). In this research, the intervention programs were intensive, incorporating a number of services for children and parents, including early childhood education, home visits and parent education, and pediatric observation for several years.

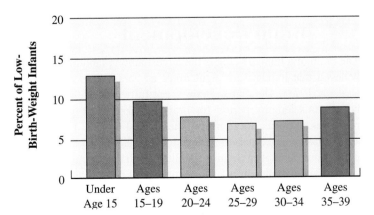

■ FIGURE 2.5
Percent of Low-Birth-Weight Infants as Percentage of All Infants Born in the United States, by Mother's Age
Source: U.S. Department of Health and Human Services (2003).

Maternal age is a contributing factor to low birth weight. A higher percent of low-birth-weight infants are born to mothers under the age of 19.

Focus on
Teaching

Is It Time for Brain-Based Education?

New research on early brain development has been the feature of numerous books, journals, magazines, and newspapers. A 1997 White House Conference called "Early Learning and the Brain" released a report detailing the importance of early brain development for child care and other social programs. Impressed by new research suggesting that classical music can improve academic learning, the former governor of Georgia, Zel Miller, convinced state legislatures to fund a program to give every newborn in the state a classical tape. Following Georgia's lead, Florida politicians proposed that child care centers receiving state funds should be required to play classical music. Michael Rutter, in his 2001 Presidential Address to the Society for Research in Child Development, referred to "misleading evangelism" during the last decade regarding reports about the extent to which early experiences determine brain development.

According to Thompson and Nelson (2001) in a renowned article, "Developmental Science and the Media," the "I Am Your Child" public information campaign organized by Rob Reiner (now known as "Parents' Action for Children") stirred increased attention to brain development. These authors suggest that this campaign, along with other events, led to widespread reports

concerning "new" research revealing the following characteristics of early brain development (believed to be previously unknown): (1) Early experiences are crucial in stimulating the development and pruning of neural synapses; (2) permanent deficits are likely if vital experiences do not occur during early critical or sensitive periods; thus, "windows of opportunity" are lost; (3) contingent nurturing is most important for early brain stimulation; and (4) neuroscientists are on the verge of significant new discoveries about early brain development with recent technological advances. This media attention has proven helpful by directing attention to the needs of young children and improvement of child care policies. And "these are valuable contributions. However, these media accounts have also tended to exaggerate how much is actually known about the developing brain, overinterpreting current scientific knowledge and overpromising its applications while also unduly narrowing public understanding of the range of important influences on brain development" (p.7). Developmentalists fear that important public interest in child development may disintegrate if parents, practitioners, and policy makers feel that they were deceived, especially if programs based on faulty interpretations of research do not show expected intellectual or social gains in children.

Brain Development

The brain of a human being is the largest among land mammals relative to body size. It is believed that humans are eight times as "brainy" as the average mammal living today (Jerison, 1973). The human brain is not fully mature until early adulthood, and scientists believe this lengthy period for brain development enables humans to acquire thought processes and skills not found in other animal species. The largest part of the human brain, and the last to develop, is the frontal lobe or cerebral cortex, shown in Figure 2.6 on page 66, which controls higher cognitive abilities such as reasoning and speech.

Brain development is a fascinating and very active area of study. Some claim that the twenty-first century will be the "century of neuroscience" (Farah et al., 2004). With the sophisticated technology for studying the human brain available today, scientists are making important discoveries about brain development, and many ideas about brain development are open for discussion and debate. As we will see, one issue of debate concerns whether or not there is a "critical period" for children's cognitive, language, social, and emotional

Thompson and Nelson (2001) state that although the significance of the first 3 years of life has been overstated, it is not a "myth" (as Bruer and others have referred to exaggerated claims about its importance for brain development; see Bruer, 1999). Instead, they suggest that parents, caregivers, educators, and therapists of children of all ages attend to the following "important news" about brain development based on research:

- Brain development can be facilitated at several developmental stages.
- Building babies' brain begins at conception, not at birth.
- Caregivers are influential not only relationally but also in the physical care, nutrition, and protections they provide to foster young brains and minds.
- Eliminating early disadvantages is important, but the plasticity of brain development means that early deprivation and harm can be treated in later years.
- Adult brains are also developing.

These conclusions may not be remarkable, but they are certainly hopeful.

Are educational practices justified on the basis of brain research? John Bruer (2002) reports other popular, misguided attempts at applying brain research to education, such as: (a) high synaptic density points to the importance of rigorous early childhood education; (b) adolescent synaptic pruning requires intensive learning to "save" synapses from elimination (the "use-it-or-lose-it" principle); (c) the brain's high neural connectivity demands integrated, experiential learning; and (d) classroom activities can and should be designed to maximize neural branching. He states that there is little scientific evidence to support these practices. Early research suggested that the young brain is more active than the adolescent and adult brain, but it is not clear that high brain activity means greater efficiency and depth of learning (Bruer, 1999, p. 656). Also, brain-based educators ignore evidence that synapse elimination (pruning) is essential for normal brain development, as we have learned. "At best, brain-based education is not more than a folk-theory about the brain and learning" (Bruer, 2002, p. 1032).

In an article about the social policy implications of brain research, Ross Thompson (1998) writes, "The mysteries of brain development are not understanding its unfolding growth (researchers learn more each day) or knowing how to promote brain development. The mystery is why, as a wise society, we do not invest more in creating the conditions that support the development of healthy minds" (p. 8).

development. As recently as 1980, scientists believed that the structure of the brain, and its development, were genetically determined. In the last several years, however, scientists discovered that experiences play a powerful role in brain development, physically determining how the brain becomes "wired." Some 10 billion nerve cells form connections after birth, and new evidence suggests that brain development occurs well into the adolescent years, and brain *reorganization* continues through much of the life span (Nelson, 2005a). In this section, we explore changes in the brain from infancy through adolescence. We also discuss the role of environmental experiences in brain development. The Focus on Teaching box on on pages 64 and 65 discusses the implications of this research for educators.

Changes in the Brain

The central nervous system is made up of the brain, the spinal cord, and nerve cells, and it controls almost every aspect of human functioning. At the center of this sophisticated control system are billions of long, thin cells called **neurons,** which are formed during the first 5 months of gestation. Neurons differ from other body cells because they are not closely packed together. There are tiny gaps between neurons, known as *synapses,* where fibers from different neurons

■ FIGURE 2.6

*Left Side of the
Human Brain*

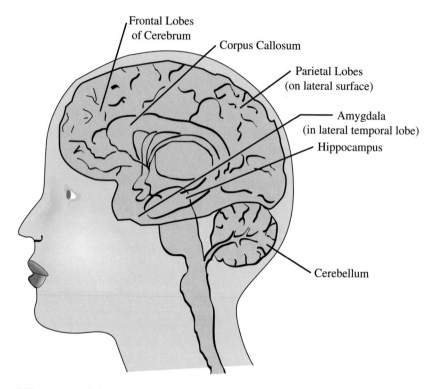

Frontal Lobes
of Cerebrum

Corpus Callosum

Parietal Lobes
(on lateral surface)

Amygdala
(in lateral temporal lobe)

Hippocampus

Cerebellum

Different parts of the brain have different functions

■ The hippocampus makes it possible to recall recent experience and new information.

■ The amygdala directs our emotional responses.

■ The frontal lobes of the cerebrum allow us to solve problems, plan ahead, understand the behavior of others, and restrain our impulses.

■ The parietal areas control hearing, speech, and language.

■ The cerebellum regulates balance, body movements, coordination, and the muscles used in speaking.

■ The corpus callosum passes information from one side of the brain to the other.

come close together but do not touch. Neurons release chemicals, called *neurotransmitters,* that cross over these gaps to communicate with other neurons (see Figure 2.7).

When a sound or image enters the senses, it is transmitted to the brain as an electrical impulse. It then travels to a region of the brain where it is interpreted and recorded by a set of neurons. The more often this same set of neurons is used due to frequent exposure to the same stimuli, the more likely a particular sound or image will be stored in long-term memory. Every memory we have is made up of thousands of these neural connections.

Research on early brain development suggests that during the early months and years of life, the brain is growing at an unprecedented rate, not to be matched in later years (Thompson, 1998). At birth, each neuron has approximately 2,500 synapses, and as many as 15,000 two years later (Nash, 1997). This initial overproduction of synapses (synaptogenesis) may be the means by which the brain is made ready to receive specific input from the environment (Nelson, 2005a). Brain development after birth involves important changes. First, the number and length of neural fibers that connect different neurons and nerve cells (dendrites and axons) increase. Figure 2.8 shows the growth of these fibers during the first 2 years of life. The dark spots are the neurons, and the thin lines are the dendrites and the axons that connect the cells. These connections allow brain cells to communicate with one another. Humans are born with more neurons than they need. It is believed that connections between neurons are formed

■ FIGURE 2.7
What Is a Neuron?

Nerve cells, or neurons, transmit information throughout the brain in the form of electrical impulses. When an impulse moves through a neuron, the cell release neurotransmitters into the synapses to communicate with other neurons.

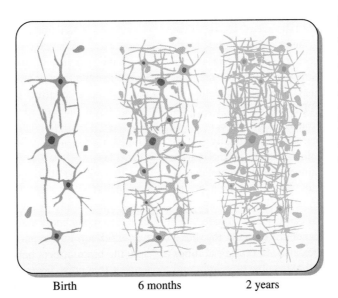

| Birth | 6 months | 2 years |

■ FIGURE 2.8
Early Brain Development
Source: Reprinted by permission of the publisher from *The Postnatal Development of the Human Cerebral Cortex,Vols I–VIII* by Jesse LeRoy Conel, Cambridge, Mass.: Harvard University Press, Copyright © 1939, 1975 by the President and Fellows of Harvard College.

each second during the first few months of life. Half of the neurons produced during prenatal development die because they fail to link to other neurons. As we will learn, the strength of connections between neurons is largely determined by activity or experience. *Pruning,* or loss of synapses, is environmentally regulated and occurs late in childhood and adolescence; it is likely that only inappropriate synapses disappear (Nelson, 2005a).

Another major change is the process of **myelination,** whereby the neurons and dendrites become coated with a fatty substance called myelin. Myelination enables neural impulses to travel faster. The changes occur rapidly in the first few years, but the process of myelination in the frontal cortex can continue into adulthood. Over the course of early development, neurons become increasingly selective and respond only to certain neurotransmitters.

Although brain growth is most rapid early in development, the brain continues to develop in childhood and adolescence. In fact, researchers have made several new discoveries about the teen brain (see Focus on Research box on page 68). As we will learn in Chapters 3 and 4, more

Focus on
Research

The Teen Brain

Much of the recent attention to research on brain development has focused on the early years of life. Recently, however, new discoveries have been made about brain development in adolescence. Contrary to the idea that the brain reaches maturity by puberty, researchers at UCLA's Lab of Neuro Imaging have discovered that the frontal lobes undergo significant changes between the ages of 10 and 12 (Begley, 2000). These areas of the brain are responsible for executive functions such as judgment, self-control, emotional regulation, and planning. Additionally, researchers have discovered that temporal lobes, which are responsible for language as well as emotional control, do not fully mature until the age of 16. Together, recent research suggests that the brain undergoes many more changes in the second decade of life than originally thought. Charles Nelson, director of the Center for Neurobehavioral Development at the University of Minnesota, explained in a PBS "Frontline" interview (2005b) that changes in the frontal cortex (especially the prefrontal area) appear to increase dramatically beginning with puberty, and probably continue to the end of adolescence. These changes affect how the frontal cortex regulates emotions in the middle part of the brain, possibly giving rise to the stereotypical mood swings and outbursts of the teenager who can cry out, "I hate you" one minute, and be calm and considerate the next. Changes in the prefrontal cortex also affect one's abilities to plan and use strategies flexibly to solve problems, and may be partially responsible for young teens' difficulties with tasks such as monitoring their schoolwork. It is also possible that adolescents take more risks, at least to some extent, because they have an immature frontal cortex.

Jay Giedd, chief of the Unit on Brain Imagining at the National Institute for Mental Health, and his colleagues have found that the cerebellum also changes well into adolescence, and may be partially responsible for enhancing physical coordination as well as processing of mental tasks. Giedd hypothesizes that this part of the brain works "like a math co-processor. It's not essential for any activity . . . but it makes any activity better. Anything we can think of as a higher thought, mathematics, music, philosophy, decision-making, social skills, draws upon the cerebellum. . . . To navigate the complicated social life of the teen and to get through these things instead of lurching seems to be a function of the cerebellum" (Sparks, 2005).

Again, researchers warn that the learning more about the *structure* of the brain does not necessarily tell us more about the *function* of the brain; discovering how parts of the brain affect *behavior* is much more complicated. Even the use of modern technologies, such as "functional" magnetic resonance imaging (fMRI), has limited use in studies with children (Rutter, 2002). Patricia Miller (2002) advises, "A cautionary note is that there is a danger that findings from neuroscience are being considered more important—more basic and explanatory—than purely behavioral findings. . . . Although neuroscientists know that showing the brain basis of behavior reflects how experience affects the brain as well as how the brain affects behavior, other people sometimes neglect this point when interpreting findings" (p. 432). The story of development is best understood through acknowledging multiple, interconnected, and equally relevant explanations (e.g., biological, behaviorial, psychological, ecological).

complex thought processes emerge in childhood and adolescence. These cognitive abilities include problem solving, strategic planning, emotion management, and searching the memory for information and events. Many of these more sophisticated thought processes are located in the cerebral cortex, which develops more slowly than other areas of the brain (see Figure 2.6 on page 66).

The brain is a living organ, and, like other biological systems, it cannot develop without adequate nutrition and protection from dangerous or toxic substances. The effects of undernutrition (lack of sufficient protein and other nutrients) on the developing brain have been studied for several decades. This research has shown that the timing of nutritional deprivation is important. In the first trimester of pregnancy, poor nutrition can negatively affect the production of neurons, whereas deprivation in late pregnancy affects the maturation of neurons. Additionally, specific nutritional deficiency, such as insufficient folic acid, can cause fetal brain damage. After birth, the developing brain is most vulnerable to nutritional deprivation within the first 2 to 3 years of life. The earlier and longer that malnutrition occurs, the greater effect on the brain (National Research Council, 2000). Similarly, the brain is most vulnerable to drugs, diseases, viruses, and other toxic substances while it is undergoing rapid growth.

However, it is important to keep in mind that the immature brain has considerable flexibility. Research suggests that it can recover from early damage or defects when periods of deprivation are followed by adequate nutrition and environmental stimulation. In Chapter 4, we will look at the success of early intervention programs in reducing the long-term impact of poverty on children's intellectual development.

Brain Development and Experience

Genetics largely influence the timing of brain development, but research from the past 5 years suggests that experience plays a more important role in shaping brain development than was previously thought (Gopnik, Meltzoff, & Kuhl, 1999; National Research Council, 2000; Thompson, 1998). Stimulation or input from the environment is important for increasing and maintaining connections between neurons. As one group of researchers described it:

> Many species seem to have evolved such that the genes need only roughly outline the pattern of neural connectivity in a sensory system, leaving more specific details to be determined through the organism's interactions with its environment. (Greenough, Black, & Wallace, 1987, p. 543)

Scientists believe that the nervous system fine-tunes itself during the course of development. Neurons are programmed to receive certain input or stimulation during the period in which the formation of synapses are at a peak; that is, certain environmental stimulation is expected (Greenough et al., 1987). This type of brain programming is called *experience-expectant*. Neurons that receive this stimulation from the environment form connections, whereas those that fail to receive the appropriate input or stimulation fade and die off. For example, a baby born with cataracts will become permanently and irrevocably blind if the condition is not treated within the first 6 months of the infant's life. The region of the brain controlling movement is also highly sensitive to input during the first 2 years. If movement is restricted, it could inhibit the formation of connections. Thus, early experiences are believed to be crucial to the wiring of the young brain. Researchers emphasize that a wide range of experiences is adequate for normal development (e.g., Nelson, 2005a; Rutter, 2002). In other words, for typically developing infants, elaborate and contrived stimulation methods are not necessary to foster brain development; natural, everyday activities such as looking at faces and splashing in the water are sufficient stimulation. However, severe deprivation, such as in the case of children raised in low-quality institutions, may hinder brain development. Rutter and O'Conner (2004) studied children who suffered physical and social neglect in Romanian orphanages from the time that they were adopted until age 6. These children were more likely than other adopted children to have cognitive deficits and problems with attachment relationships with their parents. The authors speculate that although the cognitive deficits might be explained by *experience-expectant* programming, the attachment difficulties might be better explained by *experience-adaptive* programming of the brain. In other words, the children's brains adapted to the deprived environment to the extent that they were not set up for forming attachments to their parents, and appeared to be comfortable going off with strangers.

However, the idea that there is a "critical period" for brain development is an issue of considerable debate. Some researchers have interpreted new research on early brain development in terms of a "windows of opportunity" metaphor. The developing brain is primed to receive certain stimulation by a particular time, and this stimulation is necessary for continued normal development. If this stimulation is not received, the window "closes." To date, much of the research in support of a critical period perspective is drawn from animal research. For example, when 1-month-old kittens are deprived of light for 3 or 4 days, the visual center of their brains begin to deteriorate. If kept in the dark for the first 2 months of life, damage to the kittens' eyesight could be permanent (Hubel & Wiesel, 1970). Studies have also shown that rats raised with toys and other stimuli grow 25 percent more synapses than rats deprived of such stimuli (Greenough et al., 1987). And rats reared with more visual stimulation have better-developed visual cortexes than rats that had little to see (Black & Greenough, 1986).

Although such research with animals suggests there is a critical period for brain development, it is not clear if the brain circuitry of humans operates the same way. Neuroscientists do not yet know the range of typical early experiences that are necessary for early brain growth in humans. The exposure to light and sound is best understood at this time. However, movement, touch, and other sensory experiences may be important as well. A recent National Research Council report, *From Neurons to Neighborhoods* (NRC, 2000), offers the following conclusion about the role of early experience in brain development:

> Scientists are far from linking specific types or amounts of experiences to the developing structure or neurochemistry of the immature human brain, and conversely, from understanding how early brain development affects the ways in which young children process the abundance of information and experiences that their environment presents to them. Answers to questions about when during development particular experiences must occur and when, in fact, timing is important and when it is not also lie, to a large extent, beyond the boundaries of current knowledge. (p. 194)

Just as neuroscientists are providing important insights into early brain development, other research findings indicate that there is a considerable degree of flexibility and plasticity in the human brain, especially in the early years of development. *Plasticity* refers to the ability of the brain to change. A lack of stimulation may slow the development of brain connections and delay the appearance of some abilities, but later stimulation can compensate for the experience of early deprivation to some extent. For example, a child who spent the first 4 years of life in a body cast will eventually learn to walk and run, but not as smoothly as a child who was able to move during those years. Similarly, children who learn a second language before the age of 10 can generally speak it without an accent, but older learners are unlikely to speak another language as if they were a native, unless it is very similar to their first language. In the latter case, existing circuits may facilitate the learning of language sounds.

As suggested earlier, it is commonly believed that the brain is most open to change during the early years of development. Neurons that are not stimulated during the peak of synapse formation may be lost forever. However, new research suggests that the brain may retain some of its ability to change and adapt well into old age (Golden, 1994). Thus, brain development occurs throughout the life span. For example, *experience-dependent* (as opposed to *experience-expectant*) learning is unique to individuals and likely involves the formation of new synaptic connections based on life experiences, such as learning a second language (e.g., Nelson, 2005a). The plasticity to form new neural connections may decline, but it does not totally disappear. Some evidence suggests that the brain works like a muscle: If it is well exercised, dendrites continue to grow. This research is opening new possibilities for the treatment of strokes, head and spinal cord injuries, and Alzheimer's disease. It may be possible to "teach an old dog new tricks," but most theorists believe that the plasticity and adaptability of a child's brain is unparalleled in the life span (Golden, 1994). Others suggest that the extent of brain plasticity and how it varies across different parts of the brain is simply unknown (e.g., Rutter, 2002).

Brain Organization and Specialization

The human brain is a highly specialized organ. Our brain is more specialized than the brain of any other mammal living today. The cerebrum of the human brain is divided into two halves by a deep fissure creating what are known as the left and right hemispheres. Researchers have known for some time that the left hemisphere controls the right side of the body, and the right hemisphere controls the left side. Each hemisphere also performs different cognitive functions. In adults, the left hemisphere largely controls verbal abilities (spoken and written language) and positive emotion, whereas the right hemisphere processes visual and spatial information as well as negative emotions, such as distress (Springer & Deutsch, 1993). John Bruer (1999) describes the left hemisphere as a serial processor that processes information in a sequential, analytical manner, whereas the right hemisphere is a parallel processor that processes information in terms of patterns and images. Some popular writers describe the "left brain" as more logical, and the "right brain" as more creative and intuitive.

Specialization of the two hemispheres is known as **brain lateralization.** It is believed that the two hemispheres may begin to specialize in their function by age 3, but researchers are still debating this point. Some researchers argue that lateralization of the brain begins before birth; whereas others argue that this process of lateralization is not complete until adolescence. There is evidence to support both arguments.

Studies of brain damage have been informative in understanding brain organization and specialization. If damage occurs in one of the hemispheres before the age of 1, the other hemisphere will take over the damaged side's function, but the child will not develop the same level of functioning as a normal child who did not experience brain damage. In addition, early research suggested that children who are less than 5 years old recovered more fully and quickly from brain damage to the left hemisphere than adults (Lenneberg, 1967). For example, a recent study showed that preschool children with a wide variety of brain injuries from the first year of life showed milder language and spatial skill deficits than did brain-injured adults. By age 5, the children's cognitive impairments had largely disappeared (Stiles, Bates, Thai, Trauner, & Reilly, 1999). It is believed that children are better able to make a fuller recovery because they are able to shift their language processing over to the right hemisphere. Adults, however, have more of their neurons committed to specialized functions, so they are not able to take over functions in the damaged regions. This argument fits with the research we discussed earlier on declines in brain plasticity.

However, new evidence has raised some important questions about the timing of brain lateralization. First, evidence suggests that brain lateralization may occur before birth when the fetal testes begin to produce testosterone. The larger amounts of testosterone in the male's fetal environment may predispose male babies toward greater specialization of cognitive functioning from birth. In addition, 2-month-old infants of both sexes respond more to sounds heard through their right ear than their left ear. By 2 years of age, children begin to show hand preferences, which may be related to one hemisphere's becoming more dominant than the other.

Recent research also suggests that both cerebral hemispheres influence more aspects of cognitive functioning than was previously thought. In a reading task, for example, the left hemisphere comprehends syntax and grammar, but the right hemisphere is better at figuring out a story's meaning and purpose. Both sides of the brain must work together to perform this activity. Brain scanning technology has shown that electrical impulses are passed between the two hemispheres during a reading task. It is believed that many other cognitive activities involve the use of both hemispheres. Much of the research that is currently taking place involves how the two sides of the brain interact and function together (Bruer, 1999; Caine & Caine, 1994).

Is there a relationship between hemispheric specialization and learning disabilities? About 60 years ago, Orton (1937) suggested that incomplete dominance of the left hemisphere leads to writing and reading disorders. Since then, considerable research has examined the role that "abnormal" patterns of hemispheric specialization might play in the explanation of learning disabilities. Some research evidence suggests that children with reading problems do not show normal lateralization patterns (Baringa, 1996). In general, however, the neurological basis of learning disabilities is not well understood at this time. However, there may be some promising breakthroughs in studies of **dyslexia** and **developmental dyscalculia** (e.g., Butterworth, 2005; Richards et al., 2005), as discussed later in the chapter.

Another common misconception is the presumed relationship between brain functioning and cognitive styles. As suggested earlier, some popular writers have argued that the left and right hemispheres of the brain process information very differently. Information processing of the left hemisphere is analytical, rational, sequential, and logical, whereas the right hemisphere is believed to be more intuitive, holistic, and emotional. Although individuals may process information in these different ways, these preferences are not necessarily tied to brain organization. At present, there is no strong scientific evidence to categorize individual differences in learning styles according to left- and right-brain hemispheric specialization (Hiscock & Kinbourne, 1987). As Bruer (1999) notes, "The fundamental problems with the right-brain versus left-brain claims that one finds in the educational literature is that they rely on our intuitions and folk theories about the brain, rather than on what brain science is actually able to tell us" (p. 653).

 # Perceptual Development

Perceptual development involves the processing of sensory information by the brain. As we just learned, the areas of the brain that interpret and respond to visual or auditory stimulation develop rapidly during the first 2 years of life. Developmentalists now believe that an infant's perceptual abilities are more advanced than was originally assumed. In this section, we explore the development of children's ability to process sensory information. As you will see, an infant quickly develops the perceptual abilities it needs to receive stimulation from the environment and to form emotional attachments.

Visual Perception

A newborn infant will gaze at an object and track it to keep it in view. However, a newborn's visual acuity (sharpness of the image) is not the same as an adult's. Infants are born legally blind, unable to see more than 7 to 8 inches in front of their faces, which is about the distance to the mother's face when a baby is nursing. A newborn infant is able to see at 20 feet what a person with perfect vision can see at 500 feet (Aslin, Jurczyk, & Pisoni, 1998). As discussed earlier, the brain region that controls vision is highly sensitive to environmental stimulation and input in the early months of development. Visual acuity improves dramatically during these months, so that infants achieve adultlike levels of vision by 12 months.

Depth perception develops after 6 months, when babies begin to move around on their own. Figure 2.9 shows the visual cliff experiment that is used to test children's depth perception (Gibson & Walk, 1960). A plate glass covers the surface of a platform to give the illusion of a dropoff. Babies who are crawling will not cross the plate glass, whereas precrawling babies will not show the same apprehension when placed on the glass. It is believed that the experience of falling and getting hurt facilitates the development of depth perception. Precrawling babies who can move around in their walkers seem to show a fear of depths as well. In short, movement (motor development) may facilitate the development of depth perception, which enables infants to move around more adaptively in a three-dimensional world.

Through a technique called the *habituation* procedure, researchers have learned a great deal about the type of visual stimulation infants prefer. Research in the 1960s revealed that infants preferred to look at stimulus displays that are novel and complex. When exposed to new sights, sounds, smells, and tastes, infants display an *orienting response.* They become quiet and attentive, and their breathing and heart rate may even slow. **Habituation** is the decrease in an infant's response to a stimulus after repeated exposure to it. For example, the infant may stop sucking a pacifier when there is a new person or new sound in the room. Using the habituation procedure, researchers can determine what stimuli are interesting and new to infants. They have learned that infants prefer human faces to other patterned stimuli. When gazing at a face, an infant tends to focus his or her attention on the eyes and facial expression, which provides important information about danger or safety in the surroundings.

By the time children enter school, they are able to systematically scan and attend to stimuli for short periods of time. At this point, they begin to exert voluntary control over their attentional processes. Developmental changes in attentional processes will be discussed again in Chapter 4.

■ FIGURE 2.9
Visual Cliff Experiment
Source: Mark Richard/Photo Edit.

Auditory Perception

What can a newborn hear? When are children able to discriminate sounds? Unlike vision, auditory perception is fairly well developed at birth. There is growing evidence that fetuses react to sound by the sixth or seventh month of prenatal development (Aslin et al., 1998). Three-day-old infants show a preference for familiar rather than unfamiliar voices, which suggests that they prefer sounds they may have heard while still in the womb. In a classic study, mothers read Dr. Seuss's *The Cat in the Hat* to their unborn children. After birth, these children responded more favorably to the book that had been read to them prenatally than to an unfamiliar book (DeCasper & Spence, 1986).

In addition to remembering familiar sounds, newborns are quite adept at discriminating between sounds. For example, young infants are able to discriminate between the sounds of *pah* and *bah*. This early ability to make subtle discriminations between sounds prepares an infant to learn the sounds of his or her language. By the time they say their first words, 2-year-old infants produce only the sounds of their native language. Auditory perception develops rapidly during infancy, but it does not reach adult levels until the elementary school years (Mauer & Mauer, 1988).

Taste, Smell, and Touch

Babies seem to be born with a "sweet tooth." They prefer sweet fluids to other tastes, and they dislike sour and bitter tastes. One interpretation of newborns' preference for sweet tastes is that they are naturally attracted to their mother's milk, which tends to have a sweeter taste than cow's milk. A preference for sweet tastes does not mean that infants should regularly drink sugar water. There is some evidence to suggest that feeding patterns in the first few years have long-term effects. For example, infants who are frequently fed sweet liquids in the first years show a preference for these liquids at age 2 (Beauchamp & Moran, 1985).

The sense of smell is also present at birth. Newborns turn away from smells like rotten eggs or ammonia, and they smile when exposed to the smell of bananas. It is believed that the sense of smell may play an important role in bonding. Researchers have shown that breast-fed babies can recognize their own mothers' smells as opposed to the smells of other lactating mothers (Cernoch & Porter, 1985). Mothers are also able to recognize the smell of their 1- or 2-day old infants (Porter, Cernoch, & McLaughlin, 1983).

Newborns are responsive to touch. If you touch a newborn's cheek it will begin to suck. This response is an automatic reflex, and one of several reflexes that enable babies to interact with their environment. Researchers also believe that touch is important for brain development. In animals, the sensation of touch releases certain body chemicals that are necessary for physical growth. For example, the licking of a mother rat influences the setting of her pups' heart rate, temperature, growth, immune system, and other physiological states. When deprived of this licking, the pups fail to grow normally.

Human touch may have the same effect on the infant's development. Studies of babies who are born prematurely support this suggestion. A preterm baby is generally placed in a plexiglass-enclosed box, called an isolette, so that the air temperature of the baby's environment can be carefully controlled. Human contact is limited because of possible infection. If preterm infants must be fed through stomach tubes, they do not receive the tactile stimulation babies normally experience during feedings. Research has shown that when preterm infants are massaged gently several times a day, they tend to grow faster than babies who do not receive this stimulation. At the end of 1 year, the massaged babies were also more advanced in motor development than the other babies (Field et al., 1986).

Research on infant attachment also supports the importance of human contact. **Attachment** is the process by which infants form strong, affectional ties with their caregivers. Generally this process begins to take place within the first 6 months of age, such that babies begin to show a preference for the people they want to be near, especially in times of stress, by 7 or 8 months. Babies who are cuddled, hugged, and handled tenderly and carefully tend to form more secure attachments with their caregivers. As will be discussed in Chapter 6, this attachment process is important for developing a basic sense of trust.

If infants can respond favorably to touch, then it is not surprising that they can also feel pain. Young infants respond to injections and circumcision by fussing and crying. Doctors no longer think that infants can be treated as if they are insensitive to pain. There is no evidence, however, that the pain experienced in routine medical care has any long-term effects on physical or emotional development.

Of course, events or objects can be simultaneously perceived by multiple senses (touch, sound, vision), which is known as **intermodal perception** (Gibson & Pick, 2000). This ability to integrate information, such as the feel, look, and sound of a favorite caregiver, begins development in infancy.

Implications for Educators

Knowledge of children's perceptual development has important implications for educators. It suggests that the developing child is attracted to stimuli that are novel and complex. Babies are attracted to colorful mobiles and patterned displays. Preschool children are attracted to picture books and enjoy finding figures of animals and other familiar objects that are hidden in larger visual displays. Older children are also attracted to colorful and stimulating displays. Walk down any elementary school hallway, and you will see art displays and samples of children's writing. It is always striking how most high school classrooms lack visual displays or attractive decorations when compared with the elementary or preschool classroom. Look around your college classroom and you will find the same. An attractive and changing classroom environment can hold the attention of learners.

It is also important for educators to understand how visual and auditory perception develops and what factors can indicate atypical development. Children and adolescents with learning disabilities may exhibit problems with auditory and visual discrimination tasks. For example, it may be difficult for a ninth grader to remember visual images and symbols, and a fourth grader may reverse letters, such as seeing and writing the letter *b* for *d*. Children with learning disabilities may also have difficultly hearing the difference between words that sound alike, such as *fit* and *fib*. In Chapter 5, we will learn that the ability to hear individual letter sounds (phonemic awareness) plays a crucial role in the development of children's reading abilities. Early intervention programs for children with special learning needs generally include activities that help to strengthen perceptual abilities.

 ## Characteristics of Children with Exceptional Needs

Many young people exhibit some type of exceptionality requiring special services beyond the general classroom. However, children with special needs should be viewed first as children with the developmental needs that all children share, and second as children with special needs. The manifestations of exceptionalities will change as a child grows, and so it is important to take a developmental perspective of students with special needs. This section focuses on some exceptionalities teachers are most likely to encounter in the regular classroom (specific learning disabilities, attention deficit hyperactivity disorder) and discusses the developmental histories and characteristics of children with these exceptionalities. Chapter 9 provides more suggestions for working with children with different needs.

Specific Learning Disabilities

Before discussing definitions and causes of learning disabilities, it is helpful to identify what a learning disability is *not*. A learning disability is *not* due to a lack of motivation or effort on the child's part, although sometimes parents and teachers treat children with learning disabilities as if they are lazy or are not trying hard enough. A learning disability is also *not* due to poor teaching; however, students with learning disabilities may tend to fare better with certain types of teaching styles and in certain classroom settings. A learning disability is *not* due to a lack of intelligence. On the contrary, students with learning disabilities demonstrate at least average potential for learning as measured by intelligence tests. Finally, a learning disability is *not* due to any temporary causes, but persists throughout the course of development. The IDEA (1990, 2004) legislation defines a *specific learning disability* as

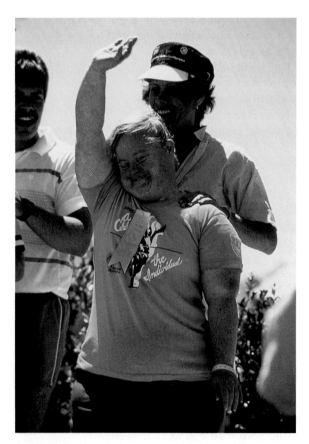

Special Olympics events enable children with mental disabilities to experience a sense of accomplishment.
Source: Jose Carrillo/Photo Edit.

A disorder in one or more of the basic psychological processes involved in understanding or in using spoken or written language, which may manifest itself in an imperfect ability to listen, think, speak, read, write, spell or to do mathematical calculations. (Federal Code Section 300.7[c][10] of 34 CFR Part 300)

A child is *not* considered to have a learning disability if learning difficulties can be attributed to visual, hearing, or motor handicaps; mental retardation; emotional disturbance; or environmental, cultural, or economic disadvantage.

Causes of Learning Disabilities

The causes of learning disabilities are difficult to determine, and often the specific cause of a child's learning disability is unclear. However, what does seem clear is that in many cases some part of the child's brain is not functioning as it should (Butterworth, 2005; Richards et al., 2005). Various possible causes have been identified, including heredity, problems during pregnancy and birth, and incidents after birth (e.g., head injuries, nutritional deprivation, exposure to toxic substances) (Hovowitz, 2006).

There is evidence that learning disabilities may be genetic, tending to run in families (Decker & DeFries, 1980; DeFries, Fulker, & LaBuda, 1987; Tallel, 2003). Learning disabilities have also been attributed to prenatal factors, such as maternal consumption of alcohol while pregnant as well as maternal smoking during pregnancy. Difficulties during the birth process resulting in a prolonged birth that decreases the oxygen supply to the fetus have also been identified as possible causes of learning disabilities. Learning disabilities have also been related to premature births and mild head injuries.

Home and child-rearing factors have also been identified as possible causes of learning disabilities. A number of home environment factors may be related to the development of learning disabilities (Hallahan & Kaufman, 2003). Some of these factors include lack of organization and structure in the home, reliance on punishment to discipline children, teenage mothers, large number of children, lack of parenting preparedness or readiness, lack of social support for the family, and so on. These factors should not be interpreted as causing learning disabilities but as related to them.

Although the exact cause of learning disabilities may not be clear, it is logical to conclude that a learning disability exists in some form before school age, at a time when such students are usually identified. During infancy, problems in arousal, attention, activity level, temperament, alertness, and tone have been noted. Between the ages of 6 and 24 months the child may exhibit delays in motor milestones, neuromuscular integrity, and fine and gross motor skill development. In the preschool years, difficulties with language development have been noted, including speech delays, articulation problems, dysfluency, and poor phonology. Between the ages of 4 and 6 years old, perceptual motor difficulties are generally exhibited in skills such as drawing, cutting, and printing letters. Between the ages of 7 and 12 years old, are common. These most often occur in the form of linguistic difficulties. The Focus on Development box on page 78 lists characteristics from the National Center for Learning Disabilities (NCLD) *Learning Disabilities Checklist*. This checklist is to help parents and educators recognize persistent patterns of behavior that may indicate a learning disability (NCLD, 2006). Characteristics are listed under the grade levels at which they usually become apparent. It is important to note that learning disabilities are pervasive (they do not come and go), persist across the life span, and impact individuals differently (Horowitz, 2006).

Children with Learning Disabilities in the School Years

Children with specific learning disabilities exhibit a wide range of academic learning problems. Some have a learning disability in only one academic area, such as reading or math. Others have difficulty in many or all academic areas. Children with specific learning disabilities also differ from one another in the level of severity. A fifth-grade student may have a mild learning disability and read at the second-grade level; or he or she may be a nonreader and have a severe learning disability that requires intensive instruction. Table 2.5 on page 80 describes different academic skill disabilities. It is important to remember that because academic skills build on one another, a student may have more than one disability at the same time. For example, the ability to read and comprehend written language will also interfere with the development of writing abilities.

Students with learning disabilities have at least average intelligence as measured by intelligence tests, yet they perform below grade level in class work and on achievement tests. Although most states use a discrepancy model—the establishment of a gap between children's intellectual abilities (IQ) and their achievement and/or performance—to identify children with learning disabilities, many researchers have noted a number of problems with this identification model (e.g., Coleman, Buysse, & Neitzel, 2006; Horowitz, 2006). Some problems include: the difficulty with measuring IQ and achievement in young children (see Chapter 4); the identification of children with achievement-IQ discrepancies that are not due to learning disabilities (e.g., inappropriate instruction, cultural or linguistic differences); and the requirement to wait until the gap is wide enough to detect (*wait-to-fail approach*). A new provision in IDEA 2004, however, releases schools from the requirement that a child must show a severe discrepancy between achievement and IQ to be identified with a specific learning disability. Thus, early intervention programs emphasize prereferral prevention and inter-

Focus on
Development

Beginning in Preschool/Kindergarten

Gross and Fine Motor Skills

- appears awkward and clumsy
- has trouble with dressing (e.g., buttons, zippers)
- creates immature artwork
- grasps pencil awkwardly, resulting in poor handwriting
- experiences difficulty using small objects with precision (e.g., Legos, puzzle pieces, scissors, tweezers)
- dislikes and avoids writing and drawing tasks

Language

- demonstrates early delays in learning to speak
- has difficulty modulating voice (e.g., too soft, too loud)
- has difficulty staying on topic
- inserts invented words into conversation
- has difficulty retelling what has just been said
- demonstrates slow and halting speech using lots of fillers (e.g., *um, you know, so*)
- mispronounces words frequently
- has difficulty rhyming
- has limited interest in books or stories
- has difficulty understanding instructions or directions

Reading

- confuses similar-looking letters and numbers
- demonstrates poor memory for printed words
- has trouble naming letters
- has problems associating letters and sounds
- has poor retention of new vocabulary
- dislikes and avoids reading

Written Language

- dislikes and avoids writing and copying
- demonstrates delays in learning to copy and write

Potential Signs of Learning Disabilities

- has difficulty remembering shapes of letters and numerals
- frequently reverses letters, numbers, and symbols

Math

- has difficulty with simple counting and one-to-one correspondence between number symbols and items/objects

Social/Emotional

- has difficulty "joining in" and maintaining positive social status in a peer group
- has difficulty with self-control when frustrated

Beginning in Grades 1–4

Gross and Fine Motor Skills

- difficulty with hand–eye coordination (e.g., piano lessons, softball)

Language

- uses vague, imprecise language and has a limited vocabulary
- uses poor grammar or misses words in conversation
- confuses words with others that sound similar
- inserts malapropisms ("slips of the tongue") into conversation
- has trouble understanding humor, colloquialisms, proverbs, idioms (note: consider regional and cultural factors)
- has difficulty with pragmatic skills

Reading

- has difficulty recognizing and remembering sight words
- frequently loses place while reading
- confuses similar-looking words (e.g., *beard/bread*)
- reverses letter order in words (e.g., *saw/was*)

- has weak comprehension of ideas and themes
- has significant trouble learning to read
- guesses at unfamiliar words rather than using word analysis skills
- reads slowly
- substitutes or leaves out words while reading

Written Language

- writing is messy and incomplete
- uses uneven spacing between letters and words
- copies inaccurately
- spells poorly and inconsistently
- has difficulty proofreading and self-correcting work

Math

- has difficulty mastering number knowledge (e.g., recognition of quantities without counting)
- has difficulty with learning and memorizing basic addition and subtraction facts
- has difficulty learning strategic counting principles (e.g., by 2, 5, 10, 100)
- has difficulty with comparisons
- has trouble telling time and conceptualizing the passage of time
- has trouble counting rapidly or making calculations

Social/Emotional

- does not pick up on other people's moods/feelings
- may not detect or respond appropriately to teasing
- has trouble knowing how to share/express feelings
- has trouble "getting to the point" in conversation (gets bogged down in details)
- has difficulty dealing with group pressure, and unexpected challenges
- confuses left and right
- often loses things

- is slow to learn new games and master puzzles
- performs inconsistently on tasks from one day to the next
- has difficulty generalizing (applying) skills from one situation to another

Beginning in Grades 5–8

Written Language

- has difficulty preparing outlines and organizing written assignments
- fails to develop ideas in writing so written work is incomplete and brief
- expresses written ideas in a disorganized way

Math

- poorly aligns numbers, resulting in computation errors
- has trouble learning multiplication tables
- has trouble interpreting graphs and charts

Social/Emotional

- has trouble setting realistic social goals
- has trouble evaluating personal social strengths and challenges
- is doubtful of own abilities, and is prone to attribute successes to luck or outside influences rather than hard work (external locus of control)
- has a poor sense of direction; easily lost or confused in unfamiliar surroundings
- finds it hard to judge speed and distance (e.g., play certain games, drive a car)
- has trouble reading charts and maps
- is disorganized and poor at planning
- has difficulty listening and taking notes at the same time

Source: Learning Disabilities Checklist, National Center for Learning Disabilities (2006), www.ld.org.

TABLE 2.5   Description of Various Academic Skill Disabilities

Developmental reading disability	This type of disability, also known as dyslexia, is quite widespread. It affects approximately 2 to 8 percent of elementary school children. Children with dyslexia have difficulty separating and distinguishing sounds in spoken words. For example, they may not be able to identify the word *sat* by sounding out the individual letters. They may also have difficulty with rhyming words, such as *ball* and *fall*. Reading disabilities are also linked to an inability to relate new words and ideas to information in memory, which makes reading comprehension difficult.
Developmental writing disability	Sometimes referred to as dysgraphia. As with reading, writing also involves various brain functions. Disabilities involving writing stem from problems with sequencing words, spelling, vocabulary, and expressive language. Children with this specific disability have difficulty composing complete, grammatical sentences.
Developmental mathematics disability	Mathematics is a complex process involving distinguishing and recognizing numbers, aligning numbers, memorizing mathematical facts, and reasoning about abstract concepts such as place value or ratios. Developmental dyscalculia (DD) describes disorders of numeracy development. Problems with numbers and basic concepts emerge in the early grades, whereas problems in the later grades are linked to reasoning.

Source: National Institutes of Mental Health (1995) and Butterworth (2005).

vention (e.g., Response to Intervention (RTI), Coleman et al., 2006). This discrepancy between intelligence and achievement may occur in one or more areas:

1. *Spoken language*—delays, disorders, or discrepancies in listening and speaking.
2. *Written language*—difficulties with reading, writing, and spelling.
3. *Arithmetic*—difficulty in performing arithmetic functions or in comprehending basic concepts.
4. *Reasoning*—difficulty in organizing and integrating thoughts.

As can be seen, a vast range of learning and behavioral characteristics are manifested by students with specific learning disabilities. In addition to cognitive problems, some students with learning disabilities have trouble with perception and motor development. They may show gross motor awkwardness, poor balance, uncoordinated movement, or poor handwriting and cutting skills. Participation in competitive sports may be particularly frustrating for some of these students.

Students with specific learning disabilities often experience social and emotional problems. Although it is not always apparent whether social and emotional problems are contributing to a student's academic difficulties, these aspects of a student's behavior usually appear to be counterproductive to learning and thus limit success. From what we know about the dependence of social interaction on communication skills, it is no surprise to find that some children with specific learning disabilities have problems with peers. Their unpopularity may be attributed to poor skills in interpreting social cues, problem solving in social situations, and verbal and nonverbal communication.

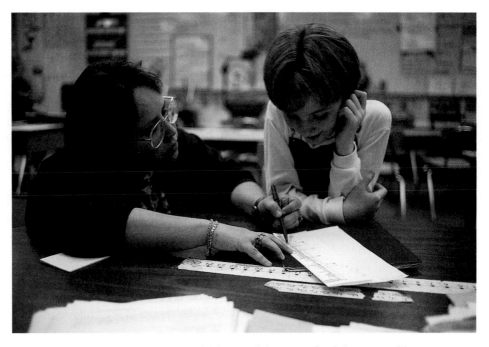

With specialized instruction, many children with learning disabilities are able to experience academic success.
Source: Joel Gordon.

As shown in the Focus on Development box on page 79, when children with specific learning disabilities succeed either academically or socially, they are likely to attribute it to factors outside of their control. This is called *external locus of control.* Students exhibiting external locus of control do not reap the positive benefits of their successes, because they do not believe their accomplishments are the result of their own abilities or efforts. Rather, they attribute them to luck, fate, or something unrelated to themselves. For example, they are likely to attribute a good grade to an easy assignment. This has direct implications for students who repeatedly experience academic failure. Over a period of time, they may apply less effort as they operate on the assumption that they are helpless to change their performance, thus perpetuating a cycle of failure. Many students lose their motivation for learning. In many cases, students avoid the tasks at which they expect to fail. Students with specific learning disabilities tend to evaluate their cognitive abilities more negatively than children without learning disabilities, and the unrelenting process of frustration and failure can erode a child's confidence in his or her abilities and skills (Vaughn & Elbaum, 1998).

As they reach adolescence, students with specific learning disabilities continue to fall further behind in academics as their deficits "manifest themselves in more subtle or controlled ways" (Deshler, 1978, p. 68). Problems in affective development persist, namely in self-concept, motivation, and social interaction (Alley & Deshler, 1979). The adolescent's need for organization and structure intensifies as curricular demands shift from learning skills to learning content at the secondary level. Oral reading becomes more problematic than silent reading, specifically, in problems with word substitution errors, fluency, comprehension, ignoring or misreading punctuation, lack of expression, and losing their place (Alley & Deshler, 1979). Poor silent and oral reading skills interfere with reading comprehension in all subject areas. Alley and Deshler (1979) also describe troublesome writing characteristics: a narrow word pool; frequent errors in spelling, capitalization, and punctuation; organizational problems; and poor monitoring of writing errors.

Attention Deficit Hyperactivity Disorder

Attention deficit hyperactivity disorder (ADHD) is a commonly diagnosed behavior disorder affecting 7 percent of school-age children (National Institutes of Health, 2000). ADHD is characterized by developmentally inappropriate levels of activity, concentration, distractibility and impulsivity. ADHD is perhaps the most frequent reason why children are referred for behavioral problems to guidance clinics. ADHD is more frequent in boys than in girls. This gender difference may be due to the fact that ADHD is more often associated with male patterns of behavior, such as aggression (Barkley, 1998; Nadeau & Quinn, 2002).

There are many myths and misconceptions about people with ADHD. Some of these views are summarized in Table 2.6. ADHD is assumed to have a neurobiological basis, and it is diagnosed according to the criteria established by the American Psychiatric Association in the *Diagnostic Statistical Manual of Mental Disorders* (DSM–IV, 1994). As described in Figure 2.10, the DSM–IV provides indicators for each of the three major characteristics: inattention, impulsivity, and hyperactivity. These indicators need to be present before the age of 7 and in more than one setting (e.g., home, school, etc.). Also, there needs to be clear evidence of a significant impairment in academic or social functioning, and these problems are not explained by other mental disorders (e.g., mood disorder, anxiety disorder, etc.). Many children exhibit some of these behaviors at

TABLE 2.6 Misconceptions about Attention Deficit Hyperactivity Disorder (ADHD)

Myth	Fact
All children with ADHD are hyperactive.	Some children with ADHD exhibit no hyperactivity and are classified as predominantly inattentive.
ADHD is a fad of recent times, with little to support it.	Reports of ADHD go back to the mid-nineteenth century. There is now an established research base on ADHD.
ADHD is primarily the result of minimal brain injury.	In most cases, there is no evidence of brain injury or damage. Most researchers believe that ADHD is the result of neurological dysfunction, which is related to hereditary factors.
Using drugs for ADHD can easily turn children into drug abusers.	There is no evidence that the use of drugs to treat ADHD leads directly to drug abuse. However, the use of prescribed drugs needs to be carefully monitored.
Because students with ADHD react strongly to stimulation, their learning environments need to be unstructured to take advantage of their natural learning styles.	Most researchers suggest a highly structured classroom for students with ADHD, especially in the early stages of instruction.
ADHD disappears in adolescence.	Researchers now believe that childhood ADHD continues into adulthood.

Source: Adapted from Hallahan & Kaufman (2000) and National Institutes of Mental Health (2000).

DSM Indicators of Inattention, Impulsivity, and Hyperactivity

A child having problems with *inattention* often:

- Fails to give close attention to details or makes careless mistakes in schoolwork, work, or other activities

- Has difficulty sustaining attention in tasks or play activities

- Does not seem to listen when spoken to directly

- Does not follow through on instructions and fails to finish schoolwork, chores, or routines (not due to oppositional behavior or failure to understand instructions)

- Has difficulty organizing tasks or activities

- Avoids, dislikes, or is reluctant to engage in tasks that require sustained mental effort (such as schoolwork or homework)

- Loses things necessary for tasks or activities

- Is easily distracted by extraneous stimuli

- Is forgetful in daily activities (pp. 83–84)

A child with problems in *impulse control* often:

- Blurts out answers before questions have been completed

- Has difficulty awaiting his or her turn

- Interrupts or intrudes on others (e.g., butts into conversations or games) (p. 84)

A child experiencing *hyperactivity* often:

- Fidgets with hands or feet or squirms in seat

- Leaves seat in classroom or in other situations in which remaining seated is expected

- Runs about or climbs excessively in situations in which it is inappropriate (in adolescents or adults, may be limited to subjective feelings of restlessness)

- Has difficulty playing or engaging in leisure activities quietly

- Talks excessively

- Acts as if "driven by a motor" and cannot remain still (p. 84)

■ FIGURE 2.10
DSM Indicators of Inattention, Impulsivity, and Hyperactivity
Source: Diagnostic and Statistical Manual of Mental Disorders (2000).

one time or another. A distinction between *expected* and *excessive* levels of attention, impulse control, and activity is made by a qualified professional, such as a child psychologist, child psychiatrist, or pediatric neurologist. A trained evaluator uses multiple measures and collects information about the child from teachers, parents, the child, and a pediatrician.

Children with ADHD do not qualify for special education simply on basis of their label. Decisions regarding educational needs and placement are made on an individual basis. Some children are found to be severely affected and are served by special education under the category of health impaired, whereas other children with ADHD qualify for special education because they have a primary disability in one of the other categories (Hallahan & Kaufman, 2003). The numbers of children with learning disabilities (LDs) who also have attention deficit hyperactivity disorder is staggering—as many as one-third (Horowitz, 2006). Researchers in the field of giftedness have suggested that some characteristics are shared between children with ADHD and those who are gifted.

Onset of ADHD

Barkley (1998) identified a number of factors associated with the early emergence and persistence of ADHD. These factors include (1) a family history of ADHD; (2) maternal smoking and/or alcohol consumption, and poor maternal health during pregnancy; (3) single parenthood; (4) low parental educational levels; (5) poor infant health or developmental delays; (6) early emergence of high activity level and demandingness in infancy; and (7) critical/directive maternal behavior in early childhood (p. 188). In a longitudinal study of children from birth to 10 years of age, Carlson, Jacobvitz, and Sroufe (1995) concluded that other than hyperactivity itself, the strongest factors associated with ADHD behaviors and the change or maintenance of those behaviors were single parenthood, level of social support for the parent, and an intrusive parenting style. Thus, it seems that a number of environmental factors may serve to maintain ADHD-type behaviors.

By the preschool years, children with ADHD present many challenges to their caregivers. Their behavior is described by parents as restless, always on the go, acting as if driven by a motor, and frequently climbing on and getting into things (Barkley, 1998). These children are more likely than typical children to suffer accidental injuries because of their impulsive behavior and thus require close monitoring and supervision. Noncompliance is common among children with ADHD, and at least 30 to 60 percent are actively defiant (Barkley, 1998). Mothers of children with ADHD are more likely to give far more commands, directions, criticism, supervision, and punishment than mothers of typical preschoolers (Barkley, 1998; Battle & Lacey, 1972; Campbell, 1990; Cohen & Minde, 1981, cited in Barkley, 1998). Difficulties with toilet training, sleep problems, and speech and/or motor delays that many ADHD children experience put further strain on the parents of children with ADHD. Parents of preschool ADHD children report much more stress in their life than do mothers of normal preschoolers or mothers of older ADHD children (Fischer, 1990; Mash & Johnston, 1982, 1983, cited in Barkley, 1998).

Is the prevalence of ADHD in children increasing? According to the National Institutes of Mental Health (NIMH, 2000), the answer to this question is not known at this time. It is clear that the number of children identified with this problem has increased over the last decade. However, this increase can be attributed to greater media interest, heightened consumer awareness, and the availability of effective treatments. Other countries are also reporting increases in the prevalence of ADHD in young people (NIMH, 2000).

ADHD in the School Years

Formal education presents a number of significant challenges to the child with ADHD. The ability to sit still, attend to instruction, inhibit impulsive behavior, and follow instructions can prove to be extremely difficult. Socially, children with ADHD find it difficult to cooperate with others, share, play well, and interact pleasantly with their peers.

Children with ADHD also may experience problems similar to those experienced by children with learning disabilities. They may have cognitive difficulties associated with memory, due to deficits

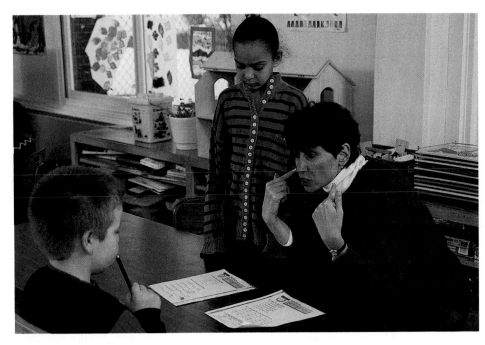

Children with ADHD often need assistance in many academic areas.
Source: Ellen B. Senisi/Photo Researchers, Inc.

in attention and problem-solving skills. They also may have difficulties using inhibitory controls to lead them through cognitive problem solving, causing an underutilization of problem-solving strategies and lower metacognitive regulation. Children with ADHD often have academic difficulties, discipline problems, and interpersonal conflicts; these problems may have more serious consequences when children reach adolescence (e.g., Barkley, 2006; Evans, Timmins, Sibley, White, Serpell, & Schultz, 2006).

By middle childhood there is also an emerging pattern of social rejection of children with ADHD because of poor social skills. The tendency for the child with ADHD to be overly active, exhibit vocal noisiness, and to touch and manipulate objects more than is normal can be aversive to others. Because of social rejection and academic failure, many children with ADHD may develop depression and a general feeling of incompetence. According to a leading expert on ADHD, approximately 40 to 60 percent may develop oppositional defiant disorders, 25 to 40 percent may develop conduct disorder and antisocial behavior between ages 7 and 10, and 20 to 35 percent may develop a reading disorder (Barkley, 1998).

Although it is often assumed that young people will outgrow their symptoms, many do not. When compared to typical adolescents, students with ADHD were more likely to have failed a grade in school (29 percent versus 10 percent), to have been suspended (46 percent versus 15 percent), or to have been expelled from school (10 percent versus 1 percent). Levels of academic achievement as measured by standardized achievement tests were significantly below normal for adolescents with ADHD in the areas of math, reading, and spelling (Barkley, 1998). Estimates indicate that up to 80 percent of youths with ADHD will continue to display symptoms of the disorder to a significant degree during adolescence and young adulthood (Barkley, 1998); however, there is a decline in the levels of hyperactivity and improvement in ability to attend and control impulsivity (Hart, Lahey, Loeber, Applegate, & Frick, 1995). Despite these improvements, new issues arise in adolescence to

Focus on
Research

Treating Children with ADHD

It is natural for teachers and parents to be concerned about the effects Ritalin and other stimulants have on children. Some worry about their side effects and long-term consequences. Many parents believe that stimulant medication can lead to drug addiction and substance abuse. Another debate is whether stimulants are prescribed unnecessarily for too many children and for children too young.

According to the U.S. National Institutes of Mental Health (2000), stimulant medications are the most thoroughly studied of all drugs used to treat children with psychiatric disorders. Stimulant use in the United States has increased substantially over the last 25 years. Numerous short-term studies have established the safety and efficacy of these medications for alleviating the symptoms of ADHD. Drug treatments are most effective when combined with intensive behavioral interventions. Careful management of medication is important when treating children with ADHD. Some children may experience insomnia and decreased appetite. Stimulant med-

ication can also become addictive if abused by adolescents and adults.

Although little information is available on the long-term effects of stimulants, there is no evidence that careful medical use is harmful for school-age children. However, according to the American Psychological Association (2000), we know little about the safety and effectiveness of medications and best treatments for very young children. When stimulant medications are taken as prescribed, they do not lead to substance abuse problems or to addiction when children are older. In fact, the evidence appears to be the opposite. Stimulants help many children to focus and to be more successful at school, home, and play. Avoiding negative experiences early in development may actually prevent addiction and other emotional problems later on. If ADHD is left untreated, young people with ADHD are a greater risk for later alcohol or substance abuse. In a study funded by the National Institutes of Mental Health and the National Institute on Drug Abuse, boys with ADHD who

further exacerbate the difficulties already being experienced. These issues include identity formation, peer group acceptance, dating, and physical development.

Children with ADHD have shown behavioral and academic improvement when a *multimodal approach* is used (Fowler, 1992). Such an approach combines educational support, psychological counseling, behavioral management at school and home, and medical management that typically involves psychostimulants, such as Ritalin and Dexedrine. Given the fact that many children with ADHD take medication, an accurate diagnosis is crucial. It is also crucial that the classroom teacher be informed of any medication a student is taking and be aware of possible side effects. Adjustments in dosage may be necessary when side effects adversely impair the child's performance. The use of stimulants to treat ADHD remains controversial. The Focus on Research box presents information on the use of stimulants and their effects on children with ADHD.

Protective Factors for Children with High-Incidence Disabilities

Thus far, our discussion of children with developmental disabilities has focused on risk factors in their lives. The Focus on Development box on page 88 summarizes these risk factors at different stages of development. In Chapter 9, we will discuss the concept of resiliency—the ability to overcome adversity and to achieve positive outcomes. Longitudinal research on children with developmental disabilities has identified several protective factors in their lives. This research has taught us many important lessons about children with high-incidence disabilities and disorders. First, the probability and severity of developmental delays and disabilities are were treated with stimulants were less likely to abuse drugs and alcohol when they got older (NIMH, 2000).

It is important to point out that there are conflicting research findings, and more research is needed to understand the effects of stimulant medication on children. However, most experts agree that stimulant medication is an effective treatment for children with ADHD when carefully supervised and combined with intensive behavioral treatments. In addition, the American Academy of Pediatrics (2001) recommends that clinicians work with parents, teachers, and other school-based professionals to monitor the progress and effectiveness of specific interventions. Desired results include:

■ improvements in relationships with parents, siblings, teachers, and peers
■ decreased disruptive behaviors

■ improved academic performance, particularly in volume of work, efficiency, completion, and accuracy
■ increased independence in self-care or homework
■ improved self-esteem
■ enhanced safety in the community (e.g., crossing streets, riding bicycles) (p. 5)

The National Resource Center on ADHD (NRC) is a government-funded information clearinghouse, recently established by the U.S. Centers for Disease Control and Prevention (CDC) and Children and Adults with Attention-Deficit/Hyperactivity Disorder (CHADD). The center presents current research findings; information on diagnosis, treatment, and intervention; and quality-of-life information about the disorder that is geared for health professionals, psychologists, educators, parents, and policy makers (see www.help4adhd.org).

Source: National Institutes of Mental Health (2000), American Academy of Pediatrics (2001), and American Psychological Association (2000, 2003).

not the same for all children. The effects of many biological risk factors (maternal smoking, premature birth, perinatal complications, etc.) diminish with the passage of time. Second, there are large individual differences among children with developmental disabilities. Developmental outcomes for most risk factors depend on the quality of care these children receive, as well as their own competencies, self-esteem, and temperamental dispositions. Most important, it emphasizes the role of teachers, psychologists, counselors, and other caring adults in the lives of these children. Supportive teachers and mentors at school can play an *enabling* role in children's lives and help reduce the negative effects of childhood disabilities and disorders.

Low-Prevalence Disabilities

Classroom teachers can expect to have at least one child in the first few years of teaching who has one of the following disabilities: severe and multiple disabilities, other health impairments, deafness or hearing impairment, physical disabilities, low vision or blindness, autism, traumatic brain injury, or deaf-blindness. These categories are summarized in the following sections.

Severe and Multiple Disabilities

Children with *severe and multiple disabilities* are characterized by two factors: they have concomitant disabilities—that is, they have two or more disabilities—and the extent of their disabilities is serious. For example, a child may have severe mental retardation and blindness, or severe emotional and behavioral disorders and physical disabilities. In most cases, children with severe and multiple disabilities are severely delayed in the areas of cognition, including adaptive behavior and language, and in physical development.

Focus on
Development

Summary of Risk Factors Associated with High-Incidence Disabilities in Children

Prenatal Period	Perinatal Period	Postnatal Period
Chromosomal abnormalities	Anoxia	Cerebral trauma
Inborn errors of metabolism	Congenital defects	Encephalitis
Harmful drugs	Disorders of delivery	Micronutrient deficiencies
Nutritional deprivation	Low birth weight	Toxic substances
Maternal infections	Infections	Family dysfunction
Metabolic disorders	Metabolic disorders	Parental mental illness
Radiation	Intracanal hemorrhage	Parental substance abuse
Toxic agents	—	Child abuse

Source: Adapted from Werner (1999).

Other Health Impairments

Children with *other health impairments* have physical limitations that interfere with their learning. They vary according to the type of impairment, the level of severity, and whether the condition is chronic (lifelong) or acute (life-threatening, but short-lived). IDEA defines children with health impairments as "having limited strength, vitality, or alertness, due to chronic or acute health problems such as a heart condition, tuberculosis, rheumatic fever, nephritis, asthma, sickle cell anemia, hemophilia, epilepsy, lead poisoning, leukemia, or diabetes that adversely affect a child's educational performance" (sec. 300.5[7]).

Deafness or Hearing Impairment

These two groups of children—deaf and hard of hearing—differ according to the degree of hearing loss. Children who are *hard of hearing* have sufficient hearing to enable them to understand speech; many require amplification of speech through a hearing aid. Children who are *deaf* cannot hear or understand speech. The extent of the disability is also affected by three essential factors: type of hearing loss, the age of onset, and the degree of residual (intact) hearing (Diefendorf, Leverett, & Miller, 1994).

Physical Disabilities

Many *physical disabilities* result from damage to the central nervous system, either the brain or spinal cord. The extent and localization of brain damage determines the child's cognitive, language, social, and physical functioning. Damage to the central nervous system, whether it involves the brain or spinal cord, typically results in either paralysis or muscle deficiencies. Physical disabilities are either congenital or acquired. Congenital disorders are present at birth (e.g., clubfoot, "brittle bones syndrome"). Acquired disorders are either due to disease (e.g., poliomyelitis, bone tuberculosis), accident (e.g., spinal cord injury), or unknown causes.

Low Vision or Blindness

Children with *low vision* cannot read newsprint-size letters, even with corrective lenses. They do have some useful visual functioning, but they require adaptations such as optical and nonoptical aids and classroom accommodations. Children who are *blind* have either 20/200 vision (seeing at 20 feet what most people see at 200 feet), or a limited field of vision (20 degrees). These children need help in using whatever residual vision remains, while also receiving adaptations such as braille materials and/or auditory tapes.

Traumatic Brain Injury

Traumatic brain injury (TBT) is an acquired injury to the brain with either open or closed head injury that has a significant impact on learning. A child's learning difficulties may be permanent or temporary, depending on the course of recovery. A child with TBI may experience difficulties with any of the following: thinking and reasoning, understanding words, remembering things, paying attention, solving problems, talking, behaving, walking and other physical activities, and learning (National Dissemination Center for Children with Disabilities, 2006). The severity and type of problem are determined by the location and extent of the brain injury.

Deaf-Blindness

Children with *deaf-blindness* have dual sensory impairments. Given the debilitating effects from hearing and vision impairments, these children have unique characteristics that separate them from those with multiple and severe disabilities. Hence, they are not categorized as severe and multiple but as deaf-blind.

Children with severe and multiple disabilities need a highly specialized educational program.
Source: *Bob Daemmrich/Stock Boston.*

The degree of integration into the general classroom depends on a child's level of cognitive development as well as the ability to communicate. For some of these children, reverse mainstreaming or partial participation will be their least restrictive environment (e.g., children with severe and multiple disabilities, deaf-blind, or low-functioning autism). For other children in low-prevalence categories, the least restrictive environment will be full-time placement in the general classroom with or without a teaching assistant (e.g., children with high-functioning autism, traumatic brain injury, or health impairments).

Given the disability category and the extent of the child's needs, specialized equipment may also be crucial for the child's learning. Advances have been made in augmentative communication systems, adaptive devices, medical technology, and vision aides.

Autism

Emerging in childhood, **autism** is a neurological disorder affecting the functioning of the brain. Autism affects three to six children in every thousand, and it is three to four times more common in boys than girls. However, girls with this disorder tend to have more severe symptoms and lower intelligence (National Institute of Neurological Disorders and Stroke, 2006).

Autism affects a person's ability to communicate, form relationships, and respond appropriately to the environment. Children's affliction can vary from mild to severe forms of autism, with 70 percent having mental retardation as a concomitant disability (Mesibov, 1991). The term *high-functioning autism* is used to describe those children who are mildly affected and tend to be placed in general classrooms.

Despite the variation in abilities, intelligence, communication skills, and psychosocial development, three primary features are common to children with autism. They have deficits in communication, both verbal and nonverbal; problems with reciprocal social interactions; and a restrictive set of activities and interests. Some children with autism are able only to parrot what they hear, a condition called *ecolahia*. As a result of brain abnormalities, many children with autism are highly attuned or even painfully sensitive to certain sounds, textures, tastes, and smells. Some children also develop fixations with specific objects, and some individuals with autism repeat certain actions over and over (i.e., flapping their hands, rocking, banging their heads). For some unexplained reason, they also like a lot of consistency in their environment, which can take the form of eating the same foods or becoming upset when a daily routine is changed.

Like the other exceptionalities discussed in this section, there is no known cure for autism. It is treated with a combination of early intervention, special education, family support, and, in some cases, medication. Intervention and educational programs can help expand these children's capacity to communicate, to learn, and to relate to others, while reducing the severity and frequency of disruptive behaviors.

 # Motor Development

When are children able to walk, hold a pencil, or hit a baseball? Motor development involves children's increasing ability to move and control their body movements. In the following sections, we explore developmental changes in children's reflexes, gross motor skills, and fine motor skills.

Newborn Reflexes

A newborn infant's movements are mainly due to innate reflexes. Sneezing, blinking, and gagging are examples of reflexes that are not consciously produced by the infant. Some of these reflexes are evident before birth. For example, sonograms show the developing infant hiccuping or sucking. Some of these responses have a protective or survival function. Crying enables the baby to signal distress, gagging prevents choking, and sucking enables infants to nurse right after birth. Some reflexes, such as blinking and gagging, are evident throughout the life span. Other reflexes, however, are present for a few months and then disappear at predictable times. These responses reappear later in development, but they are then under the voluntary control of the child. At birth, physicians routinely check an infant's reflexes. If a certain reflex is missing or present for a longer time than it should be, it may signal a neurological problem.

Development of Gross Motor Skills

Gross motor skills involve the movement of the head, body, legs, arms, and large muscles. The Focus on Development box on page 92 presents the sequence of development in this area. Remember that every child follows a universal as well as a unique timetable of development.

Perhaps the most significant change for children and their parents is the emergence of locomotion skills. Once infants can move about on their own, their environment greatly expands. Crawling generally appears around 8 to 10 months. By 13 months, some infants are able to climb up stair steps, but coming back down is a different matter. The appearance of crawling places new demands on parents, such as removing fragile objects from surfaces the child can reach, covering electrical outlets, securing cupboards with baby locks, and closing off stairways. Most parents "baby proof" their home by the time their baby is 6 months old, if not sooner.

Between 10 and 15 months, children begin to walk. Because their head and trunk are larger than their legs, they walk with their legs apart and toes pointed inward for balance. Children are affectionately called toddlers at this age because their steps are short and uncertain, and they toddle from side to side. As their bodies lengthen and become less top-heavy between the ages of 4 and 7, their walk begins to resemble that of an adult. By age 3, children can run, jump, and ride a tricycle.

During the preschool years, children's muscles grow stronger, and their physical coordination improves. Now they can throw a ball without losing their balance, hop on one foot, and run more smoothly. By age 5, most children can catch a ball with two hands, turn somersaults, and skip. Children's running, jumping, throwing, and coordination continues to improve in middle childhood. If you observe a group of late elementary school children playing on the playground, you will see fancy footwork in skip rope or hopscotch; games of dodgeball, kickball, or softball; or activities requiring a great deal of agility and balance, such as walking on narrow ledges or hanging upside down on the monkey bars. Consider, in comparison, the level of coordination and balance needed for skateboarding. Few 6- and 7-year-olds can perform this complicated feat.

The effective performance of some motor activities also depends on improvements in certain cognitive skills. To hit a ball, for example, a child must choose the appropriate time to swing the bat. The child must judge the speed of the ball, formulate an appropriate response, and allow time for the plan of action to reach the muscles (Cratty, 1986). Young elementary school children usually swing the ball too early or too late. For this reason, T-ball, a modified version of baseball using a pitching machine, may be more appropriate for younger elementary school children than baseball. Similarly, kickball should precede instruction in soccer, basketball, or football (Thomas, 1984).

Development of Fine Motor Skills

The advent of walking in the second year frees up the hands for the development of **fine motor skills,** the skills that involve small body movements. Activities such as pouring milk, cutting food with a knife and fork, drawing, assembling a puzzle, writing, working at a computer, and playing a musical instrument all involve fine muscle coordination and control. As with gross motor skills, this development is a continuous and gradual process. The development of fine motor skills also follows a universal sequence, but each child has his or her own individual timetable.

Reaching and grasping are among the first fine motor movements to appear. Around 5 months, an infant is able to grasp and hold objects, but hand and eye coordination is very limited. The infant can hold a bottle with two hands but may have difficulty guiding it to his or her mouth. This type of coordination must wait for myelination of those areas of the brain that coordinate eye and hand movements. By the end of the first year the pincer grasp appears. The infant can use the thumb and index finger to pick up small objects, such as blocks, buttons, or puzzle pieces. Once the pincer grasp develops, the infant's ability to manipulate objects greatly expands. By age 2, infants can turn knobs and faucets and play with screw-type toys. The ability to assemble simple

UNDERSTANDING CHILDREN
*Strategy 3.6:
Observation of Gross
Motor Skills in School
Settings*

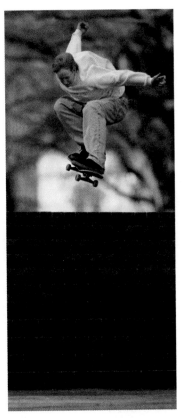

As this high school student is demonstrating, motor skills, coordination, and balance are well developed by adolescence.
Source: Jim Bounds/News & Observer.

Focus on
Development

Sequence of Motor Skills Development

Age	Description of Skill
Birth to 6 months	Exhibits many reflexes Reaches for objects Rolls from front to back Holds head up when on stomach
6 to 12 months	Demonstrates fewer reflexes Sits up Creeps and crawls Stands holding on Pincer grasp matures
12 to 18 months	Begins to walk Climbs up stairs Throws objects
18 to 24 months	Begins to run Shows hand preference Turns pages a few at a time Can stack 4 to 6 blocks Gains control over bowels Holds spoon, feeds self
24 to 36 months	Jumps Begins to ride tricycle Can kick a ball forward Can throw a ball with two hands Gains control over bladder Walks up and down steps without assistance Begins to undress

UNDERSTANDING
CHILDREN
*Strategy 3.5:
Observation of
Children's Handwriting
and Drawing Skills*

puzzles and to hold large crayons, paintbrushes, or marker pens develops during the preschool years (ages 3 to 5).

By age 5 or 6, most children are able to copy simple geometric shapes, manipulate buttons and zippers, and, perhaps, tie their own shoes. They can also print the alphabet, the letters in their name, and numbers from 1 to 10 with reasonable clarity, although writing tends to be quite large and not well organized on the paper. When children first begin to write, they reverse many letters (e.g., *b* and *d* or *w* and *m*). These letter reversals are normal and generally disappear by the age of 8 or 9. Children generally master uppercase letters first, because vertical and horizontal movements are easier to control. By age 7, children begin to form letters of uniform height and space and to use lowercase letters. These improvements indicate that they are ready to master cursive writing.

Between the ages of 10 and 12, children begin to show manipulative skills similar to those of adults. They can perform crafts, type at a keyboard, play musical instruments, and work puzzles with tiny little pieces almost as well as any adult.

3 to 4 years	Masters running
	Walks up stairs alternating steps
	Can button large buttons
	Can catch large ball
	Holds pencil between thumb and first two fingers
4 to 5 years	Can dress self
	Walks down stairs alternating steps
	Can gallop
	Catches ball
	Can cut on straight line with scissors
	Can thread beads, but not needle
	Can walk across balance beam
	Begins to hold writing tool in finger grip
5 to 6 years	Can button small buttons
	Can hop 8 to 10 steps on one foot
	Can connect zipper on a coat
	Might be able to tie shoes
	Plays ball games
6 to 7 years	Can skip 12 or more times
	Can ride a bicycle
	Can throw ball in adult manner
8 years and onward	Skips freely
	Rides bike easily
	Writes individual letters

Source: After Thomas (1984) and Conner (2003).

When do children begin to show a preference for using their right or left hand? Hand dominance does not generally appear until age 5 or later. Most toddlers begin to show a preference for one hand while performing an activity such as reaching, but they can perform most activities with either hand. By age 5, more than 90 percent of all children show a hand preference, but they can still be taught to use their nonpreferred hand. In the past, lefties were encouraged to use their right hands by misguided parents and teachers who believed that not using the right hand was a handicap. Researchers now believe that brain specialization and lateralization leads to handedness. A strong hand preference reflects the greater capacity of one side of the brain to carry out a skilled motor action. For right-handed children, the left side of the brain is the dominant cerebral hemisphere. Once brain specialization becomes firmly established, it is more difficult for children to use their nonpreferred hand for writing, painting, and so on. It is interesting that most left-handed people are ambidextrous; that is, they can perform some activities as skillfully with their left as with their right hand. Moreover, contrary to past beliefs, there is some evidence to suggest that left-handed and ambidextrous people tend to have superior verbal and mathematical abilities (Benbow, 1986).

Gender Differences in Motor Development

Girls tend to walk earlier than boys because the female skeleton is slightly more mature at birth. By the early childhood years, however, boys outperform girls on most gross motor tasks, such as jumping, kicking, and throwing. Girls, on the other hand, tend to have better flexibility, balance, foot locomotion, and small muscle coordination (Roberton, 1984). Differences begin to appear in preschool and extend into middle childhood and beyond.

What explains these differences? Some of the sex differences may be attributable to differences in body size. However, boys do not gain superiority in physical and muscular strength until after puberty. Many researchers believe that the environment plays a large role in the development of boys' and girls' gross motor skills. From an early age, boys are encouraged to run, jump, climb, and engage in rough-and-tumble play and other forms of play fighting and competitive play (e.g., football) more than girls. These patterns are found across cultures, and may be explained by tendencies to practice competitive skills during human evolution (Geary, 2004). Parents also hold higher expectations for boys' than girls' athletic performance, and their children internalize these messages about their abilities (Eccles & Harold, 1991). As early as kindergarten, girls report that they have less ability at sports than do their male classmates. Also, elementary school girls perceive physical activities, such as sports, as more appropriate for boys than girls (Pel'lett & Harrison, 1992). By sixth grade, girls are less likely than boys to devote time to sports or athletic activities (Eccles & Harold, 1991). Theorists believe that gender differences in gross motor skills are likely to disappear with the greater participation of girls in sports and athletics during childhood and adolescence. Gender differences in some motor skills seem to be more related to practice, experience, and interest than to innate differences (Roberton, 1984). In general, studies show that children are more likely to participate and sustain vigorous physical activity if they feel competent and enjoy it (e.g., Conner, 2003).

Schools and Physical Activity

Children or adolescents with poor motor skills may avoid physical activities and become sedentary. We will learn later how low physical activity is an important contributor to childhood obesity. A young person's motor skills may also influence his or her peer relations and choice of activities. Youngsters who are skilled may be asked by their peers to participate in games, sports, and other physical activities. Peer relations have an important influence on feelings of self-esteem and self-worth. Finally, physical activity is associated with children's abilities to concentrate on cognitively demanding tasks.

How can schools help facilitate the development of motor skills? Play and physical activity is the medium by which children and adolescents develop their physical abilities. The American Academy of Pediatrics (2001) states that infant exercise programs are unnecessary. Early childhood teachers need to provide ample opportunities for children to engage in large motor activities, such as running, riding tricycles, climbing, block building, jumping, and so on. The National Association for the Education of Young Children (NAEYC) recommends that programs for toddlers and preschoolers provide daily indoor and outdoor activities that exercise children's large muscles (Bredekamp, 1997). Most preschools and kindergartens have areas for children to engage in large motor activities. These areas need to be well supervised to prevent injuries and accidents. It is also important that the preschool classroom provide activities that will develop fine motor skills, such as sand play, drawing, painting, playing with puzzles, play dough, and so on.

As children move into the elementary school years, they are better able to sit and attend for longer periods of time. However, periods of concentrated work need to be distributed over the course of a school day. In Japanese and Taiwanese schools, primary-grade children have a 10-minute break from classwork every 40 to 50 minutes (Stevenson & Lee, 1990). Research has shown that regular breaks for physical activity and social interactions can increase rather than decrease young elementary school children's attention to demanding cognitive tasks (Pellegrini, Huberty, & Jones, 1995; Pellegrini & Smith, 1998). Even older children and young adolescents are not able to sit and concentrate for long periods of time. They also need plenty of opportunities to stretch, move their bodies, and engage in social interactions (see the Focus on Teaching on page 96).

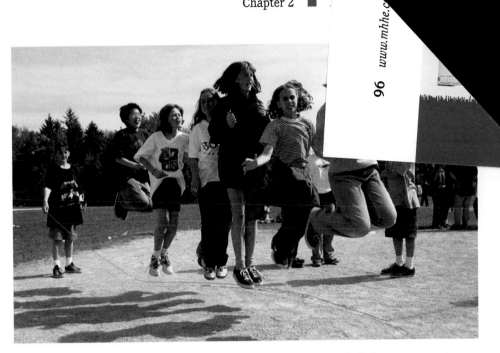

Regular breaks for physical activity and social interactions can help improve attention and concentration during classroom activities.
Source: Bill Wittman.

UNDERSTANDING CHILDREN
Strategy 3.3:
Observation of School Day Activity; Strategy 3.7: Playground Environment Checklist/Rating Scale; Strategy 3.8: Observation of Playground Behaviors

As we will learn later, childhood obesity has been on the rise for the last 15 years. One of the contributing factors to this increase is the lack of regular physical activity. A recent report indicated that 38 percent of Americans do not exercise regularly, despite a national health campaign to raise public awareness about the many health benefits associated with physical activity (Centers for Disease Control and Prevention, 2002). Even fewer adolescents exercise on a regular basis. In 1999, 53 percent of eighth graders and 45 percent of twelfth graders reported that they exercised on a regular basis. Also, boys report consistently exercising or participating in sports more often than girls (Bachman, Johnston, & O'Malley, 1999). An accepted standard for appropriate physical activity for school-age children is 30 minutes of moderate to vigorous activity, 3 days a week (e.g., Conner, 2003).

Safety Concerns

As motor skills develop and children begin to spend more time away from the careful supervision of parents, the incidence of accidental injuries rises. As stated earlier, elementary school children are still acquiring the cognitive abilities they need to make judgments of speed and timing. Injury is the leading killer of children in all industrialized countries, accounting for almost 40 percent of all deaths among children ages 1 to 14 (United Nations Foundation, 2001). Injuries that require medical attention or restrict activity affect more than 20 million children and adolescents and cost $17 billion annually for medical care (Danseco, Miller, & Spicer, 2000). In fact, accidents are the number-one cause of childhood death in the United States. The average child has twice the chance of dying an accidental death before the age of 10 than dying from a disease.

Focus on
Teaching

The emphasis on accountability in education, most recently associated with the No Child Left Behind (NCLB) Act of 2001, has led to reorganization of some school schedules so that academic instructional time is maximized and time for other activities, such as recess and physical education, is reduced. The trend toward reducing recess time has been found in some national surveys. For example, one national survey showed that only 70 percent of kindergarten classrooms sampled had recess (e.g., Pellegrini, 2005). A decline in recess periods is also reported for primary and secondary schools in England. It is difficult to determine the actual amount of time children spend in recess in the United States because the way that it is defined and implemented varies dramatically across school districts. Not all schools report having recess, and even within individual schools, times and duration of recess varies (Pellegrini, 2005). Pellegrini argues that *unstructured, playful* recess is important for enhancing children's attention to schoolwork, social adjustment, and academic achievement, as well as their physical health.

Role of Physical Activity in Schools

The provision of *structured* time for physical activity in school, such as physical education classes, is also important. The National Association for Sport and Physical Education (NASPE) recently conducted a survey with a nationally representative sample of 500 youth (ages 12–17) and 1,000 adults. About half of the parents (with children age 6–17) and teens reported that they did not have daily physical education classes. The majority of respondents suggested that physical education does not interfere with academic needs. Interestingly, about 40 percent of the teens suggested that they liked physical education classes because they provide opportunities to have exercise and get fit. The NASPE recommends that school districts fulfill the NCLB-mandated Wellness Policies for Physical Activity by providing: daily physical education in grades K–12, daily recess during elementary grades, physical activity opportunities before and after school, use of school facilities outside of school hours, and safe routes to and from school (i.e., to encourage walking, biking).

For this reason, parents and children need information on how to prevent childhood injuries. Many elementary schools now provide classes on bicycle safety as part of the physical education program. The use of reflectors on bikes and helmets can substantially reduce a large proportion of the bicycle-related deaths that occur each year. Children and adolescents should also be required to wear helmets and protective gear for skating and skateboarding. (Safe Kids, 2007).

Sports Participation

Another major area of concern is the effect of children's participation in organized sports. There are now baseball, soccer, and football leagues for children as young as 4 and 5 years old. Although these activities provide children an opportunity to develop their motor skills, to learn how to be a team player, and to cope with failure, far too many children are pushed into competitive sports before their motor skills have significantly matured. One result is that some children lose interest in athletic activities at an early age. Some experts argue that the most appropriate time for the introduction of team sports is when children are able to engage in cooperative play at about the age of 6 or 7. Furthermore, some children are seriously injured when they play sports before they are physically ready. The American Academy of Pediatrics (AAP, 2001) discourages team sports for children under the age of 6. For these reasons, most physical education programs in the elementary grades are replacing competitive sports with ones that encourage children to be physically active but not competitive.

There is still some debate concerning the effects of interscholastic or intramural sports participation for older children and adolescents. Many parents and teachers worry that athletics can take time away from studying and other extracurricular pursuits. However, most studies reveal that the effect of sports participation on academic achievement is either slight or negligible (Buoye, 1998). In fact, there is growing evidence that athletic participation can have many positive benefits for students. For example, two large-scale national studies (*High School and Beyond* and the *National Educational Longitudinal Study of 1988*) reported positive relations between sports participation and academic achievement for high school students (Bouye, 1998; Marsh, 1993). Findings also suggested that relations are stronger for individual sports (swimming, track, wrestling, etc.) than for team sports (basketball, football, and baseball), after controlling for individual characteristics (e.g., ethnicity, socioeconomic status, gender) and previous achievement. Research also suggests that nonorganized sports, such as swimming, walking, bicycling, jogging, and golfing, may be more likely to become "life sports" (AAP, 2006).

Other studies suggest that the benefits of sports participation may extend beyond academics for samples of female and minority students. In a review of research on athletic experiences of ethnically diverse girls, Jeanne Weiler (1998) reported positive benefits for self-esteem, confidence, and career aspirations. Girls who participated in sports also had a lower risk for dropping out of school and lower rates of sexual activity and pregnancy.

Similarly, studies of minority youth suggest that high school sports participation can lead to increased self-confidence, peer popularity, and school engagement (Jordon, 1999). Participation in multiracial teams can also facilitate positive cross-ethnic relations within schools (Slavin & Madden, 1999). However, it is important to note that studies of minority youth have not consistently reported positive effects for various measures of school achievement. Barring socioeconomic differences, these results raise the possibility that minority athletes are not receiving the same level of academic challenge and support as their white peers. Researchers speculate that stereotypes about the intellectual abilities of different minority groups as well as athletes ("dumb jocks") may doubly shortchange minority athletes in the classroom (Melnick & Sabo, 1992, p. 290).

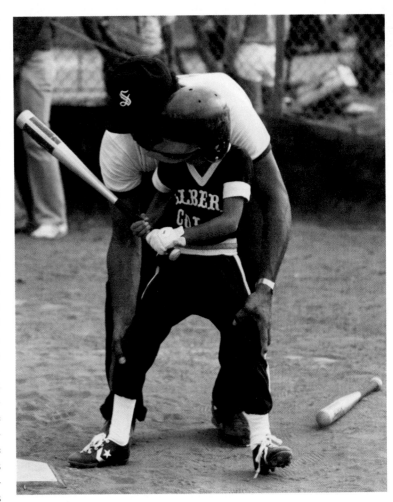

Sports participation can have many positive benefits, such as increased self-confidence.
Source: © Stephanie Maze/CORBIS.

Physical Growth

Changes in Weight and Height

The average infant weighs approximately 7.5 pounds at birth. Consequently, infancy is characterized by rapid growth. During the first year, an infant's weight will triple, to 20 to 24 pounds, and the baby will grow to 20 to 30 inches. The infant's physical growth follows two basic principles. First, growth is characterized by a **cephalocaudal pattern.** It starts at the head and proceeds downward; thus, the infant's brain, neck, and trunk develop before the legs. Second, growth is also characterized by a **proximal-distal pattern,** in which development begins in the center and proceeds outward. Accordingly, the organs develop before the arms or hands. Weight gain slows in the second year, but the infant will continue to add inches. By the end of the second year, infants are 50 percent of their adult height, but only one-fourth their adult weight (Tanner, 1978). At birth, the infant's head is surprisingly large relative to other parts of the body. As the infant's height increases, the head decreases in its proportion to the overall body.

Physical growth slows down during the preschool and elementary school years. Between ages 2 and 5, most children gain about 6 or 7 pounds per year. Preschoolers also gain about 2 to 4 inches per year. This pattern continues until puberty, so that children who are entering adolescence are about twice as heavy and a foot taller than they were as preschoolers. Elementary schoolchildren tend to look much thinner than younger children because of their added height.

It is interesting to note that the average American is growing taller today. By 1977, the average American had gained 2.5 to 3 inches in height since the early eighteenth century, and it is believed that this trend is continuing. Also, it appears that young people are attaining their adult height at an earlier age than before. One hundred years ago people did not reach their adult height until their early or mid-20s. Today, many 16- or 17-year-olds are taller than their parents. This shift in normative patterns of development is called a **secular trend.** Historical changes in growth patterns are due to improved nutrition and health conditions. We will learn that a secular trend also characterizes the onset of puberty.

Variations in Physical Size

Heredity plays a very important role in determining a child's shape and size. From the age of 2 years on, the parents' heights are good predictors of their children's heights. Ethnic background as well tends to be a good predictor of physical size. In general, children from North America, northern Europe, and Africa are the tallest in the world. Children from South America and Asia tend to be smaller. Within the United States, African American children tend to be taller than children of European, Asian, or Hispanic descent. Also, girls tend to be slightly taller than boys from age 2 until about 9, when boys

During the preschool years, children gain between 2 to 4 inches in height each year.
Source: Rachel Epstein/Photo Edit.

catch up. However, weight and muscle mass are about the same for boys and girls before puberty. As suggested earlier, with equal training and experience, girls can be as good athletes as boys in the elementary school years.

Unfortunately, variations in physical size can lead some children to be judged as less mature than other children. For example, younger children, who tend to be physically small relative to their classmates, are more likely than older children in the same grade to be retained in elementary school, because they are perceived as less mature. Achievement and adjustment problems can also emerge when children and adolescents are too physically mature for their grade level. As mentioned earlier, these young people are likely to seek out older friends who are more mature.

Physical attractiveness is another factor that can influence our judgments of other people. Adults tend to more positive attributes and characteristics (e.g., intelligence, leadership ability, social competence) for physically attractive versus unattractive children. Studies of children reveal the same patterns (Langlois & Stephen, 1981). Children prefer attractive peers and find unattractive peers unacceptable. One study showed that even preschool children rated attractive peers as friendlier, smarter, and better behaved than less attractive peers (Langlois & Stephen, 1981). Moreover, research on young children reveals that being attractive is more important for girls' than boys' acceptance by their peers (Vaughn & Langlois, 1983). Even more disturbing, a recent study revealed that girls who were judged by their peers and teachers as unattractive in middle school received lower grades, and 5 years later were more likely to drop out of school and to become teenage mothers than were attractive girls (Cairns & Cairns, 1994). This research raises important concerns about the effects of physical attractiveness on interpersonal relations in the classroom. In the introductory vignette, we saw the critical role that physical attractiveness played in Lisa's life. It is important to recognize how cultural stereotypes of physical attractiveness may be shaping the way we evaluate and relate to children.

Nutrition, Sleep, and Development

Nutrition is a core element of well-being throughout the life span. Good nutrition is particularly important for young children because of its role in fostering positive developmental outcomes (cognitive, social, physical), and in establishing healthy eating habits throughout the life span (Leavitt, Tonniges, & Rogers, 2003). Nutritional deficiencies usually occur in conditions of poverty, particularly in developing countries. There are several ways to define malnutrition, including low height-for-age (stunting) and low weight-for-height (wasting), and low weight-for-age (a combination of stunting and wasting). The timing, duration, and severity of a period of malnutrition may be critical in determining its effect on children's long-term development. Some researchers propose that poor nutrition in early childhood may be particularly deleterious because it reduces physical activity and attentiveness; thus children are less likely to explore and receive stimulation from the environment, which in turn contributes to cognitive deficits (Leavitt et al., 2003). Research has found that malnutrition in childhood has negative effects on motor, intellectual, and behavioral, as well as social and emotional development; however, if children move out of poor environments and receive intervention, they can improve (Grantham-McGregor, Ani, & Fernald, 2001). Small long-term benefits are found if mothers in pregnancy and their children received nutritional supplementation. Also, studies show that breast-feeding provides a small benefit (Grantham-McGregor et al., 2001).

Less severe problems are associated with short-term food deprivation—reduced dietary intakes, skipping breakfast, or feelings of hunger. The Community Childhood Hunger Identification Project estimated that 8 percent of U.S. children under 12 years are hungry and 21

UNDERSTANDING CHILDREN
*Strategy 3.1:
Observations of Body Growth and Physical Development*

UNDERSTANDING CHILDREN
*Strategy 3.2:
Perception of Attractiveness Interview*

percent are at risk for hunger (Kleinman et al., 1998). Many children come to school without breakfast. Several studies have examined the effects of school breakfast programs on children's performance in school, and have found positive effects on problem solving, memory and math tasks, on-task behavior, creativity, physical perseverance, and attendance, as well as limited improvement in overall school achievement (reviewed in Grantham-McGregor et al., 2001). Researchers suggest that integrated interventions, including educational and nutritional components, are necessary for noticeable improvements in overall achievement.

Comprehensive intervention programs involve: incorporating instruction about basic healthy eating habits in the curriculum (see USDA's Food Guide Pyramid for children ages 6–11, Figure 2.11; school personnel modeling healthy food choices; providing healthy school lunches and snacks; and parental involvement (e.g., Pyle, Sharkey, Yetter, Felix, Furlong, & Poston, 2006). These are sometimes accompanied by a focus on increasing students' physical activity in school (see Focus on Teaching: The Role of Physical Activity in Schools on page 96).

Sleep is also a vital component of health and well-being, and affects children's development and their lives at school. Some experts believe that proper sleep allows for the needed "exercise" and repair of neural connections (e.g., Tonninges & Leavitt, 2003). According to the National Institute of Neurological Disorder and Stroke (NINDS, 2000), studies have shown that adequate sleep is also necessary for healthy immune and nervous system functioning; it is hypothesized that neural patterns repeated during deep sleep aid in memory coding and learning. Furthermore, researchers have also discovered that important growth hormones are released in children and young adults as they sleep.

As is widely known, infants' sleeping habits are often erratic until they are 1 to 2 years of age, when children without sleeping problems more closely resemble those of adults and sleeping during the day decreases (e.g., Tonninges & Leavitt, 2003). A dangerous sleep problem for infants is sudden infant death syndrome (SIDS). Recent health campaigns urging caregivers to place infants on their backs to sleep (supine sleeping) have dramatically reduced SIDS cases in the United States (AAP Task Force on Infant Sleep Position and Sudden Infant Death Syndrome, 2000). Some young children can experience sleep difficulties, such as nightmares, night terrors, irregular sleep patterns, and separation anxiety.

In general, however, children's biological clocks allow them to go to sleep in the evening when they need to and wake up fresh and energetic until the preteenage years (10–12 years), when they are naturally inclined to perk up at night when they should be getting sleepy (Carskadon, 1999). These and other study findings reported by the National Sleep Foundation (2005) have drawn attention to the plight of sleep-deprived teens and how changing school start times can help (see Focus on Research on page 102). Studies show that adequate sleep, along with good nutrition and other factors, is vital for optimal performance in learning (e.g., Siegel, 2001).

Onset of Puberty

Puberty refers to the period in which a young person becomes capable of sexual reproduction. This period of development involves many physical changes that typically stretch out for many years. The changes include: (a) a rapid acceleration in growth, (b) the development of primary sex characteristics, (c) development of secondary sex characteristics, (d) changes in body composition, and (e) changes in circulatory and respiratory systems.

What Causes Puberty to Begin?

To parents, and the teens themselves, puberty may seem to come rapidly, but it is actually a slow and gradual process. Puberty is activated by changes in the level of sex hormones—*androgens*

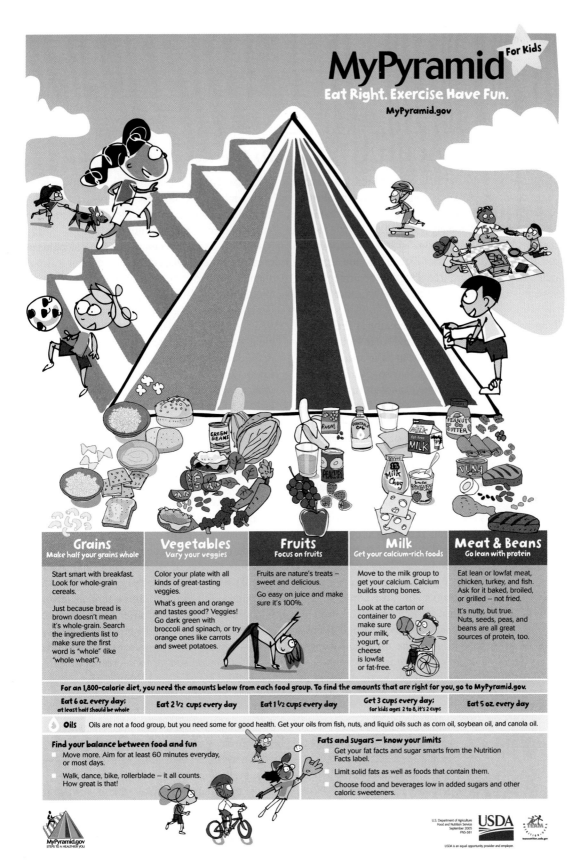

MyPyramid For Kids
Eat Right. Exercise. Have Fun.
MyPyramid.gov

Grains	Vegetables	Fruits	Milk	Meat & Beans
Make half your grains whole	**Vary your veggies**	**Focus on fruits**	**Get your calcium-rich foods**	**Go lean with protein**
Start smart with breakfast. Look for whole-grain cereals. Just because bread is brown doesn't mean it's whole-grain. Search the ingredients list to make sure the first word is "whole" (like "whole wheat").	Color your plate with all kinds of great-tasting veggies. What's green and orange and tastes good? Veggies! Go dark green with broccoli and spinach, or try orange ones like carrots and sweet potatoes.	Fruits are nature's treats – sweet and delicious. Go easy on juice and make sure it's 100%.	Move to the milk group to get your calcium. Calcium builds strong bones. Look at the carton or container to make sure your milk, yogurt, or cheese is lowfat or fat-free.	Eat lean or lowfat meat, chicken, turkey, and fish. Ask for it baked, broiled, or grilled – not fried. It's nutty, but true. Nuts, seeds, peas, and beans are all great sources of protein, too.

For an 1,800-calorie diet, you need the amounts below from each food group. To find the amounts that are right for you, go to MyPyramid.gov.

Eat 6 oz. every day; at least half should be whole	Eat 2 ½ cups every day	Eat 1 ½ cups every day	Get 3 cups every day; for kids ages 2 to 8, it's 2 cups	Eat 5 oz. every day

Oils Oils are not a food group, but you need some for good health. Get your oils from fish, nuts, and liquid oils such as corn oil, soybean oil, and canola oil.

Find your balance between food and fun
- Move more. Aim for at least 60 minutes everyday, or most days.
- Walk, dance, bike, rollerblade – it all counts. How great is that!

Fats and sugars — know your limits
- Get your fat facts and sugar smarts from the Nutrition Facts label.
- Limit solid fats as well as foods that contain them.
- Choose food and beverages low in added sugars and other caloric sweeteners.

U.S. Department of Agriculture
Food and Nutrition Service
September 2005
FNS-381

USDA

USDA is an equal opportunity provider and employer.

MyPyramid.gov
STEPS TO A HEALTHIER YOU

■ FIGURE 2.11
My Pyramid for Kids
Source: U.S. Department of Agriculture.

101

Focus on
Research

Do Adolescents Need More Sleep?

Any parent can describe the difficulty of waking a sleepy teenager to catch an early morning bus or a carpool ride. First-period high school teachers often find themselves in front of a group of teenagers nodding off to sleep. Many people attribute adolescents' sleep deprivation to a busy social life, to late nights of listening to music, or to lax parents who do not enforce a regular bedtime. However, researchers have discovered there is more to the story.

Sleep patterns change fundamentally at the transition to adolescence. Adolescents tend to go to bed later, and their natural time to fall asleep is around 11 P.M. Adolescents also tend to sleep less as they mature, but sleep requirements do not decline in adolescence. It is estimated that adolescents need at least $8\frac{1}{4}$ hours of sleep to function adequately, or $9\frac{1}{4}$ hours to maintain optimal alertness during the day (Carskadon, 1999). Developmental changes in sleep patterns are found not only in North America but also in Australia, Europe, and South America. Many researchers believe that internal changes in the circadian timing system may delay the timing of sleep behavior in adolescents (Carskadon, 1999). Controlled by light signals, circadian rhythms are synchronized to a 24-hour day and function as an internal biological clock to control wake and sleep cycles.

Changes in adolescents' sleep cycles raise some interesting questions for schools. In most communities, high schools have the earliest starting times, followed by middle schools, then elementary schools. Younger children tend to go to school later. The transition to high school can require a change in starting time from 8:30 A.M. to 7:30 A.M. Some high schools begin as early as

7:15 A.M. These early starting times may be "out of sync" with adolescents' sleeping patterns. Even with a regular bedtime of 11 P.M., most adolescents average only 6 to 7 hours of sleep on school nights.

Sleep deficits increase daytime sleepiness and decrease alertness. One study showed that it is possible for a small group of tenth-grade students to fall asleep in an average of 3.4 minutes when tested at 8:30 A.M. (Carskadon, 1999). This same pattern was found in patients with the sleep disorder called narcolepsy! Insufficient sleep is associated with memory lapses, attention deficits, depressed moods, irritability, and slow reaction times (Dahl, 1999). Sleep deprivation can also undermine adolescents' abilities to perform complex cognitive tasks, such as those involving abstract reasoning. These conditions are not optimal for learning.

Educators rarely consider these biological changes in sleep patterns when formulating school policies. Generally, school schedules are based on bus schedules, sports programs, and so on.

However, sleep researchers are encouraging schools to adjust their starting times to accommodate the biological needs of sleepy adolescents. The National Sleep Foundation (NSF) has been helpful in informing the public about results of such studies, and about results in school districts that have been successful in changing the start times. For example, some schools in Virginia, Kentucky, and Connecticut, after overcoming obstacles to initiate changes, eventually reported benefits of later start times—ranging from increases in sleep, alertness, and attitudes toward school to decreases in traffic accidents (NSF, 2005).

and *estrogens.* Although we generally associate androgens with male characteristics and estrogens with female characteristics, both hormones are produced and present in both sexes. The level of sex hormones, and hormones in general, is controlled by the pituitary gland, which is under the control of the hypothalamus at the base of the brain. The pituitary gland is like a master hormone-secreting gland, whereas the hypothalamus is like a thermostat that monitors and regulates levels of hormones in the body.

Prior to puberty, the hypothalamus is "set" to maintain low levels of sex hormones circulating in the body. However, the hypothalamus appears to lose some of its sensitivity to sex hormones at puberty. The cause of this change is not well understood (Grumbach, Roth,

Kaplan, & Kelch, 1974), but it triggers the pituitary gland to secrete hormones that cause the adrenal glands and gonads (testes in males and ovaries in females) to increase the concentration of sex hormones—estrogen in females and testosterone in males. The rate of increase is sex specific. At puberty, the production of estrogen is much higher in females (8 times the level of childhood) than males, whereas the production of testosterone is much higher in males (18 times the level of childhood) (Malina & Bouchard, 1991).

In both male and female adolescents, changes in levels of sex hormones stimulate the development of primary and secondary sex characteristics. *Primary sex characteristics* involve changes in the gonads (testes and ovaries) and the development of eggs and sperm. *Secondary sex characteristics* involve changes in genitals and breasts, and the growth of facial, pubic, and body hair. In females, estrogen is crucial to the maturation of the reproductive system, including the ovaries, fallopian tubes, and uterus. It is also involved in breast development and in the onset of ovulation and mensturation. In males, testosterone affects the development of the penis, testes, and other organs of the reproductive system.

When Does Puberty Begin?

There is considerable variability in the onset of puberty. Developmental norms published in the early 1970s indicated that the average age of onset was 10 to 12 years for girls and 12 to 14 years for boys (Tanner, 1978). These norms, however, were established based on a small sample of children growing up in British orphanages during the 1960s. For girls, puberty may have been delayed due to poor nutrition. Moreover, children of different ethnic and racial backgrounds were not studied at this time.

A large U.S. study examined the onset of puberty in 17,077 girls, aged 3 to 12 years (Herman-Giddens et al., 1997). This study defined the onset of puberty as the development of breasts and/or public hair. As Figure 2.12 below shows, girls can begin puberty well before the age of 10. In fact, 15 percent of white girls and 48 percent of African American girls had started puberty by age 8. Although signs of physical maturity can begin well before the age of 10, the average age of onset of menstruation has changed little since the 1960s. For white girls, the average is 12.8 years; it is 6 months earlier for African American girls.

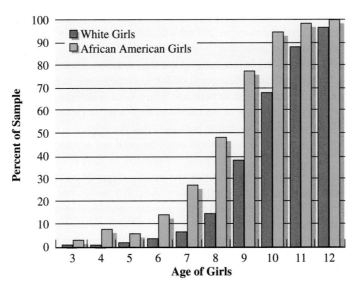

■ FIGURE 2.12
Ethnic Differences in Onset of Puberty

By 8 years of age, 15 percent of white girls and 48 percent of African American girls have started to develop breasts and/or pubic hair.

Because girls begin puberty earlier than boys, school dances are a little awkward.
Source: News & Observer.

Ethnic differences in the onset of puberty are not well understood at this time. Researchers believe that diet, genetics, environment, and even latitude may play a role. Nevertheless, it is important for educators to remember that it is not "abnormal" for girls to show signs of puberty in the middle to late elementary school years. The early onset of puberty raises some interesting questions concerning a preteen's ability to understand and cope with these changes. As we will discuss later, early maturation can have negative consequences for girls.

It is also important to point out that some adolescents may start and finish their pubertal changes before their peers of the same sex even begin their changes. As we will learn later, adolescents can experience adjustment problems if they begin puberty much earlier or later than their peers. As shown in the Focus on Development box, developmental norms based on Tanner's research indicated that the sequence of change was different for females and males. Therefore, we will consider each sex separately.

As discussed, the first sign of puberty in girls is the elevation of the breast or the appearance of pubic hair. During the middle stages of puberty, girls experience a height spurt. At the peak of puberty, girls grow about 3.5 inches per year and add another foot or so to their height before the end of the growth spurt. Most of their physical growth occurs in their torso, rather than their legs. **Menarche,** the beginning of the menstrual cycle, is generally the last physical change to occur in puberty. Hence it is wrong to assume that the beginning of the menstrual cycle marks the beginning of puberty in girls. Many other important changes have already occurred.

On the average, boys begin puberty 2 years later than girls. This 2-year difference can explain some of the tension in gender relations among young adolescents. The first signs of puberty in males are changes in their genitalia, accompanied by the appearance of pubic

Focus on Development

Sequence of Change at Puberty

	GIRLS		BOYS
Age	**Characteristics**	**Age**	**Characteristics**
8 to 13	Growth of breasts	10 to 13.5	Growth of testes
8 to 14	Growth of pubic hair	10 to 15	Growth of public hair
9.5 to 14.5	Height spurt	11 to 16	Height spurt
10 to 16.5	Menarche	11 to 14.5	Growth of penis, change of voice, facial hair

Source: After Tanner (1978).

hair. Approximately 1 year later, the growth spurt begins. Next come changes in the size of the penis, development of facial and body hair, and a gradual lowering of the voice.

We have focused so far on the pubertal changes associated with sexual reproduction. Clearly, adolescents are concerned with these changes as well, but there are many other physical changes taking place in the adolescent body. The growth spurt is accompanied by increases in muscle mass and body fat, adding weight to the adolescent body. In general, muscle tissue grows faster in boys than in girls. Body fat increases for both males and females, but the rate of fat accumulation is greater and faster for girls, especially during the period just before the onset of puberty. By the end of adolescence, boys have a higher muscle-to-fat ratio (3:1) than do girls (5:4). The rapid increase in body fat often causes girls to become overly concerned about their weight, especially in a society that values thinness. In extreme cases, this concern can take the form of excessive dieting and bulimia or anorexia nervosa. We will discuss the development of eating disorders in a later section.

As the adolescent body grows, there are also changes in the size and capacity of the heart and lungs. The magnitude of changes is greater in males than in females. Compared with girls, boys have greater physical strength, higher blood hemoglobin, more red blood cells, better exercise tolerance, and greater ability for neutralizing the chemical products of muscular exercise (e.g., lactic acid) by the end of adolescence (Peterson & Taylor, 1980). These factors may help explain sex differences in athletic ability in late adolescence, but biological differences are only part of the story. Differences in diet and exercise also play a role (Smoll & Schutz, 1990).

In summary, puberty is a dramatic period of physical development, second only to infancy. It involves changes in weight, height, and secondary sex characteristics. It also affects almost every vital organ, including, as we learned earlier, the brain. Research in the last decade also suggests that puberty can affect the sleep patterns of adolescents. The Focus on Research box describes this research and its educational implications.

Psychological Impact of Puberty

For adolescents, puberty involves more than just physical changes. Puberty often leads to changes in adolescents' self-image, self-confidence, family relations, moods, relations with the opposite sex, and many other behaviors. The ways in which adolescents react to puberty is a complicated story. The nature and timing of pubertal changes seem to be important in predicting the effects of puberty, but young people's reactions to puberty are also shaped by the larger society. Consider the ways in which adolescents are portrayed in the media. They are often depicted as sex-crazed, rebellious, troubled, indecisive, moody, and so on. You have to look long and hard to find a positive image of adolescents in the media. These images reflect cultural stereotypes, and they not only shape the way adult society reacts to young people, but also influence the adolescents themselves.

Adolescence has been called the "gangly years." An adolescent's body seems to be all out of proportion. In the early stages of puberty, feet, hands, and even legs can appear out of proportion to the adolescent's torso. This is, in fact, the case. Parts of the adolescent's body are maturing at different rates. In general, the hands and feet will grow before the torso and shoulders. Variations in growth can lead to feelings of clumsiness and awkwardness, which can negatively affect an adolescent's self-image until some kind of balance is restored.

Adolescents are often portrayed as moody. They can be happy and friendly one moment, and angry or sad the next. Many adults attribute the emotional fluctuations to "raging hormones." A recent review of this research suggested that adolescents may experience intense mood swings, but the links between hormones and moods are *not* particularly strong (Buchanan, Eccles, & Becker, 1992). It is difficult to identify one single source for these mood changes, because adolescents are experiencing so many changes (physical development, school transitions, new cognitive abilities), as well as increased concentrations of hormones at the same time (Buchanan et al., 1992) along with the changes in the brain discussed earlier.

There is some evidence to suggest that the rapid increase of hormones in the early stages of puberty can lead to increased irritability, impulsivity, aggression (in boys), and depression (in girls), but these effects are generally moderated by environmental events. For example, increases in hormonal levels in early adolescence may lead to depressed moods in girls, but stressful events such as problems with friends, school, and family members play a much more influential role in explaining the development of depression in adolescent girls (Brooks-Gunn & Warren, 1989). The adolescent's social setting also plays a role in his or her moodiness. Over the course of a day, most adolescents go through many mood changes (Csikszentmihalyi & Larson, 1984). They are happy at lunch, excited with friends, bored in school, and angry if treated unfairly by a teacher. In other words, their moods fluctuate as they change activities. Because adolescents change activities and settings more frequently than adults do, this may account for their greater moodiness.

Adolescents are also viewed as rebellious and uncontrollable. Is there research evidence to support this view of adolescents? Most studies find some disruption in the parent and child relationship during puberty (Buchanan et al., 1992). As children enter adolescence, they report fewer positive feelings toward their parents, less communication with their parents, and more conflict on a daily basis. For example, a recent study showed that early menarche was associated with more conflict with mothers and with more family stress in late childhood (Kim & Smith, 1998). Conflict tends to be greater among adolescents and their mothers (Paikoff & Brooks-Gunn, 1991), perhaps because they spend more time together. The intensity and frequency of conflict appear to be greatest at the peak of puberty. However, as we will learn in Chapter 8, these conflicts tend not to be serious.

Because there is a great deal of individual variation in puberty, the increased conflict is not related to age per se. Most theorists believe that this increased conflict stems from the adolescent's need for more independence and for a greater say in family decisions. If parents are not able to relinquish some of their control, this could lead to rebellious behavior. It is safe to say that in most families, the onset of puberty brings about some imbalance in the parent and child relationship. Rebellious behavior is more common among parents and adolescents who have a history of conflict. When there are positive parent-child relations, balance is usually restored as parents and their adolescents renegotiate roles, rules, and expectations. The implications for teachers are clear. Teachers of adolescents can also expect more conflict if they are not willing or able to allow students to have some independence or control in the classroom.

Effects of Early and Late Physical Maturity

As mentioned earlier, there is considerable individual variability in the onset of puberty. Some youngsters can begin puberty at age 7 or 8, whereas others may not begin puberty until age 14 or 15. Although adjusting to adolescence can be difficult for most adolescents, it is particularly stressful for young people who mature earlier or later than their peers. Adolescents are very much aware of whether or not they are early or late for their age. Interestingly, adolescents' *perceptions* of themselves as early or late have a stronger impact on their reactions than the actual timing of puberty (Dubas, Graber, & Peterson, 1991).

The effects of early and late physical maturation are different for girls and boys. Early maturity in girls is particularly problematic, because the average girl matures 2 years earlier than boys. Consequently, an early-maturing girl is out of sync with both male and female age-mates.

Early physical maturity in girls can have some positive consequences, but it also poses some risks. Initially, early maturity can enhance girls' peer relations, popularity, and social competence. Early-maturing girls are also less dependent on parents than their late-maturing peers (Simmons & Blyth, 1987). However, early maturity in girls can lead to a number of emotional difficulties, including low self-esteem, poor self-image, depression, anxiety, and eating disorders (Aro & Taipale, 1987; Ge, Conger, & Elder, 1996; Simmons & Blyth, 1987). Early-maturing girls are also more likely to engage in deviant behavior, to have problems in school, and to experience early sexual intercourse (Caspi & Moffitt, 1991; Magnusson, Stattin, & Allen, 1985). These problem behaviors are more likely to occur in girls with a prior history of difficulties (Caspi & Moffitt, 1991). Additionally, the negative effects of early maturity are accentuated when combined with other significant transitions such as a change in schools, a geographical move, or a family divorce or remarriage (Simmons & Blyth, 1987).

What explains the negative consequences of early maturity for girls? The lowered self-esteem of early-maturing girls may be related to their body types. Early-maturing girls tend to be heavier than their girlish, late-maturing peers. As a result, their bodies no longer fit the current feminine ideal of thinness that our culture so highly values. Early-maturing girls are also more likely to associate with older peers, which can lead them to engage in actions they are not emotionally prepared to handle, such as early dating and sexual activity, drinking, and deviant behaviors. School involvement tends to be lower among early-maturing girls who have older friends, begin to date early, and engage in early sexual activity (Magnusson et al., 1985). Early-maturing girls who choose not to associate with older peers or engage in these behaviors are less likely to experience long-term social adjustment problems. Thus, the effects of early maturity are partly due to the company girls choose to keep.

What about boys? Is early maturity also associated with negative consequences for boys? Studies conducted some years ago revealed that early maturity has many positive consequences for boys. During high school, early-maturing boys are more self-assured, more popular, and more likely to be chosen as leaders than late-maturing boys (Mussen & Jones, 1957). Early-maturing boys tend to have more favorable self-images, fewer psychological problems, and higher peer popularity than late-maturing boys (Graber, Lewinsohn, Seeley, & Brooks-Gunn, 1997). As with girls, cultural ideals play an important role in how early-maturing boys react to their physical changes. Their physical appearance is moving closer to the cultural ideal of a tall, muscular male body. In contrast to girls, then, an early-maturing boy is more likely to react positively to his physical changes.

However, like their female counterparts, early-maturing boys who choose to affiliate or "hang out" with older peers are at greater risk for engaging in deviant or antisocial activities (Andersson & Magnusson, 1990; Duncan, Ritter, Dornbusch, Gross, & Carlsmith, 1985; Silbereisen, Petersen, Albrecht, & Kracke, 1989). For example, studies in the United States and Europe show that early-maturing boys who develop friendships with older peers are more likely to be truant, to experiment with drugs and alcohol, to have school problems, and to engage in early sexual activities (Magnusson et al., 1985).

Other data reveal that late maturity in boys may be advantageous for some reasons. At age 30, early-maturing males tend to be more conforming, more traditional in their gender role, and less creative than their late-maturing male peers (Livson & Peskin, 1980). It is believed that early-maturing males are pushed into adult roles before they have an opportunity to experiment with different roles and identities. In a way, the greater adjustment problems early-maturing males face in adolescence may lead them to develop coping skills that are useful in adulthood.

As implied in this discussion, the effects of early and late maturity are influenced by a young person's social and cultural context. A New Zealand study revealed that the effects of early maturity in girls are less likely to be found when girls attend single-sex, instead of coeducational, schools (Caspi, Lyman, Moffitt, & Silva, 1993). Similarly, the effects of early maturity are different for girls depending on whether they are attending an elementary or middle school, with early-maturing girls experiencing more difficulty in middle school because they are experiencing multiple transitions (Blyth, Simmons, & Zakin, 1985). Coeducational and middle schools also increase the opportunities of early-maturing girls to engage in deviant behavior. Additionally, the effects of early and late maturity would have less impact on both sexes if our society did not place such a high premium on physical appearance and attractiveness. Parents and teachers can help young people make the transition to adolescence by preparing them for the changes that will take place (e.g., many children go through a "chubby" phase just before their height spurt) and by diminishing the importance of physical appearance. It is important to help young people recognize that individuals have many qualities that make them special, unique, and attractive.

 ## Special Health and Safety Concerns

In this last section, we examine several health problems that can occur in childhood or adolescence. As you know, young people today face a number of risks and challenges, including drug use, early sexual experimentation, and AIDS, to name just a few. The

- In 2001, almost half of the total number of enrollees in Medicaid were children under age 19.

- In 2002, 425,493 babies were born to girls ages 15 to19, a birthrate of 43 per 1,000 girls.

- In 2002, an estimated 2,209,000 children ages 12–17 were dependent on or abusing illicit drugs or alcohol.

- Co-occurring mental health and substance abuse disorders are increasingly prevalent in youth; of youth treated for substance abuse disorders, 80–85% also have a mental health disorder.

- In 2003, 1,687,814 children under age 18 were arrested; of these arrests, 25,531 were for violent crimes and 11,501 were for possession of a weapon.

- A 2001 census showed that 104,413 children are housed in juvenile correction facilities in the United States.

- In 2001, 1,890 children under age 20 committed suicide in the United States, a rate of 2.6 per 100,000 children.

■ FIGURE 2.13
Concerns of Children and Adolescents Today
Source: Child Welfare League of America, 2005.

Centers for Disease Control and Prevention (CDC, 2004) identify six major health risk behaviors that typically emerge during childhood and adolescence: unhealthy dietary behaviors, inadequate physical activity, tobacco use, alcohol and other drug use, sexual behaviors that contribute to pregnancy and sexually transmitted diseases (STDs), and behaviors that contribute to unintentional injuries and violence. Figure 2.13 presents a portrait of the health and safety concerns of children and adolescents in the early twenty-first century. From this figure, it is easy to conclude that many young people are indeed in jeopardy. However, it is important to remember that the problems documented here do not include a majority of adolescents. Although their numbers are growing, only a minority of youths find it difficult to make a healthy transition into adulthood. Developmentalists now recommend looking at indexes of well-being from a strengths-based approach (e.g., Pollard & Rosenberg, 2003). Some attributes promoting safety and security are introduced at the end of the chapter.

We turn now to four major health issues facing young people: eating disorders, substance abuse, adolescent sexuality and pregnancy, and depression and suicide. These health problems were selected because schools can play an important role in prevention and intervention efforts. The Focus on Research box on page 110 describes how a sense of school connection can help protect adolescents from harm.

UNDERSTANDING CHILDREN
Strategy 3.9: Visit with the School Nurse

Eating Disorders

As we have seen, there is considerable individual variation in young people's height and weight during childhood and adolescence. Although most youngsters are able to maintain a weight within the normal range for their height, some children and adolescents may

Focus on
Research

Protecting Adolescents from Harm

Numerous studies have documented the various conditions that can lead to health-compromising behaviors in adolescents. Some health risk behaviors (cigarette smoking, alcohol use, weapon-related violence, etc.) appear to be disproportionately high among adolescents of color, lower-income adolescents, and those living in single-parent homes. In addition, low grades, low self-esteem, having repeated a grade in school, and working 20 or more hours per week are all positively associated with risky behaviors in adolescents. Consistent with research on early maturity, being "out of sync" with peers can also place young people at risk. Both male and female adolescents who perceive themselves as looking *older* than their peers initiate sexual intercourse at a younger age, and they have a higher likelihood of using cigarettes, alcohol, and marijuana. They are also more likely to participate in violence and to experience emotional distress, including suicide ideation, than adolescents who view themselves as age-appropriate. Interestingly, these patterns were found for those adolescents who perceived themselves as looking older, not younger, than their age-mates (Resnick et al., 1997).

Having identified important risk factors, researchers are now turning to the home, school, and individual characteristics that help protect young people from harm. Results from the *National Longitudinal Study of Adolescent Health* (Resnick et al., 1997) showed that one of the significant protective factors for adolescents is their sense of connection to parents, families, or other caring adults. Adolescents who feel loved and wanted by family members are less likely to engage in risky behaviors. The importance that adolescents place on prayer and religion is also a significant protective factor in their lives.

More important for educators, the adolescents' sense of school connectedness functions as an important protective factor in their lives. *School connectedness* was defined as the degree to which adolescents (a) feel their teachers treat students fairly, (b) feel close to people at school, and (c) feel part of their school. Other studies of adolescents also show that participation in school activities and academic achievement can reduce risky behaviors (Cairns & Cairns, 1994; Eccles & Barber, 1999; Mahoney, 2000). Using a national data set, one group of researchers found that after controlling for race and poverty status, tenth graders who reported spending *no* time in school-sponsored activities were 49 percent more likely to use drugs, 37 percent more likely to become teen parents, and 35 percent more likely to have smoked cigarettes compared to students who spend 1 to 4 hours weekly in extracurricular activities (Zill, Nord, & Loomis, 1995). However, involvement in school activities may not lower rates of binge drinking (Eccles & Barber, 1999).

Studies of risk and protective factors in adolescents' lives underscore the need for school environments that enhance young people's ability to cope with difficult and challenging circumstances in their lives. This capacity is known as **resiliency.** Schools that help adolescents develop their talents and a positive identity, that provide opportunities for meaningful participation, and that promote caring relationships among students and teachers are resiliency-building environments (Henderson & Milstein, 1996). It is important for schools to focus on adolescents' well-being and healthy development, rather than on problem behaviors.

develop eating disorders that have serious physical and psychological implications. In this section, we briefly consider the causes and consequences of three different types of eating disorders: obesity, anorexia, and bulimia nervosa.

Obesity

In the last 30 years, Americans have become increasingly preoccupied with their weight. At the same time, the percentage of young people who are overweight has more than doubled in the last 30 years (see Figure 2.14). About 16 percent of young people aged 6

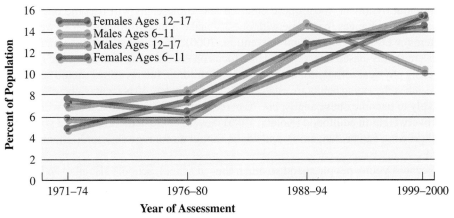

Percent of Overweight Youths in the United States, by Age and Gender
Source: U.S. Department of Health and Human Services (2003).

Overweight is defined as body mass index (BMI) at or above sex- or age-specific 95th percentile BMI cutoffs for children ages 6–11 and for adolescents ages 12–17.

to 19 years are overweight today (Centers for Disease Control and Prevention, 2002). Not only is childhood obesity on the rise, but it is also occurring at a younger and younger age. In addition, about one-third of youth may be considered at risk for overweight (Pyle et al., 2006). Obesity is the most common eating disorder among young people today.

Obesity is defined as a greater than 20 percent increase over average body weight for the child's age, sex, and body build (Behrman Kliegman, 1990). Because childhood obesity has increased so rapidly in the last 30 years, we know the problem is not simply genetic: The gene pool has not changed rapidly during the course of this epidemic. A number of factors contribute to childhood obesity, including heredity, unhealthy diet, lack of exercise, and, in some cases, abnormal metabolism or family trauma. There is growing recognition that television watching is also associated with weight problems. While watching television, children see a steady stream of junk food commercials, eat more snacks, and burn fewer calories (Gortmaker, Dietz, Chueng, 1990). In fact, some evidence suggests that television viewing places children in a relaxed state, which lowers their metabolism below the normal level (Klesges, 1993). Many of these same factors contribute to obesity in adulthood as well.

The rise in childhood obesity is also attributed to low physical activity. As we learned earlier, American children spend far less time in physical activity at school than children in other countries. A 1997 survey of adolescents indicated that more than 36 percent did not regularly participate in any rigorous physical activity. Approximately 51 percent were not enrolled in physical education classes, and daily participation in physical education classes had dropped from 42 percent in 1991 to 27 percent in 1997 (Centers for Disease Control and Prevention, 2000).

Obesity has serious consequences for children and adolescents. It is associated with respiratory and orthopedic problems as well as diabetes. Childhood obesity can also result in increased blood pressure and high cholesterol, which are risk factors for cardiovascular disease in adults. Recent studies reveal that cardiovascular disease can be detected as early as age 8 (Harrell et al., 1996). Because of societal definitions of attractiveness, obese children and adolescents also experience teasing, ridicule, and rejection from peers. As a result, they can develop low self-esteem, depression, and behavioral problems (Strauss, Smith, Frame, & Forehand, 1985; Pyle et al., 2006). Childhood obesity becomes a vicious cycle in which low self-esteem and social isolation contribute to overeating, keeping the young person overweight.

Without treatment, most obese children and adolescents will become obese adults. The metabolic changes that come with obesity make it more difficult to lose weight later (Centers for Disease Control and Prevention, 2000). The most successful treatment programs are family-based interventions that focus on encouraging healthy eating habits and increasing physical activity for both parents and children. Interventions should begin early, before unhealthy eating habits are established. Approximately 40 percent of obese 7-year-olds are likely to become obese adults, but 70 percent of overweight adolescents will continue to be overweight in adulthood (Kolata, 1986). Severe or crash dieting while a young body is still growing can be dangerous, and adults should discourage children's attempts in this regard.

Because young people spend so much time at school, schools also play an important role in improving students' eating habits and in promoting physical activity. A number of school-based interventions for promoting healthy weight have been implemented. The most successful programs combine behavior management counseling, teaching children how to identify healthy foods and avoid unhealthy foods, implementing daily physical activities, and involving parents (Pyle et al., 2006). Some examples are the *Pathways* program, developed for American Indian children; the *Be Smart Program* based on Bandura's social learning theory, developed for children age 5 to 7 years in the United Kingdom; the *Eat Well and Keep Moving Program,* developed for fourth and fifth graders; and the *Planet Health* program for sixth and seventh graders. These programs have shown a variety of positive, short-term effects on children's knowledge about nutrition and physical activity and some (but not all) targeted behaviors (e.g., physical activity, healthy eating); however, we know less about the sustainability of these programs and their long-term effects.

Anorexia and Bulimia Nervosa

At the other end of the continuum are youngsters who are seriously underweight. The eating disorder **anorexia nervosa** mainly affects adolescent girls between the ages of 14 and 18. Girls with this disorder lose between 25 percent and 50 percent of their body weight through excessive dieting and exercise. A large number of anorexic girls will also develop **bulimia nervosa,** an eating disorder in which one goes on an eating binge and then vomits or uses laxatives as a way of purging the body. Whereas anorexia nervosa is common among adolescent girls, bulimia tends to be common among older teens and young adults. It is estimated that anorexia affects from 0.5 to 1 percent of teenage and young women, and bulimia from 1 to 3 percent (Centers for Disease Control and Prevention, 2000). Women are 8 to 10 times more likely to suffer from anorexia or bulimia than are men.

As with obesity, anorexia and bulimia result from a complex interplay of many different factors, including biological changes, familial relations, and the larger society (Manley, Rickson, Standeven, 2000). As you know, physical attractiveness and self-esteem are strongly linked in childhood and adolescence, especially for girls. For many girls and women, it is extremely difficult to meet society's definition of physical attractiveness. Female models, often considered to have the ideal body type, are 9 percent taller and 16 percent thinner than the average woman (Wolf, 1991). Even the most well-adjusted female will have difficulty meeting this standard. Unfortunately, girls who are at most risk for eating problems are those who most often accept society's definition of the ideal female body. For example, white adolescent girls are more likely to be dissatisfied with their bodies than African American girls, who are less likely to define beauty in terms of the size of a

Helping Students with Eating Disorders

If teachers suspect that a student may have an eating disorder, but he or she has not been diagnosed, they should consider the following strategies:

- Express concern to the student and a willingness to help, while still respecting his or her need for autonomy and privacy.
- Do not force the student to eat.

Source: Manly et al. (2000).

- Find out where to go for support, and encourage the student to seek help.
- Observe, describe, and document eating behaviors of concern across times and across settings.
- Consult with the school-based team regarding referral to other experienced professionals for a thorough assessment.

woman's waistline. African American girls believe it is better to be a little overweight than underweight (Becker, Yanek, Koffman, & Bronner, 1999; Ingrassia, 1995). Another characteristic of anorexics is that they are typically perfectionists who are model students with high standards for their behavior and performance. Unlike anorexics, who tend to be highly controlled, bulimic young women are impulsive and perceive themselves as out of control. Bulimics are also at greater risk than anorexics for developing substance abuse problems.

Both anorexia and bulimia, if left untreated, have serious consequences. Each is a compulsive disorder that begins as a strategy to control weight but then takes on a life of its own. Anorexia can result in malnutrition, stunted growth, hair loss, disruption of the menstrual cycle, and extreme sensitivity to the cold. Nearly 20 percent of anorexic girls inadvertently starve themselves to death. Bulimia can result in malnutrition, dental problems, and electrolytic imbalances that can trigger heart attacks as well as cause life-threatening damage to the throat and stomach. Both disorders can be associated with low self-esteem and depression.

Treatment of anorexia and bulimia requires professional help. Teachers who are concerned about a student should consult with a health professional at their school (nurse, social worker, psychologist, or counselor) to obtain information about the referral process. The Focus on Teaching box includes some strategies teachers may use if they suspect one of their students has an eating disorder that has not yet been diagnosed.

Treatment of anorexia and bulimia may be lengthy and difficult for both the students and their families. Generally, treatment involves a combination of individual and family therapy. Girls with these disorders tend to have a distorted view of their body image. Anorexics believe they are too fat, even when they are visibly underweight, and they do not believe their eating habits are abnormal. Bulimics are generally aware of their abnormal eating patterns, but they lack the ability to control their impulses. Consequently, bulimia is generally easier to treat than anorexia through family and individual therapy. Anorexia generally requires hospitalization as the initial step. Medical treatment must be accompanied by family therapy focused on changing parent–child interactions and expectations.

Substance Abuse

It is commonly believed that drug problems among young people are at an epidemic level in the United States. Research on substance abuse among young people has focused on the use of alcohol, cigarettes, inhalants (glue and paint thinner), and illegal drugs such as marijuana, amphetamines, LSD, and cocaine. During the 1980s, substance abuse was the focus of considerable public attention. From 1975 to the early 1990s, there were significant declines in use of cigarettes, alcohol, stimulants, and marijuana. However, researchers believe that these patterns are beginning to reverse themselves. As Figure 2.15 shows, the use of illicit drugs (e.g., marijuana, hallucinogens, cocaine, heroin, etc.) increased among adolescents from the early to the mid-1990s. In 1998, it began to show a downturn (Johnston, Bachman, & O'Malley, 1999). *Substance abuse* is defined as frequent or excessive use of a drug. Rates of substance abuse depend on the substance. The three most commonly used substances are cigarettes, alcohol, and marijuana.

Cigarette smoking is one of the most preventable causes of death in the United States. Research evidence suggests that those individuals who initiate smoking in adolescence have a high likelihood of continuing to smoke into adulthood (U.S. Department of Health & Human Services, 2000). Additionally, youths who smoke are more likely to drink alcohol and use illicit drugs than their nonsmoking peers. Daily smoking among high school students has been increasing steadily through the 1990s, and smoking is most prevalent among white adolescents. Between 1992 and 1997, the percentage of high school seniors who reported smoking on a daily basis increased from 17 percent to 25 percent. Approximately 9 percent of eighth graders and 16 percent of tenth graders reported smoking on a daily basis. It is estimated that one in four high school students smoke cigarettes (Centers For Disease Control and Prevention, 2005a). This figure does not include young people who use smokeless tobacco. Almost 90 percent of adults who die from smoking-related illnesses started smoking as teens.

Along with cigarette smoking, many young people smoke marijuana, and it is the most commonly used illicit drug. The number of high school students who have smoked marijuana increased from about 14 percent in 1991 to 27 percent in 1999; however, use decreased to about 20 percent in 2005 (Centers For Disease Control and Prevention, 2005b).

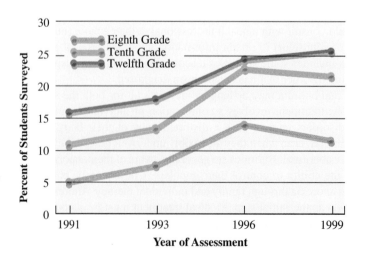

■ FIGURE 2.15
Percent of High School Students Reporting Use of Any Illicit Drug in Previous 30 Days
Source: After Johnston et al. (1999).

The use of other illegal drugs is less frequent. In 1999, 17 percent of high school seniors had tried amphetamines, 14 percent had tried hallucinogens (e.g., LSD), and 10 percent had tried cocaine (Johnston et al., 2000).

Alcohol use among adolescents is also of considerable concern. In 1999, 51 percent of high school seniors reported using alcohol at least once in the last week, and 31 percent reported engaging in binge drinking (drinking five or more alcoholic drinks in a row) during the past 2 weeks (Johnston et al., 2000). Additionally, this study indicated that one-half of the eighth-grade students surveyed had tried alcohol, and one-fourth had been drunk. A study of youth risk behaviors indicated that 10 percent of high school students reported they had driven after drinking alcohol, and 29 percent reported they had ridden with a driver who had been drinking alcohol (Centers For Disease Control and Prevention, 2005c).

As mentioned, substance abuse is associated with many different problems, and the consequences become more severe with greater use. It is important to distinguish between occasional experimentation and frequent use. Most young people will experiment with alcohol, cigarettes, and perhaps other drugs. Drug use becomes problematic when it is frequent and excessive. Young people who abuse drugs or alcohol are more likely to experience problems in school. In fact, dramatic changes in school performance are often a symptom of substance abuse. Drug and alcohol abuse is associated with loss of sleep, chronic fatigue, depression, and other psychological problems. Substance abusers also place themselves at risk for developing long-term health problems, such as cancer, heart disease, respiratory problems, and kidney or liver damage. Moreover, drugs and alcohol are often implicated in fatal or near-fatal accidents (e.g., automobile crashes, falls, and drownings) involving young people.

Most young people first experiment with drugs and alcohol in their teenage years, so childhood and adolescence are important times to encourage the prevention of substance abuse. One of the greatest risks for substance abuse in adolescence or adulthood is early exposure. Research suggests that adolescents who have not experimented with alcohol or marijuana before the age of 21 are unlikely to ever use drugs (Kandel & Logan, 1984). Efforts to prevent substance abuse must begin early, while children are in elementary school, and most drug prevention programs are, in fact, provided in school settings (Dryfoos, 1990). Research suggests that the risk of substance abuse for a student who attends a school in which illegal drugs are kept, used, or sold is at twice the risk of a student in a drug-free school.

Most prevention programs have targeted the "gateway" drugs—alcohol, tobacco, and marijuana. Project Dare (Drug Awareness Resistance Education) is a popular school-based program that is taught in over 75 percent of school districts and focuses on teaching students to resist peer pressure and that educates young people about the health dangers of substance use. It is also clear that efforts to keep schools free of drugs can reduce the rates of substance abuse among young people. However, there is growing recognition that a variety of strategies are needed. The most successful programs are ones that are not only implemented in the schools but also involve the adolescents' peers, parents, and community. Efforts to prevent substance abuse must also start early, perhaps in late elementary school, and continue on an annual basis through the middle and high school years.

Adolescent Sexuality and Pregnancy

As a consequence of popular culture and society's relaxed attitudes about sexuality, many researchers believe that young people are dealing with sexual issues at a younger age than ever before. A 1999 survey of students indicated that approximately 40 percent of ninth graders nationwide report having had sexual intercourse, and this figure rises with each grade. By the twelfth grade, 65 percent of teens report having had sexual intercourse. Males are more sexually active than females at each of the grade levels surveyed (U.S. Department of Health and Human Services, 2002). There are also ethnic differences in young people's sexual behavior, as shown in Figure 2.16. A higher percent of African American and Hispanic adolescents are sexually active than white adolescents. Additionally, 24 percent of African American adolescents report having had intercourse by age 13, compared with 9 percent of Latinos and 6 percent of whites (Blum et al., 2000). Research also indicates that 19 percent of students in grades 9 to 12 have already had sexual intercourse with four or more partners (Warren, Harris, & Kann, 1995). Without a doubt, sex is very much a part of the adolescent experience.

The consequences of adolescent sexuality are well known. Compared with adults, adolescents are at a higher risk for acquiring sexually transmitted diseases (STDs), including HIV. The most common STDs are chlamydia, gonorrhea, and herpes simplex. Both chlamydia and gonorrhea can be treated with antibiotics, but left untreated these diseases can lead to serious health problems, including infertility. There is no known cure for herpes simplex, and this disease results in sores, blisters, fever, headaches, and fatigue that can last for up to 4 days. This disease is also highly infectious. Overall, approximately two-thirds of all STDs occur in people under the age of 15 (Carroll & Wolpe, 1996). The risk of infection from human immunodeficiency virus (HIV), which leads to AIDS, is also substantial in adolescence, because teens are more likely to engage in risky behaviors associated with this disease, such as unprotected intercourse, multiple sex partners, and intravenous drugs.

To date, however, the problem that has received the most attention is adolescent pregnancy. Pregnancy rates have declined for women between the ages of 15 and 19 years by 15 percent since 1991, when teen pregnancy rates had reached their peak. However, more than 900,000 adolescents become pregnant each year. The United States now has the highest rate of teenage pregnancy in the industrialized world. In the mid 1990s, rates were twice as high as in England or Canada, and eight times as high as in Japan (Singh & Darroch, 2000). In the United States, teen pregnancy rates vary by ethnic background. In 1999, pregnancy rates

■ FIGURE 2.16
*Percent of U.S.
Adolescents Reporting
Sexual Intercourse*
Source: Adapted from Blum
et al. (2000).

were more than twice as high among non-Hispanic blacks and Hispanic teens as among non-Hispanic white teens (U.S. Department of Health and Human Services, 2003).

Along with pregnancy rates, teenage birth rates have been steadily declining and have fallen 18 percent since 1991. In 2002, there were approximately a half million births to adolescents 15 to 19 years of age (Child Welfare League of America, 2005). Teenage parenthood has adverse effects on the life chances of young people and their babies. Teenage mothers are likely to drop out of high school, and almost half will never finish. Because only a small percentage of teenage mothers marry and stay married to the child's father, many women must rely on public assistance. Early childbearing is one of the strongest factors associated with poverty and welfare dependency.

Babies born to adolescent mothers are likely to be low-birth-weight babies due to poor nutrition or poor prenatal care. As discussed previously, these babies will experience many difficulties in early infancy. By the preschool and elementary years, learning and psychosocial problems are generally evident in the offspring of teenage mothers. In adolescence, children of teenage mothers have more achievement and discipline problems than children of older mothers do. Many of these problems are attributed to the low socioeconomic and educational levels of the teenage mothers. Unfortunately, poor academic achievement (including dropping out), discipline problems, and low socioeconomic status place the girls of teenage mothers at risk for an early pregnancy, and the cycle repeats itself. Improving schools in general is important, as youth are more likely to become pregnant in schools with high rates of poverty and social disorganization (Kirby, 2000a). On the positive side, greater attachment to school and plans to attend college decrease the chances of sexual risk-taking (e.g., Kirby, 2002a).

Experts agree that the leading causes of adolescent pregnancies are lack of sex education and lack of access to reliable contraceptives. School-based efforts to prevent adolescent pregnancies have been disappointing at best. If taught at the secondary level, these programs are too late. Moreover, most sex education programs focus on the biological aspects of sex and ignore the emotional and ethical issues involved. Many public school districts that have a policy to teach sex education require educators to teach abstinence as the preferred or only option outside of marriage (Alan Guttmacher Institute, 1999; Kirby, 2002b). Reviews of research indicate that there is little sound scientific evidence that these programs delay sexual intercourse (Kirby, 2002b), and may inadvertently lead youth to unprotected sex (American Psychological Association, 2005). Such programs provide little protection for those adolescents already engaged in sexual activity. Additionally, most school-based sex education programs totally ignore the needs of homosexual youths, who have one of the highest rates of suicide among adolescents.

There are a number of ways schools can improve their sex education programs. First, it is important to recognize that most teenage pregnancies are unintended and unwanted. Second, efforts to increase young people's knowledge about sex, contraceptives, pregnancy, and sexually transmitted diseases must begin early. Some parents and policy makers are reluctant to provide this information because they fear it will encourage sexual promiscuity. In fact, fifteen years of research shows that comprehensive sexuality education programs for youth—that provide information, encourage abstinence, promote appropriate condom use (for those who are sexually active), encourage fewer sexual partners, and teach sexual communication skills—delay the onset of sexual intercourse as well as reduce HIV-risk behavior (American Psychological Association, 2005). Furthermore, sex education programs should be designed to teach decision-making skills and interpersonal assertiveness (e.g., how to say "no" under peer pressure) and values clarification to equip them with the knowledge and skills necessary to negotiate safer sex (Conner & Dewey, 2003). The most successful adolescent pregnancy prevention programs combine education about sexuality with school-based health clinics, where students can obtain contraceptives and learn to use them effectively (Children's Defense Fund, 1996). This last recommendation is perhaps the most controversial of all, but the one with the greatest impact.

Depression and Suicide

Although many children and adolescents experience feelings of sadness and loneliness, a small number suffer from chronic depression. **Depression** is an affective disorder that is characterized by disturbances in cognitive and behavioral functioning. Common symptoms of childhood depression are the inability to concentrate, feelings of hopelessness, weight changes, sleep problems, inactivity or overactivity, slowed thinking, lack of motivation, low energy and fatigue, inability to have fun, and thoughts of death (American Psychiatric Association, 1994). Depression is often difficult to diagnose in children because sleep disturbances and appetite changes are relatively frequent for this group. However, most clinicians and researchers believe that some form of childhood depression exists, even if it is difficult to diagnose. If any of the symptoms discussed here persist longer than 2 or 3 weeks, the child should be referred for professional help.

Some researchers have also argued that depressive disorders are not possible until adolescence, when children are cognitively able to reflect on their inner thoughts and feelings. Consistent with this view, depression is twice as frequent in adolescence as in childhood (Compas, Ey, & Grant, 1993). Approximately 20 to 25 percent of adolescents report mild feelings of depression, and 4 percent are severely depressed (National Institutes of Mental Health, 2000). By adolescence, depression is more common among girls than boys. Researchers believe that the higher rate of depression in girls is mostly due to gender-role expectations. Interestingly, girls with a highly feminine gender-role identity are more likely to experience depression than are those with a masculine or androgynous gender-role identity (Petersen et al., 1993). Another explanation for the gender difference in depression is that girls are more likely than boys to experience multiple transitions (changes in body, family, school, etc.) early in adolescence, when they have less-effective coping strategies. In *Reviving Ophelia,* Mary Pipher (1994), a clinical psychologist who works with teenage girls, writes, "Girls are under more stress in the 1990s; they have less varied and effective coping skills to deal with that stress, and they have fewer internal and external resources on which to rely" (p. 158). She observes that young women often deal with this pain by harming themselves through self-mutilation (e.g., burning, cutting, or piercing themselves), like Lisa, in the introductory vignette, which has been on the rise in recent years.

Like other health concerns discussed in this section, depression has serious consequences. It is associated with poor school achievement, substance abuse, juvenile delinquency, anxiety and eating disorders, and suicidal ideation. Without treatment, depressed children and adolescents have a high likelihood of becoming depressed adults.

In extreme cases, depression can lead to suicide. It is estimated that six children and youths a day commit suicide (Children's Defense Fund, 2000). In 1999, 25 percent of female adolescents and 14 percent of male adolescents in grades 9 to 12 had seriously considered attempting suicide, according to the Youth Risk Surveillance Study by the Centers for Disease Control and Prevention (Centers for Disease Control and Prevention, 1999). Suicide is close behind homicide as the second leading cause of death among young people. Rates of adolescent suicide are higher among Native Americans than other ethnic groups. Also, homosexual youths are at greater risk than heterosexual youths for suicide (Remafedi, 1999). Whereas girls make more suicide attempts than boys, more boys die in suicide attempts, because they use more effective methods for taking their lives (e.g., hanging or gunshot).

What can cause a young person to take his or her life? Several factors increase the risk of suicide in young people. As mentioned previously, depression and substance abuse are associated with an increased risk. Other risk factors are family stress, parental rejection, and family disruption. A family history that includes psychiatric or depressive disorders is also a risk factor. Sadly, access to a firearm is associated with an increased risk. Some researchers believe that increases in adolescent suicide rates can be partly attributed to the increased availability of firearms in the last 20 years. Additionally, adolescents who have attempted suicide once are at risk for attempting it again (Garland & Zigler, 1993).

Contrary to popular belief, suicide is rarely an impulsive reaction to a distressing event, such as a divorce or a romantic breakup. Young people who take their lives generally first make appeals for support from friends, family, and teachers. There are also several early signs that should not be ignored. Suicidal teens may give away their prized possessions, say good-bye to friends, show disregard for their personal safety, and become preoccupied with death. Some reports suggest that adolescents may be absent from school for long periods of time before they commit suicide. Several risk factors associated with adolescent suicide are summarized in Figure 2.17. Most schools now provide group counseling when a student in a school has committed suicide. Through group discussions, school officials hope to reduce the risk of cluster suicides, which involve an unusually high number of suicides within a particular geographic location or time period. There is a higher risk of cluster suicides among young people.

A teacher may be one of a few people in a child's life who can recognize or respond to these appeals for help. If you suspect a young person is contemplating suicide, you should take the person seriously. Ask direct questions (Are you planning to hurt yourself? How will you do it?) in a calm manner. Encourage the young person to talk about his or her feelings and listen carefully. You should then contact a health professional in your school (school nurse, guidance counselor, or social worker) who can provide further assistance. Most

Risk Factors of Adolescent Suicide

- Sudden decline in school attendance and achievement, especially in above-average students

- History of substance abuse, conduct problems, or affective disorders

- Poor coping skills and deficits in interpersonal skills

- Family turmoil and instability

- History of sexual abuse

- A humiliating or shameful event, such as an arrest, breakup of romantic relationship, or school or work failure

- Access to firearms

- Exposure to suicidal behavior

- Feelings of hopelessness and preoccupation with death

■ FIGURE 2.17
Risk Factors of Adolescent Suicide
Source: After Garland & Zigler (1993).

Focus on
Development

Prevention Strategies for Schools and Society

Infants (ages 0–3)

Society

- deconcentrate lower-income housing
- reduce income inequality

Childhood (ages 3–11)

School

- social development training
- preschool enrichment programs (e.g., Head Start)
- bullying prevention programs
- school policies to prevent injuries
- use of protective equipment in sports

Society

- public information campaigns to promote prosocial norms
- reduce levels of media violence
- develop a "culture of safety"
- educate drivers to share the road

Adolescence (ages 12–19)

School

- home–school partnership programs to promote parental involvement
- mentoring
- academic enrichment programs
- education to promote healthy relations with the opposite sex and decrease dating violence
- social development training in anger management, social skills, and problem solving
- develop and enforce school safety policies
- insist on the use of protective gear in sports

Society

- reduce levels of media violence
- public information campaigns to promote prosocial norms
- educational incentives for at-risk disadvantaged high school students
- enforce laws prohibiting illegal transfers of guns to youth
- support bicycle and motorcycle helmet laws
- support restrictions on access to alcohol

Source: Modified from Sleet & Mercy (2003).

communities also have crisis hotlines that can provide professional help. It is important that you assist the young person in getting professional help. Thoughts or attempts of suicide may be a trial run for the real thing.

Although our discussion of depression and suicide has focused on individual treatment, researchers believe that schools can play a much larger role in preventing these problems. Programs that promote social competence, problem-solving skill training, coping strategies for stress, and basic mental health education may provide the best prevention of all. According to Ann Garland and Edward Zigler (1993), "These types of programs are truly primary prevention and would address many of the current social problems" (p. 177).

Development of Well-Being in School

Schools, like other ecological contexts, support healthy development of children and adolescents and prevent risky behavior. "Individuals, families, communities, workplaces, schools, and other social institutions are important partners in creating a 'culture of safety' for children" (Sleet & Mercy, 2003). Sleet and Mercy suggest a number of research-based prevention strategies for homes, schools, community, and society. These suggestions for how schools and society can foster the safety and well-being of infants, children, and adolescents were shown in the Focus on Development box on the previous page.

■ Chapter Summary

Prenatal Development

■ Developmental processes begin at the moment of human conception. The period from conception to birth is called prenatal development. This period of development is mainly directed by genetic influences and follows a universal pattern.

■ Genes and chromosomes are the basic building blocks of human life. Each cell contains 23 pairs of chromosomes, which are composed of DNA structures containing thousands of genes.

■ Most genetic disorders are caused by recessive genes. Common genetic disorders include hemophilia, sickle-cell anemia, PKU, muscular dystrophy, congenital diabetes, and cystic fibrosis. Some genetic disorders are caused by abnormal chromosomes. Down syndrome and fragile-X syndrome are two conditions caused by an extra or a damaged chromosome. Both conditions affect the mental and physical development of the child.

■ The genes a person inherits from both parents determine the person's genotype for a particular trait. The expression of these traits is called a phenotype. If the environment does not facilitate the expression of a particular trait (e.g., high intelligence) then the genotype and phenotype will differ. The concept of reaction range defines the degree to which the environment can affect the expression of genes.

■ Prenatal development is divided into three major stages. During the germinal period (first 2 weeks after conception), the fertilized egg travels down the fallopian tube and attaches itself to the uterine wall. In the embryonic period (weeks 2 to 8), all the basic structures of the child-to-be are formed. This prenatal stage is particularly vulnerable to environmental agents because of the rapid development of new organs and systems. During the fetal period (8 weeks to birth), the fetus increases in size and weight. Most babies are born between 38 and 42 weeks.

■ Although prenatal development is mainly guided by genetic influences, exposure to dangerous environmental agents or conditions can disrupt this process. Alcohol, nicotine, drugs, radiation, and environmental pollutants can have a negative effect on prenatal development and must be avoided during pregnancy. The fetus is most vulnerable to environmental influences in the early stages of pregnancy when body structures and major organs are developing.

■ A premature birth or low birth weight are risk factors in a child's development. Premature births and low birth weights are caused by poor nutrition, poor prenatal care, and environmental agents such as nicotine, alcohol, and drugs. In elementary school, children with a low birth weight are more likely than children of normal birth weight to have mild learning disabilities, attention problems, poor concentration, language delays, and asthma.

Brain Development

■ The human brain is not fully mature until early adulthood. Brain development after birth involves increases in the number and length of neural fibers that connect nerve cells, deposits of a fatty substance (myelin) on neural fibers that enables impulses to travel faster through the brain, and pruning.

- The human brain is open to change (plasticity), especially in early development. Researches also report significant changes in the brain during adolescence.
- The infant brain quickly develops the perceptual abilities it needs to process and interpret information from the five senses.

Children with Exceptional Needs

- Educators are likely to encounter children with specific learning disabilities and attention deficit hyperactivity disorder (ADHD) in the classroom. The IDEA legislation defines a specific learning disability as "a disorder in one or more of the basic psychological processes involved in understanding or in using spoken or written language, which may manifest itself in an imperfect ability to listen, think, speak, read, write, spell, or to do mathematical calculations."
- Learning disabilities are influenced by heredity, problems during pregnancy, and incidents after birth.
- Children are often identified with learning disabilities during the elementary years, but there are efforts to identify and intervene earlier during the preschool years.

Motor Development

- Motor development involves children's increasing ability to move and to control their body movements. A newborn's movements are mainly due to innate reflexes, such as sucking, choking, and grasping. Gross motor skills that involve the movement of head, body, legs, and arms develop first. Fine motor skills develop in the preschool years. Gender differences in gross and fine motor skills are evident in childhood due to differences in socialization experiences.
- Play is the medium by which children develop their motor skills. Preschool and young elementary school children need daily activities that exercise their large muscles and help develop their fine motor skills. Older elementary children are able to sit for longer periods of time, but they also need frequent periods of activity. As motor skills are developing, children's play activities need careful supervision. Accidents are the number-one cause of childhood deaths.

Physical Growth

- Infancy is characterized by a rapid period of growth. In the elementary school years, physical growth slows down, although children continue to gradually add weight and height to their bodies.
- Children's physical size and attractiveness can influence how they are perceived by others. Children and adults attribute more positive attributes and characteristics to physically attractive than unattractive children. Children who are physically attractive also have more positive peer relations.
- Puberty begins between the ages of 10 and 12 for girls and 12 and 14 years for boys. Within each sex, there is considerable individual variability in the timing of puberty, but the sequence of change is universal. The changes that occur in puberty primarily prepare the body for sexual reproduction, but the development of secondary characteristics is only one of many changes that are taking place. There are changes in the skeleton, muscles, and vital organs.
- Puberty can pose adjustment problems for adolescents. It often leads to changes in the adolescent's self-image, self-confidence, social relations, moods, and so on. Parts of the body mature at different rates, which can make adolescents feel clumsy and awkward. Adolescents are moody, but there is little evidence to suggest that their mood swings are caused by "raging hormones."
- Early and late maturity have different effects for girls than for boys. Early maturity in girls can lead to low self-esteem, depression, anxiety, and eating disorders. If early-maturing girls seek out the company

of older peers, it can also lead to risk behaviors such as drinking, early sexual activity, and delinquency. Early-maturing boys tend to have the advantage in terms of their self-esteem, popularity, and leadership skills. However, if they associate with older peers, they may also be at risk for engaging in deviant or antisocial behavior. In general, recent studies suggest that late-maturing boys and girls experience fewer adjustment problems in the long run than do early maturers.

Nutrition and Sleep

■ Psychologists and educators are attending more to how children's and adolescents' eating and sleeping habits may affect their learning and adjustment in school. Some effective school-based intervention programs incorporate nutrition education, increased physical activities, and parent involvement.

Special Health and Safety Concerns

■ Young people, especially adolescents, face many health and safety risks. Most young people are able to make a healthy transition to adulthood, but the numbers of young people who are at risk for serious health problems are increasing.

■ Obesity is the most common eating disorder. A number of factors contribute to childhood obesity, including heredity, an unhealthy diet, lack of physical activity, and television viewing. Obese children experience peer rejection, low self-esteem, and other behavioral problems. They also have a high likelihood of becoming obese adolescents and adults. Schools can help obese children by encouraging healthy eating habits, eliminating junk food, increasing physical activity, and reducing stereotypes of overweight people.

■ Anorexia and bulimia nervosa affects 3 percent of adolescent and young women. The girls who are most at risk for these eating disorders are those who have accepted society's definition of feminine attractiveness. Both anorexia and bulimia are associated with low self-esteem and depression, and can be life-threatening if left untreated. Medical treatment is generally accompanied by family therapy focused on changing parent–child interactions and expectations.

■ The four most frequently abused substances among young people today are tobacco, alcohol, marijuana, and inhalants. Young people who abuse alcohol and drugs experience problems in school as well as psychological and health problems. Childhood and adolescence is an important time for the prevention of substance abuse. The most successful prevention programs educate young people about the risk of drug use but also promote interpersonal skills and self-esteem.

■ Sex is very much a part of the adolescent experience. Adolescents begin to experiment with their sexuality earlier than ever before. The leading causes of sexual risk behaviors are lack of sex education and lack of access to contraceptives. Comprehensive sex education programs have proven to be effective in delaying the onset of sexual intercourse and reducing some risk behaviors.

■ A small number of children and adolescents suffer from chronic depression. Depression is more prevalent in adolescents than children, due to the adolescent's ability to be self-reflective and self-critical. In extreme cases, depression can increase a young person's risk of suicide, which is now the second leading cause of death among young people. Researchers believe that schools must play a larger role in preventing these problems. Prevention efforts should focus on improving social skills, teaching stress management strategies, and promoting basic mental health.

■ Schools can foster a healthy sense of well-being in children and adolescents through a variety of means, including facilitating home–school partnerships, providing nutritional education, implementing bullying prevention programs, and enforcing safety policies.

■ Key Terms

anorexia nervosa *(p. 112)*
attachment *(p. 75)*
autism *(p. 89)*
brain lateralization *(p. 71)*
bulimia nervosa *(p. 112)*
cephalocaudal pattern *(p. 98)*
chromosomes *(p. 51)*
depression *(p. 118)*
developmental dyscalculia *(p. 72)*
dizygotic twins *(p. 53)*
Down syndrome *(p. 53)*

dyslexia *(p. 72)*
fine motor skills *(p. 91)*
fragile-X syndrome *(p. 55)*
genotype *(p. 55)*
gross motor skills *(p. 90)*
habituation *(p. 73)*
intermodal perception *(p. 75)*
low birth weight *(p. 62)*
menarche *(p. 104)*
mitosis *(p. 57)*
monozygotic twins *(p. 53)*

myelination *(p. 67)*
neurons *(p. 65)*
obesity *(p. 111)*
phenotype *(p. 56)*
polygenetic traits *(p. 51)*
proximal-distal pattern *(p. 98)*
puberty *(p. 100)*
reaction range *(p. 56)*
resiliency *(p. 110)*
secular trend *(p. 98)*
teratogen *(p. 59)*

■ Activities

1. Observe three different age groups (e.g., kindergarten, third grade, and fifth grade) playing outside at a local school. Use the following checklist to record the various motor skills exhibited by each age group. After collecting your observations, describe the age differences you observed. Give specific examples of behaviors you observed to support your assessment of each age group. Were most of the students "on time" in their motor development, according to the information in the Focus on Development box on page 92? Were some students more or less advanced for their age group? Did you observe any gender differences in students' motor skills? How would you account for these gender differences?

Motor Skill Checklist

Age _____

Skill _____

Exhibited	**Not Exhibited**
a. Runs well	
b. Climbs well	
c. Shows good balance	
d. Hops on one foot	
e. Skips well	
f. Gallops	
g. Climbs by alternating feet	
h. Kicks ball well	
i. Throws ball well	
j. Catches ball well	

2. Design an outside play area for elementary school children to promote the development of gross motor skills. Your design should include play equipment for younger as well as older children. In designing your play area, be sure to consider safety and supervision concerns.

3. As you know, society's definitions of physical attractiveness affect the way variations in children's physical size are perceived. For this activity, choose a particular age group and observe the social interactions of students who are either tall or short for their age. Observe how these children are treated by others as well as what personality characteristics they exhibit (e.g., leadership abilities, shyness, impulsiveness, etc.). After collecting your observations, analyze the patterns you observed. Were tall and/or short students treated differently? What personality characteristics did they exhibit? Were there gender differences in the patterns you observed?

How do your observations help you understand the ways cultural stereotypes of physical attractiveness may shape the way people evaluate and relate to children?

4. Interview three girls and three boys who are between 13 and 16 years old. Ask them to respond to the following questions:

a. What do you think is your best feature?
b. What do others tell you is your best feature?
c. What do you think is your worst feature?
d. What would you like to change about yourself?

Following the interviews, analyze the students' responses for themes about their body image. Do girls or boys have a more positive body image? Do girls' responses show a preoccupation with weight? What concerns do the boys express about their body image? How do your results compare with the research on the psychological impact of puberty?

Cognitive Development: Piaget's and Vygotsky's Theories

THESE TWO LESSONS OCCURRED IN A SIXTH-GRADE SCIENCE CLASS AND *a kindergarten class. We will learn in this chapter how teachers can help students construct knowledge of complex concepts.*

Sixth Grade Teacher:	Can someone tell me whether the water today boiled more or less quickly than before?
Student:	More quickly.
Teacher:	Why? Who has some ideas?
Student:	Particles are more separated.
Teacher:	Okay; let's think about density. Is tap water more or less dense than boiled water? What happens to water when it boils?
Student:	There are bubbles.
Student:	It evaporates.
Teacher:	Is the water turning into gas?
Student:	Yes.
Teacher:	Would that make the water more or less dense?
Student:	Less dense.
Teacher:	Okay; think about two pots of beans. If you have one pot with just a little bit of beans and a pot with a lot of beans, which pot would take longer to boil?
Student:	The pot with a lot of beans.
Teacher:	Why?
Student:	It's more dense.
Teacher:	Okay; let's talk about temperature. At what temperature did the tap water boil? What about the already boiled water? What did you see? Maybe we first need to come to some consensus about boiling. Who can give me a definition?
Student:	When the water starts to bubble.
Student:	When there is steam.
Teacher:	Okay; if we get steam, what is the boiling water doing? Is it changing states?
Student:	It's changing into gas.
Teacher:	Okay; now did the boiling occur at a higher or lower temperature with the already boiled water?
Student:	Higher.
Teacher:	Who can tell me why?
Student:	It's less dense.
Teacher:	Why?
Student:	It's got less stuff in it.
Teacher:	Okay; can anyone give us a general rule about the relationship between density and boiling?
Student:	The less dense the solution, the longer it takes to boil.
Teacher:	Good. Now let's think about some other solutions. What about salt water?
Student:	It's more dense.
Kindergarten Teacher:	Why are there so many different languages?
Lisa:	Because some people don't know these other languages.
Kim:	They can't talk the way we talk.

Eddie:	Maybe when people are born they choose the language they want to know and then they go to a special place to learn it. I mean their mother chooses.
Andy:	Like a child could tell his mother and father to take him to a place where they can learn French if they are French.
Warren:	God gives people all the sounds. Then you can tell you're in a different place because it sounds different.
Wally:	When you're little you try to think of what the name of something is and people tell you.
Eddie:	Oh, yeah. Your mother tells you. You come out of her stomach and she talks English to you and she tells you the name for everything.
Deana:	If you live in a different country, there's a different language there. Wherever you were born you talk in that language.
Warren:	Wherever your mother was born.
Teacher:	Your mother was born in China, Warren, but you speak English.
Deana:	Because he never lived in China.
Warren:	I'm going to Chinese school Saturdays when I'm six.
Eddie:	Someone has to teach you. My brother didn't know one word when he was born. Not even my name.
Earl:	When I was little, I said "ca-see."
Rose:	What does that mean?
Earl:	"Take me in the car." Now I know every word.
Rose:	Me too.
Teacher:	Akemi was born in Japan and she speaks Japanese. How are you learning all these English words now, Akemi?
Akemi:	I listen to everybody.

Source: Reprinted by permission of the publisher from Wally's Stories: Conversations in the Kindergarten by Vivian Gussin Paley, pp. 116–117, Cambridge, Mass.: Harvard University Press, Copyright © 1981 by the President and Fellows of Harvard College.

The first conversation is from a sixth-grade science class. The students have just completed an experiment in which they observed and recorded the temperature of and the time it took to boil a solution of previously boiled water. The teacher expected the students to compare these data with the information they collected from a similar experiment with tap water. At the end of an activity, the teacher and students discuss the results together.

Do you think the sixth graders demonstrate a good understanding of the experiment at the beginning of discussion? Not really. Although the students make some very good observations about the experiment, few are able to give a scientific explanation for what they observed. The teacher and students *construct* this understanding jointly. The teacher does not give the students the answers but helps the students think through the experiment by posing questions, linking new information to familiar experiences, giving feedback, and so forth. We will learn that this teacher is providing a *scaffold* to guide the students' thinking. By the end of the discussion, the teacher and students have come to a shared understanding of the experiment, and the students are able to apply this learning to new problems (e.g., What about alcohol and salt water?).

In the second scenario, the kindergarten teacher and her students are engaging in a similar endeavor—attempting to better understand an abstract question. The question concerning different languages was derived from kindergarteners' own curiosities and pursued through the teacher's and other students' prompts. Vivian Paley, a well-known teacher and the author in this case, notes that Wally's comment helped connect the children to their own concrete experiences of learning language as little children; thus, they became more logical. Piaget's theory anticipates such development in reasoning as children transition into middle childhood. Vygotsky's theory helps us understand the social processes that propel this development.

These teachers are using what is known as a **constructivist approach.** The simple proposition underlying this approach is that children must construct their own understandings of the world in which they live. Knowledge is not something teachers can directly transmit to learners. The information must be mentally acted on, manipulated, and transformed in order to have meaning for the learner. However, as the examples illustrate, the teacher helps guide this knowledge construction process through focusing attention, posing questions, and stretching children's thinking. The teacher's role is to help students rethink their ideas by asking questions they would not generally think about on their own. According to a constructivist point of view, learning involves structural changes in the way children think about their world.

Constructivism is the basis for many current reforms in education. Both the National Council for Teachers of Mathematics and the National Science Teachers Association have called for classrooms where problem solving, "hands-on" experimentation, concept development, logical reasoning, and authentic learning are emphasized. Similarly, advocates of whole-language approaches to reading and language arts also stress the importance of authentic learning in which students are immersed in a language-rich environment in meaningful and productive ways.

In this chapter, we examine the developmental theories that provide the developmental foundations for a constructivist approach to learning. Constructivism is theoretically grounded in the developmental research of Piaget and Vygotsky. Piaget's theory can help teachers understand how children reason or think about their world at different ages. Vygotsky's theory can help teachers understand the social processes that influence the development of children's intellectual abilities; this perspective is sometimes labeled **social constructivist.** Both theories have important implications for teaching.

Piaget's Theory of Cognitive Development

Jean Piaget had a major impact on the way we think about children's development. Before Piaget's theory was introduced, children were generally thought of as passive organisms who were shaped and molded by their environment. Piaget taught us that children act as "little scientists," trying to make sense of their world. They have their own logic and ways of knowing, which follow predictable patterns of development as children biologically mature and interact with the world. By forming mental representations of their world, children are able to act on and influence their environment as much as their environment influences them.

Piaget was born in Switzerland in 1896. As a child, he was extremely bright and inquisitive. By the age of 10, he published his first scientific paper; he received his first job as a curator of the mollusk collection at the Geneva museum by the age of 15. He received his Ph.D. in natural sciences 6 years later. Piaget continued to develop his scholarship in many areas, including sociology, religion, and philosophy. While studying philosophy, he became intrigued with epistemology, or how knowledge is obtained. This question led him to study philosophy and psychology at the Sorbonne, where he met Theodore Simon, who, at the time, was developing the first intelligence test for children. Simon persuaded Piaget to assist him in collecting age norms for his test items. It was through this work that Piaget began to explore children's reasoning processes. He became intrigued with the fact that individual children often had very different reasons for the answers they chose. For example, two children might say a tree is alive but explain their answers differently. One child may say it is alive because it moves, while another may say it's alive because it makes seeds. Through a set of procedures, which became known as the *clinical interview method* (see Chapter 1), Piaget explored the reasoning processes underlying children's correct and incorrect answers. His fascination with children's knowledge acquisition processes helped sustain a 60-year career in child development research. By the end of his career, Piaget had published more than 40 books and 200 articles on child psychology.

Piaget was an early constructivist theorist in psychology. He believed that children actively construct their own knowledge of the environment using what they already know to interpret new events and objects. Piaget's research focused primarily on how children acquire knowledge as they develop. That is, he was not so interested in *what* children know as he was in *how* they thought about problems and solutions. He believed cognitive development involved changes in a child's ability to reason about his or her world.

Key Concepts in Piaget's Theory

Cognitive Stages

Piaget was a stage theorist who divided cognitive development into four major stages: sensorimotor, preoperations, concrete operations, and formal operations. At each stage of development, children's thinking is assumed to be *qualitatively* different from their thinking at other stages. According to Piaget, cognitive development involved not simply quantitative changes in facts and skills but rather major transformations in the way children organize knowledge. Once children have entered a new cognitive stage they do not revert to an earlier form of reasoning or functioning.

Piaget proposed that cognitive development occurs in an invariant sequence. That is, all children proceed through the four stages of cognitive development in the same sequence. It is not possible to skip or miss a stage. Piaget's stages are generally related to specific age ranges, but there is a great deal of individual and cultural variation in the amount of time children may spend in a particular stage. We will examine the cognitive characteristics of each stage in a later section.

Development as Changes in Knowledge Structures

Piaget believed that all people, even infants, begin to organize their knowledge of the world into what he called *schemata* or *schemes*. **Schemes** are sets of physical actions, mental operations, concepts, or theories people use to acquire and organize information about their world. Young children primarily know their world through physical actions they can perform, whereas older children and adults can perform mental operations and use symbol systems (e.g., language) to acquire knowledge about their world. As children progress through Piaget's stages, they become increasingly able to use complex and abstract schemes for organizing knowledge. Cognitive development involves not just the construction of new schemes, but the reorganization and differentiation of existing schemes.

Piaget distinguished between three types of knowledge. **Physical knowledge** is knowing the attributes of objects, such as their number, color, size, and shape. Other examples of physical knowledge may include the observations that some objects roll and other do not, that some objects float and others do not, or that length of string can effect how fast objects on a pendulum move back and forth. Physical knowledge is acquired by acting on objects, experimenting, and observing reactions.

Logico-mathematical knowledge involves the mental construction of relationships. For example, logico-mathematical knowledge involves the understanding that a certain number of objects (which can be observed and counted) also represents a more abstract concept such as number. The number "eight" is an abstract concept that cannot be derived from experience. Also, groups of 10 objects can make up larger numbers such as 50 or 100. Logico-mathematical knowledge is also evident in the understanding that a mathematical problem such as $4 + 4$ can also be represented by $2 + 2 + 2 + 2$. Whereas physical knowledge is derived from observing and experimenting, logico-mathematical knowledge involves mental constructions, or a **reflective abstraction.** Figure 3.1 shows children's representation of the number "eight" in Piaget's theory. In this example, the eight apples, tallies, and circles are concrete and observable (physical knowledge), but the number "eight" is a form of logico-mathematical knowledge because it is a concept that needs to constructed by the child from social knowledge. Unlike tallies and pictures that children can use to express their understanding of eight, the spoken word or sign for eight is taught (Kamii, 2000).

In this way, Piaget's theory also recognized the importance of **social knowledge** that is derived in part through interactions with others. Examples of this form of knowledge are mathematical words and signs (e.g., "+" for addition), languages, musical notations, as well as social and moral conventions, such as turn taking in conversations, ways of initiating interactions, how to play a game, or how to respond to another person in distress.

Principles of Development

Organization and Adaptation In Piaget's theory two basic principles guide children's intellectual development. The first of these principles is organization, which Piaget believed

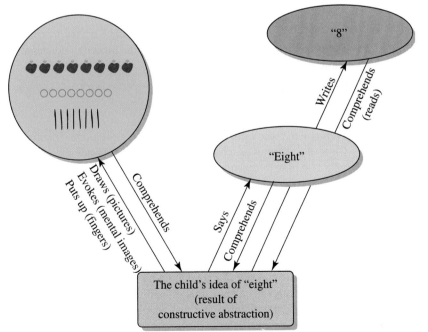

■ FIGURE 3.1
A Child's Representation of "Eight" in Piaget's Theory
Source: After Kamii (2000).

is an innate predisposition in all species. As children mature, they integrate simple physical patterns or mental schemes into more complex systems. The second guiding principle is **adaptation.** According to Piaget, all organisms are born with the ability to adapt their mental structures or behavior to fit environmental demands.

Assimilation and Accommodation   Piaget used the terms *assimilation* and *accommodation* to describe how children adapt to their environment. Through the process of **assimilation** children mold new information to fit their existing schemes. For example, a young child who has never seen a donkey may refer to it as a pony with long ears. Assimilation is not a passive process; it often involves actively modifying or transforming new information to make it fit prior knowledge. When this new information is consistent with what the child already knows, a state of equilibrium or balance is achieved. All the pieces of information fit together. When new information does not fit into an existing scheme, the child may alter his or her old way of thinking or acting to fit the new information. The process of changing existing schemata is called **accommodation.** In the example given here, the child may form a new scheme when he or she learns that the animal is not a pony but a donkey. Accommodation is most likely to occur when the information is only slightly discrepant with the child's existing schemes. If the information is too discrepant, accommodation may not be possible, because the child does not have any mental structures for interpreting this information. Recall that in the introductory vignette, children were initially having difficulty accommodating the information about learning different languages; the ideas were too discrepant from their everyday experiences. Wally's comment, however, shifted the discussion so that they were able to relate to their own learning of language when they were little (existing schemas). According to Piaget, the processes of assimilation and accommodation are closely intertwined and explain changes in cognition throughout the life span.

Can you think of an example of assimilation and accommodation from your own learning experiences? As you are reading this material, you should be using what you already know about children's development to make sense of the new information. However, you may need to adjust some of your ideas as you acquire new information. For example, you may have learned elsewhere that infants are incapable of symbolic thought. As you will see, Piaget's theory teaches us that a form of symbolic thought begins to emerge during the second year. Therefore, in order to develop a more sophisticated understanding of infancy, you would need to change your existing knowledge of infant development to incorporate (accommodate) this new information.

Development Processes

If cognitive development represents changes in children's cognitive structures or schemata, what causes those developmental changes? As an interactional theorist, Piaget viewed development as a complex interaction of innate and environmental factors. According to Piaget, the following four factors contribute to children's cognitive development:

- Maturation of inherited physical structures
- Physical experiences with the environment
- Social transmission of information and knowledge
- Equilibration

Equilibration is a unique concept in Piaget's theory that refers to our innate tendency to keep our cognitive structures in balance. Piaget maintained that states of disequilibrium or imbalance are so intrinsically dissatisfying that people are compelled to alter their cognitive structures in order to restore balance. Equilibration is thus a form of self-regulation in

Stages in Piaget's Theory of Cognitive Development

Focus on Development

Stage	Approximate Age Range	Characteristics
Sensorimotor The Active Child	Birth through $1\frac{1}{2}$ to 2 Years	Infants develop goal-directed behavior, means-ends thinking, and object permanence.
Preoperations The Intuitive Child	2 through 5 to 7 Years	Children can use symbols and words to think. Intuitive problem solving, but thinking limited by rigidity, centration, and egocentrism.
Concrete Operations The Practical Child	5 to 7 through 11 to 12 Years	Children develop logical operations for seriation, classification, and conservation. Thinking tied to real events and objects.
Formal Operations The Reflective Child	11 to 12 Years and Onward	Children develop abstract systems of thought that allow them to use propositional logic, scientific reasoning, and proportional reasoning.

Piaget's theory. By altering and adjusting our cognitive structures we maintain organization and stability in our environment. We also reach a higher level of cognitive functioning as a result of this equilibration process.

Stages of Cognitive Development

Piaget proposed that cognitive development followed an invariant sequence from infancy through adolescence. The four stages of development are: (1) sensorimotor stage, (2) pre-operational stage, (3) concrete operational stage, and (4) formal operational stage. The Focus on Development box summarizes characteristics of each stage. As we will discuss later, child development researchers today question several aspects of Piaget's theory. For instance, questions have been raised about the ages associated with each stage. We will learn that children may be able to perform some cognitive operations earlier or later than Piaget originally proposed. Theorists have also raised questions about the stagelike nature of children's thinking. When children are making a transition into a new stage, they often exhibit characteristics of the new and old stage at the same time. We will first discuss the four stages, then consider the limitations of Piaget's theory.

Sensorimotor Stage

During the **sensorimotor stage,** children acquire schemes for two basic competencies: (1) goal-directed behavior and (2) object permanence. Piaget regarded these schemes as the building blocks of symbolic thinking and human intelligence.

Development of Goal-Directed Behavior   One defining characteristic of the sensorimotor period is an infant's clear progression toward goal-directed actions. At birth, a child's behavior is largely controlled by reflexes. Babies are born with the ability to suck, grasp, cry, and move their bodies, which allows them to assimilate physical experiences. For example, a young child learns to differentiate hard from soft objects by sucking on them. Within the first few months, new behaviors are added. Thumb-sucking, for instance, is a chance occurrence that, once discovered, is repeated over and over, because it is a pleasant sensation for the baby. It is initiated by the child with a specific goal in mind. Piaget referred to this set of intentional or goal-directed actions as **circular reactions.**

By the end of the first year, a child begins to anticipate events and combines previously acquired behaviors to achieve those goals. At this point, infants are no longer repeating accidental events but are initiating and selecting a sequence of actions to obtain a specific goal. Piaget first observed this sequence of behavior when he placed his 10-month-old son's favorite toy under a pillow. His son paused, batted the pillow away, and grabbed the toy. He combined several actions to get what he wanted.

At the end of the sensorimotor period, children begin to experiment with new ways of accomplishing their goals when a problem cannot be solved with existing schemata (such as looking, reaching, and grasping). If, for example, a child's toy is out of reach under the sofa, the child may crawl around to the back of the sofa to retrieve it. Rather than continuing to

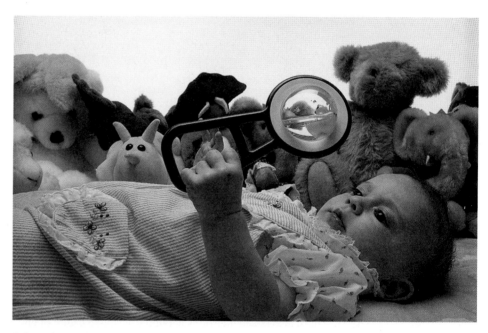

Infants learn through acting on objects. By simply changing the position of the rattle, this infant is experimenting with cause-and-effect relations.
Source: Mike Malyszko/Stock Boston.

apply existing schemata, the child is now able to mentally construct new solutions to problems. For Piaget, the invention of new problem-solving methods marked the beginning of truly intelligent behavior. Although children continue to solve problems through trial and error for many more years, some of this experimentation can now be carried out internally through mental representation of action sequences and goals.

Development of Object Permanence   Another important development that occurs in the sensorimotor period is object permanence. **Object permanence** involves the knowledge that objects continue to exist even when they can no longer be seen or acted on. As adults, we know a missing shoe continues to exist even though we cannot see it. We search the closet, check under the bed, and finally find it under the sofa in the living room. Young infants act differently when objects disappear from their sight. They act as though the object no longer exists.

A child's concept of object permanence can be studied in a number of different ways. As described here, one way is to hide a child's favorite toy under a pillow or blanket while the child watches. Young infants (1 to 4 months) may visually track the object to the spot where it disappears but show no awareness of the object once it is no longer visible. Piaget explained that at this age, objects have no reality or existence for children unless directly perceived. Because the child's only way of knowing objects is through their reflexive actions, an object no longer exists if it cannot be sucked, grasped, or seen. In other words, the child is not yet able to form a mental representation of this object.

The first glimmer of object permanence emerges around 4 to 8 months. The child will now search for an object if it is partially visible but needs some perceptual cue to remember the object continues to exist. Between 8 and 12 months, a child's behavior indicates that he or she understands an object continues to exist even though it cannot be seen. Children will now actively search for hidden objects by combining several sensorimotor schemes, such as looking, crawling, and reaching, into goal-directed actions.

Some researchers have questioned Piaget's findings on object permanence (Baillargeon, 1987; 2004). Recent evidence suggests that a mental representation of objects may appear as early as 4 months. Other researchers claim that babies may understand that objects are permanent, but may lack the memory skills to remember the location of the object or the motor skills to carry out the actions needed to find the object. Nevertheless, most theorists agree that the ability to construct mental images of objects within the first year of development is a significant achievement.

Preoperational Stage

The ability to think about objects, events, or people in their absence marks the beginning of the preoperational stage. From about 2 years old, children demonstrate an increased ability to use symbols—gestures, words, numbers, and images—to represent real objects in their environment. They can now think and behave in ways that were not possible before. They can use words to

During the preschool years, pretend play represents real events in children's lives.
Source: ©Bettman/CORBIS.

communicate, use numbers to count objects, engage in make-believe play, and express their ideas about the world through drawings. Although the ability to represent objects and events symbolically is a significant advance, preoperational thinking is limited in a number of ways. Piaget used the term **preoperational stage** because preschool children lack the ability to do some of the logical operations he observed in older children. Before examining the limitations of preoperational thinking, let's consider the important cognitive advances of this stage.

Representational Thinking   During the preoperational stage, children can use symbols as a tool to think about their environment. The ability to use a word (e.g., *cookies, milk*) to stand for a real object that is not present is called *symbolic* or **representational thinking.** Piaget suggested that one of the earliest forms of representational thinking was deferred imitation, which first appears toward the end of the sensorimotor period. **Deferred imitation** refers to the ability to repeat a simple sequence of actions or sounds several hours or days after they were originally produced. Piaget (1962) observed the following example of deferred imitation with his daughter:

> Jacqueline (1 year, 4 months) has a visit from a 1.5-year-old boy whom she used to see from time to time, and who, in the course of the afternoon, got into a terrible temper. He screamed as he tried to get out of the playpen and pushed it backward, stamping his feet. Jacqueline stood watching him in amazement, never having witnessed such a scene before. The next day, she herself screamed in her playpen and tried to move it, stamping her feet lightly several times in succession. (p. 62)

Several new examples of representational thinking appear during the preoperational stage. The preschool years are often considered the "golden age" of symbolic or imaginary play (Singer & Singer, 1976; 2005). Symbolic play begins with simple sequences of behavior using real objects, such as pretending to drink from a cup or to eat with a spoonlike object. By 4 years of age, children can invent their own props, make up a story line, and assume various social roles. Consider how these 4-year-olds are learning to negotiate social relationships in the following example of pretend play from Vivian Gussin Paley's (1988) *Bad Guys Don't Have Birthdays:*

Barney:	Keep makin' gold. You're the walkout guards and the goldmakers. Don't forget, I'm the guard that controls the guns.
Frederick:	But we control the guns when you sleep.
Barney:	No. You make the gold and I control the guns. Anyway, I'm not sleeping, because there's bad guys coming. Calling all guards! Stuart get on. You wanna be a guard? Bad guys! They see the ship because it's already in the sun.
Mollie:	No bad guys, Barney, the baby is sleeping.
Barney:	There hasta be bad guys, Mollie. We gots the cannons.
Mollie:	You can't shoot when the baby is sleeping.
Barney:	Who's the baby? We didn't say a baby.
Mollie:	It's Christopher. Come on, baby Starlite. Lie down over here.
Barney:	Say no, Christopher. You can be the Boy Scout brother. Say no, say no.
Christopher:	I gotta shoot bad guys for awhile, okay, Mollie? (p. 19)

UNDERSTANDING CHILDREN
*Strategy 4.1:
Observation of
Cognitive Processes
Revealed in Play*

For the most part, children's pretend play reflects real events in their lives (e.g., playing house, going to the store, going on a trip), but pretend play involving fantasy and superhero characters is very appealing to young children as well. As discussed in the Focus on Teaching box, developmentalists are concerned about reduced time for play in and out of the classroom. Many experts believe that pretend play is important for the development of children's

The Value of Fantasy Play in School

Dorothy and Jerome Singer's recently authored book, *Imagination and Play in the Electronic Age* (2005), reviews what is currently understood about the potential of various forms of play for children's development. They focused, in particular, on the value of symbolic or pretend-fantasy play, which reaches its peak from ages 3 to 6 but continues throughout life. Although fantasy play in the form of acting out roles and speaking aloud fades in middle childhood, it does not disappear, and may take place when children are out of sight of adults, such as in the formation of secret clubs and codes. Fantasy play may also reappear in later childhood and adolescence in forms that children think are socially acceptable, such as in acting in school plays, writing stories, and participating in other forms of art or music. Children's and adolescents' creations and actions in the role of various characters in computer simulation games and chat rooms may also be a form of fantasy play (and may have some positive and negative influences on development).

These authors recognize that play is sometimes not valued by educators, but argue for the benefits of guided imaginary play for teaching cognitive and social skills in school. For example, teachers can provide cues to help elaborate the script for playing the "store" game. They cite studies showing that play, guided by the teacher, fosters literacy development in preschoolers as well as primary-grade students (e.g., language use, story comprehension, reading, writing). Dramatic play can also help older elementary children learn skills to deal with conflicts with adults and peers. Singer and Singer (2005) caution that educators should not over-help children with play scripts. Although qualified adult facilitators can encourage and foster children's creativity, this play should be primarily child-initiated. They suggest, instead, that "in school, it can take place for a few minutes during each play period, and the teacher can use guided play with different children each time. If this were a part of the curriculum over the year, we believe that much incidental learning could take place in an atmosphere of enjoyment so that children would be motivated to repeat the games on their own and, in effect, practice the new words and activities naturally" (pp. 146–147). Furthermore, research suggests that children involved in a child-initiated curriculum perform better academically in later grades than those from more traditional, academically oriented early education programs.

Other experts are also concerned about the devaluing and limiting of play. For example, within the popular book and PBS program *Raising Cain*, psychologists such as Michael Thompson urge parents and educators to allow safe superhero play of boys, as a means of expressing feelings and imaginations, without being overly concerned with violent themes that may be involved.

There is no evidence connecting superhero play to violent behavior in later development. Furthermore, researchers argue that fantasy play may help children to work through issues related to power and control (Carlsson-Paige & Levin, 1995). Banning superhero play from the classroom or playground can send the message to children that they need to hide their interests from adults, and teachers may lose an opportunity to help children express concerns about power and control. Thus, educators can help children learn from their superhero friends. There are resources available to help teachers support and use superhero play effectively in the classroom (see Greenberg, 1995; Gronlund, 1992; Levin, 1994).

Another resource for incorporating play into the curriculum is the work of Vivian Paley, introduced at the beginning of this chapter. Paley has long been recognized for her use of fantasy play, storytelling, and acting (drama) as a means of relating to children and enhancing their literacy and social skills and moral development in the classroom. She has received many awards for her teaching and writing of numerous books, including the 2004 Outstanding Educator in the English Language Arts Award. Her most recent book, *The Child's Work: The Importance of Fantasy Play* (2004), has received many accolades, including one from Howard Gardner, "At a time when policymakers are attempting to convert the preschool years into basic training for school, master teacher Vivian Paley reminds us that fantasy play is the essential, irreplaceable curriculum of the first years . . ." (Gardner, 2004). In Paley's own words, "To express ideas is the most profoundly human act of all. The simple need to communicate is, after all, the basis of community, and of education itself. Tell me your story and I'll tell you mine; we'll put all our stories on a pretend stage and then we'll know who we are" (Koshewa, 2002, p. 9).

137

language and cognitive and social skills. (e.g., Pellegrini, 2005; Pellegrini & Blatchford, 2000; Singer & Singer, 2005). It also helps to foster their creativity and imagination.

Piaget believed that the development of representational thinking enables children to acquire language. The preschool years are a period of rapid language development, with most children saying their first words around their second birthday and increasing their vocabulary to approximately 2,000 words by the age of 4. We will discuss language development in detail in Chapter 5; for now, it is important to understand its connection to representational thinking. When babies first begin to talk, they use words that refer to ongoing activities and events and immediately present desires. During the preoperational period, children begin to use words in a truly representational way. Rather than focusing exclusively on ongoing activities or immediate desires, children begin to use words to stand for absent objects and past events (Ginsburg & Opper, 1988). In other words, children use words to refer to events they are not experiencing directly. Piaget believed that representational thinking facilitates the rapid development of language in the preoperational period. That is, thinking precedes language development in Piaget's view.

During the preoperational period, children also begin to represent their world through pictures and images, leading some experts to refer to children's art as the "silent language." By studying children's art, we can learn much about their thinking and feelings. For example, 2- and 3-year-old children, when asked what they are drawing or painting, are likely to respond, "I'm just drawing." By age 3 or 4, however, children begin to combine marks to make squares, crosses, circles, and other geometric shapes. Children enter the representational stage of drawing around the age of 4 or 5. They draw houses, animals, people, cartoon characters, and other objects. Their figures may represent real objects in their environment or fantasy characters they have heard about or seen. The Focus on Development box shows this developmental progression in children's drawings. As they develop, children add more and more detail to their drawings, including words that tell the story line. By the time they enter kindergarten, some children can write their own names. Now, printed words as well as pictures can stand for a real object in a child's environment.

Number Concepts   Along with an increased ability to use words and images as symbols, children begin to use numbers as a tool for thinking during the preschool years. Piaget argued that children do not acquire a true concept of numbers, or *numerosity*, until the concrete operational stage when they begin to develop logical reasoning, and can understand that the number of items remains unchanged even though they have been rearranged, at about 6 years (Butterworth, 2005). However, recent research has indicated that some basic number principles begin to appear during preoperations. Research by Rochel Gelman and her associates (Gelman, 1990; Gelman & Gallistel, 1978; Gelman & Meck, 1983) suggests that some 4-year-olds can understand the following basic principles of counting: (a) any array of items can be counted; (b) each item should be counted only once; (c) numbers should be assigned in the same order; (d) the order in which objects are counted is irrelevant; and (e) the last spoken number word is the number of items in that set. Preschool children also have some basic understanding of number relationships. Most 3- and 4-year-olds, for example, know that 3 is more than 2. In addition, preschool children seem to have an intuitive understanding of addition and subtraction. Children begin to relate their understandings of small and large numerosities with number word meanings between 4 and 5 years of age (e.g., Spelke, 2005).

Although preschoolers are beginning to understand basic number concepts, it is important to keep in mind that they will make plenty of counting errors. They may skip numbers (e.g., 1, 2, 3, 5), miss items while counting, and so on. In addition, most preschool and early elementary children have difficulty counting large groups of disorganized items (Baroody, 1987). It is also difficult for preschool children to count beyond 10 in English, because the teen-number

Developmental Progression
of Children's Drawings

Focus on
Development

Level of Development	Age Range	Characteristics
Placement stage	Age 32 months	(scribbles)
Basic shapes	Age 42 months	(circle)
Design stage	Age 40 and 47 months	(combination design)
Pictorial stage	Age 45 months	(sun)
Pictorial stage	Age 48 to 60 months	(humans)

Source: After Kellogg (1970).

words do not follow their 1 to 10 counterparts. Learning to count beyond 10 is easier for children who speak Japanese, Chinese, or Korean (see Focus on Research box on page 140).

Intuitive Theories   Young children are known for their curiosity and inquisitiveness. During the preschool years, children begin to form **intuitive theories** about natural phenomena. Piaget (1951) interviewed young children to find out how they explained events, such as the origins of trees, the movement of clouds, the beginning of the sun and moon, and the concept of life. He found that young children's conceptions of the world are characterized by **animism;**

Focus on
Research

Learning Place Value: Does Language Make a Difference?

International comparisons of mathematics achievement consistently show large differences in favor of Asian students. Research studies have shown that the superior performance of Asian students in abstract counting and in understanding place value may already be apparent by the first grade. Differences in children's understanding of number concepts may be due to differences in the number words. In most languages, the numbers 1 to 10 are arbitrary, and the numbers after 20 have a regular pattern (twenty-one, thirty-two, etc). English, French, and Swedish children have a difficult time learning the number words from 11 to 20, because the teen-numbers do not match their 1 to 10 counterparts. In Japanese, the numbers from 11 to 20 follow a regular pattern, and they are composed of "ten" plus the single number. For example, in Japanese the number 10 is *juu* and the number 2 is *ni*. The word for twelve is *juu-ni* ("ten-two"). The number words for 11 to 20 also follow this pattern in Chinese and Korean.

Do the number words for 11 to 20 give Asian children an advantage in learning to count? Studies show no differences in children's counting performance through the age of 3 when learning is focused on acquiring the first 10 number words. However, around the time children begin to learn the teen words large differences appear. Learning to count beyond 10 is considerably easier for children who speak some Chinese, Japanese, or Korean because the number words for 11 to 20 follow a regular pattern (e.g., "ten-one," "ten-two," etc.). In addition, studies reveal that Asian children have less difficulty than U.S. children in understanding place value because the number names in their languages explicitly state each number's composition ("ten-five"). By the time Asian children are 6 years old, they have little difficulty making models of multidigits using 10 blocks and units. For example, they can represent the number 54 with 5 ten blocks and 4 unit blocks. In contrast, U.S. children showed a preference for representing whole numbers in terms of individual units rather than units of 10. Asian number words may help children in those countries to learn place value at a younger age than U.S. children who, even by the third grade, have difficulty identifying correctly the value of numerals in different positions (e.g., in the ones place, tens place, and hundreds place).

This research has important implications for education. To help children acquire a sense of number and place value, teachers might use counting words that resemble Asian languages, such "ten-one," "ten-two," "ten-three" as a different way of saying *eleven, twelve,* and *thirteen.* Children also need opportunities to work with math manipulatives that provide opportunities to organize large numbers of items into units of 10s.

Source: Adapted from Miura, Okamoto, Kim, Steere, & Fayol (1993).

that is, they do not distinguish between animate (living) and inanimate (mechanical) objects, and they attribute intentional states and human characteristics to inanimate objects. For example, a 3-year-old may say that the sun is hot because it wants to keep people warm or that trees lose their leaves because they want to change the way they look. Rocks, trees, fires, rivers, cars, and bicycles are all judged to have lifelike characteristics because they move. The following example illustrates this animistic thinking, according to Piaget:

> Zimm (7 years, 9 months; child's responses in italics). Is a cat alive? *Yes.* A snail? *Yes.* A table? *No.* Why not? *It can't move.* Is a bicycle alive? *Yes.* Why? *It can go.* Is a cloud alive? *Yes.* Why? *It sometimes moves.* Is water alive? *Yes, it moves.* Is it alive when it does not move? *Yes.* Is a bicycle alive when it isn't moving? *Yes, it's alive, even when it doesn't move.* Is a lamp alive? *Yes, it shines.* Is the moon alive? *Yes, sometimes it hides behind the mountains.* (Piaget, 1951, p. 199)

In constructing their beliefs, children draw on their own personal experiences and observations. The term *intuitive* is often applied to the preoperational stage, because the child's reasoning is based on immediate experiences, and may not be open to conscious reflection (e.g., Torff & Sternberg, 2001). However, intuitive conceptions are certainly not limited to this stage.

Interestingly, recent studies reveal that children's intuitive understandings of their physical and biological concepts are a little more sophisticated than Piaget believed. In the area of physics, research suggests that young children have a naive understanding of the atomic theory of matter—that objects are composed of tiny bits of matter (Carey, 1991). Four-year-olds understand that you cannot pour water into a box that is already filled with a steel block. Preschoolers can also attribute the snuffing out of a candle to a fan that was turned on rather than one turned off. Other research suggests that preschool children have also developed concepts about the earth's shape, the movement of the planets, and so on. Along these same lines, toddlers and preschoolers have acquired some rudimentary biological conceptions as well. Preschool children can distinguish inanimate from living objects, contrary to Piaget's suggestion, and they are beginning to develop an understanding of biological properties. Recent research suggests that preschool children recognize that plants, like people, can grow, heal, and decompose (Wellman & Gelman, 1998). Preschool children also have a rudimentary understanding of inheritance (e.g., Gelman, 2003). They expect, for example, that animals of the same family share certain physical properties. Additionally, they understand that an infant calf that comes from a cow will grow up "to moo" and "to have a straight tail," even if it is raised among pigs. However, this does not mean that young children have a sophisticated sense of biological inheritance. Recent cross-cultural studies indicate that children continue to learn distinctions between inherited and learned traits and behaviors through middle childhood (e.g., Astuti, Solomon, & Carey, 2004).

Young children have many misconceptions of their intuitive physical and biological worlds that can have a lasting influence on their learning. When children are presented factual information in school, this information is often assimilated into the naive or commonsense theories they have already formed about the world. For example, Eaton, Anderson, and Smith (1984) found that after 6 weeks of science lessons on light and vision, most of the fifth graders in their study held onto their naive conceptions: We see things because light shines on them and brightens them. According to these researchers, the teachers seemed to do everything right in presenting scientific explanations, but they did not directly confront their students' naive conceptions of light. Figure 3.2 on page 142 lists other examples of children's naive theories in science. These schemes for explaining natural events may persist, unless children's naive conceptions are confronted directly. Thus, children's intuitive conceptions can both help and hinder the teaching-learning process from an educator's perspective (Torff & Sternberg, 2001).

Just as children begin to develop theories of the external world during the preoperational period, they also begin to develop theories about the internal world of the mind. Piaget (1962) proposed that children confuse mental and real events. This confusion was most evident when children were asked to explain the origins of dreams (e.g., Where do dreams come from?). For preoperational thinkers, dreams are external events that can be seen by other people. Piaget used the term **realism** to describe the young child's tendency to confuse physical and psychological events.

Current research indicates that preschoolers' knowledge of the mind is more sophisticated than Piaget originally suggested (Wellman & Gelman, 1998). According to Henry Wellman (1990), most 3-year-olds understand that internal wishes and desires can cause a person to act a certain way. Most 3- to 5-year-olds also know it's not possible to touch or eat cookies that are in a person's dreams, and they know dreams can be about impossible events, such as a dog flying (Wellman & Estes, 1986). When asked to name things the mind can do, 4- and 5-year-olds say that the mind can think, remember, and dream. By this age, children can also distinguish between their own knowledge and that of others (Wellman,

■ FIGURE 3.2

*Elementary School
Students' Naive
Conceptions in Science*
Sources: After Driver,
Guesne, & Tiberghien
(1985) and Hyde & Bizar (1989).

Elementary School Students' Naive Conceptions in Science

- Sugar ceases to exist when placed in water.

- Clouds or the earth's shadow causes the phases of the moon.

- Plants get their food from the soil.

- Light travels farther at night than in the day.

- Shadows are made out of matter.

- Heavier objects fall faster.

- Electric current is used in a light bulb.

- The world is flat.

- Coldness causes rust.

- If you add warm water to an equal amount of warm water, you get water that is twice as warm.

1990). Children's awareness of their own and others' thoughts and feelings is often made evident in their sociodramatic (pretend) play, especially as they move in and out of and communicate about their roles (e.g., Fromberg, 2001).

Although children are beginning to develop a theory of mind in the preoperational stage, they have a very limited understanding of thinking processes and memory. Preschool children, for example, believe they can remember everything they see and hear. Between the ages of 8 and 10, children begin to acquire what is known as *metacognitive knowledge.* **Metacognition** is "thinking about thinking," and it plays a very important role in children's cognitive development during the middle childhood and adolescent years. It is this explicit awareness of one's own theories that distinguishes mature scientific thinking from intuitive theories (Kuhn & Pearsall, 2000). We will discuss how metacognition influences children's cognitive development when we explore information processing theories.

Limitations of Preoperational Thinking   So far we have discussed the important advances in children's thinking during the preoperational period. Let's turn to some of the limitations of preoperational thinking. The three main cognitive limitations of this stage are egocentrism, centration, and rigidity of thinking. **Egocentrism** refers to the tendency to "perceive, understand, and interpret the world in terms of the self" (P. Miller, 1993, p. 53). This egocentrism is particularly evident in the conversations of preschoolers. Because young children are unable to take the perspective of others, they make little effort to modify their speech for the listener. Three-year-olds seem to have what are called **collective monologues,** in which their remarks to each other are unrelated. By 4 and 5 years of age, children begin to show some ability to adjust their communication to the perspective of their listeners.

Piaget and Inhelder (1956) used the famous mountain task to study the egocentrism of young children. A model of a landscape containing three mountains was placed on top of a table with four chairs arranged around the table. For the study, a child sat in one chair and was asked to choose from a group of drawings the one that best described how the mountains might look to a person sitting in another chair. This study found that most children under the age of 7 or 8 picked the drawing that showed how the mountains looked to them, not how the mountain might look to someone sitting in another chair.

Some researchers have claimed that the mountain task is not a fair test of children's perspective-taking abilities. To do this task, children must be able to rotate objects in a spatial arrangement. When a simplified form of this task is used, preschoolers seem to be less egocentric than Piaget claimed. For example, most 3-year-olds understand that if a picture of an object is held vertically facing them, they can see the depicted object, but someone sitting opposite them cannot, as Figure 3.3 shows. This later research suggests that an understanding that two people can have different perspectives of the same object develops between the ages of 3 and 4 (Flavell, 1985, 2004).

Another limitation of preoperational thinking is *centration*. **Centration** means that young children tend to focus or center their attention on only one aspect of a stimulus. Other features of the stimulus are ignored. As will be discussed later, centration explains why children have difficulty performing conservation tasks. Suppose you show a 4-year-old two identical glasses containing the same amount of water and then pour the contents of one glass into a tall, thin glass. When asked, "Which glass has more?" the child will focus on the height of the water and choose the taller glass. Other dimensions of the glass, such as its width, will be ignored.

This example illustrates another limitation of preoperational thought. Young children's thinking tends to be very rigid. In the previous example, the child is focusing on "before" and "after" states rather than the transformation process. With development, children's thinking becomes less rigid, and they begin to consider how transformations (pouring the contents of one glass into another glass) can be reversed. The ability to mentally reverse operations is a characteristic of the next stage of cognitive development known as *concrete operations*.

Until children have developed some mental operations, such as reversibility, they tend to base their judgments of quantity on perceptual appearances rather than reality. If a glass looks like it has more water, young children assume it has more. Flavell and his associates (Flavell, Green, & Flavell, 1986) studied children's understanding of appearances and reality. They found that the ability to distinguish appearance from reality develops between the ages of 3 and 5. When 3-year-olds are shown a sponge that looks like a rock, they believe

UNDERSTANDING
CHILDREN
Strategy 4.3:
Perspective-Taking and
Others' Intentions

Which child can see the cat?

■ FIGURE 3.3
Perspective-Taking Task

it really is a rock. If a cloth smells like an orange, then it is an orange. This tendency to confuse reality and appearances is what makes Halloween a scary event for most 3-year-olds and some 4-year-olds. If a person looks like a monster, then that person must be a monster! By age 5, most children begin to distinguish between appearances and reality.

Concrete Operational Stage

In the elementary years, children begin to use mental operations and logic to think about events and objects in their environment. For example, if asked to arrange a set of five sticks according to size, concrete operational thinkers can mentally compare the objects and then draw logical inferences about the correct order without physically performing the actions. This ability to use logic and mental operations allows concrete operational children to approach problems more systematically than a preoperational child.

According to Piaget, several advances in children's thinking take place during the **concrete operational** stage. First, their thinking appears to be less rigid and more flexible. The child understands that operations can be mentally reversed or negated. That is, you can change a stimulus, such as the water poured into the thin beaker, back to its original state by reversing the action. Along these same lines, the child's thinking appears to be less centrated and egocentric. The grade-school child can attend to several characteristics of a stimulus at the same time. Rather than focusing exclusively on static states, the child is now able to make inferences about the nature of transformations. Finally, concrete operational thinkers no longer base their judgments on the appearances of things.

Let's take a closer look at the three types of mental operations or schemes children use to organize and make sense of their world during concrete operations: seriation, classification, and conservation.

During concrete operations, children begin to sort, organize, and classify objects according to common attributes.
Source: Mary Kate Denny/Photo Edit.

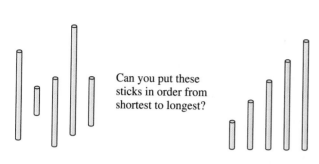

Can you put these sticks in order from shortest to longest?

In concrete operations, children can order a series of sticks according to size

Seriation   Seriation involves the ability to order objects in a logical progression, such as from shortest to tallest. **Seriation** is important for understanding the concepts of numbers, time, and measurement. For example, most preschoolers have a limited concept of time. In their minds, 2 minutes is the same as 20 minutes or 200 minutes. In contrast, elementary school children can order concepts of time in terms of increasing or decreasing quantity. For them, 20 minutes is fewer than 200 minutes, but more than 2 minutes.

In one of his experiments, Piaget asked children to order a series of sticks like the ones shown in Figure 3.4. At ages 3 and 4, children can find the longest and shortest sticks. They seem to understand the *logical rule of progressive change*—that is, items can be ordered in terms of increasing and decreasing size—but they have difficulty constructing an ordered sequence of three or more sticks. To succeed at this task, the children must perform two mental operations simultaneously. They must select the appropriate stick by thinking about how long or short it is in relation to the sticks already used as well as to those that remain. Preschool children are unable to perform this task because they focus on one dimension at a time (i.e., their thinking is centrated). The ability to coordinate two pieces of information simultaneously develops gradually during the early elementary years, when children's thinking begins to be characterized less by centration.

In order to solve seriation problems, children must also apply the *logical rule of transitivity*. Part of the problem for young elementary children is that they do not understand that objects in the middle of a series are both shorter and longer than others. Older children can mentally construct relations among objects. They can infer the relationship between two objects by knowing its relationship to a third. For example, if they know stick A is shorter than stick B, and stick B is shorter than stick C, then A must be shorter than C. This answer is a logical deduction based on the rule of transitivity (A > B and B > C, thus A > C). According to Piaget's theory, an understanding of transitivity is acquired between the ages of 7 and 11.

Classification   In addition to seriation, Piaget believed that classification skills are central to the development of concrete operations. **Classification** is another way children can impose order on their environment by grouping things and ideas according to common elements. Classification is a skill that begins to emerge in early childhood. Toddlers and preschoolers can generally group objects according to a single dimension, such as size or color. However, it is not until the concrete operational period that children classify objects according to multiple dimensions or understand relations between classes of objects. Piaget described two different types of classification systems that develop during middle childhood as matrix and hierarchical classification.

Matrix classification involves classifying items by two or more attributes, as shown in Figure 3.5 on page 146. We already know that preschool children can group objects according to single dimensions. What would happen, however, if you gave a group of children objects of different shapes *and* colors to sort? Piaget found that young preschool children sort

UNDERSTANDING
CHILDREN
*Strategy 4.5: Classes
and Relations Tasks*

■ FIGURE 3.5
*Matrix
Classification Task*

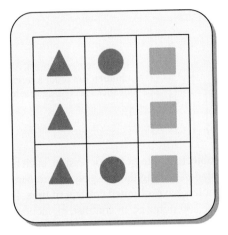

What is the color and what is the
shape of the missing object?

things correctly along one dimension, either shape or size. A slightly more advanced pre-school child might then subdivide each of the color groups along the second dimension. This behavior suggests that children are in a transition stage. They *notice* more than one dimension but are unable to coordinate this information. By age 8 or 9, children will demonstrate the ability to sort objects using two dimensions simultaneously.

Piaget believed that centration places a greater constraint on younger than on older children's classification skills. Young children tend to group things based on their similarities; differences between objects are typically ignored. Older children are able to consider how objects may be similar and different at the same time. The ability to classify objects according to two dimensions also requires *reversibility* in thinking. This ability to mentally reverse an operation allows a child to first classify an object by one dimension (color) and then reclassify it by a second attribute (shape or size). Older elementary school children are able to handle this problem, because they are becoming more flexible in their thinking.

During the later elementary school years, children also begin to use **hierarchical classification** systems for imposing order on their environment. Such classification systems are used to organize information about geology, biology, astronomy, history, physics, music, and so forth. By sixth grade, for instance, children are expected to know that all matter is composed of molecules, and each molecule is made up of atoms, which carry different units of protons, electrons, and neutrons. The child must also be able to reason about hierarchical relations in order to understand number concepts. For example, the number 5 is part of a set that also includes the numbers preceding it (1, 2, 3, and 4). The number 1 can be divided into several different parts (halves, quarters, tenths, etc.), and the number 100 is made up of 10 groups of tens. During the concrete operational stage, children begin to understand hierarchical relations.

The standard test for assessing children's understanding of hierarchies is the *class inclusion* task. A child is shown pictures of two different animals, say three dogs and seven cats, and then asked, "Are there more cats or more animals?" (see Figure 3.6). Most 5- and 6-year-olds say there are more cats. They typically compare the subclasses (dogs and cats) and do not grasp that they make up a larger class (animals). To answer correctly, children have to think about the subsets in relation to the whole. Around the age of 8 or 9, children begin to base their responses on the *logical rule of class inclusion*. They now understand that a total collection of items must be larger than any one of its subparts and use this

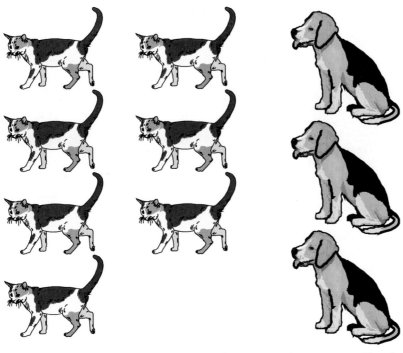

■ FIGURE 3.6
*Are There More
Cats or Animals?*

Preschool children respond that there are more cats, because they compare the two groups. They do not understand that each group also belongs to a large class (animals).

logical operation to organize information in class inclusion problems. Before children have acquired an understanding of class inclusion, they may have difficulty understanding part-whole relations in math, science, reading, and many other subjects.

Conservation According to Piaget's theory, the ability to reason about conservation problems is the major hallmark of the concrete operational stage. **Conservation** involves the understanding that an entity remains the same despite superficial changes in its form or physical appearance. During the concrete operational stage, children no longer base their reasoning on the physical appearance of objects. They recognize that a transformed object may seem to have more or less of the quantity in question, but it may not. In other words, appearances can be misleading.

UNDERSTANDING
CHILDREN
*Strategy 4.4:
Conservation Tasks*

Piaget examined children's understanding of five types of conservation: number, liquid, substance (mass), length, and volume. Examples of these conservation tasks are shown in the Focus on Development box on page 148. Although these tasks differ with respect to the dimension that is to be conserved, the basic paradigm is the same. In general, a child is shown two identical sets of objects, such as identical rows of coins, identical amounts of clay, or identical glasses of water. After the child agrees that the objects are the same, one object is transformed in a way that changes its appearance but not the basic dimension of interest. For example, in the conservation-of-number task, one row of coins is shortened or lengthened. The child is allowed to observe this transformation. The child is then asked to state whether the dimension of interest (quantity, mass, area, etc.) is still the same.

Children who have entered the concrete operational stage will reply that the set of objects is still the same. One object may look bigger, longer, or heavier, but the two objects are really the same. According to Piaget, children use three basic mental operations to perform conservation tasks: *negation, compensation,* and *identity.* These mental operations are

Focus on Development

Children's Understanding of Conservation Problems

CONSERVATION SKILL	BASIC PRINCIPLE	TEST FOR CONSERVATION SKILLS	
		Step 1	Step 2
Number (Ages 5 to 7)	The number of units in a collection remains unchanged even though the units are rearranged in space.	Two rows of pennies arranged in one-to-one correspondence	One of the rows elongated or contracted
Substances (Ages 7 to 8)	The amount of a malleable, plasticlike material remains unchanged regardless of the shape it assumes.	Modeling clay in two balls of the same size	One of the balls rolled into a long, narrow shape
Length (Ages 7 to 8)	The length of a line or an object from one end to the other end remains unchanged regardless of how it is rearranged in space or changed in shape.	Strips of cloth placed in a straight line	Strips of cloth placed in altered shapes
Area (Ages 8 to 9)	The total amount of surface covered by a set of plane figures remains unchanged regardless of the position of the figures.	Square units placed on top of each other	Square unit rearranged
Weight (Ages 9 to 10)	The heaviness of an object remains unchanged regardless of the shape that it assumes.	Units placed on top of each other	Units placed side by side
Volume (Ages 12 to 14)	The space occupied by an object remains unchanged regardless of a change in its shape.	Displacement of water by object placed vertically in the water	Displacement of water by object placed horizontally in the water

Source: After Vander Zanden (1993).

reflected in the ways an 8-year-old might explain why the amount of water in two different glasses remained the same:

"You could pour it back and it will be the same." (*negation*)

"The water goes up higher, but the glass is skinnier." (*compensation*)

"You just poured it, nothing was added or taken away." (*identity*) (P. Miller, 1993, p. 57)

Between the ages of about 7 and 11, children acquire the mental operations needed to think about the transformations represented in conservation problems. When children can reason logically about number, mass, and volume without being confused by physical appearances, they are capable of *reflective abstraction*. They can separate the invariant characteristics of stimuli (e.g., weight, number, volume) from how the object may appear to them.

The acquisition of the mental operations used to perform conservation tasks does not take place at the same time in all areas. Children's understanding of conservation problems follows a developmental sequence (see the Focus on Development box on page 148). Children generally acquire the ability to conserve numbers between the ages of 5 and 7. The ability to conserve area and weight develops between the ages of 8 and 10. Most children are unable to perform conservation-of-volume tasks until 10 or 11 years. Piaget referred to this inconsistency of children's thinking within a stage as **horizontal decalage.**

Formal Operational Stage

Having the ability to handle problems such as seriation, classification, and conservation, children from about 11 or 12 years old begin to develop a coherent system of formal logic. By the end of the concrete operational period, they have the cognitive tools for solving many types of logical problems, for understanding conceptual relations among mathematical operations (e.g., $15 + 8 = 10 + 13$), and for ordering and classifying bodies of knowledge. During adolescence, the mental operations that emerged in previous stages are organized into a more elaborate system of logic and abstract ideas.

The most important change that occurs during the formal operations stage is that children's thinking shifts from the *real* to the *possible* (Flavell, 1985). Older elementary school children can reason logically but only about people, places, and things that are tangible and concrete. In contrast, adolescents can think about things they have never experienced (e.g., "When you read this story, try to imagine what it might have been like to be a slave in the 1850s."); they can generate ideas about events that never happened (e.g., "What would Europe be like today if Germany had won World War II?"); and they can make predictions about hypothetical or future events (e.g., "Suppose the federal government passed a bill to ban the death penalty. What would happen to the crime rate?"). Older adolescents can discuss complex social and political issues involving abstract ideas such as human rights, equality, and justice. They can also reason about proportional relations and analogies, solve algebraic equations and geometric proofs, and analyze the inherent validity of an argument.

The ability to think abstractly and reflectively occurs during the **formal operational** stage. In the following sections, we look at four key characteristics of formal operational thinking: propositional logic, scientific reasoning, combinatorial reasoning, and reasoning about probabilities and proportions.

Propositional Logic Adult mental operations correspond to a certain type of logical operation called *propositional logic,* which Piaget believed was central to formal operational thinking. **Propositional logic** involves the ability to draw a logical inference based on the relationship between two statements or premises. In everyday language, propositional logic can be expressed in a series of if/then statements. Consider the following example:

> If babies are older than adults;
>
> And babies are older than children;
>
> Then adults are older than children.

The *conclusion* is factually correct but invalid, because it *does not follow* from the information that preceded it. David Moshman and Bridget Franks (1986) found that elementary school children tend to evaluate the above conclusion on the basis of its factual truth rather than the validity of the argument. As children enter formal operations, however, they begin to consider the inherent validity of the argument, regardless of its factual truth. The conclusion may be factually correct, but some adolescents would question the validity of the argument.

For formal operational thinkers, the validity of the argument has to do more with the way the statements are related than with the truthfulness of the content. According to Piaget, formal operational reasoning involves thinking about the logical relationships among propositions. Formal operational thinkers seem to understand that logical arguments have a "disembodied, passionless life of their own, at least in principle" (Flavell, 1985, p. 101).

Many types of problem-solving situations involve the use of propositional logic. Solving algebra problems, for example, involves the ability to think about propositional statements (e.g., $x + 2y = 11$; if $y = 1$, then $x =$ _____?). Propositional logic is also essential for reasoning about scientific problems, such as determining how to classify an animal or plant (e.g., If all mammals nurse their young and this animal nurses its young, then it must be a mammal.).

Good writers, lawyers, politicians, and teachers use propositional logic when they want to argue a point. When adolescents acquire this ability, be prepared. They not only become

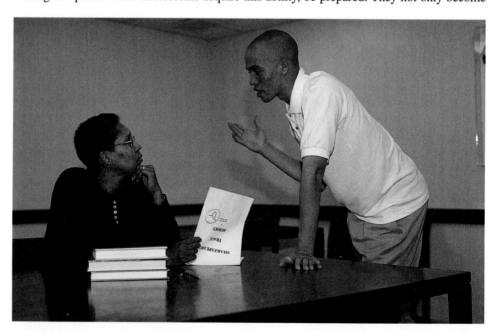

As adolescents acquire formal logic, they become more skilled at debating issues, such as why they deserve a higher grade on a test.
Source: Cleve Bryant/Photo Edit.

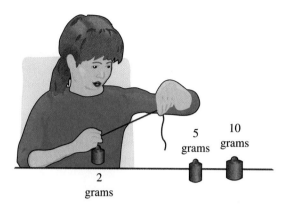

What makes the pendulum swing faster? The four factors involved are the length of the string, the weight of the pendulum, the height from which the pendulum is released, and the force with which the pendulum is pushed.

more argumentative, but also better arguers. They can find the fallacies in your logic and come back with the appropriate counterargument.

Scientific Reasoning   As adolescents develop their use of propositional logic, they approach problems in a more systematic manner. They can form hypotheses, determine how to test each one against the facts, and rule out those that prove to be wrong. Piaget called the ability to generate and test hypotheses in a logical and systematic manner **hypothetico-deductive thinking.**

To study the development of this type of thinking, Piaget used the pendulum task shown in Figure 3.7. In this experiment, a child is given a rod from which strings of different lengths are suspended. Different-size weights can be easily attached to each string. The child is shown how the pendulum works, and then asked which of four factors—length of string, weight of object, force of push, or height of drop—is responsible for the speed at which the pendulum swings. They are allowed to experiment with the apparatus before stating their answer.

What do you think the correct answer is? How would you approach this problem? The first step is to generate a hypothesis or make a prediction. Concrete operational thinkers are able to use this problem-solving strategy. The next step involves testing the hypothesis. This step generally separates the concrete from the formal operational thinker. The trick is to change one of the problem's factors or variables while holding all others constant. Concrete operational thinkers often get off to a good start but fail to test all possible combinations. They may also change more than one variable at the same time (e.g., the string and the weight). Because they do not approach the problem systematically, concrete operational thinkers often draw the wrong conclusion when there are multiple variables to consider. In contrast, the formal operational thinker typically thinks about all possible combinations of variables. In this example, there are 16 different combinations that should be considered to draw the correct conclusion. The correct answer, of course, is the length of string. *A short string makes the pendulum go faster, regardless of all other factors.*

Combinatorial Reasoning   Another characteristic of formal operations is the ability to think about multiple causes. Suppose you give elementary and secondary students four plastic chips of different colors and ask them to put the chips together in as many different ways as possible. Children are likely to combine only two chips at the same time. Few will be able to do this task in any systematic way. Adolescents, on the other hand, may develop

Two of the clear liquids in the four beakers when combined with liquid
g produce a yellow solution. How would you solve this problem?

▩ FIGURE 3.8
Chemistry Task

a way of representing all the possible combinations, including combinations of three and four chips. They are also more likely than children to produce these combinations systematically. This process is known as **combinatorial reasoning.**

Piaget and Inhelder (1956) used a chemistry experiment to study children's and adolescents' ability to use combinatorial logic. Figure 3.8 shows this experiment, in which children must combine liquids from different bottles to create a yellow solution. When the liquids from two bottles are combined with the g liquid, the solution turns yellow. Liquid from one of the bottles has no effect, and liquid from a fourth bottle can turn the solution clear. Concrete operational children generally take a drop of liquid from each of the four bottles and combine it with the g liquid one by one. If nothing happens, they think they have exhausted all possibilities. If they are told to combine liquids, they may do so but not in a systematic way. Formal operational thinkers go beyond testing each liquid one at a time. They combine the liquids systematically (1 + 2 + g, 1 + 3 + g, 1 + 4 + g, etc.), until they find the combination that turns the solution yellow when g is added. Some adolescents may even go on to speculate about which liquids would combine to turn the solution clear again.

Reasoning About Probabilities and Proportions   Elementary-aged children generally have a limited understanding of probability. Piaget's theory helps to explain why. Figure 3.9 shows a bubble gum machine with 30 red balls and 50 yellow balls. If a child inserts a coin into the machine, which color gumball is most likely to come out? A concrete operational thinker is likely to say "yellow," because there are more yellow than red balls. This child focuses on the absolute difference between the two quantities. Formal operational thinkers will mentally represent the problem differently. They will think about the problem in terms of the ratio of red to yellow balls. Adolescents are more likely to say that the child has a higher likelihood of getting a yellow ball, because there is a higher proportion of yellows to reds. A ratio is not something a person can see; it is an inferred relationship between two quantities. This example illustrates how concrete and formal thinkers may answer a question the same way, but they use a qualitatively different system of logic.

Some theorists contend that Piaget's research may have overestimated the ability of adolescents to reason about proportions. There is some evidence to suggest that even adults

■ FIGURE 3.9
Ratio Task

If you insert a coin, which color
gumball is most likely to come out?

may not use a proportional reasoning strategy when solving practical problems. In one study, researchers asked 50 women in a supermarket to judge which of two sizes of the same product was a better buy (Capon & Kuhn, 1979). One bottle of garlic powder contained 1.25 ounces and sold for 41 cents, whereas the second bottle contained 2.37 ounces and sold for 77 cents. The women were given pencil and paper and told to justify their responses. The most direct way to do this problem is to compute the price of garlic powder per ounce for each bottle, and then compare the amounts. This strategy involves reasoning about proportions, which, according to Piaget's theory, is a characteristic of formal operations. Capon and Kuhn's supermarket study reported that fewer than 30 percent of the women used a proportional reasoning strategy when comparing products. Most used a subtraction strategy, and justified their response by saying, "With the bigger one you get 32 more ounces for 36 more cents." Others just relied on previous experience and justified their choices by simply saying, "The bigger one is always better or cheaper." This study concluded that many adults may be unable to use formal operations when solving real-world problems.

This finding will not surprise most high school teachers. Most know that their students have difficulty with tasks involving more abstract forms of reasoning. It is estimated that only 30 to 40 percent of high school students in American schools can solve formal operational tasks (Keating, 1990). The development of formal operations is greatly influenced by cultural expectations and experiences. Formal operational thinking is more prevalent in societies that emphasize mathematical and technical skills. Even within scientifically oriented countries such as the United States, some groups of students have greater experience with mathematical and scientific thinking than others. The Focus on Development box on page 154 shows some typical developments in children's and adolescents' mathematical and scientific thinking affected by educational and cultural experiences.

Limitations of Piaget's Theory

Piaget's theory is one of the most widely cited and discussed theories of cognitive development. Piaget helped to alter the course of research on children's development, and is still today widely considered to be the most influential developmental theorist (e.g., Dixon,

Focus on
Development

Development of Mathematical and Scientific Thinking

	Math and Number Concepts	Science
Early Childhood (Preschool/ Kindergarten)	▪ 4- to 5-year-olds begin to understand basic number concepts (e.g., counting) and relation between number words and larger/smaller numerosities (e.g., 4 is more than 2) ▪ 4- to 5-year-olds begin to understand **inversion** as it applies to set of objects (e.g., a set remains the same if 2 objects are removed and 2 are added) ▪ difficulty with understanding mathematical **equality**	▪ ask scientific questions and form intuitive theories naïve about natural phenomenon ▪ influenced more by coincidental events and by external appearances than older children
Middle Childhood (Elementary)	▪ 6- to 9-year-olds become faster at solving inversion problems in numerical form ($a + b - b$) ▪ developing understandings of equality in problems such as $4 + 5 + 6 = \_\_\_ + 6$; 8- to 9-year-olds often answer 15	▪ with instructional assistance, can learn the rationale for experimental comparisons that vary only by one factor at a time ▪ difficulty with interpreting experimental results inconsistent with prior beliefs; improve with practice
Early Adolesence (Middle School)	▪ from 11 years, demonstrate better conceptual understandings of equality, and of the inversion principle— ignoring the particular value of b in ($a + b - b$) ▪ developing understandings of underlying principles to help solve decimal fractions, algebra problems, etc.	▪ improve conduct of experiments, such as varying one variable at a time, and drawing valid inferences ▪ scientific reasoning improves with age, but difficulties remain
Middle and Late Adolescence (High School)	▪ continue to build conceptual understanding of variables, function, etc. ▪ apply algebra to solve contextualized problems	▪ scientific reasoning improves with age, but impediments remain in adolescence and adulthood (e.g., reasoning bias, misconceptions, making inappropriate conclusions from scientific evidence)

Source: Siegler & Alibali (2005).

2004; Flavell, 1996). Once researchers viewed development through Piaget's eyes, they could no longer see a child as a passive organism molded and shaped by the environment (P. Miller, 1993). Although Piagetian research continues to influence the way we think about children, in recent years his theory has generated substantial controversy and criticism. Indeed, Piaget considered himself a primary revisionist of his own theory, and continued to make modifications throughout his life (Miller, 2002.) Questions have been raised about (a) his research methods, (b) the stagelike nature of children's thinking and the universality of Piaget's stages, and (c) the adequacy of explanations for developmental transitions (Flavell, 1985; P. Miller, 1993, 2002).

Concerns About Research Methods

Many contemporary theorists believe that Piaget underestimated younger children's abilities due to the research methods he used. As stated earlier, the tasks he used were highly complex and cognitively demanding, many requiring sophisticated verbal skills. Critics have argued that children may have the ability to perform problems at higher cognitive levels but may lack the verbal skills to demonstrate their competence. Thus, when nonverbal measures are used to test for the presence or absence of key concepts, the results differ from those reported by Piaget. In the infancy section, for example, we discussed recent research suggesting that object permanence may appear earlier than Piaget claimed. We also reviewed research suggesting that 3- and 4-year-old children can perform simple visual perspective-taking tasks (see discussion of egocentrism on pages 142 and 143).

In another experiment, Rochel Gelman (1972) found that 3-year-olds were able to understand number conservation tasks when more familiar language and a small number of objects were used. In Gelman's experiment, 3-year-olds were shown two different plates. One plate contained three toy mice and the other plate contained two mice. The children were told to pick the "winner" plate and the "loser" plate. Children consistently identified the plate with three mice as the "winner." After children demonstrated they could correctly identify the winner and loser plates, the experimenter "magically" changed the winner plate by taking away the middle mouse or by pushing the mice closer together. When the children viewed the plates again, they acted surprised. Some asked where the missing mouse had gone. More important, they defined the winner plate by the number of mice on it rather than by the length of the row. When the three mice in the row were pushed together, they still called it the winner. This study supports some contemporary theorists' suggestions that children's cognitive abilities in both infancy and childhood were underestimated by Piaget (Gelman & Baillargeon, 1983). Others, however, suggest that these simpler tasks may reveal precursors to the more advanced concepts Piaget was attempting to identify (P. Miller, 2002).

Concerns About the Nature of Development

Piaget has received the most criticism for his ideas about the qualitative nature of cognitive development. Some theorists have questioned whether changes in children's cognitive systems are as "fundamental, momentous, qualitative, and stagelike as Piaget suggested" (Flavell, 1985, p. 82). Researchers have also argued that the equilibration model is inadequate for explaining advances in cognitive development. There are no precise statements as to what cognitive activities actually take place during the process of assimilation, accommodation, and equilibration (Flavell, 1985; P. Miller, 1993; Siegler, 1991). However, translations of Piaget's later work indicate that he was attempting to improve descriptions of these developmental processes, and was placing less emphasis on steplike stages (e.g., Dawson-Tunik, Fischer, & Stein, 2004; P. Miller, 2002).

FOCUS ON
Development

Structures in Case's Theory of Cognitive Development

Stage/Structure	Characteristics
Sensorimotor (Birth to 1½ years)	Mental representations consist of sensory input and action responses are physical movements. (e.g., Seeing a snake and running away.)
Interrelational or Representational (1½ to 5 years)	Mental representations and actions consist of concrete images. (e.g., Creating a mental image and drawing of snake.)
Logical or Dimensional (5 to 11 years)	Mental representations are abstract and can be transformed in simple ways. (e.g., Realizing nondangerous snakes and how to handle.)
Central Conceptual Structures* ■ unidimensional (about 6 years) ■ bidimensional (about 8 years) ■ integrated (about 10 years)	
Formal or Abstract (11 to 19 years)	Abstract representations can be transformed in complex ways. (e.g., Realizing problems living with snakes and engaging in community education efforts.)

Source: Case & Okamoto (1996) and Siegler & Alibali (2005).

*Note: A similar developmental sequence (uni- to bi- to integrated bidimensional) is expected for understanding particular concepts within each major stage.

Considerable research now suggests that stagelike changes in children's thinking appear to be causally linked to more gradual and quantitative sorts of changes in children's attentional and memory capacities. This research suggests that young children may be unable to perform some Piagetian tasks because they fail to attend to the relevant dimensions, to encode the appropriate information, to relate information to existing knowledge, to retrieve the appropriate solution from memory, and so forth (Siegler, 1991). When young children are trained to use these cognitive processes more effectively, age differences in children's performances on Piagetian tasks begin to disappear. For example, nonconservers as young as 4 years old can perform conservation tasks when they are trained to attend to the relevant dimensions (Gelman, 1969). Other research suggests that concrete operational children can be trained to solve formal operational problems (Siegler, Robinson, Liebert, & Liebert, 1973). However, this learning may not transfer to other types of formal operational tasks.

Although training studies call into question the qualitative nature of developmental changes, the issue of stages in children's cognitive development remains controversial (Flavell, 1985; Siegler & Alibali, 2005; Miller, 2002). Some theorists contend that a stage theory of cognitive development may still be viable (Case, 1985, 1988; Case & Okamoto, 1996). An additional issue of concern for contemporary theorists is the universality of Piaget's stages. As stated earlier, it is estimated that only a small minority of adolescents reach Piaget's formal operational stage. The development of formal operations seems to be influenced by cultural expectations and experiences. We will explore the role of culture further in the next section on the contributions of Vygotsky's theory.

Neo-Piagetian Theories

Neo-Piagetian theories have attempted to add greater specificity to developmental changes, while maintaining the basic assumptions of Piaget's theory (e.g., knowledge is actively constructed, cognitive changes are stagelike, etc.). These theories have begun to look at the role of children's information processing capabilities in explaining structural changes in children's thinking. The Focus on Development box on page 156 presents Robbie Case's cognitive development model. This model links structural changes (movement from stage to stage) to the development of cognitive strategies and memory processes. Within each of the four stages are substages or levels—unidimensional, bidimensional, and integrated bidimensional (elaborated)—showing the cyclical nature of cognitive development (e.g., Flavell, 1996). For example, in studies of storytelling, Case and Okamoto (1996) found that 6-year-old children typically created a story around the intentions of one central character (unidimensional or uniintentional), 8-year-olds created two or more event sequences with one leading to goal satisfaction (bidimensional or bi-intentional), and 10-year-olds integrated multiple motives to satisfy goals into a complex, organized plot (integrated). These researchers found a similar developmental sequence in children's representations of spatial relations. Figure 3.10 on page 158 shows Chinese children's drawings at the (a) predimensional level, with no concern with spatial relations; (b) unidimensional level, with placement of objects into a single dimension; (c) bidimensional level; with placement in both foreground and background; and (d) integrated bidimensional, with creation of a coherent picture.

Case and his colleagues have proposed that domains of knowledge, such as thinking about space, number, or social interactions, are represented in *central conceptual structures.* These are less general than Piaget's structures but more general than a single task. For example, learning about stories or spatial relations on one kind of task, along with increases in information processing capacity, can foster development of understandings within that domain (i.e., changes in central conceptual structures from uni- to bidimensional). Thus, development can sometimes appear to be stagelike if changes in several conceptual structures occur simultaneously (developmental spurts). Case's theory is just one of many that attempt to integrate Piagetian and information processing theories (see also Fisher, 1980; Fisher & Bidell, 1998; Flarell, 1996).

Core-Knowledge Theories

As mentioned previously, some developmentalists argue that Piaget (and Vygotsky) underestimated young children's cognitive abilities, and that they are not as perception-bound as once believed. Children's somewhat sophisticated reasoning about concepts—such as living things, inanimate objects, and the mind—at a young age have led some theorists to propose that children are born with innate capabilities or mental structures. These capacities allow children to organize a great deal of knowledge about the world that is basic for survival and

■ FIGURE 3.10

Children's Representations of Spatial Relationships

Source: "The Role of Central Conceptual Structures in the Development of Children's Thought," by R. Case & Y. Okamoto, 1996, *Monographs of the Society for Research in Child Development, 61(1–2),* Fig. 26, (p. 139).

everyday interactions. This proposal is similar to Chomsky's explanation for children's rapid abilities to acquire language (see Chapter 5). **Core-knowledge** theorists assume that these basic capabilities are *domain specific,* or limited to organizing knowledge about certain areas. Some theorists (sometimes referred to as *theory theorists*) propose that children organize their understanding of important domains into informal or naïve theories, especially of physics (knowledge of objects), biology (knowledge of plants and animals), and psychology (knowledge of people) (e.g., Wellman & Gelman, 1998). Children's initial "theories" may emerge very young (before 3 years), particularly concerning understandings of people's intentions and desires (theory of mind) (e.g., Gelman, 2003). Children, like scientists, use their theories to explain and predict their world. For example, a preschooler might try to make sense of his teacher's behavior (looking for the book that he had in his lap) by inferring that she *wanted* or *intended* to begin storytime and that she *believed* it was somewhere else. It is important to remember, however, that children's theories are naïve, everyday "folk" theories, not mature scientific theories (Miller, 2002). Later in life, children develop understandings of their social and physical worlds well beyond their initial theories.

One educational implication of research inspired by this perspective, mentioned previously, is that children (and adults) often resist giving up their naïve theories (see Figure 3.2 on page 142), tending to ignore disconfirming evidence or make adaptations in their conceptions rather than give them up. Teachers may have to focus on helping children give up their old theories, such as "the world is flat," before introducing new ones. Another implication may be that children can begin to develop deeper understandings of concepts in areas such as science at a younger age than previously assumed (Gelman & Brenneman, 2004).

The core-knowledge perspective differs from Piaget's approach primarily in its assumptions that children's theories are domain-specific and separate from each other, and that children's ability to construct these theories is innate and emerges early in life. However, these theorists share similar views with Piaget of children as "little scientists" who actively construct their knowledge of the world, are limited by their current knowledge, and make progress when confronting challenges to their existing mental structures (Miller, 2002).

Conclusions About Piaget's Theory

Despite the criticisms discussed here, most theorists believe that Piaget captured many of the major trends in children's thinking (Flavell, 1996; Miller, 2002). Flavell (1996) concludes that "I think we are more in danger of underappreciating Piaget than overappreciating him, for much the same reason that fish are said to underappreciate the virtues of water. That is, many of Piaget's contributions have become so much a part of the way we view cognitive development nowadays that they are virtually invisible" (p. 202). Most preschool children are unable to consistently consider more than one dimension of a stimulus object, to think about relations, or to take the perspective of another person. Older elementary school children can think logically about relations, perform mental operations, and reflect on their own thinking processes, but they are unable to solve hypothetical problems in their heads or to approach problems in a systematic way, especially when multiple steps are involved. Adolescents are better able to use complex symbol systems, to analyze the inherent logic of an argument, and to draw inferences from multiple pieces of evidence, even when there is some conflicting information. Simply put, Piaget taught us that children do not see and think about the world as adults do.

Educational Implications

Much of Piaget's research focused on children's development of logical, scientific, and mathematical concepts. Although Piaget reflected on the general educational implications of his research, he refrained from making specific educational recommendations. Eleanor Duckworth (1987), a student of Piaget's, has aptly described perceived difficulties with applying his theory in her classic article titled, "Either We're Too Early and They Can't Learn It, or We're Too Late and They Know It Already: The Dilemma of Applying Piaget." Nevertheless, Piaget's research on children's intellectual development inspired major curriculum reforms. Piaget's theory of cognitive development had a major impact on preschool education (DeVries, 1990). The National Association of Young Children (NAEYC) developed and published teaching guidelines that incorporated Piaget's ideas about children's development (Bredekamp & Copple, 1997). Piaget's theory also serves as the theoretical rationale for constructivist, discovery, inquiry, and problem-oriented teaching approaches in today's classrooms. The Focus on Research box on page 160 describes a constructivist approach to teaching and learning mathematics that incorporates learning principles from Piaget's theory. In this section, we discuss the implications of this theory for teaching.

Focus on Cognitive Processes

One of the most important contributions of Piaget's work concerns the purposes and goals of education. Piaget was critical of educational approaches that emphasized the transmission and memorization of ready-made information. Such approaches, he argued, discourage children from learning to think for themselves and from developing confidence in their own thinking processes. In Piaget's view, "learning how to learn" should serve as the major

Focus on
Research

Learning and Teaching Mathematics: A Constructivist Approach

Piaget was very critical of the teaching of mathematics. In his view, mathematics was being taught as a set of ready-made rules and formulas. When math is taught this way, children acquire very little understanding of mathematical concepts and rules. As a result, they are unable to explain problem solutions. When asked, for example, to explain why they do the steps of a long-division problem, most fourth graders reply, "I don't know, my teacher told me to do it this way."

Terry Wood, Paul Cobb, and Erna Yackel (1992) developed a set of mathematical activities for second-grade children that were based on constructivist principles of teaching and learning. These activities were subsequently used in 10 second-grade classrooms for a full year. The mathematical activities could be solved in a variety of ways. The children worked on the problems in pairs so that they could share ideas, justify answers, and resolve conflicting points of view. As children worked on problems collaboratively, the teacher observed and listened. When appropriate, the teacher intervened to offer suggestions to challenge ideas and to probe the children's thinking. Small-group work was then followed by a whole-class discussion. In this setting, children explained and shared their problem solutions. The goal of this whole-class discussion was to construct some shared meaning of the mathematical problem and its solution. The following excerpt illustrates how the class developed a "shared" understanding of commutativity:

Teacher:	*Okay. Can we stop a minute boys? I think we have all agreed on something that I want to get clear. We all agree that 3 times 6 is 18?*
Children:	*Yes.*
Teacher:	*And we agree 6 times 3 is 18?*
Children:	*No. No. Yes. (Children begin to talk.)*
Matt:	*But I will count on my fingers. (He goes to front.) Watch. Six plus 6 is 12.*
Teacher:	*Let's listen.*
Matt:	*So that's 2 (holds up two fingers for the two 6s) and then add 6 more on. Six (putting his thumb up then pausing to think) 12–13, 14, 15, 16, 17, 18 (counts on, using his other hand).*
Teacher:	*Okay we have agreed on that, haven't we?*
Children:	*Yeah.*
Teacher:	*We've agreed that 3 times 6 is 18 and that 6 times 3 is 18, so is it possible to switch them around and still come up with the same answer?*
Children:	*Yes.*
Teacher:	*I think we have pretty much agreed on that, haven't we?*
Children:	*Yes.*

At the end of the school year, researchers assessed how well children in the problem-oriented mathematics curriculum performed on a standardized achievement test (Wood et al., 1992). When compared with children who had traditional textbook instruction in mathematics, children in the problem-oriented classes did just as well on computational tests, but they scored higher on tests that measured mathematical concepts and applications. In addition, children in the problem-oriented classes were more likely to report that understanding and collaboration leads to success in mathematics, whereas children in the traditionally taught mathematics classes reported that success depended on conforming to the ideas of others, being neat, and working quietly.

focus of education, so that children can become creative, inventive, and independent thinkers. Education should "form not furnish" children's minds (Piaget, 1969, pp. 69–70).

A similar focus on the process of learning is advocated by other contemporary cognitive developmental theorists. For example, educational programs based on core-knowledge or domain-specific theories emphasize helping children develop their scientific thinking processes as they engage in explorations. For example, the Preschool Pathways to Science (PrePS) is a science and math program developed for preschoolers with its basis in domain-specific theories and constructivist approaches (Gelman & Brenneman, 2004). This program employs practices also consistent with those advocated in National Academy of Science publications, such as *How People Learn: Brain, Mind, Experience, and School* (Brown, Bransford, & Cocking, 2000). Teachers attempt to build on children's relevant knowledge in science, for example, by engaging them in hands-on science activities using the language and skills of science (e.g., observing, predicting, checking). In a simple example, a teacher introduces an apple, asks children to *observe* its features with all senses, *predict* what will happen when they cut it open (records their predictions), and then asks children to *check* their predictions. These words and processes are used repeatedly as children investigate their natural world.

Focus on Exploration

The second most important contribution of Piaget's research is the idea that knowledge is constructed from the child's own physical and mental activities. Piaget (1964) taught us that knowledge is not something that can simply be given to children.

> Knowledge is not a copy of reality. To know an object, to know an event, is not simply to look at it and make a mental copy or image of it. To know an object is to act on it. To know is to modify, to transform the object, and to understand the process of this transformation, and as a consequence to understand the way the object is constructed. (p. 8)

Piaget's theory of intellectual development has also greatly influenced mathematics and science education. Current reform efforts in these areas are guided by constructivist views of teaching and learning that are based in part on Piaget's theory. Consistent with Piaget's views, the new curriculum standards in mathematics and science education emphasize that knowledge is not simply transmitted. Students must have opportunities to experiment, to question, and to create their own meaning through their own physical and mental activities. The curriculum standards also emphasize the important role of peer interactions in children's cognitive development. Students need opportunities to share, discuss, and argue different points of view. Moreover, reform efforts in mathematics and science emphasize the role of teachers in choosing appropriate learning activities, guiding learning, and stimulating children's reasoning processes. The Focus on Teaching box on page 163 presents a high school biology lesson that incorporates Piaget's principles of learning.

Focus on Social Interactions

Another important contribution of Piaget's research to education concerns the role of social interactions in children's cognitive development. Piaget (1976) emphasized, "No real intellectual activity can be carried out in the form of experimental actions and spontaneous investigations without free collaboration among individuals, that is to say, among students" (pp. 107–108). For younger children, social interactions play an important role in the reduction of egocentrism. For older children, especially adolescents, interactions with peers and adults are a natural source of cognitive conflict. Through interacting with others, children clarify their views, obtain conflicting opinions, and reconcile their ideas with those of others. We see this activity occurring in the opening vignettes. The equilibration processes described previously are often set into motion when children do not agree with one another.

Social interactions can also help children develop an awareness and understanding of others. Teachers and parents can facilitate perspective-taking skills by asking children to explain how they feel when they are hurt or injured by another child. When negotiating conflict, adults can help children generate and evaluate different solutions to problems. Role-taking and simulation activities are also helpful for helping children understand the perspective of others. Children's literature may be helpful as well. Adults can ask children how different characters feel about different events or to act out how a character may be feeling. Discussion and reading groups for adolescents can help them to understand that others may have feelings like them.

The Importance of Play

Piaget's theory also emphasizes the important role of play in children's development. Play is a natural way for children to learn. It is through play that children learn about the world and how to master the environment. Play is also an important window into children's cognitive and social development. Researchers indicate that forms of children's play follow Piaget's stages of cognitive development. Infants play by exploring and manipulating objects, such as shaking a rattle or kicking a mobile in their crib. Preschoolers engage in pretend, socio-dramatic, or fantasy play, such a pretending to be a firefighter or going on a trip. Children in the primary grades engage in a good deal of fantasy play, but as they mature they begin to prefer organized games with rules. By late childhood, children have moved away from time spent in dramatic play to games that are group oriented. Play may involve organized sports, board games, or simply hanging out with friends and listening to music.

Although children's play is often not taken seriously by adults, it has many important benefits, as discussed in the earlier Focus on Teaching box on page 137. "The Value of Fantasy Play in School." In infancy, play can stimulate brain development and provide the foundation for understanding causality. Through symbolic play, children express and represent their ideas, thoughts, and feelings. Play also helps to develop skills in abstract thinking, problem solving, perspective taking, and persistence. In addition to supporting cognitive development, play has many important benefits for children's language, social, emotional, and physical development. As Maria Montessori so wisely observed, "Play is the child's work."

The Role of Learning

Although Piaget's ideas about development have influenced educational theory, one dimension of his theory remains controversial. Piaget (1964) argued that "learning is subordinated to development and not vice-versa" (p. 17). Piaget's theory represents a fundamental departure from the view that learning can stimulate development. Behaviorists such as Edward Thorndike and B. F. Skinner, for example, assert that learning new information or skills can result in higher levels of cognitive functioning. As will be discussed presently, Vygotsky (1978) also proposed that "properly organized learning results in mental development and sets in motion a variety of developmental processes that would be impossible apart from learning" (p. 90). For Piaget, the stage of development limits what children can learn and how they learn. It is not possible to accelerate development through learning experiences. The following statement (Duckworth, 1964) makes this point very clear.

> The goal in education is not to increase the amount of knowledge, but to create the possibilities for the child to invent and to discover. When we teach too fast, we keep the child from inventing and discovering himself. . . . Teaching means creating the situations where [mental] structures can be discovered; it does not mean transmitting structures which may be assimilated at nothing other than the verbal level. (p. 3)

Unfortunately, Piaget's view on the relationship of development to learning is often interpreted to mean that the teaching of certain skills and subjects should be delayed until the

Focus on Teaching

Learning Genetics Through Inquiry

Mrs. Johnson is planning a semester unit on how traits are inherited from one generation to the next. She believes that many important learning goals of her school's science program can be met in this unit. Mrs. Johnson wants to provide students with opportunities to understand basic principles of transmission genetics. She also wants them to appreciate how using a *mental model* is useful for understanding. She wants her students to engage in and learn the processes of inquiry as they develop their mental models, and she also wants them to understand the effect of transmission genetics on their lives and on society.

Selecting an appropriate computer program to simulate genetic events is important, because simulation will be key. In reviewing several programs, she noted several common features. Each simulation allows students to select parental phenotypes and make crosses. Offspring are produced quickly by all programs. The student will be able to simulate many generations of crosses in a single class period.

All the programs are open-ended—no answer books are provided to check answers. All the programs allow students to begin with data and to construct a model of

elements and processes of an inheritance program. Students will work in teams to develop their inheritance models. Mrs. Johnson also plans to obtain reprints of Mendel's original article for students to read early in the unit. In addition to using the simulations and reading, Mrs. Johnson wants her students to be working with living organisms. She has ordered yeast strains, fruit flies, and Fast Plants. She has prepared units in genetics using each of these organisms and has adapted the units to meet the needs of the students. As the unit progresses, a genetics counselor from a local hospital will talk to the class about common genetic disorders and how such disorders are diagnosed and treated.

For the final project, each student will become an "expert" in one inherited disorder and prepare a report that discusses its inheritance pattern, symptoms, frequency, and effects. Students will present their findings as a poster, presentation, or report to be shared with their classmates and parents. Mrs. Johnson has also actively gathered information from organizations, such as March of Dimes, so students, if they choose, can become involved in service organizations focused on a particular genetic disorder.

Source: From National Academy of Sciences (1996).

child is "mentally ready." It is important to keep in mind that Piaget recognized social interactions as a factor that stimulated children's development. Piaget's point was that external stimulation of thinking can only succeed if it provokes the child to engage in assimilation and accommodation processes. It is the child's own efforts to resolve a conflict that takes him or her to a new level of cognitive functioning. Children can certainly memorize that $2 + 18 = 20$, but do they really understand that the 1 in 18 stands for ten? The Focus on Research box on page 164 describes how teaching simple algorithms such as "carrying" and "borrowing" while children are acquiring an understanding of place value can undermine the development of their numerical reasoning.

According to Piaget, a better approach would be to ensure that students have numerous opportunities to group and count objects before problems are presented in a symbolic or abstract form. The task for teachers is to probe their students' current level of understanding and to determine the prerequisite experiences students need to move to a higher level of understanding. This interpretation implies that teachers should not simply wait until children are "mentally ready" to learn. They should adjust their instructional tactics to meet the levels of cognitive development they encounter.

Focus on
Research

Reinventing Arithmetic in the Primary Grades

For 20 years, Constance Kamii has observed children doing math lessons in the early primary grades. Her book *Young Children Reinvent Arithmetic* (Kamii, 2000) uses Piaget's theory to explain how children acquire number concepts. Consistent with a constructivist approach, Kamii believes that mathematical knowledge is *"constructed (created) by each child from within, in interaction with the environment"* (Kamii, 2000, p. 3). Kamii's research has shown that teaching children algorithms can "unteach" place value. This conclusion is based on interviews with three classes of second graders. One of the teachers taught algorithms (i.e., carrying and borrowing), but two did not. At the end of the school year, children were asked to solve the following problem without paper or pencil: 7 + 52 + 186 = _____. Children in the no-algorithm classes produced the highest number of correct answers (45 percent), and the algorithm classes produced the lowest number (12 percent). By analyzing children's *incorrect* answers, Kamii began to see the harmful effects of algorithms. Children in the algorithm classes gave answers that were not reasonable (e.g., 29, 30, 198, 938, 989, etc.) in relation to the addends given. Kamii explained that answers in the 900s were obtained by adding 7 to the 1 of 186, and carrying one from another column. Answers smaller than 186 were obtained by adding all the digits as one: 7 + 5 + 2 + 1 + 8 + 6. In contrast, incorrect answers in the no-algorithm classes were reasonable. The children in these classes began by adding 50 to 180, then adding the 1s. They appeared to be using good number sense (i.e., the answer could not be smaller than one of the addends).

Kamii argues that encouraging young children to use algorithms to solve arithmetic problems can prevent them from developing number sense. It encourages them to give up their thinking about numbers. Adults understand that the 5 in 52 stands for 50, but children who are still acquiring a sense of place value think that the 5 means five. In this way, algorithms can "unteach" place value. Kamii has developed a series of videotapes for teaching numerical concepts using Piaget's theory:

Kamii, C. (1989). *Double-column addition: A teacher uses Piaget's theory.* [Videotape]. New York: Teachers College Press.

Kamii, C. (1990). *Multidigit division. Two teachers using Piaget's theory.* [Videotape]. New York: Teachers College Press.

Kamii, C., & Clark, F. B. (2000). *First graders dividing 62 by 5.* [Videotape]. New York: Teachers College Press.

Kamii and her colleagues have also examined the use of manipulatives for teaching mathematics (Kamii, Lewis, & Kirkland, 2001). Based on their observations of primary-grade children's behavior in classrooms, they provide the following suggestions: (a) tangrams can be useful for spatial reasoning if children are encouraged to solve problems on their own; (b) counters (in the form of interesting items, such as pretend cookies, etc.) can be helpful in introducing children to addition and subtraction and word problems, but should not be used in overly prescriptive ways that interfere with children's thinking or their use of other inventions such as tally marks, drawing, or fingers; and (c) board games with cards (e.g., Leftovers), can also be useful, if children are allowed to devise their own notations to help them (e.g., writing and crossing out numbers). These researchers caution educators about the misuse of manipulatives, such as balances and Unifix Cubes, that can interfere with numerical thinking. They conclude, "In short, the mathematics we want children to learn does not exist *in* manipulatives. It develops as children think, and manipulatives are useful or useless depending on the quality of thinking they stimulate" (p. 30).

Source: After Kamii (2000) and Kamii, Lewis, & Kirkland (2001).

Vygotsky's Theory of Cognitive Development

Lev Vygotsky (1896–1934) was a major figure in Russian psychology. Vygotsky provided a theory of children's development that was greatly influenced by the historical events of his time. Following the Russian Revolution in 1917, leaders of the new Soviet society emphasized the role of each person in transforming society through labor and education. Vygotsky constructed a psychological theory of development that fit the view of this new Soviet state.

Vygotsky's theory stresses relations between the individual and society. He asserted that it is not possible to understand a child's development without some understanding of the culture in which the child is raised. Vygotsky believed that an individual's thinking patterns are not primarily due to innate factors but are products of cultural institutions and social activities. Adult society has a responsibility to share its collective knowledge with younger and less advanced members in order to promote intellectual development. Through social activities, children learn to incorporate cultural tools such as language, counting systems, writing, art, and other social inventions into their thinking. Cognitive development occurs as children internalize the products of their social interactions. According to Vygotsky's theory, both the history of the child's culture and the history of the child's own experiences are important for understanding cognitive development. This tenet in Vygotsky's theory represents a cultural-historical or sociocultural view of children's development. Vygotsky stressed that development could only be understood by looking at the *mutual* influences of individual, interpersonal, and cultural-historical factors on one another (e.g., Rogoff, 2003; Scrimsher & Tudge, 2003).

Vygotsky's career as a psychologist was brief, due to his premature death at age 38 from tuberculosis. During his 10-year career, however, Vygotsky wrote more than 100 books and articles. His most influential book, *Thought and Language,* was not published until the year of his death. From 1936 to 1956, Vygotsky's work was banned in the Soviet Union, because it contained references to Western psychologists. Consequently, Vygotsky's work did not become widely available to researchers until the 1960s, almost 30 years after his death.

In the last two decades, Vygotsky's influence on developmental psychology has steadily grown. His views regarding the social context of learning also have a major impact on educational practices today. See the Focus on Research box, "Learning Arithmetic in Context" on page 166. In the next sections, we consider the major contributions of Vygotsky's theory for understanding children's cognitive development and learning in the classroom.

Key Concepts in Vygotsky's Theory

Social Origins of Thought

Vygotsky is considered one of the earliest critics of Piaget's theory of cognitive development. In Vygotsky's view, knowledge is not individually constructed, as Piaget proposed, but socially *co-constructed* between people as they interact. Social interactions with more knowledgeable peers and adults provide the main vehicles for intellectual development. For Vygotsky, knowledge is not located in the environment nor in the child. Rather, it is situated in a particular social or cultural context. In other words, Vygotsky believed that individual mental processes, such as remembering, problem solving, or planning, have a social origin (Wertsch & Tulviste, 1992).

Focus on
Research

Learning Arithmetic in Context

A group of British and Brazilian researchers studied the computational skills of 9- to 15-year-old street vendors in Brazil. In many Brazilian towns, it is common for younger sons and daughters of street vendors to help their parents at the market. Adolescents may develop their own businesses to sell roasted peanuts, popcorn, coconut milk, or corn on the cob. These researchers found that children and adolescents develop sophisticated arithmetic skills in the context of buying and selling, but they are unable to perform the same mathematical operations when they are presented out of context. For example, a typical interview with a 12-year-old street vendor in the market might go like this (Carraher, Carraher, & Schliemann, 1985):

Customer:	*How much is one coconut?*
Child:	*35 cruzerios.*
Customer:	*I would like ten. How much is that?*
Child:	*(pause) Three will be 105, with three more, that will be 210. (pause) I need four more. That is . . .(pause) 315. I think it is 350.*

After the interviewers posed a number of such questions, the children were given a paper and pencil and asked to solve identical problems. For example, they were asked: $35 \times 10 =$ _____? The math operation that was performed on the street was also represented in a word problem: Each banana costs 12 cruzerios. Mary bought 10 bananas. How much did she pay altogether?

The results of this interesting study showed that when mathematical problems were embedded in real-life contexts (e.g., buying and selling), they were solved at a much higher rate than the same problems presented out of context. Children correctly answered the context-specific question 98 percent of the time. When the same operation was embedded in a word problem, children correctly solved the problem 73 percent of the time. In contrast, children correctly solved the mathematical operation with no context 37 percent of the time.

The results of this study show that context can have an important influence on whether or not children are able to use their existing mathematical knowledge. The children in this study were unable to use the computational strategies they used while selling on the streets for solving problems in school-type situations. This study raises questions about teaching mathematics as a set of conventions and routines that are divorced from children's daily problem-solving activities.

According to Vygotsky, children are born with elementary mental abilities such as perception, attention, and memory. As they interact with more knowledgeable peers and adults, these "innate" abilities are transformed into higher mental functions. More specifically, Vygotsky believed that cognitive development involves the internalization of functions that first occur on what he called a *social plane*. **Internalization** refers to the process of constructing an internal representation of external physical actions or mental operations. James Wertsch (1985) described Vygotsky's ideas about the social origins of cognition in this way:

> An important point to note about Vygotsky's ideas on the social origins of cognition is that it is at this point that he uses the notion of *internalization*. He is not simply claiming that social interaction leads to the development of the child's abilities in problem solving, memory, etc.; rather, he is saying that the *very means* (especially speech) used in social interactions are taken over by the individual child and internalized. Thus, Vygotsky is making a very strong statement here about internalization and the social foundations of cognition. (p. 146; italics added)

A good example of this internalization process may be observed when an adult reads to a young child. For instance, a parent may point to objects on a page and count off "one," "two," "three," and so forth. The next time this parent and child read the book together, the child may point to the pictures and try to count the objects on his or her own. A very young child will have difficulty remembering the order of number tags, so the parent is likely to say the number words too. In the Vygotskian sense, the child is internalizing a way of using numbers to give meaning to a set of objects. When children begin to count off objects in the absence of a parent's prompts or assistance, then they have truly made this external operation their own. The counting operation has become a part of the children's own internal organization, and it is carried out without the support of others.

Tools for Thought

Similar to Piaget's way of thinking, Vygotsky defined cognitive development in terms of qualitative changes in children's thinking processes. However, he described these developmental changes in terms of the technical and psychological tools children use to make sense of their world. Technical tools are generally used to change objects or to gain mastery over the environment, whereas psychological tools are used to organize or control thought and behavior.

In the example described previously, the child is learning to use a counting system as a way of ordering objects. Numbers, words, and other symbol systems are different examples of psychological tools. Other examples include systems of logic, social norms and conventions, theoretical concepts, maps, plans, literary forms, or drawings. Some examples of technical tools include pencil and paper, protractors, machines, scales, hammers, and so on. According to Vygotsky, every culture has its own set of technical and psychological tools that are passed on to children through social interactions. For example, Gauvain (2001) studied how mothers assist their children with using plans or directions that accompany toys and games. These cultural tools in turn shape the mind.

What are some other ways children's thinking is molded by society? In the early 1900s, for instance, mothers taught their daughters to churn butter and to weave cloth by the time they reached puberty. Few young women today learn these skills. Before the availability of inexpensive calculators, students of all ages were required to memorize arithmetic facts, including square roots of numbers. Most schools today allow students to use calculators in mathematics and science classes. Currently, another technological tool, the computer, is becoming more and more common in classroom and home environments. It is interesting to consider how computers are influencing the way children and adolescents think.

Language and Development

For Vygotsky, language is the most important psychological tool influencing children's cognitive development. In Vygotsky's (1962) words, "The child's intellectual development is contingent on mastering the social means of thought, that is, language" (p. 24). He identified three different stages in children's use of language: social, egocentric, and inner speech.

In the first stage, **social speech,** language is used primarily for communicative functions. Thought and language have separate functions. Children enter the next stage of development, **egocentric speech,** when they begin to use speech to regulate their behavior and thinking. For example, many 5- and 6-year-old children talk aloud to themselves as they work on various tasks. Because children are not trying to communicate with others, these self-verbalizations are viewed as private rather than social speech. At this point in development, speech begins to serve an intellectual as well as communicative function. Berk and Garvin (1984) observed the following examples of *private speech* in an Appalachian mission school for low-income children aged 5 to 10 years old.

> [Student] O. Sits down at the art table and says to himself, "I want to draw something. Let's see. I need a big piece of paper. I want to draw my cat."

[Student] C., working in her arithmetic workbook says out loud to no one in particular, "Six." Then counting on her fingers she continues, "Seven, eight, nine, ten. It's ten, it's ten. The answer's ten." (p. 277)

In Vygotsky's last stage of speech development, **inner speech,** children internalize egocentric speech. They use language internally to guide their thinking and behavior. At this stage, children can think about problem solutions and action sequences by manipulating language "in their heads."

Zone of Proximal Development

One of the most important contributions of Vygotsky's theory to psychology and education is the *zone of proximal development.* Vygotsky (1978) was interested in children's *potential* for intellectual growth rather than their *actual* level of development. The **zone of proximal development** includes those functions that are in the process of developing but not yet fully developed.

> The zone of proximal development defines those functions that have not yet matured but are in the process of maturation, functions that will mature tomorrow but are currently in an embryonic state. These functions could be termed the "buds" or "flowers" of development rather than the "fruits" of development. The actual development level characterizes mental development retrospectively, while the zone of proximal development characterizes mental development prospectively. (pp. 86–87)

In practice, the zone of proximal development represents the gap between what children can do on their own and what they can do with the assistance of others, as illustrated in Figure 3.11. For example, a 6-year-old might have difficulty assembling a model airplane alone, but with the assistance and guidance of an older, more experienced sibling, the child can successfully complete the task.

In the example presented at the beginning of the chapter about boiling tap water, the students are acquiring a more sophisticated understanding of their science experiment with the teacher's guidance. Note that the teacher is not telling students what they should learn from the experiment. He is guiding their thinking through the use of questions ("What happens when the water is boiled?") and prompts ("Think about density."). At the end of the discussion, the students can use what they learned from the experiment to make hypotheses about other liquids. As a result, the students are thinking about the experiment at a level that was not evident when they were carrying out the experiment on their own. The kindergarten teacher is also interacting with children to stimulate ideas about learning languages ("How are you learning all these English words now?").

■ FIGURE 3.11
Zone of Proximal Development
Source: After Hamilton & Ghatala (1994).

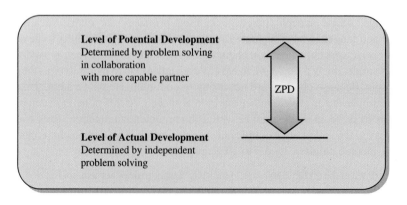

Level of Potential Development
Determined by problem solving in collaboration with more capable partner

ZPD

Level of Actual Development
Determined by independent problem solving

Vygotsky assumed that interactions with adults and peers in the zone of proximal development help children to move to a higher level of functioning. We will examine how adults can help learn from and "build scaffolds" for children when we consider the educational implications of Vygotsky's theory.

Contrasts Between Piaget's and Vygotsky's Theories

There are several important differences in the basic assumptions of Vygotsky's and Piaget's theories. Both theorists agree that knowledge must be mentally constructed by the child, but Vygotsky placed a much stronger emphasis on the role of social interactions in this construction process. To Vygotsky, the construction of knowledge is not an individual process. In James Wertsch's (1999) words, cognition does not only go on "within the skin" (p. 311). Rather, it is primarily a social process in which higher mental functions are products of socially mediated activity. Collaborative learning and problem solving are the main vehicles of cognitive change.

Compared with Piaget, Vygotsky also placed a stronger emphasis on culture in shaping children's cognitive development. As children develop, they learn to use tools for thought that are valued by their culture. There are no universal patterns of development because cultures emphasize different kinds of tools, intellectual skills, and social conventions. The intellectual skills needed for survival in a highly technical society differ from those needed for survival in a largely agrarian society.

Another important difference between Piaget's and Vygotsky's views concerns the importance placed on learning. As we know, Piaget believed that cognitive development limits what children are capable of learning from social experiences. It is not possible to accelerate development through learning experiences. Although Vygotsky (1978) agreed that learning is not the same as development, he argued that "learning is a necessary and universal aspect of the process of developing culturally organized, specifically human, psychological functions" (p. 90). Vygotsky believed instruction (both formal and informal) by more knowledgeable peers or adults is at the heart of cognitive development. Vygotsky believed that learning precedes development.

In addition, Vygotsky's zone of proximal development offers a very different view of readiness than the one provided by Piaget's theory. According to Piaget, children's readiness for learning is defined by their existing level of competence and knowledge. If a teacher attempts to teach a concept or operation before a child is mentally ready, it can result in what Piaget called "empty learning." In contrast, Vygotsky (1978) argued that instruction should be directed toward children's potential level of development, the level of competence they can demonstrate with the assistance and guidance of others. In his words, "The only 'good learning' is that which is in advance of the child's development" (p. 89).

Finally, Vygotsky and Piaget had very different opinions about the role of language in development. In Piaget's view, the egocentric speech of young children reflects the child's inability to take the perspective of others. It plays no useful role in their development. Thinking processes develop from children's actions on objects, not from talking. Vygotsky, on the other hand, thought that egocentric speech is an extremely important developmental phenomenon. He believed that egocentric speech helps children organize and regulate their thinking. When children talk to themselves, they are trying to solve problems and think on their own. According to Vygotsky, egocentric speech, or private speech, is the means by which children move from being regulated by others (other-regulated) to being regulated by their own thinking processes (self-regulated). Egocentric speech has both an intellectual and a self-regulatory function for young children.

Limitations of Vygotsky's Theory

Vygotsky's theory helps us to understand how cognition and learning is a social collaborative process with others (Rogoff, 1998, 2003). This theory represents a radical departure from Piaget's emphasis on cognition as an individual activity, and, as described next, it has important implications for education. Nevertheless, Vygotsky's theory has some important limitations that need to be considered. First, Vygotsky's theory places much less emphasis on physical maturation or innate biological processes than most other developmental theories. We have learned that development involves a complex interaction of genetic and environment influences. Additionally, little attention was given to what is meant by learning and development in this perspective. In Vygotsky's view, development involves changes in the child's participation in social activities; however, the cognitive processes that enable this transformation to occur have not been clearly specified. For example, what cognitive changes enable the child to move from an assisted reader to an independent reader? As discussed in Chapter 5, this transformation involves attention and memory processes, as well as social interactions that support reading efforts.

Current Sociocultural Perspectives

Developmentalists continue to work on a coherent "family" of sociocultural theories and studies inspired by Vygotsky (Rogoff, 2003). These approaches are referred to as sociohistorical, cultural-historical, or cultural-context theories. In the emerging sociocultural perspective, there is agreement that "people contribute to the creation of cultural processes and cultural processes contribute to the creation of people" (Rogoff, 2003, p. 51). According to Barbara Rogoff, this view is complemented by the related theories of John Dewey (introduced in Chapter 1), especially when applied to the understanding of children's development in school. The "community of learners" philosophies and programs (discussed later in the chapter), emphasizing active involvement of children and adults in learning together (collaboration), are rooted in these ideas.

Educational Contributions of Vygotsky's Theory

Vygotsky regarded education as central to the development of children (Moll, 1990). In the introduction to Vygotsky's *Thought and Language* (1962), Jerome Bruner wrote, "Vygotsky's conception of development is at the same time a theory of education" (p. v). Although seven of Vygotsky's first eight writings in psychology (written between 1922 and 1926) addressed educational issues, his work is only beginning to have a significant impact on education in the United States (Moll, 1990; Newman, Griffin, & Cole, 1989; Tharp & Gallimore, 1989). This section examines the educational implications and applications of Vygotsky's theory.

The Role of Private Speech

In Vygotsky's theory, **private speech** serves an important self-regulatory function. It is the means by which children guide their own thinking and behavior. Children engage in overt self-regulatory speech before they use covert, inner speech. As children make this transition in the early grades, they need learning activities that permit them to talk aloud as they are solving problems and completing tasks.

Observations of children in classroom settings provide clear support for Vygotsky's claim that private speech plays an important role in learning. For example, Berk and Garvin (1984) observed the frequency and variety of private speech among 5- to 10-year-olds in a school setting. They observed an average of 30 private utterances per hour. Interestingly, there were no age differences in the quantity of private speech observed, and, for all age groups, private speech increased when students completed cognitively demanding tasks without an adult present. In another study, Berk (1986) observed the frequency of private speech in first- and third-grade mathematics classes. She reported that nearly 98 percent of the children talked aloud to themselves as they worked on math problems. Furthermore, this task-related private speech was positively related to mathematics achievement in the early grades.

As children mature, task-related vocalizations are gradually transformed into quiet whispers until they are internalized as inner speech. Private speech in the form of self-guiding statements or reading aloud declines by the age of 10. However, some studies suggest that older students can continue to benefit from the use of self-instructional strategies, especially if they lack an ability to regulate their behavior or thinking.

Donald Meichenbaum's (1977) program of **cognitive behavior modification** uses self-regulatory speech to help children control and regulate their behavior. Children are taught self-regulatory strategies that can be used as a verbal tool to inhibit impulses, control frustration, and promote reflection. The training program generally begins with an adult performing a task while talking aloud (*cognitive modeling*). Next, a child performs the same task under the guidance of an adult who encourages the child to talk aloud as he or she works on the task (*overt guidance*) and reinforces the child for using the modeled strategies. When children in this program become proficient in the use of cognitive strategies and overt self-instructions, they are encouraged to perform the task while guiding their behavior by way of whispering the instructions to themselves (*faded self-guidance*) or by internal speech (*covert self-instruction*). Following is an example of a training protocol for a line-drawing task that was first modeled by an adult and eventually used by a child (Meichenbaum & Goodman, 1971):

> Okay, what is it that I have to do? You want me to copy the picture with the different lines. I have to go carefully and slowly. Okay, draw the line down, down, good; then to the right, that's it; now down some more and to the left. Good. I'm doing fine so far. Remember, go slowly. Now back up again. No, I was supposed to go down. That's okay. Just erase the line carefully. . . . Good. Even if I make an error I can go on slowly and carefully. I have to go down now. Finished. I did it! (p. 117)

Self-instructional training has been used successfully to improve self-management skills and self-control in impulsive and aggressive children (Camp, Blom, Hebert, & van Doornick, 1977; Manning, 1988; Neilans & Israel, 1981). These techniques also show promise for improving children's writing skills, reading comprehension, and mathematics achievement (Harris & Graham, 1985; Meichenbaum & Asarno, 1978; Schunk & Cox, 1986). In sum, considerable research suggests that private speech is a valuable tool for learning. Because private speech is important for the development of self-regulatory processes, teachers need to model self-instructional strategies and encourage students' use of task-related verbalizations when they are having difficulty in the classroom.

The Importance of Adult Guidance

Vygotsky's theory emphasized the critical role of adults in guiding and supporting children's intellectual development. Through the social guidance provided by others, children can function at a higher level of development, their zone of proximal development. Several researchers have studied the processes by which adults guide children's participation in the zone of proximal development. We will examine two different but closely related conceptions of this social process—guided participation and scaffolding.

Barbara Rogoff (1990) used the term **guided participation** to describe the mutual involvement between children and their social partners in collective activities. Guided participation has three phases: choosing and structuring activities to fit the skills and interests of children, supporting and monitoring children's participation in activities, and adjusting the level of support provided as children begin to perform the activity independently. The goal of guided participation is to transfer responsibility for the task from the skilled partner to the child.

Rogoff and her colleagues (1984) observed many examples of guided participation in a study of mothers assisting 6- and 9- year-old children to perform two different classification tasks in the laboratory. The tasks resembled either a home activity (i.e., sorting food items onto shelves) or a school activity (i.e., sorting photographs of objects into abstract categories). The mothers used a variety of techniques to guide their children's participation in these activities. For example, some mothers connected the food sorting task to putting groceries away at home. Other mothers used subtle gestures (pointing, looking, etc.) and verbal cues to guide their child's participation.

Most significantly, Rogoff and her colleagues found that mothers adjusted their level of support according to their perceptions of the child's ability to handle the task. For example, mothers of 6-year-olds provided more formal instruction in the school task than mothers of 8-year-olds. Age differences in the level of support provided by mothers were less evident in the more familiar home task. In addition, as the children showed they could handle more of the task on their own, the mothers provided less instruction, but when the children began to make errors, this instructional support reappeared. This sensitive adjustment of support is perhaps the most significant aspect of guided participation, because it enables the child to gradually assume more responsibility for managing the activity.

Rogoff's notion of guided participation is closely related to the concept of *scaffolding.* Jerome Bruner and his associates (Wood, Bruner, & Ross, 1976) introduced this term before Vygotsky's work was widely known in the United States. Similar to guided participation, **scaffolding** refers to the process by which adults provide support to a child who is learning to master a task or problem. When adults scaffold a task or problem, they perform or direct those elements of the task that are beyond the child's ability.

Scaffolding can take the form of verbal or physical assistance. For example, a father who is building a birdhouse with his 7-year-old daughter might help guide her hands while she saws and nails the pieces of wood. The daughter is not able to perform these activities on her own, but with her father's assistance, she can participate meaningfully in the activity. At a later point, the father may assist his daughter in another woodworking task by providing verbal reminders ("Remember how I taught you to hold the hammer.") or by providing feedback ("This piece of wood needs to be sanded some more before you paint it."). With practice and time, the daughter will learn to perform woodworking activities more and more independently.

In a classic study, Wood et al. (1976) studied an adult's role in helping a child move from joint to independent problem solving. Female tutors, who were given no special training, were asked to build a pyramid from interlocking wooden blocks with 3-, 4-, and 5-year-old children. By observing this joint problem-solving activity, the researchers identified six important elements of the scaffolding process: recruitment, demonstrating solutions, simplifying the task, maintaining participation, providing feedback, and controlling frustration.

Scrimsher and Tudge (2003) argue, however, that although this scaffolding practice may be effective, it is much more of a teacher-directed approach to teaching and learning than was meant by Vygotsky. Instead, the process of teaching and learning (the Russian term, *obuchenie*) is far more collaborative.

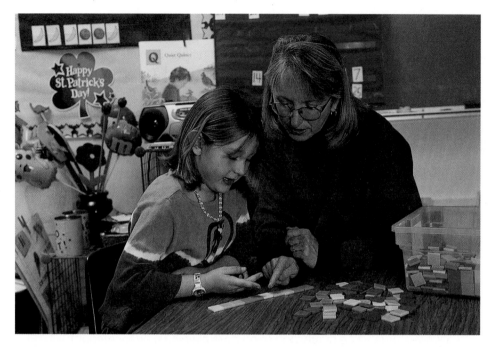

Vygotsky's theory of development emphasizes the importance of adults in guiding and supporting children's learning. Less guidance is needed as children learn to perform activities on their own.
Source: David Young-Wolff/Photo Edit.

> From the teacher's side, this not only involves guidance and careful discernment of what a child knows and needs to know, but also the necessity to learn from the child. From the child's side, there is a history of making sense of the world in a particular way and being motivated to try to understand it better. Teaching/learning that leads to development thus occurs . . . through a collaborative relationship. (pp. 299–300)

One example of a collaborative process in the classroom can be seen in the Kamehameha Elementary Education Program (KEEP; Tharp & Gallimore, 1988). In this program, teachers and students are expected to learn from one another. For example, in reading comprehension lessons, teachers and students engage in **instructional conversations,** a communicative style similar to that of parents and children. Teachers begin with inviting children to relate a text to their own experiences, because KEEP requires that teachers inquire about what children know and listen attentively. (This literacy activity is described in more detail in Chapter 5.) They assist children's learning through the "thoughtful, reflective tailoring of assistance" while engaging in activities and discussions with children; this assistance is provided through a number of means, including those briefly described in Figure 3.12 on page 174.

The following excerpt from an observation of a primary UK teacher and her students illustrates the use of some means of assistance (modeling of scientific processes) while engaged in a "mystery substance" collaborative activity.

Teacher:	What about this stuff?. . .
Child:	It looks like a liquid.
Teacher:	It looks like a liquid? Why does it look like a liquid?
Child:	It's wet.

Means of Assisting Performance

- **Modeling.** The teacher offers behavior for students to imitate through live actions, words, pictures, etc. Cognitive strategies can also be modeled, such as searching a text for evidence that bears on a question, examining the evidence, and drawing a conclusion.

- **Managing contingency.** The teacher offers rewards (e.g., praise) to develop existing behaviors (cannot be used to develop new behaviors).

- **Feeding-back.** The teacher informs students of the quality or accuracy of their learning.

- **Instructing.** In response to student efforts, the teacher tells students what to do next (to move through the zone of proximal development).

- **Questioning.** The teacher asks questions to prompt higher-order thinking, or to direct the course of assistance.

- **Cognitive structuring.** The teacher provides a structure for thought or action (assists students with organizing content or experiences). One type involves organizing perception (e.g., by explaining a phenomenon); another type involves facilitating metacognition (e.g., how to remember, rules for accumulating evidence).

Teacher:	It feels wet.
Child:	It looks like a liquid even though it looks hard.
Child:	It's a bit hard.
Child:	Even though it's sticky.
Teacher:	But you can cut it can't you? Like a solid. . .
Child:	I cut it and then it went back in to the shape.
Teacher:	Oh look! She cut it, but it didn't keep its shape.
Child:	I think it might be a liquid. (Watt, 2002, p. 177)

In summary, the concepts of guided participation, scaffolding, and instructional conversation were inspired by Vygotsky's theory of development. Keep in mind, however, that teachers need to gradually pass more and more control of the activity to the child. By relinquishing control, the teacher learns with children, enabling them to engage in independent and self-regulated learning and "rouses minds to life" (Tharp & Gallimore, 1988).

Reciprocal Teaching

One of the best applications of Vygotsky's theory is the **reciprocal teaching (RT)** model developed by Annemarie Palincsar and Ann Brown (1984). The model was originally designed to help poor readers acquire comprehension skills. In this program, teachers and students take turns being the discussion leader. Through collaborative learning dialogues, children learn how to regulate their own reading comprehension. The reciprocal teaching procedure has been used successfully with both elementary and secondary school students.

The program starts out with adults or teachers serving as the leaders and modeling how to lead the discussion. The leader is responsible for asking questions that require students to summarize material, detect inconsistencies, and make predictions about what will happen next. Students carry out simpler aspects of the task while observing and learning from the adult. As the students develop their comprehension skills, the teacher increases his or her demands, requiring students to participate at slightly more challenging levels. Eventually, students assume the leader's position, and the teacher acts more as a coach than as a model. During the course of training, student questions become more and more sophisticated. The Focus on Research box on page 177 compares the quality of reciprocal teaching dialogue on day 3 and day 13 of the program.

Palincsar and Brown's instructional program incorporates several features of Vygotsky's theory. First, group discussions allow less-competent students to perform at levels slightly above their current level of competence or at their zone of proximal development. Second, the learning situation is carefully scaffolded by the adult. The teacher continues to push for deeper understanding and to provide instructional support for less-able students but then "fades into the background when students demonstrate they can take over" (Brown & Campione, 1990, p. 119). Finally, the meaning of the text is socially negotiated and constructed in the context of group discussions.

Early studies reported by Palincsar and Brown (1984) indicate that the reciprocal teaching procedure leads to substantial improvements in seventh-grade students' comprehension skills. Additionally, the students maintained the effects of the program for at least 8 weeks. Even more important, the training generalized to other subject areas. The students who participated in the program showed a better understanding of the science and social studies materials they read in their classroom. Thus, the internalization of strategies learned in the reciprocal teaching program allowed students to better monitor and regulate their comprehension in other learning situations as well.

In a more recent review of research with at-risk readers in grades 1 through 8, Brown (1997) reported that in study after study, participants in RT groups improved their abilities to comprehend text, and even maintained their advantages after a year. These RT practices are now incorporated as reading components within larger programs referred to as Fostering Communities of Learners (FCL). FCL classrooms incorporate four major underlying ideas: (a) *agency,* taking control of one's thinking; (b) *reflection,* making sense of what one learns (metacognition); (c) *collaboration,* sharing resources with others; and (d) *culture,* intentionally designing classroom environments (the way of life) to foster community (e.g., Bruner, 1996). These ideas are explained in more detail in Chapter 4. The purpose of these programs is to help children "think deeply about serious matters" (Brown, 1997, p. 399) based on what is known about development of children's thinking in the domains educators wish to foster.

The Role of Peer Interactions

Both Piaget and Vygotsky emphasized the importance of peers in children's cognitive development. Following Piaget's theory, children can influence each other's cognitive development when they say or do something that is in conflict with the other child's thinking. Cognitive conflict leads children to restructure their thinking (*accommodate*) in order to restore a balance (*equilibration*). By comparison, researchers examining peer interactions from a Vygotskian perspective have argued that children influence each other's development through the process of collaboration (Tudge & Rogoff, 1989). The following example illustrates how one student can help guide the thinking of another student while working on a lever task in fifth-grade science.

Vygotsky's theory emphasizes the importance of collaborative learning experiences with peers.
Source: Creatas/Jupiterimages.

Hank:	Ready? Do you want to hold the lever?
Lester:	Yeah.
Hank:	Now, let's wait a sec. Let's make sure that we're setting everything up right. Now, that [spring scale] goes on the 4 and the block goes on 5. [Lester begins adjusting the scale.]
Hank:	I'll tell you when it's level. You just have to pull. You have to pull real hard. OK. A little bit more, pull a little bit more. OK, stop. You got it. Great. (Jones & Carter, 1994, pp. 613–614)

From a Vygotskian perspective, collaborative problem solving among peers offers some of the same experiences for children as adult–child interactions. When children work jointly on problems, they must come to some mutual understanding of the problem, procedures, and solution. Children use speech to guide each other's activities, and these social interactions are gradually internalized as tools for regulating independent problem-solving efforts in the future.

To study the processes by which peers influence learning and development, Jonathan Tudge (1993) paired nonconservers with conservers on a mathematical balance beam problem. The results showed that the less competent partner improved significantly on the balance beam task when paired with a peer who could reason about the problem at a more advanced level. This study also suggested that the less competent partner needed to adopt the reasoning of the more competent partner while performing the task. That is, mere exposure to a higher level of thinking did not lead to improvements in the less competent partner's use of problem-solving rules. Of even greater importance was the finding that there were some circumstances under which children's thinking may be adversely affected by a peer. This decline is most likely to occur when children are not provided any feedback

UNDERSTANDING
CHILDREN
*Strategy 4.12:
Instructional
Interactions with
Teachers and Students.*

Examples of Reciprocal Teaching Dialogue: Day 3 and Day 13 of Training

Day 3

TEXT (read silently):
Can Snakes Sting with their Tongues? No—snakes' tongues are completely harmless. They're used for feeling things and for sharpening the snakes' sense of smell. Although snakes can smell in the usual way, the tongue flickering in the air picks up tiny particles of matter. These particles are deposited in two tiny cavities at the base of the nostrils to increase the snake's ability to smell.

1. A: Do snakes' tongues sting?
2. K: Sometimes.
3. A: Correct. This paragraph is about do snakes sting with their tongue, and different ways that the tongue is used and the senses of smell.
4. T: Are there any questions?
5. C: Snakes' tongues don't sting.
6. T: Beautiful! I thought, boy, I must have been doing some fast reading there because I missed that point. A, could you ask your question again?
7. A: Do snakes' tongues really sting?
8. T: Now, A, since you have asked the question, can you find in that paragraph where the question is answered?
9. A: No, snakes' tongues are completely harmless.
10. T: So we'll try again. Can you generate another question that you think a teacher might ask?

Source: After Palincsar & Brown (1984).

11. A: What are the tongues used for?
12. T: Good!

Day 13

TEXT (read silently):
The second oldest form of salt production is mining. Unlike early methods that made the work extremely dangerous and difficult, today's methods use special machinery, and salt mining is easier and safer. The old expression "back to the salt mine" no longer applies.

1. L: Name two words that often describe mining salt in the old days.
2. K: Back to the salt mines?
3. L: No. Angela?
4. A: Dangerous and difficult.
5. L: Correct. This paragraph is about comparing the old mining of salt and today's mining of salt.
6. T: Beautiful.
7. L: I have a prediction to make.
8. T: Good.
9. L: I think it might tell when salt was first discovered, well, it might tell what salt is made of and how it's made.
10. T: O.K. Can we have another leader?

L = Indicates discussion leader
T = Indicates adult teacher
A, B, C, K, and L are seventh-grade students with reading comprehension skills 2 years below grade level.

---

after working on a problem or when they are not confident about their reasoning. Under these conditions, children's thinking may be negatively influenced by social interactions that are slightly behind their current level of thinking (Tudge, 1993).

Although Tudge's study provides support for Vygotsky's ideas about the cognitive benefits of peer interactions, it also suggests that teachers need to carefully structure the conditions under which children work together. In a review of Vygotskian research related to the effects of peer interactions on development, Tudge and Rogoff (1989) conclude:

1. Young children may show limited cognitive benefits from peer interactions, because they are unable to provide each other the type of scaffolded assistance or guidance that older children and adults can provide.

Focus on
Teaching

Applying Piaget's and Vygotsky's Theories in the Classroom

Applications of Piaget's Theory

- Provide opportunities for play.
- Provide opportunities for students to communicate through symbols—art, writing, drama, mathematical formulas, and so on.
- Provide a range of real-world experiences to serve as foundations for building new concepts, and provide opportunities for children to choose activities of interest to them.
- For young learners, use concrete objects, visual aids, and other teaching tools (e.g., videotapes, counters) for teaching abstract and unfamiliar concepts.
- Provide opportunities for students to explore, experiment, apply knowledge, and engage in hands-on learning.
- Ask students to explain their reasoning and help them to find inconsistencies. Suggest alternative explanations to consider.
- Provide opportunities for students to express opinions, discuss, debate, and receive feedback from peers.

Applications of Vygotsky's Theory

- Use guided participation in which students can be apprentices in learning. Use modeling and verbal cues to guide students' learning, gradually giving the students more responsibility for carrying out the learning activity on their own.
- Model "thinking aloud" when problem solving with students, and encourage students to "talk themselves" through challenging problems.
- Provide opportunities for students to collaborate on learning activities together. Peers are important role models for problem solving, and learning is facilitated when there are opportunities to explain ideas and resolve controversies with other students. Interactions with equal or more skilled peers have the most positive benefits.
- Engage in learning and assessment activities within the *zone of proximal development*. Provide sufficient instructional supports (cues, suggestions, assistance) for performing challenging tasks. Gradually withdraw support when students are able to perform tasks their own.

2. Adult–child interactions may be more beneficial than peer interactions when children are first learning new skills or concepts.
3. Peer interactions are most effective when partners must achieve a shared understanding of a topic or problem and work toward a shared goal.

Studies of school-age children's behaviors while constructing a board game together indicate that effective peer interactions (in terms of evolving game complexity) are also somewhat dependent on children's abilities to coordinate their own and others' perspectives (Bearison & Dorval, 2002). These researchers, along with others, note that these interactions can be explained by complementary notions proposed by Piaget and Vygotsky.

Putting Piaget's and Vygotsky's Theories Together: Construction and Collaboration

We have examined important distinctions between Piaget's and Vygotsky's theories; now it is time to consider some common themes in this last section. As we have discussed, both theories serve as the foundation for constructivist approaches in education. The Focus on Teaching box on page 178 presented some ways the two theories can be applied in the classroom. Piaget and Vygotsky both believed that cognitive development involved changes in children's abilities to represent knowledge in terms of more abstract forms such as symbols, logical rules, principles, concepts, and so forth. Both theorists also emphasize that children are not passive recipients of knowledge and recognized the value of play and activity for cognitive development. Piaget focused on how children constructed knowledge by ordering, transforming, and reorganizing existing knowledge, whereas Vygotsky described how children constructed internal representations of mental operations learned through social interactions with adults and peers. Shayer (2003) contends that Piaget and Vygotsky had reached almost identical positions regarding child development in his provocative article titled, "Not Just Piaget, not Just Vygotsky, and Certainly Not Vygotsky as Alternative to Piaget." Other developmentalists would not make quite so bold a claim, but do recognize their compatibility (e.g., DeVries, 2000; Miller, 2002). Both theories maintain that teachers serve as important organizers, stimulators, guides, and supporters of learning. Constructivist educators often take advantage of both Piaget's and Vygotsky's thinking, in conjunction with recent research findings on the development of conceptual thinking and everyday cognition, to guide their practice.

Learning Communities for Children and Educators

Many developmentalists, from constructivist and sociocultural perspectives, criticize the current organization of most schools based on the "factory" or "assembly-line" model of instruction (e.g., Cole, Cole, & Lightfoot, 2005; Dewey, 1916; Rogoff, Paradise, Arauz, Correa-Chavez, & Angelillo, 2003; Rogoff, Turkanis, & Bartlett, 2001; Tharp & Gallimore, 1988), based to some extent on behaviorist views of development (see Chapter 1). Characteristics of this model include: (a) segregating children from the daily activities of the adults in their community; (b) isolating skills from their use in daily or productive activities; (c) grouping large numbers of children by age to provide standard instruction in a steplike progression, usually by a single adult (teacher); and (d) attempting to motivate children by grading their performance (e.g., Rogoff et al., 2001). Even the physical arrangements of typical classrooms across the world look similar, with the teacher standing at the front or sitting at a desk facing children sitting in parallel rows. These arrangements, combined with assumption that the teacher is the primary authority figure with the goal to transmit information to children, lead to a method of communicating that is unusual outside of school (although it is sometimes used). This method is sometimes referred to as *instructional discourse;* a common form is the *recitation script* in which the teacher initiates an exchange by asking a question, one student replies, and the teacher provides feedback (Cole et al., 2005; Rogoff et al., 2003). This school-based way of communicating may be especially foreign to children from some cultural groups (see further discussion in Chapter 5).

The assembly-line form of instruction contrasts with collaborative approaches practiced in innovative schools, such as those espoused by John Dewey (1916). Collaborative approaches are characterized by children's *intent participation,* in which they "observe and listen with intent concentration and initiative, and their collaborative participation is expected when they are ready to help in shared endeavors" (Rogoff et al., 2003, p. 176). A comparison of these major traditions by Rogoff and her colleagues is shown in Figure 3.13 on page 180.

■ FIGURE 3.13

Comparison of Approaches for Organizing Learning
Source: After Rogoff, et al. (2003).

	Intent Participation Community of Learners	Assembly-line Instruction
Participation Structure	Collaborative, horizontal with flexible responsibilities	Hierarchical, with fixed roles
Roles	Experienced people guide while participating	Experts manage and divide tasks, without participating; learners receive info
Learning	Occurs through observation during participation in shared endeavors	Occurs through lessons, exercises, outside of purposeful endeavors
Motivation	Inherent in importance of activity; steps related to purpose understood	Connected to extrinsic rewards, threats; purpose of steps is often unknown
Communication	Occurs through joint action, words, and gestures about needed information	Occurs mainly in words; questions to quiz learners
Assessment	Occurs during shared endeavors to aid learning	Occurs separately from learning, to test receipt of information

From their viewpoint, these traditions are not completely separate from one another, and constructivist educational practices share more features with the intent participation form, and recitation practices with the assembly-line form.

Rogoff and classroom teachers Bartlett and Turkanis (2001) describe collaborative practices in an innovative public elementary school, referred to as "the OC" in their book *Learning Together: Child and Adults in a School Community.* Characteristics of the learning environment in this school include multiage classrooms, integrated curriculum generated by the needs and interests of students, and use of parents (and students) as co-educators. Teachers use the state curriculum as a general guide for highlighting the concepts children learn, but learning in the classroom goes beyond these guidelines, focusing on "Big Ideas." Big Ideas connect across the curriculum and involve understanding patterns in the world and ways of learning about them, such as *learning involves problem solving* (in academic and interpersonal domains), and language, mathematics, and science are ways of *communicating about ideas.* The book provides details about how such a learning community is created. Many similar constructivist and collaborative approaches are currently being implemented in public and private schools, as well as in after-school programs, museums, parks, and other learning environments. For example, Fusco (2001) investigated how adolescents in an urban after-school program learned about the process and relevance of science through their creation of a garden for the community.

Central to the community of learners approach is the pursuit of real-world questions based on children's existing understandings. This means that educators must attend carefully to children's behavior and development, as the teachers in the introductory vignettes showed us. Japanese educators make this a priority in their collaborative observations and discussions about "live" classroom lessons, such as a science activity involving lifting a heavy weight (Lewis, Perry, & Murata, 2006). As one teacher explained, the primary benefit of these lesson studies was "developing the eyes to see children" (Lewis, et al., 2006, p. 7). This chapter focused on "seeing" the cognitive development of children and adolescents through the eyes of two keen observers, Piaget and Vygotsky.

■ Chapter Summary

Constructive Approaches to Education

■ Piaget's and Vygotsky's theories of cognitive development provide the psychological foundations for constructivist approaches to teaching and learning.

■ Piaget argued that cognitive development involves major transformations in the way knowledge is organized. Vygotsky believed that cognitive development represents changes in the cultural tools children use to make sense of their world.

Piaget's Theory of Cognitive Development

■ Piaget proposed that two basic principles guide children's intellectual development: organization and adaptation. As children mature, their knowledge schemes are integrated and reorganized into more complex systems that are better adapted to their environment. Adaptation of knowledge schemes occurs through the process of assimilation and accommodation.

■ Piaget proposed that development follows an invariant sequence. The early childhood years are characterized by two stages. During the sensorimotor period, children acquire schemes for goal-directed behavior and object permanence. In the preoperational stage, children begin to use words, numbers, gestures, and images to represent objects in their environment.

■ The elementary and secondary school years are characterized by two additional stages. During the concrete operational stage, children begin to use mental operations to think about events and objects in their environment. The mental operations that appear in this stage are classification, seriation, and conservation. In the last stage of cognitive development, formal operations, adolescents and adults can think about abstract objects, events, and concepts. They develop the ability to use propositional logic, inductive and deductive logic, and combinatorial reasoning. Formal operational thinkers are also able to reflect on their own thinking processes.

■ Core-knowledge theories share some constructivist principles with Piagetian theory, but differ in beliefs about how children develop understandings of important domains of knowledge (e.g., psychology, physics, biology) early in life and separately from one another.

■ Neo-Piagetian theories have attempted to add greater specificity to Piaget's theory, while maintaining its basic assumptions that cognitive development is qualitative and stagelike. Neo-Piagetian theorists examine the role of children's information processing capabilities in explaining developmental changes.

■ Piaget's theory and other constructivist approaches have inspired major curriculum reforms, and they continue to have an important influence on education practice today. Among Piaget's major contributions to education are the ideas that (a) knowledge must be actively constructed by the child; (b) educators should help children learn how to learn; (c) learning activities should be matched to the child's level of conceptual development; and (d) peer interactions play an important role in the child's cognitive development. Piaget's theory also emphasizes the role of teachers in the learning process as organizers, collaborators, stimulators, and guides.

Vygotsky's Theory of Cognitive Development

■ When compared with Piaget, Vygotsky places a stronger emphasis on social interactions. Knowledge is not individually constructed, but co-constructed between two people. Remembering, problem solving, planning, and abstract thinking have a social origin.

■ In Vygotsky's theory, elementary cognitive functions are transformed into higher mental functions through interactions with more knowledgeable adults and peers. Internalization refers to the process of constructing an internal (cognitive) representation of physical actions or mental operations that first oc-cur in social interactions. Through internalizing elements of social interactions, children develop ways of regulating their own behavior and thinking.

■ Vygotsky described developmental changes in children's thinking in terms of the cultural tools they use to make sense of their world. Technical tools are generally used to change objects or to gain mastery over the environment, whereas psychological tools are used to organize behavior or thought. Vygotsky be-lieved that language was the most important psychological tool that influences children's cognitive de-velopment. The history of both the culture and the child's experiences are important for understanding cognitive development.

■ Vygotsky used the term *zone of proximal development* to refer to the difference between what children can do on their own and with the assistance of others. If an adult or peer carefully provides an appropri-ate level of support and guidance, children are generally able to perform at a higher level than they can perform at on their own. Vygotsky assumed that interactions with adults and peers in the zone of prox-imal development help children move to higher levels of mental functioning.

■ Vygotsky's writings are beginning to have a major impact on education in the United States. Among the major educational contributions of Vygotsky's theory are the role of private speech in cognitive development, the importance of guided participation, and the role of peer interactions in cognitive development.

Putting Piaget's and Vygotsky's Theories Together: Construction and Collaboration

■ Constructivist and sociocultural perspectives, inspired by Piaget and Vygotsky, shape many current prac-tices and proposals for improving teaching and learning in schools. This influence is seen vividly in "community of learners" programs.

■ Key Terms

accommodation *(p. 132)*
adaptation *(p. 132)*
animism *(p. 139)*
assimilation *(p. 132)*
circular reactions *(p. 134)*
centration *(p. 143)*
classification *(p. 145)*
cognitive behavior modification
    (p. 171)
collective monologues *(p. 142)*
combinatorial reasoning *(p. 152)*
concrete operations *(p. 144)*
conservation *(p. 147)*
constructivist approach *(p. 129)*
core knowledge *(p. 158)*
deferred imitation *(p. 136)*
egocentricism *(p. 142)*
egocentric speech *(p. 167)*

equilibration *(p. 132)*
formal operations *(p. 149)*
guided participation *(p. 172)*
hierarchical classification
    (p. 146)
horizontal decalage *(p. 149)*
hypothetico-deductive thinking
    (p. 151)
inner speech *(p. 168)*
instructional conversations *(p. 173)*
internalization *(p. 166)*
intuitive theories *(p. 139)*
logico-mathematical knowledge
    (p. 131)
matrix classification *(p. 145)*
metacognition *(p. 142)*
neo-Piagetian theories *(p. 157)*
object permanence *(p. 135)*

physical knowledge *(p. 130)*
preoperational stage *(p. 136)*
private speech *(p. 170)*
propositional logic *(p. 150)*
realism *(p. 141)*
reciprocal teaching (RT) *(p. 174)*
reflective abstraction *(p. 131)*
representational thinking *(p. 136)*
scaffolding *(p. 172)*
schemes *(p. 130)*
sensorimotor stage *(p. 134)*
seriation *(p. 145)*
social constructivist *(p. 129)*
social knowledge *(p. 131)*
social speech *(p. 167)*
zone of proximal development
    (p. 168)

■ Activities

1. Piaget used many different tasks to study children's logic while performing operations such as seriation, classification, and conservation. The purpose of this activity is to examine how elementary school children of different ages perform Piagetian tasks. Three simple tasks are described next. Using these tasks, individually test two kindergartners and two third graders, and then compare their responses. Be sure to ask children to explain their responses, to get at their logic and reasoning. If you do these activities at school, you will need the teacher's permission. After collecting your data, answer the following questions: (a) Which tasks were the kindergarten and third-grade children able to solve correctly? (b) How do the kindergarten children's responses reflect the limitations of preoperational thinking? (c) What types of cognitive operations did the third-grade students use in solving the problems? (d) How did your observations help you understand Piaget's theory of cognitive development?

Task 1: Seriation

Use 5 to 10 sticks or strips of paper that vary in length from 1 to 10 inches. Begin by asking students to place 3 sticks in order, then 5 sticks, and add 2 more sticks until the student is unable to perform the task. Be sure to mix up the sticks each time, and record the students' responses.

Task 2: Conservation of Number

Use 12 coins of the same denomination (all pennies or dimes). Place six coins in one row about a half inch apart, and place the other six coins below the first row. Ask the students if the number of coins in each row is the same or different, and then ask, "How do you know?" Next, spread out the coins in the first row, so that each coin is several inches from the others. Ask the students again if the number of coins in each row is the same or different. Again ask, "How do you know?" and record the students' responses.

Task 3: Multiple Classification

Cut out geometric shapes (triangles, squares, and circles) from red, blue, and yellow construction paper (three colors per shape). Ask the students to sort the cutouts that go together into different piles. Record how the students sort the cutouts. Now, ask the students if there is another way the cutouts can be sorted, and record how they do the second sort.

2. Observe two or three small groups of children working on a common task. Record the way in which the children help one another to perform the task. After completing your observations, answer the following questions.

   a. Did you see evidence of the students directing, monitoring, or assisting one another?

   b. How did the children negotiate roles? Did one student assume responsibility for leading the activity?

   c. Did you see evidence of scaffolding by the children or teacher? If so, describe some examples of this scaffolding.

   d. How did this activity help you understand Vygotsky's concept of the zone of proximal development?

3. Obtain permission to observe an elementary or secondary classroom (any subject) in a local school. Observe three to four lessons in each classroom, and identify the questions or problems that pose difficulty for the students. Describe the problems in your observational notes. After collecting your observations, use Piaget's theory of cognitive development to analyze the problems students encountered in their lessons. Use the following questions to analyze your notes:

   a. How are the problems related to limitations in the students' concrete or formal operational thinking?

   b. What type of instructional support or scaffolding was available to help students when they were having difficulty?

   c. How did this observation help you understand different aspects of concrete or formal operational thinking?

4. To assess students' formal operational thinking, individually test two middle school students and two high school students using the Piagetian tasks described next. Be sure to use mixed-gender groups at each level. Ask students to think aloud as they do the problems, and record their responses. If you do these tasks in a local school,

you will need the teacher's permission. After collecting your data, answer the following questions:

a. How did the students approach each task? Did they have a systematic plan that considered all possible solutions or combinations. In task 1, did they systematically manipulate each variable and test its effect?

b. What differences did you observe between the responses of the younger and older adolescents? Did you see evidence of formal operational reasoning in either group, both groups, or neither group of adolescents? Do your observations support Piaget's theory?

c. Did you find evidence of gender differences in students' responses? How would you account for these findings?

Task 1: Pendulum Problem

For this task, you will need three different lengths of string and four different weights that can be attached to the string. Instruct your students to experiment with the string and weights in order to determine which variable(s) makes the pendulum go faster or slower. They should consider four variables: the length of the string, the different weights, the force of the initial push, and the height at which they let go of the pendulum.

Task 2: Sandwich Combinations

For this task, you need to write on a piece of paper four different breads (white, rye, sourdough, and wheat), four different meats (ham, beef, turkey, and salami), and four different spreads (mayonnaise, mustard, butter, and ketchup). For each sandwich, they can only use one bread, one meat, and one spread. Ask your students to figure out how many different sandwich combinations they can make. The students may want to use pencil and paper for this task.

Cognitive Development: Information Processing and Intelligence Theories

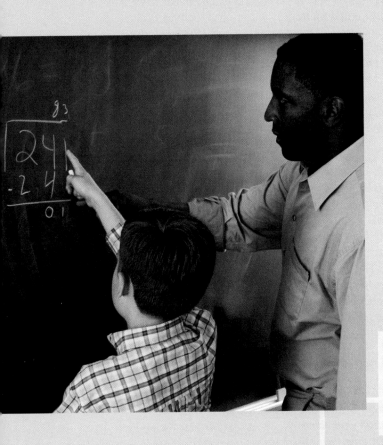

T
HE FOLLOWING EXCERPTS ARE ADAPTED FROM AN ONGOING *conversation between a teacher and her second-grade students about learning science.*

Teacher:	What's the best way to learn about science?
Child:	Have a science instructor.
Child:	Science projects.
Child:	I like to see pictures . . . not just people telling. And it is neat how people can share ideas. Like, some of my friends have weird ideas. Ulp! I don't mean they're stupid. I think they are silly, but then I think about it, and it makes sense.
Child:	Read books.
Child:	Have a scientist here.
Child:	Have a movie.
Child:	We could have an hour or 30 minutes and **do** things about science. Then we can write about it and tell it.
Child:	I think we should do experiments . . .
Teacher:	How would you do experiments?
Child:	We could have a center and probably make a book about it.
Child:	We could get paper and everyone can make a picture of what happens. [Model making is proposed.]
Child:	I'm putting together a Challenger [space shuttle] kit. It really helps me understand the engine and how it works . . .
Teacher:	What is science?
Child:	Learning.
Child:	Science is what you're thinking about and what you discover.
Child:	You go on trips and try to see what happens . . . you put a straw in water and . . .
Child:	One thing I like in science is things from the past.
Child:	Maybe we can put all the information in the computer.
Teacher:	How will you know if the information is accurate?
Child:	Get different books and read them and get models and compare.
Child:	Why would you want to go to more than one thing?
Child:	Computers don't know everything.
Child:	To see if everyone thinks the same thing, and if they do, it's probably true.
Teacher:	Should I teach science like reading?
Children:	NO.
Child:	We should really do it in life. . . . Scientists aren't inside doing worksheets. They are out in the world finding things.
Teacher:	Do scientists write things?
Child:	They write after their experiments.
Teacher:	So you want to write afterward?
Child:	We could write lists of what we want to do and then do them and then write it . . . and then tell it.
Teacher:	Sometimes writing things down means you don't forget.
Child:	And you could keep those ideas and that would tell you what children think about.

Source: From John Nicholls & Susan Hazzard, Education as Adventure: Lessons From Second Grade, *New York: Teachers College Press, 2001 (p. 92–93).*

This classroom conversation illustrates an important aspect of children's cognitive development—their developing (metacognitive) abilities to reflect on thinking and learning, including their memory limitations and use of effective learning strategies. Assuming their interests and emerging abilities, the teacher was able to engage children in a preliminary discussion about a complex topic: the learning of science.

How do children develop specific mental processes and abilities? How do students become independent learners? How are individual differences in students' mental abilities assessed? Are some students naturally more able than others? If not, what explains variations in children's cognitive development? These questions are the focus of this chapter. We will examine the contributions of information processing and intelligence theories to research on children's development. If you recall, neither Piaget nor Vygotsky provided a fine-grain analysis of a child's cognitive system. The two theories described in this chapter help specify the cognitive processes and mental abilities children use to make sense of their world.

The chapter begins with a discussion of information processing theories. This perspective focuses on developmental changes in children's attention, memory, problem-solving skills, knowledge base, and metacognitive skills. As students progress in school, greater demands are placed on them to remember large amounts of information, to recall it quickly and effortlessly, and to learn independently. Information processing theories can help teachers understand the limitations, constraints, and potential of a child's information processing system. It can also help teachers identify learning difficulties that involve problems in attention, memory, and information retrieval.

 # Information Processing Theories

In the last 30 years, information processing theories have become the leading strategy for studying children's cognitive development (Klahr & MacWhinney, 1998). These theories claim that cognitive development involves changes in content, structure, and processing of information. This approach to studying cognition was greatly influenced by advances in computer technology in the early 1960s. With the invention of digital computers, psychologists began to view the human mind as a symbol-manipulating system. Like computers, people must manipulate symbols and transform inputs into outputs. Both computers and people are limited with regard to the amount of information they can attend to, process, and act on at one time. Not all information processing theorists use computer processing as a metaphor for explaining mental activity in the same way (as depicted in the model in Chapter 1). However, these theorists share the assumption that thinking involves active processing of information, and try to explain exactly how thinking processes work, step by step, in particular situations (online functioning). Developmentalists also try to explain how children's processes advance with age and how they are limited. In other words, they are interested in discovering "both how children of given ages have come as far as they have and why they have not gone further" (Siegler, 1998, p. 64). In this view, children develop cognitive abilities as they gradually overcome processing limitations (e.g., speed, memory capacity) and think or solve problems more efficiently (with new knowledge and strategies).

First, we look at the fixed structure (organization) and components of the information processing system that influence thinking in almost all situations and determine its limits. Then we describe some of the means or specific mental processes that are used more variably by individuals in particular situations, allowing them to flexibly respond to their environments.

Structure and Components of the Information Processing System

Information processing theorists focus on the flow of information through the cognitive system. The basic structures and processes included in most information processing models were described in Chapter 1. The information processing system begins with inputs into the cognitive system from any of the sense modalities, such as the ears, the eyes, and the fingers. This information is retained for a very brief period of time—only a few milliseconds—in the **sensory memory.** There is a separate sensory register for each sense. Information will be lost from the system unless it is recognized or interpreted. We often use previously learned information to interpret or make sense of sensory inputs.

Once information is interpreted, it passes into **short-term memory,** a component of the information processing system that holds information while we consciously work on it some more. The fact that information in short-term memory is consciously manipulated in some way has led some researchers to refer to this structure as *working memory.* Adults can store a limited amount of information, perhaps five to nine pieces of information, for 15 to 30 seconds in short-term memory. Because short-term memory has a limited capacity, a person must perform certain cognitive operations on new information in order to remember it for a longer period of time. For example, we can generally remember a phone number for more than 30 seconds if we repeat it over and over. We may be able to remember this information still longer if we can form a mental image of it or relate it to existing information, such as the year of an important event or a birthday.

Information that is transformed or organized in some way moves into **long-term memory.** This component of the cognitive system has a large capacity and presumably stores information indefinitely. During retrieval, information from sensory memory and long-term memory may be brought together in working memory to perform various cognitive and problem-solving activities. For example, an adolescent may recall previous car problems as he or she attempts to diagnose a strange engine noise. In other words, "what we remember is what we understand and retrieval means reconstructing that understanding" (Kuhn, 2000, p. 22).

An alternative model is the level-of-processing theory. Rather than focusing on different types of memory stores (sensory registers, short-term memory, long-term memory), this theory proposes that differences in the level or amount of information processing determines how long and how well it will be remembered (Craik & Lockart, 1972). When information is processed at the shallow level, little mental energy is expended and, consequently, it will be remembered for only a short time. Skimming or repeating information is an example of shallow processing. In contrast, when considerable mental effort is expended organizing or altering information in a way that makes it more meaningful, it is processed at a deeper level and is generally remembered longer. Organizing information into categories or separating it into manageable chunks as we do with phone numbers is an example of deep processing. According to the level-of-processing model, what is remembered is determined by the amount of mental effort expended and by the kinds of operations applied to it.

Developmental Processes

The digit-span task is widely used to estimate children's working memory capacities. An adult reads a random set of numbers (e.g., 7-2-10-8-1-3-9) to the child at a rate of one per second. The child is then asked to repeat the sequence in the same order. Depending on the child's age, the adult would begin with a three-digit sequence and add a digit until the

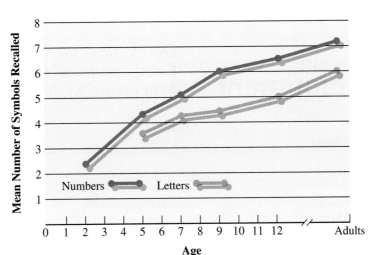

■ FIGURE 4.1
*Improvement with Age
in Memory Span
for Numbers and Letters*
Source: After Dempster (1981).

child's limit is reached. Figure 4.1 shows how children's improvement on the digit-span task improves with age. In general, memory-span studies show that the average 4- or 5-year-old can repeat about four items, the average 9- or 10-year-old can repeat six, and the average adult can repeat seven items (e.g., Schneider & Pressley, 1997). Like memory capacity, processing speed also develops with age. On a variety of cognitive tasks (e.g., naming objects), 4- and 5-year-old children are generally one-third as fast as adults, and 8- and 9-year-olds are about half as fast as adults (Kail, 2000).

What explains this improvement? Does the physical size of children's storage structures expand so they can store more information? Using the computer analogy, the hypothesis implies that cognitive development represents improvements in children's "hardware." That is, children acquire a larger and faster central processing unit. A second hypothesis is that older children have developed better procedures for processing and storing information. In computer terminology, they acquire more sophisticated "software" to run the information processing system. Recent studies indicate that how efficiently one processes information *is* critical for the development of working memory and thinking (Demetriou, Christou, Spanoudis, & Platsidou, 2002).

Although theorists are not yet able to rule out biological explanations, most of the research in the last 20 years has focused on developmental changes in the strategies and knowledge children apply to information. The following sections examine developmental changes in attention, memory, content knowledge, metacognition, and learning strategies. The Focus on Development box on page 190 summarizes the developmental changes that take place in three aspects of the information processing system.

Development of Attention

Early theories defined attention in terms of a general mental capacity of the child (Gibson & Rader, 1979). The term *attention span* is often used in this regard. Studies indicate that attention span increases during the preschool years (Ruff, Capozzoli, & Weissberg, 1998). For example, research on the television program *Sesame Street* has revealed significant improvements in children's attention from 1 to 4 years of age (Anderson & Levin, 1976). This research further suggests that children's attention is highly variable. That is, children's attention to *Sesame Street* was greater in the presence of some program features (e.g., women, puppets, and animation) and lower in the presence of others (e.g., adult men, animals, and

Focus on
Development

Developmental Changes in Components of Information Processing System

Source of Development	Early Childhood	Middle Childhood	Adolescence
Attention Processes	Focus on salient features of objects. Experience difficulty distinguishing between relevant and irrelevant information.	Selective attention develops. Focus on central information. Gradual automatization of basic skills and information.	Ability to divide attention between more than one activity at the same time. Strategic use of attention strategies.
Memory Strategies	Use memory scripts and simple rudimentary strategies.	Acquisition and increasing use of organization and rehearsal strategies.	Use elaboration strategies and more strategic use of memory strategies. Able to retrieve information from memory with fewer prompts.
Metacognition	Little knowledge of learning and memory processes.	Understand that memory is limited. Begin to use strategies to increase comprehension and retention of information.	Better able to reflect on learning processes and to effectively apply metacognitive knowledge.

still drawings). In addition, children were less attentive when attractive toys were placed in the room or the program content was too abstract. The research on *Sesame Street* illustrates how difficult it is to draw any firm conclusions about how long children can attend at a given age, because so much depends on the nature of the stimulus object, the child's physical and motivational state, and the surrounding circumstances.

Current research no longer defines attention as a general mental capacity but, rather, as a set of behaviors and processes. Good attention involves perceiving what is relevant to the task at hand (Gibson & Radar, 1979). From this perspective, it would be a mistake to define attention solely as some mental capacity of the child. Attention involves "extracting information from ongoing events in an active, selective, and economical way" (Gibson & Radar, 1979, p. 3).

Developmental changes primarily involve learning how to make better and more efficient use of existing perceptual and attentional processes. Some of the more important changes include the ability to make fine discriminations between stimulus objects, the development of automaticity and selective attention, and the ability to exert control over attentional processes. Consistent with the definition of attention presented here, most learners are able to deploy their attention in a planned, strategic, and efficient manner and inhibit irrelevant information by adolescence.

For example, in order to learn numbers and letters, children must be able to compare symbols in terms of their similarities and differences. Older children are better able to discriminate between letters, because they can visually scan material more systematically. Figure 4.2 shows a set of pictures used to study children's visual scanning. Elaine Vurpillot (1968) asked 4- and 8-year-olds to determine whether or not the house on the left was identical to the one on the right. Using a camera to record children's eye movements during the task, this study showed that older children more often looked back and forth between corresponding windows in the two houses and more often proceeded down a column or across a

Young children are able to attend to puzzle tasks that are highly engaging.
Source: *James L. Shaffer/Photo Edit.*

row within a house. In other words, they systematically analyzed the pair of houses. The 4-year-olds, in contrast, were more likely to state their answers after viewing only about half the windows in the two houses. In short, young children's visual exploration of stimulus objects was much more haphazard. In middle childhood, children are better able to direct their attentional processes.

Automaticity and Selective Attention   Automaticity is another factor that plays an important role in the development of children's attentional processes. **Automaticity** is defined as the gradual elimination of attention in the processing of information. As children gain experience with certain objects and problem-solving tasks, less effort is needed in the early stages of information processing. For example, experienced readers can recognize letters and words with very little mental effort. Decoding skills have been mastered and can be performed without thinking. When is the last time you had to decode a word, sound out letters, or figure out the meaning of a word? If you have ever tried to learn a foreign language, you can appreciate the demands placed on children's attentional processes during the early stages of reading. It involves effort and hard work, and it is difficult to do for long periods of time. As children gain experience and acquire knowledge, fewer cognitive resources are expended in the picking up of information.

■ FIGURE 4.2
Developmental Changes in Scanning Strategies
Source: After Vurpillot (1968).

With increases in age, children become better able to focus their attention on task-relevant information and to ignore irrelevant information. This process is called **selective attention.** This developmental change allows children to use their limited cognitive resources more efficiently. Researchers use what are known as incidental learning tasks to study the development of selective attention in children (Hagen & Hale, 1973; Miller & Weiss, 1981). In these studies, children are typically shown pictures with pairs of objects, such as a familiar animal paired with a common household object. The child is then told he or she will be asked to recall one member of each pair later on (e.g., the animals). The animals, then, are the central learning stimuli, and the other item in each pair serves as the incidental learning stimulus. Because the child's attentional capacity is limited, the most efficient way to approach the task is to attend only to the animals (the central learning stimuli) and to ignore information that is not relevant to the task. After each picture is presented, the child is asked first to recall the central stimuli (e.g., the animal in the pair). The experimenter then asks the child to recall the information he or she was suppose to ignore (i.e., the incidental objects).

Figure 4.3 shows the general pattern of findings from early studies of children's selective attention. As you can see, the processing of relevant information continues to improve well into the high school years, whereas decreases in incidental learning do not occur until about the age of 11 or 12. Recent studies also show that older children devote a higher proportion of their processing capacity to relevant material, whereas younger children do not effectively filter out irrelevant and distracting information (e.g., Kail, 2002). Compared with older children, young children spend more of their mental effort attending to irrelevant information rather than concentrating on the central features of the lesson or text. Likewise, older children become more efficient users of study time.

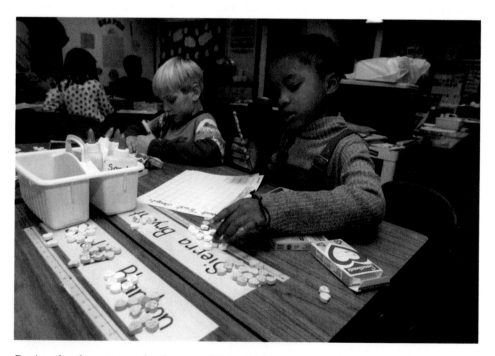

During the elementary school years, children gain more control over attentional processes needed for independent learning activities in the classroom.
Source: *Chris Seward/News & Observer.*

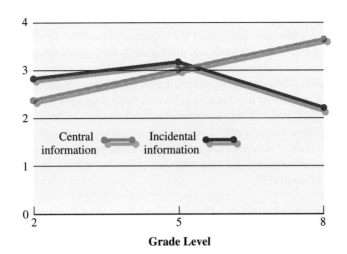

■ FIGURE 4.3
Recall of Central and Incidental Information, Selective Attention Task
Source: After Miller & Weiss (1981).

With the development of selective attention, the older child is gaining more voluntary control over his or her attentional processes. Like adults, they can consciously force themselves to focus on certain stimuli and to ignore distracting stimuli. Older children are also better able than younger children to broaden or narrow their attention according to the task demands (Flavell, 1985). Because different learning tasks may require different attentional strategies, this flexibility is advantageous for learning.

Memory Processes

According to some information processing theories (and neo-Piagetion theories), only a small amount of information can be kept in working memory at any one time. For young children, it may be difficult to engage in complex learning activities because the task itself overloads their memory capacities. Learning to read, for example, is a highly complex cognitive activity. As mentioned earlier, children must remember the distinctive feature of each letter and associate it with a specific sound. To make sense of this information, children must associate letter patterns with other information stored in memory. Ever greater demands are placed on children's memory processes as they progress in school. To perform successfully on an essay test, for instance, high school students must be able to recall and hold in working memory letter formations, correct spellings, rules of grammar and punctuation, and content knowledge.

Memory development has been one of the more active areas of research in developmental psychology (Kuhn, 2000). Memory processes begin to develop early in infancy. Within a few days of birth, breast-fed infants can recognize the smell of their mother's breast milk. This rather amazing feat implies that infants must have some way of storing the smell of their mothers' breast milk in order to recall it. Memory processes are also involved in forming emotional attachments to people. Without some ability to form a mental image of a caregiver, infants would not show signs of distress or cry when their mother or father leaves the room. Similarly, looking for hidden objects involves memory processes. In order to search for a ball that has rolled under a chair, a young toddler must have some mental image of that object after it disappears. By 5 months of age, infants can recognize previously seen stimulus material (objects, faces, numbers, shapes, etc.) as long as 2 weeks after the material was first presented.

Memory processes continue to improve through the preschool years. Young children often recall information in the form of a script. These **memory scripts** are mental representations of frequently repeated events in children's everyday life (Nelson & Hudson, 1988). Two- and 3-year-olds can easily recall the sequence of events in familiar routines such as eating breakfast, brushing their teeth, and getting ready for bed (Wellman, 1988). For example, a script for going to a restaurant might include driving to the restaurant, waiting to be seated, ordering food, waiting for food, eating, and paying for the food as you leave. Events are recalled in a very logical and orderly sequence. For children, these scripts help to increase the predictability of events in their world. When scripts are violated, young children may become upset and confused. Children's scripts provide interesting insights into how information is organized and remembered early in development. By the end of the preschool years, children can recall familiar stories, experiences, and events that are of interest to them as well as most adults (Flavell, 1985; P. Miller, 1993).

Encoding Strategies   During the preschool and early elementary years, children begin to use memory strategies to *encode* or place into memory information that is abstract, unfamiliar, or not meaningful. To store this type of information, a child must do something special to the material in order to remember it (Miller, 1993). What children do is apply some type of *memory strategy*. Suppose you were asked to remember the following list of items. What would you do?

apple	chair	goat
dog	potato	table
orange	lamp	bird
bed	cat	cabbage

Some people may repeat the items over and over again. This memory strategy is known as *rehearsal*. Others will try to group together the items into meaningful categories such as food, animals, and furniture. Researchers refer to this memory strategy as *organization*. Another group of people will try to construct a mental image of the items. This memory strategy is an example of *elaboration*. In terms of the levels of processing model described earlier, rehearsal is an example of shallow processing, whereas both organization and elaboration involve a deeper processing of information.

   Rehearsal strategies, the first kind of memory strategy to appear, are generally used when verbatim recall of information is required (Siegler, 1998). Research indicates that children younger than 6 or 7 years use rehearsal strategies less often than older children. In a classic study, John Flavell and his colleagues (Flavell, Beach, & Chinsky, 1966) showed that 10 percent of kindergartners, 60 percent of second graders, and 85 percent of fifth graders used a verbal rehearsal strategy in performing a memory task. Another study indicated that children who spontaneously rehearsed the information to be remembered recalled more of the items after a planned delay than those who did not (Keeney, Cannizzo, & Flavell, 1967). The second study also showed that nonrehearsers could be taught to rehearse with a minimum of instruction and that using this strategy increased their level of recall to that of the spontaneous rehearsers.

   Developmental changes in children's use of **organizational strategies** parallels those found in research on rehearsal strategies. These memory strategies entail grouping items or information into a form that is easier to remember. In the classroom, organizational strategies can take several different forms, including organizing ideas into an outline, searching for relationships between ideas, identifying the main ideas in a segment of text, and grouping items into categories. In general, these strategies enhance memory and understanding, because children are actively transforming the learning material in some way that is meaningful to them. In Piagetian terms, they are *assimilating* the information. Children younger than 6 years old use organizational strategies less frequently and effectively than 9- and

10-year-olds and older children. Because organizational strategies are more complex than rehearsal strategies, they generally emerge later in development.

Elaboration strategies involve adding to the information to make it more meaningful and easier to store. For example, one fourth-grade teacher uses the image of a hamburger to help students remember the components of a good paragraph. Figure 4.4 illustrates this mental image. Other examples of elaboration strategies include relating information to existing knowledge, translating information into one's own words, providing concrete examples of abstract concepts, and summarizing the main ideas of a story or chapter. Compared with rehearsal and organizational strategies, the spontaneous use of elaboration strategies appears much later in development. Studies indicate that elaboration strategies are primarily used by adolescents (Sneider & Bjorklund, 1998).

Retrieval Strategies   The research we have reviewed so far has focused on the strategies children and adolescents use to move information into short- or long-term memory. How is information retrieved from memory? Are there developmental differences in the types of strategies children use to retrieve information from their memory? Researchers distinguish between recognition and recall tasks.

Retrieval strategies refer to the cognitive operations a learner might use to recover information from memory (Flavell, 1985). Like the strategies children use to encode information (rehearsal, organization, and elaboration), retrieval strategies vary in complexity and sophistication. One of the simplest forms of a retrieval strategy is not to give up efforts to recall information just because it does not immediately come to mind. Research suggests that older children tend to be more exhaustive in their memory searches, whereas younger children may give up the search after only a few items are retrieved (Flavell, 1985).

In addition, older children tend to be more systematic and deliberate in their memory searches than younger children are. For example, Keniston and Flavell (1979) asked subjects from grades 1, 3, 7, and college to write down on a small card each alphabet letter the experimenter named. After 20 letters were written down in a random order, the cards were taken away and the subject was asked to write down the same letters on a large sheet of paper. The most effective memory strategy is to go through the alphabet in one's head and write down the letters you recognize from before. This simple strategy changes a difficult free-recall task into an easy recognition task. The researchers found that older children were more likely to use this retrieval strategy spontaneously. Younger children could use the strategy when they were told to do so, but they did not think of it on their own. These and other study findings indicate that young children may benefit from adult hints or retrieval cues more than older children (Sneider & Bjorklund, 1998).

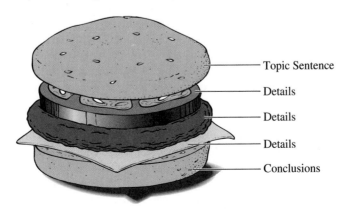

Topic Sentence
Details
Details
Details
Conclusions

■ FIGURE 4.4
Hamburger-Helper Paragraph

Summary of Memory Development Much of what develops in the area of memory consists of learning to encode and retrieve information more selectively, deliberately, systematically, and flexibly, depending on the task at hand. Some theorists say that children become more strategic learners; that is, they use cognitive strategies to enhance their learning, with age and experience (Paris, Lipson, & Wixson, 1983). Children aged 10 to 12 and older are more likely to remember information in part because they organize and elaborate on the information in ways that make it personally meaningful. Older children are also better able to conduct thorough searches of their memory, and they can recall information with fewer prompts and cues. This does not mean, however, that development proceeds smoothly. As we will see, children may think of good strategies that do not help them remember (utilization deficiency), and may use a variety of strategies that are more or less helpful for the same task (e.g., Miller, 2002). Effective strategy use may depend, to some extent, on development of memory capacity as well as prior knowledge, metacognition, and metamemory, as discussed next.

Deanna Kuhn (2000) suggests that we think about memory in terms of the following questions:

- What to know? (knowledge)
- What does it mean? (comprehension)
- How to know? And manage knowing? (strategies, metacognition)
- Why know? (context and purpose)

Knowledge and Comprehension

Older children certainly know more about their world than younger children. What role does a child's existing knowledge play in the development of the information processing system? In general, the more that children know about a particular topic, the easier it is for them to interpret and store related information in a meaningful and memorable way (Flavell & Wellman, 1977). Put another way, children are more likely to remember things that fit with what they know and comprehend, such as a child-oriented story, or a familiar activity.

In a classic study, Michelene Chi (1978) demonstrated the effects of knowledge on memory processes by studying adult's and children's recall of chess pieces. This study had an interesting twist. The researcher recruited six children from the third to eighth grades who had participated in chess tournaments and six adults who knew how to play chess but were not good at the game. She then showed both groups a picture of a chessboard with pieces arranged as they might appear during an actual game. She also administered a standard test of memory span (see Figure 4.5). When asked to reconstruct chess pieces from memory, the child experts recalled more pieces than the adults who were novices at the game. However, as expected, the adults outperformed the children on the memory test. Chi's findings illustrate the influence of prior knowledge on memory. If children are highly knowledgeable in a certain area, their memory capacities may equal or even surpass those of less knowledgeable adults.

Chi's study was one of many **expert versus novice studies.** Researchers have compared the thinking and problem-solving processes of experts and novices in tennis, soccer, and physics. Regardless of the domain or the participants' ages, more knowledgeable individuals are better able than novices to group or organize information in meaningful patterns. For example, research on both children (Chi, 1978) and adults (Chase & Simon, 1973) has shown that chess experts organize chess pieces into familiar patterns, whereas novices tend to remember the location of individual pieces. In addition, experts tend to relate facts and information to higher-level concepts more than novices do (Chi, Feltovich, & Glaser, 1981). Expert and novice studies suggest that advances in children's thinking

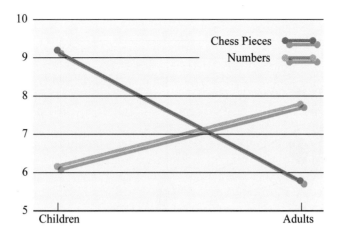

■ FIGURE 4.5
Children's and Adults'
Recall of Numbers
and Chess Pieces
Source: After Chi (1978).

processes are explained by quantitative changes in knowledge as well as by qualitative changes in how knowledge is structured and organized.

Evidence suggests that even young children can have highly integrated knowledge structures for topics of great interest to them. Chi and Koeske (1983) studied how one 4-year-old boy organized his knowledge of dinosaurs. While most children are fascinated with dinosaurs, this child knew the names of more than 40 dinosaurs. However, he seemed to know more about some dinosaurs than others. By asking the boy a series of questions on six separate occasions, the researchers were able to "map" his knowledge of dinosaurs. Figure 4.6 on page 198 presents a graphic representation of the findings.

As shown here, the boy seemed to know more about armored dinosaurs than giant plant eaters. Notice the difference in the number of characteristics and links between pairs of dinosaurs on the left and right sides of the figure. The lines indicate which pairs were linked in the child's memory. On all six recall tasks, for instance, the child mentioned stegosaur and triceratops together in a consecutive order, prompting the conclusion that he had better recall of the armored dinosaurs, because they were closely linked in his knowledge network. Recalling one of the dinosaurs facilitated the recall of others associated with it.

To summarize, children's prior knowledge can influence memory processes in a number of different ways. As children acquire knowledge, they are better able to identify relevant information and to organize it in meaningful ways. It is important to emphasize that simply increasing children's knowledge of facts (about dinosaurs, birds, etc.) does *not* necessarily lead to greater recall. Recent studies indicate that children may have to organize these facts in meaningful ways before recall improves (e.g., Miller, 2002). Having a more highly integrated or structured knowledge base, then, results in faster processing of information, more effective use of deep processing strategies, and more efficient use of cognitive resources (Alexander, 1996; Bjorklund, Muir-Broaddus, & Schneider, 1990).

Metacognition and Strategy Use

As discussed in Chapter 3, **metacognition** refers to children's knowledge and understanding of their own cognitive capabilities and thinking processes. With age and experience, children acquire knowledge of how tasks, strategies, and learner characteristics affect recall and learning (Flavell, 1985). We see evidence of children's developing abilities to reflect on their thinking and learning processes in the introductory vignette. Children use this metacognitive knowledge to choose more effective memory and learning strategies. For this reason, developmental changes in children's metacognition play an important role in school learning.

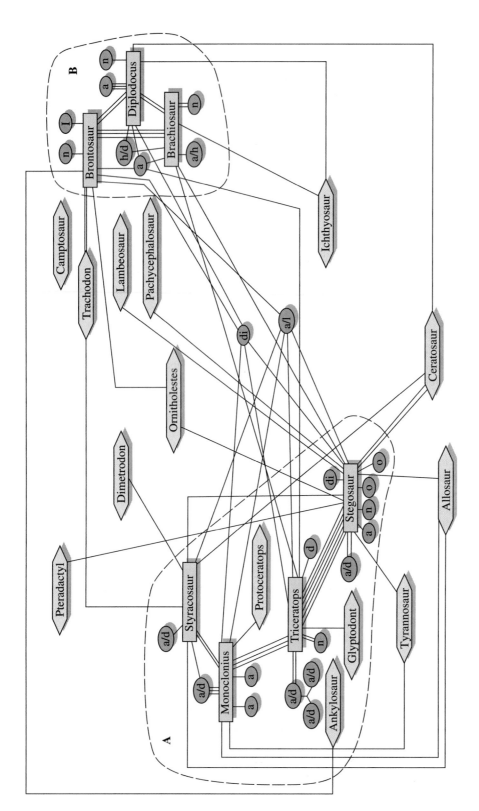

■ FIGURE 4.6

Child's Concept Map of Dinosaurs

Source: After Chi & Koeske (1983).

This concept map represents an 8-year-old's knowledge of dinosaurs. Dinosaurs in Group A are armored, whereas the ones in Group B are plant eaters. Multiple lines between dinosaurs indicate that the names are closely linked in the child's semantic network. The small letters indicate what the child knows about the dinosaur: appearance (a), defense mechanism (d), diet (di), nickname (n), habitat (h), and locomotion (l).

Much of a child's knowledge about cognition is acquired between the ages of 5 and 10 (Siegler, 1998). One aspect of metacognition that improves significantly during the elementary years is **metamemory**, or knowledge about memory. Preschool and kindergarten children tend to believe they cannot forget things they see or hear, whereas children beyond age 6 know they can forget (Kreutzer, Leonard, & Flavell, 1975). When asked how many of 10 items they can remember, young children believe they can remember all 10. The responses of older children suggest they view their memory capabilities as more limited. Further, older elementary school children understand reasonably well that relearning something is easier than learning it for the first time (Kreutzer et al., 1975) and that the longer one studies something the longer it will be remembered (Yussen & Bird, 1979). Children also improve abilities to identify "good" versus "bad" reasoning (e.g., use of evidence to draw conclusions, mental effort) during these critical middle childhood years (Amsterlaw, 2006). Other important metacognitive developments, such as understanding controllability of mental states and attentional processes, emerge later in childhood and early adolescence (e.g., Flavell, Green, & Flavell, 1998).

There are age-related improvements in children's knowledge of how a particular learning strategy can enhance recall or comprehension. In an early interview study, elementary school children were asked to describe some different ways they could remember to take their ice skates to school the next morning (Kruetzer et al., 1975). Older children were able to think of more things they could do to remember than younger children. Interestingly, the most commonly mentioned strategies were external aids, such as asking their mothers to remind them or writing themselves a note.

Paris, Lipson, and Wixon (1983) offer a more complicated view of strategy knowledge. They describe developmental changes in children's *declarative, procedural,* and *conditional knowledge* about learning strategies. That is, as children develop they learn not only what strategies are available to help them (*declarative knowledge*) but also how they should be applied (*procedural knowledge*) and why they are effective in specific situations (*conditional knowledge*). Paris and Winograd (1990) maintain that young children may know what strategies to use but lack knowledge of how to apply the strategy in various situations or how to evaluate its effectiveness (utilization deficiency).

Siegler (2004a) proposes that children gradually learn to adapt their strategy choices to better solve problems in his *overlapping waves theory.* Siegler and his colleagues have conducted many studies showing that children often use several different approaches to solve the same problem, and do not consistently use a superior strategy when they initially discover it. For example, adolescents may rely more and more on systematic procedures to conduct science experiments, just as children come to gradually rely on logic to solve conservation problems. According to this view, cognitive change occurs when children: (a) acquire new strategies, (b) increasingly use relatively superior strategies, (c) increasingly choose adaptive strategies for tasks, and (d) execute strategies effectively.

In summary, several age-related changes in metacognitive knowledge can affect how children approach learning tasks. As children develop, they acquire a greater understanding that there are limits to what can be remembered (person knowledge), that some learning tasks require more cognitive effort than others (task knowledge), and that certain strategies can aid the recall of information (strategy knowledge). Generally, this "knowing how to know" begins to appear during the preschool years, but it is slow to develop, because it requires the ability to consider one's own cognitive processes as objects of thought and reflection (Flavell & Wellman, 1977). It is also believed that age-related improvements in metacognition may be due to the large amount of information older children and adolescents are expected to remember in school (Siegler, 1998).

UNDERSTANDING CHILDREN
Strategy 4.10: Memory Awareness and Self-Monitoring

UNDERSTANDING CHILDREN
Strategy 4.7: Arithmetic Strategies

Context and Purpose

In this section, we turn to the question "Why know or remember?" Culture encourages children to "acquire some strategies more than others and give them an opportunity to practice these valued strategies" (Miller, 2002, p. 244). Developmentalists have more recently examined how social interaction influences children's memories and strategy use. For example, researchers have looked at how others' attitudes and questions influence children's recall of meaningful events (e.g., Siegler, 2004b). Other researchers have examined how children react to each others' strategy explanations. Study results suggest that children's strategy use may partly depend on their peers' enthusiasm and their abilities to generate ideas together (think about each others' thinking).

The purpose or motivation for acquiring strategies is also recognized in the "Good Information Processing" model, proposed by Pressley, Borkowski, Schneider, and their colleagues (Schneider & Bjorklund, 1998). This model emphasizes the interaction of several factors mentioned so far—memory capacity, knowledge, motivation—in the development of strategies and metacognitive processes. It also highlights the role of parents and educators in the acquisition of these processes, described in the following steps:

1. Children learn advantages of strategies, taught by parents and teachers, through practice. Children expand *specific strategy knowledge* when they encounter more strategies in stimulating home and school environments.
2. Children learn how strategies are related by teachers demonstrating similarities and differences of multiple strategies in a domain *(relational knowledge)*.
3. Children recognize the value of being strategic, leading to *general strategy knowledge*. They learn to attribute successful learning outcomes to strategy efforts, and acquire *metacognitive* processes (i.e., cognitive monitoring strategies appropriate for the task). (Schneider & Bjorklund, 1998, p. 441)

Pressley and his colleagues have illustrated how to incorporate "good information processing" in educational settings. The Transactional Strategies Instruction (TSI) approach presented in Chapter 5 is one example.

Self-Regulated Learning

With the development of metacognitive knowledge, children begin to regulate and control their own learning activities. Some theorists refer to this process as **self-regulated learning** (Paris & Winograd, 1990; Zimmerman, 1990). According to Zimmerman (1990), self-regulated learners can "plan, set goals, organize, self-monitor, and self-evaluate at various points during the process of knowledge acquisition" (pp. 4–5). The ability to learn independently is important for children's success in school. By high school, students spend a good deal of class time learning from textbooks, listening to lectures, and studying on their own.

UNDERSTANDING CHILDREN
Strategy 4.11: Planning and Problem-Solving

When are students able to regulate and control their own learning? Research suggests that the answer to this question depends on the learning task and the students' prior knowledge (Brown, Bransford, Ferrara, & Campione, 1983). However, there are some clear developmental trends in students' use of planning, monitoring, and evaluation strategies in learning situations.

Much research has focused on the strategies students use while studying and reading on their own. Between the fifth and eighth grades, children show a significant increase in their reported use of planning, sequencing, and goal-setting strategies (Zimmerman & Martinez-Pons, 1990). Additional evidence suggests that elementary and middle school students tend to use passive rather than active strategies for remembering text (Brown & Smiley, 1978). For example, when given extra time to study, younger students favor rereading the learning material, whereas high school students tend to take notes or underline passages. Furthermore, when asked to summarize or outline text, elementary and middle school students tend to copy words verbatim rather than connecting ideas, arranging information by topic clusters, or stating information in their own words (Brown et al., 1983). Most students are not able to adequately summarize a typical fifth-grade text until well into the high school years.

Comprehension monitoring is an essential component of self-regulated learning. Skilled learners monitor their comprehension as they study or read and take corrective action when they fail to comprehend (Brown et al., 1983). Elementary school children tend to underestimate their level of mastery on learning tasks and how much time they need to study in order to achieve mastery (Pressley & Ghatala, 1990). In addition, elementary school children are less likely than older students to monitor their comprehension while reading. If a younger reader can decode and make sense of individual words, he or she continues reading (Baker & Brown, 1984). Older students are better able to detect inconsistencies and confusion when they read. When comprehension falters, they adjust their strategies accordingly. For example, they may reread confusing passages, look up a word in the dictionary, look for meaning in the surrounding context, or slow down until comprehension is restored. These comprehension-monitoring skills continue to develop well into adolescence.

Putting Theories Together (Again)

Before discussing the specific implications of information processing research for educational practices, it is important to point out what this approach shares in common with Piaget's and Vygotsky's theories of cognitive development. First, all three views emphasize that learners must play an active role in the learning process. In information processing approaches, this activity involves selectively attending, interpreting, and organizing information; using cognitive strategies; and building webs of connected knowledge. Like Piaget and Vygotsky, information processing theorists also emphasize that learning is the construction of meaning. Students come to the classroom with a range of experiences, beliefs, skills, and concepts, and this prior knowledge plays a role in how new information is interpreted, organized, and remembered. Finally, "learning how to learn" is central to the development of cognition. In information processing theory, this process involves becoming a strategic learner, critical thinker, and skilled problem solver.

Implications of Information Processing Theories for Teaching

Having identified some common themes across different theories of cognitive development, what are the specific implications of information processing research for educational practices? The Focus on Teaching box on page 202 summarizes several ways information processing theory can be applied in the classroom.

In order to increase alertness and attentiveness, it is important to create a classroom environment that is secure, attractive, novel, and stimulating. Posing unexpected problems, changing the displays on bulletin boards, and introducing variety into the schedule can capture students' attention. As we learned in Chapter 2, it is difficult for students of all ages to maintain high levels of concentration. Physical movement and activity can help increase students' concentration (Pellegrini et al., 1995).

The findings from research on the development of selective attention suggest that young elementary school students may have difficulty differentiating relevant from irrelevant information. They may also have difficulty when tasks require a shift in attention—say,

Focus on
Teaching

*Applying Information-Processing
Theories in the Classroom*

Attention Strategies	Memory Strategies	Metacognitive Skills and Self-Regulated Learning
Introduce learning material by relating information to students' interests or by asking questions to stimulate interest.	For young learners, use charts, visual aids, and songs to help children remember routines or basic information such as numbers and letters.	Provide opportunities for students to set their own goals, and monitor their progress toward those goals.
Use novelty, variety, and unexpected problems to capture students' attention, but minimize unnecessary distractions.	Present information in an organized way and cue important information to be remembered.	Model and help students learn strategies for focusing and controlling attention.
Provide opportunities for physical movement and activity to help increase students' concentration.	Help students relate information to what they already know. Model strategies for organizing and trieving information.	Help students learn strategies such as outlining, summarizing, making concept maps, and connecting ideas.
Help students identify salient dimensions, main ideas, or key features of information.	Encourage students to use concept maps, outlines, or pictures to help them organize information in ways that are meaningful.	Encourage students to monitor and check their comprehension as they read and learn.
Use questions, outlines, study guides, and visual aids to help cue attention and keep students focused.	Encourage students to use elaboration strategies such as teaching information to a peer, relating it to their own experiences, or applying it to real-life situations.	Model and teach strategies students can use when they experience difficulty, such as rereading the directions, dividing problems into smaller tasks, trying different strategies, seeking help from books, and seeking assistance from others.
Use instructional methods and formats that will hold students' interests.	Ask students to help review and summarize information in lessons. Review key concepts or information regularly.	
Recognize developmental and individual differences in attention, and adjust assignments accordingly.	When students experience difficulty remembering information, provide retrieval cues that relate information to what the students already know.	For older learners, provide assignments that require independent learning, and provide the necessary guidance for students to complete them on their own.

from a central idea to peripheral topics or from a broad to a narrow focus. In such situations, teachers will need to help students focus their attention on the most relevant features of learning tasks. When complex or unfamiliar learning tasks are introduced, even high school students may experience difficulty identifying the significant features that require special attention. Some discussion of the activity beforehand may guide students' attention to relevant aspects of the task. Outlines and study guides may also help cue students' attention, as can the use of advance organizers that connect new information to students' prior knowledge. For younger students, it may be important to color-code or highlight important information. For example, a new letter or number symbol can be highlighted or can be written in a different color to cue attention. Additionally, teachers can use questions and feedback to help students stay focused on relevant aspects of the learning task.

Research on the development of memory processes offers additional suggestions for educational practices. It is important for teachers to recognize that students, especially younger ones, are limited in terms of the amount of verbal or visual information they can process. Most of the memory strategies we discussed do not develop until after the age of 6. However, younger children form scripts to help them remember routines and expectations. Songs and fingerplays can also help young children remember important information such as numbers or letters. These activities are a form of rehearsal.

As with brain development, the principle of "use it or lose it" applies to memory processes. Practice and use increases the strength of a particular memory record, and it facilitates the process of automaticity. For example, in the next chapter, we will learn that when children begin to recognize many words on sight, they are on their way toward becoming fluent readers. Similarly, "expert" physicists can easily recognize and encode technical terms that most of us could not interpret or comprehend without a great deal of cognitive effort. Accordingly, students need opportunities to practice newly learned material to increase both its strength and familiarity in memory.

Does this suggestion mean that students should simply memorize facts and information? The current thinking on this question is that some information (e.g., letter sounds, sight words, addition facts, multiplication tables, etc.) needs to be readily accessed with minimal effort to enable higher levels of cognitive processing. For example, solving long-division problems takes more cognitive effort when students have not learned simple multiplication facts. The problem can be solved, but similar to the reading example given earlier, most of the student's thinking processes are focused on doing multiplication, rather than understanding the concept of long division. The same applies to more complex tasks such as writing. As I finish this paragraph, for instance, I am not thinking about how to spell familiar words or where to place my fingers on the keyboard. My thinking is focused on what I am trying to communicate.

Because memory capacities are limited, it is also important for teachers to help children organize their learning experiences. To help students separate essential from nonessential details, teachers need to introduce lessons with a set of guiding questions or goals. In other words, teachers need to provide a "road map" for the lesson to help students sequence and organize the learning material. Teachers also need to help students make connections between new information and what they already know. Through questioning, teachers can help students retrieve information that is relevant for understanding the new material.

Additionally, research on memory suggests that teachers need to promote the deep processing of information. Deep processing is facilitated by the use of organizational and elaboration strategies that involve transforming the learning material in meaningful ways. Examples of organizational strategies are clustering information into categories, identifying relationships between ideas or concepts, or connecting information to existing knowledge. Concept maps like the one shown in Figure 4.7 on page 204 are often used to help students

■ FIGURE 4.7

*A Fourth Grader's Map
of Geometric Concepts*
Source: After Baroody &
Bartels (2000).

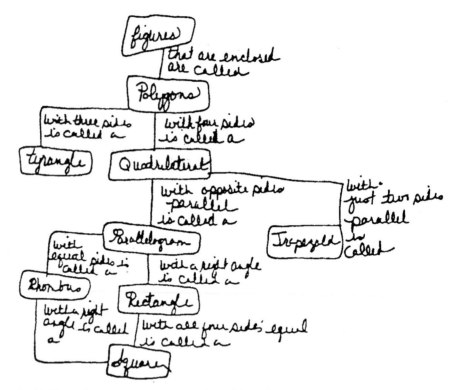

As this figure shows, a concept map consists of three elements: (1) concepts are written inside loops, boxes, rectangles, or other shapes; (2) linking lines show connections between concepts; and (3) linking phrases describe the relationship between concepts. Concept-mapping can promote meaningful learning in the classroom because the process enables students to actively construct relationships between concepts. To correctly place a trapezoid in the above figure, students must recognize that a trapezoid is a four-sided shape and, thus, a type of quadrilateral.

organize information in terms of meaningful categories. Outlines are another way students can organize knowledge into meaningful categories. It is important to point out that when students do their own organization, it has a stronger effect on recall than when teachers provide that organization (McDaniel, Waddill, & Einstein, 1988). Elaboration strategies involve imposing meaning on learning material. Organizing information into meaningful categories can aid in that process, but elaboration can take other forms as well. It can include restating new material in one's own words, explaining or teaching the material to someone else, creating a visual or mental image of the material, or applying information to real-world situations. The use of journals in which students can draw or write about what they are learning can help in the deep processing of learning material.

As you know, the development of metacognition enables learners to regulate and control their learning or to become self-regulated learners. Numerous classroom-based programs have been developed to train students in metacognitive skills and cognitive strategies. Instructional programs have focused on the development of planning, organization, and comprehension strategies. Research suggests that explicit strategy instruction can be beneficial for less-advanced learners (Schunk, 2000). However, explicit strategy instruction is most beneficial when students also learn when and how to use the strategy effectively and why the strategy is helpful. In other words, explicit strategy instruction is most beneficial to learners after the instructional program ends, when it emphasizes *what, when, why,* and *how.* Research also suggests that interventions of this type need a good deal of scaffolded instruction to ensure that internalization of the strategy takes place.

Research on the development of basic cognitive processes is having a major impact on education today. Research on the development of attention and memory can help teachers diagnose learning problems. Students with learning disabilities often experience problems with attention and memory. Researchers draw on information processing theories to develop classroom interventions or accommodations for these students. Additionally, information processing approaches have been used to design instructional interventions to help children with poor reading or writing skills (Block & Pressley, 2002).

Many theorists believe that educators need to go beyond the teaching of specific skills to developing a culture of thinking and learning in the classroom (Bruner, 1996; Tishman, 1995). An excellent illustration is a *community of learners* approach, introduced in Chapter 3, blending social constructivist and information processing views of cognitive development to help create a school environment (Brown & Campione, 1994). A community of learners is structured around several key learning principles (Brown, 1997):

- **Agency.** Both teachers and learners routinely engage in the search for meaning and understanding. The *strategic* nature of learning is emphasized.
- **Collaboration.** Both teachers and students must share in developing and sustaining the community of learning. Teachers help guide students to deeper levels of understanding, but learning is a shared and joint activity. Cooperative and collaborative learning among students is also commonplace. These activities not only have an important learning function (children share their expertise and take responsibility for their learning), but also strengthen the collaborative structures of the classroom.
- **Reflection.** The classroom is designed to stimulate active exchange of ideas and discourse. Students are encouraged to ask themselves, "Do I understand?" or to say, "That doesn't make sense to me." Discussion, analysis, and critique are all valued practices in this community.
- **Deep discipline inquiry.** Students engage in disciplined inquiry on a central theme that can sustain in-depth research over time. Students need opportunities to reason about serious matters at the upper limits of their capabilities. Deep discipline inquiry involves reasoning with research and evidence, seeking expert advice, and sharing results and ideas with others.

Every classroom has a culture of some sort. The classroom culture influences the ways students and teachers interact and their shared understanding of what is valued and acceptable. In a community of learners, learning is negotiated and shared as a way of life.

Intelligence Theories and Cognitive Development

So far our discussion of cognitive development has focused on cognitive differences among different age levels. It is important to keep in mind that there is a wide range of variation in children's cognitive abilities within a particular age group. In any third-grade classroom, for example, there will be children reading at a fourth- or fifth-grade level as well as children who are just starting to read on their own. What might explain these cognitive differences within an age group? Do some children simply have more innate ability for learning than others? Are these differences related to children's early learning experiences? How might differences in children's home environment contribute to their cognitive development?

In this section, we discuss how researchers assess and explain individual differences in cognitive development. **Psychometric** or **intelligence theories** attempt to identify the processes that explain individual differences revealed on cognitive measures, such as intelligence tests. Central to this discussion is the question of how much heredity and environment each contribute to individual differences in intelligence. This question has been hotly debated for decades, and it continues to be a subject of much controversy. In 1994, the publication of *The Bell Curve* by Richard Herrnstein and Charles Murray sparked considerable debate, because the authors claimed that social problems such as high school dropout, teenage pregnancy, infant mortality, unemployment, crime, poverty, and even "broken homes" were a function of innate intelligence. Because research on heredity and intelligence is so extensive, we will limit our discussion of individual differences in cognitive development to the following questions:

- How are individual differences in cognitive development measured?
- How is intelligence defined?
- How does the environment influence intellectual development?
- What can parents do to enhance their child's intellectual development?
- How do schools influence children's intellectual development?

Key Concepts

Assessing Cognitive Differences

The most common methods of assessing individual differences in cognitive development are standardized tests of intelligence and academic achievement. These tests yield scores that provide an index of the person's intellectual performance relative to other people of the same chronological age. The use of standardized tests of intelligence to study individual differences in cognitive development is known as the *psychometric approach.* If you recall, Piaget focused on individual differences in the quality of children's thinking. Information processing theorists focus on individual differences in children's attentional processes, encoding and retrieving strategies, and metacognitive knowledge. In contrast, psychometricians focus on what and how much children know and what explains individual differences. Some argue that individual differences in cognitive development can be measured and quantified through the use of standardized tests.

Alfred Binet, a French psychologist, published the first intelligence test in 1904. Binet claimed that a person's intellectual ability could be inferred from his or her performance on a series of cognitive tasks. Binet and his student Theodore Simon assembled a series of cognitive tasks that measured such things as memory for numbers, attention, reading comprehension, mathematics reasoning and computation skills, and general information (knowledge of numbers, days of the week, coins, etc.). The tasks were graded in difficulty and linked to chronological age.

Binet and Simon developed their measure as a practical device for identifying children who needed special help in school (Gould, 1981). They were responsible for introducing the concept of mental age (MA). This score represents the number of test items a child gets correct, which is then compared with the average number of items children of the same age get correct. A 10-year-old who can answer as many answers correctly as the average 12-year-old has a mental age of 12. Later, a German psychologist, William Stern, introduced the **intelligence quotient (IQ),** which represents a score obtained by dividing a child's mental age score by the child's chronological age (CA) and multiplying by 100 (e.g., IQ = MA/CA = 100). If a child has a score of 100, his or her performance is average

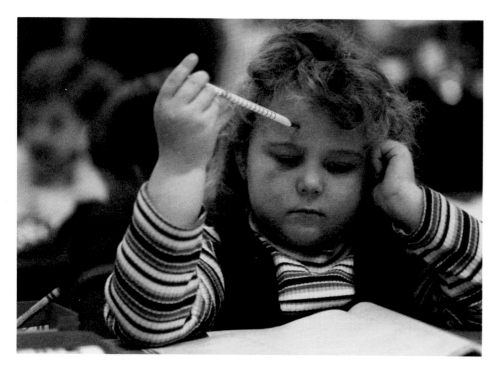

An important issue of debate is when schools should begin testing children. Should children in the early elementary grades take standardized tests?
Source: Chris Seward/News & Observer.

for that age. Scores above 100 indicate that a child is above average for that age, whereas scores below 100 indicate that a child is below average.

Conceptions of Intelligence

Despite the fact that IQ tests have been around for nearly 100 years, there is no widely accepted definition of intelligence (Neisser et al., 1996). Because Binet and Simon's IQ test yielded a single score, this assessment procedure is assumed to represent a unitary conception of intelligence. That is, intelligence is considered to be a general cognitive ability. As you will see, many intelligence tests are based on this unitary conception of intelligence. However, this view of intelligence is beginning to lose ground to a more multidimensional conception in which intelligence is defined in terms of several different mental abilities or intellectual competencies. Furthermore, conceptions of intelligence vary considerably across cultural groups (Rogoff, 2003).

UNDERSTANDING CHILDREN
Strategy 4.13: Interview with a Teacher; Views of Intelligence

Before we discuss different conceptions of intelligence, it is important to distinguish between intelligence tests and *achievement tests.* Intelligence tests are thought to measure a child's ability to learn or to apply information in new ways. These tests assess learning that results from a wide variety of experiences. Most intelligence tests are individually administered by a trained examiner. Two of the most widely used intelligence tests will be described in the following section. An achievement test, on the other hand, is designed to measure what children have gained from instruction at home or at school. Test items stress the mastery of factual information. These tests are generally group administered by teachers, and they provide a way of comparing children in different instructional programs or tracking children's academic progress over time. Although intelligence tests and achievement tests are generally viewed as distinct assessment instruments, we will point out some overlap between them.

Single-Factor Conceptions of Intelligence   Traditional approaches to intelligence testing define intelligence as a single ability or capacity. Lewis Terman of Stanford University, who was responsible for bringing Binet and Simon's testing methods to the United States, defined intelligence as an ability to think in abstract terms. He translated and revised Binet's test, then standardized it on a large sample of children and adults. The revised test, called the *Stanford-Binet Intelligence Scale,* was first published in 1916, and it became the standard for IQ tests (Gould, 1981). Terman and his followers argued that a **general intelligence,** called *g,* under-lies all cognitive functioning. Someone with a high score on Terman's test is expected to do well on all intellectual tasks.

Multiple-Factor Conceptions of Intelligence   More than 70 years ago, Charles Spear-man (1927) argued that intelligence represents a *g,* or general factor, and a number of *s,* or specific ability, factors. In 1938, Louis Thurston suggested that intelligence was composed of seven separate skills that included perceptual speed, numerical facility, word fluency, in-ductive reasoning, and memory. Later, J. P. Guildford (1967) concluded that intelligence consists of 120 different factors, and he developed a test to assess 75 of these.

Research in the 1970s proposed that there are basically two kinds of intelligence, known as crystallized intelligence and fluid intelligence (Catell, 1971). **Crystallized intelligence** is assessed by measures of word fluency, general information, and vocabulary and verbal com-prehension. In contrast, **fluid intelligence** involves speed of information processing, memory processes, ability to detect relationships, and other abstract thinking skills. Research suggests that fluid intelligence improves until the early adult years, then slowly declines, whereas crys-tallized intelligence continues to improve well into the adult years (Horn, 1985).

The question of whether intelligence represents a general capability or multiple abilities remains unresolved today. In 1985, Robert Sternberg introduced the **triarchic model of in-telligence.** He defined intelligence as "mental activity directed toward purposive adaptation to, and selection and shaping of, real world environment relevant to one's life" (p. 45). His theory attempts to integrate aspects of the information processing and psychometric approaches, as well as cognitive developmental (Piagetian) and sociocultural approaches.

According to Sternberg's theory, there are three major components of intelligent behavior. The first component, **componential intelligence,** draws heavily on information processing theory. It involves such skills as the ability to allocate mental resources, to encode and store information, to plan and monitor, to identify problems, and to acquire new knowledge. The second component, **experiential intelligence,** involves the ability to cope with new situations in an effective, efficient, and insightful manner. Experiential intelli-gence is involved in diagnosing why a computer program might not run. The third compo-nent of Sternberg's model is called **contextual intelligence.** It involves the ability to adapt to a changing environment or, more important, to shape that environment to capitalize on one's abilities or skills. In Sternberg's view, this component of intelligence involves the ap-plication of intelligence to everyday problems, or what he called **practical intelligence.** An intelligent person, according to Sternberg, is one who can use his or her skills effectively in a particular environment. Figure 4.8 lists what Sternberg saw as the principal abilities that underlie intelligent behavior. At present, however, there are few standardized measures that assess these components of intelligence. In a recent reflection on intelligence tests, Sternberg, Grigorenko, and Kidd (2005) note, ". . . it is especially important that we acknowledge that we have nothing even vaguely close to a 'tape measure' of intelligence" (p. 47).

Multiple Intelligences   Another multiple-factor view of intelligence is Howard Gardner's (1999) theory of **multiple intelligences.** Like Sternberg, Gardner questions traditional measures of intelligence that are narrow in their focus. Gardner proposed that there are at least

Principal Characteristics of Intelligent Behavior

- Recognizing and defining the nature of a problem

- Deciding on the processes needed to solve the problem

- Sequencing the processes into an optimal strategy

- Deciding on how to represent problem information

- Allocating mental and physical resources to the problem

- Monitoring and evaluating one's solution processing

- Responding adequately to external feedback

- Encoding stimulus elements effectively

- Inferring relations between stimulus elements

- Mapping relations between relations

- Applying old relations to new situations

- Comparing stimulus elements

- Responding effectively to novel tasks and situations

- Effectively automizing information processing

- Adapting effectively to the environment in which one resides

- Recognizing one's strengths and weaknesses

- Selecting environments as needed to achieve a better fit of one's abilities and interests to the environment

- Shaping environments to increase one's effective use of one's abilities and interests

■ FIGURE 4.8
Principal Characteristics of Intelligent Behavior
Source: After Sternberg (1984) and Sternberg & Grigorenko (2000).

eight different types of intelligences, and possibly more. He further suggests that each intelligence has its own form of perception, memory, and learning. Gardner believes that each intelligence has a unique developmental history, and it may be governed by a distinct region of the brain. He also believes that cultural values, historical changes, and learning opportunities have a great influence on the abilities of individuals to develop and express their intellectual strengths. In Gardner's view, we are currently entering a new century in which people need to be adept at manipulating symbols and adapting to change. At the turn of the twentieth century, a naturalist intelligence was critical for an economy dependent on farming, fishing, and hunting.

Table 4.1 on page 210 presents the eight intelligences identified by Gardner. Linguistic, logical-mathematical, and spatial intelligences are generally assessed by traditional measures of intelligence. Gardner argues that people also show special abilities in bodily kinesthetic, interpersonal, intrapersonal, and naturalistic domains. For example, dancers and athletes

TABLE 4.1 Gardner's Eight Intelligences

Intelligence	End States	Core Components
Logical-mathematical	Scientist Mathematician	Sensitivity to and capacity to discern logical or patterns; ability to handle long chains of reasoning
Linguistic	Poet Journalist	Sensitivity to sounds, rhythms, and meaning of words; sensitivity to the different functions of language
Musical	Composer Musician	Abilities to produce and appreciate rhythm, pitch, and timbre; appreciation of different forms of musical expressiveness
Spatial	Navigator Sculptor	Capacities to perceive the visual-spatial world accurately and to perform transformations on one's initial perceptions
Bodily kinesthetic	Dancer Athlete	Abilities to control one's body movements and to handle objects skillfully
Interpersonal	Therapist Salesperson	Capacities to discern and respond appropriately to the moods, temperaments, motivations, and desires of other people
Intrapersonal	Person with detailed, accurate self-knowledge	Access to one's own feelings and the ability to discriminate among them to guide behavior; knowledge of one's own strengths, weaknesses, desires, and intelligences
Naturalistic	Botanist Farmer Veterinarian	Ability to discriminate among living things (plants, animals) as well as demonstrate a sensitivity toward other features of the natural world (e.g., rocks, cloud formations, etc.)

Source: After Gardner & Hatch (1989) and Checkley (1997).

generally have a great ability to move their bodies through space (bodily kinesthetic intelligence); good teachers, social workers, and psychotherapists seem particularly adept at understanding the feelings, motives, and moods of others (interpersonal intelligence). Veterinarians, botanists, and farmers are skilled in observing, understanding, and appreciating the natural world, or what Gardner calls naturalistic intelligence. It is also possible for individuals to show strengths in two or more areas. Novelists, for example, generally make use of heightened linguistic and interpersonal intelligences.

Gardner's ideas about multiple intelligences are being applied in many schools and classrooms today. His theory has helped teachers to understand that there are different ways of being "smart" and that it is important to foster all kinds of intelligences, not just verbal or mathematical abilities. According to Gardner, teachers should follow the Chinese adage "Let a hundred flowers bloom" (Gardner, 1999, p. 89).

Summary

There is no one definition of intelligence. As we will see, most intelligence tests today yield more than one score, so it is possible to compare children's intellectual functioning across different domains. These profiles are useful for assessing a child's intellectual strengths and weaknesses. For the most part, the tests used in schools today emphasize children's linguistic, mathematical, and analytical abilities. They reflect the type of intellectual abilities our culture values. Multifaceted views of intelligence offer new ways of conceptualizing children's intellectual abilities. It is hoped that such views will help educators see intelligent behavior in all children in one form or another. We will discuss some of the practices based on these views at the end of this section. The important point to remember is that different students show intelligence in different ways.

Measures of Intelligence

The Stanford-Binet Intelligence Scale (Roid, 2003; Thorndike, Hagen, & Sattler, 1986) is the most widely used intelligence test. The Stanford-Binet Intelligence Scale, Fifth Edition (SB5) measures five cognitive factors in both verbal and nonverbal domains: fluid reasoning, knowledge (crystallized ability), quantitative reasoning, visual-spatial processing, and working memory. Rather than a single score, the scale now yields 10 profile scores, as well as a composite score for the test as a whole. See Figure 4.9 on page 212 for a description of the subtests in the revised Stanford-Binet test. Many of the new features of the SB5 were developed to aid in the assessment of preschool children, individuals with mental retardation, and individuals with intellectual giftedness (Roid & Barram, 2004).

Another widely used test is the Wechsler Intelligence Scale for Children—Third Edition (WISC—III) (Wechsler, 1991) for children between the ages of 8 and 18. The design of this scale was influenced by the earlier Stanford-Binet, but it places less emphasis on children's verbal skills. The WISC—III contains 10 subtests divided into two separate scales. The verbal scales assess vocabulary, digit-span memory, general comprehension, basic facts, and arithmetic knowledge and reasoning. The performance scales, on the other hand, measure spatial orientation, perceptual abilities, and problem-solving skills that are thought to be less dependent on verbal skills, formal education, and other cultural factors. Wechsler's scale thus yields a separate score for verbal and performance IQ as well as a full-scale IQ based on the combined scores.

Although the WISC—III yields two separate IQ scores, Wechsler defined intelligence as a unitary construct. It is "the aggregate or global capacity of the individual to act purposively, to think rationally, and to deal effectively with his environment" (Wechsler, 1958, p. 7). The WISC—III is valuable for diagnostic purposes because it distinguishes between a child's verbal and performance abilities. A child who does well on the performance scale but poorly on the verbal scale may have poor language skills. Conversely, a child who performs well on the verbal scale but poorly on the performance scale may have perceptual or spatial orientation problems.

The Stanford-Binet Intelligence Scale and WISC—III are the most reliable, best validated, and most widely used intelligence tests we have today. Both tests are individually administered by a trained examiner. Composite scores on these tests are viewed as estimates of general intelligence, or *g*.

There are also intelligence tests for infants and young children. The best-known assessment is the Bayley Scales of Infant and Toddler Development (Bayley, 1969, 1993), recently expanded by Greenspan, Harrison, and Oakland. The Bayley-III (2006) assesses the cognitive, language, motor, socioemotional, and adaptive-behavior development of children ages 1 to 42 months. This instrument is primarily used as a tool to identify developmental delays in these five domains.

Interpreting an IQ Score

Whether an IQ test yields one or several scores, it is assumed that these scores represent some estimate of a child's cognitive ability relative to other children of the same age. As mentioned earlier, an IQ score is the ratio of the child's mental age to chronological age.

Subtest Descriptions of the Stanford-Binet Intelligence Scale

Verbal

Fluid Reasoning: Early reasoning (e.g., picture reasoning), classic verbal absurdities and verbal analogies

Knowledge: Vocabulary. Includes toys, identification of body parts, and classic word definitions

Quantitative Reasoning: Verbal quantitative reasoning items, tapping number concepts, problems solving, and figural-geometric problems

Visual Spatial Reasoning: Position and direction problems, requiring explanation of directions, identifying spatial relations in pictures, etc.

Working Memory: Memory for sentences, last word procedure (recalling the last word of a series of questions)

Nonverbal

Fluid Reasoning: Object series/matrices, includes sequential reasoning items

Knowledge: Procedural knowledge, involving gestures; picture absurdities

Quantitative Reasoning: Nonverbal quantitative reasoning, tapping number concepts, problems solving, and figural-geometric problems

Visual Spatial Reasoning: Form board and patterns, making designs from form board pieces

Working Memory: Delayed response (e.g. hiding an object under a cup), block span (block-tapping procedure)

Most intelligence tests today use a scoring procedure that results in a deviation IQ score. These scores have a mean of 100 points and a standard deviation of 15 or 16 points, depending on the test. A **standard deviation** is a measure of the average amount scores vary from the mean. The smaller the standard deviation, the more scores cluster around the mean. Deviation IQ scores are based on a normal distribution or bell curve, like the one shown in Figure 4.10. The mean is at the midpoint of this distribution, and 95 percent of all scores are within two standard deviation units above or below the mean (i.e., between 70 and 130).

Using the deviation IQ score procedure, children with raw scores that match the average for their age group receive an IQ score of 100. Half of the children (50 percent) score below 100, and half score above 100. On the WISC—III, children with raw scores one standard deviation (15 points) above the mean receive an IQ score of 115. These children perform better than 84 percent of children their age. In contrast, 84 percent of same-aged children perform better than children with an IQ score of 85, one standard deviation

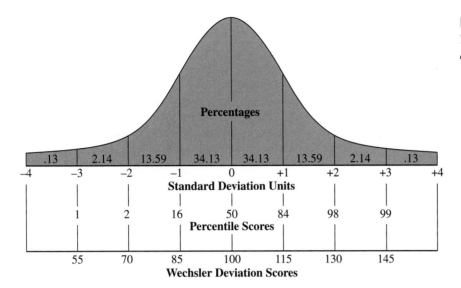

(15 points) below the mean. In a normal distribution, most children's scores fall within one standard deviation above or below the mean (between 85 and 115 on the WISC—III). Very few children will have scores more than two standard deviations from the mean.

The most vocal critics have argued that intelligence tests are biased against anyone who does not come from white, Anglo-American, middle-class, English-speaking families. To perform well on an IQ test, they claim, children must have a good deal of familiarity with middle-class culture and good standard-English verbal skills. As we will see, African American, Latino, and poor children generally do not perform as well on standardized tests as white middle-class children. Stephen Ceci (1990) argued that many children who perform poorly on traditional IQ tests may demonstrate more sophisticated cognitive abilities in more familiar domains. Tests such as the Kaufman Assessment Battery (Kaufman & Kaufman, 1983) have been developed to minimize cultural bias. On these tests, gaps in the performances of white and minority children are considerably smaller. Therefore, teachers should use caution when traditional IQ measures are employed to assess children from different socioeconomic, cultural, and language backgrounds.

IQ and School Achievement

An IQ test is alleged to predict everything from mental health to job performance (Ceci, 1991). Some psychologists have claimed that intelligence tests have even helped to win wars (Gould, 1981). However, for a number of researchers, IQ scores are simply viewed as relatively good predictors of success in school, at least in American culture (Ceci, 1991, Ceci & Williams, 1997).

Studies repeatedly show that IQ scores are correlated with various measures of school achievement (Ceci, 1990, 1991; Ceci & Williams, 1997; Geary, 2005). Children with higher IQ scores typically do better on standardized tests of academic achievement, have higher school grades, and complete more years of school. Correlations between IQ scores and measures of school achievement are in the range of 0.40 to 0.60, not a perfect correlation but certainly a substantial one. Because these are correlational data, they should not be interpreted to mean that intelligence causes a child to do well or poorly in school. In fact, considerable evidence suggests that schooling plays an important causal role in the development of intelligence, at least as it is currently defined and assessed (Ceci, 1990). We will discuss this evidence later on.

To summarize, a child's IQ score is best thought of as an indicator of how well that child will do in school. Under optimal testing conditions, an intelligence test can help diagnose learning problems or areas in which children need special instructional assistance. Intelligence tests are not measures of innate ability, creativity, or even complex reasoning (Ceci, 1991). Furthermore, IQ scores are not very good predictors of social success, mental health, or personality. An IQ score provides information about what intelligence tests were originally intended to measure—namely, a child's ability to perform in school.

Developmental Changes in Intelligence

How much does a child's IQ score change during development? If we know a child's IQ score at age 5, how well can we predict his or her score at age 15 or 18? Will a bright kindergartener be at the top of her class when he or she graduates from high school? Questions concerning the **stability of IQ** have been of interest to psychologists for some time (Bloom, 1964) because they shed light on the nature–nurture issue. If IQ scores are relatively stable over time, then the environment is presumed to have little influence on intellectual development. If, however, IQ scores vary a great deal from infancy to adulthood, then the environment must play a more significant role than heredity.

Are IQ scores fixed at birth? On the basis of the evidence so far, the answer to this question is not straightforward. On the one hand, research suggests that IQ scores are fairly stable from middle childhood onward (Brody, 1992; Kopp & McCall, 1982). On the other hand, there seems to be considerable individual variation. Evidence suggests that some children's IQ scores can vary as much as 20 to 30 points from age 2 to 17 (McCall, Applebaum, & Hagarty, 1973). More recent studies indicate that this variance is more modest, up to 13 points (e.g., Brody 1992). Furthermore, there are individual differences in these patterns of IQ change. While some children show steady increases, others show increases at certain ages and then declines later in development. Currently, most researchers believe that individual differences in these patterns of change are related to aspects of a child's home or school environment. The next section examines some of these influences more closely.

Genetic Influences

Studies of biological twins are a valuable source of information concerning how genetic and environmental factors influence intelligence. In Chapter 2, you learned that monozygotic twins have the same genotype, whereas dizygotic twins are born from two separate eggs fertilized at the same time by different sperm. Researchers compare these two different sets of twins to estimate the heritability of intelligence. **Heritability** refers to "the proportion of observed variance for a behavior that can be ascribed to genetic differences among individuals in a particular population" (Plomin, 1989). The key word in this definition is *population*. A heritability index is a statistic that applies to a population, rather than a trait or an individual (e.g., She inherited her mathematical abilities from her mother.).

What can twin studies tell us about the heritability of intelligence? Recent data suggest that 50 percent of the variation in intelligence within a population can be attributed to genetic differences between people (Plomin, 1990b). Studies show that the correlation between IQ scores for monozygotic twins is around 0.86, whereas the correlation for dizygotic twins is around 0.60; the correlation between IQ scores for monozygotic twins reared apart (0.72) is higher than that for dizygotic twins reared together (0.60)

(Bouchard & McGue, 1981; Plomin & DeFries, 1980). When monozygotic twins are reared apart they are generally adopted shortly after birth. Because the monozygotic twins are raised in different environments, this finding offers strong support for the genetic position. The twins did not share the same environment; hence, any similarity in their intelligence must be due to their similar genotypes.

Recent longitudinal studies with twins and adopted/biological siblings show that genetic influences are variable during early childhood, suggesting that ". . . the biological underpinnings of general cognitive ability are not fixed at birth but continue to change along with the still developing brain" (Bishop et al., 2003, p. 45). However, these studies show that by 10 or 11 years of age, genetic influences on intelligence become stronger. In other words, adolescents' (and adults') IQs are more predictable from their biological parents' IQs than children's (Ferrari & Sternberg, 1998).

Sandra Scarr and her associates (Scarr, 1992 and 1996; Scarr & McCartney, 1983) have developed a model of gene-environmental relations that is useful for understanding why children's IQs may become increasingly influenced by their genotypes as they get older. As described in Table 4.2, there are three types of genotype-environment effects. At a young age, two processes are operating. The first is called a *passive* gene-environment effect. Parents pass on their genes to their offspring and provide an environment for development that is influenced by their own heredity. In this case, it is difficult to disentangle the influence of nature and nurture because the parents' genes are correlated with the child's, as well as with the rearing environment. However, the genotypes of children begin to mold the environment through a second gene-environment effect called *evocative*. Different genotypes evoke different reactions for the social and physical environment. A happy baby elicits more positive responses than a temperamental or passive one. Similarly, a very verbal preschooler elicits more social interactions with adults and peers than a shy preschooler. The responses these different children receive from their environment shape their development in ways that correlate with their genotype. For example, the shy child has fewer opportunities to develop social skills. At older ages, an *active* gene-environment effect emerges when children begin to choose friends and activities that fit their genetic tendencies. For example, the shy child may choose to spend time in solitary activities that again

TABLE 4.2	Types of Genes □ Environmental Effects
Passive	Parents pass on their genes to their children and provide an environment based on a shared genetic heredity. For example, parents of a child with high verbal abilities are likely to create a literacy-rich environment. Parents' and children's genes are correlated early in development.
Evocative	Children's genotypes (i.e., temperament, verbal abilities, sex, etc.) evoke different reactions and responses from their environment. Children play a role in shaping and creating their environments. For example, a happy child is likely to evoke positive responses from caregivers, which reinforces a pleasant disposition.
Active	With maturity, children and adolescents choose environments that complement and fit their genetic tendencies. For example, a highly social adolescent is likely to choose friends who are outgoing and enjoy social activities.

Source: After Scarr & McCartney (1983).

limit his or her opportunities to develop social skills. This tendency to choose an environment that complements our heredity is know as **niche-picking** (Scarr & McCartney, 1983). Thus, with age and increasing independence, genetic factors become more important in development because they shape the environments we create for ourselves.

Currently, most theorists believe that genetic factors establish the upper and lower limits, or reaction range (see Chapter 2), of intellectual development. For the most part, intelligence is malleable, and the reaction range defines the degree to which the environment can affect intellectual development. The environment has a stronger influence on children with high intellectual potential but a limited effect on those with low intellectual potential. As the next section will show, educational experiences at home and at school play an important role in the formation, maintenance, and modification of children's intellectual development.

Environmental Influences on Cognitive Processes and Intellectual Development

Few child development researchers today question the influence of the environment on children's intellectual development. As we learned in Chapter 2, the lack of adequate nutrition and exposure to toxic substances can have a negative effect on early brain development. Also, according to Scarr and McCartney's model, children's intellectual development is strongly influenced by the home environment during infancy and early childhood when they are under the direct influence of parents. As children mature, schools and peers also begin to play a role in their intellectual socialization. Furthermore, the powerful role of environment may be reflected in findings that IQ scores in general have increased over time (Neisser, 1997). In this section, we examine the influence of the home environment and schooling experiences on children's intellectual development.

The Home Environment and Parenting Behavior   We have already discussed how IQ scores begin to stabilize by late childhood. For this reason, numerous studies have focused on the influence of learning experiences in the early childhood years, when parents can have a substantial impact on their children's intellectual development. Research examining the influence of the home environment on cognitive development is primarily concerned with the factors responsible for the establishment of intellectual competence (Bjorklund, 1995). Many of these studies have used the Home Observation for Measurement of the Environment (HOME) scale developed by Betty Caldwell and Robert Bradley (1978) to characterize the quality of a child's early learning environment. Categories from the HOME scale assess such things as the mother's responsiveness, discipline style, and involvement with the child; the organization of the environment; the availability of appropriate learning materials; and the opportunity for daily stimulation. New versions of the HOME scale assess family environments of preschoolers, school-age children, and adolescents (e.g., Bradley, Corwyn, McAdoo, & Cole, 2001). (See Chapter 8 for sample items.)

Studies indicate that each of the HOME categories relates positively to children's IQ scores from 6 months to 5 years (Bradley & Caldwell, 1984). Two subscales in particular show consistent and strong relations to IQ scores. Children whose mothers are more responsive and regularly provide stimulating learning activities have scored higher on IQ measures. Furthermore, HOME scores for 2-year-olds relate to their IQ scores and math and reading achievement at age 11 (Olson, Bates, & Kaskie, 1992). Note that children's early

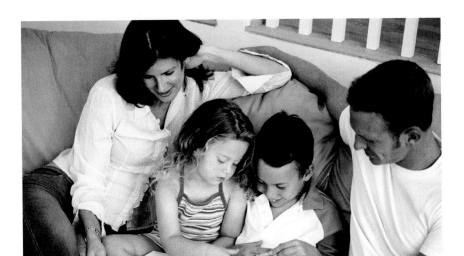

Parents have a positive influence on their children's intellectual development when they provide learning materials in a warm, responsive environment.
Source: Banana Stock/Punch Stock.

experiences are not only related to their level of IQ but also to changes in their IQ over time. These findings have now been replicated across six different longitudinal studies, in which the HOME scale was used to study a combined sample of 931 children and their families (Bradley et al., 1989).

Numerous studies have examined the effects of home and family influences on children's early cognitive development. The findings are fairly consistent across studies and suggest that parents have a positive influence on their child's early intellectual development when they provide appropriate play and learning materials, encourage exploration and stimulate curiosity, and create a warm, responsive, and supportive environment (Baharudin & Luster, 1998; Belsky, 1981).

How can parents help to maintain the benefits of early learning experiences? What can research tell us about the effects of the home environment and parenting practices on children's later intellectual development? Although research evidence strongly suggests that the home and family play an important role in the establishment and maintenance of children's intellectual abilities, a few issues need further discussion. First, much of the research on the home environment and parenting practices has focused on interactions between the mother and child. Researchers have only recently begun to study the effects of fathers on children's abilities (see Chapter 8). Second, it is important to keep in mind that measures of home environment are not totally free of genetic influences. As discussed earlier, parents with a high IQ may provide a better organized environment or more stimulating learning materials. Similarly, a child's genetic characteristics, such as alertness or temperament, may elicit different reactions from the environment. For example, some children may be more responsive to intellectual stimulation than others, thereby reinforcing parental efforts to provide such stimulation. It is important to remember that children affect their environment as much as their environment affects them. The research on parent–child relations underscores the point made earlier that it is nearly impossible to separate genetic and environmental influences (see Chapter 8).

However, research conducted by the NICHD Early Child Care Network (e.g., 1998, 2000, 2002, 2003a, 2005b) has attempted to disentangle these influences. For example, a recent study by this research group (2005b) examined the influences of maternal sensitivity and stimulation (using the HOME scale) on children's cognitive processes. Findings showed positive relationships between mothers' behaviors and their first graders' attention (maintenance and control) and memory (both short and long term). Notably, researchers reported that these findings cannot be explained by shared intelligence of mothers and children (to the extent that maternal vocabulary controls for heritability). Interestingly, researchers also noted that these results were found although children spent substantial time cared for by someone else in their early years. Thus, mothers appear to influence their children's cognitive development beyond contributing their genes! Furthermore, based on other study findings, these researchers suggest that experiences throughout childhood are important for cognitive outcomes, not just the first few years of life (see Chapter 2, Focus on Teaching box on page 64).

The Effects of Poverty and Early Intervention   We have discussed how intellectual competence is established and maintained through experiences in the home. We now turn to research concerning the degree to which children's intellectual development is influenced by poverty and can be modified through early intervention. It is clear that an appropriate level of stimulation, structure, and support is important for optimal intellectual development. Many factors associated with poverty, such as poor nutrition, low maternal education, unemployment, inadequate living conditions, limited educational opportunities, and poor health, can all raise the risk of poor intellectual development (Sameroff, Seifer, Barocas, Zax, & Greenspan, 1987). Even after accounting for maternal education, poverty has negative effects on children's IQ (Duncan, Yeung, Brooks-Gunn, & Smith, 1998). Is it possible to reverse, or at least offset, the negative effects of a poor home environment on children's intellectual development?

During the 1960s, a number of compensatory educational programs were implemented to offset the negative effects of poverty on children's intellectual development. One of the best-known efforts is Project Head Start, a federally funded program for children from low-income families. Established in 1965, Head Start programs provided preschool children with intensive educational experiences, as well as social, medical, and nutritional services. Most of the programs also include a parent education and involvement component. Head Start began as a summer program, grew into a full-year program for 4-year-olds, then continued as Project Follow Through, a compensatory education program for the first 3 years of elementary school (Oden, Schweinhart, & Weikart, 2000). Early Head Start has evolved to provide services for low-income families with infants and toddlers, beginning with prenatal care.

Head Start programs for 3- and 4-year-old children can have a lasting influence on development.
Source: *Cindy Charles/Photo Edit.*

Early evaluations of Head Start indicated that almost all programs were able to produce short-term gains in IQ scores. A study of 14 projects showed an IQ increase of approximately 7.42 points (Lazar, Darlington, Murray, Royce, & Snipper, 1982). During kindergarten and first grade, children who attended Head Start performed better on measures of cognitive development than comparable groups of children who had not attended Head Start programs. However, Head Start children lost their advantage as they grew older. By ages 10 and 17, few significant differences were found in the IQ scores of children who did or did not participate. Additionally, evaluations of Project Follow Through showed no enduring changes in IQ scores for its participants. Thus, initial studies concluded that there were no lasting changes in IQ test scores associated with participation in any compensatory education program.

Despite these early findings, researchers and educators were not willing to dismiss the potential benefits of early intervention for economically disadvantaged children. A survey of 14 longitudinal studies of children who participated in Head Start programs during the 1960s reported several positive but delayed effects of the intervention (Lazar et al., 1982). As compared with comparable groups of children who did not participate in the program, Head Start graduates scored higher on reading and mathematics achievement tests in elementary school, and they were less likely to be retained a grade or to receive special education services. Moreover, as teenagers, Head Start participants were less likely to drop out of high school and were more likely to attend college than those who did not participate. In view of this later evidence, researchers now believe that high-quality preschool educational programs, such as Head Start, have long-term effects such as increases in achievement, socialization, motivation, and parental involvement in school. However, the data on raising scores in IQ tests is less clear (Barnett & Boocock, 1998). The Focus on Research box on page 220 describes a highly successful early childhood program for low-income children, the High/Scope Perry Preschool Project, that has documented effects well into adulthood.

Although most Head Start programs typically enroll 3- or 4-year-old children, a few intervention programs have focused on infants (Garber, 1988; Ramey & Campbell, 1984), including the Early Head Start program. One of the most successful intervention programs for infants was the Carolina Abecedarian Project, in which participants began before they were 3 months old and continued to the age of 8 (Ramey & Campbell, 1991). The children who participated in this program were 98 percent African American and were judged to be at serious risk for school failure on the basis of family income, maternal IQ and educational level, a history of poor school achievement among older siblings, and other family problems. Participants were randomly assigned to a treatment or control group. The intervention, which enrolled four cohorts of children between 1972 and 1977, occurred in two phases. For the first 5 years, children in the treatment group attended a full-time day care program that promoted the development of motor, cognitive, language, and social skills. When children entered elementary school, a parent education component was implemented to increase parental involvement in the children's education at school.

Evaluations of the Carolina Abecedarian Project were done on a regular basis. Figure 4.11 on page 221 shows that children who participated in the intervention began to outperform control children on IQ tests beginning at age 2. Children in the treatment group maintained their advantage in IQ through preschool and elementary school and high school (Campbell, Kameu, Pungello, Miller-Johnson, & Burchinal, 2001). At ages 12 and 15, adolescents in the treatment group were achieving better in school, especially in the areas of reading, writing, and general knowledge, and achievement differences favoring the treatment group were still evident at age 15 and 21 (Campbell, et al., 2002, Campbell & Ramey, 1993, Campbell, Ramey, Pungello, Sparling, & Miller-Johnson, 2002). Interestingly, evaluations of this project showed that school-age interventions alone were not associated with enhanced school achievement or IQ scores. Rather, the low-income African American children in this project seemed to benefit the most from the early phase, but school-age treatment helped maintain benefits, especially for reading.

Focus on
Research

The High/Scope Perry Preschool Project

Since the early 1960s researchers have been following 123 children who participated in the High/Scope Perry Preschool Project at the ages of 3 or 4. All of the children were African American and were from the same neighborhood in Ypsilanti, Michigan. The mothers of these children had completed an average of 9.5 years of school, and half were on welfare at the onset of the program. The children were randomly assigned to two different groups at the beginning of the project. One group served as the control, and these children did not receive the preschool program. The other group received a high-quality early childhood program based on the child development principles of Jean Piaget. It included activities and social interactions that promoted children's active, constructivist learning and development (Hohmann & Weikart, 1995). The program consisted of 2.5 hours of preschool experience, 5 days a week for 7.5 months over a 2-year period. Teachers also visited each mother and child at home for 90 minutes per week during the school year. Both groups were assessed annually from ages 3 to 11, at ages 14 to 15, at age 19, and at age 27. During the school years, information was collected on school achievement, special education placement, attitudes, classroom behavior, and self-reported delinquency. For the adult assessments, information was collected on years of school completed, employment, public assistance, and criminal records.

Longitudinal data collected over 25 years revealed that the High/Scope program improved children's school achievement, reduced their years in special education placement and compensatory education programs, and increased their graduation rates and years of school completed. Compared with the control group, program participants had lower rates of self-reported delinquency at age 14, and they were less likely to be chronic juvenile offenders at age 19. The latest assessment at age 27 noted these differences favoring the preschool participants:

- Higher monthly earnings
- Higher percentages of home ownership
- Higher levels of schooling completed
- Lower numbers receiving public assistance
- Fewer arrests

Given these long-term benefits, it is estimated that a high-quality early childhood program, like the Perry Preschool Project, can save taxpayers $7.16 for every $1.00 invested, due to savings in special education and remediation programs and welfare assistance, as well as gains in economic productivity. *Quality* in this preschool program was defined by the following dimensions:

- A developmentally appropriate, active learning curriculum
- Systematic and ongoing staff development, training, and supervision
- A strong parent involvement and inclusion components
- A reasonable child–adult ratio, appropriate assessment procedures, and supportive administration

Source: Oden, Schweinhart, & Weikart (2000) and Schweinhart & Weikart (1997).

In summary, outcomes from carefully designed early intervention programs suggest that it is possible to modify the course of intellectual development for low-income children. The results of the Carolina Abecedarian Project further suggest that earlier and longer treatments may have more powerful and longer-lasting influences on intellectual development than preschool or school-age interventions alone (Campbell et al., 2001, 2002; Helms, Sparling, & Ramey, 1998; Ramey & Campbell, 1991). According to the project originators, Ramey and Ramey (2004), findings suggest that seven types of early experiences are essential for intellectual development and school success: (1) encouraging exploration, (2) mentoring of basic skills, (3) "celebrating" developmental advances, (4) practicing and expanding of new skills, (5) protecting from inappropriate social disapproval (e.g., teasing) and punishment, (6) providing rich and responsive communication opportunities, and (7) guiding and limiting behavior (p. 473).

■ FIGURE 4.11

IQ Scores of Children in the Carolina Abecedarian Project

Source: After Campbell et al. (2001).

Race, Ethnicity, and Intelligence

As described in Chapter 1, a disproportionate number of African American and Hispanic American children are from low-income families. Poor children experience a number of conditions that can negatively affect their cognitive development, such as poor nutrition, inadequate health care, overcrowded living conditions, low parental education, and chronic stress. Poor children also receive a poorer quality of education because they attend schools in poor communities. When differences in children's socioeconomic background and home environment are controlled, performance gaps on IQ tests narrow, but do not totally disappear (Brooks-Gunn, Klebanov, Smith, Duncan, & Lee, 2003; Suzuki & Valencia, 1997). In general, performance gaps between whites and blacks on IQ tests are approximately 15 points, or one standard deviation unit. IQ gaps are generally smaller between white and Hispanic populations (Williams & Ceci, 1997). It is important to note the overlaps in score distributions, despite the point gap. Differences in IQ scores are found by age 3 and remain constant until adulthood (Brody, 1992).

Sternberg, Grigorenko, and Kidd (2005) remind us that IQ tests are not "culture fair" and focus on measuring analytic abilities and past learning, which can be the result of differences in many factors, including motivation and educational opportunities. (An exception is dynamic tests, discussed later in the chapter.) Also, IQ tests do not generally assess creative, practical, and other abilities that experts and laypersons consider important in their conceptions of intelligence, as we have seen. These researchers also argue that when group differences in IQ or achievement tests are found among children socially labeled as white, black, Hispanic, and Asian, the extent of the differences and what groups they favor depend on what is tested. For example, using Sternberg's contemporary measures of analytical, creative, and practical intelligence, studies show higher scores for European and Asian Americans on tests of analytical thinking (similar to traditional IQ measures), but different patterns on tests of creative and practical thinking. Sternberg, Grigorenko, and Kidd (2005) argue further that researchers have not yet identified yet a single gene contributing to either IQ or academic achievement. Thus, they conclude that, "the statement that racial differences in IQ or academic achievement are of genetic origin is, when all is said and done, a leap of imagination" (p. 57).

Schooling Influences on Intellectual Development

How important is schooling for children's intellectual development? In Chapter 1, we discussed the ways formal schooling can shape young children's reasoning and thinking abilities. However, we have just seen that the cognitive benefits of early intervention may not extend into the school years. Does schooling have only a limited impact on older children's intellectual development, as these findings seem to suggest?

The available evidence suggests that children's educational experiences affect their intellectual development well beyond infancy and early childhood. In a recent review article, Ceci (1991) organized and presented several different types of evidence to support this claim.

- There are strong correlations between IQ and years of school completed. After controlling for socioeconomic status and other background variables, this correlation ranges between 0.60 and 0.80. Individuals who stay in school longer have higher IQ scores.
- Children who are truant or frequently absent from school have lower IQ scores than children who attend school regularly.
- A South African study showed that children experience a 5-point deficit in IQ scores for every year their schooling is delayed.
- A Swedish study of high school dropouts and graduates indicated that there was a loss of 1.8 IQ points for each year of high school that was not completed.
- Children experience a small but substantial decline in IQ scores over the summer months, with low-income children showing the largest decline, possibly because their summer activities do not resemble those found in school. Children who engage in schoollike activities over the summer do not show the June to September IQ drop.
- A study of African American children who migrated from poor, segregated schools in Georgia to better-quality schools in Philadelphia between World Wars I and II showed that children gained about one-half an IQ point for each year they attended the northern school.

Some of the strongest evidence of the impact of schooling on children's intellectual development can be found in studies that use the cut-off method to study early cognitive development (see Chapter 1). If intellectual development is mostly controlled by maturational or biological processes, then we would expect to find children's IQ scores to be influenced more by age than by years of schooling. If you recall, studies show that first-grade children with early birthdates (before the cut-off date for school entry) perform better than their slightly younger peers who had started school 1 year later.

To summarize, a number of studies emphasize the important influence of schools on children's intellectual development. Children who start school earlier, remain in school longer, and attend higher-quality schools generally perform better on IQ tests. Because much of the data cited in this section are from correlational studies, it is not possible to draw firm conclusions about cause-and-effect relations. It is suggested here that the quantity and quality of school leads to increases in IQ. Of course, it is equally possible that genetically intelligent people are encouraged to start school earlier, remain in school longer, and attend better schools. However, Ceci (1990) argued that schooling is most likely to influence children's performance on IQ tests, because schools teach the information and various perceptual, memory, and problem-solving skills that are needed to perform well on IQ tests. In other words, aspects of intelligence are learned at school.

Individual Differences in Intellectual Abilities

Giftedness

Many different terms are used to describe individuals who have unique talents or gifts, including *genius, creative, gifted,* and *talented.* Psychologists are currently leaning toward a broad definition of **giftedness,** as *unusually high ability in any area* (general IQ or domain-specific ability) (e.g., Winner, 2000). Some argue that equal attention should be given to individuals' *creativity* or original ideas (e.g., Renzuli, 2004), *motivation* or "rage to master" (e.g., Winner, 1996), and different *modes of thinking* or information processing (e.g., Sternberg & Clickenbeard, 1995). Ellen Winner (2000), an expert on giftedness, summarizes current thinking in the field, "The strong drive that accompanies giftedness, the posing of challenges, the mastery orientation, and the ability to make discoveries independently together suggest that gifted children do not just develop more rapidly than others, but develop and think differently from others" (p. 154). She suggests, however, that researchers need to establish whether high ability is *always* accompanied by qualitative motivation and cognitive differences.

Subotnik (2006) proposes a developmental perspective on giftedness. She argues that giftedness *develops* when children's intellectual potential is recognized and nurtured through provision of appropriate challenges in the elementary years. In middle school, as parents and teachers have less influence on decision making and use of time, gifted young adolescents' "hunger" (or motivation) for learning and intellectual stimulation plays a larger role. By the end of high school, older adolescents' discovery of domains of ability and interest will influence their potential as gifted adults. Implications of this developmental model are discussed at the end of this section.

The majority of children with special gifts and talents served in schools are the academically gifted. In most states, the criteria for giftedness require a minimal IQ score (usually 130) and above-average academic achievement (usually 2 years above grade level), referred to as "schoolhouse giftedness" (Renzuli, 2004). Reflecting more contemporary conceptions of giftedness, in some states, children have been identified through nonstandardized methods, such as classroom teacher nomination and observation of outstanding skills and talents. By expanding identification practices beyond standardized intelligence and achievement tests, schools are including more children from culturally and linguistically diverse backgrounds. They are also including children with other disabilities, particularly those with learning disabilities. Some children are both gifted and learning disabled. They tend to be highly intelligent but have a specific learning disability in one academic area coupled with poor organizational skills. It is estimated that approximately 3 percent to 5 percent of the school population in the United States falls into the category of gifted, but this number depends on the definition of gifted used (Hallahan & Kauffman, 2000).

Origins of Giftedness As with other types of exceptionalities, both genetic and environmental factors play a role in the development of giftedness. In a recent review of this research, Ellen Winner (2000) reports that there is some evidence to suggest that children with mathematical gifts show enhanced brain activity in their left hemisphere when asked to recognize faces, a task that is typically done in the right hemisphere. Also, people who are gifted in mathematics, visual arts, and music are disportionately left-handed. Studies also show that mathematically and musically gifted individuals have a more bilaterial, symmetrical brain organization than usual. Other evidence suggests that giftedness in mathematics is associated with a disproportionate incidence of language-related learning disorders and with immune disorders. Interestingly, recent studies have shown that adolescents with dyslexia are especially talented in global (holistic) visual-spatial processing (Von-Karoli, Winner, Gray, & Sherman, 2003). Taken together, studies suggest that giftedness in some areas may be due to atypical brain organization, which may in turn be due to testosterone effects on the brain during prenatal development.

Although this evidence of biological influences cannot be dismissed, it is important to recall our discussion of variations in intellectual abilities. Researchers have not yet identified the genes associated with different cognitive abilities. Some researchers have argued that individuals with special gifts and talents are not necessarily genetically endowed. There is some evidence to suggest that giftedness in any domain is due to hard work or deliberate practice. For example, studies show that expertise in piano, violin, chess, bridge, and athletics is directly related to the amount of deliberate practice (Ericsson, Krampe, & Tesch-Romer, 1993). Benjamin Bloom (1985) showed that eminent adults did not achieve their level of talent without a long and intensive period of training, which often began in early childhood with supportive and encouraging caregivers. However, Bloom's account also suggests that prior to intensive training, children demonstrated an usual ability in a particular area that teachers and parents recognized as special.

As suggested, a child's skills need to be recognized and supported. Numerous studies have identified ways in which the special talents of children are nurtured by their home environment. Parents of gifted children typically have high expectations for their children and model hard work and achievement themselves (Bloom, 1985; Csikszentmihalyi, Rathunde, & Walen 1993; Gardner, 1993). They also encourage their children to explore and provide home activities related to their child's developing talent, but teaching is informal and occurs in a variety of settings. Later on, they would seek out teaches or formal learning opportunities to further develop their child's abilities. Overall, the home environment of children with special talents is stimulating, warm, supportive, directive, and rewarding, regardless of the child's ethnic or socioeconomic backgrounds (Hallahan & Kauffman, 2000; Winner, 2000).

Characteristics of Children with Special Gifts and Talents   Clark (1992) compiled a list of various characteristics found in children who are academically gifted. Each child shows some but not all of the characteristics in cognition, language, and affective domains listed in Figure 4.12. Both preschool and school-age students with a special gift or talent will be more advanced in a particular area than their age-mates. They can also have strong verbal skills, superior intellectual abilities, and well-developed sensory awareness. Students with special gifts and talents may also be above average in adaptive behavior, leadership skills, and self-sufficiency. They also have a deep intrinsic interest or "rage to master" the domain in which they are talented, and it is difficult to tear them away from the computer, the art center, or a math book. This intense drive needs to be nurtured, not destroyed. If reasonably challenged, most students with special gifts remain interested and engaged in school.

The peer relations of academically gifted students have been an issue of some concern. Although gifted students may spend more time alone developing their talents, they report a preference for being with others and having peer contact (Csikszentmihalyi et al., 1993). Although there are exceptions, they are well liked by their peers. They are sensitive to the feelings of others and concerned about interpersonal relations and moral issues. However, students who are profoundly gifted (IQs over 180) may experience social or emotional problems. Extreme levels of giftedness can lead to social isolation. Profoundly gifted children are known to hide their talents to increase their peer popularity (Winner, 2000).

Clark's Characteristics of Giftedness

Cognitive Characteristics

- Extraordinary quantity of information

- Unusual retentiveness

- Advanced comprehension

- Unusually varied interests and curiosity

- Ability to generate original ideas and solutions (pp. 38–39)

Language Characteristics

- Strong verbal skills

- Highly developed receptive language and written language

- Well-developed sensory awareness

- Vulnerable to "Cartesian split," "a lack of integration between mind and body" (p. 43)

Affective Characteristics

- An evaluative approach toward self and others

- Persistent, goal-directed behavior

- Unusual sensitivity to the expectations and feelings of others

- Heightened self-awareness, accompanied by feelings of being different

- Earlier development of an inner locus of control and satisfaction

- Unusual emotional depth and intensity

- High expectations of self and others, often leading to high levels of frustration with self, others, and situations

- Advanced level of moral judgment

- Advanced cognitive and affective capacity for conceptualizing and solving social problems (pp. 40–43)

Source: After Clark (1992).

As they enter adolescence, students who are academically gifted have qualities that help them cope with many of the challenges presented during this developmental period. Yet, they are vulnerable to some special difficulties. The social disadvantages that result from being perceived by peers and teachers as "different" can undermine their personal growth. For example, their preference for independent learning may be misinterpreted by teachers as "oppositional" and by peers as "elitist." Ethnic minorities, particularly males, tend to be underrepresented in classes for the gifted and talented. Once placed in gifted programs or advanced placement courses, minority students risk rejection from peers of the same ethnic background, as well as from white students and teachers who do not understand them. Many African American students hide their academic abilities by being the classroom clown, suppressing effort, or dropping out (Ford, 1996). Strong negative social implications have also been documented in gifted girls, who are subject to conflicting gender-role expectations and stereotypes (Kerr, Colangelo, & Gaeth, 1998). Some evidence suggests that gifted girls are more likely than their male counterparts to suffer from low self-esteem, depression, and other psychosomatic symptoms (Gross, 1993).

Educational Concerns and Programs   Currently, there is considerable debate concerning how best to serve children with special gifts and talents. One issue of concern is that most school systems focus on academically gifted and talented students. If students demonstrate superior artistic, musical, or athletic abilities, these talents tend to be nurtured and supported through existing physical education and arts programs offered by schools. When

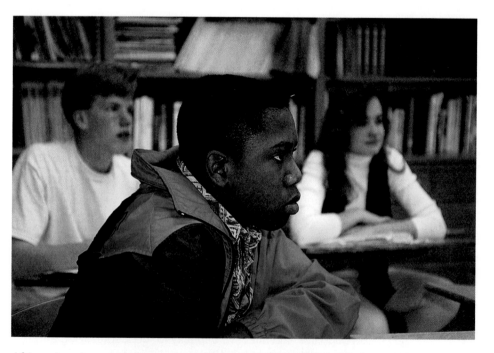

African American students represent 16 percent of the public school population but make up only 8 percent of those enrolled in gifted programs. Experts believe that this discrepancy is due to screening procedures and cultural stereotypes.
Source: *Jeff Greenberg/Photo Edit.*

schools experience budget difficulties, these programs are generally the first ones to be "downsized" or eliminated altogether.

Most school systems do not test for academic giftedness until the third or fourth grades. Advocates of early intervention argue that preschoolers with special gifts need to receive educational programs appropriate for their abilities, especially if they are from low-income families or have disabilities. Another issue concerns testing and screening procedures. Standardized tests measure a narrow range of abilities, notably those needed to succeed in school. Teacher nominations may be biased due to cultural or gender stereotypes. As previously mentioned, ethnic minority students tend to be underrepresented in gifted programs. For example, African American students constitute 16 percent of the public school enrollment but make up only 8 percent of those enrolled in gifted programs (Hallahan & Kauffman, 2000). Girls, on the other hand, tend to be overrepresented in programs for the gifted and talented in elementary school, but underrepresented in mathematics and science courses for high-ability students at the high school or college levels (Eccles, 1995). The Focus on Teaching box on the next page presents a set of multicultural and diversity issues that need to be considered in programs for academically gifted and talented students.

Once they are identified, there are a wide variety of plans for educating students with special needs and talents. Some schools offer *enrichment programs,* in which students are offered additional experiences without placing them in a higher grade. *Acceleration* is another approach that involves moving a student ahead of his or her age in one or more curriculum areas or grade levels. In some schools teachers who are certified in gifted education co-teach and/or consult with classroom teachers. The Focus on Teaching box on page 228 shows various ways that content in social studies can be adjusted for middle school students who are gifted. Learning centers can be developed that include challenging, higher-order thinking skill activities. Some schools provide **mentorship programs** that pair a student with an adult who shares a common interest or vocation. For example, the APA's Center for Gifted Education Policy teams talented adolescents with top thinkers in a variety of fields (Smith, 2003). In addition, secondary-level programs are offered in special honors courses, advanced placement classes, elective courses, and summer institutes that recruit students statewide.

We return to Subotnik's (2006) suggestions for fostering the development of giftedness:

- Provide all children with an enriched early childhood education.
- Search for those demonstrating exceptional potential in childhood.
- Provide children and adolescents with exceptional potential with highly challenging work and teachers with appropriate expertise.
- Always encourage hunger for and commitment to excellence.
- Guide older adolescents with great potential to explore preferred domains of talent and interest.
- Encourage development of unique styles and personal skills that may contribute to making our lives better or more beautiful.

Mental Retardation

The most distinctive characteristic of mental retardation is deficient intellectual functioning (Zigler, 2002). Students with mental retardation differ from their same-age classmates in their levels of intelligence and adaptive behavior. Adaptive behavior consists of those skills that enable a person to live socially productive life. The American Association on Mental

Focus on
Teaching

Multicultural and Diversity Considerations in Education Programs and Services for the Gifted

1. What is the school district's philosophy of gifted education and definition of giftedness?
   - In what ways are the philosophy and definition inclusive? Exclusive? To what extent are the strengths of black (and other minority) students represented in the definition?
   - Does the gifted education program reflect community needs? Are students retrofitted to the program or is the program reflective of student needs?
   - Have contemporary definitions of giftedness been adopted and/or modified for use with racially and culturally diverse students?

2. Is the gifted program reflective of community demographics?
   - To what extent is there diversity relative to gender, race, and socioeconomic status?
   - What discrepancies, if any, exist among the community, school, and gifted program demographic characteristics?
   - Is there evidence of increasing among professionals and students in the gifted programs?

3. Are there opportunities for continuing professional development in gifted and multicultural education?
   - Are faculty and other school personnel encouraged and given opportunities by administrators to participate in workshops, conferences, university courses, and so forth? Do administrators attend such professional development training? Do

personnel seek or willingly take advantage of these opportunities?
   - What are the indications of multicultural commitment? For instance, does a library exist for teachers and students that contains up-to-date multicultural resources (e.g., newsletters, journals, books)?

4. Are assessment practices equitable?
   - Are the measures used valid and reliable for the student population?
   - what biases exist relative to the selection process?
   - How are instruments administered (individually or in a group)?
   - Which instruments appear to be most effective at identifying the strengths of minority students?
   - Is a combination of quantitative and quantitative assessment practices used? If so, is one type given preference or higher weight than the other?
   - What are the primary purposes of assessment?
   - Are personnel trained to administer and interpret test results?
   - In what ways are students' learning styles accommodated relative to test administration and instructions?
   - To what extent are students' home language, culture, and background reflected in the tests?
   - Are tests biased in favor of verbal students, higher-SES students, or white students?

Source: After Ford (1996).

Retardation (AAMR, 2002) defines **mental retardation** as "a disability characterized by significant limitations both in intellectual functioning and in adaptive behavior as expressed in conceptual, social, and practical adaptive skills." Children and adolescents with mental retardation have difficulties with conceptual skills (such as receptive and expressive language, reading and writing, and money concepts), social skills (such as interpersonal skills, following rules, responsibility, and gullibility), and practical skills (such as daily living and occupational skills).

Levels of intelligence and adaptive behavior vary, and children are usually classified in schools as mild, moderate, or severe/profound retarded on the basis of IQ scores. A child with mild mental retardation may be reading at the second-grade level and performing basic mathematical computations, whereas a child of the same age with severe/profound

Reuben

Reuben Murray is a gregarious 18-year-old whose interests include weight lifting, listening to music with his friends, and "hanging out at the mall." In addition to attending high school, he has a part-time position as a bagger for a major grocery chain and participates in a monthly self-advocacy group for people with developmental disabilities.

Reuben is also a popular and frequent guest lecturer on the university circuit. Speaking to graduate-level students in the fields of special education and medicine, he readily shares his insights and experiences. During a recent presentation, when asked what makes a "good" teacher, Reuben replied, "They're the ones who help me so I can learn."

From the time he was 4 months old, Reuben has received special education services. These began with an early developmental program that focused on stimulation activities for implementation in the home. For the past few years, Reuben and his parents have been concerned with transition issues—preparing Reuben for independent living and working in the community. On graduation, one of his goals is to move from his parents' home and "live with two or three other guys." Together with The Arc, a parent–professional advocacy organization, his parents are helping him attain this goal.

Reuben has Down syndrome, also known as Trisomy #21, a chromosomal condition that occurs in 1 of every 800 to 1,000 children who are born in our country each year. It is caused by the production of an additional #21 chromosome.

retardation may not be toilet-trained, may be unable to dress himself, and may use the vocabulary of a 1-year-old. Figure 4.13 contains a brief description of Reuben, an adolescent with mild retardation.

According to AAMR (2002), an important purpose for describing limitations of individuals is to develop a profile of needed supports. With appropriate personalized supports over a sustained period of time, children and adolescents with mental retardation will generally improve functioning in their everyday lives. Common areas of personalized support include:

- **Communication.** Individuals must receive support to improve their communication and social interactions and reduce their challenging behaviors.
- **Assistive technology.** Individuals must have access to services, devices, and training to assist them with mobility, communication, and self-determination.
- **Personal assistance.** Adults (and parents of children under 21) should be able to hire (and fire) assistants to help them perform everyday activities and exercise control over their lives.

A collaborative team needs to plan and monitor the quality and effectiveness of these supports.

Factors Contributing to Mental Retardation Mental retardation has both genetic and environmental causes. As discussed in Chapter 2, genetic abnormalities such as Down syndrome, fragile-X syndrome, and Tay–Sachs disease result in mental retardation. Infections in the mother such as rubella (German measles), syphilis, and herpes simplex can cause mental retardation in their children. Fetal alcohol syndrome and low birth weight are also associated with mental retardation, as well as loss of oxygen during the birth process. Infections in the child, such as meningitis, encephalitis, and pediatric AIDS, are other causes of mental retardation. Additionally, poverty, family instability, and low parental education are associated with mental retardation. Currently, however, experts are able to pinpoint the causes of mental retardation in only about 10 to 15 percent of the cases (Hallahan & Kauffman, 2000).

Characteristics of Children and Youth with Mental Retardation   Table 4.3 summarizes and compares the level of functioning of children classified as mildly (89 percent), moderately (6 percent), and severely (5 percent), retarded. As you can see, homogeneity within this category of exceptionality is more the exception than the rule. Since intellectual development and language development are closely related, language difficulties are found in most children with mild or moderate retardation. Other common characteristics among children with mental retardation are shared by children with other disabilities: inattention, memory problems, low self-esteem, external locus of control, and difficulties generalizing newly learned skills. Children with mental retardation also have difficulty making and keeping friends. Social problems are evident as early as preschool (Kasari & Bauminger, 1998).

Our knowledge of developmental issues in adolescents with mental retardation is minimal, because the focus has been on programming needs rather than on developmental processes (Rowitz, 1998). As a group, these adolescents need assistance in socialization, personal skills, vocational preparation, transition into the community, independent adult living, and functional math and reading skills.

Educational Programs for Students with Mental Retardation   Educational programs differ by the severity of the mental retardation. When children with mental retardation are placed in the regular classroom, teachers collaborate with special educators, speech language therapists, occupational and physical therapists, and vocational education teachers to provide support. Areas that may be in need of support are as follows:

- Functional academics (e.g., balancing a checkbook, ordering from a menu, planning a bus trip, reading sings)
- Home-living skills (e.g., laundering clothes, cooking meals)

TABLE 4.3   Comparison of Levels of Retardation

Characteristics	Mild**	Moderate	Severe/Profound
I.Q	50–70	35–50	Below 35
Mental age range*	7–11 yrs.	2–7 Yrs.	6 mo–2 yrs.
Cognitive level	Concrete operational	Preoperational	Sensory motor
Primary areas in need of support	Functional academics	Home-living	Self-care skills***
	Communication	Self-care skills	Communication
		Communication	

*Mental age score tells us that a child can perform tasks that most children can accomplish at a particular age level. It does not tell us anything about emotional, physical and social needs. For example, a 12-year-old child with a mental age of 65 can be expected to have the potential for, learning exhibited in most 6-year-olds. However, he or she will not be similar to a 6-year-old in his or her psychosocial needs, interest level, or physical development.

**The majority of children with mild mental retardation share common areas of difficulty with children with learning disabilities and emotional or behavioral disorders (Hallahan & Kauffman, 1977; Heward & Orlansky, 1988; Strichard & Gottlieb, 1982).

***Since the majority of children with severe/profund mental retardation have multiple disabilities (including significant health and physical impairments) they require intensive levels of support in these areas.

- Self-care skills (e.g., toileting, grooming, hygiene)
- Communication—understanding and expressing verbally (e.g., sing language, spoken word, written word) and nonverbally (e.g., facial expression, touch gestures)

Means for assisting children and adolescents with special needs in the classroom are described in Chapter 9.

Teaching for Thinking

Contemporary information processing and intelligence theories have inspired the creation of a number of "teaching-for-thinking" programs to help students succeed at school. For example, the Practical Intelligence for Schools (PIFS) program was developed by Robert Sternberg and his colleagues at Yale University and Howard Gardner and the Harvard Project Zero group at Harvard University. PIFS incorporates principles from triarchic and multiple intelligence theories (discussed earlier in the chapter), and was designed to help students: (a) develop a sense of their own intellectual profile, such as understanding their learning strategies and intellectual strengths and weaknesses; (b) develop an understanding of the structure and learning of academic subjects; and (c) view school as a complex social system (Sternberg & Ben-Zeev, 2001).

PIFS is currently used as an intervention with sixth- and seventh-grade students—at a time when many make the transition from elementary to middle school and need to assume more responsibility for their learning. The program helps students through enhancing their understanding of their own motives and interests, the purpose of school tasks, the importance of organizational and self-regulatory skills, the study requirements for different subjects, and the practices of cognitive monitoring. (The introductory vignette illustrates teacher–student discussions about some of these topics.) PIFS curriculum includes lessons on reading, writing, homework, and test taking that can be incorporated into regular classroom activities. Figure 4.14 on page 232 provides some sample curriculum activities from PIF. The program has been used in urban, rural, and suburban schools in several states. A study evaluating the effectiveness of the program at two school sites with students from diverse backgrounds showed that PIFs enhanced students' practical and academic skills (Williams, Blythe, White, Li, Gardner, & Sternberg, 2002). These findings suggest that acquiring insights about cognitive and metacognitive processes contributes to adolescents' real-world learning and school achievement. Thus, the authors argue for a broad-based approach to identifying school-based competence, that include areas such as practical intelligence.

Innovative preschool and elementary programs have also been developed based on multiple intelligence (MI) theory. Some rich case studies illustrating the best of MI practices (according to Gardner) are described in Kornhaber, Fierros, and Veenema's (2004) book. For example, in one elementary school, children learned about the local town history through an archaeological project. To do this, they worked with amateur archaeologists and a local museum curator to carry out an excavation of one of the town's abandoned outdoor shipyards. They examined and organized their findings, and prepared them for exhibition in the local museum. This is an example of interdisciplinary collaboration—similar to experiences in the "community of learners" programs previously described—that exploited and fostered many intellectual competencies and interests. Gardner (2004) concludes, "At the heart of MI theory is the belief that each individual has a rich and differentiated mind; that no two persons have exactly the same cognitive configuration; and that education is most likely to be successful if it pays attention to these individual differences in the course of fashioning curriculum, pedagogy, and assessment" (p. xiii).

■ FIGURE 4.14

Sample Discussion Questions and Activities from the Practical Intelligence for School (PIFS) program.

Source: Adapted/condensed from the PIF Expository Writing chapter (Williams, Blythe, White, Li, Gardner, & Sternberg, 2002).

Lesson 3.2 Using Past Experiences in Writing

Central Themes: Knowing Self, Knowing Process

Synopsis: Journal writing, discussion, and brainstorms to help students reflect on their past experiences with writing and on the extracurricular interests and strengths that might help them in their writing.

Connections to Other Lessons: Writing Lesson 3.7 Choosing a Format; Reading Lesson 2.3: Personal Reading Profiles; Homework Lesson 4.6: Making It More Interesting and Personal

Activities:

1. Students refer to their list of different types of writing (brainstormed earlier) to answer questions such as the following (in their journals).

   - What kind of writing do you like the most? What is easiest or most enjoyable about doing that kind of writing?
   - What circumstances make it hard for you to write?
   - What do you like to write about?
   - Do you prefer the writing assignments in some subjects?

2. Teachers talk with students about the things they find easiest and hardest about writing, and discuss trends across the class (e.g., writing outside school is easier).

3. Students refer to their self-profile journals to see how they can incorporate their interests, experiences, and strengths into their writing assignments.

4. Teachers select a report topic, and have students think of ideas for a writing assignment that could incorporate a personal interest or area of expertise.

5. Students share their own ideas, and help individuals relate their interests to the topic.

6. Students discuss advantages and disadvantages of choosing unusual topics.

7. Students follow up the writing assignment by writing in their journals about how they related their interests to the topic.

Current Issues in School Learning

Group Differences in Cognitive Performance

Standardized tests of academic achievement are often used to examine group differences in cognitive abilities. This section examines recent research on ethnic and gender differences. We will also briefly discuss some possible explanations for the differences that are reported. Most researchers believe that ethnic and gender variations in cognitive abilities are due largely to socialization experiences and cultural conditions.

Ethnic Differences

As discussed in Chapter 1, the ethnic and racial composition of American schools is rapidly changing. Over two-thirds of the students enrolled in U.S. public schools are likely to be a member of an ethnic minority group by the year 2010. The changing racial and ethnic backgrounds of America's schoolchildren will have profound implications for education in the future. Research indicates that children from minority ethnic groups score lower on many tests of cognitive ability than do their non-Hispanic, white classmates. The major exceptions to this pattern are Asian American children, who tend to perform better on tests of quantitative abilities than white children.

Gaps in achievement test scores show little change from first to twelfth grade (Jencks & Phillips, 1998). Some evidence suggests that the black-white performance gap is narrowing. According to several reviews (Jencks & Phillips, 1998; Jones, 1984; Williams & Ceci, 1997), reading and mathematics performance measured by the National Assessment of

The school population is becoming more and more ethnically diverse. Ethnic differences in achievement are found as early as first grade.
Source: Frank Siteman/Stock Boston.

Educational Progress showed a decline in the white-black difference from 1971 to 1980 at each age of assessment (9, 13, and 17 years). Some estimates indicate that the gaps had narrowed by 25 to 50 percent depending on subject area and grade level (Williams & Ceci, 1997). This decline is due to rises in the average level of performance by African American students. Recent data (2004) indicate that gaps continue to narrow to some extent (NAEP, 2005). The verbal and quantitative subtests of the Scholastic Aptitude Test (SAT), which is taken by college-bound high school seniors, also shows a decline in the white-black gap over the last 25 years. In this case, declines are due to decreases in the performance of white students and increases in the performance of African American students.

In science, achievement gaps are considerably larger, and there has not been much change in the size of the achievement gap from the early 1980s. However, recent NAEP data (2004) indicate that gaps in science scores are beginning to narrow in fourth grade (but not in eighth and twelfth grade, NAEP, 2005).

The major exception to the achievement patterns of ethnic minority students is Asian Americans, who generally outperform Anglo-American classmates on tests of mathematical reasoning, spatial abilities, and numerical skills (Sue & Okazaki, 1990). Even children of Southeast Asian boat people, who arrive at school with little knowledge of English and Western culture, are able to excel in mathematics within a short period of time (Caplan, Choy, & Whitmore, 1992). The Focus on Research box on page 235 describes some of the factors that contribute to the high academic achievement of Asian American students.

One of the major shortcomings of research on racial and ethnic differences in cognitive abilities is that it fails to examine differences within ethnic groups. There are often wide differences within as well as between ethnic groups. For example, there are differences in the achievement levels of Chinese Americans, Filipino Americans, and Vietnamese Americans that are masked when students are treated as one homogeneous group of Asian Americans. In addition, research indicates that recent immigrants tend to achieve better in school than American-born ethnic minority students (Spencer & Dornbusch, 1990). Girls perform better on tests of cognitive abilities than boys in some ethnic groups. Also, few studies have disentangled social class and ethnic differences. Middle-income African American students perform better on cognitive tests than their lower-income peers.

Because most schools reflect a white middle-class culture, ethnic minority children experience a number of problems when they enter school. Non-English-speaking children struggle the most, because they must master a new language before they can fully participate in learning activities in most schools. Even if children speak English, they may use speech patterns of a particular ethnic, social, or regional group, called social dialects, that white teachers find unacceptable. Because some dialects are viewed as linguistically inferior to more standard speech patterns, a dialect can affect teachers' judgments of children's abilities, their learning potential, and how they should be grouped for instruction (Harrison, 1985). Teachers who expect problems with children on the basis of judgments of their dialects are more likely to treat these children differently in the classroom, which may, in turn, influence children's feelings of competence, self-worth, and motivation to learn.

The way teachers ask questions in school can also cause problems for children who are not from the dominant culture. According to Shirley Brice Heath (1983), parents in some African American communities do not ask questions that have an obvious answer unless the child is being disciplined. Additionally, children are taught not to ask or answer personal questions. In school, however, teachers often ask "known-answer" questions ("What color is your shirt?") and personal questions ("Where does your mother work?"). When

Achievement Patterns of Asian American Students

Ethnic differences in educational achievement and school success are well documented. One of the most interesting findings in this research literature is the relatively high academic performance of some Asian American groups during the last 40 years (Chen & Stevenson, 1995; Okagaki & Frensch, 1998; Sue & Okazaki, 1990). On the average, Asian Americans are perform better in U.S. schools than do African Americans and Hispanic Americans, even though they experience racial prejudice and discrimination (Sue & Okazaki, 1990). For college-bound students, the grade point averages of Asian Americans are often higher than that of Anglo-Americans. Moreover, the superior performances of Asian American students emerges during the transition to junior high school, when most students' grades decline (Fulgini, 1997b).

What explains the exceptional achievement of Asian American students in U.S. schools? There is no evidence that these differences are explained by genetic or socioeconomic factors (Sue & Okazaki, 1990). Much of the evidence instead suggests that the values and child-rearing practices of Asian families play a very important role. Compared to other ethnic groups, Asian parents are more likely to believe that success in life is associated with educational achievement (Okagaki & Frensch, 1998). In addition, Asian parents teach their children that success is in their own hands. All children can succeed in school if they work hard (Chen & Stevenson, 1995; Stevenson & Stigler, 1992). More important, Asian parents emphasize a family-based orientation to achievement. Achievement is viewed as a way to repay one's parents for their sacrifices (Slaughter-Defoe, Nakagawa, Takanishi, & Johnson, 1990).

As a result of socialization practices at home, Asian American students value school achievement, and they worry about the possible negative consequences of not doing well in terms of their parents' disappointment and future occupational choices (Steinberg, Dornbusch, & Brown, 1992). In fact, some evidence suggests that a fear of failure may be an important motivating factor for Asian American students (Eaton & Dembo, 1997). They also spend more time on homework and significantly less time socializing and watching television than other students (Caplan, Choy, & Whitemore, 1992; Fuligini & Stevenson, 1995). Additionally, Asian American students tend to believe that the only way they can succeed in mainstream American society is through educational achievement, and they pay less of a price for their superior performance than other ethnic groups in terms of depression, anxiety, or stress (Crystal et al., 1994). In contrast, African American and Hispanic American students tend to believe that educational achievement will have less occupational payoff for them within a prejudiced society (Ogbu, 1978).

African American children take a long time to respond, teachers infer that they have a hearing or comprehension problem: "I would almost think some of them have a hearing problem; it is as though they don't hear me ask a question. I get blank stares to my questions" (pp. 107–108).

There are many other examples of cultural differences in behaviors and customs that can influence an ethnic minority child's success in school. In many cultures, group achievement is valued over individual success. Children of these cultures (e.g., Native American, Mexican American, Asian American) may resist competing with others for grades and other incentives that are used to motivate and reward students in school. They may also feel uncomfortable when their individual achievements are publicly recognized. Certain Native American communities do not express feelings through facial expressions or maintain eye contact in verbal exchanges with adults. These cultural differences can lead to adjustment and achievement problems for ethnic minority students if the behaviors are interpreted as unacceptable, inappropriate, or "odd" by teachers or peers.

The achievement problems of racial and ethnic minority students are compounded by a school's **ability grouping** or **tracking** systems. In elementary school, children are generally grouped according to their ability for reading and mathematics. Frequently this ability grouping occurs within the classroom, but some elementary schools may assign students to classes based on their achievement levels. This process is known as between-class ability grouping or tracking. Most high schools have college preparatory, general, or vocational tracks. In general, students who are placed in low-ability groups during elementary school remain in those tracks through high school. Research indicates that a disproportionate number of ethnic minority students, not including Asian Americans, are placed in lower-ability groups or classes. Considerable evidence suggests that ability grouping and tracking systems can severely limit minority children's learning and achievement opportunities for the following reasons (Oakes, 1995; Oakes & Stuart, 1998):

■ There are clear differences in the quality of instruction across ability groups. Teachers of low-ability classes place little emphasis on problem-solving and inquiry skills. Compared to higher-ability classes, there is a stronger emphasis on rote memorization, basic skills, and remediation in low-ability classes. Teaching for higher-order thinking is more likely to occur in high-ability than low-ability classes.
■ Students in low-ability classes are often taught by less-experienced teachers.
■ Students in low-ability classes are likely to be perceived as slow and incompetent, which can lower self-esteem and motivation.
■ Tracking systems determine the courses students can take in high school, which in turn affects students' eligibility for college.

On the basis of this evidence, it is not surprising that ability grouping and tracking tend to accentuate rather than diminish preexisiting ability differences among racial or ethnic groups. Unfortunately, it appears that students inside or outside the mainstream culture who need the most help and encouragement in school are often assigned to classes where instruction is likely to be the poorest and the least motivating.

To summarize, most theorists believe that the underachievement of ethnic minority students in American schools is due to a combination of social and economic factors. A disproportionate number of ethnic minority students are from low-income families and attend schools in poor communities. At school, ethnic minority students experience adjustment and academic problems due to the white middle-class culture of their schools. Their problems are further complicated by ability and tracking systems that can severely restrict learning opportunities and educational aspirations. Creating a positive learning environment for students of all racial and ethnic backgrounds will involve changes in the curriculum, the organization and culture of schools, the attitudes and beliefs of school staff, and the way students are currently taught and evaluated. We will discuss some strategies for achieving these objectives at the end of the chapter.

Gender Differences

Look inside any high school physics or calculus class today, and you are likely to find more boys than girls present. At the lower grade levels, more boys than girls are diagnosed as having reading problems and are placed in the low reading groups. Most people argue that these performance differences simply reflect innate mental abilities. Boys are thought to be good at spatial and mathematical tasks, whereas girls are assumed to have good verbal skills. Are there differences in the cognitive abilities of women and men? If so, when do these differences in cognitive abilities appear in development? Because most standardized IQ tests are constructed to remove gender bias, most studies report no overall differences in IQ scores (Brody, 1992). Gender-related differences in scores are limited to specific skill areas. Early studies reported a small female advantage on tests of verbal abilities and a male advantage on tests of spatial skills and mathematical abilities (Maccoby & Jacklin, 1974). Current research also examines differences in students' science abilities along gender lines.

Verbal Abilities   In their classic book *The Psychology of Sex Differences*, Eleanor Maccoby and Carolyn Jacklin (1974) wrote, "Female superiority on verbal tasks has been one of the most solidly established generalizations of the field of sex differences" (p. 74). Verbal tasks can include anything from speech fluency to reading comprehension. Consistent with Maccoby and Jacklin's assertion, studies published before 1973 reveal a minor female advantage of approximately one-fifth a standard deviation on verbal assessments (Hyde & Linn, 1988). Since 1974, however, the male-female discrepancy has declined to about one-tenth a standard deviation, indicating no reliable gender difference in verbal abilities. A few studies have shown that females tend to perform better on tests of verbal fluency and males on verbal analogies (Spelke, 2005). Moreover, there is little variation in gender effects across different age groups. Thus, most researchers now believe there is a negligible difference in verbal abilities between sexes (Caplan, 1999; Hedges & Nowell, 1995; Hyde, 2005; Hyde & Linn, 1988).

Spatial Abilities   **Spatial skills** are believed to contribute to gender-specific abilities in mathematics and science performance (Linn & Hyde, 1989). Examples of spatial problem-solving tasks include identifying hidden objects embedded in a complex design, the ability to rotate two- or three-dimensional objects in space, and the ability to reason about spatially presented information. Research in this area, however, yields no clear pattern of findings with regard to gender differences. In a 1985 review, Marcia Linn and Anne Petersen (1985) reviewed 127 gender effects in spatial abilities. Their analysis revealed that performance differences favoring males was most measurable for tasks that involved mental rotation of two- or three-dimensional objects. (A mental rotation task is shown in Figure 4.15 on page 238.) A 1995 review of gender differences in spatial abilities reports similar findings (Voyer, Voyer, & Bryden, 1995). Recent studies indicate that females remember spatial locations of objects better, and males remember the geometric arrangement of an environment better (e.g., Halpern, 2002; Spelke, 2005). Some studies report gender differences in spatial abilities before adolescence. However, the evidence also suggests that the magnitude of the discrepancy for some spatial tests has declined from one-third to one-tenth a standard deviation since 1974. Researchers argue that a gender effect of this magnitude can be eliminated by instructional intervention. Furthermore, there is little evidence to support the assertion that students' abilities to perform mental rotation tasks are related to their mathematics and science performance (Linn & Hyde, 1989).

Mathematical Abilities   Differences measured between genders in students' mathematics abilities depend on a student's age and the type of test used (Hyde, Fennema, & Lamon,

■ FIGURE 4.15
Example of a Mental Rotation Task
Source: After Linn & Peterson (1985)

Standard

1   2   3   4

A mental rotation item. Respondents are asked to identify the two responses that show the standard in a different orientation.

1990). During elementary and middle school, girls generally outperform boys on tests of computational skills. No gender-attributable differences in students' algebra and basic mathematics knowledge have been measured. Among high school students, boys score slightly higher on tests of mathematics reasoning and problem solving (primarily word problems). However, on most standardized tests of mathematics achievement for older adolescents and young adults, the gender gap is closing. For example, recent data from the 2004 National Assessment of Educational Progress (NAEP) showed no significant gender differences in mathematics performance at ages 9, and small differences at age 13 (4 points) and age 17 (3 points) (NAEP, 2005). Tests show differences between female and male performances, especially for the SAT—M (Gallagher & Kaufman, 2005). Some researchers, however, attribute this anomaly to the content and format of the SAT—M, which tends to favor males (Linn & Hyde, 1989; Gallagher & Kaufman, 2005). It is interesting to note here that girls receive higher grades than boys in mathematics and take equally demanding classes in high school (Gallagher & Kaufman, 2005). Even within mathematically gifted populations, where boys generally outperform girls on standardized achievement tests, girls receive higher math grades. Female superiority in math grades is often overlooked in mathematical ability research (Halpern, 1997).

Science Abilities   Differences by gender in students' science abilities are not consistent across age groups and content areas. On general tests of science achievement, there are few gender-related performance differences at the elementary school level. Differences in science abilities between girls and boys begin to occur in middle school and increase as students progress in school. By high school, studies reveal gender differences of about one-third of a standard deviation, and the magnitude of this difference depends on the content area. Gender differences are more evident in the physical sciences, whereas no gender differences in achievement are found for the biological sciences (Hyde & McKinley, 1997). Recent NAEP data indicate a narrowing of the gender gap in science achievement since the 1980s (NCES, 2000); however, in 2005, male students in grades 4, 8, and 12 continued to outscore female students by a few points (NCES, 2005). Other evidence indicates that men outnumber women by a margin of seven to one among individuals who do perform extremely well (top 5 percent) on standardized tests of science achievement (Hedges & Nowell, 1995).

Conclusions About Gender Differences   It is difficult to draw any firm conclusions about gender differences in cognitive abilities. Measurable ability differences between sexes depend on the age of the subjects, the content area, and the type of cognitive measure used. In most areas, these ability differences are declining. Although this section's focus has been on performance differences between boys and girls, it is important to keep in mind the considerable overlap in all students' abilities. Some girls can outperform the majority of boys on mathematical tasks, and some boys can do better than most girls on verbal tasks. Most researchers view girls and boys as more similar than different in their cognitive abilities, leading Hyde (2005) to propose the *gender similarities hypothesis.* As one researcher put it, "We can predict very little about an individual's mental abilities based on his or her sex" (Kimura, 1989).

Research suggests that girls approach computers as a tool, whereas boys approach them as toys.
Source: James L. Shaffer/Photo Edit.

Biological Explanations   Researchers who favor biological explanations point to hormone levels and brain organization. There is growing evidence that hormone levels can influence women's and men's performance on cognitive tasks. Recent evidence suggests that women's abilities to perform certain cognitive or motor tasks fluctuates over their menstrual cycle. Similarly, men's performance on visual-spatial tasks fluctuates with daily variations in testosterone. Also, studies show that testosterone treatment for men with low levels of this hormone can improve their spatial ability performance (Halpern, 1997).

Another popular theory states that the female brain is less lateralized than the male brain. By *lateralized,* researchers mean that each of the two cerebral hemispheres performs a special set of functions (for review, see Chapter 2). New technologies have enabled researchers to perform brain scans while men and women are performing different cognitive tasks. By monitoring changes in the blood flow to different areas of the brain, researchers have found that women tend to use both sides of the brain while performing spelling and mental rotation tasks. Men, on the other hand, primarily use their left hemisphere for spelling tasks and their right hemisphere for spatial tasks. It is believed that this lateralization in brain functioning enables men to perform highly specialized visual-spatial tasks better. Currently, however, there is not agreement among researchers on this assertion (Halpern, 1997).

The search for biological causes to explain gender differences in cognitive functioning is likely to continue for some time. At present, the influence of hormonal levels and brain lateralization on cognitive functioning is not well understood. Even if there are innate causes to explain gender differences in cognitive functioning, the influence at birth of environmental and learning experiences can alter the brain's biochemistry and physiology. Perhaps the strongest evidence against the biological argument is that gender-related performance differences in some spatial perception tasks can be eliminated through instructional intervention (Conner, Shackman, & Serbin, 1978). More important, if biological factors were the strongest influence on ability, we would expect to see gender differences in children's cognitive abilities early in development, which is not the case (Spelke, 2005).

Environmental Explanations   Researchers who favor environmental explanations focus on the socialization experiences of boys and girls in a number of different contexts. In Chapter 6, we will discuss research on sex-role socialization, the process by which children acquire the knowledge, skills, and traits appropriate for their gender.

Collectively, studies of children's early socialization into gender roles indicate that boys are encouraged to engage in activities that help develop spatial skills, mathematical reasoning, and problem solving, whereas girls are encouraged to develop their verbal and interpersonal skills (Lytton & Romney, 1991). We will touch on gender-role socialization within the family again in Chapter 8, including the family conditions that lead children to develop less-sex-stereotypic attitudes.

Along these same lines, American parents also communicate different expectations for achievement to their sons and daughters. For example, Anglo-American parents expect their sons more than their daughters to attain an advanced graduate degree (Adelman, 1991). Studies of high school students also reveal that Anglo-American parents are more likely to encourage their sons rather than their daughters to take advanced high school courses in mathematics, chemistry, and physics (Eccles, Jacobs, & Harold, 1991; Jacobs, Chin & Bleeker, 2006). Gender differences in parental expectations for their sons' and daughters' achievement in mathematics and reading are found as early as the first grade (Lummis & Stevenson, 1990), and parental expectations can have enduring effects on young people's educational & occupational pursuits (Jacobs et al., 2006).

It is clear that gender socialization begins at home. What role might schools play in this process? Unfortunately, much evidence suggests that schools serve to reinforce or strengthen gender differences in students' skills and interests (Meece, 1987). Two major reports, *How Schools Shortchange Girls* (Wesley College Center for Research on Women, 1992) and *Failing at Fairness: How Schools Cheat Girls* (Sadker & Sadker, 1995), identified ways in which schools help to reproduce gender inequities in society.

- Women constitute a majority of classroom teachers, but they are underrepresented in administrative positions. Also, a higher number of men than women teach advanced mathematics and science classes in high school. Such staffing patterns teach students who can lead and who is good at math or science.
- Masculine images and interests continue to be overrepresented in curriculum materials, particularly in mathematics and science. A male bias is also evident in computer programs and testing materials.
- Boys receive considerably more attention than girls in the classroom, which reinforces a perception of male dominance and importance. High-ability girls receive the least amount of attention of all groups.
- When asking complex, abstract, or open-ended questions, teachers call on boys more frequently than girls. They also wait longer for boys than girls to answer questions and provide more detailed feedback to boys than to girls. These differences are most pronounced in mathematics and science classes.
- Approximately 90 percent of the criticism girls receive for schoolwork is directed at the intellectual quality of their work, compared with 50 percent for boys. When boys are criticized, they are often told their poor performance is due to lack of effort. Girls are less likely to receive this message from teachers.

- When classes are divided into ability groups, boys with high mathematics achievement scores are more likely than girls with similar scores to be assigned to high-ability groups.
- When boys and girls work on projects together, girls are more likely to watch and listen while boys perform the activity.
- Girls respond more favorably to a cooperative rather than competitive classroom environment, but few classrooms emphasize cooperation and collaborative efforts.
- Student reports of sexual harassment are increasing. In most cases, boys are harassing girls, which can affect girls' participation in class, school attendance, and study habits.

As this analysis indicates, sex-role messages pervade almost every aspect of children's schooling experiences. It is important to point out that gender differences in teachers' behaviors may be due to how boys and girls behave in the classroom. As discussed earlier in this chapter, people evoke certain reactions from their environment. Boys may be called on more frequently than girls because they are more active or assertive. Despite the source of these exchanges in the classroom, the result is that as young women progress in school they are less likely than men to take advanced courses in mathematics and science. Research also indicates that when differences in course enrollment patterns are controlled, gender differences in mathematics achievement in late adolescence and young adulthood decrease substantially or disappear altogether (Adelman, 1991; Oakes, 1990).

What Can Schools Do? Current Perspectives on Multicultural Education, Learning, and Assessment

Clearly, schools need to make a better effort to create learning environments that provide equal resources, encouragement, and opportunities to girls and boys of all backgrounds. The subtle and not-so-subtle negative messages students receive in school about their abilities and future careers must be changed.

Multicultural Education

Most teacher preparation programs now offer courses on multicultural education. According to James Banks (1994), multicultural education has two important goals: (1) to increase educational equality and opportunity for all students, regardless of their culture, race, ethnicity, gender, religion, social class, or exceptionality; and (2) to promote positive intergroup attitudes and values, so that all students can function more effectively in a pluralistic society and an international community. To achieve these objectives, multicultural education will need to go beyond the study of Native American cultures at Thanksgiving or celebrations of Black History Month, Cinco de Mayo, and Women's History Week. Multicultural education is conceptualized broadly as a field consisting of five dimensions (Banks, 2004). Brief definitions of these dimensions are as follows:

- **Content integration:** Using examples and content from a variety of cultures and groups to illustrate key concepts in a subject.
- **The knowledge-construction process:** Helping students to understand, investigate, and determine how implicit cultural perspectives within a discipline influence the ways in which knowledge is constructed.
- **An equity pedagogy:** Modifying teaching in ways to foster the academic achievement of students from diverse racial, cultural, and social-class backgrounds.

Focus on
Teaching

Eight Characteristics of Multicultural Schools

1. Teachers and school administrators have expectations for all students and positive attitudes toward them. They also respond to them in positive and caring ways.
2. The formalized curriculum reflects the experiences, cultures, and perspectives of a range of cultural and ethnic groups as well as of both genders.
3. Teaching styles match the learning, cultural, and motivational styles of the students.
4. Teachers and administrators show respect for the students' first language and dialects.
5. Instructional materials used in the school show events, situations, and concepts from the perspec-

tives of a range of cultural, ethnic, and racial groups.
6. Assessment and testing procedures used in the school are culturally sensitive and result in students of color being represented proportionately in classes for the gifted and talented.
7. The school culture reflects cultural and ethnic diversity.
8. School counselors have high expectations for students from different racial, ethnic, and language groups and help all students to set and to realize positive career goals.

Source: After Banks (1994).

- **Prejudice reduction:** Characterizing and modifying students' racial attitudes.
- **An empowering school culture and social structure:** Creating a school culture that empowers students from diverse groups through examination of its components (such as grouping practices, disproportionality in achievement, and the interaction of the staff and students across ethnic and racial lines) (Banks, 2006).

Banks proposes that this conception of multicultural education makes clear that it is for *all* students. Creating culturally compatible schools will involve radical changes in the curriculum materials, the organization of schools, the attitudes and beliefs of school staff, the school culture, and the ways students are currently taught and assessed. The Focus on Teaching box lists eight characteristics of multicultural schools identified by Banks (1994).

A focus on how we use and interpret assessments, such as intelligence and achievement tests, is also seen in Lisa Delpit's (2003) inspiring lecture on how to improve the education of poor, African American students.

> In closing, we *can* educate all children if we truly want to. To do so, we must first stop attempting to determine their capacity. We must be convinced of their inherent intellectual capability, humanity, and spiritual characters. We must fight the foolishness proliferated by those who believe that one number can measure the worth and drive the education of human beings, or that predetermined scripts can make for good teaching, Finally, we must learn *who* our children are—their lived culture, their interests, and their intellectual, political, and historical legacies . . . we must create Perry's "intentional communities" designed around a counternarrative—one that affirms Black brilliance both to the students themselves and to their communities. Then, we can begin to educate the inheritors of the planet. (p. 20)

Assessment and Learning

Shepard (2000) asks a practical question related to the use of assessments in school, "How should what we do in classrooms be changed so that students and teachers look to assessment as a source of insight and help instead of its being the occasion for meting out reward and punishment?" (p. 12). To achieve such a transformation, Shepard proposes that we need to make assessments more useful, more helpful in learning, and *change the social meaning of evaluation.* Many educational researchers agree that good use of assessments based on contemporary cognitive theories can promote learning (e.g., Committee on the Foundations of Assessment, 2001; Popham, 2005). In particular, Popham (2005) argues that teachers should use assessments to *make better decisions.*

Theorists have sometimes distinguished between two types of assessments. **Static assessments** generally provide information about the present state and existing skills of students to teachers (and others). In contrast, **dynamic assessments** involve two-way interactions between students and teachers, tap into students' developing processes, and provide them with feedback. According to Sternberg and Grigorenko (2002), there are two main types of dynamic testing: the sandwich format and the cake format. The sandwich format involves a pretest and posttest and instruction in between. The sandwiched instruction provides students with opportunities to see which skills they have and have not mastered. This feedback may be more implicit in a group-testing situation and explicit in an individual-testing situation. In the cake format, the educator presents a sequence of progressively more challenging tasks to a student, providing continuous feedback, until the student either solves the problem or gives up. In this way, dynamic assessments are tests of learning potential; thus, some refer to these as *learning assessments*. Researchers are currently investigating how such dynamic assessments in contemporary teaching-learning approaches affect students' cognitive processing and learning.

Promising results are found with the use of approaches such as the Cognitively Guided Instruction (CGI) approach developed by Carpenter, Fennema, and colleagues (Committee on Foundations of Assessment, 2001) to foster children's thinking about arithmetic. In this approach, teachers "read and react" to ongoing events in real time and modify instruction as they continually assess children's learning. In this type of program "assessment is woven seamlessly into the fabric of instruction" (p. 231). The interweaving of assessment and instruction is also seen within communities of learners and with the use of computer-based tutors. This leads us to the next section, which discusses the role of computers in children's and adolescents' learning.

Computers and Learning

The use of computers is rapidly becoming a routine part of children's lives. Among households with children ages 2 to 17, home computer ownership went from 48 percent in 1996 to 70 percent in 2000 (Woodard & Gridina, 2000). Surveys also reveal that nearly twice that number of children have access to computers at school (Becker, 2000). As with other technological innovations, researchers are interested in the effects of computers on children's activities and development. In this section, we will consider how computers are changing what and how children learn. We will begin with a discussion of who has access to computers, then turn to their influence on learning and school achievement. Research is also beginning to identify the impact of computers on children's social development and emotional well-being (Wartella & Jennings, 2000), but discussion of this research is beyond the scope of this chapter.

Use of Computers

One issue of concern is *who* has access to computers. It is generally believed that there is a growing digital divide separating children from different socioeconomic groups in the United States. On the whole, surveys reveal that children between the ages of 2 and 17 spend approximately 1.5 hours per day using the computer or playing video games (Becker, 2000). When this figure is added to hours of television viewing, children with access to computers or video games are spending, on average, 4 to 5 hours per day in front of a television screen or a computer monitor (Stranger & Gridina, 1999). Children's access to computers at home is greatly influenced by family income; this disparity is often referred to as the "digital divide." In 2003, only 47 percent of low-income students had access to a home computer, compared with 97 percent of high-income households (U.S. Census Bureau, 2005). There are also significant socioeconomic differences in the quality of children's computer access. Children from more-affluent homes are more likely than lower-income children to have access to computers that have a CD-ROM drive, a printer, and a modem for Internet access (Becker, 2000).

How do young people use their home computers? Household surveys indicate that home computers are used for both school-related and recreational purposes. Figure 4.16 shows age differences in how young people use their home computers. As shown here, students' use of home computers for school assignments, electronic mail, Internet, and word processing increases with age. There is a higher use of computers at home when parents or siblings have computer experience and when students have access to computers at school. Wartella, Caplovitz, and Lee (2004) report age differences in the use of time on computers. Younger children (ages 0–8) prefer and spend more time playing educational games than older children (ages 9–12) and adolescents. Adolescents spend more time on the computer in general than children, and they spend the most time on the Internet and playing video games.

Children from higher socioeconomic backgrounds use a broader range of computer applications than lower-income children, even when parents have the same level of work-based experiences with computers (Becker, 2000). Although concerns have been expressed about gender differences in computer literacy, a 1997 study found similar patterns of home computer use by boys and girls (Becker, 2000). There were only small differences in the use of computer games (75 percent for boys and 68 percent for girls) and for word processing (36 percent for boys and 41 percent for girls). As the array of computer applications increases, gender differences in home computer use are expected to decrease.

For many young people, school provides the greatest access to computers. A greater number of children and adolescents have access to computers at school than at home, especially among lower-income groups. Since the 1980s, the number of computers in American schools has grown steadily. Whereas half of schools nationwide had no computer in 1983, all schools were equipped with at least one computer by 1998 (Becker, 2000) and by 1999, 95 percent had access to the Internet. Additionally, students in low-income schools are equally likely to have access to computers as students in high-income schools. However, there are important differences in the availability of high-quality computer equipment, sophisticated software, and high-speed Internet access. When these factors are taken into account, schools with the highest proportion of students from low-income families are 1 to 2 years behind middle-income schools, and even farther behind schools serving high-income families (Becker, 2000).

Computers in low- and high-income schools tend to be used for different purposes. A 1998 nationwide survey of teachers indicated that lower-income students used computer applications for remediation or practicing skills, whereas higher-income students used computer applications for research, analyses, and written expression (Becker, 2000). For

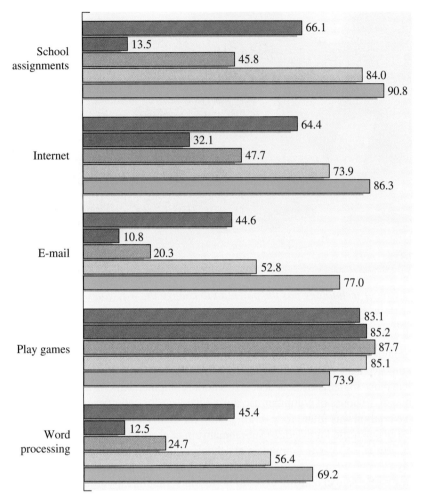

■ FIGURE 4.16
Types of Computer Use at Home for Children 3 to 17 Years by Age: 2003
Source: U.S. Census Bureau, Current Population Survey, October 2003.

this reason, experts have argued that economic disparities in students' access to enriched learning opportunities with technology are increasing (Shields & Behrman, 2000).

Effects of Computers on Learning and School Achievement

Although computers are more widely used by young people today than ever before, it is not clear that this technological innovation is making them "smarter" (Subrahmanyam, Kraut, Greenfield, & Gross, 2000). Let's first consider the use of home computers. Young people use different computer applications, but computer games in particular are designed in ways that emphasize *visual* rather than *verbal* information processing. Some evidence suggests that these interactive games can enhance children's spatial skills, but may not generalize to other contexts (Lee & Huston, 2003). If related to spatial problem-solving skills, such programs should be beneficial for more abstract forms of mathematics, but few studies have examined this possible link.

A few studies indicate that computer use at home can enhance school achievement (Subrahmanyam et al., 2000). However, as we know, children's access to and use of computers are tied to their parents' income levels. Studies have not adequately controlled for these influences. With this caveat in mind, one longitudinal study that tracked seventh

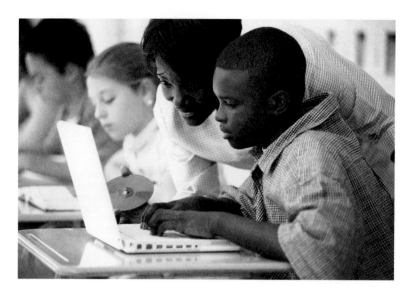

Computer technology has the potential to change the way young people learn in school.
Source: Creatas/Punch Stock.

through twelfth graders showed that students with computers at home had higher grade point averages (GPAs) and, more specifically, better grades in English and mathematics than those students without access to a home computer. Among those students who reported at least 10 hours of computer use during the year for activities unrelated to a class, a positive relation was found for overall grades, for math and English grades, and for scores on a test of scientific knowledge (Subrahmanyam et al., 2000).

How is access to computers at school influencing learning? Computer technology today clearly has the potential to change the way young people learn in school. Students can now participate in real-life expeditions to Mars, rain forests, archeological digs, coral reefs, or jungles. The Global Learning and Observations to Benefit the Environment (GLOBE) program, introduced by Vice President Gore in 1992, connected more than 3,800 schools around the world to scientists studying the environment. Teachers and students collected environmental data in their local areas and worked with scientists to analyze environmental problems (Gore, 1992). Computer programs such as ThinkerTools enable middle school students to visualize the concepts of velocity and acceleration (White, 1993), and computer software is available to help students visualize and explore geometric and algebraic concepts online. There are also computer tools that enable students to choreograph plays and to examine cultural artifacts from ancient civilizations. Interactive storybooks are available to help first graders learn basic reading skills, and various multimedia applications exist to provide opportunities for older students to actively construct presentations that reflect their knowledge and understanding of a particular subject matter or topic. Lastly, computer technology is providing new ways for children with special needs to learn in the regular classroom environment (Roshelle, Pea, Hoadley, Gordin, & Means, 2000).

Although these computer applications have the potential to enhance students' learning, information on their effectiveness is fairly limited. Researchers propose that interactive media may foster children's metacognitive abilities (i.e., thinking about their learning strategies) by helping them organize information, adapt the material to their abilities, and receive continuous feedback. However, few studies have demonstrated how such interactive processes enhance this learning (Wartella et al., 2004). Much of the research to date has focused on math and science, and on middle and high school students. In general, the strongest evidence for positive effects are computer applications that use a constructivist approach and that emphasize conceptual understanding and higher-order thinking skills. One nationwide study, for example, showed that highly interactive software that promotes active engagement and participation was more effective than drill-and-practice software in increasing mathematics achievement in fourth and eighth graders (Weglinsky, 1998). However, software applications that emphasized repetitive skill practice improved students' performance on basic skill tests (Kulik, 1994).

As with any curriculum innovation, the positive benefits of computer technology for student learning are influenced by many different factors, including teacher training, administrative support, state and local curriculum standards, and assessment procedures. And, of course, live teachers who provide flexible and sensitive assistance (Committee on Foundations of Assessment, 2001) to meet the minds of children and adolescents cannot be replaced.

■ Chapter Summary

Information Processing Theories

- Information processing and intelligence theories help specify the cognitive processes and mental abilities that change with development. Information processing theories focus on developmental changes in children's abilities to encode, store, and retrieve information, whereas intelligence theories focus on individual differences in children's cognitive abilities within age groups.
- According to information processing theorists, important developmental changes occur in children's attentional processes, memory strategies, content knowledge, and metacognitive knowledge. As children mature, they become more selective and efficient in their use of attentional, memory, and learning strategies. As a result, they can remember larger amounts of information for longer periods of time.

Developmental Changes in Cognitive Processes

- Memory processes are evident early in development. By the preschool years, children can recall familiar stories, experiences, routines, and events. During the early and late elementary years, children begin to use memory strategies to encode information that is unfamiliar. Rehearsal strategies appear first, followed by organization and elaboration strategies.
- With development, children can recall information with fewer prompts or cues. They can also search their memory in a more systematic, selective, and strategic manner.
- Children's existing knowledge can influence attentional and memory processes. Expert versus novice studies indicate that a highly integrated knowledge base results in faster processing of information, more effective use of encoding strategies, and more efficient use of cognitive resources.
- Metacognition refers to children's knowledge and understanding of their own thinking processes. As children develop, they acquire a greater understanding that there are limits to what can be remembered, some learning tasks require more cognitive effort than others, and certain strategies can aid the recall of information.
- Age-related changes in metacognitive knowledge also facilitates the development of self-regulated learning. Self-regulated learners can plan, organize, monitor, and evaluate their own learning activities. Evidence indicates that children show a significant increase in their use of self-regulated learning strategies in later elementary grades. However, study strategies, such as comprehension and monitoring, continue to develop well into adolescence.

...

- Teachers need to make a greater effort to teach specific cognitive strategies, to provide information concerning their usefulness in learning, and to suggest when strategies may be useful for other learning situations.

Intelligence Theories

- There is considerable variability in children's cognitive abilities within any age group. Standardized tests of intelligence or achievement are used to assess individual differences in cognitive development. Intelligence tests are thought to measure a child's ability to use information in new ways or potential to learn, whereas achievement tests measure what children have gained from instruction at home or school.
- There is no agreed-on definition of intelligence. Some theorists have argued that intelligence represents a general or global intellectual capacity, whereas others have argued that intelligence represents several independent skills or abilities. Most intelligence tests used today yield a profile of a child's intellectual abilities.
- As children develop, the stability of their IQ scores increases. By middle childhood, IQ scores are reasonably good predictors of adult IQ.

Developmental Influences

- Most researchers focus on how environmental factors interact to influence intellectual development. Genes may set the upper and lower limits for intellectual development, but the environment may explain variations in development within that range.
- Several aspects of the home environment can influence early intellectual development. Research indicates that parents can have a positive influence on their children's cognitive development when they provide appropriate stimulation and play materials, encourage exploration and stimulate curiosity, and create a warm, supportive, and responsive environment.
- Early intervention can help offset the negative effects of a poor home environment. Evidence suggests that earlier and longer interventions may have a stronger impact on children's intellectual functioning.
- Formal schooling is another important aspect of the environment that influences children's intellectual development. Children who start school earlier, remain in school longer, and attend higher-quality schools have higher IQ scores. Theorists argue that schooling influences IQ scores because schools teach the type of information and skills children need to perform well on intelligence tests.
- Individual differences in intellectual functioning are examined. New perspectives on the development of giftedness and functioning of children with mental retardation are highlighted.
- A number of "teaching for thinking" educational programs have been developed on the basis of information processing and intelligence theories, such programs involve new ways to consider the role of assessment in learning.

Group Differences in Cognitive Abilities

- Most researchers believe that ethnic differences in students' IQ and achievement test scores are due to social and economic factors. When differences in socioeconomic background are controlled, performance gaps narrow but do not completely disappear. Some factors that contribute to the lower performance of ethnic minorities on mental tests include language or dialect differences, a school culture that favors white, middle-class students, and tracking systems that limit minority children's learning and achievement opportunities in school.
- Gender differences in students' cognitive abilities are less evident today than 20 years ago.
- Efforts to explain gender differences in cognitive abilities focus on biological and environmental influences. The influence of hormones and brain organization on cognitive functioning is not well understood. Therefore, most researchers focus on differences in children's socialization experiences. There is considerable evidence that boys and girls are treated differently and encouraged to pursue different activities at home. Research has also documented the numerous ways boys and girls are treated differently at school.

■ Schools need to make a better effort to create learning environments that provide equal resources, encouragement, and opportunities for boys and girls of all backgrounds. Multicultural education programs are designed to promote equal educational opportunities and to increase positive intergroup attitudes and values. Creating a positive learning environment for all students will involve radical changes in curriculum materials, the organization and culture of schools, the attitudes and beliefs of school staff, and the ways students are currently taught and assessed.

Computers and Learning

■ Computers are becoming a routine part of children's lives, but access to high-quality computers and software is tied to family income.

■ Students' use of computers for school-related purposes increases with age. There are similar patterns of computer use for girls and boys today.

■ Research on the effects of computers on students' learning is fairly limited. Computer programs tend to have the greatest impact when they use a constructivist approach and emphasize higher-order thinking skills.

■ Key Terms

ability grouping *(p. 236)*
automaticity *(p. 191)*
componential
   intelligence *(p. 208)*
contextual intelligence *(p. 208)*
crystallized intelligence *(p. 208)*
dynamic assessments *(p. 243)*
elaboration strategies *(p. 195)*
experiential intelligence *(p. 208)*
expert versus novice
   studies *(p. 196)*
fluid intelligence *(p. 208)*
general intelligence *(p. 208)*
giftedness *(p. 223)*

heritability *(p. 214)*
intelligence quotient
   (IQ) *(p. 206)*
intelligence theories *(p. 206)*
long-term memory *(p. 188)*
memory scripts *(p. 193)*
mental retardation *(p. 228)*
mentorship programs *(p. 227)*
metacognition *(p. 197)*
metamemory *(p. 199)*
multiple intelligences *(p. 208)*
niche-picking *(p. 216)*
organizational strategies *(p. 194)*
practical intelligence *(p. 208)*

psychometric theories *(p. 206)*
rehearsal strategies *(p. 194)*
retrieval strategies *(p. 195)*
selective attention *(p. 192)*
self-regulated learning *(p. 200)*
sensory memory *(p. 188)*
short-term memory *(p. 188)*
spatial skills *(p. 237)*
stability of IQ *(p. 214)*
standard deviation *(p. 212)*
static assessments *(p. 243)*
tracking *(p. 236)*
triarchic model of
   intelligence *(p. 208)*

■ Activities

1. A digit-span test is often used to assess children's memory processes. Using the following list of digits, test four individuals of different ages (a 4-, 7-, 12-, and 20-year-old). Present each digit approximately 1 second apart. Start with line 1, and work your way up until the person recalls less than half the list. For each list, record the number of digits the person recalled correctly. If you interview children at school, you will need the permission of the teacher. In analyzing your data, consider the following questions:
(a) Were there age differences in memory span? What was the nature of the differences observed? (b) What accounts for these differences? What else might account for the differences? (c) How does this exercise help you to understand developmental changes in memory?

Digit-Span Test	Number Correct
1. 3	
2. 5 - 9	
3. 1 - 6 - 8	
4. 2 - 4 - 7 - 0	
5. 3 - 9 - 4 - 1 - 8	
6. 9 - 4 - 3 - 7 - 8 - 5	
7. 1 - 2 - 6 - 3 - 7 - 9 - 0	
8. 7 - 5 - 1 - 8 - 6 - 2 - 4 - 9	

2. Study skills increase with age. For this activity, interview an upper-elementary student, a middle school student, and a high school student about their study skills. Ask each student the following questions:

   a. Tell me about the last test you had in this class.

   b. How well did you do on the test?

   c. Did you do anything special to prepare for the test?

   d. If you got stuck on a problem or question, what did you do?

   e. Did you do anything special before you turned in your test?

   After collecting your interview data, compare the responses of your students. Were there age differences in the types of strategies students use in preparing for a test, getting unstuck, or reviewing their test? What was the nature of these differences? What might explain these differences? How did this exercise help you to understand developmental changes in learning strategies?

3. Observe two lessons (any subject) in two classrooms at different grade levels (e.g., fifth and seventh grade). While observing each lesson, record the following:

   a. Describe any teacher instruction related to a specific strategy students can use to complete the assignment. Examples might include: read the directions carefully, think about a prior assignment, use a particular reading or mathematical skill, use aids or resources in the classroom, ask a friend for assistance, check over answers, make a plan, organize thoughts, take some notes, etc.

   b. Describe the teacher's rationale for using the strategy (i.e., what was it supposed to accomplish?).

   c. Describe what the teacher said or did to remind students to use the strategy. After collecting your observation data, answer the following questions:

      - What type of strategy instruction did each teacher provide?
      - How did the strategy instruction differ across subject areas or grade levels?
      - How often did the teacher provide a rationale for using a particular strategy?
      - How did this exercise help you understand the ways teachers can facilitate the development of learning strategies in the classroom?

4. Racial or gender biases in curriculum materials can affect students' learning. For this activity, analyze two current textbooks (any subject or grade level) for social stereotypes. First, examine the degree to which women and minorities are represented in the texts you selected. Who are the main characters? Whom do you see in the pictures? Next, analyze the characteristics of the women and minorities. Are the men strong and active and the women weak and passive? Are ethnic minorities depicted as leaders and competent? Describe the roles and occupations of the characters. In your opinion, are these texts appealing to females and minorities? Do they strengthen or weaken social stereotypes? What would you do as a teacher to counteract racial or gender stereotypes in curriculum materials?

5. Review computer software for different age groups (preschool, elementary, etc.). Analyze the software in terms of its ability to support the cognitive skills that are emerging at that point in development. To what extent does each program emphasize drill-and-practice versus problem solving? Examine the programs for their attractiveness to different gender and ethnic groups. Which of the computer software programs would you recommend to teachers? Include a rationale for your explanation.

Language and Literacy Development

H ALLIE CIRINO, A TEACHER AND PARTICIPANT IN TEACHER-RESEARCH *groups with Eleanor Duckworth, writes the following journal entry concerning her work with three students of various writing abilities from the same class: Anne (age 5), James (age 5), and June (age 6). The children were from well-educated families.*

Anne and James were present during this week's writing time; June was absent. Anne opened her writing book and announced, "I'm going to make a jungle!"

Curious about whether Anne had a story line in her mind or simply a topic idea, I asked, "What is going to happen in your jungle?"

Anne replied, "I'm not telling you; I just want to write it," and she began drawing a tree. Then Anne said, "Guess what I'm writing?"

"I thought you said you were writing about a jungle?" Anne nodded in the affirmative.

James, watching and listening to Anne, said, "I know a monkey named Curious George. He comes from a jungle in Africa." Anne nodded and continued to illustrate trees, and James started to draw a tree as well...

Anne looked up from her writing and said, "Everything June writes she knows." (I wondered if Anne was reading my mind!)

"What do you mean?" I asked.

"June always knows all the letters for everything."

"Well, June is a little older than you," I told Anne. "She has a little more experience with writing than you do and she tries to be helpful. The more times that you write a word, the easier it is to remember how to write it the next time. Think about your name, Anne. Do you need to sound out the letters of your name every time you write it?"

Anne laughed, "No!" She then started to write about her illustration with the words "this is." Anne always wrote the word this *with the single letter z. As she wrote her z she said, "I never have to think about how to write the word this because I know it's a letter z." It is likely that Anne was comparing her writing ability to June's: knowing letters without having to think about them.*

"Adults write the word this *differently," I mentioned to Anne, "but I know what you mean when you write the letter z." This was the first time Anne called her z a z; in the past, she always called it a "zig-zag."*

Anne stopped writing and said, "I want to draw more on my picture before I write anymore." Did Anne need to develop ideas through her drawing before she could write?

James finished his illustration, and I asked him what he had drawn next to his tree. He pointed to a long rectangle and said, "This is a piece of wood." He pointed to a second, similar rectangle and said, "And this is a ladder." James then wrote, "ZANS iS WWDN AD A REN." He read aloud, "This is wood and a tree."

"Why is there wood and a tree?" I asked.

In answer, James wrote, "BKNZ G T B AA REN HOS," and read, "because it's going to be a tree house." In the first sentence, when James was writing, and he came to the word tree, *he sounded it out aloud. He was stuck on the tr blend and eventually wrote an R. When he came to writing* tree *the second time, he started sounding aloud again, then turned to me and asked, "How do you write* tree?"

"You've already written it once, James," I prompted, to see if he could find the word and apply it.

"Oh, yeah." James read through his piece, pointing at each word as he read, until he came to the word tree. *He kept his finger on it and wrote it down again...*

In this session, Anne seems to have picked up the strategy of writing words to go with her drawings, as June and James have done. Her drawings were still the most important part of her writing; she would feel the need to finish drawing before she could write. Her drawings were her text, and the words she now wrote were there to support her text.

James began really reading during this session. For the first time he pointed to the words he had written and read them. For the first time he decided how to write a word by seeing how it had been written before (admittedly, by himself). And for the first time he started writing in complete sentences and leaving spaces between his words. He connected Anne's writing to literature via his comment about knowing Curious George, a monkey who lives in a jungle. James seemed to exhibit more enthusiasm about his writing than he had been showing. He was usually more subdued, but became quite bubbly when something piqued his interest. (Cirino, 2001, pp. 81–83)

Lisa Schneider, another teacher and participant in teacher-research groups with Eleanor Duckworth, shares her story about studying a poem, "miss rosie," with six first-year high school students. The students were from diverse racial and ethnic groups, and were from the lowest English skill levels in the school; four of the students were learning English as their second or third language. The following are brief excerpts:

Nildo:	*See: This is weird. This is weird. I don't get it. What is she doing?*
Marco:	*It's just dumb.*
Maddie:	*That part, the last part don't make no sense. When it says, "when I watch you you brown bag of a woman," first she's talking about sitting next to a [pause] wrapped up like garbage and then...*
Juana:	*Now she changed to the brown bag or whatever she's saying.*
James:	*It's supposed to be one main thing.*
Maddie:	*That's right.*

Nildo, continuing the shaping begun by Maddie, focused on the last few lines, building a more specific theory:

Nildo:	*"I stand up to your destruction [sic]." That's what I don't get. Why would* _____*?*
Juana:	*"I stand up/through your destruction/I stand up."*
Nildo:	*Almost two paragraphs over that, it's like sad. And this one is beautiful, talking about a beautiful woman, and then they say, "I stand up to your destruction"* _____ *Oh, I see it, I get it now. O yeah.*
LS:	*What did you just get?*
Nildo:	*No, I have an idea, I don't know* _____ *[others talking]*
LS:	*Let him tell his idea and then other people can respond to it, OK?*
Nildo:	*Maybe this person who wrote the poem is like a friend—or something like that—and she, like, she'll be beside her when something goes wrong? Something like that . . .*

What followed I can only describe as a burst of energy. They started to articulate theories that were somehow catalyzed by their focus on the two conflicting descriptions in the poem. All the theories were attempts at reconciling these descriptions. (Schneier, 2001, pp. 48–51)

From Tell Me More: Listening to Learners Explain, *by E. Duckworth (Ed.), 2001, New York: Teachers College Press.*

As these vignettes illustrate, children and adolescents use language to express themselves creatively, to make meaning, and to interact with others. The vignettes also illustrate how students develop confidence and capacities to engage with text, and how perceptive teachers can help foster such literacy skills. Language mediates and facilitates mental growth, but it also builds social relationships. Even though some students have limited language and literacy skills, they are able to fully participate in these literacy experiences with support from others. For example, the "ah ha's" or deeper understandings that the students experience—Anne connecting sounds to letters, James identifying words in sentences, and Nildo making sense of a poem—were all enhanced through guided social interactions.

Teachers who understand the way language develops initially can provide a better and more natural language learning environment. This holds true for both acquiring written language abilities and extending spoken language abilities. However, the relationships between these language processes are complex: Do children acquire speech or are they biologically hardwired for language? If speaking develops without formal instruction, why don't reading and writing develop similarly? Will every child in a literate culture learn to read and write? What determines who becomes literate? Does a child who is bilingual learn differently than one who is monolingual? We will explore these issues in this chapter.

What Is Language and Literacy?

Most commonly, we think of literacy as the ability to read and write. Being able to read print and to produce written words are regarded by our culture as important skills. Often whether a person can work productively in society depends on his proficiency with reading and writing. Why are reading and writing so valuable? We know that in young children language develops alongside cognition, each process mutually enhancing the other. **Language,** on the other hand, is a symbolic system: a series of sounds or gestures in which the words *freedom, ball*, and *Mommy* can represent an idea, an object, a person. Such symbolic representation eventually becomes the medium through which we think. Imagine what it would be like to think without language. Is that even possible?

In this text, we define **literacy** as the ability to construct and express meaning through reading, writing, and discussing texts (Snow, 2005). In short, literacy can be thought of as a set of language-based skills that allows us to comprehend a text, whether the newspaper or a classic novel. In addition, to function in our increasingly complex society, individuals must develop critical literacy, the ability to use written language to solve problems and to communicate (Calfee, 1994; MacWhinney & Bornstein, 2003). But is literacy limited only to printed texts? With the advent of electronic technology, including computers and video capabilities, our culture's conception of what it means to be literate has expanded. In an essay entitled "Rethinking Literacy," Elliot Eisner (1991) pointed out that literacy now extends beyond print to include other systems for constructing meaning and communicating with others: "Literacy is not limited to text. . .[but] relates to the ability to construe meaning, in any of the forms used in the culture to create and convey meaning" (p. 125). Multiple literacies, those associated with music, visual images, dance and theater, as well as computers and other technological literacies, all depend on the mind's ability to use symbols to represent and to communicate about thoughts or experiences.

Although spoken language is crucial for the development of cognition, written language provides additional benefits for thought. Writing enables us to fix ideas permanently to a printed page, or onto a computer file, so that we don't have to rely on memory alone. Being able to read and write enables people to communicate with each other across space and time. With the use of technologies such as electronic mail, the amount of information that can be produced and exchanged by written (visual) forms far exceeds that which is possible when spoken language is the only available medium. The term *literate thinking* has been coined to describe "the ability to think and reason like a literate person, *within a particular society*" (Langer, 1991, p. 11). In order to participate fully, individuals need to develop ways of thinking (such as analysis and synthesis) that are associated with the uses of literacy in their particular culture. But no single culture is monolithic or uniform. Rather, individuals belong to various subcultures, which means that several literacies are being learned, practiced, and enjoyed at any one time.

In this chapter, we will discuss the role of language in child development, including cognitive as well as social dimensions. Can a child develop emotionally or intellectually without language? How does language affect human development? Although psychologists have devised different theories about the relationship between language and cognition, all agree that language is a medium for thinking and learning, because it is a system for representing or symbolizing our experiences. However, languages fundamentally are social systems. Everyone who learns and speaks the English language agrees that the sound of *cat* [kaet], for instance, means a small furry house pet. From a social perspective, this shared knowledge enables communication: We describe experiences, exchange information, make plans, discuss ideas, create stories, and build personal bonds through conversational routines.

In every culture, language is fundamental. Increasingly, it is common for a culture to be multilingual—in which people speak two or more languages. As we have discussed, approximately 19 percent of all school-aged children speak a language other than English at home (National Center for Education Statistics, 2005a). Instead of being English-dominant, these and many other children in the next generation will grow up bilingual. In addition to being multilingual, children will increasingly develop in an environment with multiple literacies. Because of the complexity of learning several languages and literacies, the process of language acquisition and development will become more extended, beginning with speech in infancy, but growing to include multiple forms of language and literacy throughout adolescence.

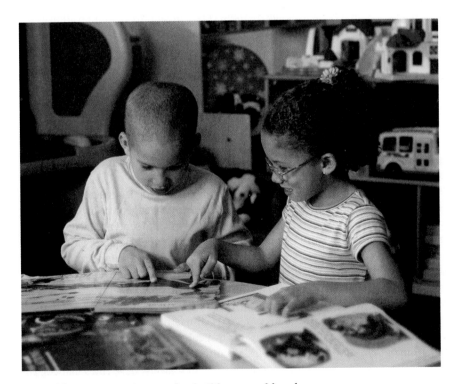

Shared literacy experiences also build personal bonds.
Source: Gaetano Images, Inc./Alamy.

By first grade, children have a great deal of experience and skill in using spoken language. They understand and appreciate the values of written language, particularly from their encounters with picture books and with the print that saturates their environment. While children will continue to develop and refine speaking skills once they enter school, it is in the area of literacy (reading and writing) that children will change most dramatically.

Perspectives on Language Development

Most children learn to speak a language without direct instruction during the first few years of life. Language enables human beings to represent objects and actions, to understand and discuss abstract ideas, to invent stories, and to exchange complex information. Many cultures develop a way of writing their language. Having a written form of language allows a culture to develop new ways of communicating, which would not be possible if only spoken language were used. Writing adds permanence to language. With writing, very long texts can be created and preserved, and texts can be repeatedly read and referenced in order to make decisions or to think through an issue. In addition, writing allows for consistency; anyone who is able to read a particular text reads exactly the same words as any other reader.

In cultures that have writing systems, children must learn to read and write their language as well as to speak it. However, these language forms develop quite differently in individuals. Spoken language is primary; all individuals (apart from those with severe impairments) learn to speak their language, but not everyone becomes literate. It is remarkable that learning to speak a language happens to everyone, whereas learning to read or write occurs only when individuals are taught these skills. In addition, children all over the world go through similar stages in acquiring spoken language. Furthermore, they appear to pay attention to certain generalizations and to ignore irregularities no matter what language (or languages) they are learning. How can we account for the universal ability of all children to learn language? And, furthermore, how do they manage it?

Various answers have been proposed. Many parents believe that their children learn language by imitating the words and sentences they hear. In addition, parents believe that reinforcing the "correct" parts of children's utterances leads to development. Yet other adults notice, often with great concern, that children create their own ways of speaking, experimenting with tenses, endings, and word order, which often do not resemble adult speech.

Although there are competing theories for *how* children develop language, we do know *what* children learn when they develop language. Learning a language is basically learning grammar. **Grammar** is not a set of prescriptions such as "don't end sentences with a preposition," but rather is "the set of rules that describe how to structure language" (Moskowitz, 1985, p. 47). Grammatical rules extend from the simplest level of combining sounds to the complex level of extended conversation. For example, word order is one rule of grammar. Speakers of English produce sentences that consist typically of a subject, a verb, and an object, put together in that order: "Carmen hit the ball." Speakers may not be conscious of these rules, but they can easily recognize a sentence that does not follow this pattern. If someone said, "Carmen the ball hit," an English speaker would be able to change the word order to make the sentence grammatically correct, although he or she may not be able to explain the underlying rule. All languages, and all dialects, have rules that control the major components of language—*phonology, semantics, syntax, pragmatics, lexicon,* and *metalinguistics.* Figure 5.1 on page 257 lists these rules.

The Major Components of Language

- **Phonology**   The sounds of a language, the rules for combining them to make words, along with stress and intonation patterns. The word bat consists of three sounds, two consonant sounds /b/ and /t/ connected with the vowel sound /ae/. The word basket has two syllables; the first syllable is stressed.

- **Semantics**   The meaning of words. Only certain strings of sounds are meaningful. Combining the sounds /r/, /t/, /a/ makes the words art and rat, but tra or rta are meaningless. Individual words carry meaning, and words can be combined into meaningful sentences, for example, "Is that picture of a rat really art?" However, words are related in complex networks and have special properties. Although both rat and art are nouns, they cannot change position and make a meaningful sentence: "Is that picture of an art really a rat?"

- **Syntax**   The way words are combined to form phrases and sentences in a language. To form a statement in English, words are arranged in the order of subject, verb, object: "The tornado destroyed the house." Syntax also determines the form of other kinds of sentences, such as questions: "What destroyed that house?" or "How did that house get destroyed?"

- **Pragmatics**   The strategies for using language appropriately in different contexts. Turn-taking rules is one strategy speakers have for structuring speech and for managing social interaction. Interrupting a speaker too soon is a pragmatic violation. Introducing topics into conversation as well as knowing how to structure a formal argument in writing constitute pragmatic knowledge.

- **Lexicon**   Vocabulary; all the words in a language for objects, qualities, actions, and events, ideas, or states of mind: flowers, unique, running, marathon, democracy, blissful.

- **Metalinguistics**   The understanding of language as language. Understanding of properties and function of language.

Theories of Language Development

Because language is so closely tied to thinking, theories of human development have also been used to describe language development. One issue we have considered in earlier chapters is the extent to which mental development depends on internal or external factors—the nature versus nurture controversy. Similarly, theories of language acquisition involve the same debate. Do children have an innate predisposition to learn language? Is language structure—the ability to produce and understand sentences—actually built into the brain? Or is language simply a special form of behavior that children learn through their parents? In order to answer these questions, we will turn our attention to what we know about human development and how different theories may illuminate our understanding of language development.

Several theories of human development were introduced in Chapter 1. Our first perspective held that development occurs naturally as the result of simple biological *maturation*, and follows a predetermined biological timetable. Second, we examined how development is shaped by the environment, a *behaviorist* perspective. Third, we discussed how development results from an *interaction* between innate and environmental factors, with the child as an active participant. Fourth, from a *contextual* perspective, we saw how both child and environment are malleable and undergoing constant change. As you read the following section, think about which perspective on language development you find most compelling.

Does Language Depend Entirely on Nurture?

Believing that the mind is a blank slate at birth, behaviorists such as B. F. Skinner (1957) attribute language development totally to environmental factors. Learning to understand and speak a language depends on the way adults nurture children. Since languages vary so considerably in sound and structure, behaviorists argue that there cannot be any innate mental program general enough to allow children to learn languages as different as Swahili and French without difficulty. Instead, behaviorists believe that language learning depends on mechanisms, such as imitation, and on operant conditioning. It is the positive and negative reinforcements that follow from one's responses to external stimuli that shape the development of language.

Here is a possible behaviorist scenario: A babbling child might produce a wide array of random sounds. Gradually, the range of sounds is reduced and shaped through adults' responses. For instance, English-speaking parents react positively to any babbling that sounds like *da da da* and *ma ma ma* for obvious reasons. Thus, the theory suggests that children learn appropriate sounds and words in reaction to their parents' reinforcement.

But what about learning how to put a sentence together or to express happiness in words? Except for very few formulas—"How are you?"—most sentences that people say are unique in terms of structure. In the course of a single day, it would be extremely unusual for any two people to use exactly the same words when speaking. Reinforcement does not account for the fact that speakers produce novel sentences, sentences they have neither said before nor heard uttered. A child could conceivably learn the words *ball* and *go* through imitation and constant parental reinforcement, but there is no way conditioning can explain the moment when the child says, "Go ball" (meaning "Go and get the ball" or "I'm going to go and get the ball"), or "Ball go" (meaning, "Look at the ball going!"). For one thing, a child would never hear a parent say either of these two-word sentences. The child who produces "Go ball" is in the process of learning how to make a grammatical sentence. However, behaviorist theory cannot explain such inductive learning.

Is Language Biologically Programmed?

No matter what the culture, children begin to learn language around the same time—between 18 and 28 months—all over the world. Some theorists believe that biological maturation is the only way to account for such regularity in the onset of language (Lenneberg, 1967). Furthermore, any language is an extremely complicated system, which consists of sets of overlapping and interrelated rules. It is not clear just how children go about learning anything this complex, especially when the underlying structures of language are not taught directly to children. According to Steven Pinker (2004a), the question concerns "how a learner can correctly generalize from a finite sample of sentences in context to the infinite set of sentences that define the language. . ." (p. 949).

So far, no research has revealed definitively the procedure by which children discover grammatical rules. Therefore, some linguists believe that an innate genetic component provides children with a chunk of the necessary grammar. If grammar is built-in, then it is simply activated as the child matures. In addition, not only does language emerge at a certain time, it also develops in a regular sequence with identifiable milestones. This aspect of language development is also considered a feature of general biological development (Aitchison, 1985). Thus, the basis for language exists within the child for biological theorists. The questions usually posed by innatists or nativists are: "What is 'built in' to the 'hardware'?" or "What does the child begin with in terms of categories, theories, grammars, or whatever?" (Nelson, 1999, p. 187).

Chomsky's View   The linguist Noam Chomsky (1957, 1965) has generated the most complete theory to describe the role of innate knowledge in language acquisition. Chomsky believes that there are universal qualities common to all languages, for instance, ways of making statements and questions, the ability to refer to past time, and ways to form negatives. Therefore, these universal qualities of language must reflect the universal, inborn, character of the human mind. In fact, Chomsky has hypothesized that children are born with a **language acquisition device (LAD),** which is programmed to recognize the universal rules or universal grammar (UG) that underlie all languages. Although the child does not have a fully formed language at birth, as the child matures, the LAD is activated, enabling the child to develop more and more complex language structures until *they reach* adult levels of ability are reached.

Searching for linguistic universals is one method of investigating the universal nature of the mind (Chomsky, 1986, 1999). Chomsky believes that particular qualities of the human mind dictate *operating principles* that all languages must follow. One such principle is called *structure-dependency*. For example, many grammatical rules depend on the fact that sentences have structure, in English and in any other language. We know that questions and statements are constructed differently. Someone might state, "I'm going to the store now," while a person out of earshot might inquire, "Are you going to the store now?" The words in a statement have to be reordered and adjusted to form a question. The auxiliary *am* not only is transformed to *are* to agree with the new subject *you*, but it also has to be moved to the front of the sentence. What Chomsky has suggested is that children approach the job of learning language *expecting* that language will have structure, a particular order, and regularity. This prior readiness and expectancy are possible only if the principle of structure dependency is already part of the child's mental makeup.

For Chomsky and others who work within this theoretical framework, the core of **syntax** or language structure of all languages is inherited. The environment plays almost no role in the innate structural theories of language development. Experience only determines *which* language a child will speak. Whatever language a child hears, whether it be Chinese or Mohawk, will be the one the child learns. Furthermore, all languages are equally learnable from a child's point of view.

Not everyone is convinced by Chomsky's work. Jerome Bruner (1982) describes the LAD as a "miraculous" version of language acquisition. Biological theories are difficult to investigate. No one can prove or disprove genetic principles. However, it is also true that linguists cannot explain definitively how children learn language. But the absence of an adequate theory to provide an alternative explanation of language development simply means more research is needed. It does not mean that Chomsky's proposals concerning innate characteristics or genetic hardwiring are true (Hockett, 1968). Chomsky's theory has several deficits. It cannot explain basic processes, such as how children acquire word meaning, or the mechanism by which the language acquisition device is triggered. However, Bruner (1982) argues that "obituaries for LAD have been premature—particularly if the view were modified . . ." (p. 3). The search for an innate, biological, or evolutionary basis for language development has not been abandoned (see Pinker, 2004b).

Current Views   In recent years, the "hot pursuit of genes for grammar, instincts for language, and special and separate neural mechanisms or 'organs' for phonology, semantics and syntax" (Bates, 2004, p. 4) has been reported in popular media and research journals. Elizabeth Bates suggests that we replace this "Swiss Army knife" metaphor for the way our brains have evolved to acquire language—as filled with specialized tools designed for specific jobs—with the *giraffe's neck* metaphor. Bates and her colleagues hypothesize that language may be a "new machine" that Nature has constructed out of old parts, just as the giraffe has developed a specialized organ that allows it to eat leaves from high tree branches from the general-purpose vertebrate neck plan that maintains its older purposes. Thus, "the uniquely human capacity for language, culture and technology may have been acquired across the course of evolution by a similar process—quantitative changes in primate abilities that bring about and insure a qualitative leap in cognition and communication" (p. 4). Bates proposes that to explain the "giraffe's neck" approach to language, we may begin with abilities that are present at birth or shortly thereafter (such as strong tendencies to orient toward social objects and capacities for cross-modal perception; see Chapter 2), and continue with examining how the entwining of these and other nonlinguistic skills leads to more sophisticated skills (such as imitation of others' actions, gestures, and sounds) or *functional infrastructures* for language. She speculates that these infrastructures may be all that is required for the construction of a LAD; furthermore, a defect in one or more of these infrastructures could have serious consequences for language learning. Thus, this speculative approach has implications for diagnosis of and intervention in communicative disorders as well as for understanding general language acquisition.

The Critical Period for Language Acquisition   In this discussion, we have assumed that every child, apart from those who suffer extreme disabilities, develops language. But do children have to be exposed to language from birth in order to learn it? Is there a critical age by which children must have acquired language if they are to learn it at all? Or is the brain so malleable and resilient that language can be acquired at any age, even if the child has been deprived and isolated from human contact for many years?

Theorist E. H. Lenneberg (1967, 1969) believes that language has a biological basis; there is a *critical period* in infancy when particular neurological faculties develop, which allows the child to learn language. The **critical period hypothesis** suggests that if certain internal or external conditions related to language development are missing, then a child will never be able to acquire language.

Since human interaction is necessary for children to develop language during the first 2 years of life, the critical period hypothesis predicts that extensive social deprivation will prevent language development. As evidence, Lenneberg points to the fact that around 18 months of age the two hemispheres of the brain begin to specialize. Each hemisphere functions to control different areas of human activity. In most people, language functions are located in the left hemisphere. But the brain is somewhat plastic, and studies of brain injuries suggest that if damage occurs in one hemisphere, in some cases the undamaged hemisphere can control new functions. But after puberty, Lenneberg noted the brain loses plasticity, because its special functions become permanent. He believed that if language is not a part of the brain's functions by this time, it never will be.

In those few cases we know of where children have endured severe isolation, their development has been retarded in all areas—cognitive, social, linguistic (Itard, 1962). Once development has been arrested, can it be restarted? Can developmentally delayed children catch up once they are no longer isolated? There is no straightforward answer to this question. Language development depends in part on the age and condition of the child at the time of isolation, the length and intensity of the deprivation, and other biological factors, such as adequate food for brain growth. Much of what we know about this topic has been learned from the case mentioned in Chapter 1 of a girl named Genie, who, for the first 14 years of her life, lived confined to a small, dark room with virtually no human contact. (For Genie's story, see Curtiss, 1977.)

Although she was 14 years old when first exposed to it, Genie did make some progress in acquiring language. However, scientists believe that she was using her right brain for language processing, which is atypical. She learned fairly quickly how to produce short sentences, but her grammar never developed much beyond the linguistic capacities of a 2½-year-old child. In contrast, her vocabulary was larger and more sophisticated than that of a young child, which indicates that her cognition developed faster than her linguistic abilities. Since Genie never developed language completely, Susan Curtiss (1977) concluded that, contrary to Lenneberg's theory, *some* degree of language acquisition is possible after the critical period.

Recently, questions concerning critical periods for language development have been addressed in two very different research camps. Neuroscientists have examined children recovering from early unilateral brain injuries, and report a high degree of neural plasticity in language learning. "Learning 'sculpts' the brain, and . . . the mechanisms that support learning in healthy children are apparently sufficient to support the development of normal language abilities in the face of early injury" (Bates et al., 2004, p. 3). Researchers studying second-language learning make similar observations about the flexibility of the brain and a fairly long "window of opportunity" for language learning. Although this window does appear to close slowly for the mastery of grammar and accent at the beginning of adolescence, this is not the case for the learning of the semantics of language (e.g., Bialystok, 2001; Bruer, 1999). Thus, although there may be sensitive periods for different aspects of language development, neuroscientists, developmentalists, and educators emphasize our adaptability and lifelong abilities for learning.

Does Language Emerge from the Interaction of Mind and Environment?

Piaget's View Arguing for a middle ground, interactional theorists such as Piaget insist that both nature and nurture contribute something to intellectual growth and language development. The child actively participates in constructing the interactions that occur between internal states and external environmental conditions. Piaget's views on language development are colored by his primary concern with understanding the developing mind of the child, as suggested by his book *The Language and Thought of the Child* (1926). Given this predisposition, it is predictable that Piaget would assume that symbolic thought is a precondition for language acquisition. During infancy, as sensorimotor schemas appear, a child is able to think symbolically. Only then is it possible for the child to understand that language functions as a system of symbols. Words can represent objects, actions, or abstract ideas; *bottle* or the more likely *baba* is a sound-symbol that represents the desired object. The relation between thoughts and words is also seen in children's use of "gone" when they achieve object permanence, and "uh-oh" or "there" when they solve problems (Gopnik & Meltzoff, 1997).

Since language depends on thought, it follows in Piaget's theory that early speech will share some of the characteristics of early thought. Although a child realizes by the end of the sensorimotor period that he or she is part of a world but has a separate self, the child's thoughts are egocentric, centered on the self. Likewise, Piaget noted that much of children's language (even for the kindergarten children he studied) had nothing to do with communication and served no obvious social function. Instead, such verbalizing mirrored the child's thinking. Piaget called instances of this kind of egocentric speech—talking in the presence of others without expecting interaction or comprehension—*collective monologues.* Here is part of an exchange between two preschool children that resembles two parallel monologues rather than conversational interaction.

Jenny: They wiggle sideways when they kiss.

Chris: (Vaguely) What?

Jenny: My bunny slippers. They are brown and red and sort of yellow and white. And they have eyes and years and these noses that wiggle sideways when they kiss.

Chris: I have a piece of sugar in a red piece of paper. I'm gonna eat it but maybe it's for a horse.

Jenny: We bought them. My Mommy did. We couldn't find the old ones. These are like the old ones. They were not in the trunk.

Chris: Can't eat the piece of sugar, not unless you take the paper off.

Jenny: And we found Mother Lamb. Oh, she was in Poughkeepsie in the trunk in the house in the woods where Mrs. Tiddywinkle lives.

Chris: Do I like sugar? I do, and so do horses.

Jenny: I play with my bunnies. They are real. We play in the woods. They have eyes. We all go in the woods. My teddy bear and the bunnies and the duck, to visit Mrs. Tiddywinkle. We play and play.

Chris: I guess I'll eat my sugar at lunch time. I can get more for the horses. Besides, I don't have no horses now. (Stone & Church, 1957, pp. 146–147)

To account for such egocentric language, Piaget looked for a cognitive explanation instead of considering social factors. He proposed that this kind of *egocentric speech* reflects the thinking that is characteristic of young children at the preoperational stage of development (see Chapter 3). At later stages of development, as Piaget observed, these monologues would eventually become dialogues, since children by then would be developmentally able to take the perspective of their listeners into consideration.

To summarize, Piaget's cognitive approach emphasizes that internal structures are fundamental but not completely deterministic. Language is not a direct result of an innate characteristic but is an ability related to cognitive maturation. Piaget's theory is interactional; there are many factors—social, linguistic, cognitive—that affect the course of development. Furthermore, these factors interact with and mutually depend on each other as well as being reciprocal. In other words, Piaget (1954) claimed that advances in language growth are constrained by cognition, but at the same time he recognized that cognitive development alone is not sufficient to ensure language development. In reacting to Chomsky's theory during a debate in 1957, Piaget asserted that the complex structures of language are not necessarily innate or learned. Instead, linguistic structures emerge as a result of the continuing interaction between a child's inner intellectual functioning and the outer social and linguistic environments. However, Piaget left the nature of this interaction unexplored, perhaps because he was more interested in how children arrive at an understanding of their physical world than of their language development.

Piaget has been criticized for underestimating social factors in development, especially the role that parents, caregivers, siblings, and other people have in affecting a child's cognitive and linguistic development. Piaget's work depicts the child acting independently to figure out the surrounding world. Other theorists believe that the child never interacts alone, but always in concert with others. Development in language and thought depends on a child's working collaboratively with other people to explore the physical and social worlds (Elliot, 1981). The possibility that intelligence may have a social origin was not something that Piaget explored. However, other researchers have attempted to study the issue of social interaction, which has led them to reinterpret some of Piaget's classic experiments (Karmiloff-Smith, 1979). Piaget used an interview method in which he relied on children's verbal responses to a set of questions as well as on informal conversation about the materials or activity at hand. It turns out that changing the way questions are worded strongly affects children's abilities to answer the questions (Sinha & Walkerdine, 1978). These findings suggest that language and cognition are deeply intertwined; language does not simply reflect the mind's functioning in any clear manner, as Piaget believed.

Current Views   Some of Piaget's views, however, have been revived in recent models of language acquisition. For example, Bloom and Tinker (2001) describe the child in the Intentionality Model as "Piaget's child," in that the focus is on *the child's contents of mind* in language-learning interactions (p. 11). They claim that in many contemporary theories of language acquisition, including biologically based theories, the children are missing! Children are depicted as merely passive receivers of physical or social cues or the locus of brain mechanisms or principles that filter information for them. Instead, these authors argue, acquiring language *takes work*—it doesn't happen easily or automatically. Children begin working at learning language from birth, and continue well into the school years. Research shows that word learning begins slowly at the end of the first year, before picking up speed toward the end of the second year. The first phrases and simple sentences then begin hesitantly, and proceed gradually and tentatively to increase in length and complexity. From this constructivist perspective (described in Chapter 3), language development emerges out of the child's engagement in new encounters and the child's efforts to connect what is already known to the new information and contradictions present in those encounters.

Does Language Development Depend on Social Interaction?

Vygotsky's View   Although Piaget felt that development involved a child's environment, he envisioned each child individually constructing a worldview based on the interaction between internal mental and external physical experiences. Piaget's theory downplays the fact that language is essentially social, and that children learn about the world in the company of others. For Vygotsky (1987), however, the social environment and surrounding culture are critical factors that motivate children's development in all areas, including the realm of language.

Vygotsky believed that thought and language originate independently but that sometime in early childhood, the two processes merge. Neither language nor thought is predominant. In addition, Vygotsky emphasized that children are born into a social community, cared for by others, and connected to the world through linguistic interactions. Psychological functions emerge in children as they interact with adults who nurture and support their efforts.

In his theory of language development, Vygotsky asserts that communicative speech develops before verbal thought. During the child's first 2 years, language and thought have independent origins. For example, children's babbling is essential to language development but does not seem critical for cognitive development. As children engage in communication, this "social speech," as Vygotsky called it, becomes "speech on its way inward." It is the precursor to verbal thought. When social speech becomes internal dialogue, a child develops what Vygotsky calls inner speech, which is the earliest form of thought mediated by language (see Chapter 3). Social speech precedes the development of inner speech; therefore Vygotsky (1962) believed that thought, in the form of inner speech, has a social origin: "Thought development is determined by language, i.e., by the linguistic tools of thought and by the sociocultural experience of the child" (p. 51).

Vygotsky's observation that language is first used by a child to communicate, and that thought emerges from internalized social speech, is the reverse of Piaget's theory. Piaget proposed that thought preceded language and that language development depended on the child's reaching new levels of cognitive development. But Vygotsky imagines the relationship between language and thought as dynamic and volatile. As language and thought develop in the child, the relationship between these two processes changes constantly. For about the first 2 years of life, language and thought develop independently, as parallel processes. But language gradually merges with thought around the age of 2, and this combination creates a unique and powerful medium. With language, individuals can internally represent objects, actions, and relationships as private thoughts and then communicate these thoughts to others. Perception, memory, and problem solving are all mental processes that depend on internalized language. One important aspect of development for Vygotsky was children's growing ability to control and direct their own behavior (see Chapter 3). Language helps children to control present action, but they can also use language to plan, order, and to some degree control their actions in the future as well (Vygotsky, 1978).

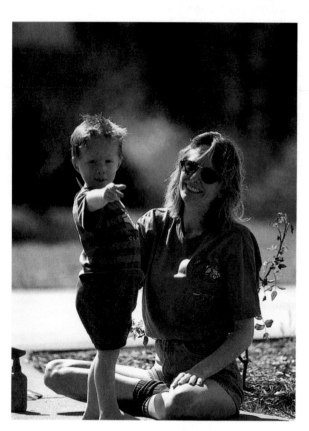

Children learn about the world in the company of others.
Source: Robert Ginn/Photo Edit.

It is important to remember that Vygotsky believed young children are capable of social and intellectual cooperation to a greater degree than Piaget ever thought was possible. Individuals are part of a community in which knowledge and practices are guided by social conventions; indeed, language itself is an agreed-on set of conventions. Vygotsky's theory of language development assumes that individuals and their thoughts are not independent of their culture but are formed through social interactions shaped by a particular culture (Vygotsky, 1978).

Current Views   Contemporary developmental psychologists have embraced aspects of Vygotsky's theory—in particular, the emphasis on the role of social activity (Nelson, 1999). For example, Jerome Bruner (1982) proposed that adults (and capable older children) arrange environments and encounters with young children in ways to *scaffold* natural language development (see Chapter 3). This interaction pattern, the **language acquisition support system (LASS)**, readies or formats the input of language for the child in a way that makes its rules more transparent to the child's LAD. "LASS, so to speak, helps LAD" (p. 5). Forms of infant-directed- speech (IDS) illustrate this process. (See the Focus on Research box, "IDS and Baby Signs.")

A related view, articulated by Barbara Rogoff (2003), focuses on the use of language as a tool for thinking. ". . . Through participation in community practices as well as in communication about them, both thinking and language develop in ways that support each other" (p. 267). These practices include narrative structures or formats that provide ways for people to express themselves in conversation and writing. For example, Japanese children are encouraged to narrate everyday events in a succinct (*haiku*-like) storytelling format. In contrast, European American children are encouraged to elaborate on a single experience, providing details about settings and emotions, even if these could be easily inferred by the listener. These distinct narrative formats may contribute to different habits of mind. Dan Slobin (cited in Bruner, 2002) expresses a similar idea: "One cannot verbalize experience without taking a *perspective,* and . . . the language being used often favors particular perspectives" (p. 73). These ideas are discussed further in the "Literacy Development" section later in this chapter.

IDS and Baby Signs

Mothers, fathers, caregivers, and even older children modify the language directed toward infants, without necessarily being aware of doing so. This type of **infant-directed speech (IDS)** or child-directed speech (CDS) (formerly referred to as *motherese* or *parentese*) is almost universal, and consists of meaningful utterances directed to the infant during everyday routines or play. It is distinguished from meaningless vocalizing toward infants that is sometimes referred to as "baby talk." IDS tends to be slower, simpler, more clearly articulated, higher in pitch, and more variable in intonation than speech directed to adults. The exaggerated intonation and slower tempo help the infant divide speech into sentences, words, syllables, and sounds (especially vowels) (De Boer, 2005). This behavior appears to facilitate children's language development by simplifying language structure. Thus, it is not surprising that infants prefer to listen to IDS rather than adult-directed speech.

A form of IDS is used in signed languages. For example, Masataka (1992) observed that deaf mothers with Japanese Sign Language as their first language communicated with their deaf infants with slower, exaggerated, repetitive signs more so than they did with their friends.

Since communication involves multiple senses—auditory, tactile, and visual (facial expressions and gestures)—adults also tend to facilitate language development by providing redundant cues, such as between words and gestures (*multimodal motherese* or *mutimodal IDS*). For example, Gogate, Bahrick, and Watson (2000) found that when European American and Hispanic American mothers taught their infants labels for novel objects, they frequently communicated by touching the infant with an object in coordination with naming and moving it. In addition, the mothers appeared to be tailoring their communication to the language level of their infants, reducing the use of motion with older infants when they apparently didn't need this redundant information. Recent research has supported the importance of nonverbal input. Pan, Rowe, Singer, and Snow (2005) found that maternal pointing gestures, mostly used to direct or discuss a joint focus of attention, had a positive effect on children's lexical growth, more so than total amount of talk.

The importance of providing multiple cues for communicating with infants has found its way to the popular press and advocates of *baby signing*. Baby signing has been described as "one of the hottest trends in child development," and a medley of organizations and businesses, such as the Baby Signing Institute and Baby Sign Language University, have sprung up in recent years, along with the production of books, videos, and DVDs to encourage and teach parents and caregivers to sign with their hearing babies. A variety of sign systems are taught, including American Sign Language (ASL) as well as other sign systems (e.g., KinderSigns). The goals are to facilitate communication with babies to reduce behavioral problems, such as

Source: ©2005 Penny Gentieu.

temper tantrums stemming from the frustration infants feel when they cannot express themselves, and to enhance their socioemotional and intellectual development. But do we have evidence to support the deliberate use of sign systems with hearing infants? Susan Goodwyn and Linda Acredolo (1998, 2000) report data from studies with infants whose parents were encouraged to use their own invented gestures along with a few target gestures. Infants in the Sign Training (gesturing) group showed greater gains in *early* language skills than infants in other groups, indicating a "jump start" in development; however, these advantages were no longer significant at age 3. The authors explain the short-term advantages in terms of the increase in parents' use of IDS, attention to their infants' interests (joint attention), and more effective scaffolding (see Chapter 3). Notably, parents also reported more positive interactions with their infants when gestures were part of their communication repertoire. For example, they felt better able to decipher and respond to infants' requests (e.g., for specific foods, such as Cheerios), feelings (e.g., hot, afraid, happy), references (e.g., monkey, zebra), and first word attempts (e.g., "tata" for "turtle").

In the end, what may matter most is that parents and caregivers attempt to attune themselves to infants in a variety of ways, as many naturally do, and feel free to use nonverbal means of communication (whether original or from an established sign system) when it is helpful. These sensitive efforts, of course, are also important for communicating with older children and those with exceptional needs.

TABLE 5.1	Different Perspectives of Language Development		
Perspective	Theorists	Major Causal Factor	
Behaviorist	Skinner	Language development is completely environmental	
Nativist	Chomsky and Pinker	Language structure depends on innate, biological characteristics of the human mind	
Interactionist (cognitive)	Piaget, Bloom, and Tinker	Language results from interaction between cognitive and environmental factors	
Interactionist (contextual)	Vygotsky, Bruner, Bates, and Rogoff	Language is constructed within a particular sociocultural context, depending on cognitive and environmental factors	

Reconciling Different Points of View

We have discussed several different ways of understanding language as it relates to cognition. Most psychologists agree that language and thought are two distinct processes, yet they are inseparable from one another. One primary distinction between theories is the degree to which biological factors (nature) versus social factors (nurture) account for language development, as shown in Table 5.1. Chomsky proposed that the LAD enables children to develop language. Piaget and Vygotsky, on the other hand, emphasized interactions between children's developing language and thought systems and their environment. Contemporary developmental theorists agree that neither nature nor nurture alone can fully explain how children acquire language. No matter how we account for the origins of language acquisition, the fact remains that language exists within a social community. Becoming a competent speaker or writer depends on the amount and quality of experience individuals have in using language to communicate.

 # Learning to Communicate

Children learn the language that they hear spoken around them. However, only being able to hear a language is not sufficient. For instance, listening to a TV will not enable a child to learn language. Being able to interact with other people who offer immediate responses is essential to language development (MacWhinney & Bornstein, 2003). So-called wild children, or children who grow up in total isolation from language and normal human interaction, do not learn language. Furthermore, no matter what a child's cultural heritage may be, he or she will acquire the language spoken by people in the immediate community. A child born of Chinese parents but adopted in infancy by English-speaking Americans will grow up speaking English.

Learning Language

In learning language, children must make sense of the sounds, gestures, and intonation patterns their parents direct toward them. When Jessie's father leans over the crib, he is already talking to his daughter. As he leans to pick her up, he accompanies his actions with words, repeating important ones such as *bottle,* and naming himself and his child.

Daddy's going to pick Jessie up.
Does Jessie need a bottle?
Oh yeah, Jessie needs a bottle.
Here! U—p we go.
Daddy's getting the bottle.

Jessie's father takes advantage of her visual attention to the bottle to label or comment on what she sees. Effective communication requires this joint attention or **intersubjectivity**—the sharing of a common focus. In other words, to succeed in influencing others (and getting what one wants) language must "connect the contents of individual minds" (Bloom & Tinker, 2001, p. 5). In order to respond, or to express a desire, Jessie needs to analyze the stream of speech in the surrounding world and select pieces to learn—those sounds that will grab her parents' attention and communicate her intentions. Parents do a good job of helping their children by emphasizing important words, speaking in a high-pitched intonation, and using many repetitions. This type of child-directed or infant-directed speech (IDS) is sometimes known as *motherese,* or more appropriately in this time of joint child-rearing, *parentese* or caretaker speech. (See also Focus on Research box on page 266.)

As Jessie's father is speaking, she must sift through a tremendous number of sounds in order to identify a word such as *bottle* and know that it signifies a particular object. When Jessie is about 10 to 11 months old, she may intentionally follow her father's gaze to discover what he is referring to—an important marker of her social and emotional growth as well as her later language development (Brooks & Meltzoff, 2005). Once the child recognizes a meaningful sound, she then must discover a way of making the sound that approximates *bottle* and of saying it with a particular kind of emphasis. And all this must happen while her parents are present to hear her request. Learning to say a single word at the right moment is the result of a great deal of analysis, effort, and construction on the child's part. We will examine several methods by which children accomplish this tremendous task.

Whether or not they realize it, parents encourage children to talk by co-constructing the content of conversations. The parent may ask questions or add a detail to a child's story. Adults rarely correct the structure of children's speech, although they may occasionally comment on the meaning or truthfulness of what children say, and they sometimes model correct pronunciation (Clark & Clark, 1977). However, adults do reinforce children's active attempts to participate in conversation.

The following exchange between mother and daughter is typical of how adults interpret the meaning of a child's utterance, while ignoring the issue of grammatical structure.

Eve:	Have that?
Mother:	No, you may not have it.
Eve:	Mom, where my tapioca?
Mother:	It's getting cool. You'll have it in just a minute.
Eve:	Let me have it.
Mother:	Would you like to have your lunch right now?
Eve:	Yeah. My tapioca cool?
Mother:	Yes, it's cool.
Eve:	You gonna watch me eat my lunch?
Mother:	Yeah, I'm gonna watch you eat your lunch.
Eve:	I eating it.
Mother:	I know you are.

Eve:	It time Sarah take a nap.
Mother:	It's time for Sarah to have some milk, yeah. And then she's gonna take a nap and you're gonna take a nap.
Eve:	And you?
Mother:	And me too, yeah. (Bellugi, 1970, p. 33)

Neither imitation nor reinforcement can account for the kind of language that Eve produces while she is speaking with her mother. At one point Eve comments, "I eating it." Among the many other things she is learning about English, Eve is at present working on verb forms and tenses. Since these forms are complex in English, Eve constructs her own way of describing present action, which leaves out the auxiliary verb *am*. Such a strategy is common among children at similar stages of language development. The important point is that Eve is making guesses about how the system works and testing out these hypotheses. A collaborative construction theory (Nelson, 1999) is powerful enough to explain three important features of language development: the rapid growth children make, the consistent patterns they produce that are not like adult structures, and the fact that learning occurs without direct instruction and in diverse circumstances that vary considerably from one child to another.

We can observe children actively constructing rules for speaking by paying attention to the way they monitor themselves and experiment with structural forms:

Laura (aged 2 years, 2 months):	Her want some more.
	Her want some more candy.
	Let's dooz this.
	Let's do this.
	Let's do this puzzle. (Laura adds nouns—*candy* and *puzzle*.) (Moskowitz, 1985, p. 59)

Older children continue to monitor and experiment to achieve new forms:

Jamie (aged 6 years, 3 months):	Who do you think is the importantest kid in the world except me?
Mother:	What did you say, Jamie?
Jamie:	Who do you think is the specialest kid in the world not counting me?
Jamie (aged 6 years, 10 months):	I figured something you might like out.
Mother:	What did you say?
Jamie:	I figured out something you might like. (Moskowitz, 1985, p. 59)

Children learn grammar—phonology, syntax, semantics, lexicon, and pragmatics—by breaking each system down into its smallest part and then developing rules for combining the parts. In the first 2 years, a child spends much time taking apart the sound system and learning sound combinations that make words. After words, children focus on structures, combining words into sentences of various kinds to communicate their intentions.

Children are very methodical language learners. They are remarkably sensitive to regularities in language that they hear around them, picking up on the joint focus of attention for adult and child (e.g., Clark, 2004) The most general rules are hypothesized first; then newer rules are added to increase precision. For instance, learning word order in English—subject, verb, object—is a more general rule than learning how to produce a present-or past-tense verb. Generally children will deal with clear-cut issues first and sort out the details later. When it comes to language, children are very inventive, as we saw in Eve's conversation. They are adept at circumventing the difficult parts of the language system while still managing to communicate.

First Words

Before they know a single word, children are communicating. Babies vocalize, changing tone and volume to convey their needs—cooing to express pleasure at seeing a parent or crying over an empty stomach. Babies babble, repeating speech sounds individually or producing long stretches of sound that seem oddly like the intonation patterns of the language spoken around them. They tend to comprehend words earlier (at about 8–10 months) than they can produce them (e.g., Bates, Devescovi, & Wulfeck, 2001). This understanding is sometimes referred to as **receptive language.**

Sometime around their first birthday, most children begin to say single words, or what adults take to be words (Bates, 1976). This onset time appears to be the same for children across the world, as documented in more than 20 languages, including sign languages (Bates et al., 2001). First words commonly refer to objects in the child's world: *ball, dada, kitty, juice.* This is not surprising, since at this age children are in the sensorimotor stage of development in which concrete knowledge is being developed (Piaget, 1952). By the time children are saying their first words, they have acquired object permanence (see Chapter 3). They understand that when a ball rolls behind a chair, it may be out of sight, but it still exists even though hidden by the chair. Children also understand something about tools—for instance, pulling the blanket closer to grab the bear resting on it—and about symbolic play—using a spoon to feed their bear some applesauce. All these abilities (object permanence, tool use, symbolic play) require the child to represent experience in some other form. Words provide such symbols. Piaget maintained that representational thinking is an important precondition for language development. Clark (2004) explains that children's conceptual representations for objects, actions, properties, and events provide a "broad cognitive basis onto which they can map words from child-direct speech" (p. 476). For example, children often rely on shape to sort objects that are similar. They might apply the word *ball* to balls first, then overextend it to apple, oranges, doorknobs, or other round objects. Or they might attend to other properties, such as size or function, in their overgeneralizations.

Although children may have fewer than a dozen words in their speaking vocabulary, they are able to use intonation, gesture, and facial expressions to impart an entire sentence's worth of meaning into a single word. **Holophrases** are single words intended to convey more complex meaning. A child may say *truck* and mean, "There's a truck" or "Give me the truck" or "I hear the garbage truck" or "The truck is driving down the road." They are trying to convey the meaning of a whole sentence in a single word, often accompanied with nonverbal actions. Adults help by interpreting children's utterances and making appropriate verbal and physical responses. Adults can foster children's development through verbal interactions such as the following.

Child: Spoon!
Adult: Down! It fell down, didn't it? Did the spoon make a noise? That was loud!

Within a few months of saying their first words, children begin combining words into two-word utterances. Although there is a great deal of variation among children, two-word utterances appear on average at 18 months of age. The progression from one- to two-word combinations is so predictable and stable that psychologists have hypothesized a cognitive limit to explain the two-word condition.

■ FIGURE 5.2
Two-Word
Utterances
Source: Bowerman (1973).

Verb and agent:	"Kendall swim."
Verb and goal:	"Writing book."
Verb and location:	"Sit pool."
Experiencer and object:	"Kimmy bike."
Location and object:	"Pillow here."
Verb and object:	"Shoe off."

Remember that children are not trying to reproduce adult sentences, which are far longer than two words, but are simply trying to communicate. In a sense, each child is constructing his or her own system, based on the language input the child is receiving from other speakers. Look at the list of 2-year-old Kendall's utterances as shown in Figure 5.2.

Two words are better than one, because children may talk about more than one role or action at a time. There are many possible variations. For instance, "Kimmy bike," or naming the experiencer and the object, is just as likely as the reverse "Bike Kimmy." Another child may name the object and then the place, "Pillow here," or the opposite, "There doggie" (Braine, 1976). These patterns are unpredictable, which demonstrates that children are constructing language individually.

Many Words

One word, two words, . . . three words? On the basis of their first utterances, it is tempting to conclude that children will keep adding a word at a time to their sentence length. But two-word combinations are the foundation for future sentences with any number of words, not just three.

Language development is fairly consistent: Children often learn a small set of single words first; then as they learn more words, they combine them into two-word utterances; then they begin producing multiple-word utterances with great speed, huge variety, and little regularity from child to child. Two strategies children appear to use are to combine smaller sequences and to embed one sequence inside another. For instance, knowing the two expressions, "Kendall swim" (agent and verb) and "sit pool" (verb and location), a child may be able to create, "Kendall swim pool." Sometimes this phase is called **telegraphic speech.** As the example shows, early telegraphic speech is typically a short, simple sentence, with primarily content words. Linking words such as *in* are omitted.

Although this expression seems rudimentary, children are acquiring new words and new functions and combining expressions so quickly that they soon begin producing complex utterances, as Andrew demonstrates:

> ***Andrew (2 years, 8 months):*** What he can ride in?
> He not taking the walls down.
> I want to open it.

Although not perfectly grammatical, Andrew is able to produce a question and indicate a negative state. Both forms are quite complex in English and, in acquiring them, children follow regular patterns. (Both these forms have been extensively studied; see Klima & Bellugi [1966] on questions and Bloom [1970] on negatives.)

Around 3 years old, children start to produce more complex sentences.

Complement:	"I want to go out."
Relative:	"The ones you've got are bigger."
Adverbial (Subordination):	"I was crying when my Mommy goed away." (Clark & Clark, 1977, p. 359)

Generally, once past the two-word phase, children from about 3 to 4 years of age expand both the structure and function of their basic language system. Structurally, word endings such as -*ed* begin to appear, as in "He kicked Teddy," and possessive forms develop, as in "My dog's bone is gone." In addition to these small refinements, children grow functionally. They are better understood by unfamiliar people, and are better able to express their feelings and ideas (NIDCD, 2000). Part of communicating effectively entails learning how to interact with listeners in increasingly sophisticated ways. For instance, 4-year-olds know that using a hedge rather than making a direct assertion will foster cooperation. Instead of saying, "That piece fits here," the child may opt to say, "*I think* that piece fits here" (Gelman & Shatz, 1976). Children are learning language on all fronts at once—not only are they improving their syntax and acquiring new vocabulary, they are also learning to argue with their peers and to solicit help from adults when they need it. They are also beginning to have fun with language, and enjoy poems and language absurdities, such as "is that an elephant on your head?" (NIDCD, 2000).

Individual Differences in Early Language Development

Although there appear to be some universal patterns in language acquisition, there are also important individual differences. This information is necessary to consider when referring to the developmental milestones listed in the Focus on Development box "Early Language Acquisition" on page 272. For example, multinational studies have shown great variation in the growth of typically developing children's vocabulary (e.g., ranging from 0–500 words at 2 years of age) within and across languages (Bates et al., 2001).

Researchers have carefully observed the natural growth of young language learners, and have described some individual differences or *styles* of children who eventually became competent speakers (without language delays or disorders). For example, Hart and Risley (1999) characterized children as "early talkers" at 15 to 18 months if they produced identifiable words in half their speech, and "late talkers" if they did so at 24 to 27 months. All the early and late talkers in their study were competent speakers by age 3. Boysson-Bardies (1999) also identified late talkers in a naturalistic study. Henri was one who skipped the typical milestones, such as babbling and the first 50 words, and started speaking with a large number of comprehensible words and word combinations when he was 20 month old. Two months later his vocabulary exploded—in one session he spoke more than 150 words in two- and three-word sentences! By 30 months, he had a huge vocabulary of sophisticated words and spoke in elaborate sentences. Apparently, he already had an organized structure for recognizing words in place well before he could (or chose to) speak them. Recent research confirms that many children whose initial language progress is slow (in terms of vocabulary and sentence length) increase their rate to catch up with typically developing peers (Feldman et al., 2005). These researchers conclude that "the rate of early language development thus appears to be an imperfect predictor of the rate of later language development and of the ultimate level of language skills in the children" (p. 866).

Other individual differences or styles have been described. Boysson-Bardies also identified children, such as Emilie, who preferred the *minimalist* strategy, trying to operate as efficiently and simply as possible. For example, Emilie initially named things that required

Focus on
Development   *Early Language Acquisition*

Age	Developmental Milestone
Birth to 6 months	Cries and coos (open vowel sounds) Recognizes human voices Responds well to high-pitched, melodic vocalizations Can distinguish *d* from *b* Varies cries to signal pain and distress
6 to 12 months	Babbles (vowel-constant sounds) Imitates voice patterns and sounds Uses voice to get attention Waves bye-bye Understands more words than can say
12 to 18 months	Uses holophrases Says first words Overextends words (apple for round objects) Uses gestures to convey meaning Shakes head to mean "no" Understands simple commands Begins to use me, you, I
18 to 24 months	Uses two-word phrases ("Mommy go") Refers to self by name Uses telegraphic speech Uses correct word order Accumulates 50 to 200 words
24 to 36 months	Begins to use word endings Uses three-word sentences Enjoys songs, rhymes, and rhythms Uses simple pronouns Continues to expand vocabulary Telegraphic speech declines Uses strategies to begin conversations Uses adjectives and adverbs Speaking vocabulary may reach about 400 words Can articulate *m, n, f, p, t, d, w*
36 months	Huge variation in vocabulary across individuals (900 to 1500 words)

Sources: West National Institutes of Mental Health 1995; Bates et al. (2001); Clark (2004).

the least possible articulatory effort, selecting adult words that contained patterns of speech that she had frequently used in her babbling. This strategy allowed her to rapidly develop a vocabulary; other minimalist strategies may not be as effective in the beginning. In contrast to this "naming things" style (or the *referential,* analytic style) is the *expressive* style observed in Simon. Simon frequently engaged in charming, "melodic conversations" with adults; however, most of the time it was impossible to relate his "very French" speech, filled with many well-articulated syllables and appropriate intonation and rhythm, to adult language. His speech eventually became more comprehensible; thus, "he entered into language with sentences and expressions" rather than single words. This style may delay lexical growth (particularly nouns), but favors social interaction ("conversation first!").

According to Boysson-Bardies, these studies show that children adopt a personal approach to language—they prefer certain hypotheses. Their choices may be influenced by their interests, caregiver styles, and the particular language that they hear (see also Bates et al., 2001). This perspective is consistent with the constructivist and intentional models of language learning described earlier. It also has practical implications for identification of communication and language disorders (discussed in the next section). Parent and teacher concerns about children who don't follow the language milestone charts exactly can be alleviated, as long as their children appear to *comprehend* language and other developmental and behavioral problems are not evident (see the Focus on Development box "Potential Danger Signals . . ." on page 280).

Children's Language After Age 5

The early stages of language acquisition have been well studied, perhaps because of children's dramatic progress in the first few years of life. For parents, no other time is as heartening as the day their child speaks the first word, or invents a name for a sibling whose own name is unpronounceable (*Rainman* for *Raymond*). Although older children's language development has been less studied, there is still a great deal that children learn about language during the school years. At 5 and 6 years old, their progress in acquiring vocabulary or in syntax may be less spectacular, but the pragmatic structures and strategies children are perfecting are vital for their later competence as adult speakers and writers. In fact, developing **communicative competence,** or learning to use language in an appropriate manner—that is, knowing what words and structures to use on what occasion—is the major area of linguistic growth during childhood, through adolescence, and continuing into adulthood (Hymes, 1974). Recent research confirms that language skills continue to develop across the first two decades of life (Dick, Wulfeck, Krupa-Kwiatkowski, & Bates, 2004).

At 5 years old, children do not make the phonological or syntactic errors typical of 3-year-olds. In English, they can distinguish between verbs that have a special form for the past tense (I *run;* I *ran*) and those that take the common *-ed* form (I *walk;* I *walked*). They know how to produce a variety of complex sentences in which two or more clauses are combined, as in the following adverbial clause example: "I ran away *when the big dog came into the yard.*" Along with syntax, children's vocabularies are also expanding rapidly. By third grade, children with well-educated parents probably have a vocabulary of approximately 12,000 words, which can grow up to 100,000 words in adulthood (Pinker, 2004b; Snow, 2005). Learning new words or extending their understanding of what a word means is a constant process. Understanding words that refer to locations, such as *beside* or *between,* is difficult conceptually, and children begin to use them reliably at about the age of 5.

In addition to sentence structure (syntax) and word meaning (semantics), school-age children's progress in social (pragmatic) uses of language develops rapidly. They are learning to engage in more sustained and effective interchanges with others. Around age 5, their delight at jokes and riddles, rhymes, and silly sounds becomes contagious. Around age 7, a child who can create a joke will have learned an important social skill, earning the respect and attention of peers. Knowing how to interrupt politely in a conversation, the rules for arguing, strategies for storytelling, and other forms of public discourse are all important parts of children's developing communicative competence.

Language into Adolescence

Once children reach middle childhood, the sound, meaning, and grammatical systems are well developed apart from a few, less commonly used forms in speech, such as relative clauses and passive sentences. They continue to develop their vocabulary; literacy experts, such as Catherine Snow (2005), propose that adolescents should know 80,000 words by the time they graduate from high school. Now that they have mastered the basics, older children focus their energies on learning how to use language, greatly expanding their range of language registers (formal and informal speech) and styles (narrative, argumentative, etc.) in both speaking and writing. In addition, school has a major impact in fostering this flexibility as well as teaching specialized knowledge about written styles.

UNDERSTANDING CHILDREN
Strategy 4.9: Use of Language: Conversations, Metaphor, and Satire

Temperamentally, any adolescent can be volatile, moody, exuberant, and restless, sometimes withdrawn but socially preoccupied with peers and dismissive of adults as authorities. At this age, teenagers use language to express their deepest emotions and thoughts. In her work teaching middle school, Nancie Atwell (1987) reported that poetry is a mode most often chosen by her eighth graders because it allows them to give shape and voice to their inner experiences. This attraction to poetry and other techniques used in creative writing, such as parody and sarcasm, is not surprising. Around the age of 11 or 12, children pass another linguistic benchmark when they perceive that meaning is multi-dimensional: Words have both literal and metaphoric definitions. Remember that young children make literal interpretations of words or texts. Fairy tales are simply entertaining and engrossing stories to an elementary age child whose thinking is very concrete. But older children develop the ability to make complex interpretations of texts. Fairy tales convey morals and messages that a middle-school-age child can articulate. Language takes on an entirely new dimension for creative expression and comprehension once the child understands how figurative language, such as metaphor, conveys meaning. Their cognitive and linguistic abilities complement each other. Adolescent students, such as Nildo, Juana, and Maddie in the opening vignette, can read a poem and afterward argue about its symbolism; they are apt to see patterns and to assess motives in events that previously had seemed straightforward. Linguistic styles proliferate at this age, especially those associated with humor: puns, quips, nonsequiturs, jokes, ad-libs, double entendres, caricatures, and imitations are common fare. Although metalinguistic *appreciation* of humor begins to emerge between 6 and 9 years of age, it is not until about 10 to 13 years of age that young adolescents offer awkward metalinguistic *explanations* of humor. These explanations become more sophisticated later in adolescence (Ashkenazi & Ravid, 1998).

By adolescence, students are extremely skilled at adapting their language to different situations. This flexibility serves two purposes: as a creative outlet and as social currency. The way we speak both reflects our individual personalities and conveys information about our relationships with other people. Imagine the conversational variety in these contexts: a 15-year-old on the phone with a close friend, a last-minute discussion between a coach and her basketball players before a big game, the small talk among a group of boys sitting on the school steps, a teenager asking to use the family car on a Saturday night. What might be some of the factors shaping speech? What social relations underlie each discourse style? Language

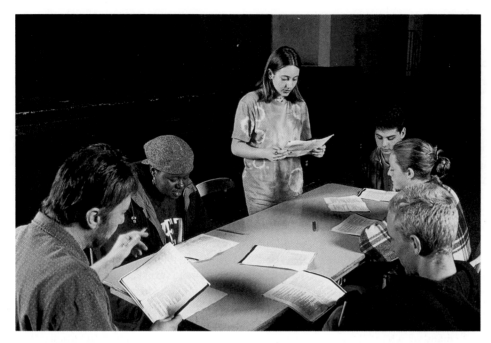

Drama and theater provide adolescents opportunities to experiment with many different language forms and linguistic styles.
Source: Michael Newman/Photo Edit.

addressed to adults will be more formal and polite compared with peers. Formality of language in tone and structure is further heightened in school contexts versus home settings. Language between peers of the same gender may be more casual and telegraphic compared with mixed-gender conversations. Language between members of an established social group, such as a neighborhood gang, may contain many special words or expressions, whose meanings are unintelligible to outsiders. Slang, or language used in casual settings to establish group solidarity and to signal group membership, is a prototypical practice during adolescence precisely because peer group socialization is so important at this age. The Focus on Research box on page 276 provides more information about the function of teenage slang.

Thus, language development through adolescence entails expanding communicative competence, since grammatical development is fairly complete. Individuals develop a repertoire of styles suited to a social context and the other participants. This ability includes knowing when and how to speak, being sensitive to appropriate topics, and adjusting style, vocabulary, and politeness levels to match the age and gender of other speakers.

Learning Two Languages

For many adults, learning to speak a second language may be regarded as an extremely difficult if not impossible task. Whether it is a college student eager to learn a foreign language for studying abroad or an adult emigrating to a new country, acquiring another language is a formidable experience. However, when we think about children learning a second language, we assume they will learn faster and more easily than any adult. A woman laments, "Oh, if only I had learned Russian from my grandmother when I was 3." Or the hopeful wish of immigrant parents for their child, "He'll learn English when he goes to school."

Focus on
Research

Teenagers and Slang

Teenagers are preoccupied with social relationships. They become acutely aware of their relations with others, particularly with their peers. Because language is a flexible system for communicating and representing individual identity, speaking styles, like clothing choices, are important emblems of teenage life. Peer-group membership is often signaled by a distinctive style or special vocabulary, especially *slang.* Slang consists of words or expressions that develop in special contexts and have particular meanings. Typically, slang is used in casual settings and is created by in-groups to include some and exclude others. Teenagers generate slang expressions that their parents, for instance, might not understand at first and would certainly never use. Every teenage generation has its own slang terms, many of which become widespread, such as *cool,* whereas other slang is very specialized. Slang words identify youth as members of the same fan community and connected to popular culture (e.g., hip-hop). Some examples are *hottie* (attractive person), *ancient* (out of style), *drama* (major concern, obsession), *crush* (person liked, but doesn't know it), and *Shut up!* (Wow!). Slang words and expressions are perpetuated in media geared toward teens, such as the once popular television show *Buffy the Vampire Slayer.* Adams (2003) expects that some items of "slayer slang" will intrude on everyday speech, and may be transformed into standard American English. There is evidence that teen slang expressions transcend their original groups and disperse through communities and even across countries (Androutsopoulos, 2002).

Schools are fertile breeding grounds for slang words and expressions, as well as for other stylistic dialects such as rap songs. Such language serves important social functions, creating ties and relationships, and should not be discouraged by parents or teachers just because it is not standard English. However, some slang words, terms, and expressions are offensive and objectionable; teachers need to use the same judgment about allowing these terms to be used publicly as they would other language, such as obscenities, in their classroom and community. Some concerns have been raised about the "maleness" of slang, and about its potential derogatory use. Research has shown that gender differences in the knowledge and use of slang may be narrowing (de Klerk, 1990; Grossman & Tucker, 1997). However, it remains the case that, although reportedly used less, more sexual and derogatory slang exists to describe women (Grossman & Tucker, 1997).

Slang is also creative work; many new words are added to English every year through the ingenuity and cleverness of the teenage mind. High school teacher Rick Ayers, inspired by the "verbal genius" of his students, created a guide to slang in 2004 with his Berkeley High School English class. His original purpose was to build students' confidence in their abilities to express themselves by allowing them to use their own language, and to foster reflection on their use of language (**metalinguistic awareness**). Students contributed words from eavesdropping on conversations, and then investigated the origins of these words. The resulting 17-page *Berkeley High School Slang Dictionary* contains several hundred words from a variety of origins (e.g., African American, Chicano, hip-hop, jazz, Yiddish). This dictionary has been the topic of several national and local news reports, and has been purchased by thousands of parents and teachers attempting to understand teens and their language. Perhaps we'll see teen inventions like *bootsy, hella, peeps,* and *nizzel* in the Merriam-Webster or Oxford American dictionaries someday. The following words, now perfectly acceptable, began as slang: *freshman, mob, dwindle,* and *glib.*

What accounts for this attitude? Is it true that children have special advantages over adults? How do children learn a second language?

Some children learn two languages from the beginning of language acquisition, whereas other children may not begin to acquire a second language until they enter school. If a child is born into a family and community in which several languages are flourishing, chances are the child will grow up **bilingual,** speaking two languages, or multilingual, speaking more than two. Remember that a child needs more than exposure to learn a language, including a second language. Just because English-speaking Canadian children can watch and listen to French TV or radio does not mean they will learn French. Interaction with other speakers for the purpose of communicating in the target language is necessary for second-language acquisition. Amazingly enough, children seem equipped to learn multiple languages simultaneously if the environment is sufficiently rich to provide the necessary linguistic interactions.

For children who are **simultaneous bilinguals,** learning two languages at the same time, their pattern of acquisition is fairly clear. At first, a child acts as if he or she is learning one language system, even though the child is being exposed to several languages. The child constructs a single system made up of combinations of features—sounds and words—from both languages. This period, called *mixed speech,* lasts until the child is about 2 years old (Imedadze, 1978). Remember that most 2-year-olds have not acquired much syntax, so combining features of two languages is not problematic. Sometimes the bilingual child will use a word from each language in producing a two-word utterance (Volterra & Taeschner, 1978) or even put a word ending from one language onto the main word of the other language (Burling, 1959). Some children know how to name an object in both languages. For instance, an 11-month-old girl with an Israeli mother and British father regularly said the word *parpar,* which means butterfly in Hebrew. She understood that the English word *butterfly* meant the same creature and could easily point to the right picture when asked in English by her father to find the butterfly in a book. But she consistently used the Hebrew word in speaking.

During the next stage, children begin to discriminate between the two languages. They start by separating the words of each language, and then they combine them according to the syntax of each language. They no longer include words from different languages in the same utterance, and they demonstrate an ability to translate from one language to another. Some studies have found that around the age of 4, children who are simultaneous bilinguals have fully separated the two languages (Volterra & Taeschner, 1978). An alternative to the *unitary* language hypothesis just described is the *differentiated* language hypothesis. Researchers adhering to the latter view point to evidence suggesting that even young bilinguals differentiate their dual lexicons from their very first words (Pettito et al., 2001). And they reach early linguistic milestones at the same time in both languages, and on the same timetable as monolinguals. Although they do simultaneously mix languages, they are not confused. They tend to mix languages like their parents, and sometimes choose their own preferred language. Children learning spoken and signed languages simultaneously follow similar paths. For a child to remain bilingual, both languages have to be in constant use throughout childhood. For most people, a language disappears if it is not actively used.

Although parents and educators are amazed by how efficiently children acquire language in the early years, a common concern about childhood bilingualism is that it may delay children's cognitive and language development. This is referred to as the *bilingual paradox.* Early research indicated that bilingual immigrant children performed more poorly on various measures of intelligence than their monolingual peers (Diaz, 1983). However, this research failed to take into account socioeconomic differences in the samples studied. More carefully controlled studies reveal that competence in two language systems can enhance mental flexibility, concept formation, and metalinguistic abilities (Bialystok, 2001; National Research Council, 1998). Additionally, children's use of their native language does not impede the acquisition of English (August & Hakuta, 1997).

We sometimes assume that children learn a second language easily simply because they are children and are predisposed to learn language. Children do seem to have an early predisposition to learn a *first* language, but it is not clear that age correlates with learning a *second* language. As we discussed earlier, research on whether or not there is a critical period for language acquisition has not proved conclusive. Even if there is a critical period for learning a first language, it does not mean there is one for a second language.

How long does it take for children to acquire a second language? The answer to this question depends on the child's age, home environment, and schooling conditions, as well as the definition of proficiency used. Studies of students with limited English proficiency in the United States have shown that it can take 1 to 3 years to acquire oral communication skills. However, it may take up to 6 to 10 years to acquire a level of English proficiency necessary for learning core subjects in school (Garcia, 2000).

Second-language learning is a complex process that is influenced by many different factors. Because of more advanced cognitive skills, older children acquire a second language at a more rapid rate than do younger school-age children (Garcia, 2000; National Research Council, 1998). Some experts also believe that second-language acquisition is faster and easier when children have mastered basic grammar structures of their first language. Thus, continued development of children's first language is important for the acquisition of a second language (National Research Council, 1998).

If older children and even adults have difficulty learning a second language, the fault may be not with age or the nature of the mind but rather with the kinds of experiences or the environment in which the second language is being learned. It is much easier for someone at any age to learn a language if they are surrounded by native speakers in a natural social context and experience the need to communicate. Adult instruction in a foreign language, which typically occurs in classrooms, is not often characterized by any of these conditions. Language is not easily learned in restricted situations with minimal interaction between students; it is learned through meaningful interactions with other speakers.

At this time in American history, there are thousands of individuals who live in the United States but do not yet speak English and millions of children ages 5 to 7 who speak English with difficulty (NCES, 2005a). While the majority are Spanish speakers, there are large numbers of Hmong, Chinese, and Vietnamese speakers (see Chapter 1). Many of these individuals will become bilingual. If a person learns English but retains his or her native language, we call this situation **successive bilingualism.** If a person already speaks one language, the stages of development in another language will be completely different. Both babbling and one- and then two-word utterances are unique features of early childhood development and will not occur when a school-age child or adult acquires a second language.

In this section, we have learned how bilinguals *acquire* several languages. In the final section of this chapter, the subject of bilingual education is discussed in greater detail.

Language and Communication Disorders

Defined as impairments in the ability to use language to communicate, *communication disorders* have much higher prevalence rates than statistics indicate. Since the federal government collects and reports head counts only for the primary disability, all those who have communication as a secondary disability are excluded from the prevalence rates for communication. When secondary disabilities are taken into account, the projected estimates of school-aged children with communication disorders vary from 3 to 5 percent (Nelson, 1993).

Causes of Language and Communication Disorders

As is the case with specific learning disabilities, language disorders develop as a result of the interaction of various biological and environmental factors. Table 5.2 outlines the various interrelated factors associated with the development of language disorders.

The acquisition of language skills is dramatic as children move from the one- to two-word utterances of toddlerhood to putting together sentences of three or more words during the

TABLE 5.2 Factors Associated with Development of Childhood Language Disorders

Central factors	Specific language disability
	Mental retardation
	Autism
	Attention-deficit/hyperactivity disorder
	Acquired brain injury
	Others
Peripheral factors	Hearing impairment
	Visual impairment
	Deaf-blindness
	Physical impairment
Mixed factors	Neglect and abuse
	Behavioral and emotional development problems

Source: After N. W. Nelson (1998).

preschool years. Language development during this period is critical to later success. IDEA stipulates that any child between the ages of 3 and 5 who needs special services should receive them. Thus, it is critical to identify children whose language development is not proceeding as expected so that the appropriate services can be provided. Some criteria for referring a child for a speech/language evaluation appear in the Focus on Development box on page 280.

Although screening may occur anytime throughout childhood, prekindergarten screening is common. Schools may use the results of early language screening to recommend that children wait a year before beginning kindergarten or that they attend a language-based developmental kindergarten class. This practice is controversial. Some see this practice as leading to early ability tracking, with children being placed in classes where there is a weaker learning environment, lowered expectations, and segregation of children in minority groups, particularly those of low socioeconomic status. However, sometimes the added boost of a year in a language-based developmental kindergarten program can provide a child with the language skills needed to be successful.

Language and Communication Disorders in the School Years

If children have not been identified prior to elementary school, teachers become the primary source of referral. Children's language disorders, however, are not always apparent to teachers. Whereas misarticulations, pronoun substitutions, and morphological immaturies are relatively easy to identify, later forms of language development, such as more complicated syntactic structures and language comprehension, are more difficult (Nelson, 1998). Damico and Oller (1980) suggest the following criteria for identifying elementary-aged children who may need to be referred for a speech/language disorder:

- *Linguistic nonfluency.* Disruption of speech production by a disproportionately high number of repetitions, unusual pauses, and excessive use of hesitation forms.
- *Revision.* Breakup of speech production by numerous false starts or self-interruptions; multiple revisions are made as if the child keeps coming to a dead end in a maze.
- *Delays before responding.* Pauses of inordinate length following communication attempts initiated by others.

Focus on
Development

- **Limitations of language expressions.** Is close to 3 years of age and produces few creative utterances that are three words or more in length.
- **Problems learning words.** Has limited receptive or expressive vocabulary and has difficulty acquiring new words to express new ideas.
- **Problems comprehending language.** Appears to rely too much on familiar contexts to understand language (shows difficulty comprehending language without gestural support or when produced by unfamiliar partners).
- **Limitations of social interaction.** Shows little interest in social interaction, except perhaps to gain adult assistance to fulfill specific desires.
- **Limitations of play.** Shows little interest in playing with peers or in combining toys and objects in imaginative symbolic play.

Source: From N.W. Nelson (1998).

Potential Danger Signals for Development of Language Disorders: Ages 3 to 5

- **Problems learning speech.** Has difficulty pronouncing words so that they are intelligible to unfamiliar adults (perfect articulation is not expected).
- **Difficulty with strategies for learning language and using language to learn.** Demonstrates unusual learning strategies for age level, such as either too much reliance on imitation (e.g., sins of echolalia) or inability to imitate the actions of others. Shows little interest in using language to learn more about language and the world (e.g., does not ask "What's that?" questions early, or "Why?" questions; which become prevalent for most children around age 4 or 5).
- **Short attention span for language-related activities.** Show little interest in sitting with an adult and looking at a book while naming and talking about the pictures or in communicating with peers.

- *Nonspecific vocabulary.* The use of expressions such as *this, that, then, he,* or *over there* without making the referents clear to the listener; also, the overuse of all-purpose words such as *thing, stuff, these,* and *those.*
- *Inappropriate responses.* The child's utterances appear to indicate that the child is operating on an independent discourse agenda, not attending to the prompts or probes of the adult or others.
- *Poor topic maintenance.* Rapid and inappropriate changes in the topic without providing transitional clues to the listener.
- *Need for repetition.* Requests for multiple repetitions of an utterance without any indication of improvement in comprehension.

Because language is critical in shaping cognitive development, students with communication disorders experience numerous academic problems in school. They can experience developmental problems in any of the following cognitive areas: metacognitive skills, placing concepts in a hierarchy, problem-solving skills, word-retrieval skills, attention, memory, and performing formal operational thought in adolescence (Larson & McKinley, 1987). Speech and language problems often coexist with reading problems and adversely affect the student's ability to understand and use language in all academic subjects (Lyon, 2002). A child with a receptive language problem may have difficulties with listening comprehension that are severe enough to interfere with the child's ability to acquire content information. A student could also have expressive language difficulties resulting in an inability to verbalize thoughts and knowledge either orally or in writing. Ensuing poor performance, on tests and in class, may lead to gross underestimations of the child's learning ability.

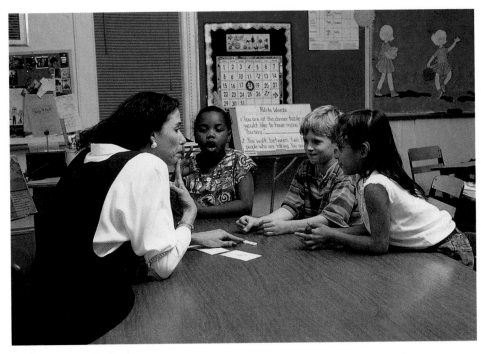

Children with communication disorders may experience problems with peer relations and social interactions.
Source: Robin L. Sachs/Photo Edit.

Language is also the primary vehicle for understanding oneself and others. It is not surprising that many students with communication disorders also experience social interaction problems because they do not understand or use nonverbal communication, do not adhere to conversational rules (e.g., turn-taking), cannot shift conversational style according to the social context, do not use effective listening skills, and cannot express their negative feelings in a nonabrasive manner (Larson & McKinley, 1987). During adolescence in particular, communication disorders persist across all domains, resulting in a "continuum of failure" in academics, peer relationships, and personal skills (Larson & McKinley, 1995, p. 64).

For children with communication disorders, the classroom teacher along with the school psychologist or speech pathologist are responsible for developing activities that encourage communication skills in the classroom. It is essential that children use specific skills in natural settings with peers so that newly learned communication skills can *generalize;* that is, children should be able to independently apply what they learn to new situations. The classroom teacher can integrate the development of learning strategies into reading, written expression, and content areas. It is also important for all who work with these children to model effective communication skills.

Some Basic Principles of Language Development

Language takes on several forms and comes in many varieties, such as the English spoken in the South, Black English dialects, and the abstract writing of legal documents. However, to understand how all forms of language develop, we need to remember a few basic concepts.

- *Language is a social phenomenon.* People living together have devised ways of interacting and communicating with each other. Children acquire whatever language or languages they hear spoken around them. The need to communicate—as when a hungry baby cries—is the primary force behind language acquisition. As children grow, they will need to learn a variety of language forms, such as slang terms particular to their peer group, the features of formal expository writing, oral storytelling styles, and creative genres, such as poetry and fiction, in order to participate fully in society.

- *Children acquire language without direct instruction and within a relative short span of time.* By the age of 7, most children have learned about 90 percent of all the language structures used by adults in their society (Daniels, 1985). They can ask questions, form negative sentences, choose appropriate pronouns, and produce complex sentence structures such as relative clauses. Besides structural knowledge, children also learn how to use language more broadly. They can conduct conversations, adjusting their language to fit their audience, such as an adult would with a 2-year-old, and can invent jokes and play word games. As children grow older, they begin to combine the structure they have learned in order to communicate more complex ideas, they gain proficiency with written language, and they acquire grace and skill in using language in a wide variety of social settings.

- *All languages are symbol systems with socially constructed rules for combining sounds into words, for making meaning with words, and for arranging words into sentences.* Children actively construct these unconscious rules through observation and hypothesis testing (Clark & Clark, 1977). They observe others and form an idea about how to express something, test their idea by speaking, and modify the end result as needed. For instance, a child might infer that adding the sound of /s/ to a word means "more than on," as in *cats.* When the child produces a nonstandard form such as "mouses," the child is testing out a hypothesis about how to make a plural noun. Eventually, through practice, the child will modify the rule to account for exceptions in English, producing *mice* as the plural form of *mouse.* Remember that a child is learning to speak by participating in social exchanges. The social context in which language is learned supports the child in producing not only well-formed utterances but also ones that are appropriate in a given situation (Elliot, 1981; Rogoff, 2003).

- *Because language is so complex, children cannot learn the system all at once.* Instead, they go through periods in which they work on learning a few things at a time, for instance, putting two words together meaningfully. When a young girl says, "Mommy sock," she is not producing a random string of words. Because her sentence is not grammatical, the child depends on the skills of her mother to interpret her words. Interacting with her mother or other adults, she gradually begins to produce sentences that approximate more closely the qualities of adult language.

- *Language comprehension (receptive language) generally comes before language production.* Children appear to understand aspects of language before they can actually talk, write, or sign.

- *Language is linked to identity.* Through language we are able to interact with others and to make sense of the world. This process allows us to develop a sense of self, to convey our private thoughts, and to share our experiences with others. The earliest efforts at symbolic formation—a child's first scribble presented to his mother, a nonsense song performed by a 2-year-old to entertain a visitor—are a child's way of establishing a sense of self in relation to others (Dyson, 1993). Our native language, with its speech and interactional patterns, connects us to our family and community, and in the process becomes a basic part of our inner selves. Language is central to our personality, "an expression and mirror of what we are and wish to be, . . . as integral to each of us as our bodies and our brains" (Daniels, 1985, p. 32).

■ *Language abilities grow by using language in meaningful contexts.* Children learn to talk by talking with others who delight in listening. This holds true not only for spoken language but also for promoting children's acquisition of literacy. Typically, spoken language is learned in home settings, whereas reading and writing are taught to children in school settings. However, just as children learned to speak because they want to interact with others, to express their thoughts and desires, so too must communication be the motivating force behind reading and writing. Too often schools teach these language skills to children using artificial tasks. For instance, a teacher may ask children to write a short paragraph describing a favorite toy. If the audience is the teacher, and if the real reason to write is only to complete the assignment, then the true purpose of writing (authentic communication) has been distorted. Instead of writing to share some personally meaningful thoughts—a central purpose of written language—children write in school mainly to demonstrate mastery for a teacher. Such tasks are often what constitute literacy instruction in school. James Britton, a British educator, calls such artificial tasks "dummy runs." He argues that children need authentic, real-life, socially meaningful reasons to speak and write. Language (speaking, reading, writing) helps children to make sense of the world. Children "must *practise* language in the sense in which a doctor 'practises' medicine, . . . and *not* in the sense in which a juggler 'practises' a new trick" (Britton, 1970, p. 130). Recall that both Piaget and Vygotsky emphasize the fact that learning is most likely to occur in meaningful contexts (see Chapter 3).

Fostering Language Development

Children do not learn language on their own. From the first moment, language is social: The mother looks into a child's eyes and pronounces her name. Granting that humans are predisposed to learn language, we also know that language development is fostered by adults and by environments that encourage communication.

First, adults assume that children will learn language. They act as if children are participants in the language game immediately. This assumption—that their children have intentions and are communicating—helps children to focus on sounds and to recognize that language is an important part of life.

Second, adults and children are partners in creating meaning and cooperate in constructing language (Ochs, Schieffelin, & Platt, 1979; Rogoff, 2003). A child may only need to point to a favorite toy car before the adult provides a long dialogue about it. Such gestures facilitate communication, and may play an important role in vocabulary growth, especially for children in low-income families (Pan et al., 2005).

Third, adult speakers structure a child's environment so that learning can occur more easily (Snow, 1986). See the Focus on Research box on page 265. They fill the world with talk. However, recent studies indicate that sheer amount of talk is not as important for development as is its richness (Pan et al., 2005). Even when a child is too young to make sounds, adults are frequently addressing their child. Adults focus on the concrete. While a child is eating, the father may point to the picture of the baby on a cereal box, allow the baby to touch the box, all the while producing a stream of talk that ensures that the child is making connections between words and things.

Some parents may also alter their intonation, adding stress and often using a higher pitch when speaking, to gain the child's attention. Middle-income American parents sometimes keep sentences short and simple, they repeat themselves endlessly, and often use a higher proportion of questions and imperatives than is typical in their everyday conversation. Some of these features are culture specific (Heath, 1983). For example, some cultures use strategies other than pitch for gaining attention. Gender plays a role, too. Mothers tend to ask more questions of their children than fathers do. But most cultures have standard strategies adults use to create a positive learning environment for their children.

Fourth, learning language continues through middle childhood and adolescence and is motivated by the desire to communicate and to engage others in the community. Conversational exchanges are embedded in natural contexts and are part of ongoing social action. Children's experiences with language are authentic acts of communication; they speak when they have something to say to an interested listener. The importance of authentic situations to ensure language learning and development at every age, from infancy through adulthood, cannot be overemphasized.

Fifth, these kinds of authentic learning experiences can be implemented in elementary and high schools to enhance language skills, such as second-language proficiency and metalinguistic awareness (see the Focus on Research box "Teenagers and Slang" on page 276).

 ## Literacy Development

In our society children are exposed to print from birth. Although children develop spoken language before they learn to read or write, they are nevertheless learning about written language from the start. A 2-year-old girl at the grocery store can recognize a box of Cheerios, her favorite cereal, demonstrating that she understands the concept of visual representation, that symbols can stand for things. On a long car trip, a 3-year-old boy shouts to his parents when he spots the "big 6" logo advertising their motel (and the pool that accompanies it). He knows that print carries meaning. Recall Anne's use of *z* (zig zag) to signify "this" in describing her picture.

Both spoken and written language are symbol systems, but each form is represented differently, speech as sound and writing as visual marks. Thus, each system has unique features that children must master. In addition, writing serves different purposes than speech in our culture. Figuring out the written system and the special functions of writing begins as soon as children are exposed to print. Early experiences may include looking at picture books, examining a blanket or favorite toy covered in letters, listening and interacting while an adult reads aloud, or scribbling on paper and telling a story. Early childhood educators once believed that young children needed to know letter names or sound–letter relationships before they were ready to read and write. But researchers and teachers now recognize that children who pretend they are reading or writing understand a great deal about literacy. For instance, long before children can translate written letters to words, they learn the basic concept that print carries meaning. Recent research indicates that oral language experiences provide a foundation for early reading skills, such as word recognition (NICHD Early Care Network, 2005a). This is a sign of **emergent literacy.** It is important to realize that certain concepts and behaviors, such as when children pretend they are translating words to print, are the basis for children's literacy when they actually do begin to read and write (Teale & Sulzby, 1986).

Emergent Reading and Writing

To learn to read and write, children must discover the *purposes* for print, the details of the *visual symbol system,* the *arbitrary conventions* for making letters and texts, and the *characteristics of different texts*—the differences between stories, letters, or grocery lists. Four-year-old

Nora holds a book on her lap ready to read. She points to the cover of *Allison's Zinnia*, by Anita Lobel (1990). Pointing to the author's name and dragging her finger across the cover from left to right, Nora pronounces in an exaggerated voice "A—lli—son's Zi—ni—a." Her mother removes her daughter's finger from the author's name and places it on the first letter of the title. Her mother reads, "Allison's Zinnia" while sliding Nora's finger under the letters. Then she says, "Allison's Zinnia! See Allison begins with A."

As a 4-year-old, Nora can make broad distinctions about print. She can identify writing or printed text from everything else on the page, such as a drawing or a picture. She points to the letters on the cover when she says the title, not to the large picture that occupies most of the cover. Nora also knows that the language found in books is special since she speaks with a loud and dramatic tone, one she doesn't adopt in a casual conversation. In addition, she is aware that print is read from left to right, as her finger sweep suggests. Her mother fosters her literacy knowledge, in particular by matching the printed to the spoken word as she helps the child point to *Allison*. Furthermore, her mother supports letter recognition and models a reading strategy by telling her to look at the first letter of a word: "Allison begins with A." So even though Nora is not able to read the print yet, she is certainly an emergent reader.

The concept of *emergent literacy* was first introduced in the early 1980s. This conception of literacy development represented a move away from the now outdated **reading readiness approach,** which emphasized a set of skills children needed to master before beginning formal reading instruction (Whitehurst & Lonigan, 1998). Emergent literacy encompasses the time from birth to age 5 or 6, and it consists of a set of "skills, knowledge, and attitudes that are presumed to be developmental precursors of reading and writing" (Whitehurst & Lonigan, 1998, p. 849). Examples of early literacy skills included identification of labels and signs in their environment, recognition of some letter–sound matches, inventive spelling, "pretend" reading, awareness of print conventions (e.g., direction and sequence of print, difference between book covers and pages, etc.), and interest in print and books (Britto & Brooks-Gunn, 2001; NAEYC, 1998). Anne demonstrated an emergent literacy skill when she attempted to use a letter (or approximation of a letter) to label her picture. Researchers who study emergent literacy have uncovered interesting links between children's early literacy experiences (storybook reading, dramatic play, exposure to print, etc.) and later reading and writing achievement (e.g., Britto & Brooks-Gunn, 2001; NAEYC, 1998; Snow, 2005). Figure 5.3 summarizes key elements of the emergent literacy perspective.

Recognizing Print

Through repeated exposures to a story read aloud, young children quickly understand that what an adult reader says is determined by the print in the book. Two-year-olds will object when a parent misreads a word or skips a line in a favorite story. Often they are capable of providing the appropriate word or sentence, or indeed of "reading" the entire book from memory. Jacob, a 2-year-old whose mother was distracted momentarily, pushed at the book impatiently and commanded that his mother "Go . . . do it . . . make the book say it." He demonstrates through his behavior his knowledge that the words are fixed in the book and that his mother knows the magic to get the book talking.

Around the age of 3 children can readily distinguish writing from other visual marks. How do children make these distinctions? In one study, children ages 3 to 6½ were shown cards on which various combinations of letters, pictures, doodles, and numbers were printed (Lavine, 1977). They were asked to make two piles of cards: writing in one pile and other nonwriting marks in another. Cards with writing were correctly identified by 80 percent of the 3-year-olds, 90 percent of the 4-year-olds, and 96 percent

■ FIGURE 5.3

Elements of the Emergent Literacy Perspective
Source: Teale & Sulzby, 1986.

Elements of the Emergent Literacy Perspective

The following findings from research on children's literacy development are central to the emergent literacy perspective:

1. Literacy development begins long before children start formal instruction. Children use legitimate reading and writing behaviors in the informal settings of home and community.

2. Literacy development is appropriate to describe what was called reading readiness. The child develops as a reader and writer. The notion of reading preceding writing, or vice versa, is a misconception. Listening, speaking, reading, and writing abilities develop concurrently and interrelatedly, rather than sequentially.

3. Literacy develops in real-life settings for real-life activities in order to "get things done." Therefore, the functions of literacy are as integral a part of learning about writing and reading during early childhood as the forms of literacy.

4. Children are doing critical cognitive work in literacy development during the years from birth to 6.

5. Children learn written language through active engagement with their world. They interact socially with adults in writing and reading situations, they explore print on their own, and they profit from modeling of literacy by significant adults, particularly their parents.

6. Although children's learning about literacy can be described in terms of generalized stages, children can pass through these stages in a variety of ways and at different ages.

of the 5-year-olds. Those children who did not yet recognize letters paid attention to several features of print in order to make their decisions. *Linearity,* the way print is arranged in rows, and variety, different shapes in the row, were two salient traits. Children who recognized letters already used that knowledge to distinguish between marks on the page and real writing.

Our understanding of children's literacy learning was greatly enhanced when three researchers, Jerome Harste, Virginia Woodward, and Carolyn Burke (1984), reported their study of preschool children's knowledge of written language. They worked with 3- to 6-year-old children; boys and girls from high-, middle-, and low-SES families; blacks and whites; and small-town and urban inner-city families. They examined children's interactions with print found in the environment—such as store signs or logos, children's scribbling, their encounters with picture books—and they observed children in experimental as well as natural settings. Their work, reported in *Language Stories and Literacy Lessons,* provides an account of what preschoolers know about literacy and what experiences foster literacy development. In one part of their study, 3-year-olds were asked both to write and to draw. They found that all children could produce "systematic and organized" marks that distinguished writing from drawing (p. 18). Terry, one 3-year-old, consistently made linear marks to indicate writing, particularly writing his name, while his drawing marks were global and circular. The researchers concluded that Terry was demonstrating, "both in form and in process, the stuff of real literacy, being invented from the inside out" (p. 18).

Interviews with kindergarten-age children reveal that by this age they can identify different kinds of reading materials and tell why people read them. In one study, 5-year-olds were shown a variety of reading materials, including picture books, magazines, calendars, and TV schedules (Weiss & Hagen, 1988). Most children in the study were able to recognize and discuss the function of different kinds of print. All except 1 of the 110 children interviewed could explain the purpose for reading storybooks, and more than 95 percent of the children understood the functions of newspapers and the telephone book. Other materials, such as shopping lists, magazines, directions, and TV guides, were recognized by about 80 percent of the children. Such knowledge arises out of children's experiences with print in their everyday life and is among the strongest preschool predictors of later reading ability (Storch & Whitehurst, 2001). Other predictors, components of emergent literacy, are described next.

Sounds and Letters

A baby's fist waving in the air was considered by Vygotsky (1978) as a precursor of writing: "Gestures . . . are writing in the air, and written signs frequently are simply gestures that have been fixed" (p. 106). When materials for marking are available, the gestures descend from the air onto a surface. Children persist in making marks and leaving visual traces, whether it is making ketchup circles on their high chair tray, using crayons on paper, or leaving finger trails in sand. These scribbles have meaning for the child who produces them whether or not an adult understands the representation.

As soon as a child realizes that writing exists—that special marks carry meaning—then the child will probably begin thinking about the connection between speaking and writing. Through play and experimentation with print as well as exposure to books and print in the environment, the child will discover print, sound, and meaning relationships.

Because written English is an **alphabetic system,** children learn that single shapes are letters and eventually that letters are linked to specific sounds. Other written systems, for example, Chinese, are based on an **ideographic system,** in which each character, or ideograph, in the script represents the meaning of an individual word. But whatever the visual system, children must learn to recognize its features and eventually to produce the script themselves.

Just as children learn the mapping principles between sound and meaning when learning to speak, so too they must learn the intricacies of linking letters to sounds and the combinations of letters into words. The ability to connect the distinctive sounds, or phonemes, in words to letters is called **phonemic awareness** (Juell, Griffith, & Gough, 1986; Perfetti, Beck, & Hughes, 1985). James demonstrates this preliminary awareness in the introductory vignette. However, such awareness does not develop easily. Children are aware of words—because a word carries meaning—long before they are self-conscious about parts of words, such as a single sound or letter. In speech, children aim to produce words even in the earliest stage, when they have only a few sounds. Paying attention to single sounds is not a process children need in order to understand spoken language (Menyuk, 1976). In learning to read and write, a child must map sounds to letters, a tremendously difficult process. For instance, the word *bat* contains three sounds (phonemes). A child learning to write *bat* has to segment the meaningful syllable *bat* into three meaningless sound parts /b/, /a/, and /t/. Furthermore, individual sounds are shaped by the surrounding sound context. Think about the word *bar*. Although only one letter is changed, the sound of /a/ is completely different in this new word. Children who speak English have difficulty matching sounds to letters because their language lacks one-to-one correspondence between sound and spelling. English has 26 letters, but the same sound may be represented by different combinations of letters such as the /f/ sound in words *phone* and *fix*. There are occasions when some letters represent no sound at all as the *gh* in *thought*. Or when the same letter sounds differently depending on its placement as the *c* in *cat* or *science*. All of these English-specific issues must be untangled by a beginning writer. We see James developing his working knowledge of sounds and letters in his invented (or phonic) spelling. This process encourages him to think actively about sound–letter relations. The temporary use of invented spelling contributes to early reading. Soon he will recognize that there are certain conventions for writing and will be interested in "correct" spellings.

Researchers have discovered that children's ability to distinguish individual phonemes is an accurate predictor of reading success (Adams, 1990; Snow, Burns, & Griffin, 1998; Whitehurst & Lonigan, 1998). The roots of phonemic awareness, according to some researchers, are sometimes found in word and rhythmic play, such as reciting nursery rhymes or skipping games (NAEYC, 1998), where children become sensitized to sound similarities in patterned, enjoyable activities. Phonemic awareness appears to have a stronger influence on the acquisition of reading skills than measures of intelligence, memory, and even social class (Whitehurst & Lonigan, 1998). Hearing individual sounds is something all speaking children can do. English speakers have many similar-sounding words—such as *bat, rat, hat, sat*—the difference between them being a single sound. But it is not just *hearing* sounds that creates phonemic awareness; rather, it is the ability to be *self-conscious* about these sounds. Anne reveals this beginning awareness when she comments on June's ability to sound out words, "everything June writes she knows . . . [She] always knows all the letters for everything." This ability to think and talk about language is called metalinguistic awareness. In other words, a child who can identify the first sound as making the difference between the words *rat* and *bat* understands a great deal about sound/print relationships.

Nora, the emergent reader we met earlier, will often "read" to her father familiar books she has memorized. Sometimes she will run her finger under the words as she "reads," imitating her parents' reading behavior. But she speaks much faster than her hand moves. In reading the title of the story "Daddy, Can You Play with Me?" she finishes speaking before her finger reaches the last word. Eventually she will begin to wonder about this mismatch, and with more experience or explanation from her parent, she will eventually understand that letters represent individual sounds and not syllables.

The Alphabet

In addition to matching sounds to letters, children also have to recognize and distinguish the letters of the English alphabet. In Chapter 4, we discussed how young children have difficulty focusing on the *distinctive features* of an object. Regarding the alphabet, children must not only learn the distinctive features of the letters but also develop the mental and perceptual processes of comparing differences between letters. For adults as well as for children, focusing on how things are different is probably more difficult and less practiced than thinking about how things are alike. Nevertheless, spoken and written language systems rely on distinctive features. The sounds of /p/ and /b/ are similar but not identical. The words *pack* and *back* when spoken aloud are only minimally distinct.

In learning the letters of the alphabet, however, children begin with similarities and ignore differences. When Matthew looked at his name, printed MATTHEW, he thought that the *M* and the *W* were the same letter, with one just upside down. After all, one cognitive principle he has learned is that even if an object is turned upside down, it remains the same thing. His toy car is still a car whether it is rolling on its wheels down the hallway or lying on its side after a crash with the wall. Eventually with experience (for example, his teachers call the letter at the end of his name a *W*), Matthew learns that orientation in space is a distinctive feature of written letters but not of three-dimensional objects.

The issue of spatial orientation may take children a while to sort out. It is common for children to write mirror images of letters and words as easily as the proper orientation. Figure 5.4 shows how Marin, a 4-year-old, writes her name as a mirror image. Such reversals may persist in the writing of 6- and 7-year-olds but will gradually disappear. In a print-rich culture such as ours, most children by the age of 5 can recognize and name the uppercase letters of the alphabet.

Learning the Conventions of Print

Language works as a form of communication because speakers agree about the way the system functions. These agreements are arbitrary. For instance, the particular combination of sounds /h/ /a/ /t/ for *hat* is not universal but was simply designated sometime in the past to mean a head covering. Likewise, grammatical rules are conventions. Speakers decided that a typical English sentence consists of a subject, verb, and object, as in, "Ralph ate the tomato." Both spoken and written forms of language have particular conventions, a kind of etiquette for performance. In conversation, speakers learn to signal the end of a turn, and to begin a new turn. Likewise, in writing, words must be spelled consistently by all writers in order to facilitate reading.

■ FIGURE 5.4
Four-Year-Old Marin Writes Her Name in Mirror Image

Literate adults may not be aware of how many conventions children must learn. For example, reading and writing progresses from left to right, not top to bottom or right to left. At the end of a line of text, the eyes return to the left side and begin scanning to the right. Words are separated by blank spaces. In the process of reading stories, adults often highlight these features of print by directing children's attention to where to begin reading and pointing to individual words (NAEYC, 1998). Margins and indentations mark paragraphs and story boundaries. Also a new reader has to notice the structural category of the sentence, a unit marked by punctuation and capitalization. In writing, sentences are well formed and grammatically complete. Written sentences are very different from the most common structures in spoken language, in which the clause or the phrase is the more basic structure. Along with new structures, new vocabulary and concepts have to be learned—*letter, word, sentence, paragraph, period*—in order for literacy learning to progress. Children must also learn how these individual structures, such as letters and words, are related. In a way, learning the conventions of writing is like solving a hierarchical classification problem, which we discussed in Chapter 3.

Conventions of Stories

Besides conventions of print format, children also must learn the various patterns of discourse forms valued in their culture, such as narratives. Telling stories is a common event in speaking, and there is a broad range of storytelling styles with flexible conventions. Although there is great variety in written stories as well, writers have developed more rigid conventions for narratives, such as the opening formula "Once upon a time . . . " or the way action or sound must be described in a dialogue, "Hiding behind a bush, Jack whispered to Megan, 'Hurry up and find the flashlight.'" Specific detail, complete sentences, and a formal tone are characteristics of written stories.

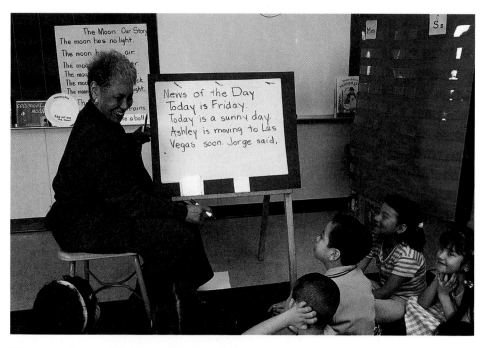

What are young children learning when they help to write stories?
Source: Michael Newmann/Photo Edit.

How do preschool children learn these conventions? Long before children can read and write, they are absorbing these written conventions through exposure to books when adults read stories aloud. Around the age of 3, children are sensitive to story markers, such as using a formulaic beginning and ending and employing the past tense to signal time shifts (Applebee, 1978). Gradually their stories become more complex and involve settings, themes, and actions that may be invented or beyond the scope of concrete experience. Children around the age of 5 or 6 are telling stories that are true narratives built around an elaborated theme with developed characters, contain some kind of action or main event, and typically end with a clear resolution to the situation. The following story, told by a 5-year-old, exhibits narrative traits very clearly.

> There was a boy named Johnny Hong Kong and finally he grew up and went to school and after that all he ever did was sit all day and think. He hardly even went to the bathroom. And he thought every day and every thought he thought up his head got bigger and bigger. One day it got so big he had to go and live up in the attic with trunks and winter clothes. So his mother bought some gold fish and let them live in his head—he swallowed them—and every time he thought, a fish would eat it up until he was even so he never thought again, and he felt much better.
>
> —Tracy H., 5 years, 8 months
> (Applebee, 1978, p. 66)

Tracy's narrative is quite sophisticated. Not only does she create the story's plot, but she uses connecting words such as *then, finally,* and *so* to link events in the story and provide time sequencing. These connectives show that the child is able to coordinate several cognitive and social factors that are characteristic of narratives (Peterson & McCabe, 1991).

Although preschool children cannot typically write their own stories, dictated narratives reveal their awareness of literate practices. The more experience they have with translations from sound to print, the easier it is for them to learn to read and write. Because they can create a narrative, they will approach reading a story with a narrative frame in mind. Having expectations about how stories proceed or being able to make predictions about characters or events greatly improves listening and reading comprehension.

Social Influences on Emergent Literacy

In a print-rich culture, literacy learning begins at birth. Children learn about reading and writing through social and linguistic interactions with others in their world. Researchers who have studied early readers and writers report that the strongest correlating factor is the nature of the home environment (Bus, van Ijzendoorn, & Pellegrini, 1995; Teale, 1978; Whitehurst & Lonigan, 1998; Yaden, Rowe, & MacGillivray, 1999). Consequently, *family literacy* has emerged as an important topic of study and policy discussion. It encompasses the natural and purposeful ways family members interact and use literacy in their homes, and the extent to which cultural heritage is reflected in these literacy activities (Britto & Brooks-Gunn, 2001). A large body of research suggests that children who are poor readers in the early elementary grades generally lack early literacy experiences at home (Beals & Detemple, 1993; Purcell-Gates, 1995; Shapiro, 1995). Children reared in poverty tend to be overrepresented in this low-literacy group (e.g., Britto & Brooks-Gunn, 2001) and often remain behind their more affluent peers through the elementary school years (National Center for Educational Statistics, 2006a; Snow, 2005). Thus, family literacy has been an integral component of some early intervention programs for low-income families, such as Even Start Family Literacy Programs.

There is a strong link between children's play experiences and emergent literacy (Yaden et al., 1999). As we discussed in Chapter 3, dramatic play is an important arena for the development of representational and language skills. Children often incorporate story characters and scripts into their play. These dramatic reenactments have a positive effect on story comprehension in kindergarten and first grade (Pellegrini & Galda, 1993; Yaden et al., 1999).

Additionally, children who learn to read early have many easy-reading materials at home and often are frequent visitors to the local library. Parents or caregivers of early readers read aloud to their children and talk with them about books and print on a daily basis. Shared book reading provides a rich source of information and opportunities to learn new vocabulary (DeLoache & DeMendoza, 1987; Pellegrini, Brody, & Seigel, 1985; Senechal & Lefevre, 2001). Snow (2005) argues that discussion and vocabulary development should be emphasized in early childhood programs, to move disadvantaged children closer to the developmental trajectory of children from highly educated families. One study showed that 5 percent of daily speech for 2-year-olds occurred in the context of storytime (Wells, 1985). Also, parents or caregivers who read themselves are modeling such behavior for their children, demonstrating that reading is purposeful and pleasurable. Early readers are early writers as well. Preschool children engage in scribbling, drawing, making letters as well as letter-like shapes, copying words, writing their names, and other simple words. A literate environment, whether it is a child care facility, a nursery school, or the home, is one in which children encounter print with authentic purposes and where adults value and participate in reading and writing themselves.

The relationship between phonemic awareness (sound and letter relationships) and reading ability is mutually enhancing, although one skill is not a prerequisite for the other. Children as young as 3 years old can exhibit signs of phonemic awareness, but it is much more common in 6-year-olds (NAEYC, 1998; Read, 1975). Phonemic awareness can be developed in a variety of ways: exposing children to sets of regular patterned words, repeated

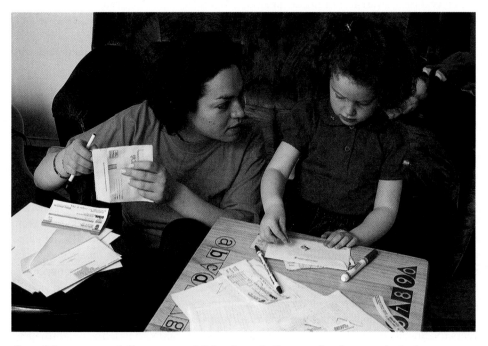

One of the strongest influences on children's early literacy development is the home environment.
Source: Laura Dwight/Photo Edit.

Development of Early Literacy

Birth to 3 Years

- Recognizes specific books by cover.
- Pretends to read books.
- Understands that books are handled in specific ways.
- Enters into book-sharing routines with primary care-givers.
- Play vocalizations gives way to rhyming language, nonsense word- play, and so forth.
- Labels objects in books.
- Comments on characters in books.
- May begin attending to specific print such as letters in names.
- Uses increasingly purposive scribbling.
- Occasionally seems to distinguish between drawing and writing.
- Produces some letter-like forms and scribbles.

3 to 4 Years

- May know that alphabet letters are a special category of visual graphics that can be individually named.
- Recognizes local environmental print.
- Knows that it is the print that is read in stories.

- Understands that different text forms are used for different functions of print (e.g., lists for groceries).
- Pays attention to separable and repeating sounds in language (e.g., Peter, Peter, Pumpkin Eater, Peter Eater).
- Is sensitive to some sequences in stories.
- Shows an interest in books and reading.
- When being read a story, connects information and events to life experiences.
- Questions and comments demonstrate understanding of literal meaning of age-appropriate story being told.
- May identify 10 alphabet letters, especially those from own name.
- Writes (scribbles) messages as part of playful activity.

Kindergarten Age

- Retells simple stories or narrative texts
- Recognizes letters and some letter–sound matches
- Understands left-to-right and top-to-bottom orientation and familiar concepts of print.
- Matches some spoken words with written words.
- Begins to write letters and some high-frequency words.

Source: Adapted from Snow, Burns, & Griffin (1998) and NAEYC (1998).

readings of familiar books with predictable sound patterns, direct phonics instruction, word-play involving rhyming games, and experimenting with writing. It is not clear from the research that any one approach to developing phonemic awareness is sufficient or effective (Mason & Allen, 1986). Providing a range of opportunities geared to children's needs is best.

However, being able to discriminate phonemes is not a necessary or sufficient condition for learning to read (Perfetti et al., 1985). On the other hand, being self-conscious about language definitely aids children in literacy learning. When a child says, "Hey, *cat* sounds like *bat*," the child is demonstrating metalinguistic awareness. Research has shown that being self-conscious about language can be enhanced simply by having more interactive experiences with print, which is good news for parents and teachers. Such awareness is not determined by reaching a particular point in children's cognitive development (Templeton & Spivey, 1980).

The Focus on Development box summarizes developmental accomplishments in a child's journey to becoming a reader and writer. This process depends heavily on social context. Frequent access to and enjoyment of a range of literacy activities, including large-print books, picture books, and books children make themselves through dictation, help literacy develop for all children. Early literacy development also depends on how parents and caregivers help children to construct meaning from their emergent reading and writing.

Focus on Teaching

Creating a Literate Environment

Young children's learning environment should be rich in print. Children are more likely to become readers and writers when they repeatedly encounter print. A *literate* classroom offers numerous opportunities for children to make use of print and practice their emerging literacy skills.

- Enable children to have access to age-appropriate, high-quality books. The class reading area should be well stocked with books, poems, and magazines. Displaying books on open shelves increases their accessibility. Books for infants and toddlers need to be sturdy and washable. Stiff cardboard is easier for young children to handle.
- Provide many types of books, including picture books, nature books, counting books, alphabet books, wordless words, and books written by the children themselves.
- Read to children daily and invite them to help choose the books. Reread favorite books.
- Prepare cozy places where children can sit and enjoy reading a book, perhaps with a friend, a stuffed animal, or a doll.
- Enable print to be visible throughout the classroom on signs, labels, alphabet letters, name tags, posters, songs, fingerplays, lists, magnetic letters, and alphabet blocks.

Oral Language Activities

Children learn vocabulary and language structures through conversations with teachers and peers. A rich vocabulary and knowledge of language structures helps with reading later on.

- Make time each day for individual conversations with children. One of the most effective ways to engage children in conversation is by joining in on their play.

Promoting Literacy Development in Early Childhood Settings

- Share with children events in your own life, and encourage them to talk about their personal experiences.
- Use high-quality books to engage children in conversations.
- Allow them to retell simple stories.

Sociodramatic Play

Through sociodramatic play, children use language to plan, organize, negotiate, and carry out the "script" of their play. Sociodramatic play involves representational thinking (letting one object stand for another), which is important in understanding abstract symbol systems.

- Include in every early childhood setting materials and spaces geared toward fantasy and creative play, such as an art center, a puppet center, a store, a nature center, a woodworking area, a housekeeping center, or an office.
- Equip play spaces with written materials that can be incorporated into children's play. Menus, catalogs, calendars, phone books, travel brochures, maps, food packages, and so forth can help children feel like readers.
- Make available writing materials for dramatic play. Children can make lists for grocery shopping in the house area, write on deposit slips for the bank, and write letters to take to the post office.

Listening Skills

The ability to hear different speech patterns and sound discriminations is essential for learning to read.

- Provide opportunities to listen to books on tapes.
- Use songs, fingerplays, poetry, and stories with rhyming words.

As we will discuss in Chapter 8, increasing numbers of young children are spending time in either a preschool or a day care setting. Preschool teachers and child care providers, therefore, play an increasingly important role in promoting early literacy development. The Focus on Teaching box describes ways of promoting children's literacy development in the preschool or day care setting.

- "Simon Says" requires children to listen to sequences of directions to play.

Phonemic Awareness

During the preschool and kindergarten years, children need to acquire an ability to think about the sounds of spoken words, independent of their meaning. It is important to help children understand the smallest meaningful units, or *phonemes,* that make up spoken words (phonemic awareness).

- Repeat readings of the same text to enable children to hear sound patterns.
- Isolate the beginning sound of words by asking children to say the sounds they hear.
- Play games that involve grouping objects by ending or beginning sounds.
- Search for objects in the room that begin or end with the same sound.
- Read books with predictable rhyming patterns and ask children to provide a new rhyming word (Dr. Seuss books are good for this purpose.)
- Sing rhyming chants and songs.
- Clap or tap out the syllables of a word.

Letter and Word Connections

To read and write, children need to distinguish letters and to connect letters to sounds.

- Provide access to letters in many different forms: alphabet blocks, wall charts, magnetic letters, letter puzzles, and so forth.
- Begin to point out distinctions between such letters as *C* and *G, b* and *d,* and *p* and *b.*

- When reading to children, point out that a sentence has many words starting with the letter *s.* Ask children to point out the words.
- When writing for children (e.g., story dictation, picture labels), sound out words and show them the letters for the sounds.
- When writing group stories, highlight words (e.g., *and, can, the*) that are repeated in sentences.

Print Awareness and Writing

Through early writing experiences, young children begin to learn many key concepts such as the function of print, uses of print, conventions of print, and phonological awareness.

- Provide access to a variety of paper, writing utensils, and materials for book making.
- Equip the art area with a variety of colored pencils, markers, pens, and paper of different sizes.
- Establish a separate writing area for children to scribble and pretend to write.
- Enable plenty of opportunities to dictate letters and stories and to have them read back to them.
- Invite children to dictate the daily schedule or menu for lunch.
- Encourage children to be "print detectives" and figure out what the words on a sign or box may say.
- When reading to children, point to the text and show children how print is read on a page (left to right, top to bottom). Also draw attention to breaks between words, uppercase and lowercase letters, and punctuation marks.

Sources: National Research Council (1999) and Neuman, Copple, & Bredekamp (2000).

Learning to Read

By the time children enter school, many are well on their way to becoming proficient readers and writers. However, between 25 and 40 percent of children in the United States encounter serious roadblocks on the way to becoming fluent and proficient readers (Snow et al., 1998). The National Assessment of Educational Progress (NAEP, 2005) Nation's Report Card indicated

Focus on Development

Development of Reading and Writing, Grades 1 to 3

What Children Can Do

What Teachers Can Do

What Parents and Family Members Can Do

Grade 1

Read and retell familiar stories

Use strategies (rereading, predicting, questioning, contextualizing) when comprehension breaks down

Use reading and writing for various purposes on their own initiative

Read orally with reasonable fluency

Use letter–sound associations, word parts, and context to identify new words

Identify an increasing number of words by sight

Sound out and represent all substantial sounds in spelling a word

Write about topics that are personally meaningful

Attempt to use some punctuation and capitalization

Support the development of vocabulary by reading daily to the children, transcribing their language, and selecting materials that expand children's knowledge and language development

Model strategies and provide practice for identifying unknown words

Give children opportunities for independent reading and writing practice

Read, write, and discuss a range of different text types (poems, informational books)

Introduce new words and teach strategies for learning to spell new words

Demonstrate and model strategies to use when comprehension breaks down

Help children build lists of commonly used words from their writing and reading

Talk about favorite story books

Read to children and encourage them to read to you

Suggest that children write to friends and relatives

Bring to a parent–teacher's conference evidence of what your child can do in writing and reading

Encourage children to share what they have learned about their writing and reading

Grade 2

Read with greater fluency

Use strategies more efficiently (rereading, questioning, and so on) when comprehension breaks down

Use word identification strategies with greater facility to unlock unknown words

Identify an increasing number of words by sight

Create a climate that fosters analytic, evaluative, and reflective thinking

Teach children to write in multiple forms (stories, information, poems)

Ensure that children read a range of texts for a variety of purposes

Teach revising, editing, and proofreading skills

Continue to read to children and encourage them to read to you

Engage children in activities that require reading and writing

Become involved in school activities

Show children your interest in their learning by displaying their written work

Write about a range of topics to suit different audiences

Use common letter patterns and critical features to spell words

Punctuate simple sentences correctly and proofread their own work

Spend time reading daily and use reading to research topics

Teach strategies for spelling new and difficult words

Model enjoyment of reading

Provide opportunities daily for children to read, examine, and critically evaluate narrative and expository texts

Visit the library regularly

Support your child's specific hobby or interest with reading materials and references

Continue to support children's learning and interest by visiting the library and bookstores with them

Grade 3

Read fluently and enjoy reading

Use a range of strategies when drawing meaning from the text

Use word identification strategies appropriately and automatically when encountering unknown words

Recognize and discuss elements of different text structures

Make critical connections between texts

Write expressively in many different forms (stories, poems, reports)

Use a rich variety of vocabulary and sentences appropriate to text forms

Revise and edit their own writing during and after composing

Spell words correctly in final writing drafts

Continue to create a climate that fosters critical reading and personal response

Teach children to examine ideas in texts

Encourage children to use writing as a tool for thinking and learning

Extend children's knowledge of the correct use of writing conventions

Emphasize the importance of correct spelling in finished written products

Create a climate that engages all children as a community of literacy learners

Find ways to highlight children's progress in reading and writing

Stay in regular contact with your child's teachers about activities and progress in reading and writing

Encourage children to use and enjoy print for many purposes (such as recipes, directions, games, and sports)

Build a love of language in all its forms and engage children in conversation

Source: After Neuman et al. (2000).

that less than one-third of our nation's students (Natioanl Center for Educational Statistics, 2006a) are proficient readers by fourth grade, and only 33 percent are proficient readers by grade 8. There are also large gaps in students' reading proficiency related to gender, race/ethnicity, parental education, and socioeconomic status. For a large number of students, the quality of reading instruction at school will determine their level of reading proficiency. Learning to read is critical for a sense of well-being. Children who cannot read well are at great risk for school and later occupational failure, and may have more restricted emotional and social lives. For these reasons, the National Institute of Child Health and Human Development (NICHD) considers reading development to reflect a public health issue (Lyon, 2002). The Focus on Development box (pp. 296–297) describes the development of children's reading and writing skills in the early elementary years, and what teachers can do to support this development.

A Beginning Reader

Seven-year-old Kevin sits with his father on the couch. He is reading the story "Pecos Bill," by Ariane Dewey (1983), aloud to his father.

Kevin:	Bill [pause] guh—guh—guh—[he stops, wiggles, sighs].
Father:	Grabbed.
Kevin:	Grabbed hold of the rat . . . rattler. The s—nake (pause) fff—fight hard . . . fighted . . . [pause] fought hard. He squeezed all the pppp—pa—h! [he yells and throws down the book].
Father:	Poison. Come on. Calm down. It's poison.
Kevin:	Poison out of the snake. I . . . I'm beat. [he repeats the phrase, this time with intonation that signals dialogue in the story] "I'm beat," The s—n . . . uh . . . rattler finally hissed.
[Story Text:	Bill grabbed hold of the rattler. The snake fought hard, but Bill fought harder. He squeezed all the poison out of the snake. "I'm beat," the rattler finally hissed. Bill coiled the snake up and put it over his shoulder.]

Reading, for Kevin, is a language process, a cognitive process, and, perhaps most important, a social process. Kevin is intent on figuring out the meaning in the story, but he cannot automatically decode or transform the written symbols into words. Because the difficult words interrupt the flow of the story, Kevin is frustrated. Nevertheless, Kevin can read the majority of the words he encounters, and with support from his father, he is able to finish reading several pages of the book. What skills has Kevin developed to become a reader? What strategies does he rely on while he is reading? What factors enable Kevin to persist with the difficult task of learning to read?

Reading involves transforming written symbols into words and combining words into phrases and sentences. As we discussed earlier, preschool children may recognize the alphabet and also know about the relationships between sounds and letters. Whereas such knowledge is essential for learning to read, it doesn't enable a child to read.

Kevin uses phonemic information—the sounds he associates with *r* and *s*—as he encounters the words *rattler* and then *snake*. But is knowledge of letters and sounds all there is to reading? Definitely not. Kevin would not have recognized either of these words if it had been isolated on a card, out of the context of the story. He is intent, first and foremost, on the meaning of the story. Having heard several versions of the tale of Pecos Bill, Kevin brings background knowledge and a set of expectations to the task of reading. Knowing about cowboys and the danger that comes from tangling with snakes helps him decode the words.

Kenneth Goodman (1976) claimed:

> Reading is a psycholinguistic guessing game. It involves an interaction between thought and language. Efficient reading does not result from precise perception and identification

of all elements, but from skill in selecting the fewest, most productive cues necessary to produce guesses (about meaning) which are right the first time. (p. 498)

Kevin demonstrates that "guessing" is a critical part of the reading process. When Kevin encounters *fought,* he first says *fight,* then self-corrects to *fought* when the verb's tense does not match up with others previously encountered in this story. Thus, getting to meaning involves paying attention to word meaning and sentence structure while simultaneously scanning a line of text and discriminating letter and word shapes. While Kevin is emotionally involved with the character and events in the story, at another level he is interacting with his father. Thus, a beginning reader has many different sources of information available, any one of which the child may draw on to keep reading (Stanovitch, 1986).

When Kevin becomes frustrated, he continues to read because his father encourages him to persist. Motivation and support from an adult reader may be the most critical factor in helping children become readers. The point of reading aloud is not so much to demonstrate that Kevin can read but for both "readers" to discover what happens to Pecos Bill. Father and son will discuss the adventure either during the reading or afterward in conversation. They are participating in a *transaction of meaning,* a relationship between the text, its author, and the readers (Rosenblatt, 1988).

Components of the Reading Process

Reading is a complex process during which the reader is translating the printed code into words, comprehending and predicting meaning, and interacting emotionally with the characters or events of the story. We will discuss each of these components separately, but it is critical to remember that these processes occur simultaneously while someone is reading.

Decoding Text

Decoding is the process that readers use to determine the oral equivalent of written words. When Kevin reads the sentence "Bill grabbed hold of the rattler," what knowledge is important? Context knowledge, phonic knowledge, and sight word knowledge are all used by readers while they are decoding. When Kevin reads the word *Bill,* he is using **context knowledge**—the surrounding text and his background knowledge—to identify the word. He knows from the title of the story that the main character is named *Bill.* But the second word, *grabbed,* is not as predictable. When he makes the sound "guh—guh—guh," Kevin is using **phonic knowledge,** or what he knows about sound–letter relationships. But phonic knowledge in English is complicated, since one letter may be pronounced several different ways. Also, phonic knowledge includes information about how the sounds of several letters blend together, for instance, the /g/ and /r/ make a fluid sound /gr/, which is much different from the "guh—guh—guh" that Kevin made.

When Kevin pauses for several seconds, his father supplies the word *grabbed.* Neither context nor phonic knowledge was strong enough to help Kevin with this difficult word. **Sight word knowledge** is the other strategy readers use to decode. In fact, mature readers decode most words automatically, without consciously thinking about other decoding strategies. In contrast, beginning readers have little or no sight word knowledge, but it will develop as their experience with reading increases.

Learning sight words is made easier by the fact that a small set of words appears frequently in standard English writing. If a reader knows by sight from 200 to 400 of the most frequently occurring words, then it is possible to recognize between 50 and 65 percent of the words in almost any reading passage (Harris & Sipay, 1990). In addition, with enough reading experience, readers will automatically recognize words that at first they must figure out using context or phonic knowledge (Stahl, 1992).

Reading specialists have identified a limited number of words that are most helpful for beginning readers to know by sight: high-frequency words such as *is, the, to, she*, and simple words with familiar meanings such as *car, come, pool, food*. Also, words that are hard to recognize by relying on phonic knowledge, such as *said, poison, one, gone*, will have to be learned as sight words, since the sound–letter relationships of these words are unreliable.

Understanding Text

Although decoding is a necessary part of the reading process, the purpose of reading is to construct meaning. Comprehension depends on the reader's ability to use syntactic, semantic, and pragmatic information in order to make sense of text. **Comprehension** is an active process in which readers strive to construct a meaningful message from text. The interactions among reader, writer, and text help readers make meaning. Many factors shape a reader's interpretation: prior knowledge of a subject; attitudes or feelings toward the characters, events, or ideas in the text; and situational knowledge. Kevin knows that the snake is speaking in the dialogue, "I'm beat." On the basis of this knowledge, he predicts *snake* as part of the next phrase "the rattler finally hissed." When he reads, "The s—n . . . uh . . . rattler . . . ," his prediction makes sense, but something else doesn't fit. As Kevin's eye tracks the text, his decoding knowledge comes into play. Before he completes the word *snake*, he self-corrects by substituting the synonym *rattler*, which matches the written text. Thus, reading comprehension depends on both the content knowledge a reader brings to the text and his decoding knowledge and skills (Anderson, Hiebert, Scott, & Wilkinson, 1985).

Becoming a Fluent Reader

UNDERSTANDING CHILDREN
Strategy 4.8: Reading Strategies and Purposes

Children who become fluent readers have mastered three important skills. They can identify printed words using connections between spellings and sounds. They can also use previous knowledge and comprehension strategies to read for meaning. Extensive reading enhances these skills by increasing children's vocabulary as well as their knowledge of the world (see Pressley, 2002a, for a review). Moreover, gaining fluency also involves rapid and automatic word recognition. In Chapter 4 we discussed the concept of automaticity. When children can automatically recognize words, it frees up more of their working memory for comprehending the meaning of the text. Figure 5.5 lists a set of characteristics that a successful reader is likely to exhibit by the end of the third grade. This summary presupposes appropriate support for literacy development at home and at school.

Approaches to Teaching Reading

No matter what beginning-reading program teachers use, children must learn how the written code works and how to construct meaning from print. Reading research conducted during the 1970s produced three theories about how to teach reading: a *skills-based approach,* a *holistic or whole-language approach*, and a *balanced approach* that combines elements of the other two. These three perspectives are reflected in the following definition, "Reading is a complex skill, a holistic act," published in the influential national report "Becoming a Nation of Readers" (Anderson et al., 1985, p. 7). Although there are many people who favor either a skills-based or holistic approach (some very strongly, hence the "reading wars" debate), a greater number of teachers are currently adopting a more comprehensive, integrated approach to teaching reading.

The *America Reads Challenge* lists a set of characteristics of successful readers at each developmental level. The checkpoints for third graders include:

- They are fluent and strategic.

- They relate what they read to what they already know.

- They monitor their comprehension.

- They learn new vocabulary from context.

- They figure out unfamiliar words with word analysis skills including phonics and context clues.

- They understand literary elements as events, characters, and settings, and they compare these elements across books.

- They recognize themes.

- They understand how genres such as fables, nonfiction, and poetry differ and can write examples of each.

- They are motivated to read.

- They have favorite authors and types of books.

- They read widely in diverse types of materials.

- They talk and write about what they read.

Skills-Based Approach

Some beginning-reading programs focus on a sequence of reading skills that children must acquire. Typically, these skills are taught directly by the teacher using an explicit, often deductive, method. Easier skills, such as *word-attack strategies* based on phonics, are taught before harder skills, such as techniques for identifying the main ideas in informational articles. Some programs are organized around a basal reading series, a collection of stories accompanied by worksheets and designed to follow a set sequence of skills. Direct instruction, in which the teacher explains, demonstrates, and then provides supervised student practice, is the most common instructional method. Often, skills are taught in isolation rather than in conjunction with reading stories or articles. When children do read texts, reading experience is thought of as an opportunity to practice new reading skills.

The skills-based approach, especially the widespread reliance on basal reading programs, has dominated reading instruction in American schools for several decades (Harste,

1989). Because reading is such a complex process, many people believed children would learn more easily if the process were broken up into small parts: words, letters, sounds. Once children learned these individual components, they could be combined and, when added together, would result in reading.

Skills-based instruction was supported by the National Reading Panel (2000) in a report based on a review of the research on early reading instruction. The panel concluded that instruction in phonics awareness and competencies, vocabulary knowledge, oral reading, and specific comprehension strategies is most effective. Critics of the report suggest that the review of literature was too narrow in scope, omitting important research on literacy development, such as the influences of family, community resources, educational television, language of instruction, school reform, and whole-language instruction (Pressley, 2002b).

Holistic Approaches

In the early 1980s, researchers and educators began to challenge the part-to-whole logic that is central to a specific skills approach (Clay, 1980; Goodman, 1986). When language is splintered into small parts, they said, its essential ingredient, meaning making, is lost. Consequently, the act of reading becomes even more difficult for children. To remedy this situation, an alternative philosophy emerged, which centered on meaning making and the need to communicate through language. These researchers believed language must remain whole if meaningful interaction and communication are to occur. The term **whole language** was promoted by Ken and Yetta Goodman to describe this perspective (1979, 1992). This approach was pervasive in the 1990s.

Several beliefs are central to a whole-language approach (Freppon & Heading, 1996). First, the purpose of language is to create and share meaning. Second, language is language, regardless of whether it is spoken or written; the same conditions that foster the acquisition of speaking work with writing. Third, language is best learned by using it in a social context for authentic purposes. As Goodman (1986) put it: "Why do people create and learn written language? They need it! How do they learn it? The same way they learn oral language, but using it in authentic literacy events that meet their needs" (p. 24). Teachers who adopt this broad philosophy must translate it by designing specific practices in their classrooms. Therefore, no two whole-language classrooms look alike.

In the whole-language approach, students are thought to develop specific reading abilities inductively, based on extensive and varied experiences with print. Literature-based reading programs promote this kind of learning (Cullinan, 1987, 1992). On the basis of interest, children choose fiction or nonfiction books of all genres to read. They may participate in book groups, or they may even write their own books. These various activities occur voluntarily and collectively, fostering a community of readers in the classroom.

Another underlying assumption of the holistic approach is the idea that spoken and written language abilities develop similarly (Weaver & Schonhoff, 1984). In other words, those factors that help children acquire spoken language are also critical in their acquisition of literacy. If children learn to speak by interacting with others in meaningful contexts, then they will need the same kind of social experiences when they are learning to read and write. Therefore, teachers should provide a context in which children have a functional need to communicate. Children should be surrounded by peers and adults who are actively engaged in authentic speaking, writing, and reading activities.

The concept of whole language has proven to be a fertile and dynamic catalyst in the field of literacy education. It has led to new teaching methods and encouraged evaluation and revision in reading curriculum and materials. However, declining achievement test scores in some schools where whole-language approaches were heavily used raised questions about this approach. Research indicates that children from low socioeconomic backgrounds in kindergarten through the third grade benefited more from basal instruction than from whole-language instruction. Perhaps most important, the notion of whole language continues to generate heated debate about how children, especially children from diverse populations, become literate. Lisa Delpit, author of *Other People's Children,* shared this observation about whole language instruction:

> In California I saw a Black child who was in a class where the kids were supposed to read a piece of literature and then respond to it. The child clearly couldn't read the selection. When asked about the situation, the teacher said, "Oh, he can't read it, but he'll get it in the discussion." Perhaps it's good that he will be able to get it in the discussion, but at the same time nobody is spending time teaching him what he also needs to learn—how to read for himself. Sometimes we have the best intentions but actually end up holding beliefs that result in lower expectations for certain students. (1991, pp. 544–545)

There is consensus among researchers that some whole-language approaches are not effective for promoting phonemic awareness and word recognition skills, especially for children already at risk for reading difficulties (e.g., Jeynes & Little, 2000). However, whole-language approaches emphasizing experiences and conversations about literature have been shown to enhance academic engagement and comprehension of ideas in text (Pressley, 2002a).

Balanced Approaches

Many teachers find that adhering too closely to either a skills-based or a whole-language approach may be too inflexible for teaching diverse groups of students and combine the two approaches (Xue & Meisels, 2004). For instance, constant attention to skills instruction bores some students. If children can already segment phonemes, why teach it? Instead of reading self-selected texts, children are sometimes forced to complete skills worksheets. On the other hand, the emphasis on self-directed learning in whole-language programs may overwhelm those students who thrive on structure and guided instruction, or who need direct instruction in reading skills. If children are unable to hear sounds in words, it is urgent that teachers help them acquire those skills.

A *balanced approach* to teaching reading is based on the assumptions that children need to be engaged in meaningful and functional literacy activities and that they need to learn specific reading skills in the process (Pressley, 1998). Balanced reading instruction combines whole-language and phonics approaches. Many reading theorists argue that phonics is one component of the reading process, but is not sufficient for developing reading proficiency; thus, it does *not* warrant instructional priority (Paris, 2005). The question is no longer whether phonics should be taught, but *how* it can be integrated into reading programs that emphasize literature, composition, inquiry, and other process-centered instruction that are common to whole-language classrooms (Freppon & Heading, 1996). This conclusion is supported by a national survey of more than 13,000 kindergartens (Xue & Meisels, 2004). Results indicated that the combination of integrated language arts (whole language) and phonics promotes children's literacy development *and* their motivation to learn. However, teachers need to adjust the balance of these approaches according to individual child characteristics, such as entering skills. For example, children with low initial literacy skills benefit from more teacher-directed, skill-based instruction, and those with high initial skills learn more with increased child-initiated, integrated arts instruction (e.g., Morrison & Conner, 2002; Xue & Meisels, 2004). The Focus on Teaching box on page 305 describes a first-grade phonics lesson embedded in the morning message. Teachers who take an integrated approach provide many authentic experiences with reading and writing, but they also use systematic direct instruction in reading skills and strategies when necessary (Spiegel, 1992).

In summary, the most successful reading teachers incorporate methods from different approaches to address the literacy needs of their students. The classrooms of effective first-grade teachers are characterized by the following (Pressley, Wharton-McDonald, Allington, Block, Morrow, 1998, p. iv):

- High academic engagement
- Excellent classroom management
- Positive reinforcement and cooperation
- Explicit teaching of skills
- An emphasis on literature
- Much reading and writing
- Matching of task demands to student competence
- Encouragement of student self-regulation
- Strong cross-curricular connections

These qualities are beautifully illustrated in case studies described in *Learning to Read: Lessons from Exemplary First-Grade Classrooms* (Pressley, Allington, Wharton-McDonald, Block, & Morrow, 2001).

Keeping Young People Engaged in Reading

The focus in the early grades is clearly *learning to read*. What happens after children have mastered the basics of reading? How do children make the shift to *reading for learning*? Clearly the amount of time young people spend reading is important for further development of their reading competencies. However, you will be surprised how little students engage in reading after the early years of school. The National Assessment of Educational Progress (NAEP) has shown that leisure reading is associated with reading achievement (National Center for Educational Statistics, 2006a). Figure 5.6 shows the percent of students, ages 9, 13, and 17 years, who report reading for fun on a daily basis. Whereas over half of 9-year-olds read for fun regularly, this figure drops to less than one-quarter of the 17-year-olds.

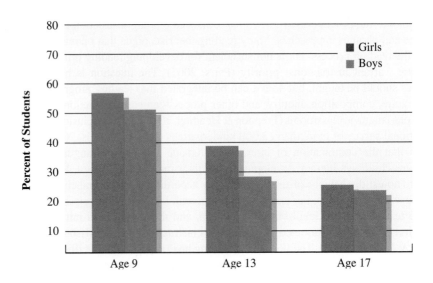

■ FIGURE 5.6
Percent of Children and Adolescents Who Read for Fun Daily
Source: U.S. Department of Health and Human Services (2000b).

Focus on Teaching

Using Embedded Phonics

Ms. Brown started the language arts lesson with a morning message, using yesterday's target pattern, —*am*. She wrote, "Sam will be 15 years young on tuesday" Then she asked the children to help her edit the message. They changed "young" to "old" and pointed out that Sam will be 7, not 15. With prompting, they agreed to capitalize the *t* in "Tuesday" and to add a period at the end of the sentence.

Ms. Brown's targeted spelling pattern for the day was —*ap*. She introduced this pattern through shared reading of a big book. During this shared reading the teacher pointed to each word of the big book as she read the story, occasionally checking the understanding of the 22 children seated cross-legged in front of her by asking a question about the story. When she came to a word containing the target pattern, *tap*, she stopped reading the story, wrote "tap" on the blackboard and asked the children what word family "tap" belonged to. Then Ms. Brown asked what other words belonged to the *ap* word family. She asked the children to spell these words to her as she wrote them on the board. The children had trouble with the *l* in *slap* so Ms. Brown had the children stretch out the sounds so that the letter /l/ was apparent.

After writing these words on the blackboard, Ms. Brown sent all but eight of the students to their seats. A strip of construction paper and a pile of alphabet letters from a bag of cereal were placed at each seat. Students were instructed to glue the letters *ap* on the construction paper and make new words by adding letters to the front. One student made *pay* and was not corrected because the teacher was busy working with the group of eight. When

students were finished with this seatwork, they were told to read independently a book of their choice.

Ms. Brown worked with the group of eight by writing yesterday's spelling pattern, —*am*, on a slate board. She elicited words with this pattern in it—*clam, slam, ram*—and wrote them down. She checked their understanding of *ram* by asking a student to use it in a sentence. Then she passed out copies of a book to each child that had the word *family* in it. The children were familiar with the story and read along with the teacher in choral reading. When they had finished, she gave them each a laminated tag board mat and laminated letters. She asked them to write some words with the *am* pattern while she listened to one of the children read. As he read, Ms. Brown kept a record of his reading miscues, prompting him to use context cues to guess the meaning of the unknown words. Finally, Ms. Brown introduced a new book to the children that contained the spelling pattern of the day, —*ap*. She previewed each page, eliciting prior knowledge from the students by asking them to expand on their interpretations of illustrations. Then she put the book in a plastic bag for each child to take home and practice reading with a partner.

With 30 minutes left for language arts, Ms. Brown began a process writing workshop on Thanksgiving activities. Students brainstormed about Thanksgiving activities while the teacher wrote down sentences that expressed their ideas. If previously taught spelling patterns appeared, she pointed them out. Once the brainstorming was complete, students wrote about their favorite Thanksgiving activity.

Source: Adapted from Snow, Burns, & Griffin (1998).

Sadly, results of recent international surveys (PIRLS, 2001) indicate that fewer U.S. 9-year-olds are reading for fun: about 35 percent report reading daily, and about 32 percent rarely read (National Center for Educational Statistics, 2004b). Most surprisingly, the 1996 National Assessment of Educational Progress indicated that adolescents reported reading fewer than five pages per day in school or for homework. As one reading researcher stated, "If they don't read much, how are they ever gonna get good?"(Allington, 1977).

How can we help young people stay engaged in reading? Many of the same principles discussed earlier apply here. Students of all ages need a literacy-rich environment, with

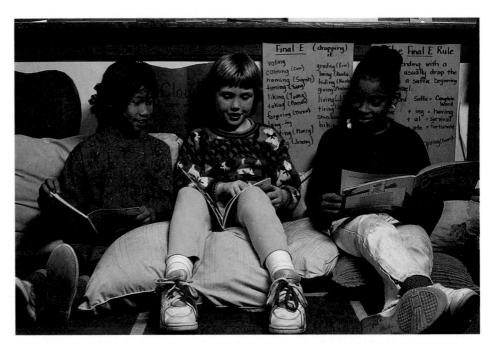

These elementary school students are enjoying a special reading time together.
Source: Jeffrey W. Meyers/Stock Boston.

plenty of opportunities to read independently and with others. It is important for young people to have a variety of reading materials to select from: paperbacks, magazines, poetry, textbooks, and so on. They need access to these materials for self-selected reading on their own. They also need meaningful reading materials related to their interests and cultural background. Reading needs to be integrated into all curriculum areas, and the use of writing should be used to support reading development.

Supporting and fostering students' motivation to read is important to keep students engaged in reading. Research shows that students who are higher in intrinsic motivation read much more than students low in motivation (Wigfield & Guthrie, 1977). Some studies show that intrinsic motivation for reading declines over the elementary years (see Wigfield, 2000). Teachers need to model positive attitudes toward reading and share favorite stories and books. Some teachers help facilitate after-school book clubs to enrich students' literacy experiences. Others have taken advantage of the popular fascination with the Harry Potter series by J. K. Rowling. Coined as "the Harry Potter effect," librarians and educators have noted how reading these books has inspired many children and adolescents to read more, including classic literature (Tigner, 2002). In addition, educators have integrated discussions about the story into other subject areas (e.g., science), as well as lessons for gifted students (Frank & McBee, 2003).

Like younger learners, older students need explicit instruction in comprehension strategies, especially as they begin to handle more complex and technical material. Studies reveal that abstract, specialized, and technical reading material decreases reading fluency, even for good readers (Chall, Jacobs & Baldwin, 1990). The International Reading Association recommends that content area teachers in the middle and secondary grades work with reading specialists to more effectively support the development of advanced reading strategies. By modeling effective reading strategies, teachers can help students maintain confidence in their reading abilities, which is strongly related to reading motivation and achievement (Wigfield, 2000).

Recommended Services for Adolescents Experiencing Difficulties with Reading

- Provide tutorial reading instruction that is part of a comprehensive program connected with subject matter.

- Assess students' reading and writing—and enable students to assess their own abilities in these areas—to plan instruction, foster individuals' control of their literacy, and immediately support learners when progress diminishes.

- Teach vocabulary, fluency, comprehension, and study strategies tailored to individuals' competencies.

- Relate literacy practices to life management issues, such as exploring careers, examining individual's roles in society, setting goals, managing time and stress, and resolving conflict.

- Offer reading programs that recognize potentially limiting forces such as work schedules, family responsibilities, and peer pressures.

■ FIGURE 5.7
Recommended Services for Adolescents Experiencing Difficulties with Reading
Source: After International Reading Association (1999).

Just as young students need special attention when they are experiencing reading difficulty, so do older students. As we discussed, national assessments indicate that only 6 percent of adolescents become advanced readers, and over 70 percent read at basic levels. These young people need services to address their reading difficulties. Figure 5.7 presents several recommendations of the International Reading Association's Commission on Adolescent Literacy.

Learning to Write

Each morning in first grade, Kevin goes to his cubby, pulls out his journal, and starts writing. This daily writing, along with many other opportunities for composing at home and school, allows Kevin a chance to express his ideas and experiences in written form. Since he is not yet proficient with spelling, he experiments as he tries to represent words with letters, as you can see in Figure 5.8 on page 308. Kevin is demonstrating development of early writing skills (expressive visible language). His "language by hand" is indirectly related to the development of his three other language systems: receptive language (listening, or "language by ear"), oral language (speaking, or "language by mouth"), and receptive visible language (reading, or "language by eye") (Berninger, 2000). These four language systems develop in overlapping, parallel waves rather than in distinct, sequential stages, and continue to develop in connection with one another throughout childhood and adolescence. Of the four systems, writing may take the longest to develop proficiently. As previously noted, many key developmental milestones in aural and oral language are achieved during early childhood (e.g., understanding and production of words and syntax) and many in reading are achieved during middle childhood (e.g., sight reading, fluency, comprehension). As we will see, some milestones in writing are also achieved during childhood (e.g., letter production, conventional spelling, beginning composition), but it is not until adolescence that key writing skills are achieved.

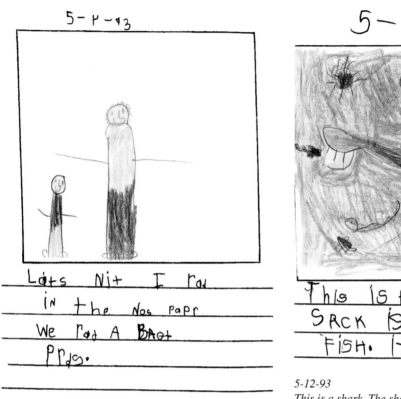

5-04-93
Last night I read in the newspaper. We read about presidents.

5-12-93
This is a shark. The shark is eating a fish. It is underwater.

■ FIGURE 5.8
First Grader Kevin's Journal Entries with Invented Spelling

Handwriting

Whereas aural language begins with the detection of speech sounds (or gestures), oral language with the production of babbles, and reading with the interaction with print, writing begins with the making of visible marks or scribbles. Children's handwriting proceeds from here, following a predictable sequence from random scribbles to zigzag lines, letter-like marks, true letters, single words, clauses, and sentences. Handwriting is distinguished from drawing from an early age (3–4 years). Handwriting and spelling are the tools for transcribing oral language into written language, and comprise the transcription component of the writing system (Berninger, 2000; Graham & Harris, 2000). Keyboarding is also a kind of second language by hand that contributes to transcription skills, especially for children with motor difficulties. Surprisingly little is known about the development of keyboarding skills considering the widespread use of computers; however, research has shown that keyboarding does not aid transcription skills of children with spelling difficulties (Berninger, Mizokawa, & Bragg, 1991). These results, along with results from other studies, indicate that handwriting (or keyboarding) and spelling are separate skills that develop independently of each other to some extent; however, they must be coordinated for optimal writing (e.g., Berninger, 2000).

Spelling Development

Focus on Development

- **Prephonemic spelling.** One early spelling is to represent a word by writing only one or two consonants, usually the initial or final consonant such as "K" for "sink," or "RT" for "rabbit."
- **Phonemic spelling.** Vowels appear along with consonants. Children attempt to match more of the sounds they hear with letters although they still focus on beginning and ending sounds: "OEN" for "ocean," or "JRAS" for "dress."
- **Transitional spelling.** With more exposure to written English, children rely less on the one-to-one correspondence strategy, and make increasing use of the alphabetic principle. They look for letter patterns or chunks common in English such as consonant-vowel-consonant patterns: "CEAP" for "keep," or "YESDDAY" for "yesterday."
- **Conventional spelling.** By 8 or 9, children spell many words according to conventional patterns, although they are not completely accurate spellers. One child showed this spelling progression: btPba, MTR, MMOSTR, MONSTUR, MONSTER.
- **Automatic spelling.** From the late elementary years, children and adolescents increasingly shift from strategic to automized spelling of common words.

Source: After Gentry (1982) and Berninger (2000).

Spelling

Children use systematic strategies in learning to spell, progressing through several overlapping phases of development (Berninger, 2000; Gentry, 1982; Read, 1975; Tremain & Bourassa, 2000). A common description of these phases, or preferred strategies at different points in development, is shown in the Focus on Development box.

As previously mentioned, when children spell words in unconventional ways they are using **invented spelling,** and these attempts should not be regarded as errors to be corrected with beginning writers (Chomsky, 1970). Instead, invented spelling is a positive sign that Kevin, Anne, and James are consciously analyzing speech sounds and print. In his journal, Kevin spells *presidents* as *Prds,* and *shark* as *srck.* When children are learning to write, ideas are more important than correct spelling. Invented spelling increases children's fluency and makes it easier for them to compose (Sowers, 1982). Contrary to the fears of many parents, it does not interfere with reading development or inhibit the development of conventional spelling. Each time children use invented spelling, they are experimenting with sound–letter relationships as well as grappling with the unpredictable aspects of English spelling. Reading specialists agree that teachers and parents should support children's use of invented spelling, recognizing that it is a transitional phase in a developmental process (Britto & Brooks-Gunn, 2001; Leu & Kinzer, 1995; Vacca, Vacca, & Grove, 1995). Language learners need freedom to experiment and construct the rules for any language system, whether it is sentence structure or conventional spelling (Henderson, 1990).

Remember that children are not learning to spell in a vacuum but in a literate environment. Teachers and parents can foster spelling development. The more children read or are exposed to printed words, the faster their approximate spellings will become conventional. Frequent writing experiences, including daily journals, ensure ample opportunity for practice and feedback. In addition, an effective spelling program teaches strategies that help children notice the generalities and patterns inherent in English (Cunningham, 1995).

Most children master transcription skills, the mechanics of writing, slowly and unevenly. Since children are coordinating cognitive and physical processes simultaneously,

■ FIGURE 5.9
*Development of
Writing Components*
Source: Berninger (2000).

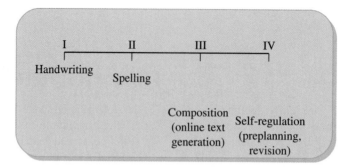

their progress may fluctuate (Graves, 1979). Focusing on the meaning of what children write instead of being excessively concerned with mechanics is the best way of encouraging young writers (Moffett, 1968). If children's attention is focused almost entirely on getting language onto paper, they will not be able to pay much attention to the other meaningful components of writing described next (see Figure 5.9). As children progress through school, their transcription skills improve (automatic spelling, fluent handwriting), making it easier to learn more complex writing skills (Graham & Harris, 2000).

Writing as Composing

The essence of writing development is learning to compose, to make meaning with printed text. There are many different reasons for writing, and a variety of genres unique to written language: stories, letters, arguments and other forms of expository writing, poetry, journals, and news writing. Teaching students to produce these diverse forms of text, each one with a special purpose, will be the ongoing goal of writing instruction from the early grades, through middle and high school, and into college.

A writer's task entails having a reason to communicate, planning content, producing some writing, and revising to fit the needs and interests of the intended audience. Composing is a complex process in which writers coordinate content and structure, while shaping language to accommodate the needs of their audience. Some elements of the writing process include *planning* (rehearsing), *drafting* (getting it down), *revising* (making changes to accommodate the reader or purpose), *editing* (attending to conventions and correctness), and *publishing* (making it public). Although we can refer to distinct parts of the writing process, writers do not experience them in any set progression, nor do they necessarily occur one at a time. Many writers are planning, drafting, and revising simultaneously. Neither do these processes proceed in a linear fashion; rather, the writing process is recursive. For example, while drafting, a writer may reread an earlier sentence and revise it before proceeding.

Berninger (2000) and her colleagues have identified developmental changes in children's compositions (text generation). When children who have not yet learned to produce true letters are asked to compose, they produce random strings of letter-like forms, draw pictures, copy words from others or materials, or refuse to write at all. (Recall that Anne, knowing few letters, focused on drawing pictures to express herself.) As soon as children can produce real letters, they begin generating text with many unconventional spellings. First graders often compose with a single clause, a complex sentence, or a few related sentences and clauses (see Kevin's journal entries in Figure 5.8). Although first graders' comments often consist of adding a simple statement of fact about a prior sentence, they also use a number of other simple formulas in their written compositions, such as stating facts or events in a sequence. Text length increases with grade level, along with the inclusion of personal evaluations, qualifications, and generalizations, particularly in junior high. Text structure also progresses from linear to hierarchical with development. Young writers often link sentences to a topic via free association; thus, the text is not psychologically coherent. Adolescent writers develop the use of several organizational levels and use more advanced narrative forms in which events are unified by a global topic sentence (see Figure 5.10 for a sample of adolescent writing). As a consequence, their writing is more psychologically coherent. They also incorporate more conventional narrative elements (e.g., problem statements, setting descriptions, character dialogue). Development of composition continues into adulthood.

Self-Regulation, Revision, and Audience

Young writers have no difficulty in finding something to say but spend much energy producing the physical marks on paper. Once the act of writing becomes easier, children become conscious of communicating with an audience. Graves (1983) reported that sometime around grades 3 and 4, children become less egocentric about their writing. That is, they no longer assume that everyone is interested in their message and become increasingly concerned about their readers' reactions. Once this happens, children are likely to begin revising their texts to match audience needs and interests.

■ FIGURE 5.10

Excerpts from an Eighth Grader's Essay

Changing Lives—One Book at a Time

How does literature help us make some of our everyday decisions? What makes certain types of literature affect us in different ways?

In the beginning of eighth grade, I read "The Diary of Anne Frank" with my language class. This book was the actual diary of a thirteen year old girl over two years of her life. This book expanded my knowledge about the Holocaust and made me realize how lucky I am to be living in the United States during this time period. Anne described the hardships that Jewish people had to face through personal experience. The book wouldn't have affected me as much if it were a biography or documentary, because it seemed much more real as a diary.

The Diary of Anne Frank also made me think about my strengths and weaknesses as a writer. Reading the work of someone else my age has made me a stronger writer. Writing is just like dancing. You learn the step or the idea in class, but only if you go home and practice will you really get it down and become better. I think this is a required lesson to be learned as we take another step towards the real world.

I also read a classic novel called Christy, by Catherine Marshall. It's about a brave nineteen year old woman who leaves her home to teach in a poor area in the Smoky Mountains. Her young students are hard to work with, but she enjoys the challenge and eventually falls in love with them. This book taught me to accept challenges and never give up. Christy's perseverance and courage paid off in the end. I learned that if I try my hardest, mine will too. The novel, Christy, is one of the reasons I decided to enroll in Pre-AP English instead of English Composition. If Christy could take on a classroom of sixty starving children with next to no education, then I could take on a classroom of thirty smart kids and a strict teacher.

Books can literally change people's lives. Getting lost in the author's world and getting to know the characters is something nothing can replace. Joining Pre-AP English 9 will lay out many paths for me as a student.

Self-regulation of writing includes planning and revising; these processes are influenced by the development of memory (see Chapter 4). Children progress from "online" planning during composing to advance planning of compositions. Their plans are more likely to control the composing process in junior high (e.g., Berninger, 2000).

Revision is a doubly difficult task since it requires the writer to step back from the text and think about it abstractly. Spontaneous revising is rare in beginning writers. The revision process also entails imagining what the needs and interests of one's readers might be. Writing programs that incorporate extensive peer review and group conferencing facilitate the development of revising abilities. Both elementary and high school students are better able to identify problems in papers written by other students than in their own work (Bartlett, 1982). Peer review develops this critical ability.

Direct feedback from a peer or teacher also eliminates some of the difficulty inherent in writing to an imagined audience. Self-regulation of the composing process requires considerable *scaffolding* until early adolescence (see Chapter 3). Teachers can guide students by "thinking aloud" during the process and by supplying graphic organizers and topics.

Syntax in Writing

Children's language development during the school years is generally marked with increased proficiency in using complex syntax, more variety in sentence structure, and longer sentences in both speaking and writing (Loban, 1976). This development is particularly critical for learning to write, since the grammatical structures typical of written language differ considerably from those used in speaking. For instance, someone telling a story aloud would use many short clauses linked together by coordinators such as *and, so,* or *but.*

> I was sitting around reading the newspaper, and I heard this scratching noise, over and over, and I just didn't want to get up, but I keep hearing it, so I went and checked to see if the cat wanted to come in, but no cat, so I sat down and started reading again.

Someone writing the same story would create discrete sentences, embed one sentence in another, and use more adjectives and adverbs.

> It was a little after five, on a rainy night. Not having had a minute to rest all day, I was savoring the soft cushions of my favorite chair and reading the evening paper. "How perfect," I thought, until a persistent and irritating scratching sound interrupted me. "Was it the cat?" I wondered, debating about whether to abandon my peace and quiet.

This example shows clearly that writing is not simply spoken language written down. Although beginning writers, between the ages of 6 and 8, rely on spoken language patterns, they gradually adapt their language to reflect the patterns and genres associated with writing (Kress, 1982). A 7-year-old wrote this story:

Scruffy

On Saturday My Dog got run over and the driver did not stop. The dog's name was scruffy and he died and then we buried him. (Kress, 1982, p. 55)

The next excerpt was written by a 12-year-old. Notice the differences in sentence structure, word choice, and genre compared with the story above.

Beaked Whales

The Beaked Whales live out in mid-ocean, where the tasty squid are found. Squid, it seems, provide most of their meals. Men do not know much about their family because even the scientists who study whales have seen very few Beaked Whales. Generally members of this family have long, narrow snouts, or "beaks." (Kress, 1982, p. 113)

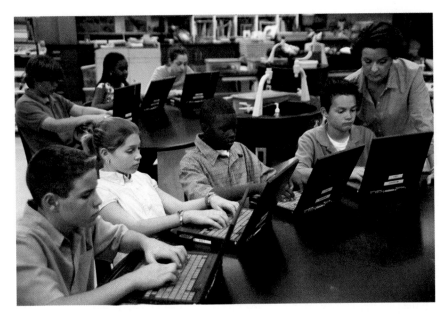

The Composing process requires scaffolding by the teacher.
Source: © Punch stock.

By middle school, children are writing expository texts (descriptive and informational writing) in addition to the narratives (stories) usually adopted by beginning writers. The sentences produced by 12-year-olds are precise, detailed, and condensed, demonstrating more syntactic and cognitive complexity than those written by younger children.

The writing of high school students reflects the same trend toward syntactic complexity. The following excerpt from a narrative by a 17-year-old demonstrates the carefully constructed and formal sentence structure typical of written texts.

> The chain of events leading to the appearance of the black shoes on the street had begun about four hours earlier. A young lady, Mary Vincent, had bought the flats at an auction late that night. Fortunately they were a little too big, for when she was suddenly dragged into a car by a couple of kidnappers, the shoes remained on the street. The crooks, being in a hurry, did not stop to pick up the flats even after they noticed Mary's stocking feet. (Loban, 1976, p. 115)

A longitudinal study of students' language from kindergarten through grade 12 showed that as children grow older they write longer clauses and embed dependent clauses more often (Loban, 1976). In particular, clauses are more complex because of changes in noun phrases found in the subjects and objects, including objects of prepositions (Hunt, 1977). For example, the subject noun phrase in this sentence written by a 17-year-old contains 15 words:

[subject noun phrase]
The chain of events leading to the appearance of the black shoes on the street

[verb phrase with prepositional phrase]
had begun about four hours earlier.

However, age alone cannot account for complicated syntax of teenage writers. Particular written genres, particularly expository forms, require grammatical complexity. For instance, tenth-grade writers in another study produced longer clauses when writing arguments than narratives (Crowhurst & Piche, 1979). Syntactic complexity is a function of the kinds of writing older students produce in the school context, along with changes in their thinking processes.

Focus on
Research

Shirley Brice Heath (1983) reported the results of a 10-year-long qualitative study of how spoken and written language is used for different purposes in two distinct but neighboring communities. Her research demonstrated that literacy practices in the home and community that matched those found in school enabled children to be successful. She studied adults' and children's language development at home and in school in two communities in the Carolina Piedmont from the late 1960s to the late 1970s. One town, Roadville, is a white, working-class community in which families have worked for four generations in the textile mills. The other town, Trackton, is a black working-class community in which families are currently working in the mills but whose previous generations once farmed the land. This work, *Ways with Words: Language, Life and Work in Communities and Classrooms*, provides startling and fascinating documentation about how language is intimately connected to race, class, gender, and culture.

Shirley Brice Heath: Ethnographer and Teacher

She discovered that historical segregation meant that each community built separate and different religious institutions, ways of communicating, worldviews, and patterns of social relations. Consequently, the way language is used to worship, for social control, and in asserting identities is distinctive to Trackton and Roadville. Both communities are literate, but each has its own traditions. Heath found that Roadville residents used writing only when they were required to; writing is seen "as an occasional necessary tool—to aid their memory, to help them buy and sell things, and sometimes to keep them in touch with family and friends" (p. 231). On the other hand, reading is considered a good thing, and residents collect reading materials for themselves and their children.

In Trackton, reading is not recognized as a special activity. Reading materials do not accumulate but are read and discarded. Reading is considered an aspect of everyday social interaction. "Trackton residents read

Form and Function

As children grow older, written language development evolves in two dimensions: expanding the variety of writing forms or styles and writing for more abstract purposes. In a literate culture, developing communicative competence includes knowing how to communicate effectively in writing in many contexts, but especially in school. Writing in the classroom serves several functions. Often, writing is used by students to learn academic content such as taking notes, writing book reports, and writing research papers. Sometimes students are asked to write in order to demonstrate what they have learned, as in the case of essay tests in a history class. In other instances, writing fosters particular kinds of thinking skills, such as analysis and interpretation, which a student would use in writing a critique of a literary work. Another function of writing is as an outlet for expression, a way for individuals to communicate ideas, emotions, and experiences, both in and outside of school. As children mature throughout middle and high school, their needs and desires change. As a result, new forms become common practices. Middle- and high-school-aged students begin to keep diaries and journals, write letters to friends, and fill notebooks with poetry. High school newspapers and literary magazines flourish as students write to serve many different social needs. It is important to remember that children learn the language forms and functions that are practiced and therefore valued by the local culture of the home, the school, the neighborhood. Not every community values language and literacy in the same way (Heath, 1983), nor are there equitable opportunities for individuals to engage in literate practices. The way we use language is also related to social factors, such as family income level, ethnic group identity, and geographical factors, as detailed in the Focus on Research box.

Once students reach high school, expository writing, especially arguments and analysis, will be dominant. In order to write well, older students' language must become more complex and abstract. A student in the middle grades may be quite comfortable producing aloud to anyone who wants to listen on the plaza, report what they have read, ask for interpretations of the written materials by the group, and enjoy the stories which invariably ensue from a report of something read." The meaning of any written materials is not interpreted individually but constructed jointly. A resident of Trackton focuses on the content of the text: "What does it say about me, or someone or something I know, and what do I do?" (p. 232).

Because of the way literacy is practiced in each community, children from Roadville and Trackton arrive at school with different ideas about writing and printed text. Trackton's children have extensive experience with the shape and style of print found on signs, cans, and in newspapers but usually are not accustomed to formal sessions devoted to reading stories. In Roadville, children are more likely to have had books read to them at bedtime and sessions with coloring books around the kitchen table. When children from both communities arrive at school, their patterns of socialization around literacy lead to very different outcomes. School is a place where structure, lessons, and clear knowledge boundaries are emphasized. Roadville children are familiar with this kind of world; what happens at home is not all that different from at school. But the children from Trackton are used to negotiating meaning together, to engaging in dramatic speaking styles, and to learning by observing and imitation, all behaviors that diverge from school values. Consequently, it is harder for the Trackton children to succeed in school and dropout rates are high, whereas the Roadville children feel more comfortable, completing high school at a higher rate. Because of her findings, Heath believes that schools must be sensitive to the literate cultures children bring with them. Teachers must be able to build cultural bridges between home and school and to link ways of being literate in school, at work, or in the home.

a narrative that centers around a plot but more than likely will struggle when writing an argument that entails the use of supporting evidence. Beginning in middle school but carrying on through the upper grades, teachers will focus on teaching written genres that have fairly abstract functions, including arguments, analysis, and problem solving. In writing a persuasive essay, a writer must coordinate several variables: producing a coherent and convincing argument, marshaling effective evidence, relating to the audience, and using a formal style. A successful essay depends on sentence and paragraph structure that is tightly structured and planned. This kind of organizational planning is difficult for high school students. However, the National Assessment of Educational Progress (NAEP) study revealed that more middle and high school students are engaging in prewriting activities, such as outlining, listing ideas, or taking notes than in earlier assessments. Results also suggest that adolescents who use prewriting activities had higher test scores than those students who did not use any visible planning (Greenwald, Persky, Campbell, & Mazzeo, 1999).

Obviously, the intellectual demands are much greater in producing expository writing than they are with narrative genres. High school writers' abilities to produce argumentative writing reflects their cognitive capacities, but such tasks can also encourage intellectual development. Russell Durst (1987) found that students who were asked to analyze a history passage did more complex thinking than those who were asked only to summarize the passage. Thus, certain kinds of writing assignments are more beneficial than others. Teachers who assign analytic writing can help students build their intellectual as well as communicative abilities.

In an extensive and now classic study of the writing abilities of children ages 11 to 18, James Britton and his colleagues (Britton, Burgess, Martin, McLeod, & Rosen, 1975) discovered that the context of school exerts a tremendous influence on how children develop as writers. (Although they studied British schools, Applebee [1981] extended these findings to American schools.) Britton and his research team categorized students' writing as personal (expressive), poetic (literary), or transactional (expository). They also identified the intended audience in each case. After analyzing more than 2,000 writing samples, they reported that 63 percent of all student writing is expository in nature. Furthermore, as students move through the upper grades, they are given less and less opportunity to produce literary (short stories, poetry) or personal writing. In addition, they found that 92 percent of all writing is produced for the teacher as audience, with 49 percent being written for the sole purpose of evaluation by the teacher.

Schools, then, have a tremendous impact on how children learn to write and what styles or genres they develop proficiently. Writing ability is tied to specific uses of writing in the home, school, and larger social settings. Despite an increased national focus on writing instruction, there has been little change in students' writing proficiency levels since 1984, when the NAEP first included a writing assessment for students at grades 4, 8, and 11. The 2002 NAEP data reveal that fewer than one-quarter of students at each grade level reach a proficient level. And only 2 percent reach an advanced level (Greenwald et al., 1999). Writing at this level is characterized by clear, complete, and detailed responses to assignments that are well organized and coherent.

To develop writers at all grade levels, two elements are essential. First, writing must be used for authentic purposes. In the larger culture, writing is used by individuals as creative expression (fiction, poetry, drama), as a means of learning (note taking, summarizing, listing), and as communication of information, thoughts, ideas (essays, newspapers, scientific studies, etc.). Accordingly, students develop as writers in school when they use writing purposefully, instead of writing only to be graded. Students who write short stories that are then published in their classroom and read by their classmates as literature experience what it feels like to be writers. They are invested in how their readers react to or interpret their work. Having readers in addition to their teacher is one way of ensuring that students write for an authentic purpose.

Second, the more students write, the more developed their writing abilities become. Early national assessments indicated that the typical high school student was producing one substantial piece of writing per month (Applebee, Langer, & Mullis, 1986). Similarly, recent evidence from the NAEP indicates that students are not asked to write multiple drafts of a paper on a regular basis. However, eighth- and twelfth-grade students had higher average writing scale scores when their teachers always asked them to write more than one draft (Greenwald et al., 1999).

Not only is practice essential, but writing in a variety of genres and styles for a range of different audiences is especially important. Outside school we use writing to accomplish many goals: to communicate, to organize, to record information, to entertain, to learn new ideas, to think. Students need experience with a range of writing genres so that they can function better in school and later in real life. However, high school students write less than younger students in all subject areas except English (Applebee et al., 1986). As a remedy, many teachers now endorse **writing across the curriculum** programs in which writing is incorporated into all subject areas from music to mathematics (Maxwell, 1996). The Focus on Teaching box lists different ways teachers can encourage student writing in meaningful ways.

To enhance writing development it is important to recall the process by which children develop spoken language. The need to communicate, an environment rich in social interchange, available and experienced adults, and hour upon hour of practice are all essential to language development. Writing, however, is more difficult and less practiced in everyday life than speaking, so teachers need to provide extra support to help students' abilities to grow. Therefore, writers need instruction and practice in the process of writing. Process-oriented teachers build in more exercises for prewriting and drafting. They use a workshop approach in which students receive regular conferences and feedback from peers as well as the teacher while they are revising their work. Although writing is a different mode from speaking, the same basic social factors are involved in all areas of language development.

Different Possible Modes of Student Writing in High School

Journals or diaries	Memos
Fiction	Poems
Fantasy	Scripts
Historical	Plays
Adventure	Radio
Science fiction	Television
Choose-your-own-adventure	Prophecies, predictions, visions
Children's books	Newspaper writing
Picture books	Articles
Dictionaries	Editorials
Fact books	Features
How-to books	Advertisements
Biographies	Proposals
Letters to real or imaginary people	Social programs
Dialogues and conversations	Grants
Thumbnail sketches	Research
People	Construction
Places	Position papers and responses
Important concepts	Reviews
Historical events	Books
Requests	Movies and TV
Applications and resumes	Recordings
Research reports	Performances
Science	Math
Observations	Word problems
Notebooks	Problem solutions
Lab reports	Practical applications
Hypotheses	Cartoons
Interviews (real or imaginary)	Debates
Photos and captions	Songs and rap
Recipes	Games and puzzles
Catalogs	Posters, displays, collages
Obituaries, epitaphs, eulogies	Instructions or directions

Source: After Tchudi & Yates (1983).

Literacy Development in the Classroom

Although we live in a literate culture, there are millions of adults in America who are not **functionally literate.** Such individuals are not able to read or write well enough to negotiate daily life. Many cannot use a phone directory, complete a job application form, or read a newspaper. Based on a national survey conducted in 2003, researchers estimated that 14 percent of the adult population had only rudimentary reading and writing skills (National Center for Educational Statistics, 2006b). Computer literacy is necessary to hold a job whether one is a clerk in an auto parts store or a personnel director for a large corporation. Bus drivers need to read street signs and city maps; assembly-line workers must read directions and interpret diagrams projected onto computer screens at their workstations. Most important, literacy is critical to democracy. To be functioning citizens, everyone must be able to read a newspaper and interpret the television news and other media in order to remain informed enough to vote thoughtfully and otherwise participate in a democratic society.

What can teachers do to ensure that every student has the best possible chance of becoming literate? Reading and writing development can be fostered in students from kindergarten through grade 12 by (a) creating language-rich classroom environments, (b) focusing on meaning and communication as the main purpose for literacy, (c) encouraging social interaction and collaboration, (d) providing explicit instruction in reading and writing strategies, and (e) using formative assessment keyed to individual growth in literacy.

A classroom environment that promotes literacy provides students with many opportunities to interact with print and nonprint sources. Listening to stories, giving oral readings of drama and poetry, reading books and magazines, viewing and discussing films and videos, and sharing book experiences are significant activities for all grade levels. Some of the books and stories children are reading should be ones they themselves have written. Publication of student writing in the classroom is vital, since student writers can experience how to produce for a real audience. Such authentic literacy tasks are critical for engagement in writing (Bruning & Horn, 2000). Sharing student writing creates a community of writers and reinforces the notion that literacy is a part of everyone's everyday life in school.

Sharing book experiences is important at all grade levels.
Source: Getty Images

Language predominates in an effective classroom, and opportunities for students to practice all modes of communication are essential. Children who are talking, reading, listening, and writing in alternating and sustained contexts are learning. Talk is especially critical in promoting concept development, developing interactional skills, and sharing knowledge in general (Wells, 1986). After all, literacy is socially constructed; individuals interacting with others is the wellspring of all language systems.

Creating and communicating meaning are the main purposes of literacy. Therefore, teachers must provide literacy activities and assignments that are both intrinsically satisfying and authentic acts of communication. Allowing children to choose their own reading materials from a wide array of styles, genres, and topics will support their individual interests. Mandated reading, which requires that every person in the class read exactly the same material in lockstep fashion, prevents individual development. Teachers should avoid practices that *confine* literacy, such as the exclusive use of basal readers in the lower grades and required reading lists of a handful of classic texts in high school English classes.

Classrooms in which collaboration is the norm will naturally reinforce the idea that literacy is socially constructed. Classroom structures should encourage collaboration in which there are many chances for students to read, write, talk, and respond to one another, such as Nildo, Marco, and Juana were able to do in their study groups. One common practice is the use of literature circles, in which students group themselves around a topic, a theme, or an individual text to read and then discuss or even write about their reactions (Harste, Short, & Burke, 1988). Books are chosen by the students, and the questions they bring to the group are student generated. Students are trained to play different roles in their circle including that of discussion leader. The teacher arranges the classroom space and materials and facilitates the groups to foster this kind of student-centered literacy. Another community-of-learners approach inspired by social constructivism is shared in compelling classroom stories written by Barbara Rogoff along with teachers, students, and parents in *Learning Together: Children and Adults in a School Community* (2001).

Social interaction in the form of response and feedback is essential for developing writers and supporting the writing process, especially during the stages of drafting and revising. Frequent teacher and peer conferences are useful for supporting developing writers. The most useful feedback involves providing specific ways to improve the organization and clarity of students' *writing,* rather than their *ideas* (Bruning & Horn, 2000).

Additionally, as we already discussed, it is important to provide explicit instruction to help students develop their reading and writing competencies. This instruction should occur within the context of meaningful learning activities. For example, teachers can teach comprehension strategies while reading storybooks. Children can be asked to retell parts of the story, predict events in the story, or make up a conclusion. Other valuable instructional approaches have been shown to be effective, such as **transactional strategies instruction (TSI).** These approaches use a combination of explicit instruction, modeling, and discussion to teach comprehension strategies. They emphasize the application of strategies and provide many opportunities for students to learn how to use strategies on their own (e.g., Pearson & Duke, 2002). Figure 5.11 displays the basic components of TSI.

Assessment of students' progress should be ongoing, occurring during the time students are actually engaged in a literacy task. By observing and interacting with students as they are reading or writing, teachers can keep anecdotal records or journals of each child's developing skills, difficulties, progress, changes, and goals (see Duckworth, 2001, for samples). *Kidwatching* is a term devised to capture the teacher's powerful role in observing children as they develop as language users (Goodman, 1978). This kind of formative assessment will ensure that teachers are intervening and instructing exactly when and where individual students

Cognitive strategies	Interpretive strategies
Thinking aloud	Character development: Imagining how a character might feel; identifying with a character
Constructing images	Creating themes
Summarizing	Reading for multiple meanings
Predicting (prior knowledge activation)	Creating literal-figural distinctions
Questioning	Looking for a consistent point of view
Clarifying	Relating text to personal experience
Story grammar analysis	Relating one text to another
Text structure analysis	Responding to certain text features, such as point of view, tone, or mood

■ FIGURE 5.11

Basic Components of TSI
Source: From "Comprehension Instruction in the Primary Grades," by P. D. Pearson & N. Duke, in C. Block & M. Pressley (Eds.), *Comprehension Instruction: Research-Based Best Practices* (2002, pp. 247–336), New York: The Guilford Press.

need it most. Because literacy is fundamental to educational achievement, it is imperative that children learn to read and write in the first few years of school. Primary-grade teachers undertake the formidable task of teaching children to read and also bear the burden of assessing those children who are not making sufficient progress. In as much as future learning and self-sufficiency depends so heavily on printed text, it is important to intervene early in the literacy acquisition process if children are failing to learn to read. The Focus on Research box on page 322 describes promising intervention programs for elementary and middle school students.

Evaluation is not the sole responsibility of teachers. Students can profit directly from reflecting on, assessing, and evaluating their own work, even in the early elementary grades, but certainly during the middle and high school years. Not only can students report on what they have learned or enjoyed, but teachers can encourage them to notice their processes and strategies while reading and writing. Keeping journals on their reading or writing process and building portfolios are both tools for keeping track of what students are reading or writing as well as for building in reflection and self-consciousness about each student's literacy development. A portfolio typically consists of a collection of a student's work over a period of time. Students select specific items for their portfolio that, in their opinion, represent their best work. By asking students to compile their own portfolios, teachers are encouraging students to make judgments about the nature and quality of their work. Portfolios can be open-ended, consisting of a wide variety of artifacts, such as a finished essay including the prewriting and drafts that led up to the final product, a videotape of the student's shared book performance, parts of a journal, notes from peer-writing conferences, story maps or other graphics, and taped oral readings. To encourage collaboration, teachers can work with students in devising the contents of a portfolio as well as in setting up criteria for evaluating its contents (Valencia, 1990; Wolfe, 1989).

Cultural Influences on Language Development

Americans think of their country as diverse, where many subcultures coexist and interact. All individuals vary along the lines of race, economics, and cultural heritage. People identify themselves variously as members of a family, a neighborhood, and a community. Language is one way that individual and community identities are created, maintained, and signaled to others. A person's language, dialect, or manner of speaking reflects features of his or her social, economic, and cultural background. Because language is so variable and plastic, it can be shaped by speakers to reflect a particular group identity. A language community can be identified in many ways: by pronunciation, such as /cah/ for *car* (New England area); by a dialect, such as the use of *be* as in "He be here" (Africanized English); or by linguistic fluency in several languages (a child who speaks Mandarin at home but English in school).

Dialects

Every person who speaks English speaks in a distinctive dialect and with an accent (Shuy, 1967). This is true whether one's family arrived from Scotland in the 1700s, from Africa in the 1800s, or from Vietnam in the 1900s. A **dialect** is a variation of a single language spoken by members of a speech community, whereas an *accent* refers to the way certain sounds are pronounced. Why do we have so many varieties of English? The answer is personal. Since language feels so basic to our identities, we usually maintain the distinct qualities of our home language even after moving away from our family and community.

However, the language variations in the United States today have created major problems for educators. For one thing, the language of instruction in schools, sometimes called **standard American English (SAE),** is often not the dialect of English spoken in children's speech communities. No matter the source of variation—whether children come from inner cities or rural settings, from insulated, culturally distinct communities such as Cuban Miami, or from newly immigrated families from Haiti—they are likely to speak a dialect of English significantly different from that studied at school. In the future, language variation in America will only increase, not diminish. In contrast, our schools are at present oriented to one standard form of English. This situation frustrates teachers and children alike who must struggle to find ways of communicating across a wide variety of language or dialect differences. Educational reform is needed in all areas. The curriculum, the materials, and the teaching methods of our schools currently are not flexible enough to accommodate the linguistic diversity of the children now attending them (Langer, 1991).

During the 1960s, differences between home and school language were blamed for many children's failures in school. For example, terms such as *culturally deprived* and *language deficient* were often used to describe children who spoke a recognizable dialect such as Black English that differed from the SAE dialect expected in school. Intensive research in the area of language variation has shown that learning is not inhibited by a person's dialect (Shuy, 1980; Smith, 1975). Dialects differ from one another, but all are rule-bound, conventional ways of speaking. Every dialect is fully capable of allowing all human experiences or thoughts to be expressed. A dialect such as Black English, for instance, is not an impoverished language form, nor is it a sloppy or ungrammatical second cousin to other English dialects (Labov, 1972; Smitherman, 1985).

Linguistically, all dialects are equally valid, but socially, not all dialects are equally valued. Dialects spoken by dominant social groups are regarded more highly than those adopted by groups with less economic or political power. The most valued dialect in America, standard American English, is the variety spoken in the Northeast and Midwest. Other distinctive dialects exist in the South, in Appalachia, in New England, in the Southwest, and on the West Coast. Black English is spoken by some but not all African Americans; it is also spoken by some European Americans, Hispanic Americans, and Asian Americans. Hispanic and Asian American dialects may not be closely tied to geographic areas but rather to cultural communities throughout the United States.

However, standard American English is the language of schooling. If children are to succeed in school today, they must learn and use standard English no matter what their home dialect is. This presents a dilemma for children and teachers alike. How are children to learn standard English if it is not their home dialect? Should a standard dialect replace a home dialect? Should teachers reject children and their schoolwork if they speak and write in a dialect other than standard English? These questions cannot be answered easily, but there are several principles to keep in mind. Above all, children's home dialects should be respected, since a person's identity and sense of self are intertwined with his or her language patterns. Instead of rejecting a child's home dialect, a teacher can help *add* standard English to the child's linguistic repertoire. Children who speak several varieties of English are said to be *bidialectal,* which helps individuals function effectively in different social settings.

Dialects in the Classroom

As the diversity of students increases, educators should expect to hear many different dialects in their classroom. It is important to remember that language develops with use. Allowing children to speak and interact at school in their home dialect or language will increase their general fluency with language and thereby develop their communication skills. In addition, the teacher can encourage competency in standard dialect by making it clear to children that acquiring a new dialect is important and by instructing them in its conventions (Delpit, 1988). For example, teachers can ask children to write two versions of the same

Focus on
Research

Characteristics of programs that are effective for students at risk for reading failure include: (a) a balance between holistic and direct skill instruction, (b) adaptability to individual student needs, (c) student engagement, and (d) an enriched environment (Manset-Williamson, St. John, Hu, & Gordon, 2002). Two well-known intervention programs share some of these features. *Reading Recovery* is a program for low-achieving readers developed by child psychologist Marie Clay. The program came to the United States in 1985 through The Ohio State University. Currently, 23 universities have established training programs for Reading Recovery teachers who serve first-grade children across the United States identified as low performing in reading and writing. Children also participate in *Descubriendo la Lectura, Reading Recovery* in Spanish.

The program provides short but concentrated periods of individual instruction on a daily basis for 12 to 20 weeks. Success rates are high, with between 70 and 80 percent of all children reading at the level of their peers by the end of the instructional period including those with limited English proficiency. The philosophy behind *Reading Recovery* ensures that teachers focus on where a child is and then builds on existing strengths, while guiding the child through reading a series of whole, predictable texts and writing self-generated sentences.

Each 30-minute session is carefully structured around each child's responses. The lessons consist in

Preventing Reading Failure

reading and rereading "little books" along with sentence writing. First, a student begins by reading a familiar short book with bright illustrations and very predictable language. While the child is reading, the teacher will keep a running record of the oral reading, noting any strategies the child is using or ignoring. The teacher will introduce a new book, looking at the pictures and asking the child to make predictions about story. They will read the new book together, and the teacher will remind the child of word-attack strategies—such as checking the beginning or final letters in a word. Or the teacher will direct the child's attention to the story content, adding context to help with word identification and comprehension. Next, the student may dictate, then write a sentence message. Often the sentence is written on tag board and cut up into individual words that are then reassembled into a sentence. Sometimes games using sight words such as *the* or *they* are played. The lessons move very quickly, and teacher and student work intensely together on a series of manageable, high-success tasks. Most important, the teacher notices and comments on the student's behavior. The goal is to move children toward independence.

However, not all children succeed in *Reading Recovery*. The program is intense but fairly brief, and it is very expensive to staff. Research has shown that if a child is not succeeding during the 20 weeks, then he or she will not profit from the program. Alternative instruction will be necessary.

story on facing pages, one in standard dialect and the other in a different dialect (Leu & Kinzer, 1995). All children, no matter which one was their home dialect, would become conscious of the differences between the two versions, and teachers will have the opportunity to value each dialect for its communicative effectiveness.

Additionally, teachers should *model* the standard English dialect used in school. Constantly intervening and correcting children's language will not promote their development of the dominant dialect. Remember that the child learning to speak does not benefit from a parent's correction of form. The child intuitively constructs the grammatical system by analyzing the language patterns he or she hears and then interacting in real exchanges. Children learn new languages or new dialects by being exposed to the target language and by frequent, meaningful interactions where they feel comfortable making mistakes. If teachers focus on correcting nonstandard speech, that teacher will succeed in silencing children rather than in promoting their language development.

Success for All is a prevention and early intervention program designed to restructure elementary schools so that all children are successful in reading, writing, and language arts. This program began as a partnership between educational researchers at Johns Hopkins University and the Baltimore City Public Schools, and it is now used in some 1,800 schools around the country. It has a companion program, *Roots and Wings,* that focuses on mathematics, science, and social studies.

Success for All was designed for schools that serve large numbers of disadvantaged students in preschool through grade 8, and is comprehensive and intensive in its approach. Prekindergarten and kindergarten classes include shared reading, telling and dramatizing of stories, thematic interdisciplinary units, and a focus on letters and the sounds of words. In the first grade, students receive *Reading Roots*, a reading program that combines phonics with the use of meaningful texts. Reading tutors are a prominent feature of the reading program. Students who experience difficulty with reading receive 20 minutes daily of one-on-one tutoring from certified teachers, many of them trained as reading specialists or special educators. Teachers and tutors communicate regularly to maintain continuity for the child. When students attain a second-grade reading level, the focus shifts to vocabulary building, decoding practice, and comprehension strategy instruction (predicting and summarizing sequences).

At every grade level, children's literature is included, and students have opportunities to discuss the meaning of the story with their classmates to develop their knowledge of story structure, as well as listening and speaking vocabulary. In addition, there is a family support team at every school, which develops programs to encourage family involvement in school programs and offers parents' strategies for helping their children at home. The team also addresses issues related to health services, attendance, and behavior problems.

Early evaluations indicated that the programs helped to boost some measures of reading achievement in the first through seventh grades. The program also helps to reduce special education placements, increase attendance, and reduce retentions. Program adaptations for Spanish bilingual students and English-language learners also show success. Researchers are continuing to monitor the effectiveness of the program using a more sophisticated experimental approach; initial findings showed that kindergarten and first graders in the program scored higher than control students on tests measuring word decoding and identification and understanding of written passages. Critics wonder whether progress shown on these measures is worth the high investment; others are impressed with the findings showing the effectiveness of school reform efforts.

Sources: Clay (2002); Reading Recovery Council (2002); Slavin & Madden (2001); and Viadero (2005).

Instead of form, teachers should focus on a child's message, providing a response that models the appropriate form (Galda, Cullinan, & Strickland, 1993). For example, if a student says, "My papa, he goed to the store," a teacher might reply, "Your papa went to the store? Why did he go to the store?" This strategy reinforces the child's success in communicating while simultaneously allowing the child to hear the appropriate verb form. Eventually, with enough exposure to alternative forms and with frequent interaction in nonthreatening, purposeful settings, children will acquire the dialect of school language (Delpit, 1990).

Language and Culture

Language varieties reflect cultural patterns and values. One dialect or language differs from another not only in terms of grammar but also in speaking styles and interaction patterns. Children behave, learn, and interact according to the values and worldviews of their culture. Thus, culture influences school achievement. In particular, there is great variability in how different cultures imagine, cultivate, and value literacy (Laquer, 1983). If there is significant discontinuity between children's home and school environments, then children can become so confused and frustrated that they are unable to participate in learning (Sleeter & Grant, 1988). Many studies, including Shirley Brice Heath's study (1983) discussed earlier, have now documented the fact that differences in classroom and home discourse patterns adversely affect the learning of children from ethnic or minority communities (Au & Mason, 1981, 1983; Erickson & Mohatt, 1982; Goldenberg, Gallimore, & Reese, 2005; Philips, 1983).

How do classroom interaction patterns affect access to school knowledge? In a traditional teacher-led classroom, a whole-group lesson works only if the participants know and adhere to the rules for turn-taking. With this kind of lesson, teachers choose the subject matter and use direct instruction (telling, showing, and guided practice) to transmit information to students. Children are expected to pay attention and to sit quietly until they are asked a question. They may not call out answers but are expected to raise their hands and speak only if they are chosen to respond. This teacher-dominated interactional model does not work equally well for all students, especially for those who are unfamiliar with this discourse pattern. Students bring the distinctive discourse patterns of their homes and communities with them into the classroom. When these patterns differ from those traditionally practiced in school, children are effectively prevented from participating.

Changing Classroom Discourse and Interaction Patterns

As we discussed in Chapter 4, multicultural education involves revising school curriculums to reflect the beliefs, traditions, and contributions of all people in an ethnically diverse society. Teachers need to understand that students' ways of speaking and interacting are inherently logical no matter how different they appear from school-based patterns. By investigating children's home cultures and finding out more about typical social interaction patterns, teachers can change their classroom to accommodate a range of behaviors.

Children's verbal participation is greater when classroom discourse patterns are similar to those used in the home or community (National Research Council, 1998). In work with Hawaiian children in the Kamehameha Early Education Program, educators devised an instructional program that incorporated the *talk story,* a Hawaiian conversational form, into classroom literacy activities (Au & Kawakami, 1985; Au & Mason, 1981). A talk story is a rambling personal narrative in which two or more speakers work together to create and jointly perform the story. A good storyteller in this culture is someone who can draw others into the conversation, not someone who can hold the floor independently. As compared with traditional classroom recitation, the talk story reflects cooperative rather than individualistic cultural values and depends on collaborative instead of monologic patterns of interaction. Because children were familiar with the simultaneous speaking, interruptions, and shared creation that occur during talk story, they participated more readily. Also, teachers were able to spend more time discussing content rather than managing the interaction.

The use of talk stories allowed children in this community to bridge home and school literacy more easily. Introducing the talk story as a school form of discourse not only ensured children's access to instruction but also changed the relationship between teachers and children. The teacher's talk became less privileged, and children and the teacher had more equal conversational rights (Au, 1993). Another way to bridge home and school is to actively engage parents in children's literacy experiences. Studies have shown, for example, that Latino kindergarteners developed skills when teachers regularly sent home literacy materials in Spanish (Goldenberg et al., 2005).

When faced with a variety of cultural patterns, teachers can also use small-group and cooperative learning formats. Reciprocal-teaching approaches, like the one discussed in Chapter 3, also change classroom discourse patterns from teacher monologues to *instructional conversations* (Palinscar & David, 1991). These more student-centered approaches permit freer, more open dialogues between all students and the teacher and among peers (McCollum, 1991; Rogoff, et al., 2001). Such interactive learning does not occur in traditional classrooms where the teacher's role is to transmit information and the students' role is to recite correct answers.

Respecting students' ways of interacting and accepting them in the classroom help to establish a multicultural climate. But students still need to learn school-based ways of speaking in order to be successful. By providing many opportunities for interaction, during which students use familiar patterns but also are exposed to the unfamiliar school-based patterns, teachers can create a composite classroom culture (Au, 1993, Pérez, 2004a). Literacy learning is enhanced when old and new language patterns are integrated.

One of the most effective ways of creating a multicultural learning environment is to bring culturally diverse reading materials into the classroom, including some written in languages other than English. Education in the United States has been English-language dominant despite the fact that we are a multicultural and multilingual society. However, beginning in the 1960s, different ethnic and minority groups (including Cuban refugees, Hispanic immigrants, and African Americans) struggled intensely for equal access to education, with the result being the emergence of bilingual education.

Bilingual Education

As we have discussed, a growing number of students are coming to school from homes where a language other than English is spoken. When these students are not proficient in English, they need more than a culturally sensitive classroom environment. They need to acquire English as their second language in order to participate in mainstream American society. How do schools best serve these children? First, it is important to know that President Johnson signed into law the Bilingual Education Act of 1968 as Title VII of the Hawkins-Stafford Elementary and Secondary Education Act. This legislation was greatly influenced by an experimental program, funded by the Ford Foundation in 1963, to use Spanish in teaching Cuban children at the Coral Way Elementary School in Dade County, Florida. The academic success of this program spurred Hispanic groups nationwide to lobby for bilingual education programs. The Bilingual Education Act of 1968 provided guidelines for curriculum development, teacher training, and program monitoring and evaluation. The law did not stipulate that these programs needed to use the students' native language. By 1971, 30 states had legislation that allowed some type of bilingual education, and 50 states had permitted it by 1983. Although the Bilingual Act was reauthorized for funding in 1988, state legislation regarding bilingual programs has been allowed to lapse, has been repealed, has suffered budget cuts, or is undergoing review.

At issue today is how our schools can best serve students with limited proficiency in English. There are many approaches for serving English-learning students (Hakuta, 1999; Pérez, 2004b). One method is **bilingual education,** in which at least two languages are used for instruction. *Transitional bilingual* programs emphasize rapid transition from instruction in the child's native language into all-English instruction. *Maintenance bilingual* programs emphasize preservation of the child's native language and continued instruction through the

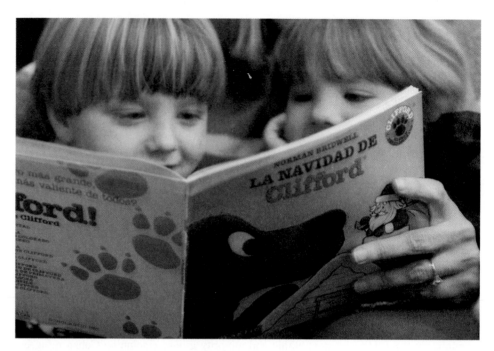

One way to create a multicultural learning environment is to include reading materials written in languages other than English.
Source: News & Observer.

elementary grades, with gradual development of English. Bilingual programs can also be characterized as *one-way* or *two-way*. One-way programs serve only limited-English-proficient (LEP) speakers; two-way or dual-language programs serve LEP and English-dominant speakers. Another popular approach is **English as a second language (ESL)** programs. Students in these programs spend time in receiving special instruction in English in special classrooms, then spend most of their day in a regular classroom. Another approach is **structured immersion,** in which children receive up to a year of intensive training in English before they are placed in an English-speaking classroom.

Although the advantages and disadvantages of each approach continue to be debated in the public policy arena, most language experts agree that some form of bilingual education is best for English-language learners. As you recall, it takes nearly 3 to 5 years to acquire oral proficiency in a language and considerably longer to gain the level of proficiency needed to learn in core subject areas (Garcia, 2000).

The most effective approaches in bilingual classrooms emphasize natural approaches to language development. Those factors that were critical in learning a first language, including active engagement, frequent experimenting, using language to communicate, and supportive adults, remain just as important in learning a second language.

Having a meaningful purpose for using language remains primary for second-language acquisition. For example, children often attempt to engage teachers and classmates in genuine communication by telling "stories" about their experiences of the previous day. Pérez and Torres-Guzmán (2002) suggest that teachers be "guided toward authenticity" by building biliteracy approaches on knowledge about children's development and their individual stories (p. 73). Talking about meaningful content is a far more effective way to practice speaking a language than working on isolated-skill exercises (Allen, 1986). Furthermore, when students are engaged in successful literacy tasks, such as storytelling or a class play, they are motivated to learn a new language.

Ideal classrooms provide language-rich environments in which bilingual learners are encouraged to interact with native speakers (Krashen & Terrell, 1983). Knowledge gained from frequent speaking and listening experiences will ease the transition to reading and writing. Teachers can organize daily classroom routines that require student leadership and participation, such as taking attendance and recording events on a class calendar (Pérez & Torres-Guzmán, 2002). Two types of informal writing have been used successfully with bilingual students: *dialogue journals,* in which students and teachers write back and forth about everyday issues, and *literature logs*, in which students record their personal reactions to reading materials (Reyes, 1995). In addition, cooperative group activities with more casual discourse patterns are beneficial. In such settings, bilingual learners gain practice speaking, they are able to participate successfully, and, consequently, their self-esteem is promoted (Long & Porter, 1985). Most important, using diverse reading materials that reflect particular cultures or individual histories will encourage bilingual learners to draw on background knowledge, making it easier to comprehend information and to participate in discussions (Au, 1993).

Creating a Positive Classroom Environment for Linguistically Diverse Students

Despite the shifting political views on bilingual education, the fact of the matter is that there is a large and growing population of students in the United States who are entering school with limited English proficiency. Also, few teacher education programs provide the necessary training for teaching linguistically diverse students. However, numerous reports in the last several years have identified a number of school- and classroom-level practices that can enhance the achievement of these students (see National Research Council, 1998; Pérez, 2004b).

At the school level, exemplary programs for English-language learners have a supportive school climate. There are high achievement expectations for all students, and their cultural and linguistic backgrounds are valued. Several teachers at these schools speak more than one language, and students are encouraged to develop and maintain their native language while becoming proficient in English. Not surprisingly, there is also strong educational leadership in exemplary schools for linguistically diverse learners. School principals play a key role in making the achievement of English-language learners a high priority. There is staff development to help all teachers, not just language specialists, to work effectively with these students. Additionally, there is a strong schoolwide commitment to involving parents in classroom and school activities and to fostering good communication between home and school. We will discuss various parent involvement strategies in Chapter 8.

At the classroom level, a number of instructional strategies can be used to raise the achievement of linguistically diverse learners. Some exemplary teaching strategies were demonstrated by Hellie and Lisa in the introductory vignettes. Other strategies are summarized in the Focus on Teaching box on page 328. As you know, there is no *one* way to teach diverse learners. Different approaches must be on page 327 used and customized for the diversity of students served and for different school conditions.

Focus on
Teaching

Effective Strategies for Teaching Linguistically Diverse Learners

- **Create truly bilingual classrooms.** Teachers provide literacy and content instruction for students in their native language while they are learning English. When children are able to learn in their native language, they are less likely to fall behind and they develop skills (e.g., decoding or comprehension skills) that can be transferred to English.

- **Incorporate dual-language strategies.** In dual-language learning environments, English-language learners learn content in their native language while learning English as a second language from English-speaking peers who are also learning a second language for enrichment. All students in this environment work toward becoming bilingual and biliterate.

- **Use integrated, whole-language approaches.** Students practice English in oral and written forms in ways that are meaningful, purposeful, engaging, and enjoyable. Rote drill-and-practice typically lacks meaning for young people. They must go beyond learning the rules of grammar to using their new language in real-life situations.

- **Use subject matter to teach language.** The learning of language cannot be separated from what is being learned. When students learn language in a functional way (similar to the way they learned their first language), the process has real meaning to them. Instead of removing an English-language learner from a lesson, that student can be paired with bilingual or monolingual students in small groups.

- **Use sheltered-language strategies.** Sheltered-language strategies make use of visuals and simple language. Similar to learning a first language, context cues and simple language structures facilitate comprehension. Teachers provide many examples and hands-on activities, so students can comprehend abstract as well as concrete instructions.

- **Practice English by solving problems in cooperative groups.** English-language learners learn more by being actively engaged in cooperative learning activities. Teachers can organize classrooms into flexible, heterogeneous, cooperative learning groups composed of native and nonnative English speakers in order to provide students with opportunities to practice English in problem-solving situations.

- **Use cross-age and peer tutoring.** Use cross-age tutoring and peer tutoring to enhance literacy and language acquisition. Research shows that learning is enhanced both for those who are tutored and for the tutors themselves. In bilingual programs, roles between the tutee and tutor can be switched depending on the content of the learning activity.

- **Respect community language norms.** Teachers demonstrate respect for each student's language and do not prevent bilingual students from alternating between English and their native language (code switching) while they work together. The most important consideration in teaching is that communication is accomplished.

- **Use thematic interdisciplinary teaching.** English-language learners learn content with greater comprehension if their learning is interdisciplinary. New learning is incremental and added to a theme the students already understand. Having a base vocabulary related to the theme enables students to make connections across disciplines.

- **Use computers and peer tutors to enhance language learning.** Teachers who create situations in which two students can use a common computer enable students to learn English as a second language more readily. Working together, students can work on problems, conduct electronic searches, create multimedia presentations, write stories, make revisions, and correct vocabulary and grammar. Simple drill-and-practice that is easier for English-language learners should be avoided.

Source: After Cole (1995).

■ Chapter Summary

Language Development

- Language acquisition is a process that researchers cannot completely explain. Several theories have been proposed, including the behaviorist, the maturationist, and the interactionist. Although each theory has limitations, the interactionist, which combines elements of the other two, provides the most comprehensive and flexible account of how children acquire language. Interactional theory proposes that language structures evolve as a result of the interplay between a child's internal mental structures and the external social world, where interaction with others is primary.

- Children acquire spoken language without direct instruction and within a relatively short time. Around the age of 2, children begin saying individual words, then combining two words, and moving on to multiple-word phrases and sentences. By the age of 7, a native speaker will know about 90 percent of the grammatical structures of English. Being social creatures, children have a natural urge to learn language in order to communicate their thoughts and desires to others.

- School-age children learn to engage in more effective interaction with others, focusing their attention on *how* to use language. Adolescents further develop their linguistic abilities and skills in adapting their language to different situations.

- If children grow up in a family or community in which two languages are spoken, then they will likely grow up bilingual. Young children are capable of learning several languages simultaneously without confusion. It may take longer for a child to construct grammars for several languages at once, but the method of acquisition and pattern of development are exactly the same for a child learning only one language. Older children and adults learning second languages experience different patterns of acquisition.

- Language and communication disorders are often identified in elementary school, and are associated with many academic problems. Classroom teachers and speech and language specialists can adapt learning activities in a natural classroom context to encourage development of skills.

Literacy Development

- Literacy is the ability to construct and express meaning through reading, writing, and discussing texts.

- In a literate culture, children learn about the characteristics and processes of reading and writing from birth, a developmental process called emergent literacy. Through experience with books, preschoolers learn that print carries meaning, recognize letters and words, and can mimic true reading by reciting memorized stories.

- Children make progress with writing and reading when they develop phonemic awareness and develop self-conscious knowledge about how the print represents spoken language, along with other skills.

- Social context has the greatest effect on whether a person becomes a proficient reader and writer. A literate environment, whether it is in a child care facility, a school, or the home, is one in which children's experiences with print are for authentic purposes and in which adults value and participate in reading and writing themselves.

- Reading is a complex process during which the reader translates print into words, comprehends and predicts meaning, and interacts emotionally with the characters or events of the story. Decoding is the process of determining equivalence with written words. Comprehension is the active process of ascribing meaning to a message. Comprehension depends on the reader's ability to use syntactic, semantic, and pragmatic information in order to make sense of what is written on the page.

- Three approaches to reading instruction are common. In the specific-skills approach, a teacher directly teaches various decoding and comprehension skills using an explicit, often deductive, method of instruction. The holistic language approach purports that children inductively learn and develop specific reading abilities based on extensive and varied experiences with print. Third, the integrated or balanced approach assumes that children must be engaged in authentic (meaningful) literacy activities but also must learn specific skills.

■ When learning to write, children first experiment with sounds and letters. Their invented spelling increases children's fluency and makes it easier for them to compose.

■ Composing is a complex process that includes planning, drafting, revising, editing, and publishing. Children normally work on the mechanical aspects of writing (e.g., spelling) before focusing on perfecting the writing process. Since revision entails considering the needs of the audience and being distanced from the text, it is the most difficult part of the process to learn. In the upper grades and high school, children become more self-regulatory and proficient with expository writing and use writing as a way of learning in the academic disciplines.

Culture and Literacy

■ A person's language, dialect, or manner of speaking reflects his or her social, economic, and cultural background. A dialect is variation of a single language spoken by members of a speech community. The language of instruction in schools, sometimes called standard American English (SAE), is often not the dialect of English spoken in children's speech communities. A teacher can help children become bidialectal and function effectively in different social settings.

■ Multicultural education refers to teaching that relies on culturally relevant materials and school curriculums that reflect the beliefs, traditions, and contributions of all people in an ethnically diverse society.

■ Children who are able to speak, read, or write some English in addition to their native language are considered bilingual learners. Many bilingual children have limited English proficiency (LEP). Some bilingual programs are designed to move children into English-dominant classrooms, whereas other programs attempt to teach English and to maintain a home language such as Spanish. Bilingual education programs reflect multicultural awareness.

■ Key Terms

alphabetic system *(p. 287)*
bilingual *(p. 276)*
bilingual education *(p. 325)*
communicative competence *(p. 273)*
comprehension *(p. 300)*
context knowledge *(p. 299)*
critical period hypothesis *(p. 260)*
decoding *(p. 299)*
dialect *(p. 320)*
emergent literacy *(p. 284)*
English as a second language (ESL) *(p. 326)*
functionally literate *(p. 317)*
grammar *(p. 256)*
holophrases *(p. 269)*

ideographic system *(p. 287)*
infant-directed speech (IDS) *(p. 265)*
intersubjectivity *(p. 267)*
invented spelling *(p. 309)*
language *(p. 254)*
language acquisition device (LAD) *(p. 259)*
literacy *(p. 254)*
language acquisition support system (LASS) *(p. 264)*
metalinguistic awareness *(p. 276)*
phonemic awareness *(p. 287)*
phonic knowledge *(p. 299)*
reading readiness approach *(p. 285)*

receptive language *(p. 269)*
sight word knowledge *(p. 299)*
simultaneous bilinguals *(p. 277)*
standard American English (SAE) *(p. 320)*
structured immersion *(p. 326)*
successive bilingualism *(p. 278)*
syntax *(p. 259)*
telegraphic speech *(p. 270)*
transactional strategies instruction (TSI) *(p. 319)*
whole language *(p. 302)*
writing across the curriculum *(p. 316)*

■ Activities

1. Children's language development is supported by interaction with others, especially with parents or caregivers. Audiotape or videotape a child between the ages of 2 and 3 in a social setting for at least an hour. (Taping several shorter sessions is also an option.) Describe or analyze the following, based on your observation.
   a. The child's stage of language development, using specific examples from your data.
   b. The role of other people in structuring or shaping the child's language. Refer to a conversation or verbal interaction between the child and adult (or older child) in addressing this issue.

2. Test out your teaching intuitions by finding a child who is just learning to read (usually a first grader). Spend three half-hour sessions with the child, if possible. In the first session, design some way of assessing the child's current decoding skills. For example, does the child know letter–sound correspondences? Then plan and teach two sessions on some aspect of decoding appropriate for the child. Try varied teaching methods, such as games, big books, physical activities, or language experience stories. (For teaching ideas, see *Language, Literacy, and the Child* [Galda et al., 1993] or *Reading and Learning to Read* [Vacca et al., 1995], or any reading methods textbook.) Tape the sessions so you have a record of what you have taught. Finally, assess what the child learned, what strategy or activity proved most helpful, and your strengths as a teacher.

3. By the time students reach middle and high school, they are writing in a variety of modes as well as writing to learn in all content areas, from math to history. Conduct a survey to discover the amount and type of writing a student accomplishes in a single school day. You can approach the survey in different ways. You might shadow a student for the day, keeping track of when, what kind, in what class, and for how much time the student writes that day. Or you might prepare a questionnaire using the modes of writing found in Figure 5.9, and survey a larger sample of students from one school for a day or even for a week. You might compile your findings with other students in your college class who are conducting the same survey. Write a brief report on the nature and extent of writing required of older students. You might compare your results with those reported by Applebee (1981).

4. As children grow older, differences between their spoken and written language become more pronounced. To discover how significant these differences are, collect spoken and written language samples from a child in either middle school or high school. Tape-record a 20-minute conversation between you and the child. Prepare for the spoken session by thinking of some questions to ask, particularly ones that will elicit extended responses. You could ask the child to tell you the plot of his or her favorite movie, book, or television show, for example. For the child's written language, ask the child for permission to copy several pieces of his or her writing from school. Book reports, descriptive essays, or literary analyses are all possibilities. Transcribe at least 5 minutes of the spoken session. Write a brief report comparing and contrasting the spoken and written samples, but consider sentence structure and word choice in particular.

5. For a class project, ask students to make up a list of any slang terms they know associated with a sport they play, a club or group they belong to, or a particular field of interest, such as computers. Students can then compare lists with both members in the same group and different groups. They can account for differences and similarities as well as make some generalizations about why slang exists.

CHAPTER

6

Self-Concept, Identity, and Motivation

CHAPTER OUTLINE

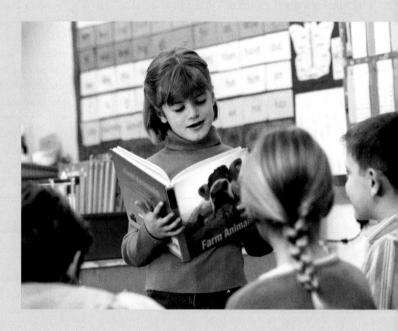

ROY WAS A 16-YEAR-OLD AFRICAN AMERICAN STUDENT IN MY *fourth-period Algebra II class. He was a very popular student and a star football and basketball player. On our first quiz, Roy made an A, showing me that he had high ability in conceptually understanding mathematics. (Today, Roy would probably say that doing well on that first quiz was his biggest mistake because after that day, I would not let him slide by.) I tried to get Roy to participate in class, but day after day he pretended to not care about his assignments. He even went so far as to pretend he did not understand what was going on in class, even though I knew fully well he understood everything we were covering. Roy stopped turning in homework and made a C on the next quiz due to skipping some of the questions. I soon contacted Roy's mother and scheduled a parent–teacher conference. During the meeting, Roy informed me that he would never participate in class or act like he could do the math because that would be too humiliating for him in front of his friends and peers. Roy and his mother asked that I stop pressuring him to explain things in front of his peers if Roy promised to complete his homework and do his best on exams. Reluctantly I agreed to these terms, and Roy passed Algebra II with an A. Although this was a positive turn-of-events for Roy, I still question whether I should have let him "act dumb" in my class. Unfortunately, Roy decided to take a lower-level mathematics class the following year. Most of his friends were in this course with him. I tried to convince Roy, his mother, and the chair of the math department that he needed to be in an upper-level math course, but I was overruled.*
—*High School Mathematics Teacher*

This description of a 10th-grade student demonstrates the difficulty adolescents experience in forming a student identity. On the one hand, Roy is very capable and his teacher recognizes and wants to support his competence and learning. On the other hand, Roy must balance his own self-perceptions with behaviors perceived as appropriate for his own ethnic group. The case clearly shows that the school and classroom environment is an important setting for the construction of one's identity, not only as a student but as a member of an ethnic group. In this chapter, we will learn that minority students sometimes experience conflict between achieving in school and minority group status. Like Roy, some students will put less effort into their studies to remain connected to an ethnic group at school. We will also learn that there are many different pathways for the development of ethnic identity. Teachers and the school environment play a very important role in helping students stay engaged and interested in learning. Roy's experiences in the classroom are an important reminder that schools teach young people more than cognitive and language skills. Schools are places where children develop a sense of self-worth, identify their strengths and weaknesses, and form an identity for the future.

Schools also play an important role in the development of children's social and emotional competence. Young people who are socially and emotionally competent have a better chance of succeeding in school and in later life (Eisenberg, Fabes, & Spinrad, 2006; Huffman, Mehlinger, & Kerivan, 2000; Miles & Stipek, 2006; Pianta, Rimm-Kaufman, & Cox, 1999; Pianta & Stulman, 2004). They exhibit confidence, self-control, motivation, and persistence. They have a positive sense of self and plans for the future. They also have good interpersonal skills that include an ability to read social and emotional cues, to take the perspective of others, and to form positive social relations.

In this chapter, we begin to consider several important aspects of children's social and emotional development. We first discuss Erikson's theory of psychosocial development as a framework for understanding the developmental needs of young people in school settings. Next, we discuss several important foundations of children's social and emotional development—forming a secure attachment, understanding and expressing emotions, and learning self-control. In later sections we explore the development of self-concept, identity, and motivation, and what role schools play in this development.

Erikson's Theory of Psychosocial Development

Developmental psychologist Erik Erikson (1963) provided a framework for understanding children's psychosocial development. The Focus on Development box provides a brief overview of this stage theory. Erikson was one of the first life-span theorists, because he believed that development is a lifelong process. Like Freud, he emphasized the importance of feelings and social relationships in a person's development. However, Erikson placed much more emphasis on social than biological influences in his theory. Although Erikson believed there are certain basic needs common to all people, he maintained that personal relationships and societal expectations influence the way we respond to those needs. For example, all infants must form a sense of trust for healthy development, but in some cultures infants spend as much time with substitute caregivers as with their own parents. Similarly, all children begin to "separate" from their caregivers when they become more mobile, but cultural norms may determine how much independence and freedom children are given at a young age.

According to Erikson's theory, children continually face new developmental tasks or issues they must somehow resolve as they mature. Erikson identified a positive and a negative outcome for each developmental stage (e.g., trust versus mistrust), and he believed that an unhealthy resolution of a particular issue could impair later development. For instance, a baby who does not develop trusting relationships during infancy may experience difficulty separating from caregivers during his or her second year. The potential for this outcome reflects Erikson's belief that the social environment largely influences how well a person's developmental needs are satisfied at each stage.

Stages of Development

Our discussion of Erikson's theory will focus mainly on the developmental stages of most concern to teachers. During infancy children must form a basic sense of trust as the foundation for later development. Children will form this trust in the first stage of development, *trust versus mistrust,* if their basic needs for food, care, and comfort are met in a sensitive and consistent manner. When children have a basic trust in their environment, they are more likely to explore and to "move away" from caregivers during the second stage of development, *autonomy versus shame and doubt.* During this stage, children require less physical contact from caregivers and begin such activities as walking, feeding, and toileting on their own. If children are unable to master some aspects of their environment or to live up to parental expectations, they may begin to doubt their ability to manage their world. In Erikson's view, infancy lays a foundation for the development of self-esteem and self-efficacy, which we will discuss later in this chapter.

Early and middle childhood are important periods for the development of self-control, initiative, and purpose. At ages 3 to 6, children attempt to resolve the conflicts associated with Erikson's third stage, *initiative versus guilt.* Developing a sense of initiative involves the "quality of undertaking, planning, and attacking a task for the sake of being active and

Erikson's Stages of Psychosocial Development

Focus on
Development

Age	Stage	Developmental Task
Birth to 1 year	Trust vs. mistrust	Children must develop a basic sense of trust or confidence that their world is predictable and safe. Their basic needs are met by sensitive and responsive caregivers.
1 to 3 years	Autonomy vs. shame and doubt	Children must develop a will of their own and sense of independence from caregivers. Their basic needs are met by caregivers who encourage independence and autonomy but do not force or shame them.
3 to 5 years	Initiative vs. guilt	Children must develop a sense of purpose and direction as their social world expands. They are asked to assume more responsibility for their actions. Their basic needs are met if caregivers do not demand too much self-control that can lead to guilt feelings when children cannot live up to parental expectations.
6 to 10 years	Industry vs. inferiority	Children must develop a capacity to work and cooperate with others as they enter school. They must direct their energies toward mastering academic skills and feeling pride in their successes. Children's basic needs are met when caregivers help them to find their special competencies.
10 to 20 years	Identity vs. role confusion	Adolescents must find out who they are, what they value, and a direction for their lives. Adolescents' basic needs are met when they are given opportunities to explore alternative options and roles for the future.
Early adulthood	Intimacy vs. isolation	Young adults must form intimate relationships with others. Intimacy involves finding oneself yet losing oneself in others. Because of early experiences, some people may not be able to form close relationships, and remain isolated from others.
Middle adulthood	Generativity vs. stagnation	Adults must find a way to give to the next generation through child rearing, caring for others, or productive work. The person who fails in these ways feels an absence of meaning in life.
Late adulthood	Integrity vs. despair	Older adults must reflect on their lives and evaluate their contributions and accomplishments and the kind of person they have been. Integrity results from feeling that life was satisfying and worth living.

on the move" (Erikson, 1963, p. 255). Preschoolers are clearly on the move, but they must learn that they cannot act on all their impulses. Young children must learn to balance their actions with those of others. However, if children are not allowed to take the initiative, or if they are constantly told what they do is wrong, they may develop a strong sense of guilt and avoid initiating actions on their own.

During the elementary school years, children develop what Erikson called a sense of industry. In the *industry versus inferiority* stage, children begin to identify their strengths and to take pleasure in their accomplishments. If children are not supported in their efforts, or if they are unable to live up to the expectations of others, they may develop feelings of inferiority or inadequacy. In later sections, we will learn that many children begin to develop more negative attitudes about their abilities and to experience declines in motivation as they move from childhood to adolescence.

Perhaps Erikson's most important theoretical contribution was his view of identity development in adolescence. During adolescence, young people enter the stage of *identity versus role confusion.* Forming an **identity** involves committing oneself to a set of beliefs, values, and adult roles. Having formed a basic sense of self, Erikson believed that young people begin to struggle with such questions as Who am I? What makes me unique? What is important to me? What do I want to do with my life? Adolescents who avoid these questions experience a state of role confusion. This "identity crisis" is undoubtedly triggered by physical changes that occur during adolescence, but society also demands that adolescents behave in new ways. They must begin to be more responsible and make decisions for themselves. In adolescence, young people must prepare for adulthood, which means figuring out what role they will play in the adult world. Although this may have seemed true when Erikson did his research in the 1940s and 1950s, more recent evidence suggests that the search for identity continues well into the adult years. Research further suggests that adolescents who commit to an identity early, without taking time to explore various options and choices, may question their commitments later on. We often make fun of adolescents who are having an identity crisis of one sort or another, but most theorists believe that young people should delay making commitments to an occupation, belief system, intimate relationship, or lifestyle until they have had an opportunity to explore different perspectives and options. Some adolescents, however, are not given the opportunity to experiment with adult roles because of family expectations or economic necessity.

Limitations and Contributions of Erikson's Theory

Erikson provides a useful framework for understanding psychosocial development. His theory helps us to understand the importance of stable and caring relationships in early development, the need for self-sufficiency and competency in the middle childhood years, and the search for identity in adolescence. However, Erikson's theory has several limitations that need to be considered. First, his theory was based on studies of men, and the focus on identity development may come later, or take a different form, for women (Gilligan, 1982; Josselson, 1987). Moreover, Erikson's theory emphasized the importance of autonomy and independence as desirable goals for development. This view of development is deeply rooted in American individualism (Rothbaum, Weisz, Pott, Miyake, & Morelli, 2000). Not all cultures encourage the development of autonomy and individualism in their young people. For example, parents of Asian, Mexican, or African American heritage are more likely to value collectivist values such as interdependence, group solidarity, and family obligations (Phinney, Ong, Madden, 2000; Triandis, 1990, 1995). European American parents encourage less interdependence in their children than do parents in collectivist cultures (Greenfield & Cocking, 1994; Greenfield, Keller, Fuligini, & Maynard, 2003; Okagaki & Sternberg, 1993).

Keeping these limitations in mind, let's consider some implications of Erikson's theory for education. First, his theory makes clear that children need a secure school environment and caring relationships with adults in order to maintain the sense of trust needed for personal development. Ideally, schools should offer students opportunities to initiate new activities and to feel a sense of accomplishment from a job well done. Students also need opportunities to find their unique strengths and to develop them. More important, students need opportunities to learn about different viewpoints and career options as they begin their search for identity. Unfortunately, schools often restrict children's personal development by undermining children's sense of competency, by reinforcing cultural stereotypes, or by limiting young people's options for the future. We will discuss some of these constraints later in the chapter.

 ## Foundations of Social and Emotional Development

Early Temperament

Look around any classroom, and you will see differences in children's activity levels, sociability, reactions to stress, and irritability. Some childhood experts believe that these behaviors reflect temperamental differences that can be traced back to early infancy. Originally, *infant temperament* referred to such observable behaviors such as activity level, regularity, moods, adaptability, responsiveness, distractibility, and attention span (Thomas & Chess, 1977). More recent studies of **temperament** have included self-regulatory processes, which involve the ability to inhibit responses, shift attention, and manage emotions (Buss & Plomin, 1984; Rothbart & Bates, 1998, 2006). While there is growing consensus about the dimensions of temperament, questions remain concerning its origins and long-term influence on development.

Alexander Thomas and Stella Chess (1977) developed one of the first influential models of infant temperament. They interviewed parents of 141 infants, and asked them to provide detailed descriptions of their infants' behaviors, routines, and moods. By analyzing parental interviews, the researchers found that behavioral patterns fell into three categories:

- The *easy child* (40 percent of sample): This infant had regular biological routines (eating, sleeping, eliminating, etc.), adapted easily to change, and displayed positive moods.
- The *difficult child* (10 percent of sample): This infant had irregular biological routines, adjusted slowly to new routines, and reacted intensely and negatively to new routines and experiences.
- The *slow-to-warm-up child* (15 percent of the sample): This child had fairly regular biological routines, showed low-to-mild reactions to new experiences, but slowly accepted them with repeated exposure.

It is noteworthy that the categories represented only 60 percent of the sample. Other children showed a combination of the different categories. Nevertheless, this pioneering research on infant temperament identified groups of children who later showed difficulty when they entered school. For example, children showing the "difficult" pattern in infancy were at greater risk than the other groups for adjustment problems in early and middle childhood. By contrast, the "easy" infants tended to show fewer of these difficulties later in development (Thomas, Chess, & Birch, 1968).

Several additional models of temperament have been introduced since this early work on temperament. Arnold Buss and Robert Plomin (1984) characterized early temperament in terms of four broad dimensions that were likely to endure into adulthood due to a high degree of heritability. The first dimension, *emotionality,* refers to the intensity of the child's negative emotional arousal, such as irritability and distress. *Activity* includes the vigor and tempo of the child's verbal and behavioral responses, and *sociability* is seen as the child's responsiveness to others. The fourth dimension, *impulsivity,* includes a broad range of behaviors such as emotional and behavioral control, discipline, and persistence (Buss, 1995).

More recent models of infant temperament, developed by Mary Rothbart and John Bates (1998, 2006), have focused on variations in reactivity and self-regulation among infants. Reactivity refers to variations in quickness, duration, and intensity of motor, emotional, and attentional responses, whereas self-regulation refers to the processes used to control, inhibit, or modulate responses to stimulation (Rothbart & Bates, 1998). Additionally, these recent conceptions of infant temperament have provided a more differentiated view of emotionality that includes (Rothbart & Bates, 1998, 2006):

- Positive affect (e.g., smiling, warmth, sociability)
- Fearful distress (e.g., anxiety, withdrawl, distress related to new situations)
- Irritable distress (e.g., fussiness, anger, frustration)

Taken together, studies of temperament have identified important differences in emotional and behavioral functioning quite early in development. Because differences are detected so early in development, temperament is believed to have some biological basis due to genetics, maturation, or early experiences (Buss & Plomin, 1984; Caspi & Shiner, 2006; Rothbart & Bates, 1998). Researchers also believe that individual differences in early temperament play a role in later development (Buss & Plomin, 1984; Caspi, 1998; Chess & Thomas, 1977; Thompson, 1999).

What are the effects of infant temperament on later emotional or social development? In general, assessments of temperament in early infancy are not very reliable in predicting the same dimension later in development. By the end of the first year, some short-term stability can be observed in certain characteristics such as fear, positive emotionality, and attention span (Thompson, 1999). In a large longitudinal study of 800 children, Caspi and Silva (1995) also found significant relations between temperament at age 3 and personality traits in adolescence. Specifically, children who were inhibited were cautious and restrained as adolescents. Some evidence also suggests that inhibited and fearful children may experience problems with social relations and with anxiety in middle childhood and adolescence (Caspi, 1998; Kagan, 1998). By contrast, those children who were impulsive, irritable, and distractible early in development were more likely to have behavioral problems such as aggression and noncompliance later on (Caspi, 1998; Eisenberg & Fabes, 1998). More recently, Bridget Hamre and Robert Pianta (2001) found that teachers' ratings of relational negativity, defined as conflict and dependency, at entry to kindergarten were related to academic and behavior measures through the eighth grade. Patterns of associations were particularly strong for children displaying problem behaviors in kindergarten and for boys in general. However, not all studies report strong continuity between early temperament and later development, and the enduring effect of early temperamental differences remains an issue of considerable debate (Caspi & Shiner, 2006; Thompson, 1999). As we have discussed previously, development is a complex interaction of genetic predispositions and environmental experiences.

In summary, it is important to understand that children differ in temperamental characteristics. Some children may be more predisposed than others to be sociable, emotionally expressive, reactive, impulsive, or withdrawn. A child who is shy or impulsive may need extra support in the classroom. The Focus on Teaching box suggests some ways teachers can help shy and withdrawn children in the classroom. As we will learn in the next section, the continuity of temperamental characteristics in children's development is significantly influenced by their interactions with caring adults and by environmental events.

Helping Shy Children in the Classroom

Shyness may be defined as a feeling of insecurity or discomfort during social situations. Symptoms of shyness include inhibition, avoidance of feared or new situations, low speaking voice, gaze aversion, nervous behaviors, and excessive smiling or nodding (Encyclopedia of Mental Health, 2001). Many children exhibit shyness at some point in their life. Common episodes of shyness occur when children enter into novel social situations, but most children overcome their shyness with continued exposure to the new experience. For example, nearly all children will exhibit symptoms of shyness on the first day of a new school year. Within a few days, however, most children become comfortable in their surroundings, feel less vulnerable, and thus lose their shy tendencies.

Shyness becomes a problem when it keeps children from engaging in social activities in which they would like to take part. Unlike introverts who prefer solitary activities, shy children state a preference for being with others and joining in social activities but are unable to do so due to feelings of self-consciousness during these episodes. Although there is no conclusive evidence tying shyness in childhood to anxiety disorders during adolescence or adulthood, most educators believe that helping younger children overcome their shyness will negate some of the adverse effects of shyness, such as having fewer friends than outgoing children and not developing or practicing appropriate social skills.

Focus on Teaching

Jere Brophy (1996), an educational researcher, has suggested some strategies for helping shy or withdrawn students in the classroom. He emphasizes using the influence of peers in addressing this issue. Opportunities for schoolwide peer involvement include cross-age tutoring and play groups as well as cooperative learning groups within the classroom. Teachers can also play a part in responding to shy children. Brophy (1995) studied how effective teachers relate to shy children in their classrooms. He found that effective teachers try to change shy students' social environment, encourage student responsiveness while minimizing angst, involve students in special activities, and talk with shy students one-on-one.

John Malouff (2000), a clinical psychologist, has also studied shyness in children and uses social learning theory as a basis for strategies that will help children overcome shyness. Some of Malouff's suggestions to parents and teachers are to (1) tell children your personal experiences about being shy, (2) inform children about the advantages of being more outgoing, (3) never label a child as shy, (4) set easily attainable goals for becoming more outgoing and chart progress, (5) model outgoing behavior, (6) praise both shy and outgoing children for outgoing behavior, and (7) give students opportunities to practice interacting with others.

Quality of Parent–Child Relations

Children's social and emotional development is firmly rooted in early relations with parents and other caregivers. In infancy, the term **attachment** is used to refer to the close, affective relationship formed between a child and one or more caregivers. Secure attachment relationships enable children to develop what Erikson called a "basic sense of trust." With rare exception, infants form an attachment with a caregiver, but not all infants form secure attachments (Ainsworth, Blehar, Waters, & Wall, 1978; Barnett & Vonda, 1999; Main & Solomon, 1990).

Mary Ainsworth was the first developmental researcher to study differences in the quality of attachments infants form with their caregivers. She created a laboratory procedure, known as the **Strange Situation,** in which a caregiver and child experience episodes of separation and reunion. At one point in the procedure, the baby is left alone, and during another separation episode, the infant is left with a stranger. On the basis of the infant's reactions to the repeated separations and reunions, Ainsworth and her colleagues (1978) distinguished three different classifications of attachment quality:

- **Securely attached**—these infants showed distress when separated from their mothers but were readily calmed or soothed by the mother's return.
- **Insecure-avoidant**—these infants appeared indifferent to the departure of their mothers from the room and avoided their mothers when they returned.
- **Insecure-resistant**—these infants displayed high levels of distress during the separation episodes but responded with ambivalence when their mothers returned.
- **Insecure-disorganized**—these infants showed the greatest degree of confusion, disorientation, and insecurity during separation and reunion episodes.

Although early attachment research focused on mother–infant attachments, it is important to emphasize that infants form attachments with fathers and other people with whom they have regular contact. In fact, most infants develop multiple attachments. Research suggests that infants show equal attachment to their mothers and fathers (Lamb, 1997). As children mature, they often develop attachments with siblings and peers. Studies of preschool children have shown that children experience a range of reactions when they are transferring to a new school or being left behind (Field, 1986). Reactions may include changes in eating and sleeping habits, as well as negative affect, increased irritability, and other symptoms associated with separation distress or loss.

What explains variations in attachment relations? Various factors have been linked to the development of secure or insecure attachment between caregivers and their infants. Perhaps the most crucial influence arises from the pattern of interactions that develops between caregiver and child. Parental warmth and responsiveness foster positive interactions and set the stage for children to develop a sense of confidence in their relationships with caregivers. Parents who are consistently available and responsive to a child's needs foster the development of secure attachment, whereas parents who are inconsistently available, unavailable, or rejecting often have insecurely attached babies (Cassidy & Berlin, 1994). These parents may have serious financial or emotional problems that make it difficult to provide for their children's needs. Changing family circumstances, such as loss of income and the experience of poverty, could undermine parenting to the point of disturbing the development of attachment (Shaw & Vondra, 1993).

As previously discussed, infants differ in their temperamental characteristics. Some babies are happy, adaptable, and calm, whereas others cry and fuss a lot, eat and sleep irregularly, and become easily distressed or upset in new situations. Consistent with this view, some evidence suggests that mothers of highly irritable infants provided less physical contact than mothers of less irritable babies (Clakins, Hungerford, & Dedmon, 2004; Van den Boom & Hoeksma, 1994). Still other evidence suggests that there is a great deal of variability in how caregivers respond to temperamentally difficult infants. The quality of care depends on other factors such as level of social support (Crockenberg, 1986) and economic hardship (Van den Boom, & Hoeksma, 1994).

Attachment relations are also shaped by the larger cultural context. In Japan, for example, young children are rarely separated from their mothers in their first year. Japanese infants respond with more distress when placed in the Ainsworth's Strange Situation because both mothers and infants have less experience with separations and reunions. Thus, researchers have recently questioned the cross-cultural validity of the attachment theory (Rothbaum et al., 2000). Conclusions about attachment relations are primarily based on white, middle-class samples from the United States. Moreover, the assumptions underlying attachment theory reflect a Western view of children's development that defines social competence in terms of separation, self-reliance, and efficacy. Attachment relations take a different form in cultures that value relatedness more than independence (Rothbaum et al., 2000). It is

Focus on Development

Attachment Classification and Later Developmental Outcomes (Ages 2 to 5)

Attachment Classification	Developmental Outcomes
Securely attached	Engages in more pretend and imaginative play Shows more flexibility in handling feelings Shows more independence and self-reliance Shows more enthusiasm and persistence in problem solving Shows greater social competence with peers and more compliance with adults Shows higher quality of friendships with peers Shows lower risk for becoming a bully or the victim of a bully
Insecurely attached	Engages in less symbolic play Less compliant with adults Less autonomous functioning More conflicts with friends Lower-quality friendships with peers Higher frequency of behavior problems Increased risk of becoming a bully or a victim of a bully

Sources: Jacabvitz & Sroufe (1987); Sroufe (1982); Sroufe, Fox, & Pancake (1983); Thompson (1998); and Troy & Sroufe (1987).

important to remember these limitations as we discuss the long-term impact of attachment relations on children's development.

What implications does a child's attachment have for later development? It is the first affectionate relationship that children form, and attachment theorists believe it serves as an important foundation for developing the self, emotions, and morality (Thompson, 1999). From early attachment relations, children begin to construct an "internal model" of the self and their social relationships that includes the roots of self-esteem and security. Securely attached children form a model of caregivers as available and responsive, and the self as worthy of care. These beliefs and expectations are "carried forward" to future relationships with other adults and with peers and siblings.

A substantial amount of research has explored the impact of attachment on children's later development in a variety of domains. Some of the findings are summarized in the Focus on Development box. In general, secure attachment measured at one point in development tends to bode well for children's later social relationships with peers, teachers, and others, whereas children identified as insecurely attached show problems in their interpersonal skills and the quality of their social relationships.

It also important to note that parent–child attachment relations are also associated with the development of competencies needed for school success. Differences in curiosity, attention, problem-solving behavior, persistence, and motivation have all been linked to the quality of children's early attachments (Birch & Ladd, 1996; Pianta & Harbers, 1996; Sroufe, 1996). Measures of school adjustment (e.g., social competence, peer popularity, and self-esteem) have also been linked to the quality of children's early attachment relations (Sroufe, 1983, 1989). For example, one study showed that boys classified as insecurely attached to their mothers were rated by their teachers as less competent and as having a greater number of

Focus on
Teaching

Teacher–Student Relations and School Adjustment

Teachers often assume a parental role with children. Like parent–child relationships, children's relations with teachers vary in quality. Some relationships are close and affectionate, whereas others are distant or conflictual (Hamre & Pianta, 2001; Howes, & Matheson, 1992; Pianta, Steinberg, & Rollins, 1995). Just as children's early attachment relations can affect later development, a growing body of research suggests that the quality of teacher–student relations can affect school adjustment and achievement.

Robert Pianta and his colleagues have studied associations between teacher–student relations and school outcomes in the school years. Using teacher reports, they found that teacher–student relations can be reliably characterized in terms of closeness, conflict, and dependency (Pianta, 1994; Pianta & Steinberg, 1992; Howes, 2000). Findings further showed that changes in teacher–student relations from year to year affected students' school adjustment. Increased conflict negatively affected school adjustment, whereas increased closeness had a positive influence. For children at high risk for grade retention or special education placement, a close teacher–student relationship functioned as a protective factor by offsetting negative consequences.

Although this research focused on the early elementary grades, students' supportive and caring relations

with teachers are essential for promoting optimal development throughout the school years. Teachers who demonstrate that they care about their students are in a better position to gain cooperation from them and to maintain students' interest in learning (Mantzicopoulos, 2005; Midgley, Feldlaufer, & Eccles, 1989; Noddings, 1992; Phelan, Davidson, & Yu, 1998). Yet studies indicate that students may experience declines in the quality of their relationships with teachers as they progress in school, which can have a negative impact on motivation, achievement, and school engagement (Feldlaufer, Midgley, & Eccles, 1988; Midgley et al., 1989; Wentzel, 1996, 2002).

How can teachers maintain good relations with students? In a study of middle school students, Kathryn Wentzel (1997) explored students' perceptions of caring, supportive teachers. The following dimensions characterized these teachers: (1) They cared about their own teaching and made a special effort to engage their students; (2) they recognized students' strengths and weaknesses, and treated students as individuals; and (3) they listened to students and showed an interest in their concerns. In general, teachers who support students' learning and achievement share many characteristics with nurturing and supportive parents.

behavior problems than boys with secure attachments (Cohn, 1990). Thus, considerable evidence suggests that children's school experiences are more productive and positive when they have a solid base of emotional security. Later in this chapter, we will learn that a *sense of relatedness* (Connell, 1990) at school is important for students adjustment, motivation, and academic engagement (see also Chapter 9).

Finally, as previously described, children form multiple attachments. In Chapter 1, we learned that roughly half of preschool-aged children (ages 3–4) are enrolled in some type of preprimary program. Kathryn Wentzel (2002) has argued that effective teachers share many characteristics with "good" parents. Consistent with this view, there is growing evidence that the quality of children's relationships with teachers plays an important role in their early and later school adjustment and achievement. Interestingly, there is a moderate degree of continuity in the quality of relationships children have with caregivers at home and at school, and positive relations with teachers help to promote school adjustment (peer competencies, ability to comply with adults, ability to work independently, etc.) from preschool through high school. The Focus on Teaching box highlights research on the role of teacher–student relations in school adjustment. A more detailed discussion of teacher–student relations is included in Chapter 9.

Understanding and Expressing Emotions

Young people experience different emotions at school. They feel happy with a good grade, they feel excited about a school production, they feel anxious about a test, they feel angry when teased, and so forth. As these examples imply, **emotions** are subjective reactions to events and experiences. They are generally experienced cognitively as pleasant or unpleasant, and are accompanied by some form of physiological change or overt behavioral response (Izard, 1991). Taking a different approach, recent theories maintain that emotions serve to energize certain actions to achieve a goal (Saarni, Mumme, & Campos, 1998). This view of emotional development, referred to as a functional approach, proposes that emotions represent responses to situational demands and serve as important regulators of behavior. For example, children express happiness when they are able to achieve a desirable goal, and display anger or distress when a desirable goal is unattainable. Table 6.1 on page 344 provides an overview of the functionalist, goal-directed view of emotional development.

Parents and children first communicate with each other through emotions. An infant cries to signal hunger, discomfort, or fear, and his or her caregivers learn to "read" these signals as they attempt to soothe and comfort the infant. As early as 2 or 3 months, infants begin to attend to different emotional responses. Ten-week-old infants respond differently to happy, sad, and angry faces—especially when the adults' voices match the facial expressions (Walker-Andrews, 1997). When experiencing new and strange situations, a 12-month-old infant may look first at a caregiver's face before taking action. Remember the visual cliff experiment described in Chapter 2? A fearful or angry look can signal a wary infant not to crawl out onto the plate glass. Studies have shown that infants' reactions to new toys or strangers are shaped by their caregivers' facial expressions (Feinman & Lewis, 1983). This process of incorporating facial cues into response sequences is known as **social referencing** (Saarni, et al., 1998). It is important to note here that the baby's use of social cues for directing responses is an early form of behavioral regulation that will continue to develop.

By the end of the second year, children show some awareness that others can have feelings different from their own. Toddlers will attempt to comfort a distressed sibling or peer. This ability to react to another person's distress is called **empathy,** and it plays an important role in the development of prosocial behaviors, such as sharing, turn-taking, and caring for others (see Chapter 7). Although 2-year-olds are capable of empathic responses, they may not respond or may not respond appropriately to another's distress. These responses are influenced, in part, by the infant's own attachment history. When parents are responsive to their child's distress, the child tends to be more responsive to the distress of others (Thompson, 1999).

During the preschool years, children's emotional understanding expands. With the development of language abilities, children have the capability to label their emotions. Older children spontaneously talk about simple feelings (e.g., "I so happy, Grandma"), as well as about the feelings of others (Saarni et al., 1998). At this age, children also understand that emotions are associated with the fulfillment of different desires. For example, the child understands that someone would feel sad if a favorite toy were lost or stolen (Harris, 1989).

Between the ages of 2 and 4, new emotional reactions emerge. Whereas the infant's emotional reactions were limited to expressions of fear, joy, anger, and surprise, which Michael Lewis calls **basic emotions,** toddlers and preschoolers can express pride, shame, and guilt, or what are known as **self-conscious emotions** (Lewis, 1992). Unlike the fundamental emotions of infancy, self-conscious emotions involve an evolving sense of self. For example, Deborah Stipek and her colleagues (Stipek, Recchia, & McClintic, 1992) found that preschool children, aged 2 to 5 years, displayed positive affect (e.g., smiling) when they

UNDERSTANDING
CHILDREN
Strategy 5.1:
Identifying Facial
Expressions and
Emotions

TABLE 6.1   Overview of Functionalist Goal-Directed View of Emotions

Emotion Family	Goal	Action Tendency	Adaptive Function
Disgust	Avoiding contamination or illness	Active rejection	Learn about substances/events/attributes to avoid contamination
Fear	Maintaining integrity of physical or psychological self	Flight; active withdrawal	Avoid danger; learn about events/attributes that are dangerous
Anger	Any end state that the person is invested in achieving	Active forward movement to eliminate obstacles	Attain different goals; learn how to overcome obstacles; communicate power/dominance
Sadness	Any end state that the person is invested in achieving	Disengagement; passive withdrawal	Conserve energy; learn which goals are realizable; encourage nurturance from others
Shame	Maintaining others' respect and affection; preserving self-esteem	Active or passive withdrawal; avoiding others; hiding of self	Behave appropriately; learn and maintain social standards
Guilt	Meeting one's own internalized standards	Outward movement; inclination to make reparation to inform others; and to punish oneself	Behave prosocially; learn/maintain moral and prosocial behavior
Pride	Maintaining the respect of oneself and others	Outward/upward movement; inclination to show/inform others about one's accomplishments	Behave appropriately, learn/maintain social standards

Source: Adapted from Saari et al. (1998), p. 239.

successfully solved a puzzle task, but they avoided looking at the experimenter when they were unsuccessful, perhaps because they anticipated a disapproving response. As preschool children develop some understanding of standards for behavior, violations of those standards can lead to feelings of shame and guilt. Parents can tell when a child has done something wrong, such as having spilled juice on a clean shirt, from the child's distressed look or avoidance of contact. As we will discuss later, self-conscious emotions play an important role in helping children to regulate their behaviors.

By middle childhood, children's understanding of emotions becomes more sophisticated. They understand that multiple emotions can be evoked by the same event or situation

(Harter & Whitesall, 1989). For example, they feel both happy and sad on the last day of school. Like adults, they also understand how a person's personality or background can shape his or her emotional reactions to a situation (Gnepp & Chilamkurti, 1988). Older children are also able to better understand the causes of specific emotions ("He's mad because he wants to play outside, and his father says he has to play inside"). Additionally, school-age children have a better understanding of the social rules of displaying emotions (Gross & Harris, 1988; Saarni et al., 1998). For example, an older elementary student understands that it is not appropriate to laugh when other students make mistakes or get in trouble. With the discovery of these social conventions for expressing emotions, children come to understand that people, including themselves, can disguise their true feelings (Saarni et al., 1998).

Adolescence brings new cognitive abilities for understanding and expressing emotions. As we discussed in Chapter 3, older adolescents are able to engage in self-reflection and to think in more complex and sophisticated ways. Consider this high school student's concerns about fitting the high-achieving Asian stereotype:

> They [whites] will have stereotypes, like we're smart . . . They are so wrong, not everyone is smart. They expect you to be this and that and when you're not . . . (shook her head) And sometimes you tend to be what they expect you to be and you just lose your identity, just lose being yourself. Become part of what . . . what somebody else want[s] you to be. And it's really awkward too! When you get bad grades, people look at you really strangely because you are sort of distorting the way they see an Asian. It makes you feel really awkward if you don't fit the stereotype. (Lee, 1996, p. 59)

Although new cognitive abilities can help adolescents interpret unpleasant experiences, they are also associated with increased self-consciousness and self-criticism. Sadly, regular feelings of pride and happiness decline when students enter adolescence (Larson & Richards, 1994). Compared with younger children, adolescents report more anxiety, loneliness, moodiness, and stress (Arnett, 1999; Buchanan et al., 1992a). Adolescents also find that their increased needs for independence and autonomy are in conflict with those of parents and other authority figures, which can heighten feelings of loneliness, frustration, and anger. Also, as discussed in Chapter 2, depression symptoms are more prevalent among adolescents than younger children (Buchanan et al., 1992; Petersen et al., 1993). Thus, many adolescents will need assistance from parents, teachers, and other caring adults in coping with these challenges.

Thus far we have discussed age differences in young people's emotional development. There are also important gender and cultural differences in these patterns of development. By the preschool years, boys express more anger whereas girls express more sadness and fearfulness (Eisenberg, Martin, & Fabes, 1996). In the elementary school years, boys are less likely than girls to express feelings of hurt, distress, and sadness (Eisenberg et al., 1988; Fuchs & Thelen, 1988). By adolescence, however, girls report greater anxiety, worry, and hopelessness than do boys, which may increase their vulnerability to depression.

Cultures also differ in terms of what feelings are acceptable, and how those feelings should be expressed (Saarni et al., 1998). For example, in Japanese and Chinese cultures, calling attention to personal success can evoke embarrassment and showing disrespect toward others can evoke intense shame (Lewis, 1992).

This section has provided a very brief overview of children's expression and understanding of emotions. The Focus on Development box on page 346 summarizes important changes in these aspects of emotional development from preschool to adolescence. In the next section, we will consider important developmental changes in children's abilities to regulate their emotions. Emotional openness and self-assertiveness are not desirable characteristics in some cultures. It is thus important to respect cultural differences in emotional responses when working with diverse groups of students.

Focus on
Development *Emotional Development*

Age Group	Emotional Development	Emotional Regulation
Infancy	Emotional awareness Basic motions[a]	Limited ability to regulate emotions; regulates emotions through approaching/avoiding situations
Early childhood 2–8 years	Able to talk about emotions Understands that others have different emotions Self-conscious emotions[b]	Uses self talk to regulate emotions Able to shift attention away from sources of frustration Uses distraction strategies to delay gratification
Middle childhood and early adolescence 8–14 years	Understands that multiple emotions can occur at same time Understands causes of emotions Understands display rules for expressing emotions	Uses both problem- and emotion-based strategies to regulate emotions Able to assess degree they can control a situation Begins to use cognitive strategies to reduce stress
Middle and late adolescence 14 to adulthood	Greater reflection on emotional states of self and others Increased moodiness Greater ability to hide true emotions	Able to evaluate consequences of different strategies for expressing/controlling emotions Greater use of cognitive strategies to control emotions Uses social support to control emotions

[a]Basic emotions are happiness, interest, surprise, fear, anger, sadness, and disgust.
[b]Self-conscious emotions are shame, embarrassment, guilt, envy, and pride.

Developing Emotional Self-Regulation

Children's abilities to exercise control over emotions play an important role in their adaptation to school settings (Howse, Calkins, Anastopoulos, Keane, & Shelton, 2003; Pianta, 1999). Even young kindergarten students are expected to control negative emotions, to persist at difficult and challenging activities, and to inhibit impulses. Some children are able to tolerate frustration, whereas others are quick to fly off the handle. In this section we examine the development of children's capacities for emotional self-regulation. Similar to the self-regulation processes discussed in earlier chapters, the development of emotional self-regulation involves the deliberate use of cognitive or behavioral strategies to achieve a desired goal, such as reducing unpleasant emotions or redirecting inappropriate behavior. Emotional self-regulation is important for establishing positive social relations, for adjusting to school life, and for learning (Eisenberg et al., 1997; Howse et al., 2003). There is also evidence to suggest that self-control functions as a protective factor to lower adolescents' risk of alcohol and drug abuse, unsafe sex, and other health and safety problems (Resnick et al., 1997).

The capacity for self-regulation is initially shaped by early interactions between caregivers and infants. Both partners must learn to respond to each other's emotions and behaviors. At first caregivers do most of the work. They are attentive to what gestures, sounds, and actions might soothe and comfort the infant. With time, however, infants become more active players in this process. Just as waving feet and arms can cause an interesting sound or visual display (Piaget's circular reactions), babies learn that their caregivers respond differently to different gestures or cries. As these patterns are established, it is possible to observe an infant wait for a caregiver's response before reacting. By delaying their response, infants are already demonstrating an ability to regulate their reactions. What an amazing feat to accomplish in the first year!

Although babies are already learning some early lessons in self-management, important advances in self-control occur between the ages of 5 and 12. These changes are in part influenced by advances in children's abilities for remembering, representing, and generalizing behavioral standards and expectations (Thompson, 1999). During the preschool years, children demonstrate an increased ability to tolerate frustration and delay gratification. For example, when a favorite toy is not available, older preschool children respond with less anger and frustration than younger children (Matas, Arend, & Sroufe, 1978; Shoda, Mischel, & Peake, 1990). In a clever set of studies using marshmallows, Walter Mishel and his colleagues found that preschool and primary-school-age children were able to delay using a variety of cognitive and behavioral strategies. A follow-up study further revealed that a preschooler's ability to resist temptation predicted coping skills in adolescence. The findings are summarized in the Focus on Research box on page 348.

By middle childhood, most children show a broader repertoire of strategies for managing their emotions. Researchers have identified two types of strategies used by older children and adolescences (Lazarus, 1999). **Problem-focused coping** involves such things as seeking information, generating different solutions, and taking action to modify the situation. On the other hand, **emotion-focused coping** includes expressing emotions, seeking solace and support from others, and avoiding stressful events. Both forms of coping are more frequently observed in older, rather than young, children.

During the elementary school years, children also show an increasing ability to assess the degree to which they can exert control over stressful events that would generally provoke anger, fear, or frustration in younger children. For example, many children with parents who cannot afford the latest style of jeans, sneakers, or cell phones risk ridicule from more economically advantaged peers. Compared to younger peers, older elementary and middle school students may be able to respond to these uncontrollable events by using cognitive strategies aimed at reducing their distress, such as concealing their emotional reactions, using distraction strategies, or redefining the situation in a way that does not provoke a negative response (Saarni et al., 2006). For most preadolescents and young adolescents, when peer pressure is strong (see Chapter 7), it is very difficult to control emotions in the moment without a lot of good coaching and modeling by adults and peers. Nevertheless, compared to preschool children, most late elementary and middle school children are developing cognitive strategies to help them regulate their emotional reactions.

During adolescence, young people use more diverse, complex, and flexible strategies for managing their emotions as compared with younger children. They may cognitively reframe the problem situation, use self-talk to calm themselves, and evaluate the consequences of different emotional responses (Campas, Conner-Smith, Saltzman, Thomsen, & Wadsworth, 2001). For example, a 15-year-old girl may decide not to confront a peer who has upset her, because it might cause her to be more upset. An added advantage for teens is the ability to discuss their emotions with others. Compared to younger children, adolescents, especially girls, are more likely to share feelings and gain support from their friends. Other

Focus on
Research

Learning to Delay Gratification

Walter Mischel and his colleagues conducted a series of studies with preschool and school-age children to trace the development of self-control strategies (e.g., Mischel, Ebbensen & Zeiss, 1972; Mischel & Mischel, 1983; Mischel & Moore, 1981). They were interested specifically in the cognitive and behavioral strategies children use to delay gratification. A standard procedure was used across the studies. Briefly, children were invited into a laboratory room at their preschool and were asked to sit at a table with a bell and reward objects (marshmallows, pretzels, or poker chips). After determining which reward was most appealing, the experimenter told the child he needed to leave the room for a few minutes and showed the child the bell to summon his return. Before leaving the room, the experimenter showed the child the reward objects—two grouped together and one apart. The experimenter then explained the delay contingency:

The child can have two rewards if he waits, but one if he rings the bell first. Thus, the child would receive two marshmallows (pretzels or chips) if he exercised control by delaying gratification.

This simple procedure provided interesting insights into children's understanding of self-control strategies. Preschool children who delayed gratification used several different strategies to help them wait. They covered their eyes, talked to themselves, played games, and so on. Elementary school children also indicated that they recognized the value of strategies that cognitively transformed the marshmallows into something less tasty, like cotton balls or clouds. Even more interesting were results of a follow-up test on a subsample of the children 12 to 14 years later. Those children who had resisted temptation at age 4 were now confident, self-reliant, and able to cope with stress as adolescents (Shoda et al., 1990).

evidence suggests that teens use music, television, computer games, and other media to help them cope with negative or stressful situations (Larson, 1995). As discussed in Chapter 2, on the negative side, teens may also use alcohol, drugs, or food to cope with stressful events.

Of course, parents and other adults are important teachers and role models for children and adolescents as they develop strategies for regulating emotions. Children tend to demonstrate more positive forms of emotional regulation when parents (a) accept children's emotions; (b) help children to express and understand their emotions; (c) provide verbal guidance in ways to respond appropriately; and (d) provide reassurance that they will become more skilled at handling stress over time (Eisenberg et al., 1998; Gottman, Katz, & Hooven, 1997; Ramsden & Hubbard, 2002). In other words, these parents and caregivers provide important guiding and scaffolding experiences, much like we discussed in Chapters 3 and 4 for cognitive development, for understanding their emotional experiences. On the other hand, children tend to be less skilled at managing their emotions when parents have difficulty expressing or controlling their own emotions, dismiss their child's emotions as unimportant, or provide little guidance in coping with stressful or upsetting situations. As suggested earlier, educators function very much like parents in children's development. In the next section, we consider ways teachers can foster children's emotional development.

Fostering Emotional Competence in the Classroom

Children learn about the nature and expression of emotions from their day-to-day interactions with people. How parents, teachers, and other adults show emotions, teach about emotions, or react to emotional experiences are all key lessons for children. In his book *Emotional Intelligence,* Daniel Goleman (1995) proposed that emotional competence may be as important as any other type of learning that takes place in school. He calls for a "schooling of emotions" that focuses on the following emotional skills: identifying, expressing, and managing emotions; controlling impulses and delaying gratification; understanding the perspective of others; and knowing the difference between feelings and actions. Many schools are beginning to take a more active role in children's emotional development.

In this section we discuss some ways teachers can foster **emotional competence**—the understanding, expression, and regulation of emotions—in the classroom. Based on developmental research, the following are several important ways educators can promote emotional competence:

■ Teachers need to create a caring, positive, and warm affective environment for students. A young person's emotional world is shaped by these day-to-day affective experiences.

■ Teachers function as important models of how to exhibit and express emotions. Through their own actions, teachers can help students expresss emotions in socially appropriate ways. Teachers can also model ways of regulating emotions, such as calming down before reacting or seeking support when stressed or frustrated.

■ It is important for teachers to discuss emotions with their students. Emotion-related language helps to increase awareness of emotional states and the intensity of feelings. Class meetings can be used to share feelings about important events or experiences. Books, stories, plays, and films can also stimulate discussions of emotional experiences.

■ Finally, explicit instruction regarding specific ways of handling emotions and stress is important. These strategies might include (a) reframing the problem situation, (b) identifying alternative actions, (c) using self-talk to calm down negative emotions, (d) seeking support and help from others, and (e) avoiding problem situations altogether.

Many of these strategies were part of a school-based prevention program, PATHS (*Promoting Alternative THinking*) in the Seattle public schools (Greenberg, Kusche, Cook, & Quamma, 1995). This program was designed to help elementary school children manage and express their emotions. It included a curriculum containing explicit lessons on affective states (Feelings Units), as well as instruction in recognizing the feelings of others and managing emotions. The stoplight graphic shown in Figure 6.1 was displayed in classrooms

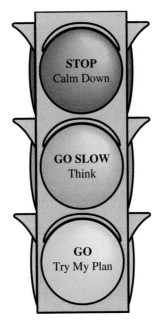

Evaluate—How Did My Plan Work?

■ FIGURE 6.1
Control Signals Poster
Source: Adapted from Weissberg, Caplan, & Bennetto (1988).

to help children bring feelings and behavior under control. Approximately 300 second and third graders completed the program, and 30 percent of the students had special learning needs. When the program was evaluated, the results showed that the program was successful in increasing children's emotional understanding and regulation (Greenberg et al., 1995). Children with behavioral problems also showed significant improvements in teacher ratings of frustration tolerance, positive peer relations, and social skills. We will examine other school-based programs for reducing aggression and antisocial behavior in the next chapter.

 # Emotional and Behavioral Disorders

Characteristics of Children with Emotional and Behavioral Disorders

Children and youths with emotional and behavioral disorders are perhaps the most problematic group of exceptional learners in the classroom. The number of children with emotional and behavioral disorders has increased dramatically in the last two decades (National Mental Health Association, 2006). The U.S. Department of Education estimates that 8 percent of the school-age population exhibits serious and persistent emotional or behavioral problems (National Center of Educational Statistics, 2005a). However, some experts believe that at least 6 to 10 percent of children and youths fall into this category (Kauffman, 1994). Children with emotional or behavioral disorders have difficulty in any of the following areas:

- Hyperactivity (short attention span, impulsiveness)
- Aggression/self-injurious behavior (acting out, fighting)
- Withdrawal (failure to initiate interaction with others, retreat from exchanges or social interaction, excessive fear or anxiety)
- Immaturity (inappropriate crying, temper tantrums, poor coping skills)
- Learning difficulties (academically performing below grade level) (NICCYD, 1994d, p. 1)

The primary characteristic of children with *emotional* or *behavioral disorders* is that their psychosocial development differs significantly from that of their same-age peers. For example, children with emotional and behavioral problems may be aggressive, defiant, withdrawn, or antisocial. All children have difficulties with their emotions and socialization at times, but these children experience them much more frequently and more intensely.

Many children with emotional and behavioral disorders have also been classified into subtypes according to diagnostic criteria in the DSM–IV (American Psychiatric Association, 1994). Figure 6.2 on page 351 lists the classifications, subtypes, and major characteristics in affective, cognitive, and physical development. Remember, these characteristics are a compilation of the various intraindividual needs found in children defined by this category. Rarely will an individual exhibit most or all of the traits presented.

Most of the problems children with emotional and behavioral disorders experience are *externalizing problems*. Their actions are overt; they may be argumentative, aggressive, antisocial, destructive, oppositional, or verbally abusive. However, some children with emotional and behavioral disorders exhibit *internalizing problems*. Internalizing behavior problems include depression, withdrawal, anxiety, obsession (repetitive and persistent thoughts), and compulsion (repetitive, ritualistic actions). Since internalizing behaviors often go undetected, children with internalizing behavior problems are not identified as frequently as those with externalizing, disruptive, antisocial behaviors.

Subtypes of Emotional or Behavioral Disorders	Possible Characteristics
Externalizing Disorder Subtypes	
Conduct disorders	Violation of social norms at school, at home, and in the community. Includes impulsivity; overt aggression (e.g., fighting, destructive toward property); covert antisocial acts (e.g., lying, stealing); temper tantrums; defying others; destroying property; running away from home.
Oppositional defiant disorders	Argumentative with adults; external locus of control (e.g., blames others); loses temper easily; intentionally annoys others; is verbally abusive or vindictive. Often coexists with conduct disorders.
Internalizing Disorder Subtypes	
Anxiety disorders	Social withdrawal; excessive worries; nervousness; tension; overestimation of the probability/severity of a feared event and underestimation of what self or others can do; physical discomfort (e.g., headaches, stomachaches, dizziness); self-consciousness.
Depressive disorders	Social withdrawal; poor school performance; suicidal ideation; chronic fatigue; low energy level; hopelessness; self-blame; self-dislike; excessive guilt; difficulty with concentration; depressed energy level. Often coexists with anxiety disorders in adolescents. Many of these characteristics are demonstrated by children who are anorexic or bulimic.

■ FIGURE 6.2
Characteristics of Subtypes of Children with Emotional or Behavioral Disorders
Source: After Coleman (1992).

Development of Emotional and Behavioral Disorders

As with other areas of development, there is no single cause for emotional and behavioral disorders. Contributing factors also depend on the particular disorder. Children with *schizophrenia* frequently, but not always, show signs of neurological abnormalities. *Tourette's syndrome,* which is characterized by multiple motor and verbal tics, is also related to a neurological disorder. Other emotional and behavioral disorders are more complex and may involve home, school, peer, and cultural influences, as well as biological factors, such as the child's temperament (Hallahan & Kauffman, 2000).

The home environment may also play a role in the development of emotional and behavioral disorders. As will be discussed in later chapters, parents who are lax in their discipline, inconsistent in dealing with misbehavior, or abusive tend to have children who are aggressive and antisocial. Chaotic or violent homes are particularly likely to place children at risk for emotional or behavioral problems. However, it is important to keep in mind that children with emotional or behavioral disorders may influence their parents as much as their parents influence them. Also, children react to their family environment in their own unique way. Not every child who is physically abused becomes aggressive or antisocial. Generally, parents of children with emotional and behavioral disorders want their children

Focus on
Research

Conduct disorders are among the most common diagnoses in mental health practice, with a prevalence of 4 to 10 percent among children and adolescents (Offord & Bennett, 1994). In order to be diagnosed with conduct disorder, a young person must manifest at least 3 of the following 15 symptoms within the last 12 months, with at least 1 occurring within the last 6 months (American Psychological Association [APA], 1994, cited in Clarizio, 1997):

I. **Aggression:** Bullies, threatens, intimidates, starts physical fights, uses a weapon that can harm others, has been physically cruel to people or animals, has stolen while confronting a victim, has forced sex on someone.

II. **Destruction of property:** Sets fires deliberately to cause serious damage, deliberately destroys property.

III. **Lying or theft:** Breaks into other's property; often cons others, lies to get things or avoids responsibility; often steals valuables without confrontation.

IV. **Serious violation of rules:** Often stays out late at night without permission, starting before age 13; has run away from home overnight at least twice; often plays hookey from school, starting before age 13.

A number of factors influence the development of conduct disorder. As was noted previously, age of onset has an impact on the course of development. While childhood onset is thought to result in long-term effects on the life course, adolescent onset conduct disorder is typically relatively short (Clarizio, 1997). Conduct disorder is three to four times more common in preadolescent boys

Diagnosis and Development of Childhood Conduct Disorders

than in preadolescent girls (Zoccolillo, 1993). However, females generally exhibit lower rates of violent behavior than males, with sexual behavior more likely to be the presenting problem for females. Also, conduct disorder has a significantly later onset in girls than in boys, with the average age of onset 13 years for girls as opposed to 7 years for boys. There also appears to be a link between intellectual performance and the development of conduct disorder. Moffitt (1990) found only a 1-point mean deficit in IQ points between adolescent delinquents and the general population, while a 17-point deficit was found for childhood-onset conduct disorder offenders.

Researchers have also identified parenting practices associated with the development of conduct disorders. These practices include harsh and inconsistent discipline, little positive parenting, and poor parental supervision of the child. These families are also characterized by a lack of reinforcement of prosocial behaviors and effective punishment for deviant behaviors, failure to set limits, and coercive parent–child interactions (Patterson, Capaldi, & Bank, 1991; Patterson, DeBaryshe, & Ramsey, 1989). The hypothesized results of this family context are children who are noncompliant and have undercontrolled behavior. Both of these characteristics are related to academic failure and rejection by members of the normal peer group. Rejection by the normal peer group and lax parental supervision have been associated with deviant peer group identification. The peer group is thought to provide the motivation, opportunity, attitudes, rationalizations, and opportunities to engage in antisocial behavior (Patterson et al., 1989).

to behave appropriately. It is better to provide support services than to blame parents for their child's problem.

The development of most emotional and behavioral disorders, however, involves a complex set of home, school, peer, and cultural influences, as well as the child's own biological characteristics such as temperament. One of the most common and troubling problems among school-age populations is **conduct disorders,** characterized by overt aggression, or disruptive or antisocial behavior. Conduct disorders are more common among boys than girls. Studies indicate that rate among boys in the general population is between 6 and 16 percent, whereas for girls the rates range from 2 to 9 percent (National Mental Health Association, 2006). The Focus on Research box above describes the diagnosis and development of conduct disorders in children and their long-term impact.

It is important for educators to remember that the school environment is a contributing factor in the development of emotional and behavioral disorders. Children who enter schools with a specific disorder can become better or worse depending on their school experiences. Discipline practices that are too lax, inconsistent, rigid, or punitive can have a negative impact. Teachers are often inadequately prepared to work with these children in their classrooms. They may reward misbehavior with special attention, which can increase the likelihood the child will misbehave again for this attention, even if it is in the form of criticism or punishment. Also, it is easy to become irritated and frustrated with these children and unintentionally model negative behaviors (rejection, hostility, etc.) that they imitate. Children with emotional or behavioral disorders often become trapped in a negative spiral interaction in the classroom (Hallahan & Kauffman, 2000). The Focus on Teaching box on page 354 describes a special educator's efforts to help a middle school student with a conduct disorder. The next section discusses some strategies for accommodating these students in the classroom.

Children with Emotional and Behavioral Disorders in the Classroom

As a group, children with emotional and behavioral disorders often experience rejection by children in the general classroom (Hollinger, 1987). Most children with emotional and behavioral disorders exhibit a lack of social-cognitive skills through hypersensitivity to social cues, misinterpretation of these cues, and inability to understand the consequences of their actions. Even when children show improvements in their social skills, their peers may continue to reject them (Zaragoza, Vaughn, & McIntosh, 1991). This continual pattern of rejection suggests that the attitudes and perceptions of children without disabilities also need to be addressed.

Most children with emotional/behavioral disorders have a low-average to average range of intelligence, although some have above-average intelligence. Approximately two-thirds have difficulties in academic areas, and the rest perform at or above grade level (Steinberg & Knitzer, 1992). Most of these children are similar to children with specific learning disabilities in that both have a pattern of poor academic performance despite an average range of cognitive ability (Scruggs & Mastropieri, 1986). The majority of children with emotional and behavioral disorders have low reading levels. Cognitive problems include lack of attention, impulsivity, and external locus of control.

Some children with emotional or behavioral disorders also exhibit difficulties in language, which could account for delays and deficiencies in psychosocial development. Language skills that may present difficulties for some children are listening comprehension, following directions, expressing thoughts and feelings, and applying rules involving morphology and syntax (Camarata, Hughes, & Ruhl, 1988).

Many children with emotional or behavioral disorders struggle during their adolescence. Low reading levels continue to plummet as they mature. In high school, they are placed in remedial or low-track classes and tend to get below-average grades (Meadows, Neel, Scott, & Parker, 1994). They are at risk for multiple forms of school failure and psychosocial difficulties including depression and suicide, failing grades, school absenteeism, poor performance on minimum competency tests, dropping out of school, substance abuse, sex-related difficulties, and delinquency (Coleman, 1992).

For children with emotional or behavioral disorders in general classrooms, classroom teachers collaborate with special educators, speech-language pathologists, and mental health professionals in addressing three major areas: management of behavior, teaching

Focus on
Teaching

After 6 years' experience as a special education teacher and having just completed a master's degree in counseling, I felt well prepared for my next challenge as a teacher. I was hired to teach the "Crisis Class," a class of 12 students identified as having severe behavior disorders. The students in the class came from six different school districts and were placed in the crisis class when they were unsuccessful in the programs for children with behavior disorders at their school.

All was going well, and then Dominick was placed in my class. He had been placed in my class after stealing the master key to all of the lockers at his middle school. He managed to pull this off despite the fact that there was a full-time assistant assigned solely to him. The first day he was scheduled to come to my class he refused to get out of his mother's car. The next day when he did come into the classroom he informed me, "I'll come here because I have to, but you can't make me do any work." And he was right.

There was a structure in place in the class whereby students could earn privileges through work completion, compliance with rules, and progress toward individual goals. Dominick wasn't interested. His first few days resulted in little work completion and much disruption in the class. I needed a different strategy. Dominick was very vocal about the fact that he didn't belong in my class or in the school. He really didn't fit in. He was of above-average intelligence, while most of the other students had some type of learning difficulty beyond their behavior disorder. Also, his family was wealthy, and most of the other students came from families with low socioeconomic status.

One day I asked Dominick what he missed most about his old school. He told me that he had been on the tennis team at his school and had been quite good. Being a part of the tennis team was what he missed the most. This knowledge became the key to Dominick's success in my class. I told Dominick (truthfully) that I had always wanted to learn how to play tennis and asked if he would be willing to give me some pointers. He agreed.

What I Learned from Dominick

The next day we both brought our tennis rackets to school. However, to be able to give me my lesson, Dominick had to earn the morning break time by completing his work and earning the required number of points on his point sheet. Dominick was successful that morning for the first time. During the morning break, we went out to the parking lot of our school and Dominick was my tennis instructor. He told me what to do and I listened and followed his instructions. For 20 minutes Dominick was in control and had the power in our relationship. He also was better at something than I was, and I demonstrated my respect for his tennis skills. This was important for Dominick. He was seeking control in his environment. Virtually all control had been taken away from him at school because of his inappropriate behavior. I believe that it had also been a long time since he had experienced a positive interaction with an authority figure in a school setting. When we returned to the classroom, he was much more willing to receive instruction from me and to comply with the classroom routines, rules, and procedures. There were still difficult days, and Dominick had not suddenly been "cured." However, we had turned a corner. By the end of the school year Dominick was being successful in my class on a regular basis. He was not yet ready to return to his old school. However, he was making positive progress, which hadn't happened in a long time.

I learned a lot from Dominick about being a teacher. He taught me the importance of getting to know my students and forming a positive relationship with them *on their terms.* I needed to explore Dominick's interests and consider what he needed from me and the class environment, as opposed to what I needed from him. I knew that he was seeking power and control, however, by talking to him I was able to find an appropriate avenue to give him control, not just of the environment but, more important, of me. It's often difficult for teachers to surrender control to students. But, when the surrendering is done appropriately, the results can be amazing.

It is important for teachers to discuss emotions with their students. These daily interactions can help students understand and handle their emotional experiences.
Source: Mary Kate Denny/Photo Edit.

social and communication skills, and providing academic support. While using nontraditional management methods for reducing inappropriate behaviors, educators also teach prosocial skills and make accommodations for academic performance. Some successful interventions are:

- Modifying learning tasks to ensure success
- Developing learning strategies
- Providing clear and consistent expectations with resulting rewards and consequences
- Involving students in goal-setting and self-evaluation
- Giving frequent feedback on performance
- Using cooperative learning and peer tutoring to structure peer interaction
- Teaching social problem-solving skills
- Direct teaching of prosocial communication skills

It is essential that people who work with children with emotional or behavioral disorders model prosocial actions themselves—demonstrating respect for diversity, self-control when frustrated, and effective interpersonal communication skills. Research by Jere Brophy and his colleagues (1986) has shown that classroom teachers who are effective with aggressive-disruptive children have developed a strong sense of self-efficacy. They are confident in their own ability to change these children. Kauffman and Wong (1991) agree.

> Teachers who maintain a high sense of self-efficacy tend to perceive their students as teachable and worthy of their attention and effort regardless of their students' low abilities and slow progress. These teachers do not perceive misbehaviors as intentional or threatening to

their authority, nor do they expect more instances of disruptive student behavior. Instead, they are likely to seek challenge, persist in the face of slow student progress, and maintain an attitude of tolerance toward difficult students. Their successes in the classroom increase self-efficacy, which, in turn, makes them likely to succeed. (p. 231)

Development of Self-Conceptions

Self-Concept and Self-Esteem

How would you describe yourself? Are you a member of a particular ethnic group? Are you strong, happy, confident, moody, shy? To what extent do you believe you are a lovable and worthy person? Answers to questions like these can tell us something about your self-concept and self-esteem. Although these two terms are frequently used interchangeably, there is an important distinction in meaning. **Self-concept** refers to the beliefs, attitudes, knowledge, and ideas people have about themselves. This self-knowledge is hierarchically organized into categories and dimensions that define the self and serve to guide behavior (Harter, 1999, 2006). For example, as will be described, adolescents have a general concept of their academic ability (e.g., "I'm a capable student") that can be broken down into different subject areas including reading, mathematics, science, and so on.

Self-esteem, on the other hand, involves an *evaluation* of our traits, abilities, and characteristics. It generally involves a global evaluation of one's overall worth as a person (Harter, 2006). According to one expert, self-esteem is "a personal judgment of *worthiness* that indicates the extent to which the individual believes himself to be capable, significant, successful, and worthy" (Coopersmith, 1967, p. 5; italics added). Thus, self-esteem involves a sense of self-acceptance and respect for oneself.

From an educational perspective, an important question concerns how children's self-perceptions relate to their school performance. As we will discuss later, perceptions of competence influence a student's motivation to learn. Children who perceive themselves as competent are generally more intrinsically motivated to learn than children with low perceived competence, and they tend to choose challenging tasks, work independently, and persist at learning tasks (Harter & Connell, 1984; Wigfield, Eccles, Schiefele, Roeser, & Davis-Kean, 2006). In addition to their motivational effects, self-concept and self-esteem affect children's actual achievement in school. As you would expect, children with high self-esteem and positive self-concepts tend to be more successful in school. Although associations between general measures of self-concept and academic performance tend to be moderate, they persist across gender, grade level, and socioeconomic groups (Hansford & Hattie, 1982; Harter, 1999). When domain-specific measures of self-concept and performance are used (e.g., one's self-concept of reading ability and one's grade in reading), the associations are even higher.

One issue of debate concerns the causal direction of the relation between self-concept and school achievement (Byrne, 1986; Calsyn & Kenny, 1977; Marsh, Byrne, & Yeung, 1999; Marsh & Yeung, 1997). It may be that high self-concept leads to high achievement, but the reverse could also be true: Children who do well in school generally feel better about themselves and their competence. Researchers generally believe that the relationship works both ways (Skaalvik, & Valas, 1999; Wigfield et al., 2006). For young children who are still forming their self-concept, academic performance may shape their perceptions of ability and feelings of self-worth. By middle school, however, the relationship between self-concept and school achievement becomes more complex. Students with high perceptions of ability may approach learning tasks with confidence, and success on those tasks may bolster their confidence (Bong & Clark, 1999; Marsh & Yeung, 1997; Wigfield & Karpathan, 1991). Once a child's sense of ability is firmly established, it can have a stronger influence on academic performance than objective measures of ability, such as grades and test scores (Eccles et al., 1983; Guay, Marsh, & Boivan, 2003; Marsh, 1990a; Marsh & Yeung, 1997; Wigfield et al., 2006). In other words, it is the child's *perception* of reality, rather than reality per se, that has the strongest influence on school performance.

Developmental Changes in Self-Concept

The self is both a cognitive and social construction process (Harter, 2006, p. 506). As discussed in previous chapters, both children and adolescents use their developing cognitive abilities to interpret and give meaning to their experiences. These same processes are at work when children construct a view of the self. As a result children's cognitive abilities can either limit or enhance their self-representations.

Children begin to think of themselves as separate individuals during the toddler period. By 21 to 24 months, children can recognize themselves in the mirror, and they begin to use such words as *me, I,* and *mine* as a way of asserting their individuality. In part, behavior attributed to the "terrible twos" is an expression of the child's emerging self and individuality.

A child's sense of self begins to emerge in the toddler years.
Source: Michael Newman/Photo Edit.

During preschool and early elementary school, children primarily describe themselves in terms of their physical characteristics, interests, actions, and other concrete labels (Damon & Hart, 1988; Harter, 1999, 2006). For example, a 4-year-old might say, "I am a boy, and I like to play with Legos." This tendency to use physical self-descriptions reflects a young child's concrete thinking abilities. That is, young children describe themselves in terms of attributes that may be physical (e.g., "I have brown hair"), active (e.g., "I can count"), social (e.g., "I have a baby brother"), or psychological (e.g., "I am nice"). However, a young child's understanding of self is very limited. Children may sometimes feel mean and sometimes feel nice, but they have difficulty coordinating these two views of themselves into a unified sense of self due to the limitations of working memory at this age (Harter, 1999, 2006). Also, children's self-evaluations during this period are unrealistically positive because young children have difficulty distinguishing between their real and ideal self. Because young children *want* to be smart, they often describe themselves as smart (Stipek, 1984). Also, preschool children lack the ability to compare themselves with others, which involves memory skills. As we discussed in Chapter 4, thinking about two events simultaneously is difficult for young children. In this case, children must think about their own attributes while also thinking about the attributes of the other person (Harter, 2006).

During the middle childhood years (8 to 12 years old), children begin to describe themselves in terms of higher-order concepts that are based on several different features of the self. For example, a 10-year-old girl might describe herself as a good student because she reads well, gets good grades, and finishes her work on time. Whereas younger children are unable to integrate opposing attributes (e.g., mean and nice), older children are able to do so. Accordingly, their self-descriptions tend to include both positive and negative characteristics (Harter, 1999). Older children are also more likely to describe themselves in terms of interpersonal and social characteristics, such as caring, loyal, trustworthy, and so forth. These self-descriptions suggest that older children are beginning to place themselves within a social context.

UNDERSTANDING
CHILDREN
Strategy 5.2:
Self-Descriptions

Older children also understand that they may have thoughts and feelings that are hidden from others. Psychologists refer to this developmental trend as the emergence of the inner or **psychological self** (Selman, 1980). It is not until adolescence, or during the formal operational period, that children begin to describe themselves in terms of abstract values, beliefs, and attitudes (Damon & Hart, 1982; Harter, 1999). Adolescents, for example, are much more likely than younger children to describe themselves in terms of a political, religious, or sexual orientation. However, young adolescents are likely to have different conceptions of themselves in relation to parents, close friends, teachers, and so forth. Discrepancies in self-perceptions across relationships and roles can cause confusion and uncertainty. These feelings are exacerbated by the adolescent's ability to reflect on internal states. As we discussed previously, adolescents can become preoccupied with their thoughts and feelings. Cognitive advances in the late adolescent years enable young people to develop a coherent and integrated representation of the self (Harter, 1999). As described next, identity formation involves defining oneself in terms of an organized system of beliefs, goals, and values. The Focus on Development box summarizes changes in self-conceptions from early childhood through late adolescence.

Along with these changes in self-conceptions, children develop a more differentiated view of the self as they mature. As early as kindergarten or first grade, children develop separate concepts of their physical, social, and cognitive abilities (Eccles, Wigfield, Harold, & Blumenfeld, 1993; Eccles, Wigfield, & Schiefele, 1998; Harter, 1998; Hattie & Marsh, 1996; Marsh, Craven, & Debus, 1991). An older student's academic self-concept may be further broken down according to success in individual subject areas, such as reading, mathematics, or science. That is to say, a student may view himself or herself as good in mathematics but not musically talented. One view of a differentiated self-concept is shown in Figure 6.3 on page 360. Teachers and parents need to remember that children's self-concepts vary across subject areas. They may have poor academic self-concepts in some subject areas but average or above-average self-concepts in others (Marsh, 1989).

Another important change that occurs during the school years is the use of social comparisons to evaluate oneself (Harter, 2006; Ruble, 1983). Whereas preschoolers may describe themselves in terms of actions (e.g., "I can run fast"), older children are much more likely to make comparative judgments of their abilities (e.g., "I am the fastest runner in the class"). Theorists believe that such comparisons help children to identify their unique characteristics and to differentiate themselves from others. However, comparisons can also produce declines in self-concept or self-esteem when children perceive themselves as less able, less socially competent, or less attractive than their peers. As we will discuss, social comparison processes in the classroom can have a very negative effect on children's concepts of ability and on their motivation to learn.

Numerous studies report that age affects children's overall and academic self-concepts. In general, there is a decline in students' overall self-concept during late childhood and

Developmental Changes in Self-Representations in Childhood and Adolescence

Focus on
Development

Age Period	Developmental Characteristics	Examples
Toddler and early childhood	Concrete observable characteristics focused on abilities, activities, and possessions. Isolated representations with no coordination or coherence.	I go to school. I can run fast. I have a baby sister.
Early to middle childhood	Simple links between traits; all-or-none thinking; typically positive representations.	I am nice and my teacher likes me. I am good at running and climbing.
Middle to late childhood	Trait labels that focus on abilities and interpersonal characteristics; social comparisons with peers. Integration of positive and negative characteristics.	I am good at math, but reading is hard for me. I have more friends than my sister.
Early adolescence	Integration of traits into simple abstractions. Focused on skills/attributes that influence interactions with others. All-or-none thinking. Don't detect inconsistencies between traits.	I am a pretty cheerful person, especially with my friends.
Late adolescence	Higher-order abstractions that reflect personal beliefs, values, and moral standards. More stable and balanced view of positive and negative standards.	People say I am moody. I am happy some days, but depressed sometimes. I am American, but I respect my Chinese heritage.

Source: After Harter (1998).

early adolescence followed by a resurgence in late adolescence and early adulthood (Eccles et al., 1993; Eccles et al., 1998; Harter, 1999, 2006; Marsh, 1989; Stipek & Mac Iver, 1989). Similarly, researchers have found that age affects children's competence perceptions in both academic (e.g., math, reading) and nonacademic (e.g., social relations, music) domains (Eccles et al., 1993; Harter, 2006; Marsh, 1989). These declines in domain-specific perceptions, particularly for mathematics, appear to be the most acute as children enter early adolescence and often continue well into adolescence (Eccles et al., 1983; Eccles et al., 1998; Wigfield, Eccles, Mac Iver, Rueman, & Midgley, 1991; Wigfield et al., 2006).

In general, children's academic self-concepts become more accurate with age. Whereas young children are likely to overestimate their abilities in certain areas, older children have a more realistic view of their abilities. That is, their self-perceptions are more highly correlated

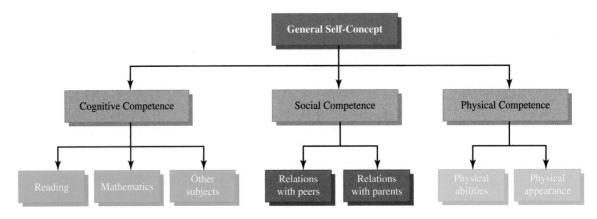

FIGURE 6.3
Hierarchical Structure of Self-Concept

UNDERSTANDING CHILDREN
Strategy 5.3: Perceptions of Competence

with grades, teacher evaluations, and other external feedback (Marsh, 1989; Stipek & Mac Iver, 1989; Wigfield et al., 2006). The increasing accuracy of children's ability perceptions is related to several factors. First, as discussed, children are better able to utilize social comparison information in judging their skills and abilities by the middle childhood years. Also, age and ability stratification in school can stimulate social comparisons among children of the same age. Further, as children's cognitive abilities mature they are better able to integrate multiple sources of information about their abilities (teacher comments, grades, etc.)

Another important change in adolescents' self-perception that teachers need to consider is their increasing ability to reflect on themselves. As adolescents become more self-reflective, they develop a greater understanding of themselves. However, this self-reflective tendency among this age group often leads to an increased sense of self-consciousness, because adolescents assume that others are also observing and evaluating them. This developmental trend can often lead adolescents to dress and act like their peers, so they won't stand out from others. It can also lead adolescents to be highly critical of themselves. Because of this heightened sense of self-consciousness, teachers should take care in singling students out in public for either special recognition or disciplinary actions. It may be more appropriate to provide such feedback in private. Gradually, as an adolescent's self-concept becomes more firmly established, he or she begins to feel more secure and less self-conscious.

Developmental Trends in Self-Esteem

As we discussed, self-esteem involves an overall evaluation of one's value or worth as a person. It is often difficult for very young children to provide an assessment of their self-esteem because of various cognitive limitations. However, this limitation does not mean that young children lack a sense of self-worth. Young children display this sense of self in behavioral terms (Harter, 2006). Children who show displays of confidence, curiosity, initiative, and independence are identified by teachers as children with high self-esteem (Harter, 1990, 1999). Also, young children with high self-esteem are able to adjust to changes and transitions, to tolerate frustration, and to handle conflict.

During the early school years, children's self-esteem generally increases as they achieve success in their peer relationships and in other areas of importance to them. Theorists believe that the contributions of specific self-appraisals to overall self-worth vary according to the degree of importance or value attached to a particular attribute (Harter,

1990). This idea dates back to the writings of William James (1892) in the late nineteenth century. James believed that individuals placed a different value on success within different domains of their lives. He further proposed that individuals compare their level of competence to their aspirations for success across different domains. The degree of congruence or discongruence determines their feelings of self-worth.

According to this view, the importance of intelligence, popularity, or physical attractiveness will determine the degree to which perceived inadequacies will affect overall evaluations of self-esteem. In a study of elementary school children (grades 3 to 6), Susan Harter (1986) found that children's evaluations of global self-worth were based upon their evaluations of how competently they could perform in areas deemed important. Interestingly, children with a high self-worth discounted the importance of domains in which they were less competent. However, children with low self-worth did not use this discounting principle in the same way.

By late childhood, global measures of self-esteem also show more stability with age. Children with high self-esteem at age 8 are likely to have high self-esteem at age 10, assuming their environment and social comparison group both remain fairly stable (Harter, 1983). In middle adolescence, global evaluations of self-worth also become more positive. Increases in self-esteem may be tied to gains in personal autonomy. Older adolescents have more opportunities to choose social or academic situations that provide positive feedback about their competencies (Harter, 1999).

Although young people's self-esteem judgments may become more stable and positive with age, important changes occur as students enter adolescence. First, recall that young people's conceptions of the self become more complex and more differentiated with cognitive maturity. This same pattern applies to self-esteem. An adolescent can have high self-esteem in relation to peer popularity but low self-esteem relative to school achievement. Until late adolescence or adulthood, there can be considerable variation in self-esteem across relational contexts (family, peer, and school), as well as experiential domains such as academic subjects, athletics, and personal appearance (Harter, 1999; Hattie, 1992). Thus, it may be misleading to describe an older child's or adolescent's self-esteem as low without knowing the particular context. Consider this adolescent girl's response to the question "How much do you like yourself?"

Students with high self-esteem show pride in their schoolwork.
Source: Banana Stock/Punchstock.

Well, I like some things about me, but I don't like others. I'm glad that I'm popular since I don't do as well as the really smart kids. That's OK, because if you're too smart you'll lose friends. So being smart is just not that important. Except to my parents. I feel like I am letting them down when I don't do as well as they want. But what's really important to me is how I look. If I like the way I look, then I really like the person I am. (Harter, 1990, p. 364)

During middle childhood, children also develop the capabilities to compare their real self with a set of desired characteristics (Harter 2006). This **ideal self** is generally constructed on the basis of social experiences. The expectations, values, and ideals of peers and adults also help to shape the content of the ideal self. When children do not measure up to their ideal self, it can lead to declines in self-esteem. A good example of this phenomenon was found in our discussion of early maturing girls in Chapter 2. As we discussed, most American girls receive consistent and clear messages that beauty is defined in terms of being "slim and trim." When early maturing girls cannot meet this cultural ideal of physical attractiveness, it leads to negative changes in self-esteem (Harter, 1993). Research shows that physical appearance is the strongest correlate of global self-worth in childhood and adolescence. These patterns were found in the United States, as well as in European and Asian countries (Harter, 1999).

School Transitions and Self-Esteem

The transition to a new school can be very stressful for many students, as we discussed previously. When students change school environments, they must adjust to new expectations and routines, as well as to unfamiliar peers and teachers. Researchers have examined how changing schools can affect students' ratings of self-esteem. In one of the first studies, Roberta Simmons and Dale Blyth (1987) compared adolescents' self-esteem in two Milwaukee public school settings. One group of students attended the same school from kindergarten to eighth grades then attended high school for 4 years (8–4 arrangement), and another grade changed schools after sixth grade and ninth grade (6–3–3 arrangement). This study showed that adolescents' self-esteem ratings were affected by these different schooling arrangements, and the effects varied by gender. Figure 6.4 shows the influence of school transitions on girls' and boys' self-esteem. As you can see, girls in the 6–3–3 showed two dramatic drops in self-esteem, whereas boys showed only one as they entered the 10th grade. In contrast, self-esteem rises for both girls and boys in the 8–4 arrangement.

Several factors seem to explain declines in students' self-esteem as they change schools. First, youngsters experience disruptions in their social networks during the change. Second, their social status also changes, as they move from being the oldest to the youngest students in their school. Third, adolescents who change schools must adjust to new school routines and social expectations, changes that often coincide with pubertal changes, especially for girls. Junior high transitions are particularly difficult, because adolescents are beginning puberty and adjusting to a new school environment at the same time. This is not the case for adolescents who remain in the same school.

Other researchers point to the effect of changes in the quality of the school environment as adolescents make the transition to junior high schools. These schools tend to be larger, more impersonal, and less sensitive to students' developmental needs than elementary schools (Anderman & Midgley, 1996; Eccles et al., 1993; Midgley, Berman, & Hicks, 1995). Such changes can produce negative outcomes for young adolescents, especially those who are already experiencing other changes or having difficulty at school or at home (Lord, Eccles, & McCarthy, 1994). Adolescents who enter schools that are more personal and smaller in size tend to experience fewer adjustment problems. Also, adolescents who remain with a stable peer group during school transitions are less likely to experience negative

■ FIGURE 6.4

Boys' and Girls' Self-Esteem Is Influenced Differently by School Transitions in Early Adolescence
Source: After Simmons & Blyth (1987).

changes in self-esteem, especially if the friendships are warm, supportive, and nurturing (Brendt, 1999). The Focus on Teaching box on page 364 summarizes some ways that teachers can enhance self-esteem in the classroom.

Interventions to Promote Positive Self-Esteem

Numerous programs have been developed to help children and adolescents with low self-esteem. Low levels of self-esteem are correlated with a range of problem behaviors, including poor school attendance and achievement, peer rejection, juvenile delinquency, loneliness, depression, teenage pregnancy, social alienation, and so forth (Haney & Durak, 1998; Harter, 1990, 1999). Intervention and treatment programs in the 1960s and 1970s focused on helping young people *feel good* about themselves. However, programs that focused on affect alone had only a limited impact on measures of global self-esteem (Harter, 1999). Positive reinforcement or praise is not enough when students are still failing in areas of importance to them.

Current efforts to help students with low self-esteem are more cognitively based. For older children and adolescents, it is helpful to explore the origins of their negative self-perceptions. Some intervention programs target attributional biases that lead students to blame themselves for their inadequacies, while crediting others for their successes. When students take responsibility for their successes, it can enhance perceptions of competence in domains of importance. Another strategy is to help students focus on domains in which they display competence and discount, as much as possible, those domains in which they feel less adequate. Because not all students can excel in a particular academic area, it is important to have broad definitions of competence. Gardner's theory of multiple intelligences reminds us that there are many ways to be smart. Finally, skill development is critical for the development of self-esteem. One of the best ways to improve students' self-esteem is to teach them the knowledge and skills that will enable them to experience real success in areas that are important to them (Bednar, Wells, & Peterson, 1995).

Focus on
Teaching

Suggestions for Enhancing Students' Self-Esteem

- Create an environment that is physically and psychologically safe for all students.
- Provide all students with an environment of encouragement and positive reinforcement.
- Accept and appreciate all students for their efforts as well as their accomplishments.
- Accept students as they are, and let them know it. Do not make acceptance conditional on behavior.
- Treat all students respectfully, as you would a family member.
- Accept the students' feelings, both positive and negative. Negative feelings are a normal part of life and need to be accepted.
- Avoid comparing students. Encourage students to compete against their previous levels of learning.

- Make standards of evaluation clear to students and help them learn to evaluate their own behavior.
- Make demands and challenges that are appropriate for the students' ages and abilities.
- Give students opportunities to make decisions, have responsibility, and experience feelings of competence and confidence.
- Encourage students to do as much as they can on their own.
- Attend extracurricular events that are important to the students, such as athletic games, recitals, plays, and debates.
- Avoid laughing at students, making jokes about students, or making sarcastic remarks to students.

Source: After Canfield (1990).

Social support can also have a positive effect on self-esteem. As we discussed, children and adolescents with warm, responsive, and nurturing parents tend to have high levels of self-esteem. For students who are experiencing disapproval, rejection, or neglect at home, a caring adult at school or in the community can help compensate for a lack of parent support. In a study of middle school students, 60 percent reported a special adult in their lives who provided various types of social support including approval, emotional support, advice, and help (Harter, 1999). Students reported that their special adults were teachers, counselors, coaches, ministers, relatives, parents of friends, or other adult friends. Big Sisters, Big Brothers, and other mentoring programs are also places young people can garner social support.

Identity Formation

In the previous sections, we discussed how children and adolescents form a sense of their competencies and self-worth. These developmental processes serve as the foundation for identity formation. As you recall, Erikson's theory maintains that *identity versus identity confusion* is the central issue that defines the adolescent. Young people needed to achieve a positive, coherent identity. Erikson's (1968) definition of identity was fairly broad:

> The wholeness to be achieved at this stage [adolescence] I have called a sense of inner identity. The young person, in order to experience wholeness, must feel a progressive continuity between that which he has come to be during the long years of childhood and that which he promises to become in the anticipated future; between that which he conceives himself to be and that which he perceives others to see in him and to expect of him. Individually speaking, identity includes, but is more than the sum of, all successive

School transitions are often difficult for young adolescents because they must adjust to new social expectations and school routines, while also adjusting to physical changes.
Source: Will & Deni McIntyre/Photo Researchers, Inc.

identifications of those earlier years when the child wanted to be, and often was forced to become, like the people he depended on. (p. 87)

For adolescents, the critical task is to select and integrate childhood identities with personal desires and societal opportunities and expectations in order to develop a sense of who they are and who they will become. According to Erikson (1968), our identity gives a sense of inner assuredness, continuity, and direction for the future, and it involves a "series of ever narrowing personal, occupational, sexual, and ideological commitments" (p. 245).

Erikson believed that the biological and social changes that occur in adolescence lead young people to reflect on their place in society, on the ways others view them, and on their options for the future. This idea fits with what we already know about adolescents. They are growing into adult bodies and assuming greater responsibility for themselves. They also are developing the cognitive abilities to engage in introspection and to contemplate the future. However, Erikson believed that social interactions as well as the social context were critical to the formation of an identity. By interacting with others, we learn about ourselves and what we ought to be. The social environment determines what sorts of identities are possible and desirable. Over the last 30 years, for example, the career options for women have changed dramatically. Women from earlier generations defined their identities in terms of commitments to marriage and family life. Many young women today postpone marriage and parenthood to pursue a career. Over 20 years ago, Erikson (1968) commented on the "prolonged adolescent" that was becoming increasingly common in industrialized societies undergoing dramatic social and economic changes. Theorists believe that Erikson's observation applies to more young people today than ever before.

Erikson wrote extensively about identity development, using a research method called psychohistory. His most famous works of psychohistory were his psychological analyses of the developmental histories of Mohandas K. Gandhi (Erikson, 1969) and Martin Luther (Erikson, 1958). Erikson's writings inspired the research of James Marcia, who investigated

■ FIGURE 6.5

Categories of Identity Status

Source: After Marcia (1966).

Commitment

	Present	Absent
Exploration Present	Identity Achievement	Moratorium
Absent	Identity Foreclosure	Identity Diffusion

identity development of young people in three areas: occupation, ideology (values and beliefs), and interpersonal relations. To determine a person's **identity status** within each domain, responses are rated on two dimensions: (1) the degree to which the person has made commitments, and (2) the degree to which the person has explored different options and alternatives.

As shown in Figure 6.5, an individual is assigned to one of four identity statuses: diffusion, moratorium, foreclosure, or achievement. Before a discussion of the characteristics of each status, it is important to point out that people do not necessarily progress through each of the categories to achieve an identity. Only one development sequence is specified. According to Erikson's theory, one must experience psychosocial moratorium before achieving an identity. Also, it is important to point out that individuals may be at different identity statuses in forming a social, occupational, or ideological identity. For example, studies reveal that young people emerge from college with a more clearly defined set of occupational plans, but with no firm ideological commitments (Waterman, 1982). Finally, individuals may reevaluate their commitments in a particular domain, even after achieving an identity. Some of you, for example, may be studying to become a teacher as a second career.

Young people who are in the *identity diffusion* category are not actively exploring potential choices, and they are unable to make any firm commitments regarding their beliefs, social relationships, or occupational plans. This identity status is correlated with low self-esteem and low self-control. It is also associated with high anxiety and high apathy (Waterman, 1999a). Individuals with a diffused identity are at greatest risk for developing psychological problems (Meeus, Iedema, Helsen, & Vollenbergh, 1999).

Young people in *identity foreclosure* have not explored different possibilities but have nonetheless committed themselves to certain choices. This category tends to be associated with conformity, conventionality, and obedience to authority (Meeus et al., 1999). Generally, youths with a foreclosed identity have a strong attachment to their parents, and they adopt their values and guidance without going through a period of exploration. Identity foreclosure tends to be associated with high levels of psychological well-being (Meeus et al., 1999).

Young people in *identity moratorium* are actively exploring different occupational plans, ideological stances, and personal relationships, but they are not ready to make any choices or commitments. When compared with those in other statuses, individuals in moratorium status tend to score lower on measures of well-being and higher on measures of anxiety and conflict with parents, but they tend to be less rigid and authoritarian (Meeus et al., 1999; Waterman, 1999a). Theorists believe that moratorium, although necessary for achieving an identity, is closest in character to an identity crisis, and it is viewed as a transitional status rather than an endpoint for identity development.

Finally, *identity achievement* describes those young people who have engaged in exploration and who have made definite personal, vocational, or ideological choices. These individuals tend to be high in self-esteem, self-control, and self-direction (Marcia, 1980). They also tend to score high on measures of academic motivation and career maturity. Consistent with Erikson's theory, these are individuals who have achieved an identity score highest on measures of psychological well-being when compared with those in other identity statuses (Meeus et al., 1999; Waterman, 1999a). In theory, these individuals have the most favorable profile for later development.

Erikson's theory proposed that identity formation defined the period of adolescence. Do empirical studies of identity development support his claim? Although exploration may begin at this age, most studies reveal that identity development extends beyond adolescence. Figure 6.6 on page 368 shows data from a study of adolescents between the ages of 10 and 18. As can be seen here, a higher proportion of high school students falls into the foreclosure and identity diffusion categories when compared with college students. These data are consistent with other studies suggesting that fewer than one-third of adolescents have achieved an overall identity by the end of high school (Meeus et al., 1999). Studies suggest that more identity exploration will occur during the college years, when young people have more opportunity and freedom to experiment with different social roles, occupations, and ideologies. However, studies reveal that a majority of young people have not reached identity achievement by age 21 (Waterman, 1999a).

Developing an Ethnic Identity

Ethnic identity refers to one's sense of identity concerning racial or ethnic group membership (Phinney, 1990). Ethnic identity is considered to vary across members of an ethnic group, and to change over time as the beliefs, values, and practices of an ethnic community evolve (Okagaki, 2006). A positively valued ethnic identity is important for a strong, positive, and stable self-identity in minority youths (Phinney & Rosenthal, 1992). An ethnic identity includes some or all of the following elements: (a) self-identification as a member of a group, (b) feelings of belonging and commitment to a group, (c) positive (or negative) attitudes toward the group, (d) a sense of shared attitudes and values, and (e) specific ethnic traditions and practices, such as language, behavior, and customs (Phinney & Rosenthal, 1992, p. 147).

Most of us in this multicultural society take pride in our ethnic heritage, whether our ancestors came from Ireland, Russia, Vietnam, Africa, Cuba, Germany, or England. Thus far, more research on the development of ethnic identity has focused on African Americans than on any other ethnic group. Moreover, few studies have differentiated among members within a particular ethnic group. For example, black youths can have either African or Caribbean ancestry, but they are generally treated as one ethnic group. Similarly, Asian American youngsters come from many different countries, each with its own language, customs, and traditions. Because our society is becoming increasingly more culturally diverse, developmental researchers are focusing greater attention on the role that ethnicity plays in children's personal and emotional development.

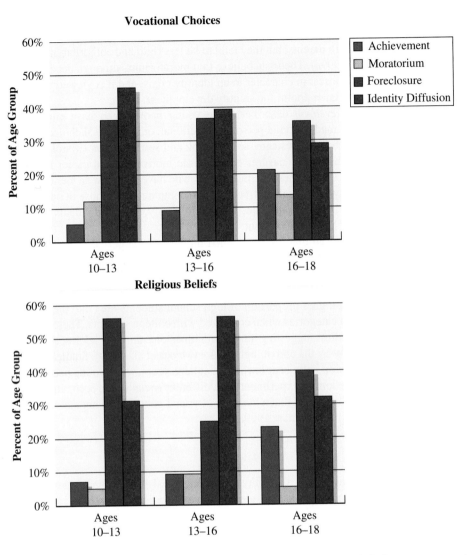

■ FIGURE 6.6
*Percent of Children
at Each Identity
Status for Vocational
Choices and Religious
Beliefs: United States*
Source: After
Waterman (1999a).

Before examining what is known in this area of development, it is important to point out distinctions between *ethnic* and *racial* identity. In the sections that follow, we will sometimes use *ethnic identity* and *racial identity* interchangeably. In part, this approach is due to new evidence that the biological basis for racial classification has been challenged in genetic studies (Smedley & Smedley, 2005). At the same time, due to enforced slavery of African Americans and the societal beliefs that maintained this system of inequality, based on socially constructed views of race for over 200 years, racial identity is often used for describing the group identity of African Americans (see Sellers, Smith, Shelton, Rowley, & Chavous [1998] for further discussion). We will use the term *racial identity* for referring to important developmental work on African American youth and *ethnic identity* for discussing multiple ethnic groups, which is consistent with recent studies of ethnic identity development (Seaton, Scottham, & Sellers, 2006).

Many psychologists and sociologists believe that a healthy racial or ethnic identity plays a positive role in development (Cross, 1991; Graham, & Hudley, 2005; Phinney, 1996; Sellers et al., 1998; Spencer, Fegley, & Harpalani, 2003). A strong connection to one's ethnic or racial group is associated with positive self-esteem (Gray-Little & Hafdahl,

2000; Rowley, Sellers, Chavous, & Smith, 1998), resiliency (Spencer et al., 2006), and psychological well being (Greig, 2003; Seaton et al., 2006). A strong ethnic identity is also associated with range of positive academic behaviors, including classroom engagement, motivation, achievement, and educational attainment (Eccles, Wong, & Peck, 2006; Graham & Hudley, 2005; Rowley, Kurtz-Costes & Cooper, in press).

In this section, we will examine the process of forming an ethnic identity and its important influence on self-esteem. Specifically, we will examine the following sorts of questions: When do people form an ethnic identity? What are the processes through which people form an ethnic identity? Do members of an ethnic minority group have more difficulty forming a coherent and integrated identity than those in the white majority?

Developing an Awareness of Ethnic Differences

Research suggests that children begin to notice racial differences among people as early as 3 years of age. By this age, children are able to correctly identify skin color and their own race or ethnicity. Much of this research is done with doll studies, in which children are asked to choose the doll that looks like a black (or a white) child and to choose the doll that looks most like them (Clark & Clark, 1940; Katz & Zalk, 1974). By age 6, white children identify with their ethnic group with a frequency of 100 percent. In contrast, African American children of the same age identify with their ethnic group at a much lower rate, approximately 70 percent to 75 percent of the time. Research in the 1960s suggested that African American children may be less likely to identify with their own race because of the negative characteristics and attributes attributed to African Americans in our society (Greenwald & Oppenheim, 1968).

However, most of these studies were conducted during the civil rights era. If racial identification studies were done today, African American children might identify with the correct doll at a much higher rate. Current studies indicate that most youths of color develop positive ethnic identities and self-concepts despite negative messages they have received from the broader society about themselves and members of their ethnic group in general (Spencer, 2006).

Ethnic Differences in Self-Concept and Self-Esteem

As you recall, Erikson believed that the development of a strong sense of competence and self-worth is critical for the formation of an identity in adolescence. Before we discuss how children form an ethnic identity, let's first review some of the research on ethnic differences in self-concept and self-esteem.

Racial and ethnic prejudices may make it difficult for ethnic minority children to develop positive feelings of competency and worth. As they grow older, ethnic minority children become painfully aware of how they are negatively evaluated by white society. Young people from various ethnic minority groups in the United States must contend with negative stereotypes, prejudices, and the lower social status of minorities. For this reason, early research assumed that ethnic minority children had poor self-concepts and low self-esteem because of their "inferior" status in white society.

We have already discussed that African American children are more likely to misidentify their ethnic group. Studies report similar results for Native Americans, and the selection of white dolls is presumed to indicate low self-esteem and self-hatred (Spencer & Markstrom-Adams, 1990). However, as suggested earlier, much of the research in this area is dated. In addition, few studies ask children their reasons for choosing the white doll. It has been suggested that children's doll preferences may reflect their understanding of power positions in the world around them (Spencer & Markstrom-Adams, 1990). In addition, children often make different selections when the experimenter is of the same ethnic background. For example, Native American children will choose the Native American doll if the experimenter is of the same tribe. This finding suggests that children may be choosing the doll they believe the white experimenter prefers them to choose. Furthermore, these studies assume that children are using white society as the source of information about their ethnicity.

In general, studies over time report little difference in white and black youths' self-concepts and self-esteem (Graham, 1994; McAdoo, 1985; Rosenberg, 1979). However, a comprehensive review of 261 studies of various ages of children, including young adults, revealed that African Americans have higher average self-esteem than their white counterparts. The advantage was particularly strong for African American girls (Gray-Little & Hafdahl, 2000). A similar pattern was not found in comparisons of Latinos and Asians with white samples. These studies generally show differences in favor of white participants (Carlson, Uppal, & Posser, 2000; Gray-Little & Hafdahl, 2000; Twenge & Crocker, 2002).

Thus far, explanations for these differing patterns of self-esteem have focused on advantages for African American youth. First, it appears that black adolescents may more effectively use their friendship networks and community for social support and acceptance (Gray-Little & Hafdahl, 1999; Greene & Way, 2005). In judging their worth or esteem, African Americans are more likely to draw on the black community as a source of comparison rather than the larger white society (Gray-Little & Hafdahl, 1999). In addition, school success is an important source of high esteem across ethnic groups. Contrary to the view that minority youth devalue the importance of education, due to perhaps their perceived lack of involvement in school activities (see Chapter 9), studies consistently show that parents of minority children stress to their children the importance of education as a way to get ahead (Eccles et al., 2006; Spencer, Noll, Stolzfus, & Harpalani, 2001; Way & Robinson, 2005.). Finally, a strong racial or ethnic identity is an important source of self-esteem among ethnic minority youth (Gray-Little & Hafdahl, 2000; Phinney, 1995; Rowley, Sellers, Chavous, & Smith, 1998; Twenge & Crocker, 2002). We turn to the processes of forming an ethnic identity next.

The Process of Forming an Ethnic Identity

The work of forming an ethnic identity generally begins in adolescence, when young people have the cognitive abilities and social experiences to consider issues related to prejudice and racism and to reflect on their own personal belief systems and values (Bernal & Knight, 1997). Ethnic identity, like any aspect of self-idenity, takes time to discover and involves experimentation with different possibilities. It is not unusual for minority adolescents to experience some type of identity crisis in which they question how they feel about their ethnic identity. This "crisis" is often triggered by an event that causes feelings of humiliation, inferiority, or rejection (Cross, 1991). In Malcom X's autobiography, for example, he attributed the beginning of his search for his ethnic identity to the day he was told by his high school counselor that he should become a carpenter rather than a lawyer, because carpentry was better suited to his race.

Jean Phinney (1989, 1990) proposed one of the most prominent models of ethnic identity development based on Marcia's status model of identity development discussed earlier. Phinney's model focuses on levels of exploration and commitment to ethnic group membership. From in-depth interviews with 91 African American, black, Hispanic, and white 10th-grade students in California, she identified the following four stages of identity states among minority youth:

- **Unexamined ethnic identity:** Some adolescents simply accept the customs and values of their culture with little exploration or question (Marcia's foreclosed status). Other adolescents are simply not interested in exploring their ethnicity, show a preference for the mainstream culture, and reflect little on their ethnicity (Marcia's diffused status).

■ **Ethnic identity search:** Adolescents in this phase of ethnic identity development are seeking to understand the meaning of their ethnicity in relation to the mainstream culture, as well as for themselves. The search process involves learning about one's ethnic heritage through reading, participating in advocacy groups, and attending cultural events.

■ **Achieved ethnic identity:** Adolescents or young people who have developed a clear and confident sense of their own identity. They have come to terms with differences between their ethnic group and the dominant culture, as well as the status of their ethnic group in the larger society (Marcia's achieved status).

About half of the minority students interviewed in this pioneering study had not explored their ethnic identity, 25 percent were involved in active exploration, and another 25 percent showed a strong commitment to their ethnic identity.

Following this initial research, Phinney (1992) developed the Multigroup Ethnic Identity Measure (MEIM), which has been used to assess the development of ethnic identity in a wide variety of groups, including African Americans, Armenians, Asian Indians, Filipinos, Latinos, Salvadorans, and Vietnamese students. Sample items from this measure are presented in Table 6.2. For the most part, studies across ethnic groups show that ethnic identity increases with age (Phinney, 1989, 1990; Seaton et al., 2006). However, ethnic identity is not a strict linear progression. Many adolescents and young adults at the explored or committed state may regress back to a less mature state of ethnic identity development when confronted with new challenges or racial discrimination (Seaton et al., 2006).

Additionally, many late adolescents form what is called *bicultural identity* (Phinney & Devich-Navarro, 1997). A bicultural identity enables ethnic minorities to go back and forth between the ethnic and dominant culture, and alternate identities as appropriate for the situation. One Chinese American adolescent described her bicultural identity this way: "I feel like I am an American, but I respect my Chinese heritage" (Phinney & Rosenthal, 1992, p. 165).

A number of questions remain concerning the development of ethnic identity. Of particular interest are factors that explain variations in ethnic identity formation. Ethnic minority youths must often live between cultures in some satisfactory way. Some may respond by rejecting their own ethnic heritage. For example, one study showed that Asian American adolescents were more likely than African Americans and Hispanic/Latinos to hold negative attitudes toward their own ethnic group (Phinney, 1993). Perhaps the strong emphasis placed on achievement and conformity in Asian American families clashes with the adolescent ideal of freedom and self-expression. An added complication is that ethnic minority youths may be rejected by their own ethnic group if they associate or identify too closely with the majority culture. For example, black students who "act white" may be called "oreos," or some other pejorative term. Recall Roy from the beginning of the chapter. He

---

TABLE 6.2 Sample Items from the Multigroup Ethnic Identity Measure (MEIM)

1. I have spent time trying to find out more about my ethnic group such as its history, traditions, and customs.
2. I am active in organizations or social groups that include mostly members of my own ethnic group.
3. I have a clear sense of my ethnic background and what it means to me.
4. I think a lot about how my life will be affected by my ethnic group membership.
5. I have a strong sense of belonging to my own ethnic group.

Source: Phinney (1992).

was having difficulty living between two cultures, and chose to downplay his abilities to gain approval from members of his ethnic group. In the following example, an African American high school student explains his ambivalence toward his academic success:

> Because they think people won't like think, if they are smart. Like my French teacher was saying—well my—she said—she was saying that I'm good and everything, right? In class, around her, want everybody to act like me. And I tried to say "No! Don't say that!," you know, 'cause I know people get mad at me and stuff. (Fordham, 1988, p. 77)

Some researchers believe that African American and Hispanic/Latino youth may hide their abilities and underachieve in school so they are not perceived as "acting white" by their ethnic group (Fordham, 1996; Fordham & Ogbu, 1986). Thus identity formation for ethnic minorities involves finding the right balance between their own ethnic background and the dominant culture.

How do ethnic minority youth form a healthy ethnic identity? Thus far, a stronger ethnic identity has been positively linked to parental educational levels, immigration status (time spent in United States), parenting discipline practices, use of ethnic language in the home, parental discussions that children about their ethnic background, peer group affiliations, and neighborhood characteristics (Ontai-Grzebik & Raffaelli, 2004; Phinney, Romero, Nava, & Huang, 2001; Supple, Ghazarian, Frabutt, Plunkett, & Sands, 2006). For educators, several other factors are also important for increasing the strength of students' ethnic identity: ethnic composition of the school or neighborhood and access to peers of the same ethnic background. For recent immigrant children and adolescents, it is important for them to identify with their country of origin (Graham & Hudley, 2005). Contrary to the view that some ethnic minority groups must reject the importance of school success, achievement in school can enhance the development of a healthy ethnic identity (Altschul, Oyserman, & Bybee, 2006; Eccles et al., 2006; Graham & Hudley, 2005; Spencer et al., 2001). For example, Tabbye Chavous and her colleagues (2003) reported that 12th-grade African American students who perceived their racial identity as central to their identity attended school more regularly, achieved higher grades, and were more likely to graduate from high school and attend college. In the next section we consider the influence of schools on ethnic identity development.

Schooling and Ethnic Identity Development

What can schools do to help students resolve their ethnic identity conflicts? Schools play a very important role in the development of a young person's ethnic identity. Middle and late adolescence is a critical period for racial identity development. If you recall, important changes in a ethnic identity development occur in part due to adolescents' increased ability to reflect on their belief systems and to think about their place in the larger society. Ethnic identity development is also a social process. Increases in adolescents' exploration of their ethnic identity partly occur due to more ethnically diverse school settings. For example, Sabine French and her colleagues (2006) report that a greater degree of identity exploration occurs when minority youth transition from ethnically homogeneous schools or neighborhoods to more diverse settings. Compared to elementary and middle schools, most high schools, unless located in urban or rural areas with highly homogeneous populations, tend to be more ethnically diverse. Thus, the transition to high school can heighten the salience of racial or ethnic differences and increase the likelihood that minority students will encounter issues concerning their ethnic status (Sellers, Chavous, & Cooke, 1998).

Unfortunately, many youth of color tend to experience more prejudice and discrimination in ethnically mixed settings (French et al., 2006). Several studies indicate that minority and immigrant youth experience discrimination from peers and teachers on a daily basis (Eccles et al., 2006; Portes & Rambaut, 2001; Quintana & Vera, 1999; Wong, Eccles, & Sameroff, 2003). It can take subtle forms such as being ignored while waiting to be called on, being suspected of cheating or receiving extra help to earn a good grade, or being singled out to be a spokesperson for one's ethnic group (Graham & Hudley, 2005; Wong et al., 2003). In many cases, discrimination takes more overt forms in schools, such as harsher disciplinary actions or exclusion of qualified minority students from gifted or advanced placement courses (Rowley, Kurtz-Costes, & Cooper, in press). Receiving lower grades than deserved and unusually harsh discipline practices are the most common experiences of mistreatment of minority youth of color in school settings. Perceptions of prejudice and discrimination can lower academic engagement, lower participation in school activities, increase problem behavior, and create a hostile learning environment for minority youth (Eccles et al., 2006; Graham & Hudley, 2005; Neblett, Phillip, Cogburn, & Sellers, 2006; Phelan et al., 1998; Rowley et al., in press; Wong et al., 2003).

Additionally, as discussed earlier, a bicultural or integrated identity is generally associated with high levels of well-being and self-esteem. If schools pressure young people to assimilate to the mainstream culture too quickly it can have negative consequences, such as alienation from school (Olneck, 1995; Spencer et al., 2001). Some minority students also cope with assimilation pressures by forming strong bonds with members of their ethnic group at school. Margaret Spencer and Carol Markstom-Adams have noted that identification with one's ethnic group can decrease academic achievement if one's ethnic group has been labeled negatively within the dominant culture. These students are at greatest risk for developing what Signithia Fordham and John Ogbu (1986) refer to as an *oppositional* identity, in which the importance of school and earning good grades is devalued. In contrast, young people who experience a modified acculturation process are less likely to form an identity in opposition to the dominant culture (Graham & Hudley, 2005).

We have learned that it is important for adolescents to maintain a connection with their ethnic group of origin. When immigrant youth are discouraged from using their native languages at school, it can hasten their assimilation into the mainstream culture and have a negative impact on ethnic identity development (Olneck, 1995). As we discussed in Chapter 4, it is important for schools to actively embrace multicultural education. Schools are most helpful to students when they respect the cultural heritage of all who attend them. This does not mean, as stated previously, that schools can simply institute international festivals or observe ethnic holidays, such as Rosh Hashanah. Every effort must be made to reduce ethnic stereotyping and to incorporate on a daily basis a sharing of the wealth of diverse ethnic cultural specifics—foods, songs, traditions, and histories.

In general, as you know, multicultural education has not been widely accepted in most schools serving ethnic minority youth. The lack of culturally relevant curriculum materials and teaching practices places added pressures on minority youth to assimilate to the mainstream culture.

Additionally, as with all students, teacher support and high expectations for achievement are important for the development of a healthy ethnic identity. Recent studies indicate that it is important for minority youth to perceive that academic success is an integral part of one's ethnic group (Altschul et al., 2006). For example, Daphne Oyserman and her colleagues (Oyserman, Harrison, & Bybee, 2001) showed that African American students reported higher academic achievement and school engagement when achievement was viewed as part of being African American. Considerable evidence suggests that parents of ethnic minority youth emphasize the importance of education for future success (Eccles et al., 2006; Okagaki, 2006). Teachers can help parents in these efforts by providing success role models for ethnic minority children and by involving parents in their children's education (see Chapter 8). Additionally, instructional practices that foster a sense of competence will help young people to develop a sense of self-confidence in their abilities and a strong ethnic identity. As discussed in a later section, these practices include providing meaningful and challenging work, as well as teacher support to maintain high levels of engagement.

Finally, ability grouping and tracking systems in schools need to be carefully examined. As discussed in Chapter 4, these institutional practices restrict the learning opportunities and educational aspirations of students placed in remedial or low-ability tracks. A disproportionate number of these students are African American or Hispanic/Latino, and fewer of these students are represented in gifted or advanced placement classes as compared to other ethnic groups (National Research Council & Institutes of Medicine, 2004; Oakes, 2005). In terms of ethnic identity development, ability grouping and tracking systems not only restrict learning opportunities, but also reinforce cultural stereotypes of the intellectual inferiority of some ethnic groups. Under these circumstances, it would be difficult for minority youth of color to view school achievement and success as an integral part of their ethnic group. To avoid systems that limit young people's achievement and identity development, it is important for teachers to learn instructional approaches that enable them to meet the needs of students who vary dramatically in their academic abilities (National Research Council & Institutes of Medicine, 2004).

In summary, schools play a very important role in the development of ethnic identity. Educators can employ several methods to help students develop a healthy ethnic identity:

- Every effort must be made to reduce racial/ethnic stereotypes, discrimination, and prejudice.
- Minority youth need opportunities to remain connected to their ethnic group of origin.
- Culturally relevant curriculum and teaching practices can lessen assimilation processes.
- Educators need to help students connect school achievement to future economic opportunities.
- School success is an integral part of ethnic identity development.

Gender-Role Conceptions

Gender is a key component of the self, and it can strongly influence our sense of self-esteem. In this section, we examine how children form *gender-role conceptions,* that is, the images we have of ourselves as males and females. Do you view yourself as sensitive, emotional, and dependent? If so, then your self-image conforms to what society defines as feminine. If you describe yourself as independent, assertive, and strong, then your self-image is consistent with the masculine ideal. Gender conceptions are important for understanding not only the self but the behavior of others. As they grow up, children use information from parents, peers, school, and the media to form theories for how men and women should behave. When certain children fail to act in a gender-typical fashion, they may be rejected or reprimanded by adults or peers (e.g., "Boys don't play with dolls!").

Developmental Trends

Children's understanding of gender categories begins early in development. They demonstrate the ability to understand labels associated with sex (e.g., he or she) by age 30 months (Ruble, Martin, & Berenbaum, 2006). In making these distinctions, young children draw heavily on

TABLE 6.3 Stereotypes of Feminine and Masculine Traits

Feminine Traits	Masculine Traits
Affectionate	Aggressive
Sensitive	Ambitious
Passive	Dominant
Emotional	Rational
Cooperative	Competitive
Dependent	Independent
Weak	Strong
Gentle	Tough
Fearful	Courageous

hair cues. People with long, curly hair, for instance, are perceived as female. By age 3, most children understand that they are a boy or a girl, and they have already begun to show gender-related preferences for toys and activities. Characteristically in American society, boys prefer trucks and blocks, and girls prefer soft, cuddly toys. Boys also engage in more rough-and-tumble play than do girls (Maccoby, 1998). At this young age, children already seem to be imitating the gender-typed behaviors and attitudes being modeled by the adults, peers, and television characters in their environment. The term *gender-typed* means that children are exhibiting a behavior that is culturally defined as appropriate for their sex. The stereotypic views of what it means to be masculine and feminine in our society are listed in Table 6.3.

Although 2- and 3-year-olds can exhibit gender-stereotypic behaviors, they have not yet acquired an understanding of **gender constancy.** Young children believe that it is possible to change one's gender by dressing or acting differently. If you recall, children have difficulty distinguishing between appearances and reality at a young age (see Chapter 3). If a person wears a rabbit costume on Halloween, he or she must be a rabbit. Similarly, young children believe that boys can become girls by wearing dresses, and girls can become boys by cutting their hair short. Boys can grow up to be mommies, and girls can become daddies, or so their thinking goes. Around the age of 4 or 5, most children acquire an understanding of gender constancy, an understanding that gender is permanent and unchangeable. Having developed a sense of gender constancy, children begin to develop a *gender-role concept.* That is, they begin to acquire an a understanding of what it means to be a boy or a girl. Boys selectively attend to male models, and girls pay closer attention to females. In other words, gender becomes a useful category for making sense of the social world. Cognitive theorists use the term **gender schema** to refer to children's knowledge of gender.

Preschool-aged children generally have a well-developed gender schema, which they use to process information. When new information does not fit the expectations of their existing schema, they transform it so that it will fit. In one study, for example, preschoolers watched videotapes of girls playing with trucks and boys playing with dolls. Several days later they were asked to recall what they saw on the videotape. The children were more likely to say that the boys were playing with trucks and the girls were playing with the dolls (Liben & Signorella, 1993). Because children begin very early to process information according to their gender schemata, it is often difficult to change sex-role stereotypes by exposing them to a few nontraditional situations (e.g., women firefighters or male nurses). Young children stubbornly cling to their gender-role concepts, because gender helps them to organize and understand themselves and others.

During early childhood, there is a marked increase in gender-typed behavior. At this age, children believe that gender norms are "immutable, inflexible, and morally right" (Huston, 1983, p. 403). Both boys and girls prefer gender-typed activities and objects over neutral ones by age 3 or 4 (Ruble et al., 2006). Studies also suggest that preschool children react negatively when peers engage in cross-gender activities (Bussey & Bandura, 1999). For example, they disapprove of boys playing with dolls and girls playing with trucks. Studies of preschool children also show that they prefer to play with same-sex friends because they share the same interests and interact in a similar way. For example, Maccoby (1998) suggests that girls prefer the company of other girls, because boys play too rough. Girls also find it difficult to influence boys. In Maccoby's view, it is the girls who stop playing with the boys. This gender segregation in peer groups further strengthens gender-typed behaviors and attitudes, as children have fewer opportunities to learn cross-gender behaviors. Research suggests that gender is more important than race or age when it comes to choosing friends (Maccoby, 1998).

Gender differences in children's interests and activities persist well into adolescence (McHale, Kim, Whiteman, & Crouter, 2004). Girls and boys show different preferences for television shows and videos (Huston & Wright, 1999). Girls spend more time on indoor tasks and chores, whereas boys spend more time outdoors (Huston, Carpenter, Atwater, & Johnson, 1986; Timmer, Eccles, & O'Brien, 1985). Girls like to read about animals, relationships, and romances more than boys, whereas boys prefer science fiction, sports, and war stories (Coles & Hall, 2002). In adolescence, girls report spending more time on personal care, socializing, and shopping, whereas boys devote more time to sports activities (Timmer, Eccles, & O'Brien, 1985). Perhaps due to opportunities afforded by Title IX legislation, girls are taking a more active role in sports in recent years, but involvement in male-typical activities declines from 8th to 10th grades (McHale, Shanahan, Updegraff, Crouter, & Booth, 2004). A recent report also raised issues concerning gender differences in adolescent's use of computer technology (American Association of University Women, 2000).

With cognitive maturity, children's gender-role conceptions become more flexible (Ruble et al., 2006). Older children and adolescents are more likely than younger children to understand that people can have both masculine and feminine traits. This blend of masculinity and femininity is known as **androgyny.** Children and adolescents who are androgynous are less likely to exhibit gender-stereotypic behaviors and attitudes. They can be assertive or sensitive, passive or active, depending on the situation. People with androgynous gender-role conceptions tend to have high self-esteem, coping skills, and life satisfaction (Huston, 1983). For this reason, many child psychologists suggest that parents, teachers, and others should encourage children to develop androgynous gender-role conceptions.

Gender Differences in Self-Perceptions

The gender-role conceptions children learn can shape their feelings of competency and self-esteem. Different competency perceptions are evident among boys and girls by early elementary school (Eccles et al., 1993) and become more marked as students get older (Eccles et al., 1983; Eccles et al., 1998; Harter, 1982; Marsh, 1989; Wigfield et al., 1991). Students' self-concepts reflect traditional sex-role stereotypes. In general, boys tend to have higher self-concepts regarding their physical ability, appearance, and math ability, whereas girls perceive themselves as more competent in reading, verbal skills, and social relationships (Eccles et al., 1983; Eccles et al., 1998; Marsh, 1989). When a general measure of academic self-concept is used, gender differences are less evident.

It is interesting that self-concept differences between adolescent boys and girls sometimes persist even though their ability differences are negligible. For example, from elementary school through college, girls have lower math self-concepts than boys, even though they generally perform equally well if not better than boys in this subject. Ability perceptions also help explain why girls strive harder to achieve in domains that use their verbal and interpersonal skills (e.g., nursing, library science, teaching, and law), and boys strive to achieve in stereotypically masculine areas (e.g., science, engineering, mechanics, and athletics) (Eccles, 1987).

Most studies also report gender differences in children's self-esteem, with boys reporting more positive feelings about themselves than girls (Kling, Hyde, Showers, & Buswell, 1999). Differences in self-esteem begin to appear in middle childhood and are most evident in early adolescence when young people are adjusting to changes in their physical appearances and social environment (Marsh, 1989). In a recent survey, 3,000 schoolchildren from across the country were asked how often they felt happy with the way they were (American Association of University Women, 1992). In elementary school, 69 percent of the boys and 60 percent of the girls responded "always true." By high school, 60 percent of the boys responded this way. However, the figures went from 60 percent to 29 percent for girls. Figure 6.7 shows these trends.

Although the AAUW study (1992) and subsequent reports (Orenstein, 1994; Pipher, 1994) gained a good deal of media attention, a recent analysis of 174 samples concluded that gender differences in self-esteem were rather small in size (Kling et al., 1999). Larger differences were found with age but did not go above one-third of a standard deviation unit, which is not considered a large effect. Furthermore, Kristen Kling and her colleagues concluded that gender differences in self-esteem were most pronounced in white samples. No significant overall gender effect was found for black samples (Kling et al., 1999).

What explains these patterns of gender differences? Many factors undoubtedly play a role. Recall that adolescent girls generally begin puberty earlier than boys, and consequently are more likely than boys to experience multiple transitions (e.g., changes in physical appearance, school settings, and social expectations) at a time when they have fewer coping strategies. Remember, too, that early maturing girls tend to be shorter and heavier than late maturers. The physical appearance of these girls is far from the present tall and slender "ideal" female body portrayed in the media, and the one they prefer. Research has shown that adolescent girls tend to prefer a body that is thinner than their own, whereas boys prefer a body that is larger than their own (Kling et al., 1999). As a result, girls who deviate from this ideal standard tend to have a poorer self-image. Researchers believe that girls—especially white girls—are more vulnerable to disturbances in self-esteem at puberty

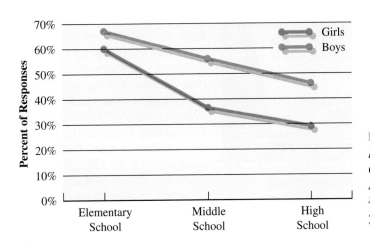

■ FIGURE 6.7
Developmental and Gender Differences in Self-Esteem
Source: After American Association of University Women (1992).

because they place more importance on this ideal of physical attractiveness than boys do (Simmons & Blyth, 1987). Evidence suggests that cultural pressures toward female thinness have intensified in the last decade (Kling et al., 1999).

Theorists also believe that cultural stereotypes play an important role in the development of girls' and boys' self-perceptions. As you will see, children begin to learn gender stereotypes at a very early age. Because "male" skills and traits tend to be more highly valued in patriarchal societies, girls who conform to traditional female stereotypes are at a greater risk for feelings of inferiority and low self-esteem. In support of this claim, research indicates that girls who view themselves as mathematically competent, a presumed masculine trait, report higher levels of self-esteem during the transition to adolescence (Wigfield et al., 1991). Other studies indicate that both male and female adolescents who have an androgynous gender-role orientation tend to report higher levels of self-esteem (Dusek, 1987; Lundy & Rosenberg, 1987) and higher levels of self-worth and scholastic achievement (Rose & Montemayor, 1994). In the next section, we examine the effects of socialization experiences on children's gender-role conceptions.

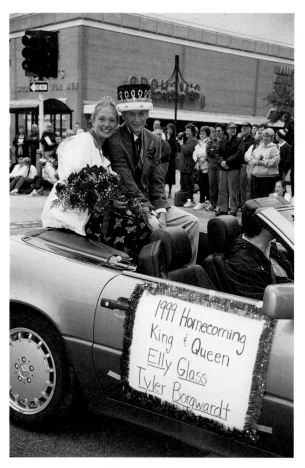

Schools are important arenas for learning and expressing gender-role behaviors. Unfortunately, schools often reinforce sex-role stereotypes.
Source: James L. Shaffer.

Gender-Role Socialization

Gender-role socialization is the process by which children learn the attitudes and behavior that society defines as appropriate for their gender. As we have seen, children have already learned a great deal about gender roles before they enter school. Theorists believe that the process of gender-role socialization begins right at birth, and then intensifies in adolescence, when young people begin to prepare for their adult roles (Hill & Lynch, 1983; Huston & Alvarez, 1990). Parents, peers, schools, and the mass media all play a role in shaping children's role conceptions (Bussey & Bandura, 1999; Ruble & Martin, 1998; Ruble et al., 2006). We briefly discuss each of these socialization influences.

Parents are extremely influential socializers of gender roles. From an early age, parents view their sons and daughters differently. They describe their newborn daughters as softer, cuter, and more delicate than their newborn sons. Baby girls are dressed in pink, dresses, lace tights, and patent-leather shoes, whereas baby boys wear blue, trousers, T-shirts, and sneakers. Even the bedrooms of infant boys and girls are decorated differently. Parents also treat their infant sons and daughters differently. They generally play in a more nurturing way with their daughters and engage in more gross motor play with their sons. Mothers are more likely to encourage autonomy and independence in their sons than in their daughters (Pomerantz & Ruble, 1998). Fathers are more likely than mothers to play with their children in a sex-stereotypic fashion, and boys receive more criticism for cross-gender behavior (e.g., playing with dolls) than girls do (Ruble & Martin, 1998).

Children also observe many examples of sex-stereotypic behavior in the home. Although gender roles are changing, the average child is still more likely to observe his or her mother cooking, cleaning, and caring for children. Fathers are observed fixing things, mowing the lawn, and driving the car. Similarly, when children are asked to do chores, girls wash the dishes and help clean the house, whereas boys mow the lawn, take out the garbage, and shovel snow (Goodnow, 1988). The average child is also likely to observe his or her mother working in traditionally "female" jobs (teaching, nursing, sales, clerical positions) and his or her father working in traditionally "male" jobs (business, trades, engineering).

Parents also hold gender-stereotypic beliefs about their children's competencies. The research of Jacquelynne Eccles and her colleagues (Eccles, 1993, 1994; Eccles & Harold, 1991; Eccles et al., 1998; Jacobs & Eccles, 1992; Yee & Eccles, 1988) has shown that parents generally subscribe to the cultural stereotype that boys are naturally better at mathematics than are girls. For example, parents of boys rated natural ability as an important reason for their son's successes in mathematics, whereas parents of girls rated effort as important (Yee & Eccles, 1988). These differences were found even when the boys and girls had equivalent abilities in mathematics. Research further suggests that parents' stereotypic beliefs have an important influence on their development of their children's achievement beliefs and self-perceptions (Alexander & Entwisle, 1988; Eccles-Parsons et al., 1982; Eccles et al., 1998; Jacobs & Eccles, 1992; Phillips, 1987).

Not all families, however, encourage or reinforce gender-typed behavior. Parents who make a conscious effort to avoid gender-stereotypic behaviors have less gender-typed children (Weisner & Wilson-Mitchell, 1990). One study showed that fathers' involvement in child care at home was associated with adolescents' approval of nontraditional roles for themselves (Williams, Radin, & Allegro, 1992). Girls without brothers or only one brother tend to have less traditional attitudes toward gender roles (Hertsgaard & Light, 1984; Levy, 1989). When there is a more egalitarian division of labor in the home (or father involvement), children show less traditional gender-role behaviors and attitudes (McHale, Crouter, & Whiteman, 2003). Additionally, adolescents of both genders in two-parent families report less traditional gender-role attitudes when their mothers are employed outside the home (Hoffman, 1989; Huston & Alvarez, 1990; Lerner, 1994).

As children grow older, they begin to spend more time with other children. The peer group is one of the most important social contexts for the socialization of gender-role behaviors and attitudes (Bussey & Bandura, 1999; Maccoby, 1998; Ruble & Martin, 1998). In fact, some experts contend that the peer group is the primary sex-role socializing agent in development (Leaper, 1994; Maccoby, 1998). By age 3, same-sex peers positively reinforce one another for showing "gender-appropriate" behavior. Preschool children who play with toys associated with the opposite sex are often ignored or teased by their peers (Fagot, 1985; Langlois & Down, 1980). Boys are particularly intolerant of other boys who engage in cross-gender play. They often voice their disapproval using expressions like, "Stop acting like a girl," or "That's for girls." Although children spend most of their time in sex-segregated peer groups, they become more tolerant of sex-role transgressions in middle childhood (Stoddart & Turiel, 1985). However, conformity to gender-role conventions becomes important again in early adolescence. Early-adolescent girls feel less free to experiment with male sex-typed activities than they did in middle childhood (Huston & Alvarez, 1990). This intensification of gender-role socialization within the peer group is partly due to dating pressures and greater cross-sex interactions. Young adolescents conform to cultural ideals of femininity and masculinity as a way of increasing their sexual attractiveness (Crockett, 1990). By late adolescence, these factors are less important, but deviation from sex-typed norms can still lead to poor peer acceptance (Huston & Alvarez, 1990).

The mass media are another source of sex-role stereotypes (Ruble et al., 2006). Although music, rock videos, films, books, and magazines are all popular forms of entertainment for children and adolescents, the effects of television on gender-role behaviors and attitudes have received the most attention (Huston & Wright, 1998). Young people spend 3 to 4 hours a day watching television (Roberts, Foehr, Rideout, & Brodie, 1999), and what they view is highly gender stereotypic (Calvert & Huston, 1987; Ruble & Martin, 1998). Children's programs tend to present more gender-stereotyped images than do adult programs. Cartoon and educational programs tend to be dominated by male characters such as Big Bird, Barney, and Spiderman. A recent study of commercials during children's programs also showed that boys appeared in greater numbers, assumed more active roles, and acted more aggressively than girls did (Ruble & Martin, 1998). Media for adolescents are also highly stereotypic in their portrayal of women and men. For example, music videos are dominated by men, and women are generally portrayed as sexual and subservient (Gow, 1996; Sommers-Flanagan, Sommers-Flanagan, & Davis, 1993). Although women are beginning to be shown in more prestigious careers on television, stereotyping of occupations for men and women continues (Signorelli & Bacue, 1999). As you might imagine, exposure to highly stereotypic messages on television can increase a young person's sex-typed beliefs and behaviors (Huston & Alvarez, 1990).

When children enter school, they encounter stereotypic curriculum materials, extracurricular activities, and staffing patterns (Bussey & Bandura, 1999; Meece, 1987; Meece & Scantlebury, 2006; Ruble & Martin, 1998). At school, children observe and learn about the adult world, and the adult images to which they are exposed may be more rigid and more polarized than those found in the larger society (Ruble & Martin, 1998). For example, women are more likely to perform traditional gender roles in schools such as caring for young children, putting on bandages, and preparing food, whereas men are more likely to manage the school and staff. A majority of high school foreign language, humanities, business education, and English teachers are female, whereas only half of science teachers are female (Weiss, Banilower, McMahon, & Smith, 2001). Students also learn important gender-role lessons from textbooks, videotapes, and computer software at school.

Teachers also tend to interact differently with boys and girls at school. At both the elementary and secondary school levels boys are called on more than girls to answer process, abstract, and complex questions. Further, compared with girls, boys also receive more acknowledgement, approval, encouragement, criticism, and corrective feedback in response to their answers (Altermatt, Jovanovic, & Perry, 1998; Brophy & Good, 1974). By high school, boys are more likely to take calculus, computer, and chemistry classes, participate in contact sports, and lead the student council. In contrast, girls are expected to excel in reading, writing, and foreign languages, to participate in the performing arts (orchestra, chorus, drama club, etc.), and to cheer for male sports teams. Numerous studies have also shown that boys and girls are treated differently in the classroom (AAUW, 1992). For example, as discussed in Chapter 4, boys receive more attention and praise for correct answers and high levels of achievement. School counselors may support and encourage boys' interests in the scientific and technological fields, but may steer young women away from those fields (Betz & Fitzgerald, 1988). Gender-biased interaction patterns not only communicate different expectations of performance but also convey different views of boys' and girls' abilities.

To summarize, children begin to learn gender-role stereotypes early in life. At home, boys and girls are encouraged to engage in sex-typed activities, and they can observe many examples of sex-stereotypic behaviors. The peer group and mass media continue this socialization process by perpetuating and reinforcing sex-role stereotypes of male and female behavior. Schools also play a significant role in the development of children's gender-role conceptions, and they have been slow in adapting to changes in the social roles of men and women. As a result, schools may be exposing children and adolescents to "masculine and feminine images that are even more rigid and more polarized than those currently held by the wider society" (Meece, 1987, p. 67).

For the most part, studies in the 1980s and 1990s argued that schools were "short-changing" girls in their development (AAUW, 1992: National Council for Women, 1998; Sadker & Sadker, 1994). Citing data documenting boys' declining achievement and status in school, recent reports have argued that educational programs to help girls achieve in schools have harmed boys (Pollock, 1998; Sommers, 2000). The Focus on Research box on page 382 summarizes recent controversies concerning the status of boys and girls in school.

Development of Achievement Motivation

Many teachers report that motivating students to learn is one of their most difficult problems. Some students are clearly self-motivated, but others show very little interest in learning, gaining new skills, or improving their abilities. Far too many students do not develop their academic abilities or talents simply because they lack the desire to do so. By adolescence, poor motivation is one of the chief contributors to the problems of student underachievement and school dropout.

Definitions of Achievement Motivation

Before exploring changes in children's motivation during the school years, we must first define what is meant by **achievement motivation.** The Latin root of the term *motivation* is the verb *movere,* which means *to move.* Achievement motivation theorists try to explain what initiates, sustains, and terminates behavior in achievement situations (Pintrich & Schunk, 1996). Unfortunately, there are numerous definitions of achievement motivation that involve defining it as an enduring psychological need, an environmentally activated state, and a set of cognitions and beliefs.

Motivation as a Psychological Need

Some motivation theorists focus on internal mechanisms, such as psychological needs. A need is an internal tension or conflict that leads a person to engage in goal-directed behavior. People have physiological, social, and psychological needs that can influence their behavior. If you recall, Erikson proposed that children have needs for security, autonomy, competence, and identity that can influence their behavior throughout childhood and adolescence.

Maslow's hierarchy of human needs is one of the best-known theories of motivation. Maslow (1970) proposed that people have lower- and higher-order needs. He conceptualized a hierarchy of human needs arranged according to the following priorities:

■ Physiological needs (hunger, thirst, sleep)
■ Safety needs (freedom from physical or psychological harm)
■ Love needs (acceptance and affection from parents, friends, etc.)
■ Esteem needs (confidence in one's abilities, mastery of environment)
■ Self-actualization needs (self-expression, creativity, curiosity, harmony with the environment)

Maslow argued that lower-order needs (physiological, safety, love) must be satisfied before higher-order needs can be pursued and expressed. If children come to school

Focus on
Research

Are Schools Failing Boys or Girls?

Are schools equitable environments for boys and girls? If not, do schools favor boys or girls? To answer these questions, researchers investigate a litany of factors that represent school achievement and psychological functioning. Depending on the frame of reference and outcome variables selected, very different conclusions can be drawn about the educational institution's ability to equally promote boys' and girls' development as they progress through school.

Educational practice, research, and policy efforts have been dominated by girls' issues, primarily due to technological advancement in the workplace coupled with the male-dominated occupational fields, especially in the scientific fields (Cooper & Weaver, 2003). For example, C. Benbow and collaborators (Benbow, Lubinski, Shea, & Eftekhari-Sanjani, 2000) conducted a 20-year follow-up investigation of 1,975 high school boys and girls ranking in the top 1 percent in mathematical ability. Findings revealed that differences in mathematical reasoning ability in high school predicted educational and occupational paths. Individuals in the sample were accomplished professionals and satisfied with their success, though as existing literature suggests, women were mainly concentrated in the humanities and men in the physical and engineering sciences. However, despite the persistent gender gap, girls are making considerable gains in mathematics and sciences. Among high school graduates in 2000, girls were more likely than boys to enroll in advanced mathematics and science courses (Coley, 2001; National Center for Education Statistics, 2005).

Over the past decade, studies revealing alarming deficits in boys' basic skills have been the catalyst for an international effort to expand the study of gender and schooling to include boys' issues (Downey & Yuan, 2005; Salomone, 2006). This shift has been coined by Weaver-Hightower as the "boy-turn," and for boys' advocates the attention is long overdue (Weaver-Hightower, 2003). Downey and Yuan's (2005) research study on gender differences in school performance revealed that at every stage in schooling, girls are producing equal or higher grades than boys in all subjects, including ones in which boys hold higher test scores. The national reading and writing report cards detail a persistent gender gap in reading and writing, with boys considerably trailing girls (National Center for Education Statistics, 2003, 2005). Other evidence research documents that lower reading ability predicted and being male predicated in-grade-retention; boys' retention rates were found to be 12.4 percentage points higher than that of girls' (McCoy & Reynolds, 1999). Further, students in the study who were retained were twice more likely to drop out of school and significantly less likely to pursue postsecondary education (Fine & Davis, 2003).

hungry, sick, or tired, they will have little interest in learning or developing their competencies. Similarly, it is difficult for children to learn if they do not feel safe or accepted at school. Maslow's theory is helpful in understanding why some children may not be motivated to develop their competencies, to try new things, or to express their creative abilities.

John Atkinson (1964) proposed that people differ in their *need to achieve,* that is, in their desire to excel in achievement situations. Other theorists have emphasized children's needs for competence and autonomy. For example, Robert White (1959) believed that such behaviors as mastery, exploration, and play were a result of a child's inherent need to deal competently with his or her environment. White labeled this disposition *effectance motivation.* He believed that this psychological need propels individuals to engage in activities from which they could derive a sense of personal mastery or competency. White believed that effectance motivation explains behaviors as diverse as a toddler learning to walk to an adolescent mastering calculus. Similarly, Edward Deci and Richard Ryan (1985) emphasized students' psychological needs for autonomy and self-determination. Like White, they believe that children strive to be causal agents in their environments.

Researchers attempt to identify school factors that can account for puzzling trends in boys' low performance in school, particularly in the humanities. Many hypotheses have been offered in popular debate; however, research verifying these theories is sparse (Weaver-Hightower, 2003). First, there is a common belief that differential rates in development leave boys in a downward academic spiral beginning in elementary school. Second, language arts curricula do not accommodate for boys' interests. Lastly, the gender of the teacher and child affect student performance and engagement.

Reading and language arts currently show the largest gender gaps throughout the school years. It is argued here that language arts curriculum do not accommodate for boys' reading interests in nonfiction and texts rich in factual information and should be expanded to include boys' interests (Salomone, 2006; Smith & Wilhelm, 2002; Taylor, 2004 2005; Weaver-Hightower, 2003). Research findings reveal that nonfiction texts were actually preferred by weaker boy readers aged 7 to 9 (Moss, 2000). Research on gender differences in writing also points to the lack of representation of boys. A New Zealand study found that boys reported more negative attitudes toward writing and less enjoyment (Hansen, 2001). Further, findings document that girls and boys reported comparable levels of confidence in their writing ability, but perceived that teachers differentially valued writing produced by boys versus girls.

Taken together, gender and education research naturally leads to the question of whether separate programs and schooling for boys and girls would be beneficial. Title IX regulations originally established in 1972 prohibited separate treatment based on gender, which prevented single-sex public schooling practices. In 2004, the Office of Civil Rights issued legislation that lifted restrictions against single-gendered schools and programs. Due to this recent change in legislation, research on the effectiveness of single-sex schooling is relatively undeveloped and currently inconclusive in the public-school sector. However, there is some evidence that single-sex programs have a positive influence on confidence, educational and career aspirations, and self-esteem (AAUW, 1998; Salomone, 2006).

Gender equity in schooling has been an important concern of educators, researchers, policy writers, and parents for many decades. The state of research indicates that debate on gender equity grows more complex and is still far from being resolved. What is clear is that the developmental needs and interests of both boys and girls should be considered simultaneously in the design of research, policy, and practice.

Children's needs for competence, autonomy, and mastery serve as the foundation for the development of intrinsic motivation. When students are intrinsically motivated to learn, they enjoy learning for the sake of learning. **Intrinsic motivation** arises from internal sources such as curiosity, interest, enjoyment, and innate strivings for mastery and growth. A student who spends hours reading a book because it is enjoyable or interesting is intrinsically motivated. The student does not need external pressures or incentives to do this task. **Extrinsic motivation,** on the other hand, arises from external contingencies. The student engages in a particular task to get a reward, to earn a high grade, to fulfill a requirement, to please someone, and so forth. When classroom activities are undertaken for these purposes, learning becomes a means to an end. The student perceives his or her behavior as controlled by external rather than internal causes, which can reduce feelings of competence and self-determination. Early studies imply that individuals are either intrinsically or extrinsically motivated to learn. However, current research suggests that for any given activity, one or both orientations may be at work (Harter, Whitesall, & Kowalksi, 1992).

In late childhood and beyond, peers have an important influence on students' motivation to learn in school.
Source: © image 100 Ltd.

Motivation as a Situational State

Other theorists conceptualize motivation as a state that is highly influenced by a particular situation. These theories focus on the *incentive* and *reinforcement* conditions within the learning situation. According to this perspective, differences in achievement motivation are explained by an individual's reinforcement history and by reward contingencies in the present situation. There is no need to consider inner thoughts, feelings, or psychological needs. Attempts to improve student motivation involve providing the appropriate rewards and incentives. Interestingly, a recent study revealed that beginning teachers generally use rewards and punishments to motivate students (Newby, 1991). More than half of their motivation strategies involved some type of external reinforcer (e.g., extra recess time, stickers, loss of privileges). Strategies that involved increasing the perceived relevance of an activity or the student's confidence to accomplish the activity occurred in less than 7 percent of the observations.

Motivation as a Set of Cognitions and Beliefs

In recent research, theorists have defined motivation as a set of cognitive beliefs and processes that are shaped both by early learning experiences and by the immediate learning situation. One cognitive model of motivation stresses the importance of students' achievement expectations and values. According to expectancy-value theories of motivation, students are more motivated to engage in learning activities when they *expect* and *want* to succeed. In other words, students ask themselves: "Am I able to do this task? Why should I want to do this task?" Numerous studies have shown that students' expectations and values are strongly related to a wide range of achievement behaviors, including task choice, persistence, and performance (Eccles, 2005, Eccles et al., 1998; Feather, 1982; Wigfield, 1994).

Another theory of motivation emphasizes the critical role of students' self-efficacy beliefs. **Self-efficacy** is defined as people's judgment of their ability to perform a task given the skills they possess and the circumstances they face (Bandura, 1986). Research suggests that self-efficacy beliefs can affect people's choice of activities, their effort, and their persistence (Bandura, 1986; Pajares, 1996; Schunk, 1991, 2002). Students who have a low sense of efficacy for accomplishing a task may avoid it, whereas those who feel capable will more readily engage in the task and persist at it longer. Students with a higher sense of efficacy are also more likely to use self-regulating learning strategies (Pintrich & Schrauben, 1992). Self-efficacy theory is very similar to expectancy-value theory because both theories emphasize the critical role of a person's judgment of his or her capabilities.

Attributional processes are believed to play an important role in the formation of expectancy and efficacy beliefs. *Attribution theories* of motivation examine how individuals interpret their successes and failures in achievement situations (Weiner, 1986). When students attribute their successes or failures to stable factors, they will expect their future performance to be similar to their current performance. If, for example, a student attributes a success (or failure) to ability, then he or she can expect to succeed (or fail) at similar tasks in the future. However, if the student attributes successes or failures to unstable factors, such as effort or luck, then the student's current performance may not be a good indicator of his or her future performance. To maintain high expectations for success, most motivation theorists believe that students should attribute their successes to high ability and attribute their failures to lack of effort (Eccles et al., 1983; Weiner, 1986).

Theories of intrinsic and extrinsic motivation also have a cognitive component. As stated previously, some motivation theorists claim that humans have a psychological need to feel self-determining or autonomous (Deci & Ryan, 1985). These theorists argue that people analyze their achievement activities in terms of the locus of causality. That is, people are intrinsically motivated when they perceive themselves as the causes of their behavior. By contrast, people are extrinsically motivated when the locus of causality is external. They perceive themselves as behaving a certain way to please others, to obtain a reward, or to avoid negative consequences. In this theory, perceptions of causality are critical for understanding achievement motivation. Activities are more intrinsically motivating when students believe they are choosing to engage in the activity by their own volition. In a later section, we will discuss the effects of rewards, incentives, and punishment on students' intrinsic motivation to learn.

Expectancy-value, self-efficacy, attribution, and intrinsic motivation theories all belong to the cognitive tradition in motivation research, because they emphasize cognitive beliefs and processes. Another theory that fits within this cognitive tradition is goal theory. *Goal theories of motivation* emphasize students' *reasons* for choosing, performing, and persisting at various achievement activities (Dweck & Elliot, 1983; Nicholls, 1994). For example, one student may spend an extra hour each night studying algebra because she wants to understand how to solve structural equations, whereas another student may study an extra hour because he wants the best grade in the class. Both of these students are motivated to study, but for different reasons.

Goal theorists have identified two types of goal orientations that influence students' achievement efforts. Distinctions between these two types of goals are quite similar to the internal and external sources of motivation described earlier. Students with an intrinsic goal orientation engage in learning activities because they want to learn something new, develop their skills, or master an activity. They are guided by what are called *task-oriented goals* or *learning-oriented goals* (Dweck & Elliot, 1983; Nicholls, 1984). Task mastery is the desired goal. In contrast, students with an *extrinsic* goal orientation engage in learning activities because they want to get a good grade, please others, obtain a reward, or avoid punishment. They are guided by goals that are extrinsic to the learning task. These students derive satisfaction from external rewards and incentives, regardless of what is learned.

Focus on
Research

Learned Helplessness in the Making

What causes students to develop a sense of mastery or helplessness in academic situations? In a study of fifth-grade students, Elliot and Dweck (1988) demonstrated that patterns of learned helplessness were elicited by different learning conditions. When the benefits of learning were emphasized by the experimenter (e.g., "Doing this puzzle will sharpen your mind"), students demonstrated a *mastery-oriented* learning pattern. When they experienced difficulty or failure, they responded by trying different problem-solving strategies, concentrating harder, and staying focused on the task. In contrast, when students were told their performance would be filmed and judged by "experts," they demonstrated a *learned helplessness* pattern, especially if they lacked confidence in their ability to perform the task. When these students experienced difficulty or failure, they responded by using less effective problem-solving strategies, giving up attempts to find more effective ways of solving the problem, expressing negative affect toward the task (e.g., "I'm going to hate this part"), and blaming themselves for failure ("I'm not good at this" or "I'm confused"). These students essentially perceived their learning problems as insurmountable and stopped trying, even though they had previously solved similar problems. Teachers can reduce learned helplessness by refraining from public forms of evaluation, by reducing testing pressures, and by providing specific feedback concerning how students can improve.

If students must compete with others for grades and recognition, this condition can evoke an orientation in which students focus on their ability to perform or to compete. These students adopt what are called *performance-oriented goals* or *ego-oriented goals* (Dweck & Elliot, 1983; Nicholls, 1984). Under these conditions, students feel successful when they receive the best grade or do well with little effort, because it implies high ability. Students with performance-oriented motivation patterns are more interested in immediate rewards than long-term learning.

Both learning- and performance-oriented students are willing to complete learning activities, but research has shown that there are important differences in the ways they approach and respond to those activities. As described in the Focus on Research box, a learning-oriented focus is associated with a *mastery-oriented* problem-solving approach, whereas students who focus on their ability to perform show a **learned helplessness** pattern. Other differences in students' achievement behavior include the following.

- Students who focus on intrinsic goals prefer challenging activities over easy tasks, because they can learn from them (Ames & Archer, 1988; Elliot & Dweck, 1988)
- With a learning-oriented focus, students are more likely to seek instrumental forms of help (e.g., asking for hints, examples, and information) that allow them to continue working on their own. When students are focused on performance goals, they prefer a more passive form of help seeking, such as having someone solve the problems for them (Aberbach & Roeser, 1993).
- With an intrinsic, learning-oriented focus, students tend to use active learning strategies that enhance conceptual understanding (e.g., reviewing material, focusing attention, setting goals, checking comprehension, and relating new information to existing information). Conversely, extrinsic goals are associated with short-term or superficial learning strategies, such as simply memorizing or rehearsing information (Ames & Archer, 1988; Graham & Golan, 1991; Meece, Blumenfeld, & Hoyle, 1988; Nolen, 1988).

The "Hidden Costs" of Rewards

Focus on
Research

Lepper, Greene, and Nisbett (1973) studied the effects of rewards on preschool children. The children were first given an opportunity to draw with magic markers. After how long each child played with the magic markers was recorded, one group of children received a reward for playing with the markers and another group received no reward. The reward was a big red ribbon with a gold star, and a piece of paper with their name on it. The children were then given another opportunity to play with the magic markers. Interestingly, the children who had received the reward did not spend as much time playing with the magic markers as the children who were not given the reward did. Moreover, the quality of the rewarded children's pictures declined once the reward was withdrawn. The researchers concluded that rewards can undermine intrinsic motivation, because children are less likely to approach or choose similar activities if they do not expect to be rewarded. That is, children come to believe that they are engaging in the task not because it is interesting or they can learn something, but because they are being rewarded. Extrinsic incentives or rewards work best when (a) students show little or no initial interest in learning, (b) they are contingent on a particular level of mastery or attainment of certain goals, (c) they are achievable by all students, and (d) they are not used to control students' behavior.

- Students who focus on their ability to perform show poor recall of information when the learning tasks require deeper levels of information processing (Benware & Deci, 1984; Graham & Golan, 1991).
- Under performance goal orientations, students may use *self-handicapping* strategies such as reducing effort, setting unrealistically high goals for themselves, or procrastinating (Anderman, Griesinger, & Westerfield, 1998; Urdan, Ryan, Anderman, & Gheen, 2002).

Why do learning and performance goals elicit these different learning patterns? Learning goals create a task focus in which students attend to the *quality* of their performance and the effort needed to succeed. Conversely, when one is focused on external rewards (praise and grades), attention is drawn away from how to do the task and is focused on its rewards. When students must compete with others for rewards or grades, they may become anxious about their ability to perform and about how they will be evaluated by others. This anxiety and worry can undermine students' concentration and impair their problem solving.

Conclusions About Motivation Theories

Motivation researchers define *motivation* in many different ways. Early theories focused on innate needs, such as the need to achieve or competence needs. Behavioral theories focused on how rewards and incentives influenced motivation. This theory of motivation is still widely applied in classrooms today. Unfortunately, research has shown that rewards and incentives can undermine students' intrinsic motivation to learn. The Focus on Research box above describes an early study of the hidden costs of rewards for student motivation.

Most contemporary theories of motivation focus on students' beliefs, values, goals, and cognitive processes. Table 6.4 on page 389 presents an overview of the various cognitive theories. Of the cognitive theories reviewed, goal theory may provide the most useful framework for teachers as it focuses on the reasons that children engage in or avoid achievement activities. In a later section, we will discuss how teachers can create an instructional environment to promote an intrinsic learning orientation in their classrooms.

UNDERSTANDING
CHILDREN
Strategy 5.13:
Observation of Student
Engagement

Focus on
Research

Illusory Incompetence

What causes some high-achieving students to experience motivational problems? Deborah Phillips and Marc Zimmerman (1990) hypothesized that some highly capable students develop unrealistically low estimates of their abilities. Phillips studied the self-perceptions and achievement aspirations of fifth- and ninth-grade students who scored above the 75th percentile on a standardized achievement test. Approximately 20 percent of fifth graders and 16 percent of ninth graders seriously underestimated their level of ability. The results also showed that approximately 28 percent of the children who underestimated their ability in fifth grade were in

the low-perceived-competence group in the ninth grade. By the ninth grade, girls mostly made up the group that underestimated their abilities. The results further showed that when compared to more confident peers, children who seriously underestimated their actual ability and children whose self-perceptions of ability declined between the fifth and ninth grade were viewed by their mothers as less capable and by both parents as not performing up to their potential. This study demonstrated that high ability does not always guarantee feelings of competence or optimal motivation. Parents help shape the way children perceive their abilities.

Individual Differences in Achievement Motivation

Why are some students confident of their ability to succeed, whereas others express serious doubts about their abilities? Why are some students more motivated to learn than others? In this section, we will examine three sources of individual differences: conceptions of ability, early learning experiences and parenting practices, and socioeconomic influences.

Ability Differences

Research suggests that students often develop unrealistic views of their abilities. We have already seen how girls are likely to underestimate their abilities in mathematics and science, whereas boys may underestimate their reading or verbal abilities. Such differences in ability perceptions can influence children's motivation to participate and to achieve in different academic domains, especially if the activity is perceived as inappropriate for one's gender.

Researchers have also examined the motivational orientations of students with different measured abilities. Their work suggests that both low and high achievers may develop motivational problems if they lack confidence in their abilities. For example, Marijo Renick and Susan Harter (1989) found that students with a diagnosed learning disability generally have more negative perceptions of their abilities, which in turn lessens their intrinsic motivation to learn. Other evidence suggests that high-ability students can have serious motivational problems if they underestimate their abilities, have low-achievement expectations, or give up easily on tasks that are well within their level of ability. The Focus on Research box describes how high-ability students can develop an illusion of incompetence. It is important to remember that even though students get good grades, they may not have the self-confidence they need to maintain a learning focus in the classroom or to take on challenging tasks.

Carol Dweck and Elaine Elliot (1983) suggest that students not only hold different *perceptions* of their abilities but also use different *conceptions* of ability for judging their

TABLE 6.4 Cognitive Theories of Achievement Motivation

Theory	Description
Expectancy-value	Emphasizes people's expectations for success and achievement values. People are highly motivated when they expect and want to do well on an achievement activity.
Self-efficacy	Emphasizes people's judgments of how well (or poorly) they will perform a task given the skills they have and the circumstances they face. People are highly motivated to achieve when they believe they can perform a task or an activity successfully.
Attribution	Emphasizes people's interpretations of their success. People are highly motivated to achieve when they attribute successes to ability and failures to lack of effort or use of appropriate strategy.
Achievement goals	Emphasizes people's reasons for engaging in achievement activities. People are highly motivated to achieve when they want to develop or demonstrate competence, but these two goal orientations are associated with very different patterns of learning. People show greater cognitive engagement in, and persistence at, achievement activities when they are learning oriented. They want to learn for the sake of learning.
Self-determination	Emphasizes people's judgments of causality. People are intrinsically motivated when they attribute their behavior to internal rather than external causes.

TABLE 6.5 Links Between Theories of Intelligence, Goals, Perceived Ability, and Learning Patterns

Theory of Intelligence	Goal Type	Dominant Concerns	Perceived Ability	Behavioral Response
Entity (ability is fixed)	Performance	Is my ability adequate?	High	Mastery
			Low	Helpless
Incremental (ability is malleable)	Learning	How can I improve?	High	Mastery
			Low	Mastery

Source: After Dweck & Leggett (1988).

competence. Some students believe that their ability level is fixed and cannot be improved through practice or effort; they have an **entity theory of ability.** Other students have an **incremental theory of ability,** because they believe they can improve their ability by investing greater effort or by trying different strategies. Dweck and Elliot maintain that these different conceptions of ability are *unrelated* to objective measures of ability such as grades or achievement test scores. Table 6.5 describes links between students' conceptions of ability, goals, and mastery-oriented versus learned helplessness behavioral patterns.

Early Learning Experiences and Parenting Practices

To explain individual differences in children's achievement motivation, many theorists focus on early learning experiences that can help children develop a sense of competence and efficacy. This research focuses on the following sorts of questions:

- Do parents encourage children from an early age to explore and to try new things?
- Do parents provide appropriate levels of support when children attempt new activities?
- Do parents provide consistent standards by which children can judge their accomplishments?
- Do parents communicate high- or low-achievement expectations to their children?
- Do parents react harshly to disappointing performances?

Early research by Susan Harter (1978) maintained that successful early learning experiences give children the confidence to deal effectively and competently with their environment. As a result, these children become intrinsically motivated. They develop an internal set of mastery standards to judge their accomplishments and a strong sense of confidence in their abilities (i.e., self-efficacy). Conversely, students whose motivation is primarily extrinsic are less likely to have developed these mastery standards early. This can occur if young children experience a history of failure or disapproval in response to their early learning efforts. Alternatively, some children are rewarded from an early age for their accomplishments, so that they become dependent on external incentives for their source of motivation.

Another area of research has examined differences in parent–child relations. This research suggests that parenting styles that are either too controlling or too permissive can damage children's motivation and achievement patterns (Bronstein, Ginsburg, & Herrera, 2005; Gonzalez, Ginsburg, & Herrera, 2005; Spera, 2005). In contrast, parenting styles that support children's independence are generally associated with higher levels of intrinsic motivation and perceived competence. Examples of supportive parenting styles might include (a) giving children input into decision making, (b) stating expectations in a suggestive rather than in a directive way, (c) acknowledging children's needs and feelings, and (d) providing choices and alternatives.

Gender Differences in Achievement Motivation

As we discussed, gender-role socialization begins quite early in children's development. By the preschool years, children sex-type activities as either masculine or feminine. And gender differences in children's perceptions of abilities are evident by the early elementary years (Eccles, 1984; Eccles et al., 1993, 1998; Eccles-Parsons et al., 1982; Harter, 1982). Cultural stereotypes, along with gender-role socialization, can have a strong impact on students' motivation to choose and to excel in different achievement domains (Meece, Glienke, & Burg, 2006).

In general, gender differences in various measures of motivation are most pronounced in gender-stereotyped domains. For example, as discussed, boys have higher competence beliefs than girls for mathematics and sports, whereas girls have higher competence beliefs than boys for reading and English (Eccles, 1984; Eccles et al., 1993; Eccles-Parsons et al., 1982; Eccles et al., 1998; Fredericks & Eccles, 2002; Marsh et al., 1991; Wigfield et al., 1991). Similar patterns emerge for children's and adolescents' achievement values. Boys value sports more than girls, whereas girls place a higher value than boys on English, social activities, and instrumental music (Eccles et al., 1993; Wigfield et al., 1991). Gender differences, favoring boys, are also found in students' valuing of science achievement (Kahle & Meece, 1984). By high school, gender differences in the valuing of mathematics appear (Eccles, 1984). There is also some evidence to suggest that girls report greater anxiety than boys about their mathematics performance (Meece, Wigfield, & Eccles, 1990), especially when they are asked to perform difficult, timed mathematics tests (Spencer & Steele, 1995). Girls' negative affective reactions can lead them to lower the value of mathematics achievement or to avoid mathematics altogether. Gender differences in students' competency beliefs and achievement values are found even when students have equivalent skills in those areas. Additionally, the magnitude of the gender effect increases after puberty, when young people begin to experience greater social pressure to conform to gender-role expectations.

According to the motivation theories we have discussed, gender differences in competency and value perceptions can affect achievement behaviors. For example, Eccles and her colleagues have shown that expectancy and value beliefs are important predictors of adolescents' enrollment and performance in mathematics (Eccles, 1984, Eccles-Parsons et al., 1982). Eccles (1984, 1987) maintains that gender differences in math-related competency and value perceptions can help explain women's underrepresentation in advanced high school mathematics and science classes. Unfortunately, this lack of advanced preparation often limits women's opportunities to pursue careers in the scientific, technological, and engineering fields.

Ethnic and Racial Differences in Achievement Motivation

As we have discussed, cultural stereotypes can also make it difficult for minority youths to develop positive perceptions of their abilities and to value their schooling experiences. There are, however, surprisingly few studies on racial and ethnic differences in students' motivation. For the most part, studies have focused on comparisons between African American and white students. In reviewing this research literature, Sandra Graham (1994) found very few ethnic or racial differences in students' need for achievement, locus of control, achievement attributions, and ability perceptions. Another analysis of this research found racial differences, favoring whites, in lower-socioeconomic-status samples and younger-age samples (Cooper & Dorr, 1995). One of the interesting patterns that emerges from this research is that African American students tend to maintain positive perceptions of their abilities, even when they are not doing as well as other students (Stevenson, Chen, & Uttal, 1990). Also, they continue to have high expectations for succeeding at tasks at which they previously failed (Graham, 1994). Further, research suggests that African American students' competence and expectancy beliefs are not predictive of their school achievement (Graham, 1994; Mickelson, 1990; Stevenson et al., 1990).

There are several possible explanations for these patterns (Graham, 1994). One possibility is that African American students are using an adaptive strategy to protect their self-esteem in the face of failure (Graham, 1994). Another possibility is that teachers tend to have lower expectations for minority students' achievement, and perceptions of differential treatment in the classroom may lead African American students to discount the feedback they receive from their teachers about their abilities. Although some studies reveal that teachers have more negative expectations for their African American and Latino students than for their white students (Dusek & Joseph, 1986; Irvine, 1990), studies have not found large differences in teachers' responses to students in the classroom (Irvine, 1990; Miller, 1995). That is, it is not clear that teachers treat minority students differently from white students as a result of their different achievement expectations.

Currently, researchers are focusing on the factors that would lead ethnic minority students to reject the importance of their school experiences for their future and for their self-worth. Sandra Graham and her colleagues (1998) used peer nominations to assess gender and ethnic group differences in young adolescents' achievement values. Participants were from a low socioeconomic background and a predominantly black middle school. There were asked to nominate children in their class they (a) admired, (b) respected, and (c) wanted to be like. The results showed that white, Latino, and African American girls nominated other girls of the same ethnicity and high achievers as the most respected and admired. Boys showed the same pattern when asked to nominate girls for the most respected and admired category. However, when nominating other males, African American boys selected low-achieving males as the most respected and admired.

The results of this peer nomination study are consistent with the idea that some minority groups may devalue academic achievement and school success. Ogbu (1992) has argued that Native, African, and Mexican Americans share a history of oppression and discrimination in the United States. To cope with the oppression, these groups develop an identity in opposition to the white, majority culture, and reject attributes valued by that culture. According to this analysis, educational achievement is associated with white culture, which leads ethnic minorities to *devalue* the importance of academic success. This pattern is particularly prevalent in minority youth, who perceive little or no relation between school achievement and access to good jobs in their community (Fordham & Ogbu, 1996).

Currently, as discussed later, the *disidentification* explanation for ethnic differences in motivation is controversial. Several studies report no evidence of disidentification with school among students of color (Eccles et al., 2006; Graham & Hudley, 2005; Spencer et al., 2001).

Another prominent explanation for ethnic differences in motivation is **stereotype threat.** Claude Steele (1992) has also argued that academic achievement has significant social costs but for different reasons. He maintains that mainstream society portrays African Americans as intellectually inferior, and a fear of confirming this negative stereotype leads African American students to "disidentify" with school by reducing their achievement efforts or by devaluing the importance of school achievement for their own feelings of self worth. The Focus on Research Box describes research on stereotype threat and its implications for educators.

These various explanations emphasize the complexity of factors that can influence the achievement motivation of ethnic minority students. For the most part, studies reveal that most ethnic minority parents and their children highly value education and have high educational aspirations (Eccles et al., 1998; Eccles et al., 2006). Additionally, recent research suggests that Afrocentric, rather than Eurocentric, values have a positive influence on academic achievement in African American youths (Spencer et al., 2001). Finally, it is important to keep in mind that there is considerable variation in achievement motivation within any ethnic group. We have already discussed gender differences within ethnic groups. In the next section, we discuss the effects of social class. Most studies of racial and ethnic differences in achievement motivation have not taken into account the influence of economic factors (Graham, 1994; Graham & Hudley, 2005; Eccles et al., 2006).

Socioeconomic Influences

Socioeconomic factors can also affect children's motivation to learn and to do well in school. The motivational problems of students from low-income families are perhaps the most complex and difficult to address for several reasons. First, compared with middle-class families, poor families have weaker resources to support their children's learning outside of school. Economically disadvantaged students often need extra help

Stereotype Threat and Student Achievement

Claude Steele, an internationally known social psychologist and professor at Stanford University, developed the theory of stereotype threat. According to Steele (1997), stereotype threat is a "social-psychological threat that arises when one is in a situation or doing something for which a negative stereotype about one's group applies" (p. 614). A person who is experiencing stereotype threat is fearful of being judged through the lens of a negative stereotype or performing in a manner that confirms the negative stereotype. Stereotype threat has a variable effect on members of any group for which a negative stereotype exist. The stereotype must be relevant to the member of the group (i.e., the person has to care about the domain) for it to become threatening, but one does not have to believe in the stereotype for it to become threatening.

Steele and his colleagues conducted multiple studies examining the effects of stereotype threat on minorities. Three main areas of interest were intelligence testing, women's mathematics performance, and disidentification. Steele found that African Americans faced stereotype threat about their groups' ability whenever they took a test that measured intelligence, including standardized tests such as the Graduate Record Exam (GRE). In one study, black and white students completed a test composed of GRE verbal questions. When the test was presented as an ability-diagnostic test, African Americans performed substantially worse, but African Americans performed equally when the test was presented as a non-diagnostic test.

Focus on
Research

It is interesting that Steele and colleagues also argued that women face stereotype threat when performing in mathematics. Spencer et al., (1999) found that women performed substantially worse on a mathematics test characterized as identifying gender differences, but performed equal to men when the test was not presented as identifying gender differences. They also found that women experienced stereotype threat more with advanced mathematics.

Following are some ways that teachers can reduce stereotype threat (Aronson, 2002; Aronson & Steele, 2005):

- De-emphasize tests as measures of cognitive abilities. Emphasize instead how tests can help teachers and administrators see how well they are helping their students to learn.
- Help students to see that their skills are improving as they progress through a course or content area.
- Help students to understand that their abilities are malleable and improvable through effort and skill development. Academic skills are not fixed traits.
- Incorporate mixed-ethnic learning groups to increase contact among ethnic groups and reduce stereotypes.
- Use cooperative learning groups to increase positive contact between ethnic groups and reduce stereotypes.
- Implement mentoring programs to help minority youth cope with racism and discrimination.

in mastering basic and advanced skills, but placement in special programs increases the risk that they will perceive themselves as slow learners. Second, the home and community socialization patterns of disadvantaged students are poorly matched to the middle-class orientations of schools. As a result, disadvantaged students frequently experience adjustment and discipline problems (Braddock & McPartland, 1993). Additionally, economically disadvantaged students have difficulty seeing the relevance and importance of schoolwork for their future goals, due to high rates of unemployment in their communities and lack of financial resources to further their education. Poor students are likely to attend schools with fewer resources for recruiting highly qualified teachers and for providing enriching educational experiences. Compounding the effects of poor school conditions, poor children live in neighborhoods with few public services, such as libraries, museums, and parks. There is also a scarcity of high-achieving role models in these communities.

As we learned in Chapter 4, early intervention programs such as Head Start are successful in improving the educational attainment of economically disadvantaged children. Some theorists believe that these programs better prepare these students for entry into school. They are able to maintain positive attitudes toward learning because they do not experience early failure in school. Thus, motivation may be an important pathway through which early intervention programs positively affect children's academic achievement and educational attainment.

UNDERSTANDING CHILDREN
Strategy 5.12: Views of Schoolwork

Developmental Trends in Achievement Motivation

Most children begin elementary school with an intrinsic desire to learn and to master new skills, which gradually fades as they progress in school. Harter (1981) reported a systematic shift from a predominantly intrinsic orientation in third grade to a more extrinsic orientation by the ninth grade. These shifts are more dramatic for some subjects than for others, but most children show significant declines in intrinsic motivation for reading, mathematics, science, and social studies by the seventh grade (Gottfried, 1985). Developmental changes in students' intrinsic motivation are generally accompanied by declining confidence and performance and by increasing anxiety (Harter & Connell, 1984). In other words, as children progress in school, they feel less intrinsically motivated to learn, more negative about their abilities, and more anxious about their school performance. Negative changes in motivation are particularly evident as students move from elementary to junior high school.

What explains the decline in students' intrinsic motivation during the school years? One explanation focuses on how students evaluate themselves at various ages. For example, kindergarten students start school with very optimistic perceptions of their abilities, with most claiming to be the smartest student in their class (Stipek, 1993). They also think that they can get smarter by just working harder. That is, young children often have an incremental view of their ability. As school learning becomes more difficult and increased effort does not always lead to success, children begin to develop a more realistic view of their abilities.

The standards children use to judge their ability also change as they progress in school. Whereas young children judge their ability in terms of effort, older children tend to rely on social standards or normative information. That is, they judge their ability in terms of how others have done, but effort has a different meaning. Compared with younger children, older children have a more differentiated conception of ability (Nicholls, 1984). By late elementary school, children understand that ability and effort are separate entities and that high effort can compensate for low ability. Thus, high effort can imply low ability if other children perform as well or better with less effort. Exhorting students to work harder is less effective at this age, because it often implies that the teacher or parent thinks the student needs to compensate for lack of ability.

These developmental changes in ability perceptions help explain declines in motivation as children grow older. Because older children measure their ability in terms of normative standards, they find it increasingly difficult to demonstrate high ability. Changes in these evaluation standards can lead students to lower their expectations for success and to feel less competent. At the same time, adolescents' increased self-awareness is likely to heighten their concerns about evaluations and their fears about "looking stupid." As a result, adolescents may show a greater ego involvement in learning activities and display the type of achievement behavior that is associated with an extrinsic motivational orientation.

A second explanation for motivational declines focuses on changes in the school environment, especially as students move from elementary to secondary school (Eccles, 2004). For example, Eccles and Midgley (1989) identified a number of ways that elementary and middle school environments differ. First, middle schools tend to be larger than elementary schools, which can disrupt peer relations and give way to feelings of anonymity and alienation. Whereas students are generally with the same teacher and peer group for most of the day in elementary school, middle school students have multiple teachers. As a result, middle school students are less likely to benefit from the types of teacher–student relations that promote learning and motivation (Wentzel, 2002). In addition, middle school classrooms are generally characterized by more whole-class instruction, more public recitation, less individualized instruction, and fewer opportunities for student choice and decision making (Eccles & Midgley, 1989). Under these conditions, students are less likely to take an active role in learning and to receive the support they need when experiencing behavioral or academic problems.

The transition to high school is a relatively new area of motivation research. Relative to elementary and middle schools, high schools are larger, more bureaucratic, more impersonal, and more academically challenging. Most high schools also use tracking systems to group students by ability and vocational aspirations. Unfortunately, a disproportionate number of low-income, black, and Hispanic students are assigned to curriculum tracks that limit future educational and economic opportunities (Oakes, 1985). Tracking systems at the high school level serve to reinforce social stratification in society rather than provide optimal education for all students regardless of ethnic, gender, or social/economic background (Lee & Bryk, 1986; Oakes, 1985). Even students performing at grade level with strong family support and positive attitudes toward school can experience difficulty navigating the transition to high school.

In summary, secondary classrooms tend to be more impersonal, formal, evaluative, and competitive than elementary classrooms. Additionally, students have fewer opportunities to manage and direct their own learning at a time when they are developing more sophisticated cognitive and problem-solving skills. Adolescent researchers argue that these grade-related changes in instructional practices lead to declines in students' ability perceptions and in their intrinsic motivation to learn (Eccles & Midgley, 1989; Eccles, 2004).

Researchers are not yet sure whether declines in intrinsic motivation are a natural consequence of cognitive and social development or a reflection of changes in the school environment. From an educational standpoint, it is important to understand both points of view. As students mature, they are better able to integrate information about their abilities from various sources, and they become anxious about their ability to handle a competitive learning environment. Such conditions make it difficult for even the best students to maintain an intrinsic orientation toward learning. We end this discussion of motivation with a Focus on Teaching box on page 396 containing some suggestions for how to create a positive motivational climate in the classroom. Other recommendations are included in Chapter 9.

Focus on
Teaching

Motivation researchers have identified a number of ways teachers can help promote an intrinsic orientation toward learning in the classroom (Ames, 1992; Brophy, 1987; Corno & Rohrkemper, 1985; Covington, 1992; Lepper & Hodell, 1989; Maehr & Midgley, 1991; Meece, 1991; Meece, Herman, & McCombs, 2003; National Research Council & The Institutes of Medicine, 2004; Nicholls, 1989). Some strategies for improving motivation in the classroom follow.

Provide Motivating Learning Activities

- Provide learning activities that are personally challenging, meaningful, and call for students' active participation in the learning process.
- Use a variety of learning activities. Even minor changes in format can have a significant impact.
- Stimulate students' curiosity by asking questions that are surprising or discrepant from students' current understanding.

Emphasize the Intrinsic Value of Learning

- Help students see the value of what they are learning for other subjects and real-life problems.
- Help students connect what they are learning to their lives outside school.
- Link learning material to current events or familiar experiences.
- Ensure that learning activities have a worthwhile instructional objective.

Promote Positive Feelings of Competency and Efficacy

- Provide feedback that lets students know they are improving their skills (e.g., "You are really getting good at multiplying fractions.").

Creating a Positive Motivational Climate in the Classroom

- Use learning activities that progressively build on one another, so students can see they are improving.
- Help students set realistic, short-term goals, so they can receive continual feedback about their progress.
- Support students' independent learning efforts.
- When students perform poorly, provide specific and informative feedback about how they can improve.

Recognize Personal Improvement

- Use improvement-oriented grading systems.
- Provide multiple opportunities for students to complete tasks.
- Use normative forms of evaluation cautiously. Avoid public forms of evaluation. If used, they should provide a way to recognize all students.

Increase Opportunities for Choice

- Let students design some learning tasks or choose how to complete a lesson.
- Let students help determine the criteria by which their assignments will be evaluated.
- Involve students in developing guidelines for classroom behavior.

Provide Opportunities for Peer Collaboration and Sense of Belonging

- Organize cooperative learning, peer tutoring, and peer interaction opportunities.
- Use a combination of heterogeneous and homogeneous grouping arrangements.
- Establish a learning environment in which differences among students are accepted and valued.

■ Chapter Summary

Erikson's Theory of Psychosocial Development

- Erikson provided a framework for understanding children's personal development. Children need a safe and secure environment in order to develop a sense of trust. They also need opportunities to initiate activities and to learn about their different strengths and options for the future.

Foundations of Social and Emotional Development

- Children differ in temperamental characteristics. Some children are predisposed to be sociable, emotionally expressive, reactive, or withdrawn. Parents, teachers, and other caregivers play an important role in the continuity of temperamental characteristics.
- Children's social and emotional development begins with early attachment relations. Children need secure attachments with parents who are warm, responsive, and caring.
- Attachments with caregivers, including teachers, can affect many behaviors important for school success, including curiosity, attention, problem-solving behavior, and persistence.
- With development, children become better interpreters of people's emotions and better able to use this information in regulating their behavior. They also become better able to express and understand complex emotions such as embarrassment, guilt, and jealousy. Gender and cultural expectations can influence what emotions are expressed and how they are expressed.
- Between the ages of 5 and 12, children show an increased ability to use cognitive and behavioral strategies for controlling impulses, tolerating frustration, and delaying gratification.
- Schools can play an important role in the development of emotional competence in the classroom. Teachers need to (1) create a positive affective environment for students, (2) model how to exhibit and express emotions, (3) discuss emotions with students, and (4) provide explicit instruction regarding how to handle emotions and stress.

Emotional and Behavioral Disorders

- Children with emotional and behavioral disorders have various difficulties in psychosocial development, either externalizing (e.g., oppositional, antisocial, aggressive) or internalizing (e.g., withdrawal, anxiety, depression) problems. Most have deficits in language and social-cognitive skills.
- The school or classroom environment plays an important role in the lives of children with emotional or behavioral disorders. Discipline practices that are too lax, inconsistent, rigid, or punitive can have a negative impact.

Development of Self-Conceptions

- Self-concept refers to a set of beliefs, attitudes, ideas, and knowledge that people have about themselves. Young children describe themselves in terms of physical traits, whereas older children and adolescents use psychological traits (e.g., intelligent, trustworthy, caring, etc.) and abstract concepts (e.g., devout Catholic). In addition, as children mature, their self-concepts become more differentiated and integrated. They see themselves as having multiple abilities, and they begin to see links between their past, present, and future selves.
- During the early school years, children's self-esteem increases as they achieve success in peer relations. The school environment plays a very important role in helping children and adolescents maintain positive self-esteem. Teachers who show concern about students, involve students in decision making, and encourage self-sufficiency can have a positive influence on self-esteem.
- Students' perceptions and evaluations of their abilities influence their performance in school. Doing well in school can bolster self-esteem, which in turn can affect how well students do in school later on.

Ethnic and Gender-Role Identity

- Children begin to develop an awareness of ethnic differences early. By age 3, children can correctly identify skin color and their own ethnic group. Because of racial prejudices and stereotypes, it may be difficult for ethnic minority children to develop positive feelings of competency and worth. Most studies today report little difference in white and African American children's self-perceptions if they are succeeding in school and are held in high regard by parents and peers.
- The work of forming an ethnic identity generally takes place in adolescence. Adolescents achieve an identity by seeking to understand the meaning of their ethnicity in relation to the mainstream culture. Many adolescents form a bicultural identity.
- Gender-role identity is a key component of the self. The gender-role concepts of young children tend to be very rigid and exaggerated. With cognitive maturity, children's gender-role concepts become more flexible and less absolute. Adolescents who have a blend of masculine and feminine traits (i.e., they are androgynous) tend to have high self-esteem, positive self-concepts, and good coping skills.
- Gender-role behaviors and attitudes are learned from the environment through the process of socialization. Parents, the mass media, and schools have an important role in gender-role socialization. Unfortunately, the images of masculinity and femininity children are exposed to at school continue to be sex-stereotypic.

Development of Achievement Motivation

- In achievement situations, motivation refers to forces that initiate, sustain, and terminate behavior. Cognitive theories of motivation emphasize the importance of efficacy beliefs, achievement values, causal attributions, and achievement goals. Goal theory may provide the most useful framework for teachers. When children are focused on learning goals, they define their competence in terms of improvement, focus on their efforts, perceive errors as a part of the learning process, attribute difficulties to lack of effort, and persist at finding the correct solution.
- The home environment is a source of individual differences in motivation. Parenting styles that support children's independence are positively associated with higher levels of perceived competence and intrinsic motivation. Also, children who view their abilities as something that can be enhanced through effort and practice have higher levels of perceived competence and intrinsic motivation.
- As children progress in school, they report lower self-perceptions of ability, less control over learning, less intrinsic motivation to learn, and more anxiety about grades and evaluation. It is believed that these changes result from both individual and environmental changes. Schools can play an important role in maintaining high levels of motivation.

■ Key Terms

achievement motivation (p. 381)
androgyny (p. 376)
attachment (p. 339)
basic emotions (p. 343)
conduct disorders (p. 352)
emotional competence (p. 349)
emotions (p. 343)
emotion-focused coping (p. 347)
empathy (p. 343)
entity theory of ability (p. 389)
ethnic identity (p. 367)

extrinsic motivation (p. 383)
gender constancy (p. 375)
gender-role socialization (p. 378)
gender schema (p. 375)
ideal self (p. 362)
identity (p. 336)
identity status (p. 366)
incremental theory of ability (p. 389)
intrinsic motivation (p. 383)
learned helplessness (p. 386)

problem-focused coping (p. 347)
psychological self (p. 358)
self-concept (p. 356)
self-conscious emotions (p. 343)
self-efficacy (p. 384)
self-esteem (p. 356)
social referencing (p. 343)
Strange Situation (p. 339)
stereotype threat (p. 392)
temperament (p. 337)

■ Activities

1. Begin to collect books and stories you can use in your classroom to help your students understand their own and others' emotions. You might consider using books written about a particular emotional issue such as shyness, friends moving away, divorce, and so forth. Be sure to choose books that are appropriate for the age group you plan to teach. Share your resource file with your classmates.

2. Interview a group of elementary and middle school students to find out about their self-concepts. Be sure to include a wide age range, say, from 7- to 14-year-olds. Ask students to describe themselves ("Tell me about yourself") and follow up with more specific questions about what they are good at and what they like about themselves. Ask them if they could change anything about themselves, what would it be? Take detailed notes on the students' responses, then analyze them according to the following questions:

   a. Did the students describe themselves according to observable characteristics (gender, physical appearance, favorite activities) or psychological traits (friendly, happy, smart)?

   b. Did the characteristics of children's self-descriptions vary by age?

   c. Did girls focus on different characteristics (e.g., physical appearance) than boys? Did girls describe themselves in less positive terms than boys?

   d. What conclusions might you draw about the students' feelings of self-esteem from the interview?

3. Interview different ages (7 to 17 years) of students to learn about their motivation to read. Before you interview students, you may try to draft some questions using what you have learned about the factors that can influence student motivation. Example questions might be:

   ■ How often do you read?

   ■ Do you like to read? Why or why not?

   ■ What kind of books do you like to read?

   ■ Do you receive much encouragement to read from your teachers, parents, or peers?

   ■ What do you think teachers should do to help motivate students to read who don't like to read?

   Analyze students' responses for the factors that influence students' motivation to read. Do some students appear to be intrinsically motivated to read, while others need external incentives and encouragement? How did students' perceptions of their ability to read influence their interest in reading? Discuss how you might use the students' responses to enhance students' intrinsic motivation to read in your classroom.

4. Interview teachers at different grade levels to gather information on motivation strategies. Ask teachers to describe the strategies they use to motivate students. How do they use rewards and incentives in their classroom? Compare teachers' strategies to the ones presented on page 396. Develop an action plan for creating a positive motivation climate in your classroom, and share it with your classmates.

CHAPTER

7

Peer Relations and Moral Development

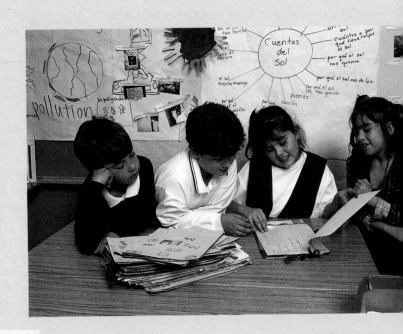

AMY IS A STUDENT IN MRS. THOMPSON'S SEVENTH-GRADE MATH CLASS. *toward the end of the class period, the students are given some time to work on their math homework, but Amy is having difficulty focusing on her work. She is seated across from Jana, who does not appear to like this arrangement. Amy tries to engage Jana in a conversation but is ignored. She then tugs on Jana's sweater, and Jana tells her, "Stop it!" Amy shows Jana her new ballpoint pen, but Jana continues to ignore her. A few seconds later, Amy stabs Jana with the pen. Jana yells, "Ow!" Mrs. Thompson looks over at Amy and tells her to get back to work. Amy ignores the teacher and waits a few seconds, then asks Mrs. Thompson if she can use the bathroom pass. Mrs. Thompson says, "No," and Amy returns to her seat. As she passes Jana, she again stabs her with the pen. Jana yells, "You'd better stop!" Amy returns to her seat, then looks around the room for several minutes. Mrs. Thompson tells the class to get ready to change classes. As the students are lining up, Amy stabs Jana with the pen very hard. Jana becomes visibly angry this time, and yells, "I told you to stop it!" Jana then pushes Amy out of line. The teacher tells Jana to go sit in her seat. Amy laughs and walks out of the room.*

How would you explain Amy's behavior? What would you want to know about this student? How might the teacher's behavior have contributed to Amy's problem? How would you respond if Amy were your student? Although the teacher in this vignette seems unbelievably "tuned out," the observation is based on events in a real classroom. Amy has apparently learned that she can get attention from others by picking on them. Generally, children like Amy have not learned socially appropriate ways of initiating and maintaining interactions with others. Unfortunately, Mrs. Thompson did not use an effective strategy for stopping Amy's behavior. Without effective and consistent guidance, students such as Amy can become increasingly noncompliant, aggressive, and difficult, which further reduces the likelihood that they will develop positive relations with others.

Children are social beings, and they must learn the patterns of social life—how to initiate social interactions, how to interpret another person's behavior, how to care for others, how to assert themselves, and so on. Although children begin learning social skills before they enter school, the classroom provides a good training ground for practicing and improving these skills. Children with good social skills generally have little difficulty making friends at school, whereas children with poor social skills often run the risk of being ignored or rejected by peers. Furthermore, children with good peer relations tend to be more successful in school. It is important, therefore, to understand the development of peer relations and social skills in order to help children form positive social relationships and function in a group.

In this chapter, we explore the development of children's abilities to relate to and care for others. We will discuss how children reason about their social world and form an understanding of its racial and ethnic diversity. We will also consider how children's social relationships with peers change over the course of development. We will also discuss why some children, such as Amy, are not able to cooperate, share, or care for others. By the end of this chapter, you will be familiar with ways that teachers can create a classroom environment that positively influences children's social and moral development.

 Understanding Others

To form social relationships, children need to develop an ability to think about the thoughts, feelings, and behaviors of others. Researchers use the term **social cognition** to refer to children's ability to think about their social world. In the previous chapter, we learned that children's social understanding begins in their early interactions with caregivers. Here the child learns that self is distinct from others and that others may have different wishes and desires. The development of children's social understanding continues well into the school years, and it plays an influential role in shaping their social relations at school. Efforts to help children with poor peer relations are often directed at helping children interpret the thoughts, feelings, and behaviors of others.

We will look at three important aspects of children's social cognition: (1) social perspective-taking skills, (2) person perceptions, and (3) race and ethnicity conceptions.

Understanding the Perspective of Others

The ability to understand the perspective of others is central to learning to relate to others. We will learn later that aggressive children often have difficulty with social problem solving, which involves taking the perspective of others and understanding the consequences of their actions on others. Interest in social perspective-taking skills can be traced back to Piaget's claim that young children are cognitively egocentric and incapable of understanding or taking the perspective of others.

Understanding the perspective of others begins in early infancy. The first step in this process is to understand that the self is distinct from others; that is, people have an independent existence. Researchers believe that this process begins to occur when infants show distress or gaze toward the door when their caregivers leave the room, but this differentiation is not fully complete until the second year. During the period known as the "terrible twos" toddlers use words such as *me* and *mine* to assert their differentiation from others. They also show signs of frustration and temper when their attempts to influence their caregivers' actions are not successful. However, toddlers can also comfort younger children in distress

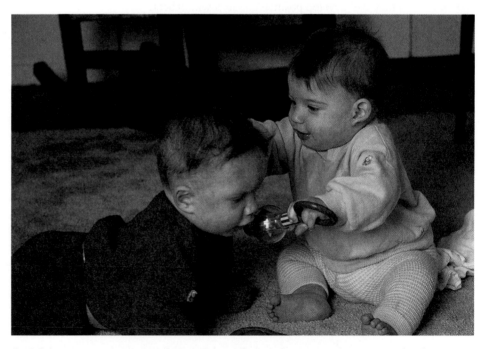

Social awareness emerges early in infancy. These infants are relating to each other through touch.
Source: Joel Gordon.

by hugging or kissing them, and they may even try to comfort an adult in pain (Zahn-Waxler, Radke-Yarrow, Wagner, & Chapman, 1992). Toddlers also respond to another's stress by getting distressed themselves. Researchers believe that this capacity to show concern for another's emotional state is important for forming social relations (Harris, 2006).

Between the ages of 3 and 5 years, children begin to develop what are known as **theories of mind** (Wellman, 1990). Just as young children work to figure out cause-and-effect relations in their physical world, they become little psychologists who try to figure out why people act the way they do. Unlike the physical world, however, the causes of human actions are not always observable. Children must make inferences about inner mental states such as beliefs, intentions, desires, and emotions (Wellman, 1990). Surprisingly, most preschool children are fairly adept at understanding some basic human psychology. By age 3, young children grasp simple causal relations between desires, outcomes, and emotions. They believe, for instance, that people will be happy when they get what they want (Wellman, 1990). They also understand that different people may have different desires. John Flavell and his colleagues found that 3-year-olds had little difficulty understanding that an adult might like coffee, even though they themselves do not (Flavell, Mumme, Green, & Flavell, 1992).

Although preschool children are making significant advances in social understanding and perspective taking, there is still much to be learned. Children under the age of 5 are known to have difficulty with what is know as **false belief** problems (Wimmer & Perner, 1983). In a simple example, a child looks into a cookie jar and finds it empty, but he finds a box of cookies inside the pantry. Now his older sister comes into the kitchen for a cookie, and the first child is asked where his sister will go to get a cookie. A preschool child will say the pantry, not the cookie jar. It is difficult for young children to understand that another person will act on beliefs that are different from their own, and thus false from their point of view. To do so, they must suppress the information they know, and assess the situation from the other person's point of view.

During the elementary school years, children make considerable advances in their understanding of the inner states of others. They understand that people do not always express what they feel, that people can have conflicting emotions or desires, and that people can even give you misleading information to deceive you (Flavell, 2000). School-age children also begin to use their inferences about internal states (desires or beliefs) to make persuasive arguments to manipulate behavior (Bartsch & London, 2000). Many parents are well aware of the persuasive arguments children will try if they want a candy bar while they are waiting to check out at the grocery store. In part, the development of social understanding in the elementary years is aided by advances in children's perspective-taking abilities.

Robert Selman (1980) identified several distinct stages in children's role-taking abilities. To study children's **perspective-taking skills,** children of different ages were asked to respond to the following social dilemma:

> Holly is an 8-year-old girl who likes to climb trees. She is the best tree climber in the neighborhood. One day while climbing down from a tall tree she falls off the bottom branch but does not hurt herself. Her father sees her fall. He is upset and asks her to promise not to climb trees anymore. Holly promises. Later that day, Holly and her friends meet Sean. Sean's kitten is caught up in a tree and cannot get down. Something has to be done right away or the kitten may fall. Holly is the only one who climbs trees well enough to reach the kitten and get it down, but she remembers her promise to her father. (Selman & Byrne, 1974, p. 805)

The researchers then asked the children their thoughts about different characters in the story. For example, they were asked:

> Does Holly know how Sean feels about the kitten?
> What will Holly's father think when he finds out?
> If Holly and her father discussed the situation, what might they decide? (Selman & Byrne, 1974, p. 805)

Focus on
Development   *Stages of Social Perspective Taking*

Levels of Social Perspective Taking	Approximate Age Range	Characteristics
Level 0: Undifferentiated and egocentric perspective taking	3 to 6 years	Children have an undifferentiated view of interpersonal situations. They are unable to recognize that other people may interpret the situation differently from them.
Level 1: Differentiated perspective taking	5 to 9 years	Children recognize that others may have different perspectives on a situation, but their interpersonal understanding is unilateral and one way. For example, they understand that giving a gift can make someone else happy, but they do not recognize that making another person happy can have a reciprocal effect.
Level 2: Reciprocal perspective taking	7 to 12 years	Children are able to put themselves in the shoes of another, and they realize others can do the same. For example, a child understands that another child may not like him because he gets the other person in trouble. Children can anticipate and consider thoughts and feelings of others.
Level 3: Mutual perspective taking	10 to 15 years	Children are able to see their own, another person's, and their mutual perspectives from the viewpoint of a third person. That is, the adolescent can step out of the immediate interaction and consider how a teacher, parent, or peer might view each individual perspective as well as their mutual perspective.
Level 4: In-depth perspective taking	12 years on	Adolescents and adults are able to understand that a person's perspective may represent a larger societal point of view. For example, adolescents are able to understand that their parents may have different perspectives because their parents' generation had different beliefs, values, and expectations.

Source: Adapted from Selman (1980).

As shown in the Focus on Development box, Selman and his colleagues found there was a developmental progression in children's role-taking skills from preschool to early adolescence. About 80 percent of preschool children were unable to recognize that people in the story would have different perspectives. When asked what the father would think, the preschool child is likely to respond, "Happy because he likes kittens." In contrast, a 10-year-old is likely to respond: "He'll be mad at first, but then when he sees the kitten he'll understand why Holly climbed the tree and will not punish her."

This research indicates that important changes in children's social perspective-taking abilities take place in the elementary school years. Most 3- and 4-year-olds have difficulty understanding that another person may have values, moral beliefs, or ideas about social rules that are different from their own. Children between the ages of 6 and 12 can put themselves in the "other's shoes" and see themselves through the eyes of others. Most elementary school children are able to consider another person's thoughts and feelings.

However, it is not until adolescence or adulthood that young people are able to think about social relationships as part of a larger social system or grasp the complexity of human behavior. For example, understanding ethnic differences involves recognizing that individuals may react a certain way because of their culture.

Additionally, as described earlier, adolescents are able to reflect on their own thoughts and feelings, and this knowledge is helpful in understanding others. Compared to younger children, they have more social experiences they can draw on to interpret people's behavior. One of the hallmarks of adolescent thinking is their ability to engage in recursive thinking (Perner & Wimmer, 1983). If you recall our earlier discussions in Chapters 3 and 4, adolescents are able to think about their thinking (metacognitive awareness). These same processes are applied to social cognition. Adolescents have the ability to think in multiple interactions as they try to understand others (e.g., He thinks that I think that . . .). Observe this 15-year-old using recursive thinking with her girlfriends:

> I wonder what he thought when I said I could not go to the movie on Thursday. I was think-
> ing we could go on Friday but he said he was busy. I should have told him my parents did
> not let me date on school nights but then I thought he would not ask me out again.

In summary, young people's understanding of others undergoes significant changes from preschool to high school. Children begin school with basic theories of human behavior, but it is difficult from them to infer what others are thinking and feeling, if these beliefs should differ from their own. Children often have difficulties forming and maintaining friendships because they are unable to understand the other person's point of view and the reasons for the other person's behavior (Le Mare & Rubin, 1987). Perspective-taking skills are associated with prosocial behaviors such as helping or sharing (Eisenberg & Fabes, 1998). When children are able to understand the thoughts and feelings of others, they are more willing to share and help. As we will learn, perspective-taking skills also play an important role in moral development.

From an educational point of view, it important for educators to help children understand the thoughts, feelings, and perspectives of others. For young children, socio-dramatic play activities, in which children try out different social roles (e.g., "mommy," "teacher," "baby sister"), allow them to act out the thoughts or feelings of others. It is also important for educators to ask children to talk about their thoughts and feelings, particularly when they may differ from the feelings of others. Research on parent–child relations has shown that such discussions can help advance social understanding (Astington & Pelletier, 1996). During group reading situations, teachers can talk about the perspectives and feelings of different characters in a story. In addition, simulation, debate, and role-play activities that involve conflict or controversy can give students practice in taking the perspectives of others. The Believing Game described in

Focus on
Teaching

Learning to Take Perspectives Through the "Believing Game"

The capacity to take on the perspective of another person is key in understanding the complexities of conflict. Developed by educator Peter Elbow and Educators for Social Responsibility, the Believing Game is a powerful tool to explore character and conflict in literature. Through the Believing Game, students will gain a greater understanding of the complexities of a controversial issue, allowing them to recognize that people have different perspectives and a "piece of the truth."

In the Believing Game, the teacher chooses a controversial issue in the news, a magazine article, a work of literature, or video clip. For example, should public schools require school uniforms for all students? The students are asked to suspend their own opinions, doubts, or facts to listen to two or three perspectives on the matter. For each perspective the steps are as follows:

1. Present the first perspective by using a speaker, an editorial, magazine, and so on. Remind students they are to approach the presentation by suspending their own beliefs about what they are hearing, watching, or reading.
2. Invite students to ask clarifying questions that will help them gain a deeper understanding of the perspective being presented.
3. Ask students to quickly jot down the essentials of the perspective presented. As they reread what they have written, ask students to check or underline what they can affirm, believe, or agree with.
4. In small groups, have students discuss and analyze the position presented. What were the facts presented?

Were there any missing facts, distortions, and so on that would raise concerns or objections? Are there any points on which most or all of the students in the group can agree? How do the values, assumptions, and opinions of the position match or conflict with your own?
5. Before presenting the next perspective, ask the students if they can agree with the assumptions, values, concerns, and recommendations that were presented. What points have been made that need to be factored into an effective solution?
6. The first five steps are repeated for each perspective presented.
7. After all perspectives are presented, debrief and review the process as a class. Possible questions to ask students include:
   - What did you learn that you did not know or were not aware of before?
   - What surprises helped you break through your own opinions and preconceptions?
   - Did the language influence or persuade you?
   - Were there values or concerns presented that were common to all perspectives?
8. As a lesson wrap-up, ask the students to write about how their thinking has changed or not changed after hearing different perspectives. How did it feel to approach a controversial issues in this way? Did the process help them to be more open-minded to positions or opinions that were different from their own? How? In what ways? How would they use this experience with their friends or outside of school?

Source: Adapted from Mertz & Miller (2001).

the Focus on Teaching Box can help middle or high school students "try on" different perspectives.

Describing Other People

In Chapter 6, we learned how children form conceptions of themselves. With development, these self-conceptions become more differentiated, complex, and abstract. We find the same pattern in children's perceptions and descriptions of other people.

Young children attend to people's observable features, such as their physical characteristics or favorite activities (Livesly & Bromley, 1973). For example, a first grader might describe her new friend in this way: "She has brown hair, and lives by me. She has one brother, and he goes to another school. We like to play together." Just as young children describe themselves in global, all-or-nothing terms, we can see the same trend in their descriptions of others. A person is either good or bad, and a good person also has many other positive traits (e.g., she is happy, friendly, and smart).

In middle childhood, children begin to move beyond surface characteristics to include more psychological traits in their descriptions. We observed this same trend in children's self-conceptions. For example, a 10-year-old may describe his classmate in this way: "He really looks weird and does silly things. I think he is really dumb and is always doing something disgusting in class." This description includes some physical traits, but it also includes some personal traits that are readily observable, such as the child's lack of ability. However, this description is vague and superficial. Researchers believe that children's person perceptions at this age are based more on how they feel about the person than about the person's actual characteristics (Ruble & Dweck, 1995). Children's perceptions of other people become more balanced later in development. The child begins to focus on those inner traits and qualities that can be observed in many situations. In other words, the child is looking for traitlike characteristics that help him or her to understand and predict a person's behavior (Flavell & Miller, 1998). The discovery of personality traits that influence behavior across settings is an important development in person perception. The use of trait terms to describe people more than doubles by the age of 8 (Ruble & Dweck, 1995).

A more differentiated and complex view of other people does not emerge until adolescence, when young people begin to see inconsistencies in their own behaviors and traits. They also begin to describe other people in terms of more subtle, abstract terms and inner dispositions. For example, a 15-year-old may describe her friend this way: "I think he only acts that way when he is around certain people . . . he really cares about people."

In summary, there are important parallels between children's self-perceptions and person perceptions. We have learned that children's descriptions shift from a focus on perceptually salient characteristics (physical appearance) to inner psychological traits and needs. For educational purposes, it is important to recognize that children's thinking about other people is very rigid and evaluative. Young children are mostly concerned with who is good or bad (Ruble & Dweck, 1995). If another child is perceived as good, many other positive traits are attributed to that person. We observed this pattern when we discussed physical attractiveness. Someone who is physically attractive is also thought to be smart, friendly, successful, and so on. We will learn next how the rigidity of children's person perceptions influences their understanding of race and ethnicity.

> UNDERSTANDING
> CHILDREN
> *Strategy 5.4: Predicting Hypothetical Classmates' Behavior*

Understanding Race and Ethnicity

A key component of person perception is understanding ethnic and racial diversity. As we have discussed, a more ethnically diverse group of children is entering schools today. For many children, their first opportunity to interact with someone from a different ethnic or racial group will occur in a school setting. **Prejudices** form when children develop a negative view of others based on their race or ethnicity. Thus, many teachers are faced with the difficult challenge of helping children to understand racial and ethnic diversity.

Social cognitive theory has been used to understand the development of children's race and ethnic conceptions (Bigler, Jones, & Lobliner, 1997; Black-Gutman & Hickson, 1996; Brown & Bigler, 2005; Quintana, 1998). The Focus on Teaching box presents a

Focus on
Teaching

Developmental Levels of Ethnic Perspective Taking

Level of Ethnic Perspective Taking	Approximate Age Range	Description	Educational Implications
Level 0: Integration of affective and perceptual understanding of ethnicity	Early Childhood, 3 to 6 years	Preschool children use physical characteristics (skin color and appearance) to classify and describe people racially. They also have pro-white racial bias and antiminority racial attitudes and prejudices that reflect wider societal views. Ethnic prejudice does not influence self-perceptions or behaviors toward other racial or ethnic groups at this age.	Young children may show strong preference for what color is used to depict skin color, and this color may not correspond to their own skin color. For example, African American children may prefer white skin. Children at this age benefit from activities that enable them to explore variations in skin color and appearance within and between racial groups. Young children may not respond positively to direct attempts to reduce racial prejudice, but it is important to present positive images of different ethnic or racial groups as concepts of social categories develop.
Level 1: Literal understanding of ethnicity and race	Middle childhood, 6 to 10 years	Children understand the permanence of racial or ethnic categorizations. Children use ancestry (e.g., My father is Chinese) and literal features of ethnicity (foods, activities, and language). A more balanced view of ethnicity emerges as children are able to think about multiple dimensions. Children have difficulty understanding prejudice and the social consequences of racial or ethnic status at this age.	Children benefit from learning about the history of different social groups, and the different customs, languages, and traditions that differentiate them. At this age, children can understand similarities and differences across and within different ethnic groups. For example, children can explore similarities and differences in families, communities, or schools. It is important for children to see positive images of their ethnic group to build ethnic pride.
Level 2: Social and nonliteral	Early Adolescence, 10 to 14 years	Young adolescents are acquiring a social	Young adolescents are able to discuss the social

| Level 2: Social and nonliteral perspective on ethnicity | Early Adolescence, 10 to 14 years | Young adolescents are acquiring a social perspective of ethnicity. They show greater awareness of the social consequences of ethnicity such as differences in houses, neighborhoods, or possessions. Young adolescents believe that ethnic similarity is important for the formation of friendships and social groups. Minority adolescents also show an awareness of ethnic bias and prejudice toward their own group, even if it is not verbally of behaviorally manifested. | Young adolescents are able to discuss the social implications of ethnicity. interventions that teach differences in languages, customs, and traditions are not as effective for this age group, because young adolescents are beyond literal definitions of ethnicity. Ethnic attitudes and prejudice are a source of conflict at this age and need to be addressed directly. Adolescents benefit from open discussions of ethnic prejudice. It is also important to emphasize interethnic similarities and to provide activities that promote intergroup cooperation. |
| Level 3: Ethnic group consciousness and ethnic identity | Adolescence, 14 years and on | Older adolescents are developing a group perspective of ethnicity. This can lead to increase in stereotyping and ethnocentricism in adolescence. Adolescents are also actively exploring their own ethnic identity. Expressions of ethnicity re related to self-perceptions rather than objective status (e.g., My parents are Mexican, but I see myself differently). | At this age, it is important to recognize ethnic differences and to provide opportunities for young people to express their ethnic identity in productive ways. Racial stereotypes and prejudices need to be discussed openly and honestly, especially when they are the source of social conflict. It is important to provide activities that promote positive interethnic relations and cooperation. |

Source: After Quintana (1998).

developmental model that teachers can use to promote ethnic awareness and understanding in their classrooms.

Ethnicity is a complex concept that many mature adults have difficulty defining and understanding. How do children develop this understanding? As we have already learned, children begin to form conceptions of gender at an early age. Young children also tend to describe people in terms of observable characteristics. Similarly, 3- and 4-year-olds are able to use skin color, hair, and other observable physical characteristics to categorize people into different racial groups (Aboud, 1998; Quintana, 1998). They can apply the labels of black and white to different pictures, dolls, and people by age 4. However, their ability to distinguish and label other ethnic groups, such as Asian Americans, Mexican Americans, and Native Americans may take longer because the distinctive features of these groups are less visible (Aboud, 1988). Children's conceptions of social groups are not stable and permanent at this point. A child might say, "I used to be white, but I went into the sun, and now I am brown" (Quintana, 1998, p. 33).

Although young children are just beginning to distinguish between racial and ethnic groups, they have already formed some racial biases and preferences. As you recall, young children process information in terms of single dimensions (e.g., length, size). They are unable to consider more than one dimension at the same time. When applied to social understanding, we find that young children tend to attribute positive attributes (e.g., friendly, kind, happy) to their own social group. This tendency may be due to the young child's desire to establish a positive social identity (Kowalski, 2003; Tajfel & Turner, 1979). (Bigler et al., 1997; Black-Gutman & Hickson, 1996; Kowalski, 2003; Quintana, 1998). However, preschool children report more positive attitudes toward whites than other ethnic groups. This pro-white attitude is found for Caucasian children as well as African Americans, Latinos, and Native Americans. What is interesting about this finding is that it appears to be unrelated to parental or peer attitudes (Quintana, 1998). Additionally, no racial bias is found in young children's preferences for playmates or social interactions. Researchers believe that young children's racial biases and preferences reflect the negative views and prejudices of the larger society. Evidence also suggests that children's pro-white attitudes may reflect their natural preference for light and bright objects at this age. Children's stories reinforce these preferences: Heroes are dressed in white, and villains all wear black. At present, the source of young children's racial attitudes are not clear.

By elementary school, children begin to form a more balanced view of ethnicity and race. Like gender, they understand the permanence of different ethnic or racial categorizations. With the development of concrete operations, children can group people into large social categories based on nonobservable features of ethnicity such as preferences for food, language, and activities (e.g., "He's Mexican because he speaks Spanish."). School-age children, who are also developing a concept of time and history, can also link ethnicity to heritage. Consequently, elementary school children have a *literal* definition of ethnicity. It is based on heritage, language spoken, and traditions (Quintana, 1998). Older children are also becoming more aware of individual differences within racial groups. It is these differences that enable the child to better predict what the person may say or do in a situation.

During the elementary school years, children become less biased in their racial attitudes. Minority children show an increase in positive attitudes toward their own group, and white children also show an increase in their positive attitudes toward minorities. At this stage of development, children are also beginning to develop an awareness of discrimination, prejudice, and racism (Brown & Bigler, 2005). For example, they describe prejudice as devaluing of an ethnic group, and discrimination as involving rights violations, racial exclusion, or negative treatment on the basis of race, as reflected in this statement of a 6-year-old (McKown, 2004, p. 611):

> . . . a long time ago, the Black people did not like the White people and the White people didn't like the Black people . . .

Additionally, African American and Latino children are more likely to be aware of racial stereotypes than European Americans (McKown & Weinstein, 2003).

During early adolescence, young people make an important transition to considering the social implications of ethnicity. Young adolescents (ages 10 to 14) show greater awareness of the social consequences of ethnicity, such as differences in houses, neighborhoods, and income. They have moved away from a literal definition to a social perspective of ethnicity. Young adolescents can now describe examples of prejudices and biases they have observed or experienced. Most significantly, young adolescents have developed an ability to understand how others may view their ethnicity. In Stephen Quintana's (1998) interviews with Mexican Americans, sixth graders were painfully aware that "Mexican kids are not the kind of kids other kids play with" (p. 38). As we have discussed previously, ethnic and racial stereotypes can make it difficult for minority youths to form a positive ethnic identity.

In adolescence, ethnic similarity becomes increasingly important in the formation of peer groups and friendships. When older adolescents are asked to describe their ethnic groups, there are more references to "us" and "we" than with younger children. It is believed that these references reflect a *group consciousness* of ethnicity that may serve as the foundation for forming an ethnic identity. Unfortunately, it tends to be associated with an increase in ethnocentrism and ethnic stereotyping in adolescence, until young people form a more "multicultural perspective of ethnicity" that involves a more sophisticated understanding of how ethnicity is only one of many dimensions of the self and others (Quintana & Vera, 1999).

Children's reasoning about ethnicity and race has important implications for educators (see the Focus on Teaching box on pages 408 and 409). Efforts to increase racial and ethnic understanding need to be sensitive to the developmental patterns we discussed. Many children may enter school with negative attitudes and prejudices toward different social groups, but young children may not respond positively to direct attempts to reduce prejudice. Children benefit more from learning about the histories, customs, and traditions of different social groups. It is also important to point out the ways social groups are similar, even though they may look, speak, or act differently. Adolescents are able to consider the social implications of race and ethnicity, such as differences in housing, income, and job opportunities. Compared with younger students, they are better able to understand the effects of racism, prejudice, and discrimination. However, efforts to de-emphasize ethnic differences may not be appropriate for youths who are developing an ethnic consciousness. Older adolescents need educators who can help them develop a healthy ethnic identity.

Schools also share an important responsibility for promoting tolerance and for reducing prejudice. Studies reveal that young people perceive and experience racial or ethnic discrimination quite frequently in and outside of school (Brown & Bigler, 2005; Fisher, Wallace, & Fenton, 2000; Wong, Eccles, & Sameroff, 2003). Additionally, more than half of hate crimes in the United States are committed by young people under the age of 21 (Heller & Hawkins, 1994). The teaching of tolerance requires that all students develop a sensitivity to the negative, discriminatory tone of racial and ethnic slurs, jokes, and stereotypes. Many schools are fostering tolerance and understanding through an antibias curriculum and innovative learning projects. For example, more than 30,000 teachers nationwide have been trained to use *Facing History and Ourselves* curriculum materials with their middle and high school students

(Heller & Hawkins, 1994). By critically examining moral questions raised by incidences of genocide (the Holocaust, Cambodia, and Armenia), these materials are designed to help young people reflect on their own identity, group membership, and obligations to others.

 # Children's Peer Relations

During the school years, children begin spending more time with their peers until, by adolescence, they spend about two-thirds of their day with classmates or friends. Adolescents consider the time they spend with their peers as the most enjoyable part of their day (Csikszentmihalyi & Larson, 1984). But parents often worry about the negative influence of peers. Problems such as drug and alcohol abuse, juvenile delinquency, and sexual promiscuity are often attributed to the negative influence of peers. However, contrary to popular belief, most studies suggest that good peer relations are *necessary* for normal psychological development. Children who are at greatest risk for developing academic problems and antisocial behaviors are those with poor peer relations. These children often have problematic family relations as well.

The Role of Peers in Children's Development

The term **peer** refers to a child of equal age or maturity. Peer relations tend to be more egalitarian and balanced than relations with parents and other adults. This equality provides a context for the development of many important interpersonal skills (Hartup, 1996). With peers, children can learn to make decisions and resolve conflict without adult intervention. The peer group also provides an opportunity to experiment with different roles and identities, and peers provide feedback that children may not get from adults. Numerous studies show that positive peer relations can enhance children's feelings of competence, efficacy, and self-worth (Parker & Asher, 1987; Parker, Rubin, Price, & DeRosier, 1995; Rubin, Bukowski, & Parker, 2006; Seguin 1999).

Peers also have an important influence on school success. We have already discussed how peers are important collaborators in learning situations. Peers help one another learn through modeling academic skills, assisting in problem solving, serving as a resource, and providing encouragement and support (Schunk & Hanson, 1985). Additionally, research suggests that peers influence how much children value achievement, how much they study, how well they perform in school, and which classes they take (Altermatt & Pomerantz, 2003; Berndt & Keefe, 1995; Eccles, Wigfield, & Schiefele, 1998; Kinderman, McCollom, & Gibson, 1996; Ryan, 2001; Wentzel & Caldwell, 1997). High-achieving students tend to associate with peers who value success in school, whereas low-achieving students are generally friends with classmates who express less interest in getting good grades (Altermatt & Pomerantz, 2003; Berndt & Keefe, 1995). Peer acceptance also promotes a sense of group belonging in school, which can promote higher school achievement (Wentzel & Caldwell, 1997). Additionally, there is evidence to suggest that peers play an important role in school adjustment. Children make a positive transition to kindergarten when they enter school with existing friends or are able to make friends easily (Ladd, 1990; Ladd & Price, 1987).

What happens when children are deprived of peer relations? Children with poor peer relations are known to experience low self-esteem, depression, poor school achievement, dropping out of school, and delinquent behavior (Parker & Asher, 1987; Parker et al., 1995; Savin-Williams & Berndt, 1990). As adults, these same children may experience mental health problems, marital instability, and erratic work lives.

In summary, peers help shape children's development in many important ways. The most common effects are:

- Peer relations provide opportunities for play and for exploring new roles.
- Peer relations provide a valuable context for learning and practicing social skills, such as social problem solving, perspective taking, and resolving conflict.
- Peer relations provide emotional and social support to enhance feelings of competency, efficacy, and self-worth.
- Peers provide valuable information about behavioral norms and expectations.
- Peer relations provide opportunities to develop close and intimate relationships with others.
- Peer relations play an important role in fostering school engagement, motivation, and achievement.

However, not all peer relations are alike. Some peer influences are not always positive. Early involvement with deviant peer groups, for example, is related to school dropout (Cairns & Cairns, 1994; Cairns, Cairns, & Neckerman, 1989). Many young people also experience peer pressure to try alcohol, to smoke cigarettes, and to engage in sexual activities. When children engage in delinquent activities for the first time (e.g., shoplifting, vandalism, truancy), it is generally in the presence of peers. Recently, peer researchers have used the term *deviancy training* when peers encourage, model, and reward aggressive or antisocial behavior in each other (Dishion, McCord, & Poulin, 1999).

Parents play an influential role in this process as well. Parents choose the neighborhoods, schools, churches, and youth organizations from which children select their friends. Parents and community members also serve as important role models. Children are more likely to try alcohol or cigarettes with their peers if they observe role models drinking or smoking (Kandel & Wu, 1995). In addition, children with poor parental relations are more susceptible to peer influences (Fletcher, Darling, Steinberg, & Dornbusch, 1995; Fuligini & Eccles, 1993). Thus, both peer and parental relations are linked to the development of problem behaviors in children and adolescents. We will explore these influences when we discuss the development of aggression in children.

Developmental Changes in Peer Relations

The development of children's peer relationships follows a predictable developmental sequence. As with other areas of development, children's peer relations show "patterns of increasing diversity, complexity, and integration" (Rubin et al., 1999, p. 633). There are developmental changes in (1) how children relate to their peers, (2) the quality of their friendships, and (3) the formation of peer groups. The Focus on Development box on page 414 summarizes developmental changes in peer relations from the preschool years through adolescence.

Infancy and Early Childhood

During infancy, children's peer interactions are limited to watching, smiling, pointing, vocalizing, and responding to another peer's behavior. When infants gain mobility and communication skills, their social exchanges become more complex.

Toddlers are much more likely to initiate play, imitate, and direct positive affection toward a playmate. Toddlers also show preferences for interacting with peers who have certain characteristics. Toddlers engage in a form of "turn-taking" with preferred playmates. They respond to their peer's overtures, then observe and respond to their responses.

UNDERSTANDING
CHILDREN
Strategy 5.10:
Observations of Social
Interactions and Play

Focus on
Development   *Development of Peer Relations*

Developmental Levels	Approximate Age Ranges	Characteristics of Peer Relations
Early Childhood	3 to 5 years	Shows preferences for certain peers: engages in turn taking with preferred peers, friendships involve doing things together
Middle childhood	6 to 10 years	Peer groups are small and selective; peer groups are same sex: peer groups have distinct social structure; friendships are based on shared values and reciprocity; concerns about social acceptance increase
Early adolescence	10 to 14 years.	Cliques of six to nine peers form; peer groups organize by sex and race; concerns about peer popularity increase; peer conformity is greatest
Late adolescence	14 to 20 years	Large organized crowds form based on reputation and stereotypes; conformity to peer pressures decline; mixed sex cliques form as interest in dating increases; friendships are characterized by intimacy, closeness, and self-disclosure.

These exchanges are evidence of a reciprocal relationship, which lays the foundation for the development of friendships (Rubin et al., 2006).

During early childhood, peer interactions become more frequent and more complex. As you know, the preschool period is an important time for the development of sociodramatic play. This form of play enables children to take on complementary roles and to come to some shared agreement as to their imaginary roles. Sociodramatic play is an important arena in which children learn to negotiate, share, take turns, and compromise. Additionally, preschool children begin to express preferences for playmates who are similar in age, sex, or behavioral tendencies. They also act differently when they are in the company of friends. They more frequently engage in both positive and negative interactions when they are with friends than with nonfriends. Interestingly, friends are more likely than nonfriends to resolve conflict through negotiation and to stay in close proximity following conflict resolution (Rubin et al., 1999).

During preschool, children's friendships are defined very concretely. A friend is someone who "likes to play dolls with me," or "plays with me a lot" (Selman, 1980). Friendships are a matter of doing the same activities together.

Elementary Years

During the elementary years, children have many more opportunities to interact with peers across a wide range of settings (e.g., school, church, home, neighborhood). Each of these contexts is associated with a different type of peer interaction. Peers must compete in some settings (i.e., sports), but cooperate in others (i.e., school).

During late childhood, there are marked changes in children's understanding of friendship. Whereas younger children's friendships were based on shared activities, older children emphasize the importance of shared rules and values. A *friendship* is a mutually agreed upon relationship in which each person responds to the other's needs and desires (Selman, 1980). In their words, a friend is someone who can "stick up for you." Older children view violations of trust—such as not telling the truth, breaking promises, or gossiping—as serious matters that can end a friendship.

Because friendships are based on mutual trust in middle childhood, school-age children may become more selective in their friendships. Girls especially tend to have a smaller network of close friends (Parker & Asher, 1993). Children's concerns about social acceptance increase in middle childhood, and disruptions in close friendships can have a serious impact on children's social adjustment. For example, friendship loss has been associated with depression and loneliness (Parker & Seal, 1996). These concerns may be related to children's abilities to compare their popularity with other children. Also, a good deal of children's gossip at this age focuses on children's social relations—who are friends, enemies, and so on. Discussions, especially among girls, can also focus on real or imagined romantic relationships with peers (Rubin et al., 1999).

UNDERSTANDING CHILDREN
Strategy 5.8: What is a Friend?

In late childhood, children begin to form **cliques.** These groups tend to be friendship-based and range in size from three to nine children of the same sex and same race (Kinderman, McCollom, & Gibson, 1995). These peer groups generally have an established social structure, with one or two members serving as the leaders. By 11 years, nearly all children are a member of a peer group, and 50 percent of their interactions take place in that context.

Adolescence

Important changes in peer relations occur in adolescence. As previously mentioned, adolescence spend one-third of their waking time with peers—double the amount of time they spend with parents and other adults (Csikszentmihalyi & Larson, 1984). Compared

During early adolescence, peer groups are organized by gender and ethnicity.
Source: Skjold Photography/Photo Edit.

with middle childhood, peer interactions are less likely to occur under the guidance and supervision of adults during adolescence.

Conceptions of friendship change in adolescence. Adolescents desire more closeness and intimacy with friends (Buhrmester, 1996). Friendships are characterized by intimate self-disclosure and provide an important source of support. During adolescence, teenagers begin to use their friends more than their parents as their trusted confidants (Fischer, Munsch, & Greene, 1996). Although adolescents tend to have fewer friends than young children, their friends tend to be more stable and enduring for psychological reasons (Cairns, Leung, Buchanan, & Cairns, 1995).

Conformity to peer norms and expectations tends to be greater in early adolescence than in childhood. Young adolescents are most susceptible to peer pressures perhaps because of their greater concerns about social acceptance at this age (Brown, 1990). Teens generally experience the greatest pressures to conform to norms concerning dress, musical preferences, and social activities (Brown, Lohr, & McClenahan, 1986). However, many teens also report that their peers exert a positive influence on their school involvement and achievement (Berdnt & Keefe, 1995; Brown et al., 1996). As previously discussed, peer pressures can lead to some unfavorable outcomes for teens who may experiment with drugs, alcohol, or sex.

The structure of peer groups also changes during adolescence. There is a general "de-grouping" of cliques in adolescence, and a more encompassing *crowd* structure emerges. Adolescent **crowds** are "reputation-based collectives of similarly stereotyped individuals who may or may not spend much time together" (Brown, 1990, p. 177). Crowds have a larger membership than cliques, and they are not particularly conducive to close interpersonal relations. In fact, an adolescent does not need to be friends with any member of the crowd to belong. The adolescent just needs to act or dress like other members of the crowd.

If you think back to your own high school experience, you can probably recall some of these crowds and their labels: the jocks, loners, brains, or nerds. As Table 7.1 shows, adolescents' descriptions of crowds in their schools tend to be highly stereotypic. It is also clear that a majority of adolescents think of themselves as normal or popular.

Being a member of a particular crowd has important consequences for the adolescent's identity. First, crowds have different social status within the schools, and students gain esteem and status by belonging to one of the prestigious crowds. In most U.S. schools, it is some variation of the "jocks" and the "populars." Members of high-status groups spend

TABLE 7.1   Description of Adolescent Crowds

Type of Crowd	Percent of Adolescents	Description of Crowd
Populars	23	Have many friends; are well known; look good; attend social events; are cool
Normals	45	Are average; go to social events for fun; don't have problems
Jocks	10	Like sports; participate in physical activities
Brains	9	Get good grades; are smart; have good academic skills
Toughs	7	Use drugs/alcohol
Loners	6	Belong to tiny groups; feel alone; are not accepted by others; do not conform

Source: After Youniss, McClellan, & Strouse (1994).

Mapping the Changes in Adolescent Crowds

David Kinney (1993) mapped the evolution of a peer group structure and the interrelations of adolescent crowds in a midwestern high school. On the basis of interviews and observations, he found that crowds evolved through three phases. As shown in Figure 7.1, the middle school social system comprised essentially two crowds: a small group of high-status "trendies" and a large group of low-status "dweebs." There was a clear boundary between the two groups. In early high school, the social systems of crowds became much more elaborate due to the broader range of extracurricular activities. The dweebs joined new crowds: "normals, "headbangers," "grits," and "punkers." The headbangers and trendies competed for top status, whereas the grits and punkers were at the bottom of the status hierarchy. There was more permeability

in the boundaries among the higher-status groups than between the higher- and lower-status groups. By late high school, peer status was no longer an important factor in differentiating crowds. Headbangers and trendies were essentially equal, and the boundary between the grits and headbangers no longer existed. In fact, a new group formed—the "grit-headbangers." During the high late school years, a number of students changed crowd affiliations. However, some crowd boundaries remained. For example, the boundary between the grits and both the trendies and punkers remained impermeable.

Kinney concluded that two factors explained changes in adolescent crowds. First, crowds need to be similar to one another in status. Second, they must also be open to forming relationships with members of different crowds.

  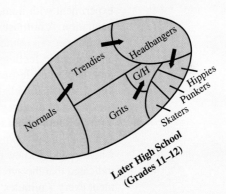

■ FIGURE 7.1
Developmental Changes in Crowd Structure
Source: After Kinney (1993).

more time with peers and friends than adolescents in low-status groups. Crowd labels also serve as a "prototype identity" for adolescents by reinforcing certain aspects of their self-conceptions (Brown, Mory, & Kinney, 1994).

Adolescent peer groups change again when young people become interested in dating. One of the first changes that occurs is when separate male and female cliques come together for a shared activity such as a school dance or party. Shortly thereafter, couples begin to form within cliques, and the crowds begin to dissolve and disappear by late adolescence. The Focus on Research box describes changes in the social system of crowds in one school.

UNDERSTANDING
CHILDREN
Strategy 5.11:
Perceptions of Social
Support

Summary of Peer Relations

Children's peers and friends play an important role in their development. As children develop, peer relations change from dyads focused on play to loosely organized crowds based on reputation and stereotypes. The peer culture of a school can either negatively or positively influence the learning environment. The influence of peers may be particularly critical during adolescence when peers fulfill needs that cannot be met by parents or other adults. Many young people report that the best part of school is spending time with their friends. Some researchers have thus argued that peers may be more important than teachers in fostering school engagement and achievement (Steinberg, Dornbusch & Brown, 1992).

Gay and Lesbian Youth

Changes in adolescents' peer relations raise some interesting questions and concerns for gay and lesbian youths. How do these young people negotiate the complexity of friendships, cliques, and crowds in adolescence? For young people who are homosexual, adolescence can be a difficult and traumatic period. They often experience considerable verbal and physical abuse from their peers, as well as social and emotional isolation from important social networks, including family and peers. Because gay and lesbian youths do not fit the heterosexual social norms of high school peer groups, they tend to experience the most negative and cruelest treatment of any social group (Bochnek & Widney, 2001).

It is estimated that 2 million youth of school age in the United States are gay, lesbian, bisexual, or transgender (GLBT; Bochnek & Widney, 2001). A large number of adolescents experiment with homosexual sex play, but for homosexual youths it is more than experimentation. A **homosexual orientation** is defined as a "consistent pattern of sexual arousal towards persons of the same gender encompassing fantasy, conscious attractions, emotional and romantic feelings, and sexual behaviors" (Remafedi, 1987, p. 332). According to reports of adult lesbians and gays, same-sex attractions may occur before the age of 15. Teens who acknowledge this attraction can often recall a period of intense anxiety when they realized that they belonged to a social group that society often portrays in derogatory terms. **Homophobia** is an irrational fear and hatred of homosexuals, and it is pervasive in American high schools. A 1999 CBS survey indicated that a third of the 11th-grade students who responded knew of incidents of harassment of gay or lesbian students. Another survey indicated that the average high school student in Des Moines, Iowa, hears an antigay comment every 7 minutes (Bochnek & Widney, 2001). The most common form of harassment is name calling, such as "faggot," "dyke," or "lesbo," often stated in front of peers. In some cases, harassment can also take the form of obscene gestures, graffiti on lockers, or even physical threats and abuse. Consider the following story a male high school student reported to Human Rights Watch (2001):

> After my art class, I needed to go up to the third floor for English, past the landing where the rednecks hung out. They tripped me. I never did anything to them. It was always "faggot," "queer"; I got pushed down the stairs.

For gay and lesbian youth, schools can be a dangerous, as well as hostile, environment. Many choose to remain silent about their homosexuality. Those who choose to "come out" as teenagers risk verbal and physical abuse. Numerous reports indicate that gay and lesbian youths have been harassed, verbally abused, and physically assaulted (McFarland & Dupuis, 2001; Savin-Williams, 1994). In his book *Breaking the Surface,* Greg Louganis, an Olympic champion diver who is gay, describes his adolescent experience with physical violence: "I got beat up often enough that it seems like a lot to me. The boys picked the fights and some of the girls cheered them on. I internalized all of it . . . I figured I must be wrong. They must be right to call me names and beat me up" (Louganis, 1995, p. 36).

Such negative experiences may account for the high rates of substance abuse among gay, lesbian, and bisexual youths. Studies reveal that approximately 60 percent of gay and lesbian adolescents abuse drugs or alcohol (Rotherman-Borus, Reid, Rosario, & Kasen, 1995; Savin-Williams, 1994). Feelings of isolation and despair can also place homosexual adolescents at greater risk than other youths for suicidal ideation, suicide attempts, and completed suicide (Remafedi, 1999). As we learned in Chapter 2, homosexual adolescents have the highest suicide rate of all young people.

Schools now have a legal responsibility to protect lesbian, gay, and bisexual youth from sexual harassment. A recent U.S. Supreme Court decision declared that school officials who ignore actions that create a sexually hostile environment for students are in violation of federal civil rights laws, and this protection extends to sexual minorities. To provide a safe educational environment for all students, many schools have developed antiharassment policies and instituted staff development programs focused on the needs of GLBT youth. Yet some school observers have stated that schools need to be more vigilant in enforcing these policies (Bochnek & Widney, 2001; Szalacha, 2003). Many GLBT youth report that teachers and administrators hear homophobic comments, but do not intervene as they should to stop them.

Peer Popularity and Rejection

As we have discussed, peer relations play an important role in fostering school engagement, motivation, and achievement. But some youth, as described, have difficulty establishing positive peer relations at school. Why do some children have so many friends and others have so

Peer rejection can have lasting consequences. Rejected children need special assistance from teachers to develop positive peer relations.
Source: Bob Daemmrich/Stock Boston, LLC.

few? Why are some children rejected? One key determinant to **peer popularity** is social competence, the ability to initiate and maintain positive interactions with others (Coie, Dodge, & Kupersmidt, 1990; Rubin et al., 1999). Popular children tend to be friendly, helpful, cooperative, good-natured, and sensitive. They also do well in school and obey the rules at home and at school. As a result, popular children have good relations with both children and adults.

Some children are neither popular nor rejected by their peers. Approximately 6 to 11 percent of elementary school children have no friends or are not nominated as friends (Rubin et al., 1999). Researchers refer to these children as **neglected peers.** They seem to be invisible in the classroom and tend to be shy and socially withdrawn (Coie et al., 1990). They do not have serious social problems, but they are not as skilled at making friends or initiating interactions as popular children. Although they spend a lot of time alone, they do not describe themselves as lonely. It is generally assumed that shy and withdrawn children are at greater risk than other children for dropping out of school or developing psychological problems later in life; however, research has not yet confirmed this hypothesis.

One of the key determinants of **peer rejection** is aggression (Coie et al., 1990; Rubin et al., 2006). Rejected children lack the social skills needed for initiating positive interactions and for resolving conflict. Peers and teachers describe rejected children as inattentive, aversive, threatening, hostile, and disruptive. As a result, rejected children are strongly disliked by most of their classmates. Aggressive children make up approximately 40 to 50 percent of the rejected children. Other children tend to be rejected because they are highly socially withdrawn, timid, and submissive (Rubin et al., 2006). Thus, there are two distinct groups of rejected children—those who are aggressive and those who are socially withdrawn and submissive. However, for older youth, aggression may not lead to peer rejection if it serves to maintain peer affiliations. Some aggressive boys are considered "tough" or "cool" by their peers (Farmer, Estell, Bishop, O'Neal, & Cairns, 2003).

As suggested earlier, peer rejection has many costs. It is associated with academic difficulties, school adjustment problems, truancy, and high school dropout. It is also a predictor of adolescent crime and delinquency. Longitudinal studies indicate that the effects of childhood rejection can last well into adulthood (Rubin et al., 2006). Rejected children who are aggressive have the greatest need for assistance in improving their peer relations.

Enhancing Peer Relations in the Classroom

Given the importance of peers in children's development, teachers need to create a classroom environment that promotes positive social relationships. How can teachers enhance peer relations? Providing preschool and primary children with play opportunities is an important training ground for social skills. Through play, children learn to understand others, to follow and lead, to express emotions, to build relationships, and to resolve problems. For elementary and secondary students, cooperative learning and peer tutoring activities can contribute to a positive peer culture in the classroom. These activities promote sharing, cooperation, and helping behaviors. Research suggests that the systematic use of cooperative learning activities can reduce the number of students who are socially isolated and improve relations between students of different ethnic and social backgrounds. Cooperative learning activities have also been found to increase student motivation and achievement (Slavin, 1995). The Focus on Teaching box on pages 422 and 423 describes ways to use cooperative learning methods in the classroom.

For neglected and rejected children, collaborative learning opportunities alone may not be enough to improve their social status in the classroom. These children may need more direct intervention in order to learn how to relate positively to others. Social skills training programs can teach unpopular children how to initiate positive interactions with peers, to make and keep

UNDERSTANDING
CHILDREN
*Strategy 5.9: Quality of
Peer Relationships*

friends, to think about the consequences of their behavior before acting, and to use nonaggressive solutions for resolving conflict. These training programs work best when teachers provide opportunities for children to practice the social skills they have learned and to receive positive responses from others when they use the skills (Berndt & Keefe, 1992). In sum, teachers can enhance children's peer relations by using a combination of cooperative learning and individual training activities in the classroom. The next sections provide some suggestions concerning how teachers can help enhance prosocial behavior and reduce aggression in their classrooms.

Development of Prosocial and Aggressive Behavior

As we have seen, popular and rejected children differ in the ways they relate to their peers. Popular children are able to share and cooperate, whereas rejected children have difficulty initiating interactions in positive ways. Let's examine how these different ways of relating to peers develop.

Development of Prosocial Behaviors

Most parents and teachers want their children to help, cooperate, and care for others. They also want their children to appreciate that other people's needs may be more important than their own. Defined as voluntary actions intended to benefit another person, **prosocial behaviors** emerge early in development when there are supportive relationships between children and caregivers (Eisenberg et al., 2006). For example, some infants react emotionally to the crying of other babies and, by the end of the second year, children will approach and try to comfort another child who is crying or upset. Two- and 3-year-olds can exhibit a wide range of prosocial behaviors including sharing, helping, and caregiving. Young children often show signs of concern, discomfort, or anxiety when they observe others in distress (Radke-Yarrow & Zahn-Waxler, 1984). These prosocial behaviors often occur spontaneously, with little prompting or encouragement from others.

Prosocial behavior increases over the elementary years. As their cognitive abilities develop, children learn to interpret what others may be feeling, thinking, and saying and to learn how their own actions affect others and themselves. As a result, they are better at anticipating how people will respond to them. They also learn to coordinate their actions with others and to work cooperatively toward a common goal. By adolescence, young people exhibit more prosocial tendencies, such as sharing, volunteering, donating, and other sympathy-related responses, than do younger children. However, there is a good deal of individual variability in young people's prosocial actions and responses (Eisenberg et al., 2006).

Why are some children more prosocial than others? There are a number of possible explanations. To some degree, genetics play a role. Twin studies reveal that prosocial behavior and empathy are more similar among identical that fraternal twins (Ruston, Fulkner, Neale, Nias, & Eysenck, 1986). We discussed how twin studies are used to establish biological influences in Chapter 2. Nancy Eisenberg and her colleagues have studied how children reason about prosocial behavior (Eisenberg et al., 2006). Because young children are not able to take the perspective of others, they do not realize the need for prosocial behavior. In elementary school, children's reasoning about prosocial behavior reflects a concern about other's people approval, as well as a desire to behave in a stereotypically "good" way. At this age, children may help others to gain approval or to do the "right thing." Beginning in late elementary school and thereafter, children begin to show a genuine concern, or empathy, for the other person's well-being. By adolescence, prosocial behaviors are guided by internalized values about helping others or by feelings of guilt or pride about one's actions.

Focus on
Teaching

Cooperative learning methods enable teachers to respond to the diverse needs of their students while at the same time promoting positive relations in the classroom. Cooperative learning takes many different forms, but most approaches involve heterogeneous groups of four or five members working together to accomplish a shared goal. Although each member of the team is individually accountable, each student must learn to depend on others for assistance. Cooperative learning methods may be used in any subject matter, from preschool through graduate school.

A number of different cooperative learning approaches have been in development. The most widely used approaches are the Jigsaw Classroom, the Student Teams Achievement Division, and a Group Investigation.

The Jigsaw Classroom (Aronson & Patnoe, 1996)

In this approach, six-member teams work on a learning task that is broken down into different parts. Each member is responsible for one part. During the first phase of the activity, members of each team who are responsible for the same part of the lesson meet to discuss their part. After mastering the material, they return to their original team to teach their part.

Student Teams Achievement Division (Slavin, 1995)

Here students are assigned to groups of four or five members to work on problems together. The teams assist one

Using Cooperative Learning to Promote Positive Peer Relations

another during the learning phases, but take individual assessments. Team scores are based on each individual member's improvement; therefore, each member can contribute to the overall goal of earning a high score. This approach has been used for projects in mathematics, reading, and social studies, and works well with students from different ability levels and in different grades.

Group Investigation (Sharan & Sharan, 1992)

In a group investigation, students work in two- to six-member teams on an independent and group assignment. The teacher chooses a topic (e.g., weather), but students get to choose an individual problem related to the topic. Students work on their problems individually and then meet with their team to integrate their findings and to develop a group report. The teacher and student jointly evaluate the group and individual projects.

Cooperative learning is perhaps one of the most extensively studied teaching approaches. Researchers have examined its influence on academic achievement, higher-order thinking, transfer and retention of learning material, moral development, social competencies, and many other outcomes (Johnson, Johnson, & Stanne, 2000; Slavin, 1995). Because cooperative learning methods were initially used in the classroom to improve intergroup relations (cross-race, cross-gender, etc.), these effects have received attention as well.

The home environment also plays an important role in the development of prosocial behavior. Children who observe prosocial behaviors modeled in the home are more likely to exhibit these behaviors in other settings, such as school. When parents are helpful and responsive, their children imitate these behaviors (Eisenberg et al., 2006). Additionally, many parents foster prosocial behaviors by providing opportunities for children and adolescents to perform routine household tasks and chores that benefit others (Grusec, Goodnow, & Cohen, 1996). It is believed that these activities sensitize young people to the needs and welfare of others.

Discipline practices also have an important influence on the development of children's prosocial behaviors. In general, parents who use reasoning and induction as a method of disciplining children tend to have children who behave prosocially (Hoffman, 2000). These parents tend to emphasize the rights and needs of others, as well as the impact of the child's behavior on others. In contrast, power tactics that involve physical punishment, physical restraint, or unexplained prohibition ("I told you not to hit!") may act as an immediate deterrent but do little to help children learn prosocial behaviors.

Although cooperative learning methods need to be carefully used in the classroom, there is general consensus about their benefits. The research clearly indicates that cooperative learning improves students' motivation to learn, interest in learning, and academic performance. It also contributes to a supportive and cooperative classroom environment. And perhaps most important, cooperative learning can improve interpersonal relations of students from different ethnic and socioeconomic backgrounds, as well as improve the social acceptance of students with learning disabilities and other handicaps (Sharan, 1980; Slavin, 1995).

David and Roger Johnson (1999), who developed a program called Learning Together, view cooperative learning methods as a vehicle for team building and for socioemotional development in the classroom. In their view, cooperative learning methods are used most effectively in the classroom when the following key elements are observed:

■ *Interdependence.* Group activities need to be structured in ways that ensure each group member's effort is required for success and each member has something unique and important to contribute. Students need to believe they sink or swim together. If there is no shared goal, there is no cooperation.

■ *Individual and Group Accountability.* Two levels of accountability need to be observed in cooperative learning approaches. The group is accountable for achieving a shared goal, and each member is evaluated in terms of his or her contribution to the group.

■ *Building Interpersonal and Small Group Skills.* Cooperative learning activities are highly complex, involving teamwork as well as individual effort. Effective cooperative learning involves helping students be good listeners, leaders, decision makers, and team members. Learning to manage conflict constructively is also important for the overall success of cooperative learning programs. It should not be assumed that students know how to work as part of a team. These skills need to be explicitly taught or modeled.

■ *Group Processes.* Group members need to discuss how the group is working together to meet its goals. The objective of these discussions is to identify ways of improving group effectiveness and relations.

When cooperative learning methods are used, careful attention needs to be given to group composition. It is best to balance groups in terms of ethnicity, gender, and ability. Teachers need to monitor groups to encourage equal participation of all members.

The research on parenting and prosocial behavior has important implications for teachers. It suggests that teachers can increase children's prosocial behaviors by modeling such behaviors, by encouraging children to share, cooperate, and help others, and by using positive discipline strategies that help students to consider the effects of their behavior on others. Students also benefit from activities in which they help others. Class projects such as tutoring younger children, reading to elderly people, building a play area, or collecting food or clothes for needy children are ways to foster a concern for the welfare of others. As discussed later service learning projects for other students has as its goal the development of social responsibility (Waterman, 1997).

Development of Aggressive Behavior

Few topics have attracted as much attention as the development of aggression in children. According to a recent national survey of high school students, 13 percent of students in grades 9 through 12 reported having been involved in a physical fight, and

Focus on
Research

Bullying Is Aggression

Data collected as part of the National Crime Victimization Study (NCVS) suggest that the number of children reporting that they were afraid of being attacked at school has declined in recent years. Nevertheless, large-scale studies indicate that between 10 and 15 percent of students, teachers, and principals feel their schools are unsafe (DeVoe et al., 2003). In addition, a significant proportion of students (5 to 9 percent) stay home from school or avoid certain places because they are afraid of being victimized (DeVoe et al., 2003). One of these students' strongest fears is peer harassment in the form of bullying.

Bullying is a subset of aggression, and is defined as a set of behaviors that is "intentional and causes physical and psychological harm to the recipient" (Smith & Thompson, 1991, p. 1). Researchers believe that bullying occurs as a way for the bully to attain social position within a peer group or have dominance over others (Espelage, Bosworth, & Simon, 2000; Olweus, 1980). Bullying behavior is most prevalent in adolescent peer groups. As adolescents make the transition to a new school environment, bullying might be one way to establish status in a new peer group (Pellegrini & Bartini, 1999). Bullies generally lack the social skills for positive

integration with peers, and they often become associated with deviant peer groups who support antisocial activities such as damaging property, fighting, and so on (Espelage et al., 2000). Boys are more likely to engage in bullying behaviors than girls; however, girls tend to use social alienation and verbal bullying as methods of intimidation. These behaviors may be more difficult to identify than the physical bullying behaviors exhibited by boys (Espelage, Mebane, and Swearer, 2004; Roberts, 2000).

Several factors contribute to the bullying behavior of youth. Because bullying is a form of aggression, it shares the same developmental course. The home environment of the bully tends to be punitive and harsh (Espelage et al., 2004). The slightest infraction may spark a verbal, emotional, and physical reaction from caregivers. Physical punishment is commonly used, and parents provide little in the way of modeling positive behaviors. Bullies spend a good deal of their time without adult supervision, and they are seldom disciplined for antisocial behavior. Researchers believe that children from these circumstances learn to gain power and status by attacking the weaknesses of others.

9 percent report being threatened or injured on school property (National Center for Educational Statistics, 2004). Although rates of youth violence have declined in recent years, violence continues to be the second leading cause of death among teenagers in the United States, and homicide is the leading cause of death for ethnic minority teens. Moreover, the tragic school shootings in recent years show that youth aggression and violence can happen anyway. As the lives of more and more families are touched by violence, policy makers and concerned citizens seek ways to stop it. Although fewer than 1 percent of all violent deaths of children occur at school, many schools are now involved in violence prevention programs.

For the purpose of our discussion, **aggression** is defined as behavior that is intentionally aimed at harming or injuring another person (Parke & Slaby, 1983, p. 50). It is important to keep in mind that not all aggression is violent in nature. Verbal abuse, destruction of property, harassment, derogatory racial or antigay remarks, obscene gestures, and even vicious gossip are different forms of aggression.

One of the most common forms of aggression in school settings is bullying behavior. Recent statistics indicate that bullying affects approximately 30 percent of American schoolchildren within any given semester (Limber & Small, 2003). **Bullying behavior** takes many

Bullying behavior has consequences for both the bully and the victim. The damage done to the victim's self-esteem may be long term and lead the victim to withdraw from school (Hanish & Guerra, 2000). For example, Dan Olweus (1993) reports that children who were bullied in middle school had low self-esteem 10 years later, and they were more likely to report social isolation and depression than peers who were not bullied. In some cases, bullying can increase aggression among victims (Hanish & Guerra, 2000). There are also long-term consequences for the bully. As they become adults, they are more likely to become involved in criminal activity and to display aggression toward spouses and children (Olweus, 1993).

Bullying is the most prevalent form of violence and aggression in schools. It often occurs in areas of the school building that are not well supervised. Attacks on the playground or in the hallway are common. To compound the problem, many victims do not report bullying incidents out of fear of additional harassment. Thus, teachers and other school personnel may not be aware that peer victimization is occurring.

What can educators do? The following are some recommended strategies:

- Many schools have adopted antibullying policies that encourage treating others with respect and care. Students need to understand that physical aggression and bullying are not acceptable ways of gaining popularity or leadership.

- Bullies need to be confronted by adults in a calm, rational way. One way to begin the conversation is to ask the student to explain the behavior (e.g., What is going on with you and David today?).

- Bullies are often sad and unhappy. Empathic listening can help identify the cognitive and affective problems associated with the bullying behavior.

- Peer–peer and student–teacher conflict can increase bullying behavior.

- Bullies need to learn alternative ways of interacting with peers. Social skills training and anger management programs have been effective in reducing bullying behavior.

- Bullying behavior is less frequent in schools that are (a) well organized, (b) supportive and low in conflict, and (c) focused on learning.

forms—embarrassing people, hitting, destroying property, ridiculing, and so on. As described in the Focus on Research box, bullying behavior has long-term consequences for both the bully and the victim. The majority of bullying incidents occur near or within school buildings, and only 25 percent of students report that their teachers intervene in bullying situations.

Current theories of childhood aggression stress the importance of both biological and environmental influences (Dodge, Coie, & Lynam, 2006; Lahey, Waldman, & McBurnett, 1999; Loeber & Stouthamer-Loeber, 1998). That is, some children may be genetically predisposed to exhibit aggressive behaviors, but there are also important family, peer, and cultural influences to consider. Once aggression becomes a significant component of a child's life, it can gain strength and become self-reinforcing because it provides children with a way to control and manipulate others (Cairns & Cairns, 1994). If left untreated, children who show an aggressive profile in kindergarten or first grade will continue to be aggressive throughout the school years (Cairns, Cairns, Neckerman, Gest, & Gariepy, 1988; Dodge et al., 2006; Olweus, 1981). Moreover, as early as first grade, childhood aggression is predictive of other problem behaviors that can occur in later development, such as poor academic achievement, peer rejection, substance abuse, truancy, and delinquent behavior (Reid, 1993).

Age-Related Changes in Aggression

There are clear differences in the form and frequency of aggression in children. Adults are often surprised when they learn that toddlers and preschoolers are often *more* aggressive than elementary-age schoolchildren. Visit any day care center, and you will see 3- and 4-year-olds quarreling or playing tug-of-war with toys and other prized possessions (Fabes & Eisenberg, 1992). To get their way, some children may hit, kick, pull hair, or bite. Physical aggression of this sort is more common among younger children because they have limited verbal and social skills. In most instances, the aggression is intended to obtain a desired object, not to hurt or to injure another person. When a child's behavior is intended to obtain an object or to protect a play space, it is known as **instrumental aggression.** If, on the other hand, the child's goal is to hurt or harm another person, it is known as **hostile aggression.**

With age, instrumental aggression declines. This decrease is due to the development of children's abilities to delay gratification (see Chapter 6). Also, as we learned earlier, older children are better able to take the perspective of others and to consider the consequences of their actions. When aggression is exhibited in elementary school and thereafter, it takes the form of hostile aggression. It is person-oriented and intended to hurt or harm the other person. Hostile aggression is much more frequent among school-aged children and adolescents than preschoolers. From about 4 years on, boys are more likely than girls to engage in physically aggressive behaviors. Despite popular movies, such as *Mean Girls*, there is no agreement among researchers that girls are more socially aggressive than boys (Dodge et al., 2006; Espelage, Mebane, & Swearer, 2004).

Rough-and-tumble play is common among young children, especially boys. The intent is not to do harm but to have fun. In contrast to fighting, the children are generally laughing and smiling.
Source: James Shaffer/Photo Edit.

Along with the developmental shift from instrumental to hostile aggression, there are also important changes in *how* aggression is expressed at different ages. Younger children with limited verbal skills tend to resolve disputes through physical aggression, but older children are more likely to use *verbal forms of aggression*. Teasing, ridiculing, and shouting are the preferred modes of aggression among older children. This developmental change in aggressive behavior is due not only to improved language skills but also to changes in adult expectations and rules. By late elementary school, most children know they should use their words and not their hands to resolve conflicts.

In some cases, verbal aggression can take the form of sexual harassment. In a recent survey of 2,064 students in grades 8 through 11, 83 percent of girls and 79 percent of boys reported they had been sexually harassed. The most common forms of harassment in schools included sexual jokes, gestures, spreading sexual rumors, or name calling (American Association of University Women, 2001). For both boys and girls, experiencing sexual harassment at school has negative and behavioral consequences, including staying home from school and cutting classes. Girls tend to report stronger negative reactions than do boys.

Causes of Childhood Aggression

Many parents and educators believe that electronic media, especially television, is a major contributor to childhood aggression. Young people watch an average of 28 hours of television per week, and 80 percent of television shows contain some form of violence (Pellman, 2000). As described in the Focus on Research box on page 428, aggressive children tend to watch more violent television programs, but the relation between television viewing and aggression is not straightforward.

The causes of aggression depend on when it emerges in development (Lahey et al., 1999; Loeber & Stouthamer-Loeber, 1998). Researchers have identified three developmental courses for aggressive behavior: (1) early onset, (2) limited duration, and (3) late onset. Most, but not all, aggressive acts during adolescence and adulthood are committed by youths who have shown a persistent pattern of aggression since childhood (Loeber & Hay, 1997). Longitudinal studies reveal that children who show an early onset of aggressive behaviors tend to have a difficult and oppositional temperament during infancy (Lahey et al., 1998). These children often come from families characterized by a number of stressful conditions (e.g., economic problems, substance abuse, marital discord, or mental health disorders), which makes it difficult for parents to set consistent limits for their children, especially if the children themselves are difficult (irritable, hyperactive, impulsive). Inconsistent or ineffective parental discipline can set in motion a *coercive family process* (Patterson, DeBaryshe, & Ramsey, 1989), and it is one of the strongest predictors of aggressive behavior in early development. Without effective guidance, the child becomes increasingly aggressive, impulsive, and noncompliant. If parents give in to such behavior, it increases the likelihood that children will respond to future requests for compliance with hostility, negativity, and resistance.

As parent–child interactions become more strained, some parents may either withdraw from the relationship or use physical punishment to bring about compliance. In either case, such parent–child interactions militate against the child's development of emotional control, academic skills, and social competence. As we will discuss in Chapter 8, parents who regularly use physical force to control people also provide an aggressive model for their children to emulate. Additionally, aggressive children receive little reinforcement when they do exhibit nonviolent, cooperative play with their siblings.

Focus on
Research

Effects of Television Violence

National surveys reveal that approximately 57 percent of American television programs between 6 A.M. and 11 P.M. contain violent images, and children's programs have the highest amount of violent content (Center for Communication and Social Policy, 1998). In most instances, perpetrators of violence go unpunished; few programs containing violence emphasize nonviolent alternatives for solving problems. The authors of this study recommended that TV producers limit violence and show negative consequences for violent acts. The study also recommended that policy makers pass federal legislation to require television manufactures to install program-blocking devices, known as *V-chips*, so that parents can limit children's viewing of violence.

What are the effects of TV violence on children? Most studies report a clear link between TV violence and aggression. For example, Bandura's (1969) early study with the Bobo doll discussed in Chapter 1 showed that preschool children who viewed a film depicting aggressive models exhibited more aggression in a free-play situation than children who did not watch the film. In another early study, Friedrich and Stein (1973) asked children to watch one of three types of television shows daily for four weeks: cartoons and other programs ("Batman") showing aggression, programs depicting prosocial themes ("Mr. Rogers' Neighborhood"), and shows with neither prosocial nor aggressive themes. Children who watched the aggressive shows displayed more aggressive behavior after the intervention than the children who viewed the other shows did. The viewing of TV violence can have long-term effects. Children with higher exposure to television violence were more aggressive 10 years later (Eron, Huesmann, Lefkowitz, & Walder, 1996; Huesmann, Moise-Titus, Podolski, & Eron, 2003; Zuckerman & Zuckerman, 1985).

As suggested here, a heavy dose of TV violence early in childhood can have harmful consequences for later development. Exposure to violence on television not only increases the likelihood of aggression but also increases children's acceptance of aggression. That is, children may become indifferent to violence. While this research suggests a clear link between TV violence and aggression, researchers are still debating cause-and-effect relations (Huston & Wright, 1998). Do aggressive children watch more aggressive TV shows? Or does violence on TV cause children, regardless of their developmental history, to become more violent? There is some evidence to suggest that aggressive children, who may have aggressive models inside and outside the home, tend to watch a greater number of television shows with aggressive themes. Also, children who show a predisposition toward aggression are more susceptible to the influence of TV violence than are children who are not aggressive.

Thus, the effects of TV violence on aggression are clearly not straightforward or simple, but there is nevertheless a strong link between the two. Over the last 20 years, children's exposure to violence in videos, movies, and computers has grown tremendously. Violence in these media sources is also associated with aggressive thoughts and feelings (Anderson & Bushman, 2002). As violence among youth continues to receive public attention, more and more pressure will be placed on television producers to eliminate or seriously reduce violence. Stay tuned.

Peers also play a role in the development of aggression. Children with an early onset of aggression tend to have fewer well-behaving peers who can serve as positive role models (Cairns & Cairns, 1994; Cairns et al., 1989; Dodge et al., 2006; Lahey et al., 1998). Aggressive children often form friendships with other aggressive or delinquent youths. These associations tend to reinforce and sustain existing problem behaviors. For youths who do not show an early pattern of aggression, the influence of deviant peers is much stronger. These associations can place nonaggressive or moderately disruptive youths on a developmental pathway toward problem behavior (criminality, police arrests, violence) in adulthood (Lahey et al., 1999; Loeber & Stouthamer-Lober, 1998). However, it is important to point out that the late onset of aggression is also associated with poor parental monitoring and high neighborhood crime rates. These environmental conditions increase the likelihood that young people will come into contact with delinquent peers (Lahey et al., 1998). Finally, some child development specialists have used social cognitive models to explain aggression in children. Aggressive children are more likely than nonaggressive children to show biases in processing and interpreting information in social situations (Crick & Dodge, 1994; Dodge et al., 2004). As with the cognitive models discussed in Chapter 4, **social information processing theory** assumes that information in social situations is processed sequentially. Figure 7.2 shows the process by which children and adolescents encode, interpret, and respond to social information. Specifically, when responding to social problems or situations, children need to go through very complex phases of cognitive stages of social information processing, while in engaged in a social interaction. The processes include:

■ Attending to and encoding relevant social information
■ Interpreting relevant social cues
■ Formulating a plan or goal for action
■ Generating strategies to achieve the chosen goal
■ Evaluating the likely success of various strategies
■ Responding to the event or situation

For aggressive children, several problems may arise while processing social events. First, for most children and adolescents in school, these events occur in busy places, such as the playground, hallway, or cafeteria—where many activities are taking place quite quickly. Unlike solving math problems, children must respond without much teacher

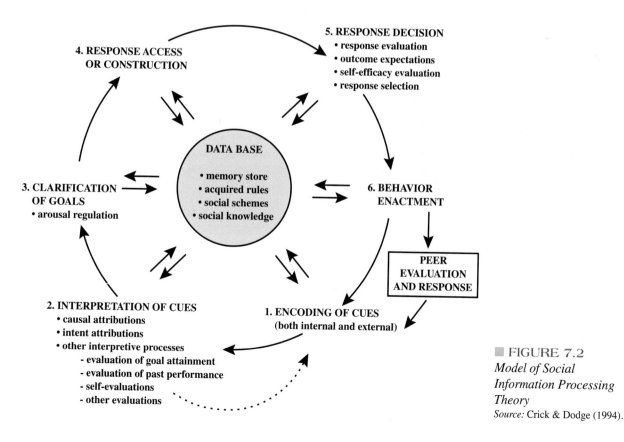

■ FIGURE 7.2
Model of Social Information Processing Theory
Source: Crick & Dodge (1994).

direction, structure, or cueing (see Chapter 4). Even under the best of circumstances, it is hard for most children to respond while in a social situation that may also evoke an emotional response, such as anger or humiliation (Lemerise & Arsenio, 2000). As we learned in Chapter 4, working memory has a limited capacity in terms of the amount of information it can process simultaneously or sequentially. When responding to social problems or situations, children or adolescents must process and interpret an array of relevant information while formulating a response to an event or situation. In most social situations, such as a school hallway, classroom, or playground, there are many activities taking place quickly and simultaneously. Therefore, young people must process information quickly and efficiently.

Using the social information processing model, researchers have found that aggressive children tend to have a **hostile attribution bias** (Crick & Dodge, 1994; Dodge et al., 2006; Graham & Hudley, 1994). Compared to nonaggressive children, they are more likely to interpret social actions as hostile, even when the intent of others is uncertain. Moreover, aggressive children tend to have difficulty finding constructive solutions to social problems. For example, they are more likely to generate "get even" strategies than nonaggressive peers, and view these actions as effective and appropriate for achieving their goals (Dodge et al., 2006). In turn, these actions are likely to elicit a hostile reaction, which serves to reinforce an aggressive child's belief in this hostility bias.

In summary, there appears to be no one single cause for aggression. It is an interplay of the child's own characteristics, family environment, peer relations, community, and culture. In the next section, we discuss how schools can help reduce aggression and violence among youth.

School Efforts to Reduce Aggression

Currently, violence prevention among youth is one of our country's top priorities. The Gun-Free Schools Act of 1994 required public schools receiving federal funding to implement mandatory expulsion rules for any student caught bringing a firearm onto school property. However, throwing troubled students out of school is not the best solution to the problem. It only increases the likelihood that they will fall further behind academically and eventually drop out of school. School expulsion also places youths at greater risk for delinquency, because they are less likely to have adult supervision (Children's Defense Fund, 1996).

Several school-based intervention programs have been successful in reducing aggression. Many schools have also implemented programs that help aggressive, socially immature children develop missing interpersonal skills. As discussed earlier, aggressive children are less likely than nonaggressive children to notice and interpret social cues correctly, to generate socially desirable responses to social problems, and to evaluate the consequences of their actions (Dodge et al., 2006). They also have difficulty carrying out nonaggressive solutions to problems. An intervention program based on this research would emphasize training to enable aggressive children and adolescents to (1) stop and think about

Many teachers today have training in conflict resolution to help young people constructively resolve interpersonal problems.
Source: Mary Kate Deny/Photo Edit.

Preventing Aggression by Promoting Social Competence

Second Step is a school-based violence prevention program geared toward children from preschool through grade 9 (Frey, Hirschstein, & Guzzo, 2000; Frey, Hirschstein, & Van Schoiack Edstrom, 2005). The program is designed to reduce aggression by promoting social competence. The curriculum is focused on three key social-emotional competencies: empathy, social problem solving, and anger management. Program lessons are taught by trained teachers twice a week in the regular classroom. Stories, puppets, videos, role play, and class discussions are used to promote key concepts. Students take an active role in solving class problems, deciding rules, and resolving conflict. "Remember the Day" activities are used at the end of the day to review and discuss certain targeted behaviors (e.g., How did you feel when you were left out?). There is also a school and family component to the program.

Initial lessons focus on empathy. Students discuss and identify different feelings, and practice communicating different feelings. This aspect of the curriculum is very similar to the PATHS program discussed in Chapter 6. Stories are used to help students understand other people's feelings. Role playing is also used to help students with perspective-taking skills (e.g., What do you say when a friend is angry?).

In the social problem-solving component of the program, students learn how to solve problems using five strategies. Students are taught to (1) identify the problem; (2) brainstorm solutions; (3) evaluate solutions by asking Is it safe? Is it fair? How might people feel? Will it work?; (4) select a solution; and (5) evaluate if the solution worked. As before, stories and role-playing activities are used to help develop these competencies.

The third component of the Second Step program is anger management. In these lessons, students are taught to recognize anger cues in their bodies—situations that "trigger" angry responses (e.g., teasing and name-calling)—and then practice strategies to bring their anger under control. These strategies may include self-talk, which involves using language to calm emotions.

Evaluations have examined the effects of the program on second- and third-grade students in 49 classes (Frey, Nolen, Van Schoiack Edstrom, & Hirschstein, 2005). Behavioral observations revealed that physical aggression decreased from fall to spring among students who were enrolled in the Second Step program. Reductions were greatest in the least structured settings—the playground and lunchroom—where aggression most frequently occurs. In addition, prosocial behavior (taking turns, sharing) increased among students from the fall to the spring term. These results provide encouraging evidence that a school-based program focused on promoting social competencies can help to reduce aggression.

social problems before reacting, (2) interpret problems accurately, (3) consider several possible solutions, and (4) evaluate the consequences of their actions. These programs are most successful when they begin early in school and involve both parents and teachers in addressing the problem behavior (Coie & Dodge, 1998).

Along with programs focused on individual groups of students, many schools have also implemented schoolwide programs for improving the social skills and interpersonal relations of all students. **Conflict resolution programs** are being used in elementary, middle, and high schools to help students solve interpersonal problems peacefully (Walker, 1995). These programs help students to (1) define the problem, (2) identify possible solutions, (3) evaluate consequences for self and others, and (4) choose solutions that benefit both sides (called *win-win* solutions). Two widely used programs of this type are (1) Teaching Students to Be Peacemakers (Johnson & Johnson, 1999), and (2) Resolving Conflict Creatively (De Jong, 1994). Both programs begin in the early grades and continue through high school.

Formal evaluations show that schoolwide conflict resolution programs are successful in reducing the frequency of aggressive behaviors and in changing cognitive processes (e.g., hostile attributions, retaliation fantasies) associated with aggression (Metris Associates, 1997; Johnson & Johnson, 2000). Another successful school-based program for reducing aggression is described in the Focus on Teaching box on page 431.

Conflict resolution and social skills programs help foster a positive school climate. Studies have identified a number of other key characteristics of schools with low levels of violent behavior (see *Early Warning, Timely Response: A Guide to Safe Schools,* Dwyer, Osher, & Wager, 1998). In these schools, there is a clear focus on academics and all students receive support in achieving high standards. There are also clear expectations for appropriate behavior, and teachers are well trained in behavior management. There is a schoolwide discipline plan that actively teaches prosocial behaviors and holds students accountable for misbehavior. Additionally, there is ample opportunity for adults to spend quality, personal time with students and to foster a sense of connection and belonging. Finally, schools with lower levels of aggression and violence maintain close ties to the families and communities they serve.

 ## Moral Development

Schools are an important training ground for children's developing conceptions of moral behavior and ethical values. At school, students are faced with moral issues almost daily. Should they return a watch found on the playground? Should they report someone cheating on an exam? Should they hit when they are angry? Should the whole class be punished when one student is bad? Should they skip school? When should a student be expelled from school? Many school subjects also present children with moral questions to discuss and debate: Should animals be used in scientific research? Should the United States have used nuclear arms in World War II? When are dissent and protest appropriate? Works such as *Huckleberry Finn, Cry the Beloved Country, The Crucible,* and *The Diary of Anne Frank* present students with moral issues to consider. In short, schools have many opportunities to teach democratic principles and ethical values such as equality, justice, honesty, civility, tolerance, and respect for life (Damon, 1999; DeVries & Zan, 1994; Lickona, 1991).

In response to public concerns about juvenile violence, schools today are placing a greater emphasis on moral education and character development. Moral judgments focus on children's understanding of fairness, justice, and the rights and welfare of others. Moral reasoning is distinct from **social convention reasoning,** which pertains to rules that help to maintain a particular social organization or system, such as a school. For example, in most schools children must learn to keep the classroom clean, to return library books on time, to raise their hand to speak, and so forth. Research indicates that both children and adolescents use different criteria for reasoning about behaviors that violate moral standards versus social conventions. Distinctions in children's moral and social conventional reasoning were observed in an observational study of elementary and junior high schools (Turiel, 2002). For events involving physical harm, the participants talked about the possible injuries to others or the unfairness of the act. In contrast, reactions to a social conventional transgression, such as leaving a candy wrapper on the cafeteria floor, focused on "rule sanctions and commands to refrain from doing the act," rather than the possible harm to others (Turiel, 2006, p. 830). This observational study clearly showed that young people were using different criteria for making social conventional and moral judgments. Moral acts, involving fairness, justice, and the welfare of others, are obligatory and not contingent on laws, authority dictates, or social consensus (Turiel, 2006). In the next section, we will draw Lawrence Kohlberg's (1969) theory of moral development to understand changes in children's conceptions of rules and fairness, and also discuss some other approaches to moral development. We will then discuss how teachers can create a classroom in which respect, responsibility, caring, and fairness are a part of the daily curriculum.

Kohlberg's Theory of Moral Development

Kohlberg's (1969) theory of moral development is based, in part, on the ideas presented in Piaget's *The Moral Judgment of the Child,* which was first published in 1932. One aspect of this study focused on how children develop respect for rules and a sense of social solidarity in the games they play among themselves. Piaget found that children progressed from *unilateral* to *mutual* respect for rules. Young children believe that rules are immutable, and terrible consequences will happen if rules are violated. As children gain experience in social interactions, particularly with peers, their understanding of rules changes. Rules are increasingly viewed as pragmatic social agreements that allow everyone to participate equally in joint activities. Respect for rules is based on a concept of cooperation: To play fair, everyone must follow the same rules. Older children believe that rules for games can be changed, but only if everyone agrees.

Kohlberg extended Piaget's theory of moral judgment. He was mainly interested in how children and adults reason about moral issues in which different perspectives and values come into play. One of the most commonly used moral dilemmas can be described as follows. Heinz's wife is dying and needs a particular drug to save her. The drug is very expensive, and the druggist who invented it will not sell it at a price Heinz can afford. Heinz becomes desperate and considers stealing the drug for his wife. Should Heinz steal the drug? Why or why not?

In listening to individual responses to Heinz's dilemma, Kohlberg was not so interested in what action should be taken as in the thought processes involved. Kohlberg believed that moral judgment was a cognitive process in which a person must identify the issues, values, and perspectives in conflict, then order them in some logical hierarchy. In the Heinz dilemma, for example, the perspectives that are in conflict are those of the shopkeeper and Heinz. The values in conflict are property rights, loyalty and duty to a spouse, and right to life. Which value takes precedence over the other?

Three Levels of Moral Judgment

Using dilemmas such as the one of Heinz, Kohlberg identified six stages of moral development that he organized into three levels. His stage theory of moral development included the following cognitive development principles from Piaget's theory: each stage involves qualitatively different modes of thinking; each stage involves a restructuring of the thought processes and structures found at earlier stages; and the stages form an invariant sequence. In Kohlberg's theory, moral development progresses from *self-centered* to *rule-oriented* to *principled reasoning.* Unlike Piaget, however, Kohlberg did not believe his stages were universal. In fact, his studies show that not all adults reach the third level of moral reasoning. Progression through Kohlberg's stages is dependent on role-taking skills, abstract thinking, and socialization experiences. The six stages of Kohlberg's model of moral development are shown in Table 7.2 on page 434.

According to Kohlberg's theory, people at the level of **preconventional moral reasoning** approach moral issues from a hedonistic perspective. They are not concerned with what society defines as the right way to behave, only with the concrete consequences of their actions. In the Heinz case, people at the preconventional level would say it is wrong for Heinz to steal because he may get caught and go to jail. Alternatively, they may say Heinz should steal the drug

TABLE 7.2   Kohlberg's Stages of Moral Reasoning

Stage	Characteristics	Child Responses to Heinz Dilemma
Level One: Preconventional	*Stage 1: Obedience-punishment orientation.* The child obeys rules to avoid punishment. *Stage 2: Instrumental and relativist orientation.* Each person needs to take care of his or her own needs.	*Pro:* Maybe he won't get caught. *Con:* He will go to jail. *Pro:* The wife needs the drug and the husband will be lonely if she dies. *Con:* The storekeeper needs the money for his store.
Level Two: Conventional	*Stage 3: "Good girl" "Nice boy" orientation.* Good people do nice things. Good behavior is what pleases other people. Intentions are important in judging goodness and badness. *Stage 4: Law and order orientation.* Good behavior is obeying laws and rules. It is important to do one's duty and respect authority.	*Pro:* He will show his wife he is a good husband. *Con:* Other people will think he is is bad. *Pro:* A husband has a duty to take care of his wife when she is sick. *Con:* It is against the law to steal.
Level Three: Postconventional	*Stage 5: Social-contract orientation.* Laws and rules exist to benefit everyone and to preserve human rights. Rules and laws are established by mutual agreement. *Stage 6: Universal ethical principle orientation.* General universal principles (justice, fairness, equality) determine what is right and wrong. Unjust laws may be broken when they conflict with moral principles.	*Pro:* The law was not intended when someone was dying. *Con:* If he steals the drug, other people who need the drug cannot buy it. *Pro:* Saving a person's life is more important than property. *Con:* He will feel guilty because he was not living up to his own moral standards.

because he would feel sad if his wife died. At this stage, children say you should obey rules and laws because you might get punished or rewarded. This type of reasoning is very common among elementary school children, and declines between the ages of 10 and 13.

At the level of **conventional moral reasoning,** children accept and obey society's rules for right and wrong behavior even when there is no punishment or reward. They look to others, especially authority figures, for guidance, and obey rules to please others and to gain their approval. Kohlberg referred to this reasoning as a "good boy/good girl" orientation. If you recall, children's prosocial behavior at this age was motivated by gaining social approval as well. Later on, when children enter the "law and order" stage, they look to society as a whole for guidelines as to what is right and wrong. At this stage, children want to be good members of society. Whereas people at the preconventional level would say it is wrong to steal because it is against the law, conventional individuals might say Heinz should steal the drug because it is what a good husband should do. This stage of moral development is very common among older elementary school children, most secondary students, and many adults.

The third level of moral judgment is called **postconventional moral reasoning.** At this level, individuals have developed their own set of ethical principles to define what is morally right and wrong. This level is rarely achieved before college, and some people never achieve it (Colby, Kohlberg, Gibbs, & Lieberman, 1983; Turiel, 1998). Postconventional individuals view rules and laws as social contracts achieved through a democratic process. Society's rules should be obeyed not because they are the "law" but because they protect basic human rights such as equality, justice, freedom, and life. Laws should be disobeyed when they are not determined through a democratic process or when they violate ethical principles. During the Vietnam War, for example, the voting age was lowered to 18 years, because 19- and 20-year-old men were being drafted in to the military before they had an opportunity to vote. Many men refused to fight in this war, because they believed it violated basic human rights, such as self-determination and the value of human life. Other powerful examples of postconventional reasoning can be found in the civil rights movement of the 1960s. In his writings and speeches, Martin Luther King, Jr., argued that people had a *moral responsibility* to challenge laws that were unjust, but they must be willing to accept the penalty. In his view, any law that degraded people was unjust. Thus, the reasoning behind King's call to change segregation laws through civil disobedience illustrated the highest level of Kohlberg's stages of moral development.

Is Moral Reasoning Linked to Behavior?

It is generally assumed that moral reasoning is linked to behavior. People who reason at Kohlberg's higher stages of moral reasoning should behave morally. In general, research evidence to support this assumption is very mixed. Consider the number of individuals who exceed the speed limit or cheat on their income taxes. The link between moral reasoning and behavior is influenced by a number of different conditions, including the presence of social sanctions and supervision that might prohibit behavior. It is also influenced by the person's ability to reflect on the behavior and consider its consequences for self and others. Some evidence suggests that moral behavior depends on the degree to which a person perceives the behavior from a moral or legalistic perspective (Bandura, 1991). For example, underage drinking and smoking may be viewed as an individual right rather than an illegal act.

For many young people, social circumstances play a very important role. As we discussed earlier in the chapter, adolescents often engage in illegal or antisocial behavior to receive the approval of their peers. Some adolescents may also reason that their moral misconduct is justified because it provides them with a sense of self-worth, protection, or satisfaction. Recently, David Moshman (2005) has argued that moral development involves the formation of a *moral identity*. In defining oneself, is it important for the youth to be a moral or ethical person? Some youths and adults have been found to regard morality as highly central to their self-identity. In developing a moral self, a young person adopts standards of right or wrong that serve as internal guides and deterrents for conduct. Adolescents who have a moral identity view themselves as someone who is committed to acting in accordance with their moral beliefs and values. In this view of moral development, adolescents refrain from engaging in behaviors that violate their moral standards in order to avoid self-condemnation.

Caring as a Moral Perspective

In her 1982 book *In a Different Voice,* Carol Gilligan challenged some of Kohlberg's ideas because they were based on men. When Kohlberg applied his scheme, women were characterized as conventional rather than postconventional thinkers, because they tended to emphasize the feelings of others. In the Heinz case, women would typically want to resolve the conflict in a way that was mutually satisfying for both parties. They had difficulty rank ordering individual rights according to some logical hierarchy. Gilligan (1982) argued that Kohlberg's view of justice was individualistic, rational, and detached. Women are socialized to take responsibility for the well-being of others. Therefore, they are likely to make moral decisions based on an **ethic of care,** which emphasizes connections between people, as well as on an **ethic of justice.** At the highest stage of Gilligan's model of moral development, individuals must balance their own needs with their responsibility to others. Gilligan's research reminds us that caring and compassion are also important aspects of moral behavior that should be encouraged and developed.

Unfortunately, Gilligan's theory is not without criticism. Some critiques claim that Gilligan's theory needed further empirical testing. Also, there is little evidence boys and girls score much differently on Kohlberg's measure of moral judgment (Turiel, 1998). However, other evidence suggests that women may focus more on issues of care when reasoning about moral dilemmas in their own lives (Jaffe & Hyde, 2000).

Nevertheless, the ethic of care serves as the foundation for Nel Noddings's ideas about caring in schools (Noddings, 1992). In Noddings's view, schools must be places where children receive care and learn to care for others. She writes, "The primary aim of every teacher must be to promote growth of students as competent, caring, loving, and lovable people" (p. 154). One of the loudest complaints of students in our schools is, "They don't care." Noddings maintains that schools must become caring communities in which children feel understood, respected, and recognized. In addition, schools must encourage a sense of caring for the self, for others, for the environment, and for the world of ideas. Such themes as war, poverty, crime, intolerance, humanity, and environmental concerns should be addressed in any subject area. Moreover, learning in the subject areas should help students confront great existential questions: What is the meaning of life? What is important? How shall I live? Caring is a crucial component of any educational program for children.

Creating a Moral Community in the Classroom

Kohlberg believed that children acquire basic moral values by participating in social institutions such as the family and school. Higher stages of moral development are generally observed in children and adolescents who come from warm and supportive homes in which parents set standards for acceptable behavior and provide reasons for *why* certain behaviors are inappropriate. These parents use an *authoritative* parenting style (see Chapter 8) and recognize that children have individual needs that should be considered in establishing and enforcing rules. More important, controversial topics and moral issues are openly discussed in these families.

In a similar way, teachers can help promote children's moral development. First, children need models of moral and prosocial behavior at school. Teachers need to establish a warm, caring, and supportive environment in which *all* children are treated with care, respect, and compassion. They need to model acceptance and respect for the feelings of others. Teachers should avoid favoritism, sarcasm, or any other behavior that embarrasses or humiliates a child (Lickona, 1991). Most important, teachers need to stop physical or verbal abuse. As we have discussed, far too many young people comment that their teachers did not respond to bullying behavior, name-calling, or derogatory ethnic or sexual remarks. All children deserve a safe and supportive school environment. In his book *The Moral Intelligence of Children*, Robert Coles writes:

> Character is ultimately who we are expressed in action, in how we live, in what we do, and so the children around us know: they absorb and take stock of what they observe, namely us— we adults living and doing things in a certain spirit, getting on with one another in our various ways. Our children add up, imitate, file away what they've observed and so very often later fall in line with the particular moral counsel we willingly or quite unself-consciously have offered them. (1997, p. 7)

Discipline practices at school can also promote or impede children's moral development. Like authoritative parents, teachers need to use an **inductive method of discipline.**

*Opportunities to participate in democratic processes are key to facilitating students'
moral development. Such experiences also promote a sense of school belonging.*
Source: Jonathan Nourok/Photo Edit.

This disciplinary method serves an educational function because it gives students reasons
for why certain behaviors are unacceptable. For example, a teacher who disciplines through
induction would point out how cheating hurts the cheater as well as other students in the
class. Discipline practices that focus on the consequences of misbehavior for self and others help children to develop self-control and self-discipline. They also promote the development of empathy, compassion, and cooperation (Maccoby & Martin, 1983). When
children are simply punished for disobedience, it does not promote the understanding that
leads to higher levels of moral development. The Focus on Teaching box on page 438
features two classroom discipline approaches that incorporate these ideas.

Another way teachers can promote moral development in the classroom is through presenting moral issues and dilemmas. Kohlberg believed that schools should incorporate moral
issues into the curriculum. As stated earlier, many school subjects present moral issues that
can be discussed. For example, the Boston Tea Party can be used to discuss protest and dissent as well as to teach values such as justice, fairness, and democracy. Many guidebooks are
available to help teachers teach values through the curriculum (see Lickona, 1991). In discussing controversial topics or moral issues, teachers need to help students consider different points of view, to share their thoughts and feelings, and to listen to one another. In this
way, class discussions can help promote perspective-taking and communication skills.

Finally, students need opportunities to participate in democratic processes. On this
point, Piaget (1965) wrote:

> How are we to bring children into the spirit of citizenship and humanity which is postulated
> by democratic societies? By the actual practice of democracy at school. It is unbelievable
> that at a time when democratic ideas enter into every phase of life, they should have been
> so little utilized as instruments of education. (p. 366)

Focus on
Teaching

Teaching Self-Discipline in the Classroom

Numerous discipline approaches are used in schools to-day. Some are based on behaviorist principles of rewards and punishments, while others emphasize the management styles of teachers (organization, monitoring, "with-itness"). The important goal of any discipline program is the development of self-discipline. Research on parenting practices (see Chapter 8) emphasizes the importance of inductive discipline approaches that enable children to understand the consequences of their actions on others, to take responsibility for their actions, and to develop decision-making skills. The following discipline approaches can be used to help children learn self-discipline in the classroom.

The Dreikurs Model: Discipline Through Democratic Teaching

In the Dreikurs model, teachers and students agree on rules and share in responsibility for establishing a class-room climate that is conducive to learning. Dreikurs refers to his approach as *democratic discipline.* Teachers spend time talking with students about how their actions affect others and about their choices of behaviors. A key element of this program is the use of *logical conse-quences* for "inappropriate" behavior choices. In Dreikurs's view, all behavior produces a corresponding result. Helping someone with his or her work has a pleas-ant or good consequence, whereas talking while others are trying to work has a negative consequence for others. When students misbehave, there should be a logical con-sequence for their action that is jointly agreed on by the students and teacher. Disturbing others means being re-moved from the group, hurting someone at recess means

no recess, and throwing paper on the floor means picking it up. The consequences are discussed, explained, and jointly agreed upon. When consequences are logical, stu-dents begin to see that their choices have certain effects. They will realize that poor choices have negative conse-quences for self and others. In Dreikurs's view, the use of logical consequences helps students learn inner disci-pline. For more information about this approach, see *Maintaining Sanity in the Classroom* (Dreikurs, 1982).

Cooperative Discipline

Dreikurs's discipline approach served as the foundation for Cooperative Discipline, developed by Linda Albert (1996). This approach also calls for a democratic style of teaching in which students are given choices and input into decision making. However, Albert's approach em-phasizes the importance of analyzing the goals of stu-dents' misbehavior. In her view, students choose to misbehave to get extra attention, to gain power, to seek re-venge, or to avoid failure. The teacher's role is to help stu-dents make better behavior choices. Albert provides specific, concrete strategies to use when students misbe-have. Albert also believes students need to be given con-tinual encouragement through what she calls Cooperative Discipline's "Three C's" approach. Teachers need to (1) help students feel *capable*, (2) *connect* positively with teachers and classmates, and (3) *contribute* significantly to the class, school, and community. Thus, the Coopera-tive Discipline approach emphasizes the importance of redirecting behavior while creating a positive classroom community for students. For more information about this approach, see *Cooperative Discipline* (Albert, 1996).

Echoing Piaget's views, Kohlberg also believed that democratic governance should be at the heart of any moral education program. Traditionally, teachers and school administrators make decisions and rules, and then impose them on students. In Kohlberg's view, this power should be shared between teachers and students. He advocated the use of community meet-ings within the school to give students greater participation in the governing process. Many teachers use class meetings for this purpose. A class meeting involves the whole class, lasts for 15 to 30 minutes, and is most effective when done regularly. Some teachers end or start the school day with a class meeting.

Class meetings can occur at any grade level. Some kindergarten teachers begin their school year by asking their students, Why do we need rules? What should the rules for this classroom be? What should happen if someone disobeys a rule? The class meeting can be used to discuss classroom rules, problems, or conflict situations, but it does not have to be limited to those topics. The class meeting can also be used to plan activities and discuss ways of improving the classroom or school environment.

Class meetings are important forums for discussing ethical issues and events inside and outside school. For example, the teacher can pose the following sorts of questions: Should animals be dissected in science classes? Should public schools provide free education to children of immigrants when money for education is scarce? Should Congress reduce spending on Social Security in order to balance the budget? In sum, class meetings help to promote a sense of community as well as an understanding and respect for the democratic process. Students learn about democracy through experiencing it firsthand.

Character Education

Character education is a direct approach to moral development that involves teaching young people core values and virtues. It has a long and controversial history in American education (Noddings, 2002). A major task for educators is to define what is "good character," and to identify its associated traits. *Character* is generally defined as the possession and demonstration of certain virtues (Noddings, 2002). Thomas Lickona (1991), a leading expert on character education, emphasizes respect and responsibility, honesty, compassion, fairness, courage, self-discipline, helpfulness, tolerance, cooperation, prudence, and democratic values. In *The Book of Virtues,* William Bennett (1993) lists responsibility, compassion, honesty, friendship, work, courage, self-discipline, perseverance, loyalty, and faith. Founded in 1993, the Character Education Partnership (CEP) lists 11 core values for any character education program, including caring, honesty, fairness, responsibility, and respect for self and others (Lickona, Schaps, & Lewis, 1998).

Character education can take many different forms. It can involve discussion groups to help young people define their own values and understand the values of others, curriculum and life skills activities to foster the development of character traits, skill training in social problem solving and conflict resolution, civic education that focuses on civil rights and responsibilities, and efforts to prevent and reduce violence. Some critics question whether virtues can be taught in the same manner as arithmetic facts (Kohn, 1997; Noddings, 2002). Most parents, however, do try to teach their children values and virtues in some direct fashion. When a parent says, "stop pulling your sister's hair because it hurts her," some direct teaching is taking place. Teachers and other adults also attempt to inculcate virtues when they comment on a child's disrespect or kindness toward others. Generally, these interactions are immediate and concrete, and include explanations and comments about the behavior. The problem with some character education programs is that character traits are taught out of context through posters, mottoes, or competitions to reward good deeds.

In general, character education works best if it permeates the young person's environment. Character education needs to be an integral component of the curriculum, discipline policies, activities, and relations among youth and school personnel. There needs to be clear consensus among all participants on the important character traits to emphasize and the definitions of those traits. Adults in the young person's social environment (staff, teachers, parents, community representatives, etc.) must model positive character traits. Additionally, character education is also most effective when it is coupled with programs, as discussed earlier, that promote interpersonal problem solving and conflict resolution. Finally, character education is most effective when young people are provided real-world experiences to practice character traits. Service learning is often used as vehicle for providing these opportunities.

Service Learning[1]

Service learning is a teaching and learning approach that integrates academic standards with meaningful community service. Discovery and self-reflection practices link curricula to the reduction of community problems. Service learning programs are intended to cause positive changes for students as well as for community recipients. Both parties should benefit from the interaction. Examples of service learning projects include designing neighborhood playgrounds, preparing food for the homeless, building wheelchair ramps, and starting recycling programs.

Participation in organized service projects helps to foster student learning and positive youth development. Young people are able to develop civic responsibility as they work for their communities. Service learning programs also contribute positively to adolescent developmental needs, such as relationship building and identity exploration, and civic responsibility. Effective service learning programs foster personal and social responsibility, increase school attendance, and improve academic skills and grades. Young people so learn important social skills such as effective communication and teamwork. Several experts agree that service learning is a particularly effective strategy for reclaiming high-risk students who are not strongly bonded to their communities (Laursen, 2003; O'Flanagan, 1997). Young people who may not otherwise get the opportunity are presented with occasions to experience success, to feel valued and helpful, and to view themselves as connected to their community.

In summary, there are a number of important ways schools can structure activities to enhance the moral and ethical development of the students they serve. In Chapter 9, we return to the role of schools in children's development. We will revisit the importance of creating schools that promote positive peer relations, emphasize care for the self and others, and allow students to feel safe and connected to their school and community.

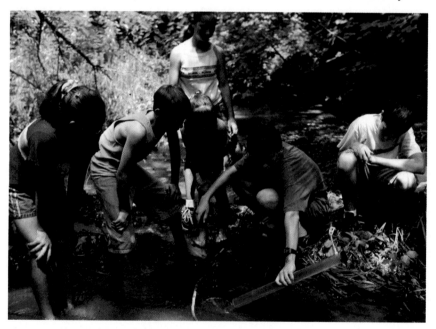

These students are collecting and testing water samples from a stream as part of a service learning project at their school.
Source: Tim McCabe, USDA.

---

[1] This section was written with the assistance of Kimberly Foreman.

■ Chapter Summary

Understanding Others

- Researchers use the term *social cognition* to describe children's understanding of other people's thoughts, feelings, and behaviors.
- Perspective taking involves the ability to take another person's point of view. Perspective-taking abilities develop gradually during the elementary school years. Children are not able to view situations or themselves from another's perspective until the late or middle childhood years. Perspective-taking abilities are important for social relations and moral development, in which other points of view must be considered.
- Between the ages of 3 and 5 years, children begin to develop theories of mind. With development, children learn to make inferences about inner mental states such as beliefs, intentions, desires, and emotions.
- Children can categorize people into racial and ethnic categories at a young age. Due to society's racial biases, young children develop a pro-white orientation that decreases in elementary school when children develop a more balanced view of ethnicity. Adolescents can think about ethnicity from a social perspective and consider its social implications (e.g., differences in housing, income, opportunities).

Peer Relations

- Peer relations are necessary for normal psychological development. Positive peer relations can influence children's feelings of efficacy, competence, and self-worth. Peers can also influence students' school achievement. When deprived of positive peer relations, children may experience low self-esteem, poor school achievement, and depression.
- Developmental changes in children's peer relations follow a predictable pattern. Young children show preferences for playmates and interactions are based on shared activities. Elementary school children prefer small peer groups of the same sex.
- The peer group structure changes in adolescence when cliques and crowds emerge. Peer conformity is highest in early adolescence.
- Approximately 2 million adolescents are gay, lesbian, bisexual, or transgender. These students are at greatest risk for harassment from peers.

Peer Popularity and Rejection

- Popular children tend to be friendly, cooperative, sensitive, and good-natured. Rejected children tend to aggressive, hostile, and disruptive. Neglected peers tend to be shy and withdrawn.
- Teachers can enhance children's peer relations in a number of ways. Cooperative learning activities are particularly effective in promoting positive peer relations, if the activities are carefully structured and monitored. Some children may need special training in how to interact positively with others and resolve conflict.
- Prosocial behaviors involve acts of caring, helping, sharing, and cooperating with others. These behaviors develop early but continue to increase in frequency as children mature cognitively and learn how their actions affect others. Parents and teachers can foster the development of prosocial behavior in children by modeling such behavior and by helping children reflect on how their behavior affects others.
- Young children use physical force to obtain an object or to get their way because they have limited social and verbal skills. This type of instrumental aggression is not intended to harm another person. Hostile aggression is more frequent among elementary and high-school-age children, and it generally takes the form of teasing, ridiculing, and shouting as children grow older.

- Bullying behavior is one of the most common forms of aggression in school settings. This form of aggression has a negative impact on the school environment, as well as long-term negative consequences for both the victim and bully.
- Most, but not all, aggressive acts in adolescence are committed by young people with a long history of aggression. The causes of aggression depend on its age of onset. Once aggression emerges as a way to control people's behavior, it is often difficult to change, because it becomes self-reinforcing.
- Schools are becoming more and more involved in efforts to reduce aggression and violence among youths. Conflict resolution and peer mediation programs are widespread. Many schools are also implementing programs to help aggressive, immature children to develop missing social skills. These programs are most successful when combined with interventions to improve academic skills and to enhance parent–child relations.

Moral Development

- Kohlberg's theory of moral development focuses on children's conceptions of rules, fairness, and justice. Preschool children believe rules should be obeyed because they lead to rewards or punishment, whereas elementary children view rules as important for maintaining social order. By late adolescence and adulthood, people begin to understand that rules are intended to help protect basic human rights such as equality, justice, and freedom.
- Gilligan argued that women are likely to make moral decisions based on an ethic of care, which emphasizes connections among people, as well as an ethic of justice. Women are socialized to care for others, and they tend to resolve moral conflicts in ways that preserve social relations and connections. Noddings argues that schools are an important place for the development of caring and compassion.
- Schools must be caring communities in which children feel understood, respected, and recognized. Schools must also help children learn how to care for themselves, others, the environment, and the world of ideas.
- Character education is becoming more popular in schools today. It is most effective as an integral component of the curriculum and school culture.
- Participation in service learning programs contributes to youth development. Young people learn important social skills such as effective communication, teamwork, and civic responsibility.

■ Key Terms

aggression *(p. 424)*
bullying behavior *(p. 424)*
character education *(p. 439)*
cliques *(p. 415)*
conflict resolution programs *(p. 431)*
conventional moral reasoning *(p. 434)*
crowds *(p. 416)*
ethic of care *(p. 435)*
ethic of justice *(p. 436)*
false belief *(p.403)*
homophobia *(p. 418)*

homosexual orientation *(p. 418)*
hostile aggression *(p. 426)*
hostile attribution bias *(p. 430)*
inductive method of discipline *(p. 436)*
instrumental aggression *(p. 426)*
neglected peers *(p. 420)*
peer *(p. 412)*
peer popularity *(p. 420)*
peer rejection *(p. 420)*
perspective-taking skills *(p. 403)*
postconventional moral reasoning *(p. 434)*

preconventional moral reasoning *(p. 433)*
prejudices *(p. 407)*
prosocial behaviors *(p. 421)*
service learning *(p. 440)*
social cognition *(p. 401)*
social convention reasoning *(p. 432)*
social information processing theory *(p. 429)*
theories of mind *(p. 403)*

■ Activities

1. Develop an observational procedure for collecting information on children's prosocial and aggressive behavior. Observe three or four elementary school children in different settings (classroom, playground, cafeteria, etc.). Try to observe children of different ages or gender. Record instances of helping, sharing, and taking turns, as well as instances of fighting, teasing, name-calling, and shouting. Be sure to record the events that preceded and followed the action. Analyze your observations for the frequency of prosocial and aggressive behaviors. Were there age or gender differences in the frequency of different behaviors? How did the setting of the observation influence children's behavior? What events tended to precede or follow acts of kindness or aggression? Discuss whether your findings fit with those described in the text.

2. Interview children of different ages about their conceptions of friendship (e.g., What is a friend?). Follow up with questions about what types of activities they like to do with their friends. How do children's conceptions of friendship change over development? Do boys and girls engage in different activities with their friends? Discuss how your findings fit with those described in the text.

3. Peer relations have an important influence on the classroom and school environment. Interview several teachers of different grade levels to ascertain their views of peer relations in their schools. Are peer groups segregated by gender, ethnicity, or social class? Is it easy or difficult for children to join different peer groups in the school? Ask teachers to describe the strategies they use to develop positive peer relations in their classroom. Share your results with classmates.

4. Interview a small group of teenagers (six to eight) of different age and gender groupings to learn about their feelings of guilt. Use the following instructions to interview each student.

We all do things we are sorry about, or that aren't nice. Sometimes we get into trouble for these things. Sometimes no one finds out. What things have you felt bad about doing? It might have been something that your parents got mad at you about, or a teacher, or maybe no one knew, but you still felt bad. . . . Write down what happened and why you felt guilty. Think of three (different) times you felt like this. (Williams & Bybee, 1994, p. 619)

After interviewing your students, analyze their responses for the nature of the incident mentioned (interpersonal problems, fights with friends or families, lying, negative thoughts about a person, fighting, neglecting responsibilities, etc.). Next, analyze the responses for age and gender differences. Were older students more concerned about violating the rights of others than about violating rules? Were they more likely to mention situations that involved the violation of ethical standards or ideals? Were girls more likely to mention situations that involved caring for others, trust, and compassion? Were boys more likely to mention issues of fairness and justice? Discuss how your results fit with research on moral development.

5. Review character education programs at the U.S. Department of Education's *What Works Clearinghouse* (http://www/whatworks.ed.gov). Divide into groups by grade level (preschool, elementary, middle school, and high school). Identify the types of social and interpersonal skills targeted and the instructional approaches used to enhance character development and prosocial skills. Drawing on your knowledge of child and adolescent development, assess the effectiveness of the programs. Which program would you choose fro your school or classroom? Provide a justification that uses your knowledge of what you learned from child and adolescent development course.

The Family: Partners in Education

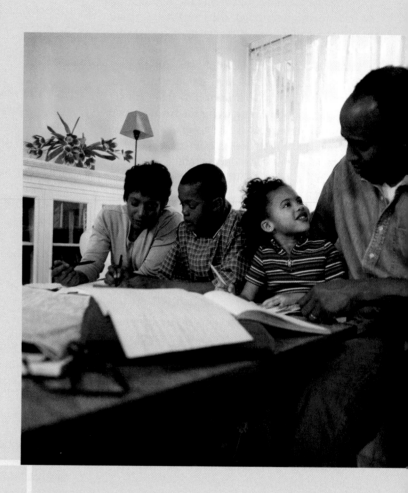

T HE FOLLOWING IS FROM AN INTERVIEW WITH A MOTHER REGARDING HER children's adjustments to school:

"The beginning of school was a bit rocky for my son. We got a call from the principal the second day of kindergarten—he kicked the teacher and yelled that he wanted to go home! You have to understand that Robbie had never done anything like that before in preschool, home, or anywhere. He was not an aggressive child—much more mild tempered. My husband and I knew that he was simply unhappy . . . and tried to make this clear in the only way that he knew how. He had been so looking forward to kindergarten . . . it just wasn't what he expected. We worked with the teacher to help Robbie adjust, and he did so quickly. We didn't receive any more phone calls like that . . . but, although he did well academically, he sometimes complained that school was 'boring.' First grade was better . . . we had a conference with his teacher at the beginning of the year, and she helped him like school better through paying attention to and encouraging him. He performed well in all subjects, but he still occasionally complained that he didn't really learn anything. I'll never forget when he stated, 'I didn't learn anything in first grade except for how to read!' I laughed and asked him if he didn't think that that was important . . . he admitted that it was. Elementary school got better and better for Robbie, especially when his teachers took the time to challenge him."

"My daughter's pathway through elementary school was much smoother! Aubrey walked to school with her best friend (a new school had just been built down the street from our house) and loved it from the very beginning. She had kind teachers who made her feel comfortable, even with her speech articulation problems. These articulation problems were common for her age (pronouncing l's and r's); she was not referred to speech therapy, and the problems nearly disappeared by second grade as expected. However, in fourth grade, her teacher noted that she was still having trouble with her r's (we hardly noticed) and suggested that a speech therapist work with her. We signed her up, and she learned how to correct the problem in two sessions! This problem has never reoccurred and we were very grateful to the teacher for intervening. It was also nice to have those services readily available at the school."

"When our family moved out of state, my husband and I were a bit worried about how the kids would adjust—but we relaxed on the first day of school when we saw more parents than kids there! We knew that this would be a good school. We met their teachers and shared our concerns about 'being new' and both promised to keep an eye on our kids and help them make friends. They kept their promises! Plus, they helped us find good after-school activities in the area. Soon, although they missed some of their 'old' friends and neighbors, our children were doing well in school and happy in their new home."

Parents are children's first teachers, and students are most successful in school when educators and teachers work together as partners, as we see happening in this vignette. In this chapter, we will learn how educators can build partnerships with parents. The chapter begins by looking at the family as a system. We will then examine variations in family structures, and ethnic differences in family values and parenting practices. We will also consider several critical issues for educators. How can teachers help children cope with family transitions, such as divorce? What are the signs of child maltreatment, and what causes it? This chapter will also provide important information on the benefits and barriers of parental involvement in education, and on the strategies schools and teachers can use to build partnerships with families.

Conceptions of the Family

Function of the Family: Socialization

The family is the child's primary source of support and nurture in early development. For many of us, our earliest memories are ones that involve a family event—a birthday party or a holiday celebration. There are also occasions when a certain sound or smell can trigger a memory of a special time shared with a grandparent. Of course, there are also memories of family conflicts and disappointments. For better or worse, according to most developmentalists, families have a lasting influence on children's development. However, some alternative perspectives have been presented, suggesting that we have exaggerated the importance of parental behavior on children's long-term development. For example, Harris (1995) argued that peer groups provide the major socializing force in children's personality development. Others, such as Steven Pinker (2002), point also to the greater role of genetic influences on psychological development.

Nevertheless, families continue to be regarded as an "early pervasive and highly influential context for socialization" (Parke & Buriel, 1998, p. 463). For centuries, families have been viewed as the social unit with primary responsibility for preparing the child to be a productive and competent member of society. This process has been termed **socialization** and concerns the rearing of children such that they may "function adequately within the requirements of the social group or groups among whom they live" (Maccoby, 1992, p. 1006). Maccoby (1992) identifies "adequate functioning" as the acquisition of those cognitive and behavioral tools that will enable individuals to (1) avoid deviant behavior, (2) contribute to the economic support of self and family, (3) form and sustain close relationships with others, and (4) be able to rear children themselves one day.

Although socialization has long been a matter of interest for child development researchers, ideas about the direction and complexity of this process have changed. Early theories of family socialization were broad, attempting to explain all of parenting and child development in a few basic principles. Parents were viewed as "all powerful" because they constructed and shaped the child's environment. For example, Sigmund Freud proposed that parents' handling of developmental tasks, such as weaning and toilet training, established lifelong patterns of thought and behavior. As we have learned, attachment theorists still view the early years of life as pivotal in establishing basic emotional and behavioral patterns. For behaviorists, such as John Watson and B. F. Skinner, successful child rearing was simply a matter of managing children's learning experiences in various circumstances so as to strengthen proper behavior and extinguish undesired behavior. However, psychoanalytic and behavioral views of the family provide a limited view of family dynamics. In fact, psychoanalytic theorists were among the first to recognize that to help an emotionally troubled child, it is necessary to change the family system (Minuchin, 1985).

The Family as a System

Most child development theorists today view family interactions as part of a highly complex system (Bronfenbrenner & Morris, 1998; Bugental & Goodnow, 1998; Cox & Paley, 1997; Sameroff, 1994). From a systems perspective, parents shape their children, but the children influence them as well. A baby's temperament, for instance, elicits different responses from caregivers, which in turn sets in motion another pattern of responses. In a systems view of the family, parent–child interactions are mutual and reciprocal.

From a family systems perspective, parents and children influence one another.
Source: © Digital Vision.

Family systems are also adaptive through processes of self-stabilization and self-organization. Families and the interactions of their members tend toward equilibrium, or homeostasis, exhibiting some resistance to change instigated by external forces. Sameroff (1994) has identified a number of family codes that help guide and organize behavior within the family system. Family beliefs, myths, stories, and rituals create a sense of history and tradition within a family and ease the day-to-day interactions of family members. However, the tendency of family systems to resist change can lead to problems when negative interaction patterns become ingrained and rigid (Katz & Gottman, 1997).

When change does occur in one element of the system, it affects the structure and functioning of the whole because of the interdependence that characterizes complex systems. The behavior of one family member affects the behavior of other family members. For example, in longitudinal studies of children with developmental disabilities, mothers' and fathers' stress levels are affected by changes in child characteristics (such as behavior problems and mastery motivation), family climate, and by parental assets (coping skills and support helpfulness) (Hauser-Cram, Warfield, Shonkoff, & Krauss, 2001). The behaviors of a parent struggling with alcoholism will influence her relationships with her children and likely their relationships with each other. Likewise, one child's exceptional performance in sports or academics will have repercussions for his parents and siblings.

From a systems perspective, the family is part of larger social systems, such as neighborhoods, communities, and cultures. These other systems can affect the interactions within a family. For example, a dangerous neighborhood can lead parents to be highly restrictive in their parenting approach to protect their children from harm (Kelly, Power, & Wimbush, 1992). Also, as we will learn, various cultures and subcultures have different expectations for children's development, which can influence how parents and children relate within the family unit.

The ecological theory of Urie Bronfenbrenner represents a systems approach for understanding family dynamics (Bronfenbrenner, 1979, 1986; Bronfenbrenner & Morris, 1998). If you recall from Chapter 1, Bronfenbrenner views children as embedded in multiple social

■ FIGURE 8.1

*Bronfenbrenner's
Ecological Model*
Source: After
Bronfenbrenner (1979).

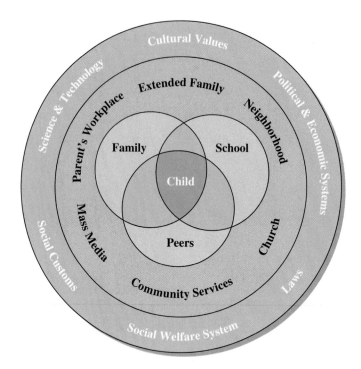

systems that interact in complex ways to influence development (see Figure 8.1). Bronfenbrenner later referred to the "**bioecological model**" to emphasize the process by which the developing characteristics of the individual and environment affect each other. In Bronfenbrenner's model, the **microsystem** is the child's immediate environment (the family, peer group, school), and the **mesosystem** is the interactions among components of the microsystem. For example, parents may meet with teachers or other school personnel to develop a management plan for a child who is having behavioral or academic problems in school.

The **exosystem** is composed of elements that may influence the child's development but only indirectly. Their impact is typically felt through their effect on elements of the microsystem, such as the family. For example, a parent's work may affect the child through its control over the amount of time the parent has for interaction with the child or through the level of economic support it provides for meeting the child's needs.

The **macrosystem** represents the larger culture and possibly subcultures in which the individual lives, including ideologies, traditions, and values. Elements of the macrosystem include regional identity, nationality, ethnicity, and religious affiliation. Children growing up in the rural, southern United States may have notably different experiences than those in the cities of the northeastern or western United States. More broadly, children living in Brazil will likely undergo a somewhat different socialization process than those living in Australia.

Family systems and their interrelationships also change over time. Bronfenbrenner refers to this level of influence as the **chronosystem.** The chronosystem represents the timing and patterning of events in an individual's life and the position of that individual's life in the larger flow of historical time. Both the child and the child's environment experience changes. For example, understanding and fostering the developing language and writing abilities of a child today will likely demand consideration of the increasing availability of electronic media for developing skills in those areas. Also, as the child progresses from preschool to adolescence, family influences give way to peers and school as important elements of the child's social environment. The ecological or "ecocultural" framework is useful for looking at how families everywhere create daily routines of family life within particular sociohistorical periods with varying support systems (Weisner, 2002, 2005). Children's experiences in these everyday activities in different families and communities provide "stepping stones" along different developmental "pathways" or trajectories (Lowe, Weisner, Geis, & Huston, 2005). Some of these different pathways will be discussed in this chapter.

In summary, conceptions of the family have changed from a simple focus on parents' effects to a complex system of interactions and processes operating at multiple levels. A child responds not only to a specific parental behavior but also to the setting, the relationship between the parent and child, and various other factors. As we will see in the next section, recent theories strive to address the broader milieu of social, economic, and cultural systems in which families and children are embedded.

 ## Variations in Family Structures

One aspect of the family system that has received much attention is the particular configuration of people who live together in a given family unit—usually called *family structure.* Numerous family structures exist in addition to the "traditional" family structure of a father, a mother, and several children. More and more children are living in single-parent households for at least part of their growing years. And many children experience a variety of family structures over the span of childhood and adolescence. Figure 8.2 provides data on some trends in family structures in the United States.

The following sections describe some of the variations in family structure and findings regarding their impact on children's developmental outcomes. Yet, even when researchers compare the development of children in specific family structures, many other factors must be examined to explain the child's development.

Two-Parent Families

In 2000, about two-thirds of children lived in married-couple family groups and about 6 percent lived in unmarried-partner (cohabitation) households (U.S. Census Bureau, 2004). Studies have shown that children living with two married parents have more daily interactions

■ FIGURE 8.2
Percentages of Children Under 18 According to Presence of Parents: 1980 to 2000
Source: U. S. Census Bureau, (2004).

Focus on
Research

The Role of Fathers in Children's Development

Increasing interest in the role of fathers in children's lives has become evident among both researchers and shapers of public policy. Consequently, more attention has been given to fathers in the research literature and in the collection and analysis of data by government agencies (Lamb, 1997; Lamb, Chuang, & Cabrera, 2005; Parke, 2004; Tamis-LeMonda & Cabrera, 1999).

Whereas earlier research on father involvement tended to focus on the simple presence or absence of the father, more recent investigations have attempted to delineate characteristics of different types of involvement. One model (Lamb, Pleck, Charnov, & Levine, 1987) suggests that father involvement can be characterized in terms of engagement (i.e., contact and interaction), accessibility

(i.e., presence and availability), and responsibility (i.e., provision of resources and meeting the child's needs). Studies conducted in the 1980s and 1990s showed that fathers were available to their children about 35 to 40 percent as much as mothers were, and were accessible about two-thirds as much (e.g., Pleck, 1997), an increase from the 1970s.

In 2002, about 19 percent of fathers provided care for at least one school-age child (ages 5–14), and about 14 percent provided care for a preschool child while the mother worked (U.S. Census Bureau, 2005a). When fathers are primary caregivers for their children, they show more affection for them, they seem more attuned to their play behavior, and the children show a preference for their fathers in stressful situations (Geiger, 1996).

together (e.g., eating, reading) and are better off in terms of material well-being than those living with unmarried parents (e.g., Acs & Nelson, 2002). These are important results to consider because family activities, such as eating and reading together, are associated with many positive child outcomes. However, many aspects of children's lives may be more affected by the number of parents and support systems available, and by the quality of relationships, than by parents' marital status alone. As we learned in Chapter 6, children's attachment relationships with mothers and fathers influence their well-being. Mothers and fathers both play important roles in fostering their children's development (see the Focus on Research box above "Role of

Family activities such as eating together are associated with positive child outcomes.
Source: Getty Images.

In terms of children's cognitive development, positive links have been noted between father involvement and children's IQ and school success in middle childhood and adolescence. Benefits accrue also for the child's social competence. For example, in a recent research review, Lamb et al. (2005) reported that positive paternal engagement predicts greater levels of social and personal maturity in children, fewer school behavior problems in boys, and more self-direction in girls. In contrast, a recent study showed that fathers' advice-giving (controlling style) predicted negative ratings of children's social competence by teachers and peers over and above mothers' advice-giving style (McDowell, Parke, & Wang, 2004). Parke (2004) concludes, "In the 21st century, fathers are clearly recognized as central players in the family and major contributors to children's social, emotional, and cognitive development" (p. 456).

It is important to recall that the family is a system of interacting members situated within a number of other social and cultural systems. The effects previously described reflect multiple intersecting processes through which father involvement impacts the child. Likewise, multiple factors interact to determine the extent of a given father's involvement with his child. Such factors include the father's mental health, his and the mother's expectations concerning his involvement in caregiving, and the level of support in the community and society for paternal involvement in the lives of children.

Fathers in Children's Development"). Furthermore, the qualities of marital or adult relationships are important predictors of mother–child and father–child relationships (e.g., Cox & Harter, 2003). Simply put, children's well-being is enhanced when their parents have healthy, happy relationships within supportive social networks and environments.

Single-Parent Families

In 2000, about 27 percent of all children under 18 lived with one parent (U.S. Census Bureau, 2004). The majority, approximately 21 percent, lived with their mother, and 5.8 percent with their father.

There are multiple pathways into single parenthood. Divorce produces the largest proportion of single parents. Other parents are widowed or assume single parenting because a spouse is out of the household due to work or incapacitation. For example, one parent may be serving in the military or is imprisoned. Also, a large number of women become single parents by having children out of wedlock. About one-third of births are to unmarried parents (Children's Defense Fund, 2004). The majority of single mothers are very young, but an increasing number of older financially capable women are choosing to become parents outside of marriage by such means as artificial insemination and adoption. These different entries into and experiences of the single-parent family affect the relationships within it and the likely outcomes for children's development. The Focus on Research box on page 452 describes difficulties associated with adolescent parenthood.

Single parents face a variety of difficulties. Of paramount concern are the experiences of role overload and economic strain

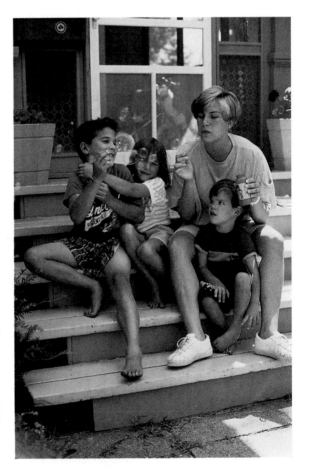

Children's experiences in single-parent families are linked to the economic and community resources available to the family.
Source: Steve Skjold/Photo Edit.

451

Focus on
Research

Over the last several years teenage pregnancy rates have been declining (Hamilton, Martin, & Sutton, 2004). The 2003 pregnancy rate for females aged 15 to 19 was approximately 41.7 per 1,000. These rates vary by ethnic group (see Figure 8.3).

Despite this trend of decreasing percentages of teenage pregnancies, the concerns faced by teenage mothers and their children warrant attention. Social and economic disadvantage, poor academic performance and educational prospects, family or community history of teenage births, and early sexual activity are among the factors thought to contribute to the likelihood of a teenage girl's becoming a mother (Brooks-Gunn & Chase-Lansdale, 1995; Rauch-Elnekave, 1994). Some of these factors are especially salient among different racial or ethnic groups. For example, African Americans report earlier sexual activity than Hispanic and European Americans, and African and Hispanic Americans are much more likely to come from socially and economically disadvantaged backgrounds. Such trends are likely to explain the differences in teen pregnancy rates shown in Figure 8.3.

Becoming a teenage parent often serves to continue the pattern of negative life circumstances for the young woman and her child. Teen mothers are more likely to drop out of school (Furstenberg, Brooks-Gunn, & Chase-Lansdale, 1989). As a result, they are often poorly prepared for finding employment and may find themselves

Teenagers as Mothers

in need of public assistance to care for their and their babies' needs (Sullivan, 1993). Consequences for children of teenage mothers may be more severe. Several studies show that attachment relationships between teen mothers and their children are more likely to be rated as insecure or disorganized as compared to low-risk populations (e.g., Lounds, Borkowski, Whitman, Maxwell, & Weed, 2005). Furthermore, high rates of insecure attachments were also found when the children were 5 years old (Lounds et al., 2005).

Higher levels of aggression and impulsive behavior and more delinquency often appear in these children (Chase-Lansdale, Brooks-Gunn, & Paikoff, 1991). Developmental and cognitive delays are also more common among children of younger mothers and may contribute to eventual academic problems including grade failure (Hetherington, 1998). And when these children become adolescents themselves, they show early sexual activity and increased risk of teen parenthood.

Prevention efforts have focused on providing accurate information to children and adolescents regarding sexuality and its risks. Schools have implemented a variety of programs employing a range of approaches, from promoting abstinence as a responsible choice to training in the appropriate and consistent use of contraceptives. Because of very strong moral and political opinions in this area, evaluations of various programs are often equivocal.

(Gongla & Thompson, 1987). Children in mother-only family groups are almost five times more likely to be living in poverty than in married-couple family groups (U.S. Census Bureau, 2004). Single parents face feelings of overwhelming responsibility as the sole caregiver and provider for their children. They must perform all of the child care tasks that can be shared in two-parent households. Even a less-involved parent in a two-parent family can provide some additional emotional and practical support to which single parents lack access. Not surprisingly, many single parents report feeling drained emotionally by their role as sole caregiver. High rates of poverty, low educational levels, and high mobility among single parents contribute additional stress.

Single Mothers

Most single parents (78 percent) are mothers. Single mothers face inordinate economic strain as a result of historical trends such as their lower levels of educational attainment,

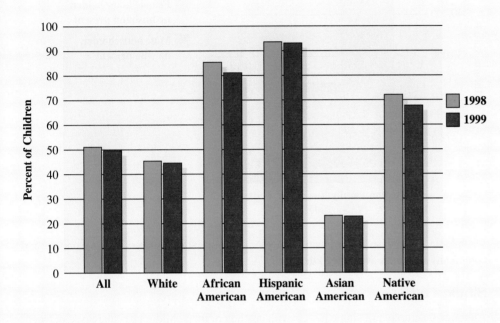

Teenage Births by Ethnicity of Mother in 1998 and 1999, per 1000 Births
Source: Curtin & Martin, (2000).

Once a teenager has become a parent, what can be done to avoid or ameliorate the negative consequences previously described? Support from the family of the teen mother can go a long way to help, especially in providing child care and training in effective parenting (Apfel & Seitz, 1991). Such support can also come from public sources such as the schools. A number of pro-grams have begun to provide child care for children of students and parenting classes for those students; these programs have had promising results. Encouraging teenage mothers to continue their education yields other obvious benefits, such as enabling them to improve their eventual employability and to forestall or even escape from disadvantaged economic circumstances.

less-developed job skills, and lower wages for jobs as compared to those performed by men (McLanahan & Sandefur, 1994). Also, single teenage mothers and single divorced mothers are especially likely to experience insufficient or decreased financial resources. Figure 8.4 on page 454 shows the levels of family income associated with different family structures.

Single mothers who work outside the home must divide their time between work and children, often neglecting their own personal needs. Such role overload coupled with eco-nomic strain can result in poorer parenting (McLoyd, 1998).

Early research on single mothers and their children focused solely on the effects of the ab-sence of a father. Studies identified a number of potentially harmful outcomes, such as behav-ior problems and less-masculine traits for boys who lacked a close father–son relationship (Biller, 1981). More recent investigations have looked at the various factors associated with the absence of a male figure in the household and children's developmental outcomes. Absence or loss of a father is associated with economic deprivation, decreased parental resources, and de-creased community resources. Each of these factors has been linked to less favorable outcomes

■ FIGURE 8.4

*Median Family Income by
Family Structure in 1999*
Source: U.S. Census Bureau,
(1999).

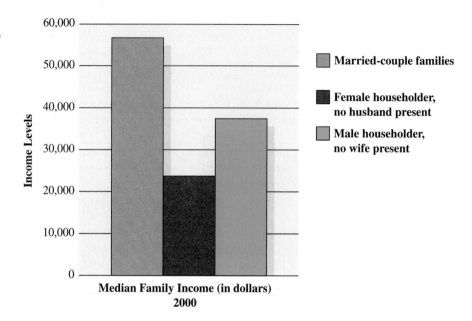

for children. Thus, the effects of a single-mother family are strongly linked to the economic and community resources available to the family.

Single Fathers

Although the number of single fathers with custody of their children has increased in recent decades, this family form still constitutes only about 22 percent of all single-parent families (U.S. Census Bureau, 2004). These single fathers also suffer role overload as they try to manage singlehandedly the roles of caregiver and provider.

Men do not face the historical economic constraints faced by women in terms of lower-status and lower-paying jobs. Consequently, single fathers tend not to suffer financially as single mothers do. They may, however, face less-optimal career options because of their parenting responsibilities. Working overtime or accepting a promotion that requires a greater time commitment at work may not be possible.

The pathway into single parenthood may affect the success and satisfaction that single fathers experience. Fathers who feel emotionally attached to their children or who question the parenting ability of their ex-partners often fight for custody. When consequently granted custody, such fathers describe the father–child relationship in very positive terms (Risman, 1986).

The age and sex of the child also play a role in the parenting of single fathers. Single fathers are more likely to parent older children. Mothers, on the other hand, more often raise infants and toddlers, who require more attention to their physical needs. Also, single fathers more often care for boys rather than girls. Fathers who raise daughters often question their parenting abilities and express concerns about providing appropriate guidance for their daughters, especially in dealing with topics such as sexuality in adolescence (Greif, 1985).

Single- and Two-Parent Families and Children's Development

Because of the stigma attached to single-parent families, much of the research has focused on expected negative outcomes for children. Moreover, most studies have focused on the effects of female-headed households. Research on the influence of single fathers on children's development is a relative new area of inquiry.

Children from single-parent families do show a greater risk of negative consequences in the areas of educational attainment and sexual activity (McLanahan & Sandefur, 1994). Children from two-parent families have higher grade point averages, test scores, and attendance records than children from single-parent families. Given these patterns, it should not seem so surprising that being from a single-parent family doubles a child's risk of dropping out of school. Children from single-parent families are also less likely to attend or eventually graduate from college. With regard to sexual activity, girls from single-parent families report earlier onset of sexual activity and show a higher rate of teenage pregnancy.

As we will see with other family effects, those just reported for children of single-parent families are not as simple as they appear. For example, race and ethnicity moderate the relationship between having a single parent and teenage pregnancy risk. Whereas coming from a single-parent family versus a two-parent family doubles the risk for European Americans and Hispanic Americans, it only increases the risk by 25 percent for African Americans (Wu & Martinson, 1993). Similarly, the risk of school dropout is different for single-parent children of different racial or ethnic backgrounds and the levels of educational attainment. Youths of highly educated white parents are three times more likely to drop out of school if they come from a single-parent home than if they come from a two-parent home.

Several other factors can influence children of single-parent families. For example, children of widowed mothers tend to resemble children of two-parent families in terms of the outcomes mentioned earlier. Also, the presence of other adults in the home, such as a grandmother, can help offset the negative consequences faced by many single-parent children (Kellam, Ensminger, & Turner, 1997).

Some of the differences found between children of single parents when compared to children raised by two parents are positive and some are negative influences. Many children of single parents assume more responsibility around the house and may be given a larger role in family decision making. When children are burdened with inappropriate adult demands in terms of household and family responsibilities, however, they may develop feelings of incompetence or resentment. Similarly, it can be emotionally demanding and detrimental if a single parent turns to a child as a confidant. On the other hand, if the increased practical and emotional responsibilities are not excessive, children may develop a stronger sense of self-sufficiency and maturity (Hetherington, 1999).

Gay and Lesbian Families

Estimates of the number of gay and lesbian parents raising children vary widely. The stigma attached to homosexuality by some segments of society leads some parents not to disclose their homosexual identity for fear of harassment of themselves or their children. Some fear legal intervention to remove their custody or visitation rights. The large number of openly homosexual parents raising children today is a recent historical phenomenon.

Disclosure or concealment of one's sexual orientation can be a key issue for many homosexual parents, as there are stresses associated with both options. Playing "straight" for friends and family out of fear of rejection, persecution, or discrimination can be emotionally taxing. One study found that lesbian mothers in stable relationships who were open about their sexual orientation were psychologically healthier than those who hid their lesbian identity (Rand, Graham, & Rawlings, 1982). Disclosure to their children seems to be more difficult for gay fathers than for lesbian mothers (Bozett, 1989). A number of other factors also affect parental decisions regarding disclosure. For example, living and working in a supportive environment in which a diversity of lifestyles is accepted and appreciated may make disclosure easier. Financial resources and ethnic background may also play a role in whether such an environment is available (Casper, Schultz, & Wickens, 1992).

There is great diversity among families with gay and lesbian parents. Most children of homosexual parents come from an earlier heterosexual union before the parent assumed a homosexual identity. However, a growing number of single and partnered gays and lesbians are choosing parenthood after assuming a homosexual identity. Options such as the use of donors or surrogates and adoption are allowing many lesbian women and gay men to become parents (Patterson, 1992). Homosexual parents also come from a variety of socioeconomic and ethnic backgrounds. Unfortunately, much of the research on gay and lesbian parents has been with a fairly homogeneous population of white, middle- to upper-middle-class, well-educated parents in urban areas. Consequently, the findings reviewed in this section should be viewed as limited in their generalizability until additional information is gathered on more diverse subgroups of homosexual parents.

As with the other "nontraditional" family structures discussed previously, much of the research on homosexual families has been either explicitly or implicitly comparative. Researchers have examined the similarities and differences between homosexual and heterosexual parents and between their respective children.

In general, gay parents and heterosexual parents are more similar than different. No differences are found between gay and heterosexual fathers on measures of their motives for parenthood, their sex-role orientation, or their involvement and intimacy with their children (Bigner & Jacobsen, 1989; Robinson & Skeen, 1982). However, lesbian mothers favor less-traditional sex-role socialization, and lesbian couples share parenting more equally than do heterosexual couples (Green, Mandel, Hotvedt, Gray, & Smith, 1986; Patterson, 1995).

Research comparing children of homosexual and heterosexual parents has focused primarily on issues of gender, sexual identity, and social adjustment. The results have revealed very few differences in outcomes for the two groups of children. No evidence for differences in gender identity or gender-role behavior has been found (Green, 1978; Green et al., 1986; Patterson, 1992). Similarly, the majority of children of both homosexual and heterosexual parents grow up to assume a heterosexual orientation (Bailey, Bobrow, Wolfe, & Mikach, 1995; Tasker & Golombok, 1997). Children of gay and lesbian parents exhibit good relations with peers and adults, and they resemble children of heterosexual parents on measures of social competence, self-concept, locus of control, and moral judgment (e.g., Patterson, 1995, 2002).

Other Family Structures and Implications for Educators

The structures of families are clearly diverse. Although a majority of children today live in two-parent families, not all children fit this pattern. We have discussed the increase in the number of single parents and gay and lesbian parents. Children may also live with aunts, grandparents, or foster parents. In 2000, approximately 1 in 12 children were living in households headed by grandparents or other relatives (Children's Defense Fund, 2005). Many of these children have no parents present in the household. These family structures are sometimes referred to as *kinship care* or *grand families,* and describe formal and informal arrangements in which grandparents or relatives raise children when their parents are unable to do so. For example, children may be removed from parental care by the state within the formal foster care system and placed with relatives. See the Focus on Research box "Grandparents as Caregivers" for more information about children's experiences in grandfamilies and how they can be supported.

It is important for teachers to be sensitive to variations in children's family circumstances. When talking about families, it might be best to use the word *parents* rather than mothers and fathers. It is also important to avoid making generalizations about single-parent families. Although these families have special challenges, the impact of this family structure on children is primarily linked to limitations in economic resources, rather than the absence of a second

Focus on
Research

Grandparents as Caregivers

More and more grandchildren are living in the homes of their grandparents. It is estimated that approximately 6 million children today are being raised by a grandparent or other relatives (Children's Defense Fund, 2004). Of those children living with their grandparents in 2000, parents were completely out of the picture for over a one-third of them. Rates vary according to race and ethnicity, however, with black children more likely to live with a grandparent than white or Hispanic children. Given reports that African American grandparents are more likely than those of other ethnicities to function as surrogate parents (Szinovacz, 1998) and that African American grandmothers in low- and moderate-income families often play a key role in child care (Pearson, Hunter, Ensminger, & Kellam, 1990), the higher rate of grandparent–grandchild co-residence for black families is not so surprising.

Grandparents may become caregivers of their grandchildren for a variety of reasons. Parents may no longer be able to provide primary care for their children as a result of death or incarceration, or they may simply abandon them. In some cases, parental mental illness, substance abuse, or child maltreatment may also lead grandparents to step in as caretakers of their grandchildren. Although legal guardianship is awarded to grandparents in many cases, sometimes these arrangements are informal, which

may lead to a number of obstacles when grandparents seek assistance for the children.

Grandparents who have assumed responsibility for rearing their grandchildren often receive little support or help from other family members. They may experience mixed feelings of anger and guilt with regard to their children's inability to parent and often feel overwhelmed by the responsibility themselves (Burton & Dilworth-Anderson, 1991; Kluger & Aprea, 1999). Many seek out help from social agencies, and hundreds of support groups have sprung up around the United States, providing everything from emotional support to political voice.

There are a number of things that educators can do to help grandfamilies. For example, educators might help caregiving grandparents by reviewing school policies that may need to be modified to accommodate them, providing information about school programs (e.g., after-school) that could lighten the caretaking load, offering referrals to health and social services as needed, and encouraging involvement in the school's activities. The grandchildren themselves could benefit from educators' acknowledgment that adjustment difficulties are possible and provide opportunities to build their resilience. Teachers and other school personnel should recognize that the children may feel "different" from peers because of their family status and should not compound the discomfort by calling attention to it.

---

parent. To increase parent involvement in school activities, special arrangements may be necessary to accommodate the busy schedules of single parents. Finally, it is important to bear in mind that the effect of various family structures on children is dependent on community resources. Schools can play an important role in strengthening family relationships.

Ethnic Diversity of Families

Along with changes in family structures, the ethnic composition of families is rapidly changing as well. For those working with children and their parents, it is important to understand the cultural values and child-rearing practices of different ethnic groups in the United States. Families play a primary role in fostering positive ethnic identities, along with other developmental assets, in their children. Extended family and secondary groups such as church, school, and volunteer organizations also play key roles in the socialization of

Grandparents may serve as primary or secondary caregivers for children.
Source: Alamy Images.

children within ethnic families (McAdoo & Martin, 2005). We examine cultural variations in this section. As is the case with any summary, the descriptions here involve generalizations; it is important to remember that great diversity exists within ethnic groups as a result of such factors as country of origin, recency of immigration, and socioeconomic status (Marín & Marín, 1991; Tanaka, Ebreo, Linn, & Morera, 1998).

African American Families

African Americans currently represent one of the largest ethnic minority groups within the United States. While significant numbers are recent immigrants from Africa or the Caribbean, the large majority are descendants of African slaves. Consequently, the experiences of African American families and children have been shaped by lingering vestiges of segregation and discrimination and a search for a positive ethnic identity (Comer & Poussaint, 1992).

Changing social and economic forces have been linked to marked changes in family life among African Americans during the past few decades. Black families in the United States have become more diverse in composition and structure than white families (Farley & Allen, 1987) as a result of such interrelated trends as decreasing employment among black males (Bowman, 1995) and declining rates of marriage (Gadsden, 1999). A majority of African American children live in mother-only households (Taylor, 1998). Also, a sizable proportion of African Americans live in urban settings in vulnerable neighborhoods where there is limited access to good schools and to secure, well-paying jobs (Gadsden, Smith, & Jordan, 1996). As can be seen in Figure 8.5, the median individual and household incomes for African Americans are significantly below the national average.

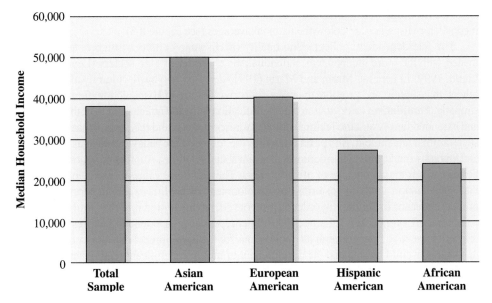

*Median Household
Income of Selected
Ethnic Groups*
Source: U.S. Census Bureau
(2000).

African American families recognize and voice concern about their poor socioeconomic situations and the public perception of them (Gadsden, 1999). Moreover, these families possess certain attributes that may serve to ameliorate the negative effects of such challenges. African Americans express high expectations for themselves, their children, and their communities (Gadsden, 1999). Child-rearing practices emphasize important traits such as assertiveness, independence, and self-confidence (Lewis, 1975). The development of spirituality and religiosity is also considered critical by African American families for promoting important coping skills to deal with difficult life experiences (McAdoo & Martin, 2005). Additionally, the African American community holds very egalitarian views of the division of labor between men and women (Scanzoni, 1985; Scott-Jones & Nelson-LeGall, 1986). African Americans also place great value on interpersonal relationships (Willis, 1992) and are more likely than whites to live in extended households made up of grandparents, uncles, aunts, cousins, godparents, and others (Farley & Allen, 1987). These extended families constitute an informal support network (Cherlin & Furstenberg, 1986; Comer & Poussaint, 1992) for the African American family and provide a range of services including monetary assistance, child care and child rearing, and emotional support (Stack & Burton, 1993). In some instances children may even be sent to live with members of the extended family, such as grandparents or aunts (McDaniel, 1994; A. Miller, 1993).

Hispanic American Families

The Hispanic population of the United States is rapidly increasing. Nearly two-thirds of this group are of Mexican origin. Puerto Rico and Cuba provide the next two largest groups followed by a variety of Central and South American countries (U.S. Census Bureau, 2000c). Many Hispanic Americans have immigrated here within the last two generations (Leyendecker & Lamb, 1999) to search for better socioeconomic circumstances and work opportunities or to escape from war or political tensions in their countries of origin. Although Hispanic families tend to be larger and divorce rates tend to be low (Zuniga, 1992), Hispanic families in the United States are more likely than non-Hispanic white families to be headed by a female with no spouse present, and Hispanics are less likely to be married than non-Hispanic whites

(U.S. Census Bureau, 2000c). As for African Americans, the median individual and household incomes for Hispanics are below the national averages (see Figure 8.5).

The interdependent, collectivistic quality of Hispanic culture is often noted and contrasted with the more independent, individualistic character of U.S. society (Leyendecker & Lamb, 1999) in general. Marín and Marín (1991) describe two basic cultural values, among others, that support and promote the more collectivist nature of Hispanic life: familialism and simpatía. **Familialism** refers to a strong identification with and attachment to both the nuclear and extended family and the feelings of loyalty, respect, duty, and reciprocity that accompany such familial attachment. **Simpatía** embodies the felt need for behaviors such as conformity and empathy that promote harmonious, pleasant social relations. Another common shared belief or value is the acceptance of life as it exists. These cultural values consequently translate into socialization goals of fostering the development of qualities such as cooperation and proper demeanor in children in order to promote social integration into the family and larger community (Leyendecker & Lamb, 1999). Interdependence in extended families may play a role as a protective force through its implications for the development of a supportive network that shares in child rearing and the development of multiple significant relationships between children and adults (Buriel & De Ment, 1997; Suarez-Orozco & Suarez-Orozco, 1994).

Hispanics may also tend to have more traditional views with regard to the roles of men and women (Leadbeater & Bishop, 1994). Male dominance and female submissiveness have been identified as common patterns in Hispanic social interactions. Whereas women are viewed as having primary responsibility for caregiving and life within the household (Zuniga, 1992), men make many of the decisions regarding the outside world. However, the level of traditionalism in gender roles is also related to levels of education and work involvement of women. Evidence suggests a range of roles is possible, including shared decision making (Mirande, 1988).

Asian American Families

Asian Americans account for approximately 4 percent of the total population of the United States. The largest proportions of Asian Americans are Chinese and Filipino, with additional substantial numbers of Japanese, Asian Indians, Koreans, and Vietnamese (U.S. Census Bureau, 2000a). More recent immigrant groups escaping political and social unrest in Southeast Asia make up smaller numbers of the Asian American total. Early Asian immigrants to the United States often served as farm workers or laborers, while in recent decades greater numbers have come in search of educational and professional job opportunities (Chan, 1992). Divorce rates are low among Asian Americans, and rates of single-parent households are comparable for Asian Americans and white Americans (U.S. Census Bureau, 2000a).

Although the median household income for Asian Americans is well above the national figure (see Figure 8.5), poverty rates are also higher for this group than for whites in the United States (U.S. Census Bureau, 2000a). Asian and Pacific Islander families tend to be larger than white families in the United States. Recency of immigration also plays a substantial role in the social and economic status of Asian Americans (Tanaka et al., 1998).

Traditional Asian culture places great emphasis on connectedness and collectivistic values (Markus & Kitayama, 1991). Consequently, there is a strong focus on family and harmony within Asian American groups. The individual is traditionally socialized to subordinate the self to the group and develop personal virtues such as patience, perseverance, restraint, and humility. Parents might be expected to sacrifice their own desires in the interest of providing the best possible opportunities for their children, while at the same time the children learn to show similar deference to the family's concerns (Chan, 1992). Education is also highly valued in many Asian cultures, and both children and parents ascribe great

Education is highly valued in Asian American families. These families often have a
special time for schoolwork in the home, and parents are highly involved in these
activities.
Source: Michael Newman/Photo Edit.

weight to effort in the pursuit of academic success (Stevenson & Lee, 1990). Thus, Asian
American parents are very involved in their children's schooling (Chao, 2000), as we
learned in Chapter 4. By doing well in school, children are seen as bringing honor to their
family and improving their own chances of job success. Such independent achievement in
the service of promoting the family's social status is encouraged (Lin & Fu, 1990). The interdependence of family members emerges also in the presence of multiple caregivers in the
traditional Asian home, where grandparents and older siblings also play a role in the socialization of young children. For example, older siblings are expected to model socially
acceptable behaviors and may be scolded for not setting a good example (Chan, 1992).

Native American Families

Native Americans (American Indian and Alaskan Native) constitute less than 1 percent of the
total population of the United States, and they are scattered among more than 300 tribes that
vary greatly in size. The largest tribes include the Cherokee, Navajo, Chippewa, Sioux, and
Choctaw, and nearly one-half of the Native American population live in the western United
States (U.S. Census Bureau, 2002). Although the majority of Native American families have
both husband and wife present, the proportion of female-headed households is higher than the
national average. Native American families also tend to be multigenerational and slightly
larger than the national average (Joe & Malach, 1992). The income levels of this group are
lower than national figures, and the poverty rate is high (U.S. Census Bureau, 2000d).

When the values and customs of Native Americans are discussed, attention must be
given to the centrality of tribal identity (Yellowbird & Snipp, 1998), as practices can vary

greatly from tribe to tribe according to historical traditions and level of contact with the larger society of the United States (Price, 1976). Nevertheless, Native Americans do share some common beliefs with regard to harmonious coexistence with nature and others (Attneave, 1982). Coupled with this focus on harmony is a tendency toward wholistic thinking, which emphasizes the interrelatedness of all things (Tharp, 1994). For a wholistic thinker, the whole must be understood as a complete functioning entity, not in terms of its individual components and their individual characteristics.

The entire Native American community plays a role in socializing children. It might not be uncommon for any member of the group to offer correction or praise to a child (Suina & Smolkin, 1994). Children are incorporated into the daily activities of the group and learn by observing and imitating adults. Much value is placed on the sharing of traditions and rituals, especially through teaching stories and oral histories. Respect for the past also appears in the reverence for elders in Native American communities; these elders play central roles in the spiritual, social, and cultural aspects of the community (Yellowbird & Snipp, 1998). Moreover, some Native Americans have described a "good Indian child" as one who shows respect to elders (Joe, 1994).

Family Influences on Development

Having addressed some of the diversity among families with regard to composition and ethnicity, we turn now to a discussion of the various ways families influence children's development. Families structure the environment in which children mature both directly and indirectly. In this section, we will discuss the characteristics of parents that foster and maintain children's adaptive development. Adaptive or positive developmental characteristics of children have been described by Lerner, Fisher, and Weinberg (2000) in terms of the *5 C's:* competence, confidence, caring, character, and connections.

Parenting Characteristics and Styles

Parents ideally strive to produce socially mature and competent children who are capable of satisfactory participation in society. How do parents accomplish this goal? Are certain behaviors more often associated with parents' effective performance of their socialization task? This section will discuss some of the various dimensions of parenting behavior that researchers have examined in their attempts to identify and understand what constitutes optimal (and less than optimal) parenting. Among the characteristics receiving attention here are warmth, responsiveness, and control, as well as constellations of parenting qualities referred to as parenting styles.

Warmth and Responsiveness

Parents who are warm, responsive, and authoritative have a positive influence on their children's school achievement.
Source: *David Young Wolff/Photo Edit.*

As with many other concepts we have discussed, parental warmth is a difficult construct to define. Yet most researchers and laypersons include in their definition of the term a level of care and acceptance expressed toward a child by a parent and contrast it with hostility. A warm parent shows affection and empathy toward a child and an interest in the child's feelings and actions. Such nurturant behaviors are positively associated with children's development of prosocial behavior and moral standards, and the presence of higher self-esteem and higher intellectual abilities (Eisenberg & Valiente, 2002; Maccoby, 1980; Schaefer, 1989; Zahn-Waxler et al., 1979). Also, the finding that children are more likely to imitate and identify with an affectionate model (Bandura, 1969) suggests a possible mechanism by which children might come to comply with and adopt parental values (MacDonald, 1992). Conversely, a lack of warmth or hostility in parent–child interactions is associated with delinquency, aggression, and a range of other problem behaviors (Hetherington & Martin, 1986; Olweus, 1980).

Responsiveness can be thought of as a parent's prompt, contingent, and appropriate reaction to a child's behavior (Bornstein & Tamis-LeMonda, 1997). Parents need to adjust their interactions to their children's temperaments and changing abilities and experiences (e.g., Bornstein, 2005). When an infant cries, a parent who checks to see what is bothering the child or what the child needs is considered responsive. Likewise, the parent who notices when his 5-year-old shows great interest in a butterfly resting on a flower and engages her in a discussion about it is exhibiting responsiveness. Parents who notice their children's signals, interpret them appropriately, and respond in a sensitive manner have children who show more optimal social and cognitive outcomes such as more secure attachment, greater social competence, more emotional expressivity, higher cognitive functioning, and more rapid language development (Bornstein, 1989; Nicely, Tamis-LeMonda, & Grolnick, 1999). Responsive parenting has also been found to predict children's resilient adjustment in the face of adversity (Wyman et al., 1999). An absence of responsiveness has been linked to an increase in the risk of disruptive behavior problems (Wakschlag & Hans, 1999).

Control and Discipline

Until children develop the ability to regulate their own behavior, the job of control falls most often on parents. Attempts to foster desired behaviors and eliminate unwanted behaviors begin early on as parents try to quiet a crying baby or to prevent the toddler's newfound walking ability from leading to a tumble down the stairs.

Parents differ in how they exert control over children. Researchers have examined the different child behavior outcomes of parents who use power-assertive versus inductive discipline techniques (Hoffman & Saltzstein, 1967; Kerr, Lopez, Olson, & Sameroff, 2004). With **power-assertive discipline,** parents attempt to influence their children's behavior by use of commands and imperatives for which no reason other than "I said so" is given. Such parents seem to coerce their children into compliance with the typically rigid rules they enforce, often by means of yelling and hitting. As discussed further in the Focus on Research box, such restrictive and hostile discipline techniques have been

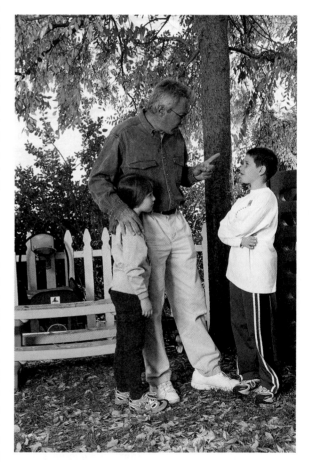

Parents who provide explanations for rules and discuss why certain behaviors are desirable or undersirable can help children learn self-discipline.
Source: Michael Newman/Photo Edit.

Focus on
Research

Is Corporal Punishment an Effective Form of Discipline?

Studies reveal that nearly all children in the United States experience some form of corporal punishment, although it may differ in frequency and severity (American Academy of Pediatrics, 1998; Strauss, 1994; Strauss & Stewart, 1999). **Corporal punishment** is defined as the use of physical punishment with the intention of causing a child to experience physical pain, but not injury, as a means of reducing an undesirable behavior (Strauss, 1994, p. 4). Forms of corporal punishment range from slapping the hand of a child about to touch a dangerous or fragile object to hitting a child with an object, such as a hairbrush, paddle, or belt.

The most common form of legal corporal punishment in the United States is spanking, which involves hitting a child with an open hand on the buttocks or extremities. In a 1995 national survey of parents, 94 percent spanked a child that year (Strauss & Stewart, 1999). About a third of the sample reported they had spanked a child under the age of 1 year. However, the frequency of spanking was highest among children aged 2 to 12 years, whereas only 14 percent of parents reported spanking their children after the age of 13 years. Boys generally experience more corporal punishment than girls, and frequency rates also differ by parental age, ethnicity, and social class (Strauss, 1994). It is important to consider the acceptance of corporal punishment by the U.S. general public in light of the growing number of countries that have adopted policies or laws prohibiting parents from using corporal punishment as a means of discipline. Current reports show that at least 16 nations have abolished

corporal punishment of children in the family (e.g., Austria, Denmark, Finland, Germany, Israel, Italy, Norway, Sweden; Epoch-Worldwide, 2006).

Is corporal punishment an effective form of discipline? The following discussion is based primarily on a meta-analysis of nearly a hundred scientific studies by Gershoff (2002) and reviews by the American Academy of Pediatrics (AAP, 1998). These reviews indicate that although corporal punishment is effective in getting children to comply immediately, it can also escalate into physical maltreatment. In other words, spanking a child for an undesirable behavior can temporarily stop or reduce a behavior, but its effectiveness decreases with subsequent use. To maintain the effectiveness of spanking over time, the intensity with which it is delivered must systematically increase. This pattern can quickly escalate into abuse (AAP, 1998). There are a number of other negative consequences that need to be considered, including the following:

- Spanking a child under the age of 18 months can cause physical injury, when the child is unlikely to understand the connection between behavior and punishment (AAP, 1998).
- Spanking provides children with aggressive models. Children who are spanked show higher rates of aggression, especially in boys (Gershoff, 2002), and delinquency in later development (AAP, 1998; Strauss, 1994).
- The frequent use of spanking creates a negative family climate of rejection. The child associates the

shown to be ineffective, and in fact lead to elevated levels of disruptive behavior problems and aggression in children (Chamberlain & Patterson, 1995; Stormshak et al., 2000). On the other hand, parents who use **inductive discipline** offer explanations for their rules and even solicit reasons from their children for why certain behaviors might be more desirable or appropriate in certain circumstances. Consequently, these children are found to engage in more prosocial behavior and to expect enhanced relations with peers (Hart, DeWolf, & Burts, 1992). Consistent with these findings, a recent study showed that boys' moral regulation (ability to refrain from wrongdoing through behavioral control) was fostered by parental discipline strategies involving warmth, use of induction, and de-emphasis on power-assertive techniques such as corporal punishment (Kerr et al., 2004).

Other issues in the discipline of children revolve around principles of reinforcement. Reinforcement of desirable behavior has been argued to be a more effective strategy to promote presence of a parent with hitting, which negatively affects the quality of the parent–child relationship.

- The use of spanking as a means of discipline undermines the effectiveness of other discipline approaches, such as reinforcing desirable behaviors, imposing logical consequences, or removing privileges.
- The use of spanking is consistently related to decreases in children's *moral internalization,* operationalized as long-term compliance, feelings of guilt following misbehavior, and tendencies to make reparations after harming others (Gershoff, 2002).

In general, child development researchers agree that corporal punishment is not an effective form of discipline. Although some suggest that the research evidence does not yet justify a "blanket injunction" against all forms of mild spanking under some circumstances for children between 18 months and puberty (Baumrind, Cowan, & Larzelere, 2002), spanking is *not* recommended. It teaches the child neither self-control nor self-discipline, and it can damage the parent–child relationship or cause injury to the child. Furthermore, it tends not to help parents further their own socialization goals for their children to continue complying when they are absent and in the future.

Of course, as we have discussed, parents need to stop undesirable behaviors when they occur. Some actions, such as touching a hot stove or biting another child, require immediate responses to stop the behavior. What are some alternatives to corporal punishment? First, it is important to protect children from potentially

dangerous or risky situations (e.g., installing safety latches on cupboards). For young children, it is best to stop a behavior with a firm "no," then remove the object from the child's hand or the child from the dangerous situation. Reasoning, verbal cues, and reprimands are ineffective for stopping undesirable behaviors in infants and toddlers.

For older children, time-out, logical consequences, or removal of privileges are effective strategies for reducing and eliminating undesirable behaviors. The logical consequence for breaking a neighbor's window is to help pay for a new one. An example of time-out is removing the child from a play or social situation for a short period of time. For older children, this strategy generally involves denying participation in activities (grounding the child for the weekend) or losing privileges (no television or computer games for a specific period of time). These three discipline strategies (logical consequences, time-out, loss of privileges) are most effective when combined with the following: (1) an immediate consequence when the behavior first occurs, (2) a consistent response when the problem behavior continues to occur, and (3) a clear but calm explanation of why the behavior is inappropriate and what consequence the child can expect when the behavior occurs. It is also important to remember that the best discipline approach is one that provides children with positive role models, parental warmth and affection, opportunities to choose and evaluate different available options, and positive reinforcement to increase desirable behaviors.

learning than punishment. Parents might attempt to forestall the appearance of unwanted behavior by providing attention and other reinforcements for positive behaviors. A child might be praised for making up his bed, for example. When less desirable behavior does appear, parents may simply ignore (i.e., withhold reinforcement from) minor inappropriate behaviors such as whining or fussiness with the effect that a child learns that such actions gain nothing. Removing a child for a short time from the situation in which his unwanted behavior is being reinforced (e.g., "time-out") has also been shown to reduce negative behaviors. All such responses, whether reinforcement for a positive behavior or discipline for a negative behavior, should be delivered in a consistent and timely fashion. Allowing a child to "get by" with unacceptable behavior sometimes or giving repeated warnings without following through on the consequences sends a confusing message and results in continued misbehavior.

■ FIGURE 8.6
Dimensions of Parenting Styles
Source: Based on Maccoby & Martin (1983).

		Levels of Acceptance/Responsiveness	
		High	**Low**
Level of Demand or Control	**High**	Authoritative	Authoritarian
	Low	Permissive-indulgent	Permissive-indifferent

Parenting Styles

None of these parenting characteristics occurs separate from the others. Parents typically show a combination of levels of warmth, responsiveness, and control. Diana Baumrind (1967a, 1971) identified some of the more common constellations of parenting behaviors, referred to as **parenting styles,** and traced some of their apparent effects on children's developmental outcomes. In Baumrind's original work, three parenting styles were identified: authoritarian, permissive, and authoritative. By examining parenting along the two dimensions of control and responsiveness, as shown in Figure 8.6, Eleanor Maccoby and John Martin (1983) provided a reformulation of Baumrind's work and further distinguished permissive-indulgent and permissive-indifferent parenting. The distinguishing characteristics of each parenting style are as follows:

- **Authoritarian parents** are high on the control dimension but low on responsiveness. Characterized by low warmth and little positive involvement with their children, these parents set rigid rules and discipline harshly with the expectation that the rules will be obeyed because of parental authority.
- **Authoritative parents** show warm, responsive involvement with their children and set appropriate and clear standards for behavior. They communicate openly with their children, providing rationales for rules and showing respect for their children's rights and opinions. In these ways, authoritative parents encourage children's autonomy and independence appropriate for their age with the result that children develop social competence.
- **Permissive-indulgent parents** are very warm and responsive to their children but place few demands or expectations on them. Rules that may exist are not clearly communicated or enforced so that children are left to make their own decisions and regulate their own behavior.
- **Permissive-indifferent parents** also leave it to their children to make their own decisions and control their own behavior by placing few demands on them, but in this case such a situation results more from neglect. Appearing emotionally detached, permissive-indifferent parents show little or no involvement in the lives of their children.

As shown in Table 8.1, each parenting style has important consequences for children's development. A number of positive child competencies are associated with authoritative parenting styles, such as self-reliance and social responsibility. As discussed in Chapter 4, an

TABLE 8.1 Parenting Styles and Children's Development

Parenting Style	Outcomes
Authoritative	Self-reliance Social responsibility Higher levels of achievement
Authoritarian	Social incompetence Anxiety about social comparison Failure to show initiative Poor communication skills Lower school performance Lower self-esteem
Permissive-indulgent	Expect to get their own way Show little respect for others Never learn to control their own behavior Lower school performance
Permissive-indifferent	Social incompetence Lack self-control Lower school performance

Source: Maccoby & Martin (1983).

authoritative parenting style also promotes intellectual development. Authoritative parenting is related to school success from early childhood through adolescence (Baumrind, 1978; Steinberg, Darling, & Fletcher, 1995). In contrast, children with authoritarian parents typically have lower grades in school and lower self-esteem. Children of indifferent-uninvolved parents tend to have the most negative profile of all. As adolescents, these children are at greatest risk for developing problem behaviors. The patterns for academic achievement shown in Table 8.1 are generally found across different ethnic groups, but European American and Hispanic American adolescents may benefit the most from authoritative parenting (Steinberg et al., 1995). Recent research also shows that these parenting dimensions (responsiveness, control) can also be applied to understanding adolescent functioning in 11 cultures across the world (i.e., groups from Africa, Asia, Europe, the Middle East, and North and South America; (Barber, Stoltz, & Olsen, 2005)). In particular, findings showed that perceived parental support was associated primarily with greater social initiative and lower depression, perceived parental psychological control with greater depression and antisocial behavior, and perceived parental behavioral control primarily with lower antisocial behavior in adolescents ages 11 to 17. The researchers conclude that these parenting dimensions are "family-level indicators of socialization conditions or states that enhance the psychological development of children" (p. 124). They suggest that we consider these dimensions in terms of broader conditions for facilitating adolescent development through professional and policy efforts—*connection* with significant others (responsiveness), *respect for individuality* (psychological control), and *regulation of behavior* (behavioral control).

Family Routines and Home Environments

As mentioned earlier, parents do more than interact with their children. They also play a role (with children) in creating a multifaceted home environment that shapes behavior and development. For example, in addition to responding to their children's emotional needs, parents also organize their living space, provide toys and books, expose them to friends, and take them on family trips. Families also develop routines that encompass these tasks and activities. According to Lowe, Weisner, Geis, and Huston (2005), children are better off if they engage in more manageable and sustainable routines, characterized by the following:

- Some balance among tasks and activities (e.g., eating, socializing, chores)
- People (e.g., mother, other kin) who are available and willing to help (social support)
- Adequate resources (e.g., money, space, tools) for the activities
- Activities are valued and desired, at least to some extent
- Participants experience greater emotional connection and engagement rather than conflict

Child care arrangements, school activities, and many other daily living activities are included in family routines.

Betteye Caldwell, and Robert Bradley and colleagues, have created several versions of the HOME (Home Observation for Measurement of the Environment) to assess family environments for children and youth: (a) between birth and 3 years (Infant-Toddler HOME); (b) between 3 and 5 years (Early Childhood HOME); (c) between 6 and 9 years (Middle Childhood HOME); and (d) between the ages of 10 and 15 (Early Adolescent HOME) (Bradley, Corwyn, Caldwell, Whiteside-Mansell, Wasserman, & Mink, 2000; Bradley, Corwyn, Burchinal, McAdoo, & Coll, 2001; Bradley, Corwyn, McAdoo, & Coll, 2001; Caldwell & Bradley, 1984). Brief descriptions of subscales for the Infant-Toddler (IT) and Early Adolescent (EA) HOME measures are shown in the Focus on Development box.

Developmentalists have been studying relations between different aspects of home environments and child outcomes for over half a century; however, it hasn't been until recently that researchers have looked comprehensively at how these environments change from infancy through adolescence (Bradley, Corwyn, Burchinal et al., 2001), and across a variety of ethnic and socioeconomic groups (Bradley, Corwyn, McAdoo et al., 2001). Recent study findings with the HOME showed, not surprisingly, that conditions, activities, and materials the children encountered change dramatically from infancy through adolescence (Bradley, Corwyn, McAdoo et al., 2001). For example, infants were more likely to be caressed than older children; young children's bids for attention were most likely to be responded to, and mothers talked to their children more in the early than in the middle years. As children got older, they were less likely to eat daily meals with both parents, and more likely to take responsibility for household chores. In addition, reading to children peaked during early childhood, and infants and adolescents had fewer books targeted especially for them. The types of toys and learning materials available changed markedly with age. Older children and adolescents were more likely to be taken to places such as museums than younger children.

Children's exposure to particular experiences in the home environment varied considerably as a function of both their ethnicity and their family income in these studies. In particular, results showed that "being poor affects nearly every aspect of children's home lives. Poverty effects were prevalent in all six environmental domains examined: from parental responsiveness to parent teaching, from the quality of the physical environment to the level of stimulation for learning present, and from the likelihood of being spanked to the likelihood of having significant contact with one's father" (Bradley, Corwyn, McAdoo et al., 2001, p. 1863). These findings are generally consistent with previous findings, but noteworthy because of their scope, and because they were based on data from thousands of cases from the NSLY database deliberately drawn to represent the U.S. population.

In a follow-up study, Bradley, Corwyn, Burchinal et al. (2001) focused on how three aspects of the home environment in particular (learning stimulation, parental responsiveness, spanking) related to developmental functioning for three major ethnic groups: European

Sample Changes in Home Environments for Young Children and Adolescents

Focus on
Development

Infant-Toddler HOME Subscales	Early Adolescent HOME Subscales
Parental Responsivity . . . responds to child's vocalizations . . . says name of person or object in "teaching style"	*Acceptance and Responsivity* . . . parent mentions a strength or accomplishment of adolescent . . . adolescent can disagree without harsh reprisals
Acceptance of Child . . .does not express overt hostility . . . or frequently interfere with child's actions	*Regulatory Activities* . . . family has a fairly predictable schedule . . . TV isn't left on continuously
Organization of the Environment . . . child is taken regularly to doctor . . . has a place for toys . . .	*Physical Environment* . . . room has wall decorations appealing to adolescent . . . house or apartment is clean
Learning Materials . . . child has age-appropriate cuddly toys or role-playing toys . . . stroller, scooter, or tricycle	*Learning Materials* . . . adolescent has access to suitable place for reading or studying . . . materials for arts and crafts and collections
Parental Involvement . . . keeps child within visual range . . . often "talks" to child	*Modeling* . . . parent reads books . . . doesn't lose temper often
Variety in Experience . . . reads stories . . . child eats meal with family regularly	*Variety of Activities* . . . family arranges to go to a museum . . . father regularly engages in outdoor activity with child
	Instructional Activities (Fostering Self-Sufficiency) . . . parent teaches adolescent independent living skills . . . monitors homework

Source: Adapted from Bradley et al. (2000) and Caldwell & Bradley (1984).

Americans, African Americans, and Hispanic Americans. They found, as expected, that for all three ethnic groups, learning stimulation was associated with early motor and social development, language competence, and achievement at almost every age. Parental responsiveness was related to early motor and social competence, consistent with what would be hypothesized on the basis of attachment theory (see Chapter 6). Also consistent with prior research, spanking and behavioral problems were related in all groups studied, and the correlations were stronger as children got older (except for in poor Hispanic families). (See also Focus on Research box on pages 464 and 465). The authors conclude that the findings support the value of attending to several aspects of children's environments simultaneously, and recommend studying their experiences in "multiple ecologies" (i.e., child care and home, school and home) as Bronfenbrenner and others do. The Early Child Care Network studies, reported later in this chapter, are other examples of how researchers examine multiple ecologies of childhood.

Parents play an important role in exposing children to different activities. This family is visiting a science museum together.
Source: Bill Aron/Photo Edit.

Developmental Changes in Family Relations

Over the course of development the relationships between parents and their children undergo considerable change. Different issues and tasks take center stage in family interactions as children mature, and the manner in which they are handled is thought, in some cases, to lay the groundwork for future development. Parents must adjust their parenting practices to the growing competencies of the child. As you might imagine, an authoritative parenting style may facilitate this process because there is more give-and-take in the parent–child relationship. Let's look at how parent–child relations change in childhood and adolescence.

Movement Toward Coregulation

As we learned in Chapter 6, the behavior of children in infancy and early childhood is mainly controlled and regulated by parents. As children mature, there is a gradual shift toward **coregulation,** whereby control is shared by parents and children (Maccoby, 1984).

In middle childhood, children begin to spend less time with their families and more time in contexts outside the home, such as in school and peer activities. Parents may spend only half as much time with children in a variety of activities, such as caregiving, reading, and playing, when they are between the ages of 5 and 12 as they did when they were younger (Hill & Stafford, 1980).

Children have also reached a point in their development where they can begin to manage their daily activities and assume responsibility for their behavior. Parents begin to expect more from them in terms of proper behavior. With children's increasing cognitive abilities, parents are able to reason with them about their behavior and its consequences. As a result, less physical discipline is used by parents of school-age children than by parents of preschoolers (Collins, Harris, & Susman, 1996).

As children demonstrate they can manage daily routines and responsibilities, there is a gradual shift in control from parents to child. Parents continue to provide broad, general guidelines for acceptable behavior while children regulate their own everyday behavior. This coregulation period provides parents with an opportunity to continue monitoring and supporting children at a distance while strengthening children's self-monitoring and decision-making skills with regard to appropriate behavioral standards. Eleanor Maccoby (1984) provides the following description of parents' and children's roles in coregulation:

> First, [parents] must monitor, guide, and support their children at a distance—that is, when their children are out of their presence; second, they must effectively use the times when direct contact does occur; and third, they must strengthen in their children the abilities that will allow them to monitor their own behavior, to adopt acceptable standards of [good] conduct, to avoid undue risks, and to know when they need parental support and guidance. Children must be willing to inform parents of their whereabouts, activities, and problems so that parents can mediate and guide when necessary. (pp. 191–192)

The process of coregulation in middle childhood prepares children for adolescence and adulthood, when they will assume responsibility for their own care and decisions.

Movement Toward Autonomy

During adolescence, parents must make further adjustments in parenting practices as young people strive for a sense of independence, or **autonomy.** If you recall, adolescence marks the beginning of a young person's search for identity. Young people are establishing themselves as separate individuals, with their own identity, values, and goals for the future.

Adolescents find themselves in a position of desiring more independence but still needing the support of their parents. And parents of adolescents are often at a point in their own lives where other concerns (e.g., work, health, care of their own parents) clamor for their attention. Consequently, the idea of yielding more responsibility to the adolescents is attractive, but parents may remain unsure of the level of autonomy to grant. This mutual ambivalence on the part of both parents and adolescents with regard to balancing dependence and independence sets the stage for adolescent–parent conflict.

Interestingly, the arguments between adolescents and their parents typically center on what could be considered fairly mundane issues of household responsibilities, finances, privileges, and issues of personal taste in areas such as music and clothing. Adolescents and their parents have very similar beliefs on the "bigger" issues of religion, politics, and problems of society (Holmbeck, 1996; Youniss, 1989). Smetana (2005) concluded a recent review of research stating that "evidence for rebellion and rejection of adult standards [by youth today] is widely overstated" (p. 70). However, the day-to-day issues of contention may seem very significant to adolescents who see them as instances in which they would like to begin exercising control over their own lives.

The frequency of adolescent–parent conflict appears to be highest in early adolescence (Laursen, Coy, & Collins, 1998). The task for parents and adolescents is to maintain a sense of closeness while roles are being renegotiated. It requires considerable mutual respect, flexibility, and openness in the parent–child relationship. Most adolescents and their parents handle this transition without excessive discord. As many as 20 percent of adolescents may experience difficulty establishing their autonomy, but a complete rupture of the parent–child relationship is rare unless there is prolonged, intense conflict (Brook, Brook, Gordon, Whitehouse, & Cohen, 1990).

In summary, an important component of the family system is that it must constantly change and adjust to the development of its members while maintaining some stability of positive routines and activities. With development, parents must adjust to the growing competencies and independence of their children. At the same time, parents may be experiencing changes in their health, job, or marital status that can make adjustments difficult to manage. The family is one of the few social systems that requires so many changes and adjustments from its members.

Sibling Relationships

Most American children will have at least one sibling. Siblings play a unique and important role in children's development. They serve as role models, playmates, teachers, and sources of emotional support. Developmentalists describe sibling relationships as "emotionally ambivalent" because typical sibling pairs are warm as well as conflicted at times (Deater-Deckard, Dunn, & Lussier, 2002, p. 572). In some families, siblings also care for younger children. Like the parent–child relationship, sibling relations also change with development.

For an older sibling, the arrival of a new baby can be both exciting and distressing. A parent's involvement with the older child will generally decline at this time. Many young children may become withdrawn, clingy, or demanding when a new baby is introduced into the family, but this distress can be avoided or reduced if parents are responsive to the older child's needs for attention and affection (Howe & Ross, 1990).

By the infant's second birthday, a sibling relationship begins to take shape. The younger child will imitate and attempt to play with the older sibling. By age 4, the young sibling will talk more to the older sibling than to his or her mother (Brown & Dunn, 1992). If they are close in age, siblings relate to each other as equals, much like peers.

Sibling conflict tends to increase during middle childhood. Some researchers believe that this conflict is due to the children's increased ability to make comparisons (Brody, Stoneman, & McCoy, 1994). One sibling may feel the other sibling is receiving more parental attention, approval, or affection, which can cause resentment. This effect may be especially strong if the father shows favoritism toward one child more than the other (Brody et al., 1994). Interestingly, a recent study showed no significant differences in sibling negativity and positivity in comparisons between intact and various stepfamilies (Deater-Deckard et al., 2002).

Though conflict may increase during the school years, siblings are also a source of companionship and support. Older siblings appear to be better teachers than friends when it comes to learning tasks (Azmitia & Hesser, 1993). However, as younger siblings mature and become more independent, they are less likely to accept direction from older brothers and sisters. As adolescents become more involved with friends, they may spend less time with siblings (Furman & Buhrmester, 1992).

The quality of sibling relationships is affected by parenting practices. Children whose parents are warm and supportive tend to develop positive sibling relationships. A similar pattern is found when there are warm, harmonious relationships between parents. In contrast, coercive, hostile, or negative relationships within the family can spill over to the sibling relationship.

UNDERSTANDING
CHILDREN
*Strategy 4.2: Guided
Participation Game:
Play with Peers and
Adults*

Birth Order Effects

Does the child's position in the family make a difference? **Birth order** has to do with the child's position in the family—first born, middle child, and so on. Numerous books and articles have been written about birth order effects in the family.

In general, many studies show birth order effects. Parents typically have higher expectations for first-born children than for later-born children, and they use stricter discipline. As a result, first-born children tend to be high achievers. They are also more conforming and obedient than their younger siblings. By the time other children arrive, parents are more realistic in their expectations and more confident in their parenting practices (Baskett, 1985). Later-born children tend to be more popular with peers (Eaton, Chipperfield, & Singeil, 1989).

Using the National Longitudinal Study of Youth (NLSY) data set, more investigators recently examined the pattern of IQ scores within and across families (Rodgers, Cleveland, van den Oord, & Rowe, 2000). The NLSY data showed that later-born siblings had lower IQ scores in comparison to their earlier-born siblings, regardless of family size. However, a negative relationship did appear between family size and IQ: Children in larger families in the NLSY data had IQ scores lower than those of children in smaller families. These findings were interpreted as demonstrating that the apparent within-family effect of birth order on intelligence is better explained by between-family factors, such as parental education and income levels.

Single-Child Families

As we have seen, sibling relationships play an important role in children's development. Children without siblings—only children—are often portrayed as selfish and spoiled. Contrary to this image, children growing up in one-child families tend to be just as socially competent and well adjusted as other children. In fact, they tend to have higher levels of self-esteem and motivation than other children. They also do better in school (Falbo, 1992). Nevertheless, being an only child does have its disadvantages. In one study, only children expressed concerns about not getting to experience the closeness of a sibling relationship and about caring for elderly parents on their own (Hawke & Knox, 1978).

Maltreatment of Children

Much of the chapter has focused so far on the ways in which families can provide support for children's positive, adaptive development with occasional identification of family circumstances that are not so beneficial. Now, however, we will address the circumstances surrounding the actual maltreatment of children, often by members of their families or family acquaintances. With knowledge of the risk factors, signs, and effects of child maltreatment, educators can better identify and more sensitively meet the needs of child victims.

Definitions of abuse and neglect are based on basic assumptions about children and the responsibilities of their caregivers. Several decades ago, it was not uncommon for young people to receive a "good strapping" to ensure their obedience. But today hitting a child with an object would be viewed as abusive. Most experts use the following definition to describe child abuse: "An abused or neglected child is a child whose physical or mental health or welfare is harmed or threatened with harm by the acts or omissions of his/her parent or other person responsible for his/her welfare" (Tower, 1992).

Child maltreatment can take different forms. **Physical abuse** includes physical injury caused by the child's caretaker, including beating, kicking, punching, burning, and so forth. By definition, the injury was not an accident. **Neglect** is a more common form of abuse, and it involves inattention to the basic needs of a child, such as food, clothing, medical care, supervision, and housing. Neglect is chronic, and generally affects all the children in the household. **Emotional maltreatment** involves rejecting a child and showing a consistent lack of concern for the child's emotional well-being. Finally, **sexual abuse** includes any contacts between the child or adult in which the child is being used for sexual stimulation. Sexual abuse may take place within the family, referred to as incest, or may involve caretakers outside the family, such as a relative, friend, or baby-sitter.

How prevalent is child abuse and neglect? In 2003, there were an estimated 900,000 victims of child maltreatment (Children's Defense Fund [CDF], 2005b). About 60 percent of the confirmed victims suffered neglect, 20 percent suffered physical abuse, 10 percent suffered sexual abuse, and 5 percent suffered psychological abuse. Tragically, only about 58 percent of these children received any postinvestigative services because of long waiting lists, unavailability of services, and other reasons (CDF, 2005b).

A number of factors have been identified that place children at increased risk for suffering maltreatment. Younger children are at greater risk than older children: Children under age 3 represent almost one-third of the victims, and half of all victims are children 7 years or younger. Children who have recurrent illnesses, who are handicapped, or who are stepchildren also have elevated risk for becoming victims of maltreatment (Daly & Wilson, 1996; Sherrod, O'Connor, Vietze, & Altemeier, 1984).

What factors lead to child maltreatment? Research has shown that often a number of factors in combination lead to physical abuse and neglect. Among those specifically identified in the literature are family stresses such as poverty and conflict, poor education, and social isolation (Coulton, Korbin, Su, & Chow, 1995; Goodman, Emery, & Haugaard, 1998; Trickett, Aber, Carlson, & Cicchetti, 1991; Zigler & Hall, 2000). Abusive parents typically have unrealistic expectations for their children and poor behavioral management skills. They tend to interpret their children's actions as willful disobedience, and they use physical force to control the child. Child abuse is one social problem that is found across education and income levels. Although much attention has been given to the idea of intergenerational transmission of maltreatment, only about 30 percent of individuals who suffered maltreatment become abusers themselves (Cicchetti & Toth, 1998).

There are serious emotional, cognitive, and social consequences for child victims (Cicchetti & Toth, 1998). Many children who are mistreated show affective scars, including sadness, fear, anger, and depression. In addition, these children may experience difficult social relations with peers as a result of their more aggressive and less cooperative behavior or their failure to initiate social contact. Such effects can spill over into a child's school functioning, leading to poorer achievement and standardized test scores as well as repetition of grades. Child victims of sexual abuse may exhibit anxious, depressed, and withdrawn affect or occasional aggressive tendencies. Precocious interest in sexual topics and seductive types of behavior have also been noted in these children (Kendall-Tackett, Williams, & Finkelhor, 1993).

Adults who work with children have a legal and ethical responsibility to report suspected child abuse. The Focus on Teaching box suggests ways educators can identify and support victims of child abuse.

Family Transitions: Divorce and Remarriage

Children tend to benefit from regularity, consistency, and continuity in family life. Regardless of their age, any change in family life can be both disruptive and upsetting to children and adolescents. In this section, we will consider the impact of two family transitions on children's development: the effects of divorce and remarriage. In both cases, the effects of family change are transmitted through changes in the parent–child relationship. Factors outside the family, such as social support and economic resources, can modify the impact of family transitions. Also, the child's own characteristics (age and gender) can play a role in this process. It is important to recognize that some children may experience multiple family transitions over the course of childhood and adolescence (e.g., a divorce may be followed by a remarriage). The effects of multiple transitions may be more enduring than those associated with a single transition (Amoto & Booth, 1991).

Helping Abused Children

Educators can contribute to both the identification and support of victims of child maltreatment and to prevention efforts. Both federal and state laws require reports of suspected child maltreatment by various professionals, including teachers. Consequently, teachers need to familiarize themselves with the warning signs of abuse and neglect. Some general indicators of child abuse and neglect are as follows:

- *Physical indicators:* Skin or bone injuries. These injuries may be concealed by clothing, as most adults recognize that abuse needs to be concealed. When there are numerous bruises at various stages of healing, abuse may be present. Injuries to the abdomen can cause swelling, tenderness, and vomiting. Head injuries result in dizziness, blackouts, retinal detachment, and, in severe cases, death.
- *Behavioral indicators:* Children who are being abused may change their behavior, becoming more aggressive, destructive, withdrawn, or uncommunicative. They may want to stay at school to avoid returning home. Children who are being abused will sometimes try to abuse other children. Fears, nightmares, and excessive concerns about cleanliness may also be symptoms of child abuse.
- *Academic performance:* Child abuse and neglect is generally associated with a sudden decline in aca-

Focus on
Teaching

demic performance or interest in learning. Maltreated children have a higher likelihood of failing or repeating a grade. Children who are hungry or who need glasses to read cannot learn, and these signs of neglect will be reflected in their school achievement.

Of course, a sudden change in behavior, affect, or academic performance does not prove that child abuse or neglect exists. However, it is important to monitor warning signs and to report this information to a school administrator, nurse, or counselor.

Because of the covert nature of child maltreatment, identification of victims can be difficult. It is no secret, however, that many children die from abuse or neglect because *no one would help or get involved.* As educators, it is important to understand your ethical and legal responsibility in reporting child abuse and neglect. For a concerned citizen, it is important to advocate for community-based services for families including parenting classes, medical care, adequate housing, job training, and quality day care programs. Additionally, educators can help stop the use of corporal punishment in our schools. If teachers and principals can use physical force to punish a child, then parents are likely to believe it is acceptable for them to do so as well.

Divorce

Approximately half of all first marriages in the United States today end in divorce, and more than 1 million children are involved in divorces each year (Kirn, 2000). Regardless of their age, divorce is difficult for both children and adults. In the years immediately after a divorce, children become more defiant, more negative, and more aggressive, depressed, or angry. If they are of school age, their school performance typically drops for at least a short time (Furstenberg & Cherlin, 1991; Hetherington, 1989; Hetherington & Clingempeel, 1992). Some children show long-term behavior problems, depression, poor school performance, acting out, low self-esteem, and later difficulties with intimate heterosexual relationships, but there is disagreement about these lasting negative effects (Hetherington, 1999; Hetherington & Kelly, 2002; Kirn, 2000; Wallerstein, Lewis, & Blakeslee, 2000).

Numerous factors have been identified as being potentially influential in the ability of children to adaptively negotiate the life transitions associated with divorce. These include (1) the child's age and gender, (2) the level of conflict between parents, (3) the custodial arrangement, (4) the income level of the custodial parent, and (5) the quality of parenting provided. Let's look at a few of these effects.

Not surprisingly, the child's age is an important factor. Children who are young at the time of their parents' divorce may experience substantial anxiety and exhibit strong emotional reactions, but their cognitive immaturity may benefit them over time. When interviewed 10 years after the divorce of their parents, adolescents in one study hardly recalled their own earlier fears or the conflict between their parents (Wallerstein, Corbin, & Lewis, 1988).

Along with age, a child's gender can also influence the effects of divorce. During the school years, the negative effects of divorce appear to be stronger for boys than for girls (Hetherington, 1989, 1991). In adolescence, however, there are signs that girls are more disrupted by a divorce than are boys. For example, early-maturing girls from divorced families, compared with their male counterparts, experience more conflict with their mothers and more difficulties in heterosexual relationships (Hetherington, 1989, 1991).

Another factor that influences children's adjustment to divorce is conflict between parents (Amato, 1993). The emotionally charged nature of separations and divorces may overwhelm the child. Children fare better in divorced families with low conflict between the separated parents (Bishop & Ingersoll, 1989; Hetherington, 1999). Children are at higher risk for adjustment problems when the parents remain embittered and hostile for a long time after the divorce (Hetherington, 1999).

There is a long-standing trend in the United States for the custody of minor children to be awarded to mothers. In the last couple of decades, more fathers have asked for and been given custody, and a growing number of divorcing parents arrange for joint custody and/or shared living arrangements in which children spend part of each week or month with each parent. Whereas some studies have found support for a custody arrangement in which children are placed with the same-sex parent (Furstenberg, 1988; Santrock & Warshak, 1986), others have found no relative benefits of same-sex parental custody over opposite-sex parental custody (Downey & Powell, 1993).

Of course the most important consideration is that children will want, and benefit from, continuing contact with their noncustodial parent. Children experience successful relationships and visitation with noncustodial parents when visitation patterns are established early, are routine, and are governed by genuine efforts to "parent," as opposed to entertain the child (Thompson & Laible, 1999).

The psychological and economic well-being of the custodial parent often rank as powerful predictors of children's postdivorce adjustment. Income plays a crucial role in the adjustment of parents and children who have experienced divorce. Fathers typically do not experience the dramatic decrease in income that mothers do following divorce (Santrock & Warshak, 1986). Approximately 60 percent of custodial mothers are awarded some level of child support. Of those, about 42 percent receive the full payment and 27 percent receive partial payment (U.S. Bureau of the Census, 2000b), but the amounts received are typically insufficient for raising children (Teachman & Paasch, 1994).

The quality of parenting typically declines in the year following divorce as parents become preoccupied with their own needs and transition issues, dealing with the depression and confusion often associated with divorce. These preoccupations inhibit the parents' ability to respond sensitively to their children. As a result, their parenting style changes, becoming almost neglectful as they fail to adequately monitor their children's behavior or set explicit rules or limits (Hetherington, 1989). This pattern may persist for several years, even after remarriage, but often, beginning in the second year after the divorce, parents grow more effective in their child-rearing practices (Hetherington & Clingempeel, 1992; Hetherington, Cox, & Cox, 1982; Hetherington, Stanley-Hagan, & Anderson, 1989).

Remarriage and Stepfamilies

Most children live in a single-parent household for approximately 5 years following a divorce. More than two-thirds of divorced parents will eventually remarry (Glick, 1989). A small minority of stepfamilies involve partners who both bring children from a previous marriage to form what is called a *blended family*. This family configuration includes a biological parent, a stepparent, and children. Figure 8.7 shows a child's portrait of her blended family. As you can see, Heather views herself as belonging to two blended families.

Remarriage often provides additional resources for promoting healthy development. There are likely to be economic benefits, especially for women who remarry, as well as added emotional and child-rearing support (Zill, 1994; Zill, Morrison, & Coiro, 1993). The new spouse who becomes involved with his or her stepchildren can share the tasks of care and supervision and may provide an additional positive adult role model in the home.

However, the addition of a new stepparent to the family can cause disruption and stress, requiring further adjustment for both adults and children who may still be attempting to deal with issues raised by divorce. Some mothers, for example, exhibit heightened conflict, disengagement, low monitoring and control, and poor communication with their children during the early months of a remarriage transition (Hetherington & Clingempeel, 1992; Hetherington & Stanley-Hagan, 1999).

Another issue facing individuals in stepfamilies is unrealistic expectations. A great deal of uncertainty often exists in stepfamilies concerning who is part of the family and what the rights and responsibilities of various members are. Attempts to force a stepfamily to fit the model of a traditional biological family can cause problems to worsen and lead to new ones (Bray & Burger, 1993). Successful adjustment seems to result when families recognize that building a family takes time and that stepparents cannot replace biological parents but must develop an alternative, perhaps nontraditional, parenting role.

Research on children in stepfamilies has followed behind research on divorced families. Children of all ages show behavior problems following remarriage of their parents. When compared to children in first marriages, children in stepfamilies appear to be less well

■ FIGURE 8.7
Heather (Age 9) and Her Blended Families

adjusted; they exhibit more behavioral and emotional problems, poorer academic achievement, lower social competence, and less social responsibility (Hetherington & Clingempeel, 1992; Hetherington & Jodl, 1994).

As with the discussion of the effects of divorce, the child's age and sex must be taken into account in discussions of what outcomes are probable. Whereas younger children are likely to eventually form an attachment to and accept a stepparent, adolescents experience more of the difficulties previously listed. In one study, children who were 9 years or older when their mother remarried displayed more problems than those whose mothers remarried when they were younger (Hetherington, 1993).

Both boys and girls show signs of emotional stress and behavioral disruption following the remarriage of their custodial parent. Over time, however, the presence of a stepfather seems to improve well-being in boys. In contrast, girls remain less warm and responsive toward stepfathers (Amato & Keith, 1991; Hetherington & Clingempeel, 1992).

Whereas a close relationship between parents in nondivorced families is related to positive child outcomes, the closer the parents' own relationship in remarried families, the more problems the children display (Hetherington, 1989). In cases in which the mother and children lived alone for some years and developed a very close relationship, the new closeness of the mother and stepfather may lead to resentment and resistance on the part of the children, setting them up for other problematic behaviors (Hetherington & Jodl, 1994).

Children's relationships with their biological parents are more positive than with their stepparents, regardless of whether a stepmother or stepfather family is involved. Even so, stepmothers are usually more involved and more active in child rearing than are stepfathers, who may remain distant and disengaged, showing little involvement or rapport with their stepchildren (Fine, Voydanoff, & Donnelly, 1993). With increasing complexity in the stepfamily structure comes increasing difficulties in the child's adjustment. The highest level of behavioral problems is typically seen in blended families in which both parents bring children from a previous marriage.

Some researchers have moved beyond simple comparisons based on family structure to examine the influence of parenting behaviors in blended families. For example, stepparents, especially stepfathers, show more punitive and critical parenting and less nurturant and responsive parenting. Such parenting patterns have been related to the lower school grades and higher rates of delinquency shown by children in these families when compared to children in two-natural-parent families (Hetherington & Clingempeel, 1992).

Positive Parenting and Helping Children Cope with Family Change

As we have noted in previous sections, children thrive best under conditions in which their needs are met with regularity and consistency. Bornstein (2005) proposes five essential "tools" for positive parenting to be considered in parenting programs (p. 170). These parenting tools are briefly summarized in Figure 8.8. However, changes in family structure and status do occur over the course of development for many children, and research on how children cope with such changes can provide useful information to educators.

Depending on whether children move as a result of a divorce or the remarriage of parents, the school may be one of the few places of continuity for them. As such, the school and school personnel can serve as supports for both the child and parents during these transitions. Providing a stable, predictable school environment may help parents and children cope while changes are occurring elsewhere. The Focus on Teaching box on page 480 discusses how educators can help children cope with family transitions.

Tools for Positive Parenting

Knowledge about Child and Adolescent Development. Parents acquire more realistic expectations of children, and skills to foster positive competencies, when they understand the patterns of physical, cognitive, emotional, and social development.

Observation Skills. Parents need observation skills to help them discover the match between their children's abilities and characteristics and ways to help them achieve development goals.

Strategies for Problem Prevention and Discipline. Parents need "creative insights" for managing their children's behavior, as well as basic knowledge and skills concerning alternative methods of discipline, including how to implement positive rewards.

Supports for Emotional, Social, Cognitive, and Language Development. Parents need to know how to take advantage of settings, routines, and activites at hand to create learning opportunities. They also need to speak and read to their children as well as present engaging solvable problems.

Personal Sources of Support. Parents need to be patient, flexible, and draw pleasure from their interactions with children. They need to understand the positive impact they can have on their children's lives though listening and taking a genuine interest in them.

▦ FIGURE 8.8
Positive Parenting
Source: After Bornstein (2005), p. 170.

 # Child Care

Since the 1960s, there has been a steady increase in the number of women entering the workforce. Due to increases in the number of women working outside the home, more and more children under the age of 5 spend part of their day being cared for by someone other than their parents. In 2002, approximately 63 percent of children received some form of early child care, whereas millions more school-age children attended after-school and summer programs while their parents worked (U.S. Census Bureau, 2004). In this section we consider the effects of child care on children's development.

Maternal Employment and Children's Development

Over the past several decades, having a working mother has become more the norm rather than the exception. It has been argued that the employment of a mother outside the home is something of an economic necessity for single-mother and minority households due to the more dire economic circumstances faced by these groups (McLoyd, 1993). Despite these trends, compared with fathers, mothers engage in more work restructuring to allow for family commitments, are more likely to follow less consistent patterns of work with more workforce entries and exits, and are more likely to work fewer hours (Karambayya & Reilly, 1992). There are also inequities in terms of household responsibilities in dual-earner families: While some fathers do increase their overall level of involvement in child care and household chores, mothers retain responsibility for the larger portion even when

Focus on
Teaching

Helping Young People Cope with Family Change

The school often plays a key role in determining how children cope with family transitions. Children spend much of their time in school, where the continuity of care can offer a stable and safe environment. Research evidence suggests that children who experience a caring and supportive school environment experience fewer adjustment problems than children who experience authoritarian, permissive, or neglectful environments (Hetherington, 1993).

Despite the high rates of divorce in the United States, there is still some stigma associated with divorce. It is not uncommon to hear adults refer to a divorced family as a "broken home." Additionally, many children's stories do not portray stepfamilies, especially stepmothers, in a favorable light. These misconceptions and stereotypes can add to children's adjustment problems. Therefore, it is important for educators not to view divorce and remarriage as having negative consequences for all children. As we have learned, many factors determine how children cope with a family transition.

As young people experience a divorce or remarriage, change in behavior is expected. Younger children may draw attention to themselves by acting out or becoming withdrawn. Older children may show more serious signs of distress, in some cases reaching the level of depression. For all children in these circumstances, lack of concentration, preoccupation, and disruption of normal schedules are likely to occur at some point.

During a family transition, students will need extra support, attention, and care at school. The following practices are effective for helping children of divorce, but are useful for other family changes as well (Freeman & Couchman, 1985; Frieman, 1993, 1997):

- Provide opportunities for students to discuss and express their feelings.
- Maintain consistent expectations and routines.
- Encourage supportive communication.
- Use curriculum materials that present positive images of different family configurations.
- Inform parents about their children's progress or difficulties.
- Encourage parents to be honest, direct, and supportive with their children.

It is also important to consult school policies regarding contact with custodial and noncustodial parents. Most schools will have policies concerning the release of children from school, parental access to records and school functions, communication responsibilities, and so forth.

Finally, it is important to inform school counselors and other support personnel when children are experiencing considerable difficulty adjusting to family changes. There are a number of individual and group counseling approaches that can help students understand their feelings, feel good about themselves and their parents, and develop new coping skills.

---

they work as much as their husbands (Pleck, 1997). And one recent study found that in "high-power" dual-career families, it is more often the wives who utilize scaling-back strategies to buffer the family from work intrusions (Becker & Moen, 1999). Such strategies include placing limits on work commitments, deciding to have a one-career family, and trading off responsibilities.

Early studies of the effects of maternal employment on children began just as women were moving into the workforce in greater numbers, and were often predicated on the expectation that there would be some detriment to children who did not have a full-time caregiver at home. But in a number of those early studies researchers discovered that the independence fostered in children who had working mothers could be beneficial and lead to higher achievement motivation, higher competence, and higher educational and occupational goals (Hock, 1978; Hoffman, 1989; Woods, 1972). Also, children of working mothers tend to have less sex-stereotyped views of gender roles. In general, much of the continuing research in this area has found similarities between children of full-time homemaker mothers and mothers employed outside the home on a range of cognitive and behavioral measures (Gottfried, Bathurst, & Gottfried, 1994; Lerner & Abrams, 1994; Richards & Duckett, 1994). These outcomes depend to some extent on the quality and stability of child care arrangements. We will examine these factors in the next section.

Evidence for some potential difficulties has been found. Children for whom maternal employment was associated with decreased monitoring of their activities are more likely to show poor school performance and to experience behavior problems (Crouter, MacDermid, McHale, & Perry-Jenkins, 1990). This illustrates a point we have made before, that understanding what influences children's development requires attention to more than whether children fall into a particular status—for example, whether their mother works outside the home or not. Instead, the context in which the family faces a particular experience and the effect of that experience on more proximal processes within the family must be explored. In this case, the mother's work status influences her ability to maintain supervision of her children, and if no other supports are present in the family or community—a grandparent or trusted neighbor, for example—to assist her in monitoring them, then adverse consequences may result.

Another example of this need to consider process and context involves the mother's attitudes about and satisfaction with her work. When a mother feels forced into employment for economic reasons and does not derive any satisfaction from the job she is doing, that will likely affect her overall mood and thereby her interactions with her children (Lerner & Galambos, 1988; Greenberger & Goldberg, 1989). Feelings of guilt, depression, or resentment could then interfere with her parenting and thereby hinder her children's adaptive development.

Early Child Care and Children's Development

A variety of arrangements are used to care for children under the age of 5 when their parents are working. In 2002, approximately 32 percent of America's infants and preschoolers were cared for by a relative, whereas 23 percent attended an organized care facility (e.g., day care center, Head Start, school). Figure 8.9 on page 482 shows the various child care arrangements. The patterns are similar across different ethnic groups (Singer, Fuller, Keiley, & Wolf, 1998).

The study of day care on children's development has a long history. However, until recently, information was rather equivocal. In 1991, the National Institute of Child Health and Human Development (NICHD) funded a comprehensive study of early child care. The study includes 1,364 mothers and newborns in 12 U.S. cities, and it examines a wide range of developmental outcomes, including attachment relations, problem behavior, emotional regulation, cognitive skills, and so on. The results thus far reveal few straightforward effects related to child care. Children in child care are just as likely to form secure attachments as children with maternal care (NICHD Early Child Care Network, 1997). Additionally, child care was not related to problem behavior such as aggression or poor self-control, regardless of the age of entry into child care (NICHD Early Child Care Network, 1998). Moreover, evidence reveals no significant effects of child care on children's cognitive and language development (NICHD Early Child Care Network, 2000). In fact, there was a slight advantage for children in child care centers, perhaps due to the increased exposure to developmentally stimulating materials and opportunities to interact with same-aged peers. Recent findings show that although the quality of the maternal caregiving context (sensitivity) was a much stronger predictor of children's cognitive and social outcomes at about 4 1/2 years of age, the quality of the child care context (e.g., adult–child interactions, climate) also mattered (NICHD Early

■ FIGURE 8.9
Who's Minding the Kids?
Source: U.S. Census Bureau
(2005a).

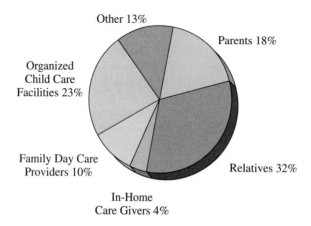

Child Care Network, 2003b). Also, these later findings showed that more hours spent in child care centers predicted some negative social outcomes (e.g., problem behavior, lower social skills, relational conflict) in first grade. Quality of the child care environments predicted children's academic functioning.

One of the most important findings of this research is that the quality of child care programs matters. Results are less favorable in lower-quality programs. What defines high-quality child care? There are a number of factors, as follows:

■ Low ratio of children to caregivers
■ Well-trained and experienced staff
■ Ample opportunities for educational, language, and social stimulation
■ Low staff turnover
■ Effective communication between parents and caregivers (Bredekamp & Copple, 1997)

The definition of low adult-to-child ratios varies by age. The National Association for the Education of Young Children (NAEYC) recommends an adult-to-child ratio of 1 to 3 for infants; 1 to 5 for children aged 1 to 2 years; 1 to 6 for children aged 2 to 3 years; and a ratio of no more than 1 to 10 for older children. Additionally, small group sizes are also important. Large groups of children with many adults is not as optimal as small groups with the same adult-to-child ratios. As with parent–child relationships, a key component of high-quality child care is warm, attentive, and responsive relationships. Unfortunately, high-quality child care is beyond the reach of many families due to its high cost and limited availability (Children's Defense Fund, 2000).

After-School Care and Children's Development

For many families, the problem of day care is resolved to some degree when children enter school. With older children, the concern is focused on the hours after school. Most schools dismiss students around 3 P.M., whereas most working parents are not able to leave work much before 5 P.M. This gap between parents' work schedules and children's school schedules can add up to 20 to 25 hours per week.

What happens to children when they leave school? Figure 8.10 shows the type of care students receive before and after school. Referred to as "latchkey children," approximately 15 percent of all children, ages 5 to 12, go home to an empty house (U.S. Census Bureau, 2004). Children left unsupervised after school often spend their time watching television.

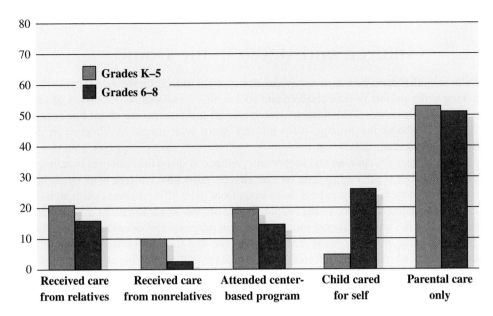

■ FIGURE 8.10
*Before- and After-School
Arrangements for
Children in Grades K–8.*
Source: National Center for
Educational Statistics (2000a).

Of even greater concern is the issue of safety. When left unsupervised, young people are more likely to engage in delinquent activities or to experiment with tobacco, alcohol, or drugs (Galambos & Maggs, 1991; Schwarz, 1999). Nearly half of all juvenile crime is committed between the hours of 2 P.M. and 8 P.M. Moreover, the U.S. Department of Justice reports that children are at greater risk for being victims of violent crime in the hours after school. Although these statistics are alarming, they do not apply to all children. Studies show that older children and adolescents can manage well on their own if they are mature, if the neighborhood is safe, if there are guidelines for emergencies, and so on (Lamb, 1998). Children and adolescents who generally spend their unsupervised time away from the home tend to be at greater risk for problem behaviors.

After-school programs can provide children with safe, supervised care. The options for after-school care may include 4-H Clubs, Boys and Girls Clubs, the YMCA, Big Brothers/Big Sisters, and church programs, to name a few. Public facilities such as libraries and community centers may provide after-school care in some communities. There is also a growing number of school-based programs. Many of these programs provide not only recreational or curricular activities, but also tutoring and enrichment programs, such as homework assistance, science clubs, or computer classes.

At issue is how much "schooling" should take place after school. Some experts argue that school-based programs that focus on academics neglect other areas of youth development. As we have discussed, young people need opportunities to participate in physical activities, to develop positive relations with adults, to engage in creative activities, and so on. If youths perceive after-school care as extended classroom time, they may lose interest in these programs.

Though evaluations of after-school programs are limited, the findings for some programs are encouraging (Dryfoos, 1999; Fashola, 1998; Posner & Vandell, 1999). For example, some school-based programs have resulted in improved school attendance, improved school achievement, and reduced high-risk behavior (Dryfoos, 1999). The effects are particularly positive for low-income children (Posner & Vandell, 1994).

Children and Media in the Home

Children's interaction with media provides an important context for their development. Just looking at the amount of time children and adolescents spend with various types of media today (e.g., television, DVD, Internet, video games) justifies this attention. For example, Figure 8.11 shows the average daily minutes spent with media by children in 2000 (Woodard & Gridina, 2000).

Not surprisingly, children and adolescents continue to spend the most time watching television, and boys watch more television than girls do. Also, poor children of all ethnic backgrounds watch more television than do children from more affluent homes. Although there are good television shows for young people, such as *Sesame Street* and *Blues Clues,* children more often watch noneducational programs or adult programs (Woodard & Gridina, 2000). This 2000 report on *Media in the Home* also showed that time with different types of media varied among children of different ages, except for in their viewing of television. Children of all ages spent the most time watching television, about 2 1/2 hours daily on average. Preschoolers spent more time watching videotapes than older children, school-age children spent the most time reading books, and adolescents spent the most time using the Internet, playing video games, and with other media types, as shown in Figure 8.12.

Since the introduction of television, concerns have been raised about its potential effects on children's intellectual development. When children are "glued" to the television for hours per day, it may leave less time for other activities. We have already discussed how television viewing may contribute to childhood obesity. There is also some evidence that television displaces leisure reading, but this association is not straightforward nor consistently found across studies (Huston & Wright, 1998). For example, one longitudinal study showed that television displaced reading as children moved from grade 3 to grade 5, but for older children, an increase in reading resulted in a decrease in television viewing (Ritchie, Price, & Roberts, 1987). Similarly, there is no strong evidence indicating that television viewing reduces time for homework (Huston & Wright, 1998).

Although many educators and parents believe that television viewing can negatively affect school achievement, this pattern is most consistently found in young people who are heavy viewers. When specific academic skills are examined, television viewing is negatively related to early reading skills, but the effect is weak and not found in older students (Huston & Wright, 1998).

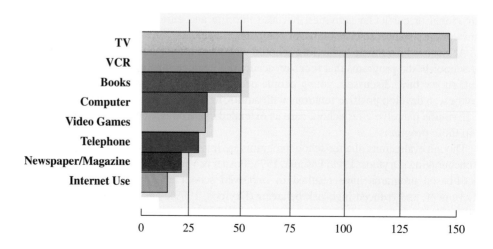

■ FIGURE 8.11

Average Daily Minutes Spent with Media by Children Ages 2–17 in 2000 (Parental Report)
Source: Woodard and Gridina (2000).

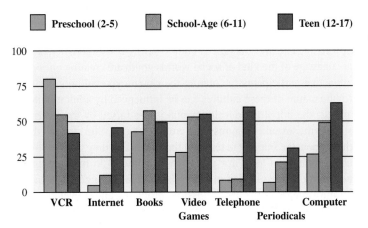

■ FIGURE 8.12
Average Daily Minutes Children Spent with Media by Child Age
Source: Woodard and Gridina (2000).

It is also important to point out that television viewing does not appear to negatively affect older children's attention span, creativity, or imagination. Several studies have examined these effects and found no conclusive evidence to support this claim (Huston & Wright, 1998). However, keep in mind some of the negative effects of heavy viewing of violent programs discussed in Chapter 7. For example, longitudinal studies show that heavy viewing of violence on television in the early years has negative effects on individuals' aggressive tendencies, even into early adulthood (Huesmann, et al., 2003). Another longitudinal study found that preschool girls (but not boys) who were frequent viewers of violent programs had lower grades in high school than infrequent viewers (Anderson, Huston, Schmitt, Linebarger, & Wright, 2001).

Other evidence suggests that high-quality programs can have positive academic benefits for all children, but especially for low-income children. *Sesame Street* is a prime example. Repeated evaluations of this program have shown that it has positive effects on children's school readiness, academic skills, and school adjustment. In a group of 2- to 5-year-olds who watched this program, improvements were found in vocabulary size, letter recognition, and math skills. These effects were not otherwise related to parent's education, income level, language spoken at home (English versus Spanish), or the overall quality of the home environment (Huston & Wright, 1998). Thus, these studies suggest that television can be an effective teacher when programs are well designed for young children. In the study following adolescents who had been studied as preschoolers, Anderson and his colleagues also found that early viewing of educational programs was associated with higher grades, reading more books, placing more value on achievement, greater creativity, and less aggression, especially for boys (Anderson et al., 2001). Children can also learn literacy and numeracy skills, as well as information about science, geography, and history.

In summary, there is little doubt that television is a part of young people's daily life. Television's positive or negative effects depend on the amount of time young people spend in front of the television, as well as on the content of the program. High-quality television programs can have positive benefits. Unfortunately, less-than-high-quality television often presents a social world that includes violence, stereotyped images, and frightening events. It is estimated that the average preschool child, who is still learning to distinguish reality from fantasy, witnesses 600 violent acts per week on television (Minow & LaMay, 1995). Studies also reveal that nearly 30 percent of the interactions in shows most popular among adolescents contain statements related to sexuality (Ward, 1995). Parental monitoring is key in reducing potential harmful influences of the media, as well as enhancing its potential positive functions.

As mentioned earlier, children, and adolescents in particular, are spending more time using the Internet. Parents, educators, and developmentalists are concerned about how to protect youth from inappropriate material. In a recent article, Patricia Greenfield (2004) drew the following conclusions from an examination of the existing research literature and her own visits to websites that cater to youth: (a) many parents are aware of children's vulnerability to advertising and are concerned about fostering consumerism (socializing materialism), but they are unaware of the kind of social worlds youth are creating online; (b) children and adolescents are active participants in creating their own cybercultures, for example, in teen chat rooms; (c) the nature of these cultures can be influenced by adult monitoring (but often they are not); and (d) the important developmental issues raised by the Internet (e.g., concerns about consumerism, sexuality, aggression) are not unique. She stresses that parents especially need to think about the Internet in terms of the values that they want to socialize, and interact with teens about their use ("pos" for parent-over-shoulder) to mitigate against potential risks, such as becoming desensitized to inappropriate sexuality, aggression, and racism. Educators can help by informing parents about possible problems and prevention approaches, as well as about constructive uses of the Internet for educational purposes.

Family Involvement in Children's Education

As we know, parents are children's first teachers. Parents have a significant impact on their children's development from birth, and this influence continues well beyond the adolescent years. As we have seen, families have the potential to create environments that prepare and support children's abilities and confidence in their learning (Fiese, 2001). Teachers today are well aware that they need to form partnerships with parents and families if they want to best meet the needs of their students. In this section, we explore (1) the benefits of parental involvement; (2) the family, school, and community characteristics that contribute to high levels of parental involvement; and (3) the most promising methods for involving parents in their children's education.

Benefits of Parent Involvement

There is general agreement among educators, researchers, and policy makers that active parental involvement in education is essential for children's and adolescents' school success (Carey, Lewis, & Farris, 1998; Comer, 2004; Epstein, 1995; Hoover-Dempsey & Sandler, 1995, 1997; Sanders & Epstein, 1998; Weiss, Dearing, Mayer, Kreider, & McCartney, 2005). But before going further, we need to define parent involvement. Parent involvement *at school* may include attending parent–teacher conferences, school programs, and engaging in volunteer activities; parent educational involvement *at home* may include helping with homework, discussing school activities, and managing children's activities (e.g., Lee & Bowen, 2006). In addition, some researchers question whether parental educational attitudes and expectations for their children should be part of this definition.

The benefits of parental involvement in education are fairly clear. There are benefits for parents, teachers, and, most of all, the students, as we gleaned from the opening vignette. When parents become involved at school, they learn ways to help and to support their children's learning at home. They also gain confidence in their own parenting abilities and in their abilities to help their children succeed in school. By becoming involved in their children's schooling, parents also reinforce the importance and value of education (Hoover-Dempsey & Sandler, 1995; Mantzicopoulos, 2003).

Through increased contact with parents, teachers can increase their understanding of their students' cultural backgrounds, needs, and strengths. They can also acquire a better understanding of the stresses their students encounter in their daily lives that affect their

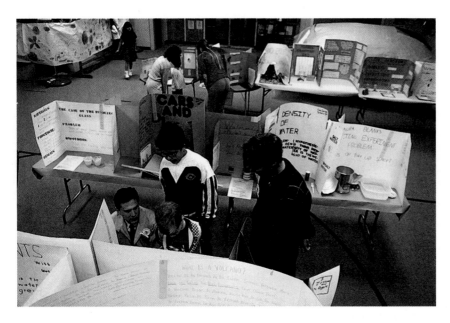

Parental involvement in school activities has important benefits for their children's learning and school adjustment.
Source: Bob Daemmrich/Stock Boston, LLC.

performance in school. Additionally, increased contact with parents can help teachers understand the goals they have for their children. One of the most consistent findings in research on parent–school relations is that "teachers have very different views of parents than parents have of themselves" (Epstein, 1996, p. 216). This knowledge base is likely to lead to (1) an increased sense of efficacy for teachers in helping parents support their children's learning, and (2) the use of effective instructional strategies in the classroom (Epstein, 1988; Haynes & Ben-Avie, 1996).

Not surprisingly, parental involvement at school has important benefits for children's and adolescents' learning. Early research suggested that parental involvement had positive effects on homework completion, student achievement, school attendance and adjustment, academic motivation, attitudes toward school, and educational aspirations, even after the effects of student ability and family economic resources are taken into account (Becher, 1984; Christenson, Rounds, & Gorney, 1992; Graue, Weinstein, & Walberg, 1983). Also, students who drop out of school report that their parents rarely attended school events or helped them with their homework (Rumberger, Ghatak, Poulos, Ritter, & Dornbusch, 1990). Recent research showed that parents' involvement at school and their educational expectations were strongly related to their elementary students' achievement (Lee & Bowen, 2006). Contrary to hypotheses, other aspects of parent involvement studied (e.g., help with homework, time management) were not always associated with student achievement.

The effects of parent involvement on students' educational outcomes are not always straightforward. Joyce Epstein (1996), a leading expert on home–school partnerships, points out that the effects may depend on the type and quality of parental involvement. If parent–teacher contact mainly focuses on academic or behavioral problems, it can lead parents to form negative expectations for their children as well as to participate less in school activities and events. Similarly, poorly designed parental involvement practices can lead to negatives outcomes for students and for schools (Epstein, 1996; Scotts-Jones, 1987).

Why Do Parents Become Involved?

Although most schools sponsor various programs and events for their children's parents, these events are not attended by all parents. The results of a 2002–2003 national survey of various programs for parents at schools are shown in Figure 8.13. The programs included open houses or back-to-school nights; sports events or field days; arts events (plays, dance, or musical performances), science fairs, or other academic events; and parent–teacher conferences. In general, as Figure 8.13 shows, parents were more likely to attend conferences with their child's teachers than any other type of school event.

Parental involvement in their children's school is influenced by a number of factors, including their belief systems, economic resources, social networks, and history with schools. It is also influenced by various teacher, school, and community characteristics, but questions concerning parental involvement are typically phrased in terms of "Why are parents not more involved in their children's education?" (Eccles & Harold, 1996). We will look at parental characteristics first, then consider school influences on parental involvement.

Parental and Familial Characteristics

Studies have shown that parental involvement is related to the parents' educational level, economic status, and family size (Dauber & Epstein, 1989). In general, parents with limited income and education are less likely to report high levels of involvement in school activities (e.g., Lee & Bowen, 2006). Parental involvement in school activities also varies by the age

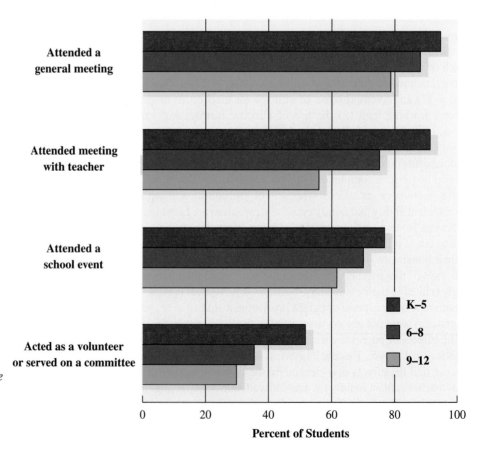

■ FIGURE 8.13
Percent of Students Whose Parents Attend a School Activity
Source: National Center for Educational Statistics (2005b).

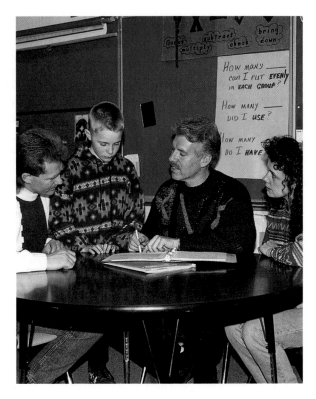

Parents want to work with teachers to enhance their children's education.
Source: James Shaffer/Photo Edit.

of the children. In general, parents attend fewer school activities as their children get older. See Figure 8.13 for national figures for parental involvement rates by grade levels.

Often ethnic minority families are less involved in their children's education at school. Many factors contribute to their low levels of parental involvement, including their own negative experiences as students (Ritter, Mont-Reynayd, & Dornbusch, 1993). Also, Rogoff (2003) points out that middle-income, educated parents often engage their children in "school-like" conversations and activities at home. Thus, well-educated parents may be more comfortable with interactions in typical U.S. school settings. Because of cultural differences, many other parents may not understand teacher expectations for getting involved in their children's education. Language barriers can compound these problems as well.

However, these family status variables alone do not fully explain parental decisions about involvement in their children's education (Hoover-Dempsey & Sandler, 1997). Many parents are able to nurture their children's school achievement even when faced with discouraging or difficult home situations. It is important, therefore, to go beyond family characteristics. Interestingly, research suggests that parental beliefs and attitudes play an important role in determining involvement in their children's schooling (Eccles & Harold, 1996; Hoover-Dempsey & Sandler, 1997). Examples include the following:

■ **Efficacy beliefs.** It is important for parents to have confidence in their abilities to help their children with schoolwork. Parents become less sure of their abilities to help children with schoolwork as the children move up in grades or take more specialized classes.

■ **Parents' perceptions of their children's abilities.** Parents' confidence in their children's ability to succeed in school, as well as their perceptions of the educational/occupational opportunities available to their children, can influence parental involvement in schooling.

- **Parents' perceptions of their role in their children's education.** It is important for parents to believe that they can play an active role in their children's education, and that their involvement can make a difference in their children's school achievement.
- **Parents' attitudes toward school.** It is important for parents to believe that the school wants them to be involved in their children's education, and that school personnel want to help, not blame, parents when their children have difficulties at school. It is important to recognize that many parents from minority and poor populations did not have positive experiences in school themselves. Parents' early experiences with schools undoubtedly influence their attitudes toward their children's schools and their willingness to participate again in those schools.
- **Compatibility of parent and school goals.** Parents undoubtedly have goals for their own children. As our society becomes more ethnically and linguistically diverse, it is critical for schools to understand that parents want their children to have an accurate representation of their culture of origin and its history.

School and Teacher Characteristics

Along with parent and family characteristics, aspects of the school environment also influence the level of parents' involvement in their children's education. In fact, many of the parent characteristics discussed previously are likely to be affected by their children's school environment.

As discussed, there is a strong relationship between the age of the child and the level of parental involvement. There is generally more parent involvement in elementary schools because the school is located close to the children's home, and children have only one teacher. The organization of middle and high schools, on the other hand, are more complex, and teachers are responsible for larger groups of students. Keeping parents informed of each student's interests and progress can become an overwhelming task. Many secondary teachers report insufficient time to implement effective parent involvement strategies, as explained in this interview:

> Every teacher is basically responsible for notifying absent students' parents everyday, but it doesn't happen because we are supposed to do this in addition to making sure the halls are cleared, in addition to the lesson plans, in addition to other responsibilities. For example, I am a second year teacher. . ., a new dad. . ., and I coach varsity sports. I find it exceedingly difficult to make the time to call. . .[I] want to, but between lesson plans, and making out final exams, it's hard. (Sanders & Epstein, 1998, p. 29)

Teachers' attitudes toward parent involvement seem to vary by grade level as well. Compared to teachers of younger students, high school teachers are less likely to encourage parent involvement. In fact, some evidence suggests that they actively discourage parent involvement unless there is a problem (Dornbusch & Ritter, 1996; Eccles & Harold, 1996; Epstein & Dauber, 1991; Hoover-Dempsey, Bassler, & Brissie, 1987). Yet research suggests that parent involvement is just as important for older students as for younger students. Parent involvement activities can positively influence students' academic achievement (Clark, 1983; Ginsburg & Hanson, 1986; Sheldon & Epstein, 2005), homework completion (Keith, Reimers, Fehrman, Pottebaum, & Aubey, 1986), and high school graduation rates (Delgado-Gaitan, 1988; Conklin & Dailey, 1981).

Encouraging Parental Involvement in Education

How can educators foster high levels of parental involvement? Traditionally, we think of parent involvement in school as attending PTA meetings, school events, and parent–teacher conferences. However, strategies for involving parents in their children's education can take

Back to School Night

Mr. Chavez is a ninth-grade English teacher at Drew Magnet School. He is preparing for back-to-school night, and hopes that more of his students' parents will attend this year than previous years. Many of his students come from single-parent families, and a large number come from homes where the first language is not English. These families are generally the hardest to reach. Mr. Chavez's school is beginning a new Family–School Partnership supported by state funds. The school plans to establish a family resource center to provide adult education classes, social services, and other family support programs. Also the school is establishing a new governance structure to give parents a strong voice in school policies and operations. During the summer, Mr. Chavez attended a continuing education program to learn new ways of working with parents of adolescents. His teacher education program provided little preservice training in this area. In fact, his college

professors stressed the importance of home visits and parent involvement for the early grades only. At the summer program, Mr. Chavez learned that these programs have important benefits for adolescents and their families as well. He also learned about changing family demographics and different techniques for fostering communication with parents.

It is almost time for parents and students to arrive, and Mr. Chavez takes one more look around his classroom. His classroom has attractive displays of literature and writing from different cultures. He has also prepared a video that shows some of the projects he hopes to do with his classes. He will also demonstrate how parents can access the school's homework hotline from their homes. Mr. Chavez recruited someone from the community to help with translation. As he places the school's new parent handbook on a table near the door, parents begin to arrive.

many different forms. Parents can support their children's learning at home and volunteer in their child's classroom. Technology can be used to link parents and children to a network for help with homework. Please see the description of Mr. Chavez's efforts to connect with parents in the Focus on Teaching box above. Mr. Chavez implemented parent involvement strategies in his classroom (videos of class projects, homework hotline), but his school as a whole was also establishing a family resource center to provide adult education classes. Some schools also have a home–school coordinator to develop outreach programs for families and children.

Joyce Epstein has developed a framework for developing effective partnerships (Epstein, 1992, 2002). This framework and sample practices are presented in the Focus on Teaching box on page 492. Epstein believes that there are many reasons for creating school and family partnerships, but the most important reason is to help young people succeed in school and in later life. In implementing parent involvement practices, it is important to remember the following (Moles, 1996, pp. 249–250):

■ Parents are the first and foremost teachers of their children.

■ Families have vast opportunities to influence children by instruction and by example.

■ All parents want their children to do well in school and have good futures.

■ Parents want to work with schools to aid their children's education.

In the next chapter, we will see how some schools have successfully integrated parents in forming school communities of learning.

Focus on
Teaching

On the basis of years of research across the country, Joyce Epstein has developed a framework for helping schools design effective school and family partnership programs. Some strategies (such as communicating, volunteering) can be implemented by individual teachers, whereas others involve the school as a whole.

Type 1: Parenting

Help all families establish home environments that support learning.

- Make home visits at transition points to elementary, middle, and secondary school.
- Hold educational programs for parents on parenting and child-rearing skills.
- Establish family support programs to help parents with health, nutrition, and other services.

Type 2: Communicating

Design effective forms of communication to reach parents.

- Hold parent–teacher conferences with each parent at least once a year.
- Use language translators for language minority families
- Send weekly or monthly folders home for review.
- Make regular phone calls, write newsletters, and use other forms of communication.

Type 3: Volunteering

Recruit and organize help and support.

- Establish school and classroom volunteer programs to assist students, teachers, administrators, and parents.
- Maintain a parent room or family center for volunteer work, meetings, and resources for families.

Source: After Epstein (2002).

Six Types of Parent Involvement

- Take annual surveys of parents to identify talents and needs.

Type 4: Learning at Home

Provide ideas to parents about how they can help children with learning at home.

- Run programs to provide parents with information on the skills required in all subjects at each grade.
- Provide information on homework policies and how parents can monitor their children's homework at home.
- Create family literacy and math programs.

Type 5: Decision Making

Include parents in school decisions and recruit parent leaders.

- Establish active PTA/PTO or other parent organizations in the school, including advisory councils and committees for curriculum, safety, and so on.
- Develop advocacy groups to work for school reform and improvements.
- Develop networks to link families to parent representatives.

Type 6: Collaborating with the Community

Identify and integrate resources and services from the community to strengthen schools, families, and student learning and development.

- Provide information on community health and other service programs.
- Inform families about mentoring and tutoring programs available in the community.
- Integrate child and family services with education.

■ Chapter Summary

Conceptions of the Family

- Families are the social unit with the primary responsibility for preparing (or socializing) the child to be a productive and competent member of society.
- A family is a highly complex system of interactions and processes operating at multiple levels. The family is embedded in larger social systems—neighborhoods, communities, and culture—that can affect interactions within the family.

Variations in Family Structures

- Though most children grow up in two-parent families, there is an increasing number of children being raised in single-parent families.
- Children from single-parent families tend to be less successful in school than children from two-parent families. The presence of economic resources and other adults in the household can offset the negative consequences of a single-parent family. Grandparents and others are also playing a major role in raising children.
- There are few differences between homosexual and heterosexual parents. Children of gay and lesbian parents exhibit good relations with peers and adults, and they resemble children of heterosexual parents on measures of social competence, self-concept, locus of control, and moral judgment.

Ethnic Diversity of Families

- African Americans currently represent the largest minority group in the United States. Child-rearing practices in African American families tend to emphasize assertiveness, independence, and self-confidence.
- The number of Hispanic American families is steadily growing. Child-rearing practices in Hispanic American families emphasize interdependence, family obligation, conformity, and cooperation.
- Asian American families also emphasize the importance of social harmony and interdependence. Asian American children are expected to do well in school to bring honor to the family.
- The traditions of Native American families differ by tribal identity. Yet most families value harmony and connectedness. The entire Native American community plays a role in raising children.

Family Influence on Development

- The family environment can be characterized in terms of routines and activities, and differences in warmth, responsiveness, and control. These dimensions form constellations of parenting behaviors, called parenting styles. There are four types of parenting styles: authoritarian, authoritative, permissive-indulgent, and permissive-indifferent.
- Authoritative parenting is associated with the most positive outcomes for children. Children of authoritative parents are self-reliant and socially responsible, and perform well in school. Children with authoritarian parents have lower self-esteem and lower achievement than children of authoritative parents. Children of permissive-indifferent parents have the most negative profile of all.
- Relationships between children and parents change over the course of development. In early development, children are regulated by parents. There is a gradual shift toward coregulation during middle childhood, whereby control is shared by parents and children. In adolescence, young people strive for independence. This period is generally characterized by minor conflict until parent and child roles are renegotiated.
- Sibling relationships play a unique and important role in children's development. Siblings serve as role models, playmates, teachers, and sources of emotional support. Like parent–child relations, sibling relationships change with development. Children whose parents are warm and responsive tend to develop positive sibling relationships.

■ Child maltreatment can take many different forms, including physical abuse, neglect, emotional maltreatment, and sexual abuse. Younger children are at greater risk for maltreatment than are older children. A number of social and economic factors contribute to child abuse, including poor parental education, family poverty and conflict, and social isolation. Child abuse has serious cognitive, emotional, and social consequences for the child.

Family Transitions: Divorce and Remarriage

■ Approximately half of first marriages end in divorce. The effects of divorce on a child are not straightforward and are related to the child's age and sex, the level of conflict between parents, the income level of the custodial parent, and the quality of the parenting provided.

■ Many children live in a blended family consisting of a biological parent, a stepparent, and children. The remarriage of a parent has both positive and negative consequences for the child. As with divorce, the effects of remarriage are shaped by the child's characteristics and the quality of parenting provided.

■ The school can provide continuity of care and stability for children experiencing a change in the family. During a family transition, young people will need extra support, attention, and care at school. It is important to maintain consistent rules and routines, and to provide opportunities for children to discuss their feelings.

Child Care

■ A large number of children under the age of 5 receive some form of early child care. Early findings on the effects of day care were equivocal. Recently, new evidence shows few negative effects of day care on children's development when children attend high-quality day care programs. Quality is defined in terms of a low ratio of children to caregivers; a well-trained staff; opportunities for educational, language, and social stimulation; and low staff turnover.

■ Many school-age children today also attend some form of after-school program. These programs are offered by churches, community organizations, and public facilities. A limited body of research suggests that school-based programs can result in improved school attendance and achievement, particularly for low-income children.

Children and Media in the Home

■ Children spend many hours today with different types of media, including TV, video games, DVDs, and the Internet. Type and time with different media changes with age.

■ Studies show that effects of media on children's development depend on the content and amount of use. Parental monitoring is important for protecting children and youth from inappropriate content.

Family Involvement in Children's Education

■ There is general agreement that active parental involvement in education is important for children's school success. When parents become involved in school activities, they devise ways of supporting their children's learning at home. Through increased contact with parents, teachers can increase their understanding of their students' cultural backgrounds, needs, and strengths.

■ Parent involvement varies by family structure and grade level. Two-parent families are more involved in their children's schooling than single parents. Also, rates of parent involvement are higher for younger than for older students. Parental beliefs and attitudes play an important role in determining whether or not parents will become involved in their child's schooling.

■ The organization of schools and teacher attitudes can encourage or discourage parental involvement. A number of effective parent involvement strategies have been identified. These include enhancing parenting skills, communicating regularly and effectively with parents, recruiting classroom volunteers, encouraging parents to help their children with learning at home, and including parents in school governance.

■ Key Terms

authoritarian parenting *(p. 466)*
authoritative parenting *(p. 466)*
autonomy *(p. 471)*
bioecological model *(p. 448)*
birth order *(p. 472)*
chronosystem *(p. 448)*
coregulation *(p. 470)*
corporal punishment *(p. 464)*

emotional maltreatment *(p. 473)*
exosystem *(p. 448)*
familialism *(p. 460)*
inductive discipline *(p. 464)*
macrosystem *(p. 448)*
mesosystem *(p. 448)*
microsystem *(p. 448)*
neglect *(p. 473)*

parenting styles *(p. 466)*
permissive-indifferent *(p. 466)*
permissive-indulgent *(p. 466)*
physical abuse *(p. 473)*
power-assertive discipline *(p. 463)*
sexual abuse *(p. 473)*
simpatía *(p. 460)*
socialization *(p. 446)*

■ Activities

1. Interview children of different ages to learn about their families. Find out what kind of activities they do with their parents and siblings. Also, ask about the activities they do with their friends. You might ask your interviewees to draw a picture of their families, and to describe what they would like to change about their families. Compare and contrast responses across the different age groups. What themes emerge regarding how children spend time with families? How do the activities differ from ones they do with friends? Are there any interesting changes with age? Discuss what you learned with your classmates.

2. Begin to develop a resource file for helping children to cope with family change. Look for books and other reading materials on divorce and re-marriage that children can read on their own. Review these materials for misconceptions about families. Collect additional professional materials on ways to support and help children who are experiencing a change in the family.

3. Interview school and community agency officials to learn more about policies and procedures concerning child maltreatment. What are you legal responsibilities as a teacher? What are the steps for reporting child maltreatment? Invite speakers to your class to discuss indicators and consequences of child abuse.

4. Interview teachers of different grade levels to gather information on parent involvement. Ask teachers to describe the strategies they use to communicate with parents, to involve them in classroom activities, and to support children's learning at home. Find out which strategies seem to be most effective. Compare the list with the ones described in Epstein's parent involvement framework (see Focus on Teaching on page 492). Share your summary with classmates.

CHAPTER

9

Supporting the Development of Children and Youth in School

CHAPTER OUTLINE

THE FOLLOWING DESCRIPTIONS ARE FROM *LEAVE NO CHILD BEHIND* (2004) by James Comer, M.D., founder of the Yale Child Study School Development Program (SDP) (introduced in Chapter 1). Public school teachers and administrators using the SDP in three major cities discuss their challenges in promoting students' academic and personal growth. These "voices from the schoolhouse" were gathered from interviews conducted by Dr. Comer in 2003 to reveal "a realistic vision." Comer's view is that ". . . the best chance for nationwide school change will come from a better public appreciation of the challenges educators face and what they will need to do their jobs well" (Comer, 2004, pp. 25–26).

One teacher from an elementary school with some of the best test scores in the state noted challenges with the press. "The newspapers focus on the schools that are doing poorly. They don't report on the ones that are doing well . . . . They don't focus on the whole child. And if you don't focus on the whole child, then all that you do instructionally falls apart." She laments that despite their successes with many children from low-income families, the media tells negative stories. "Things are not right when you can't get praise in good schools. It's bad for the morale of teachers in schools serving poor children . . . . It is one of the reasons there is so much teacher turnover in many schools" (Comer, 2004, p. 28). This situation is also bad for the morale of the children and their parents.

Along with not feeling celebrated, educators noted the lack of resources for helping students with chaotic family lives and health problems. "Our kids come to school two years behind the professional-class kids, a year behind the working-class kids. And they move often—across town and in and out of the country. We need programs and people who are going to **go all out** for them. And many do, but the best are recruited away . . ." (Comer, 2004, p. 39).

Another major challenge noted was having to follow dictates based on misunderstandings about what children need and how they learn. One educator remarked, "Show me the evidence that 'test them and they will learn' will work. I can show them the evidence of programs right here in this district which improve learning and overcome low self-esteem, the effects of lean learning environments, and poor teacher attitudes. But we can't keep such programs going. Why not fund our successful programs rather than dictate?" (p. 40).

Despite these challenges, SDPs have flourished. Educators are "going all out" for their students. Hundreds of U.S. schools serving many low-income students have adopted this model, which has at its heart a focus on understanding child and youth development. A few anecdotes illustrate this progress:

A principal relates the story about 12-year-old Joey (pseudonym), who arrived at a U.S. school in 2000 from another country where he had been placed with kindergarteners because of his special learning needs. The child study team assigned to review his case discovered that in addition to his lack of social skills, he had a rare form of disability that confused information that he processed visually (see Chapter 4). He was placed in a nurturing fourth-grade teacher's class, and on the baseball team to learn how to interact with peers. At the end of the year when his team won the baseball competition, his classmates held him up on their shoulders and "rah-rah-ed" him; it was the first time Joey smiled. The principal exclaimed, "You should see him now: he's in our fifth-grade special education class, and he's getting outside occupational therapy, physical therapy, and

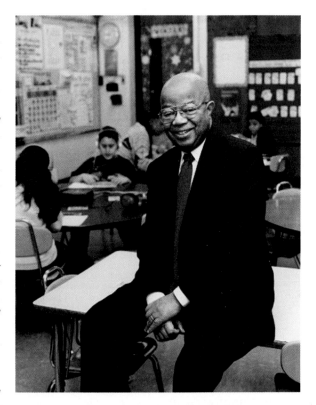

Dr. James Comer, Founder of the Yale Child Study Development Program, vsits a classroom using the School Development Program.
Source: Yale Medicine/Terry Dagradi.

psychological services. He's reading on a second-grade level, he comes to school every day, and he smiles all the time" (Comer, 2004, pp. 46–47).

In addition to the clear rise in achievement test scores in schools using the Comer Process, students are also receiving fewer suspensions from school and are demonstrating more respect for their teachers and fellow students. In some schools, such improvement in behavior may be in part due to requiring students who hurt others (including their feelings) to engage in Acts of Kindness. This is no simple action. For example, one principal explains that if a boy pulls a chair out from under a girl, and she falls and gets hurt and embarrassed, the boy must perform Acts of Kindness for this girl for 2 weeks. He must bring her lunch to her table, clean up and remove the tray after she is done, carry her book bag from class to class, and hold the door open for her. If the girl says, "we're friends now," the boy can stop these activities and the apology is accepted. The principal explains, "I make them go through Acts of Kindness because I feel that they have civil and ethical responsibilities" (Comer, 2004, p. 48).

As you recall from Chapter 1, the Comer Process or Comer Model creates a school environment that takes into account the needs of the whole child, drawing from developmental and educational theories. Dr. Comer argues that "development and learning are inextricably linked" (Comer, 2004, p. xiv). For children to learn, schools must meet six integrated developmental needs: physical, cognitive, psychological, linguistic, social, and ethical. Evidence shows that the process is working for many students, even in inner-city schools, where their academic performance is above the national average and their behavior shows progress in their emotional wellness and social and moral development as well.

The focus on fostering the development of the whole child is central to the Comer Process, as he puts it simply, "good child and youth rearing and development . . . simultaneously produce good test scores" (Comer, 2004, p. xiv). The SDP is committed to helping parents, educators, and policy makers create learning environments that support children's

■ FIGURE 9.1

The Developmental Pathways Panel. The Comer Process promotes growth along all of the six pathways critical to children's learning and development.
Source: From Joyner et al. (2004).

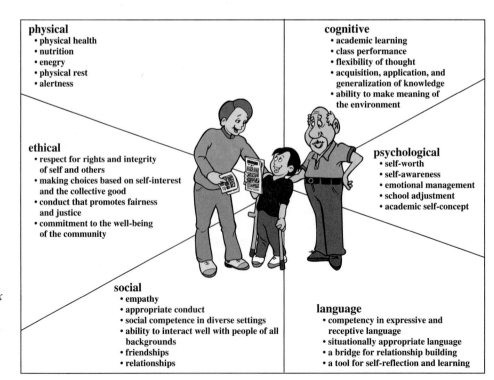

physical
• physical health
• nutrition
• enegry
• physical rest
• alertness

cognitive
• academic learning
• class performance
• flexibility of thought
• acquisition, application, and generalization of knowledge
• ability to make meaning of the environment

ethical
• respect for rights and integrity of self and others
• making choices based on self-interest and the collective good
• conduct that promotes fairness and justice
• commitment to the well-being of the community

psychological
• self-worth
• self-awareness
• emotional management
• school adjustment
• academic self-concept

social
• empathy
• appropriate conduct
• social competence in diverse settings
• ability to interact well with people of all backgrounds
• friendships
• relationships

language
• competency in expressive and receptive language
• situationally appropriate language
• a bridge for relationship building
• a tool for self-reflection and learning

and adolescents' development along *all* of the six critical pathways illustrated in Figure 9.1. One of the major premises is that children's most meaningful learning occurs through supportive relationships with caring adults, and that parents, staff, and community members must interact collaboratively and sensitively with one another in order to bring out the best in children. We have seen this theme echoed throughout this text.

In this final chapter, we briefly reexamine some teacher and school characteristics that foster student learning and development. We look at the critical role of teacher–student relationships. We follow with a discussion of the teacher's role in identifying special learning needs of children and adolescents, and how to accommodate these needs. Finally, we return to look at schools and classrooms in terms of their quality characteristics and processes, and the roles that educators can play in advocating for children and youth.

Why Educators Study Development

A Return to the Ecological Perspective

Gates (2004) describes the Comer Process in the following terms:

> . . . the school, the family, and the neighborhood are united in a seamless web of reinforcement and constructive reaffirmation, literally day to day, unobtrusively yet decidedly ever-present in the very fabric of a continuous education process, one not relegated merely to the classroom. (p. xiii)

This quote should remind the reader of the **ecological perspective** on human development introduced in Chapter 1. Bronfenbrenner points out that humans create the conditions for living that in turn create the potential to "make human beings human." Educators, parents, policy makers, and developmentalists and other professionals working with children, youth, and families are—together—capable of creating school environments that nurture students' development and potential as human beings.

The influence of the ecological perspective is vividly portrayed in the recent "marriage" between Comer's School Development Program and Edward Zigler's School of the 21st Century (21C). This new model, referred to as CoZi (for Comer-Zigler), combines the SDP goals of creating a strong school community with the 21C goals of starting early with young children and their parents. Thus, CoZi offers year-round child care and family support services in a school governed by representatives in the community. Based on a needs assessment, these services may also include adult education, social services, and health services. CoZi is unique because it incorporates the organizational structure of the SDP—bringing teachers, parents, child care, and service providers together—to share information and make plans (see Figure 9.2 on page 500). Understanding children's development is at the heart of all planning and decision making. This organizational structure puts into practice the solutions Bronfenbrenner proposed for fostering human development through creating linkages between families, schools, community services, and other systems. The first link that we will focus on is between children and their teachers.

Teacher–Student Relations

The quality of children's relationships with their teachers is recognized as an important contributor to school adjustment and success (e.g., Birch & Ladd, 1997; Hamre & Pianta, 2001; Pianta, 1999; Pianta & Stuhlman, 2004; Stuhlman, & Pianta, 2002). Similar to parent–child relationships, the quality of teacher–child relationships in the early elementary years may

■ FIGURE 9.2
*Schoolhouse Model of the
Comer Process*
Source: From Joyner et al.
(2004).

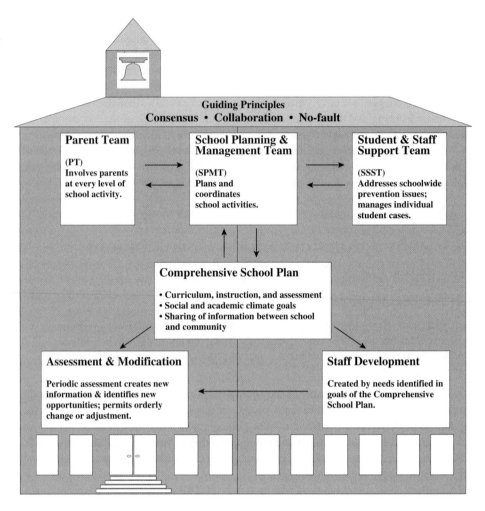

predict students' later social and emotional competencies, which in turn contribute to their school success. Children probably do not form attachments to their teachers in the same way they do with parents (e.g., Kesner, 2000; see Chapter 6). However, Pianta (1999) explains that supportive relationships with teachers can meet children's emotional needs, allowing them to regulate their behavior and develop skills necessary for dealing with peer and academic demands in school. For example, one study showed that improved or secure teacher–student relations in kindergarten were related to competent behavior and fewer problems in first grade (Pianta & Nimentz, 1991). Similarly, another study showed that conflicts with kindergarten teachers predicted decreases in prosocial behavior and increases in aggressive behavior with peers (Birch & Ladd, 1998).

Furthermore, the quality of the relationship students have with teachers in the early school years is related to the quality of their relationships with future teachers (e.g., Howes & Hamilton, 1993). Children who have chronic conflicts in relationships with teachers demonstrate less motivation and liking for school than those with close relationships with teachers, and are at increased risk for poor academic achievement (e.g., Ladd & Burgess, 2001). In contrast, positive relationships with teachers can buffer or protect children at risk for school failure (e.g., Burchinal, Peisner-Feinberg, Pianta, & Howes, 2002; Lynch & Cicchetti, 1992). Thus, there is mounting evidence to suggest that the quality of early teacher–student relationships may forecast later school experiences and achievement. However, developmentalists emphasize that other interpersonal aspects of the early school years also contribute to later school success (Pianta, 2006; Pianta & Stuhlman, 2004), such as the development of peer relationships (Flook, Ullman, & Repetti, 2005) and parent–teacher relationships. Students' concurrent relationships with teachers are also significant.

The importance of teacher–student relationships is not limited to the early years of schooling. For example, McCombs and Laeur (1997) found that middle school teachers' perceptions of their positive relationships with students predicted student reports of self-efficacy, use of active learning strategies, and motivation to learn (curiosity and task mastery). In addition, Wentzel (1997, 1998) found that young adolescents' perceived support from teachers predicted their school motives and pursuit of goals. Furthermore, in a later study, Wentzel (2002) found that lack of nurturance on the part of teachers was a consistent negative predictor of sixth graders' academic performance and social behavior; this relationship was similar for African American and European American students, and for boys and girls. Thus, teacher–student relationships continue to play a role in student motivation and achievement throughout the school years.

Teacher–Student Relations, Classroom Management, and Pedagogy

What are qualities of positive teacher–student relationships and interactions? Some developmentalists have characterized relationships in terms of their closeness (warmth) and conflict, as mentioned earlier. Others describe teacher–student interactions in terms of teachers' emotional support (interpersonal relations), discipline (management), and instruction (pedagogy) (e.g,. Pianta, La Paro, Cox, Payne, & Bradley, 2002). Another way to address this question is to ask children and adolescents themselves. Research conducted with students in the elementary (e.g., Daniels, Kalkman, & McCombs, 2001; Daniels & Perry, 2003; Weinstein, 1983) and middle grades (e.g., Wentzel, 1997) describes similar qualities of good teachers. These qualities include (Daniels, Beaumont, & Doolin, 2002):

- Caring (warm, friendly)
- Responsive (provides academic assistance/feedback when requested)
- Fair (distributes attention and rewards in a fair manner)
- Personal (knows students as individuals, including background and interests)
- Interesting (provides stimulating activities)
- Individualizes instruction (provides appropriate challenges, choices)
- Manages classroom effectively (provides clear instructions and appropriate systems for maintaining discipline and accomplishing tasks)

Note how student perceptions of teachers include aspects of their personal relationships and other aspects of their teaching, including classroom management and pedagogy.

Carol Weinstein (1998) asked a similar question of prospective elementary and secondary teachers concerning what they might do to indicate that they care about students. Although most emphasized establishing positive interpersonal relationships with students, others also defined caring in terms of pedagogy and classroom management. Figure 9.3 on page 502 shows the kinds of responses provided. Educational psychologists also include the creation of positive teacher–student and peer relationships in definitions of effective classroom management (e.g., Emmer & Stough, 2001).

UNDERSTANDING CHILDREN
Strategy 5.5: What is a Good Teacher? and Strategy 5.6: Quality of Relationship with Teacher

Prospective Teachers' Views of What It Means to Care for Students

Interpersonal

- Treat all students with respect.
- Ask them about themselves.
- Let them know they can confide in you.
- Let them know that you understand.
- Show them you're not perfect either.

Pedagogy

- Offer a variety of materials and ways to teach.
- Allow students to participate to some extent in choosing what they want to learn.
- Be willing to slow down if necessary.
- Establish convenient out of school time for extra help.
- Give students a chance to talk (give opinions, ask questions, debate, etc.) during lessons.

Management

- Ask for student input into rules.
- Do not put students down; criticize their behavior (not them).
- Explain why you are reprimanding a student.

■ FIGURE 9.3

Prospective Teachers' Views of What It Means to Care for Students.
Source: After Weinstein (1998).

Comprehensive views of classroom management also include the importance of understanding students' psychological and learning needs, and the flexible use of instructional methods that respond to these needs. This understanding is portrayed in the Focus on Development box, which describes a fifth-grade teacher's teaching practices. This "teacher story" also illustrates an important point introduced in Chapter 1: Teachers' views on child development matter! Research demonstrates that teachers' developmental perspectives influence their interactions with students and classroom practices (e.g., Daniels & Shumow, 2003). As we will see, teachers' attitudes toward included children also matter (see the Focus on Research box on page 506.). In the next section, we attend to how teachers can adapt instruction for children and adolescents with special learning needs.

Teaching Students with Special Learning Needs

The Role of a Classroom Teacher

Most classrooms contain some students with identified exceptionalities as well as others who are experiencing problems that have not been identified. The classroom teacher, who is responsible for meeting the diverse needs of all students, may need to access special education for assistance and instructional support. In order to obtain these services, the

A Development-Driven Classroom Culture

Rhona Weinstein (2002) describes Mrs. Kay's creation of a "development-driven achievement culture" in her fifth-grade classroom. According to Dr. Weinstein, Mrs. Kay's practices stem from her worldview of children's development and learning. Mrs. Kay believes that children's intelligence is malleable (incremental view) and multidimensional (recall Gardner and Sternberg's theories). This is reflected in her varied lessons and activities, as well as in her assessments. She believes that knowledge is socially constructed in interactions between teachers, students, and the material, and that her role is to meet children where they are and stretch their cognitive abilities by providing essential scaffolding (recall Vygotsky's theory). Her beliefs about subject-matter learning emphasize the teaching of complex thinking skills (e.g., critical analysis of literature, mathematical problem solving) concurrently with teaching decoding skills, math facts, and grammar. Her teaching strategies reflect high expectations for all students, varied methods and performance opportunities, and flexible and interest-based grouping.

Mrs. Kay's views of children's social and emotional development are also revealed in her practices.

Focus on Development

For example, she attempts to foster child agency, self-regulation, and self-reflection in her approaches to classroom management and problem solving. She creates a cooperative climate for students and their parents in the classroom and school, featuring "trust, humor, responsiveness to individuality, and the nurturing of community" (Weinstein, 2002, p. 142).

Weinstein comments, "here the *development* of student ability is taken seriously—and most important, the teacher takes responsibility for helping children keep up and move up" (2002, p. 142). She contrasts this view with those held by educators who believe that there are limits in students' capacities to learn, leading to the creation of "selection-driven" achievement cultures—in which high achievers are pressed to keep their status and low achievers are repetitively taught lower-order skills. In her book, *Reaching Higher: The Power of Expectations in Schooling*, she describes children's lives in "development-driven" (like Mrs. Kay's) and "selection-driven" achievement cultures. As a student of development, can you imagine what these children's different experiences in school might be like?

classroom teacher must take an active role in the five stages of decision making: prereferral, referral, evaluation, **individualized education plan (IEP)** development, and placement. These stages and their corresponding responsibilities are described here. The Focus on Teaching box on page 504 provides a list of specific tasks for the classroom teacher at each stage.

In addition to these roles, secondary school (middle and high school) teachers play a crucial part in preparing their students for the transition to adult life. Transition services are required for students by age 16 and recommended as early as age 14. As members of the transition planning team, secondary teachers are involved in designing IEPs that specify the curricular components and modifications necessary for successful attainment of postsecondary goals. Along with the other transition team members, they share responsibility for teaching the prerequisite academic and adaptive skills. Given the poor economic and social outcomes for adolescents and adults with exceptionalities (e.g., high dropout rates and low employment rates), the need for effective transition plans and services is acute.

We now discuss some broad recommendations for teaching children with exceptionalities, appropriate for all ages, ranging from young children to those attending high school. Many of these recommended practices—learning centers, computer-assisted instruction, and peer tutoring—were initially designed for general education students and later adapted

Focus on
Teaching

Prereferral Stage

Meet with parents to discuss your concerns (document attempts to contact parents).

Identify possible modifications.

Develop a plan for implementing modifications.

Document student performance (collect samples of student work, test papers, behavioral observations, anecdotal records, etc.).

Gather information from student records (health, previous referrals/testing, attendance, grade retention).

Interview parents, previous teachers, and current professionals who work with the child.

Meet with the team to brainstorm additional modifications, evaluate effectiveness, and/or determine if special education should be considered.

Referral Stage

Provide documentation of modifications/interventions and evidence of success/failure.

Provide documentation of student strengths and needs in:

- Academics (e.g., divergent thinking, problem solving, content areas, handwriting, memory, reading).

Tasks for the Classroom Teacher During the Decision-Making Stages

- Behavior (e.g., activity level, independent skills, emotional state, self-concept, attention, peer relations).
- Communication skills (e.g., language proficiency, speech articulation, written expression, oral expression, listening comprehension).
- Physical characteristics (e.g., physical complaints, sensory impairments, fine motor and gross motor skills).

Evaluation Stage

Continue to collect samples of student work in skill areas and subjects that need attention.

Continue to record observations and anecdotes of student behavior.

Present evaluation information to team members.

Ask questions for clarification if unfamiliar terms are used, particularly professional jargon.

Ask for a written copy of the test report, if none is provided.

Collaborate with the team to determine the following:

- Does performance on standardized tests correspond to classroom performance? If no, why not? Which performance measures are more relevant and why?
- Do evaluation data match eligibility criteria?
- Will the child benefit from special education? If so, how?

---

for children with exceptional needs. Adapting these and other teaching strategies to the learning needs of an increasingly heterogeneous group of students necessitates that teachers acquire a broad repertoire of personal characteristics and professional skills. A brief review of some of the more important personal and professional competencies follows.

Teacher Competencies

What competencies are needed to teach a diverse range of students? Mercer and Mercer (1989) reviewed studies that addressed this question and identified eight principles that seemed to characterize the teaching styles of the most competent teachers. They found that the most competent teachers:

1. Frequently use *direct instruction;* that is, they actively lead student activities, present demonstrations, structure practice opportunities, and provide feedback
2. Emphasize *academic instruction,* so that their students are actively engaged in academic tasks most of the time
3. Structure activities so that students experience *high rates of success*
4. Provide specific *feedback* on correct and incorrect student responses
5. Create a *positive atmosphere* that recognizes student accomplishments

IEP Stage

State the goals, objectives, modifications, and evaluation methods that pertain to the general classroom.

Listen to each others' proposed plans and incorporate them into a written form that is a joint effort.

Discuss how evaluation methods will correspond to grading practices.

Placement Stage

Collaborate with the team to determine the following:

■ What is the least restrictive environment most appropriate for this child?

■ What are the advantages/disadvantages of recommending this placement?

■ What related services (speech therapy, physical therapy, etc.) are needed to support his or her learning?

■ To what extent can professionals team together and provide services in the general classroom, rather than remove the child from the class? Who is responsible for which objectives?

If a "pull-in" approach is used, maximize the effectiveness of both educators:

■ Schedule weekly planning time when both educators can collectively plan lessons.

■ Use creative co-teaching arrangements.

One teach–one "drift"—One person teaches while the other monitors and assists students.

Station teaching—Instructional content is divided into two parts: each person teaches his or her part to half of the class. The student groups are then rotated. Each group receives instruction from both people.

Instruct and outline—One person teaches while the other writes an outline that follows the presentation.

■ Prevent communication problems by practicing effective listening skills.

If a student is not succeeding in his or her current placement despite modifications, document all intervention efforts and initiate referral procedures for possible change of placement.

Source: After Schulz, Carpenter, & Turnbull (1991)

6. Promote student *motivation* through support and encouragement
7. Maintain student *attention* by redirecting them when they are off-task
8. Actively *enjoy* their work and celebrate their students' success

In addition to these personal characteristics and professional skills, competent teachers need a repertoire of general teaching strategies that will accommodate a range of student abilities and needs in the general classroom. Some of these practices focus on **teacher-directed learning** activities, others are **peer-directed,** and still others are self-directed. A greater number of students with special learning needs are being educated in general education classrooms for at least half of the school day. As described in the Focus on Research box on page 506, a teacher's expertise and skills to deliver appropriate instruction for students with special learning needs can affect the degree to which these students are accepted or rejected.

Teacher-Directed Learning

Teacher-directed activities include both instructional methods and classroom accommodations that are planned and implemented by the teacher. Examples of teacher-directed instructional methods are reciprocal instruction, scaffolding, test-teach-test-retest (mastery learning),

Focus on
Research

Teachers' Attitudes Toward Included Students with Mild and Severe Disabilities

The number of students with disabilities who spend at least half of the school day in a general education classroom has increased. Inclusion rates for students with both mild and severe disabilities are also increasing. Thus, general education teachers are assuming more and more responsibility for the education of students with disabilities.

Numerous studies indicate that positive outcomes for students with disabilities are consistently associated with inclusion (Cook, Semmel, & Gerber, 1999; Klinger, Vaughn, Hughes, Schumm, & Elbaum, 1998). General education teachers often lack the training needed to support the learning of students with mild and severe disabilities in their classroom. Additionally, these students often experience high rates of rejection or poor acceptance by nondisabled peers (Vaughn & Elbaum, 1999).

Recently, researchers have begun to study the attitudes of teachers toward included students (Cook, 2001; Cook et al., 1999; Cook, Tankersley, Cook, & Landrum, 2000). Early studies had identified four attitudinal categories that typify teachers descriptions and interactions with students (Brophy & Good, 1974; Good & Brophy, 1972; Silberman, 1971). Students nominated for the *attachment category* generally receive more praise, less criticism, and more process questions from their teachers than their classmates (Good & Brophy, 1972). Those students who fall into the *concern category* also receive a larger share of positive interactions in the classroom, and

teachers "push them to do their best" (Good & Brophy, 1972, p. 621). In contrast, students in the *indifferent category* are often overlooked in the classroom, and they have fewer and briefer interactions with teachers than their classmates. Students in the *rejection category* have the most negative interactions with their teachers. Nominated because of attitudinal, behavioral or academic problems, these students generally receive more criticism focused on behavior and fewer instructional opportunities than other students (Good & Brophy, 1972; Silberman, 1971).

In a recent study, Bryan Cook (2001) explored teachers' attitudes of attachment, concern, indifference, and rejection in relation to students with mild and severe disabilities. Seventy elementary school teachers with included students (totaling 173) were asked to respond to the following questions: If you could keep one student another year for the sheer joy of it, whom would you pick? If you could devote all your attention to a child who concerns you a great deal, whom would you pick? If a parent were to drop by for a conference, whose child would you be least prepared to talk about? If your class was to be reduced by one child, whom would you be relieved to have removed? Teachers were asked to nominate at least three students from their classes to each category, and they were asked to consider, as well, students who spent only part of their day in their classroom.

modeling, concept attainment, direct instruction, learning centers, and computer-assisted instruction. Our discussion of teacher-directed learning will focus on how diversity can be addressed by learning centers, computer-assisted instruction, and classroom accommodations.

Learning Centers

Learning centers provide a way to individualize instruction for all children. Traditional learning centers contain multilevel materials and activities that cover a range of objectives, skills, and interests. Their primary purpose is to teach skills acquisition. Center activities are typically described on task cards, and student progress is measured in terms of skill mastery or acquisition. These activities are beneficial for a range of learners, because they can be completed at the child's own pace and level, independent of others. The tasks generally require different modes of response, tapping a variety of learning strengths and interests. For example, a first-grade learning center on plants may have puzzles, experiments, art

The results showed that included students were overrepresented in three attitudinal categories. The severity of disability also influenced teachers' nominations, but not as predicted. Only 12 of the 173 students were nominated for the attachment category, and a very small number of these students had severe or obvious disabilities (e.g., physical impairments, mental retardation, multiple disabilities, etc.). The remaining students were nominated for the concern (64 percent), indifferent (28 percent), and rejection (38 percent) categories. As discussed, students in the *attachment* and *concern* categories are the most likely to receive the instructional support needed to succeed in the inclusion classroom. Although a high number of included students were nominated for the concern category, it is not clear that the teachers interviewed in this study had the expertise and competencies to use their concern to create a meaningful and appropriate learning environment for these students. Cook speculates that a lack of knowledge and ability to meet the needs of students with disabilities also explained the large number of students assigned to the indifference and rejection categories. These students are least likely to receive the instructional support they need in the inclusive classroom. Interestingly, students with mild or hidden disabilities (e.g., specific learning disabilities) were overrepresented in the indifference and rejection categories. Because these students are not physically different from nondisabled students, teachers do not adjust their expectations. When students with mild or hidden disabilities violate these expectations, teachers respond negatively because they pose unexpected instructional or classroom management problems. Cook argues that a severe and obvious disability protects children from rejection because atypical behavior and performance are anticipated and expected. In other words, there was an excuse or explanation for their behavior.

Research on teachers' attitudes toward included students has several important implications for teacher education and for educational policy. First, it is critical that general education teachers receive training in special education, applied behavioral analysis, and classroom management. Second, it is important to consider teachers' attitudes toward inclusion, as well as their training and knowledge of appropriate instructional strategies for students with mild and severe disabilities, when making placement decisions. It is also important to encourage, if not require, collaboration between general and special educators to assure that appropriate instruction is provided.

Source: Cook (2001).

projects, an assortment of books, and worksheets. In addition, learning center tasks generally range from lower-order thinking (e.g., labeling the parts of a plant, identifying seeds) to higher-order thinking (e.g., comparing growth rates, evaluating the effects of sunlight).

Another type of learning center is an interest development center (Burns, 1985). Interest centers are open-ended and exploratory, not driven by objectives and skills. The purpose is to "expose children to a broadened base of knowledge" and encourage them to apply research skills in pursuing their interests (Burns, 1985, p. 42). The centers contain videotapes, records, filmstrips, journals, books, audiotapes, pamphlets, and written suggestions for experimenting and exploring various topics.

Computer Technology

Teachers report that computer technology can help level the playing field for students with special learning needs in the regular classroom (Hasselbring & Glaser, 2000). In fact, for children with visual and hearing impairments, it may be the only way these children can be included in

A teacher adapts instruction for students with different learning needs.
Source: James Shaffer/Photo Edit.

the regular classroom, unless the teacher has specialized training. For the academically gifted and talented, the Internet expands their learning opportunities well beyond the classroom walls.

Computer-assisted instruction (CAI) has been available for several years. It can be used to support the learning of children with exceptional needs in many ways: tutorials, enrichment activities, recording of student progress, enhancement of memorization skills, and support of written expression. Although CAI has been effective in producing gains in academic achievement, children still require teacher monitoring while using the computer. Children can also engage in CAI activities in cooperative learning groups. Okolo, Bahr, and Rieth (1993) reviewed studies in which the effectiveness of CAI combined with cooperative learning groups was compared with CAI used individually. They found that children's academic performance increased significantly when they used CAI in the cooperative learning groups rather than individually. The researchers also noted that the students made social gains.

Computer software can also be used to support the development of various writing and language skills. Hunt-Berg, Rankin, and Beukelman (1994) described the following: speech synthesis with pronunciation editing and visual highlighting of read text; spell checking; spelling assistance that signals incorrect spellings; spelling modifications; word dictionaries, prewriting support (e.g., brainstorming activities, guidelines for specific writing styles, and outliners); grammar correction, and tutorials. Research indicates that children with disabilities related to written expression are more likely to revise and edit their work on a word processor than on handwritten drafts (Hasslebring & Glaser, 2000). Word-processing software is also beneficial for students who have difficulty writing legibly.

Hyperlinks and multimedia environments also appear to have benefits for students with special learning needs. Hyperlinks enable students to access electronically linked information with a click of a mouse. As you might expect, students with disabilities are more likely to perform electronic than text-based searches for information. With hypertext, students can click on words they do not recognize or understand and receive immediate assistance. Multimedia software can help enhance students' conceptions of ideas by using visual imagery and sound effects. These technologies are particularly effective for students with learning disabilities. Multimedia software also enables students with disabilities to collaborate on meaningful learning projects with other students. However, as we discussed in Chapter 4, these technologies are most effective when they actively engage students in the learning process.

For students with auditory, visual, or communication impairments, technology is opening new avenues for learning. The specialized technology of augmentative or alternative communication (ACC) devices makes it possible for students with no speech or with poor speech to communicate with others. Video captioning and captioned education programs are helping students with learning disabilities to read. Optical character recognition (OCR) technology can scan and read text aloud. This technology allows students with visual impairments greater access to various learning materials and to read them independently.

In sum, many many new computer technologies are now available to create new learning opportunities for students with special learning needs (e.g., see Male 2003, for a comprehensive review). However, widespread use of these technologies is limited by cost and inadequate teacher training (Hasselbring & Glaser, 2000). Additionally, many school systems today must seek external funding for complex technical equipment, due to limited resources from state and federal agencies.

Classroom Accommodations

Classroom accommodations are minor modifications that can be easily implemented in the general classroom to target students' specific needs. Accommodations may target problems in learning (such as test taking, auditory perception, visual perception, fine motor skills) or problems in behavior that impede learning (such as inattention, acting inappropriately, inability to adjust to change, and lack of self-esteem).

Some common behavioral problems warrant additional accommodations. For example, some children engage in disruptive, inappropriate behavior in an attempt to obtain peer attention. In such cases, any one of a variety of accommodations may help. The teacher could avoid paying attention to (reinforcing) disruptive behavior by any of the following means: attending only to the appropriate behavior, teaching conflict resolution, teaching social skills, or modeling appropriate ways to gain another's attention.

Transitions from activity to activity and from class to class are other areas of difficulty for many children. They may spend too much time gathering and organizing their materials, or they may seem agitated during the transition. Some students have difficulty focusing their attention after the transition, whereas others may persevere on the previous task, refusing to leave it for the new task.

For children experiencing self-concept concerns accommodations that develop self-esteem are needed. In these cases, the teacher can do the following: plan activities that allow the student to demonstrate his or her strengths; use frequent and specific positive reinforcement (e.g., "I like the way you didn't give up, even though this task was challenging

Adaptations with technology are helping children with learning disabilities achieve success in the regular classroom.
Source: Stephen McBrady/ Photo Edit.

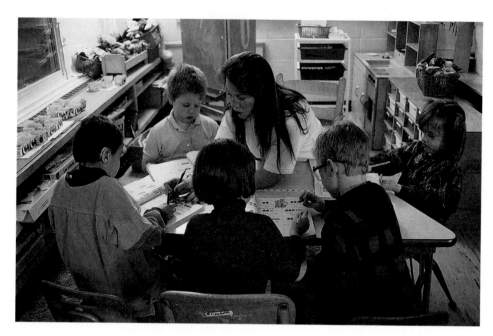

Cooperative learning activities such as this one are one way of accommodating exceptional learners in the regular classroom.
Source: Ellen B. Senisi/Photo Researchers.

for you. You really stuck to it!"); support the student in identifying and developing interests and strengths; structure tasks for success by breaking them down into smaller, more manageable units.

Many local school districts and state departments of education provide extensive lists of classroom accommodations that are typically included on the child's IEP. The possibilities are virtually endless and beyond the scope of this chapter.

Peer-Directed Learning

In addition to learning from their teachers, children naturally learn from one another. Examples of ways teachers can structure student interaction are cooperative learning, peer tutoring, or a buddy system (Wood, 1993). Peer-directed learning is particularly useful for children who need to develop social skills.

Cooperative Learning

Cooperative learning has been the most successful and popular technique for integrating exceptional children into general classrooms. In cooperative learning, heterogeneous groups of four to six children join together to accomplish a mutual goal. Tasks are divided so that each child contributes, using a particular talent or skill to create a group product (e.g., a multimedia project on explorers, a worksheet containing mathematical computations). Students work interdependently while the teacher monitors individuals. While working together, students communicate ideas, share resources, support one another, resolve conflicts that may emerge, and evaluate each person's contribution.

Cooperative learning can be used for all academic areas and with any learner. It has been successful with every exceptionality, including with children having severe and multiple disabilities (Salisbury, Palombaro, & Hollowood, 1993) and children who are deaf-blind (Downing & Eichinger, 1990). We discussed cooperative learning as a method for improving peer relations in Chapter 7.

Peer Tutoring

Tutors may be selected from the same class (same-age tutors), or across grade levels (cross-age tutors). A variety of possible tutorial arrangements are possible. Children with disabilities can serve as cross-age tutors of younger children without disabilities. Children without disabilities can serve as same-age or cross-age tutors of children with disabilities. Three-way tutorials among same-age children with disabilities have been successfully used to develop reading skills (Harris & Aldridge, 1983).

Peer tutoring is not intended to supplant teacher instruction, but to supplement it. An ideal use of tutorials is to serve as practice sessions for reviewing, reinforcing, and evaluating skills and concepts that have been introduced by the teacher. Careful selection, training, and planning is required before tutorial sessions. Goals, objectives, and evaluation criteria are essential ingredients. Despite the initial time investment, many teachers find that the long-term benefits of peer tutoring are rewarding for both the tutor and tutee. "The advantages associated with peer tutoring are that it encourages social acceptance, enables explanation of assignments in student terms, increases the tutor's own learning (through teaching)" (Wood, 1993, p. 193).

Buddy System

In this system, teachers assign a "buddy" for children who benefit from a one-on-one relationship. This could be any child, but typically buddies are used for children with emotional and behavioral disorders, sensory impairments, physical disabilities, or severe and multiple disabilities. It is essential that buddies be given specific instructions as to the amount and type of assistance they are to provide. The purpose of a buddy is to provide assistance in learning, behavior, or general classroom functioning. For example, buddies can help by taking class notes, explaining directions for assignments, reading difficult material, offering encouragement during stressful incidents, retrieving materials, or dictating test items.

Self-Directed Learning

In this section we focus on ways children can be more involved and accountable for directing their own learning. These activities teach children how to learn on their own. The purpose is to actively involve the learner, increase self-knowledge, and facilitate generalization of what has been learned. Two strategies for accomplishing this objective are learning strategies training and self-management instruction.

Learning Strategies Training

Learning strategies are the mental schemes students use to memorize, solve problems, plan, and organize their learning. As discussed in Chapter 4, cognitive strategies that help acquire and structure information can be directly taught to children who are experiencing academic problems. Strategy training is most beneficial for adolescents who are developmentally ready to spontaneously apply the strategies they have learned (Alley & Deshler, 1979). Examples of some learning strategies are mnemonics and SQ3R.

Mnemonics (Mastropieri & Scruggs, 1994) are used to improve memory and to recall important concepts by linking unfamiliar information to familiar information. There are several different mnemonic methods, two of which are described here. Keyword mnemonics can be applied to teaching new vocabulary words. For example, to learn that dahlia is a type of flower, the word *dahlia* is first recorded to the keyword *doll. Doll* is a good keyword for *dahlia* because it sounds like the first part of *dahlia* and is easily pictured. The learner is then shown (or asked to imagine) a picture of the keyword and the referent interacting; in this case, the student perhaps can picture a doll sniffing a flower. It is important that the keyword be associated with the referent in the picture and not simply pictured with it. Thus, although a picture containing a doll and a flower may not be sufficient to facilitate the association, a doll sniffing, picking, or otherwise interacting with the flower is more likely to facilitate the association. Finally, the retrieval process should be explicitly described to the student: "When you hear the word *dahlia,* remember the keyword *doll,* remember the picture of the doll, and think of what else was in the picture. The doll sniffing the flower means that dahlia is a kind of flower." (pp. 172–173).

Letter strategies (Mastropieri & Scruggs, 1994) are used to recall lists or categories of information. *Acronyms* are a type of letter strategy in which each letter represents the first letter of a word in the list. An example is *homes,* an acronym for memorizing the Great Lakes: *H*uron, *O*ntario, *M*ichigan, *E*rie, and *S*uperior. Another letter strategy recommended by Mastropieri and Scruggs (1994) is making an *acrostic,* using some of the letters to form a motto or title. As an example, they use an acrostic for memorizing the planets in the solar system, "'My very educated mother just served us nine pizzas,' stands for Mercury, Venus, Earth, etc." (p. 271).

SQ3R is used to acquire study skills essential to comprehending written information. *SQ3R* is an acronym for the following five-step process (Strichart, 1993):

- **Survey.** Skim the titles, headings, subheadings, subtitles, chapter introduction and summary, graphs, and figures.
- **Question.** Turn headings into questions *(who, what, where, when, why, how).* Try to answer the questions.
- **Read.** Read the content for the purpose of answering the questions, highlight the answers, and write them down.
- **Recite.** First, read the question and answer aloud. Then, read the question and state the answer without seeing it. Practice these steps a few times.
- **Review.** Practice the recitation steps every day, for at least 3 days. Practice more often if necessary.

Self-Management Instruction

Self-management instruction has been effective in improving a variety of behaviors, ranging from increasing attention (on-task behavior), to increasing accuracy of academic work, to reducing disruptive behavior. Self-management techniques are systematically taught and include the following: self-instruction, self-monitoring, and self-evaluation. **Self-instruction** teaches a child to use private speech to guide himself through a task in a step-by-step manner. Following is an example of a child with attention and impulse control problems who has been taught to apply self-management techniques while completing independent seatwork. Before using this strategy, he rushed through his work, overlooked some of the items, and produced too many errors. Now, while working at his desk, he engages in an inner dialogue:

"What is it I have to do? I have to concentrate, think only of my work. Be careful, look at one at a time. Good—I got it! Am I following my plan . . . did I look at each one? That's okay . . . even if I make an error I can back up and go slowly." (Harris, 1982, p. 6)

Self-monitoring teaches a child to record his or her performance. Using the preceding example, a child could self-monitor by checking off each worksheet item as he completed it. **Self-evaluation,** the third technique, teaches how to evaluate one's own performance. In our example, the child could tally the number of checked items as well as record the accuracy of his answers. He could compare these results to his target goal of attaining a minimum accuracy of, say, 85 percent. For additional reading, Bauer and Sapona (1991) give in-depth coverage on methods for teaching self-management skills.

Schooling and Development

Fostering Resiliency in Children and Adolescents

Schools play an important role in fostering in young people. As discussed in earlier chapters, resiliency is commonly defined as a person's ability to develop competence in the face of adversity and hardship (Masten & Coatsworth, 1998). In other words, resilience is characterized as "good outcomes in spite of serious threats to adaptation or development" (Masten, 2001). We have learned that families can promote children's positive development when they provide close affectionate relationships, models of appropriate behavior, and support and supervision. However, we have also learned that family circumstances can sometimes threaten children's well-being and healthy development. See the Focus on Research box on page 514 for ways children, schools can help promote resilient actions. A favorite teacher or a coach can become an important role model for children experiencing difficulty at home or needing extra attention. The resiliency-building capacity of schools is a relatively new area of research (Henderson & Milstein, 1996). In this section, we will examine how schools can foster resiliency in youth, regardless of family circumstances.

Resilient youth have a number of defining characteristics (Henderson & Milstein, 1996; Masten, 2001; Masten & Coatsworth, 1998; Werner & Smith, 1992). The ones most commonly mentioned across research studies include:

- **Social competence.** Resilient children have easygoing dispositions, and they easily adapt to different situations. They are socially skilled and able to attract the attention, support, and affection they need from peers, parents, and other adults.
- **Cognitive competence.** Resilient children have good problem-solving and intellectual abilities. They take initiative, set realistic goals, and monitor their progress. They are also resourceful in seeking help from others and in avoiding risky or harmful circumstances.
- **Positive self-perceptions.** Resilient children are confident in their abilities to succeed. They have a sense of purpose and foresee a positive future for themselves.

It is also important to emphasize that resiliency is not just a list of individual child traits and characteristics—it is process (Henderson & Milstein, 1996; Luthar, 2003). Resiliency is learned and supported in families, schools, and communities.

Masten (2001) concludes a review of research on resilience with the statement:

> Resilience does not come from rare and special qualities, but from the everyday magic of ordinary, normative human resources in the minds, brains, and bodies of children, in their families and relationships, and in their communities. (p. 235)

However, we must ensure that this "ordinary magic" is available. A study conducted by Gutman, Sameroff, and Cole (2003) examined influences of child characteristics (e.g., intelligence,

Focus on
Research

Beating the Odds

One of the pioneering studies of childhood resilience was conducted by Emmy E. Werner and Ruth Smith (1992) on the Hawaiian island of Kauai. They followed the development of 698 infants from their birth in 1955 through their early thirties. Approximately half of the infants grew up in poverty, and one of six was diagnosed with a physical or mental handicap before the age of 2. By age 10, two-thirds of the high-risk infants had developed serious learning or behavioral problems. Twenty-two of these children (13 males and 9 females) had been diagnosed with a learning disability, which included ADHD in this study. By grade 12, most of this group had a history of poor academic performance and serious underachievement. At ages 17 and 18, they also scored significantly lower than their peers on measures of socialization and responsibility, achievement motivation, and self-assurance. Only one in four of the children diagnosed as learning disabled showed a more positive profile by age 18. These young people attributed their successful adaptation to the "sustained emotional support of family members, peer friends, or

elders who bolstered their self-esteem" (p. 21). In contrast, most of the other teens with learning disabilities stated that special education teachers, counselors, and mental health professions were of "little help."

In the course of following these individuals into adulthood, the researchers made some interesting discoveries. By adulthood, the life course of individuals with childhood learning disabilities had significantly improved. No one was unemployed or dependent on public assistance. As adolescents, roughly two-thirds of the sample had a delinquency record or a serious mental health problem. At age 32, less than 10 percent had criminal records or persistent mental health problems. And by age 40, three out of four individuals with childhood learning disabilities were judged to be making an "adequate to good" adaptation to the demands of work, marriage, and family life (p. 21). There were several different clusters of protective factors operating in the lives of these individuals:

■ Cluster 1 included temperamental characteristics of the individual that helped him or her to elicit positive

mental health) on academic progress throughout the school years (grades 1 through 12). Results showed that children's characteristics were significant in promoting grades, but not their commitment to school (i.e., number of absences). Furthermore, these characteristics did not *protect* children who were at high risk. As shown in Figure 9.4, school absences showed a steady upward turn for high-risk students. Based on these findings, the authors suggest that alleviating social risks in children's lives is more effective than focusing solely on strengthening children's personal characteristics.

How can schools foster resiliency? Any effort that increases young people's social skills, cognitive abilities, and self-perceptions helps to foster resiliency. Research has identified a number of school characteristics that can foster resiliency and positive development (Bernard, 1991; Comer, 1984, 2004; Henderson & Milstein, 1996; Rutter, Maughan, Mortimore, Ouston, & Smith, 1979):

■ **Encourage strong commitment and connections to school.** Numerous studies show that a positive connection to the school environment or to teachers functions as a protective factor in young people's lives. Youths who report strong attachment to their schools are less likely to engage in problem behaviors and to drop out of school. When schools are safe, supportive, and caring communities, young people are more likely to form a connection to school.

■ **Set and communicate high expectations.** Research on both successful schools and youth resiliency emphasizes the importance of setting high expectations for all students.

responses from a variety of caring persons: parents, teachers, friends, spouses, and coworkers.

■ Cluster 2 included special skills and talents as well as the motivation to use efficiently whatever abilities they had; faith that the odds could be overcome; realistic educational and vocational plans; and regular chores and domestic responsibilities assumed as children and teenagers.

■ Cluster 3 included characteristics and caregiving styles of parents, especially the mother, that reflected competence and fostered self-esteem in their offspring, and structures and rules in the household that gave their children a sense of security.

■ Cluster 4 consisted of supportive adults who fostered trust and acted as gatekeepers for the future. Among these "surrogate" parents were grandparents, elder mentors, youth leaders, and members of church groups.

■ Cluster 5 consisted of openings of opportunities to major life transitions—from high school to the workplace, from civilian to military life, from single to married status and parenthood—that put the life trajectories of the majority of individuals with learning disabilities on the path to successful adult adaptation.

It is unfortunate that this list of protective factors does not include schooling experiences. These findings underscore the important role schools need to play in fostering self-esteem and efficacy, creating supportive relationships, engendering a sense of security and trust, developing competencies, and providing new opportunities for the future. Werner and Smith's study of Kauaian children teaches us that a substantial number of children with developmental disabilities and disadvantages can "beat the odds" when they have various protective factors from which they can draw.

Source: Adapted from Werner & Smith (1992).

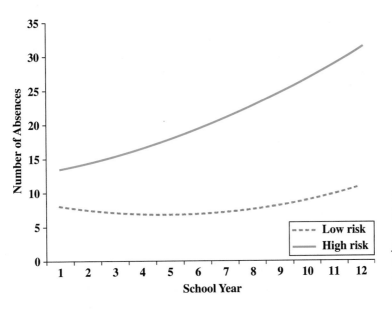

■ FIGURE 9.4

Number of Absences from 1st Grade to 12th Grade for Students with High and Low Risk
Source: From Gutman, Sameroff, & Cole (2003).

Schools with high expectations for behavior and achievement have lower rates of delinquency, drug use, teen pregnancy, and other problem behaviors. Through relationships that convey high expectations, students learn to believe in themselves.

- **Provide meaningful learning opportunities.** Schools that foster young people's resiliency provide opportunities to engage in meaningful learning activities that are related to their interests, culture, and developmental levels. Young people need opportunities for problem solving, goal setting, critical inquiry, self-reflection, and helping others. Grouping practices need to be inclusive and to promote cooperation and shared responsibility for learning.
- **Opportunities for participation.** Young people need opportunities for meaningful involvement and participation within the school. They need opportunities for leadership, for helping others, and for determining policies that affect them. Participation in athletics, extracurricular activities, and school governance can foster a sense of belonging and connection for young people.

In summary, children grow up in many overlapping worlds: families, peers, schools, and communities. Each context has its own set of risk and protective factors. Schools have the power and resources to promote the development of competency and resiliency in youth. We will look further at components of successful schools in the next section.

 ## Schools Make a Difference

Creating Successful Schools for Children

Recognition of the multiple influences on children's success in school has led to a renewal of efforts to create new connections between schools, families, and neighborhoods to improve student learning (Blank, Shah, Johnson, Blackwell, & Ganley, 2005). Some of these efforts are based on the belief that children and youth develop best within loving families and under the protection of safe, supportive communities. "Full-service" (Zigler & Hall, 2000) or "21st-century community schools" have been established, built on John Dewey's (1902) vision of the school as center of the community along with contemporary developmental perspectives discussed in this text. The CoZi model described earlier is an example. According to Blank and his colleagues (2005), several factors fuel the growth of the community schools approach to education today: (a) demographic changes (e.g., increases in ethnic minority populations), (b) parent and neighborhood concerns (e.g., about low levels of student performance), (c) public engagement (e.g., schools reaching out to the community for help), (d) the after-school movement (e.g., recognition that children need safe places for activities and extra learning opportunities after school), and (e) "challenges at the schoolhouse door" (e.g., family problems, poverty, mental health problems, violence). Enhanced awareness that quality early childhood programs also contribute to school success also may play a role (Zigler & Hall, 2000). These factors, along with the recognition that we have common goals and interests in the development of children and youth, require that schools and communities work together to achieve those goals.

The Coalition for Community Schools (2000) has developed a framework and vision for designing schools across the country. It is not considered a "model" but a resource to be used to help decide what will work in individual communities. Such a community school, operating in a public school building, might be open year-round and provide services to students, families, and community members before and after school (e.g., family resource center, health clinic, child care). The school curriculum is expected to use the assets and problems of the community as a primary resource to engage student learning. It is difficult to estimate the number of schools using this framework because of the uniqueness of the various approaches; however, recent reports show a rise in the number of schools with after-school programs and health centers.

The Coalition (2003) recently established five essential conditions for learning based on research:

Condition 1. The school has a core instructional program with qualified teachers, a challenging curriculum, and high standards and expectations for students.

Condition 2. Students are motivated and engaged in learning—both in school and in community settings, during and after school.

Condition 3. The basic physical, mental, and emotional health needs of children and their families are recognized and addressed.

Condition 4. There is mutual respect and effective collaboration among parents, families, and school staff.

Condition 5. Community engagement, together with school efforts, promotes a school climate that is safe, supportive, and respectful and that connects students to a broader learning community.

We expect that these conditions for learning and development will sound familiar to the reader. Some reports show promising improvements in achievement, attendance, and parental involvement, as well as reductions in suspensions, high-risk behaviors, and neighborhood violence in community schools (e.g., Blank et al., 2005; Dryfoos, 2000).

Another way to look at what works in schools is to examine their components. Researchers have systematically examined the effects of structural and process components on student outcomes. Studies on *structural* components of elementary schools have shown that factors such as class size, teacher–child ratios, and teacher preparation are associated with children's academic and social outcomes (Bogard & Takanishi, 2005). Research on *process* components in schools and classrooms shows that factors such as teacher sensitivity and the quality of teacher–child interactions are also related to child outcomes. Pianta (2007) argues that the process features—how teachers teach, speak, and interact with children—tend to be more robust predictors of children's learning and development relative to structural features.

For example, research shows that qualities of classroom instruction and teacher--student relations influence children's achievement and motivation in the early elementary grades. For example, Deborah Stipek and her colleagues (Stipek et al., 1998; Stipek, Feiler, Daniels, & Milburn, 1995) have contrasted the effects of didactic versus child-centered instruction. A **didactic instructional approach** is defined by those teachers who provide high levels of direct instruction and who play a central role in selecting activities, providing instruction, and defining rules. The focus of instruction is basic-skill and factual-knowledge acquisition. On the other hand, teachers using a **child-centered instructional approach** serve as partners in children's learning, providing direction and guidance to help children develop their knowledge while providing opportunities for children to take responsibility for their own learning. Teacher–student relations are characterized by warmth, nurturance, and support.

Children actively participate in learning experiences with the guidance of a teacher.
Source: ThinkStock/PunchStock.

Research contrasting these different approaches has not provided consistent support for either approach on children's motivation and learning in the early grades (Hamre & Pianta, 2005; Rutter & Maughan, 2002; Stipek et al., 1995, 1998). Not surprisingly, Stipek and colleagues reported (1995, 1998) that children taught by didactic methods made significant gains in reading skills, whereas children in the child-centered classes outperformed their counterparts on problem solving, oral language, and conceptual grouping tasks. Only marginal differences were found for mathematics achievement. With regard to motivation, differences were found related to achievement expectancies, negative affect, compliance, and discipline. For these measures, the differences favored children taught by child-centered methods. Thus, a didactic instructional approach in the early years of elementary school has motivational costs that need to be considered in relation to children's academic gains.

The National Association of Education of Young Children (NAEYC) advocates for educational approaches that are similar to the child-centered approach just described. Based on developmental theory and research, The NAEYC formulated a Position Statement in 1997 describing principles of **developmentally appropriate practice** for programs serving children from birth to age 8. Table 9.1 on pages 519–521 provides examples of appropriate practices for children in the preschool and primary-grade years derived from these principles (Bredekamp & Copple, 1997). Note that this table includes policy recommendations for assisting children with making transitions between teachers and settings. One critical transition is from home and preschool to elementary school.

Creating Successful Schools for Young Adolescents

The middle school years are a critical turning point in young people's lives. Early adolescence is an important time for youth to adjust to a rapidly changing body, learn new cognitive skills, form positive social relationships, develop a positive sense of self, and forge a

TABLE 9.1 Examples of Developmentally Appropriate Practices

	Appropriate Practices for 3- Through 5-Year-Olds	Appropriate Practices for 6- Through 8-Year-Olds
Creating a Caring Community of Learners *Promoting a positive climate for learning*	**Ex.** Teachers help children learn how to establish positive, constructive relationships with adults and other children. *Fostering a cohesive group and meeting individual needs* **Ex.** Responsiveness to differences in children's abilities and interests is evident in the curriculum, adults' interactions, and the environment. Teachers bring each child's home culture and language into the shared culture of the school so that children feel accepted.	**Ex.** Children learn personal responsibility, how to develop constructive relationships, and respect for individual and cultural differences. *Building a democratic community* **Ex.** Class meetings occur regularly and children participate in group decision making. Children work on group activities, such as a school recycling project.
Teaching to Enhance Development and Learning *Environment and schedule*	**Ex.** Teachers prepare a learning environment that fosters children's initiative, active exploration of materials, and sustained engagement with other children and adults.	**Ex.** Teachers plan so that children can learn through active involvement in various learning experiences with each other, with adults, and with a variety of materials.
Teaching strategies	**Ex.** Teachers extend children's thinking and learning within child-initiated activities by posing problems, asking questions, making suggestions, adding complexity to tasks, and providing information, materials, and assistance as needed	**Ex.** Teachers use a variety of active, intellectually engaging strategies, including posing problems, asking thought-provoking questions, adding complexity to tasks, and engaging in reciprocal discussion in which they take children seriously.
Motivation and guidance	**Ex.** Teachers draw on children's curiosity and desire to make sense of their world to motivate them. Teachers facilitate the development of social skills, self-control, and	**Ex.** Teachers draw on children's eagerness to make sense of the world and to acquire competence by engaging them in interesting and challenging learning

(Continued)

TABLE 9.1   Examples of Developmentally Appropriate Practices (Continued)

	self-regulations by using positive guidance techniques.	experiences . . . Teachers promote children's development of respect for others, conscience, and self-control through positive guidance techniques, such as involving children in setting rules for social living and conflict resolutions, redirecting behavior, etc.
Learning experiences	**Ex.** Teachers plan a variety of concrete learning experiences with materials and people relevant to children's own life experiences. Materials include blocks, books, dramatic-play props, art materials, science tools, etc.	
Language and communication	**Ex.** Teachers encourage children's developing language by talking with them throughout the day, engaging them in conversations about real experiences, projects, and current events, and they respond to children's initiatives.	
Constructing Appropriate Curriculum *Integrated curriculum*	**Ex.** Content from various disciplines, such as math, science, or social studies, is integrated through themes, projects, play, and other learning experiences.	**Ex.** The curriculum is organized and integrated so that children acquire deeper understandings of key concepts, skills, and tools of inquiry of each subject area, so as to be able to and see apply their knowledge, connections between disciplines. Field trips and visits from community resource people are planned to enable children to do direct investigation (e.g., social studies project involving operating a store).
The continuum of development and learning	**Ex.** The curriculum plan is designed to help children explore and acquire tools of inquiry of the various disciplines in ways that are comprehensible for their age. For example, science experiences include exploration and direct observation.	
Coherent, effective curriculum and content	**Ex.** Teachers use a variety of approaches to develop children's *language and literacy skills* through meaningful experiences, such as listening to and reading stories, taking field trips, dictating stories, participating in dramatic play, etc.	**Ex.** Children have numerous opportunities to read or hear high-quality children's literature and nonfiction for pleasure and information; discuss readings; draw, dictate, and write about their experiences; plan and implement projects involving

TABLE 9.1 (Continued)

	Opportunities to develop *aesthetic expression* through art and music, *gross and fine motor skills* through play, and *self-help skills* are provided daily.	research at suitable levels of difficulty, etc. Math skills and meaningful problem solving are fostered through play, projects, and situations of daily living. Social studies topics are the focus on in-depth work for an extended time period. Science is a major part of the curriculum, building on children's interests. Art, music, drama, dance, and other fine arts are the explicit focus of study at times. Physical education and health and safety projects are integral parts of the curriculum.
Assessing Children's Learning and Development	**Ex.** Teachers use observational assessment of children's progress, examination of their work samples, and documentation of their development and learning to plan and adapt curriculum, identify children who may have a learning problem, and communicate with parents.	**Ex.** Teachers assess each child's learning progress primarily through written records of observation and evaluation of work samples collected systematically. Results are used to improve and individualize instruction. Teachers involve children in evaluating and revising their own work. Teachers solicit parent's knowledge about children's learning.
Reciprocal Relationships with Parents	**Ex.** Teachers work in partnerships with parents, communicating regularly to build mutual understanding and ensure that children's needs are met.	**Ex.** Teachers view parents as partners in the educational process, and have time for periodic conferences. Parents' visits to school are welcomed at all times.
Policies	**Ex.** The program ensures continuity of care and relationships among adults and children over a given day and across many months and even years.	**Ex.** Children are assigned to a primary teacher and remain in relatively smalls groups. The classroom teacher works with any specialists who supplement the regular program and colleagues who have special expertise. Teachers assist children in making transitions from one grade or group to the next.

Source: After Bredekamp & Copple (1997).

personal code of ethics and morality (Eccles & Midgley, 1989; Jackson & Davis, 2000). As discussed earlier in this chapter, negative changes in children's motivation, achievement, and social adjustment often occur with the transition to middle school. In a groundbreaking report, *Turning Points: Preparing American Youth for the 21st Century* (Carnegie Council on Adolescent Development, 1989), a group of educators, researchers, policy makers, and media leaders concluded that middle schools are "potentially society's most powerful force to recapture millions of youths adrift" (p. 32).

There is now considerable consensus on the characteristics of successful schools for young adolescents (Carnegie Council on Adolescent Development, 1989; Jackson & Davis, 2000; Lipsitz, Mizell, Jackson, & Austin, 1997; Meece, et al., 2003; Midgley & Edelin, 1998; National Middle School Association, 1995). Several key recommendations of the most recent report of the Carnegie Foundation of New York, *Turning Points 2000,* for ensuring the success of young adolescent learners are outline as follows:

- **Organize relationships for learning to create a climate of intellectual development and a caring community of shared educational purpose.** Large schools should be divided into smaller learning communities, with teams of teachers and students as the underlying organizational structure. Students' viewpoints on issues are valued, respected, and nurtured, as they negotiate and forge their new ways of viewing themselves. Team efforts should have a common goal of building a strong learning community, where students feel safe, connected, and supported, as well as encouraged to achieve high standards of excellence.
- **Teach a curriculum grounded in rigorous, public academic standards for what students should know and be able to do, relevant to the concerns of adolescents and based on how students learn best**. Considerations of both excellence and equity should guide every decision regarding what will be taught. Curriculum should be based on content standards and organized around concepts and principles. At the same time, young adolescents are *active* learners. They enjoy learning activities that provide opportunities to engage in problem solving, inquiry, and applying knowledge to their lives outside of school. Classroom activities that involve passive forms of learning, such as lecturing and memorizing facts, can negatively affect class engagement. Flexible scheduling enables students to participate in collaborative learning and inquiry- or project-based instruction.
- **Use instructional methods designed to prepare all students to achieve higher standards and become lifelong learners.** To be effective, instruction should mesh with three other aspects of teaching and learning: the standards and resulting curriculum outlining what students should learn; the assessments students will use to demonstrate their knowledge and skills; and the needs, interests, and learning styles of the students themselves. Classes should include students of diverse needs, achievement levels, interests, and learning styles; instruction should be differentiated to take advantage of the diversity of students.
- **Opportunities to learn with and from peers.** Young adolescents thrive on opportunities to learn with peers. Cooperative and collaborative learning in the middle-grades classroom has important academic, motivational, and social benefits. By working with others, students have opportunities to discuss, explain, justify, and receive feedback from others. With young adolescents, teachers may need to assign roles for group members (e.g., leader, recorder, resource finder, reporter, etc.) and carefully monitor groups to encourage equal participation.
- **Schoolwide policies and efforts that foster health, wellness, and safety.** Schools that foster physical and psychological safety facilitate the development of resiliency in young people. Specialized professionals, as well as teachers, should be

Focus on
Research

Why Do Students Leave School?

Recent data places the current national high school dropout rate at 10.3 percent (National Center for Educational Statistics, 2006). This figure can range as high as 23 percent for Hispanic students, and blacks are nearly twice as likely as whites to drop out of school. Approximately two-thirds of high school dropouts leave school before the 10th grade (National Center for Educational Statistics, 2001). Consequently, the ninth grade is a particularly critical transition. Students who experience severe academic and behavioral difficulties in the first year of high school are at elevated risk for high school dropout, and if retained in ninth grade, the probability of dropout is even greater (Letgers & Kerr, 2001).

For many young adolescents, the pathway to high school dropout begins in elementary or middle school when the experience difficulty keeping up with their peers, behavioral problems, or difficulty "fitting in" with the school environment. Sociologists Karl Alexander and Doris Entwisle (1988) refer to high school dropout as a process rather than an event. Older nonwhite minorities, male, and low-income students are at greater risk for early high school dropout than other students (Wehlage & Rutter, 1986). Grade retention, low academic performance, frequent school absences, antisocial peers, and deviant behavior also play a role in shaping the pathway toward leaving high school (Rumberger, 2001).

Although family and student characteristics may predispose certain groups toward dropping out of school, there is general agreement among scholars that the high school environment plays a critical role as well. For example, using national data from the High School and Beyond study in the early 1980s, Wehlage and Rutter (1986) reported that students who dropped out of high school viewed teachers as uninterested in students, and school

discipline as ineffective and unfair. Studies of ethnic minority youth also document how unsupportive teacher relations, discriminatory practices, noninclusive curriculum materials, and inappropriate instructional methods can undermine the academic achievement and school engagement of ethnic minority students (Eccles, Wong, & Peck, 2006; Meece & Kurtz-Costes, 2001). In contrast, Lee and Burkam (2003) found that students are less likely to drop out of schools that enroll greater than 1,500 students, offer more challenging and fewer remedial courses, and encourage positive relations between teachers and students. Similarly, using a motivation model of high school completion, Hardre and Reeve (2002) reported how rural students were less likely to formulate plans to drop out when school environments engendered feelings of support, belonging, competence, and self-determination (see Chapter 6). Taken together, these findings are consistent with the view that some high schools create conditions that "push out" students (Cairns & Cairns, 1994; Fine, 1991).

High school reform is currently in the national spotlight, and many efforts are targeting the ninth-grade transition. Letgers and Kerr (2001) compiled a set of practices to promote ninth-grade success. The strategies included smaller learning communities (e.g., career or first-year academies), extra instruction or academic coaching in core subjects as needed, special seminars to help students learn social or academic skills needed to be successful in high school, homeroom advisory groups, student-centered teaching approaches (e.g., cooperative or project-based learning), and elimination of tracking systems. Many of these strategies characterize high school environments that also foster high levels of student engagement and motivation (National Research Council & The Institutes of Medicine, 2004).

readily available to offer the assistance young people need in negotiating adjustments in and outside of school. Middle schools, in partnership with community agencies, should provide health education as well as access to medical and mental health services.

■ **Involve parents and communities in supporting student learning and healthy development.** Schools and families need to collaborate to provide continuity in expectations and services. Communication between home and school is essential to

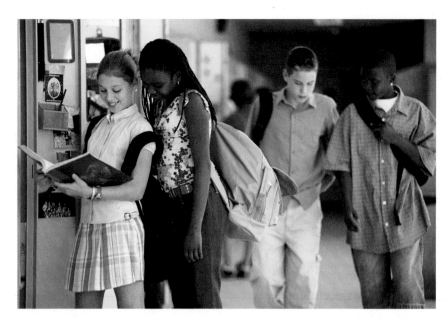

Students feel safe, connected, and supported in successful schools.
Source: Creatas/PunchStock.

monitor and support students' schoolwork and progress and to expand learning opportunities beyond regular school hours and outside school walls. (Jackson & Davis, 2000, pp. 23–24; National Middle School Association, 1995, Rural Early Adolescent Learning, 2004)

Many of these recommendations are also included in the National Middle School Association's *This We Believe: Developmentally Responsive Middle Level Schools* (1995). Included in this document is the recommendation that educators of middle school students have a shared vision, set high expectations for all students, and serve as an advocate for their students. Together, the recommendations discussed in this section provide a framework for what works best for helping young adolescent learners achieve success.

Creating Successful Schools for High School Students

As students enter high school, they encounter a large school environment, a complex social setting, a diverse student body, and a wide range of curriculum choices and extracurricular activities. As described earlier, many young people encounter difficulty navigating the transition to high school (Eccles, 2004). For example, current reports indicate that only 32 percent of adolescents leave high school qualified to attend 4-year colleges (Green & Foster, 2003), and one-third of high school students who attend colleges need remedial education courses (National Center of Education Statistics, 2003). A large number of high school students report that they are not very interested in school or motivated to learn (National Research Council & The Institutes of Medicine, 2004; Steinberg, 1996). Additionally, approximately 70 percent of all students in public high schools today graduate with a high school diploma, and these figures differ greatly by ethnicity. A study of the class of 2002 showed that 78 percent of white students graduated from high school, while 56 percent of African American and 52 percent of Latino students did (Greene, 2005). Furthermore, approximately two-thirds of high school dropouts will leave before the 10th grade (National Center of Education Statistics, 2001).

While family and student characteristics can predispose certain groups toward dropping out of school, there is general consensus among scholars that the high school environment itself plays a critical role. For example, an early study reported that students who dropped out of high school viewed teachers as uninterested and school discipline as ineffective or unfair (Wehlage & Rutter, 1986). See the Focus on Research box on page 523 for more information about why students leave school. Other evidence suggests that students are less likely to drop out of schools that (a) enroll fewer than 1500 students, (b) offer challenging and fewer remedial courses, and (c) encourage positive relations between teachers and students (Lee & Burkam, 2003).

Due to large numbers of high school students who leave school unprepared to further their education or to enter the workplace, high school reform is currently in the national spotlight. Over the past years, states, public agencies, and private foundations, such as the Bill and Melinda Gates Foundation, have been investing billions in raising high school graduate rates and increasing college preparedness. Current research emphasizes the importance of comprehensive schoolwide reform to be successful in achieving results, especially for the most challenging students. In 2004, a national panel of experts identified several dimensions of successful schools for adolescents (National Research Council & The Institutes of Medicine, 2004 (pp. 1–9)). The key dimensions included:

- **Create small learning communities that foster personalized and continuous relationships between teachers and students.** Supportive personal relationships are critical in promoting and maintaining student engagement and learning. School personnel need to promote an environment of trust and respect, where disrespectful behavior among students is not tolerated.
- **Maintain high academic standards for all students.** A critical norm that must be shared by all school personnel is that all students, regardless of ability levels and socioeconomic backgrounds, can learn and improve their achievement. An intellectual climate that challenges students and communicates high expectations for learning is essential.
- **Provide support and resources to help all students achieve high standards of excellence.** Support can be provided through individualized instruction, tutoring, and summer programs for students to help them progress in their skills.
- **High school courses and instructional methods must be designed in ways that increase adolescent engagement and learning.** Students stay engaged in learning when instruction is varied and appropriately challenging for them, when they are active learners, and when instruction draws on students' preexisting understandings, interests, cultures, and real-world experiences.
- **Use ongoing assessments of students' understanding and skills to monitor the effectiveness of curriculum and instructional practices, and students' progress.** Tests that are used to evaluate students need to assess high-level critical thinking, conceptual understanding, and application of knowledge.
- **Both formal and informal tracking by ability should be eliminated.** Alternative strategies such as differentiated instruction, computer-based instruction, peer teaching, and co-teaching with special education or language specialist should be utilized rather than tracking programs.
- **Draw on parents, religious institutions, and other community resources to enrich the high school curriculum and help students see the real-world meaningfulness of school learning.** It is particularly important to develop connections with health and social services in the community to facilitate students' access to the services they need.

■ **School guidance and counseling responsibilities need to be distributed among school staff, supported by school counselors and other professionals.** It is important for school personnel to serve as advocates for students, and to connect them to the guidance, psychological, and social services they need.

As you may have noticed, many of the recommendations suggested for older adolescents are quite similar to those needed by their younger peers. Even as they approach young adulthood, older adolescent learners need knowledgeable, skilled, and caring adult relationships; a school curriculum that is challenging, meaningful, and relevant to their lives; a school environment that promotes a sense of belonging and connection; and strong links to the community for services that meet their nonacademic needs. Unlike middle schools, high schools often assume a greater responsibility for preparing youth for the transition to postsecondary education and employment. Upward Bound and service learning programs, as well as career academies, have been helpful in this regard (Kemple, 2001; Myers & Schirm, 1999; National Research Council & The Institutes of Medicine, 2004). Nevertheless, throughout the research on secondary schools is the underlying theme that the social context of schools matters just as much as curriculum and instruction in the overall success of adolescent learners. What also emerges is the idea that school personnel must assume *collective responsibility* for the learning and well-being of all students (Lee, 2001; National Research Council & The Institutes of Medicine, 2004). Some school reform advocates argue that this responsibility extends beyond local school officials to state, business, and political leaders, as well as postsecondary institutions. This view is best summarized by a recent call for action from the 2005 National Education Summit on High Schools:

> This action agenda to ensure the readiness of our high school students for college, work, and citizenship is ambitious, but the need for action has never not been more clear or urgent. . . . We must not let the difficulty of the task sway us from taking the right course. We owe it to our youth and our nation to redesign the American high school and make it a cutting-edge institution again. The future health of our economy and democracy depends on our answering this call to action. (Conklin, Curran, & Gandal 2005, p. 21)

Conclusion: Successful Schools

There is national consensus on the need for twenty-first-century schools to offer more than academic instruction to foster success in school and life for all children (e.g., Greenberg et al., 2003). We have learned that we must be careful about focusing too narrowly on fostering academic achievement without simultaneously attending to children's social and emotional development (e.g., Elias, Zins, Graczyk, Weissberg, 2003; Elkind, 2005; Greenberg et al., 2003). This method simply doesn't work. Schools are increasingly expected to implement effective educational approaches that promote academic success, enhance health, and prevent behavioral problems. Fortunately, as we have seen, there are school reform models available today demonstrating positive influences in the lives of children and adolescents. We have seen that it is possible for twenty-first-century schools—with the support of educators, families, communities, policy makers, and others in the ecosystem—to educate students to become knowledgeable, thoughtful, caring, responsible, healthy, and contributing citizens. It is not easy. In the next section, we will introduce educators to some excellent professional organizations and resources to aid in this difficult, but worthy and satisfying, endeavor.

Teachers play an important role in advocating on the behalf of their students.
Source: Comstock/PictureQuest.

Child Advocacy and Resources

Teachers as Advocates for Children and Youth

Children are seldom able to advocate for themselves, so adults must step up to safeguard and improve their welfare. Teachers advocate for children and youth naturally as part of their role, sometimes without acknowledging that this is what they do. **Child advocates** are "those who press for reforms that will result in better lives for children, or for the maintenance of the status quo in areas in which children are being well served by existing policies and practices" (Zigler & Hall, 2000, p. 39). Advocates can be individuals or groups, and can be involved at any level—local, state, or federal—at which decisions regarding practices and policies affecting children and families are made. They might be concerned with improving the well-being of children in general, or they may be concerned with a single issue, such as policies for identifying and serving the needs of gifted children and youth. Without advocacy, there can be no changes in the ways that educational institutions operate (Zigler & Hall, 2000). Some individual or group must ensure that representatives responsible for policy making and the general public become aware of a need or problem and press for improvements.

The largest volunteer child advocacy association in the United States is the national Parent Teacher Association (PTA), with over 6 million members. The PTA cooperates with many national education, health, safety, and child advocacy groups to bring a "powerful voice to speak on behalf of every child while providing the best tools for parents to help their children be successful students" (PTA, 2006). The PTA is open to all adults who care about children (e.g., parents, grandparents, teachers, school administrators, mentors, caregivers, community leaders) and works to help children succeed academically and personally in schools. State and national PTAs also bring current information about issues affecting children to public attention through websites and other avenues, and provide excellent resources for teachers.

Teachers can also get involved in advocating for children and youth in simple ways, without taking much precious time away from other responsibilities. One method is to get involved in "pajama politics"—a term coined by Pam Fielding, president of a grassroots advocacy consulting firm E-Advocates, to describe how citizens can make a difference in the legislative process at any time from the comfort of their homes. For example, the National Education Association (NEA) can alert members by e-mail about proposed legislation and direct them to the Legislative Action Center on the website, where they can send ready-made messages to their representatives. Personal experiences can also be included in these messages. A recent article in *NEA Today*, titled "The E-Mail That Roared," relates an inspiring anecdote about a teacher who shared her experiences with a struggling third grader who was just beginning to learn English. She did not anticipate that her story would be read by NEA President Reg Weaver as part of testimony urging Congress to modify No Child Left Behind (NCLB) (Long, 2006). This is just one way that educators who care passionately about their students can make a difference. These opportunities are also provided through other professional organizations; a few are briefly introduced next.

Resources for Teachers

The *National Education Association (NEA)*, www.nea.org, is the nation's largest teacher organization, with 3.2 million members in 2006. As mentioned, this association provides opportunities for educators (including prospective teachers), parents, and others to become aware of and respond to current issues affecting children and youth in schools. The NEA also provides a wealth of resources for effective teaching.

The *National Association for the Education of Young Children (NAEYC)*, www.naeyc.org, is the world's largest association working on behalf of young children, with nearly 100,000 members in 2006. NAEYC is dedicated to enhancing the well-being of children, with a focus on improving the quality of educational and developmental services for children from birth through age 8. It provides opportunities for advocacy and professional development as well as resources and guidelines for implementing developmentally appropriate practices.

The *National Middle School Association (NMSA)*, www.nmsa.org, represents educators and community leaders throughout the world who are committed to the educational and developmental needs of young adolescents. The NMSA provides a voice, key resources, and professional development opportunities for middle-level educators.

The *National Dissemination Center for Children with Disabilities (NICHCY)*, www.nichcy.org, serves the nation with a central source of information on disabilities in children and youth. It also provides current information about IDEA and NCLB as they relate to children with disabilities, and research as it applies to effective educational practices and intervention services. In addition, educators and parents can locate resources and other related organizations through this website.

The *Center for Psychology in Schools and Education (CPSE)*, www.apa.org/ed/cpse, serves as a liaison between the American Psychological Association (APA) and other educational and scientific organizations and federal agencies. The mission of CPSE includes generating public awareness, advocacy, and research to enhance educational and developmental opportunities for students at all levels of schooling. For example, it provides information about attributes for school success, including the "other 3 R's: Resilience, Responsibility, and Reasoning," as well as resources to assist educators with teaching gifted children and adolescents. The APA also provides a wealth of information on current issues affecting children, youth, and families via www.apa.org/topics/topicchildren.

The *Collaborative for Academic, Social, and Emotional Learning (CASEL)*, www.casel.org, provides information and resources for enhancing children's success in school and life based on current research. CASEL focuses on the promotion of social, emotional, and academic learning in preschool through high school. Educators can also find out about how other schools are effectively implementing SEL practices through this source.

The *Yale Child Study Center* provides information about two school reform efforts discussed in this text: the *Comer School Development Program* (www.med.yale.edu/comer) and the *School of the 21st Century* (www.yale.edu/bushcenter/21C). Details about the principles and practices in model schools are made available, as well as professional development opportunities and products to assist with implementing effective practices.

Rethinking Schools, www.rethinkingschools.org, offers insightful articles and publications on critical education issues along with opportunities for teachers to network.

The *What Works Clearinghouse (WWC)*, www.whatworks.ed.gov, was established in 2002 by the U.S. Department of Education's *Institute of Educational Sciences (IES)* to provide educators, policy makers, and the public with a central informational source of scientific evidence on what works in education. Reviews of studies on effective educational interventions (programs, products, practices, and policies) are available on a variety of topics, such as reading interventions, English-language learning, middle school math curricula, dropout prevention, and character education.

■ Chapter Summary

Why Educators Study Development

- Teacher and school characteristics that foster student learning can be development can be examined from an ecological perspective. Model programs based on an understanding of children's development, such as comer's School Development Program, have enhanced student academic performance and social behavior.
- Teacher–student relationships impact student adjustment and achievement throughout the school years. Teacher–student interactions are affected by classroom management contexts and teacher views of development.

Teaching Students with Special Learning Needs

- The process of identifying and serving children with exceptional needs occurs in stages—namely, prereferral, referral, evaluation, individualized education plan (IEP), placement, and review. As a member of a multidisciplinary team, a classroom teacher plays an active role throughout the decision-making process.
- In order to teach a diverse group of learners, teachers must have a repertoire of teaching strategies, including learning centers, computer-assisted instruction, classroom accommodations, cooperative learning, peer tutoring, buddy systems, learning strategies training, and self-management instruction.

Schooling and Development

- Schools play an important role in fostering resiliency in youth. Any effort that enhances children's cognitive abilities, social competence, and self-esteem builds resiliency. Schools can foster resiliency by encouraging a strong connection to school, communicating high expectations, providing meaningful learning opportunities, and encouraging participation.

■ Qualities of successful community schools and developmentally appropriate classroom practices for children and adolescents have been identified, such as small learning communities, instruction linked to real-world experiences, and support from a variety of professionals.

Child Advocacy and Resources

■ Teachers are natural child advocates, and have access to a variety of resources and support systems. Many state and national professional and parent organizations offer assistance as well as information.

■ Key Terms

child advocates *(p. 527)*
child-centered instructional approach *(p. 517)*
computer-assisted instruction (CAI) *(p. 508)*
developmentally appropriate practice *(p. 518)*

didactic instructional approach *(p. 517)*
ecological perspective *(p. 499)*
individualized education plan (IEP) *(p. 503)*
learning centers *(p. 506)*
peer-directed learning *(p. 505)*

self-evaluation *(p. 513)*
self-instruction *(p. 512)*
self-monitoring *(p. 513)*
teacher-directed learning *(p. 505)*

■ Activities

1. Conduct informal interviews with one or two students from elementary, middle, and high school levels. Ask students to describe qualities of a good teacher ("What is a good teacher like?"). Analyze responses in terms of the qualities mentioned in the "Teacher–Student Relations" section of this chapter. Compare your interviewees' responses with those of your classmates. Did the teacher qualities described differ by age or school level?

2. Interview a teacher about the accommodations he or she makes to assist children with special learning needs. Inquire about a range of teacher-directed, peer-directed, and self-directed instructional activities and their effectiveness.

3. Review the examples of developmentally appropriate practices provided in Table 9.1 of this chapter. Observe an elementary school classroom for several hours on at least two different occasions, and describe the extent to which some of the practices you observed fit the examples shown in the table.

4. Visit the National Middle School Association's website (www.nmsa.org) or the National Education Association's website (www.nea.org). Provide a list of resources helpful for implementing *one* of the key recommendations for creating successful schools for young or older adolescents described in this chapter.

Glossary

A

ability grouping   The practice in elementary school of grouping children according to their presumed academic ability; thought by some, when not used in conjunction with other grouping possibilities, to stigmatize and limit children's potential, particularly minority students, at an early age; see *tracking*.

accommodation   A term used by Piaget to describe how children change existing schemes by altering old ways of thinking or acting to fit new information in their environment; contrast with *assimilation*.

achievement motivation   An internal mechanism that energizes, directs, and terminates achievement behavior; explained by theorists variously as an enduring psychological need, an environmentally activated state, or a set of cognitions and beliefs.

action research   Research conducted by teachers, administrators, and other change agents in the school to improve the educational environment for their students. The goal of action research is to understand a specific problem or to improve teaching practices within a specific classroom or school setting.

adaptation   One of two basic principles referred to by Piaget as invariant functions; the ability of all organisms to adapt their mental representations or behavior to fit environmental demands; contrast with *organization*.

adolescent egocentrism   A cognitive limitation emerging in adolescence, characterized by difficulty distinguishing thoughts about one's own thinking from thinking about the thoughts of others. This limitation may manifest itself in heightened self-absorption and self-consciousness.

age norms   The estimated age, often established by *cross-sectional studies,* at which certain psychological or behavioral characteristics emerge.

aggression   Behavior that is intentionally aimed at harming or injuring another person; see *instrumental aggression, hostile aggression*.

alphabetic system   The structure of some languages, including English, whereby single shapes in the written language make up letters, which in turn, are linked to specific sounds; contrast with *ideographic system*.

amniotic sac   A structure present at implantation of the zygote that begins to function and mature during the embryonic period. See *placenta*.

androgens   Sex hormones generally associated with male characteristics, yet produced and present in both sexes.

androgyny   A blend of masculine and feminine traits that develops gradually as young people mature and become more flexible in their attitudes toward *gender-typed behaviors* through encounters with new activities and interests.

animism   According to Piaget, children's inclination during the *preoperational stage* to attribute intentional states and human characteristics to inanimate objects.

anorexia nervosa   An eating disorder, mainly affecting adolescent girls between the ages of 14 and 18, characterized by a 25 to 50 percent loss in body weight through excessive dieting and exercise; usually treated with a combination of hospitalization and family counseling.

assimilated   A personal attitude and stance of a minority member characterized by adopting the norms, attitudes, and behaviors of the dominant culture and rejecting one's ethnic or racial culture.

assimilation   A term used by Piaget to describe how children mold new information to fit their existing schemes in order to better adapt to their environment; contrast with *accommodation*.

attachment   The close, affective relationship formed between a child and one or more caregivers.

attention deficit hyperactive disorders (ADHD)   Behavior, diagnosed by a qualified professional, characterized by inattention, impulsivity, and unusual or excessive activity.

attribution theory   A cognitive theory of motivation that examines how individuals interpret their successes and failures in achievement situations.

authentic assessment   A currently preferred performance assessment method with the underlying principle that students are more apt to understand a concept that has real-life application.

authoritarian parenting   A parenting style characterized by rigid rules and often unrealistic expectations for children; contrast with *authoritative* and *permissive.* It is high on the demand/control dimension but low on acceptance/responsiveness. It is also characterized by low warmth and little positive involvement. Rigid rules are set with the expectation they will be followed due to parental authority.

authoritative   A parenting style characterized by high levels of warmth, acceptance, and responsiveness as well as reasonable expectations for children and firmly enforced rules; contrast with *authoritarian* and *permissive.*

authoritative parenting   A style of parenting characterized by warm, responsive involvement, and the setting of appropriate and clear standards for behavior. The child's autonomy is encouraged by providing rationales for rules and showing respect for his or her rights and opinions.

autism   A lifelong developmental disability that is neurologically based and affects the functioning of the brain; disabilities vary from mild to severe and include deficits in verbal and nonverbal communication, problems with reciprocal social interaction, and a restrictive set of activities and interests.

automaticity   A factor in the development of children's attentional processes whereby familiarity with an object or task allows them to use it or perform without thinking.

Autonomy   The ability to be independent and self-motivated; to control and assume responsibility for one's own actions.

B

basic emotions   Fundamental emotional reactions or expressions that are limited to fear, joy, anger, and surprise; contrast with *self-conscious emotions.*

basic sense of trust   In Erikson's theory, the first stage of psychosocial development, in which infants must form a sense that their caregivers and their environment are safe, secure, and predictable; establishes a foundation for confidence in one's self. See Table 6.1.

behavioral geneticist   Scientists who study the degree to which psychological traits, such as sociability, aggression, and mental abilities, are inherited.

biculturalism   The maintaining of ties of both the dominant and ethnic culture and developing an identity that allows the child to alternate between dominant and ethnic identities depending on the situation.

bidilectal   An ability to speak several varieties of English, including *SAE* and a home *dialect.*

bilingual   The ability to speak two languages.

bilingual-bicultural program   A learning program focused on producing balanced learners who are competent in both English and their home language; contrast with *transitional bilingual program.*

bilingual education   A perspective or approach to teaching children that uses at least two languages during instruction, usually a child's native language and the second language the child is acquiring.

binge drinking   Drinking five or more alcoholic drinks in a row.

birth order   The child's position in the family, whether born first, second, last, and so forth.

blended family   A family configuration that includes a biological parent, stepparent, and child. It is formed when two partners bring together children from a previous marriage.

blind   Those who have either 20/200 vision or a 20 percent or less field of vision; see *low vision.*

bulimia nervosa   An eating disorder characterized by binge eating followed by vomiting or use of laxatives to purge the body; more common among older teens and young adults. This disorder generally is associated with a distorted body image and an inability to control one's impulses; treatable through family and individual therapy.

bullying behavior   The most common form of aggression, often taking the form of embarrassing people, hitting, destroying property, and ridiculing.

C

case study   A research design for in-depth investigation of a person or small group of individuals; not a reliable source for generalized statements beyond those investigated in the study.

causal relationship   When the results of a study indicate there is a systematic cause-and-effect result between two factors.

centration   A developmental limitation present during the *preoperational stage* that makes young children focus their attention on only one aspect, usually the most salient, of a stimulus.

cephalocaudal   One of two patterns characterizing growth in infancy; growth begins at the head and proceeds downward. As a result, the infant's brain, neck, and trunk develop before the legs.

character education   A direct approach to teaching core values and virtues, such as responsibility, respect, honesty, cooperation, and compassion.

child-centered instructional approach   An instructional approach whereby teachers serve as facilitators and partners in children's learning by guiding their learning and enabling them to take greater and greater responsibility for their learning; contrast with *didactic instructional approach.*

chromosomes   The structures that carry the genes; composed of long threadlike molecules of deoxyribonucleic acid (DNA).

chronosystem   Term used by Bronfenbrenner to refer to involving the timing and patterning of events in an individual's life and the position of that individual's life in the larger flow of historical time.

circular reactions   Piaget's term for patterns of behavior during the *sensorimotor stage* that are repeated over and over again as goal-directed actions.

class inclusion   A concept acquired during the *concrete operational stage* that involves children's understanding of hierarchies; knowledge that objects in a subcategory (tulips) must be smaller than the superordinate category (flowers).

classical conditioning   A behavioral principle of learning by which a new response is learned through the pairing of two stimuli. The response that naturally occurs in the presence of one stimulus (food) that begins to occur following the presentation of a second stimulus (bell) when the two stimuli are repeatedly paired.

classification   A mental operation achieved during the *concrete operational stage* that allows children to impose order on their environment by grouping things and ideas according to common elements.

clinical interview method   An interview technique attributed to Piaget of probing children's reasoning processes; a way of combining *performance assessments* and *interviews.*

clique   A small peer group, generally same sex and same race, that has a clear social structure with one or two members serving as leaders.

code-switching   A personal attitude and stance, usually by a minority member, characterized by successful shuttling between the dominant and one's ethnic or racial culture.

coercive family process   A family dynamic characterized by inconsistent, ineffective, or punitive parental discipline during early development that leads to aggressive behavior in children.

cognitive behavior modification   Meichenbaum's developmental program that helps children control and regulate their behavior; children are taught self-regulatory strategies to use as a verbal tool to inhibit impulses, control impulses and frustration, and promote reflection.

collective monologue   A characteristic conversational pattern of preschoolers who are unable to take the perspective of others and thus make little effort to modify their speech for their listener so that remarks to each other seem unrelated.

communication disorders   Specific impairments in speech and/or language.

communicative competence   Learning to use language in an appropriate manner; knowing what words and structures to use on what occasion. This is the major area of linguistic growth during childhood, through adolescence, and continuing into adulthood.

compensation   One of three basic mental operations including *negation* and *identity* needed to perform Piagetian *conservation* tasks; a form of *reversibility* that involves an understanding that one operation can compensate for the effects of another operation. In Piaget's *conservation* of liquid task, the height of one glass can compensate for the breadth of another glass.

componential intelligence   One of three components of intellectual behavior in Sternberg's *triarchic model of intelligence* involving such skills as the ability to allocate mental resources, to encode and store information, to plan and monitor, to identify problems, and to acquire new knowledge; contrast with *experimental intelligence* and *contextual intelligence.*

comprehension   An active process in which readers strive to construct a meaningful interpretation of written or oral information.

computer-assisted instruction (CAI)   Instructional assistance provided by computer software or specialized devices such as alternative communication devices or optical character recognition; type of instruction often used to support children with special needs in the regular education classroom.

concrete operational stage   The period of life from 7 to 11 years old when, Piaget believed, children's thinking becomes less rigid, and they begin to use mental operations, such as *classification, conservation,* and *seriation* to think about events and objects in their environment.

conditional knowledge   Children's understanding about why learning strategies are effective in specific situations; contrast with *declarative knowledge* and *procedural knowledge.*

conduct disorders   A pattern of behaviors characterized by overt aggression, disruptive or antisocial behavior, and/or serious violations of rules. Caused by a complex set of environmental and biological influences, the behavior pattern causes serious impairments in social and academic function.

conflict resolution program   School-based intervention program designed to help students acquire the skills they need to resolve conflict; components include defining the problem, brainstorming about possible solutions, and choosing solutions that benefit both sides (called win-win solutions).

conservation A mental operation in the *concrete operational stage* that involves the understanding that an entity remains the same despite superficial changes in its form or physical appearance.

constructivist approach An approach to learning purporting that children must construct their own understandings of the world in which they live. Teachers guide this process through focusing attention, posing questions, and stretching children's thinking; information must be mentally acted on, manipulated, and transformed by learners in order to have meaning.

context knowledge A *decoding* strategy; using the surrounding text and one's background knowledge to identify an unknown word; contrast with *phonic knowledge* and *sight word knowledge.*

contextual intelligence One of three components of intellectual behavior in Sternberg's *triarchic model of intelligence* involving the ability to adapt to a changing environment or to shape the environment to capitalize on one's abilities or skills; contrast with *componential intelligence* and *experiential intelligence;* also see *practical intelligence.*

conventional level According to Kohlberg, the second level of moral judgment, characterized by individuals who accept society's rules for right and wrong and obey authority figures; contrast with *preconventional level* and *postconventional level.*

core-knowledge theories A type of cognitive theory that attempts to explain the sophistication of young children's reasoning about domains important for survival and everyday interactions, such as living things (biology), inanimate objects (physics), and the mind (psychology). Children use core-knowledge theories to predict and explain their world.

corporal punishment Use of physical punishment with the intention of causing a child to experience physical pain, but not injury; used as a means for reducing or eliminating undesirable behavior in children.

corregulation Control of behavior shared by parents and children; develops in middle childhood.

correlational coefficient The statistic that measures the strength of relations between two measures (e.g., self-esteem and school achievement); expressed in a positive or negative ratio from 1.0 to +1.0.

correlational study A widely used design for developmental research studying what different factors influence one another or go together; such studies are not able to test cause-and-effect hypotheses.

critical literacy The ability to use written language to solve problems and to communicate.

critical period (1) Periods of development during which certain basic structures are formed or a child is most vulnerable or responsive to environmental influences. (2) Lenneberg's hypothesis that language development has a biological basis and there is a time in infancy when particular neurological faculties develop. It states that if certain internal or external conditions related to language development are missing, then a child will never be able to acquire language.

cross-sectional study A study that gathers information simultaneously on one or more aspects of development among children of different age groups.

cross-sequential study A study that follows a group of different-aged children for 2 or 3 years; can reliably identify antecedents and stability of behavior patterns during the course of the study.

crowds The largest adolescent group that is made up of individuals with similar reputations and stereotyped identities that is not conducive to close interpersonal relations.

crystallized intelligence In intelligence theories, one of two kinds of intelligence that develops from learning experiences; measured by word fluency, general information, and vocabulary and verbal comprehension; contrast with *fluid intelligence.*

cumulative deficit effect A phenomenon found in some studies showing that under poor environmental conditions, differences in IQ scores among races increase with age.

D

deaf Those who cannot hear or understand speech; see *hard of hearing.*

deaf-blindness A condition characterized by the unique debilitating effects of hearing and vision impairments.

declarative knowledge Children's understanding about what learning strategies are available to help them; contrast with *procedural knowledge* and *conditional knowledge.*

decoding The process that readers use to determine the oral equivalent of written words.

deferred imitation A Piagetian concept in *representational thinking* in which children are able to repeat a simple sequence of actions or sounds after the sequence is observed; an early form of *representational thinking.*

deoxyribonucleic acid (DNA) Long threadlike molecules that twist around to form a double helix and make up chromosomes; believed to contain about 100,000 genes, the basic units of heredity; see *dominant gene* and *recessive gene.*

dependent variable   The outcome measure or variable in a research study.

depression   An affective disorder characterized by disturbances in cognitive and behavioral functioning that last longer than 2 or 3 weeks; symptoms include an inability to concentrate, feelings of hopelessness, weight changes, an inability to have fun, and thoughts of death.

development   The systematic and successive changes that follow a logical or orderly pattern over a long period of time and enhance a child's adaptation to the environment.

developmental dyscalculia   A condition or disorder that causes difficulty in mathematics; a deficit in the processing of numerical and arithmetic information related to neurological impairments.

developmentally appropriate practices   A phrase used to describe teaching strategies, curricula, discipline practices, learning approaches, classroom environments, and interpersonal relationships that promote children's development at all ages.

dialect   A variation of a single language spoken by members of a speech community; contrast with *accent;* see *social dialect.*

didactic instructional approach   An instructional approach defined by high levels of teacher instruction, structure, and control; teachers play a central role in selecting activities, instructing students, and determining classroom rules; contrast with *child-centered instruction;* see also *direct instruction* and *teacher-directed instruction.*

direct instruction   A teaching strategy in which the teacher explains, demonstrates, and then provides supervised practice for a learning task.

discontinuous process   The emergence of drives, needs, and cognitive processes in a series of discrete stages of maturation that influence the way a child relates to the environment; psychoanalytic and cognitive development (Piagetian) theories argue that development is a series of discrete stages.

dizygotic twins   Two siblings who come from separate eggs that are released at the same time from an ovary and are fertilized; also known as fraternal twins.

dominant gene   A gene inherited from one parent, such as brown hair, that will mask the expression of a *recessive gene* from the other parent.

down syndrome   A genetic disorder of varying degree that is due to the presence of an extra twenty-first chromosome or a piece of one, causes a range of physical and mental handicaps, and occurs in 1 out of 800 live births. Mothers over the age of 35 have an increased risk of conceiving a child with this disorder, because of their longer exposure to environmental substances. The presence of this abnormality can be detected through the genetic screening process of amniocentesis in the fourth month of pregnancy.

dynamic assessment   A type of assessment that assesses a child's learning potential and developing processes through the use of progressively more challenging and continuous feedback; a type of assessment used to assess a child's learning potential; contrast with *static assessment.*

dyslexia   A condition that causes difficulty with reading or writing in spite of normal or above-average cognitive abilities.

E

ecological perspective   Bronfenbrenner's contextual or systems model of development that embeds the developing child in nested layers of social systems, from the family and school to the larger cultural, economic, and historical contexts.

ectoderm   The outermost layer of the embryonic structure that will develop into the nervous system and skin.

effectance motivation   According to White, an inherent need that propels individuals to engage in activities from which they can derive a sense of personal mastery or competence.

egocentric speech   One of three stages of children's use of language identified by Vygotsky, during which children begin to use speech to regulate their behavior and thinking through spoken-aloud self-verbalizations; contrast with *social speech* and *inner speech.*

ego-oriented goals   See *performance-oriented goals.*

egocentrism   The tendency to think about, see, and understand the world from one's own perspective; an inability to see objects or situations from another's perspective.

elaboration   A memory encoding strategy in which one forms a personally meaningful mental image of items to be remembered.

embryonic period   The second stage of prenatal development marked by the implantation of the *zygote* and lasting from weeks 2 to 8, during which all the basic structures of the child (the central nervous system, the skeleton, and the internal organs) are established and begin to function.

emergent literacy   The concept that literacy learning is ongoing from birth.

emotion-focused coping   A coping strategy that involves expressing emotions, seeking solace and support from others, and avoiding stressful situations.

emotional competence   The understanding, expression, and regulation of emotions. Also called emotional intelligence.

emotional maltreatment   Rejection and consistent lack of concern for another's emotional well-being.

emotional or behavior disorders   Characterized by significantly different psychosocial development from one's peers, including hyperactivity, aggression, withdrawal, immaturity, and learning difficulties.

empathy   The ability to know and feel another person's emotional state.

encode   To process information and place into memory through the use of cognitive strategies such as *elaboration, organization,* and *rehearsal.*

endoderm   The innermost layer of the embryonic structure that will develop into the digestive tract and vital organs.

English as a second language (ESL)   A special language-learning program for nonnative speakers that focuses narrowly on learning the target language.

entity theory of ability   A theory of intelligence, proposed by Dweck, whereby students believe their ability level is fixed and cannot be improved through practice or effort; contrast with *incremental theory of ability.*

episodic memory   Long-term memory storage of personal or autobiographical events or information, as well as information about the place, time, and order of events.

equilibration   Piaget's concept that refers to our innate tendency of self-regulation to keep our mental representations in balance by adjusting them to maintain organization and stability in our environment through the processes of *accommodation* and *assimilation.*

estrogens   Sex hormones generally associated with female characteristics, yet produced and present in both sexes; crucial to the maturation of the reproductive system, breast development, and the onset of ovulation and menstruation in females.

ethic of care   Gilligan's argument that women are socialized to take responsibility for the well-being of others and therefore emphasize connections between people as well as justice.

ethnic identity   Refers to one's sense of self concerning racial or ethnic group membership.

ethnicity   Refers to a group of people, such as Japanese, Cuban, or Italian, who share a common nationality, cultural heritage, and language; contrast with *race.*

event sampling   A technique used to record observations of a certain selected behavior, such as aggression.

exceptionality   An umbrella term to describe all who receive special education—children with disabilities as well as children who are gifted.

exosystem   In Bronfenbrenner's theory, the system that influences the child's development only indirectly.

expectancy-value theory   A cognitive model of motivation stressing that individuals are more apt to engage in and persist at learning activities when they expect and want to succeed.

experiential intelligence   One of three components of intellectual behavior in Sternberg's *triarchic model of intelligence* involving the ability to cope with new situations in an effective, efficient, and insightful manner; contrast with *componential intelligence* and *contextual intelligence.*

experimental study   After careful selection and matching on a number of variables, participants are randomly assigned to either an experimental or a control group to measure any difference between the groups for a particular outcome, known as the dependent variable; any significant variance between the two groups' outcome measure would support the hypothesis that the treatment caused the outcome.

expert versus novice studies   A research paradigm that shows that more knowledgeable individuals are better able than novices to group or organize information in meaningful patterns and suggests that advances in children's thinking processes are explained by both quantitative changes in their thinking processes and qualitative changes in how knowledge is organized.

external locus of control   A pattern of attributing events to factors outside one's control; a characteristic of children with learning disabilities; see *locus of causality.*

externalizing problems   The kinds of difficulties a majority of children with emotional and behavioral disorders experience, including argumentative, aggressive, antisocial, and destructive actions; contrast with *internalizing problems.*

extrinsic motivation   A need to learn or act that rises from external contingencies, such as winning an award, parental demands, or to achieve a high grade; contrast with *intrinsic motivation.*

F

false belief problems   Social situations that present difficulties for young children because they are not able to understand that another person will act on beliefs that differ from their own are false from their point of view.

familialism   The strong identification with and attachment to both the nuclear and extended family, and the feelings of loyalty, respect, duty, and reciprocity that accompany such familial attachment.

family structure   The configuration of people who live together in a given family unit.

feeling of inferiority   In Erikson's fourth stage of psychosocial development, children 7 to 11 years old can develop negative attitudes about their abilities and competencies if a parallel internal *sense of industry* is not encouraged (see Table 6.1).

fetal period The third and longest stage of prenatal development, from 8 weeks until birth, during which time the fetus increases in size; eyelids, fingernails, taste buds, and hair form; and the respiratory system matures to enable breathing after birth.

fine motor skills Involve small body movements and small muscle coordination and control.

fluid intelligence In intelligence theories, one of two kinds of intelligence that reflects innate cognitive abilities; measured by the speed of information processing, memory processes, ability to detect relationships, and other abstract thinking skills; contrast with *crystallized intelligence.*

formal logic The development during the *formal operational stage* of the cognitive tools for solving many types of logical problems; examples are *propositional* and *hypothetico-deductive thinking.*

formal operational stage The period of life between 11 and 12 years of age and onward, during which, Piaget believed, children begin to apply formal rules of logic and gain the ability to think abstractly and reflectively; thinking shifts from the real to the possible; see *formal logic.*

fragile-X syndrome A genetic disorder more common in male than female offspring due to the presence of an X chromosome that appears to be pinched or very thin in one area and is likely to break during cell division. May cause mild retardation in females; will cause varying degrees of retardation in males and is associated with both physical (cleft palate, eye disorders) and mental (hyperactivity) deficits. This disorder can be detected through genetic screening.

functionally literate Able to read and write well enough to negotiate daily life.

G

gender constancy The understanding by around age 4 or 5 that one's sex is permanent and cannot be altered by changes in clothing, hairstyle, or activities.

gender-role conceptions The images we have of ourselves as males and females.

gender-role identity Children's perceptions of themselves as a female or male.

gender-role socialization The process by which children learn the attitudes and behavior that society defines as appropriate for their gender; see *gender-typed behavior.* Same as sex-role socialization.

gender schema Children's understanding of gender and gender-role expectations.

gender-typed behavior Preferences demonstrated by the age of 3 for choosing toys and activities; can be influenced by stereotypical social values.

general intellectual factor In intelligence theories, the idea that a general ability factor (g) underlies all intellectual functioning. Someone with a high general intelligence is expected to do well on all intellectual tests.

generalizability An important determination, in judging the quality of a study, of whether or not the findings apply or do not apply to groups other than the one studied.

gene A unit of the chromosome by which hereditary characteristics are transmitted.

genotype A person's genetic characteristics as determined by the genes a person inherits from both parents for any particular trait; contrast with *phenotype.*

germinal period The first stage of prenatal development, encompassing the first 2 weeks of fetal development. The fertilized egg rapidly divides, travels down the fallopian tube to the uterus, and prepares for implantation.

giftedness Individuals identified with a minimal IQ score of about 130 and above-average academic achievement, usually 2 years above grade level.

goal theory of motivation A cognitive theory of motivation that emphasizes students' personal reasons for choosing, performing, and persisting at various achievement levels.

grammar Language rules that extend from the simplest level of combining sounds to the complex level of extended conversations including phonology, semantics, syntax, pragmatics, and the lexicon; see Figure 5.1.

gross motor skills Involve the movement of the head, body, legs, arms, and large muscles; see Table 2.7.

guided participation Rogoff's term used to describe transferring responsibility for a task from the skilled partner to the child in a mutual involvement between the child and the partner in a collective activity. Steps include choosing and structuring activities to fit the child's skills and interests, supporting and monitoring the child's participation, and adjusting the level of support provided as the child begins to perform the activity independently.

H

habituation procedure A technique researchers use to study infant memory by assessing changes in the intensity of infants' responses to various forms of stimulation over a period of time.

hand dominance A preference for using either the right or left hand that develops around the age of 5 for more than 90 percent of all children.

hard of hearing   Those who have sufficient hearing to enable them to understand speech; may require amplification of speech through a hearing aid; see *deaf.*

heritability   The proportion of observed variance for a behavior that can be ascribed to genetic differences among individuals in a particular population; a population statistic that applies only to the sample from which it is derived.

hierarchial classification   A mental operation learned during the *concrete operational stage* that allows children to organize concepts and objects according to how they relate to one another in a building-block fashion. For example, all matter is composed of molecules and molecules are made up of atoms, which in turn are made up of protons, electrons, and neutrons.

holophrases   Refers to single words intended to convey more complex meaning; typically utilized by children aged 18 to 24 months.

homophobia   An irrational fear and hatred of homosexuals.

homosexual orientation   Consistent sexual attraction toward persons of the same gender that includes fantasies, conscious attraction, romantic feelings, or sexual behaviors.

horizontal decalage   Piaget's term for children's inconsistency in thinking within a developmental stage; explains why, for instance, children do not learn *conservation* tasks about numbers and volume at the same time.

hostile aggression   In 3- and 4-year-old children, behavior that is intended to hurt or harm another person; see *aggression.* Contrast with *instrumental aggression.*

hostile attribution bias   The tendency of some aggressive children to interpret social situations as personally threatening or hostile, even when the intentions of other actors are unclear.

hypothalamus   A structure at the base of the brain that controls the pituitary gland.

hypothesis   A statement of prediction derived from a theory that has not yet been tested.

hypothetico-deductive thinking   A form of *formal logic* achieved during the *formal operational stage* Piaget identified as the ability to generate and test hypotheses in a logical and systematic matter.

I

ideal self   The image of the self created during middle childhood that is developed by comparing one's real self to a set of desired characteristics, including the expectations, values, and ideals of peers and adults.

identity   (1) In Piaget's theory, one of three basic mental operations including *negation* and *compensation* needed to perform *conservation* tasks; involves an understanding of cognitive constancy, that people, objects, and quantities remain unchanged despite changes in appearance. (2) In Erikson's theory, the fifth stage of psychosocial development when adolescents commit themselves to a set of beliefs, values, and adult roles in forming a basic sense of self. If adolescents are unable to explore alternative roles and options, they will experience a parallel internal state of *role confusion;* see Table 6.1.

identity achievement   Marcia's term for an adolescent's determination of definite goals or choices after having explored different options.

identity foreclosure   The state adolescents are in when they have not explored different possibilities but have committed to specific choices.

identity moratorium   Marcia's term for an adolescent's exploration of different occupational plans, ideological stances, and personal relationships when she or he is not ready to make a choice or commitment.

identity versus identity confusion   In Erikson's theory, the central issue that defines adolescence whereby the adolescent must feel his identity informed by his past, future, and current identities, and how he sees himself and how others see him.

ideographic system   The structure of some languages, including Chinese, whereby each character in the written language represents the meaning of an individual word; contrast with *alphabetic system.*

imaginary audience   The belief that one is constantly being watched and evaluated, which is an expression of adolescent egocentrism, defined by Elkind as resulting from the inability of adolescents to distinguish between their thoughts about themselves and their thoughts about others.

incremental theory of ability   A theory of intelligence, proposed by Dweck, whereby students believe their ability level can improve through a greater investment of effort or by trying different strategies; contrast with *entity theory of ability.*

independent variable   A variable or factor hypothesized to influence a particular outcome or result in a research study.

individual Educational Plan (IEP)   A written plan developed by teachers, school specialists, and parents to address the specific needs of children with disabilities.

inductive discipline   A discipline technique in which parents offer explanation for their rules and ask children to reflect on their behavior; helps children develop self-control and self-discipline.

infant attachment   The process by which infants form strong affectional ties with their caregivers; generally takes place within the first 6 months of age and is important for the development of a basic sense of trust that can have long-term effects on an infant's later emotional and cognitive development.

infant mortality   A term referring to the number of infants that die within the first year of life; often caused by a short gestation period or low birth weight.

inner speech   One of three stages of children's use of language identified by Vygotsky, during which children internalize their self-verbalizations and are able to manipulate language in their heads to think about problem solutions and action sequences. A self-regulatory process by which children guide their own thinking and behavior; also called private speech; contrast with *social speech* and *egocentric speech.*

insecure-avoidant attachment   In Ainsworth's theory, a behavior pattern in which infants appear indifferent to the departure of their mothers and avoid them when they return. Distinguished from secure attachment.

insecure-disorganized attachment   Another form of insecure attachment in which infant shows disorientation and contradictory behavior in Ainsworth's Strange Situation. Distinguished from secure attachment.

insecure-resistant attachment   In Ainsworth's theory, a behavior pattern in which infants show high levels of distress upon separation, but ambivalence when parents return.

instructional conversations   A collaborative process between teachers and students used to teach reading comprehension. The teachers invite children to relate the text to their own experiences, then assist children in understanding the text by providing feedback, modeling, questioning, organizing the content, and so on.

instrumental aggression   In young children, behavior that is intended to obtain an object, to protect a play space, or to get one's way; behavior that is not intended to hurt or harm another person; see *aggression.* Contrast with *hostile aggression.*

instrumental conditioning   See *operant conditioning.*

intelligence quotient (IQ)   Represents a score obtained by comparing a child's *mental age* score with other children's of the same chronological age; currently determined through a deviation IQ score procedure.

intelligence theories   A theory that focuses on how cognitive processes explain individual differences in children's performance on intelligence tests and other cognitive measures; see also *psychometric theories.*

interactional perspective   A theory that supports the interplay of innate and environmental influences on a child's development.

intercoder reliability   See *interobserver reliability.*

intermodal perception   The ability to integrate information across the five senses (e.g., auditory, tactile, and visual cues).

internalization   Vygotsky's term for the process of constructing a mental representation of external physical actions or cognitive operations that first occur through social interaction.

internalizing problems   The kinds of problems some children with emotional and behavioral disorders experience, including depression, withdrawal, anxiety, and obsession; contrast with *externalizing problems.*

interobserver reliability   A reliability estimate used in interview and observation studies whereby more than one person observes or codes the same events and a percentage of agreement is computed to guard against subjective interpretations and judgments; also called *intercoder reliability.*

interview   A *self-report* measure in which subjects are asked a standard set of questions.

intraindividual variation   The unique pattern of strengths and needs related to each child's physical, cognitive, social, and emotional growth; see *interindividual variation.*

intrinsic motivation   A desire to learn or act that arises from internal sources of curiosity, interest, enjoyment, and innate strivings for mastery and growth; contrast with *extrinsic motivation.*

intuitive theory   Piaget's explanation for young children's attempts to explain natural phenomena by using their personal experiences; characterized by *animism.*

invented spelling   Unconventional ways children spell words in their early attempts at writing.

L

language   A symbolic system in which a series of sounds make words to represent an idea, an object, or a person and eventually becomes the medium through which we think.

language acquisition device (LAD)   Chomsky's idea that children are born with a mechanism in their brains that enables them to recognize the universal rules that underlie all languages and the structure and grammar of their native language.

lateralization   Specialization of the two hemispheres of the brain.

lateralized   A theory about cognitive functioning suggesting that each of the two cerebral hemispheres of the brain, the left side and the right side, performs a special set of functions and becomes the dominant center of brain functioning.

learned helplessness   A feeling of helplessness that develops when one encounters difficulty or failure, especially in situations when one does not have control. This reinforces low self-confidence.

learning centers   Structured areas in the classroom set aside to provide multilevel activities to address a broad range of interests, skills, and objectives; a teaching method used to provide individualized instruction in the classroom.

learning-oriented goals   Outcome desired because of the child's intrinsic interest in learning something new.

limited English proficiency (LEP)   A minimal knowledge of *Standard American English (SAE);* often characteristic of nonnative speakers.

literacy   Constructed meaning; meaning created through the interaction of reader or writer and written text.

literate environment   A place in which children encounter print with authentic purposes and adults value and participate in reading and writing.

literate thinking   The ability to think and reason like a literate person within a particular society; see *literacy.*

locus of causality   In *attribution theory,* the motivational source, either internal or external, to which people attribute their actions or achievements.

logical rule of class inclusion   A mental operation achieved during the *concrete operational stage* that allows children to understand the relationship of something's whole to its parts; see *class inclusion.*

logical rule of progressive change   The understanding that develops during the *concrete operational stage* that various stimuli can be ordered in terms of increasing and decreasing size.

logical rule of transitivity   The understanding that develops during the *concrete operational stage* that objects in the middle of a series are both shorter and longer than others; a necessary concept in solving *seriation* problems.

logico-mathematical knowledge   In Piaget's theory, the type of knowledge consisting of the mental construction of relationships involved in the concrete operations of seriation, classification, and conservation, as well as various formal operations that emerge in adolescence.

longitudinal study   A study that collects different types of data (e.g., early experiences, education, personality characteristics) on a regular basis and tracks the development of a group of children over a number of years.

long-term memory   A component of the information processing system into which information passes from *short-term memory* if it has been transformed or worked on in some personally meaningful way; has a large capacity, and can store information indefinitely.

low birth weight   Many premature and some full-term babies who weigh less than 5.5 pounds or 2,500 grams at birth.

low vision   Those who cannot read newsprint-size letters, even with corrective lenses; see *blind.*

M

macrosystem   In Bronfenbrenner's model, the larger culture and possibly subculture in which the individual lives— including ideologies, traditions, and values. Elements of the macrosystem include regional identity, nationality, ethnicity, and religious affiliation.

marginality   Living within a dominant culture but remaining estranged or alienated from it.

mastery oriented   When the desired outcome is the ability to perform, rather than attainment of new knowledge.

matrix classification   In Piaget's theory, a concept achieved during the *concrete operational stage* that involves ordering items by two or more attributes, such as by both size and color.

memory script   A mental representation of often-repeated events in a child's daily life; a basic method for organizing and interpreting familiar experiences.

memory strategy   A cognitive operation, such as repeating a list of items over and over again, that will help one to remember abstract, unfamiliar, or meaningless information.

menarche   The beginning of a girl's menstrual cycle; generally the last physical change to occur in puberty.

mental age (MA)   The score represented by the number of test items a child gets correct that was formerly used in calculating an IQ score; see *intelligence quotient.*

mental retardation   Characterized by a lower than normal level of intelligence and developmental delays in specific adaptive behavior.

mesoderm   The middle layer of the embronic structure that will become the skeleton and muscles.

mesosystem   In Bronfenbrenner's model, interactions among components of the microsystem.

metacognition   Knowledge about one's own thinking; involves an understanding of how memory works, what tasks require more cognitive effort, and what strategies facilitate learning; plays an important role in children's cognitive development during the middle childhood years and in the development of self-regulated learning.

metalinguistic awareness   The ability to think and talk about the relationship between print and sound in a language; for instance, a child's ability to identify the first sound as making the difference between the words *rat* and *bat.*

metamemory   Knowledge about memory; improves with development. See also *metacognition.*

microsystem   In Brofenbrenner's model, the child's immediate environment (the family, peer group, school).

mitosis   The process through which chromosomes produce duplicate copies of themselves and divide into new cells; each new cell has 23 pairs of chromosomes.

mixed speech   A single language system lasting until about 2 years of age in which a *simultaneous bilingual* combines features of both languages he or she is exposed to.

monozygotic twins   Two siblings who come from the same fertilized egg and contain the same genetic instructions; also known as identical twins.

motherese   A type of child-directed speech also known as parentese in which parents or caregivers modify language they direct toward their children from birth; thought to assist children's language development by simplifying structure to make language acquisition simpler.

multidimensional conception of intelligence   The concept that intelligence represents several different mental abilities or intellectual competencies; contrast with *unitary conception of intelligence*.

multilingual   The ability to speak more than two languages.

myelin   The fatty substance that coats neurons and dendrites to enable *myelination*.

myelination   The second of two changes during brain development after birth; the process during which neurons and dendrites become coated with a fatty substance *(myelin)* to enable neural impulses to travel faster.

N

natural experiment   Studies that use natural settings (home, school, playground) in which to study children to avoid skewing experimental evidence due to overly controlled laboratory-like settings that do not resemble the real world.

naturalistic observation   An observation situation that uses real-life environments in which to collect data; see *natural experiment*.

need to achieve   In motivation theory, a person's desire to excel in achievement situations.

negation   In Piaget's theory, one of three basic mental operations including *compensation* and *identity* needed to perform *conservation* tasks; a form of *reversibility* that involves an understanding that operations can be undone (negated) or can have an inverse relationship (subtraction is the inverse of addition).

negative identity   A possible outcome for ethnic or racial minority young people who fail to establish a strong sense of self and reject their community's values as well as those of the dominant culture.

neglect   A form of child abuse involving inattention to basic needs such as food, clothing, and medical care.

neglected peers   Children who are seldom chosen as work or play partners by their peers.

neo-Piagetian theories   Cognitive theories that add greater specificity to Piaget's theory of development while adhering to the basic assumptions of his theory. Case's neo-Piagetian theory links stage-like changes in knowledge to the development of cognitive and memory strategies.

neurons   Long thin cells within the central nervous system, different from other cells because they are not closely packed, that are formed during the first 5 months of gestation.

neurotransmitters   Chemicals released by *neurons* that cross over *synapses* in the central nervous system to communicate with other neurons.

niche-picking   The tendency of older children to choose an environment that compliments their heredity as part of the active gene-environment effect described by Sandra Scarr and her associates.

O

obesity   A greater than 20 percent increase over average body weight for an individual's age, sex, and body build; contributing factors can be heredity, unhealthy diet, lack of exercise, abnormal metabolism, and family trauma.

object permanence   Piaget's term for an infant's understanding during the *sensorimotor stage* that objects continue to exist even when they can no longer be seen or acted on.

operant conditioning   A behavioral principle of learning through which behavior is increased or extinguished by rewards and punishments; same as *instrumental conditioning*.

organization   (1) In Piaget's theory, one of two basic principles referred to as invariant functions that guide children's intellectual development; the innate predisposition to integrate simple physical patterns or mental schemes into more complex systems; contrast with *adaptation*. (2) In information processing theory, a memory encoding strategy in which one tries to group items to be remembered into meaningful categories.

P

parenting style   Common patterns of parenting styles including authoritarian, permissive, and authoritative.

partial participation   A teaching approach in which a student from a separate special classroom spends time in the general classroom engaged with activities modified to fit his or her abilities; see *reverse mainstreaming.*

peer A person equal in age, rank, or maturity to another person.

peer-directed learning An instructional approach that allows children and adolescents to learn from one another; examples include cooperative learning, peer tutoring, and the buddy system.

peer popularity A popular peer is one whose presence or opinion is sought after by others of the same age; the key determinants are the abilities to initiate and to maintain positive interactions with others.

peer rejection Ignoring or avoiding those who are strongly disliked by their peers; those rejected are often inattentive, aversive, threatening, hostile, and disruptive.

performance assessment A method of collecting information that measures children's ability to perform specific cognitive or physical tasks correctly.

performance-oriented goals One type of achievement goal identified by motivation theorists, whereby students are motivated to achieve by a desire to demonstrate high ability or to avoid negative evaluations of ability; same as ego-oriented goals. Contrast with *task-oriented goals.*

permissive-indifferent parenting A style of parenting in which children are left to make their own decisions and regulate their own behavior that often results from or leads to neglect.

permissive-indulgent A style of parenting in which parents are very warm and responsive, and put few demands or expectations on their children. Rules are not clearly communicated or enforced, leaving children to make their own decisions and regulate their own behavior.

permissive parenting A parenting style characterized by a lack of rules and expectations for children and by inconsistent discipline; contrast with *authoritative* and *authoritarian.*

personal fable A second aspect of adolescent egocentrism that follows from the belief in an imaginary audience, resulting in an increased concern about appearance and behavior as an expression of one's uniqueness and sense of self-importance.

perspective-taking skills One of the important aspects of the development of social cognition that involves being able to imagine what others may be thinking and feeling.

phenotype A person's observable physical and behavioral characteristics; when individuals receive a recessive gene from one parent and a dominant gene from another, their *genotype* will be different from their phenotype.

phonemic awareness The ability to connect the distinctive sounds, or phonemes, in words to letters.

phonic knowledge A *decoding* strategy; the rules for combining sounds to make words and the stress and intonation patterns of a language (Figure 5.1); contrast with *context knowledge* and *sight word knowledge.*

physical abuse Purposeful bodily injury caused by another.

physical disabilities Congenital or acquired disabling conditions that result from damage to the central nervous system, either to the brain or the spinal cord.

physical knowledge One of three types of knowledge as described by Piaget; knowing the attributes of objects such as their number, color, size, and shape; knowledge is acquired by acting on objects, experimenting, and observing reactions.

pincer grasp Develops at the end of the first year of life as an infant learns to use the thumb and index finger to pick up small objects.

pituitary gland A small endocrine gland near the base of the brain responsible for the release of hormones affecting growth.

placenta A structure present at implantation of the zygote that begins to function and mature during the embryonic period. This structure, the *umbilical cord,* and the *amniotic sac* make up the life-support system for the developing embryo.

plasticity The ability of the brain, especially in the early years of development, to change.

polygenetic traits Human characteristics, such as intelligence, skin color, and height, that result from the combination or interaction of two or more genes.

postconventional level According to Kohlberg, the third level of moral judgment, characterized by individuals who develop their own set of principles to define what is morally right and wrong; contrast with *preconventional level* and *conventional level.*

power assertive discipline A discipline style in which parents attempt to control their children's behavior by use of commands and imperatives based solely on their authority.

practical intelligence Sternberg's theory that an intelligent person can use skills effectively in a particular context; involves applying *contextual intelligence* to everyday problems; see Figure 4.8.

pragmatics of language The strategies for using language appropriately in different contexts, such as turn-taking, interrupting, beginning a new topic appropriately; see Figure 5.1.

preconventional level According to Kohlberg, the first level of moral judgment, characterized by individuals who approach moral issues from a hedonistic or pleasure-oriented perspective; contrast with *conventional level* and *postconventional level.*

prejudice   Unfounded negative feelings toward a person because of his or her membership in a group.

prenatal development   The time from conception to birth; follows a universal sequence that is mainly directed by genetic influences but also can be affected by environmental factors.

preoperational stage   The period of life from 2 to 7 years old when, Piaget believed, children demonstrate an increased ability to use symbols (gestures, words, numbers) to represent real objects in their environment.

primary sex characteristics   Changes in the gonads (testes and ovaries) and the development of eggs and sperm stimulated by a change in the levels of sex hormones in male and female adolescents during puberty.

private speech   See *inner speech.*

problem-focused coping   A coping strategy that involves seeking information, generating different solutions, and taking action to modify a situation; contrast with *emotion-focused coping.*

procedural knowledge   Children's understanding about how learning strategies should be applied; contrast with *declarative knowledge* and *conditional knowledge.*

propositional logic   A form of *formal logic* achieved during the *formal operational stage* that Piaget identified as the ability to draw a logical inference between two statements or premises in an "if-then" relationship.

prosocial behavior   Actions stemming from an appreciation that others' needs are as important or more important than one's own; supportive actions, such as sharing, helping, and care giving.

proximal-distal   One of two patterns characterizing growth in infancy; development begins in the center and proceeds outward. As a result, the organs develop before the arms or hands.

psychological need   An internal tension or conflict that leads to or influences a person's goal-directed behavior.

psychological self   A developmental gain during which adolescents begin to understand that they have an inner self—thoughts and feelings hidden from others unless they share them.

psychometric theories   Theories that focus on how cognitive processes explain individual differences in children's performance on intelligence tests and other cognitive measures; see also *intelligence theories.*

puberty   Refers to the period in which a young person becomes capable of sexual reproduction; the average age of onset for girls is 10 to 12 years old and for boys, 12 to 14 years old.

Q

qualitative changes   The emergence of discrete competencies and behaviors during different stages of development. Those theorists who view development as discontinuous.

quasi-experimental studies   A type of research design that utilizes comparison groups without random assignment. Also known as a causal-comparative design.

questionnaire   A *self-report* measure that contains carefully written questions for subjects to answer; a very common method of data collection.

R

race   Refers to a group of people, such as African Americans or Asian Americans, who share biologically transmitted traits that are defined as socially significant, such as skin color or hair texture; contrast with *ethnicity.*

rating scale   A form of questionnaire or interview in which research subjects are asked to rate themselves or others on a set of dimensions, such as aggression, temperament, and intelligence.

reaction range   A concept used by researchers to understand an individual's unique, genetically determined response to environmental influences. Genes may determine the upper and lower boundaries for development, but the reaction range defines the degree to which the environment can affect development.

reading readiness approach   An outdated conception of literacy development that emphasized a set of skills children needed to master before beginning formal reading instruction; contrast with *emergent literacy.*

realism   According to Piaget, children's inclination during the *preoperational stage* to confuse physical and psychological events in their attempts to develop theories of the internal world of the mind.

recall memory   A form of information retrieval that involves the free recall of information without any cues or prompts to aid the process; requires more cognitive effort than *recognition memory;* children display better recall memory as they get older.

recessive gene   A gene inherited from one parent, such as blond hair, not always expressed, because its genetic directions are masked by a *dominant gene* of the other parent. A child needs to inherit a recessive gene from each parent for the gene to be expressed.

reciprocal determinism   Defined by Bandura's social learning theory as a bidirectional relationship between a child and his or her social environment; children have as much an influence on their environment as it has on them.

reciprocal teaching Palincsar and Brown's learning model designed to help poor readers acquire comprehension skills. Teachers and students take turns being the discussion leader, and through collaborative learning dialogues, students learn how to regulate their own understanding of what they are reading.

recognition memory A basic form of information retrieval that involves recognizing a familiar stimulus when it is seen, heard, or experienced again; requires less cognitive effort than *recall memory* tasks; infants are able to display recognition memory by attending more to an unfamiliar than a familiar stimulus.

reflective abstraction A concept that allows children to use information they already have acquired to form new knowledge; begins to emerge during the *concrete operational stage* but is more characteristic of adolescent thinking.

rehearsal The first memory encoding strategy to be learned, involving the repetition of information over and over again to assist with recall.

reinforcement A repeated response to an action in which individuals modify their behavior on the basis of the expected response.

reliability The consistency or precision of a measurement when repeated under similar circumstances; can be tested by administering the same test several times within a short interval of time (e.g., a few weeks) to check the consistency of results over time.

representational thinking A Piagetian concept that develops during the *preoperational stage* in which children gain the ability to use words to stand for real objects.

research design The plan or structure of an investigation, which is determined in part by the investigator's research question.

resiliency The capacity of young people to cope with difficult and challenging circumstances in their lives to develop competence.

retrieval strategy Any of the cognitive operations a learner might use to recover information from memory.

reverse mainstreaming A teaching approach in which students from the general classroom spend some time in the separate special classroom, interacting with children with disabilities in learning activities; see *partial participation.*

reversibility A concept achieved during the *concrete operational stage* that allows children to mentally reverse operations; involves an understanding that actions can be undone and is important for understanding *conservation* problems.

role confusion In Erikson's fifth stage of psychosocial development, adolescents can experience uncertainties about themselves and their future if they are unable to explore different roles and options; contrast with *identity.*

S

scaffolding The process by which adults provide support to a child who is learning to master a task or problem by performing or directing those elements of the task that are beyond the child's ability.

scheme Also referred to as schema (pl. schemata) in some research areas; in Piaget's theory, the physical actions, mental operations, concepts, or theories people use to organize and acquire information about their world.

script See *memory script.*

secondary sex characteristics Changes in genitals, breasts, and the growth of facial, pubic, and body hair stimulated by a change in the level of sex hormones in male and female adolescents during puberty.

secular trend A shift in normative patterns of development exemplified in today's average adult height and the onset of puberty.

securely attached In Ainsworth's theory, infants who are distressed by parental separation and easily comforted by the parent upon return. Distinguished from insecure attachment.

selective attention A development that allows children to focus their attention on task-relevant information and ignore irrelevant information so they use their cognitive resources more efficiently.

self-concept The beliefs, attitudes, knowledge, and ideas people develop or construct about their personality, physical skills, and mental abilities; see *self-esteem.*

self-conscious emotions Feeling such as pride, shame, and guilt requiring a connection between one's actions and feelings that involve an evolving sense of self; generally emerges between the ages of 2 and 4.

self-control Being able to control negative emotions, persist at difficult and challenging activities, and inhibit impulses.

self-determination In motivation theory, the ability to act independently and to choose one's own course of action.

self-efficacy In motivation theory, an individual's judgment of personal ability to perform a task given the skills he or she possesses and the circumstances he or she faces; according to Bandura, shaped by prior experience, peer models, and corrective feedback.

self-esteem Personal evaluation of one's own traits, abilities, and characteristics; a judgment of one's own worth, value, or competence; see *self-concept.*

self-evaluation   A learning strategy that teaches children to evaluate their own performance as they progress through or end a learning activity.

self-instruction   A learning strategy that teaches children to use private or inner speech to guide themselves through a task in a step-by-step manner; see *inner speech.*

self-monitoring   A learning strategy that teaches children to check and track their own progress through a learning task; effective strategy for children with special learning needs.

self-regulated learning   Children's increasing regulation and control of their own learning processes due to their development of their metacognitive knowledge.

self-report   A method of collecting information in which individuals being studied report on themselves through *questionnaires, rating scales,* or *interviews.*

semantic memory   Long-term memory storage of information, skills, and concepts of a general nature. Much of what is learned in school is included in semantic memory.

semantics   The meaning of words; only certain strings of sounds are meaningful as words and words are related in complex networks and have special properties; see Figure 5.1.

semiotic functioning   See *representational thinking.*

sense of guilt   In Erikson's third stage of psychosocial development, children 3 to 6 years old can develop guilt feelings if their caregivers demand too much self-control or initiative; contrast with *sense of initiative.*

sense of industry   In Erikson's theory, the fourth stage of psychosocial development in which children 7 to 11 years old must begin to identify their strengths and to take pleasure in their accomplishments; if they are unsupported in their mastery efforts, a parallel internal *feeling of inferiority* or inadequacy may develop. See Table 6.1.

sense of initiative   In Erikson's theory, the third stage of psychosocial development in which children 3 to 6 years old develop a sense of purpose and direction and learn to balance their actions with the demands of others. If children are unable to live up to parental expectations, a parallel *sense of guilt* will develop; see Table 6.1.

sensorimotor stage   The period of life from birth to 2 years old when children acquire what Piaget believed are the building blocks of symbolic thinking and human intelligence—schemes for two basic competencies, goal-directed behavior, and *object permanence.*

sensory register   According to information processing theories, the place where information is stored in the cognitive process for a few milliseconds until it is recognized or lost; each sense has its own sensory register.

separation   The rejection of the dominant culture by the minority, who then only associates with members of his or her own minority group.

seriation   In Piaget's theory, the understanding that develops during the *concrete operational stage* that involves the ability to order objects in a logical progression, such as from shortest to tallest; important for understanding the concepts of number, time, and measurement.

service learning   A form of character education that involves meaningful community service to teach civic responsibility and to foster positive youth development; examples include designing neighborhood playgrounds, preparing food for the homeless, and recycling programs.

sex chromosome   The twenty-third chromosome; humans have two types, X and Y; females have two X chromosome, and males have an X and a Y chromosome.

sex-linked characteristic   Some recessive traits carried on the female *sex chromosome,* such as baldness, color blindness, and hemophilia; generally expressed in male rather than female offspring.

sex-role socialization   The process by which children acquire the knowledge, skills, and traits appropriate for their gender.

sexual abuse   Contacts between the child and adult in which the child is being used for sexual stimulation.

short-term memory   A component of the information processing system into which information passes and is held for a brief period of time once it has been interpreted or encoded in terms of prior knowledge; also known as working memory; contrast with *long-term memory.*

sight word knowledge   A *decoding* strategy; the developing recognition and understanding through exposure of the meaning of words; contrast with *context knowledge* and *phonic knowledge.*

simpatía   The felt need for behaviors, such as conformity and empathy, that promote harmonious, pleasant social relations.

simultaneous bilingual   Learning several languages at the same time.

social cognition   A Piagetian concept defined as knowledge about people, including their thoughts, feelings, and actions.

social comparison   A developmental change that occurs during the school years as children begin to compare themselves with others in terms of actions or abilities.

social constructivist   An approach to learning and teaching based on Vygotsky's theory of development.

social convention reasoning   Children's understanding of the rules, customs, and rituals that govern social interactions and organizations, such as turn-taking, dress styles, and table manners.

social desirability   A tendency of individuals to overestimate desirable behavior and underestimate undesirable behavior on *self-report* measures.

social dialect   Speech patterns of a particular ethnic, social, or regional group.

social information processing theories   A view based on information processing theory that information in social situations is encoded, interpreted, evaluated, and responded to in a sequential manner.

social knowledge   In Piaget's theory, this type of knowledge is derived in part through interactions with others. Examples of this knowledge include mathematical words and signs, languages, musical notations, as well as social and moral conventions.

social referencing   The process of incorporating facial cues into response sequences in infants.

social speech   One of three stages of children's use of language identified by Vygotsky that is used primarily for communicative purposes in which thought and language have separate functions; contrast with *egocentric speech* and *inner speech.*

socialization   The social processes in which a child is prepared to be a productive and competent member of society.

stability of IQ   In intelligence theories, the degree to which an IQ score remains constant over time; central to the *heritability* of intelligence issue. For instance, if IQ is not stable over time, researchers could point to the influence of environmental factors in the outcome of people's intellectual potential.

standard American English (SAE)   The language of instruction in schools.

standard deviation   A statistical estimate used with IQ scores that represents the average amount individual scores within a sample vary from the mean.

standardized tests of intelligence   The most common method of assessing individual differences in cognitive development; referred to as the psychometric approach.

static assessment   A type of assessment teachers and other educational professionals can use that provides information about the present state of children's existing skills; contrast with *dynamic assessment.*

statistically significant   When the relation between two measures is stronger than would have been predicted by chance.

stereotype threat   A person is experiencing stereotype threat when he or she is fearful of performing an academic task or test in a manner that would confirm negative social stereotypes of one's gender or ethnic group. This condition can lead students to devalue the importance of academic success or to invest less effort in their academic studies.

strange Situation   Ainsworth's procedure for assessing behaviors of caregivers and children; used to establish quality of attachment.

strategic learner   Any learner who uses cognitive strategies (attention, encoding, memory, and retrieval) to enhance his or her learning.

structured immersion   A method for serving English-learning students in which children receive up to a year of intensive training in English before they are placed in an English-speaking classroom.

structured observation   An observation situation that uses a carefully controlled setting and standardizes the conditions under which data are collected.

submersion   A "sink or swim" approach to teaching students with limited proficiency in English in which learners are placed into a monolingual, English classroom without any instructional support.

substance abuse   Frequent or excessive use of a drug, including cigarettes, alcohol, and marijuana.

successive bilingualism   A person who learns the dominant language (English) but retains his or her native language as well (Spanish); the stages of language development will be different from *bilingual* or *multilingual* learners; see *mixed speech.*

synapses   The tiny gaps between *neurons* in the central nervous system where fibers from different neurons come close together but do not touch and *neurotransmitters* cross over.

syntax   The structure of language; the way words are combined to form phrases and sentences.

T

task-oriented goals   One type of achievement goal identified by motivation theorists, similar to *intrinsic motivation,* whereby students are motivated to achieve by a desire to improve or develop their competencies; same as learning-oriented goals. Contrast with *performance-oriented goals.*

teacher-directed instruction   Activities, instructional practices, and classroom accommodations planned and implemented by the teacher; see *direct instruction.*

telegraphic speech   Early speech that is characterized by typically short, simple sentences composed primarily of content words: "Kendall swim pool."

temperament An infant's characteristic style of responding to the environment; includes activity level, predictability, and emotionality; believed to be early component of personality development.

teratogen Any environmental substance or disease (alcohol, caffeine, radiation, caustic chemicals, chicken pox, AIDS) that can have an adverse effect on a fetus during prenatal development.

testosterone Hormone affecting the development of the penis, testes, and other organs of the reproductive system in males.

test-retest reliability A measure used to determine the consistency of a test's results; see *reliability.*

theories of mind Children's naïve or intuitive psychological theories about the causes of human behavior; inferences children make about inner mental states such as beliefs, intentions, desires, and emotions.

theory A set of general rules, assumptions, propositions, and principles used to explain facts; a developmental theory provides a framework for observing, interpreting, and explaining children's changes over time.

theory of multiple intelligences Gardner's proposal that there are at least seven different intelligences: linguistic, logical-mathematical, musical, spacial, bodily-kinesthetic, interpersonal, and intrapersonal; see Table 4.1.

time sampling A technique used to record on a coding sheet all observations listed that happen within a predetermined length of time, say, within a 5-minute time frame.

tracking The ongoing practice in middle and high schools of grouping students according to their presumed academic ability; thought by some to limit learning and achievement opportunities due to the kinds and quality of instruction and to students' resulting low motivation and self-esteem; see *ability grouping.*

traumatic brain injury (TBI) An acquired injury to the brain from either an open or closed head injury that has significant impact on learning, including problem solving, speech and motor abilities, psychosocial behavior, and information processing; learning difficulties may be permanent or temporary, depending on the location and extent of the injury.

triangulation The use of multiple data collection methods to compare findings across sources and to find consistent patterns.

triarchic model of intelligence Sternberg's concept that intelligence is divided into contextual, experiential, and componential subcomponents; see *componential intelligence, contextual intelligence,* and *experiential intelligence;* see also *multidimensional conception of intelligence.*

U

umbilical cord A structure present at implantation of the zygote that begins to function and mature during the embryonic period. See *placenta.*

V

validity The degree to which a research instrument or test accurately measures what it claims to measure.

W

whole language A language philosophy characterized by a set of beliefs, including the beliefs that the purpose of language is to create and share meaning; that language is language, regardless of whether it is spoken or written; and that language is best learned by using it in a social context for authentic purposes.

working memory See *short-term memory.*

writing across the curriculum A program approach in which writing is incorporated into all subject areas, from music to mathematics.

Z

zone of proximal development A concept in Vygotsky's theory regarding children's potential for intellectual growth rather than their actual level of development; the gap between what children can do on their own and what they can do with the assistance of others (see Figure 3.10).

zygote The human cell that is formed by the union of the female egg and male sperm and contains one set of 23 chromosomes from the mother and another set of 23 chromosomes from the father.

References

AAUW Educational Foundation Commission on Technology, Gender and Teacher Education. (2000). *Tech-Savvy: Educating Girls in the New Computer Age*. Washington, DC: American Association of University Women Educational Foundation.

Aber, J. L., Jones, S. M., Brown, J. L., Chaundry, N., & Samples, F. (1998). Resolving conflict creatively: Evaluating the developmental effects of a school-based violence prevention program in neighborhood and classroom context. *Development and Psychopathology, 10*, 187–213.

Aberbach, A., & Roeser, R. (1993, April). Motivational influences on fifth graders' help-seeking strategy use in math classrooms. Paper presented at the annual meeting of the American Educational Research Association, Atlanta, GA.

Aboud, F. E. (1988). *Children and prejudice*. New York: Blackwell.

Acs, G., & Nelson, S. (2002). The kids are alright? Children's well-being and the rise in cohabitation. Urban Institute. Available online at http://www.urban.org/url.cfm?ID=310544.

Adams, M. (2003). Do you speak American? Words that shouldn't be? Sez who? Slayer slang: Buffy and company changes how teens talk. A lot. Retrieved August 2005 from http://www.pbs.org/speak/words/sezwho/buffy/.

Adams, M. J. (1990). *Beginning to read: Thinking and learning about print*. Cambridge, MA: MIT Press.

Ainsworth, M. D., Blehar, M., Waters, E., & Wall, S. (1978). *Patterns of attachment*. Hillsdale, NJ: Erlbaum.

Aitchison, J. (1985). Predestinate grooves: Is there a preordained language "program"? In V. P. Clark, P. A. Eschholz, & A. F. Rosa (Eds.), *Language: Introductory readings* (pp. 90–111). New York: St. Martin's Press.

Albert, L. (1996). *Cooperative discipline*. Circle Pines, MN: American Guidance Service.

Alexander, K. L., & Entwisle, D. R. (1988). Achievement in the first 2 years of school: Patterns and processes. *Monographs of the Society for Research in Child Development, 53*(2, Serial No. 218).

Alexander, K. L., Entwisle, D. R., & Drauber, S. L. (1995). *On the success of failure: A reassessment of the effects of retention in the primary grades*. New York: Cambridge University Press.

Alexander, K. L., Natriello, G., & Pallas, A. (1985). For whom the school bell tolls: The impact of dropping out on cognitive performance. *American Sociological Review, 50*, 409–420.

Alexander, P. A. (1996). The past, present, and future of knowledge research: A reexamination of the role of knowledge in learning and instruction. *Educational Psychologist, 31*, 89–92.

Allen, V. (1986). Developing contexts to support second language acquisition. *Language Arts, 64*, 61–67.

Alley, G., & Deshler, D. (1979). *Teaching the learning disabled adolescent: Strategies and methods*. Denver: Love.

Allington, R. L. (1977). If they don't read much, how they ever gonna get good? *Journal of Reading 21*, 37–61.

Altermatt, E. R., Jovanovic, J., & Perry, M. (1998). Bias or responsivity? Sex and achievement-level effects on teachers' classroom questioning practices. *Journal of Educational Psychology, 90*(3), 516–527.

Altermatt, E. R., & Pomerantz, E. M. (2003). The development of competence-related and motivational beliefs: An investigation of similarity and influence among friends. *Journal of Educational Psychology, 95*, 111–123.

Altschul, I., Oyserman, D., & Bybee, D. (2006). Racial-ethnic identity in mid-adolescence: Content and change as predictors of academic achievement. *Child Development, 77*, 1129–1520.

Amato, P. R. (1993). Children's adjustment to divorce: Theories, hypotheses, and empirical support. *Journal of Marriage and the Family, 55*, 23–38.

Amato, P. R., & Booth, A. (1991). Consequences of parental divorce and marital unhappiness for adult well-being. *Social Forces, 69*, 895–914.

Amato, P. R., & Keith, N. (1991). Parental divorce and adult well-being: A meta-analysis. *Journal of Marriage and the Family, 53*, 43–58.

American Academy of Pediatrics. (1998). Guidance for effective discipline (RE9740). *Pediatrics, 101*(4), 723–728.

American Academy of Pediatrics. (2001). Clinical practice guideline: Treatment of the school-aged child with attention-deficit/hyperactivity disorder. *Pediatrics, 108*, 1033–1044.

American Academy of Pediatrics, Council on Sports Medicine and Fitness, & Council on School Health. (2006, 2000). Policy statement: Active healthy living: Prevention of childhood obesity through increased physical activity. *Pediatrics, 117*, 1834–1842.

American Academy of Pediatrics & Task Force on Infant Sleep Position and Sudden Infant Death Syndrome. (2000). Changing concepts of sudden infant death syndrome: Implications for infant sleeping environment and sleep position, *Pediatrics, 105*, 650–656.

American Association on Mental Retardation. (2002). The AAMR definition of mental retardation. American Association on Intellectual and Developmental Disabilities. Retrieved January 2007 from http://www.aamr.org/Policies/faq_mental_retardation.shtml.

American Association of University Women. (1992). *The AAUW report: How schools shortchange girls*. Washington, DC: Author and National Education Foundation.

American Association of University Women. (2001). *Hostile hallways II: Bullying, teasing, and sexual harassment in school.* Washington, DC: Author.

American Association of University Women Educational Foundation. (1998). *Gender gaps: Where schools still fail our children.* Washington, DC: Author.

American Psychiatric Association. (1994). *Diagnostic and statistical manual of mental disorders* (4th ed.). Washington, DC: Author.

American Psychological Association. (2000). APA testimony on ADHD treatment. APA Public Policy Office. Retrieved July 2006 from http://www.apa.org/ppo/issues/pchilrit.html.

American Psychological Association. (2003). Check out a one-stop resource on ADHD. *Monitor on Psychology, 34*, 10.

American Psychological Association. (2005). Research shows that abstinence-only programs have limited effectiveness and unintended consequences. Retrieved July 2006 from http://apa.org/releases/sexeducation.html.

Ames, C. (1992). Classrooms: goals, structures, and student motivation. *Journal of Educational. Psychology, 84,* 261–271.

Ames, C., & Archer, J. (1988). Achievement goals in the classroom: Students' learning strategies and motivation processes. *Journal of Educational Psychology, 80,* 260–267.

Amey, C., & Campbell, F. (1991). Poverty, early childhood education, and academic competence: The Abcederian experiment. In A. Huston (Ed.), *Children reared in poverty* (pp. 190–221). New York: Cambridge University Press.

Amsterlaw, J. (2006). Children's beliefs about everyday reasoning. *Child Development, 77,* 443–464.

Anderman, E. M., Griesinger, T., & Westerfield, G. (1998). Motivation and cheating during early adolescence. *Journal of Educational Psychology, 90,* 84–93.

Anderman, E. M., & Midgely, C. (1996). Changes in achievement goal orientation after the transition to middle school. Paper presented at the Biennial Meeting of the Society for Research on Adolescence, Boston, MA.

Anderson, C. A., & Bushman, B. J. (2002). The effects of media violence on society. *Science, 295,* 2377–2379.

Anderson, D., Huston, A., Schmitt, K., Linebarger, D., & Wright, J. (2001). Early television viewing and adolescent behavior. *Monographs of the Society for Research in Child Development, 66*(1, Serial No. 264).

Anderson, D., & Levin, S. (1976). Young children's attention to "Sesame Street." *Child Development, 47,* 806–811.

Anderson, R. C., Hiebert, E. H., Scott, J. A., & Wilkinson, I. A. G. (1985). *Becoming a nation of readers: The report of the commission on reading.* Washington, DC: National Institute of Education.

Andersson, T., & Magnusson, D. (1990). Biological maturation in adolescence and the development of drinking habits and alcohol abuse among young males: A prospective longitudinal study. *Journal of Youth and Adolescence, 19,* 33–42.

Androutsopoulos, J. (2002). Do you speak American? Words that shouldn't be? Sez who? Born in the USA: The global spread of American slang. Retrieved August 2005 from http://www.pbs.org/speak/words/sezwho/globalslang/.

Anglin, J. M. (1993). Vocabulary development: A morphological analysis. *Monographs of the Society for Research in Child Development, 58*(Serial No. 238).

Apfel, N. H., & Seitz, V. (1991). Four models of adolescent mother-grandmother relationships in black inner-city families. *Family Relations, 40,* 421–429.

Applebee, A. N. (1978). *The child's concept of story.* Chicago: University of Chicago Press.

Applebee, A. N. (1981). *Writing in the secondary school.* Urbana, IL: National Council for Teachers of English.

Applebee, A., Langer, J., & Mullis, I. (1986). *Writing trends across the decade, 1974–84.* Princeton, NJ: Educational Testing Service.

Applebee, A., Langer, J., & Mullis, I. (1988). *Who reads best: Factors related to reading achievement in grades 3, 7, and 11.* Princeton, NJ: Educational Testing Service.

Applebee, A., Langer, J., Mullis, I., & Jenkins, L. (1990). *The writing report card, 1984–88. Findings from the nation's report card.* The National Assessment of Educational Progress. Princeton, NJ: Educational Testing Service.

Archambault, R. (1964). *John Dewey on education: Selected writings.* New York: Modern Library.

Arnett, J. (1992). Reckless behavior in adolescence: A developmental perspective. *Developmental Review, 12,* 339–373.

Arnett, J. J. (1999). Adolescent storm and stress reconsidered. *American Psychologist, 54,* 317–326.

Aro, H., & Taipale, V. (1987). The impact of timing of puberty on psychosomatic symptoms among fourteen- to sixteen-year-old Finnish girls. *Child Development, 58,* 261–268.

Aronson, E., & Patnoe, S. (1996). *The jigsaw classroom* (2nd ed.). Boston: Addison-Wesley.

Aronson, J. (2002). Stereotype threat: Contending and coping with unnerving expectations. In J. Aronson (Ed.), *Improving academic achievement* (pp. 281–304). Boston: Academic Press.

Aronson, J., & Steele, C. M. (2005). Stereotypes and the fragility of human competence, motivation, and self-concept. In C. Dweck & E. Elliot (Eds.), *Handbook of competence and motivation.* New York: Guilford.

Ashkenazi, O. & Ravid, D. (1998). Children's understanding of linguistic humour: An aspect of metalinguistic awareness. *Current Psychology of Cognition, 17,* 367–387.

Ashworth, K., Hill, M., & Walker, R. (1994). Patterns of childhood poverty: New challenges for policy. *Journal of Policy Analysis and Management, 13,* 658–680.

Aslin, R. N., Jurczyk, P. W., & Pisoni, D. B. (1998). Speech and auditory processing during infancy: Constraints on and precursors to language. In W. Damon (Gen. Ed.), D. Kuhn (Vol. Ed.), & R. Stiegler (Vol. Ed.), *Handbook of child psychology, Vol. 2: Cognition, perception, and language* (pp. 147–198). New York: John Wiley.

Astingon, J., & Jenkins, J. (1999). A longitudinal study of the relation between language and theory of mid development. *Developmental Psychology, 35,* 1311–1320.

Astington, J. W., & Pelletier, J. (1996). The language of mind: Its role in teaching and learning. In D. R. Olson & N. Torrance (Eds.), *The handbook of education and human development* (pp. 593–620). Oxford: Blackwell.

Astuti, R., Solomon, G., & Carey, S. (2004). Constraints on conceptual development: A case study of the acquisition of folkbiological and folksociological knowledge in Madagascar. *Monographs of the Society for Research in Child Development, 69*(Serial No. 277).

Atkinson, J.W. (1964). *An introduction to motivation.* Princeton, NJ: Van Nostrand.

Attneave, C. (1982). American Indians and Alaska Native families: Emigrants in their own homeland. In M. McGoldrick, J. Pearce, & J. Giordano (Eds.), *Ethnicity and family therapy* (pp. 55–83). New York: The Guilford Press.

Au, K. (1993). *Literacy instruction in multicultural settings.* Fort Worth, TX: Harcourt Brace Jovanovich.

Au, K., & Kawakami, A. (1985). Research currents: Talk story and learning to read. *Language Arts, 62,* 406–411.

Au, K., & Mason, J. (1981). Social organizational factors in learning to read: The balance of rights hypothesis. *Reading Research Quarterly, 17,* 115–152.

Au, K., & Mason, J. (1983). Cultural congruence in classroom participation: Achieving a balance of rights. *Discourse Processes, 6,* 145–167.

August, D., & HaKuta, K. (1997). *Improving schooling for language minority children.* Washington, DC: National Academy Press

Ayers, R. (2004). *Berkeley High School slang dictionary.* Berkeley, CA: North Atlantic Books.

Azmitia, M., & Hesser, J. (1993). Why siblings are important agents of cognitive development: A comparison of siblings and peers. *Child Development, 64,* 430–444.

Baharudin, R., & Luster, T. (1998). Factors related to the quality of the home environment and children's achievement. *Journal of Family Issues, 19*(4), 375–403.

Bailey, D., & Nelson, D. (1995). The nature and consequences of fragile X syndrome. *Mental Retardation and Developmental Disabilities Research Reviews, 1,* 238–244.

Bailey, J. M., Bobrow, D., Wolfe, M., & Mikach, S. (1995). Sexual orientation of adult sons of gay fathers. *Developmental Psychology, 31,* 124–129.

Baillargeon, R. (1987). Young infants' reasoning about the physical and spatial properties of a hidden object. *Cognitive Development, 2,* 179–200.

Baillargeon, R. (1994). Physical reasoning in young children: Seeking explanations for impossible events. *British Journal of Developmental Psychology, 12,* 9–33.

Baillargeon, R. (2004). Infants' reasoning about hidden objects: Evidence for event-general and event-specific expectations. *Developmental Science, 7,* 391–424.

Baillargeon, R., Spelke, E. S., & Wasserman, S. (1985). Object permanence in 5-month-olds. *Cognition, 20,* 191–208.

Baker, L., & Brown, A. L. (1984). Metacognitive skills and reading. In P. D. Pearson (Ed.), *Handbook of reading research* (pp. 353–394). New York: Longman.

Bandura, A. (1969). Social learning theory of identifactory processes. In D. A. Goslin (Ed.), *Handbook of socialization theory and research* (pp. 213–262). Chicago: Rand-McNally.

Bandura, A. (1986). *Social foundations of thought and action: A social cognitive perspective.* Englewood Cliffs, NJ: Prentice Hall.

Bandura, A. (1989). Social cognitive theory. In R. Vasta (Ed.), *Annuals of child development* (Vol. 6, pp. 1–60). Greenwich, Conn.: JAI Press.

Bandura, A. (1991). Social cognitive theory of moral thought and action. In J. L. Gewirtz, & W. M. Kurtines (Eds.), *Handbook of moral behavior and development, Vol. 1: Theory; Vol. 2: Research; Vol. 3: Application* (pp. 45–103). Hillsdale, NJ: Erlbaum.

Bandura, A., Ross, D., & Ross, S. (1963). Imitation of film-mediated aggressive models. *Journal of Abnormal and Social Psychology, 66,* 3–11.

Banks, J. (1994a). *An introduction to multi-cultural education.* Boston: Allyn & Bacon.

Banks, J. (1994b). *Multiethnic education: Theory and practice* (3rd ed.). Boston: Allyn & Bacon.

Banks, J. (2004). *Cultural diversity and education: Foundation, curriculum, and teaching* (5th ed.) Boston: Pearson/Allyn and Bacon.

Barber, B., Stolz, H., & Olsen, J. (2005). Parental support, psychological control, and behavioral control: Assessing relevance across time, culture, and method. *Monographs of the Society for Research in Child Development, 70*(Serial No. 282).

Baringa, M. (1996). Learning defect identified in the brain. *Science, 273,* 867–868.

Barkley, R. (2006). About ADHD—A fact sheet by Dr. Barkley. Retrieved January 2007 from http://www. russellbarkley.org/adhd-facts.htm.

Barkley, R. A. (1998). *Attention-deficit hyperactivity disorder: A handbook for diagnosis and treatment* (2nd ed.). New York: Guilford Press.

Barnes, D. (1989). "Fragile X" syndrome and its puzzling genetics. *Science, 243,* 171–172.

Barnett, D., & Vonda, J. I. (1999). Atypical patterns of early attachment: Theory, research, and current directions. In J. I. Vonda & D. Barnett (Eds.), Atypical attachment in infancy and early childhood among children at developmental risk. *Monographs of the Society in Child Development, 64*(3, Serial No. 258), 1–24.

Barnett, W. S., & Boocock, S. S. (1998). *Early care and education for children in poverty: Promises, programs, and long-term results* (SUNY series, Youth Social Services, Schooling, and Public Policy; SUNY series, Early Childhood Education). Albany: State University of New York Press.

Baroody, A. (1987). *Children's mathematical thinking.* New York: Teachers College Press.

Baroody, A., & Bartels, B. (2000). Using concept maps to link mathematical ideas. *Mathematics Teaching in the Middle Schools, 5*(9), 604–609.

Barr, H. M., Streissguth, A. P., Darby, B. L., & Sampson, P. D. (1990). Prenatal exposure to alcohol, caffeine, tobacco, and aspirin: Effects on fine and gross motor performance in 4-year-old children. *Developmental Psychology, 26,* 339–348.

Bartlett, E. J. (1982). Learning to revise: Some component processes. In M. Nystrand (Ed.), *What writers know: The language, process, and structure of written discourse.* New York: Academic Press.

Bartsch, K., & London, K. (2000). Children's use of mental state information in selecting persuasive arguments. *Developmental Psychology, 36,* 352–365.

Baskett, L. M. (1985). Sibling status effects: Adult expectations. *Developmental Psychology, 21,* 441–445.

Bates, E. (1976). *Language and context: The acquisition of pragmatics.* New York: Academic Press.

Bates, E. (2004). Explaining and interpreting deficits in language development across clinical groups: Where do we go from here? *Brain and Language, 88,* 248–253.

Bates, E., Devescovi, A., & Wulfeck, B. (2001). Psycholinguistics: A cross-language perspective. *Annual Review of Psychology, 52,* 369–396.

Battle, E. S., & Lacey, B. (1972). A context for hyperactivity in children, over time. *Child Development, 43,* 757–773.

Bauer, A., & Sapona, R. (1991). *Managing classrooms to facilitate learning.* Upper Saddle River, NJ: Prentice Hall.

Baumrind, D. (1967a). Child care practices anteceding three patterns of preschool behavior. *Genetic Psychology Monographs, 75,* 43–88.

Baumrind, D. (1967b). Current patterns of parental authority. *Genetic Psychology Monographs, 75,* 43–88.

Baumrind, D. (1971). Current patterns of parental authority. *Developmental Psychology Monographs, 4,* 1–102.

Baumrind, D. (1978). Parental disciplinary patterns and social competence in children. *Youth & Society, 9,* 239–276.

Baumrind, D., Cowan, P., Larzelere, R. (2002). Ordinary physical punishment: Is it harmful? Comment on Gershoff (2002). *Psychological Bulletin, 128,* 580–589.

Bayley, N. (1969). *The Bayley scales of infant development.* New York: Psychological Corporation.

Bayley, N. (1993). *Bayley scales of infant development* (2nd ed.). San Antonio, TX: The Psychological Corporation, Harcourt Assessment.

Bayley, N. (2006). Bayley scales of infant and toddler development (3rd ed.; Bayley–III). San Antonio, TX: The Psychological Corporation, Harcourt Assessment. Retrieved September 2006 from http://harcourtassessment.ca/HAIWEB/Cultures/en-us/dotCom/Bayley-III.com+Home.htm.

Beals, D. E., & DeTemple, J. M. (1993). Home contributions to early language and literary development. In D. Lea and C. Kenzer (Eds.), *Examinary central issues in literary research theory and practice: Full second yearbook of the National Reading Conference* (pp. 207–216). Chicago: National Reading Conference, Inc.

Beals, D. E., DeTemple, J. M., & Dickinson, D. K. (1994). Talking and listening that support early literacy development of children from low-income families. In D. K. Dickinson (Ed.), *Bridges to literacy: Children, families, and schools.* Cambridge, MA: Blackwell.

Bearison, D., & Dorval, B. (2002). *Collaborative cognition: Children negotiating ways of knowing.* Westport, CT: Ablex.

Beauchamp, C. K., & Moran, M. (1985). Acceptance of sweet and sour tastes in 2-year-old children. *Appetite, 5,* 291–305.

Becher, R. M. (1984). *Parent involvement: A review of research and principles of successful practice.* Urbana-Champaign, IL: ERIC Clearinghouse on Elementary and Early Childhood Education. (ERIC Document Reproduction Service No. ED 247-032)

Becker, D. M., Yanek, L. R., Koffman, D. M., & Bronner, Y. C. (1999). Body image preferences among urban African Americans and whites from low income communities. *Ethnicity and Disease, 9*(3), 377–386.

Becker, H. J. (2000). Who's wired and who's not: Children's access to and use of computer technology. *The future of children: Children and computer technology,* Vol. 10, 44–75.

Becker, P. E., & Moen, P. (1999). Scaling back: Dual-earner couples' work-family strategies. *Journal of Marriage and the Family, 61,* 995–1007.

Bednar, R. L., Wells, M. G., & Peterson, S. R. (1995). *Self-esteem* (2nd ed.). Washington, DC: American Psychological Association.

Begley, S. (1999). Shaped by life in the womb. *Newsweek, 134*(13), 50–57.

Begley, S. (2000). Getting inside a teen brain. *Newsweek, 135*(9), 58–59.

Behrman, R., & Kliegman, R. (1990). *Nelson essentials of pediatrics.* Philadelphia: W. B. Saunders.

Bellugi, U. (1970). Learning the language. *Psychology Today, 4,* 33.

Belsky, J. (1981). Early human experience: A family perspective. *Developmental Psychology, 17,* 2–23.

Bempechat, J., & Drago-Severson, E. (1999). Cross-national differences in academic achievement: Beyond etic conceptions of children's understandings. *Review of Educational Research, 69,* 287–314.

Benbow, C. (1986). Physiological correlates of extreme intellectual precocity. *Neuropsychologia, 24,* 719–725.

Benbow, C. (1992). Academic achievement in mathematics and science of students between 13 and 23: Are there differences among students in the top one percent of mathematical ability? *Journal of Educational Psychology, 84,* 51–61.

Benbow, C. P., Lubinski, D., Shea, D., & Eftekhari-Sanjani, H. (2000). Sex differences in mathematical reasoning ability at age 13: Their status 20 years later. *Psychological Science, 11*(6), 474–480.

Bender, B., Linden, M., & Robinson, A. (1987). Environment and developmental link in children with sex chromosome abnormalities. *Journal of the Academy of Child and Adolescent Psychiatry, 26,* 499–503.

Bennet, W. J. (1993). *The book of virtues: A treasury of great moral stories.* New York: Simon and Schuster.

Benware, C., & Deci, E. L. (1984). Quality of learning with an active versus passive motivational set. *American Educational Research Journal, 21,* 755–765.

Berk, L. (1986). Relationship of elementary school children's private speech to behavioral accompaniment to task, attention, and task performance. *Developmental Psychology, 22,* 671–680.

Berk, L., & Garvin, R. (1984). Development of private speech among low-income Appalachian children. *Developmental Psychology, 20,* 271–286.

Berliner, D., & Biddle, B. (1995). *The manufactured crisis. Myths, fraud, and the attack on America's public schools.* New York: Addison Wesley.

Bernal, M., & Knight, G. (1997). Ethnic identity of Latino children. In J. Garcia & M. Zea (Eds.), *Psychological interventions and research with Latino populations* (pp. 15–38). Newton, MA: Allyn & Bacon.

Bernard, B. (1991). *Fostering resiliency in kids: Protective factors in the family, school, and community.* Portland, OR.: Western Regional Center for Drug-Free Schools and Communities, Northwest Educational Laboratory.

Berndt, T. (1999). Friends' influence on students' adjustment to school. *Educational Psychologist, 34,* 15–28.

Berndt, T. F., & Keefe, K. (1995). Friends' influence on adolescents' adjustment to school. *Child Development, 66,* 1312–1329.

Berndt, T. J. & Keefe, K. (1992). Friends' influence on adolescents' perceptions of themselves in school. In D. H. Schunk & J. Meece (Eds.), *Student perceptions in the classroom* (pp. 51–73). Hillsdale, NJ: Erlbaum.

Berninger, A., Mizokawa, D., & Bragg, R. (1991). Theory-based diagnosis and remediation of writing disabilities. *Journal of School Psychology, 29,* 57–79.

Berninger, V. (2000). Development of language by hand and its connections with language by ear, mouth, and eye. *Topics in Language Disorders, 20,* 65–84.

Bertalanffy, L. von (1968). *General systems theory.* New York: Braziller.

Betz, N. E., & Fitzgerald, L. F. (1988). *The career psychology of women.* Orlando, FL: Academic Press.

Bialystok, E. (2001). *Bilingualism in development: Language, literacy, and cognition.* New York: Cambridge University Press.

Bigler, R., Jones, L., & Lobliner, D. (1997). Social categorization and the formation of intergroup attitudes in children. *Child Development, 68,* 530–543.

Bigner, J. J., & Jacobsen, R. B. (1989). Parenting behaviors of homosexual and heterosexual fathers. In F. W. Bozett (Ed.), *Homosexuality and the family* (pp. 173–186). New York: Harrington Park Press.

Biller, H. B. (1981). Father absence, divorce, and personality development. In M. E. Lamb (Ed.), *The role of the father in child development* (pp. 489–552). New York: John Wiley.

Birch, S., & Ladd, G. (1996). Interpersonal relationships in the school environment and children's early school adjustment. In J. Juvonen & K. Wentzel (Eds.), *Social motivation: Understanding children's school adjustment* (pp. 199–225). New York: Cambridge University Press.

Birch, S., & Ladd, G. (1997). The teacher-child relationship and children's early school adjustment. *Journal of School Psychology, 35,* 61–79.

Birch, S., & Ladd, G. (1998). Children's interpersonal behaviors and the teacher-child relationship. *Developmental Psychology, 34,* 934–946.

Bishop, E., Cherny, S., Corley, R., Plomin, R., DeFries, J., & Hewitt, J. (2003). Development genetic analysis of general cognitive ability from 1 to 12 years in a sample of adoptees, biological siblings, and twins. *Intelligence, 31,* 31–49.

Bishop, S. M., & Ingersoll, G. M. (1989). Effects of marital conflict and family structure on the self-concepts of pre- and early adolescents. *Journal of Youth and Adolescence, 18,* 25–38.

Bissex, G. (1980). *GYNS AT WRK: A child learns to write and read.* Cambridge, MA: Harvard University Press.

Bjorklund, D. F. (1995). *Children's thinking: Developmental function and individual differences.* New York: Brooks/Cole.

Bjorklund, D. F., Muir-Broaddus, J. E., & Schneider, W. (1990). The role of knowledge in the development of strategies. In D. F. Bjorklund (Ed.), *Children's strategies: Contemporary views of cognitive development* (pp. 93–128). Hillsdale, NJ: Erlbaum.

Black, B., & Greenough, W. (1986). Induction of pattern in neural structure by experience. In M. Lamb, A. Brown, & B. Rogoff (Eds.), *Advances in developmental psychology* (Vol. 4, pp. 1–41). Hillsdale, NJ: Erlbaum.

Black-Gutman, D., & Hickson, F. (1996). The relationship between racial attitudes and social-cognitive development in children: An Australian study. *Developmental Psychology, 32,* 448–456.

Blank, M., Shah, B., Johnson, S., Blackwell, W., Ganley, M. (2005). Reforming education: Developing 21st-century community schools (pp. 227–246). In R. Lerner, F. Jacobs, & D. Wertlieb (Eds.), *Applied developmental science: An advanced textbook.* Thousand Oaks, CA: Sage.

Block, C., & Pressley, M. (2002). Comprehension instruction: Research-based best practices. New York: The Guilford Press.

Bloom, B. (1964). *Stability and change in human characteristics.* New York: John Wiley.

Bloom, B. (1985). *Developing talent in young people.* New York: Ballantine.

Bloom, L. (1970). *Language development: Form and function in emerging grammars.* Cambridge, MA: MIT Press.

Bloom, L., & Tinker, E. (2001). The intentionality model of language acquisition: Engagement, effort, and the essential tension in development. *Monographs of the Society for Research in Child Development, 66*(4), Serial No. 267.

Blum, R. W., Beuhring, T., Shew, M., Bearinger, L. H., Sieving R. E., & Resnick, M. D. (2000). The effects of race/ethnicity, income and family structure on adolescent risk behaviors. *American Journal of Public Health, 90*(12), 1879–1884.

Blumsack, J., Lewandowski, L., & Waterman, B. (1997). Neurodevelopmental precursors to learning disabilities: A preliminary report

from a parent survey. *Journal of Learning Disabilities, 30,* 228–237.

Blyth, D., Simmons, R., & Zakin, D. (1985). Satisfaction with body image for early adolescent females: The impact of pubertal timing within different school environments. *Journal of Youth and Adolescence, 14,* 207–225.

Board on Children and Families. (1995). Immigrant children and their families: Issues for research and policy. *The Future of Children, 5,* 72–89.

Boateng, F. (1990). Combating deculturalization of the African-American child in the public school system. In K. Lomotey (Ed.), *Going to school. The African-American experience.* Albany: State University of New York Press.

Bochnek, M., & Widney, B. (2001). Hatred in the hallway: Violence and discrimination against lesbian, gay, bisexual, and transgender students in U.S. schools. New York: Human Rights Watch. Available online at http://www.hrw.org/reports/2001/uslgbt/toc.htm.

Bogard, K., & Takanishi, R. (2005). PK–3: An aligned and coordinated approach to education for children 3 to 8 years old. *SRCD Social Policy Report, 19,* 3–21.

Bong, M., & Clark, R. (1999). Comparison between self-concept and self-efficacy in academic motivation research. *Educational Psychologist, 34,* 139–153.

Booth, A., & Dunn, J. (1996). *Family-school links: How do they affect educational outcomes.* Mahwah, NJ: Erlbaum.

Borko, H., & Putnam, R. T. (1996). Learning to teach. In D.C. Berliner & R. C. Calfee (Eds.), *Handbook of educational psychology* (pp. 673–708). New York: Macmillian.

Bornstein, M. (1989). *Maternal responsiveness: Characteristics and consequences.* San Francisco, CA: Jossey-Bass.

Bornstein, M., (2005). Positive parenting and positive development in children. In R. Lerner, F., Jacobs, & D. Werlieg (Eds.), *Applied development science: An advanced textbook* (pp. 155–178). Thousand Oaks, CA: Sage.

Bornstein, M., & Tamis-LeMonda, C. S. (1997). Maternal responsiveness and infant mental abilities: Specific predictive relations. *Infant Behavior and Development, 20,* 283–296.

Bosworth, K., Espelage, D. L., & Simon, T. R. (1999). Factors associated with bullying behavior in middle school students. *Journal of Early Adolescence, 19*(3), 341–362.

Bouchard, T., Jr., & McGue, M. (1981). Familial studies of intelligence: A review. *Science, 212,* 1055–1059.

Bowerman, M. (1973). *Early syntactic development: A cross-linguistic study with special reference to Finnish.* Cambridge, England: Cambridge University Press.

Bowlby, J. (1969). *Attachment and loss: Vol. 1. Attachment.* New York: Basic Books.

Bowman, P. (1995). Coping with provider role strain: Adaptive cultural resources among black husband-fathers. *Journal of Black Psychology, 16*(2), 1–21.

Boyd, B. (1997). Teacher response to superhero play: To ban or not to ban? *Childhood Education, 74,* 23–28.

Boysson-Bardies, B. (1999). *How language comes to children: From birth to two years.* Cambridge, MA: Bradford, The MIT Press.

Bozett, F. W. (1989). Gay fathers: A review of the literature. *Journal of Homosexuality, 18,* 137–162.

Bracey, G. (1995). *Final exam: A study of the perpetual scrutiny of American education: Historical perspectives on assessment, standards, outcomes, and criticism of U.S. public schools.* Bloomington, IN: TECHNOS Press.

Braddock, J., & McPartland, J. (1993). Education of early adolescents. *Review of Research in Education, 19,* 135–170.

Bradley, R., & Caldwell, B. (1984a). 174 children: A study of the relationship between the home environment and early cognitive development in the first five years. In A. W. Gottfried & A. E. Gottfried (Eds.), *The home environment and early cognitive development.* New York: Academic Press.

Bradley, R., & Caldwell, B. (1984b). The HOME inventory and family demographics. *Developmental Psychology, 20,* 315–320.

Bradley, R., & Caldwell, B. M. (1984c). The relation of infants' home environments to achievement test performance in first grade: A follow-up study. *Child Development, 55,* 803–809.

Bradley, R., Corwyn, R., Burchinal, M., McAdoo, H., & Coll, C. (2001b). The home environments of children in the United States part II: Relations with behavioral development through age thirteen. *Child Development, 72,* 1868–1886.

Bradley, R., Corwyn, R., Caldwell, B., Whiteside-Mansell, L., Wasserman, G., & Mink, I. (2000). Measuring the home environments of children in early adolescence. *Journal of Research on Adolescence, 10,* 247–288.

Bradley, R., Corwyn, R., McAdoo, H., & Coll, C. (2001a). The home environments of children in the United States part 1: Variations by age, ethnicity, and poverty status. *Child Development, 72,* 1844–1867.

Bradley, R. H., Caldwell, B. M., & Rock, S. L. (1988). Home environment and school performance: A ten-year follow-up and examination of three models of environmental action. *Child Development, 59,* 852–867.

Bradley, R. H., Caldwell, B. M., Rock, S. L., Ramey, G. T., Barnard, K. E., Gray, G., Hammond, M. A., Mitchell, S., Gottfried, A. W., Siegel, L., & Johnson, D. L. (1989). Home environment and cognitive development in the first 3 years of life: A collaborative study involving six sites and three ethnic groups in North America. *Developmental Psychology, 25,* 217–235.

Braine, M. D. S. (1976). Children's first word combinations. *Monographs of the Society for Research in Child Development, 41*(Serial No. 164).

Bransford, J., Brown, A., & Cocking, R. (Eds.). (2000). *How people learn: Brain, mind, experience, and school.* Commission on Behavioral and Social Science and Education, National Research Council. Washington, DC: National Academy Press.

Braumind, D. (1967). Child care practices anteceding three patterns of preschool behavior. *Genetic Psychology Monographs, 75,* 43–88.

Braverman, P. K. (2000). Sexually transmitted diseases in adolescents. *Medical Clinics of North America, 84*(4), 869–889, vi–vii.

Bray, J. H., & Burger, S. H. (1993). Developmental issues in stepfamilies research project: Family relationships and parent-child interactions. *Journal of Family Psychology, 7,* 76–80.

Bredekamp, S., & Copple, C. (1997). *Developmentally appropriate practice in early childhood programs.* Washington, DC: National Association for the Education of Young Children.

Brendt, T. J. (1999). Friends' influence on students' adjustment to school. *Educational Psychologist, 34,* 15–29.

Britto, P., & Brooks-Gunn, J. (2001). The role of family literacy environment in promoting young children's emerging literacy skills. *New Directions for Child and Adolescent Development, 92,* 1–7. San Francisco: Jossey-Bass.

Britton, J. (1970). *Language and learning.* New York: Penguin Books.

Britton, J., Burgess, T., Martin, N., McLeod, A., & Rosen, J. (1975). *The development of writing abilities* (pp. 11–18). London: Macmillan Education.

Brody, G. H., & Flor, D. L. (1998). Maternal resources, parenting practices, and child competence in rural, single-parent African American families. *Child Development, 69,* 803–816.

Brody, G. H., Stoneman, A., & McCoy, J. K. (1994). Forecasting sibling relationships in early adolescence from child temperaments and family processes in middle childhood. *Child Development, 65,* 771–784.

Brody, N. (1992). *Intelligence.* New York: Academic Press.

Bronfenbrenner, U. (1979). *The ecology of human development: Experiments by nature and design.* Cambridge, MA: Harvard University Press.

Bronfenbrenner, U. (1986). Ecology of the family as a context for human development: Research perspectives. *Developmental Psychology, 22,* 723–742.

Bronfenbrenner, U. (1993). Ecological systems theory. In R. Wozniak, & K. Fisher (Eds.), *Specific environments: Thinking in contexts* (pp. 3–44). Hillsdale, NJ: Erlbaum.

Bronfenbrenner, U., & Morris, P. A. (1998). The ecology of developmental processes. In W. Damon (Gen. Ed.) & R. M. Lerner (Vol. Ed.), *Handbook of child psychology: Vol. 1. Theoretical models of human development* (pp. 993–1028). New York: John Wiley.

Bronstein, P., Ginsburg, G. S., & Herrara, I. S. (2005). Parental predictors of motivational orientation in early adolescence: A longitudinal study. *Journal of Youth and Adolescence, 34,* 599–575.

Brook, J. S., Brook, D. W., Gordon, A. S., Whiteman, M., & Cohen, P. (1990). The psychological etiology of adolescent drug use: A family interactional approach. *Genetic, Social and General Psychology Monographs, 116,* 110–267.

Brooks, R., & Meltzoff, A. (2005). The development of gaze following and its relation to language. *Developmental Science, 8,* 535–543.

Brooks-Gunn, J., Britto, P. R., & Brady, C. (1999). Struggling to make ends meet: Poverty and child development. In M. E. Lamb (Ed.), *Parenting and child development in "nontraditional" families* (pp. 279–304). Mahwah, NJ: Erlbaum.

Brooks-Gunn, J., & Chase-Lansdale, P. L. (1995). Adolescent parenthood. In M. H. Bornstein (Ed.), *Handbook of parenting: Vol. 3. Status and social conditions of parenting* (pp. 113–149). Mahwah, NJ: Erlbaum.

Brooks-Gunn, J., Klebanov, P., Smith, J., Duncan, G., & Lee, K. (2003). The black-white test score gap in young children: Contributions of test and family characteristics. *Applied Developmental Science, 7,* 239–252.

Brooks-Gunn, J., & Warren, M. (1989). Biological and social contributions to negative affect in young adolescent girls. *Child Development, 60,* 40–55.

Brophy, J. (1986). *On motivating students.* (Occasional paper No. 101). East Lansing, MI: Institute for Research and Teaching, Michigan State University. (ERIC Document Reproduction Service No. ED 276 724)

Brophy, J. (1995). *Elementary Teachers' perceptions of and reported strategies for coping with twelve types of problem students.* East Lansing, MI: Institute for Research on Teaching, Michigan State University. (ERIC Document Reproduction Service No. ED 389 390)

Brophy, J. (1996). Working with shy or withdrawn students. ERIC Clearinghouse on Elementary and Early Childhood Education website. Retrieved March 9, 2001 from http://ericps.edu.uiuc.edu/eece/pubs/digests/1996/brop-s96.html. (ERIC Document Reproduction Service No. EDO-PS-96-14)

Brophy, J. (2004). *Motivating students to learn* (2nd ed.). Mahwah, NJ: Erlbaum.

Brophy, J., & Good, T. (1974). *Teacher-student relationships: Causes and consequences.* New York: Holt, Rinehart, & Winston.

Brown, A. (1997). Transforming schools into communities of thinking and learning about serious matters. *American Psychologist, 52,* 399–413.

Brown, A. L., Bransford, J. D., Ferrara, R. A., & Campione, J. C. (1983). Learning, remembering, and understanding. In W. Damon (Series Ed.), J. H. Flavell (Vol. Ed.), & E. M. Markman (Vol. Ed.), *Handbook of child psychology: Vol 3. Cognitive develop-ment* (pp. 77–166). New York: John Wiley.

Brown, A. L., & Campione, J. C. (1990). Communities of learning and thinking, or a context by any other name. In D. Kuhn (Ed.), *Developmental perspectives on teaching and learning thinking skills* (pp. 108–126). Basel, Switzerland: Karger.

Brown, A. L., & Campione, J. C. (1994). Guided discovery in a community of learners. In K. McGilly (Ed.), *Classroom lessons* (pp. 229–270). Cambridge, MA: MIT Press.

Brown, A. L., & Smiley S. S. (1978). The development of strategies to study text. *Child Development, 49,* 1076–1088.

Brown, B. (1990). Peer groups and peer culture. In S. S. Feldman & G. R. Elliot (Eds.), *At the threshold: The developing adolescent* (pp. 171–196). Cambridge, MA: Harvard University Press.

Brown, B., Mory, M. S., & Kinney, D. (1994). Casting adolescent crowds in a relational perspective: Caricature, channel, and context. In R. Montemayor, G. R. Adams, & T. P. Gulotta (Eds.), *Personal relationships during adolescence. Advances in adolescent development* (Vol. 6, pp. 123–168). Thousand Oaks: CA: Sage.

Brown, B. B., Lohr, M. J., & McClenahan, E. L. (1986). Early adolescents' perceptions of peer pressure. *Journal of Early Adolescence, 6,* 139–154.

Brown, C. S., & Bigler, R. S. (2005). Children's perceptions of discrimination: A developmental model. *Child Development, 76,* 533–553.

Brown, J. H., & Dunn, J. (1992). Talk with your mother or your sibling? Developmental changes in early family conversations about feelings. *Child Development, 63,* 336–349.

Brown, J. R., & Dunn, J. (1996). Talk with your mother or your sibling? Developmental changes in early family conversation about feelings. *Child Development, 67,* 789–802.

Brown, R. (1973). *A first language: The early stages.* Cambridge, MA: Harvard University Press.

Bruer, J. (1999). *The myth of the first three years: A new understanding of early brain development and life long learning.* New York: Free Press.

Bruer, J. (2002). Avoiding the pediatricians' error: How neuroscientists can help educators (and themselves). *Nature Neuroscience Supplement, 5,* 1031–1033.

Bruer, J. T. (1999). In search of brain-based education. *Phi Delta Kappan, 80,* 649–657.

Bruner, J. (1982). The formats of language acquisition. *American Journal of Semiotics, 1,* 1–16.

Bruner, J. (1996). *The culture of education.* Cambridge, MA: Harvard University Press.

Bruner, J. (2002). *Making stories: Law, literature, life.* New York: Farrar, Straus & Giroux.

Bruning, R., & Horn, C. (2000). Developing motivation to write. *Educational Psychologist, 35,* 25–38.

Bryant, B. K., & Crockenberg, S. B. (1980). Correlates and dimensions of prosocial behavior: A study of female siblings with their mothers. *Child Development, 51,* 529–554.

Bryant, D., Clifford, R., & Peisner, E. (1991). Best practices for beginners: Developmental appropriateness in kindergarten. *American Educational Research Journal, 28,* 783–803.

Buchanan, C. M., Eccles, J. S., & Becker, J. B. (1992). Are adolescents the victims of raging hormones?: Evidence of activational effects of hormones on moods and behavior in adolescence. *Psychological Bulletin, 111*(1), 62–107.

Buchannan, C. M., Eccles, J. S., Flanagan, C., Midgley, C., Feldlaufer, H., & Harold, R. (1990). Parents' and teachers' beliefs about adolescents: Effects of sex and experience. *Journal of Youth and Adolescence, 19,* 363–394.

Buchanan, C. M., Maccoby, E. E., & Dornbusch, S. M. (1992). Adolescents and their families after divorce: Three residential arrangements compared. *Journal of Research in Adolescence, 2*(3), 261–291.

Bugental, D. B., & Goodnow, J. J. (1998). Socialization processes. In W. Damon (Gen. Ed.) & N. Eisenberg (Vol. Ed.), *Handbook of child psychology: Vol. 3. Social, emotional, and personality development* (pp. 389–462). New York: John Wiley.

Buhrmester D. (1996). *Need fulfillment, interpersonal competence, and the developmental contexts of early adolescent friendship.* In W. Bukowski, A. Newcomb, &. W. Hartup (Eds.), *The Company They Keep* (pp. 158–185). New York: Cambridge University Press.

Buoye, A. (1998). Differentiating the effects of industrial and team sports participation on students' grade. Unpublished master's thesis, Notre Dame University, South Bend, IN.

Burchinal, M., Peisner-Feinberg, E., Pianta, R., & Howes, C. (2002). Development of academic skills from preschool through second grade: Family and classroom predictors of development trajectories. *Journal of School Psychology, 40,* 415–436.

Bureau of the U.S. Census. (1984). *Conditions of Hispanics in America today.* Washington, DC: U.S. Government Printing Office.

Bureau of the U.S. Census. (1987). *The Hispanic population in the United States: March 1986 and 1987.* Washington, DC: U.S. Government Printing Office.

Buriel, R., & De Ment, T. (1997). Immigration and sociocultural change in Mexican, Chinese, and Vietnamese American families. In A. Booth, A. C. Crouter, & N. Landale (Eds.), *Immigration and the family* (pp. 165–200). Mahwah, NJ: Erlbaum.

Burling, R. (1959). "Proto-Bodo." *Language, 35,* 433–453.

Burns, G. L. (1995). *Child and adolescent disruptive behavior inventory–parent rating scale version 1a.* Washington State University.

Burton, L., M., & Dilworth-Anderson, P. (1991). The intergenerational roles of aged black Americans. *Family Review, 6,* 311–330.

Bus, A. G., van Ijzendoorn, M. H. & Pellegrini, A. (1995). Joint book ready makes for success in learning to read: A meta-analysis on intergenerational transmission of Literacy. *Review of Educational Research, 65,* 1–21.

Buss, A., & Plomin, R. (1984). *Temperament: Early developing personality traits.* Hillsdale, NJ: Erlbaum.

Buss, A. H. (1995). *Personality: Temperament, social behavior, and the self.* Boston: Allyn & Bacon.

Bussey, K., & Bandura, A. (1999). Social cognitive theory of gender development and differentiation. *Psychological Review, 106,* 676–713.

Butterworth, B. (2005). The development of arithmetical abilities. *Journal of Child Psychology and Psychiatry, 46,* 3–18.

Byrne, B. M. (1986). Self-concept academic achievement relations: An investigation of dimensionality, stability, and causality. *Canadian Journal of Behavioral Science, 18,* 173–186.

Caine, R. N., & Caine, G. (1994). *Making connections: Teaching and the human brain.* New York: Addison Wesley.

Cairns, R. B., & Cairns, B. D. (1994). *Lifelines and risks: Pathways of youth in our time.* New York: Cambridge University Press.

Cairns, R. B., Cairns, B. D., & Neckerman, H. J. (1989). Early school dropout: Configurations and determinants. *Child Development, 60,* 1437–1452.

Cairns, R. B., Cairns, B. D., Neckerman, H. J., Gest, S. D., & Gariepy, J. L. (1988). Social networks and aggressive behavior: Peer support or peer rejection? *Developmental Psychology, 24,* 815–823.

Cairns, R. B., Leung, M. C., Buchanan, L., & Cairns, B. D. (1995). Friendships and social networks in childhood and adolescence: Fluidity, reliability, and interrelations. *Child Development, 66,* 1330–1345.

Caldwell, B. M. (1973). Infant day care—the outcast gains respectability. In P. Robey (Ed.), *Child care—who cares? Foreign and domestic infant and early childhood development policies.* New York: Basic Books.

Caldwell, B. M., & Bradley, R. H. (1984). *Home observation for measurement of the environment.* Little Rock: University of Arkansas.

Calfee, R. (1994). Critical literacy: Reading and writing for a new millennium. In N. Ellsworth, C. Hedley, & A. Baratta (Eds.), *Literacy: A redefinition* (pp. 19–38). Hillsdale, NJ: Erlbaum.

Calkins, S. D., Hungerford, A., & Dedmon, S. E. (2004). Mothers' interactions with temperamentally frustrated infants. *Infant Mental Health Journal, 25,* 219–239.

Calsyn, R., & Kenny, D. (1977). Self-concept of ability and perceived evaluations by others. Cause or effect of academic achievement. *Journal of Educational Psychology, 69,* 136–145.

Calvert, S. L., & Huston, A. C. (1987). Television and children's gender schemata. In L. S. Liben & M. L. Signorella (Eds.), *Children's gender schemata* (pp. 75–88). San Francisco: Jossey-Bass.

Camarata, S. M., Hughes, C. A., & Ruhl, K. L. (1988). Mild/moderate behaviorally disordered students: A population at risk for language disorders. *Language, Speech and Hearing Services in Schools, 19,* 191–200.

Camp, B. W., Blom, G., Hebert, F., & van Doornick, W. (1977). "Think Aloud": A program for developing self-control in young aggressive boys. *Journal of Abnormal Psychology, 5,* 157–169.

Campbell, F. A., & Ramey, C. T. (1993, March). Mid-adolescent outcomes for high risk students: An examination of the continuing effects of early intervention. Paper presented at the biennial meeting of the Society for Research in Child Development, New Orleans, LA.

Campbell, F. A., & Ramey, C. T. (1994). Early intervention on intellectual and academic achievement: A follow-up study of children from low-income families. *Child Development, 65*(2), 684–698.

Campbell, F., Ramey, C., Pungello, E., Miller-Johnson, S., & Burchinal, M. (2001). The development of cognitive and academic abilities: Growth curves from an early childhood educational experiment. *Developmental Psychology, 37,* 231–242.

Campbell, F., Ramey, C., Pungello, E., Sparling, J., & Miller-Johnson, S. (2002). Early childhood education: Young adult outcomes from the Abecedarian Project. *Applied Developmental Science, 6,* 42–57.

Campbell, J. R., Hombo, C. M., & Mazzeo, J. (2000). *NAEP 1999 trends in academic progress: Three decades of student performance.* Washington, DC: U.S. Department of Education, Office of Educational Research and Improvement.

Campbell, S. B. (1990). *Behavior problems in preschool children.* New York: Guilford Press.

Campoy, R. (2005). *Case study analysis in the classroom. Becoming a reflective teacher.* Thousand Oaks, CA: Sage Publications.

Canfield, J. (1990). Improving students' self-esteem. *Educational Leadership, 48,* 48–50.

Caplan, N., Choy, M., & Whitmore, J. (1992, February). Indochinese refugee families and academic achievement. *Scientific American, 266,* 36–42.

Caplan, P. J., & Caplan, J. B. (1999). *Thinking critically about research on sex and gender* (2nd ed.). New York: Addison Wesley Longman.

Capon, N., & Kuhn, D. (1979). Logical reasoning in the supermarket: Adult females' use of a proportional reasoning strategy. *Developmental Psychology, 15,* 450–452.

Carey, N., Lewis, L., & Farris, E. (1998). *Parent involvement in children's education: Efforts by public elementary schools.* National Center for Education Statistics Statistical Analysis Report. (ERIC Document Reproduction Service No. ED416027)

Carlson, E. A., Jacobvitz, D., & Sroufe, L. A. (1995). A developmental investigation of inattentiveness and hyperactivity. *Child Development, 66,* 37–54.

Carlsson-Paige, N., & Levin, D. E. (1995). Can teachers resolve the war-play dilemma? *Young Children, 50,* 62–63.

Carnegie Council on Adolescent Development. (1989). *Turning points: Preparing American youth for the 21st century.* Washington, DC: Carnegie Council on Adolescent Development.

Carraher, T., Carraher, D., & Schliemann, A. (1985). Mathematics in the streets and in the schools. *British Journal of Developmental Psychology, 3,* 21–29.

Carrasquillo, A. (1993). Whole native language instruction for limited-English-proficient students. In A. Carrasquillo & C. Hedley (Eds.), *Whole language and the bilingual learner* (pp. 3–19). Norwood, NJ: Ablex.

Carskadon, M. (1999). When worlds collide. Adolescent need for sleep versus societal demands. *Phi Delta Kappan, 80*(5), 348–353.

Casanova, U. (1995). Bilingual education: Politics or pedagogy? In O. Garcia & C. Baker (Eds.), *Policy and practice in bilingual education* (pp. 15–24). Bristol, PA.: Multilingual Matters.

Case, R. (1985). *Intellectual development: A systematic reinterpretation.* New York: Academic Press.

Case, R. (1998). The development of conceptual structures. In W. Damon (Series Ed.), D. Kuhn (Vol. Ed.), & R. Siegler (Vol. Ed.), *Handbook of child psychology: Vol. 2: Cognition, perception, and language* (5th ed., pp. 745–800). New York: John Wiley.

Case, R., & Okamoto, Y. (1996). The role of central conceptual structures in the development of children's thought. *Monographs of the Society for Research in Child Development, 61*(Serial No. 246).

Casper, V., Schultz, S., & Wickens, E. (1992). Breaking the silences: Lesbian and gay parents and the schools. *Teachers College Record, 94,* 109–137.

Caspi, A. (1998). Personality development across the life course. In W. Damon (Series Ed.) & N. Eisenberg (Vol. Ed.), *Handbook of child psychology, Vol. 3. Social, emotional, and personality development* (pp. 311–388). New York: John Wiley.

Caspi, A., Lynam, D., Moffitt, T., & Silva, A. (1993). Unraveling girls' delinquency: Biological, dispositional, and contextual contributions to adolescent misbehavior. *Developmental Psychology, 29,* 19–30.

Caspi, A., & Moffitt, T. (1991). Individual differences and personal transitions. The sample case of girls at puberty. *Journal of Personality and Social Psychology, 61,* 157–168.

Caspi, A., & Shiner, R. (2006). Personality development. In W. Damon & R. M. Lerner (Editors-in-Chief) & N. Eisenberg (Vol. Ed.), *Handbook of child psychology. Vol. 3. Social, emotional, and personality development* (pp. 300–365). New York: John Wiley.

Caspi, A., & Silva, P. A. (1995). Temperamental qualities at age 3 predict personality traits in young adulthood: Longitudinal evidence from a birth cohort. *Child Development, 66,* 129–161.

Cassidy, J., & Berlin, L. J. (1994). The insecure/ambivalent pattern of attachment: Theory and research. *Child Development, 65,* 971–991.

Cattell, R. B. (1971). *Abilities: Their structure, growth, and action.* Boston: Houghton Mifflin.

Ceci, S. (1990). *On intelligence . . . more or less: A bioecological treatise on intellectual development.* Englewood Cliffs, NJ: Prentice Hall.

Ceci, S. (1991). How much does schooling influence general intelligence and its cognitive components? A reassessment of the evidence. *Developmental Psychology, 27,* 703–722.

Ceci, S., & Williams, W. (1993). Schooling, intelligence, and income. *American Psychologist, 52,* 1051–1058.

Center for Communication and Social Policy. (Ed.). (1998). *National television violence study* (Vol. 2). Newbury Park, CA: Sage.

Center for Human Resources. (1999, July). *Summary report. National evaluation of Learn and Serve America.* Report preparted for the National Corporation for National Service. Waltham, MA: Brandeis University. Retrieved October 23, 2004, from http://www. learnandserve.org/.

Centers for Disease Control and Prevention (CDC). (1994, August 29). Zidovudine for the prevention of HIV transmission from mothers to infants. *Morbidity and Mortality Weekly Report, 43,* 577–581.

Centers for Disease Control and Prevention (CDC). (2002). *Prevalence of overweight among children and adolescents: United States, 1999–2002.* National Center for Health Statistics.

Centers for Disease Control and Prevention (CDC). (2005a). *Healthy youth! Health topics: Tobacco use.* National Center for Chronic Disease Prevention and Health Promotion. Washington, DC: U.S. Department of Health and Human Services.

Centers for Disease Control and Prevention (CDC). (2005b). *Trends in the prevalence of marijuana, cocaine, and other illegal drug use.* National Youth Risk Behavior Survey (YRBSS): 1991–2005. Washington, DC: U.S. Department of Health and Human Services.

Centers for Disease Control and Prevention (CDC). (2005c). *Healthy youth! Health topics: Alcohol and drug use.* National Center for Chronic Disease Prevention and Health Promotion. Washington, DC: U.S. Department of Health and Human Services.

Cernoch, J. M., & Porter, R. H. (1985). Recognition of maternal axillary odors by infants. *Child Development, 56,* 1593–1598.

Chall, J. S., Jacobs, V. & Baldwin, L. (1990). *The reading crisis: Why poor children fall behind.* Cambridge, MA: Harvard University Press.

Chamberlain, P., & Patterson, G. R. (1995). Discipline and child compliance in parenting. In M. H. Bornstein (Ed.), *Handbook of parenting: Vol. 4. Applied and practical parenting* (pp. 205–226). Mahwah, NJ: Erlbaum.

Chan, S. (1992). Families with Asian roots. In E. W. Lynch & M. J. Hanson (Eds.), *Developing cross-cultural competence* (pp. 121–150). Baltimore: Paul H. Brookes Publishing Company.

Chao, R. (2000). Cultural explanations for the role of parenting in the school success of Asian-American children. In R. Taylor & M. Wang (Eds.), *Resilience across contexts: Family, work, culture, and community.* Mahwah, NJ: Erlbaum.

Chao, R. K. (1994). Beyond parental control and authoritarian parenting style: Understanding Chinese parenting through the cultural notion of training. *Child Development, 65,* 1111–1119.

Chase, W. G., & Simon, H. A. (1973). Perception in chess. *Cognitive Psychology, 4,* 55–81.

Chase-Lansdale, L., Brooks-Gunn, J., & Paikoff, R. L. (1991). Research and programs for adolescent mothers: Missing links and future promises. *Family Relations, 40,* 396–403.

Chavkin, N. F. (Ed.). *Families and schools in a pluralistic society.* Albany: State University of New York Press.

Chavous, T. M., Bernat, D. H., Schmeelk-Cone, K., Caldwell, C. H., Kohn-Wood, L., & Zimmerman, M. A. (2003). Racial idenity and academic attainment among African American adolescents. *Child Development, 74*(4), 1076–1090.

Checkly, K. (1997, September). The just seven . . . and the eighth. A conversation with Howard Gardner. *Educational Leadership,* pp. 8–13.

Chen, C., Lee, S., & Stevenson, H. (1996). Long-term prediction of academic achievement of american, Chinese, and Japanese adolescents. *Journal of Educational Psychology, 88,* 750–759.

Chen, C., & Stevenson, H. (1995). Motivation and mathematics achievement: A comparative study of Asian-American, Caucasian-American, and East Asian high school students. *Child Development, 66,* 1215–1234.

Chen, C., Stevenson, H., Haywood, C., & Burgess, S. (1995). Culture and academic achievement: Ethnic and cross-national differences. In P. Pintrich & M. Maehr (Eds.), *Advances in motivation and achievement. Culture, motivation and achievement* (Vol. 9, pp. 119–152). Greenwich, CT: JAI Press, Inc.

Chen, X., Hastings, P. D., Rubin, K. H., Chen, H., Cen, G., & Stewart, S. L. (1998). Child-rearing attitudes and behavioral inhibition in Chinese and Canadian toddlers: A cross-cultural study. *Developmental Psychology, 34,* 677–686.

Cherlin, A. J., & Furstenberg, F. F. (1986). *The new American grandparent: A place in the family, a life apart.* New York: Basic Books.

Chess, S., & Thomas, A. (1977). Temperamental individuality from childhood to adolescence. *Journal of American Academy of Child Psychiatry, 16,* 218–226.

Chess, S., & Thomas, A. (1984). *Origins and evolution of behavior disorders.* New York: Brunner/Mazel.

Chi, M. T. H. (1978). Knowledge structure and memory development. In R. Siegler (Ed.), *Children's thinking: What develops?* Hillsdale, NJ: Erlbaum.

Chi, M. T. H., Feltovich, P. J., & Glaser, R. (1981). Categorization and representation of physic problems by experts and novices. *Cognitive Science, 5,* 121–152.

Chi, M. T. H., & Koeske, R. D. (1983). Network representation of a child's dinosaur knowledge. *Developmental Psychology, 19,* 29–39.

Child Welfare League of America. (2005). National Fact Sheet 2005. Retrieved July 2005 from http://www.cwla.org/ advocacy/default.htm.

Children's Defense Fund. (1996). *Yearbook 1996. The state of American's children.* Washington, DC: Author.

Children's Defense Fund. (1999). *Yearbook 1999. The state of American's children.* Washington, DC: Author.

Children's Defense Fund. (2000). *Yearbook 2000. The state of American's children.* Washington, DC: Author.

Children's Defense Fund. (2004). Key facts about American children. Available online at http://www. childrensdefense.org.

Children's Defense Fund. (2005a). Kinship care families (grandfamilies). Available online at http://www.childrensdefense.org.

Children's Defense Fund. (2005b). *The state of America's children 2005.* Washington, DC: Author.

Chomsky, N. (1957). *Syntactic structures.* The Hague, The Netherlands: Mouton.

Chomsky, N. (1965). *Aspects of the theory of syntax.* Cambridge, MA: MIT Press.

Chomsky, C. (1970). Reading, writing, and phonology. *Harvard Educational Review, 40,* 297–309.

Chomsky, N. (1986). *Knowledge of language: Its nature, origin and use.* New York: Praeger.

Chomsky, N. (1999). On the nature, use, and acquisition of language. In W. Ritchie & T. Bhatia (Eds.), *Handbook of child language acquisition* (pp. 33–54). San Diego, CA: Academic Press.

Christenson, S., Rounds, R., and Gorney, D. (1992). Family factors and student achievement: An avenue to increase students' success. *School Psychology Quarterly, 7,* 178–206.

Cicchetti, D., & Toth, S. L. (1998). The development of depression in children and adolescents. *American Psychologist, 53,* 221–241.

Cirino, H. (2001). Journal journeys: An exploration with young writers. In D. Duckworth (Ed.), *Tell me more: Listening to learners explain* (pp. 79–92). New York: Teachers College Press.

Clarizio, H. F. (1997). Conduct disorder: Developmental considerations. *Psychology in the Schools, 34,* 253–265.

Clark, B. (2002). *Growing up gifted* (4th ed.). Upper Saddle River, NJ: Merrill/Prentice Hall.

Clark, E. (2004). How language acquisition builds on cognitive development. *Trends in Cognitive Sciences, 8,* 472–478.

Clark, H., & Clark, E. (1977). *Psychology and language.* New York: Harcourt Brace Jovanovich.

Clark, K. B., & Clark, M. K. (1940). Skin color as a factor in racial identification of Negro pre-school children. *Journal of Social Psychology, 2,* 154–167.

Clark, L. A., Kochanska, G., & Ready, R. (2000). Mothers' personality and its interaction with child temperament as predictors of parenting behavior. *Journal of Personality and Social Psychology, 79,* 274–285.

Clark, M. L. (1991). Social identity, peer relations, and academic competence of African American adolescents. *Education and Urban Society, 24*(1), 41–52.

Clark, R. (1983). *Family life and school achievement: Why poor black children succeed or fail.* Chicago: University of Chicago Press.

Clark, V. P., Eschholz, P. A., & Rosa, A. F. (1985). *Language: Introductory readings.* New York: St. Martin's Press.

Clarke, S. C. (1995). Advance report of final marriage statistics, 1989 and 1990. *Monthly Vital Statistics Report, 43*(12), suppl. (DHHS Publication No. [PHS] 95-1120). Hyattsville, MD: National Center for Health Statistics.

Clay, M. (2002). *An observation study of early literacy achievement* (2nd ed.). Portsmouth, NH: Heinemann.

Clay, M. M. (1980). *Reading: The patterning of complex behavior* (2nd ed.). Portsmouth, NH: Heinemann.

Clay, M. M. (1985). *The early detection of reading difficulties* (3rd ed.). Portsmouth, NH: Heinemann.

Clay, M. M. (1991). *Becoming literate: The construction of inner control.* Portsmouth, NH: Heinemann.

Coalition for Community Schools. (2000). *Community schools: Partnerships for Excellence.* Washington, DC: Institute for Educational Leadership.

Coalition for Community Schools. (2003). *Making the difference: Research and practice in community schools.* Washington, DC: Institute for Educational Leadership.

Cohen, B. (1980). *Issues related to transferring reading skills from Spanish to English.* Bilingual Education Paper Series. New York: Research & Development.

Cohen, F. (1984). *Clinical genetics in nursing practice.* Philadelphia: Lippincott.

Cohen, N. J., & Minde, K. (1981). The "hyperactive syndrome" in kindergarten children: Comparison of children with pervasive and situational symptoms. *Journal of Child Psychology and Psychiatry, 24,* 443–455.

Cohn, D. A. (1990). Child-mother attachment of six-year-olds and social competence at school. *Child Development, 61,* 152–162.

Coie, J. D., & Dodge, K. A. (1983). Continuities and changes in children's sociometric status. A five-year longitudinal study. *Merrill-Palmer Quarterly, 29,* 261–282.

Coie, J. D., & Dodge, K. (1998). Aggression and antisocial behavior. In W. Damon (Series Ed.) & N. Eisenburg (Vol. Ed.), *Handbook of child development, Vol. 3. Social, emotional and personality development* (pp. 779–862). New York: John Wiley.

Coie, J. D., Dodge, K., & Kuperschmidt, J. B. (1990). Peer group behavior and social status. In S. K. Asher & J. D. Coie (Eds.), *Peer rejection in childhood* (pp. 17–59). New York: Cambridge University Press.

Colby, A., Kohlberg, L., Gibbs, J., & Lieberman, M. (1983). A longitudinal study of moral judgment. *Monographs of the Society for Research in Child Development, 481*(Serial No. 200).

Cole, M. (2006). Culture and cognitive development in phylogenetic, historical, and ontogenetic perspective. In W. Damon & R. M. Lerner (Editors-in Chief), & D. Kuhn & R. Siegler (Vol. Eds.), *Handbook of child psychology. Volume two: Cognition, perception, and language* (pp. 636–683). New York: John Wiley.

Cole, M., Cole, S., & Lightfoot, C. (2005). *The development of children* (5th ed.). New York: Worth Publishers.

Cole, R. (1995). *Educating everybody's children. Diverse teaching strategies for diverse learners.* Alexandria, VA: Association for Supervision and Curriculum Development.

Coleman, M. (1992). A comparison of how gifted/LD and average/LD boys cope with school frustration. *Journal for the Education of the Gifted, 15,* 239–265.

Coleman, M., Buysse, V., & Neitzel, J. (2006). *Recognition and response: An early intervention system for young children at-risk for learning disabilities: Research synthesis and recommendations.* Chapel Hill, NC: FPG Child Development Institute, University of North Carolina at Chapel Hill.

Coles, M., & Hall, C. (2002). Gendered reading: Learning from children's reading choices. *Journal of Research on Reading, 25,* 96–108.

Coles, R. (1997). *The moral intelligence of children.* New York: Random House.

Coley, R. J. (2001). *Differences in the gender gap: Comparisons across racial/ethnic groups in education and work.* Princeton, NJ: Educational Testing Service.

Collins, W. A., Harris, M. L., & Susman, A. (1996). Parenting during middle childhood. In M. H. Borstein (Ed.), *Handbook of parenting: Vol 1. Children and parenting* (pp. 65–90). Mahwah, NJ: Erlbaum.

Collins, W. A., Maccoby, E. E., Steinberg, L., Hetherington, E. M., & Bornstein, M. H. (2000). Contemporary research on parenting: The case for nature and nurture. *American Psychologist, 55,* 218–232.

Comer, J. (1984). Home–school relationships as they affect the academic success of children. *Education and Urban Society, 16,* 323–337.

Comer, J. (1985). The Yale–New Haven Primary Prevention Project: A follow-up. *Journal of the American Academy of Child Psychiatry, 24,* 154–160.

Comer, J. (1989). Educating poor minority children. *Scientific American, 259*(9), 42–48.

Comer, J. (2004). *Leave no child behind: Preparing today's youth for tomorrow's world.* New Haven, CT: Yale University Press.

Comer, J. O., & Haynes, H. D. (1999). The dynamics of school change: Response to the article, "Comer's School Development Program in Prince George's County, Maryland: A theory-based evaluation," by Thomas D. Cook et al. *American Educational Journal, 36*(3), 599–607.

Comer, J. P., Haynes, H. D., Joyner, E. T., & Ben Avie, M. (1996). *Rallying the whole village: The Comer process for reforming education.* New York: Teachers College Press.

Comer, J. P., & Poussaint, A. F. (1992). *Raising black children.* New York: Penguin Books.

Committee on the Foundations of Assessment. (2001). *Knowing what students know: The science and design of educational assessment.* Washington, DC: National Academy Press.

Compas, B., Ey, S., & Grant, K. (1993). Taxonomy, assessment, and diagnosis of depression during adolescence. *Psychological Bulletin, 114,* 323–344.

Compas, B. E., Connor-Smith, J. K., Saltzman, H., Thomsen, A. H., & Wadsworth, M. (2001). Coping with stress during childhood and adolescence: Problems, progress, and potential in theory and research. *Psychological Bulletin, 127,* 87–127.

Conger, R., Conger, K., Elder, G., Lorenz, F., Simons, R., & Whitbeck, L. (1992). A family process model of economic hardship and adjustment of early adolescent boys. *Child Development, 63,* 526–541.

Conklin, K. D., Curran, B. K., & Gandal, M. (2005). *2005 National Education Summit on High Schools.* Washington, DC: Achieve Inc. and National Governors Association. Available online at http://www.nga.org.

Conklin, M. E., & Dailey, A. R., (1981). Does consistency of parental encouragement matter for secondary students? *Sociology of Education, 54,* 254–262.

Connell, J. P. (1990). Context, self, and action: A motivational analyses of self-system processes across the life span. In D. Cicchetti & M. Beeghly (Eds.), *The self in transition: Infancy to childhood.* Chicago: University of Chicago Press.

Conner, J. (2003). Physical activity and well-being. In M. Bornstein, L. Davidson, C. Keyes, & K. Moore (Eds.), *Well-being: Positive development across the life course* (pp. 65–80). Mahwah, NJ: Erlbaum.

Conner, J., & Dewey, J. (2003). Reproductive health. In M. Bornstein, L. Davidson, C. Keyes, & K. Moore (Eds.), *Well-being: Positive development across the life course* (pp. 99–108). Mahwah, NJ: Erlbaum Associates.

Conner, J. M., Schackman, M., & Serbin, L. A. (1978). Sex-related differences in response to practice on a visual-spatial test and generalization to a related test. *Child Development, 49,* 24–29.

Cook, B. G. (2001). A comparison of teachers' attitudes toward their included students with middle and severe disabilities. *The Journal of Special Education, 34,* 203–213.

Cook, B. G., Semmel, M. I., & Gerber, M. M. (1999). Attitudes of principals and special education teachers toward inclusion: Critical differences of opinion. *Remedial and Special Education, 20,* 199–207, 256.

Cook, B. G., Tankersley, M., Cook, L., & Landrum, T. J. (2000). Teachers' attitudes toward their included students with disabilities. *Exceptional Children, 67,* 115–135.

Coon, H., Fulker, D., DeFries, J. C., & Plomin, R. (1990). Home environment and cognitive ability of 7-year-old children in the Colorado Adoption Project: Genetic and environmental etiologies. *Developmental Psychology, 26,* 459–468.

Cooper, H., & Dorr, N. (1995). Race comparisons on need for achievement: A meta-analytic alternative to Graham's narrative review. *Review of Educational Research, 65,* 483–508.

Cooper H., Nye, B., Charlton, K., Lindsay, J. & Greathouse, S. (1996). The effects of summer vacation on achievement test scores: A narrative and meta-analysis review. *Review Educational Research, 66,* 227–269.

Cooper, J., & Weaver, K. D. (2003). *Gender and computers. Understanding the digital divide.* Mahwah, NJ: Lawrence Erlbaum.

Coppersmith, S. (1967). *The antecedents of self-esteem.* San Francisco: W. H. Freeman.

Corno, L., & Rohrkemper, M. (1985). The intrinsic motivation to learn in classrooms. In C. Ames & R. Ames (Eds.), *Research on motivation in education: The classroom milieu* (Vol. 2, pp. 53–84), New York: Academic Press.

Coulton, C. J., Korbin, J. E., Su, M., & Chow, J. (1995). Community level factors and child maltreatment rates. *Child Development, 66,* 1262–1276.

Council of Chief State Officers. (2002). *Interstate New Teacher Assessment and Support Consortium (INTASC).* Washington, DC: Author. Retreived August 21, 2006, from http://www.ccsso.org/projects.

Covington, M. V. (1992). *Making the grade: A self-worth perspective on motivation and school reform.* New York: Cambridge University Press.

Cox, M., & Harter, K. (2003). Parent–child relationships. In M. Bornstein, L. Davidson, C. Keyes, & K. Moore (Eds.), *Well-being: Positive development across the life course* (pp. 191–204). Mahwah, NJ: Erlbaum.

Cox, M. J., & Paley, B. (1997). Families as systems. *Annual Review of Psychology, 48,* 243–267.

Craik, F. I. M., & Lockhart, R. S. (1972). Levels of processing: A framework for memory research. *Journal of Verbal Learning and Verbal Behavior, 12,* 599–607.

Crain-Thoreson, C., & Dale, P. S. (1992). Do early talkers become early readers? Linguistic precocity, preschool language, and emergent literacy. *Developmental Psychology, 28,* 421–429.

Cramer, C., & Davidhizar, R. (1999). FAS/FAE: impact on children. *Journal of Child Health Care, 3*(3), 31–54.

Cratty, B. J. (1986). *Perceptual and motor development in infants and children* (3rd ed.). Englewood Cliffs, NJ: Prentice Hall.

Crick, N. R., & Dodge, K. A. (1994). A review and reformulation of social-information processing mechanisms in children's social adjustment. *Psychological Bulletin, 115,* 74–101.

Crnic, K., & Greenberg, M. (1987). Maternal stress, social support, and coping: Influences on early mother-child relationships. In C. Boukydis (Ed.), *Research on support for parents and infants in the postnatal period* (pp. 25–40). Norwood, NJ: Ablex.

Crockenberg, S. B. (1986). Are temperamental differences in babies associated with predictable differences in caregiving? *New Directions in Child Development, 31,* 53–73.

Crosbie-Burnett, M., & Helmbrecht, L. (1993). A descriptive study of gay male stepfamilies. *Family Relations, 43,* 394–399.

Cross, J. E., Jr. (1991). *Shades of black: Diversity in African American identity.* Philadephia: Temple University.

Crouter, A. C., MacDermid, S. M., McHale, S. M., & Perry-Jenkins, M. (1990). Parental monitoring and perceptions of children's school performance and conduct in dual- and single-earner families. *Developmental Psychology, 23,* 649–657.

Crowhurst, M., & Piche, G. L. (1979). Audience and mode of discourse effects on syntactic complexity in writing at two grade levels. *Research in the Teaching of English, 13,* 101–109.

Crystal, D. S., Chen, C., Fuligini, A. J., Hsu, C. C., Ko, H. J., Kitamura, S., & Kimura, S. (1994). Psychological maladjustment and academic achievement: A cross-cultural study of Japanese, Chinese, and American high school students. *Child Development, 65,* 738–753.

Csikszentmihalyi, M., & Larson, R. (1984). *Being adolescent: Conflict and growth in the teenage years.* New York: Basic Books.

Csikszentmihalyi, M., & Rathunde, K., & Walen, S. (1993). *Talented teenagers: The roots of success and failure.* New York: Cambridge University Press.

Cullinan, B. E. (1987). *Children's literature in the reading program.* Newark, DE: International Reading Association.

Cullinan, B. E. (1992). *Invitation to read: More children's literature in the reading program.* Newark, DE: International Reading Association.

Cummings, M. E., & O'Reilly, A. W. (1997). Fathers in family context: Effects of marital quality on child adjustment. In M. E. Lamb (Ed.), *The role of the father in child development* (pp. 49–65). New York: John Wiley.

Cunningham, A. E., & Stanovich, K. E. (1991). Tracking the unique effects of print exposure in children: Associations with vocabulary, general knowledge, and spelling. *Journal of Educational Psychology, 83,* 264–274.

Cunningham, P. M. (1995). *Phonics they use: Words for reading and writing.* New York: HarperCollins.

Curtin, S., & Martin, J. (2000). Births: Preliminary data for 1999. *National Vital Statistics Reports, 48*(14). Washington, DC: U.S. Department of Health and Human Services, Centers for Disease Control and Prevention.

Curtiss, S. (1977). *Genie: A psycholinguistic study of a modern-day "wild child."* New York: Academic Press.

Dahl, R. E. (1999). The consequences of insufficient sleep for adolescents, *Phi Delta Kappan, 80*(5), 354–359.

Daly, M., & Wilson, M. (1996). Violence against stepchildren. *Current Directions in Psychological Science, 5,* 77–81.

Damico, J., & Oller, J. W., Jr. (1980). Pragmatic versus morphological/syntactic criteria for language referrals. *Language, Speech, and Hearing Services in Schools, 11,* 85–94.

Damon, W. (1999). Moral development of children. *Scientific American, 281,* 72–79.

Damon, W. & Hart, D. (1982). The development of self-understanding from infancy through adolescence. *Child Development, 53,* 841–864.

Damon, W., & Hart, D. (1988). *Self-understanding in childhood and adolescence.* New York: Cambridge University Press.

Danesco, E., Miller, T., & Spicer, R. (2000). Incidence and costs of 1987–1994 childhood injuries. Demographic breakdowns. *Pediatrics, 105*(2), 27.

Daniels, D., Beaumont, F., & Doolin, C. (2002). *Understanding children. An interview and observation guide for educators.* Boston: McGraw-Hill.

Daniels, D., Kalkman, D., & McCombs, B. (2001). Young children's perceptions of learning and teacher practices in different classroom contexts: Effects on motivation. *Early Education and Development, 12,* 253–273.

Daniels, D., & Perry, K. (2003). "Learner-centered" according to children. *Theory into Practice, 42*(2), 102–108.

Daniels, D., & Shumow, L. (2003). Child development and classroom teaching: A review of the literature and implications for educating teachers. *Journal of Applied Developmental Psychology, 23*(5), 495–526.

Daniels, H. A. (1985). Nine ideas about language. In V. Clark, P. Eschholz, & A. Rosa (Eds.), *Language: Introductory readings* (pp. 18–36). New York: St. Martin's Press.

Dauber, S. L. & Epstein, J. L. (1989). *Parents' attitudes and practices of involvement in inner-city elementary and middle schools.* (CREMS Report 33). Baltimore, MD: Johns Hopkins University, Center of Research on Elementary and Middle Schools.

Dauber, S. L., & Epstein, J. L. (1993). Parents' attitudes and practices of involvement in inner-city elementary and middle schools. In N. F. Chavkin (Ed.), *Families and schools in pluralistic society* (pp. 53–71). Albany: State University of New York Press.

Dawson-Tunik, T., Fischer, K., & Stein, Z. (2004). Do stages belong at the center of developmental theory? A commentary on Piaget's stages. *New Ideas in Psychology, 22,* 255–263.

Deater-Deckard, K., Dunn, J., & Lussier, G. (2002). Sibling relationship and social-emotional adjustment in different family contexts. *Social Development, 11,* 571–590.

deBoer, B. (2005). Infant directed speech and evolution of language. In M. Tallerman (Ed.), *Evolutionary prerequisites for language* (pp. 100–121). Oxford: Oxford University Press.

DeCasper, A. J., & Spence, M. J. (1986). Prenatal maternal speech influences newborns' perception of speech sounds. *Infant Behavioral Development. 9,* 133–150.

Deci, E. L., & Ryan, R. R. (1985). *Intrinsic motivation and self-determination in human behavior.* New York: Plenum Press.

Decker, S. N., & DeFries, J. C. (1980). Cognitive abilities in families with reading disabled children. *Journal of Learning Disabilities, 13,* 517–522.

Dee, T. (nd). Teachers and gender gap in student achievement. Retrieved October 27, 2006, from http://www.swarthmore.edu/SocSci/tdee1/Research/jhrforthcoming.pdf.

DeFries, J. C., Fulker, D. W., & LaBuda, M. C. (1987). Evidence for a genetic etiology in reading disability of twins. *Nature, 537–539.*

DeGarmo, D. S., Forgatch, M. S., & Martinez, C. R., Jr. (1999). Parenting of divorced mothers as a link between social status and boys' academic outcomes: Unpacking the effects of socioeconomic status. *Child Development, 70,* 1231–1245.

DeJong, W. (1994). *Building the peace: The resolving conflict creatively program.*

Washington, DC: U.S. Department of Justice, National Institute of Justice.

DeKlerk, V. (1990). Slang: A male domain? *Sex Roles, 22,* 589–606.

Delgado-Gaitan, C. (1988). The value of conformity: Learning to stay in school. *Anthropology and Educational Quarterly, 19*(4), 354–381.

Delgado-Gaitan, C., & Trueba, H. (1991). *Crossing cultural borders.* New York: Falmer Press.

DeLoache, J. S., & DeMendoza, O. A. P. (1987). Joint picture book interactions of mothers and one-year-old children. *British Journal of Developmental Psychology, 5,* 11–123.

Delpit, L. (2003). Educators as "seed people" growing a new future. *Educational Researcher, 7,* 14–21.

Delpit, L. D. (1988). The silenced dialogue: Power and pedagogy and educating other people's children. *Harvard Educational Review, 58,* 280–298.

Delpit, L. D. (1990). Language diversity and learning. In S. Hynds & D. L. Rubin (Eds.), *Perspectives on talk and learning.* Urbana, IL: National Council for Teachers of English.

Demetriou, A., Christou, C., Spanoudis, G., & Platsidou, M. (2002). The development of mental processing: Efficiency, working memory, and thinking. *Monographs of the Society for Research in Child Development, 67*(Serial No. 268).

Dempster, F. N. (1981). Memory span: Sources of individual and developmental differences. *Psychological Bulletin, 89,* 63–100.

Denham, S. (1998). *Emotional development in young children.* New York: Guilford Press.

Deshler D. (1978). Psycho-educational aspects of learning disabled adolescents. In L. Manss, L. Goodman, & J. L. Wickerholt (Eds.), *Teaching the learning disabled adolescent* (pp. 47–74). Boston: Mifflin.

DeVoe, J. F., Peter, K., Kaufman, P., Ruddy, S., Miller, A., Planty, M., Snyder, T. D., & Rand, M. (2003). *Indicators of school crime and safety: 2003.* Report by National Center of Education Statistics and the Bureau of Justice Statistics. Available online at http://www.ojp.usdoj.gov/bjs/pub/pdf/iscs03.pdf.

DeVries, R. (1990). *Constructivist early education: Overview and comparisons with other programs.* Washington, DC: National Association for the Education of Young Children.

DeVries, R. (2000). Vygotsky, Piaget, and education: A reciprocal assimilation of theories and educational practices. *New Ideas in Psychology, 18,* 187–213.

DeVries, R., & Zan, B. (1994). *Moral classrooms, moral children: Creating a constructivist atmosphere in early education.* New York: Teachers College Press.

Dewey, A. (1983). *Pecos Bill.* New York: Mulberry Books.

Dewey, J. (1902, July). The school as social center: An address delivered before the National Council of Education, Minneapolis, Minnesota. *Elementary School Teacher, 3,* 73–86.

Dewey, J. (1916). *Democracy and education.* New York: Macmillan.

Diaz, R. M. (1983). Thought and two languages: The impact of bilingualism on cognitive development. *Review of Research in Education, 10,* 23–54.

Dick, F., Wulfeck, B., Krupa-Kwiatkowski, M., & Bates, E. (2004). The development of complex sentence interpretation in typically developing children compared with children with specific language impairments or early unilateral focal lesions. *Developmental Science, 7,* 360–377.

Diefendorf, A. O., Leverett, R. G., & Miller, S. M. (1994). Hearing impairment. In S. Adler & D. A. King (Eds.), *Oral communication problems in children and adolescents* (pp. 141–164). Boston: Allyn & Bacon.

Dishion, T. J., McCord, J., & Poulin, F. (1999). When interventions harm: Peer groups and problem behavior. *American Psychologist, 54,* 755–764.

Dixon, W. (2004). *Twenty studies that revolutionized child psychology.* Upper Saddle River, NJ: Merrill/Prentice Hall.

Dodge, K, Coie, J., & Lynam, D. (2006). Aggression and antisocial behavior in youth. In W. Damon & R. M. Lerner (Editors-in-Chief) & N. Eisenberg (Vol. Ed.), *Handbook of child psychology. Vol. 3. Social, emotional, and personality development* (pp.719–788). New York: John Wiley.

Dorman, G. J. (1984). *How to multiply your baby's intelligence.* Garden City, NY: Doubleday.

Dornbusch, S., & Ritter, P. (1996). Parents of high school students: A neglected resource. *Educational Horizons, 66*(2), 75–77.

Dornbusch, S., Ritter, P., & Steinberg, L. (1991). Community influences on the relation of family statuses to adolescent school performance: Difference between African-American and non-Hispanic whites. *American Journal of Education, 99,* 543–567.

Downey, D., & Yuan, A. (2005). Sex differences in school performance during high school: Puzzling patterns and possible explanations. *Sociological Quarterly, 46,* 299–321.

Downey, D. B., & Powell, B. (1993). Do children in single-parent households fare better living with same-sex parents? *Journal of Marriage and the Family, 55,* 55–71.

Downing, J., & Eichinger, J. (1990). Instructional strategies for learners with dual sensory impairments in integrated settings. *The Journal of Association for Persons with Severe Handicaps, 15*(2), 98–105.

Dreikurs, R. (1982). *Maintaining sanity in the classroom.* New York: Harper & Row.

Driver, R., Gruesne, E., & Tiberghein, A. (1985). *Children's ideas in science.* Philadelphia: Open University Press.

Dryfoos, J. (1990). *Adolescents at risk: Prevalence and prevention.* New York: Oxford University Press.

Dryfoos, J. (1994). *Full-service schools: A revolution in health and social services for children, youth, and families.* San Francisco: Jossey Bass.

Dryfoos, J. (1999). The role of school in children's out-of-school time. *The Future of Children. When School Is Out, 9*(2), 117–132.

Dryfoos, J. (2000). *Evaluation of community schools: Findings to date.* Washington, DC: Coalition for Community Schools. Available online at http://www.communityschools.org/Resources/evalcontents.html.

Dubas, J., Graber, J., & Petersen, A. (1991). A longitudinal investigation of adolescents' changing perceptions of pubertal timing. *Developmental Psychology, 27,* 580–586.

DuBors, D. L., Tevendale, H. D., Burk-Braxton, C., Suenson, L., & Hardesty, J., (2000). Self-system influences during early adolescence: Investigation of an integrature model. *Journal of Early Adolescent,* 12–43.

Duckworth, E. (1964). Piaget rediscovered. In R. Ripple & V. Rockcastle (Eds.), *Piaget rediscovered* (pp. 1–5). Ithaca, NY: Cornell University Press.

Duckworth, E. (1987). *"The having of wonderful ideas" and other essays on teaching and learning.* New York: Teachers College Press.

Duckworth, E. (2001). *Tell me more: Listening to learners explain*. New York: Teachers College Press.

Duncan, G., Yeung, W., Brooks-Gunn, J., & Smith, J. (1998). How much does poverty affect the life changes of children? *American Sociological Review, 63*, 406–423.

Duncan, G. J., & Brooks-Gunn, J. (1997). *Consequences of growing up poor*. New York: Sage.

Duncan, G. J., & Brooks-Gunn, J. (2000). Family poverty, welfare reform, and child development. *Child Development, 71*, 188–196.

Duncan, G. J., & Rogers, W. (1988). Longitudinal aspects of childhood poverty. *Journal of Marriage and the Family, 50*, 1007–1021.

Duncan, P., Ritter, P., Dornbusch, S., Gross, R., & Carlsmith, J. (1985). The effects of pubertal timing on body image, school behavior, and deviance. *Journal of Youth and Adolescence, 14*, 227–236.

Durst, R. (1987). Cognitive and linguistic demands of analytic writing. *Research in the Teaching of English, 21*, 347–376.

Dusek, J., & Joseph, G. (1986). The bases of teacher expectations: A meta-analysis. *Journal of Educational Psychology, 75*, 327–446.

Dusek, J. B. (1987). *Adolescent development and behavior*. Englewood Cliffs, NJ: Prentice-Hall.

Dweck, C. S., & Elliott, E. S. (1983). Achievement motivation. In P. H. Mussen (Gen. Ed.) & E. M. Hetherington (Vol. Ed.), *Handbook of child psychology: Vol. IV. Social and personality development* (pp. 643–691). New York: John Wiley.

Dweck, C. S., & Leggett, E. L. (1988). A social cognitive approach to motivation and personality. *Psychological Review, 95*, 256–273.

Dwyer, K., Osher, D., & Wager, C. (1998). *Early warning, tiimely response: A guide to safe schools*. Washington, DC: U.S. Department of Education. Available online at http:// www.ed.gov/goffices/OSERS/OSEP/earlywrn.html.

Dyson, A. H. (1993). *Social worlds of children learning to write in an urban primary school*. New York: Teachers College Press.

Eaton, J., Anderson, C., & Smith, E. (1984). Students' misconceptions interfere with science learning: Case studies of fifth-grade students. *Elementary School Journal, 64*, 365–379.

Eaton, M. J., & Dembo, M. H. (1997). Differences in the motivational beliefs of Asian American and non-Asian students. *Journal of Educational Psychology, 89*(3), 433–440.

Eaton, W. O., Chipperfield, J. G., & Singeil, C. E. (1989). Birth order and activity level in children. *Developmental Psychology, 25*, 668–672.

Eccles, J. S. (1984). Sex differences in achievement patterns. In T. Sonderegger (Ed.), *Nebraska Symposium on Motivation* (pp. 97–132). Lincoln: University of Nebraska Press.

Eccles, J. S. (1985). Why doesn't Jane run? Sex differences in educational and occupational patterns. In F. D. Horowitz & M. O'Brien (Eds.), *The gifted and talented: A developmental perspective* (pp. 251–295). Washington, DC: APA Press.

Eccles, J. S. (1987). Gender roles and women's achievement-related decisions. *Psychology of Women Quarterly, 11*, 135–172.

Eccles, J. S. (1993). School and family effects on the ontogeny of children's interests, self-perceptions and activity choices. In R. Dienstbier & J. E. Jacobs (Eds.), *Developmental perspectives on motivation* (Vol. 40, pp. 145–208). Lincoln: University of Nebraska Press.

Eccles, J. S. (1994). Understanding women's educational and occupational choice. *Psychology of Women Quarterly, 18*, 585–609.

Eccles, J. S. (2004). School, academic motivation, and stage-environment fit. In R. M. Lerner and L. Steinberg (Eds.), *Handbook of adolescent psychology* (2nd ed., pp. 125–154). Hoboken, NJ: John Wiley.

Eccles, J. S. (2005). Subjective task value and the Eccles et al. model of achievement-related choices. In A. J. Elliot & C. S. Dweck (Eds.), *Handbook of competence and motivation* (pp. 105–121). New York: Guilford Press.

Eccles, J. S., Adler, T. F., Futterman, R., Goff, S. B., Kaczala, C. M., Meece, J. L., & Midgley, C. (1983). Expectancies, values, and academic behaviors. In: J. T. Spence, (Ed.), *Achievement and achievement motivation* (pp. 75–146). San Francisco: W. H. Freeman.

Eccles, J. S., & Barber, B. L. (1999). Student council, volunteering, basketball, or marching band: What kind of extra-curriculum involvement matters? *Journal of Adolescent Research, 14*, 10–43.

Eccles, J. S., & Harold, R. D. (1991). Gender differences in sport involvement: Applying the Eccles' expectancy-value model. *Journal of Applied Sport Psychology, 3*, 7–35.

Eccles, J. S., & Harold, R. D. (1993). Parent-school involvement during the early adolescent years. *Teachers College Record, 94*(3), 568–587.

Eccles, J. S., & Harold, R. D. (1996). Family involvement in children's and adolescents' schooling. In A. Booth & J. Dunn (Eds.), *Family school links* (pp. 3–34). Mahwah, NJ: Erlbaum.

Eccles, J. S., Jacobs, J., & Harold, R. (1991). Gender role stereotypes, expectancy effects, and parents' role in the socialization of gender differences in self-perceptions and skill acquisition. *Journal of Social Issues, 46*, 182–201.

Eccles, J. S., Lord, S., & Midgley, C. (1991). What are we doing to early adolescents: The impact of educational contexts on early adolescents. *American Journal of Education, 99*, 521–542.

Eccles, J. S., & Midgley, C. M. (1989). Stage/environment fit: Developmentally appropriate classrooms for early adolescents. In R. E. Ames & C. Ames (Eds.), *Research on motivation in education: Goals and cognitions* (Vol. 3, pp. 139–186). New York: Academic Press.

Eccles, J. S., Midgley, C. M., Wigfield, A., Buchanan, C. M., Reuman, D., Flanagan, C., & Mac Iver, D. (1993). Development during adolescence. The impact of stage-environment fit on young adolescents; experiences in schools and in families. *American Psychologist, 48*(2), 90–101.

Eccles, J. S., Wigfield, A., Harold, R. D., & Blumenfeld, P. (1993). Age and gender differences in children's self- and task perceptions during elementary school. *Child Development, 64*, 830–847.

Eccles, J. S., Wigfield, A., & Schiefele, U. (1998). Motivation to succeed. In W. Damon (Series Ed.) & N. Eisenberg (Vol. Ed.), *Handbook of child psychology: Vol. 3. Social, emotional, and personality development* (5th ed., pp. 1017–1095). New York: John Wiley.

Eccles, J. S., Wong, C., & Peck, S. (2006). Ethnicity as a social context for the development of African-American adolescents. *Journal of School Psychology, 44*, 407–426.

Eccles-Parsons, J., Adler, T. F., & Kaczala, C. M. (1982). Socialization of achievement attitudes and beliefs: Parental influences. *Child Development, 53,* 322–339.

Echols, L. D., West, R. F., Stanovich, K. E., & Zehr, K. S. (1996). Using children's literacy activities to predict growth in verbal cognitive skills: A longitudinal investigation. *Journal of Educational Psychology, 88,* 296–304.

Edelsky, C., Altwerger, B., & Flores, B. (1991). *Whole language: What's the difference?* Portsmouth, NH: Heinemann.

Edin, K., & Lein, L. (1997). *Making ends meet: How single mothers survive welfare and low-wage work.* New York: Sage.

Eisenburg, N., & Fabes, R. A. (1998). Prosocial development. In. W. Damon (Series Ed.) & N. Eisenburg (Vol. Ed.), *Handbook of child psychology, Vol. 4. Socialization, personality, and social development* (pp. 701–778). New York: John Wiley.

Eisenberg, N., Fabes, R. A., Shepard, S. A., Guthrie, I. K., Murphy, B. C., & Resier, M. (1999). Parental reactions to children's negative emotions: Longitudinal relations to quality of children's social functioning. *Child Development, 70,* 513–534.

Eisenberg, N., Fabes, R., & Spinrad, T. L. (2006). Prosocial development. In W. Damon & R. M. Lerner (Editors-in-Chief) & N. Eisenberg (Vol. Ed.), *Handbook of child psychology. Vol. 3. Social, emotional, and personality development* (pp. 646–718). New York: John Wiley.

Eisenberg, N., Guthrie, I. K., Fabes, R., Reiser, M., Murphy, B., Holgren, R. et al. (1997). The relations of regulation and emotionality to resiliency and competent social functioning in elementary school children. *Child Development, 68,* 295–311.

Eisenburg, N., Martin, C. L., & Fabes, R. A. (1996). Gender development and gender effects. In D. C. Berliner & R. C. Calfee (Eds.), *The handbook of educational psychology* (pp. 358–396). New York: MacMillan.

Eisenberg, N., & Valiente, C., (2002). Parenting and children's prosocial and moral development. In M. Bornstein (Ed.), *Handbook of parenting: Vol. 5. Practical parenting* (2nd ed., pp. 111–142). Mahwah, NJ: Erlbaum.

Eisner, E. W. (1991). Rethinking literacy. *Educational Horizons, 69,* 120–128.

Elias, M., Zins, J., Graczyk, P., & Weissberg, R., (2003). Implementation, sustainability, and scaling up of social-emotional and academic innovations in public schools. *School Psychology Review, 32,* 303–320.

Elkind, D. (1967). Egocentrism in adolescence. *Child Development, 38,* 361–375.

Elkind, D. (1981). *The hurried child: Growing up too fast too soon.* Reading, MA: Addison Wesley.

Elkind, D. (2005). Early childhood amnesia: Reaffirming children's needs for developmentally appropriate programs. *Young Children, 60,* 38–40.

Elliot, A. J. (1981). *Child language.* Cambridge, England: Cambridge University Press.

Elliott, E. S., & Dweck, C. S. (1988). Goals: An approach to motivation and achievement. *Journal of Personality and Social Psychology, 54,* 5–12.

Emery, R. E. (1999). *Marriage, divorce, and children's adjustment* (3rd ed.). Newbury Park, CA: Sage.

Emmer, E., & Stough, L. (2001). Classroom management: A critical part of educational psychology. *Educational Psychologist, 36,* 103–113.

Encyclopedia of Mental Health. (2001). *Shyness.* San Diego, CA: Academic Press. Retrieved March 9, 2001, from http://www.shyness.com/encyclopedia.html.

Ensminger, M., & Alexander, K. (1993). Paths to high school graduation or dropout: A longitudinal study of first-grade cohorts. *Sociology of Education, 65,* 95–113.

Entwisle, D., & Alexander, K. (1993). Entry into school: The beginning school transition and educational stratification in the United States. *Annual Review of Sociology, 19,* 401–423.

Entwisle, D., & Hayduk, L. (1982). *Early schooling: Cognitive and affective outcomes.* Baltimore: Johns Hopkins Press.

Entwisle, D., & Stevenson, H. W. (1987). Schools and development. *Child Development, 58,* 1149–1150.

Epoch-Worldwide. (2006). Discipline and the law. Center for Effective Discipline. Available online at http://www.stophitting.com/laws.

Epstein, J. (1987). Parent involvement: What research says to adjustments. *Education and Urban Society, 19*(2), 119–136.

Epstein, J. (2002). School, family, and community partnerships: Caring for the children we share. In J. Epstein, J. Sanders, B. Simon, K. Salina, N. Jansorn, & F. Van Voorhis (Eds.), *School, family, and community partnerships* (2nd ed.). Thousand Oaks, CA: Corwin.

Epstein, J. L. (1988). How do we improve programs for parent involvement? *Educational Horizons, 66,* 58–59.

Epstein, J. L. (1992). School and family partnerships. In M. Aikin (Ed.), *Encyclopedia of educational research* (6th ed., pp. 1139–1151). New York: MacMillan.

Epstein, J. L. (1995). School/family/community partnerships: Caring for the children we share. *Phi Delta Kappan, 76*(9), 701–712.

Epstein, J. L. (1996). Perspectives and previews on research and policy for school, family, and community partnerships. In A. Booth & J. Dunn (Eds.), *Family school links: How do they affect educational outcomes?* (pp. 209–246). Mahwah, NJ: Erlbaum.

Epstein, J. L., & Connors, L. J. (1992). Six types of involvement in the middle grades and high schools. *The Practitioner, 18*(4), 1–8.

Epstein, J. L., & Dauber, S. L. (1991). School programs and teacher practices of parent involvement in inner-city elementary schools. *Elementary School Journal, 91,* 289–305.

ERIC Clearinghouse on Handicapped and Gifted Students. (1990). Giftedness and the gifted: What's it all about? *ERIC Digests* (#E476). Reston, VA: Author.

Erickson, F., & Mohatt, G. (1982). Cultural organization of participant structures in two classrooms of Indian students. In G. D. Spindler (Ed.), *Doing the ethnography of schooling: Educational anthropology in action* (pp. 132–174). New York: Holt, Reinhart & Winston.

Ericsson, K. A., Krampe, R., & Tesch-Romer, C. (1993). The role of deliberate practice in the acquisition of expert performance. *Psychological Review, 100,* 363–406.

Erikson, E. H. (1958). *Young man Luther: A study of psychoanalysis and history.* New York: Norton.

Erikson, E. H. (1963). *Childhood and society.* New York: Norton.

Erikson, E. H. (1968). *Identity: Youth and crisis.* New York: Norton.

Erikson, E. H. (1969). *Gandhi's truth: On the origins of militant nonviolence.* New York: Norton.

Eron, L. D., Huesman, L. R., Lefkowitz, M. M., & Walder, L. O. (1996). Does television violence cause aggression? In D. F. Greenberg (Ed.), *Criminal careers*

(Vol. 2, pp. 311–321). Aldershot, England: Darmouth Publishing.

Espelage, D., Bosworth, K., Karageorge, K., & Daytner, G. (1996, August). Family environment and bullying behaviors: Interrelationships and treatment implications. Paper presented at the annual meeting of the American Psychological Association, Toronto, Canada.

Espelage, D., Bosworth, K., & Simon, T. (2000). Examining the social context of bullying behaviors in early adolescence. *Journal of Counseling and Development, 78,* 326–333.

Espelage, D. L., Mebane, S. E., & Swearer, S. M. (2004). Gender differences in bullying: Moving beyond mean level differences. In D. Espelage and S. Swearer (Eds.), *Bullying in American schools: A social-ecological perspective on prevention and intervention* (pp. 15–35). Mahwah, NJ: Erlbaum.

Evans, S., Timmins, B., Sibley, M., White, L., Serpell, Z., & Schultz, B. (2006). Developing coordinated, multimodal, school-based treatment for young adolescents with ADHD. *Education and Treatment of Children, 29,* 359–378.

Fabes, R. A., & Eisenberg, N. (1992). Young children's coping with interpersonal anger. *Child Development, 63,* 116–128.

Fagot, B. I. (1985). Beyond the reinforcement principle: Another step toward understanding sex role development. *Developmental Psychology, 21,* 1092–1104.

Falbo, T. (1992). Social norms and the one-child family: Clinical and policy implications. In F. Boer & J. Dunn (Eds.), *Children's sibling relationships* (pp. 71–82). Hillsdale, NJ: Erlbaum.

Farah, M., Illes, J., Cook-Deegan, R., Gardner, H., Kandel, E., King, P., Parens, E., Sahakian, B., & Wolpe, P. (2004). Neuroconitive enhancement: What can we do and what should we do? *Nature Reviews, 5,* 421–425.

Farley, R., & Allen, W. (1987). *The color line and the quality of life in America.* New York: Oxford University Press.

Farmer, T., Estell, D., Bishop, J., O'Neal, K., & Cairns, B. (2003). Rejected bullies or popular leaders? The social relations of aggressive subtypes of rural African American early adolescents. *Developmental Psychology, 39,* 992–1004.

Fashola, O. (1998). *Review of extended-day and after-school programs and their effectiveness.* (Report No. 24). Baltimore: Johns Hopkins University, Center for Research on the Education of Students Placed at Risk.

Feather, N. T. (1982). Human values and the prediction of action: An expectancy-valance analysis. In N. T. Feather (Ed.), *Expectations and actions: Expectancy-value models in psychology* (pp. 263–289). Hillside, NJ: Erlbaum.

Federal Interagency Forum on Child and Family Statistics. (2000). *America's children: Key national indicators of well-being, 2000.* Washington, DC: U.S. Government Printing Office.

Federal Interagency Forum on Child and Family Statistics. (2005). *America's children: Key national indicators of well-being, 2005.* Washington, DC: U.S. Government Printing Office. Available online at http://www.childstats.gov.

Feinman, S., & Lewis, M. (1983). Social referencing at ten months: A second order effect on infants' responses to strangers. *Child Development, 54,* 878–887.

Feldlaufer, H., Midgley, C., & Eccles, J. S. (1988). Student, teacher, and observer perceptions of the classroom before and after the transition to junior high school. *Journal of Early Adolescence, 8,* 133–156.

Feldman, H., Dale, P., Campbell, T., Colborn, D., Kurs-Laskey, M., Rockette, H., & Paradise, J. (2005). Concurrent and predictive validity of parent reports of child language at ages 2 and 3 years. *Child Development, 76,* 856–868.

Fenzel, L. M. (2000). Prospective study of changes in global self-worth and strain during the transition to middle school. *Journal of Early Adolescence, 20,* 93–116.

Ferrari, M., & Sternberg, R. (1998). The development of mental abilities and styles. In W. Damon (Editor-in-Chief) & D. Kuhn & R. Siegler (Vol Eds.), *Handbook of child psychology: Vol. 2,* (5th ed., pp. 899–946). New York: John Wiley.

Ferreiro, R., & Teberosky, A. (1982). *Literacy before schooling.* Portsmouth, NH: Heinemann.

Field, T. M. (1990). *Infancy.* Cambridge, MA: Harvard University Press.

Field, T. M., Schanberg, S. M., Scafidi, F., Bauer, C. R., Vega-Lahr, N., Garcia, R., Nystrom, J., & Kuhn, C. M. (1986). Effects of tactile/kinesthetic stimulation on preterm neonates. *Pediatrics, 77,* 654–658.

Fiese, B. (2001). Family matters: A systems view of family effect on children's cognitive health. In R. Sternberg & E. Grigorenko (Eds.), *Environmental effects on cognitive abilities* (pp. 39–57). Mahwah, NJ: Erlbaum.

Fine, J. G., & Davis, J. M. (2003). Grade retention and enrollment in post-secondary education. *Journal of School Psychology, 41*(6), 401–411.

Fine, M. (1991). *Framing dropouts: Notes on the politics of an urban high school.* Albany: State University of New York Press.

Fine, M. A., Voydanoff, P., & Donnelly, B. W. (1993). The relations between parental control and warmth and child well-being in stepfamilies. *Journal of Family Psychology, 7,* 222–232.

Fischer, J. L., Munsch, J., & Greene, S. M. (1996). Adolescence in intimacy. In G. R. Adams & R. Montemayor (Eds.), *Psychosocial development during adolescence* (Vol. 8, pp. 95–129). Thousand Oaks, CA: Sage.

Fisher, K., & Bidell, T. (1998). Dynamic development of psychological structures in action and thought. In R. Lerner (Ed.), *Handbook of child psychology: Vol 1. Theoretical models of human development* (5th ed., 467–561). New York: John Wiley.

Fischer, M. (1990). Parenting stress and the child with attention deficit hyperactivity disorder. *Journal of Clinical Child Psychology, 19,* 337–346.

Fisher, C. B., Wallace, S. A., & Fenton, R. E. (2000). Discrimination distress during adolescence. *Journal of Youth and Adolescence, 29,* 679–695.

Fisher, K. (1980). A theory of cognitive development: The control and construction of hierarchies of skills. *Psychological Review, 87,* 477–531.

Fix, M., & Passel, J. S. (1994). *Immigration and immigrants: Setting the record straight.* Washington, DC: Urban Institute.

Flaks, D. K., Ficher, I., Masterpasqua, F., & Joseph, G. (1995). Lesbians choosing motherhood: A comparative study of lesbian and heterosexual parents and their children. *Developmental Psychology, 31,* 105–114.

Flavell, J. (1985). *Cognitive development* (2nd ed.). Englewood Cliffs, NJ: Prentice Hall.

Flavell, J. (1996). Piaget's legacy. *Psychological Science, 7,* 200–203.

Flavell, J. (2004). Theory-of-mind development: Retrospect and prospect. *Merrill-Palmer Quarterly, 50,* 274–290.

Flavell, J., Beach, D., & Chinsky, J. (1966). Spontaneous verbal rehearsal in memory task as a function of age. *Child Development, 37,* 283–299.

Flavell, J., Green, F., & Flavell, E. (1998). The mind has a mind of its own: Developing knowledge about mental uncontrollability. *Cognitive Development, 13,* 127–138.

Flavell, J. H. (2000). Development of children's knowledge about the mental world. *International Journal of Behavioral Development, 24,* 15–23.

Flavell, J. H., Green, F. L., & Flavell, E. (1986). Development of knowledge about the appearance-reality distinction. *Monographs of the Society of Child Development, 51*(1, Serial No. 22).

Flavell, J. H., & Miller, P. H. (1998). Social cognition. In D. Kuhn & R. S. Siegler (Eds.), *Handbook of child psychology: Vol. 2. Cognition, perception, and language* (pp. 851–898). New York: John Wiley.

Flavell, J. H., Mumme, D. L., Green, F. L., & Flavell, E. R. (1992). Young children's understanding of different types of beliefs. *Child Development, 63,* 960–977.

Flavell, J. H., & Wellman, H. M. (1977). Metamemory. In R. V. Kail & J. W. Hagen (Eds.), *Perspectives on the development of memory and cognition.* Hillsdale, NJ: Erlbaum.

Fletcher, A., Dailiry, N. E., Steinburg, L., & Dornbusch, S. M. (1995). The company they keep: Relation of adolescents' adjustment and behavior to their friends' perception of authoritative parenting in the social network. *Developmental Psychology, 31,* 300–310.

Flook, L, Ullman, J., & Repetti, R. (2005). Classroom social experiences as predictors of academic performance. *Developmental Psychology, 41,* 319–327.

Florio-Ruane, S. (1985). Creating your own case study. Unpublished manuscript, Michigan State University.

Ford, D. Y. (1996). *Reversing under-achievement among gifted black students: Promising practices and programs.* New York: Teachers College Press.

Fordham, S. (1988). Racelessness as a factor in black students' school success: Pragmatic strategy or pyrrhic victory? *Harvard Educational Review, 58,* 54–84.

Fordham, S. (1996). *Blacked out dilemmas of race, identity, and success at Capitol Hill.* Chicago: University of Chicago Press.

Fordham, S., & Ogbu, J. (1986). Black students' school success: Coping with the "burden of 'acting white.'" *The Urban Review, 18*(3), 176–206.

Forness, S. R., Kavale, K. A., & Walker, H. M. (1999). Identifying children at risk for antisocial behavior: The case for comorbidity. In R. Gallimore, L. P. Bernheimer, D. L. MacMillan, D. L. Speece, & S. Vaughn (Eds.), *Developmental perspectives on children with high-incidence disabilities.* Mahwah, NJ: Erlbaum.

Fox, G. L., & Kelly, R. F. (1995). Determinants of child custody arrangements at divorce. *Journal of Marriage and the Family, 57,* 693–708.

Frank, A., & McBee, M. (2003). The use of *Harry Potter and the Sorcerer's Stone* to discuss identity development with gifted adolescents. *The Journal of Secondary Gifted Education, 15,* 33–38.

Fredericks, J. A., & Eccles, J. S. (2002). Children's competence and value beliefs from childhood through adolescence: Growth trajectories in two male-sex-typed domains. *Developmental Psychology, 38,* 519–533.

French, S. E., Seldman, E., Allen, L., & Aber, J. L. (2006). The development of ethnic identity during adolescence. *Developmental Psychology, 42*(1), 1–10.

Frey, K. S., Hirschstein, M. K., & Guzzo, B. A. (2000). Preventing aggression by promoting social competence. *Journal of Emotional and Behavioral Disorders, 8,* 102–112.

Frey, K. S., Hirschstein, M. K., & Van Schoiack Edstrom, L. (2005). The *Steps to Respect* program uses a multilevel approach to reduce playground bullying and destructive bystander behaviors. In D. L. White, M. K. Faber, & B. C. Glenn (Eds.), *Persistently safe schools 2005* (pp. 47–56). Washington, DC: Hamilton Fish Institute, George Washington University.

Frey, K. S., Nolen, S. B., Van Schoiack Edstrom, L., & Hirschstein, M. K. (2005). Effects of a school-based social-emotional competence program: Linking children's goals, attributions and behavior. *Journal of Applied Developmental Psychology, 26,* 171–200.

Friedrich, L. K., & Stein, A. H. (1973). Aggressive and prosocial television programs and the natural behavior of preschool children. *Monographs of the Society for Research in Child Development, 38*(4, Serial No. 151), 1–63.

Frieman, B. B. (1993). Separation and divorce: Children want their teachers to know—meeting the emotional needs of preschool and primary school children. *Young Children, 48*(6), 58–63.

Frieman, B. B. (1997). Two parents—two homes. *Educational Leadership, 54*(7), 23–25.

Fromberg, D. (2001). The intuitive mind and early childhood education: Connections with chaos theory, script theory, and theory of mind. In B. Toriff and R. Sternburg (Eds.), *Understanding and teaching the intuitive mind* (pp. 93–114). Mahwah, NJ: Erlbaum.

Fuchs, D., & Thelen, M. H. (1988). Children's expected interpersonal consequences of communication their affective state and reported likelihood of expression. *Child Development, 59,* 1314–1322.

Fuligni, A. J. (1997). The academic achievement of adolescents from immigrant families: The roles of family background, attitudes, and behavior. *Child Development, 68,* 351–363.

Fuligini, A. J., & Eccles, J. S. (1993). Perceived parent-child relationships and early adolescents' orientations toward peers. *Developmental Psychology, 29,* 622–632.

Fuligni, A. J., & Stevenson, H. W. (1995). Time use and mathematics achievement among American, Chinese, and Japanese high school students. *Child Development, 66,* 830–842.

Furham, S. (1988). Racelessness as a factor in black students' school success: Pragmatic strategy or phyrric victory? *Harvard Educational Review, 58,* 54–84.

Furman, W., & Buhrmester, D. (1992). Age and sex differences in perception of networks of personal relationships. *Child Development, 63,* 103–115.

Furstenberg, F. F., Jr. (1988). Child care after divorce and remarriage. In E. M. Hetherington & J. D. Arasteh (Eds.), *Impact of divorce, single-parenting, and stepparenting on children* (pp. 245–261). Hillsdale, NJ: Erlbaum.

Furstenberg, F. F., Jr., Brooks-Gunn, J., & Chase-Lansdale, L. (1989). Teenaged pregnancy and child bearing. *American Psychologist, 44,* 313–320.

Furstenberg, F. F., Jr., & Cherlin, A. J. (1991). *Divided families: What happens to children when parents part.* Cambridge, MA: Harvard University Press.

Furstenberg, F. F., Jr., & Nord, C. W. (1985). Parenting apart: Patterns of childrearing after marital disruption. *Journal of Marriage and the Family, 47,* 893–904.

Fusco, D. (2001). Creating relevant science through urban planning and gardening.

Journal of Research in Science Teaching, 38, 860–877.

Gadsden, V. L. (1999). Black families in intergenerational and cultural perspective. In M. E. Lamb (Ed.), *Parenting and child development in "nontraditional" families* (pp. 221–246). Mahwah, NJ: Erlbaum.

Gadsden, V. L., Smith, R. R., & Jordan, W. J. (1996). The promise of desegregation: Tendering expectation and reality in achieving quality schooling. *Urban Education, 31*(4), 381–402.

Galambos, N. L., & Maggs, J. L. (1991). Out-of-school care of young adolescents and self-reported behavior. *Developmental Psychology, 27,* 644–655.

Galda, L., Cullinan, B. E., & Strickland, D. S. (1993). *Language, literacy, and the child.* Fort Worth, TX: Harcourt Brace.

Gallagher, A., & Kaufman, J. (2005). *Gender differences in mathematics.* New York: Cambridge University Press.

Garber, H. (1988). *The Milwaukee project: Preventing mental retardation in children at-risk.* Washington, DC: American Association on Mental Retardation.

Garcia, E. E. (1994). "Hispanic" children: Effective schooling practices and related policy issues. In N. Ellsworth, C. Hedley, & A. Baratta (Eds.), *Literacy: A redefinition* (pp. 77–87). Hillsdale, NJ: Erlbaum.

Gardner, H. (1983). *Frames of mind: The theory of multiple intelligences.* New York: Basic Books.

Gardner, H. (1993). The relationship between early giftedness and later achievement. In G. R. Bock & K. Ackrill (Eds.), *The origins and development of high ability* (pp. 175–182). New York: John Wiley.

Gardner, H. (1999). *Intelligence reframed multiple intelligences for the 21st century.* New York: Basic Books.

Gardner, H. (2004a). Backcover of Paley, V. (2004). *A Child's Work: The Importance of Fantasy Play.* Chicago, IL: University of Chicago Press.

Gardner, H. (2004b). Foreword: A practical theory. In M. Kornhaber, E. Fierros & S. Veenema (Eds.), *Multiple intelligences: Best ideas from research and practice* (pp. xi–xiii). Boston: Allyn & Bacon.

Gardner, H., & Hatch, T. (1989). Multiple intelligences go to school. *Educational Researcher, 18,* 4–10.

Garland, A., & Zigler, E. (1993). Adolescent suicide prevention. *American Psychologist, 48,* 169–182.

Gates, H. J. (2004). Foreword. In J.Comer, *Leave no child behind: Preparing today's*

youth for tomorrow's world. New Haven, CT: Yale University Press.

Gauvain, M. (2001). Cultural tools, social interaction and the development of thinking. *Human Development, 44,* 126–143.

Ge, X., Conger, R. D., & Elder, G. H. (1996). Coming of age too early: Pubertal influences on girls' vulnerability to psychological distress. *Child Development, 67,* 3386–4000.

Geary, D. (2004). Evolution and developmental sex differences. In D. Kenrick & C. Luce (Ed.), *The functional mind: Readings in evolutionary psychology.* Boston: Allyn & Bacon.

Geary, D. (2005). *The origin of mind: Evolution of brain, cognition, and general intelligence.* Washington, DC: American Psychological Association.

Geiger, B. (1996). *Fathers as primary caregivers.* Westport, CT: Greenwood.

Gelman, R. (1969). Conservation acquisition: A problem of learning to attend to relevant attributes. *Journal of Experimental Child Psychology, 7,* 167–187.

Gelman, R. (1972). Logical capacity of very young children: Number invariance rules. *Child Development, 43,* 75–90.

Gelman, R., & Baillargeon, R. (1983). A review of Piagetian concepts. In J. Flavell & E. Markman (Eds.), *Handbook of child psychology: Cognitive development, Vol. 3* (pp. 167–230). New York: John Wiley.

Gelman, R., & Brenneman, K. (2004). Science learning pathways for young children. *Early Childhood Research Quarterly, 19,* 150–158.

Gelman, R., & Gallistel, C. R. (1978). *Children's understanding of number.* Cambridge, MA: Harvard University Press.

Gelman, R., & Meck, E. (1983). Preschoolers' counting: Principles after skills. *Cognition, 13,* 343–359.

Gelman, R., & Shatz, M. (1976). Appropriate speech adjustments: The operation of conversational constraints on talk to two-year-olds. In M. Lewis & L. Rosenblum (Eds.), *Conversation, interaction, and the development of language.* New York: John Wiley.

Gelman, S. (2003). *The essential child: Origins of essentialism in everyday thought.* Oxford University Press.

Gentry, R. (1982). An analysis of the developmental spellings in *Gnys at Wrk. The Reading Teacher, 36,* 192–200.

Gershoff, E. (2002). Corporal punishment by parents and associate child behaviors and

experiences: A meta-analytic and theoretical review. *Psychological Bulletin, 128,* 539–579.

Gesell, A., & Ilg, F. (1946). *The child from five to ten.* New York: Harper Brothers.

Gesell, A., Ilg, F., & Ames, L. (1956). *Youth: The years from ten to sixteen.* New York: Harper Brothers.

Gibson, E., & Pick, A. (2000). *An ecological approach to perceptual learning and development.* London: Oxford University Press.

Gibson, E., & Radar, N. (1979). Attention: The perceiver as performer. In G. Hale & M. Lewis (Eds.), *Attention and cognitive development* (pp. 1–22). New York: Plenum.

Gibson, E. J., & Walk, R. D. (1960). The "visual cliff." *Scientific American, 202,* 64–71.

Gilligan, C. (1982). *In a different voice.* Cambridge, MA: Harvard University Press.

Ginsburg, A., & Hanson, S. (1986). *Gaining ground: Values and high school success.* Washington, DC: U.S. Department of Education.

Ginsburg, G. S., & Bronstein, P. (1993). Family factors related to children's intrinsic/extrinsic motivational orientation and academic performance. *Child Development, 64,* 1461–1474.

Ginsburg, H., & Opper, S. (1988). *Piaget's theory of intellectual development* (3rd ed.). Englewood Cliffs, NJ: Prentice Hall.

Gleason, J., Berko, J., & Weintraub, S. (1976). The acquisition of routines in child language. *Language in Society, 5,* 129–136.

Glick, P. C. (1989). Remarried families, stepfamilies, and stepchildren: A brief demographic profile. *Family Relations, 38,* 24–27.

Gnepp, J., & Chilamkurti, C. (1988). Children's use of personality attributions to predict people's emotional and behavioral reactions. *Child Development, 59,* 743–754.

Gogate, L., Bahrick, L., & Watson, J. (2000). A study of multimodal motherese: The role of temporal synchrony between verbal labels and gestures. *Child Development, 71,* 878–894.

Goldberg, M. F. (1997, March). Maintaining a focus on the child. *Phi Delta Kappan,* pp. 557–559.

Golden, D. (1994, July). Building a better brain. *Life Magazine,* pp. 62–70.

Goldenberg, C., Gallimore, R., & Reese, L. (2005). Using mixed methods to explore Latino children's literacy development. In T. Weisner (Ed.), *Discovering successful pathways in children's development: Mixed methods in the study of childhood and family life* (pp. 21–46). Chicago, IL: The University of Chicago Press.

Goleman, D. (1995). *Emotional intelligence. Why it can matter more than IQ.* New York: Bantam.

Golombok, S., & Tasker, F. L. (1996). Do parents influence the sexual orientation of their children? Findings from a longitudinal study of lesbian families. *Developmental Psychology, 32,* 3–11.

Gongla, P. A., & Thompson, E. H., Jr. (1987). Single-parent families. In M. B. Sussman & S. K. Steinmetz (Eds.), *Handbook of marriage and the family* (pp. 397–418). New York: Plenum.

Gonzalez, A. R., Holbein, M. F. D., & Quilter, S. (2002). High school students' goal orientations and their relationship to perceived parenting styles. *Contemporary Educational Psychology, 27,* 450–470.

Good, T., & Brophy, J. (1972). Behavioral expression of teacher attitudes. *Journal of Educational Psychology, 63,* 617–624.

Goodlad, J. (1984). *A place called school.* New York: McGraw-Hill.

Goodman, G. S., Emery, R. E., & Haugaard, J. J. (1998). Developmental psychology and law: Divorce, child maltreatment, foster care, and adoption. In W. Damon (Gen. Ed.), I. E. Sigel (Vol. Ed.), & K. A. Renninger (Vol. Ed.), *Handbook of child psychology: Vol. 4. Child psychology in practice.* New York: John Wiley.

Goodman, K. (1976). Reading: A psycholinguistic guessing game. In H. Singer & R. Ruddell (Eds.), *Theoretical modes and processes of reading* (2nd ed., pp. 497–508). Newark, DE: International Reading Association.

Goodman, K. (1986). *What's whole in whole language?* Portsmouth, NH: Heinemann.

Goodman, K. (1992). I didn't found whole language. *The Reading Teacher, 46,* 188–199.

Goodman, K., & Goodman, Y. (1979). Learning to read is natural. In L. B. Resnick & P. S. Weaver (Eds.), *Theory and practice of early reading* (Vol. 1). Hillsdale, NJ: Erlbaum.

Goodman, Y. (1978). Kid-watching: An alternative to testing. *National Elementary Principal, 10,* 41–45.

Goodnow, J. J. (1988). Parents' ideas, actions and feelings: Models and methods from developmental and social psychology. *Child Development, 59,* 286–320.

Goodwyn, S., & Acredolo, L. (2000). Impact of symbolic gesturing on early language development. *Journal of Nonverbal Behavior, 24,* 81–103.

Gopnik, A., & Melzoff, A. (1997). *Words, thoughts, and theories,* Cambridge, MA: Bradford, The MIT Press.

Gopnik, A., Meltzoff, A., & Kuhl, P. (1999). *The scientist in the crib: Minds, brains and how children learn.* New York: William Morrow.

Gore, J. M. (1992). What can we do for you! What can 'we' do for 'you' ? Struggling over empowerment in critical and feminist pedagogy. In C. Luke & J. M. Gore (Eds.), *Feminism and critical pedagogy.* New York: Routledge.

Gortmaker, S., Dietz, W., & Cheung, L. (1990). Inactivity, diet, and the fattening of America. *Journal of the American Dietetic Association, 90,* 1247–1252.

Gottfried, A. E. (1985). Academic intrinsic motivation in elementary and junior high school students. *Journal of Educational Psychology, 77,* 631–645.

Gottfried, A. E., Bathurst, K., & Gottfried, A. W. (1994). Role of maternal and dual-earner employment status in children's development: A longitudinal study from infancy through early adolescence. In A. E. Gottfried & A. Gottfried (Eds.), *Redefining families: Implications for children's development* (pp. 55–97). New York: Plenum Press.

Gottman, J. M., Katz, L. F., & Hooven, C. (1997). *Meta-emotion.* Hillsdale, NJ: Erlbaum.

Gould, S. J. (1981). *The mismeasure of man.* New York: W. W. Norton & Company, Inc.

Gow, J. (1996). Reconsidering gender roles on MTV: Depictions in the most popular music videos of the early 1990s. *Communication Reports, 9,* 151–161.

Graber, J. A., Lewinsohn, P. M., Seeley, J. R., & Brooks-Gunn, J. (1997). Is psychopathology associated with the timing of pubertal development? *Journal of the American Academy of Child and Adolescent Psychiatry, 36,* 1768–1776.

Graham, S. (1984). Communicating sympathy and anger to black and white children: The cognitive (attributional) consequences of affective cues. *Journal of Personality and Social Psychology, 47,* 40–54.

Graham, S. (1994). Motivation for African Americans. *Review of Educational Research, 64,* 55–117.

Graham, S. & Golan, S. (1991). Motivational influences on cognitive: Task involvement, ego involvement, and depth of information processing. *Journal of Educational Psychology, 83,* 187–196.

Graham, S., & Harris, K. (2000). The role of self-regulation and transcription skills in writing and writing development. *Educational Psychologist, 35,* 3–13.

Graham, S., & Hudley, C. (1994). Attributions of aggressive and nonaggressive African American male early adolescents. A study of construct accessibility. *Developmental Psychology, 28,* 731–740.

Graham, S., & Hudley, C. (2005). Race and ethnicity in the study of motivation and competence. In A. J. Elliot & C. S. Dweck (Eds.), *Handbook of competence and motivation* (pp. 392–413). New York: Guilford Press.

Graham, S., Taylor, A. Z., & Hudley, C. (1998). Exploring achievement values among ethnic minority early adolescents. *Journal of Educational Psychology, 90,* 606–620.

Grant, C. A., & Gomez, M. L. (1996). *Making schooling multicultural: Campus and classroom.* Englewood Cliffs, NJ: Prentice Hall.

Grantham-McGregor, S., Ani, C., & Fernald, L. (2001). The role of nutrition in intellectual development. In R. Sternberg, & E. Grigorenko (Eds.), *Environmental effects on cognitive abilities* (pp. 119–148). Hillside, NJ: Erlbaum.

Graue, M. E., Weinstein, T., & Walberg, H. J. (1983). School-based home instruction and learning: A quantitative analysis. *Journal of Educational Research, 76*(6), 351–360.

Graves, D. H. (1979). What children show us about revision. *Language Arts, 56,* 312–319.

Gray-Little, B., & Hafdahl, A. R. (2000). Factors influencing racial comparisons of self-esteem: A quantitative review. *Psychological Bulletin, 126*(1), 26–54.

Green, R. (1978). Sexual identity of 37 children raised by homosexual or transsexual parents. *American Journal of Psychiatry, 135,* 692–697.

Green, R., Mandel, J. B., Hotvedt, M. E., Gray, J., & Smith, L. (1986). Lesbian mothers and their children: A comparison with solo parent heterosexual mothers and their children. *Archives of Sexual Behavior, 15,* 167–184.

Greenberg, J. (1995). Making friends with the Power Rangers. *Young Children, 50,* 60–61.

Greenberg, M., Kusche, C. A., Cook, E. T., & Quamma, J. (1995). Promoting emotional competence in school-aged children: The Effects of the PATHS curriculum. *Development and Psychopathology, 7,* 117–136.

Greenberg, M., Weissberg, R., O'Brien, M., Zins, J., Fredericks, L., Resnik, H., & Elias, M. (2003). Enhancing school-based prevention and youth development through coordinated social, emotional, and academic learning. *American Psychologist, 58,* 466–474.

Greenberger, E., & Goldberg, W. A. (1989). Work, parenting and the socialization of children. *Developmental Psychology, 25,* 22–35.

Greene, J. (2005, February). *Public high school graduation and college readiness rates in the United States: 1991–2002.* Education Working Paper No. 8. New York: Manhattan Institute for Policy Research. Available online at http://www.manhattan-institute.org.

Greene, M. L., & Way, N. (2005). Self-esteem trajectories among ethnic minority adolescents: A growth curve analysis of the patterns and predictors of change. *Journal of Research on Adolescence, 15*(2), 151–178.

Greenfield, P. (2004). Developmental considerations for determining appropriate Internet use guidelines for children and adolescents. *Journal of Applied Developmental Psychology, 25,* 751–762.

Greenfield, P., & Cocking, R. (1994). *Cross-cultural roots of minority child development.* Hillsdale, NJ: Erlbaum.

Greenfield, P. M., Keller, H., Fuligini, A., & Maynard, A. (2003). Cultural pathways through development. *Annual Review of Psychology, 54,* 491–490.

Greenough, W. T., Black, J. E., & Wallace, C. S. (1987). Experience and brain development. *Child Development, 58,* 539–559.

Greenwald, H., & Oppenheim, D. (1968). Reported magnitude of self-misidentification among Negro children: Artifact? *Journal of Personality and Social Psychology, 8,* 49–57.

Greif, G. L. (1985). *Single fathers.* Lexington, MA: Heath.

Greig, R. (2003). Ethnic identity development: Implications for mental health in African-American and Hispanic adolescents. *Issues in Mental Health Nursing, 24,* 317–331.

Grinsberg, R. W. (1998). Silenced voices inside our schools. *Initiatives, 58,* 1–15.

Grolnick, W. S., & Ryan, R. M. (1989). Parent styles associated with children's self-regulation and competence in school. *Journal of Educational Psychology, 81,* 143–154.

Gronlund, G. (1992). Coping with Ninja Turtle play in my kindergarten classroom. *Young Children, 48,* 21–25.

Gross, D., & Harris, P. L. (1988). False beliefs about emotion: Children's understanding of misleading emotional displays. *International Journal of Behavioral Development, 11,* 475–488.

Grossman, A., & Tucker, J. (1997). Gender differences and sexism in the knowledge and use of slang. *Sex Roles, 37,* 101–110.

Grumbach, M., Roth, J., Kaplan, S., & Kelch, R. (1974). Hypothalamic-pituitary regulation of puberty in man: Evidence and concepts derived from clinical research. In M. Grumbach , G. Gave, & F. Mayer (Eds.), *Control of onset of puberty.* New York: John Wiley.

Grusec, J. E., Goodnow, J. J., & Cohen, L. (1996). Household work and the development of concern for others. *Developmental Psychology, 32,* 999–1007.

Guay, F., Marsh, H., & Boivan, M. (2003). Academic self-concept and academic achievement: Developmental perspectives on their causal ordering. *Journal of Educational Psychology, 95,* 124–136.

Guilford, J. P. (1967). *The nature of human intelligence.* New York: McGraw-Hill.

Gutman, L., Sameroff, A., & Cole, R. (2003). Academic growth curve trajectories from 1st grade to 12th grade: Effects of multiple social risk factors and preschool child factors. *Developmental Psychology, 39,* 777–790.

Hack, M., Klein, N., & Taylor, G. (1995). Long-term developmental outcomes of low birth weight infants. *The Future of Children, 5,* 176–196.

Hagen, J., & Hale, G. (1973). The development of attention in children. In A. Pick (Ed.), *Minnesota symposium on child psychology, Vol. 7* (pp. 117–140). Minneapolis: University of Minnesota Press.

Hagerman, R. J., & Silverman, A. C. (1991). *Fragile X syndrome: Diagnosis, treatment, and research.* Baltimore: Johns Hopkins University Press.

Hakuta, K. (1986). *The mirror of language.* New York: Basic Books.

Hakuta, K. (1999). The debate on bilingual education. *Developmental and Behavioral Pediatrics, 20,* 36–37.

Hakuta, K., & Garcia, E. E. (1989). Bilingualism and education. *American Psychologist, 44,* 374–379.

Hakuta, K., & Gould, L. J. (1987). Synthesis of research on bilingual education. *Educational Leadership, 44,* 38–45.

Hale-Benson, J. (1990). Visions for children: Educating black children in the context of their culture. In K. Lomotemy (Ed.), *Going to school: The African-American experience.* Albany: State University of New York Press.

Hallahan, D. P., & Kauffman, J. M. (2000). *Exceptional learners. Introduction to special education* (8th ed.). Boston: Allyn & Bacon.

Halpern, D. (2002). Sex differences in achievement scores: Can we design assessments that are fair, meaningful, and valid for girls and boys? *Issues in Education, 8,* 1–19.

Hamilton, B., Martin, J., & Sutton, P. (2004). Birth: Preliminary data for 2003. *National Vital Statistics Reports, 53.* Centers for Disease Control and Prevention. Available online at http://www.cdc.gov/nchs/data/nvsr.

Hamilton, R., & Ghatala, E. (1994). *Learning and instruction.* New York: McGraw-Hill.

Hamre, B., & Pianta, R. (2001). Early teacher-child relationships and the trajectory of children's school outcomes through eighth grade. *Child Development, 72,* 625–638.

Hamre, G., & Pianta, R. (2005). Can instructional and emotional support in the first-grade classroom make a difference for children at risk of school failure? *Child Development, 76,* 949–967.

Haney, P., & Durlak, J. (1998). Changing self-esteem in children and adolescents: A meta-analytic review. *Journal of Clinical Child Psychology, 27,* 423–433.

Hanish, L., & Guerra, N. (2000). Children who get victimized at school: What is known? What can be done? *Professional School Counseling, 4*(2), 113–119.

Hanrich, C. C., Brown, J. L., & Aber, J. L. (1999). Evaluating the effectiveness of school-based violence prevention: Developmental approaches. *Social Policy, Report,* Vol. XIII, Society for Research in Child Development.

Hansen, S. (2001, July). Boys and writing: Reluctance? Reticence? Or rebellion?.

Paper presented at the Annual Meeting of the Education Research Network, Spetses, Greece.

Hansford, B. C., & Hattie, J. A. (1982). The relationship between self and achievement/ performance measures. *Review of Educational Research, 52,* 123–142.

Hardre, P., & Reeve, J. (2003). A motivational model of rural students' intentions to persist in, versus drop out of, high school. *Journal of Educational Psychology, 95,* 347–356.

Harjo, S. S. (1993). The American Indian experience. In H. P. McAdoo (Ed.), *Family ethnicity: Strength in diversity* (pp. 199–207). Newbury Park, CA: Sage.

Harman, D. (1987). *Illiteracy: A national dilemma.* New York: Cambridge University Press.

Harrell, J., McMurray, R., Bangdiwala, S., Frauman, A., Gansky, A., & Bradley, C. (1996). The effects of a school-based intervention to reduce cardiovascular disease risk factors in elementary school children: The cardiovascular health in children (CHIC) study. *The Journal of Pediatrics, 128,* 797–805.

Harris, A. J., & Sipay, E. R. (1990). *How to increase reading ability* (9th ed.). New York: Longman.

Harris, D. (1982). Communication interaction processes involving nonvocal physically handicapped children. *Topics in Language Disorders, 2,* 21–37.

Harris, J. (1995). Where is the child's environment? A group socialization theory of development. *Psychological Review, 102,* 458–489.

Harris, J. R. (1998). *The nurture assumption: Why children turn out the way they do.* New York: The Free Press.

Harris, K., & Graham, S. (1985). Improving learning disabled students' composition skills: Self-control strategy training. *Learning Disability Quarterly, 8,* 27–36.

Harris, P. (2006). Social cognition. In W. Damon (Series Ed.), D. Kuhn (Vol. Ed.), & Robert Siegler (Vol. Ed.), *Handbook of child psychology: Vol. 2. Cognition, perception, and language* (5th ed., pp. 811–858). New York: John Wiley.

Harris, P. L. (1989). *Children and emotion: The development of psychological understanding.* Oxford: Basil Blackwell.

Harrison, J. (1985). Functions of language attitudes in school settings. *Language in Society, 22,* 1–21.

Harste, J. (1989). *New policy guidelines for reading: Connecting research and practice.* Urbana, IL: National Council for Teachers of English.

Harste, J., Short, K., & Burke, C. (1988). *Creating classrooms for authors: The reading writing connection.* Portsmouth, NH: Heineman.

Harste, J., Woodward, V., & Burke, C. (1984). *Language stories and literacy lessons.* Portsmouth, NH: Heinemann.

Hart, B., & Risley, T. (1999). *The social world of children: Learning to talk.* Baltimore, MD: Brookes Publishing.

Hart, B., & Risley, T. R. (1992). American parenting of language-learning children: Persisting differences in family-child interactions observed in natural home environments. *Developmental Psychology, 28,* 1096–1105.

Hart, C. H., DeWolf, D. M., & Burts, D. C. (1992). Linkages among preschoolers' playground behavior, outcome expectations, and parental disciplinary strategies. *Early Education and Development, 3,* 265–283.

Hart, C. H., DeWolf, D., Wozniak, P., & Burts, D. C. (1992). Maternal and paternal disciplinary styles: Relations with preschoolers' playground behavioral orientations and peer status. *Child Development, 63,* 879–892.

Hart, E. L., Lahey, B. B., Loeber, R., Applegate, B., & Frick, P. J. (1995). Developmental changes in attention-deficit hyperactivity disorder in boys: A four-year longitudinal study. *Journal of Abnormal Child Psychology, 23,* 729–750.

Harter, S. (1978). Effectance motivation reconsidered: Toward a developmental model. *Human Development, 21,* 34–64.

Harter, S. (1981). A new self-report scale of intrinsic versus extrinsic orientation in the classroom: Motivational and informational components. *Developmental Psychology 17,* 300–312.

Harter, S. (1982). The Perceived Competence Scale for Children. *Child Development, 53,* 87–97.

Harter, S. (1983). Developmental perspectives on the self-system. In E. M. Hetherington (Ed.) & P. H. Mussen (Series Ed.), *Handbook of child psychology. Socialization personality and social development* (Vol. 4, pp. 275–385). New York: John Wiley.

Harter, S. (1986). Processes underlying the construct, maintenance, and enhancement of the self-concept in children. In J. Seils & A. Greenwald (Eds.), *Psychology perspectives on the self, Vol. 3,* (pp. 137–181). Hillsdale, NJ: Erlbaum.

Harter, S. (1990). Causes correlates and the functional role of global self-work: A lifespan perspective. In R. Steinberg & J. Kolligian, Jr. (Eds.) *Competence considered* (pp. 67–97). New Haven, CT: Yale University Press.

Harter, S. (1993). Causes and consequences of low self-esteem in children and adolescents. In R. F. Baumeister (Ed.), *Self-esteem: The puzzle flow self-regard.* (pp. 87–116). New York: Plenum Press.

Harter, S. (1998). The development of self-representations. In W. Damon (Series Ed.), & N. Eisenberg (Vol. Ed.), *Handbook of child psychology. Vol. 3: Social, emotional and personality development* (pp. 553–618). New York: John Wiley.

Harter, S. (1999). *The construction of the self.* New York: Guilford Press.

Harter, S. (2006). The self. In W. Damon & R. Lerner (Editors-in-Chief) & N. Eisenberg (Vol. Ed.), *Handbook of child psychology. Vol. 3: Social, emotional and personality development* (pp. 505–570). New York: John Wiley.

Harter, S., & Connell, J. P. (1984). A model of children's achievement and related self-perceptions of competence, control, and motivational orientation. In J. G. Nicholls (Ed.), *The development of achievement motivation* (Vol. 3, pp. 219–250). Greenwich, CT: JAI Press.

Harter, S., & Whitesall, N. (1989). Developmental changes in children's understanding of single, multiple, and blended emotional concepts. In C. Saarni, & P. Harris (Eds.), *Children's understanding of emotions* (pp. 81–116). Cambridge, England: Cambridge University Press.

Harter, S., Whitesall, N., & Kowalski, P. (1992). Individual differences in the effects of educational transitions on young adolescents' perception of competence and motivational orientation. *American Educational Research Journal, 29,* 77–807.

Hartup, W. W. (1996). The company they keep: Friendships and their developmental significance. *Child Development, 67,* 1–13.

Hartup, W. W., & Stevens, N. (1999). Friendships and adaptation across the lifespan. *Current Directions in Psychological Science, 8*(3), 76–79.

Harwood, R. L., Miller, J. G., & Irizarry, N. L. (1995). *Culture and attachment: Perceptions of the child in context.* New York: Guilford Press.

Hasslebring, T. S., & Glaser, C. H. W. (2000). Use of technology to help students with special needs. *Future of Children. Children and Computer Technology,* Vol. 10, pp. 102–122. Available online at http://www. futureofchildren.org.

Haston, A. C., & Wright, J. C. (1998). Mass media and children's development. In I. Sejel (Vol. Ed.), K. A. Renninjer (Vol. Ed.), & W. Damon (Editor-in-Chief), *Handbook of Child Psychology* (5th ed., pp. 999–1058) New York: John Wiley.

Hattie, J. (1992). *Self-concept.* Hillsdale, NJ: Erlbaum.

Hattie, J., & Marsh, H. W. (1996). The relationship between research and teaching—a meta-analysis. *Review of Educational Research, 66,* 507–542.

Hauser-Cram, P., Warfield, M., Shonkoff, J., & Krauss, M. (2001). Children with disabilities: A longitudinal study of child development and parent well-being. *Monographs of the Society for Research in Child Development, 66* (Serial No. 266).

Hawke, S., & Knox, D. (1978). The one-child family: A new life style. *Family Coordinator. 27,* 215–219.

Hayman, N., & Comer, J. (1990). Helping black children succeed: The significance of some social factors. In K. Lomotey (Ed.), *Going to school: The African-American experience.* Albany: State University of New York Press.

Haynes, N., & Ben-Avie, M. (1996). Parents as full partners in education. In A. Booth and J. Dunn (Eds.), *Family school links: How do they affect educational outcomes?* (pp. 45–56). Mahwah, NJ: Erlbaum.

Heath, S. B. (1983). *Ways with words: Language, life, and work in communities and classrooms.* Cambridge, England: Cambridge University Press.

Hedges, L., & Nowell, A. (1995). Sex differences in mental test scores, variability, and numbers of high scoring individuals. Science, *269,* 41–45.

Heller, C., & Hawkins, J. (1994). Teaching tolerance: Notes from the front line. *Teachers College Record, 95,* 337–369.

Henderson, E. (1990). *Teaching spelling.* Boston: Houghton Mifflin.

Henderson, N., & Milstein, M. M. (1996). *Resiliency in schools: Making it happen for students and educators.* Thousand Oaks, CA: Corwin Press.

Herman-Giddens, M., Slora, E., Wasserman, R., Bourdony, C., Bhapkar, M., Koch, G., & Hasemeier, C. (1997). Secondary sexual characteristics and menses in young girls seen in office practice: A study from the Pediatric

Research in Office Settings Network. *Pediatrics, 88,* 505–512.

Herrnstein, C., & Murray, C. (1994). The bell curve: Intelligence and class structure in American life. New York: Free Press.

Hertsgaard, D., & Light, H. (1984). Anxiety, depression, and hostility in rural women. *Psychological Reports, 55,* 673–674.

Hetherington, E. M. (1989). Coping with family transitions: Winners, losers, and survivors. *Child Development, 60,* 1–14.

Hetherington, E. M. (1991). The role of individual differences and family relationships in children's coping with divorce and remarriage. In P. A. Cowan & E. M. Hetherington (Eds.), *Family transitions* (pp. 165–194). Hillsdale, NJ: Erlbaum.

Hetherington, E. M. (1993). An overview of the Virginia longitudinal study of divorce and remarriage with a focus on early adolescence. *Journal of Family Psychology, 7,* 1–18.

Hetherington, E. M. (1998). Social capital and the development of youth from nondivorced, divorced, and remarried families. In A. Collins (Ed.), *Relationships as developmental contexts: The 29th Minnesota symposium on child psychology.* Hillsdale, NJ: Erlbaum.

Hetherington, E. M. (1999). Should we stay together for the sake of the children? In E. M. Hetherington (Ed.), *Coping with divorce, single parenting, and remarriage: A risk and resiliency perspective.* Mahwah, NJ: Erlbaum.

Hetherington, E. M., & Clingempeel, W. G. (1992). Coping with marital transition. *Monographs of the Society for Research in Child Development, 57*(2–3, Serial No. 227).

Hetherington, E. M., Cox, M., & Cox, R. (1982). Effects of divorce on parents and children. In M. Lamb (Ed.), *Nontraditional families* (pp. 233–288). Hillsdale, NJ: Erlbaum.

Hetherington, E. M., & Jodl, K. M. (1994). Stepfamilies as settings for child development. In A. Booth & J. Dunn (Eds.), *Stepfamilies: Who benefits? Who does not?* (pp. 55–79). Hillsdale, NJ: Erlbaum.

Hetherington, E. M., & Martin, B. (1986). Family interaction. In H. C. Quay & J. C. Werry (Eds.), *Psychopathological disorders of childhood* (3rd ed., pp. 332–390). New York: John Wiley.

Hetherington, E. M., & Parke, R. D. (1993). *Child psychology: A contemporary view.* New York: McGraw-Hill.

Hetherington, E. M., & Stanley-Hagan, M. M. (1995). Parenting in divorced and remarried families. In M. H. Bornstein (Ed.), *Children and parenting* (Vol. 4). Hillsdale, NJ: Erlbaum.

Hetherington, E. M., & Stanley-Hagan, M. M. (1999). Stepfamilies. In M. E. Lamb (Ed.), *Nontraditional families.* Hillsdale, NJ: Erlbaum.

Hetherington, E. M., Stanley-Hagan, M. M., & Anderson, E. R. (1989). Marital transitions: A child's perspective. *American Psychologist, 44,* 303–312.

Hetherington, M., & Kelly, J. (2002). *For better or worse. Divorce reconsidered.* New York: Norton.

Heusmann, L. R., Eron, L. D., Lefkowitz, M. M., & Walder, L. O. (1984). Stability of aggression over time and generations. *Developmental Psychology, 20,* 1120–1134.

Heusmann, L. W., Moise-Titus, J., Podolski, C., & Evon, L. (2003). Longitudinal relations between children's exposure to TV violence and their aggressive and violent behavior in young adulthood: 1977–1992. *Developmental Psychology, 39,* 201–221.

Hiebert, E. H. (Ed.). (1991). *Literacy for a diverse society: Perspectives, practices, and policies.* New York: Teachers College Press.

Hill, C. R., & Stafford, F. P. (1980). Parental care of children: Time diary estimate of quantity, predictability, and variety. *Journal of Human Resources, 15,* 219–239.

Hill, J., Brooks-Gunn, J., & Waldfogel, J. (2003). Sustained effects of high participation in an early intervention for low-birth-weight premature infants. *Developmental Psychology, 39,* 730–744.

Hill, J. P., & Lynch, M. E. (1983). The intensification of gender-related role expectations during early adolescence. In J. Brooks-Gunn & A.C. Petersen (Eds.), *Girls at puberty: Biological and psychosocial perspectives* (pp. 201–228). New York: Plenum.

Hines, M. (1990). Gonadal hormones and human cognitive development. In J. Balthazart (Ed.), *Brain and behaviour in vertebrates 1: Sexual differentiation, neuroanatomical aspects, neuro-transmitters and neuropeptides* (pp. 51–63). Basel, Switzerland: Karger.

Hirsch, B. J., & Rapkin, B. D. (1987). The transition to junior high school: A longitudinal study of self-esteem, psychological symptomatology, school life, and social support. *Child Development, 58,* 1235–1243.

Hiscock, M., & Kinbourne, M. (1987). Specialization of the cerebral hemisphere: Implications for learning. *Journal of Learning Disabilities, 20,* 130–142.

Hoch, J. (1985). Remodeling old models of intelligence. In B. B. Wolman (Ed.), *Handbook of intelligence* (pp. 267–300). New York: John Wiley.

Hock, E. (1978). Working and nonworking mothers with infants: Perceptions of their careers, their infants' needs, and satisfaction with mothering. *Developmental Psychology, 4,* 37–43.

Hockett, C. (1968). *The state of the art.* (J. Linguarum, series minor, 73). The Hague, The Netherlands: Mouton.

Hoff-Ginsberg, E. (1991). Mother-child conversation in different social classes and communicative settings. *Child Development, 62,* 782–796.

Hoffman, L. W. (1989). Effects of maternal employment on the two-parent family. *American Psychologist, 44,* 283–292.

Hoffman, M. L. (1994). Discipline and internalization. *Developmental Psychology, 30,* 26–28.

Hoffman, M. L. (2000). *Empathy and moral development: Implications for caring and justice.* Cambridge, England: Cambridge Press.

Hoffman, M. L., & Saltzstein, H. D. (1967). Parent discipline and the child's moral development. *Journal of Personality and Social Psychology, 5,* 45–57.

Hohmann, M., & Weikart, D. (1995). *Educating young children: Active learning practices for preschool and child care programs.* Ypsilanti, MI: High/Scope Educational Foundation.

Hollinger, J. (1987). Social skills for behaviorally disordered children as preparation for mainstreaming: Theory, practice, and new directions. *Remedial and Special Education, 8,* 17–27.

Holloway, S. D., Kashiwagi, K., Hess, R. D., & Azuma, H. (1986). Causal attributions by Japanese and American mothers and children about performance in mathematics. International *Journal of Psychology, 21,* 269–286.

Holmbeck, G. N. (1996). A model of family relational transformations during the transition to adolescence: Parent-adolescent conflict and adaptation. In J. A. Graber & J. Brooks-Gunn (Eds.), *Transitions through adolescence: Interpersonal domains and context* (pp. 167–199). Mahwah, NJ: Erlbaum.

Hoover-Dempsey, K., & Sandler, H. (1995). Parental involvement in children's education: Why does it make a difference? *Teachers College Record, 97,* 310–331.

Hoover-Dempsey, K., & Sandler, H. (1997). Why do parents become involved in their children's education? *Review of Educational Research, 67,* 3–42.

Hoover-Dempsey, K. V., Bassler, O. C, & Brissie, J. S. (1987). Parent involvement: Contributions of teacher efficacy, school socioeconomic status, and other school characteristics. *American Educational Research Journal, 24,* 417–435.

Horowitz, S. (2006). Asking the experts: Sheldon Horowitz. PBS Parents: Struggling to learn. Retrieved July 2006 from http:// www.pbs.org/parents/strugglingtolearn/asking_horowitz.html.

Howe, N., & Ross, H. S. (1990). Socialization perspective taking and the sibling relationship. *Developmental Psychology, 26,* 160–165.

Howes, C. (2005). Social-emotional classroom climate in child care, child-teacher relationships, and children's second grade peer relations. *Social Development, 9,* 191–204.

Howes, C., & Hamilton, C. (1993). The changing experience of child care: Changes in teacher and teacher-child relationships and children's social competence with peers. *Early Childhood Research Quarterly, 8,* 15–32.

Howes, C., & Matheson, C. C. (1992). Contextual constraints on the concordance of mother-child and teacher-child relationships. In R. C. Pianta (Ed.), *New directions in child development, Vol. 57. Relationships between children and non-parental adults* (pp. 25–90). San Francisco: Jossey-Bass.

Howes, C., & Wu, F. (1990). Peer interactions and friendships in an ethnically diverse school setting. *Child Development, 61,* 537–541.

Howse, R. B., Calkins, S. D., Anastopoulos, A. D., Keane, S. P., & Shelton, T. L. (2003). Regulatory contributors to children's kindergarten achievement. *Early Education and Development, 14,* 101–119.

Hubel, D. H., & Wiesel, T. N. (1970). The period of susceptibility to the physiological effects of unilateral eye closure in kittens. *Journal of Physiology, 206,* 419–436.

Huffman, L. C., Mehlinger, S. L., & Kerivan, A. S. (2000). Risk factors for academic and behavioral problems at the beginning of school. In *Off to a good start: Research on the risk factors for early school problems and selected federal policies affecting children's social and emotional development and their readiness for school.* Chapel Hill: University of North Carolina, Frank Porter Graham Child Development Center.

Huggins, S. L. (1989). A comparative study of self-esteem of adolescent children of divorced lesbian mothers and divorced heterosexual mothers. In F. W. Bozett (Ed.), *Homosexuality and the family* (pp. 123–135). New York: Harrington Park Press.

Human Genome Project. (2004). Human genome information. Retrieved July 2006 from http://www.ornl.gov/sci/techresources/Human_Genome/home.shtml.

Human Rights Watch. (2001). *Hatred in the hallways. Violence and discrimination against lebian, gay, bisexual, and transgender students in U.S. schools.* New York: Author. Retrieved October 2006 from http://www.hrw.org/reports/2001/uslgbt/toc.htm.

Hunt, K. (1977). Early blooming and late blooming syntactic structures. In C. Cooper & L. Odell (Eds.), *Evaluating writing: Describing, measuring, judging* (pp. 91–106). Urbana, IL: National Council for Teachers of English.

Hunt-Berg, M., Rankin, R. L., & Beukelman, D. R. (1994). Ponder the possibilities: Computer-supported writing for struggling writers. *Learning Disabilities Research and Practice, 9,* 169–178.

Hunter, C. S. J., & Harman, D. (1979). *Adult illiteracy in the United States.* New York: McGraw-Hill.

Hussar, W. J., & Bailey, T. M. (2006). *Projections of education statistics to 2015.* (NCES 06-084). U.S. Department of Education, National Center for Education Statistics. Washington, DC: U.S. Government Printing Office.

Huston, A. C. (1983). Sex typing. In P. H. Mussen (Series Ed.) & E. M. Hetherington (Vol. Ed.), *Handbook of child psychology: Vol. 4. Socialization, personality, and social development* (4th ed., pp. 387–467). New York: John Wiley.

Huston, A. C., & Alvarez, M. M. (1990). The socialization context of gender role development in early adolescence. In R. Montemayor, G. R., Adams, & T. P. Gullotta (Eds.), *Advances in adolescent development: Vol. 2. From childhood to adolescence: A transitional period?* (pp. 156–182). Newbury Park, CA: Sage.

Huston, A. C., Carpenter, C. J., Atwater, J. B., & Johnson, L. M. (1986). Gender, adult structuring of activities and social behavior in middle childhood. *Child Development, 57,* 1200–1209.

Huston, A. C., & Wright, J. C. (1998). Mass media and children's development. In W. Damon (Series Ed.), I. Sigel (Vol. Ed.), & A. Renniger (Vol. Ed.), *Handbook of child psychology, Vol. 4, Child psychology in practice* (pp. 999–1058). New York: John Wiley.

Hyde, A., & Bizar, M. (1989). *Thinking in context: Teaching cognitive processes across the elementary school curriculum.* New York: Longman.

Hyde, J. (2005). The gender similarities hypothesis. *American Psychologist, 60,* 581–592.

Hyde, J. S., Fennema, E., & Lamon, S. J. (1990). Gender differences in mathematics performance: A meta-analysis. *Psychological Bulletin, 107,* 139–155.

Hyde, J. S., & Linn, M. (1988). Gender differences in verbal ability. A meta-analysis. *Psychological Bulletin, 104,* 53–69.

Hyde, J. S., & McKinley, N. M. (1997). Gender differences in cognition: Results from meta-analyses. In P. J. Caplan, M. Crawford, J. S. Hyde, & J. T. E. Richardson (Eds.), *Gender differences in human cognition* (pp. 30–51). New York: Oxford University Press.

Hymel, S., Comfat, C., Schoreit-Reichl, K., & McDougall, P. (1996). Academic failure and school dropout: The influence of peers. In J. Juvonen & K. R. Wentzel (Eds.), *Social maturation: Understanding children's school adjustment.* New York: Cambridge Press.

Hymes, D. (1974). *Foundations in sociolinguistics.* Philadelphia: University of Pennsylvania Press.

Imedadze, N. V. (1978). On the psychological nature of child speech formation under condition of exposure to two languages. In E. M. Hatch (Ed.), *Second language acquisition: A book of readings.* Rowley, MA: Newbury House.

Ingrassia, M. (1995, April 24). The body of the beholder. *Newsweek,* pp. 66–67.

Institute for Children and Poverty. (2005). *Homeless in America, part two: A statistical reader.* New York: White Tiger Press.

International Association for the Evaluation of Educational Achievement. (1997). *Science achievement in the middle school years.* U.S. Department of Education, National Center for Educational Statistics. Washington, DC: U.S. Government Printing Office.

International Reading Association. (1999). Adolescent literacy: A position statement. Retrieved January 2007 from http://www.reading.org/downloads/positions/ps1036_adolescent.pdf.

Irvine, J. (1990). *Black students and school failure. Policies, practices, and prescriptions.* New York: Praeger.

Itard, J. (1962). *The wild boy of everyone.* New York: Appleton-Century-Crofts.

Izard, C. E. (1991). *The psychology of emotions.* New York: Plenum.

Jackson, A. W., & Davis, G. A. (2000). *Turning points 2000: Educating adolescents in the 21st century.* New York: Teachers College Press.

Jacobs, J. E., Chin, C. S., & Bleeker, M. M. (2006). Enduring links: Parents' expectations and their young adult children's gender-typed occupational choices. *Educational Research and Evaluation, 12,* 395–408.

Jacobs, J. E., & Eccles, J. S. (1992). The impact of mothers' gender-role stereotypic beliefs on mothers' and childrens' ability perceptions. *Journal of Personality and Social Psychology, 63,* 932–944.

Jacabvitz, D., & Sroufe, L. A. (1987). The early caregiver-child relationship and attention deficit disorder with hyperactivity in kindergarten: A prospective study. *Child Development, 58*(6), 1488–1495.

Jaffe, S. R., & Hyde, J. S. (2000). Gender differences in moral orientation. A meta-analysis. *Psychological Bulletin, 126,* 703–706.

James, W. (1948). *Psychology.* New York: World Book. (Original publication, 1890)

Jencks, C., & Phillips, M. (1998). The black-white test score gap: An introduction. In C. Jencks & M. Phillips (Eds.), *The black-white test score gap* (pp. 1–51). Washington, DC: Brookings Institution Press.

Jerald, C. D., & Orlofsky, G. F. (1999). Raising the bar on school technology. *Education Week, 19,* 58–108.

Jerison, H. J. (1973). *Evolution of the brain and intelligence.* New York: Academic Press.

Jeynes, W., & Littell, S. (2000). A meta-analysis of studies examining the effect of whole language instruction on the literacy of low-SES students. *Elementary School Journal, 101,* 21–33.

Joe, J. R. (1994). Revaluing Native-American concepts of development and education. In P. M. Greenfield & R. R. Cocking (Eds.), *Cross-cultural roots of minority child development* (pp. 107–114). Hillsdale, NJ: Erlbaum.

Joe, J. R., & Malach, R. S. (1992). Families with Native American roots. In E. W. Lynch & M. J. Hanson (Eds.), *Developing cross-cultural competence* (pp. 89–119). Baltimore: Paul H. Brookes Publishing Company.

Johnson, D. W., & Johnson, R. T. (1999). *Learning together and alone: Cooperative, competitive, and individualistic learning* (5th ed.). Boston: Allyn & Bacon.

Johnson, D. W., & Johnson, R. T. (2000). Teaching students to be peacemakers: Results of twelve years of research. Unpublished manuscript, University of Minnesota.

Johnson, D. W., Johnson, R. T., & Stanne, M. B. (2000). Cooperative learning methods: A meta-analysis. Unpublished manuscript, University of Minnesota.

Johnston, L., Bachman, J., & O'Malley, P. (1999). *Monitoring the future.* Ann Arbor, MI: Institute for Social Research.

Jones, G., & Carter, G. (1994). Verbal and nonverbal behavior of ability-grouped dyads. *Journal of Research on Science Teaching, 31,* 603–619.

Jones, L. (1984). White-black achievement differences. *American Psychologist, 39,* 1207–1213.

Jones. S. M., & Dindia, K. (2004). A meta-analytic perspective on sex equity in the classroom. *Review of Educational Research, 74*(4), 443–471.

Jordon, W. (1999). Black high school students' participation in school-sponsored sports activities: Effects on school engagement and achievement. *Journal of Negro Education, 68*(1), 54–71.

Josselson, R. (1988a). *Finding herself: Pathways to identity development in women.* San Francisco: Jossey-Bass.

Josselson, R. (1988b). The embedded self: I and thou revisited. In D. K. Lapsley & F. C. Power (Eds.), *Self, ego, and identity: Integrative approaches* (pp. 91–106). New York: Springer-Verlag.

Juell, C., Griffith, P., & Gough, P. (1986). The acquisition of literacy: A longitudinal study of children in first and second grade. *Journal of Educational Psychology, 78,* 243–255.

Kagan, D. (1992). Implications of research on teacher belief. *Educational Psychologist, 27,* 65–90.

Kagan, J. (1998). Biology and the child. In W. Damon (Series Ed.) & N. Eisenberg (Vol. Ed.), *Handbook of child psychology, Vol. 3. Social, emotional, and personality development* (pp. 177–236). New York: John Wiley.

Kahle, J. B., & Meece, J. L. (1984). Research on girls in science: Lessons and applications. In D. Gabel (Ed.), *Handbook of research on science teaching* (pp. 1559–1610). Washington, DC: National Science Teachers Association.

Kail, R. (2000). Speed of information processing: Developmental change and links to intelligence. *Journal of School Psychology, 38,* 51–61.

Kail, R. (2002). Developmental change in proactive interference. *Child Development, 73,* 1703–1714.

Kamii, C. (2000). *Young children reinvent arithmetic. Implications of Piaget's theory.* New York: Teachers College Press.

Kamii, C., Lewis, B., & Kirkland, L. (2001). Manipulatives: When are they useful? *The Journal of Mathematical Behavior, 20,* 21–31.

Kandel, D., & Logan, J. (1984). Patterns of drug use from adolescence to young adulthood, I: Periods of risk for initiation, continued use, and discontinuation. *American Journal of Public Health, 74,* 660–666.

Kandel, D., & Wu, P. (1995). The contributions of mothers and fathers to the intergenerational transmission of cigarette smoking in adolescence. *Journal of Research on Adolescence, 5,* 225–252.

Kaplan, D., Damphouse, K., & Kaplan, H. (1996a). Mental health implications of not graduating from high school. *Journal of Experimental Education, 62,* 105–123.

Kaplan, D., Damphouse, K., & Kaplan. H. (1996b). Moderating effects of gender on the relationship between not graduating from high school and psychological dysfunction in young adulthood. *Journal of Educational Psychology, 88,* 760–774.

Karambayya, R., & Reilly, A. H. (1992). Dual earner couples: Attitudes and actions in restructuring work for family. *Journal of Organizational Behavior, 13,* 585–601.

Karmiloff-Smith, A. (1979). *A functional approach to child language: A study of determiners and reference.* Cambridge, England: Cambridge University Press.

Kasari, C., & Bauminger, N. (1998). Social and emotional development in children with mental retardation. In J. A. Burack, R. M. Hodapp, & E. Zigler (Eds.), *Handbook of mental retardation and development* (pp. 411–433). New York: Cambridge University Press.

Katz, L. F., & Gottman, J. M. (1997). Buffering children from marital conflict and dissolution. *Journal of Clinical Child Psychology, 26,* 157–171.

Katz, P. A., & Zalk, S. R. (1974). Doll preferences: An index of racial attitudes. *Journal of Educational Psychology, 5,* 663–668.

Kaufman, A., & Kaufman, N. (1983). *Kaufman assessment battery for children: Administration and scoring manual.* Circle Pines, MN: American Guidance Service.

Kauffman, J. M. (1994). Places of change: Special education's power and identity in an era of educational reform. *Journal of Learning Disabilities, 27,* 610–618.

Kauffman, J. M., & Wong, K. L. H. (1991). Effective teachers of students with behavioral disorders: Are generic teaching skills enough? *Behavioral Disorders, 16,* 225–237.

Keating, D. (1990). Adolescent thinking. In S. Feldman & G. Elliot (Eds.), *At the threshold: The developing adolescent* (pp. 54–90). Cambridge, MA: Harvard University Press.

Keeney, T., Cannizzo, S., & Flavell, J. (1967). Spontaneous and induced verbal rehearsal in a recall task. *Child Development, 38,* 953–966.

Keith, T. Z., Reimers, T. M., Fehrman, P. G., Pottebaum, S. M., & Aubey, L. W. (1986). Parental involvement, homework, and TV time: Direct and indirect effects on high school achievement. *Journal of Educational Psychology, 78*(5), 424–434.

Kellam, S. G., Ensminger, M. E., & Turner, R. J. (1997). Family structure and the mental health of children. *Archives of General Psychiatry, 34,* 1012–1022.

Kelley, M. L., Power, T. G., & Wimbush, D. D. (1992). Determinants of disciplinary practices in low-income black mothers. *Child Development, 63,* 573–582.

Kellogg, R. (1970). *Analyzing children's art.* Mountain View, CA: Mayfield.

Kemple, J. J. (2001). *Career academies: Impacts on students' initial transitions to post-secondary education and employment.* New York: Manpower Demonstration Research Corporation.

Kendall-Tackett, K. A., Williams, L. M., & Finkelhor, D. (1993). Impact of sexual abuse on children: A review and synthesis of recent empirical studies. *Psychological Bulletin, 113,* 164–180.

Keniston, A., & Flavell, J. (1979). A developmental study of intelligent behavior. *Child Development, 50,* 1144–1152.

Kerr, B., Colangelo, N., & Gaeth, J. (1988). Gifted adolescents' attitudes toward their giftedness. *Gifted Child Quarterly, 32,* 245–247.

Kerr, D., Lopez, N., Olson, S., & Sameroff, A. (2004). Parental discipline and externalizing behavioral problems in early childhood: The roles of moral regulation and child gender. *Journal of Abnormal Child Psychology, 32,* 369–383.

Kesner, J. (2000). Teacher characteristics and the quality of child-teacher relationships. *Journal of School Psychology, 38,* 133–150.

Kim, K., & Smith, P. K. (1998). Childhood stress, behavioral symptoms and mother-daughter pubertal development. *Journal of Adolescence, 21*(3), 231–240.

Kimura, D. (1989, November). Monthly fluctuations in sex hormones affect women's cognitive skills. *Psychology Today,* 63–66.

Kinderman, T. A., McCollam, T. L., & Gibson, E., Jr. (1996). Peer networks and students' classroom engagement during childhood and adolescence. In K. Wentzel & J. Juvonen (Eds.), *Social motivation: Understanding children's school adjustment* (pp. 279–312). New York: Cambridge University Press.

Kindler, A. (2002, May). *Survey of the states' limited English proficient students & available educational programs and services 1999–2000 summary report.* Washington, DC: National Clearinghouse for English Language Acquisition and Language Instruction Educational Programs. Retrieved July 1, 2006, from http://www.ncela.gwu.edu/policy/states/reports/seareports/0001/sea0001.pdf.

Kinney, D. (1993). From "nerds" to "normals": Adolescent identity recovery within a changing social system. *Sociology of Education, 66,* 21–40.

Kirby, D. (2002a). The impact of schools and school programs upon adolescent sexual behavior. *The Journal of Sex Research, 39,* 27–33.

Kirby, D., (2002b). Effective approaches to reducing adolescent unprotected sex, pregnancy, and childbearing. *The Journal of Sex Research, 39*, 51–57.

Kirn, W. (2000, September 25). Should you stay together for the kids? *Time, 156*, 75–82.

Klahr, D., & MacWhinney, B. (1998). Information processing. In W. Damon (Editor-in-Chief), D. Kuhn (Vol. Ed.), & R. S. Siegler (Vol. Ed.), *Handbook of child psychology: Vol. 2*, (5th ed., pp. 631–678). New York: John Wiley.

Kleinman, R., Murphy, J., Little, M., Pagano, M., Wehler, C., Regal, K., & Jellinek, M. (1998). Hunger in children in the United States: Potential behavioral and emotional correlates. *Pediatrics, 101*, 1–3.

Klesges, R. (1993). Effects of television on metabolic rate: Potential implications for childhood obesity. *Pediatrics, 19*(2), 281–286.

Klig, K. C., Hyde, J. S., Showers, C. J., & Buswell, B. N. (1999). Gender differences in self-esteem: A meta analysis. *Psychological Bulletin, 125*, 470–500.

Klima, E., & Bellugi, U. (1966). Syntactic regulation in the speech of children. In J. Lyons & R. Wales (Eds.), *Psycholinguistics papers* (pp. 183–208). Edinburgh, Scotland: Edinburgh University Press.

Kling, K. C., Hyde, J. S., Showers, C. J., & Buswell, B. N. (1999). Gender differences in self-esteem: A meta-analysis. *Psychological Bulletin, 125*, 470–500.

Klinger, J., Vaughn, S., Hughes, M., Schumm, J., & Elbaum, B. (1998). Academic outcomes for students with and without disabilities in inclusive classroom. *Learning Disabilities Research and Practice, 13*, 153–160.

Kluger, M. P., & Aprea, D. M. (1999). Grandparents raising grandchildren: A description of the families and a special pilot program. *Journal of Gerontological Social Work, 32*, 5–17.

Kohlberg, L. (1969). Stage and sequence: The cognitive-developmental approach to socialization. In D. A. Goslin (Ed.), *Handbook of socialization theory and research* (pp.347–480). Chicago: Rand McNally.

Kohn, A. (1997). How not to teach values: A critical look at character education. *Phi Delta Kappan, 78*(6), 428–439.

Kolata, G. (1986). Obese children: A growing problem. *Science, 232*, 20–21.

Kopp, C. B., & McCall, R. B. (1982). Predicting later mental performance for normal, at-risk, and handicapped infants. In P. B. Baltes & O. G. Brim (Eds.),

Life-span development and behavior (Vol. 4). New York: Academic Press.

Kornhaber, M., Fierros, E., & Veenema, S. (2004). *Multiple intelligences: Best ideas from research and practice*. Boston: Allyn & Bacon.

Koshewa, A. (2002, October/November). Acting out: Drama as social action: Interview with Vivian Paley. *Talking Points*, 7–9.

Kowalski, K. (2003). The emergence of ethnic and racial attitudes in preschool aged children. *Journal of Social Psychology, 143*, 677–690.

Kozol, J. (1985). *Illiterate America*. New York: Anchor/Doubleday.

Kozol, J. (1991). *Savage inequalities: Children in America's schools*. New York: Crown.

Krashen, S. D., & Terrell, T. D. (1983). *The natural approach: Language acquisition in the classroom*. New York: Pergamon Press.

Kress, Gunther. (1982). *Learning to write*. London: Routledge & Kegan Paul.

Kreutzer, M. A., Leonard, C., & Flavell, J. H. (1975). An interview study of children's knowledge about memory. *Monographs of the Society for Research in Child Development, 40*(1, Serial No. 159).

Kubow, P. K., Wahlsstrom, K. L., & Bemis, A. (1999). Starting time and school life: Reflections from educators and students. *Phi Delta Kappan, 80*(5), 366–371.

Kuhn, D. (2000). Does memory development belong on an endangered topic list? *Child Development, 71*, 21–25.

Kuhn, D., & Pearsll, S. (2000). Developmental origins of scientific thinking. *Journal of Cognition and Development, 1*, 113–129.

Kulik, J. (1994). Meta-analytic studies of findings on computer-based instruction. In E. Baker & H. O'Neil (Eds.), *Technology assesment in education and training*, New York: Erlbaum.

Labov, W. (1972). *The logic of nonstandard English. Language in the inner city: Studies in the black English vernacular*. Philadelphia: University of Pennsylvania Press.

Ladd, G., & Burgess, K. (2001). Do relational risk and protective factors moderate the links between childhood aggression and early psychological and school adjustment? *Child Development, 72*, 1579–1601.

Ladd, G., & Price, J. (1987). Predicting children's social and school adjustment

following from preschool to kindergarten. *Child Development, 58*, 1158–1189.

Ladd, G. W. (1990). Having friends, keeping friends, making friends and being liked by peers in the classroom: Predictors of children's early adjustment? *Child Development, 61*, 1081–1100.

Lahey, B. B., Loeber, R., Quay, H. C., Applegate, B., Shaffer, D., Waldman, I., Hart E. L., McBurnett, K., Frick, P. J., Jensen, P. S., Dulcan, M. K., Canino, G., & Bird, H. R. (1998). Validity of DSM-IV subtypes of conduct disorder based on age of onset. *Journal of the American Academy of Child and Adolescent Psychiatry, 37*, 435–442.

Lahey, B. B., Waldman, I. D., & McBurnett, K. (1999). Annotation: The development of antisocial behavior: An integrative causal model. *Journal of Child Psychology and Psychiatry, 40*, 699–682.

Lamb, M., Chuang, S., & Cabrera, N. (2005). Promoting child adjustment by fostering positive paternal involvement. In R. Lerner, F. Jacobs, & D. Werlieg (Eds.), *Applied development science: An advanced textbook* (pp. 179–200). Thousand Oaks, CA: Sage.

Lamb, M. E. (1997). *The role of the father in child development* (3rd ed.). New York: John Wiley.

Lamb, M. E. (1998). Nonparental child care: Contex, quality, correlates, and consequences. In W. Damon (Series Ed.), I. Siegel (Vol. Ed.), & A. Renniger (Vol. Ed.), *Handbook of child psychology, Vol. 4*, (pp. 73–134). New York: John Wiley.

Lamb, M. E., Pleck, J. H., Charnov, E. L., & Levine, J. A. (1987). A biosocial perspective on paternal behavior and involvement. In J. B. Lancaster, J. Altman, A. Rossi, & L. R. Sherrod (Eds.), *Parenting across the lifespan: Biosocial perspectives* (pp. 11–42). New York: Academic Press.

Landry, S. H., Smith, K. E., Swank, P. R., & Miller-Loncar, C. L. (2000). Early maternal and child influences on children's later independent cognitive and social functioning. *Child Development, 71*, 358–375.

Langer, J. (1991). Literacy and schooling: A sociocognitive perspective. In E. H. Hiebert (Ed.), *Literacy for a diverse society* (pp. 9–27). New York: Teachers College Press.

Langlois, J., & Stephen, C. (1981). Beauty and the beast: The role of physical attractiveness in peer relationships and social behavior. In S. Brehm, S. Kassin, & S. Gibbons (Eds.),

Developmental social psychology: Theory and research (pp. 152–168). New York: Oxford University Press.

Langlois, J. H., & Downs, A. C. (1980). Mothers, fathers, and peers as socialization agents of sex-typed play behaviors in young children. *Child Development, 51,* 1237–1247.

Laosa, L. M. (1990). Psychosocial stress, coping, and development of Hispanic immigrant children. In F. C. Serafica, A. I. Schwebel, R. K. Russell, P. D. Isaac, & L. B. Myers (Eds.), *Mental health of ethnic minorities* (pp. 38–65). New York: Praeger.

Laquer, T. W. (1983). Toward a culture ecology of literacy in England, 1600–1850. In D. P. Resnick (Ed.), *Literacy in historical perspective* (pp. 43–57). Washington, DC: Library of Congress.

Larsen, L. J. (2004). *The foreign-born population in the United States: 2003.* Current Population Reports, P20-551. Washington, DC: U.S. Census Bureau.

Larson, R. (1995). Secrets in the bedroom: Adolescents private use of media. *Journal of Youth and Adolescence, 24,* 535–550.

Larson, R., & Richards, M. H. (1994). *Divergent realities: The emotional lives of mothers, fathers, and adolescents.* New York: Basic Books.

Laursen, B., Coy, K. C., & Collins, W. A. (1998). Reconsidering changes in parent–child conflict across adolescence: A meta-analysis. *Child Development, 69,* 817–832.

Laursen, E. K. (2003). Creating community through service. *Reclaiming Children and Youth, 11*(4), 240–241.

Lavine, L. (1977). Differentiation of letterlike forms in pre-reading children. *Developmental Psychology, 13,* 89–94.

Lazar, I., Darlington, R., Murray, H., Royce, J., & Snipper, A. (1982). Lasting effects of early education: A report from the Consortium for Longitudinal Studies. *Monographs of the Society for Research in Child Development, 47*(Serial No. 195).

Le Mare, L. J., & Rubin, K. H. (1987). Perspective taking and peer interaction: Structural and developmental analyses. *Child Development, 58,* 306–315.

Leadbeater, B. J., & Bishop, S. J. (1994). Predictors of behavior problems in preschool children of inner-city Afro-American and Puerto Rican adolescent mothers. *Child Development, 65,* 638–648.

Leaper, C. (Ed.). *Childhood gender segregation: Cause and consequences.* San Francisco: Jossey-Bass.

Leavitt, C., Tonniges, T., & Rogers, M. (2003). Good nutrition: The imperative for positive development. In M. Bornstein, L. Davidson, C. Keyes, & K. Moore (Eds.), *Well-being: Positive development across the life course* (pp. 35–50). Mahwah, NJ: Erlbaum.

Lee, J., & Bowen, N. (2006). Parent involvement, cultural capital, and the achievement gap among elementary school children. *American Educational Research Journal, 43,* 193–218.

Lee, J., & Huston, A. (2003). Educational televisual media effects. In E. Palmer & B. Young (Eds.), *Faces of televisual media: Teaching, violence, and selling to children* (2nd ed., pp. 83–106). Mahwah, NJ Erlbaum.

Lee, S. (1996). *Unraveling the "model minority" stereotype. Listening to Asian American youth.* New York: Teachers College Press.

Lee, V., & Bryk, A. (1986). Curriculum tracking as mediating the social distribution of high school achievement. *Journal of Education Psychology, 78,* 81–395.

Lee, V., Loeb, S., & Lubeck, S. (1998). Contextual effects of prekindergarten classes for disadvantaged children on cognitive development: The case of chapter 1. *Child Development, 69,* 479–494.

Lee, V., & Marks, L. (1990). Sustained effects of the single-sex secondary school experience on attitudes, behaviors, and values in college. *Journal of Educational Psychology, 82,* 578–590.

Lee, V. E. (2001). *Restructuring schools for equity and excellence: What works.* New York: Teachers College Press.

Lee, V. E., & Burkam, D. T. (2003). Dropping out of high school: The role of school organization and structure. *American Educational Research Journal, 40,* 353–394.

Lefkowitz, M. M., Eron, L. D., Walder, L. O., & Huesmann, L. R. (1977). *Growing up to be violent: A longitudinal study of the development of aggression.* New York: Pergamon.

Lemerise, E., & Arsenio, W. F. (2000). An integrated model of emotion processes and cognition in social information processing. *Child Development, 71,* 107–118.

Lemonick, M. (2000). Teens before their time. *Time, 156*(18), 67–74.

Lenneberg, E. H. (1967). *Biological founda-tions of language.* New York: John Wiley.

Lenneberg, E. H. (1969). On explaining language. *Science, 164,* 635–643.

Leopold, W. F. (1954). *A child's learning of two languages.* Georgetown University Round Table on Languages and Linguistics, 7, pp. 19–30. Reprinted in E. M. Hatch (Ed.), *Second language acquisition: A book of readings.* Rowley, MA: Newbury House, 1978.

Lepper, M. R., Greene, D., & Nisbett, R. E. (1973). Undermining children's intrinsic interest with extrinsic reward. *Journal of Personality and Social Psychology, 28,* 129–137.

Lepper, M. R., & Hodell, M. (1989). Intrinsic motivation in the classroom. In C. Ames & R. Ames (Eds.), *Research on motivation in education: Vol. 3. Goals and cognitions* (pp. 73–105). New York: Academic Press.

Lerner, J. V. (1994). *Working women and their families.* Thousand Oaks, CA: Sage.

Lerner, J. V., & Abrams, L. A. (1994). Developmental correlates of maternal employment influences on children. In C. B. Fisher & R. M. Lerner (Eds.), *Applied developmental psychology.* New York: McGraw-Hill.

Lerner, J. V., & Galambos, N. L. (1988). The influences of maternal employment across life: The New York Longitudinal Study. In A. E. Gottfried & A. W. Gottfried (Eds.), *Maternal employment and children's development: Longitudinal research* (pp. 59–83). New York: Plenum.

Lerner, R., Fisher, C., & Weinberg, R., (2000). Toward a science for and of the people: Promoting civil society through the application of developmental science. *Child Development, 71,* 11–20.

Letgers, N., & Kerr, K. (2001, January). Easing the transition to high school: An investigation of reform practices to promote ninth grade success. A paper prepared for Civil Rights Project at Harvard University's Graduate School of Education and Achieve, Inc., Cambridge, MA. Retrieved May 23, 2006, from http://www.civilrightsproject. harvard.edu/research/dropouts/ letgerskerr.pdf.

Leu, D., & Kinzer, C. (1995). *Effective reading instruction* (3rd ed.). Englewood Cliffs, NJ: Merrill.

Levin, D. E. (1994). *Teaching young children in violent times: Building a peaceable classroom.* Cambridge, MA: Education for Social Responsibility.

Levine, S. C., Huttenlocher, J., Taylor, A., & Langrock, A. (1999). Early sex differences in spatial skill. *Developmental Psychology, 35*(4), 940–949.

Levy, G. D. (1989). Relations among aspects of children's social environments, gender schematization, gender role knowledge, and flexibility. *Sex Roles, 21,* 803–823.

Lewis, C., Perry, R., & Murata, A. (2006). How should research contribute to instructional improvement? The case of lesson study. *Educational Researcher, 35,* 3–14.

Lewis, D. (1975). The black family: Socialization and sex roles. *Phylon, 36,* 221–237.

Lewis, M. (1992). *Shame: The exposed self.* New York: Free Press.

Leyendecker, B., & Lamb, M. E. (1999). Latino families. In M. E. Lamb (Ed.), *Parenting and child development in "nontraditional" families* (pp. 247–262). Mahwah, NJ: Erlbaum.

Liben, L. S., & Signorella, M. L. (1993). Gender-schematic processing in children: The role of initial interpretations of stimuli. *Developmental Psychology, 29,* 141–149.

Lichter, D. T., & Johnson, K. M. (2006). Emerging rural settlement patterns and the geographic redistribution of America's new immigrants. *Rural Sociology, 71*(1), 109–131.

Lickona, T. (1991). *Educating for character: How our schools can teach respect and responsibility.* New York: Bantam Books.

Lickona, T., Schaps, E., & Lewis, C. (1998). *Eleven principles of effective character education.* Washington, DC: Character Education Partnership.

Limber, S. P., & Small, M. A. (2003). State laws and policies to address bullying in schools. *School Psychology Review, 32,* 445–455.

Lin, C-Y. C., & Fu, V. R. (1990). A comparison of child-rearing practices among Chinese, immigrant Chinese, and Caucasian-American parents. *Child Development, 61,* 429–433.

Linney, J., & Seidman, E. (1989). The future of schooling. *American Psychologist, 44,* 343–348.

Lipsitz, J., Mizell, M. H., Jackson, A. W., & Austin, L. M. (1997). Speaking with one voice: A manifesto for middle grades reform. *Phi Delta Kappan, 78,* 533–540.

Livesly, W. J., & Bromley, D. B. (1993). *Person perception in childhood and adolescence.* New York: John Wiley.

Livson, N., & Peskin, H. (1980). Perspectives on adolescence from longitudinal research. In J. Abelson (Ed.), *Handbook of adolescent psychology* (pp. 47–98). New York: John Wiley.

Lloyd, D. (1976). Prediction of school failure from third-grade data. *Educational Psychological Measurement, 38,* 1193–1200.

Loban, W. (1976). *Language development: Kindergarten through grade 12.* Urbana, IL: National Council for Teachers of English.

Lobel, A. (1990). *Allison's zinnia.* Fairfield, NJ: Greenwillow Books.

Locke, J. (1902). *Some thoughts on education.* Cambridge, MA: Cambridge University Press.

Loeber, R., & Hay, D. F. (1997). Key issues in the development of aggression and violence from childhood to early adulthood. *Annual Review of Psychology, 48,* 371–410.

Loeber, R., & Stouthamer-Loeber, M. (1998). Development of juvenile aggression and violence: Some common misconceptions and controversies. *American Psychologist, 53,* 242–259.

Long, C. (2006, October). The e-mail that roared. NEA Today. National Education Association. Available online at http://www.nea.org/neatoday/0610.

Long, M., & Porter, P. (1985). Group work, interlanguage talk, and second language acquisition. *TESOL Quarterly, 19,* 207–228.

Lord, S. E., Eccles, J. S., & McCarthy, K. (1994). Surviving the junior high school transition. Family processes and self-perceptions as protective and risk factors. *Journal of Early Adolescence, 14,* 162–199.

Louganis, G. (1995). *Breaking the surface.* New York: Random House.

Lounds, J., Borkowski, J., Whitman, T., Maxwell, S., & Weed, K. (2005). Adolescent parenting and attachment during infancy and early childhood. *Parenting: Science and Practice, 5,* 91–118.

Lowe, E., Weisner, T., Geis, S., & Huston, A. (2005). Child-care instability and the effort to sustain a working daily routine: Evidence from the New Hope ethnographic study of low-income families. In C. Cooper, C. Coll, T. Bartko, H. Davis, & C. Chatman (Eds.), *Developmental pathways through middle childhood: Rethinking contexts and diversity as resources* (pp. 121–144). New York: Erlbaum.

Lu, M. C., Lin, Y. G., Prietto, N. M., & Garite, T. J. (2000). Elimination of public funding of prenatal care for undocumented immigrants in California: A cost/benefit analysis. *American Journal of Obstetrics and Gynecology, 182* (Pt. 1), 233–239.

Lummis, M., & Stevenson, H. W. (1990). Gender differences in beliefs and achievement: A cross-cultural study. *Developmental Psychology, 26,* 254–263.

Lundy, A., & Rosenberg, J. A. (1987). Androgyny, masculinity and self-esteem. *Social Behavior & Personality, 15,* 91–95.

Luster, T., & McAdoo, H. (1995). Factors related to self-esteem among African American youths: A secondary analysis of the High/Scope Perry Preschool data. *Journal of Research on Adolescence, 5,* 451–468.

Luthar, S. (Ed.). (2003). *Resilience and vulnerability.* New York: Cambridge University Press.

Lynch, M., & Cicchetti, D. (1992). Maltreated children's reports of relatedness to their teachers. In R.C. Pianta (Ed.), *Beyond the parent: The role of other adults in children's lives* (Vol. 57, pp. 81–108). San Francisco: Jossey-Bass.

Lytton, H., & Romney, D. (1991). Parents' sex-related differential socialization of boys and girls: A meta-analysis. *Psychological Bulletin, 109,* 267–296.

Lyon, G (2002). Reading development, reading difficulties, and reading instruction educational and public health issues. *Journal of School Psychology, 40,* 3–6.

Lyons, J. J. (1995). The past and future directions of federal bilingual education policy. In O. Garcia & C. Baker (Eds.), *Policy and practice in bilingual education* (pp. 1–14). Bristol, PA.: Multilingual Matters.

Lyons, T. A. (1983). Lesbian mothers' custody fears. *Women and Therapy, 2,* 231–240.

Maccoby, E. (1984). Socialization and developmental change. *Child Development, 55,* 317–328.

Maccoby, E. (1998). *The two sexes: Growing up apart, coming together.* Cambridge, MA: Belknap Press.

Maccoby, E. E. (1980). *Social development: Psychological growth and the parent–child relationship.* New York: Harcourt Brace Jovanovich.

Maccoby, E. E. (1984). Middle childhood in the context of the family. In W. A. Collins (Ed.), *Development during middle childhood: The years from six to twelve.* Washington, DC: National Academy Press.

Maccoby, E. E. (1992). The role of parents in the socialization of children: An historical overview. *Developmental Psychology, 28,* 1006–1017.

Maccoby, E. E., & Martin, J. (1983). Socialization in the context of the family: Parent–child interactions. In E. M. Hetherington (Ed.) & P. H. Mussen (Series Ed.), *Handbook of child psychology. Vol. 4, Socialization, personality, and social development* (pp. 1–101). New York: John Wiley.

Maccoby, E. E., & Mnookin, R. H. (1992). *Dividing the child: Social and legal dilemmas of custody.* Cambridge, MA: Harvard University Press.

Maccoby, M. E., & Jacklin, C. N. (1974). *The psychology of sex differences.* Palo Alto, CA: Stanford University Press.

MacDonald, K. (1992). Warmth as a developmental construct: An evolutionary analysis. *Child Development, 63,* 753–773.

MacWhinney, B., & Bornstein, M. (2003). Language and literacy. In M. Bornstein (Ed.), *Well-being: Positive development across the life course* (pp. 331–340). Mahwah, NJ: Erlbaum.

Madden, N., Salvin, R., Karweit, N. Dolan, L., & Wasik, B. (1993). Success for all: Longitudinal effects of a restructuring program for inner-city elementary schools. *American Educational Research Journal, 30,* 123–148.

Maehr, M. L., & Midgley C. (1991). Enhancing student motivation: A school-wide approach. *Educational Psychologist, 26,* 399–427.

Magnusson, D., Stattin, H., & Allen, V. (1985). Biological maturation and social development: A longitudinal study of some adjustment processes from mid-adolescence to adulthood. *Journal of Youth and Adolescence, 14,* 267–283.

Mahoney, J. L. (2000). School extracurricular activity participation as a moderator in the development of antisocial patterns. *Child Development, 71*(2), 502–516.

Main, M., & Solomon, J. (1990). Procedures for identifying infants as disorganized/disoriented during the Ainsworth strange situation. In M. Greenberg, D. Cicchetti, & E. M. Cummings (Eds.), *Attachment in the preschool years: Theory, research and intervention* (pp. 121–160). Chicago: University of Chicago Press.

Male, M. (2003). *Technology for inclusion: Meeting the special needs of all students* (4th ed.). Boston: Allyn & Bacon.

Malina, R. M., & Bouchard, C. (1991). *Growth, maturation, and physical activity.* Champaign, IL: Human Kinetics.

Manley, R., Rickson, H., & Standeven, B. (2000). Children and adolescents with eating disorders: Strategies for teachers and school counselors. *Intervention in School and Clinic, 35,* 228–231.

Manning, B. H. (1988). Application of cognitive behavior modification: First and third graders' self-management of classroom behavior. *American Educational Research Journal, 25,* 193–212.

Manset-Williamson, G., St. John, E., Hu, S., & Gordon, D. (2002). Early literacy practices as predictors of reading related outcomes: Test scores, test passing rates, retention, and special education referral. *Exceptionality, 10,* 11–28.

Mantzicopoulos, P. (2003). Flunking kindergarten after Head Start: An inquiry into the contribution of contextual and individual variables. *Journal of Educational Psychology, 95,* 268–278.

Marcia, J. E. (1980). Identity in adolescence. In J. Adelson (Ed.), *Handbook of adolescent psychology* (pp. 159–187). New York: John Wiley.

Marcia, J. E. (1996). Development and validation of ego-identity status. *Journal of Personality and Social Psychology, 3,* 551–558.

Mariani, M., & Barkley, R. S. (1997). Neuropsychological and academic functioning in preschool children with attention deficit hyperactivity disorder. *Developmental Neuropsychology, 13,* 111–129.

Marín, G., & Marín, B. V. (1991). *Research with Hispanic populations.* Newbury Park, CA: Sage.

Marjoribanks, K. (1987). Ability and attitude correlates of academic achievement: Family group differences. *Journal of Educational Psychology, 79,* 171–178.

Markus, H. R., & Kitayama, S. (1991). Culture and the self: Implications for cognition, emotion, and motivation. *Psychological Review, 98,* 224–253.

Marsh, H. (1993). The effects of participation in sport during the last two years of high school. *Sociology of Sport Journal, 10,* 18–43.

Marsh, H., Byrne, B., & Yeung, A. S. (1999). Casual order of academic self-concept and achievement: Reanalysis of a pioneer study and revised recommendations. *Educational Psychologist, 34,* 155–167.

Marsh, H., & Yeung, A. S. (1997). Causal effects of academic self-concept on academic achievement: Structural equation models of longitudinal data. *Journal of Educational Psychology, 89,* 41–54.

Marsh, H. W. (1988). Casual effects of academic self-concept on academic achievement: A reanalysis of Newman (1984). *Journal of Experimental Education, 56,* 100–103.

Marsh, H. W. (1989). Effects of attending single-sex and coeducational high schools on achievement, attitudes, behavior, and sex differences. *Journal of Educational Psychology, 81,* 70–85.

Marsh, H. W. (1990a). Causal ordering of academic self-concept and academic achievement: A multiwave, longitudinal panel analysis. *Journal of Educational Psychology, 82,* 646–656.

Marsh, H. W. (1990b). A multidimensional, hierarchical model of self-concept: Theoretical and empirical justification. *Educational Psychology Review, 2,* 77–172.

Marsh, H. W. (1990c). The structure of academic self-concept: The Marsh/Shavelson model. *Journal of Educational Psychology, 82,* 623–636.

Marsh, H. W., Craven, R. G., & Debus, R. (1991). Self-concepts of young children 5 to 8 years of age: Measurement and multidimensional structure. *Journal of Educational Psychology, 83,* 377–392.

Masataka, N. (1992). Motherese in a signed language. *Infant Behavior and Development, 15,* 453–460.

Mash, E. J., & Johnston, C. (1982). A comparison of mother-child interactions of younger and older hyperactive and normal children. *Child Development, 53,* 1371–1381.

Mash, E. J., & Johnston, C. (1983). Sibling interactions of hyperactive and normal children and their relationship to reports of maternal stress and self-esteem. *Journal of Clinical Child Psychology, 12,* 91–99.

Maslow, A. H. (1954). *Motivation and personality.* New York: Harper & Row.

Maslow, A. H. (1970). *Motivation and personality.* New York: Harper and Row.

Mason, J., & Allen, J. B. (1986). A review of emergent literacy with implications for research and practice in reading. In E. Rothkopf (Ed.), *Review of research in education* (pp. 3–47). Washington, DC: American Education Research Association.

Massachusetts Governor's Commission on Gay and Lesbian Youth. (1993). *Making schools safe for gay and lesbian youth: Breaking the silence in schools and in families.* Boston: Author.

Masten, A. (2001). Ordinary magic: Resilience processes in development. *American Psychologist, 56,* 227–238.

Masten, A. S., & Coatsworth, J. D. (1998). The development of competence in favorable and unfavorable environments: Lessons from research on successful children. *American Psychologist, 53,* 205–220.

Mastropieri, M. A., & Scruggs, T. E. (1994). Issues in intervention research: Secondary students. In S. Vaughn & C. Bos (Eds.), *Research in learning disabilities: Theory, methodology, assessment, and ethics* (pp. 130–145). New York: Springer Verlag.

Matas, L., Arend, R. A., & Scroufe, L. A. (1978). Continuity of adaptation in the second year: The relationship between quality of attachment and later competence. *Child Development, 49,* 547–556.

Mauer, D., & Mauer, C. (1988). *The world of the newborn.* New York: Basic Books.

Maxwell, R. J. (1996). *Writing across the curriculum in middle and high schools.* Needham Heights, MA: Allyn & Bacon.

Mayes, L., & Fahy, T. (2001). Prenatal drug exposure and cognitive developmemt. In R. Sternberg & E. Grigorenko (Eds.). *Environmental effects on cognitive abilities* (pp. 189–211). Mahwah, NJ: Erlbaum.

McAdoo, H., & Martin, A. (2005). Families and ethnicity. In R. Lerner, F. Jacobs, & D. Werlieg (Eds.), *Applied development science: An advanced textbook* (pp. 141–154). Thousand Oaks, CA: Sage.

McAdoo, H. P. (1985). Racial attitudes and self-concept of young black children over time. In H. P. McAdoo and J. L. McAdoo (Eds.), *Black children: Social, educational and parental environments* (pp. 213–242). Beverly Hills, CA: Sage Publications.

McCaul, E. J., Donaldson, G. A., Colsdarci, T., & Davis, W. (1992). Consequences of dropping out of school: Findings from the high schools and beyond. *Journal of Educational Psychology, 85,* 198–207.

McCollum, P. (1991). Cross-cultural perspectives on classroom discourse and literacy. In E. Hiebert (Ed.), *Literacy for a diverse society* (pp. 108–121). New York: Teachers College Press.

McCombs, B., & Lauer, P. (1997). Development and validations of the learner-centered battery: Self-assessment tools for teacher reflection and professional development. *Professional Educator, 20,* 1–20.

McCoy, A. R., & Reynolds, A. J. (1999). Grade retention and school performance: An extended investigation. *Journal of School Psychology, 37*(3), 273–298.

McDaniel, A. (1994). Historical racial differences in living arrangements of children. *Journal of Family History, 19,* 57–77.

McDaniel, M. A., Waddill, P. J., & Einstein, G. O. (1988). A contextual account of generation effect: A three factor theory. *Journal of Memory and Language, 25,* 521–536.

McDowell, D., Parker, R., & Wang, S., (2003). Differences between mothers' and fathers' advice-giving style and content: Relations with social competence and psychological functioning in middle childhood. *Merrill-Palmer Quarterly, 49,* 55–76.

McFarland, W., & Dupuis, M. (2001). The legal duty to protect gay and lesbian students from violence in school. *Professional School Counseling, 4*(3), 171–179.

McHale, S. M., Crouter, A. C., & Whiteman, S. D. (2003). The family contexts of gender development in childhood and adolescence. *Social Development, 12,* 125–148.

McHale, S. M., Kim, J., Whiteman, S., & Crouter, A. C. (2004). Links between sex-typed time use in middle childhood and gender development in early adolescence. *Developmental Psychology, 40,* 868–881.

McHale, S. M., Shanahan, L., Updegraff, K. A., Crouter, A. C., & Booth, A. (2004). Developmental and individual differences in girls' sex-typed activities in middle childhood and adolescence. *Child Development, 75,* 1575–1593.

McKown, C. (2004). Age and variation in children's thinking about the nature of racism. *Applied Developmental Psychology, 25,* 597–617.

McKown, C., & Weinstein, C. (2003). The development and consequences of stereotypes consciousness in middle childhood. *Child Development, 74,* 498–515.

McLanahan, S., & Sandefur, G. (1994). *Growing up with a single parent: What hurts, what helps?* Cambridge, MA: Harvard University Press.

McLoyd, B. (1990). The impact of economic hardship on black families and children. Psychological distress, parenting, and socioeconomic development. *Child Development, 61,* 311–346.

McLoyd, V. (1993). Employment among African-American mothers in dual-earner families: Antecedents and consequences for family life and child development. In J. Frankel (Ed.), *The employed mother and the family context* (pp. 180–226). New York: Springer.

McLoyd, V., Jayaratne, T., Ceballo, R., & Borquez, J. (1994). Unemployment and work interruption among African-American single mothers: Effects on parenting and socio-emotional functioning. *Child Development, 65,* 562–589.

McLoyd, V. C. (1998). Socioeconomic disadvantage and child development. *American Psychologist, 53,* 185–204.

McNeill, D. (1966). Developmental psycholinguistics. In F. Smith & G. A. Miller (Eds.), *The genesis of language: A psycholinguistic approach* (pp. 15–84). Cambridge, MA: MIT Press.

Meadows, N. B., Neel, R. S., Scott, C. M., & Parker, G. (1994). Academic performance, social competence, and mainstream and nonmainstreamed students with serious behavioral disorders. *Behavioral Disorders, 19,* 170–180.

Meece, J. L. (1987). The influence of school experiences on the development of gender schemata. In L. Liben & M. Signorella (Eds.), *Children's gender schemata (New Directions for Child Development,* No. 38, pp. 57–74). San Francisco: Jossey-Bass.

Meece, J. L. (1991). The classroom context and children's motivational goals. In M. Maehr & P. Pintrich (Eds.), *Advances in achievement motivation research* (Vol. 7, pp. 261–285). New York: Academic Press.

Meece, J. L. (2003). Applying learner-centered principles to middle school education. *Theory into Practice, 42,* 109–116.

Meece, J. L., Anderman, E. M., & Anderman, L. H. (2006). Classroom goal structure, student motivation, and academic achievement, *Annual Review of Psychology, 57,* 487–503.

Meece, J. L., Blumenfeld, P. C. & Hoyle, R. (1988). Students' goal orientations and cognitive engagement in classroom activities. *Journal of Educational Psychology, 80,* 514–523.

Meece, J. L., Glienke, B. B., & Burg, S. (2006). Gender and motivation. *Journal of School Psychology, 44,* 351–373.

Meece, J. L., Herman, P., & McCombs, B. (2003). Relations of learner-centered teaching practices to adolescents' achievement goals. *International Journal of Educational Research, 39,* 457–475.

Meece, J. L., & Kurtz-Costes, B. (2001). Introduction: The schooling of ethnic minority children and youth. *Educational Psychologist, 36,* 1–8.

Meece, J. L., Scantlebury, K. (2006). Gender and schooling: Progress and persistant barriers. In J. Worell & C. D. Goodheart (Eds.), *Handbook of girls' and women's psycological health. Gender and well-being across the life span.* New York: Oxford University Press.

Meece, J. L., Wigfield, A., & Eccles, J. (1990). Predictors of math anxiety and its consequences for young adolescents' course enrollment intentions and performance in mathematics. *Journal of Educational Psychology, 82,* 1–11.

Meeus, W., Iedema, J., Helsen, M., & Vollebergh, W. (1999). Patterns of adolescent identity development: Review of literature and longitudinal analysis: *Development Review, 19,* 591–621.

Meichenbaum, D. (1977). *Cognitive-behavior modification: An integrative approach.* New York: Plenum Press.

Meichenbaum, D., & Asarno, J. (1978). Cognitive behavioral modification and metacognitive development: Implications for the classroom. In P. Kendall & S. Hollon (Eds.), *Cognitive-behavioral interventions: Theory, research, and procedures* (pp. 11–33). New York: Academic Press.

Meichenbaum, D., & Goodman, J. (1971). Training impulsive children to talk to themselves: A means of developing self-control. *Journal of Abnormal Psychology, 77,* 115–126.

Melnick, M., & Sabo, D. (1992). Educational effects of interscholastic athletic participation on African-American and Hispanic youth. *Adolescence, 27*(106) 295–308.

Menyuk, P. (1976). Relations between acquisition of phonology and reading. In J. T. Guthrie (Ed.), *Aspects of reading acquisition.* Baltimore, MD: Johns Hopkins University Press.

Mertz, G., & Lieber, C. M. (2001). Suggestions for using the Believing Game. Educators for Social Responsibility. Available online at http://www.esrnational. org/sp/we/uw/believe.htm.

Metris Associates. (1999). *Evaluation of RCCP in Newark, NJ public schools.* New York: Author.

Meyer, D. K. (1993). What is scaffolded instruction? Definitions, distinguishing features, and misnomers. In D. J. Leu & C. K. Kinzer (Eds.), *Examining central issues in literacy research, theory, and practice: Forty-second yearbook of the National Reading Conference,* pp. 41–54. Chicago: National Reading Conference.

Mickelson, R. A. (1990). The attitude-achievement paradox among black adolescents. *Sociology of Education, 63,* 44–61.

Midgley, C., Anderman, E. M., & Hicks, L. (1995). Differences between elementary and middle school teachers and students: A goal theory approach. *Journal of Early Adolescence, 15,* 90–113.

Midgley, C., & Edelin, K. (1998). Middle school reform and early adolescent well-being: The good news and the bad. *Educational Psychologist, 33,* 195–206.

Midgley, C., Feldlaufer, H., & Eccles, J. S. (1989). Changes in teacher efficiency and student self- and task-related beliefs during the transition to junior high school. *Journal of Educational Psychology, 81,* 247–258.

Miles, S., & Stipek, D. (2006). Contemporaneous and longitudinal associations between social behavior and literacy achievement in a sample of low-income elementary school children. *Child Development, 77,* 103–117.

Miller, A. (1993). Social science, social policy, and the heritage of African American families. In M. B. Katz (Ed.), *The "Underclass" debate: Views from history* (pp. 254–289). Princeton, NJ: Princeton University Press.

Miller, P. (1993). *Theories of developmental psychology* (3rd ed.). New York: Freeman.

Miller, P. (2002). *Theories of developmental psychology* (4th ed.). New York: Worth.

Miller, P., & Weiss, M. (1981). Children's attention allocation, understanding of attention, and performance on the incidental learning task. *Child Development, 52,* 1183–1190.

Miller, S. A. (1988). Parents' beliefs about children's cognitive development. *Child Development, 59,* 259–285.

Miller, S. A. (1995). Parents' attributions for their children's behavior. *Child Development, 66,* 1557–1584.

Mills, G. E. (2001). *Action research: A guide for the teacher researcher.* Columbus, OH: Merrill.

Milunsky, A. (1989). *Choices, not chance.* Boston: Little, Brown.

Minnow, N., & LaMay, C. (August 6th, 1995). Abandoned in the wasteland: Children, television and the First Amendment Report for the Federal Communications Commission. *Detroit Free Press,* Magazine Section, pp. 12–16.

Minuchin, P. (1985). Families and individual development: Provocations from the field of family therapy. *Child Development, 56,* 289–302.

Minuchin, P., & Shapio, E. (1983). The school context for social development. In P. Mussen (Series Ed.) & E. M. Hetherington (Vol. Ed.), *Handbook of Child Development* (pp. 197–276). New York: John Wiley.

Mirande, A. (1988). Chicano fathers: Traditional perceptions and current realities. In P. Bronstein & C. P. Cowan (Eds.), *Fatherhood today: Men's changing role in the family* (pp. 93–106). New York: John Wiley.

Mischel, H. N., & Mischel, W. (1983). The development of children's knowledge of self-control strategies. *Child Development, 54,* 603–619.

Mischel, W., Ebbensen, E. B., & Zeiss, A. R. (1972). Cognitive and attentional mechanisms in delay of gratification. *Journal of Personality and Social Psychology, 21,* 204–218.

Mischel, W., & Moore, B. (1980). The role of ideation in voluntary delay of symbolically presented rewards. *Cognitive Therapy and Research, 4,* 211–221.

Miura, I., Okamoto, Y., Kim, C., Steere, M., & Fayol, M. (1993). First graders' cognitive representation of number and understanding of place value: Cross-national comparisons—France, Japan, Sweden, and the United States. *Journal of Educational Psychology, 85,* 24–30.

Moely, B., Hart, S., Leal, L., Santulli, K., Koa, N., Johnson, T., & Hamilton, L. (1992). The teacher's role in facilitating memory and study strategy in the elementary school classroom. *Child Development, 63,* 653–672.

Moffett, J. (1968). *A student-centered language arts curriculum, grades K–13: A handbook for teachers.* New York: Houghton Mifflin.

Moffitt, T. (1990). Juvenile delinquency and attention-deficit disorder: Developmental trajectories from age 3 to 15. *Child Development, 61,* 893–910.

Moffitt, T., Lynam, D., & Silva, P. (1994). Neuropsychological tests predicting persistent male delinquency. *Criminology, 32,* 277–300.

Moles, O. C. (1996). New national directions in research and policy. In A. Booth, & J. Dunn (Eds.), *Family-school links. How do they affect educational outcomes?* (pp. 247–254). Mahwah, NJ: Erlbaum.

Moll, L. (1990). *Vygotsky and education: Instructional implications and applications of sociohistorical psychology.* New York: Cambridge University Press.

Morrison, F., & Connor, C. (2002). Understanding schooling effects on early literacy: A working research strategy. *Journal of School Psychology, 40,* 493–500.

Morrison, F., Smith, S., & Dow-Ehrensberger, M. (1995). Education and cognitive development: A natural experiment. *Developmental Psychology, 34,* 789–799.

Moshman, D. (2005). *Adolescent psychological development. Rationality, morality, and identity* (2nd ed.). Mahwah, NJ: Erlbaum.

Moshman, D., & Franks, B. (1986). Development of the concept of inferred validity. *Child Development, 57,* 153–165.

Moskowitz, B. (1985). The acquisition of language. In V. P. Clark, P. A. Eschholz, & A. Rosa (Eds.), *Language: Introductory readings* (pp. 45–73). New York: St. Martin's Press.

Moss, G. (2000). Raising boys' attainment in reading: Some principles for intervention. *Reading, 34*(4), 101–106.

Munio, G., & Adams, G. (1977). Ego identity formation in college students and working youth. *Development Psychology, 13,* 523–524.

Mussen, P., & Jones, M. (1957). Self-conceptions, motivations, and interpersonal attitudes of late- and early-maturing boys. *Child Development, 28,* 243–256.

Mutas, L., Arend, R., & Sroufe, L. A. (1978). Continuity of adaptation in the second year: The relationship between quality of attachment and later competence. *Child Development, 49,* 542–556.

Myers, D. E., & Schirm, A. L. (1999). *The impacts of Upward Bound final report for Phase I of the national evaluation* (MPR Reference No. 8046-515). Washington, DC: U.S. Department of Education.

Nadeau, K., & Quinn, P. (2002). The history of AD/HD—an unexamined gender bias. In P. Quinn & K. Nadeau (Eds.), *Gender issues and ADHD: Research, diagnosis, and treatment* (pp. 22–23). Silver Springs, MD: Advantage Books.

National Academy of Science. (1996). *National science education standards.* Washington, DC: National Academy Press.

National Assessment of Educational Progress. (1981). *Reading, thinking, and writing: Results from the 1979–80 national assessment of reading and literature.* Denver, CO: National Assessment of Educational Progress.

National Assessment of Educational Progress. (NAEP). (2005). The Nation's Report Card 2005 assessment results. Retrieved September 2006 from http://nces.ed.gov/nationsreportcard.

National Association for the Education of Young Children. (1998). Learning to read and write: Developmentally appropriate practices for young children: A joint position statement of the International Reading Association and the NAEYC. *Young Children, 53,* 30–46.

National Association for Sport and Physical Education. (2006). Local school wellness policies—An opportunity to make a difference. Retrieved July 2006 http://www.aahperd.org/naspetemplate. cfm?template=5wellness.html.

National Center for Educational Statistics. (1993). *The condition of education.* Washington, DC: U.S. Department of Education, Office of Education Research and Improvement.

National Center for Educational Statistics. (1995a). *The condition of education.* Washington, DC: U.S. Department of Education, Office of Education Research and Improvement.

National Center for Educational Statistics. (1995b). *Third international mathematics and science study, videotape classroom study, 1995–1996.* Washington, DC: U.S. Department of Education, Office of Research and Educational Improvement.

National Center for Educational Statistics. (1997). *Digest of educational statistics, 1997.* Washington, DC.: U.S. Government Printing Office.

National Center for Educational Statistics. (1998). *The condition of education.* Washington, DC: U.S. Department of Education, Office of Educational Research and Improvement.

National Center for Educational Statistics. (1999). *Digest of educational statistics, 1999.* Washington, DC: U.S. Government Printing Office.

National Center for Educational Statistics. (2000a). *America's kindergarteners. Findings from the Early Childhood Longitudinal Study, Kindergarten Class of 1998–99.* Washington, DC: U.S. Department of Education, Office of Educational Research and Improvement.

National Center for Educational Statistics. (2000c). *National Assessment of Educational Progress (NAEP), 1999 long-term trend assessment.* Washington, DC: U.S. Department of Education, Office of Education and Improvement.

National Center for Educational Statistics. (2000d). *The condition of education.* Washington, DC: U.S. Department of Education, Office of Educational Research and Improvement.

National Center for Educational Statistics. (2001). *Dropout rates in the United States: 2000.* Washington, DC: U.S. Department of Education, Institute of Education Sciences.

National Center for Educational Statistics. (2003a). *The Nation's Report Card: Writing 2002* (NCES 2003–529). Washington, DC: U.S. Department of Education, Institute of Education Sciences.

National Center for Educational Statistics. (2003b). *Remedial education at degree-granting post-secondary institutions in fall 2000.* Washington, DC: U.S. Department of Education, Institute of Education Sciences.

National Center for Educational Statistics. (2004a). *Highlights from the Trends in International Mathematics and Science Study (TIMSS) 2003.* U.S. Department of Education, Institute of Education Sciences. Washington, DC: U.S. Government Printing Office. Available online at http://nces.ed.gov/timss/results03.

National Center for Educational Statistics. (2004b). PIRLS 2001: Choice of activities outside of school. Retrieved August 2005 from http://nces.ed.gov/pubs2004/pirlspub/13.asp?nav=4.

National Center for Educational Statistics. (2004c). NAEP 2004. Trends in academic progress. Retrieved July 1, 2006, from http://nces.ed.gov/nationsreportcard/nde/.

National Center for Educational Statistics. (2005a). *Digest of educational statistics, 2004.* U. S. Department of Education, Institute of Education Sciences. Washington, DC: U.S. Government Printing Office. Available online at http://nces.ed.gov/programs/digest/d05.

National Center for Educational Statistics. (2005b). *The Nation's Report Card. NAEP 2004 trends in academic progress: Three decades of student performances in reading and mathematics.* Washington, DC: U.S. Department of Education, Institute of Education Sciences.

National Center for Educational Statistics. (2005c). *Parent and family involvement in Education: 2002–2003* (NCES 2005-043). Washington, DC: U.S. Department of Education, Institute of Education Sciences.

National Center for Educational Statistics. (2006a). *The Nation's Report Card: Reading 2005* (NCES 2006–451). Washington, DC: U.S. Government Printing Office.

National Center for Educational Statistics. (2006b). National Assessment of Adult Literacy (NAAL) demographics. Retrieved January 2007 from http://nces.ed.gov/ NAAL/index.asp.

National Center for Learning Disabilities. (2006). Learning disabilities checklist. Retrieved April 2006 from http:// www.LD.org.

National Council for Research on Women. (1998). *The girls report. What we know and need to know about growing up female.* New York: Author.

National Dissemination Center for Children with Disabilities (NICHCY). (2006, May). Traumatic brain injury. *NICHCY Disability Fact Sheet-No. 18.*

National Governor's Association. (2000). Teacher supply and demand: Is there a shortage? Retrieved June 30, 2006, from http://www.nga.org/cda/files/000125TEAC HERS.pdf.

National Institute of Child Health & Human Development Early Child Care Research Network. (2004). Trajectories of physical aggression from toddlerhood to middle childhood. *Monographs of the Society for Research in Child Development, 69*(4, Serial No. 2780.).

National Institute on Deafness and Other Communication Disorders (NIDCD). (2000). *Speech and language: Developmental milestones.* NIH Publication # 00-4781. Retrieved August 2005 from http://www.nidcd.nih.gov/ health/voice/speechandlanguage.asp.

National Institute of Neurological Disorders and Stroke. (2000). Brain basics: Understanding sleep (NIH Publication N. 98-3440-c). Bethesda, MD: National Institutes of Health.

National Institutes of Health. (2000). *AIDS in infants and children.* Bethesda, MD: Author.

National Institutes of Mental Health. (1995). *Learning disabilities.* Bethesda, MD: Author.

National Institutes of Health. (1998, November). *Diagnosis and Treatment of Attention Deficit Hyperactivity Disorder. NIH Consensus Statement.* Bethesda, MD: Author.

National Institutes of Mental Health. (2000). *Attention deficit hyperactivity disorder: Questions and answers.* Bethesda, MD: U.S. Department of Health and Human Services.

National Mental Health Association. (2006). Fact sheet: Conduct disorders. Retrieved November 2006 from http://www.nmha. org/infoctr/facsheets/74.cfm.

National Middle School Association. (1995). *This we believe. Developmentally responsive middle level schools.* Columbus, OH: National Middle School Association.

National Reading Panel (NRP). (2000). *Teaching children to read: An evidence-based assessment of the scientific research literature on reading and its implications for reading instruction.* Report of the National Reading Panel submitted to Congress February 1999.

National Research Council. (1996). *National science standards.* Washington, DC: National Academy Press.

National Research Council. (1997). *The new Americans. Economic, demographic and fiscal effects of immigration.* Washington, DC: National Academy Press.

National Research Council. (1999). *Starting out right: A guide to promoting children's reading success.* Washington, DC: Author.

National Research Council. (2000). *From neurons to neighborhoods.* Washington, DC: National Academy Press.

National Research Council & The Institutes of Medicine. (2004). *Engaging schools: Fostering high school students' motivation to learn.* Washington, DC: The National Academy Press.

National Sleep Foundation. (2005). Sleepiness in teens: Not just a side effect of growing up. A look at how changing school start times can help! *Sleep Matters, 7,* 3.

Natriello, G., McDill, E. L., & Pallas, A. M. (1990). *Schooling disadvantaged children: Racing against catastrophe.* New York: Teachers College Press.

Natriello, G., Pallas, A. M., & McDill, E. (1986). Taking stock: Renewing our research agenda on the causes and consequences of dropping out. *Teachers College Record, 87,* 430–440.

Neblett, E. W., Jr., Philip, C. L., Cogburn, C. D., & Sellers, R. M. (2006). African American adolescents' discrimination experiences and academic achievement: Racial socialization as a cultural compensatory and protective factor. *Journal of Black Psychology, 32,* 199–218.

Needle, R. H., Su, S. S., & Doherty, W. J. (1990). Divorce, remarriage, and adolescent substance use: A prospective longitudinal study. *Journal of Marriage and the Family, 52,* 57–169.

Nash, J. M. (1997, February 3). Fertile minds. *Time. 149*(5), 48–56.

National Academy Press. (1996). *National science standards.* Washington, DC: Author.

Neisser, U. (1997). Never a dull moment. *American Psychologist, 52,* 79–81.

Neisser, U., Boodoo, G., Bouchard, T. J., Jr., Ceci, S. J., Halpern, D. F., Loehlin, J. C., Perloff, R., Sternberg, R. J., & Urbina, S. (1996). Intelligence: Knowns and unknowns. *American Psychologist, 51,* 77–101.

Nelson, C. (2005a). Neural development and lifelong plasticity. In R. Lerner, F. Jacobs, & D. Werlieb (Eds.), *Applied developmental science: An advanced textbook* (pp. 31–60). Thousand Oaks, CA: Sage.

Nelson, C. (2005b). Frontline: Inside the teenage brain: Interview with Charles Nelson. Retrieved August 2005 from http://www.pbs.org/wgbh/pages/frontline/ shows/teenbrain/interviews/nelson.html.

Nelson, K. (1999). The developmental psychology of language and thought. In M. Bennett (Ed.), *Developmental psychology: Achievements and prospects.* Philadelphia: Psychology Press.

Nelson, K., & Hudson, J. (1988). Scripts and memory: Functional relationships in development. In F. Weinert & M. Perlmutter (Eds.), *Memory development: Universal changes and individual changes* (pp. 147–168). Hillsdale, NJ: Erlbaum.

Nelson, N. W. (1998). *Childhood language disorders in context: Infancy through adolescence.* Boston: Allyn & Bacon.

Nettle, E. B. (1998). Stability and change in the beliefs of student teachers during practice teaching. *Teaching and teacher education, 2,* 193–204.

Newby, T. (1991). Classroom motivation: Strategies of first-year teachers. *Journal of Educational Psychology, 83,* 195–200.

Newman, D., Griffin, P., & Cole, M. (1989). *The construction zone: Working for cognitive change in school.* New York: Cambridge University Press.

Nicely, P., Tamis-LeMonda, C. S., & Grolnick, W. S. (1999). Maternal responsiveness to infant affect: Stability and prediction. *Infant Behavior and Development, 22,* 103–117.

NICHD and Early Child Care Network. (1997). The effects of infant child care on infant-mother attachment security: Results of the NICHD study of early child care. *Child Development, 68*(5), 860–879.

NICHD and Early Child Care Network. (1998). Early child care and self-control, compliance, and problem behavior at twenty-four and thirty-six months. *Child Development, 69*(4), 1145–1172.

NICHD and Early Child Care Network. (2000). The relation of child care to cognitive and language development. *Child Development, 71,* 960–980.

NICHD and Early Child Care Research Network. (2002). Early child care and children's development prior to school entry: Results from the NICHD Study of Early Child Care. *American Educational Research Journal, 39,* 133–164.

NICHD and Early Child Care Research Network. (2003a). Do children's attention processes mediate the link between family predictors and school readiness? *Developmental Psychology, 39,* 581–593.

NICHD and Early Child Care Research Network. (2003b). Social functioning in first grade: Associations with earlier home and child care predictors and with current classroom experiences. *Child Development, 74,* 1639–1662.

NICHD and Early Child Care Research Network. (2005a). Pathways to reading: The role of oral language in the transition to reading. *Developmental Psychology, 41,* 428–442.

NICHD and Early Child Care Research Network. (2005b). Predicting individual differences in attention, memory, and planning in first graders from experiences at home, child care, and school. *Developmental Psychology, 41,* 99–114.

Nicholls, J. G. (1984). Achievement motivation: Conceptions of ability, subjective experience, task choice, and performance. *Psychological Review, 91,* 328–346.

Nicholls, J. G. (1989). *The competitive ethos and democratic education.* Cambridge, MA: Harvard University Press.

Nicholls, J., & Hazzard, S. (1993). *Education and adventure: Lessons from second grade.* New York: Teachers College Press.

Noddings, N. (1992). *The challenge to care in schools.* New York: Teachers College Press.

Noddings, N. (2002). *Educating moral people. A caring perspective to character education.* New York: Teachers College Press.

Nolen, S. B. (1988). Reasons for studying: Motivational orientations and study strategies. *Cognition and Instruction, 5,* 269–287.

North Carolina Department of Public Instruction. (1998). *Public school enrollment data.* Raleigh, NC: Author.

Oakes, J. (1985). *Keeping track: How schools structure inequality.* New Haven, CT: Yale University Press.

Oakes, J. (1990). Opportunities, achievement, and choice: Women and minorities. In C. Cazden (Ed.), *Review of research in education* (Vol. 16, pp. 153–222). Washington, DC: American Educational Research Association.

Oakes, J. (1991). Limiting opportunity: Student race and curricular differences in secondary vocational education. *American Journal of Education, 91,* 801–820.

Oakes, J. (1995). Two cities' tracking and within-school segregation. *Teachers College Record, 96*(4), 681–691.

Oakes, J. (2005). *Keeping track: How schools structure inequality.* New Haven, CT: London: Yale University Press.

Oakes, J., & Stuart, A. (1998). Detracking for high student achievement. *Educational Leadership, 55*(6), 38–42.

Ochs, E., Schieffelin, B., & Platt, M. (1979). Propositions across utterances and speakers. In E. Ochs & B. Schieffelin (Eds.), *Developmental pragmatics* (pp. 251–268). New York: Academic Press.

Oden, S., Schweinhart, S., & Weikart, D. (2000). *Into adulthood. A study of the effects of Head Start.* Ypsilanti, MI: High/Scope Educational Research Foundation.

O'Flanagan, B. (1997). Creating purpose through service. *Reclaiming Children and Youth, 11,* 240–241.

Ogbu, J., & Fordham, S. (1986). Black students' school success: Coping with the "burden of acting white." *Urban Review, 18,* 176–206.

Ogbu, J. (1978). *Minority achievement and caste.* San Diego, CA: Academic Press.

Ogbu, J. (1987). Variability in minority school performance: A problem in search of an explanation. *Anthropology & Education Quarterly, 18,* 508–523.

Ogbu, J. (1988). Literacy and schooling in subordinate cultures: The case of black Americans. In E. Kintgen, B. Kroll, & M. Rose (Eds.), *Perspectives on literacy,* (pp. 227–242). Carbondale, IL: Southern Illinois University Press.

Ogbu, J. U. (1992). Understanding cultural diversity and learning. *Educational Researcher, 21*(8), 5–14.

Okagaki, L. (2006). Ethnicity and learning. In P. Alexander and P. Winne (Eds.), *Handbook of educational psychology* (pp. 615–634). Mahwah, NJ: Erlbaum.

Okagaki, L., & Frensch, P. A. (1998). Parenting and children's school achievement: A multiethnic perspective. *American Educational Research Journal, 35*(1), 123–144.

Okagaki, L., & Sternberg, R. (1993). Parental beliefs and children's school performance. *Child Development, 64,* 36–56.

Okolo, C. M., Bahr, C. M., & Rieth, H. J. (1993). A retrospective of computer-based instruction. *Journal of Special Education Technology, 12*(1), 1–27.

Olneck, M. R. (1995). Immigrants and education. In J. A. Banks & C. A. M. Banks (Eds.), *Handbook of research on multicultural education* (pp. 310–327). New York: Macmillan.

Olson, S., Bates, J., & Kaskie, B. (1992). Caregiver-infant interaction antecedents of children's schoolage cognitive ability. *Merrill-Palmer Quarterly, 38,* 309–330.

Olweus, D. (1980). Familial and temperamental determinants of aggressive behavior in adolescent boys: A casual analysis. *Developmental Psychology, 16,* 644–666.

Olweus, D. (1981). Continuity in aggressive and inhibited withdrawn behavior patterns. *Psychiatry and Social Services, 1,* 141–159.

Olweus, D. (1993). Victimization by peers: Antecedents and long-term outcomes. In K. H. Rubin & J. B. Asendorpf (Eds.), *Social withdrawal, inhibition, and shyness in childhood* (pp. 315–341). Hillsdale, NJ: Erlbaum.

O'Malley, J. M. (1982). *Children's English and services study: Educational and needs assessment for language minority children with limited English proficiency.* Rosslyn, VA: Inter-American Research Associates.

Ontai-Grzebik, L. L., & Raffaelli, M. (2004). Individual and social influences on ethnic identity among Latino young adults.

Journal of Adolescent Research, 19(5), 559–575.

Orenstein, P. (1994). *School girls: Young women, self-esteem, and the confidence gap.* New York: Bantam Doubleday Dell Publishing Group, Inc.

Orenstein, P. in Association with the American Association of University Women. (1994). *School girls: Young women, self-esteem, and the confidence gap.* New York: Anchor Books, Doubleday.

Orlofsky, J. L. (1997). Sex role orientation, identity, formative, and self-esteem in college men and women. *Sex Roles, 3,* 561–374.

Orton, S. T. (1937). *Reading, writing, and speech problems in children.* New York: Norton.

Oyserman, D., Harrison, K., Bybee, D. (2001). Can racial identity be promotive of academic efficacy? *International Journal of Behavioral Development, 25,* 379–385.

Paikoff, R., & Brooks-Gunn, J. (1991). Do parent–child relationships change during puberty? *Psychological Bulletin, 110,* 47–66.

Paivis, A. (1971). *Imagery and verbal processes.* New York: Holt, Rinehart, and Winston.

Pajares, F. (1966). Self-efficacy beliefs in academic settings. *Review of Educational Research 66,* 543–578.

Paley, V. (1981). *Walley's stories: Conversations in kindergarten.* Cambridge, MA: Harvard University Press.

Paley, V. (2004). *A child's work: The importance of fantasy play.* Chicago, IL: University of Chicago Press.

Paley, V. G. (1988). *Bad guys don't have birthdays.* Chicago: University of Chicago Press.

Palinscar, A. S., & Brown, A. L. (1984). Reciprocal teaching of comprehension-fostering and comprehension-monitoring activities. *Cognition and Instruction, 1,* 117–175.

Palinscar, A. S., & David, Y. M. (1991). Promoting literacy through classroom dialogue. In E. Hiebert (Ed.), *Literacy for a diverse society* (pp. 122–140). New York: Teachers College Press.

Pan, A., Rowe, M., Singer, J., & Snow, C. (2005). Maternal correlates of growth in toddler vocabulary production in low-income families. *Child Development, 6,* 763–782.

Paris, S. (2005). Reinterpreting the development of reading skills. *Reading Research Quarterly, 40,* 184–202.

Paris, S., & Jacobs, J. (1984). The benefits of informed instruction for children's reading awareness and comprehension. *Child Development, 55,* 2083–2093.

Paris, S. G., Lipson, M. Y., & Wixon, K. (1983). Becoming a strategic reader. *Contemporary Educational Psychology, 8,* 293–316.

Paris, S. G., & Winograd, P. W. (1990). How metacognition can promote academic learning and instruction. In B. J. Jones & L. Idol (Eds.), *Dimensions of thinking and cognitive instruction* (pp. 15–51). Hillsdale, NJ: Erlbaum.

Parke, R. (2004). Fathers, families, and the future: A plethora of plausible predictions. *Merrill-Palmer Quarterly, 50,* 456–470.

Parke, R. & Buriel, R. (1998). Socialization in the family: Ethnic and ecological perspectives. In W. Damon (Series Ed.) & N. Eisenberg (Vol. Ed.), *Social, emotional and personality development. Vol. 3. Handbook of child psychology* (pp. 463–552). New York: John Wiley.

Parke, R., & Slaby, R. G. (1983). The development of aggression. In E. M. Hetherington (Ed.), *Handbook of child development, Vol. 4. Socialization, personality and social development* (4th ed., pp. 547–641). New York: John Wiley.

Parker, J. G., & Asher, S. R. (1987). Peer relations and later adjustment: Are low-accepted children at risk? *Psychological Bulletin, 102,* 357–389.

Parker, J. G. & Asher, S. R. (1993). Friendship and friendship quality in middle childhood: Links with peer group acceptance and feelings of loneliness and social dissatisfaction. *Developmental Psychology, 29,* 611–621.

Parker, J. G., Rubin, K. H., Price, J., & DeRosier, M. E. (1995). Peer relationships, child development, and adjustment: A developmental psychopathology perspective. In D. Cicehetti & D. Cohen (Eds.), *Developmental psychopathology, Vol. 2. Risk, disorder, and adaptation* (pp 96–161). New York: John Wiley.

Parker, J. G., & Seal, J. (1996). Forming, losing, renewing, and replacing friendships: Applying temporal parameters to the assessment of children's friendships experiences. *Child Development, 67,* 2248–2268.

Patterson, C. (1995). Families of the lesbian baby boom: Parent's division of labor and children's adjustment. *Developmental Psychology, 31,* 115–123.

Patterson, C. (2002). Lesbian and gay parenthood. In M. Bornstein (Ed.), *Handbook of parenting* (2nd ed.; Vol. 3): *Biology and ecology of parenting* (pp. 317–338). Erlbaum.

Patterson, C. J. (1992). Children of lesbian and gay parents. *Child Development, 63,* 1025–1042.

Patterson, C. J., & Chan, R. W. (1999). Families headed by lesbian and gay parents. In M. E. Lamb (Ed.), *Nontraditional families.* Hillsdale, NJ: Erlbaum.

Patterson, G. R., Capaldi, D., & Bank, L. (1991). An early starter model for predicting delinquency. In D. J. Pepler & K. H. Rubin (Eds.), *The development and treatment of childhood aggression* (pp. 139–168). Hillsdale, NJ: Erlbaum.

Patterson, G. R., DeBaryshe, B. D., & Ramsey, E. (1989). A developmental perspective on antisocial behavior. *American Psychologist, 44,* 329–335.

Pearson, J. L., Hunter, A. G., Ensminger, M. E., & Kellam, S. G. (1990). Black grandmothers in multigenerational households: Diversity in family structure and parenting involvement in the Woodlawn community. *Child Development, 61,* 434–442.

Pearson, P., & Duke, N. (2002). Comprehension instruction in the primary grades. In C. Block & M. Pressley (Eds.), *Comprehension instruction: Research-based best practices* (pp. 247–260). New York: The Guilford Press.

Pellegrini, A. (2005). *Recess: Its role in education and development.* Mahwah, NJ: Erlbaum.

Pellegrini, A., & Bartini, M. (1999). A longitudinal study of bullying, victimization, and peer affiliation during the transition from primary school to middle school. Paper presented at the 107th American Psychological Association Conference, Boston, MA.

Pellegrini, A., & Blatchford, P. (2001). *The child at school: Interactions with peers and teachers.* New York: Oxford University Press.

Pellegrini, A. D., Brody, G. H., & Seigel, I. E. (1985). Parents' book reading habits with their children. *Journal of Educational Psychology, 77,* 332–340.

Pellegrini, A. D., & Galda, L. (1993). Ten years after: A reexamination of symbolic play and literacy research. *Reading Research Quarterly, 28,* 162–175.

Pellegrini, A. D., Huberty, P., & Jones, I. (1995). The effects of recess timing on children's playground and classroom behaviors. *American Educational Research Journal, 32,* 845–864.

Pellegrini, A. D., & Smith, P. K. (1998). Physical activity play: The nature and function of a neglected aspect of playing. *Child Development, 69*(3), 577–598.

Pellett, T. L., & Harrison, J. M. (1992). Children's perceptions of the gender appropriateness of physical activities: A further analysis. *Play and Culture, 5,* 305–313.

Pellman, H. (2000). What parents need to know about children and the media. *Pediatrics, 18,* 4–6.

Perez, B. (Ed.). (2004a). *Sociocultural contexts of language and literacy* (2nd ed.). Mahwah, NJ: Erlbaum.

Perez, B. (2004b). Becoming biliterate: A study of two-way bilingual immersion education. Mahwah, NJ: Erlbaum.

Perez, B., & Torres-Guzman, M. (2002). *Learning in two worlds: An integrated Spanish/English biliteracy approach* (3rd ed.). Boston: Allyn & Bacon.

Perfetti, C., Beck, I., & Hughes, C. (1985). Reading acquisition and beyond: Decoding includes cognition. *American Journal of Education, 93,* 40–60.

Perie, M., & Moran, R. (2005). *NAEP 2004 trends in academic progress: Three decades of student performance in reading and mathematics.* U.S. Department of Education, National Center of Educational Statistics. Washington, DC: Government Printing Office. Available online at http:// nces.ed.gov/ nationsreportcard/pubs/2005.

Perner, J., & Wimmer, H. (1985). "John thinks that Mary thinks that . . .": Attribution of second order false beliefs by 5–10 year old children. *Journal of Experimental Child Psychology, 39,* 437–471.

Petersen, A., Compas, B., Brooks-Gunn, J., Stemmler, M., Ey, S., & Grant, K. (1993). Depression in adolescence. *American Psychologist, 48,* 155–168.

Petersen, A., & Taylor, B. (1980). The biological approach to adolescence: Biological change and psychological adaptation. In J. Adelson (Ed.), *Handbook of adolescent psychology* (pp. 117–155). New York: John Wiley.

Peterson, C., & McCabe, A. (1991). Linking children's connectives use and narrative macrostructure. In A. McCabe & C. Peterson (Eds.), *Developing narrative structure.* Hillsdale, NJ: Erlbaum.

Petitto, L., Katerelos, M., Levy, B., Gauna, K., Tetreault, K., & Ferraro, V. (2001). Bilingual signed and spoken language acquisition from birth: Implications for mechanisms underlying early bilingual language acquisition. *Journal of Child Language, 28,* 453–496.

Phelan, P., Davidson, A. L., & Yu, H. C. (1998). *Adolescents' worlds: Negotiating family, peers, and schools.* New York: Teachers College Press.

Philips, S. U. (1983). *The invisible culture: Communication in the classroom and community on the Warm Springs Indian Reservation.* New York: Longman.

Phillips, D., & Zimmerman, M. (1990). The developmental course of perceived competence and incompetence among competent children. In R. J. Sternberg & J. Kolligian (Eds.), *Competence considered* (pp. 41–66). New Haven, CT: Yale University Press.

Phillips, D. A. (1987). Socialization of perceived academic competence among highly competent children. *Child Development, 58,* 1308–1320.

Phinney, J. (1992). The Multigroup Ethnic Identity Measure: A new scale for use with adolescents and young adults from diverse groups. *Journal of Adolescent Research, 7,* 156–176.

Phinney, J. (1993). A three-stage model of ethnic identity development. In M. E. Bernal, & G. P. Knight (Eds.), *Ethnic identity: Formation and transmission among Hispanics and other minorities.* Albany: State University of New York Press.

Phinney, J. (1995). Ethnic identity and self-esteem: A review and integration. In A. Padilla (Ed.), *Hispanic psychology: Critical issues in theory and research* (pp. 57–70). Thousand Oaks, CA: Sage.

Phinney, J. (1999, May). *Ethnic families in southern California: Change and stability in multicultural settings.* Symposium presented at the Western Psychological Association Annual Convention, Irvine, CA.

Phinney, J., & Devich-Navarro, M. (1997). Variation in bicultural identification among African American and Mexican American adolescents. *Journal of Research on Adolescence, 7,* 3–32.

Phinney, J. S. (1989). Stages of ethnic identity development in minority group adolescents. *Journal of Early Adolescence, 9,* 34–49.

Phinney, J. S. (1990). Ethnic identity in adolescents and adults: A review of research. *Psychological Bulletin, 108,* 499–514.

Phinney, J. S. (1996). Understanding ethnic diversity: The role of ethnic identity. *American Behavioral Scientist, 40,* 143–152.

Phinney, J. S., Romero, I., Nava, M., & Huang, D. (2001). The role of language, parents and peers in ethnic identity among adolescents in immigrant families. *Journal of Youth and Adolescence, 30*(2), 135–153.

Phinney, J. S., & Rosenthal, D. A., (1992). Ethnic identity in adolescence: Process, context, and outcome. In G. R. Adams, T. P. Gullotta, & R. Montemayer (Eds.), *Adolescent identity formation* (pp. 145–172). Newbury, CA.: Sage.

Piaget, J. (1926). *The language and thought of the child.* London: Routledge & Kegan Paul.

Piaget, J. (1951). *The child's conception of the world.* New York: The Humanities Press.

Piaget, J. (1952). *The origins of intelligence in children.* New York: International Universities Press.

Piaget, J. (1962). *Play, dreams, and imitation in children.* New York: Norton.

Piaget, J. (1964). Development and learning. In R. Ripple & V. Rockcastle (Eds.), *Piaget rediscovered* (pp. 7–20). Ithaca, NY: Cornell University Press.

Piaget, J. (1965). *The moral judgment of the child.* Hommondsworth: Penguine Books. (Original work published 1932).

Piaget, J. (1967). *Six psychological studies.* New York: Random House.

Piaget, J. (1969). *Science of education and the psychology of the child.* New York: Viking.

Piaget, J. (1976). *Judgment and reasoning in the child.* Totowa, NJ: Littlefield, Adams.

Piaget, J., & Inhelder, B. (1956). *The child's conception of space.* London: Routledge & Kegan Paul.

Pianta, R. (1999). *Enhancing relationships between children and teachers.* Washington, DC: American Psychological Association.

Pianta, R. (2007). Preschool is school, sometimes. *Education Next, No. 1.* Retrieved January 2007 from http://www. hoover.org/ publications/ednext/4612287.html.

Pianta, R., La Paro, K., & Bradley, R. (2002). The relation of kindergarten classroom environment to teacher, family, and school characteristics and child outcomes. *Elementary School Journal, 102,* 225–238.

Pianta, R., La Paro, K., Payne, C., Cox, M., & Bradley, R. (2002). The relation of kindergarten classroom environment to teacher, family, and school characteristics and child outcomes. *Elementary School Journal, 102,* 225–238.

Pianta, R., & Nimetz, S. (1991). Relationships between teachers and children: Associations with behavior at home and in the classroom. *Journal of Applied Developmental Psychology, 12,* 379–393.

Pianta, R. C. (1994). Patterns of relationships between children and kindergarten teachers. *Journal of School Psychology, 32,* 15–32.

Pianta, R. C. (1999). *Enhancing relationships: Between children and teachers.* Washington, DC: American Psychological Association.

Pianta, R. C. (2006). Schools, schooling, and developmental psychopathology. In D. Cicchetti & D. J. Cohen (Eds.), *Developmental psychopathology. Vol. 1: Theory and method* (2nd ed., pp. 494–529). Hoboken, NJ: John Wiley.

Pianta, R. C., & Harbers, K. (1996). Observing mother and child behavior in a problem-solving situation at school entry: Relations with academic achievement. *Journal of School Psychology, 34,* 307–322.

Pianta, R. C., Rimm-Kaufman, S. E., & Cox, M. J. (1999). Introduction: An ecological approach to the kindergarten transition. In R. C. Pianta & M. J. Cox (Eds.), *The transition to kindergarten* (pp. 3–12). Baltimore, MD: Paul H. Brookes Publishing Company.

Pianta, R. C., & Steinberg, M. (1992). Relationships between children and kindergarten teachers from the teachers' perspective. In R. C. Pianta (Ed.), *Beyond the parent: The role of other adults in children's lives* (pp. 61–80). San Francisco: Jossey-Bass.

Pianta, R. C., Steinberg, M., & Rollins, K. (1995). The first two years of school: Teacher-student relationships and deflections in children's classroom adjustment. *Development and Psychopathology, 7,* 297–312.

Pianta, R. C., & Suhlman, M. W. (2004). Teacher-child relationships and children's success in the first years of school. *School Psychology Review, 33,* 444–458.

Pilkington, N. W., & D'Augelli, A. R. (1995). Victimization of lesbian, gay, and bisexual youth in community setting. *Journal of Community Psychology, 23,* 34–56.

Pinker, S. (1994). *The language instinct: How the mind creates language.* New York: William Morrow.

Pinker, S. (2002). *The blank slate: The modern denial of human nature.* New York: Viking Penguin.

Pinker, S. (2004a). Clarifying the logical problem of language acquisition. *Journal of Child Language, 31,* 949–953.

Pinker, S. (2004b). Language as an adaptation to the cognitive niche. In D. Kenrick & C. Luce (Eds.), *The functional mind: Readings in evolutionary psychology.* Boston: Allyn & Bacon.

Pinnell, G., DeFord, D., & Lyons, C. (1988). *Reading recovery: Early intervention for at-risk first graders.* Arlington, VA: Educational Research Service.

Pintrich, P., & Schunk, D. (1996). *Motivation in education: Theory, practice, and applications.* Englewood Cliffs, NJ: Merrill.

Pintrich, P. R., & Schrauben, B. (1992). Students' motivational beliefs and their cognitive engagement in classroom academic tasks. In D. Schunk & J. Meece (Eds.), *Student perceptions in the classroom: Causes and consequences* (pp. 149–183). Hillsdale, NJ: Erlbaum.

Pipher, M. (1994). *Reviving Ophelia: Saving the selves of adolescent girls.* New York: Ballantine Books.

Pleck, J. H. (1997). Paternal involvement: Levels, sources, and consequences. In M. Lamb (Ed.), *The role of the father in child development* (pp. 66–103). New York: John Wiley.

Plomin, R. (1989). Environment and genes: Determinants of behavior. *American Psychologist, 44,* 105–111.

Plomin, R. (1990a). *Nature and nurture.* Pacific Grove, CA: Brooks/Cole.

Plomin, R. (1990b). The role of inheritance in behavior. *Science, 248,* 183–188.

Plomin, R. (2005). Finding genes in child psychology and psychiatry: When are we going to be there? *Journal of Child Psychology and Psychiatry, 46,* 1030–1038.

Plomin, R., & DeFries, J. (1980). Genetics and intelligence: Recent data. *Intelligence, 4,* 15–24.

Plomin, R., DeFries, J., & Loehlin, J. (1977). Genotype-environmental interaction and correlation in the analysis of human behavior. *Psychological Bulletin, 24,* 738–745.

Pollard, E., & Rosenberg, R. (2003). The strength-based approach to child well-being: Let's begin with the end in mind.

In M. Bornstein, L. Davidson, C. Keyes, & K. Moore (Eds.), *Well-being: Positive development across the life course* (pp. 13–22). Mahwah, NJ: Erlbaum.

Pollock, W. (1998). *Real boys.* New York: Henry Holt.

Pomerantz, E. M. & Ruble, D. N. (1998). The role of maternal control in the development of sex differences in child self-evaluative factors. *Child Development, 69,* 458–478.

Popham, J. (2005). *Classroom assessment: What teachers need to know* (4th ed.). Boston: Allyn & Bacon.

Porter, R. H., Cernoch, J. M., & McLaughlin, F. J. (1983). Maternal recognition of neonates through olfactory cues. *Physiology and Behavior, 30,* 151–154.

Portes, A. (1997). Immigration theory for a new century: Some problems and opportunities. *International Migration Review, 31,* 799–825.

Portes, A., & Rumbaut, R. G. (2001). *Legacies: The story of immigrant second generation.* Berkley: University of California Press.

Portes, P. R. (1999). Social and psychological factors in the academic achievement of children of immigrants: A cultural history puzzle. *American Educational Research Journal, 36,* 489–507.

Posner, J. K., & Vandell, D. (1994). Low income children's after-school care: Are there beneficial effects of after-school programs? *Child Development, 65,* 440–456.

Posner, J. K., & Vandell, D. L. (1999). After-school activities and the development of low-income urban children: A longitudinal study. *Developmental Psychology, 35,* 868–879.

Pressley, M. (1998). *Reading instruction that works: The case for balanced teaching.* New York: Guilford Press.

Pressley, M. (2002a). Effective beginning reading instruction. *Journal of Literacy Research, 34,* 165–188.

Pressley, M. (2002b). *Reading instruction that works: The case for balanced teaching,* (2nd ed.). New York: Guilford Press.

Pressley, M., Allington, R., Wharton-McDonald, R., Block, C., & Morrow, L. (2002). *Learning to read: Lessons from exemplary first-grade classrooms.* New York: Guilford Press.

Pressley, M., & Ghatala, E. S. (1990). Self-regulated learning: Monitoring learning from text. *Educational Psychologist, 25,* 19–34.

Pressley, M., Wharton-McDonald, R., Allington, R., Block, C. C., & Morrow, L. (1998). *The nature of effective first grade literacy instruction.* (CELA Research Rep. No. 11007). Albany State University of New York at Albany, The National Center on English Learning and Achievement. Available online at http://cela.albany.edu/1stgradelit/index.html.

Price, J. A. (1976). North American Indian families. In C. H. Mindel & R. W. Haberstein (Eds.), *Ethnic families in America: Patterns and variations* (pp. 248–270). New York: Elsevier.

Prior, M. (2000). Does shy-inhibited temperament in childhood lead to anxiety problems in adolescence? *Journal of the American Academy of Child and Adolescent Psychiatry, 39*(4), 461–468.

Puma, M. J., Jones, C. C., Rock, D., & Fernandez, R. (1993). *Prospects: The congressionally mandated study of educational growth and opportunity. Interim report.* Bethesda, MD: Abt Associates.

Purcell Gates, V. (1995). *Other people's words: The cycle of low literacy.* Cambridge, MA: Harvard University Press.

Pyle, S., Sharkey, J., Yetter, G., Felix, E., Furlong, M., & Poston, W. (2006). Fighting an epidemic: The role of schools in reducing childhood obesity. *Psychology in the Schools, 43,* 361–376.

Quintana, S. (1998). Children's developmental understanding of ethnicity and race. *Applied and Preventive Psychology, 7,* 27–45.

Quintana, S. (1999). Role of perspective-taking abilities and ethnic socialization in development of adolescent ethnic identity. *Journal of Research on Adolescence, 9*(2), 161–184.

Quintana, S. M., Vera, E. M. (1999). Mexican-American children's ethnic identity, understanding of ethnic prejudice, and parental ethnic socialization. *Hispanic Journal of Behavioral Sciences, 21,* 387–404.

Radke-Yarrow, M., & Zahn-Waxler, C. (1984). Root, motives, and patterns in children's prosocial behavior. In E. Staub, D. Bar-Tal, J. Karylowski, & J. Reykowski (Eds.), *Development and maintenance of prosocial behavior* (pp. 81–99). New York: Plenum Press.

Ramey, C., & Ramey, S. (2004). Early learning and school readiness: Can early intervention make a difference? *Merrill-Palmer Quarterly, 50,* 471–491.

Ramey, C. T., & Campbell, F. A. (1984). Preventive education for high-risk children: Cognitive consequences of Carolina Abecedarian Project. *American Journal of Mental Deficiency, 88,* 515–523.

Ramey, C. T., & Campbell, F. A. (1991). Poverty, early childhood education, and academic competence: The Abecedarian experiment. In A. C. Huston (Ed.), *Children in poverty: Child development and public policy* (pp. 190–221). New York: Cambridge University Press.

Ramsden, S., & Hubbard, J. (2002). Family expressiveness and parental emotional coaching: Their role in children's emotion regulation and aggression. *Journal of Abnormal Child Psychology, 30,* 657–667.

Rand, C., Graham, D. L. R., & Rawlings, E. I. (1982). Psychological health and factors the court seeks to control in lesbian mother custody trials. *Journal of Homosexuality, 8,* 27–39.

Rank, M. R., & Hirschl, T. A. (1999). The economic risk of childhood in America: Estimating the probability of poverty across the formative years. *Journal of Marriage and the Family, 61,* 1058–1067.

Rauch-Elnekave, H. (1994). Teenage motherhood: Its relationship to undetected learning problems. *Adolescence, 29,* 91–104.

Raudenbush, S., Rowan, B., & Cheong, Y. (1993). Higher order instructional goals in secondary schools: Class, teacher, and school influences. *American Educational Research Journal, 30,* 523–553.

Read, C. (1975). *Children's categorization of speech sounds in English* (National Council for Teachers of English Research Report No. 17). Urbana, IL: National Council for Teachers of English.

Reading Recovery Council. (2002). Reading Recovery Results 2001–2002. National Data Evaluation Center, The Ohio State University College of Education. Columbus, Ohio. Retrieved June 2005 from http://ndec.reading-recovery.org.

Reeve, J. (2006). Teachers as facilitators: What autonomy-supportive teachers do and why their students benefit. *The Elementary School Journal, 106*(3), 225–236.

Reeves, J. R. (2006). Secondary teacher attitudes toward including English-language learners in mainstream

classrooms. *Journal of Educational Research, 99,* 131–142.

Reid, J. (1993). Prevention of conduct disorders before and after school entry: Relating interventions to developmental findings. *Development and Psychology, 5,* 243–262.

Remafedi, G. (1999). Sexual orientation and youth suicide. *Journal of the American Medical Association, 282*(13), 1291–1292.

Remafedi, G. J. (1987). Adolescent homosexuality: Psychosocial and medical implications. *Pediatrics, 79,* 331–337.

Renick, M. J., & Harter, S. (1989). Impact of social comparisons on the developing self-perceptions of learning disabled students. *Journal of Educational Psychology, 81,* 631–638.

Renzulli, J. (Ed.). *Identification of students for gifted and talented programs.* Thousand Oaks, CA: Corwin Press.

Resnick, M. D., Bearman, P. S., Blum, R. W., Bauman, K. E., Harris, K. M., Jones, J., Tablro, J., Beuhring, T., Sieving, R. E., Shew, M., Ireland, M., Bearinger, L. H., & Udry, J. R. (1995). Protecting adolescents from harm. Findings from the National Longitudinal Study of Adolescent Health. *Journal of the American Medical Association, 278*(10), 823–832.

Reyes, M. de la Luz. (1995). A process approach to literacy using dialogue journals and literature logs with second language learners. In O. Garcia & C. Baker (Eds.), *Policy and practice in bilingual education* (pp. 200–215). Bristol, PA: Multilingual Matters.

Reynolds, A. J., & Wahlberg, H. J. (1991). A structural model of science achievement. *Journal of Educational Psychology, 83,* 97–107.

Richards, M. H., & Duckett, E. (1994). The relationship of maternal employment to early adolescent daily experiences with and without parents. *Child Development, 65,* 225–236.

Richards, T., Berninger, V., Nagy, W., Parsons, A., Field, K., & Richards, A. (2005). Brain activation during language task contrasts in children with and without dyslexia: Inferring mapping processes and assessing response to spelling instruction. *Educational and Child Psychology, 22,* 62–80.

Richardson, V. (1996). The role of attitude and belief in learning to teach. In J. Sikula, T. Buttery, & E. Guyton (Eds.), *Handbook of research on teacher education* (2nd ed., pp. 102–119). New York: MacMillan.

Risman, B. J. (1986). Can men "mother"? Life as a single father. *Family Relations, 35,* 95–102.

Ritchie, D., Price, V., & Roberts, D. F. (1987). Television, reading, and reading achievement: A reappraisal. *Communication Research, 14,* 292, 315.

Ritter, P. L., Mont-Reynaud, R., & Dornbusch, S. M. (1993). Minority parents and their youth: Concern, encouragement, and support for school achievement. In N. F. Chavkin (Ed.), *Families and schools in a pluralistic society* (pp. 107–120). Albany: State University of New York.

Roberton, M. A. (1984). Changing motor patterns during childhood. In J. Thomas (Ed.), *Motor development during childhood and adolescence* (pp. 48–90). Minneapolis, MN: Burgess.

Roberts, D. F., Foehr, U. G., Rideout, V. J., & Brodie, M. (1999, November). *Kids and media @ the new millenium.* Menlo Park, CA: Kaiser Family Foundation.

Roberts, W. B. (2000). The bully as victim: Understanding bully behaviors to increase effectiveness of interventions in bully-victim dyad. *Professional School Counseling, 4*(2), 148–155.

Robinson, B. E., & Skeen, P. (1982). Sex-role orientation of gay fathers versus gay nonfathers. *Perceptual Motor Skills, 55,* 1055–1059.

Rodgers, J. L., Cleveland, H. H., van den Oord, E., & Rowe, D. C. (2000). Resolving the debate over birth order, family size, and intelligence. *American Psychologist, 55,* 299–612.

Roeser, R., Eccles, J. S., & Sameroff, A. J. (2000). School as a context of early adolescents' academic and social-emotional development: A summary of research findings. *The Elementary School Journal, 100,* 443–471.

Roeser, R., Midgley, C., & Urban, T. (1996). Perceptions of the school psychological environment and early adolescents' psychological and behavioral functioning in school: The mediating role of goals and belonging. *Journal of Educational Psychology, 88,* 408–422.

Rogler, L. (1994). International migrations: A framework for directing research. *American Psychologist, 49,* 710–718.

Rogoff, B. (1981). Schooling and the development of cognitive skills. In H. C. Triandis & A. Heron (Eds.), *Handbook of cross-cultural psychology* (Vol. 4, pp. 233–294). Boston: Allyn & Bacon.

Rogoff, B. (1990). *Apprenticeship in thinking: Cognitive development in social context.* New York: Oxford University Press.

Rogoff, B. (1998). Cognition as a collaborative process. In D. Kuhn & R. S. Siegler (Series Eds.), & W. Damon (Ed.), *Cognition, perception and language. Vol. 2, Handbook of child psychology* (5th ed., pp. 679–744). New York: John Wiley.

Rogoff, B. (2003). *The cultural nature of human development.* New York: Oxford University Press.

Rogoff, B., Ellis, S., & Gardner, W. (1984). Adjustment of adult–child instruction according to child's age and task. *Developmental Psychology, 20,* 193–199.

Rogoff, B., & Morelli, G. (1989). Perspectives on children's development from cultural psychology. *American Psychologist, 44,* 343–348.

Rogoff, B., Paradise, R., Arauz, R., Correa-Chavez, M., & Angelillo, C. (2003). Firsthand learning through intent participation. *Annual Review of Psychology, 54,* 175–203.

Rogoff, B., Turkanis, C., & Bartlett, L. (2001). *Learning together: Children and adults in a school community.* New York: Oxford University Press.

Roid, G. (2003). *Standford-Binet Intelligence Scales* (5th ed.). Itasca, IL: Riverside.

Roid, G., & Barram, A. (2004). *Essentials of Stanford-Binet Intelligence Scales (SB5).* New York: Wiley.

Romo, H. D., & Falbo, T. (1996). *Latino high school graduation: Defying the odds.* Austin: University of Texas Press.

Roschelle, J. M., Pea, R. D., Hoadley, C. M., Gordin, D. N., & Means, B. M. (2000). Changing how and what children learn in school with computer-based technologies. *The Future of Children. Children and Computer Technology, Vol. 10,* 76–101.

Rose, A. J., & Montemayor, R. (1994). The relationship between gender role orientation and perceived self-competency in male and female adolescents. *Sex Roles, 31,* 579–595.

Rosenberg, M. (1979). *Conceiving the self.* Malabar, FL: Robert. E. Kriegen.

Rosenberg, R. N., & Pettigrew, J. W. (1983). Genetic neurological diseases. In R. N. Rosenberg (Ed.), *The clinical neurosciences* (pp. 33–165). New York: Churchill Livingston.

Rosenblatt, L. M. (1988). *Writing and reading: The transactional theory* (Tech. Rep. No. 416). Urbana, IL: Center for the Study of Reading.

Ross, S., Smith, L., Casey, J., & Slavin, R. (1995). Increasing the academic success of disadvantaged children: An examination of alternative early intervention programs. *American Educational Research Journal, 32,* 73–800.

Rothbart, M. K., & Bates, J. E. (1998). Temperament. In W. Damon & N. Eisenberg (Eds.), *Handbook of child psychology, Vol. 3, Social, emotional, and personality development* (5th ed., pp. 105–176). New York: John Wiley.

Rothbart, M. K., & Bates, J. E. (2006). Temperament. In W. Damon and R. M. Lerner (Eds.), *Handbook of child psychology. Vol. 3: Social, emotional, and personality development* (6th ed., pp. 99–166). New York: John Wiley.

Rothbaum, F., Weisz, J., Pott, M., Miyake, K., & Morelli, G. (2000). Attachment and culture: Security in the United States and Japan. *American Psychologist, 35,* 1093–1104.

Rothenberg, D. (1996). *Grandparents as parents: A primer for schools* (Report No. EDO-PS-96-8). Urbana, IL: ERIC Clearinghouse on Elementary and Early Childhood Education. (ERIC Document Reproduction Service No. ED 401 044)

Rotherman-Borus M., Reid, H., Rosario M., & Kasen, S. (1995). Determinants of safer sex patterns among gay/bisexual male adolescents. *Journal of Adolescence, 18,* 3–15.

Rotheram-Borus, M. S., Rosaris, M., Van Russem, R., Reid, H., Gellis, R. (1995). Prevalence, course, and predictors of multiple problem behaviors among gay and bisexual male adolescents. *Developmental Psychology, 31,* 75–85.

Rousseau, J. (1911). *Emile.* New York: Dutton.

Rowitz, L. (1988). The forgotten ones: Adolescence and mental retardation. *Mental Retardation, 26,* 115–117.

Rowley, S. A., Kurtz-Costes, B., & Cooper, S. (in press). The role of schooling in ethnic minority achievement and attainment. In J. Meece & J. Eccles (Eds.), *Handbook on schools, schooling, and development.* Mahwah, NJ: Erlbaum.

Rowley, S. A., Sellers, R. M., Chavous, T. M., & Smith, M. S. (1998). The relationship between racial identity and self-esteem in African-American college and high school students. *Journal of Personality and Social Psychology, 74,* 715–724.

Rubin, K., Bukowski, W., & Parker, J. (2006). Peer interactions, relationships, and groups. In W. Damon & R. M. Lerner (Editors-in-Chief) & N. Eisenberg (Vol. Ed.), *Handbook of child psychology. Vol. 3. Social, emotional, and personality development* (pp. 571–645). New York: John Wiley.

Rubin, K., Coplan, R. J., Nelson, L. J., Cheah, C. L., & Legace-Seguin, D. G. (1999). Peer relationships in childhood. In M. H. Bornstein & M. E. Lamb (Eds.), *Developmental psychology* (4th ed., pp. 451–503). Hillsdale, NJ: Erlbaum.

Rubin, K. H., Nelson, L. J., Hastings, P., & Asendorpf, J. (1999). The transaction between parents' perceptions of their children's shyness and their parenting styles. *International Journal of Behavioral Development, 23*, 937–958.

Ruble, D., & Dweck, C. S. (1995). *Self-conceptions, person conceptions, and their development.* In N. Eisenberg (Ed.), *Social development* (pp. 109–139). Thousand Oaks, CA: Sage.

Ruble, D., Martin, C. L., & Berenbaum, S. (2006). Gender development. In W. Damon & R. M. Lerner (Editors-in-Chief) & N. Eisenberg (Vol. Ed.), *Handbook of child psychology. Vol. 3. Social, emotional, and personality development* (pp. 858–932). New York: John Wiley.

Ruble, D. N. (1983). The development of social comparison processes and their role in achievement-related self-socialization. In E. T. Higgins, D. N. Ruble, & W. W. Hartup (Eds.), *Social cognition and social development: A socio-cultural perspective* (pp. 134–157). New York: Cambridge University Press.

Ruble, D. N., & Martin, C. L. (1998). Gender development. In W. Damon (Series Ed.), & N. Eisenberg (Vol. Ed.), *Handbook of child psychology: Vol. 3. Social, emotional, and personality development* (pp. 933–1016). New York: John Wiley.

Rueda, R. (1986). Metacognition and passing: Strategic interactions in the lives of students with learning disabilities. *Anthropology and Education Quarterly, 17*, 145–165.

Ruff, H. A., Capozzoli, M., & Weissberg, R. (1998). Age, individuality, and context as factors in sustained visual attention during the preschool years. *Developmental Psychology, 34*(3), 454–464.

Rumberger, R. W. (2001, January). Why students drop out of school and what can be done. Paper prepared for the Civil Rights Project at Harvard University's Graduate School of Education and Achieve, Inc., Cambridge, MA. Retrieved May 23, 2006, from http://www. civilrightsproject. harvard.edu/research/ dropouts/rumberger.pdf.

Rumberger, R. W., Ghatak, R., Poulos, G., & Ritter, P. L., & Dornbusch (1990). Family influences on dropout behavior in one California high school. *Sociology of Education, 63*, 283–299.

Rural Early Adolescent Project. (2004). *Supporting and encouraging effective transitions.* Chapel Hill: National Research Center of Rural Education Support, University of North Carolina.

Rushton, J., Fulker, D. W., Neale, M. C., Nias, D. K. B., & Eysenck, H. J. (1986). Altruism and aggression: The heritability of individual differences. *Journal of Personality and Social Psychology, 50*, 1192–1198.

Rutter, M. (1983). School effects on pupil progress. Research findings and policy implications. *Child Development, 54*, 1–29.

Rutter, M. (2002). Nature, nurture, and development: From evangelism through science toward policy and practice. *Child Development, 73*, 1–21.

Rutter, M., & Maughan, B. (2002). School effectiveness findings 1979–2002. *Journal of School Psychology, 40*, 451–475.

Rutter, M., Maughan, B., Mortimore, P., Ouston, J., & Smith, A. (1979a). *Secondary schools and their effects on children.* Cambridge, MA: Harvard University Press.

Rutter, M., O'Connor, T., & the English and Romanian Adoptees (ERA) Study Team. (2004). Are there biological programming effects for psychological development? Findings from a study of Romanian adoptees. *Developmental Psychology, 40*, 81–94.

Ryan, A. M. (2001). The peer group as a context for the development of young adolescent motivation and achievement. *Child Development, 72*, 1135–1150.

Saarni, C., Campos, J. J., Camras, L. A., & Witherington, D. (2006). Emotional development: Action, communication, and understanding. In W. Damon & R. M. Lerner (Editors-in-Chief) & N. Eisenberg (Vol. Ed.), *Handbook of child psychology, Vol. 3: Social, emotional, and personality development* (6th ed., pp. 226–299). New York: John Wiley.

Saarni, C., Mumme, D. L., & Campos, J. J. (1998). Emotional development: Action, communication, and understanding. In W. Damon (Series Ed.) & N. Eisenberg (Vol. Ed.), *Handbook of child psychology, Vol. 3: Social, emotional, and personality development* (5th ed., pp. 237–309). New York: John Wiley.

Sadker, M., & Sadker, D. (1995). *Failing at fairness: How America's schools cheat girls.* New York: Touchstone Press.

Safe Kids. (2007). Facts about childhood recreational injuries. Retrieved January 2007 from http://www.usa.safekids.org/ content_documents/Rec_tips.pdf.

Sagi, A., Donnell, F., van Ijzendoorn, M. H., Mayseless, O., & Aviezer, O. (1994). Sleeping out of home in a kibbutz communal arrangement: It makes a difference for infant-mother attachment. *Child Development, 65*, 992–1004.

Salisbury, C. L., Palombaro, M. M., & Hollowood, T. M. (1993). On the nature and change of an inclusive elementary school. *Journal of the Association for Persons with Severe Handicaps, 18*(2), 75–84.

Salomone, R. C. (2006). Single-sex programs: Resolving the research conundrum. *Teachers College Record, 108*(4), 778–802.

Sameroff, A. J. (1994). Developmental systems and family functioning. In R. D. Parke & S. G. Kellam (Eds.), *Exploring family relationships with other social contexts* (pp. 199–214). Hillsdale, NJ: Erlbaum.

Sameroff, A. J., Seifer, R., Barocas, R., Zax, M., & Greenspan, S. (1987). Intelligence quotient scores of 4-year-old children: Social-environmental risk factors. *Pediatrics, 79*, 343–350.

Sanders, M., & Epstein, J. (1998, August). *School-family-community partnerships in middle and high schools from theory to practice* (CRESPAR Report No. 22). Baltimore, MD: Johns Hopkins University, Center for Research on the Education of Students Placed at Risk.

Santrock, J. W., & Warshak, R. A. (1986). Development, relationships, and legal/clinical considerations in father-custody families. In M. E. Lamb (Ed.), *The father's role: Applied perspectives.* New York: John Wiley.

Savin-Williams, R. (1994). The disclosure to families of same-sex attractions by lesbian, gay, and bisexual youths. *Journal of Research on Adolescence, 3*, 49–68.

Savin-Williams, R. C., & Berndt, T. J. (1990). Friendship and peer relations. In S. S. Feldman & G. R. Elliott (Eds.), *At the threshold: The developing adolescent* (pp. 277–307). Cambridge, MA: Harvard University Press.

Scanzoni, J. (1985). Black parental values and expectations of children's occupational and educational success: Theoretical implications. In H. P. McAdoo & J. McAdoo (Eds.), *Black children: Social, educational, and parental environments* (pp. 113–122). Beverly Hills, CA: Sage.

Scarr, S. (1992). Developmental theories for the 1990s: Development and individual differences. *Child Development, 63*, 1–19.

Scarr, S. (1996). How people make their own environments: Implications for parents and policy makers. *Psychology, Public Policy, and Law, 2*, 204–228.

Scarr, S., & McCartney, K. (1983). How people make their own environments: A theory of genotype environmental effects. *Child Development, 54*, 424–435.

Schaefer, E. S. (1989). Dimensions of mother-infant interaction: Measurement, stability, and predictive validity. *Infant Behavior and Development, 12*, 379–393.

Schickendanz, J. (1986). *More than the ABCs: The early stages of reading and writing.* Washington, DC: National Association for the Education of Young Children.

Schneider, B., & Stevenson, D. (1999). *The ambitious generation: America's teenagers, motivated, but directionless.* New Haven, CT: Yale University Press.

Schneider, S., & Pressley, M. (1997). *Memory development between two and twenty* (2nd ed.). Mahwah, NJ: Erlbaum.

Schneider, W., & Bjorklund, D. (1998). Memory. In W. Damon (Editor-in-Chief) & D. Kuhn & R. Siegler (Vol. Eds.), *Handbook of child psychology: Vol. 2,* (5th ed., pp. 467–522). New York: John Wiley.

Schneier, L. (2001). Apprehending poetry. In D. Duckworth (Ed.), *Tell me more: Listening to learners explain* (pp. 42–78). New York: Teachers College Press.

Schon, I. (1985). *Books in Spanish for children and young adults: An annotated guide.* Metuchen, NJ: Scarecrow Press.

Schon, I. (1986). *Basic collection of children's books in Spanish.* Chicago: American Library Association.

Schulz, J. B., Carpenter, C. D., & Turnbull, A. P. (1991). *Mainstreaming exceptional students: A guide for classroom teachers.* Boston: Allyn & Bacon.

Schunk, D. H. (1991). Self-efficacy and academic motivation. *Educational Psychologist, 26*, 207–231.

Schunk, D. H. (2000). *Learning theories. An educational perspective* (3rd ed.). Upper Saddle River, NJ: Merrill/Prentice Hall.

Schunk, D. H., & Hanson, A. R. (1985). Peer models: Influence on children's self efficacy and achievement. *Journal of Educational Psychology, 77*, 313–322.

Schunk, D. S., & Cox, P. D. (1986). Strategy training and attributional feedback with learning disabled students. *Journal of Educational Psychology, 78*, 201–209.

Schwarz, W. (1996). *A guide to choosing an after-school program: For parents/about parents.* New York: ERIC Clearinghouse on Urban Education.

Schwarz, N. (1999). Self-reports: How the questions shape the answers. *American Psychologist, 54*, 93–105.

Schweinhart, L. J., & Weikert, D. (1997). *Lasting differences: The High/Scope Perry Preschool Curriculum Comparison study through age 23.* (Monographs of the High/Scope Educational Research Foundation, 12). Ypsilanti, MI: High/Scope Press.

Scott-Jones, D. (1984). Family influences on cognitive development and school achievement. *Review of Research in Education, 11*, 259–304.

Scott-Jones, D. (1987). Mother-as-teacher in the families of high- and low-achieving low-income black first graders. *Journal of Negro Education, 56*, 21–34.

Scott-Jones, D. (1995). Parent–child interactions and school achievement. In B. A. Ryan, G. R. Adams, T. P. Gullotta, R. P. Weisberg, & R. L. Hampton (Eds.), *The family-school connection: Theory, research and practice* (Vol. 2, pp. 75–107). Thousand Oaks, CA: Sage.

Scott-Jones, D., & Nelson-LeGall, S. (1986). Defining black families: Past and present. In E. Seidman & J. Rappaport (Eds.), *Redefining social problems* (pp. 83–100). New York: Plenum.

Scrimsher, S., & Tudge, J. (2003). The teaching/learning relationship in the first years of school: Some revolutionary implications of Vygotsky's theory. *Early Education and Development, 14*, 293–312.

Scruggs, T. E., & Mastropieri, M. A. (1986). Academic characteristics of behaviorally disordered and learning disabled children. *Behavioral Disorders, 11*, 184–190.

Seaton E. K., Scottham K. M., & Sellers, R. M. (n.d.). The status model of racial identity development in African American adolescents: Evidence of structure, trajectories, and well-being. *Child Development, 77*, 1416–1426.

Segalowitz, S. J., & Lawson, S. (1995). Subtle symptoms associated with self-reported mild head injury. *Journal of Learning Disabilities, 28*, 309–319.

Seginer, R. (1983). Parents' educational expectations and children's academic achievements: A literature review. *Merrill-Palmer Quarterly, 29*, 1–23.

Seitz, S., & Stewart, C. (1975). Imitations and expansions: Some developmental aspects of mother-child communication. *Developmental Psychology, 11*, 763–768.

Sellers, R. M., Smith, M. A., Shelton, J. N., Rowley, S. A., & Chavous, T. (1998). Multidimensional model of racial identity: A reconceptualization of African-American racial identity. *Personality and Social Psychology Review, 2*, 19–39.

Selman, R. (1980). *The growth of interpersonal understanding.* New York: Academic Press.

Selman, R. L., & Byrne, D. F. (1974). A structural-developmental analysis of levels of roletaking in middle childhood. *Child Development, 45*, 803–806.

Sènèchal, M., & Cornell, E. H. (1993). Vocabulary acquisition through shared reading experiences. *Reading Research Quarterly, 28*, 360–375.

Sènèchal, M., & LeFevre, J. (2001). Storybook reading and parent teaching: Links to language and literacy development. In P. Britto & J. Brooks-Gunn (Eds.), *The role of family literacy environment in promoting young children's emerging literacy skills* (pp. 39–52). San Francisco: Jossey-Bass.

Sènèchal, M., LeFevre, J., Hudson, E., & Lawson, E. P. (1996). Knowledge of storybooks as a predictor of young children's vocabulary. *Journal of Educational Psychology, 88*, 520–536.

Shapiro, J. (1995). Home literacy environment and young children's literacy knowledge and behavior. In W. Linek & E. Sturtevant (Eds.), *Generations of literacy: Seventeenth yearbook of the College Reading Association* (pp. 288–300). Harrisonburg, VA: College Reading Association.

Sharan, S. (1980). Cooperative learning in small groups: Recent methods and effects on achievement, attitudes and ethnic relations. *Review of Educational Research, 50*, 241–271.

Sharan, S., Foot, H., Morgan H. M., & Shute, R. H. (1990). Cooperative learning and helping behavior in the multi-ethnic classroom. In *Children helping children.* New York: John Wiley.

Sharan, S., & Sharan, S. (1992). *Expanding cooperative learning through group investigation.* New York: Teachers College Press.

Sharp, D., Cole, M., & Lave, C. (1979). Education and cognitive development: The evidence from experimental research. *Monographs of the Society for Research in Child Development, 44*(1–2, Serial No. 178).

Shaw, D. S., & Vondra, J. I. (1993). Chronic family adversity and infant attachment security. *Journal of Child Psychology and Psychiatry and Allied Disciplines, 34*, 1205–1215.

Shayer, M. (2003). Not just Piaget; not just Vygotsky, and certainly not Vygotsky as *alternative* to Piaget. *Learning and Instruction, 13*, 465–485.

Sheilds, M. K., & Behrman, R. E. (2000). Children and computer technology: Analysis and recommendations. *The Future of Children: Children and Computer Technology*, Vol 10, 4–30.

Sheldon, S., & Epstein, J. (2005). Involvement counts: Family and community partnerships and mathematics achievement. *The Journal of Educational Research, 98*, 196–206.

Shepard, L. (2000). The role of assessment in a learning culture. *Educational Researcher, 29*, 4–14.

Sherman, A. (1997). *Poverty matters: The cost of child poverty in America.* Washington, DC: Children's Defense Fund.

Sherrod, K. B., O'Connor, S., Vietze, P. M., & Altemeier, W. A., III. (1984). Child health and maltreatment. *Child Development, 55*, 1174–1183.

Shields, C. M., & Oberg, S. L. (1999). What can we learn from the data? Toward better understanding of the effects of multitrack year-round schooling. *Urban Education, 24*, 125–155.

Shine, J. H. (1997). The relationship between blame attribution, age and personality characteristics in inmates admitted to Grendon Therapeutic Prison. *Personality and Individual Differences, 23*(6), 943–947.

Shiono, P., & Behrman, R. (1995). Low-birth-weight: Analysis and recommendations. *The Future of Children, 5*, 4–18.

Shoda, Y., Mischel, W., Peake, P. (1990). Predicting adolescent cognitive and self-regulatory competencies from preschool delay of gratification: Identifying diagnostic conditions. *Developmental Psychology, 26*, 978–986.

Shumow, L., Vandell, L., & Kang, K. (1996). School choice, family characteristics, and home-school relations: Contributions to school achievement? *Journal of Educational Psychology, 99*, 451–460.

Shuy, R. (1967). *Discovering American dialects.* Urbana IL: National Council for Teachers of English.

Shuy, R. (1980). Vernacular black English: Setting the issues in time. In M. F. Whiteman (Ed.), *Reactions to Ann Arbor: Vernacular black English and education.* Arlington, VA: Center for Applied Linguistics.

Siegler, R. (1998). *Children's thinking* (3rd ed.). Upper Saddle River, NJ: Prentice-Hall.

Siegler, R. (2004a). Learning about learning. *Merrill-Palmer Quarterly, 50*, 353–368.

Siegler, R. (2004b). Turning memory inside out. *Developmental Review, 24*, 469–475.

Siegler, R., & Alibali, M. (2005). *Children's thinking* (4th ed.). Upper Saddle River, NJ: Prentice Hall.

Siegler, R. S., Robinson, M., Liebert, D. E., & Liebert, R. M. (1973). Inhelder and Piaget's pendulum problem: Teaching preadolescents to act as scientists. *Developmental Psychology, 9*, 97–101.

Signorelli, N., & Bacue, A. (1999). Recognition and respect: A content analysis of prime-time television characters across three decades. *Sex Roles, 40*, 527–544.

Silbereisen, R., Petersen, A., Albrecht, H., & Kracke, B. (1989). Maturational timing and the development of problem behavior: Longitudinal studies in adolescence. *Journal of Early Adolescence, 9*, 247–268.

Silberman, M. L. (1971). Teachers' attitudes toward elementary school students. *Journal of Educational Psychology, 60*, 402–407.

Simmons, R. et al. (1987). The impact of cumulative change in early adolescence. *Child Development, 5*, 1220–1234.

Simmons, R., Black, A., & Zhou, Y. (1991). African-American versus white children and the transition into junior high school. *American Journal of Education, 99*, 481–520.

Simmons, R., & Blyth, D. (1987). *Moving into adolescence. The impact of pubertal change and school context.* Hawthorne, NY: Aldine de Gruyter.

Simons, R. L., Lin, K.-H., Gordon, L. C., Conger, R. D., & Lorenz, F. O. (1999). Explaining the higher incidence of adjustment problems among children of divorce compared with those in two-parent families. *Journal of Marriage and the Family, 61*, 1020–1033.

Singer, D., & Singer, J. (2005). *Imagination and play in the electronic age.* Cambridge, MA: Harvard University Press.

Singer, J. D., Fuller, B., Keiley, M. K., & Wolf, A. (1998). Early child-care selection: Variation by geographic location, maternal characteristics, and family structure. *Developmental Psychology, 34*, 1129–1144.

Singer, J. L., & Singer, D. G. (1976). Imaginative play and pretending in early childhood. In A. Davids (Ed.), *Child personality and psychopathology* (pp. 69–112). New York: John Wiley.

Singh, S., & Darroch J. (2000). Adolescent pregnancy and childbearing: Levels and trends in developed countries. *Family Planning Perspectives, 32*, 14–23.

Sinha, C. G., & Walkerdine, V. (1978). Conservation: A problem in language, culture and thought. In N. Waterson & C. Snow (Eds.), *The development of communication.* London: John Wiley.

Skaalvik, E. M., & Valas, H. (1999). Relations among achievement, self-concept, and motivation in mathematics and language arts: A longitudinal study. *The Journal of Experimental Education, 67*, 135–149.

Skinner, B. F. (1957). *Verbal behavior.* New York: Appleton-Century-Crofts.

Slaughter-Defoe, D. T., Nakagawa, K., Takanishi, R., & Johnson, D. J. (1992). Toward cultural/ecological perspectives on schooling and achievement in African- and Asian-American children. *Child Development, 61*, 363–383.

Slavin, R., & Madden, N. (2001). *One million children: Success for all.* Thousand Oaks, CA: Corwin.

Slavin, R. E. (1994). *Using team learning* (4th ed.). Baltimore, MD: Johns Hopkins University, Center for Research on Elementary Schools.

Slavin, R. E. (1995). *Cooperative learning: Theory, research, and practice* (2nd ed.). Boston: Allyn & Bacon.

Slavin, R. E., Karweit, R. E., & Madden, N. L. (1989). *Effective programs for children at risk.* Boston: Allyn & Bacon.

Slavin, R. E., & Madden, N. A. (1999). School practices that improve race relations. *American Educational Research Journal, 16*(2), 169–180.

Sleet, D., & Mercy, D. (2003). Promotion of safety, security, and well-being. In M. Bornstein, L. Davidson, C. Keyes, & K. Moore (Eds.), *Well-being: Positive development across the life course* (pp. 81–98). Mahwah, NJ: Erlbaum.

Sleeter, C. E., & Grant, C. A. (1987). An analysis of multicultural education in the United States. *Harvard Review, 57,* 421–444.

Sleeter, C. E., & Grant, C. A. (1988). *Making choices for multicultural education: Five approaches to race, class, and gender.* Columbus, OH: Merrill.

Smedley, A., & Smedley, B. (2005). Race as biology is fiction, racism as a social problem is real: Anthological and historical perspectives on the social construction of race. *American Psychologist, 60,* 16–26.

Smetana, J. (2005). Adolescent-parent conflict: Resistance and subversion as developmental process. In L. Nucci (Ed.), *Conflict, contradiction, and contrarian elements in moral development and education.* Mahwah, NJ: Erlbaum.

Smith, D. (2003). Cultivating otherwise untapped potential. *APA Monitor on Psychology, 34.* Retrieved September 2006 from http://www.apa.org/monitor/may03/cultivating.html.

Smith, M., & Wilhelm, J. (2002). *Reading don't fix no Chevys: Literacy in the lives of young men.* Portsmouth, NH: Heinemann.

Smith, M. L., & Shepard, L. A. (1988). Kindergarten readiness and retention: A qualitative study of teachers' beliefs and practice. *American Educational Research Journal, 25,* 307–333.

Smith, N. B. (1975). Cultural dialects: Current problems and solutions. *The Reading Teacher, 29,* 137–141.

Smith, P. K., & Thompson, D. (1991). Dealing with bully/victim problems in the U.K. In P. K. Smith and D. Thompson (Eds.), *Practical approaches to bullying* (pp. 1–2). London: Fulton.

Smitherman, G. (1985). "It bees dat way somtime": Sounds and structures of present-day black English. In V. Clark, P. Eschholz, & A. Rosa (Eds.), *Language* (4th ed., pp. 552–568). New York: St. Martin's.

Smoll, F., & Schutz, R. (1990). Quantifying gender differences in physical performance: A developmental perspective. *Developmental Psychology, 26,* 360–369.

Snow, C. (1986). Conversations with children. In P. Fletcher & M. Garman (Eds.), *Language acquisition: Studies in first language development* (pp. 69–89). Cambridge, England: Cambridge University Press.

Snow, C. (2005). From literacy to learning. *Harvard Education Letter*, July/August.

Snow, C., Burns, M. S., & Griffin, P. (1998). *Preventing reading difficulties in young children.* Washington, DC: National Academy Press.

Society for Research in Child Development. (1990, Winter). *Report of the Committee for Ethical Conduct in Child Development Research,* pp. 5–7. Ann Arbor, MI: Author.

Sommers, C. H. (2000). *The war against boys. How misguided feminism is harming our young men.* New York: Simon & Schuster.

Sommers-Flanagan, R., Sommers-Flanagan, J., & Davis, B. (1993). What's happening on music television? A gender role content analysis. *Sex Roles, 28,* 745–753.

Sousa, D. (1995). *How the brain learns. A classroom teacher's guide.* Reston, VA: National Association of Secondary Principals.

Sowers, S. (1982). Six questions teachers ask about invented spelling. In T. Newkirk & N. Atwell (Eds.), *Understanding writing* (pp. 47–54). Boston: Northeast Regional Exchange.

Spangenberg-Urbschat, K., & Pritchard, R. (1994). Kids come in all languages: Reading instruction for ESL students. Newark, DE: International Reading Association.

Spearman, C. (1927). *The abilities of man.* New York: Macmillan.

Spelke, E. (2005). Sex differences in intrinsic aptitude for mathematics and science? A critical review. *American Psychologist, 60,* 950–958.

Spencer, M., & Dornbusch, S. M. (1990). Challenges in studying minority youth. In S. Feldman & G. Elliot (Eds.), *At the threshold: The developing adolescent* (pp. 255–276). Cambridge, MA: Harvard University Press.

Spencer, M., Steele, C., & Quinn, D. (1999). Stereotype threat and women's math performance. *Journal of Experimental Social Psychology, 35,* 4–28.

Spencer, M. B. (2006). Revisiting the 1990 *Special Issue on Minority Children*: An editorial perspective 15 years later. *Child Development, 5,* 1149–1154.

Spencer, M. B., Fegley, S. G., & Harpalani, V. (2003). A theoretical and empirical examination of identity as coping: Linking coping resource to the self-processes of African American youth. *Applied Developmental Science, 7,* 181–188.

Spencer, M. B., Harpalani, V., Cassidy, E., Jacobs, C., Donde, S., Gross, T. et al. (2006). Understanding vulnerability and resilience from a normative development perspective: Implications for racially and ethnically diverse youth. In D. Chicchetti & E. Cohen (Eds.), *Handbook of development and psychopathology* (pp. 627–672). New York: John Wiley.

Spencer, M. B., Noll, E., Stoltzfus, J., & Harpalani, V. (2001). Identity and school adjustment: Revisiting the "acting white" assumption. *Educational Psychologist, 36,* 21–30.

Spiegel, D. L. (1992). Blending whole language and systematic direct instruction. *The Reading Teacher, 46,* 38–47.

Spinks, S. (2005). Adolescent brains are works in progress: Here's why. Frontline: Inside the teenage brain: Work in progress. Retrieved August 2005 from http://www.pbs.org/wgbh/pages/frontline/shows/teenbrain/work/adolescent.html.

Spring, J. (1994). *The American school. 1642–1993* (3rd ed.). New York: McGraw-Hill.

Springer, S. P., & Deutsch, G. (1993). *Left brain, right brain.* New York: Freeman.

Sroufe, L. A. (1982). Attachment and the roots of competence. In H. E. Fitzgerald & T. H. Carr (Eds.), *Human development: Annual editions.* Guilford, CA: Duskin.

Sroufe, L. A. (1983). Infant-caregiver attachment and patterns of adaptation in preschool. The roots of maladaptation and competence. In M. Perlmutter (Ed.), *Minnesota symposium in child psychology* (Vol. 16, pp. 41–81). Minneapolis: University of Minnesota Press.

Sroufe, L. A. (1989). Pathways to adaptation and maladaption: Psychopathology as developmental deviation. In D. Cicchetti (Ed.), *Rochester Symposium on Developmental Psychopathology, Vol. 1: The emergence of a discipline* (pp. 13–40). Hillsdale, NJ: Lawrence Erlbaum.

Sroufe, L. A. (1996). *Emotional development: The organization of emotional life in early years.* New York: Cambridge Press.

Sroufe, L. A., Fox, N. E., & Pancake, V. R. (1983). Attachment and dependency in developmental perspective. *Child Development, 54,* 1615–1627.

Stack, C. B., & Burton, L. (1993). Kinscripts. *Journal of Comparative Family Studies, 24,* 157–170.

Stahl, S. A. (1992). Saying the "p" word: Nine guidelines for exemplary phonics instruction. *The Reading Teacher, 45,* 618–625.

Stanovich, K. E. (1986). Matthew effects in reading: Some consequences of individual differences in the acquisition of literacy. *Reading Research Quarterly, 16,* 360–407.

Steele, C. (1992). Race and the schooling of black Americans. *The Atlantic Monthly, 269*(4), 68–78.

Steele, C. (1997). A threat in the air: How stereotypes shape intellectual ability and performance. *American Psychologist, 52,* 613–629.

Steele, C., & Aronson, J. (1995). Stereotype threat and the intellectual test performance of African Americans. *Journal of Personality and Social Psychology, 69*(5), 797–811.

Steinberg, L. (1996). *Beyond the classroom: Why school reform has failed and what parents need to do.* New York: Simon & Schuster.

Steinberg, L., Darling, N., & Fletcher, A. C. (1995). Authoritative parenting and adolescent adjustment: An ecological journey. In P. Moen, G. H. Elder, & K. Lüscher (Eds.), *Examining lives in context: Perspectives on the ecology of human development* (pp. 423–466). Washington, DC: American Psychological Association.

Steinberg, L., Dornbusch, S. M., & Brown, B. B. (1992). Ethnic differences in adolescent achievement. An ecological perspective. *American Psychologist, 47,* 723–729.

Steinberg, Z., & Knitzer, J. (1992). Classrooms for emotionally and behaviorally disturbed students: Facing the challenge. *Behavioral Disorders, 17,* 145–156.

Sternberg, R. (1984). How can we teach intelligence? *Educational Leadership,* 38–48.

Sternberg, R. (1985). *Beyond IQ: A triarchic theory of human intelligence.* New York: Cambridge University Press.

Sternberg, R., & Ben-Zeev, T. (2001). *Complex cognition: The psychology of human thought.* New York: Oxford University Press.

Sternberg, R., & Clinkenbeard, P. (1995). The triarchic model applied to identifying, teaching, and assessing gifted children. *Roeper Review, 17,* 225–236.

Sternberg, R., & Grigorenko, E. (2000). *Teaching for successful intelligence: To increase student learning and achievement.* Arlington Heights, IL: A&B SkyLight.

Sternberg, R., & Grigorenko, E. (2002). *Dynamic testing: The nature and measurement of learning potential.* Cambridge University Press.

Sternberg, R., Grigorenko, E., & Kidd, K. (2005). Intelligence, race, and genetics. *American Psychologist, 60,* 46–59.

Stevenson, H. W., Chen, C., & Uttal, D. (1990). Beliefs and achievement: A study of black, white, and Hispanic children. *Child Development, 61,* 508–523.

Stevenson, H. W., & Lee, S. (1990). Contexts of achievement: A study of American, Chinese, and Japanese children. *Monographs of the Society for Research in Child Development, 55*(1–2, Serial No. 221).

Stevenson, H. W., & Sigler, J. W. (1992). *The learning gap: Why our schools are failing and what we can learn from Japanese and Chinese education.* New York: Simon & Schuster.

Stigler, J., Gallimore. R., & Hiebert, J. (2000). Using video surveys to compare classrooms and teaching across cultures: Examples and lessons for the TIMSS video studies. *Educational Psychologist, 35,* 87–100.

Stigler, J., Gonzales, P., Kawanka, T., Knoll, S., & Serrano, A. (1999). *The TIMSS videotape classroom study: Methods and findings from an exploratory research project on eighth-grade mathematics instruction in Germany, Japan, and the United States.* Washington, DC: U.S. Department of Education, National Center for Educational Statistics.

Stigler, J., & Hiebert, J. (1999). *The teaching gap: Best ideas from the world's teachers for improving education in the classroom.* New York: Free Press.

Stiglitz, E. (1990). Caught between two worlds: The impact of a child on the lesbian couple's relationship. *Women and Therapy, 10,* 99–116.

Stiles, J., Bates, E. A., Thai, D., Trauner, D., & Reilly, J. (1999). Linguistic, cognitive, and affective development in children with prenatal and perinatal focal brain injury: A ten-year overview from the San Diego Longitudinal Project. In C. Rovee-Collier (Eds.), *Advances in infant research* (Vol. 13), Norwood, NJ: Ablex.

Stipek, D. (1984). Sex differences in children's attributions for success and failure on math and spelling tests. *Sex Roles, 11,* 969–981.

Stipek, D. (1993). *Motivation to learn: From theory to practice* (2nd ed.). Needham Heights, MA: Allyn & Bacon.

Stipek, D. (2002). Good instruction is motivating. In A. Wigfield & J. S. Eccles (Eds.), *Development of achievement motivation* (pp. 310–334). New York: Elsevier Press.

Stipek, D., Feiler, R., Byler, P., Ryan, R., Milburn, S., & Salmon, J. (1998). Good beginnings: What difference does the program make in preparing young children for school? *Journal of Applied Developmental Psychology, 19,* 41–66.

Stipek, D., Feiler, R., Daniels, D., & Milburn, S. (1995). Effects of different instructional approaches on young children's achievement and motivation. *Child Development, 66,* 209–223.

Stipek D., & MacIver, D. (1989). Developmental change in children's assessment of intellectual competence. *Child Development, 60,* 521–538.

Stipek, D., Recchia, S., McClintic, S. (1992). Self-evaluation in young children. *Monographs of the Society for Research in Child Development, 57*(1, Serial No. 226).

Stoddart, T., & Turiel, E. (1985). Children's concepts of cross-gender activities. *Child Development, 56,* 1241–1252.

Stone, J. L., & Church, J. (1957). *Childhood and adolescence: A psychology of the growing person.* New York: Random House.

Storch, S., & Whitehurst, G., (2001). The role of family and home in the literacy development of children from low-income backgrounds. In P. Britto & J. Brooks-Gunn (Eds.), *The role of family literacy environment in promoting young children's emerging literacy skills. New directions for child and adolescent development, 92* (pp. 53–72). San Francisco: Jossey-Bass.

Stormshak, E. A., Bierman, K. L., McMahon, R. J., Lengua, L. J., & The Conduct Problems Prevention Research Group. (2000). Parenting practices and child disruptive behavior problems in early elementary school. *Journal of Clinical and Child Psychology, 29,* 17–29.

Stranger, J. D. F., & Gridina, N. (1999). Media in the home 1999: The fourth annual survey of parents and children.

Philadelphia: Annenbery Public Policy Center, University of Pennsylvania.

Strauss, C., Smith, K., Frame, C., & Forehand, R. (1985). Personal and interpersonal characteristics associated with childhood obesity. *Journal of Pediatric Psychology, 10,* 337–343.

Strauss, M. A. (1994). *Beating the devil out of them. Corporal punishment in American families.* New York: Lexington Books.

Strauss, M. A., & Stewart, J. H. (1999). Corporal punishment by American parents: National data on prevalence, chronicity, severity, and duration, in relation to child and family characteristics. *Clinical Child and Family Psychology Review, 2*(2), 55–70.

Strichart, S. S. (1993). *Teaching study strategies to students with learning disabilities.* Boston: Allyn & Bacon.

Strickland, D. S., & Morrow, L. M. (1989). Developing skills: An emergent literacy perspective. *The Reading Teacher, 43,* 82–83.

Stronge, J. H., & Reed-Victor, E. (2000). *Educating homeless children.* Larchmont, NY: Eye on Education.

Stuhlman, M., & Pianta, R. (2002). Teachers' narratives about their relationships with children: Association with behavior in classrooms. *School Psychology Review, 31,* 148–164.

Stuhlman, M., & Pianta, R. (2004). Teachers' narratives about their relationships with children: Association with behavior in classrooms. *School Psychology Review, 31,* 148–164.

Suarez-Orozco, C., & Suarez-Orozco, M. M. (1994). The cultural psychology of Hispanic immigrants. In T. Weaver (Ed.), *Handbook of Hispanic cultures in the United States, Vol. 2: Anthropology* (pp. 129–146). Houston, TX: Arte Publico Press.

Subotnik, R. (2006). A developmental view of giftedness: From *being to doing.* APA Center for Gifted Education Policy. Retrieved August 2006 from http://www.apa.org/ed/view_giftedness.pdf.

Subrahmanyam, K., Kraut, R. E., Greenfield, P. M., & Gross, E. F. (2000). The impact of home computer use on children's activities and development. *The Future of Children. Children and Computer Technology, Vol. 10,* 123–144.

Sue, S., & Okazaki, S. (1990). Asian-American educational achievements: A phenomenon in search of an explanation. *American Psychologist, 45,* 913–920.

Suina, J. H., & Smolkin, L. B. (1994). From natal culture to school culture to dominant society culture: Supporting transitions for Pueblo Indian students. In P. M. Greenfield & R. R. Cocking (Eds.), *Cross-cultural roots of minority child development* (pp. 115–130). Hillsdale, NJ: Erlbaum.

Sullivan, M. L. (1993). Culture and class as determinants of out-of-wedlock childbearing and poverty during late adolescence. *Journal of Research on Adolescence, 3,* 295–316.

Summerville, M., & Kaslow, N. (1993, March). Racial differences in psychological symptoms, cognitive style, and family functioning in suicidal adolescents. Paper presented at the biennial meeting for the Society for Research in Child Development, New Orleans, LA.

Supple, A. J., Ghazarian, S. R., Frabutt, J. M., Plunkett, S. W., & Sands, T. (2006). Contextual influences on Latino adolescents' ethnic identity and academic outcomes. *Child Development, 77,* 1427–1433.

Suzuki, L., & Valencia, R. (1997). Race-ethnicity and measured intelligence: Educational implications. *American Psychologist, 52,* 1103–1114.

Szalacha, L. A. (2003). Safer sexuality diversity climates: Lessons learned from an evaluation of Massachusetts Safe Schools Program for gay and lesbian students. *American Journal of Education, 110,* 58–88.

Szinovacz, M. (1998). Grandparents today: A demographic profile. *The Gerontologist, 38,* 37–52.

Tajfel, H., & Turner J. (1979). An integrative theory of intergroup conflict. In W. Austin & S. Worchel (Eds.), *The social psychology of intergroup relations* (pp. 94–109). Monterey, CA: Brooks/Cole Publishers.

Tallal, P. (1980). Auditory temporal perception, phonics, and reading disabilities in children. *Brain Language, 9,* 182–198.

Tallal, P. (2003). Language learning disabilities: Integrating research approaches. *Current Directions in Psychological Science, 12,* 206–211.

Tamis-LeMonda, C. S., & Cabrera, N. (1999). Perspectives on father involvement: Research and social policy. *Social Policy Report, 13*(2), 1–26.

Tanaka, J. S., Ebreo, A., Linn, N., & Morera, O. F. (1998). Research methods: The construct validity of self-identity and its psychological implications. In L. C. Lee & N. W. S. Zane (Eds.), *Handbook of*

Asian American psychology (pp. 21–79). Thousand Oaks, CA: Sage.

Tanner, J. (1978). *Fetus into man: Physical growth from conception to maturity.* Cambridge, MA: Harvard University Press.

Tasker, F. L., & Golombok, S. (1997). *Growing up in a lesbian family: Effects on child development.* New York: Guilford Press.

Taylor, B. M., Fryre, B. L., & Marayama, G. H. (1990). Time spent reading and reading growth. *American Education Research Journal, 27,* 351–372.

Taylor, D. L. (2004/2005). "Not just boring stories": Reconsidering the gender gap for boys. *Journal of Adolescent and Adult Literacy, 48*(4), 290–298.

Taylor, R. L. (1998). Black American families. In R. L. Taylor (Ed.), *Minority families in the United States* (pp. 19–45). Upper Saddle River, NJ: Prentice Hall.

Tchudi, S., & Yates, J. (1983). *Teaching writing in the content areas: Senior high school.* Washington, DC: National Education Association.

Teachman, J. D., & Paasch, K. M. (1994). Financial impact of divorce on children and their families. *The Future of Children, 4,* 63–83.

Teale, W., & Sulzby, E. (Eds.), (1986). *Emergent literacy.* Norwood, NJ: Ablex.

Teale, W. H. (1978). Positive environments for learning to read: What studies of early readers tell us. *Language Arts, 55,* 922–932.

Templeton, S., & Spivey, E. (1980). The concept of word in young children as a function of level of cognitive development. *Research in the Teaching of English, 14,* 265–278.

Terman, L. (1925). *Genetic studies of genius, Vol. 1: Mental and physical traits of a thousand gifted children.* Stanford, CA: Stanford University Press.

Terman, L., & Oden, M. H. (1959). *Genetic studies of genius, Vol. 4: The gifted group at midlife.* Stanford, CA: Stanford University Press.

Tharp, R., & Gallimore, R. (1988). *Rousing minds to life: Teaching, learning, and schooling in social context.* New York: Cambridge University Press.

Tharp, R. G. (1989). Psychocultural variables and constants: Effects on teaching and learning in schools. *American Psychologist, 44,* 349–359.

Tharp, R. G. (1994). Intergroup differences among Native Americans in socialization and child cognition: An ethnogenetic analysis. In P. M. Greenfield & R. R. Cocking (Eds.), *Cross-cultural roots of* *minority child development* (pp. 87–105). Hillsdale, NJ: Erlbaum.

Thomas, A., & Chess, S. (1977). *Temperament and development.* New York: Brunner/Mazel.

Thomas, A., Chess, S., & Birch, H. C. (1968). *Temperament and behavior disorders in children.* New York: New York University Press.

Thomas, J. R. (1984). Children's motor skill development. In J. R. Thomas (Ed.), *Motor development during childhood and adolescence* (pp. 91–104). Minneapolis: Burgess.

Thompson, M. (2006). Raising Cain: Boys in focus: Meet the experts. Retrieved August 2006 from http://www.pbs.org/ opg/rasiningcain/experts.html.

Thompson, R., & Nelson, C. (2001). Developmental science and the media: Early brain development. *American Psychologist, 56,* 5–15.

Thompson, R. A. (1998). Early brain development and social policy. *Policy and Practice in Public Human Services, 56,* 66–77.

Thompson, R. A. (2000). The legacy of early attachments. *Child Development, 71*(1), 145–152.

Thompson, R. A., & Laible, D. J. (1999). Noncustodial parents. In M. E. Lamb (Ed.), *Parenting and child development in "nontraditional" families* (pp. 103–123). Mahwah, NJ: Erlbaum.

Thorndike, R., Hagen, E., & Sattler, J. (1986). *The Stanford-Binet Intelligence Scale: Guide for administering and scoring* (4th ed.). Chicago: Riverside Publishing.

Tigner, S. (2002). Harry Potter and the good life. Center for the Advancement of Ethics and Character (CAEC), Boston University. Retrieved July 2005 from http://www. bu.edu/education/caec/files/potter.htm.

Timmer, S. G., Eccles, J., & O'Brien, K. (1985). How children use time. In F. Juster & F. P. Stafford (Eds.), *Time, goods, and well-being* (pp. 353–382). Ann Arbor, MI: Institute for Social Research

Tonniges, T., & Leavitt, C. (2003). Preventive health care in early childhood and throughout the life span. In M. Bornstein, L. Davidson, C. Keyes, & K. Moore (Eds.), *Well-being: Positive development across the life course* (pp. 51–64). Mahwah, NJ: Erlbaum.

Torff, B., & Sternberg, R. (2001). Intuitive conceptions among learners and teachers. In B. Torff & R. Sternberg (Eds.),

Understanding and teaching the intuitive mind (pp. 1–3). Mahwah, NJ: Erlbaum.

Tower, C. C. (1992). *The role of educators in the prevention and treatment of child abuse and neglect.* Washington, DC: U.S. Department of Health and Human Services.

Treiman, R., & Bourassa, D. (2000). The development of spelling skill. *Topics in Language Disorders, 20,* 1–18.

Triandis, H. (1990). Cross-cultural studies of individualism and collectivism. In J. Berman (Ed.), *Nebraska symposium on motivation, Vol. 37: Cross-cultural perspectives* (pp. 41–133). Lincoln: University of Nebraska Press.

Triandis, H. (1995). *Individualism and collectivism.* Boulder, CO: Westview.

Trickett, P. K., Aber, J. L., Carlson, V., & Cicchetti, D. (1991). Relationship of socioeconomic status to the etiology and developmental sequence of physical child abuse. *Developmental Psychology, 27,* 148–158.

Troy, M., & Sroufe, L. A. (1987). Victimization among preschoolers: Role of attachment relationship history. *Journal of the American Academy of Child and Adolescent Psychiatry, 26*(2), 166–172.

Tudge, J. (1993). Processes and consequences of peer collaboration: A Vygotskian analysis. *Child Development, 63,* 1364–1379.

Tudge, J., & Rogoff, B. (1989). Peer influences on cognitive development: Piagetian and Vygotskian perspectives. In M. H. Bornstein & J. S. Bruner (Eds.), *Interaction in human development* (pp. 17–40). Hillsdale, NJ: Erlbaum.

Turiel, E. (1998). The development of morality. In W. Damon (Series Ed.) & N. Eisenberg (Vol. Ed.), *Handbook of child psychology: Vol. 3. Social, emotional, and personality development* (5th ed., pp. 863–932). New York: John Wiley.

Turiel, E. (2002). *The culture of morality: Social development, context, and conflict.* Cambridge, England: Cambridge University Press.

Turiel, E. (2006). The development of morality. In W. Damon & R. M. Lerner (Editors-in-Chief) & N. Eisenberg (Vol. Ed.), *Handbook of child psychology. Vol. 3. Social, emotional, and personality development* (pp. 789–857). New York: John Wiley.

Twenge, J. M., & Crocker, J. (2002). Race and self-esteem: Meta-analyses comparing

whites, blacks, Hispanics, Asians, and American Indians and comment on Gray-Little and Hafdahl. *Psychological Bulletin, 128*(3), 371–408.

United Nations Foundation. (2001, February). *A league table of child deaths by injury in rich countries.* Innocenti Report Card, 2. Florence, Italy: UNICEF Innocenti Research Centre.

United States Department of Agriculture. (2006). MyPyramid for Kids. Retrieved July 2006 from http://www. mypyramid.gov.

Urban Institute. (2000). One in five U.S. children are children of immigrants. Available online at http://www.urban. org/news/press/CP_000911.html.

Urdan, T., Ryan, A. M., Anderman, E. M., & Gheen, H. H. (2002). Goals, goal structures, and avoidance behaviors. In C. Midgley (Ed.), *Goals, goal structures, and patterns of adaptive learning.* Hillsdale, NJ: Erlbaum.

U.S. Department of Education, Planning and Evaluation Service, Elementary and Secondary Education Division. (2002). *The Education for Homeless Children and Youth Program: Learning to succeed.* Washington, DC: Author.

U.S. Census Bureau. (1993a). *We the Americans: Asians* (Series WE-3). Washington, DC: U.S. Government Printing Office.

U.S. Census Bureau. (1993b). *We the First Americans* (Series WE-5). Washington, DC: U.S. Government Printing Office.

U.S. Census Bureau. (1999). *Statistical abstract of the United States* (119th ed.). Washington, DC: U.S. Government Printing Office.

U.S. Census Bureau. (2000a). *The Asian and Pacific Islander population in the United States: March 1999* (Current Population Reports, Series P20-529). Washington, DC: U.S. Government Printing Office.

U.S. Census Bureau. (2000b). *Child support for custodial mothers and fathers: 1997* (Current Population Reports, Series P60-212). Washington, DC: U.S. Government Printing Office.

U.S. Census Bureau. (2000c). *The Hispanic population in the United States: March 1999* (Current Population Reports, Series P20-527). Washington, DC: U.S. Government Printing Office.

U.S. Census Bureau. (2000d). *Poverty in the United States: 1999* (Current Population Reports, Series P60-210). Washington, DC: U.S. Government Printing Office.

U.S. Census Bureau. (2002, February). *The American Indian and Alaska Native Population: 2000*. (Census Bureau Special Report C2KBR/01-15). Washington, DC: U.S. Government Printing Office.

U.S. Census Bureau. (2004). *Children and the households they live in: 2000*. (Census 2000 Special Reports, CENSR-14). Washington, DC: U.S. Government Printing Office.

U.S. Census Bureau. (2005a). *Who's minding the kids? Child care arrangements: Winter 2002*. (Current Population Reports, P70-101). Washington, DC: U.S. Government Printing Office.

U.S. Census Bureau. (2005b, October). *Computer and Internet use in the United States: 2003*. (Current Population Reports P23-208). Washington, DC: U.S. Government Printing Office.

U.S. Centers for Disease Control and Prevention. (1996). Guidelines for school health programs to promote lifelong healthy eating. *Morbidity and Mortality Weekly Report, 45,* 3.

U.S. Department of Education. (1991). *The condition of bilingual education in the nation: A report to the Congress and the president*. Washington, DC: U.S. Department of Education.

U.S. Department of Education. (1999). Twenty-first annual report to Congress on the implementation of the Individuals with Disabilities Education Act. Washington, DC: Author.

U.S. Department of Health and Human Services. (2000a). *Child maltreatment 1998: Reports from the states to the National Child Abuse and Neglect Data System*. Washington, DC: U.S. Government Printing Office.

U.S. Department of Health and Human Services. (2000b). *Trends in the well-being of America's children and youth 2000*. Washington, DC: Author.

U.S. Department of Health and Human Services. (2003). *Trends in the well-being of America's children and youth 2003*. Washington, DC: Author.

U.S. Department of Labor & U.S. Department of Education. (1988). *The bottom line: Basic skills in the workplace*. Washington, DC: Office of Public Information, Employment and Training Administration, U.S. Department of Labor.

Vacca, J. A., Vacca, R., & Grove, M. K. (1991). *Learning to read* (2nd ed.). New York: HarperCollins.

Vacca, J. A., Vacca, R. T., & Grove, M. K. (1995). *Reading and learning to read* (2nd ed.). New York: HarperCollins.

Vacca, R. T., & Rasinski, T. V. (1992). *Case studies in whole language*. Fort Worth, TX: Harcourt Brace Jovanovich.

Valencia, S. (1990). Assessment: A portfolio approach to classroom reading assessment: The whys, whats, and hows. *The Reading Teacher, 44,* 338–340.

Van den Boom, D. C., & Hoeksma, J. B. (1994). The effect of infant irritability on mother-infant interaction: A growth-curve analysis. *Developmental Psychology, 30,* 590.

Vander Zanden, J. (1993). *Human development* (5th ed.). New York: McGraw-Hill.

Vaughn, B., & Langlois, J. (1983). Physical attractiveness as a correlate of peer status and social competence in preschool children. *Developmental Psychology, 19,* 561–567.

Vaughn, S., & Elbaum, B. (1999). The self-concepts and friendships of students with learning disabilities: A developmental perspective. In R. Gallimore, L. P. Bernheime, D. L. MacMillian, D. L. Speece, & S. Vaughn (Eds.), *Developmental perspectives on children with high-incidence disabilities* (pp. 81–110). Mahwah, NJ: Erlbaum.

Viadero, D. (2005, May). Long-awaited study shows "Success for All" gains. *Education Week, 24,* S3. Retrieved June 2005 from http://www.edweek.org.

Volterra, V., & Taeschner, T. (1978). The acquisition and development of language by bilingual children. *Journal of Child Language 5,* 311–326.

von Karolyi, C., Winner, E., Gray, W., & Sherman, G. (2003). Dyslexia linked to talent: Global visual-spatial ability. *Brain and Language, 85,* 427–431.

Voyer, D., Voyer, S., & Bryden, M. P. (1995). Magnitude of sex differences in spatial abilities: A meta-analysis and consideration of critical variables. *Psychological Bulletin, 117,* 250–270.

Vurpillot, E. (1968). The development of scanning strategies and their relation to visual differentiation. *Journal of Experimental Child Psychology, 6,* 632–650.

Vygotsky, L. S. (1962). *Thought and language*. Cambridge, MA: MIT Press.

Vygotsky, L. S. (1978). *Mind in society: The development of higher psychological processes*. Cambridge, MA: Harvard University Press.

Vygotsky, L. S. (1987). Thinking and speech. In *The collected works of L. S. Vygotsky, Vol. 1: Problems of general psychology* (N. Minick, trans.). New York: Plenum Press.

Wakschlag, L. S., & Hans, S. L. (1999). Relation of maternal responsiveness during infancy to the development of behavior problems in high-risk youths. *Developmental Psychology, 35,* 569–579.

Walker, D. (1995). School violence prevention. *Eric Digest, Number 94*. Eugene, OR: ERIC Clearinghouse on Educational Management.

Walker-Andrews, A. S. (1997). Infants' perception of expressive behavior: Differentiation of multimodal information. *Psychological Bulletin, 121,* 437–456.

Wallerstein, J. S., Corbin, S. B., & Lewis, J. M. (1988). Children of divorce: A 10-year study. In E. M. Hetherington & J. D. Arasteh (Eds.), *Impact of divorce, single parenting, and stepparenting on children*. Hillsdale, NJ: Erlbaum.

Wallerstein, J. S., Lewis, J. M., & Blakeslee, S. (2000). *The unexpected legacy of divorce: A 25-year landmark study*. New York: Hyperion.

Ward, L. M. (1995). Talk about sex: Common themes about sexuality in prime-time television programs children and adolescents view most. *Journal of Youth and Adolescence, 24,* 595–616.

Warren, C., Harris, W., & Kann, L. (1995). *Adolescent health: State of the nation—pregnancy, sexually transmitted diseases and related risk behaviors among U.S. adolescents* (Monograph Series No. 2). Atlanta: Centers for Disease Control and Prevention, Division of Adolescent and School Health, Surveillance and Evaluation Research Branch.

Wartella, E., Caplovitz, A., & Lee, J. (2004). From Baby Einstein to Leapfrog, from Doom to The Sims, from instant messaging to Internet chat rooms: Public interest in the role of interactive media in children's lives. *SRCD Social Policy Report, 18,* 3–17.

Wartella, E. A., & Jennings, N. (2000). Children and computers: New technology—old concerns. *Future of children. Children and Computer Technology, Vol. 10,* 31–42.

Washington, V. (1988). The black mother in the United States: History, theory, research, and issues. In B. Birns & D. F. Hay (Eds.), *The different faces of motherhood* (pp. 185–213). New York: Plenum.

Waterman, A. (1982). Identity development from adolescence to adulthood: An extension of theory and review of research. *Developmental Psychology, 18,* 341–358.

Waterman, A. (1999a). Identity, the identity statuses, and identify status development: A contemporary statement. *Developmental Review, 19,* 591–621.

Waterman, A. (1999b). Issues of identity formation revisited: United States and the Netherlands. *Developmental Review, 19,* 462–479.

Waterman, A. S. (1997). An overview of service learning and the role of research and evaluation in service-learning programs. In A. S. Waterman (Ed.), *Service learning* (pp. 4–24), Mahwah, NJ: Erlbaum.

Watt, D. (2002). Assisting performance: A case study from a primary science classroom. *Cambridge Journal of Education, 32,* 165–182.

Weare, K. (2004). *Developing the emotionally literate school.* Thousand Oaks, CA: Sage Publications Inc.

Weaver, P., & Schonhoff, F. (1984). *Subskill and holistic approaches to reading instruction* (3rd ed.). New York: Longman.

Weaver-Hightower, M. (2003). The "boy turn" in research on gender and education. *Review of Educational Research, 73*(4), 471–498.

Wechsler, D. (1958). *The measurement and appraisal of adult intelligence* (4th ed.). Baltimore: Williams & Wilkins.

Wechsler, D. (1991). *Wechsler intelligence scale for children* (3rd ed.). San Antonio: Psychological Corporation.

Weglinsky, H. (1998). *Does it compute? The relationship between educational technology and student achievement in mathematics.* Princeton, NJ: ETS Policy Information Center. Available online at http://www.ets.org/research/pic/technology.html.

Wehlage, G., & Rutter, R. (1986). Dropping out: How much do schools contribute to the problem? *Teachers College Record, 87,* 374–392.

Wehlage, G., Rutter, R., Smith, G., Lesko, N., & Fernandez, R. (1989). *Reducing the risk: Schools as communities of support.* New York: Falmer Press.

Weiler, J. (1998). The athletic experiences of ethnically diverse girls. *ERIC/CUE Digest.* New York: ERIC Clearhouse in Urban Education.

Weiner, B. (1979). A theory of motivation for some classroom experiences. *Journal of Educational Psychology, 71,* 3–25.

Weiner, B. (1986). *An attributional theory of motivation and emotion.* New York: Springer-Verlag.

Weinstein, C. (1998). "I want to be nice, but I have to be mean": Exploring prospective teachers' conceptions of caring and order. *Teaching and Teacher Education, 14,* 153–163.

Weinstein, R. (1983). Student perceptions of schooling. *Elementary School Journal, 83,* 287–312.

Weinstein, R. (2002). *Reaching higher: The power of expectations in schooling.* Cambridge, MA: Harvard University Press.

Weir, R. H. (1962). *Language in the crib.* The Hague, The Netherlands: Mouton.

Weisner, T. (2002). Ecocultural understanding of children's developmental pathways. *Human Development, 45,* 275–281.

Weisner, T. (2005). *Discovering successful pathways in children's development: New methods in the study of childhood and family life.* Chicago: University of Chicago Press.

Weisner, T. S., & Wilson-Mitchell, J. E. (1990). Nonconventional family life-styles and sex-typing in six-year olds. *Child Development, 61*(6), 1915–1933.

Weiss, H., Dearing, E., Mayer, E., Kreider, H., McCartney, K. (2005). Family educational involvement: Who can afford it and what does it afford? In C. Cooper, C. Coll, T. Bartko, H. Davis, & C. Chatman (Eds.), *Developmental pathways through middle childhood: Rethinking contexts and diversity as resources* (pp. 17–39). Hillside, NJ: Erlbaum.

Weiss, I., Banilower, E., McMahon, K., & Smith, P. (2001). *Report on the 2000 national survey of science and mathematics education.* Chapel Hill, NC: Horizon Research.

Weiss, M. J., & Hagen, R. (1988). A key to literacy: Kindergarteners' awareness of the functions of print. *The Reading Teacher, 41,* 574–578.

Weissberg, R. P., Caplan, M. Z., & Bennetto, L. (1988). *The Yale-New Haven social problem-solving (SPS) program for young adolescents.* New Haven, CT: Yale University Press.

Wellman, H. (1988). The early development of memory strategies. In F. Weinert & M. Perlmutter (Eds.), *Memory development: Universal changes and individual differences* (pp. 3–29). Hillsdale, NJ: Erlbaum.

Wellman, H., & Estes, D. (1986). Early understanding of mental entities: A reexamination of childhood realism. *Child Development, 57,* 910–923.

Wellman, H., & Gelman, S. (1998). Enabling constraints for cognitive development and learning: Domain specificity and epigenesis. In W. Damon (Series Ed.), D. Kuhn (Vol. Ed.), & R. Siegler (Vol. Ed.), *Handbook of child psychology, Vol. 2: Cognition, perception, and language* (5th ed., pp. 575–630).

Wellman, H. M. (1990). *The child's theory of mind.* Cambridge, MA: MIT Press.

Wells, G. (1985). *Language development in the preschool years.* New York: Cambridge University Press.

Wells, G. (1986). *The meaning makers: Children learning language and using language to learn.* Portsmouth, NH: Heinemann.

Wenglinsky, H. (1998). *Does it compute? The relationship between educational technology and student achievement.* Princeton, NJ: Educational Testing Service.

Wentzel, K. (1996). Social goals and social relationships as motivators of school adjustment. In J. Juvonen & K. R. Wentzel (Eds.), *Social motivation: Understanding children's school adjustment* (pp. 226–248). New York: Cambridge University Press.

Wentzel, K. (1997). Student motivation in middle school: The role of perceived pedagogical caring. *Journal of Educational Psychology, 89,* 411–419.

Wentzel, K. (1998). Social support and adjustment tin middle school: The role of parents, teachers, and peers. *Journal of Educational Psychology, 90,* 202–209.

Wentzel, K. (2002). Are effective teachers like good parents? Teaching styles and student adjustment in early adolescence. *Child Development, 73,* 287–301.

Wentzel, K., & Caldwell, K. (1997). Friendship, peer acceptance, and group membership: Relations to academic achievement in middle school. *Child Development, 68,* 1198–1209.

Werner, E. E. (1999). Risk and protective factors in the lives of children with high-incidence disabilities. In R. Gallimore, L. P. Bernheimer, D. L. MacMillan, D. Speece, & S. Vaughn (Eds.), *Developmental perspectives on children with high-incidence disabilities* (pp. 15–32). Mahwah, NJ: Erlbaum.

Werner, E. E., & Smith, R. S. (1992). *Vulnerable but invincible: A study of resilient children.* New York: McGraw-Hill.

Wertsch, J. (1985). *Vygotsky and the social formation of mind.* Cambridge, MA: Harvard University Press.

Wertsch, J. (1999). Cognitive development. In M. Bennett (Ed.), *Developmental psychology: Achievement and prospects* (pp. 309–321). Philadelphia: Psychology Press.

Wertsch, J., & Tulviste, P. (1992). L. S. Vygotsky and contemporary developmental psychology. *Developmental Psychology, 28,* 548–557.

Wesley College Center for Research on Women. (1992). *American Association of University Women Report: How schools shortchange girls.* Washington, DC: AAUW.

White, R. W. (1959). Motivation reconsidered: The concept of competence. *Psychological Review, 66,* 297–335.

Whitehurst, G. J., Lonigan, C. J. (1998). Child development and emergent literacy. *Child Development, 68,* 848–872.

Wierson, M., & Forehand, R. (1992). Family stressors and adolescent functioning: A consideration of models for early and middle adolescents. *Behavior Therapy, 23,* 671–688.

Wigfield, A. (1994). Expectancy-value theory of achievement motivation: A developmental perspective. *Educational Psychology Review, 6,* 49–78.

Wigfield, A. (2000). Facilitating children's reading motivation. In L. Baker, M. J. Dreher, & J. Guthrie (Eds.), *Engaging young readers.* New York: Guilford Press.

Wigfield, A., Eccles, J., Mac Iver, D., Reuman, D., & Midgley, C. (1991). Transitions at early adolescence: Changes in children's domain-specific self-perceptions and general self-esteem across the transition to junior high school. *Developmental Psychology, 27,* 552–565.

Wigfield, A., Eccles, J. S., Schiefele, U., Roeser, R., & Davis-Kean, P. (2006). Development of achievement motivation. In N. Esienberg (Ed.), *Handbook of child psychology. Volume 3. Social, emotional and personality development* (6th ed., pp. 933–1002). Hoboken, NJ: John Wiley.

Wigfield, A., & Guthrie, J. (1997). Relations of children's motivation for reading to the amount and breadth of their reading. *Journal of Educational Psychology, 89,* 420–432.

Wigfield, A., & Karpathian, M. (1991). Who am I and what can I do? Children's self-concepts and motivation in achievement situations. *Educational Psychologist, 26,* 233–261.

Williams, C., & Bybee, J. (1994). What do children feel guilty about? Developmental and gender differences. *Developmental Psychology, 30,* 617–623.

Williams, E., Radin, N., & Allegro, T. (1992). Sex-role attitudes of adolescents raised primarily by their fathers. *Merrill-Palmer Quarterly, 38,* 457–476.

Williams, W., Blythe, T., White, N., Li, J., Gardner, H., & Sternberg, R. (2002). Practical intelligence for school: Developing metacognitive sources of achievement in adolescence. *Developmental Review, 22,* 162–210.

Williams, W., & Ceci, S. (1997). Are American becoming more or less alike? Trends in race, class, and ability differences in intelligence. *American Psychologist, 52,* 1226–1235.

Willis, W. (1992). Families with African American roots. In E. W. Lynch & M. J. Hanson (Eds.), *Developing cross-cultural competence* (pp. 121–150). Baltimore, MD: Paul H. Brookes Publishing Company.

Wimmer, H., & Perner, J. (1983). Beliefs about beliefs: Representation and constraining function of wrong beliefs in children's understanding of deception. *Cognition, 13,* 103–128.

Winner, E. (1996). *Gifted children: Myths and realities.* New York: Basic Books.

Winner, E. (2000). The origins and ends of giftedness. *American Psychologist, 55,* 159–169.

Wolf, N. (1991). *The beauty myth: How images of beauty are used against women.* New York: William Morrow.

Wolfe, D. P. (1989, April). Portfolio assessment: Sampling student work. *Educational Leadership,* pp. 35–39.

Wong, C., Eccles, J. S., & Sameroff, A. (2003). The influence of ethnic discrimination and ethnic identification on African American adolescents' school and socioemotional adjustment. *Journal of Personality, 71,* 1197–1232.

Wood, D., Bruner, J. S., & Ross, G. (1976). The role of tutoring in problem solving. *Journal of Child Psychology and Psychiatry, 17,* 89–100.

Wood, J. (1993). The professional development of teachers as facilitators of computer mediated collaborative learning. In T. Nunan (Ed.), *Distance education futures, 11th Biennial Forum ASPESA* (pp. 93–104). Adelaide: University of South Australia.

Wood, T., Cobb, P., & Yackel, E. (1992). Change in learning mathematics: Change in teaching mathematics. In H. Marshall (Ed.), *Redefining student learning: Roots of educational change.* Norwood, NJ: Ablex.

Woodard, E., & Gridina, N. (2000). *Media in the home: The fifth annual survey of parents and children.* Pennsylvania: The Annenberg Public Policy Center of the University of Pennsylvania.

Woods, N. B. (1972). The unsupervised child of the working mother. *Developmental Psychology, 6,* 14–25.

Wrobel, G. D. (1999). The impact of school starting time on family life. *Phi Delta Kappan, 80*(5), 360–365.

Wu, L., & Martinson, B. (1993). Family structure and the risk of premarital birth. *American Sociological Review, 58,* 210–232.

Wyman, P. A., Cowen, E. L., Work, W. C., Hoyt-Meyers, L., Magnus, K. B., & Fagen, D. B. (1999). Caregiving and developmental factors differentiating young at-risk urban children showing resilient versus stress-affected outcomes: A replication and extension. *Child Development, 70,* 645–659.

Xue, Y., & Meisels, S. (2004). Early literacy instructions and learning in kindergarten: Evidence from the early childhood longitudinal study—kindergarten class of 1998–1999. *American Educational Research Journal, 41,* 191–229.

Yaden, D., Rouge, D., & MacGellivency, L. (1999). *Emergent literacy: A polyphony of perspectives.* (Report Number 1-005). Michigan: University of Michigan, Center for the Improvement of Early Reading Achievement.

Yee, D., & Eccles, J. C. (1988). Parent perceptions and attributions for children's math achievement, *Sex Roles, 19,* 317–333.

Yellowbird, M., & Snipp, C. M. (1998). American Indian families. In R. L. Taylor (Ed.), *Minority families in the United States* (pp. 226–248). Upper Saddle River, NJ: Prentice Hall.

Youniss, J. (1989). Parent-adolescent relationships. In W. Damon (Ed.), *Child development today and tomorrow* (pp. 379–392). San Francisco: Jossey-Bass.

Youniss, J., McCellen, J. A., & Strouse, D. (1994). "We're popular, but you are snobs": Adolescents describe their crowds. In R. Montemayor, G. R. Adams, & T. P. Gallota (Eds.), *Personal relationships during adolescence* (pp. 102–122). Thousand Oaks, CA: Sage.

Yussen, S. R., & Bird, J. E. (1979). The development of metacognitive awareness in memory, communication, and attention. *Journal of Experimental Child Psychology, 28,* 502–508.

Zahn-Waxler, C., Radke-Yarrow, M., & King, R. A. (1979). Child-rearing and children's prosocial initiations toward victims of distress. *Child Development, 50,* 319–330.

Zahn-Waxler, C., Radke-Yarrow, M., Wagner, E., & Chapman, M. (1992). Development of concern for others. *Developmental Psychology, 28,* 126–136.

Zaragoza, N., Vaughn, S., & McIntosh, R. (1991). Social skills interventions and children with behavior problems: A review. *Behavioral Disorders, 16,* 260–275.

Zigler, E. (2002). Looking back 40 years and seeing the person with mental retardation as a whole person. In H. Switzky (Ed.), *Personality and motivational differences in persons with mental retardation.* Mahwah, NJ: Erlbaum.

Zigler, E., & Hall, N. (2000). *Child development and social policy: Theory and applications.* Boston: McGraw-Hill.

Zigler, E., & Hall, N. W. (1989). Physical child abuse in America: Past, present, and future. In D. Cicchetti & V. Carlson (Eds.), *Child maltreatment: Theory and research on the causes and consequences of child abuse and neglect.* New York: Cambridge University Press.

Zill, N. (1994). Understanding why children in stepfamilies have more learning and behavior problems than children in nuclear families. In A. Booth & J. Dunn (Eds.), *Stepfamilies: Who benefits? Who does not?* (pp. 97–106). Hillsdale, NJ: Erlbaum.

Zill, N., Morrison, D. R., & Coiro, M. J. (1993). Long-term effects of parental divorce and parent child relationships, adjustment, and achievement in young adulthood. *Journal of Family Psychology, 7,* 91–103.

Zill, N., Nord, C. W., & Loomis, L. S. (1995). *Adolescent time use, risky behavior and outcomes: An analysis on national data.* Rockville, MD: Westat.

Zimmerman, B. J. (1990). Self-regulated learning and academic achievement: An overview. *Educational Psychologist, 25,* 3–18.

Zimmerman, B. J., & Martinez-Pons, M. (1990). Student differences in self-regulated learning: Relating grade, sex, and giftedness to self-efficacy and strategy use. *Journal of Educational Psychology, 82,* 51–59.

Zoccolillo, M. (1993). Gender and the development of conduct disorder. *Development and Psychopathology, 5,* 65–78.

Zuckerman, D. M., & Zuckerman, B. S. (1985). Television's impact on children. *Pediatrics 75,* 233–240.

Zuniga, M. E. (1992). Families with Latino roots. In E. W. Lynch & M. J. Hanson (Eds.), *Developing cross-cultural competence* (pp. 151–179). Baltimore, MD: Paul H. Brookes Publishing Company.

Credits

Photo Credits (Chapter Openers)

Text Credits

CHAPTER 1   Opening vignette, p. 2: From *Case Study Analysis in the Classroom, Becoming a Reflective Teacher*, by Renee Campoy, 2005, Thousand Oaks, CA: Sage Publications. Copyright © 2005. Reprinted by permission Sage Publications, Inc.

Fig. 1.1, p. 6: From *Model Standards for Beginning Teacher Licensing, Assessment, and Development: A Resource for State Dialogue*, by the Council of Chief State School Officers, 1992, Washington, DC: Author.

Fig. 1.9, p. 17: Copyright © The Children's Defense Fund, 2000. All rights reserved.

Focus on Teaching, p. 38: From "The Use of Technology to Enhance Mathematics Achievement" by Clem Annice, 2000, in Geoffrey E. Mills (Ed.), *Action Research, A Guide for the Teacher Researcher* (pp. 70–71), Upper Saddle River, NJ: Merrill/Prentice Hall. Reprinted with permission of Merrill/Prentice Hall, Inc.

Fig. 1.18, p. 44: From *Guidelines for Conducting Research with Children*, by the Society for Research in Child Development Committee on Ethical Conduct in Child Development Research, 1990. Reprinted with permission.

CHAPTER 2   Opening vignette, p. 50: From *School Girls: Young Women, Self-Esteem and the Confidence Gap* (pp.108–109), by P. Orenstein, 1994, New York: Anchor Books, Doubleday.

Fig. 2.1, p. 52: From M. M. Grumbach, University of California, San Francisco. Reprinted by permission.

Fig. 2.8, p. 67: Reprinted by permission of the publisher from *The Postnatal Development of the Human Cerebral Cortex, Vols I–VIII,* by Jesse LeRoy Conel, 1939/1975, Cambridge, MA: Harvard University Press. Copyright © 1939, 1975 by the President and Fellows of Harvard College.

Fig. 2.10, p. 83: Reprinted with permission from *Diagnostic and Statistical Manual of Mental Disorders* (4th ed.), American Psychiatric Association, 2000, Washington, DC: Author. Copyright © 2000, American Psychiatric Association.

CHAPTER 3   Opening vignette, pp. 127–128: From *Wally's Stories: Conversations in the Kindergarten* (pp. 116–117), by Vivian Gussin Paley, 1981, Cambridge, MA: Harvard University Press. Copyright © 1981 by the President and Fellows of Harvard College. Reprinted with permission.

Excerpt, p. 136: From "*Barney: Keep Making Gold . . .*", by V. Paley, 1988, in *Bad Guys Don't Have Birthdays* (p. 19), Chicago: University of Chicago Press. Reprinted by permission of The University of Chicago Press.

Focus on Development, p. 139: From *Analyzing Children's Art*, by Rhonda Kellog, 1968/1970, Mountain View, CA: Mayfield. Copyright © 1968, 1970 by Rhoda Kellogg. Reprinted by permission of The McGraw-Hill Companies.

Focus on Research, p. 140: From "First Graders' Cognitive Representation of Number and Understanding of Place Value: Cross-National Comparisons—France, Japan, Korea, Sweden, and the United States," by L. Miura, Y. Okamoto, C. Kim, M. Steer, & M. Fayol, 1993, *Journal of Educational Psychology*, Vol. 85, pp. 24–29, American Psychological Association. Reprinted with permission.

Fig. 3.10, p. 158: From "The Role of Central Conceptual Structures in the Development of Children's Thought," by R. Case & Y. Okamoto et al., 1996, *Monographs of the Society for Research in Child Development, 61*(1–2), Fig 26, p. 139, Blackwell Publishing.

Focus on Teaching, p. 163: From "Genetics," in *National Science Education Standards* (pp. 64–66), by the National Academy of Sciences, 1996, Washington, DC: Author. Copyright © 1996 by the National Academy of Sciences. Reprinted with permission.

Focus on Research, p. 177: From "Reciprocal Teaching of Comprehension-Fostering and Comprehension-Monitoring Activities," by Annemarie Sullivan Palincsar & Ann L. Brown, 1984, *Cognition and Instruction, 1*(2), p. 161. Copyright © 1984 by Lawrence Erlbaum Associates, Inc. Reprinted by permission of Annemarie Palincsar.

Name Index

A

Aber, J. L., 474
Aberbach, A., 386
Aboud, F. E., 410
Abrams, L. A., 481
Acredolo, L., 266
Acs, G., 450
Adams, M., 276
Adams, M. J., 288
Adelman, 241
Ainsworth, M., 339, 340
Aitchison, J., 258
Albert, L., 438
Albrecht, H., 108
Aldridge, 511
Alexander, K., 8, 379, 523
Alexander, P. A., 197
Alibali, M., 154, 156, 157
Allegro, T., 379
Allen, J. B., 293
Allen, L., 326
Allen, V., 107
Allen, W., 458, 459
Alley, G., 81, 511
Allington, R. L., 304, 305
Altemeier, W. A., 474
Altermatt, E. R., 380, 412
Altschul, I., 372, 373
Alvarez, M. M., 378, 379, 380
Amato, P. R., 476, 478
Ames, C., 386, 396
Ames, L., 22
Amoto, 474
Amsterlaw, J., 199
Anastopoulous, A. D., 346
Anderman, E. M., 362, 387
Anderson, C. A., 428
Anderson, D., 189, 485
Anderson, R. C., 300
Andersson, T., 108
Androutsopoulous, J., 276
Angelillo, C., 179
Ani, C., 99
Apfel, N. H., 453
Applebaum, 214
Applebee, A., 315

Applegate, B., 85
Aprea, D. M., 457
Arauz, R., 179
Archer, J., 386
Arend, R. A., 347
Arnett, J., 345
Aro, H., 107
Aronson, E., 422
Aronson, J., 393
Asarno, J., 171
Asher, S. R., 412, 415
Ashkenazi, O., 274
Aslin, R. N., 72, 74
Astington, J. W., 405
Astuti, R., 141
Atkinson, J., 382
Atwell, N., 274
Au, K., 324, 325, 328
Aubey, L. W., 490
August, 277
Austin, L. M., 522
Ayers, R., 276
Azmitia, M., 472

B

Bachman, J., 95, 114
Bacue, A., 380
Baharudin, R., 217
Bahr, C. M., 508
Bahrick, L., 266
Bailey, D., 55
Bailey, J. M., 456
Baldwin, L., 306
Bandura, A., 24, 26, 34, 376, 378, 379, 380, 383, 428, 435
Banilower, E., 380
Bank, L., 352
Banks, J., 241, 242
Barber, B., 110, 467
Baringa, M., 72
Barkley, R., 84, 85
Barnes, D., 55
Barnett, D., 339
Barnett, W. S., 219
Barocas, R., 218
Baroody, A., 138, 204

Barr, H. M., 61
Barram, A., 211
Bartels, B., 204
Bartlett, L., 179, 180
Bartsch, K., 403
Bassler, O. C., 490
Bates, E., 71, 216, 259–260, 261, 269, 271, 272, 273, 338
Bates, J., 338
Bathurst, K., 481
Battle, E. S., 84
Bauer, A., 513
Bauminger, N., 230
Baumrind, D., 465, 467
Bayley, N., 211
Beach, D., 194
Beals, D. E., 291
Bearison, D., 178
Beauchamp, C. K., 74
Beaumont, F., 2, 501
Becher, R. M., 487
Beck, I., 287
Becker, D. M., 113
Becker, H. J., 243, 244
Becker, J. B., 106
Becker, P. E., 480
Bednar, R. L., 363
Behrman, R., 62, 63, 111
Bellugi, U., 268, 270
Belsky, J., 217
Ben-Avie, M., 4, 487, 498, 500
Benbow, C., 93, 384
Bender, B., 55
Bennett, W., 439
Bennetto, L., 355
Benware, C., 386
Ben-Zeev, 231
Berenbaum, 374
Berk, L., 170, 171
Berlin, L. J., 340
Berliner, D. C., 10
Berman, 362
Bernal, M., 370
Bernard, B., 516
Berndt, T., 412, 421
Berninger, V., 307, 308, 310, 312
Betz, N. E., 380

Subject Index